W9-DFB-003

University Casebook Series

May, 1993

ACCOUNTING AND THE LAW, Fourth Edition (1978), with Problems Pamphlet (Successor to Dohr, Phillips, Thompson & Warren)

George C. Thompson, Professor, Columbia University Graduate School of Business.

Robert Whitman, Professor of Law, University of Connecticut.

Ellis L. Phillips, Jr., Member of the New York Bar.

William C. Warren, Professor of Law Emeritus, Columbia University.

ACCOUNTING FOR LAWYERS, MATERIALS ON (1980)

David R. Herwitz, Professor of Law, Harvard University.

ADMINISTRATIVE LAW, Eighth Edition (1987), with 1993 Case Supplement and 1983 Problems Supplement (Supplement edited in association with Paul R. Verkuil, Dean and Professor of Law, Tulane University)

Walter Gellhorn, University Professor Emeritus, Columbia University.

Clark Byse, Professor of Law, Harvard University.

Peter L. Strauss, Professor of Law, Columbia University.

Todd D. Rakoff, Professor of Law, Harvard University.

Roy A. Schotland, Professor of Law, Georgetown University.

ADMIRALTY, Third Edition (1987), with 1991 Statute and Rule Supplement

Jo Desha Lucas, Professor of Law, University of Chicago.

ADVOCACY, see also Lawyering Process

AGENCY, see also Enterprise Organization

AGENCY—PARTNERSHIPS, Fourth Edition (1987)

Abridgement from Conard, Knauss & Siegel's Enterprise Organization, Fourth Edition.

AGENCY AND PARTNERSHIPS (1987)

Melvin A. Eisenberg, Professor of Law, University of California, Berkeley.

ANTITRUST: FREE ENTERPRISE AND ECONOMIC ORGANIZATION, Sixth Edition (1983), with 1983 Problems in Antitrust Supplement and 1992 Case Supplement

Louis B. Schwartz, Professor of Law, University of Pennsylvania.

John J. Flynn, Professor of Law, University of Utah.

Harry First, Professor of Law, New York University.

BANKRUPTCY, Third Edition (1993)

Robert L. Jordan, Professor of Law, University of California, Los Angeles.

William D. Warren, Professor of Law, University of California, Los Angeles.

BANKRUPTCY AND DEBTOR–CREDITOR LAW, Second Edition (1988)

Theodore Eisenberg, Professor of Law, Cornell University.

UNIVERSITY CASEBOOK SERIES—Continued

COMMERCIAL TRANSACTIONS—Principles and Policies, Second Edition (1991)

Alan Schwartz, Professor of Law, Yale University.
Robert E. Scott, Professor of Law, University of Virginia.

COMPARATIVE LAW, Fifth Edition (1988)

Rudolf B. Schlesinger, Professor of Law, Hastings College of the Law.
Hans W. Baade, Professor of Law, University of Texas.
Mirjan P. Damaska, Professor of Law, Yale Law School.
Peter E. Herzog, Professor of Law, Syracuse University.

COMPETITIVE PROCESS, LEGAL REGULATION OF THE, Revised Fourth Edition (1991), with 1991 Selected Statutes Supplement

Edmund W. Kitch, Professor of Law, University of Virginia.
Harvey S. Perlman, Dean of the Law School, University of Nebraska.

CONFLICT OF LAWS, Ninth Edition (1990), with 1992 Supplement

Willis L. M. Reese, Professor of Law, Columbia University.
Maurice Rosenberg, Professor of Law, Columbia University.
Peter Hay, Professor of Law, University of Illinois.

CONSTITUTIONAL LAW, CIVIL LIBERTY AND INDIVIDUAL RIGHTS, Second Edition (1982), with 1992 Supplement

William Cohen, Professor of Law, Stanford University.
John Kaplan, Professor of Law, Stanford University.

CONSTITUTIONAL LAW, Ninth Edition (1993), with 1993 Supplement

William Cohen, Professor of Law, Stanford University.
Jonathan D. Varat, Professor of Law, University of California, Los Angeles.

CONSTITUTIONAL LAW, Twelfth Edition (1991), with 1993 Supplement (Supplement edited in association with Frederick F. Schauer, Professor, Harvard University)

Gerald Gunther, Professor of Law, Stanford University.

CONSTITUTIONAL LAW, INDIVIDUAL RIGHTS IN, Fifth Edition (1992) (Reprinted from CONSTITUTIONAL LAW, Twelfth Edition), with 1993 Supplement (Supplement edited in association with Frederick F. Schauer, Professor, Harvard University)

Gerald Gunther, Professor of Law, Stanford University.

CONSUMER TRANSACTIONS, Second Edition (1991), with Selected Statutes and Regulations Supplement

Michael M. Greenfield, Professor of Law, Washington University.

CONTRACT LAW AND ITS APPLICATION, Fourth Edition (1988)

Arthur Rosett, Professor of Law, University of California, Los Angeles.

CONTRACT LAW, STUDIES IN, Fourth Edition (1991)

Edward J. Murphy, Professor of Law, University of Notre Dame.
Richard E. Speidel, Professor of Law, Northwestern University.

CONTRACTS, Sixth Edition (1993)

John P. Dawson, late Professor of Law, Harvard University.
William Burnett Harvey, Professor of Law and Political Science, Boston University.
Stanley D. Henderson, Professor of Law, University of Virginia.

CONTRACTS, Fourth Edition (1988)

E. Allan Farnsworth, Professor of Law, Columbia University.
William F. Young, Professor of Law, Columbia University.

CONTRACTS, Selections on (statutory materials) (1992)

CONTRACTS, Second Edition (1978), with Statutory and Administrative Law Supplement (1978)

Ian R. Macneil, Professor of Law, Cornell University.

COPYRIGHT, PATENTS AND TRADEMARKS, see also Competitive Process; see also Selected Statutes and International Agreements

COPYRIGHT, PATENT, TRADEMARK AND RELATED STATE DOCTRINES, Revised Third Edition (1993), with 1991 Selected Statutes Supplement and 1981 Problem Supplement

Paul Goldstein, Professor of Law, Stanford University.

COPYRIGHT, Unfair Competition, and Other Topics Bearing on the Protection of Literary, Musical, and Artistic Works, Fifth Edition (1990), with 1993 Statutory and Case Supplement

Ralph S. Brown, Jr., Professor of Law, Yale University.
Robert C. Denicola, Professor of Law, University of Nebraska.

CORPORATE ACQUISITIONS, The Law and Finance of (1986), with 1992 Supplement

Ronald J. Gilson, Professor of Law, Stanford University.

CORPORATE FINANCE, Brudney and Chirelstein's Fourth Edition (1993)

Victor Brudney, Professor of Law, Harvard University.
William W. Bratton, Jr., Professor of Law, Rutgers University, Newark.

CORPORATION LAW, BASIC, Third Edition (1989), with Documentary Supplement

Detlev F. Vagts, Professor of Law, Harvard University.

CORPORATIONS, see also Enterprise Organization and Business Organization

CORPORATIONS, Sixth Edition—Concise (1988), with 1993 Case Supplement and 1992 Statutory Supplement

William L. Cary, late Professor of Law, Columbia University.
Melvin Aron Eisenberg, Professor of Law, University of California, Berkeley.

CORPORATIONS, Sixth Edition—Unabridged (1988), with 1993 Case Supplement and 1992 Statutory Supplement

William L. Cary, late Professor of Law, Columbia University.
Melvin Aron Eisenberg, Professor of Law, University of California, Berkeley.

CORPORATIONS AND BUSINESS ASSOCIATIONS—STATUTES, RULES, AND FORMS, 1993 Edition

CORRECTIONS, see Sentencing

CREDITORS' RIGHTS, see also Debtor–Creditor Law

CRIMINAL JUSTICE ADMINISTRATION, Fourth Edition (1991), with 1993 Supplement

Frank W. Miller, Professor of Law, Washington University.
Robert O. Dawson, Professor of Law, University of Texas.
George E. Dix, Professor of Law, University of Texas.
Raymond I. Parnas, Professor of Law, University of California, Davis.

CRIMINAL LAW, Fifth Edition (1992)

Andre A. Moenssens, Professor of Law, University of Richmond.
Fred E. Inbau, Professor of Law Emeritus, Northwestern University.
Ronald J. Bacigal, Professor of Law, University of Richmond.

CRIMINAL LAW AND APPROACHES TO THE STUDY OF LAW, Second Edition (1991)

John M. Brumbaugh, Professor of Law, University of Maryland.

CRIMINAL LAW, Second Edition (1986)

Peter W. Low, Professor of Law, University of Virginia.
John C. Jeffries, Jr., Professor of Law, University of Virginia.
Richard C. Bonnie, Professor of Law, University of Virginia.

CRIMINAL LAW, Fifth Edition (1993)

Lloyd L. Weinreb, Professor of Law, Harvard University.

CRIMINAL LAW AND PROCEDURE, Seventh Edition (1989)

Ronald N. Boyce, Professor of Law, University of Utah.
Rollin M. Perkins, Professor of Law Emeritus, University of California, Hastings College of the Law.

CRIMINAL PROCEDURE, Fourth Edition (1992), with 1993 Supplement

James B. Haddad, late Professor of Law, Northwestern University.
James B. Zagel, Chief, Criminal Justice Division, Office of Attorney General of Illinois.
Gary L. Starkman, Assistant U.S. Attorney, Northern District of Illinois.
William J. Bauer, Chief Judge of the U.S. Court of Appeals, Seventh Circuit.

CRIMINAL PROCESS, Fifth Edition (1993), with 1992 Supplement

Lloyd L. Weinreb, Professor of Law, Harvard University.

CRIMINAL PROCESS, PART ONE—INVESTIGATION (1993) (Reprint of Chapters 1–6 of Weinreb's CRIMINAL PROCESS, Fifth Edition)

CRIMINAL PROCESS, PART TWO—PROSECUTION (1993) (Reprint of Chapters 7–18 of Weinreb's CRIMINAL PROCESS, Fifth Edition)

DAMAGES, Second Edition (1952)

Charles T. McCormick, late Professor of Law, University of Texas.
William F. Fritz, late Professor of Law, University of Texas.

DECEDENTS' ESTATES AND TRUSTS, see also Family Property Law

DECEDENTS' ESTATES AND TRUSTS, Eighth Edition (1993)

John Ritchie, late Professor of Law, University of Virginia.
Neill H. Alford, Jr., Professor of Law, University of Virginia.
Richard W. Effland, late Professor of Law, Arizona State University.
Joel C. Dobris, Professor of Law, University of California, Davis.

DISPUTE RESOLUTION, Processes of (1989)

John S. Murray, President and Executive Director of The Conflict Clinic, Inc., George Mason University.
Alan Scott Rau, Professor of Law, University of Texas.
Edward F. Sherman, Professor of Law, University of Texas.

DOMESTIC RELATIONS, see also Family Law

DOMESTIC RELATIONS, Second Edition (1990), with 1993 Supplement

Walter Wadlington, Professor of Law, University of Virginia.

EMPLOYMENT DISCRIMINATION, Third Edition (1993)

Joel W. Friedman, Professor of Law, Tulane University.
George M. Strickler, Professor of Law, Tulane University.

EMPLOYMENT LAW, Second Edition (1991), with 1992 Statutory Supplement and 1992 Case Supplement

Mark A. Rothstein, Professor of Law, University of Houston.
Andria S. Knapp, Visiting Professor of Law, Golden Gate University.
Lance Liebman, Professor of Law, Harvard University.

ENERGY LAW (1983), with 1991 Case Supplement

Donald N. Zillman, Professor of Law, University of Utah.
Laurence Lattman, Dean of Mines and Engineering, University of Utah.

ENTERPRISE ORGANIZATION, Fourth Edition (1987), with 1987 Corporation and Partnership Statutes, Rules and Forms Supplement

Alfred F. Conard, Professor of Law, University of Michigan.
Robert L. Knauss, Dean of the Law School, University of Houston.
Stanley Siegel, Professor of Law, University of California, Los Angeles.

ENVIRONMENTAL POLICY LAW, Second Edition (1991)

Thomas J. Schoenbaum, Professor of Law, University of Georgia.
Ronald H. Rosenberg, Professor of Law, College of William and Mary.

EQUITY, see also Remedies

EQUITY, RESTITUTION AND DAMAGES, Second Edition (1974)

Robert Childres, late Professor of Law, Northwestern University.
William F. Johnson, Jr., Professor of Law, New York University.

ESTATE PLANNING, Second Edition (1982), with 1985 Case, Text and Documentary Supplement

David Westfall, Professor of Law, Harvard University.

ETHICS, see Legal Ethics, Legal Profession, Professional Responsibility, and Social Responsibilities

ETHICS OF LAWYERING, THE LAW AND (1990)

Geoffrey C. Hazard, Jr., Professor of Law, Yale University.
Susan P. Koniak, Professor of Law, University of Pittsburgh.

UNIVERSITY CASEBOOK SERIES—Continued

FEDERAL RULES OF CIVIL PROCEDURE and Selected Other Procedural Provisions, 1993 Edition

FEDERAL TAXATION, see Taxation

FIRST AMENDMENT (1991), with 1993 Supplement

William W. Van Alstyne, Professor of Law, Duke University.

FOOD AND DRUG LAW, Second Edition (1991), with Statutory Supplement

Peter Barton Hutt, Esq.
Richard A. Merrill, Professor of Law, University of Virginia.

FUTURE INTERESTS (1970)

Howard R. Williams, Professor of Law, Stanford University.

FUTURE INTERESTS AND ESTATE PLANNING (1961), with 1962 Supplement

W. Barton Leach, late Professor of Law, Harvard University.
James K. Logan, formerly Dean of the Law School, University of Kansas.

GENDER DISCRIMINATION, see Women and the Law

GOVERNMENT CONTRACTS, FEDERAL, Successor Edition (1985), with 1989 Supplement

John W. Whelan, Professor of Law, Hastings College of the Law.

GOVERNMENT REGULATION: FREE ENTERPRISE AND ECONOMIC ORGANIZATION, Sixth Edition (1985)

Louis B. Schwartz, Professor of Law, Hastings College of the Law.
John J. Flynn, Professor of Law, University of Utah.
Harry First, Professor of Law, New York University.

HEALTH CARE LAW AND POLICY (1988), with 1992 Supplement

Clark C. Havighurst, Professor of Law, Duke University.

HINCKLEY, JOHN W., JR., TRIAL OF: A Case Study of the Insanity Defense (1986)

Peter W. Low, Professor of Law, University of Virginia.
John C. Jeffries, Jr., Professor of Law, University of Virginia.
Richard C. Bonnie, Professor of Law, University of Virginia.

IMMIGRATION LAW AND POLICY (1992)

Stephen H. Legomsky, Professor of Law, Washington University.

INJUNCTIONS, Second Edition (1984)

Owen M. Fiss, Professor of Law, Yale University.
Doug Rendleman, Professor of Law, College of William and Mary.

INSTITUTIONAL INVESTORS (1978)

David L. Ratner, Professor of Law, Cornell University.

INSURANCE, Second Edition (1985)

William F. Young, Professor of Law, Columbia University.
Eric M. Holmes, Professor of Law, University of Georgia.

INSURANCE LAW AND REGULATION (1990)

Kenneth S. Abraham, University of Virginia.

UNIVERSITY CASEBOOK SERIES—Continued

INTERNATIONAL LAW, see also Transnational Legal Problems, Transnational Business Problems, and United Nations Law

INTERNATIONAL LAW IN CONTEMPORARY PERSPECTIVE (1981), with Essay Supplement

Myres S. McDougal, Professor of Law, Yale University.
W. Michael Reisman, Professor of Law, Yale University.

INTERNATIONAL LEGAL SYSTEM, Third Edition (1988), with Documentary Supplement

Joseph Modeste Sweeney, Professor of Law, University of California, Hastings.
Covey T. Oliver, Professor of Law, University of Pennsylvania.
Noyes E. Leech, Professor of Law Emeritus, University of Pennsylvania.

INTRODUCTION TO LAW, see also Legal Method, On Law in Courts, and Dynamics of American Law

INTRODUCTION TO THE STUDY OF LAW (1970)

E. Wayne Thode, late Professor of Law, University of Utah.
Leon Lebowitz, Professor of Law, University of Texas.
Lester J. Mazor, Professor of Law, University of Utah.

JUDICIAL CODE and Rules of Procedure in the Federal Courts, Students' Edition, 1993 Revision

Daniel J. Meltzer, Professor of Law, Harvard University.
David L. Shapiro, Professor of Law, Harvard University.

JURISPRUDENCE (Temporary Edition Hardbound) (1949)

Lon L. Fuller, late Professor of Law, Harvard University.

JUVENILE, see also Children

JUVENILE JUSTICE PROCESS, Third Edition (1985)

Frank W. Miller, Professor of Law, Washington University.
Robert O. Dawson, Professor of Law, University of Texas.
George E. Dix, Professor of Law, University of Texas.
Raymond I. Parnas, Professor of Law, University of California, Davis.

LABOR LAW, Eleventh Edition (1991), with 1993 Statutory Supplement and 1992 Case Supplement

Archibald Cox, Professor of Law, Harvard University.
Derek C. Bok, President, Harvard University.
Robert A. Gorman, Professor of Law, University of Pennsylvania.
Matthew W. Finkin, Professor of Law, University of Illinois.

LABOR LAW, Second Edition (1982), with Statutory Supplement

Clyde W. Summers, Professor of Law, University of Pennsylvania.
Harry H. Wellington, Dean of the Law School, Yale University.
Alan Hyde, Professor of Law, Rutgers University.

LAND FINANCING, Third Edition (1985)

Norman Penney, late Professor of Law, Cornell University.
Richard F. Broude, Member of the California Bar.
Roger Cunningham, Professor of Law, University of Michigan.

LAW AND MEDICINE (1980)

Walter Wadlington, Professor of Law and Professor of Legal Medicine, University of Virginia.

Jon R. Waltz, Professor of Law, Northwestern University.

Roger B. Dworkin, Professor of Law, Indiana University, and Professor of Biomedical History, University of Washington.

LAW, LANGUAGE AND ETHICS (1972)

William R. Bishin, Professor of Law, University of Southern California.

Christopher D. Stone, Professor of Law, University of Southern California.

LAW, SCIENCE AND MEDICINE (1984), with 1989 Supplement

Judith C. Areen, Professor of Law, Georgetown University.

Patricia A. King, Professor of Law, Georgetown University.

Steven P. Goldberg, Professor of Law, Georgetown University.

Alexander M. Capron, Professor of Law, University of Southern California.

LAWYERING PROCESS (1978), with Civil Problem Supplement and Criminal Problem Supplement

Gary Bellow, Professor of Law, Harvard University.

Bea Moulton, Professor of Law, Arizona State University.

LEGAL ETHICS (1992)

Deborah Rhode, Professor of Law, Stanford University.

David Luban, Professor of Law, University of Maryland.

LEGAL METHOD (1980)

Harry W. Jones, Professor of Law Emeritus, Columbia University.

John M. Kernochan, Professor of Law, Columbia University.

Arthur W. Murphy, Professor of Law, Columbia University.

LEGAL METHODS (1969)

Robert N. Covington, Professor of Law, Vanderbilt University.

E. Blythe Stason, late Professor of Law, Vanderbilt University.

John W. Wade, Professor of Law, Vanderbilt University.

Elliott E. Cheatham, late Professor of Law, Vanderbilt University.

Theodore A. Smedley, Professor of Law, Vanderbilt University.

LEGAL PROFESSION, THE, Responsibility and Regulation, Second Edition (1988)

Geoffrey C. Hazard, Jr., Professor of Law, Yale University.

Deborah L. Rhode, Professor of Law, Stanford University.

LEGISLATION (1993)

William D. Popkin, Professor of Law, Indiana University at Bloomington.

LEGISLATION, Fourth Edition (1982) (by Fordham)

Horace E. Read, late Vice President, Dalhousie University.

John W. MacDonald, Professor of Law Emeritus, Cornell Law School.

Jefferson B. Fordham, Professor of Law, University of Utah.

William J. Pierce, Professor of Law, University of Michigan.

PROCEDURE (1988), with Procedure Supplement (1991)

Robert M. Cover, late Professor of Law, Yale Law School.
Owen M. Fiss, Professor of Law, Yale Law School.
Judith Resnik, Professor of Law, University of Southern California Law Center.

PROCEDURE—CIVIL PROCEDURE, Sixth Edition (1990), with 1993 Supplement

Richard H. Field, late Professor of Law, Harvard University.
Benjamin Kaplan, Professor of Law Emeritus, Harvard University.
Kevin M. Clermont, Professor of Law, Cornell University.

PROCEDURE—CIVIL PROCEDURE, Successor Edition (1992)

A. Leo Levin, Professor of Law Emeritus, University of Pennsylvania.
Philip Shuchman, Professor of Law, Rutgers University.
Charles M. Yablon, Professor of Law, Yeshiva University.

PROCEDURE—CIVIL PROCEDURE, Fifth Edition (1990), with 1993 Supplement

Maurice Rosenberg, Professor of Law, Columbia University.
Hans Smit, Professor of Law, Columbia University.
Rochelle C. Dreyfuss, Professor of Law, New York University.

PROCEDURE—PLEADING AND PROCEDURE: State and Federal, Sixth Edition (1989), with 1993 Case Supplement

David W. Louisell, late Professor of Law, University of California, Berkeley.
Geoffrey C. Hazard, Jr., Professor of Law, Yale University.
Colin C. Tait, Professor of Law, University of Connecticut.

PROCEDURE—FEDERAL RULES OF CIVIL PROCEDURE, 1993 Edition

PRODUCTS LIABILITY AND SAFETY, Second Edition (1989), with 1993 Case and Statutory Supplement

W. Page Keeton, Professor of Law, University of Texas.
David G. Owen, Professor of Law, University of South Carolina.
John E. Montgomery, Professor of Law, University of South Carolina.
Michael D. Green, Professor of Law, University of Iowa.

PROFESSIONAL RESPONSIBILITY, Fifth Edition (1991), with 1993 Selected Standards on Professional Responsibility Supplement

Thomas D. Morgan, Professor of Law, George Washington University.
Ronald D. Rotunda, Professor of Law, University of Illinois.

PROPERTY, Sixth Edition (1990)

John E. Cribbet, Professor of Law, University of Illinois.
Corwin W. Johnson, Professor of Law, University of Texas.
Roger W. Findley, Professor of Law, University of Illinois.
Ernest E. Smith, Professor of Law, University of Texas.

PROPERTY—PERSONAL (1953)

S. Kenneth Skolfield, late Professor of Law Emeritus, Boston University.

PROPERTY—PERSONAL, Third Edition (1954)

Everett Fraser, late Dean of the Law School Emeritus, University of Minnesota.
Third Edition by Charles W. Taintor, late Professor of Law, University of Pittsburgh.

PROPERTY—INTRODUCTION, TO REAL PROPERTY, Third Edition (1954)

Everett Fraser, late Dean of the Law School Emeritus, University of Minnesota.

PROPERTY—FUNDAMENTALS OF MODERN REAL PROPERTY, Third Edition (1992)

Edward H. Rabin, Professor of Law, University of California, Davis.
Roberta Rosenthal Kwall, Professor of Law, DePaul University.

PROPERTY, REAL (1984), with 1988 Supplement

Paul Goldstein, Professor of Law, Stanford University.

PROSECUTION AND ADJUDICATION, Fourth Edition (1991), with 1993 Supplement

Reprint of Chapters 11–26 of Miller, Dawson, Dix and Parnas's CRIMINAL JUSTICE ADMINISTRATION, Fourth Edition.

PSYCHIATRY AND LAW, see Mental Health, see also Hinckley, Trial of

PUBLIC UTILITY LAW, see Free Enterprise, also Regulated Industries

REAL ESTATE PLANNING, Third Edition (1989), with Revised Problem and Statutory Supplement (1991)

Norton L. Steuben, Professor of Law, University of Colorado.

REAL ESTATE TRANSACTIONS, Third Edition (1993), with Statute, Form and Problem Supplement (1993)

Paul Goldstein, Professor of Law, Stanford University.
Gerald Korngold, Professor of Law, Case Western Reserve University.

RECEIVERSHIP AND CORPORATE REORGANIZATION, see Creditors' Rights

REGULATED INDUSTRIES, Second Edition (1976)

William K. Jones, Professor of Law, Columbia University.

REMEDIES, Third Edition (1992)

Edward D. Re, Professor of Law, St. John's University.
Stanton D. Krauss, Professor of Law, University of Bridgeport.

REMEDIES (1989)

Elaine W. Shoben, Professor of Law, University of Illinois.
Wm. Murray Tabb, Professor of Law, Baylor University.

SALES, Third Edition (1992)

Marion W. Benfield, Jr., Professor of Law, Wake Forest University.
William D. Hawkland, Professor of Law, Louisiana State Law Center.

SALES (1992) (Reprinted from Commercial Law) Third Edition (1992)

Robert L. Jordan, Professor of Law, University of California, Los Angeles.
William D. Warren, Professor of Law, University of California, Los Angeles.

SALES AND SECURED FINANCING, Sixth Edition (1993)

John Honnold, Professor of Law Emeritus, University of Pennsylvania.
Steven L. Harris, Professor of Law, University of Illinois.
Charles Mooney, Jr., Professor of Law, University of Pennsylvania.
Curtis R. Reitz, Professor of Law, University of Pennsylvania.

SALES LAW AND THE CONTRACTING PROCESS, Second Edition (1991) (Reprinted from Commercial Transactions) Second Edition (1991)

Alan Schwartz, Professor of Law, Yale University.
Robert E. Scott, Professor of Law, University of Virginia.

SALES TRANSACTIONS: DOMESTIC AND INTERNATIONAL LAW (1992)

John Honnold, Professor of Law Emeritus, University of Pennsylvania.
Curtis R. Reitz, Professor of Law, University of Pennsylvania.

SECURED TRANSACTIONS IN PERSONAL PROPERTY, Third Edition (1992) (Reprinted from COMMERCIAL LAW, Third Edition (1992))

Robert L. Jordan, Professor of Law, University of California, Los Angeles.
William D. Warren, Professor of Law, University of California, Los Angeles.

SECURITIES REGULATION, Seventh Edition (1992), with 1993 Selected Statutes, Rules and Forms Supplement, and 1993 Cases and Releases Supplement

Richard W. Jennings, Professor of Law, University of California, Berkeley.
Harold Marsh, Jr., Member of California Bar.
John C. Coffee, Jr., Professor of Law, Columbia University.

SECURITIES REGULATION, Second Edition (1988), with Statute, Rule and Form Supplement (1991)

Larry D. Soderquist, Professor of Law, Vanderbilt University.

SECURITY INTERESTS IN PERSONAL PROPERTY, Second Edition (1987)

Douglas G. Baird, Professor of Law, University of Chicago.
Thomas H. Jackson, Dean of the Law School, University of Virginia.

SECURITY INTERESTS IN PERSONAL PROPERTY, Second Edition (1992)

John Honnold, Professor of Law Emeritus, University of Pennsylvania.
Steven L. Harris, Professor of Law, University of Illinois.
Charles W. Mooney, Jr., Professor of Law, University of Pennsylvania.

SELECTED STANDARDS ON PROFESSIONAL RESPONSIBILITY, 1993 Edition

SELECTED STATUTES AND INTERNATIONAL AGREEMENTS ON UNFAIR COMPETITION, TRADEMARK, COPYRIGHT AND PATENT, 1991 Edition

SELECTED STATUTES ON TRUSTS AND ESTATES, 1992 Edition

SOCIAL RESPONSIBILITIES OF LAWYERS, Case Studies (1988)

Philip B. Heymann, Professor of Law, Harvard University.
Lance Liebman, Professor of Law, Harvard University.

SOCIAL SCIENCE IN LAW, Second Edition (1990)

John Monahan, Professor of Law, University of Virginia.
Laurens Walker, Professor of Law, University of Virginia.

TAXATION, FEDERAL INCOME (1989)

Stephen B. Cohen, Professor of Law, Georgetown University.

TAXATION, FEDERAL INCOME, Second Edition (1988), with 1993 Supplement (Supplement edited in association with Deborah H. Schenk, Professor of Law, New York University)

Michael J. Graetz, Professor of Law, Yale University.

TAXATION, FEDERAL INCOME, Seventh Edition (1991)

James J. Freeland, Professor of Law, University of Florida.
Stephen A. Lind, Professor of Law, University of Florida and University of California, Hastings.
Richard B. Stephens, late Professor of Law Emeritus, University of Florida.

TAXATION, FEDERAL INCOME, Successor Edition (1986), with 1993 Legislative Supplement

Stanley S. Surrey, late Professor of Law, Harvard University.
Paul R. McDaniel, Professor of Law, Boston College.
Hugh J. Ault, Professor of Law, Boston College.
Stanley A. Koppelman, Professor of Law, Boston University.

TAXATION, FEDERAL INCOME, OF BUSINESS ORGANIZATIONS (1991), with 1993 Supplement

Paul R. McDaniel, Professor of Law, Boston College.
Hugh J. Ault, Professor of Law, Boston College.
Martin J. McMahon, Jr., Professor of Law, University of Kentucky.
Daniel L. Simmons, Professor of Law, University of California, Davis.

TAXATION, FEDERAL INCOME, OF PARTNERSHIPS AND S CORPORATIONS (1991), with 1993 Supplement

Paul R. McDaniel, Professor of Law, Boston College.
Hugh J. Ault, Professor of Law, Boston College.
Martin J. McMahon, Jr., Professor of Law, University of Kentucky.
Daniel L. Simmons, Professor of Law, University of California, Davis.

TAXATION, FEDERAL INCOME, OIL AND GAS, NATURAL RESOURCES TRANSACTIONS (1990)

Peter C. Maxfield, Professor of Law, University of Wyoming.
James L. Houghton, CPA, Partner, Ernst and Young.
James R. Gaar, CPA, Partner, Ernst and Young.

TAXATION, FEDERAL WEALTH TRANSFER, Successor Edition (1987)

Stanley S. Surrey, late Professor of Law, Harvard University.
Paul R. McDaniel, Professor of Law, Boston College.
Harry L. Gutman, Professor of Law, University of Pennsylvania.

TAXATION, FUNDAMENTALS OF CORPORATE, Third Edition (1991)

Stephen A. Lind, Professor of Law, University of Florida and University of California, Hastings.
Stephen Schwarz, Professor of Law, University of California, Hastings.
Daniel J. Lathrope, Professor of Law, University of California, Hastings.
Joshua Rosenberg, Professor of Law, University of San Francisco.

TAXATION, FUNDAMENTALS OF PARTNERSHIP, Third Edition (1992)

Stephen A. Lind, Professor of Law, University of Florida and University of California, Hastings.
Stephen Schwarz, Professor of Law, University of California, Hastings.
Daniel J. Lathrope, Professor of Law, University of California, Hastings.
Joshua Rosenberg, Professor of Law, University of San Francisco.

TAXATION OF CORPORATIONS AND THEIR SHAREHOLDERS (1991)

David J. Shakow, Professor of Law, University of Pennsylvania.

UNIVERSITY CASEBOOK SERIES—Continued

TAXATION, PROBLEMS IN THE FEDERAL INCOME TAXATION OF PARTNER-SHIPS AND CORPORATIONS, Second Edition (1986)

Norton L. Steuben, Professor of Law, University of Colorado.
William J. Turnier, Professor of Law, University of North Carolina.

TAXATION, PROBLEMS IN THE FUNDAMENTALS OF FEDERAL INCOME, Second Edition (1985)

Norton L. Steuben, Professor of Law, University of Colorado.
William J. Turnier, Professor of Law, University of North Carolina.

TORT LAW AND ALTERNATIVES, Fifth Edition (1992)

Marc A. Franklin, Professor of Law, Stanford University.
Robert L. Rabin, Professor of Law, Stanford University.

TORTS, Eighth Edition (1988)

William L. Prosser, late Professor of Law, University of California, Hastings.
John W. Wade, Professor of Law, Vanderbilt University.
Victor E. Schwartz, Adjunct Professor of Law, Georgetown University.

TORTS, Third Edition (1976)

Harry Shulman, late Dean of the Law School, Yale University.
Fleming James, Jr., Professor of Law Emeritus, Yale University.
Oscar S. Gray, Professor of Law, University of Maryland.

TRADE REGULATION, Third Edition (1990), with 1993 Supplement

Milton Handler, Professor of Law Emeritus, Columbia University.
Harlan M. Blake, Professor of Law, Columbia University.
Robert Pitofsky, Professor of Law, Georgetown University.
Harvey J. Goldschmid, Professor of Law, Columbia University.

TRADE REGULATION, see Antitrust

TRANSNATIONAL BUSINESS PROBLEMS (1986)

Detlev F. Vagts, Professor of Law, Harvard University.

TRANSNATIONAL LEGAL PROBLEMS, Third Edition (1986), with 1991 Revised Edition of Documentary Supplement

Henry J. Steiner, Professor of Law, Harvard University.
Detlev F. Vagts, Professor of Law, Harvard University.

TRIAL, see also Evidence, Making the Record, Lawyering Process and Preparing and Presenting the Case

TRUSTS, Sixth Edition (1991)

George G. Bogert, late Professor of Law Emeritus, University of Chicago.
Dallin H. Oaks, President, Brigham Young University.
H. Reese Hansen, Dean and Professor of Law, Brigham Young University.
Claralyn Martin Hill, J.D., Brigham Young University.

TRUSTS AND ESTATES, SELECTED STATUTES ON, 1992 Edition

TRUSTS AND WILLS, see also Decedents' Estates and Trusts, and Family Property Law

UNFAIR COMPETITION, see Competitive Process and Business Torts

UNIVERSITY CASEBOOK SERIES—Continued

WATER RESOURCE MANAGEMENT, Fourth Edition (1993)

A. Dan Tarlock, Professor of Law, IIT Chicago–Kent College of Law.

James N. Corbridge, Jr., Chancellor, University of Colorado at Boulder, and Professor of Law, University of Colorado.

David H. Getches, Professor of Law, University of Colorado.

WOMEN AND THE LAW (1992)

Mary Joe Frug, late Professor of Law, New England School of Law.

WILLS AND ADMINISTRATION, Fifth Edition (1961)

Philip Mechem, late Professor of Law, University of Pennsylvania.

Thomas E. Atkinson, late Professor of Law, New York University.

WRITING AND ANALYSIS IN THE LAW, Second Edition (1991)

Helene S. Shapo, Professor of Law, Northwestern University.

Marilyn R. Walter, Professor of Law, Brooklyn Law School.

Elizabeth Fajans, Writing Specialist, Brooklyn Law School.

University Casebook Series

EDITORIAL BOARD

DAVID L. SHAPIRO
DIRECTING EDITOR
Professor of Law, Harvard University

EDWARD L. BARRETT, Jr.
Professor of Law Emeritus, University of California, Davis

ROBERT C. CLARK
Dean of the School of Law, Harvard University

OWEN M. FISS
Professor of Law, Yale Law School

GERALD GUNTHER
Professor of Law, Stanford University

THOMAS H. JACKSON
Provost University of Virginia

HARRY W. JONES
Professor of Law, Columbia University

HERMA HILL KAY
Dean of the School of Law, University of California, Berkeley

PAGE KEETON
Professor of Law, University of Texas

ROBERT L. RABIN
Professor of Law, Stanford University

CAROL M. ROSE
Professor of Law, Yale University

CASS R. SUNSTEIN
Professor of Law, University of Chicago

SAMUEL D. THURMAN
Professor of Law Emeritus, University of Utah

WATER RESOURCE MANAGEMENT

A Casebook in Law
and
Public Policy

FOURTH EDITION

By

A. DAN TARLOCK
Professor of Law, IIT Chicago-Kent College of Law

JAMES N. CORBRIDGE, JR.
Chancellor, University of Colorado at Boulder, and Professor of
Law, University of Colorado School of Law

DAVID H. GETCHES
Professor of Law, University of Colorado School of Law

Westbury, New York
THE FOUNDATION PRESS, INC.
1993

COPYRIGHT © 1971, 1980, 1988 THE FOUNDATION PRESS, INC.
COPYRIGHT © 1993 By THE FOUNDATION PRESS, INC.

> 615 Merrick Ave.
> Westbury, N.Y. 11590–6607
> (516) 832–6950

All rights reserved
Printed·in the United States of America

Library of Congress Cataloging-in-Publication Data
Tarlock, A. Dan, 1940–
   Water resource management : a casebook in law and public policy /
A. Dan Tarlock, James N. Corbridge, Jr., David H. Getches. — 4th
ed.
     p.   cm. — (University casebook series)
   Rev. ed. of: Water resource management / by Charles J. Meyers . . .
[et al.]. 3rd ed. 1988.
   Includes index.
   ISBN 1–56662–068–6
   1. Water resources development—Law and legislation—United
States—Cases. 2. Water—Law and legislation—United States—Cases.
I. Corbridge, James N. II. Getches, David H. III. Title.
IV. Series.
KF5568.W38 1993
346.7304'691—dc20
[347.3064691]   93–19095

T., C. & G. Water Man. 4th Ed. UCS

*Eventually, all things merge into one,
and a river runs through it.*

NORMAN MACLEAN

SPECIAL DEDICATION

This edition is specially dedicated to the late Charles J. Meyers, one of the original two authors. "Charlie" excelled at life and law. He was a master teacher, a writer of lucid, penetrating prose and an endlessly fascinating conversationalist. Those of us privileged to know him were the beneficiaries of his charm, his energy and his freely given insights as well as his penetrating, blunt and all too often accurate critical assessments of an idea or piece of work. After a distinguished career at Texas, Columbia, and Stanford, where he served as dean between 1976–81, Dean Meyers entered private practice in Denver, Colorado where he remained until his death. The following summary of his accomplishments is adapted from Tarlock, Tribute, 29 Natural Resources J. 328 (1989).

Charlie Meyers was the leading water law scholar of his generation until he died, too early, just short of his sixty-third birthday in July of 1988. The collective loss of his scholarship and wisdom is irreplaceable, but his contributions to water law and policy endure.

Charlie's involvement with water law began at the top. In the late 1950s, while teaching at Columbia he served as Special Master Rifkind's law clerk in Arizona v. California, and used his experience to author a meticulous study of the allocation of the Colorado River from the 1922 Compact to Arizona v. California. Meyers, The Colorado River, 19 Stan.L.Rev. 1 (1966). He consistently advocated a presumption of state rather than federal allocation primacy, and he was an even more forceful advocate of the position that the principal function of the law should be to define exclusive property rights in natural resources so that the operation of markets could be triggered. Between 1971 and 1972, Charlie was the assistant legal counsel to the National Water Commission, and its final report, *Water Policies for the Future* (1973), is his most enduring scholarly legacy to the field.

Water Policies for the Future is the most comprehensive and forward-looking examination of water policy issues ever written and is even more relevant now than it was in 1972. Charlie's influence on the final report is pervasive. He was a forceful advocate of incorporating efficiency principles into water allocation. As he put it two decades ago, "[t]he fundamental message of the Commission's Report was that the days of subsidized agricultural water development are over, that existing supplies should be made subject to reallocation, and that reallocation should be effected through the mechanism of market transfers." The current debates about the future of western water allocation build on the themes sounded in the report.

*

PREFACE

This is the fourth edition of a casebook first published i𝑟
Charles J. Meyers and A. Dan Tarlock, *Water Resource Manage*
book was conceived by the late Charles J. Meyers, law professor ⌣
dinaire at the Texas, Columbia and Stanford Law Schools, in the la⌣
1960s. A second edition was prepared in 1980 mainly by Professor Tarlock, though Professor Meyers remained the guiding spirit behind the
book until he entered private practice in 1981. A tribute to Charlie pre-
cedes this Preface.

Water Resource Management was substantially revised in 1988 by
the three present authors. The first edition was prepared in the twilight
of the Reclamation Era. By contrast, the revision represented by the
third edition encompassed the elements of the remarkable transition from
the era of subsidized water development to an era of comprehensive management and reallocation of water resources for consumptive use, commodity production, evironmental protection, and community sustainability. This thoroughly revamped fourth edition emphasizes the integration
of these trends into the mainstream of water law.

Water law—more than other areas of law—is the product of specific
ecnomic and cultural circumstances. The legal, administrative and political institutions that have developed can only be understood in this context. The transition from the Reclamation Era to an era of management
and reallocation has been characterized by: the expanded assertion of
public rights in water; greater concern for efficient water management;
the federal government's role as regulator rather than developer; water
marketing, including proposals for interstate markets and exchanges;
mounting public concern over water pollution, especially of groundwater;
and a new recognition that surface waters and associated groundwater
play a crucial role in biodiversity maintenance. Furthermore, water is
increasingly understood as an integrating resource that links development and preservation demands. Water decisionmaking is becoming the
crucible for achieving equity as well as economic and ecological health in
resource use-essential goals for a sustainable society. We have attempted
to synthesize and incorporate these changing circumstances and forces
throughout the eight chapters of the fourth edition.

One of the endearing qualities of water law is that it enjoys a rich
history and literature. We believe that students benefit from an appreciation of this tradition and therefore include historical background throughout the book. We also introduce some of the scientific, technical and
economic aspects of water allocation and use, including the most current
available data. We have been selective in choosing from among the available materials for the fourth edition, however. A comprehensive bibliography of the field of water law and policy appears in Appendix B at the
end of the book for those who wish to explore the subject further.

We place a greater emphasis in this edition on statutory systems
than in prior editions. Plainly, in both riparian and prior appropriation
jurisdictions, water is allocated and administered according to statutes,

vii

generally providing for permits to represent water rights. While we believe that the subject should not be taught without reference to principles rooted in history, students will quickly realize that there is little practice any more under those principles apart from their embodiment in statutes. We have bolstered the materials on public interest issues under state and federal laws. An emphasis will also be detected on the importance and special difficulties of obtaining and using water by and for municipalities.

The first two editions of the book devoted a separate chapter to water pollution because the federal programs were new and students lacked familiarity with them. As environmental law became a basic law school course, and was taken by most students interested in natural resources, we dropped the separate chapter in the third edition and integrated pollution issues into several chapters to reflect the growing relationship between quantity and quality issues. The fourth edition retains this approach and strengthens the integration of water quantity and quality considerations.

New cases have been added to this edition and dated or prolix materials have been ruthlessly pruned. The past five years have produced fundamental changes in the politics of water allocation. Many of these changes are not yet reflected in the case law and thus significant new developments are captured by adding relevant textual material, notes of recent legislative activity, and scholarly commentary.

Many of the changes in the concept, content and organization of this edition were made in response to suggestions and constructive criticisms of our colleagues around the country. We are especially grateful for the suggestions, oral and written, of Professors Robert E. Beck, Michael C. Blumm, Harrison C. Dunning, Corwin W. Johnson, Ralph W. Johnson, John D. Leshy, George W. Pring, Mark S. Squillace, Albert W. Stone, and Charles F. Wilkinson. In several cases, these colleagues submitted excerpts or text revisions for which we are enormously grateful. While we have tried to follow faithfully their ideas and recommendations, not all were compatible with one another or with our basic concepts. Thus, we give them all credit for improving our work while we assume full blame for its deficiencies.

We have broadened the earlier editions' national orientation, reflecting the fact that water issues are not limited to the West's perceived scarcity. We believe that the book can be adapted to courses taught from the perspective of any region, humid or arid. Blocks of material can be included or omitted to suit the needs of the teacher. Cross-referencing facilitates presenting the chapters in a different order if the instructor so chooses.

Our profound expression of gratitude to the law student research team at the University of Colorado School of Law is well-deserved and heart-felt, yet inadequate to convey how important they were to us in preparation of the manuscript. Patricia Moore's excellent editing and quality control stand out prominently. Research, drafting, and long hours of proofreading were contributed by Kevin Clarke, Michael Connor, and

PREFACE

Erich Schwiesow. Bill Hugenberg, Suzanne Fairchild Carlson, and Patrick Teegarden all researched, collected materials, and worked on revisions of portions of the casebook. Ted Kowalski and Bart Miller assisted with the final editing.

We enjoyed the generous support of the Rocky Mountain Mineral Law Foundation through its scholarship and Grants Program. The Foundation's financial contribution was amply supplemented by Dean Gene R. Nichol of the University of Colorado School of Law and by Dean Richard Matasar of the IIT Chicago-Kent College of Law. We thank the Foundation and Deans Nichol and Matasar for their extraordinary assistance.

To us, water law is a fascinating blend of the history of human settlement of inhospitable areas, deep policy analysis and hard law. We hope that the students and teachers who do us the honor of using this book will find as much pleasure from these materials as we have found in preparing them and that they will share our love of this subject.

J.N.C.
D.H.G.
A.D.T.

Boulder, Colorado
May, 1993

*

ACKNOWLEDGMENTS

We have reproduced portions of the following publications and wish to express our appreciation to the copyright holders and others for permission to reprint them. Except as noted, permission was granted by the copyright holder.

Robert H. Abrams, *Replacing Riparianism in the Twenty-First Century*, 36 Wayne L.Rev. 93–98 (1989). Copyright © 1989 by the Wayne State University Law School.

William Ashworth, Nor Any Drop to Drink, 19–20, 25–26 (1982). Copyright © 1982 by William Ashworth.

Sarah F. Bates, David H. Getches, Lawrence J. MacDonnell & Charles F. Wilkinson, Searching Out the Headwaters: Change and Rediscovery in Western Water Policy 4–8 (1993). Copyright © 1993 by Island Press.

William Blomquist, Dividing the Waters: Governing Groundwater in Southern California 146–50 (1992). Copyright © 1992 by ICS Press.

F. Lee Brown & Helen M. Ingram, Water and Poverty in the Southwest: Conflict, Opportunity and Challenge 79–80 (1987). Copyright © 1987 by the Arizona Board of Regents. Reprinted with permission of the University of Arizona Press.

Conservation Foundation, America's Water: Current Trends and Emerging Issues 34–35, 42–43, 47–48 (1984). Copyright © 1984 by the Conservation Foundation.

Deborah A. de Lambert, Comment, *District Management for California Groundwater*, 11 Ecology L.Q. 373, 391–93 (1984). Copyright © 1991 by Ecology Law Quarterly.

Joseph W. Dellapenna, 1 Waters and Water Rights § 6.01(c) (1991 ed.). Copyright © 1991 by The Michie Company.

Tim De Young, *Some Thoughts of Governing Special Districts*, in Discussion Papers on Irrigation Water Supply Organizations 49–61 (Occasional Papers Series 1991). Copyright © 1991 by the Natural Resources Law Center, University of Colorado School of Law.

Harrison C. Dunning, *The "Physical" Solution in Water Law*, 57 U.Colo.L.Rev. 445 (1986). Copyright © 1986 by the University of Colorado Law Review, Inc. Reprinted with permission also from Harrison Dunning.

Mohamed T. El-Ashry & Diana C. Gibbons, *The West in Profile*, in Water and Arid Lands of the Western United States 12–14 (Mohamed T. El-Ashry & Diana C. Gibbons, eds., 1988). Copyright © 1988 by the Cambridge University Press.

Kenneth D. Frederick, ed., Scarce Water and Institutional Change 7–11 (1986). Copyright © 1986 Resources for the Future, Washington, D.C.

ACKNOWLEDGMENTS

Kenneth D. Frederick, Water Resources in America's Renewable Resources: Historical Trends and Current Challenges 66–67 (Kenneth D. Frederick & Roger A. Sedjo eds., 1991).

David H. Getches, *Competing Demands for the Colorado River*, 56 U.Colo.L.Rev. 413, 415–20 (1985). Copyright © 1985 by the University of Colorado Law Review, Inc.

David H. Getches, *From Ashkabad, To Wellton-Mohawk, To Los Angeles: The Drought in Water Policy*, 64 U.Colo.L.Rev. 523, 525, 548–52 (1993). Copyright © 1993 by the University of Colorado Law Review, Inc.

David H. Getches, Water Allocation During Drought in Arizona and Southern California: Legal and Institutional Responses 1–3 (Occasional Papers Series, January 1991). Copyright © 1991 by the Natural Resources Law Center, University of Colorado School of Law.

David H. Getches, *Water Planning: Untapped Opportunity for the Western States*, 9 J. of Energy L. & Pol'y 1, 18–25, 33–35 (1988). Copyright © 1988 by the Journal of Energy Law and Policy.

David H. Getches, Lawrence J. MacDonnell, & Teresa A. Rice, Controlling Water Use: The Unfinished Business of Water Quality Protection 91–120 (1991.) Copyright © 1991 by the Natural Resources Law Center, University of Colorado School of Law.

Eva Morreale Hanks, *The Law of Water in New Jersey*, 22 Rutgers L.Rev. 621, 627–32 (1968). Copyright © 1968 by Rutgers-The State University.

Jack Hirshleifer, James C. DeHaven & Jerome W. Milliman, Water Supply: Economics, Technology and Policy 36–42, 59–64 (1960). Copyright © 1960 by the RAND Corporation.

Lawrence J. MacDonnell, *Transferring Water Uses in the West*, 43 Okla.L.Rev. 119 (1990). Copyright © 1990 by Oklahoma Law Review.

John McInerney, *Natural Resource Economics: The Basic Analytical Principles in the Economics of Environmental and Natural Resources Policy*, 1976 J. of Agric. Econ. 30–40.

Frank E. Maloney, Sheldon J. Plager & Fletcher N. Baldwin, Water Law and Administration: The Florida Experience 172–73 (1968). Copyright © 1968 by the Trustees of Indiana University. Reprinted with permission of Indiana University Press and Sheldon J. Plager.

John R. Mather, Water Resources: Distribution, Use, and Management 8, 294–305 (1984). Copyright © 1984 by V. H. Winston & Sons, Inc.

Charles J. Meyers, *The Colorado River*, 19 Stan.L.Rev. 1, 39–43, 51–53 (1966). Copyright © 1966 by Charles J. Meyers.

Taylor O. Miller, Gary D. Weatherford, and John E. Thorson, The Salty Colorado 24–26, 30–31, 36–39, 41–45, 51–52, 65, 72–75, 77 (1986). Copyright © 1986 by the Conservation Foundation and the John Muir Institute.

ACKNOWLEDGMENTS

National Academy of Sciences, Water Transfers in the West: Efficiency, Equity, and the Environment 30–34, 38–39, 234–43, 257–59 (1992). Copyright © 1992 by the National Academy of Sciences. Reprinted with permission of the National Academy Press.

Mark Obmascik, *Soaked in Big Water Deal*, The Denver Post, July 20, 1992. Copyright © 1992 by The Denver Post.

Organization for Economic Cooperation and Development, State of the Environment 1991, 54 (1991). Copyright © 1991 by the Organization for Economic Cooperation and Development, Publications and Information Center.

Carol M. Rose, *Energy Efficiency in the Realignment of Common-Law Water Rights*, 19 J. Legal Studies 261, 273 (1990). Copyright © 1990 by the University of Chicago. All rights reserved.

Bonnie Colby Saliba & David B. Bush, Water Markets in Theory and Practice 1–33 (1987). Copyright © 1987 by Bonnie Colby. Published by Westview Press.

Joseph L. Sax, *The Constitution, Property Rights, and the Future of Water Law*, 61 U.Colo.L.Rev. 257 (1990). Copyright © 1990 by the University of Colorado Law Review, Inc.

George William Sherk, *Eastern Water Law: Trends in State Legislation*, 9 Va.Envtl.L.J. 287 (1990). Copyright © 1990 by the Virginia Environmental Law Journal Association.

Steven J. Shupe, *Water in Indian Country: From Paper Rights to a Managed Resource*, 57 U.Colo.L.Rev. 561, 577 (1986). Copyright © 1986 by the University of Colorado Law Review, Inc. Reprinted with permission also from Steven Shupe.

A. Dan Tarlock, *The Endangered Species Act and Western Water Rights*, 20 Land & Water L.Rev. 1 (1985). Copyright © 1985 by the University of Wyoming. Reprinted with permission of the Land & Water Law Review.

A. Dan Tarlock, *The Law of Equitable Apportionment Revisited, Updated and Restated*, 56 U.Colo.L.Rev. 381, 385–400 (1985). Copyright © 1985 by the University of Colorado Law Review, Inc.

A. Dan Tarlock, Law of Water Rights and Resources § 3.14 (1989). Copyright © 1993 by Clark Boardman Callaghan. Reprinted with permission. Original, printed in *Law of Water Rights & Resources*. 1–800–221–9428 for order information.

Frank J. Trelease, *New Water Legislation: Drafting for Development, Efficient Allocation and Environmental Protection*, 12 Land & Water L.Rev. 385–87, 409–16 (1977). Copyright © 1977 by the Land and Water Law Review. Reprinted with permission also from Mrs. Frank J. Trelease and George E. Radosevich.

Richard W. Wahl, Markets for Federal Water: Subsidies, Property Rights, and the Bureau of Reclamation 27–46 (1989). Copyright © 1989 by Resources for the Future.

ACKNOWLEDGMENTS

Charles F. Wilkinson, Crossing the Next Meridian 286–91 (1992). Copyright © 1992 by Island Press.

Charles F. Wilkinson, *The Headwaters of the Public Trust: Some Thoughts on the Source and Scope of the Traditional Doctrine*, 19 Envtl.L. 425, 428–31 (1989). Copyright © 1989 by Environmental Law.

World Resources Institute, 1992 Information Please Environmental Almanac 86, 100–02. Copyright © 1992 by World Resources Institute. Reprinted by permission of Houghton Mifflin Co. All rights reserved.

SUMMARY OF CONTENTS

TABLE OF CONTENTS

TABLE OF CONTENTS

TABLE OF CONTENTS

APPENDICES

TABLE OF CASES

Principal cases are in italic type. Non-principal cases are in roman type. References are to Pages.

xxvii

*

WATER RESOURCE MANAGEMENT

*

Chapter One

WATER LAW: AN OVERVIEW

This evening, as I write, the sun is going down, and the shadows are settling in the canyon. The vermilion gleams and roseate hues, blending with the green and gray tints, are slowly changing to somber brown above, and black shadows are creeping over them below; and now it is a dark portal to a region of gloom—the gateway through which we are to enter on our voyage of exploration tomorrow. What shall we find?

John Wesley Powell, The Exploration of the Colorado River 15 (1875, abridged ed. U. of Chicago Press, 1957).

Water has played an essential role in the opening and development of the North American continent. While colonial settlers primarily used water for navigation and transportation of goods, developments in agricultural irrigation and mining soon expanded the demand on our nation's water. For much of the twentieth century water development has been of pervasive importance. Billions of dollars, mostly federal, have been invested in multiple use projects that provide flood control, navigation, recreation, fish and wildlife, and hydroelectric power benefits as well as agricultural, municipal and industrial water supplies. These investments were essential to opening much of the West to habitability and economic viability. Public investment has also financed municipal water delivery and storage systems throughout the nation. Water facilities developed or expanded since the turn of the century serve virtually every corner of the country. As the nation has reached maturity, the need for building major new projects has declined.

The satisfaction of most of America's basic water development needs has coincided with a drastic decline in the availability of public capital. Furthermore, there is a growing national consciousness of the value of maintaining base flows in many waterways for pollution control and wildlife protection. Indeed, the public insists on preserving some waterways in their undeveloped condition for recreational purposes or simply to protect a natural heritage that includes some free-flowing streams, undammed canyons, pristine lakes, open shores, wild rivers, and native fish populations.

Strong public sentiment for environmental protection and political pressures for reducing government spending have led to new approaches to meeting the demands for water for population growth. Better management of water resources is becoming the focus of most water allocation institutions. Non-structural solutions to water supply problems such as reuse and conservation are less costly and less environmentally intrusive. In addition, protecting existing water qual-

1

ity and cleaning up tainted water sources free up supplies that would be "consumed" by pollution. Careful planning can prevent supply problems by predicting growth in demand and taking action to reallocate supplies, manage demand, and, where necessary, seek new sources of supply. Water law and policy operate to solve these problems.

The central issue of water resources law and management is not the allocation of a finite depleting supply, as it is with oil and gas, but rather a geographic and temporal mismatch of supply and demand. As the materials on pages 4–15, infra, show, areas of high municipal, agricultural, and industrial water demand often coincide with areas of low precipitation, particularly in the western and southwestern United States. A nearly pathological fear of drought has moved people in these areas to create water institutions that anticipate and avoid conflicts among competing demands in times of shortage. This has prevented major catastrophes during recent dry cycles in most of the arid regions. But increasingly serious water supply problems are ironically being felt in the humid eastern states where political inattention to water needs and decentralized allocation systems have allowed growth in demand to overtake available supplies.

In recent years, water quality and the protection and enhancement of environmental and amenity values have emerged as major water issues. Pollution of streams and lakes and contamination of groundwater render these sources less useful. Consequently, our legal institutions began to struggle with the task of integrating these concerns with systems that respect the existing rights and historic use patterns established in an earlier era. Legal systems for dealing with water quality bear little relationship to water allocation law. The former field was originally a minor area of tort law and is now dominated by federal laws; the latter is controlled by diverse state statutory and case law based primarily on the creation and protection of exclusive property rights.

There is an emerging awareness that the quality of water is linked to the quantity available for use. For example, contamination forecloses most uses of ground and surface water. The popular desire for clean water has led to a complex administrative structure to control waste disposal, pollution from municipal, agricultural, and industrial users, groundwater contamination, and the increasingly serious problem of unsafe hazardous waste storage and disposal. This structure remains largely separate from water allocation institutions.

Public uses for water—nominally a public resource—are increasingly drawn into competition with entrenched private uses. Water uses may be conveniently divided into instream (or "in situ") and offstream uses. Instream uses include transportation, hydroelectric power generation, recreation, fish and wildlife, and aesthetics. They are typically considered "public uses." Offstream uses include agricultural irrigation, and municipal, industrial, and domestic water supply, and more often than not they are subject to private rights.

There have always been tensions between private rights and public uses, as well as conflicts among private users. For example, farmers and ranchers contest municipalities and industries over scarce supplies. At another level, states argue amongst themselves and with the federal government for control of both interstate and intrastate waters. Indian tribes assert their rights as independent sovereigns and as beneficiaries of a "trust" relationship with the federal government. All these conflicts continue, but the public-private, instream-offstream conflicts are becoming especially heated. Meanwhile, many of the public-private clashes are being resolved through innovative market transactions.

The broad interests of the public to use water bodies (for navigation, recreation, or enjoyment of the amenity and ecological values of lakes and streams), as contrasted with the rights of individual or corporate land owners and water users, are creating burgeoning concerns for the law and opportunities for advocates.

To deal with conflicts among water users, three types of water law systems arose in the United States. The first of these, the riparian system of the eastern states, assigns rights to water use to land owners, and requires equal sharing among users in times of shortage. The appropriation system, dominant in the West, by contrast, allows the severance of water use rights from land ownership, and allocates available water in order of priority, so that senior appropriators may be satisfied during dry periods at the expense of juniors. Ten semi-arid states on either side of the arid intermountain West, however, use a hybrid system which contains elements of both appropriation and riparian law. These states initially adopted the common law but largely abandoned it to cope better with the problems of anticipated droughts and interbasin transfers. In these hybrid systems, with their built-in tension between the two underlying doctrines, the appropriation system generally predominates. Whichever underlying theoretical system may prevail, most states have departed from doctrine to establish systems of allocating rights to water use by permits issued by state water management agencies and the accompanying administrative process. Colorado is the sole western jurisdiction in which a permit system has not been imposed. The role of water management agencies in shaping the underlying doctrines will be explored in the chapters ahead.

In examining water law in its historical setting, the student should keep in mind that the values assigned to various water uses by society—and therefore by the courts—have changed over the past century and a half. Early legislators and judges had a narrower, more utilitarian view than would be generally acceptable today. As a result, legal protections for instream uses, aesthetic concerns, and public recreational values are relatively new.

The pioneering water developers—the nineteenth century canal companies, miners, and irrigators, and the twentieth century municipal and hydroelectric project builders—were great dreamers and doers. The less dramatic modern tasks of adjusting institutional responses to technological change, economic exigency, and evolving social values are nonetheless vitally important to the nation's future well-being.

As in the past, it is not overstatement to suggest that the law's handling of conflicts over water has been, and may continue to be a life and death matter. Evidence of mighty conflicts of the past can be found in the legal literature, from logging Maine's pine forests (see Dwinel v. Barnard, 28 Me. (15 Shep.) 554 (1848)), to making the thirsty desert of the Southwest bloom. At one time Arizona mobilized its National Guard to prevent the construction of Parker Dam on the Colorado River. See Arizona v. California, 292 U.S. 341 (1934). Small water rights also have been acquired and defended with zeal and intensity. The first reported water dispute in the Montana courts was a criminal case. A miner sought to assert as a defense to his prosecution for shooting another man the fact that the victim had cut off water running through a gulch that he had been using to work the mining claim. Territory of Montana v. Drennan, 1 Mont. 41 (1868). Indeed, many a water dispute, historical and modern, has been settled in the local cemetery.

Finally, it is worth stressing that water law has a history, lore, and romance of its own, and a well-documented one at that, as the bibliographical information in Appendix B, page 915, infra, shows.

A. THE WATER RESOURCE: SUPPLY AND DEMAND

1. Water Supply

Water is present in many different forms everywhere on earth. Most of the globe's surface, in fact, is covered with water. This water is not all available for human use, however, as most of it is tied up in non-potable forms as oceans (97.5% of the total water resource), glaciers and ice caps (1.8%) and in soil or rocks (0.6%). The remaining forms of water—in lakes, rivers, vegetation, and the atmosphere—contain less than 0.5% of the total. "Vast quantities of water are available on the earth but only tiny amounts are available in fresh water form in areas where a population needs to exist." John R. Mather, Water Resources: Distribution, Use, and Management 11 (1984).

The United States has copious water. Our renewable water supply in the lower forty-eight states is approximately 1,400 billion gallons per day (bgd), about fourteen times the national consumptive use of water. Our water supply problems arise, however, from unequal distribution of water throughout the country, as well as from changing demands of water users.

Figure 1.   Average annual precipitation in the United States

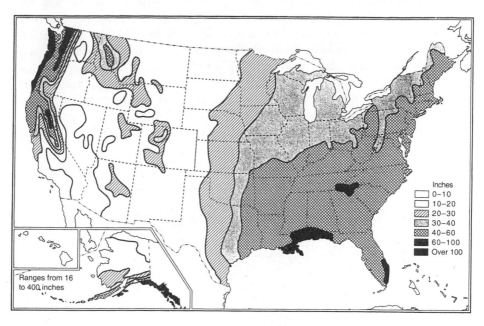

Source: U.S. Water Resources Council (1978, vol. 1).

Precipitation is the source of virtually all freshwater, and regional variations in climate accounts for much of the unequal distribution of our water.   As shown in Figure 1, rainfall is heaviest in the Pacific Northwest, southern Appalachian Mountains, and along the Gulf Coast. The western Great Plains and the Rocky Mountain areas, on the other hand, are the driest regions.   The average annual rainfall in the lower forty-eight states is thirty inches per year, with variations from less than four inches in parts of the Southwest to over 100 inches in coastal regions of the Pacific Northwest.   Some parts of Hawaii receive over 400 inches of rainfall annually.

Unequal geographic distribution of water is a worldwide phenomenon, but North America is much better situated than most other continents.   Furthermore, the effects are exacerbated in areas where the population creates demands disproportionate to supplies.   Worldwide runoff averages approximately 30,800 bgd, which greatly exceeds the estimated 2,030 bgd in worldwide demand.   However, on a continental basis, Asia with 59% of the world's population has only 29.4% of the water supply, and Africa with 10.4% of the world's population has 9.4% of the water supply.   James W. Moore, Balancing the Needs of Water Use 3 (1989).   The well-documented severe water shortage in Africa illustrates the impact of unequal regional distributions of water.

Water is not a static resource.   In economic terms, it is a "flowing," not a stock resource (some aquifers excepted).   Therefore, any description of its distribution must include its constant movement in the hydrologic cycle:

Water constantly circulates from the sea, to and through the atmosphere, to the land, and eventually returns to the sea by streamflow and to the atmosphere (by way of transpiration and evaporation) from the sea and land surfaces. This circulation pattern is termed the "hydrologic cycle" and is often described as a gigantic distillation machine. This movement of water and moisture is driven by energy from the sun and involves a number of interrelated processes, such as precipitation, evaporation, surface runoff, and groundwater flow; it also involves a variety of geochemical and biological processes.

Figure 2.   Hydrologic cycle

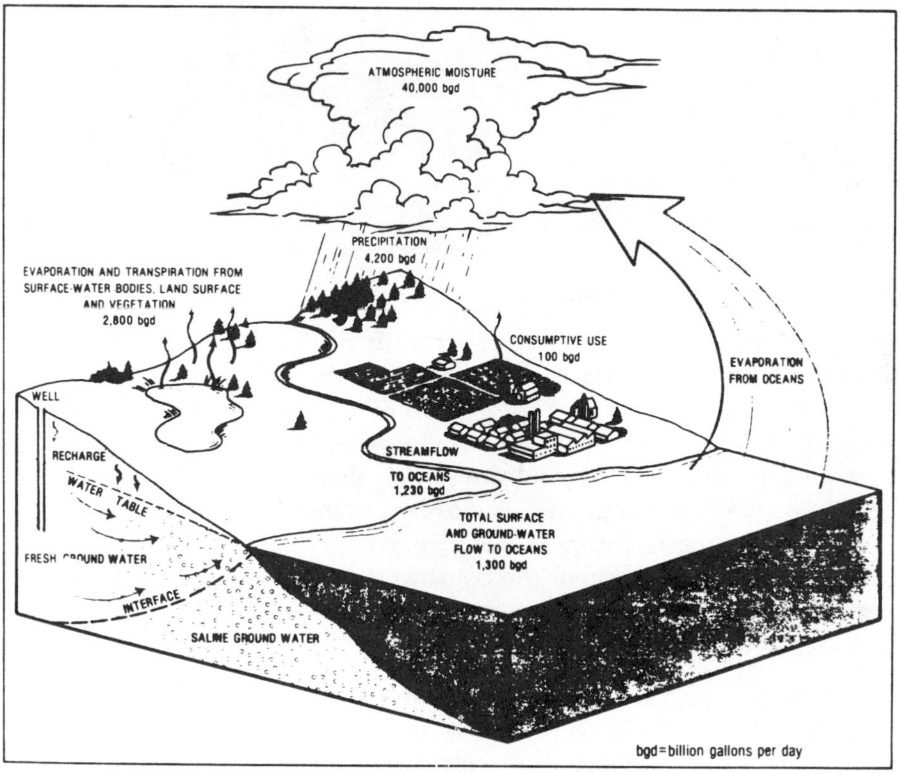

ATMOSPHERIC MOISTURE
40,000 bgd

PRECIPITATION
4,200 bgd

EVAPORATION AND TRANSPIRATION FROM
SURFACE-WATER BODIES, LAND SURFACE
AND VEGETATION
2,800 bgd

CONSUMPTIVE USE
100 bgd

EVAPORATION
FROM OCEANS

WELL

RECHARGE

WATER TABLE

STREAMFLOW
TO OCEANS
1,230 bgd

FRESH GROUND WATER

TOTAL SURFACE
AND GROUND-WATER
FLOW TO OCEANS
1,300 bgd

INTERFACE

SALINE GROUND WATER

bgd=billion gallons per day

Source: U.S.G.S. National Water Summary 1983—Hydrologic Events and Issues 9 (1983).

The magnitude of the quantities of water transported by the hydrologic cycle is illustrated by the gross water budget of the coterminous United States, as shown in [Figure 2.] Of the approximately 40,000 billion gallons per day (bgd) of water vapor that pass over the conterminous United States, about 4,200 bgd falls as precipitation. About two-thirds of this precipitation (2,800 bgd) is returned to the atmosphere through evapotranspiration—loss of water from a land area through transpiration of plants and evaporation from the soil and water surfaces. The remaining 1,400 bgd, depending upon the properties of the land surface, soils, and vegetation, discharges directly to streams, lakes, or to the ocean, or seeps into the ground, where it goes into storage and subsequently discharges to surface water bodies. During its journey to the ocean, some of this water is withdrawn from aquifers and streams for various uses by man, returned to its source (usually to streams), and withdrawn again several times. These uses and reuses of water involve the total withdrawal of approximately 380 bgd of freshwater, of which about 100 bgd is consumptively used. The total amount of water that returns to the ocean is about 1,300 bgd.

United States Geological Survey, National Water Summary 8 (1983).

2. Water Demand

WORLD RESOURCES INSTITUTE, THE 1992 INFORMATION PLEASE ENVIRONMENTAL ALMANAC
100–02 (1992).

Consider the "typical" North American family of four. In the bathroom alone, this family uses an average of 188 gallons of water each day. Elsewhere in the house, the same family uses 35 gallons per day doing the laundry, 15 for dishwashing, and 5 in the utility sink. All told, the family uses 243 gallons of water per day, not including water for cooking or for outdoor uses such as watering the lawn and washing the family automobile.

In addition to these direct, domain uses, we use water indirectly, in the production of many common products. At the service station, for instance, every gallon of gasoline pumped into the family car takes 7 to 25 gallons of water to manufacture. In 1985, industrial and mining activities used the equivalent of 30,800 million gallons of water per day for each resident of the United States. Some other industrial water uses are:

- one pound of steel takes 35 gallons of water to produce;
- one Sunday newspaper takes 280 gallons to produce;
- and one new car takes 100,000 gallons to produce.

Agriculture in the United States uses about 600 gallons per capita per day. To produce just one egg, for instance, a farmer uses 40 gallons of water.

Other sectors also use enormous amounts of water. In 1985, the thermo-electric power industry in the United States used 131,000 million gallons of water per day to feed and cool its turbines.

* * *

Total annual domestic water use in Canada amounted to 1,960 cubic yards (1,500 cubic meters) per person in 1990. The average U.S. resident used 2,825 cubic yards (2,161 cubic meters) per person. In Europe, water use is approximately one-half that of Canada.

Figure 3 shows a comparison of different countries with respect to annual water withdrawal (from both ground and surface water sources) per capita. The United States has the highest withdrawal rate at over 2000 m^3 (7.6 million gallons) per person annually.

Figure 3.   Water Withdrawal

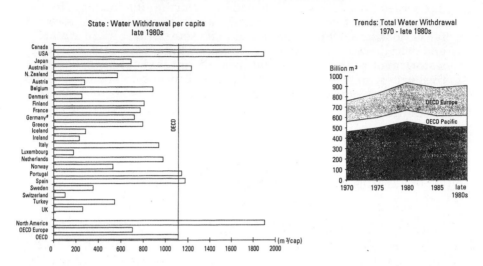

State : Water Withdrawal per capita late 1980s

Trends: Total Water Withdrawal 1970 - late 1980s

ote: a) Includes western Germany only.

Source: Organization for Economic Cooperation and Development, The State of the Environment 54 (1991).

Demand for water varies over time, and is affected by such diverse factors as population concentration, changing demands for products, public attitudes toward conservation and environmental protection, development of new power and energy sources, the costs of obtaining alternative supplies of water, and the level of public financial subsidies for water use.   Projections of water demand are notoriously inaccurate, in part because of the impossibility of predicting these factors and their impact on water demand.   Thus, water resource managers usually predict future demands by examining past and current uses of water and then applying population and economic forecasts.

Water use can be consumptive or nonconsumptive.   Nonconsumptive uses are generally those that occur without removing water from the stream, (e.g. outdoor recreation such as fishing and boating, hydroelectric power generation, navigation, fish and wildlife habitat, ecosystem maintenance, waste assimilation, and conveyance of water to downstream points of diversion).   Some water diverted from the stream is also used essentially for nonconsumptive purposes, such as cooling, washing, conveyance of other water, hydraulic power, and sewage dilution.

Table 1.   Offstream Water Use for the Lower Forty-eight States, 1985

(billions of gallons per day)

Category of Use	Withdrawals		Consumptive use	
	Fresh	Saline	Fresh	Saline
Domestic	23.9		5.6	
Commercial	6.8		1.2	
Irrigation	135.9		73.7	
Livestock	4.3		2.4	
Industrial	27.9	3.5	4.2	1.0
Mining	2.7	0.8	0.7	0.3
Thermoelectric	130.4	53.0	4.3	1.8
Public use and losses	3.8			
Total	336.3 *	57.3	92.1	3.1

* The figures do not add to total due to independent rounding.

Source: Wayne B. Solley, Charles F. Merk, and Robert Pierce, **Estimated Use of Water in the United States in 1985,** U.S. Geological Survey Circular 1004 (1988).

MOHAMED T. EL-ASHRY & DIANA C. GIBBONS, *THE WEST IN PROFILE*, IN WATER AND ARID LANDS OF THE WESTERN UNITED STATES 12–14

(Mohamed T. El–Ashry & Diana C. Gibbons, eds., 1988).

Consumptive use for irrigation is the largest single water use in the United States, often reaching 90 percent of total water consumption in western states.

Agricultural water use has the highest consumption-to-withdrawal ratio, which means that relatively more of the water diverted from streams or aquifers evaporates from the soil or transpires from crops instead of returning to the sources for reuse. This ratio averages about 60 percent, compared to 25 percent in municipal use and 0–25 percent in industrial use.

Nationally, irrigation is a significant factor in the success and size of the agricultural economy. Although irrigated farms make up only one-seventh of all agricultural lands, they contribute more than one-fourth of the total value of crop production. Irrigated acreage increased from about 4 million in 1890 to nearly 60 million in 1977, and about 50 million of these acres are located in the 17 western states. Although the total acreage under irrigation in the United States is still growing, this growth is concentrated in southeastern states and elsewhere.

The most important determinant of the total number of irrigated acres is undoubtedly the overall crop price index. When national or international supply and demand cause the prices of food and fiber to fall, acreage decreases as well. Thus, unless crop prices rise substantially, water demand for agriculture in the West is not expected to grow. In fact, Bureau of Reclamation data show a sustained decline in irrigated acres in the West since 1979 (with the exception of 1982) and an increase since 1966 in land used for purposes other than crop production (for example, residential, commercial, and industrial purposes). In many areas, irrigated agriculture is threatened by urban encroachment. In metropolitan Phoenix the trend is evident, and on the front range of Colorado a string of cities from Colorado Springs to Fort Collins has advanced into formerly agricultural and grazing lands.

* * *

Much of the water supplied to irrigators originates in state or federal (Bureau of Reclamation) water projects subsidized by taxpayers. When combined with use-it-or-lose-it provisions in state water law and restrictions on use and on the size and timing of return flow, these subsidies are a disincentive to conserving surface water. As long as water is cheap, it will be used inefficiently. And if farmers cannot consider the opportunity cost of retaining water for irrigation, perhaps because resale or leasing is prohibited, they have no reason to make sure that the economic return to the water used for growing crops approaches that in alternative uses.

An exception to the norm of low water prices is the use of groundwater for irrigation. Farmers who rely on groundwater merely pump the water as needed, subject to state laws on pumping rates and well spacing. Because energy costs comprise the bulk of water-procurement costs for these farms, the rise in energy prices since 1974 has eroded profit margins and forced some farmers to conserve water. In many places, the conservation effect of higher energy prices is compounded by the need to go to ever-greater pumping depths as underlying aquifers are mined. As the costs of pumping groundwater have become prohibitive in places, most notably in parts of Texas and central California, the productivity of water use has increased. More efficient pumps and irrigation systems have become economical to install, and management practices have been adapted to the increased water scarcity. Rising water costs have also triggered shifts to higher-value crops and to crops that need less water to grow. When water costs make irrigated crop production less profitable, irrigated acreage finally reverts back to dryland farming, or it is abandoned. In the High Plains of Texas overlying the Ogallala aquifer and in other isolated areas of the West, this shift is already occurring.

WILLIAM ASHWORTH, NOR ANY DROP TO DRINK
19–20, 25–26 (1982).

Overall, those states west of the hundredth meridian grew at a rate two and one half times faster than their Eastern cousins. And since the West is so much drier than the East, this means that the actual per-capita amount of rain which fell in the vicinity of each U.S. citizen decreased over this period at a rate far faster than the population increase alone would indicate. We have water; but we are rapidly and methodically moving ourselves away from it. And in the process, we are creating severe and sometimes unsolvable problems. Our Sun Belt cities grow; but it is rain, not sun, that we must have in order to provide water.

As the population has shifted westward, so has the agriculture that supports it. As late as 1920, a full fifty percent of all U.S. crops were grown east of the tier of states—North Dakota to Texas—that contains the hundredth meridian. Today, that amount has shrunk to less than thirty-four percent. But because crops cannot grow on the West's tiny rainfall, this westward shift in agriculture has led to a veritable explosion in irrigation. Between 1940 and 1980, irrigated acreage in the West more than doubled, with some areas—western Kansas, for example—showing increases of as much as three thousand percent.

All this, of course, has put a tremendous overburden on the West's scanty water resources. But not all water distribution problems are found in the West; even the rain-rich East is showing signs of the kinds of stress caused by not having enough water in the right places. The reason, here, is not too little water for a given locality, but too many people.

Despite the westward movement, most of our population still lives in the East, clumped into cities that have simply outgrown their ability to efficiently supply water at the rates their citizens demand it. New York City's use figure, for example, is 190 gallons per person per day; with a population of 7.4 million and a rainfall of forty-two inches a year, this means that even if the city could collect and utilize every drop that fell—instead of the one drop in three that is closer to reality—it would still need a catchment basin ten miles wide and nearly one hundred miles long merely to keep up with daily demand. Other cities in the East and the South—Boston, Philadelphia, Washington, Atlanta—are experiencing similar difficulties. The problems caused by the concentration of water demand can lead to other problems, many of them severe. New York's financial crisis has been caused at least partially by the capital demands made on the city's government by the need to maintain and expand the water system. Groundwater withdrawal from beneath Orlando, Florida, has opened great caverns in the earth, and Orlando has begun collapsing in upon itself; Houston, with the same problem but different underlying geology, is slowly sinking into the sea.

――――

Two water supply problems are related to changing demands: limited surface water supplies and groundwater overdraft. The extent of surface water supplies in the Midwest and Southwest is shown in Figure 4. Depletion of low natural streamflows can adversely affect instream water uses. The Lower Colorado River, for example, has an average flow of 1,550 million gallons per day (mgd), although the optimal flow for fish habitats in the river is 6,864 mgd.

Figure 4. Areas Affected by Inadequate Water Supply*

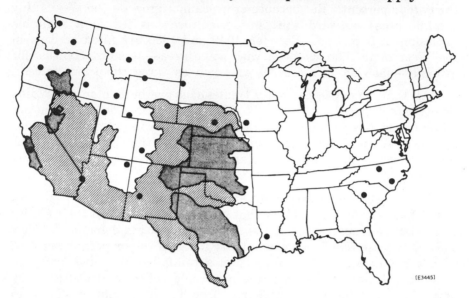

[E3445]

* Hatched areas show where streamflows are 70% depleted in average or dry years; dotted areas show where streamflows are 70% depleted in dry years only. Black dots indicate places with inadequate supply to support conflicting offstream and instream uses.

Figure 5.   Areas Affected by Significant Groundwater Overdraft *

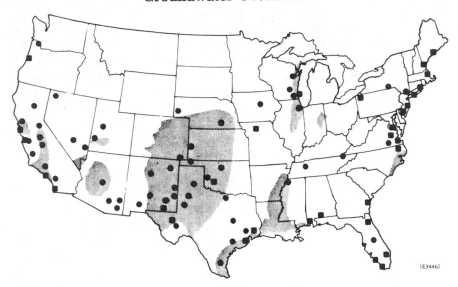

[E3446]

* Black dots indicate areas of declining groundwater levels; black squares indicate places where saline water intrusion into fresh water is occurring.

Source: John R. Mather, Water Resources: Distribution, Use. and Management 386 (1984)

Figure 5 shows the second problem related to our changing water demand, groundwater overdraft.

Groundwater volumes for the nation as a whole equal about 50 years of surface runoff (well in excess of the total capacity of all of the lakes and reservoirs of the nation including the Great Lakes). Yet, in certain areas, especially in the Great Plains from southern Nebraska to western Texas, in parts of central Arizona and California, and along the southern portion of the Mississippi River valley, significant groundwater overpumping is occurring even now and will continue into the future (Fig. [5]). Eight of the 106 water resources subregions have critical overpumping problems at the present time while 30 more have moderate problems and 22 others have minor overpumping problems. Thus, more than half of the water resources subregions are experiencing some sort of over-pumping problems at the present which may become more serious in the future as demand for fresh water increases.

John R. Mather, Water Resources: Distribution, Use and Management 385 (1984).

KENNETH D. FREDERICK, WATER RESOURCES, IN AMERICA'S RENEWABLE RESOURCES: HISTORICAL TRENDS AND CURRENT CHALLENGES

66–67 (Kenneth D. Frederick & Roger A. Sedjo eds. 1991).

Meeting Future Water Demands

Increasing affluence, leisure time, and population tend to increase the demand for water and water services. Development and adoption of more water-efficient technologies can temper or even reverse the growth in demand for agricultural, domestic, commercial, industrial, and other withdrawal uses. Indeed, the decline in the quantities of water withdrawn for irrigation and thermoelectric uses from 1980 to 1985 probably is attributable in part to improvements in water-use efficiency. But technology is not likely to offer any suitable and comparable substitutes for such instream services as fish and wildlife habitat, water-based recreation, and the amenities of natural waterways. As the search for clean sources of energy intensifies, hydroelectric power becomes more attractive relative to many of the alternative sources of power. Increasing incomes as well as a growing appreciation for the potential values that can be provided by improving streamflows in some areas are likely to increase demands for these instream services faster than the rate of population growth.

Actual water use, of course, will be limited by available supplies and how they are allocated among competing uses. Effective supplies are influenced by investments to control flows, by uses that alter the quality or long-term availability of water, by technological changes, and by management of supply systems. Investments in new dams and reservoirs can increase effective supplies for offstream use, but the costs of these supplies are high relative to the prices people are accustomed to paying for water, and these investments are likely to have adverse effects on instream uses. Interbasin transfers can move water from low-value to high-value uses, but they do not add to total supplies. Moreover, the institutional obstacles to such transfers are increasing as potential exporters become more aware of the environmental and other opportunity costs associated with the loss of water. Groundwater supplies are being mined in a number of areas, and the potential for contamination threatens the utility of both groundwater and surface water in many locations.

Another element that may affect the balance of future water supplies and demand is greenhouse warming, which is associated with increasing atmospheric concentrations of carbon dioxide and other trace gases such as nitrous oxide, methane, chlorofluorocarbons, and tropospheric ozone. If the globe does indeed get warmer, the hydrologic cycle will accelerate. Globally, this will mean increased rates of evaporation and increased precipitation. A warming of 2 to 5 degrees Celsius (the range expected to result from an equivalent doubling of carbon dioxide) is expected to increase average global precipitation and evaporation by 7 to 15 percent. Regional impacts are likely to include changes in precipitation and runoff patterns, evapotranspiration rates, and the frequency and intensity of storms. The impact of higher temperatures on annual runoff is likely to be adverse in arid areas; the impact on seasonal streamflow patterns will be greatest in areas such as northern California, where precipitation currently comes largely in the form of winter snowfall and runoff comes largely from spring and summer snowmelt.

The possibility of greenhouse warming adds uncertainty to the future supply and demand for water. The hydrologic impact on any particular region is unknown, but could be severe because of increased hydrologic uncertainty and the fact that the existing infrastructure, management practices, and patterns of use are predicated on the existing climate and will almost certainly be less well adapted to a new hydrologic regime. Additional infrastructure has been the traditional means of responding to water problems, and this approach might help prevent climate-induced flooding or shortages. Such investments would be costly, however, and, in the absence of a clearer idea of the nature of climatic changes, may be of little value.

The high costs of developing additional storage and the large uncertainties regarding regional hydrologic changes suggest the importance of exploring both the technological alternatives for increasing the quantity and quality of available supplies and the opportunities for increased flexibility in managing and allocating limited supplies. Lower-cost sources of supply, improved management of existing supplies, and greater flexibility in the allocation of limited water supplies in response to changing conditions are desirable goals even in the absence of climate change; the uncertainty associated with the possibility of a greenhouse warming gives added weight to these objectives.

NOTE: WATER MEASUREMENT

Water is measured by different units, depending on the purpose: storage capacity, consumption, streamflow rates or rainfall determination. For example, the basic unit of storage capacity measurement or consumption is the "acre-foot." One acre-foot is enough water to cover one acre of land to a depth of one foot, and is equivalent to 325,851 gallons. This is about enough water to supply the domestic needs of five people for one year at a rate of 180 gallons per person per day. Water flowing in a stream is measured by "cubic feet per second" (cfs); one cubic foot per second equals 7.48 gallons of water per second. Rainfall is measured by inches of precipitation, and often is expressed as inches per year. One inch of rain over an acre of land delivers 27,200 gallons of water. Large-scale descriptions of water supply frequently use the terms "million gallons per day" (mgd) or "billion gallons per day" (bgd). Finally, there is an older measurement of water flow encountered infrequently, the "miner's inch" or "statutory inch." Used by California miners in the 1800s, the miner's inch is measured by allowing water to flow at a specified pressure through an orifice of a specified size. The amount of water represented by a miner's inch varies among states from 0.02 cfs to 0.028 cfs. A table showing common water measurement equivalents and metric conversion factors is found in Appendix A, page 914), infra.

3. Water Quality

WORLD RESOURCES INSTITUTE, THE 1992 INFORMATION PLEASE ENVIRONMENTAL ALMANAC
86–95, 98–99 (1992).

Roots of Our Water Problem

When compared to that of other industrialized countries, U.S. and Canadian water use per person is high [see Figure 3].

But burgeoning urban populations and farm use are draining water supplies, thus increasing the value of water. All across the continent, water availability is becoming an issue. Well drillers must dig ever deeper to find water in the Midwest. New Yorkers are building bigger reservoirs to meet expanding needs. In Florida, seawater has encroached upon the fresh groundwater that is a major resource for its cities. Massive amounts of chemical fertilizers and pesticides used in that state's citrus groves have seeped down into these underground freshwater reserves.

A new generation of water pollutants has created the second major issue. Toxic materials threaten water supplies once considered pure if they contained no disease-carrying bacteria or viruses. But the U.S. Environmental Protection Agency (EPA) now considers toxic pollution in drinking water supplies to be one of the greatest environmental hazards in America. EPA, mandated by Congress to enforce the nation's drinking water laws and protect the public from contaminated water supplies, has been criticized for failure to enforce required water quality standards and for not reporting to the public the failure of municipal water companies to meet standards.

In 1974, passage of the U.S. Safe Drinking Water Act extended federal standards to most community water systems. But water quality was found to be worse than previously thought. In the 1980s, scientists found "new" toxic materials throughout the water system, even in underground supplies. A study by the National Wildlife Federation found that community water systems serving more than 40 million people had violated federal water quality standards over 100,-000 times between October 1986 and September 1987. Only 2 percent of the violators had to face any government action or fines.

High levels of bacteria, which can cause immediate and often severe health effects, have been eliminated from municipal drinking water supplies. Other pollutants originate when pesticides are applied to farmland; others come from manufacturing and mining. Not until 1986 did legislators amend the Safe Drinking Water Act to regulate these newly recognized contaminants.

Water shortages and the discovery of pervasive pollutants have sparked a new concern for water conservation and protection. The focus now is on using less water, recycling industrial water, and finding ways to make agriculture more water-efficient. Citizen groups have put notices on storm drains to raise public awareness and prevent thoughtless dumping of oil and other materials into the water supply. Bottled drinking water has surged in popularity as worried consumers seek to protect themselves from potentially fouled municipal supplies.

* * *

Sources of Water Pollution

Water pollution sources include municipal (home and business), industrial, nonpoint (which simply means the source is broad and cannot be easily pinpointed as can a wastewater pipe draining into a stream, for example), and land dredging and filling practices, which stir up sediments.

One primary nonpoint source of water pollution is pesticide, fertilizer, and other chemical runoff from farmland. Forestry practices, construction, and mining are also important contributors to nonpoint pollution. According to EPA, nonpoint sources are responsible for 65 percent of pollution in degraded rivers and for 76 percent of pollution in degraded lakes [see Figure 6]. In estuaries, nonpoint pollution makes up 45 percent of the problem.

Figure [6] Nonpoint Pollution Sources Affecting Streams

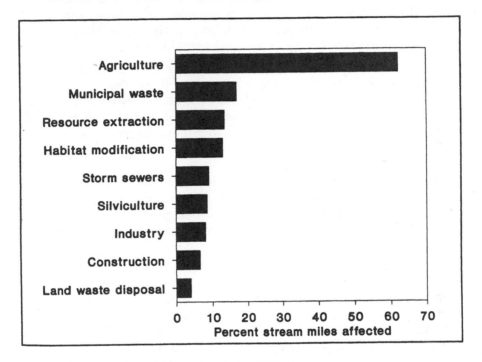

Source: U.S. Environmental Protection Agency, 1990.

Endangered Groundwater

* * *

The same pollutants that foul surface waters make their way underground by many routes. In addition to seepage of pesticides, herbicides, and toxic wastes from trash dumped illegally into rivers, ditches, and lakes, as many as 10,000 underground gasoline tanks in the United States may be leaking petroleum products into the soil. Other contaminants include salts leached from the soil by agricultural irrigation and de-icing salts used on roads and airport runways in colder regions. Because these sources are located beneath the Earth's surface, their problems are harder to treat than are problems with surface water pollution. Prevention of further pollution is often the only realistic policy.

* * *

Dealing With Foul Water

The first water-pollution issue faced by most societies has been waterborne diseases caused by untreated sewage dumped into lakes and rivers. In North America, we have spent millions of dollars on sewage treatment plants to eliminate this public health problem. The 1991 cholera epidemic in South America was a reminder that sewage and water treatment are, first of all, essential to our health, not an environmental luxury.

In the 1960s and 1970s, scientists realized that enormous amounts of phosphates from laundry detergents were damaging lakes and rivers. These common household products contained chemicals that spurred aquatic plant growth, or the process of eutrophication.

A lake undergoing eutrophication contains a high amount of nutrients that spur growth of algae to such a point that they absorb available oxygen and close out sunlight, both necessary for other water species to exist. When phosphates were dumped into surface waters on a massive scale, huge natural systems were endangered.

The Great, Troubled Lakes

In the early 1970s, Lake Erie and Lake Ontario were so overgrown with algae that oxygen shortages killed entire populations of fish. Befouled municipal water supplies also tasted and smelled bad. This was a critical problem for the Great Lakes, which contain roughly 20 percent of the world's fresh surface water.

The Great Lakes have suffered from development, industry, and dam building along the shores, and from the dumping of toxic industrial compounds. Even in lake regions more distant from factories and urban areas, a significant amount of pollutants have drifted on air currents and settled. According to EPA, air currents bring pesticides, including DDT, to the Great Lakes from as far away as Central America. Industrial chemicals and metals, including mercury and cadmium, also find their way to the lakes via the atmosphere. Approximately 90 percent of the polychlorinated biphenyls (PCBs) in Lake Superior drift there on air currents.

The International Joint Commission (IJC), a U.S./Canadian advisory group responsible for the boundary waters, has been at work since 1973. According to the IJC, 362 toxic chemicals affect the lake ecosystems—not only the water, but the plants, fish, and mammals that live there as well. At least 35 million people live in the Great Lakes region, and many are warned not to eat the local fish.

During the past 10 years, improved wastewater treatment plants and bans on phosphate detergents have decreased phosphate output significantly. Phosphorus dumped into Lake Erie dropped from roughly 18,500 metric tons (20,400 tons) in 1976 to 11,100 metric tons (12,200 tons) in 1986. Lake Ontario phosphorus inputs fell from 12,700 metric tons (18,700 tons) to 9,600 metric tons (10,600 tons) over the same period. These drops were largely a result of better municipal water treatment, according to the U.S. Council on Environmental Quality.

Despite these drops, both lakes still suffer from phosphate loadings that come from nonpoint sources, especially fertilizer runoff from farms.

* * *

Danger in a Drinking Glass

Since the Clean Water Act was passed in 1972, the standards for drinking-water quality have improved dramatically. EPA has provided funds to more than 5,000 treatment facilities for improvements. The act requires secondary water treatment to remove 85 percent of major pollutants and suspended particles in used water and sewage. Some plants achieve even better results. In 1972, 85 million people in the United States had access to water that had undergone secondary treatment. By 1988, that number had increased to 143 million people.

In 1990, the EPA completed a five-year survey of pesticides in drinking-water wells. The first country-wide study of its kind, this National Survey of Pesticides included tests for pesticides and nitrates at levels EPA considers a health concern in more than 1,300 wells, some from each state. EPA identified over 1,000 possible drinking-water contaminants, including inorganic substances such as cadmium, mercury, selenium, and arsenic; and organic materials such as paint thinners, glues, dyes, and pesticides. Many of these chemicals can cause cancer, as well as nerve damage, kidney disease, and other diseases, including rare effects such as the "blue baby syndrome" in newborns, which is caused by nitrates and nitrites.

In general, EPA reported that the percentage of wells containing pesticides was low, but rural domestic wells, in particular, were often affected by one or more pesticides. Nitrates and nitrites were more commonly present in all types of wells sampled, at levels EPA considers a health concern.

A 1986 amendment to the 1974 Safe Drinking Water Act directed EPA to prepare a list of drinking-water standards for maximum allowable contaminant levels. The list includes pesticides and herbicides, nine inorganic substances, and radium and overall radioactivity. Secondary standards are set for nontoxic materials that affect taste and tooth color and cause pipe corrosion.

Many substances are in the process of being listed and are being tested for their presence in municipal water systems. In the summer of 1991, four pesticides were listed. Regulations on testing for radon in water supplies are expected sometime in 1993.

B. ECONOMIC ISSUES

Water is a scarce resource that must be allocated among competing uses. Because water is essential to sustain life and welfare, issues of fair distribution arise. Water allocation issues range from the criteria for the assignment and transfer of property rights to the standards by which public investment in water development and flood control projects and water quality and environmental protection regulation should be evaluated. The following excerpts raise some of these fundamental economic issues.

JOHN A. McINERNEY, NATURAL RESOURCE ECONOMICS: THE
BASIC ANALYTICAL PRINCIPLES IN THE ECONOMICS OF
ENVIRONMENTAL AND NATURAL RESOURCES POLICY
IN ECONOMICS OF ENVIRONMENTAL AND
NATURAL RESOURCES POLICY

30–40 (J.A. Butlin ed. 1981).

The field of natural resource economics

* * *

If economics is to be functional as an applied discipline in this area,
to serve as a guide to policy choices rather than as an exercise in
intellectual tidiness, it needs to identify problem situations and group
them into types which share some common thread in economic terms.
The commonality between problems of land use, wildlife conservation,
energy supplies and pollution is not meaningfully revealed by appealing
to their connection with some natural processes which originated before
man. It can, however, be found if we start from the idea of natural
resources having a fixed initial availability—i.e. they exist as *stocks*.
Clearly every resource exists as a given stock at a particular point in
time, but a natural resource has one of two main distinguishing
features. Either

    1. The maximum stock of the resource that could be utilised
is totally fixed, having been predetermined before man commenced
any economic activity; or

    2. To the extent that the available stock changes, it does so at
a "natural" biological or biochemical rate; this rate may not be
constant over time, but biological or biochemical factors will prescribe a maximum rate of change (certainly with respect to increases in stock) that is outside of man's control.

The first characteristic is shared by resources such as the land
area, metal ores, fossil fuels, scenic amenity, and other resources of a
geophysical nature. The second characteristic is exemplified by forests,
fish stocks, natural fauna and flora, fresh (as opposed to polluted) air
and water supplies, and the other resources of a biological nature.
Human labour, too, might seem to fit into this second category, but
from the economic (and social) point of view the problems of labour
utilisation and natural resource utilisation are very different. It is to
the economic aspects, therefore, that we must turn to finally delimit
the natural resource area. Because of their stock characteristics, the
essence of natural resources as a branch of applied economics is the
central problem of *intertemporal allocation*—deciding how much of the
existing stock of resource should be designated for use (consumption)
now, and how much should be left *in situ* for the future. Although
many other considerations may have to be introduced it is this focal
problem, and the analytical techniques necessary to handle it, that
provide the basis for "natural resource economics" as a distinct area of
study. We may therefore define this area as *the study of society's
choices in the intertemporal allocation of resources (or resource services)*

derived from stocks which are either fixed or are changing at "natural" rates. This definition illustrates the three key features of the subject which serve to distinguish it from the study of other economic problems:

    1. The problems are to be viewed at a societal as opposed to an individual level, and therefore attention is focused largely on social choice rather than the private choice that occupies so much of microeconomic theory.

    2. Time considerations are of central importance to the analytical frameworks employed; there can be no entirely static theory of natural resource economics (although static aspects do enter in the form of the allocation of resources amongst competing uses at any one point in time—the bread and butter of traditional microeconomics).

    3. The constraints on social choice are imposed by factors which are ultimately outside the control of man, for either the maximal resource stocks are immutably fixed, or change at rates which are not man-made.

From all this it is evident that the social choices to be made are fundamentally choices about the rate at which resource stocks are to be depleted or "used up"—i.e. they are consumption choices. Alternatively, since in choosing how much of a given stock to use one is by the same token deciding how much should be left untouched, we may equally view the situation as one of determining the optimal conservation policy. This emphasizes that "conservation" is controlled utilisation, a dynamic concept, as distinct from "preservation", which is static.

    McInerney analyzes natural resources allocation using an intertemporal choice approach—how much of the resource stock to consume now and how much to retain for the future. This model reflects the level of time preference, which is the rate at which future consumption will be sacrificed for current consumption. Economists have devoted much effort to establish economics as a "positive science." This requires the separation of "hard" efficiency from "soft" equity issues. Value-laden issues such as inter-generational justice make many economists uncomfortable. The value quagmire is usually avoided by the artificial condition of superimposing a societal indifference map (between current and future consumption) on the consumption possibility frontier (total amount of the natural resource stock available for consumption). In this way, the optimal resource use is determined. If a price is established that reflects the *real* cost to society of current consumption, then the operation of resource policy can be left to the market to decide—as adequate resource retention for the future will be brought about on its own with no need for artificial restrictions of resource demand.

JACK HIRSHLEIFER, JAMES C. DeHAVEN AND JEROME
W. MILLIMAN, WATER SUPPLY: ECONOMICS,
TECHNOLOGY AND POLICY
36–42 (1960).

Granted that competition for the use of existing supplies of a resource like water exists, what principles or criteria are available to enable us to conclude that a given proposed division or allocation of the supplies is desirable or undesirable? And, second, what institutions or processes of decision will tend to lead to good allocations and so should be favored as against possible procedures or practices that tend to lead to defective allocations? One branch of human study has been devoted to the exploration of these questions—the science or field of learning known as economics. It is evidently not immediately clear to all, however, just how economic principles are to be applied to water-resource problems. In fact, perusal of the public press reveals that this ignorance is not limited to any special or backward group but is prevalent among legislators, government executives, scientists, engineers, businessmen, and public-spirited citizens when they come to deal with water-resource problems. Among the criteria bandied about in public discussions on the allocation of water supplies are such phrases as "fair shares," "reasonable requirements," "needs," "beneficial uses," etc.; in some cases these can only be regarded as noises with emotive content used as substitutes for rational analysis.

1. *Efficiency Effects and Distribution Effects*

The economic effects of any proposed policy can be divided under two headings: the effects on *efficiency* and the effects on *distribution*. Efficiency questions relate to the size of the pie available; distribution questions, to who gets what share. More formally, we can think of the pie as representing the national income or community income. Someone may propose reducing income taxes in the upper brackets on the ground that the high rates now effective there seriously deter initiative and enterprise and so reduce national income; he is making an efficiency argument that the present taxes reduce the size of the national pie. Someone else may point out that such a change will help large taxpayers as against small—a distributional consideration. In the field of water supply it is possible to find examples in the West where a certain amount of water could produce goods and services more highly valued in the market place if it were shifted from agricultural to industrial uses—this is an efficiency argument. On the other hand, this shift may hurt the interests of farmers or of their customers, employees, or suppliers while helping industrial interests—all distributional considerations.

Now economics can say something of the distributional consequences of alternative possible policies, but what it says stops short of any assertion that any man's interests or well-being can be preferred to another's. The fact that economics has nothing to say on such matters does not mean, of course, that nothing important can be said. Ethics as a branch of philosophy and the entire structure of law (which to some extent embodies or applies ethical thought) are devoted to the consideration of the rights and duties of man against man, and many propositions arising out of such thought may well command almost unanimous consent in our society. Ethics may say that no one should be permitted to starve, and law that no one should be deprived of property without due process, but these are propositions outside economics.

Most of what the existing body of economic thought has to say concerns the *efficiency* effects—the effects on size of the pie—of alternative possible policies or institutional arrangements. There is, of course, a sense in which enlarging the size of the pie may be said to be good for the eaters as a group irrespective of the distribution of shares. This sense turns upon the *possibility* of dividing the enlarged pie in such a way that everybody benefits. If such a distribution of the gain is not adopted, there may or may not be good reason for the failure to do so, but the reason is presumed to be legal or ethical and so outside the sphere of economic analysis. Economics alone cannot give us answers to policy problems; it can show us how to attain efficiency and what the distributional consequences are of attaining efficiency in alternative possible ways, but it does not tell us how to distribute the gain from increased efficiency.

It is true that it is often the case that the efficiency and distributional consequences of a proposed change cannot be so neatly separated. Any particular change in the direction of efficiency will involve a certain intrinsic distribution of gains and losses, and in practice it may be unfeasible to effect a redistribution such that everyone gains. Nevertheless, we feel that a presumption in favor of changes increasing the national income is justified, while conceding that this presumption can be defeated if there are irreparable distributive consequences that are sufficiently offensive on ethical or legal grounds.

Nothing is more common in public discussions of economic affairs, however, than a consideration of distributive effects of any change to the utter exclusion of the efficiency question. The agricultural price-support policy, for example, is usually and fruitlessly discussed pro and con in terms of the interests of farmers versus the interests of consumers and taxpayers. But a policy of expensive storage of perishing commodities to hold them out of human consumption is, obviously, inefficient. Concentration upon the efficiency question might readily suggest solutions that would increase the national income and would help consumers and taxpayers a great deal while hurting farmers relatively little or not at all.

2. *The Principle of Equimarginal Value in Use*

Suppose for simplicity we first assume that the stock or the annual flow of a resource like water becomes available without cost, the only problem being to allocate the supply among the competing uses and users who desire it. Economic theory asserts one almost universal principle which characterizes a good or efficient allocation—the principle we shall here call "equimarginal value in use." The *value in use* of any unit of water, whether purchased by an ultimate or an intermediate consumer, is essentially measured by the *maximum* amount of resources (dollars) which the consumer would be willing to pay for that unit. *Marginal* value in use is the value in use of the last unit consumed, and for any consumer marginal value in use will ordinarily decline as the quantity of water consumed in any period increases. The principle, then, is that the resource should be so allocated that all consumers or users derive equal value in use from the marginal unit consumed or used.

An example of the process of equating marginal values in use may be more illuminating than an abstract proof that this principle characterizes efficient allocations. Suppose that my neighbor and I are both given rights (ration coupons, perhaps) to certain volumes of water, and we wish to consider whether it might be in our mutual interest to trade these water rights between us for other resources—we might as well say for dollars, which we can think of as a generalized claim on other resources like clam chowders, baby-sitting services, acres of land, or yachts. My neighbor might be a farmer and I an industrialist, or we might both be just retired homeowners; to make the quantities interesting, we will assume that both individuals are rather big operators. Now suppose that the last acre-foot of my periodic entitlement is worth $10 at most to me, but my neighbor would be willing to pay anything up to $50 for that right—a disparity of $40 between our marginal values in use. Evidently, if I transfer the right to him for any compensation between $10 and $50, we will both be better off in terms of our own preferences; in other words, the size of the pie measured in terms of the satisfactions yielded to both of us has increased. (Note, however, that the question of whether the compensation should be $11 or $49 is purely distributional.)

But this is not yet the end. Having given up 1 acre-foot, I will not be inclined to give up another on such easy terms—water has become scarcer for me, so that an additional amount given up means foregoing a somewhat more urgent use. Conversely, my neighbor is no longer quite so anxious to buy as he was before, since his most urgent need for one more acre-foot has been satisfied, and an additional unit must be applied to less urgent uses. That is, for both of us marginal values in use decline with increases of consumption (or, equivalently, marginal value in use rises if consumption is cut back). Suppose he is now willing to pay up to $45, while I am willing to sell for anything over $15. Evidently, we should trade again. Obviously, the stopping point is where the last (or marginal) unit of water is valued equally (in terms of the greatest amount of dollars we would be willing to pay) by the two of us, based on the use we can make of or the benefit we can derive from the last or marginal unit. At this point no more mutually advantageous trades are available—efficiency has been attained.

Generalizing from the illustration just given, we may say that the principle of equimarginal value in use asserts that an efficient allocation of water has been attained when no mutually advantageous exchanges are possible between any pair of claimants, which can only mean that each claimant values his last or marginal unit of water equally with the others, measured in terms of the quantity of other resources (or dollars) that he is willing to trade for an additional unit of water.

What institutional arrangements are available for achieving water allocations that meet the principle of equimarginal value in use? Our example suggests that rationing out rights to the available supply will tend to lead to an efficient result if trading of the ration coupons is freely permitted; this is true so long as it can be assumed that third parties are unaffected by the trades. More generally, any such vesting of property rights, whether originally administrative, inherited, or purchased, will tend to an efficient solution if trading is permitted. (The question of the basis underlying the original vesting of rights is a serious and important one, but it is a distributional question.) A rather important practical result is derived from this conclusion if we put the argument another way: however rights are vested, we are effectively *preventing* efficiency from being attained if the law forbids free trading of those rights. Thus, if our ration coupons are not transferable, efficiency can be achieved only if the original distribution of rights was so nicely calculated that equimarginal value in use prevailed to begin with and that thenceforth no forces operated to change these values in use. As a practical matter, these conditions could never be satisfied. Nevertheless, legal limitations on the owner's ability to sell or otherwise transfer vested water rights are very common. While at times valid justification at least in part may exist for such limitations (one example is where third parties are injured by such transfers), it seems often to be the case that these prohibitions simply inflict a loss upon all for no justifiable reason. * * *

It is important to note here that the market price of water rights or ration coupons, if these can be freely traded, will tend to settle at (and so to measure) the marginal value in use of the consumers in the market. Any consumer who found himself with so many coupons that the marginal value in use to him was less than market price would be trying to sell some of his rights, while anyone with marginal value in use greater than market price would be seeking to buy. The process of trading equates marginal value in use to all, and the going market price measures this value. This proposition is of very broad validity, being in no way restricted to the commodity water. It is true, technical qualifications aside, that market price measures marginal value in use to its consumers for any commodity in which free trading is permitted and perfect rights can be conveyed.

Another possible institutional device for allocating water supplies of a community would be to establish, say, a municipal water-supply enterprise which would sell water, the customers being free to take any amount desired at the price set. The principle of equimarginal value in use then, setting aside possible complications, indicates a certain pattern of pricing: the price should be equal for all and at such a level that the customers in the aggregate use up all the supply. The reason for this pattern being the best is the same as that discussed earlier: if one individual had the privilege of buying units of water for $10 when another had to pay $50, mutually advantageous trading could take place if the water (or rights to it) could be transferred. If trading possibilities are ruled out, the marginal value in use would be $10 for the favored customer and $50 for the other—the former is taking so much in terms of his needs or desires that he is employing the marginal unit of water for very low-value purposes, while high-value uses are being deprived because water is so scarce to the other customer. The efficiency effects of trading can be achieved simply by setting the price to the two customers equal at such a level that the combined demands will take the supply in hand. Since the customer is permitted to purchase any desired amount, he will continue to buy additional units so long as the marginal value in use to him exceeds the price he must pay, marginal value in use being defined in terms of the price he is willing to pay for an additional unit. Evidently, he will stop purchasing where marginal value in use equals the price—and so, if the price is equal to all customers, marginal value in use will be equal to all. Then no mutually advantageous trading will be possible, so that we have achieved an efficient allocation of the water resource.

Note that there will be a distributional consequence of the removal of a privilege to buy water at a preferential price—the former holder of the privilege will lose as compared with all others. The attainment of efficiency in the new situation means that it is *possible* to insure that everyone is better off.[8] But whether it is or is not desirable to provide the compensation required to balance the loss of the formerly preferred customers is a distributional question.[9]

Our discussion of the principle of equimarginal value in use has led to two rules of behavior necessary if efficiency is to be achieved in different institutional contexts: (1) If rights to water are vested as property, there should be no restrictions on the purchase and sale of such rights, so long as third parties are unaffected. (2) If water is being sold, the price should be equal to all customers. This second rule was derived, however, under a special assumption that the water became available without cost. More generally, there will be costs incurred in the acquisition and transport of water supplies to customers; taking costs into account requires a second principle for pricing of water in addition to the principle of equimarginal value in use.

3.   *The Principle of Marginal-Cost Pricing*

In our previous discussion we assumed that a certain volume or flow of water became available without cost, the problem being to distribute just that amount among the potential customers. Normally,

---

8. Following up the example above, suppose that the common price is set at $30. Then every unit no longer purchased by the preference customer had a marginal value in use to him less than $30 (but more than the price he was previously paying, $10). That same unit must have a marginal value in use to its new purchaser of more than $30. Evidently, for each such unit there is an increase in the marginal value in use as a result of the transfer, and this increase can be divided among the preference customer, the non-preference customer, and the water-supply enterprise so that all gain.

9. From the distributional point of view, the sale of vested rights automatically insures that no one loses (since otherwise he would not participate in a voluntary exchange) in the process of attaining efficiency. The elimination of special purchase privileges, on the other hand, does necessarily involve redistribution. Even in the former case, though, the question naturally arises as to the fairness of the original vesting of rights.

there will not be such a definite fixed amount but rather a situation in which another unit could always be made available by expending more resources to acquire and transport it, that is, at a certain additional or marginal cost. The question of where to stop in increasing the supplies made available is then added to the question just discussed of how to arrange for the allocation of the supplies in hand at any moment of time.

From the argument developed earlier about the allocation of a certain given supply, we can infer that, whatever the price may be, it should be equal to all users (since otherwise employments with higher marginal values in use are being foregone in favor of employments with lower values). Suppose that at a certain moment of time this price is $30 per unit. Then, if the community as a whole can acquire and transport another unit of water for, say, $20, it would clearly be desirable to do so; in fact, any of the individual customers to whom the unit of water is worth $30 would be happy to pay the $20 cost, and none of the other members of the community is made worse off thereby. We may say that, on efficiency grounds, additional units should be made available so long as any members of the community are willing to pay the additional or marginal costs incurred. To meet the criterion of equimarginal value in use, however, the price should be made equal for all customers. So the combined rule is to make the price equal to the marginal cost and equal for all customers.

One important practical consideration is that, because of differing locations, use patterns, types of service, etc., the marginal costs of serving different customers will vary. We will discuss these matters in detail in a later chapter, but at this point it is of some interest to know in principle how this problem should be handled. The correct solution is to arrange matters so that for each class of customers (where the classes are so grouped that all customers *within* any single class can be served under identical cost conditions) the prices should be the same and equal to marginal cost. *Between* classes, however, prices should differ, and the difference should be precisely the difference in marginal costs involved in serving the two.

Consider, for example, a situation in which there are two customers, identical in all respects except that one can be served at a marginal cost of $10 per unit and the other at $40—perhaps because the latter has a hilltop location and requires pumped rather than gravity service. If they are both charged $10, the community will be expending $40 in resources to supply a marginal unit which the latter customer values at $10; if they both are charged $40, the former customer would be happy to lay out the $10 it costs to bring him another unit. The principle of equimarginal value in use which dictates equal prices was based on the assumption that costless transfers could take place between customers, but in this case any transfer from the gravity to the pumped customer involves a cost of $30. Another way to look at the matter is to say that the commodity provided is not the same: the customer who requires pumped water is demanding a more costly commodity than the gravity customer.

Where water is sold to customers, therefore, the principles we have developed indicate that customers served under identical cost conditions should be charged equal prices and that the commodity should be supplied and priced in such a way that the price for each class of service should equal the marginal cost of serving that class. Where marginal costs differ, therefore, prices should differ similarly.

4. Allocation With Complementary Uses

The analysis above was based entirely upon the assumption that demands for water are competitive. While the competition of different uses for water is the most important fact of life which needs to be appreciated, it is true that certain uses are complementary rather than competitive. For example, suppose that a certain quantum of water may be diverted from a river for irrigation, after which we may assume that it is lost to ocean or atmosphere—or, alternatively, the water may be allowed to flow in the riverbed so as to be of value first for hydropower and then for industrial uses downstream. Here the power and industrial demands are complementary to each other, but jointly they are in competition with the use of the water for irrigation.

Our simple rules of equimarginal value in use and marginal-cost pricing are valid among uses that are competitive. Where demands are complementary instead, it is necessary to *add* the marginal values in use of the members of the complementary group to determine a joint marginal value in use for comparison with the marginal values in use of other, competitive, demands or with marginal cost. Thus in our example above water should be divided between the agricultural and the allied hydropower and industrial uses in such a way that the marginal value in use for irrigation equals the *sum* of the marginal values in the power and industrial uses. Or, if we are considering procurement of new water for, or sale of water to, the power-industrial combination, the principle is to equate marginal cost to the sum of the marginal values in use of the two allied uses.

BONNIE COLBY SALIBA AND DAVID B. BUSH, WATER
MARKETS IN THEORY AND PRACTICE

1–33 (1987).

* * *

Desirable Characteristics of Allocation Processes

When water becomes economically scarce, conflicts over access begin to develop and a water allocation process of some kind must evolve. Water is said to be economically scarce when there is no longer enough available to allow all users to have as much as they want without giving up something else of value in order to obtain it. Where water is abundant, there is no reason for anyone to pay to obtain it since more can be used without giving up something else and there is little reason to develop rules for water use and allocation. However, water is economically scarce in areas of the West where undeveloped water supplies and unappropriated water rights are no longer readily available. Decisions must therefore be made about who will have access to water and under what conditions.

* * * Howe et al.[1] outline six characteristics desirable in water allocation processes:

1. There should be flexibility so as to allow water to be shifted in location, season and purpose of use in response to changing social and economic conditions.

2. There should be secure expectations of water availability for established right holders, giving water users a basis for making long-term investment and planning decisions.

3. Opportunity costs associated with water use and transfer must be accounted for by water right holders so that their decisions are based on a complete assessment of costs and benefits. Opportunity costs are the stream of net benefits that are foregone when one resource use alternative is chosen over other alternatives.

4. Collective values related to water must be incorporated into the allocation process so that water use and transfer decisions reflect not only private interests but also broader social values.

5. Predictability of the allocation process helps water users know what to expect and to adjust gradually to changes. Prevailing requirements (the "rules of the game") should be clear and not subject to unanticipated changes.

6. Fairness requires that uncompensated costs must not be imposed on third parties and the public, and that water transfers are noncompulsory.

How Does Market Allocation Compare?

Howe et al. have argued that market processes meet the above six criteria better than alternative allocation processes—administrative or judicial reassignment of water rights, for instance. They note that markets guarantee flexibility and security of water rights since all rights holders are permitted to participate in the market but none are required to do so. The opportunity to buy and sell forces rights holders to consider water's opportunity cost. Transactions are fair in the sense that buyers and sellers will only participate if they believe they have something to gain. Markets allocate economically scarce water resources by compelling buyers to evaluate the benefits of acquiring additional quantities of water at the expense of foregoing something else of value.

Reliance on market processes is consistent with the belief that individuals are the best judges of their own well-being and have the right to make economic decisions in pursuit of their own self-interest.

1. Charles W. Howe, Dennis R. Schurmeier, and W. Douglass Shaw, *Innovative Approaches to Water Allocation: The Po-* *tential for Water Markets,* 22 Water Resources Research 438–445 (1986).

Markets disperse the capacity to make resource allocation decisions among individuals who control resources. In a "free" market, resource ownership is primarily vested in private individuals and firms and the role of government is limited to facilitating individual decision-making through clarification and enforcement of property rights and contractual agreements.

Individual writers have displayed a wide range of opinions about the appropriateness of the market as a water allocation mechanism. Howe et al. recognize the inherent weaknesses of market processes but suggest ways in which these weaknesses can be strengthened. Tregarthen asserts that there is general agreement among economists that the market is capable of allocating water rights, and that the market is constrained by rules that limit its efficiency because jurists and policy-makers don't perceive the virtues of an unfettered market which are so apparent to economists. Quinn notes that very few water transfers resemble a "pure" market transaction in which water is treated like other routinely exchanged commodities and that in those situations which do approach the market paradigm, serious implementation issues have had to be addressed and overcome. Nunn et al. argue that even though rural-to-urban market transfers may appear economically efficient and involve willing sellers, there are significant hidden costs and social impacts not adequately reflected in market transactions. Brown and Ingram emphasize the social consequences of market transfers, quoting a member of the Tohono O'odham tribe on the leasing of tribal water rights. ". . . [M]oney," he said, "is just spent and the people are left with nothing. With water, there is something in the future." [8] To appreciate this wide spectrum of opinion on market transfers, it is important to understand the competitive market model for resource allocation and then to explore how actual water market processes differ from this model.

* * *

A perfectly functioning market would ensure that transfers occur automatically whenever the net benefits from a transfer are positive. Beneficial reallocations take place when a change in demand stimulates a change in marginal values. Under the competitive market model, when marginal values are not equal among water users, gains from an exchange are possible and a transfer between willing buyers and sellers will bring marginal values back into equilibrium.

Three conditions must be satisfied for a buyer and seller to consummate a water transfer:

1. The buyer must expect the returns from the water rights purchase (which may be contributions to some production process, investment returns or returns to real estate development) to exceed all costs associated with the purchase including the price paid to the seller, water storage, treatment and conveyance costs, and legal costs to implement the transfer.

---

8. The tribal reservation is adjacent to the City of Tucson and has been the subject of large scale land and water development proposals.

2. The seller must receive a price offer that equals or exceeds the return he gives up and that covers any costs he has incurred in transferring the water. A farmer, for instance, must consider the net returns to water in irrigation, any decreases in the value of his land, improvements and equipment due to reduced water available for irrigation, and expected appreciation in the value of the water right over time.

3. The buyer must view a market purchase of water rights as an economically attractive method of obtaining water relative to other possibilities—such as contracting for public project water or hooking up to a water service organization.

These conditions can be summarized in the following two inequalities:

Buyer's Returns —Buyer's Costs Associated with Transfer	>	Returns Foregone by Seller	+	Seller's Costs Associated with Transfer
Buyer's Costs Associated with Transfer	<	Costs of Alternative Means of Obtaining Water Supplies		

Use of these conditions to evaluate a particular proposed transfer requires that all returns and costs be expressed in comparable units, such as discounted present value.[15]

The description of the market process thus far has assumed fixed water supplies. A competitive market could also, hypothetically, ensure that an efficient quantity of water is provided. Economic efficiency requires that another unit of water be supplied whenever the cost of supplying it is less than the benefits generated by supplying it, and only then. This implies that the optimal quantity is that for which the marginal cost of supplying an additional increment of water equals exactly the marginal value of that additional increment. For quantities less than the optimum, benefits of supply expansion exceed the costs, while for quantities greater than the optimum, water supplies are too expensive at the margin and this results in net losses. Profit-maximizing suppliers of water would respond to increases in the marginal value of water by providing more water, up to the quantity where marginal costs rise as high as marginal value. The costs of supplying an additional unit of water can be expressed as a marginal cost function which indicates the change in the total cost of providing water resulting from an incremental change in the quantity of water supplied.

* * *

To summarize, a competitive market creates and maintains production, consumption and exchange patterns that cannot be improved upon

---

15. The costs and returns of a water transfer typically are spread over a number of years. In order to determine whether returns outweigh costs, the stream of costs and returns over time must be reduced to a single number. The present value concept explicitly recognizes the time value of money by converting a stream of payments over time into the current worth of that stream of payments at a particular interest (or discount) rate.

by any alternative arrangement given current technology, preferences and wealth distribution.

Deviations From the Competitive Market Model

Water markets, along with markets for many goods and services, are not perfectly competitive and deviate significantly from the model just described. These deviations, often referred to as market failure, will be discussed in four broad categories which are briefly defined in this chapter. * * * A fifth category, equity and collective values, will also be introduced although it is related to the distributional impacts rather than the economic efficiency of market water transfers, and so is not typically considered a market failure in the economics literature.

External Effects of Market Activities

When water use and transfer decisions have impacts on individuals who were not party to the decision process or transfer negotiations, some values are affected that are not considered in buyers' and sellers' decisions. These third-party effects are termed "externalities." They occur because property rights in water are difficult to completely specify and make exclusive—the mobile nature of water makes third-party impacts almost inevitable. When water use and transfer decisions involve externalities, prices no longer convey accurate information about opportunity costs. In particular, market transactions fail to account for costs imposed on third-parties and thus market prices fail to reflect these costs.

Public Goods Characteristics of Water Resources

Some water uses can provide benefits to more than one individual simultaneously, a characteristic called nonrivalry or joint consumption. It may also be difficult to limit benefits received to those who pay for them, a characteristic called nonexcludability. The benefits generated by water use for urban greenbelts and parks and the aesthetic and recreation value of water on public lands are both nonrival and nonexcludable. Since the market allocates goods by excluding those who will not pay the going price, the nonexcludability characteristic means that market prices cannot effectively allocate water for these uses. To further complicate matters, even if exclusion were possible, to exclude individuals from the benefits of nonrival goods would reduce the total value that these water uses can generate. Uses of water which have public good characteristics cannot be efficiently allocated through market processes, either because it is impractical to charge a price (due to nonexcludability) or because it is not desirable to exclude individuals who benefit from the water use at zero cost to others (due to nonrivalry).

Imperfect Competition

When individual buyers or sellers can influence market prices, a market is characterized as imperfectly competitive. Under these circumstances, prices may no longer reflect the marginal value of water in alternative uses and may not provide market signals that result in efficient water use and transfer. Imperfect competition can arise for a number of reasons, two of which are relevant to this discussion. First, because supply or distribution costs typically decrease on a per acre-foot basis as the quantity of water provided by a particular organization increases, larger providers may undercut smaller providers resulting in a small number of water suppliers or distributors who have power over price. The second reason, often related to the first, is public policies which affect the number of prospective water providers. Public policies often result in only one water service company or one irrigation project serving an area. If these organizations participate in market transfers, their control over local water resources may influence market outcomes.

Risk, Uncertainty and Imperfect Information

The efficiency of competitive markets assumes accurate information is available on water quality, availability, and costs of supply over time so that individuals may decide how much supply uncertainty is acceptable to them and at what price. Opportunities for redistributing risk exist when some water users are willing to pay more than others to protect themselves against supply shortfalls. The consequences of water shortages for a city may be more serious than the consequences of water shortages for an irrigator. A market potentially could distribute the risks of supply shortfalls between those willing to bear some risks if they are compensated for doing so—irrigators, for example—and those willing to pay to protect themselves from supply uncertainty—cities or industrial users. Examples of risk sharing in water markets include city purchases of options to use irrigation water rights in drought years. Markets to redistribute risk typically are incompletely developed due to uncertainty about the nature of the risk and asymmetric information which could allow parties which have special information on the nature of the risk to take advantage of any risk allocation process.

Equity and Conflict Resolution

Policymakers may intervene in market allocation processes in pursuit of objectives such as redistribution of economic gains from water use, settlement of water right conflicts, revenue generation to repay water project costs, public control over strategic water resources and enhancement of specific interest groups' objectives. Public policies can affect the efficiency of market processes. Public policies which affect the cost of water to specific users may impair the ability of the market price system to reflect accurately opportunity costs and to induce efficient water use. An example is the longstanding federal policy of subsidizing irrigators. Providing water to irrigators at less than the marginal cost of supplying that water prevents farmers from accounting for the full opportunity costs of irrigation water use. As a result, marginal values of water in irrigation may be less than the marginal costs of providing irrigation water and may also be less than water's marginal value in alternative uses.

The Potential for Inefficiency in Market Transfers

While the competitive market model has a number of attractive features, both the nature of real world markets, with the imperfections described, and the nature of water resources suggest that water markets will not necessarily ensure efficient use and transfer of water. Young summarizes characteristics of water itself which make it difficult and costly for market processes to efficiently allocate water. Since water is highly mobile (it flows, evapotranspires and seeps), it is difficult to define and measure property rights in water. Supply can be highly variable across seasons, years and locations, and water quality varies as well. The diversity of uses to which water can be put, along with the mobility of water, create interdependencies among water users. Many off-stream uses of surface water, such as irrigation, return a proportion of water diverted back to the stream system and these return flows are used by downstream users. Transfer of a water right can change these return flow patterns and affect water availability for downstream users. Water has instream values related to recreation, fish and wildlife, and aesthetics. Instream and offstream water values come into conflict when water is diverted at locations and in seasons for which instream values are high.

* * *

Summary

Competitive markets have many desirable attributes but the interdependencies and public goods characteristics associated with water resources imply that a perfectly competitive market is not a feasible water allocation process.

C. WATER AND THE LAW

THE CONSERVATION FOUNDATION, AMERICA'S WATER:
CURRENT TRENDS AND EMERGING ISSUES

34–35, 42–43, 47, 48 (1984).

Many experts agree that most water problems do not result primarily from physical limitations or technical inadequacies. Water shortages, while growing in number and seriousness, are still fairly unusual. And, certainly, technical means are available for dealing with most contamination problems—at least of surface water. But, as in the case of energy, water problems could be compounded as a result of imprudent and misguided human choices. Such choices typically are shaped by market imperfections and by unwise government policies, including narrow-purpose programs, long-established subsidies, and inappropriate legal constraints. Because many of today's water crises stem largely from government policies and human desires and habits rather than physical or technological limitations, crises over water often are susceptible to, and prevented by, changes in the ways legal, political, economic, and social institutions deal with water. The real question is whether the institutional adjustments necessary to respond to conditions of increased scarcity can be made before it is too late.

Such changes, necessary as they may be, generate bitter conflict. Farmers, urbanites, industrialists, professional and sport fishers, environmentalists, and officials of different states all find themselves competing for water, the purity and availability of which suddenly carry a high price. Water administrators and legislators accustomed to distributing largess to appreciative constituencies now find that the limited availability of both water and money forces decisions that outrage various parties. In short, water allocation and treatment programs developed under conditions of surplus and subsidy must adapt to conditions of mounting shortages and heated competition.

Water problems, obviously, are most likely to be noticed when they become tangible—be they manifested as groundwater pollution in New Jersey, flooding along the Colorado River, groundwater depletion in Illinois, or the drying up of the Everglades Swamp in Florida. These situations may worsen, and others, less pressing now, are likely to erupt. But underlying all these specific problems are some generic issues relating to water use and management in the United States. Three of the most fundamental issues are: For what purposes are supplies of water to be used? Who should decide how to allocate water? Who should pay for water investments?

SCARCE WATER AND INSTITUTIONAL CHANGE
7–11 (Kenneth D. Frederick ed. 1986).

Water Law

Water is not treated like any other resource. The states reserve the power and prerogative to establish the institutions for allocating all the waters within their boundaries not encumbered by federal law or interstate compact. The states grant water use rights based on either a common law doctrine that calls for all users to cut back in time of shortage or a system in which the earliest users have the most senior rights. In almost all cases, water is treated as a free commodity; charges are not made for extracting water from surface or groundwater sources, but only for the costs of moving the water. The rights to the water, however, are often constrained in ways that limit or at least raise doubts about the legality of transfers to other uses and users.

The earliest state laws controlling surface waters were based on the common law doctrine of riparian rights, which grants the owner of land adjacent to a water body the right to use the water. Riparian rights are inseparable from the land and are constrained to uses that are "reasonable" and do not unduly inconvenience other riparian owners. There is no priority of use, so all riparian owners must share in curtailing use in time of shortage. Riparian doctrine still underlies the water codes of almost all the relatively water-abundant eastern states.

In regions where streams are less numerous and their flows smaller and less reliable, extensive development required diverting water beyond riparian lands with greater assurance of availability. Consequently, the seventeen western states adopted the doctrine of prior appropriation as the basis of their water laws. Under this doctrine, water is allocated according to the principle of "first in time, first in right." Thus, the holders of senior water rights have priority over all subsequently acquired rights, and the full burden of any water shortage is borne by the holders of the most junior rights.

Appropriative rights eliminate a major obstacle to water transfers and markets by breaking the link between water and land. However, a variety of legal provisions in states using the appropriation doctrine inhibit the creation of well-defined, transferable property rights in water. Appropriative rights are acquired by diverting water from a stream and putting it to some beneficial use; the right originates only at the point of diversion and is contingent upon continued beneficial use. The acquired right can be sold or transferred, but the right is limited to use (not ownership) of the water, and there may be restrictions as to how and where it can be used. Twelve western states specify a ranked preference of use that allows preferred uses (municipal and domestic first, often followed by agriculture) to supersede water rights destined for less-preferred uses in time of scarcity. And the right to transfer water to other uses and locations is complicated by the fact that return flows are public property, freed for appropriation by downstream users.

State laws and institutions guiding the allocation and use of water have evolved over time in response to new conditions. However, * * * changes enabling institutions to deal efficiently with water scarcity have lagged well behind need. Most of the laws and institutions remain more appropriate for an era when water was in actuality as well as in law a free resource. These provisions served their regions reasonably well when new demands could be met by developing new supplies. But their shortcomings are apparent when there is need to apportion existing supplies among alternative uses or respond to short-term shortages.

FRANK J. TRELEASE, NEW WATER LEGISLATION: DRAFTING FOR DEVELOPMENT, EFFICIENT ALLOCATION AND ENVIRONMENTAL PROTECTION

12 Land & Water L.Rev. 385–87, 409–16 (1977).

The Need for New Laws

In today's rapidly changing world many water lawyers find themselves faced with a task that puts them to a challenging test. Each an expert in the application and administration of an existing system of water law, some are called upon to write new laws that will replace that system while others are asked to transplant their systems to new and unfamiliar ground. Once practitioners of an obscure specialty, water lawyers have been pushed to prominence by an immense surge of interest in their subject. Nations all over the world, in developed and developing stages, in tropical and temperate zones, with arid and humid climates, are reexamining their laws which regulate water allocation and use and are calling on local experts and consultants from afar to recommend needed changes.

The overshadowing cause of this interest is, of course, the increase in world population, which everywhere adds to needs for urban supplies, rural domestic use, and food production. A contributing factor is industrial growth, including the processing of minerals, food and textiles for all the world's peoples. With industrialization comes a higher standard of living and a concomitant increase in the per capita consumption of water that compounds the problem. Arid countries seek to make their land more productive or to produce higher valued crops, those subject to rainy and dry seasons to stretch the growing season and add a new annual crop. In humid zones once plentiful water supplies are now subject to local and intermittent shortages, caused not only by increased urban and industrial uses but by new demands for supplemental irrigation to smooth out the vagaries of seasonal rainfall and eliminate losses from periodic droughts. Investors in multimillion dollar enterprises and international agencies underwriting large projects now seek from the law the security once supplied by a seemingly inexhaustible stock of water. Where supplies are scant and almost wholly put to use, pressures of new demands require greater efficiency in use and legal mechanisms to shift water from less productive uses to new and more desirable applications. All these demands on a finite quantity of water are met with a counter-pressure that arises from our new-found concern for preservation of environmental and ecological values and that operates to diminish the available supply.

The laws at hand to manage and meet these demands and conserve the supply are in many cases left over from simpler days. Time has overtaken laws which give developers or property owners a free hand, and advances in knowledge and technology have outdated many early types of control. The search for new sources leads to groundwater, to transdivide importation, to storage and distribution schemes of undreamed size, and existing laws may have no provisions for regulating these sources or enabling such projects.

To meet these needs new water laws must be drafted. They must be designed not only to facilitate and achieve efficient allocation of resources and environmental protection, but in many cases they must also help to achieve social and national goals. Each law must fit a particular set of physical and climatological conditions and be compatible with local historical and cultural backgrounds. This is a difficult task and a challenging assignment for the draftsmen.

* * *

There are at least five ways of [allocating and distributing a fixed supply of water]. One is to enforce strict temporal priority, as exemplified by American prior appropriation. Another is to apply equal sharing enforced by proportionate reduction, as among some riparian irrigators. A third is to follow a statutory list of preferences, giving priority according to a fixed ranking of the values of different uses. A fourth is to distribute the water as determined by administrative discretion based on various economic and social factors. A fifth is to put up the water for sale or auction, as practiced in some Moslem communities.

T., C. & G. Water Man. 4th Ed. UCS—4

Since the criterion for the law is efficiency in obtaining maximum net benefits from water use, each of these must be evaluated against that standard before an intelligent choice can be made. *Prima facie,* each seems to have advantages and disadvantages. Temporal priority gives security, but it may sometimes seem to discriminate rather arbitrarily among people who are essentially similarly situated, and the earliest uses may not be the best ones. Sharing may be equitable among many farmers, but not if some have orchards or vineyards and others grow annual field crops, and a variable supply may be completely unsatisfactory for a factory or a mine. Statutory lists may reflect prevailing notions of relative values, but they may embody obvious diseconomies or prevent the comparison of the relative merits of individual uses. Even if they do prefer the most efficient uses, they operate so that the rich get richer and the poor get poorer. Bidding on the water market would seem to insure that the water goes to those who can produce the most from it, but it can lead to speculation and gouging, and to enrichment of those who hold a monopoly on water rather than those who work with it.

This leaves administrative control, and a number of water lawyers have thought this to be the ideal. Their theory is to place all the water in the hands of a wise administrator, let him put it where it will do the most good, let him prorate, let him reduce the supply or suspend the rights of some so that others may receive the water.

Those who advocate administrative distribution in case of shortage may urge that with this method the public interest, or the environment, can be protected. But it must be remembered that all of this has been taken care of in the initial allocation of rights. To understand the workings of administrative distribution, it must be very clearly kept in mind that all we are talking about is water already allocated to private use, that the state and its administrators have issued permits for its use, that every use is beneficial, and that all uses can be made in times of water plenty. It must be remembered that all minimum flow requirements are met, that all other environmental factors are protected, and that the state water plan is observed or even furthered. The public interest stands neutral, and the only question is, which people get to use the water.

* * *

In my preferred solution, temporal priority is the starting point, but only that.

* * *

Teclaff, in his survey of 57 countries, tells us that seniority in use is the most common of all bases for distributing water among users. In its most explicit form, prior appropriation exists not only in 19 American states, but also in the four western provinces of Canada, in Taiwan (China), Iran, Rhodesia, Zambia and the Philippines. There are strong elements of it in several South American countries. The 1963 British Water Resources Act creates a "protected right" indistinguishable from an appropriation, though enforced in an unusual roundabout manner.

Protection based on temporal priority is to some degree implicit in many other laws. Before state controls came into being, customary water rights, held from time immemorial or for prescriptive periods, were everywhere protected. When state authority to use water was instituted, the notion that a state should not make successive grants of the same water to different people appeared in most such laws. Permits, licenses or concessions, whatever they may be called, are not to be issued to the detriment of existing uses in most of the Spanish American countries, in several of the eastern United States, in Tanzania, and in Italy. Practically every new water code has given some sort of group preference to uses in existence when the code was adopted.

Some evidence indicates a subliminal recognition of priority even where the law is specifically to the contrary. The natural flow theory of 19th century English riparianism has been said to have been a protection of mill owners, a law designed to keep the wheels of the Industrial Revolution turning. The reasonable use theory of American riparian law is applied to require several types of adjustments which enable several riparian uses to coexist, but a recent study of the cases shows that when two uses are truly incompatible the American courts almost invariably hold that a new use is unreasonable if it takes the water supply of an existing user. Empirical studies show the existence of a sort of "practical priority" in some American states, where riparians with theoretical rights to share in a stream voluntarily refrain from taking water after their neighbors have first captured the available supply. Even under modern statutes that subject the allocation and distribution of water to administrative discretion, the administrators in Great Britain, Kenya and Mexico have eased their burden by issuing permits that authorize the withdrawal of water only when there is a surplus over the needs of existing users.

ROBERT H. ABRAMS, REPLACING RIPARIANISM IN THE TWENTY–FIRST CENTURY
94 Wayne L.Rev. 93 (1989).

Riparianism has been the universal water law of the East for two centuries. The doctrine has served the region well largely because the demand on the water resource has rarely exceeded supply. However, the East is now facing both unprecedented demand and changing climatic conditions that will cause chronic water shortages. Riparianism lacks a reliable method of allocating water uses in times of shortage. Therefore, a search for alternatives to the venerable doctrine must begin. This Article is the final part of a trilogy that outlines the need for a radical departure from riparianism. It proposes to replace riparianism with a hierarchical permit-based water rights system that features transferable permits. The new system will function both in times of ample water supply and in times of water shortage.

I. REJECTING PRIOR APPROPRIATION AND EXISTING EASTERN ADMINISTRATIVE SYSTEMS

Before presenting the proposed permit system, the inappropriateness of two other water allocation methods as alternatives to riparianism, prior appropriation and administrative permit systems, must be briefly discussed to show that a better alternative is needed. In the arid West, where water shortages are common, prior appropriation replaced riparianism and became the dominant water law. Riparianism's rules of sharing in times of shortage did not offer a sufficiently secure right to water use. To overcome this insecurity, Western water law developed a temporal appropriation system ("first in time, first in right") that erected a quantifiable set of annual usufructuary rights that were far more precise than the rights granted under riparianism. Thus, one might suppose that prior appropriation could successfully replace riparianism in any region facing water shortfalls because its allocative system was designed for water-short areas.

Beyond security of right, two additional aspects of prior appropriation are particularly attractive: (1) its doctrinal promise to avoid waste and promote conservation; and (2) its ability to permit marketing of the water rights that results in the transfer of water from low value uses to high value uses. Both of these features foster efficient use of the water, allowing maximum utilization. Under scrutiny, the expected failure of riparianism on these two counts is not total, nor is the expected exemplary performance of prior appropriation patent. These findings challenge the supposition that prior appropriation is the cure for riparianism and spark the search for still better alternatives.

Waste avoidance and conservation are vital to water-short regions, and the governing water law doctrines must reflect the importance of these practices. Riparianism views a wasteful use as unreasonable, and therefore enjoinable, if it harms another user. More important, in the ad hoc nature of riparian decisionmaking, the presence or absence of conservation efforts can be used to determine whether an otherwise reasonable riparian use is being undertaken in a reasonable fashion during a time of shortage. Prior appropriation guards against waste as a facet of the beneficial use inquiry. Only the amount of water put to a beneficial use is protected; for example, in an irrigation application, water that is applied in excess of the amount needed for the crop can be allocated to another user. In virtually all prior appropriation states, however, the waste doctrine is not strictly applied. One commentator noted that "[prior appropriation] actually encouraged the development of inefficient techniques in areas where greed and speculation were commonplace; the greater the appropriation, the greater the water right claimed * * *. Only in cases of extreme wastefulness have courts required that irrigation appropriations conform to customary practices of the region."[4]

The second claimed attraction of prior appropriation systems as an improvement on riparianism is the transferability of the water rights. Riparianism's penchant for trying to accommodate competing users through sharing of the shortage offers little promise to a user in a

4. Shupe, *Waste in Western Water Law: A Blueprint for Change,* 61 Or.L.Rev. 483, 486 (1982). Conformity to local custom is hardly a standard that inspires extensive conservation efforts. See, e.g., Tulare Irr. Dist. v. Lindsay–Strathmore Irr. Dist., 3 Cal.2d 489, 45 P.2d 972 (1935) (condoning transmission loss of almost half of diverted water as consistent with custom).

water-short area that water use will continue without diminution. The user cannot increase the certainty of continued water by purchasing additional water rights because none of the coriparians can exclude others from the use of the water. Each riparian will sell the usufructuary right of withdrawal for whatever price it will bring. Low value and high value water users alike have correlative rights, and there is no guarantee that in time of shortage the uses curtailed will be the low, rather than the high, value uses. Riparianism thus impedes the creation of a meaningful water market.[5]

In contrast, prior appropriation offers the user an opportunity to purchase a senior water right, thereby ensuring more secure water receipt. This buying and selling of water rights leads to the possibility of creating a functioning water market in which the price of water not only measures the cost of its provision, but also reflects its value as a productive scarce resource. Unfortunately, prior appropriation's record of fostering water transfers that move scarce water to more valuable uses merits only faint praise. Appropriative water rights, despite creating a quantified set of usufructuary priorities capable of supporting efficiency-enhancing transfers, are not readily marketable commodities that can be transferred easily to their highest use. The doctrine has always permitted transfers, but the transfers are limited by the "no harm on transfer" rule, which requires deference to the security of the rights of downstream junior water users who depend on making use of water that is withdrawn, but not consumed, by upstream seniors. The no harm rule limits transfers to those in which the disparity in values of the water to the transferee and transferor is sufficiently great to overcome what are almost always very high transaction costs.

Beyond the false promises of efficient water use and marketing of water rights, a final objection to importing prior appropriation to the East is the doctrine's neglect of instream uses, a systemic weakness that is of particular concern in the Eastern United States. The doctrinal insistence that a usufructuary right could only be perfected by a physical diversion of water from the watercourse, and thereafter applying the diverted water to a beneficial use, made it impossible to obtain rights to protect instream flows needed to support recreation or fish and wildlife habitat. Within the last two decades, this shortcoming of appropriation law has been addressed by state governments with statutes that protect instream flows. These statutes mark a departure from appropriation toward a managerial system that accommodates the broader spectrum of interests in ways that are more nearly riparian in flavor. Thus, what is sensibly under consideration as an alternative to

---

5. Only in the setting of a public utility clothed with the right of eminent domain can riparianism support a form of water marketing. In times of shortage, the condemned water users will be without the right to insist that the water utility share the shortage. The utilities can pass on the cost of the purchased security of right as part of the price of the water delivered to their customers, but there is little evidence that those water suppliers use their power to charge a price to spur conservation. See Center for Great Lakes, *Reassessing Water,* 6 Great Lakes Rep. July–Aug. 1989, at 1. By the same token, in times of water abundance, water supply organizations are unlikely either to ration, refuse water to potential customers, or promote conservation, for fear of angering the public they serve and the regulatory authority that oversees their operations.

riparianism, although flying the banner of prior appropriation, is instead a potpourri of appropriation and regulation. This raises the question of whether it would be preferable to build a replacement for riparianism on a regulatory platform that grows out of riparian, rather than appropriation, traditions.

A more attractive path for improving riparianism is to overlay some government regulation on the traditional pattern of unbridled private decisionmaking and common-law judicial review that has determined water use patterns in the Eastern United States. Two riparian states, Iowa and Florida, have adopted far-reaching permit systems; sixteen other riparian jurisdictions have supplemented their common law with some kind of regulatory system. Although their standards for permit issuance are linguistically similar to the common-law doctrine, these systems typically require some form of administrative issuance of permits for the allocation of surface waters. The systems are thus a significant departure from riparianism because the permit applications are reviewed prospectively before the use is initiated. States can therefore avoid user conflicts before they arise by refusing a permit, conditioning a permit grant, or taking actions that reduce the overall demand for water. These systems are more sensitive than prior appropriation because the permitting agency is empowered to consider the impact of the permit on competing uses, including instream uses of the water, and can control the duration of the permit. Permits, like other methods that quantify uses, allow easy introduction of price-induced conservation methods such as a withdrawal and/or consumption fee on a per unit basis. However, most states have been slow to adopt such fees.

Three evident drawbacks of a standard permit system are its rigidity, its tendency to overregulate, and its lack of articulated policy objectives. Permits in the typical Eastern systems are user specific and are not transferable separate from the land that is benefitted by the use. The system is hyperactive—even users who are not part of the allocation problem are forced to participate in government regulation. Finally, the existing systems offer little guidance to state agencies. Administrative decisions, like their riparian common-law forebearers, continue to be made on an ad hoc basis with little regard for integrated water system management.

The foregoing critique of prior appropriation systems and the bulk of the current permit systems has tried to show that in many ways those systems do not effectively manage the water resource. Neither pose so attractive an alternative to riparianism that adoption is imminent. If a better alternative can be fashioned, the time to act is now, for "damages can be lessened if societies utilize a strategy of proactive risk management rather than one of reactive crisis management." Ideally, integrated intergovernmental long-range water planning might well be the optimal initial proactive step. Comprehensive planning, however, is both a lengthy and expensive process that too often fails to yield the definitive guidance needed to support a coherent resource management system. The need is for a mechanism that is less cumbersome to implement, yet has the capacity to respond to escalating pressure on the water resource. The instrumentalist theory of water law comes to the fore by identifying the principal objective sought— giving legal protection to the most important uses of the water.

SARAH F. BATES, DAVID H. GETCHES, LAWRENCE J. MACDON- NELL & CHARLES F. WILKINSON, SEARCHING OUT THE HEADWATERS: CHANGE AND REDISCOVERY IN WESTERN WATER POLICY

4–8, (1993).

The root difficulty with preserving the status quo is that western water is governed by one of the most outmoded collections of rules found anywhere in American public policy. The society that created the current system well over a century ago saw the rivers of the American West through a particular lens: Water was a commodity that needed to be removed from the river channel and "put to use." Water left wild and flowing in the channel was "wasted." Extravagant government expenditures to impound and transport water were justi- fied in the name of "conservation."

This single-minded focus on the extraction of water at any cost was overwhelmingly successful in achieving the objectives of official nine- teenth-century policy: to encourage American citizens to settle the broad, dry, and inhospitable western lands. The federal and state governments made western water development—dams, reservoirs, transmountain tunnels, pipelines, and canals—a first-line priority and laid out a sprawling program of subsidies that led to engineering triumph after engineering triumph. The human effort and ingenuity were extraordinary, and the benefits were many, whether measured by solid farming and ranching communities, construction jobs, or the museums and symphonies of the region's urban centers.

* * *

There are other new perceptions. Westerners now view water as more than a commodity. They see western rivers and lakes, like the mountains, forests, and wide-open spaces, as public assets of inestima- ble value. By and large, today's populace came west, not to wrestle an existence out of a harsh land, but to capture the privilege of living, working, and raising their families in a blessed place. To do that requires some water development, but it does not require the radical posture that water policy adopted and has held since the middle nineteenth century.

The western water regime has caused serious, deeply embedded problems. The most pressing problems—for example, vanishing Pacific salmon in Washington, overtapped groundwater in Arizona—may vary, and the severity may differ, but all western states share an essential commonality of aridity and scarcity when it comes to water. That is logical and inevitable, for water policy in every western state traces to the same era and the same attitudes.

While there is no definitive, formal, West-wide inventory of the region's mounting water problems, * * * the necessary starting point is to understand the depth of the chasm between western water policy and what the modern West demands of it. The following episodes, like many others that we will describe in the pages to come, represent the West's challenges:

- The National Marine Fisheries Service, warning that 100 stocks of salmon and steelhead have become extinct and that most of the remaining runs are in danger, has put the chinook salmon and four other runs on the threatened species list for most of the rivers of Washington, Oregon, and Idaho. In 1991 the American Fisheries Society expressed concern for survival of 214 native naturally spawning salmon and steelhead stocks in California, Oregon, Washington, and Idaho.

- In the early 1980s thousands of birds were poisoned in the Kesterson National Wildlife Refuge by irrigation drainage waters tainted with toxic levels of selenium leached from the water-logged fields of California's Central Valley Project, a federally financed water supply project built in the 1940s that has encouraged large expansion of irrigated agriculture in the San Joaquin Valley.

- The future of the Pyramid Lake Band of Paiute Indians is in jeopardy because it depends on the fate of Pyramid Lake and its fishery. Beginning in the early twentieth century, a federally subsidized dam and canal system began diverting more than half of the water from the Truckee River in Nevada to another watershed to grow alfalfa. Congress has approved a last-ditch attempt to resuscitate the Truckee River system recognizing that insufficient water remains in the Truckee to stabilize Pyramid Lake, which has no other source and has already dropped 70 feet and lost one-fourth of its surface area. The cui-ui, a fish species unique to the Truckee River–Pyramid Lake system, is on the federal threatened species list, and the Lahontan cutthroat trout survives only through a hatchery program.

- Beaches deep in the Grand Canyon—sand deposited perhaps a millennium ago—are being scoured away by bursts of water released from Glen Canyon Dam to generate cheap electric power during the hours of the day when it is most in demand in southwestern cities. With the sand goes the habitat of plants, animals, and fish, as well as recreational opportunities for thousands of people.

- In 1961 an international incident erupted when Colorado River water delivered to Mexico under a treaty became too salty to irrigate crops after being used north of the border. In response, the United States has spent a billion dollars on salinity control measures, half of that sum for a desalination plant to clean up water spoiled by irrigation and return it to the river. These measures were intended to avoid any reduction in irrigation in the United States, but the Bureau of Reclamation estimates additional palliatives will be needed in less than a decade.

- Stretches of Montana's blue-ribbon Gallatin River are drained dry each summer by irrigation in spite of the area's heavy economic dependence on recreation from West Yellowstone to Bozeman.

- According to the U.S. Geological Survey, the million-year-old Ogallala Aquifer, underlying eight states (Wyoming, Colorado, South Dakota, Nebraska, Kansas, Oklahoma, Texas, and New Mexico), is in dire jeopardy. The nation's largest deposit of groundwater could be depleted, its stores beyond the economic reach of most pumpers, in only sixty years.

- A 1992 Wyoming state court ruling prevents the tribes of the Wind River Reservation from dedicating the reservation's water rights (though recognized in 1988 as being the oldest and largest in the watershed) to maintain and restore natural stream flows. This means that trout populations managed by the tribal wildlife department cannot be rehabilitated to meet the growing demands for recreation on the eastern side of the Wind River Range. Meanwhile, nearby non-Indian irrigators extract Wind River water and, like growers across the West, pour it on their fields in profligate amounts, using outmoded flood irrigation methods that are wasteful and inefficient by any modern standard.

- Metropolitan Denver has obtained water rights on rivers in western Colorado without making any payment to the state or federal governments, and has transported the water under the Continental Divide for urban use, away from communities on the Western Slope. Half of all the water in the Denver area, as in other cities in the West, is used for lawns and other exotic landscaping.

These and similar episodes throughout the West are explained by the narrow perspective of traditional western water law. Water policy shuts out large segments of the population and, with them, a set of ideals for how water should be used. Rigid patterns of water allocation that made sense generations ago now create divisiveness, bad economic results, and destruction of aquifers, rivers, lakes, and wildlife. The outmoded way of governing water fails to respond to the whole community.

CHARLES F. WILKINSON, CROSSING THE NEXT MERIDIAN
286–91 (1992).

Setting water policy right in a relatively short time is a realistic objective, and it can be done without taking draconian measures. Ironically, one of the greatest aids in correcting the excesses of western water development is those excesses themselves. The West is so extravagantly overbuilt—so much water has been developed, and so many water users are so wasteful—that the water supplies in the present system, if used sensibly, can meet most or all future needs for the foreseeable future without investment in more structural alternatives, such as substantial dams and stream diversions. * * *

The starting point, then, is that the current situation affords an extraordinary amount of flexibility, a powerful ability to create new supplies of water from existing supplies. * * *

The possibilities of reallocation without undue hardship are so great in part because the waste and excessive use are so great. The technology is available to save huge quantities of water in both urban and agricultural settings. In the cities, low-flush toilets and water-saving, or xeriscape, landscaping in new homes can be used. On the farms, water can be conserved with ditch lining; low-energy precision sprinklers, which "spoon-feed" water under low pressure to crops through hoses that drop from elevated pipes; laser-leveling of fields, which prevents pooling, seepage, and runoff; or drip or trickle irrigation, which applies water to the root systems of crops through pipes placed in furrows.

Water conservation in the West, however, has barely begun. Even though, as noted, there have been some advances and even though the benefits are undeniable—one study concludes that the modest objective of a 7 percent reduction in agricultural use would support a 100 percent increase in all other uses—resistance is deep and profound. Some of the objections deserve respect. Lining a canal system with cement or installing a precision-application sprinkler system requires a large capital expenditure. In addition, leaky earthen canals sometimes support cottonwood trees and other vegetation; lining the canals to prevent water loss may reduce or eliminate wildlife habitat for small animals. Economic and environmental concerns, therefore, require a selective approach to conservation. The deeper problem, however, lies with the old attitudes, the idea that the water developers control the rivers: "It's their water, and they'll do with it as they please." They get the support of silence from the state engineers' offices and the state legislatures. The silence translates into inaction and the preservation of the *status quo.* As one Bureau of Reclamation official said of water users in the Middle Rio Grande Conservancy District, "Flood irrigation is the old-time practice and irrigators are not about to change it."

Yet changes are in the wind, enough movement to make a person believe that the West is entering a period of transition for western water. Perhaps we are nearing the point when we will heed the call of Wallace Stegner, who has understood the West and its aridity better than anyone since John Wesley Powell:

> [W]here is the democratic, Jeffersonian, agrarian society the West hoped to become and once approximated? Every one of them, to establish and keep control of the waters of life, became an oligarchy. That is what the West is now, an elite of landowners and water experts on the top, an army of migrant aliens, most of them illegals, on the bottom * * *.
>
> The West cannot carry what it has lifted * * *.
>
> We need a Redeemer. We need a Congress that will say no to any more water boondoggles in the West. We need a moratorium on boosters and developers and raiders who can't or won't see the consequences of their acts. We need to scale down our expectations and advise a lot of hopeful immigrants that what they seek is not here.
>
> For in creating the modern West we have gone a long way toward ruining this magnificent and fragile habitat. And as Marcus Aurelius said a long time ago, what is bad for the beehive cannot be good for the bee.

The outlines of a program to answer Stegner's call are not hard to sketch. First and foremost, states should adopt phased-in conservation programs to require reduced consumption and diversion of water. Over time, the current high level of waste can be significantly reduced through installing affordable and available technology that would permit more efficient use of the water resources.

The conservation effort should emphasize the pricing of water. Water pricing should be applied in two situations: the first, already used by some municipal water suppliers, would replace the flat rates now employed with a graduated price structure that requires a higher per-unit cost for high-volume users. Commentators draw a direct connection between the current rate structures in western cities, which are too low and are based on a flat rate, and the high per capita water use in the urban West.

Pricing should also be applied in another, even more fundamental, setting. From the beginning, as one manifestation of their control over the rivers, water users have enjoyed the perquisite of free water—they have never paid any fee to the state or federal government for the right to use water.

Governments ought to receive revenues when public water is put to private use, just as they do when other public resources are used for extractive purposes. The charge, which should be levied on every water developer for every acre-foot diverted, should be nominal at first but should gradually be increased to a higher, but still reasonable, level. Such a charge at the front end would encourage conservation at all levels. Further, since all elements of a conservation policy must be acutely sensitive to the needs of individual water users, especially struggling farm and rural communities, all or part of this charge for water diversions could be placed in a conservation fund to assist in paying for conservation measures—a recognition that today conservation means saving water, not building more water projects.

A new approach toward western water also should respond to the existing public consensus and incorporate a heavy, near-absolute presumption against new dams and other structural alternatives. The West is currently so overbuilt that few, if any, new dams are necessary. The current antipathy against dams has begun to inspire some conservation efforts; the stronger and more absolute the official declaration that dams are not needed, the quicker and stronger will be the response of looking to non-structural alternatives. We have already harvested enough April rivers. Now we need to put those April rivers to much more efficient use.

Again, these approaches will not be draconian. They will be phased in and will come easily and naturally. Remember, the lords of yesterday provide ironic assistance: the West has slipped into such a profligate use of water that a relatively small percentage of savings will free up large amounts of water. * * *

Conservation programs will accomplish little if they are not complemented by programs to allocate the conserved water. If nineteenth-century prior appropriation is simply allowed to run its course, as it still does on most western rivers, the saved water will simply be captured by whichever private interest is next in line. It will still be mostly business as usual.

The basic approach should be to put teeth in Elwood Mead's old Wyoming idea that appropriations should be allowed only if they are in the public interest. This means that we should make provision for river use just as we have become accustomed to doing for land use. Future water uses (including uses of conserved water) should be allowed only if consistent with a state or local government plan that defines the public interest.

* * *

There are other necessary parts of an effective reform movement. The legacy of Owens Valley ought to be the adoption of laws protecting basins of origin, usually rural river valleys, from water projects that benefit water users, usually urban land developers in other regions. The heart of the laws should be the requirement that no out-of-basin use can even be considered unless the water developer in the other basin has put in place a comprehensive water conservation program. This would prevent unnecessary raids on other communities.

* * *

Last, water decision making needs to be opened up. Western water has long been the province of "experts," mostly engineers and lawyers. Professionals from many other disciplines—economists, historians, biologists, sociologists, political scientists, and ecologists are just a few— have much to offer to water policy. So, too, does the generalist, the conscientious citizen, have much to offer in this field, where a fresh look is so critical. These changes should be made at two levels. State water policy boards with citizen members should be created, and in those few states that already have them, their membership should be further diversified. The same approach should be taken for personnel in the state administrative offices. Policy in the national forests went wrong in part because the Forest Service is dominated by foresters. The engineering mentality has been one factor in making water policy one-sided in favor of building and extractive uses. It is now clear that there is more in our rivers than we are allowed to see through the lens with which our policies view them.

DAVID H. GETCHES, FROM ASHKABAD, TO WELLTON– MOHAWK, TO LOS ANGELES: THE DROUGHT IN WATER POLICY

64 Colo.L.Rev. 523, 548–52 (1993).

Water policy in the United States is typically little more than a description of legal systems in which a few interests control historically imbedded rights. Policies in other areas express goals for society; laws are then shaped to achieve them. Thus, criminal laws attempt to preserve order, deter misconduct, remove dangerous people from society, treat victims fairly, and so on. The goals of water policy tend to be confined to respecting existing rights and rewarding development. Western states are lately realizing that economic stability, human health, ecological balance, and survival of urban and rural communities all have a nexus in water. Widening public concerns over the untoward effects of "lawful" water uses has led to some modest reforms in water laws. The response, however, falls short of a comprehensive water policy.

* * *

There are strong pressures for improving the capacity of water law to come to grips with alternatives and consequences of water use. So-called water policy reformers are focused on modest trimming and repair work on the system. They tend to be fixed on palliatives: adding incentives to make water use more efficient, building in some public interest review criteria into water decisions, considering third-party effects of water transfers, and merging water quality control with water allocation. They urge changing reclamation law to improve efficiency and to make project water more easily transferable.

All these so-called reforms are making a difference, and they are tremendously important. But they are neither new nor enough. Reasonable "reforms" have been pressed for years. Nearly all can be traced to the early, landmark work of Gilbert White and others; many are found in the National Water Commission's 1973 report. The ideas are, at last, in the mainstream of western policy, with the central issue being how best to package and incorporate them in the existing legal system. But governments still have not confronted the root cause of water problems: the absence of a comprehensive water policy. Such a policy admits that major commitments of water usually commit people and places to extraordinary consequences and it integrates these water decisions with broader social and resource decisions.

* * *

Realization of a comprehensive, integrated approach to water policy requires new institutions that respond to wide communities of interest. Regional and international bodies must be formed with the mandate of integrating water decisions and their consequences with the aspirations of society in the area affected by the decision. The boundaries of watersheds should be the presumptive starting point, and we should look outward from there.

* * *

"Policy" should be stated in terms of broad, long-term goals. A water policy, thus, should not be "to preserve and protect existing rights," but should be in terms of society's goals. Those goals should be more inclusive than "to promote agriculture," or "to accommodate urban expansion." Imagine an economic policy or foreign policy or air quality goal so simplistic and narrow. Plainly, there are multiple effects to be assessed, and there must be multiple objectives to be coordinated within any water policy. A comprehensive policy seeks to achieve ends like economic security and stability, ecological integrity, and a satisfying quality of human life.

* * *

Major water commitments should trigger a thorough examination of alternatives and consequences. As water development becomes more difficult and expensive we should pause longer and think harder about its consequences. Water policy should not simply be the handmaiden of the proponents of growth and development. It should search and account for the consequences of each new decision that gives information back to decisionmakers who are politically responsible to the public.

Chapter Two

RIPARIAN LAW

A. COMMON LAW DEVELOPMENT
TYLER v. WILKINSON

Circuit Court, Dist. of Rhode Island, 1827.
24 F.Cas. 472.

Bill in equity [by Ebenezer Tyler and others against Abraham Wilkinson and others] to establish the right of the plaintiffs to a priority of use of the waters of Pawtucket river.

* * *

STORY, CIRCUIT JUSTICE.   * * *

The river Pawtucket forms a boundary line between the states of Massachusetts and Rhode Island, in that part of its course where it separates the town of North Providence from the town of Seekonk. It is a fresh water river, above the lower falls between these towns, and is there unaffected by the ebb or flow of the tide. At these falls there is an ancient dam, called the lower dam, extending quite across the river, and several mills are built near it, as well on the eastern as on the western side of the river. The plaintiffs, together with some of the defendants, are the proprietors in fee of the mills and adjacent land on the eastern bank, and either by themselves or their lessees are occupants of the same. The mills and land adjacent, on the western bank, are owned by some of the defendants. The lower dam was built as early as the year 1718, by the proprietors on both sides of the river, and is indispensable for the use of their mills respectively. There was previously an old dam on the western side, extending about three quarters of the way across the river, and a separate dam for a saw-mill on the east side. The lower dam was a substitute for both. About the year 1714 a canal was dug, or an old channel widened and cleared on the western side of the river, beginning at the river a few rods above the lower dam, and running round the west end thereof, until it emptied into the river about ten rods below the same dam. It has been long known by the name of "Sergeant's Trench," and was originally cut for the passage of fish up and down the river; but having wholly failed for this purpose, about the year 1730 an anchor-mill and dam were built across it by the then proprietors of the land; and between that period and the year 1790, several other dams and mills were built over the same; and since that period more expensive mills have been built there, which are all owned by some of the defendants. About thirty years before the filing of the bill, to wit, in 1792, another dam was built across the river at a place above the head of the trench, and about 20 rods above the lower dam; and the mills on the upper dam, as well as those on Sergeant's trench, are now supplied with water by proper flumes, &c. from the pond formed by the upper dam. The proprietors of this last dam are also made defendants.

* * *

The principal points, which have been discussed at the bar, are, first, what is the nature and extent of the right of the owners of Sergeant's trench; and, secondly, whether that right has been exceeded by them to the injury of the plaintiffs.

* * *

Primá facie every proprietor upon each bank of a river is entitled to the land, covered with water, in front of his bank, to the middle thread of the stream, or, as it is commonly expressed, usque ad filum aquæ. In virtue of this ownership he has a right to the use of the water flowing over it in its natural current, without diminution or obstruction. But, strictly speaking, he has no property in the water itself; but a simple use of it, while it passes along. The consequence of this principle is, that no proprietor has a right to use the water to the prejudice of another. It is wholly immaterial, whether the party be a proprietor above or below, in the course of the river; the right being common to all the proprietors on the river, no one has a right to diminish the quantity which will, according to the natural current, flow to a proprietor below, or to throw it back upon a proprietor above. This is the necessary result of the perfect equality of right among all the proprietors of that, which is common to all. The natural stream, existing by the bounty of Providence for the benefit of the land through which it flows, is an incident annexed, by operation of law, to the land itself. When I speak of this common right, I do not mean to be understood, as holding the doctrine, that there can be no diminution whatsoever, and no obstruction or impediment whatsoever, by a riparian proprietor, in the use of the water as it flows; for that would be to deny any valuable use of it. There may be, and there must be allowed of that, which is common to all, a reasonable use. The true test of the principle and extent of the use is, whether it is to the injury of the other proprietors or not. There may be a diminution in quantity, or a retardation or acceleration of the natural current indispensable for the general and valuable use of the water, perfectly consistent with the existence of the common right. The diminution, retardation, or acceleration, not positively and sensibly injurious by diminishing the value of the common right, is an implied element in the right of using the stream at all. The law here, as in many other cases, acts with a reasonable reference to public convenience and general good, and it is not betrayed into a narrow strictness, subversive of common sense, nor into an extravagant looseness, which would destroy private rights. The maxim is applied, "Sic utere tuo, ut non alienum lædas."

But of a thing, common by nature, there may be an appropriation by general consent or grant. Mere priority of appropriation of running water, without such consent or grant, confers no exclusive right. It is not like the case of mere occupancy, where the first occupant takes by force of his priority of occupancy. That supposes no ownership already existing, and no right to the use already acquired. But our law annexes to the riparian proprietors the right to the use in common, as an incident to the land; and whoever seeks to found an exclusive use, must establish a rightful appropriation in some manner known and admitted by the law. Now, this may be, either by a grant from all the proprietors, whose interest is affected by the particular appropriation, or by a long exclusive enjoyment, without interruption, which affords a just presumption of right. By our law, upon principles of public convenience, the term of twenty years of exclusive uninterrupted enjoyment has been held a conclusive presumption of a grant or right.

* * *

With these principles in view, the general rights of the plaintiffs cannot admit of much controversy. They are riparian proprietors, and, as such, are entitled to the natural flow of the river without diminution to their injury. As owners of the lower dam, and the mills connected therewith, they have no rights beyond those of any other person, who might have appropriated that portion of the stream to the use of their mills. That is, their rights are to be measured by the extent of their actual appropriation and use of the water for a period, which the law deems a conclusive presumption in favor of rights of this nature. In their character as mill-owners, they have no title to the flow of the stream beyond the water actually and legally appropriated to the mills; but in their character as riparian proprietors, they have annexed to their lands the general flow of the river, so far as it has not been already acquired by some prior and legally operative appropriation. No doubt, then, can exist as to the right of the plaintiffs to the surplus of the natural flow of the stream not yet appropriated. Their rights, as riparian proprietors, are general; and it is incumbent on the parties, who seek to narrow these rights, to establish by competent proofs their own title to divert and use the stream.

* * *

In this view of the matter, the proprietors of Sergeant's trench are entitled to the use of so much of the water of the river as has been accustomed to flow through that trench to and from their mills (whether actually used or necessary for the same mills or not), during the twenty years last before the institution of this suit, subject only to such qualifications and limitations, as have been acknowledged or rightfully exercised by the plaintiffs as riparian proprietors, or as owners of the lower mill-dam, during that period. But here their right stops; they have no right farther to appropriate any surplus water not already used by the riparian proprietors, upon the notion, that such water is open to the first occupiers. That surplus is the inheritance of the riparian proprietors, and not open to occupancy.

* * *

[If] there be a deficiency, it must be borne by all parties, as a common loss, wherever it may fall, according to existing rights; that the trench proprietors have no right to appropriate more water than belonged to them in 1796, and ought to be restrained from any further appropriation; and that the plaintiffs to this extent are entitled to have their general right established, and an injunction granted.

It is impracticable for the court to do more, in this posture of the case, than to refer it to a master to ascertain, as near as may be, and in conformity with the suggestions in the opinion of the court, the quantity to which the trench owners are entitled, and to report a suitable mode and arrangement permanently to regulate and adjust the flow of the water, so as to preserve the rights of all parties.

In respect to the question of damages for any excess of the use of the water by the trench owners, beyond their right, within six years next before the filing of the bill, I have not thought it my duty to go into a consideration of the evidence. It is a fit subject, either for a reference to a master, or for an issue of *quantum damnificatus,* if either party shall desire it.

The decree of the court is to be drawn up accordingly; and all further directions are reserved to the further hearing upon the master's report, &c. Decree accordingly.

NOTE: THE HISTORY OF RIPARIAN DOCTRINE

Tyler v. Wilkinson is the foundation American riparian case. According to Samuel C. Wiel, the great early twentieth century treatise writer and water law scholar, it was "the first expression * * * of the familiar notation of 'riparian' in reference to rights in watercourses." Samuel C. Wiel, *Waters: American Law and French Authority,* 33 Harv.L.Rev. 133, 136 (1919). *Tyler* and an English case decided a few years later, Mason v. Hill, 5 B. & Ad. 1, 110 Eng.Rep. 692 (1833), provoked a lively twentieth century academic dispute about the historical roots of riparian rights. Wiel posited that modern riparian doctrine was grounded in civil, more particularly French, law. He argued that French ideas were more welcome in the United States than those of England, and that Justice Story and Chancellor Kent had borrowed their "riparian doctrine" from the Code Napoleon, which states that property rights accrue to those with property adjacent to a watercourse and that water must be returned to its ordinary course after being used. Two more recent scholars, Arthur Maas and Hiller B. Zobel, have argued that English common law was the true source of riparianism as we know it. They theorize that English common law had developed riparianism over centuries and that Justice Story and Chancellor Kent built upon both English and American precedent to create riparian law. Arthur Maas and Hiller B. Zobel, *Anglo–American Water Law: Who Appropriated the Riparian Doctrine?,* 10 Pub.Pol. 109 (1960). This is difficult to document in reported English decisions.

Professor Carol M. Rose of Yale Law School has shown the opposite in her research. Theoretically, as the scarcity of a natural resource increases, property rights will become more individualized and articulated. History reveals, however, that in Britain, as water resources became scarcer, the status quo favoring ancient, established uses prevailed until the late eighteenth century. Carol M. Rose, *Energy and Efficiency in the Realignment of Common–Law Water Rights,* 19 J.Legal Stud. 261 (1990).

An evolutionary view of property rights would suggest that this no-change approach occurs only in a zone between a perceived plenty and an increased demand that threatens to make a given resource scarce. Accordingly, no-change doctrines may crumple when the resource comes under more serious pressure. But the seventeenth- and eighteenth-century watercourse law tells us that the no-change approach may also be fairly stable, at least under certain conditions.

These conditions are, first, that rivalries are relatively infrequent; second, that they involve one-on-one conflicts so that, in the normal case, it is fairly easy to negotiate reallocations from the baseline of no-change property allocation; third, that it is relatively easy to go elsewhere if negotiation fails; and finally, that the actual use of the resource is fairly stable over time so that one can reasonably presume that an established use is the most valuable one. All these conditions combined to maintain a certain stability in the doctrinally rigid water law of preindustrial Britain. It was stable precisely because the legal arrangements did not matter very much and were marginal to most ordinary behavior.

Id. at 273.

When the conditions above no longer existed and new uses were deemed the most valuable ones by the industrialized nation, Britain moved to an occupancy system that favored the first person to alter a stream from its natural condition. By the early nineteenth century, the law in England and in the eastern United States had developed a form similar to that of prior appropriation in the western United States today. Such a system worked well while the typical water dispute involved few parties in areas with abundant water supplies.

The Massachusetts courts, then, were well on the way to an occupancy regime similar to that which would emerge in the American West. The first person to install works for utilizing the power of the fall would be entitled to keep that power, either against a prior unimproving user—however ancient his use—or against a subsequent improver along the same watercourse.

* * *

[A] major difference between ancient use and occupancy doctrines lay in their implicit assessment of the relative value of water uses: ancient use assumed that the use in place for many years was superior, whereas occupancy assumed that the first capital expenditure marked the more valuable use.

But what was not different was that the occupancy cases, like the older ancient-use cases, took place in a microcontext of one-on-one conflicts between owners of neighboring sites. Until the middle of the nineteenth century, the leading Massachusetts occupancy cases were backflow cases, and these almost certainly involved few parties: usually a downstream neighbor with a new dam and an upstream neighbor whose earlier waterwheel was swamped by the new dam. In these two-party site-use conflicts, whether governed by ancient use or by occupancy, it should have been relatively easy for most parties to organize a bargain, particularly before a new mill was constructed. Indeed, the cases themselves show that, in both Britain and America, fall-line riparian owners entered quite complex contractual arrangements for the distribution of given sites' waterpower.

Id. at 280.

Both ancient use and occupancy functioned well while transaction costs were low. When flow interruptions and pollution problems dramatically increased transaction costs, the law quickly adapted. A new system of correlative rights appeared in New York at the turn of the nineteenth century. This system was labeled riparianism twenty years later in *Tyler v. Wilkinson,* and gave riparians equal rights to use a watercourse. Riparianism was well suited to areas where water power, not consumption, was the major use. According to Rose, Britain and Massachusetts soon followed in New York's footsteps as their industrialization demanded water allocation with minimal transaction costs. Thus, they all moved from a more individualized property system to a common property system. While the movement toward common property discounts Rose's theoretical construct, she concludes that the subject matter of disputes and low consumptive uses account for the variation.

BROADBENT v. RAMSBOTHAM

Court of the Exchequer, 1856.
11 Ex. 602, 156 Eng.Rep. 971.

The plaintiff is the owner and occupier of a mill at Clough Bottom, in the township of Longwood, in the parish of Huddersfield. It has existed as a mill for fifty years, and is situate upon a natural stream called Longwood Brook, the waters of which have, during all that time, been used by the occupiers of the mill for working the mill by water power, and carrying on in it the business of a manufacturer of woollen cloths.

* * *

The defendant Atkinson is the occupier of a farm in the said township, called Petty Royds farm, on the north-west side of the range called Nettleton Hill. The defendant Dr. Ramsbotham is the receiver and manager of that estate for the owner, who is an infant ward in Chancery.

The natural state of the surface of Petty Royds farm is very uneven, and has much needed draining. Parts of it had been partially, but imperfectly, drained by the tenants, before making the drain which led to the present action. In some of the closes lodgments of water and boggy places had existed, and horses when crossing over the close called Longbottom had sunk in. The farm of Petty Royds is chiefly used as a dairy-farm, in which the tenant kept about sixteen head of cattle.

From the sides of the hills called Pighill Wood and Pendle Hill, which lie to the west of Petty Royds farm buildings, the natural flow of water is northward, until it reaches the Longwood Brook; and all water passing over the lands which lie on the west side of the farm buildings naturally flows northward into that brook. * * *

On the west side of the farm buildings there formerly existed a well of water distant seventy yards from the farm house. This well was supplied by a subterraneous flow of water out of the ground, and from it the farm house was supplied with water. The well was about two feet deep and about one yard broad and wide. In seasons of a great supply of water there was an overflow from this well, which ran northward to the Longwood Brook. The water of this well the former occupants of the farm and of the neighbouring cottages used for domestic purposes as spring water.

Adjoining the south side of this well was a swamp, extending over an area of about sixteen perches, occasioned by a slight elevation of the surface towards the north, which obstructed the escape of any water which had once found its way there. * * *

Some time previous to 1851 the defendant Atkinson had partially drained portions of Longbottom, and in that year he applied to Dr. Ramsbotham to have a main drain cut for the purpose of carrying off the water from the upper portion of that close, and improving this part of the farm. Dr. Ramsbotham gave Atkinson authority to make the drain. * * *

Atkinson's object in continuing the drain to the west of the stone watering places was to carry water from the west side of the farm buildings for the supply of those watering places on the east of them, and was not intended by him for agricultural purposes. * * *

The drain from the spot occupied by the stone watering places east of Petty Royds farm yard down Duck Holes and Longbottom and through Lower Woods is a good and useful agricultural drain, for the purpose of relieving the ground and subsoil of those closes of lodgments of water and swamps, which in parts extended to a great depth, as it will serve as a master drain into which collateral drains can find an outlet for more completely draining these parts of the farm of Petty Royds.

The effect produced by the part of the drain which is carried from the stone troughs to the west through the elevated ground upon the natural flow of the streams of water which escaped to the northward into Longwood Brook from the well on the west side of the farm house, is to divert the water of the streams and to intercept the water which before ran into and under ground there near this well and was there discharged northwards, and to carry these waters away down to the east by the south side of the farm house. The surface of the swamp near the well on the west side of the farm buildings, as it existed before the cutting of the drain, has been filled in and raised, and the well itself has been filled up and leveled and does not now exist.

* * *

ALDERSON, B. * * * Now, we think that this water, both that which overflows and that which sinks in, belongs absolutely to the defendant on whose land it arises, and is not affected by any right of the plaintiff. The right to the natural flow of the water in Longwood Brook undoubtedly belongs to the plaintiff; but we think that this right cannot extend further than a right to the flow in the brook itself, and to the water flowing in some defined natural channel, either subterranean or on the surface, communicating directly with the brook itself. No doubt, all the water falling from heaven and shed upon the surface of a hill, at the foot of which a brook runs, must, by the natural force of gravity, find its way to the bottom, and so into the brook; but this does not prevent the owner of the land on which this water falls from dealing with it as he may please and appropriating it. He cannot, it is true, do so if the water has arrived at and is flowing in some natural channel already formed. But he has a perfect right to appropriate it before it arrives at such a channel. In this case a basin is formed in his land, which belongs to him, and the water from the heavens lodges there. There is here no watercourse at all. If this water exceeds a certain depth it escapes at the lowest point, and squanders itself (so to speak) over the adjoining surface. The owner of the soil has clearly a right to drain this shallow pond and to get rid of the inconvenience at his own pleasure. We have no doubt, therefore, that, as to this source of feeding the Longwood Brook, the plaintiff has no title. The same may be said of the swamp of sixteen perches, which is merely like a sponge fixed (so to speak) on the side of the hill, and full of water. If this overflows it creates a sort of marshy margin adjoining; and there is apparently no course of water, either into or out of it, on the surface of the land. As to the subterranean course communicating with this swamp, which must no doubt exist, it is sufficient to say, that they are not traceable, so as to shew that the water passing along them ever reaches Longwood Brook. This falls, therefore, into the same category, or rather is a stronger instance of the rule before mentioned. * * *

* * * The water falling from heaven on the side of a hill, we have before said, may be appropriated, though not after it has once arrived at a defined natural watercourse; and here the question is, whether this water in its first origin, and before it has arrived at any definite natural watercourse conveying it onwards towards Longwood Brook, has not been intercepted by the defendant's drain, and so appropriated by him; and we think it has. For what are the facts? The water in dispute is only the overflow of a well, and the well is now prevented from overflowing. But when before it did overflow it ran into a ditch (the lowest adjoining ground) made artificially, and for a different purpose, running beside a hedge. This was no natural defined watercourse. After this, it squandered itself over a swamp made by the feet of cattle treading about, and it is not till long after this, that what still remained of it found its way into what may there perhaps be correctly

called a definite natural watercourse, receiving this and probably other water from other sources also.   * * *

Judgment for the defendants.

NOTE

In *Broadbent v. Ramsbotham,* the good and useful agricultural drain constructed by one Atkinson did so relieve the ground and subsoil of Petty Royds farm of waters in lodgments and boggy places (which in parts extended to great depth) that Longwood Brook was deprived of water that, in its natural course, would have been available to Broadbent's mill situated upon the brook at Clough Bottom. The Chancellor, atop his woolsack, denied Broadbent's right to command the full, natural flow of all waters. Did the Chancellor, indeed, do equity? Why did not Broadbent have a right to the water from the heavens lodged, albeit temporarily, upon Petty Royds farm, but destined for Longwood Brook? Were not those waters part of the natural flow of Longwood Brook? Of what consequence was it that Petty Royds farm had much needed drainage? Should the portion of the water used by Atkinson for the supply of watering places, not carried off for agricultural drainage, be treated differently?

NOTE: DIFFUSED SURFACE WATERS

As in *Broadbent v. Ramsbotham,* courts have generally held that water that is not in a natural watercourse is not subject to riparian rights. These waters are classified as diffused surface waters. The classification not only defeats the rights of lower landowners to the natural flow, but also gives rise to potential rights in landowners who capture diffused surface waters on their lands.

Assume that water naturally drains across the lands of A. If A desires to subdivide the land and construct a small artificial lake maintained by an earthen dam, what right does A have to use the water which A formerly was glad to see drain to B, a lower owner? If the court chooses to classify the water as diffused surface water the general rule is that the landowner across whose land the water flows may capture the water and, once collected, the water becomes private property. If the court decides the water is flowing in a natural watercourse, the upper owner may have to share it with the lower under the law of riparian rights (or it may be subject to prior appropriation).

Judicial classifications vary for "[n]either the judicial definition of 'water course,' nor any definition, can draw a sharp line where nature has not." Report submitted by the Legislature Research Council Relative to Rights to Surface and Sub–Surface Water in Massachusetts 29 (1957). Diffused surface waters are often defined merely by example— rain and melted snow—or in the negative—not in a watercourse. The Restatement (Second) of Torts employs both criteria, defining diffused surface waters as: "water from rain, melting snow, springs or seepage, or detached from subsiding floods, which lies or flows on the surface of the earth but does not form part of a watercourse or lake." Restatement (Second) of Torts § 846 (1979).

A useful discussion of the factors that courts consider is found in South Santa Clara Valley Water Conservation Dist. v. Johnson, 41 Cal.Rptr. 846 (Cal.App.1964), in which a lower water district sued to enjoin an upper landowner from capturing runoff because the lower owner claimed riparian rights to at least part of the waters:

> [W]e find a variety of definitions as to what constitutes a watercourse. In Los Angeles Cemetery Ass'n v. City of Los Angeles, 103 Cal. 461, 464–465, 37 P. 375, 376, we find this definition: "There must be a stream usually flowing in a particular direction, though it need not flow continually. It may sometimes be dry. It must flow in a definite channel, having a bed, sides, or banks, and usually discharge itself into some other stream or body of water. It must be something more than a mere surface drainage over the entire face of a tract of land, occasioned by unusual freshets or other extraordinary causes. It does not include the water flowing in the hollows or ravines in land, which is the mere surface water from rain or melting snow, and is discharged through them from a higher to a lower level, but which at other times are destitute of water. Such hollows or ravines are not, in legal contemplation, watercourses." * * *

> However, as to the difficulty of applying this definition, we find the following statement:

> > " 'While it is ordinarily defined as a stream, containing a definite bed, banks and channel, which flows into some other river, stream, lake or the sea, none of those characteristics is an absolute fixed factor. A watercourse may exist even though it serves as a mere channel by means of which a particular watershed is drained, and although it may be dry in certain seasons * * *.' "

Phillips v. Burke, 133 Cal.App.2d 700, 703, 284 P.2d 809, 811 * * *

> Thus, we are left with a somewhat nebulous concept, the only concrete element of which seems to be the requirement of definite bed, banks, and channel. As to the definition of a watercourse which the trial judge applied in deciding in favor of defendants, it appears from the findings that he relied heavily on the concept of the presence or absence of a bed, bank, and channel. The court specifically found that there was no live stream with established banks and bed and channel leading into the said reservoir. Its finding that no name exists for the gullies or ravines leading into the reservoir is immaterial on the issue of the existence of a watercourse. We can find no authority which considers the presence or absence of a name in determining whether a watercourse in fact exists. * * *

> As for the finding that the reservoir "is fed only by the runoff of waters in the time of heavy rainfall from the natural drainage of waters resulting solely from said rainfall," this fact, in and of itself,

does not negate the existence of a watercourse because the runoff from the annual rainfall can constitute a watercourse. The critical factor in determining whether water consisting of the runoff from the usual and recurring rainfall constitutes a watercourse is whether or not it runs in a well-defined channel. * * *

What practical reasons exist for excluding certain waters from controls under the legal regime (whether riparian or appropriation) adopted by a state for water allocation? Would it not lead to better reliability for owners of water rights and greater efficiency in the use of water resources for all waters to be under the prevailing law of water allocation?

Rules allowing landowners to control surface waters upon their lands are related to the need for drainage of lands to dispose of excess waters, a typical problem exemplified in *Broadbent*. A substantial body of law has developed concerning the liability of an upper landowner for damage caused to a lower landowner by drainage or avoidance of waters flowing across the upper landowner's land. Generally, one cannot obstruct or divert the water of a natural watercourse so as to cause damage to another. Johnson v. Whitten, 384 A.2d 698 (Me.1978). The rule historically differed in some jurisdictions if diffused surface waters were involved.

Most of the litigated cases involve the issue of whether an improving landowner is liable for altering established drainage patterns thus causing damage to other property. As in *Broadbent,* the purpose may be to drain saturated lands so that water would be useful for agriculture. Other situations include attempts to protect improvements such as buildings from surface flows, and construction on land (including paving) that alters drainage. Though typically it is an upper landowner who causes harm by draining water to a lower landowner, there are cases in which a lower landowner obstructs or dams flowing water so that it floods upper land. Some cases involve the diversion or obstruction of water in a natural watercourse, in which case rights of lower riparians to the flow may be implicated.

Initially, there were two diametrically opposed rules to determine the liability of a landowner who altered surface drainage patterns, the common enemy rule and the civil law rule.

The common enemy rule gave an improving surface owner the privilege to divert surface drainage as needed to make the land useful. The upper landowner was not liable if improvements or drainage systems caused damage to lower landowners. The opportunities for disregard of the right of lower landowners to use their property fully, for the sake of the upper landowners created a situation in which the respective rights of the owners were out of balance. Thus, in nearly all jurisdictions following the common enemy rule it has been modified to require considerations of reasonableness.

The civil law rule imposed a servitude of natural drainage on lower property owners but prohibited the upper owner from altering natural drainage patterns. E.g., Gross v. Connecticut Mutual Life Ins. Co., 361 N.W.2d 259 (S.D.1985). All owners had reciprocal duties to prevent harm to others. Carried to its logical conclusion, the rule could prevent all development that had any significant effect on development. A building or parking lot or drainage from a field needed for farming all change the natural drainage pattern. Therefore, courts have modified the rule to allow reasonable alterations of drainage patterns. Under the civil law rule the upper landowner could alter the flow of a natural watercourse so long as the flow remained in the watercourse. This rule can have important consequences for irrigators. Similarly, a lower landowner who fills in the channel of a watercourse cannot claim protection from the actions of an upper landowner who discharges greater flows from a newly developed spring into the old channel, which would have been adequate to pass all the water. Smith v. King Creek Grazing Ass'n, 671 P.2d 1107 (Idaho App.1983).

By incorporating principles of reasonableness, the two rules operate similarly in practice. The reasonable use rule found in Restatement (Second) of Torts §§ 822–831, 833 is effectively the rule in most states. See, e.g., Keys v. Romley, 412 P.2d 529 (Cal.1966); Gutierrez v. Rio Rancho Estates, Inc., 605 P.2d 1154 (N.M.1980). Under this approach, an upper owner has a qualified privilege to improve but also has a duty to minimize alteration of natural drainage patterns. Differences in application of reasonableness rules may continue, however, based on whether a state traces its rule to the common enemy doctrine or the civil law doctrine.

Special rules may apply where waters are captured, stored, and discharged. A high duty of care attaches to the impoundment of water on one's land. Some states follow English common law and impose absolute liability for harm caused by the artificial storage of water, such as by flooding when a dam breaks. Rylands v. Fletcher, L.R. 3 H.L. 330 (1868); Cities Service Co. v. State, 312 So.2d 799 (Fla.App. 1975). Many other states require proof of negligence. The "act of God" defense has been frequently asserted in negligence actions, but courts have rejected it if the dam operator failed to design the facility to accommodate foreseeable floods. Barr v. Game, Fish and Parks Comm'n, 497 P.2d 340 (Colo.App.1972).

STRATTON v. MT. HERMON BOYS' SCHOOL

Supreme Court of Massachusetts, 1913.
216 Mass. 83, 103 N.E. 87.

Rugg, C.J. The plaintiff, the owner of a mill upon a small stream, sues the defendant, an upper riparian proprietor upon the same stream, for wrongful diversion of water therefrom to his injury. The material facts are that the defendant owns a tract of land through which the stream flows and upon which also is a spring confluent to the stream. Upon this land it has established pumping apparatus whereby it diverts about 60,000 gallons of water each day from the spring and stream to another estate belonging to it and not contiguous to its land adjacent to this stream, but located about a mile away in a different watershed, for the domestic and other uses of a boys' school with dormitories, gymnasium and other buildings and a farm. The number of students increased from 363 in 1908 to 525 in 1911, while the number of teachers, employés and other persons on the estate was over 100. During the latter year there were kept on the farm 103 cattle, 28 horses and 90 swine. There was a swimming pool, laundry, canning factory and electric power plant, for the needs of all of which water was supplied from this source. There was evidence tending to show that this diversion caused a substantial diminution in the volume of water which otherwise in the natural flow of the stream would have come to the plaintiff's land and in the power which otherwise might have been developed upon his wheel by the force of the current.

* * *

The common-law rights and obligations of riparian owners upon streams are not open to doubt. Although the right to flowing water is incident to the title to land, there is no right of property in such water in the sense that it can be the subject of exclusive appropriation and dominion. The only property interest in it is usufructuary. The right of each riparian owner is to have the natural flow of the stream come to his land and to make a reasonable and just use of it as it flows through his land, subject, however, to the like right of each upper proprietor to make a reasonable and just use of the water on its course through his land and subject further to the obligation to lower proprietors to permit the water to pass away from his estate unaffected except by such consequences as follow from reasonable and just use by him. This general principle, simple in statement, often gives rise to difficulties in its application. What is a reasonable and just use of flowing water is dependent upon the state of civilization, the development of the mechanical and engineering art, climatic conditions, the customs of the neighborhood and the other varying circumstances of each case. To some extent often the amount and character of the flow may be modified by such use, for which, even though injurious to other proprietors, no action lies. A stream may be so small that its entire flow may be abstracted by the ordinary domestic uses of a farmer. Its bed may be so steep that its reasonable utilization for the generation of power requires its impounding in numerous reservoirs. But whatever the condition, each riparian owner must conduct his operations reasonably in view of like rights and obligations in the owners above and below him. The right of no one is absolute but is qualified by the existence of the same right in all others similarly situated. The use of the water flowing in a stream is common to all riparian owners and each must exercise this common right so as not essentially to interfere with an equally beneficial enjoyment of the common right by his fellow riparian owners. Such use may result in some diminution, obstruction or change in the natural flow of the stream, but such interference cannot exceed that which arises from reasonable conduct in the light of all circumstances, having due regard to the exercise of the common right by other riparian owners. In the main, the use by a riparian owner by virtue of his right as such must be within the watershed of the stream, or at least that the current of the stream shall be returned to its original bed before leaving the land of the user. This is implied in the term "riparian." It arises from the natural incidents of running water. A brook or river, so far as concerns surface indications, is inseparably connected with its watershed and owes the volume of current to its area. A definite and fixed channel is a part of the conception of a water course. To divert a substantial portion of its flow is the creation of a new and different channel, which to that extent defeats the reasonable and natural expectations of the owners lower down on the old channel. Abstraction for use elsewhere not only diminishes the flow of the parent stream but also increases that which drains the watershed into which the diversion is made, and may injure thereby riparian rights upon it. Damage thus may be occasioned in a double aspect. The precise point whether riparian rights include diversion in reasonable quantities for a proper use on property outside the watershed has never been decided in this commonwealth. There are numerous decisions in other jurisdictions to the effect that the rights of a riparian proprietor do not extend to uses on land outside the watershed. These were made in cases where actual perceptible damages were wrought by the diversion.

There are numerous expressions to the effect that the rights of riparian ownership extend only to use upon and in connection with an estate which adjoins the stream and cannot be stretched to include uses reasonable in themselves, but upon and in connection with nonriparian estates.

These principles, however, are subject to the modification that the diversion, if for a use reasonable in itself, must cause actual perceptible damage to the present or potential enjoyment of the property of the lower riparian proprietor before a cause of action arises in his favor * * *. The question in such a case is not whether the diversion, being for a legitimate use, is in quantity such as is reasonable, having regard to all the circumstances, as it is in cases of distinctly riparian uses, but only whether it causes actual damage to the person complaining.

* * * Nor is this inconsistent with the decisions which hold that there may be recovery even though there is no present actual damage, provided an injurious effect may be produced upon the lower estate by the acquirement of right through lapse of time.

The distinction is between a diversion which causes a present or potential injury to the lower estate for a valuable use and one which cannot produce such a result. * * *

The governing principle of law in a case like the present is this: A proprietor may make any reasonable use of the water of the stream in connection with his riparian estate and for lawful purposes within the watershed, provided he leave the current diminished by no more than is reasonable, having regard for the like right to enjoy the common property by other riparian owners. If he diverts out of the watershed or upon a disconnected estate the only question is whether there is actual injury to the lower estate for any present or future reasonable use. The diversion alone without evidence of such damage does not warrant a recovery even of nominal damages.

The charge of the court below was not in conformity to this principle. It would have permitted the recovery of nominal damages in any event, quite apart from the possibility of real injury to the plaintiff. But the defendant has suffered no harm by this error. The verdict of the jury was for substantial damages and there was ample evidence to support such a conclusion.

NOTES

1. The rigid, common law rule was that any use of water on nonriparian land may be enjoined. In *Stratton* water was clearly being used on nonriparian land, yet the court opined that there would be no restriction on nonriparian uses by the riparian owner absent proof of actual injury to other riparians. Here the plaintiff showed injury and recovered damages. What are the consequences of denying an injunction (or nominal damages where there is no harm)? Does the court's approach amount to granting a private right of condemnation to riparians as against one another? Is the result, and the analysis used to reach it, any different from that which would be used if all the uses were on riparian lands?

2. In determining the reasonableness of a use of water on nonriparian lands, does it matter how much land the user owns that is riparian to a stream? Could a landowner with a tiny parcel of riparian land, only large enough to accommodate diversion works, take water for an enormous tract of nonriparian land? If so, why should it matter that the user is only technically a riparian? Does it make any practical difference to other riparians whether it is a riparian or a nonriparian who uses water on nonriparian land? Should courts liberalize the requirement that the user be a riparian?

3. The plaintiff in *Stratton* had an independent ground for objecting to the defendant's use beyond the fact that it was on nonriparian land. The water was being applied in another watershed. Why should it matter that water is used in a watershed apart from the stream of origin? Is there a modern rationale for the watershed limitation beyond protection of downstream return flows for the benefit of present and future consumptive uses? See Lynda Butler, *Allocating Consumptive Water Rights in a Riparian Jurisdiction: Defining the Relationship Between Public and Private Interests*, 47 U.Pitt.L.Rev. 95, 111–117 (1985).

Some lands actually abut more than one stream. If so, might water then be withdrawn from stream A and applied to a portion of the tract that lies within the watershed of stream B? Does it matter if both streams join together to form a large stream and therefore that the land is all in the watershed of the larger stream? In Anaheim Union Water Co. v. Fuller, 88 P. 978 (Cal.1907), the Santa Ana River ran from east to west, consisting in its eastern reaches of two forks that joined to form the mainstream. Defendant's parcel of land lay athwart both forks, and plaintiff's land was downstream from defendant's, on the north fork and upstream from the confluence of the two forks. Defendant diverted water from the north fork over a ridge into the watershed of the south fork, where the water was used for irrigation. The court held that plaintiff may enjoin the diversion, explaining the purpose of the watershed rule:

> The principal reasons for the rule confining riparian rights to that part of lands bordering on the stream which are within the watershed are, that where the water is used on such land it will, after such use, return to the stream so far as it is not consumed, and that as the rainfall on such land feeds the stream, the land is, in consequence, entitled, so to speak, to the use of its waters. Where two streams unite, we think the correct rule to be applied, in regard to the riparian rights therein, is that each is to be considered as a separate stream, with regard to lands abutting thereon above the junction, and that land lying within the watershed of one stream above that point is not to be considered as riparian to the other stream.

Id. at 980. Compare Rancho Santa Margarita v. Vail, 81 P.2d 533 (Cal.1938), where plaintiff was a riparian located below the junction of the two branches on which the defendant owned land. It was held that the plaintiff could not complain of the defendant's use of water outside of one of the two tributary watersheds because the plaintiff failed to show injury. There was no actual injury to the plaintiff in *Anaheim* either; the non-watershed use was sufficient ground for an injunction. The difference between the two cases seems to be that in 1928 California adopted a constitutional amendment imposing a reasonable use rule. Making any non-watershed use actionable would be inconsistent with the amendment which states that "because of the conditions prevailing in this State the general welfare requires that the water resources of the state be put to beneficial use to the fullest extent * * *." Calif. Const., art. X, § 2 (quoted in full at pages 147–48, infra).

Apparently there was another ground for the result in *Anaheim*. The court also applied the "source of title" rule to hold that the land in the south fork watershed had once been severed by conveyances from the land in the north watershed and, though later it came back into common ownership, it was technically "nonriparian." See the note on the unity of title and source of title rules, page 68, infra.

4. Can a riparian use a natural stream as a conduit to transport water to a point where it would be extracted and used? In Alburger v. Philadelphia Elec. Co., 535 A.2d 729 (Pa.1988), a public utility sought to discharge water diverted from the Delaware River into a small, non-navigable creek, where it would be transported to a nuclear power plant and there used for cooling and water supply for surrounding towns. The court enjoined the transport of foreign water as exceeding the flowage easement that the company had, as an upstream riparian, over the lands of downstream riparians.

In Okaw Drainage Dist. v. National Distillers and Chemical Corp., 882 F.2d 1241 (7th Cir.1989), National Distillers pumped groundwater and transported it down the Kaskaskia River in central Illinois for use at its alcohol plant and for resale to nearby towns. The water flowed through a stretch of the river maintained by the district, which opposed the use of the stream as a conduit because it interfered with farmland drainage along the banks by eroding the banks and raising the level of the river. The district argued that National's continued use of the ditch was a nuisance. Judge Posner refused to issue an injunction because the plaintiff failed to present any evidence to offset the balance of equities which favored the downstream municipal purchasers of the flow.

An 1882 Illinois case, not cited by the court in *Okaw,* does hold that a mill owner who diverted water placed in the Des Plaines River by a transbasin diversion into the canal (the reversal of the Chicago River from Lake Michigan to the Mississippi drainage basin) was liable for injuries suffered by a mill owner between the point of diversion and use. Defendants argued in part that the augmented flow was artificial water, but the court reasoned that it became part of the natural flow because it was abandoned. Druley v. Adam, 102 Ill. 177 (1882).

NOTE: WHO IS A RIPARIAN?

Land Abutting a Watercourse

In the riparian system, only the owners of lands abutting a watercourse are entitled to use the water. Several complications lurk behind this apparently straightforward statement. The first is the meaning of "abutting." Most courts hold that one claiming riparian rights must own land that reaches the high water mark of the waterbody; occasionally ownership to the low water mark is required. Riparian rights might be seasonal depending on the water level of the watercourse at peak versus low flow periods. Turner v. James Canal Co., 99 P. 520 (Cal.1909).

Determining the exact location of these boundaries may prove troublesome, especially where tidal waters are involved. These complexities are discussed in Borax Consol. Ltd. v. Los Angeles, 296 U.S. 10 (1935) and Frank E. Maloney and Richard C. Ausness, *The Use and Legal Significance of the Mean High Water Line in Coastal Boundary Mapping,* 53 N.C.L.Rev. 185 (1974). A riparian normally need not own submerged lands to claim rights, but for some purposes—the right to fill, for instance—ownership of the bottom of the waterbody may be required. Typically, these situations are limited to non-navigable waters, because private ownership of navigable bottoms below the high or low water mark is subject to public uses, pages 405–18, infra.

Once the appropriate boundary of the watershed is established, the next task is to determine whether the tract of land in question reaches it. The calls of the deed must be examined, to ascertain the intent of the grantor. Where bottom ownership is required, the landowner is assisted by the common law presumption that "absent an express reservation by the grantor, a conveyance of riparian property conveys title to the thread of the stream unless a contrary intention appears or is clearly inferrable from the terms of the deed." Nilsson v. Latimer, 664 S.W.2d 447, 449 (Ark.1984). The rule also applies to lakes, where the landowners' correlative rights are technically classified as "littoral" rights. Bottom ownership is ordinarily determined by extending property lines from the points at which they touch the high water mark to

the center of the lake. Determining the boundaries of bottom ownership of irregular lakes can be a challenge to the surveyor's art. See
Curtis M. Brown, *et al.,* Evidence and Procedures for Boundary Location 247–75 (2d ed. 1981).

Nature of Interest in Riparian Land

Must the person claiming riparian rights show fee title, or may a
lessee be a riparian? What if the fee owner of riparian land conveys
rights to an easement, the exercise of which necessarily involves the
assertion of riparian privileges? Is the easement holder the "owner" of
the riparian rights? See the discussion of Burkart v. Fort Lauderdale,
168 So.2d 65 (Fla.1964), at page 140 infra.

"Source of Title" and "Unity of Title" Rules

A major limitation on water use under the riparian system may
relate to the derivation of title to the land. Even though land appears
to be riparian, it may be considered nonriparian under the "source of
title" rule. This rule, and the more inclusive "unity of title" rule are
discussed in Peter W. Davis, *Australian and American Water Allocation
Systems Compared,* 9 Boston C.Indus. and Comm.L.Rev. 647, at 680–82
(1968):

> Two major doctrines have emerged defining just which land
> that abuts a stream is to be considered riparian land. The "source
> of title" test states that water may be used only on land which has
> been held as a single tract throughout its chain of title. This
> means that any nonabutting portions of the original tract which
> have been severed forever lose their riparian character unless a
> contrary intention is manifested. Reuniting such severed tracts
> with the abutting tract will not reestablish their riparian status.*
> The total amount of riparian land under this rule cannot be
> enlarged by the purchase of contiguous back tracts.

> Another rule followed in some states, the "unity of title" rule,
> provides that any tracts contiguous to the abutting tract are
> riparian if all of them are held under single ownership regardless
> of the times when the various tracts were acquired. This means

---

* The author here cites, *inter alia,* Boeh-
mer v. Big Rock Irr. Dist., 48 P. 908 (Cal.
1897). In justifying the application of the
unity of title rule, the court says (48 P. at
910):

* * * [I]t has been the policy of the general government to subdivide the public
domain into small tracts, and to dispose of
them as such, and for the purpose of carrying out such policy restricted the right of
entry under the homestead and pre-emp-
tion laws to one hundred and sixty acres.
Even in its grants to railroads, by granting
alternate sections, it prevented the acquisition from the government of large bodies of
contiguous lands, and a similar policy is
pursued by the state in disposing of state
lands. * * *

In the case at bar the stipulation is that
these fourteen quarter sections were granted each by a separate patent, each patent
being based upon a separate entry, and
these fourteen quarter sections therefore
constitute fourteen distinct tracts of land,
and mere contiguity cannot extend a riparian right which is appurtenant to one quarter section to another, though both are now
owned by the same person.

An additional explanation for the adoption of the rule in California was the policy
of that state to enlarge the amount of
water available for appropriation and prescription. [Eds. Note]

that a riparian proprietor may enlarge the amount of his riparian land by purchasing contiguous back tracts within the watershed. The general rule that water may not be diverted to lands outside the watershed of the originating stream follows from the rule that water diverted for any extraordinary purpose must be returned to the stream above the next lower riparian's land.

The difference in the amount of land available for riparian water use under these two rules can be considerable. A recent study in northwestern Wisconsin indicates that the "unity of title" test would encompass 64 percent more land than the "source of title" test. This substantial increase results from the fact that most farms today have different boundaries than the original farms and that many back tracts have changed hands.

Although riparianism generally restricts use of water to riparian land, there is considerable authority for the proposition that in many instances water may be used by riparians on nonriparian land. These cases, admittedly the minority rule, state that water may be diverted to and used on nonriparian land provided that lower riparians are not damaged. Two states in this group allow use on nonriparian land even though riparians are damaged if the use is reasonable. To the contrary is the majority rule that riparian rights may not be exercised on nonriparian land. Many eastern states have not decided which rule to follow.

Place-of-use restrictions have not yet raised any obvious problems in the East, where development of industry has been concentrated at streamside. The problem of locational restrictions probably will be more relevant for the East if irrigation becomes prevalent, or if severe water shortages should occur.

California, where expansion of riparian rights is disfavored because new water rights may be obtained under the appropriation system, applies the "source of title" rule. As stated in Anaheim Union Water Co. v. Fuller, 88 P. 978, 980 (Cal.1907), discussed at pages 65–66, supra: "If the owner of a tract abutting on a stream conveys to another a part of the land not contiguous to the stream, he thereby cuts off the part so conveyed from all participation in the use of the stream and from riparian rights therein, unless the conveyance declares the contrary." This suggests a means of ameliorating the sweeping, sometimes harsh effect of the source of title rule.

Professor Farnham has reviewed the theories of riparian ownership from an eastern perspective. He argues that the humid states should not adopt the source of title rule because "the policy in aid of which these practices were inaugurated—the policy against concentration of land ownership in too few hands—should not now be pursued in the East in view of the economic and scientific factors currently affecting agriculture," and recommends legislation that would require only that the land be both within the watershed of the stream and a reasonable distance from the stream. William F. Farnham, *The Permissible Extent of Riparian Land,* 7 Land & Water L.Rev. 31, 54 (1972).

NOTE

Can theories that limit the amount of land that can be classified as riparian be justified today because they tend to make more water available for instream uses such as recreation and fish and wildlife preservation? As a means of making more water available for downstream uses? Some states, such as California, have dual systems of water rights; riparian rights are available to those who own land along a stream, and appropriative rights are available for others. Is there a greater justification for a restrictive definition of riparian land in dual system states?

KUNDEL FARMS v. VIR–JO FARMS, INC.

(Court of Appeal of Iowa, 1991).
467 N.W.2d 291.

Kundel Farms (Kundel) and Vir–Jo Farms (Vir–Jo) are adjoining landowners. Kundel owns land to the east, north, and west of Vir–Jo. A dispute arose between the parties concerning a fence between their properties. In 1987, at Vir–Jo's request, Lake Township Fenceviewers inspected the property and issued an order. The fenceviewers ordered Kundel to repair and maintain 100 rods of fence and ordered Vir–Jo to repair and maintain 116 rods of fence.

Kundel appealed the fenceviewers' order to district court. Kundel claimed the westerly fifty-five rods of fence it was ordered to maintain are solely on its property and, therefore, outside the jurisdiction of the fenceviewers. Kundel refused to abide by the fenceviewers' order. Vir–Jo repaired the entire fence at its own expense. Vir–Jo repaired this fifty-five rods of fence.

During the same time period, Vir–Jo filed an equity action against Kundel in the district court. Vir–Jo claimed Kundel was obstructing the natural waterflow over its land.

The fence and water disputes were consolidated by the court and, by request of the parties, submitted to a master pursuant to Iowa Rules of Civil Procedure 207–214. The master filed his report finding: 1) the fenceviewers' order was void due to their lack of jurisdiction over a non-partition fence located solely on Kundel's land; and 2) Vir–Jo failed to show Kundel's alterations of the embankment substantially harmed Vir–Jo's land.

* * *

Vir–Jo has cross-appealed the district court's denial of its petition to have Kundel restore the dam in Crane Creek to its original level when Kundel bought the property in 1978. At that time, a thirty-six-inch steel culvert at creek bed level allowed the creek to flow through the dam. The dam itself is actually a causeway traversing a low-lying swampy portion of Kundel's land. This low-lying area extends down into Vir–Jo's property.

The dam as presently constructed has two fifteen or eighteen inch steel culverts. The first is about two feet above the creek bed level.

The second is about nine inches or so above the first. There is no question the positioning and decreased diameter of the present culverts substantially affect the flow of water onto Vir–Jo's servient property.

* * *

Now, each riparian owner has a right to use the water of a surface stream for ordinary or natural uses, and, under certain circumstances, for artificial uses, such as for irrigation and the like; and the better law seems to be that he may use the water for his natural and ordinary wants, regardless of the effect upon other proprietors on the stream; that is, as we understand the rule, one riparian proprietor may, for his natural wants, if necessary, use all of the water in a surface stream, to the exclusion of every other such proprietor, certainly so as against the other proprietor using the water for artificial purposes. In case, however, such a proprietor puts the water to an extraordinary or artificial use, he must do so in such a manner as not to interfere with its lawful use by others above or below him upon the same stream. As to extraordinary or artificial uses, the rights of all proprietors on the stream are equal; and the artificial use is held to be always subordinate to the natural use. If there is not water enough to more than supply the natural wants of the several riparian owners, none can use the water from the stream for artificial purposes. Ordinary or natural uses have been held to include the use for domestic purposes, including household purposes, such as cleansing, washing, and supplying an ordinary number of horses or stock with water, and it is said that natural uses are limited to the purposes above stated. Now, what is a reasonable use of the water of a surface stream for artificial purposes? Clearly, such a use as permits the return of the water used to the stream in its natural channel, without corruption or sensible diminution in quantity. By this is not meant that all the water must be returned to the stream, because in the use some will necessarily be lost or wasted. What is or constitutes such reasonable use must be determined in view of the size and capacity of the stream, the wants of all other proprietors, the fall of the water, the character of the soil, the number of proprietors to be supplied, and all other circumstances.

* * *

Vir–Jo desires to use the water in Crane Creek for watering stock and other agricultural purposes. Kundel uses the water to make a wetland so four hunters may rent the land for $1,000 a year. While we find neither use unreasonable, creating a wetland for hunting certainly is an artificial use. As such, Vir–Jo's natural use of the stream to water his livestock takes precedence.

The two foot minimum depth of Kundel's pond will substantially diminish the flow of water onto Vir–Jo's property, especially in drier years. Also, the smaller size of the two pipes and their relative height will further diminish the flow.

We determine Kundel's alteration of the previously agreed upon thirty-six-inch culvert to be impermissible in light of the diminished flow of water to servient properties. Kundel is ordered to return the dam to the former dimensions, with a thirty-six-inch culvert set at creek bed level.

We reverse the trial court on this issue.

NOTE

Under riparian law, domestic or "natural" uses have always enjoyed a preference over other uses, which the courts refer to as "artificial." In distinguishing between the two, the court in an Illinois case, Evans v. Merriweather, 4 Ill. (3 Scam.) 492, 495 (1842) noted:

> * * * it is proper to consider the wants of man in regard to the element of water. These wants are either natural or artificial. Natural are such as are absolutely necessary to be supplied, in order to his existence. Artificial, such only as, by supplying them, his comfort and prosperity are increased. To quench thirst, and for household purposes, water is absolutely indispensable. In civilized life, water for cattle is also necessary. These wants must be supplied, or both man and beast will perish.

Compare the analysis offered by Roscoe Pound, one of the seminal figures in American jurisprudence, when he was a young commissioner in his native Nebraska:

> This subject has been confused needlessly by the unfortunate use of the words "natural" and "ordinary" in this connection to distinguish those uses which the common law does not attempt to limit, and "artificial" or "extraordinary" to designate those which are required to be exercised within reasonable bounds. It is no doubt true that irrigation is a very natural and a very ordinary want and that use of a stream for such purpose is natural and ordinary in semiarid regions. But such is not the question. The law does not regard the needs and desires of the person taking the water solely to the exclusion of all other riparian proprietors, but looks rather to the natural effect of his use of water upon the stream and the equal rights of others therein. The true distinction appears to lie between those modes of use which ordinarily involve the taking of small quantities, and but little interference with the stream, such as drinking and other household purposes, and those which necessarily involve the taking or diversion of large quantities and a considerable interference with its ordinary course and flow, such as manufacturing purposes.

Meng v. Coffey, 93 N.W. 713, 717–18 (Neb.1903).

The domestic preference has generally not been extended to municipalities or other large institutional suppliers. See Pernell v. Henderson, 16 S.E.2d 449 (N.C.1941). The question of municipal supply is further considered in Chapter Six.

MASON v. HOYLE
Supreme Court of Errors of Connecticut, 1888.
56 Conn. 255, 14 A. 786.

* * * The plaintiff Mason, during all that time, has owned and operated a saw-mill, grist-mill, and wagon-shop, with machinery driven

wholly by water-power, under a head and fall of about eight feet, supplied from a small pond owned by him, covering not over an acre and a half, and raised by a dam across the bed of the stream. About eighteen inches only upon the top of this pond, when full, is available for power. When the flow of water into the pond is scant, but adequate for the purpose, the ordinary practice at this mill has been to run the machinery until the pond is drawn down some six or eight inches from the top, and then cease running till it fills again, when the use is resumed as before. This privilege is an ancient one. [The water uses of other plaintiffs were described.] The machinery and business at each is and has been such that the ordinary flow of the stream, during the dry seasons of the year, as they ordinarily occur, would (except for the acts of the defendant mentioned hereafter) have been ample to continue the business, and meet its ordinary demands. The defendant Hoyle, since the year 1875, has been owner and possessor of land, mills, and mill privileges in the town of Willington, on the same stream, next above the mill of the plaintiff Mason, and about four hundred and fifty rods therefrom, which are and long have been used for the manufacture of woolen goods. The privilege consists of a head and fall of twenty feet, the water being drawn onto the wheel directly from a small pond near the mills, which is supplied by means of a canal or ditch connecting with a larger pond or reservoir, owned by him, about a quarter of a mile above, on the same stream, where there is an additional fall, when the reservoir is full, of about eleven feet; and some five acres are covered with the water. The dam at the reservoir was repaired and enlarged by the defendant about the year 1881. In addition to water-power, the defendant has at his mills a steam-boiler and engine, capable of driving his machinery independently of the water-wheel, but it is so arranged that it may be used with facility, and without detriment to the business, in connection with the water-power. As a usual thing, for eight or nine months of each year, extending from September or October to May or June following, there has been flowing in the river an ample supply of water for all the privileges and mills thereon, and during such periods there has been no complaint, or ground of complaint, against the defendant, or any other mill-owner, as to the mode of using the water; but during the remaining three or four months, between May and October, (subject to a few exceptions in extraordinary seasons,) the supply of water has been comparatively small. And during such dry seasons the amount of machinery to be driven at the defendant's mill has been and is greatly disproportionate to the diminished capacity of the stream, and it has been impossible for the defendant, at such times, to run all his machinery by water-power alone, except for a small part of the time. The mill and privilege now owned by the defendant was owned and occupied by other parties, for the same purposes, many years before the defendant obtained the same. These prior owners and occupants, during the season of deficient supply of water, as a general rule, used steam and water power in connection; and in this way the water naturally flowing in the stream was allowed to pass regularly to the several privileges of the plaintiffs, furnishing a supply sufficient to meet the ordinary demands of their business; so that no complaint was made by them, or either of them. But about the year 1881 the defendant adopted a practice in this respect different from that of his predecessors, and during the season of the year when the water supply has been inadequate for his use he has been in the habit of shutting his gates, wholly or partially, so that the water would accumulate in his reservoir, meanwhile running his machinery wholly by steam-power from two to five days, until there was an accumulation of water in his reservoir sufficient to run by water-power alone continuously for five or six hours; and, after so running, he would return again to the exclusive use of steam, and continue, as before, the alternative use of steam and water power. By these means the defendant has detained, for periods varying from two to five days in the week, and for many weeks, during the dry season of each year, substantially all the natural flow of the stream, except so much as he required daily for washing wool and cloth, and for his boiler, (which usually has been much less than the natural flow of the stream;) and then, by the use of water-power alone, for periods of five or six hours a day, once or twice during the week, and sometimes oftener, the water has flowed from his wheel in quantities far in excess of the natural flow of the stream during such seasons, which has resulted in quickly filling the small ponds of the plaintiffs, and then running to waste over their several dams. * * *

LOOMIS, J. The rule that now obtains in all jurisdictions, as recognized by all the authorities, is that the use made by mill-owners of a stream must, in its relation to other mill-owners on the same stream, be a reasonable use. The rule is obviously one that applies solely to the relation of the several occupants of the stream among themselves. Where one mill-owner is the sole occupant, there is in law no limitation upon his use. The rule being that of reasonable use, the application of the rule becomes a matter for each particular case. The question, while in some sense a mixed question of law and fact, is yet essentially a question of fact. Whether the use be reasonable must depend less upon any general rule than upon the particular circumstances. But there are certain conditions essential to a reasonable use so long recognized by common consent, or so obviously just, that we may safely generalize with regard to them. In the first place, the use must be as near as possible an equal use, or, rather, an equal opportunity to use. "Equity delighteth in equality." Every owner improving a mill privilege has a right to consider the law as protecting him against any unfair use by any other owner who may establish a mill above him. The term "unfair use" is the equivalent of "unreasonable use." When the owner above him has established his mill, he is bound, not merely by this obvious rule of the stream, but by another more general rule of universal application, that no one may so use his own as to injure the property of another. This golden rule of the law is not, of course, to be taken literally; for where there is a concurrent use of water, and at the same time a deficiency, the use of one will, to some extent, injure another. In the next place, a reasonable use is one adapted to the character and capacity of the stream. Indeed, there is no other factor of so much importance that comes into the question as that of the capacity of the stream; and, in determining this capacity, its condition throughout the year is to be considered. * * * In the next place, a reasonable use must permit the water to flow in its accustomed way, so far as this can be done, and a beneficial use, though a limited one, be made of the reduced stream, each riparian mill-owner having his fair proportion. It is the right of every mill-owner, large or small, on the stream, that the water be allowed to run in its usual way, except where detained by another to secure his fair proportion of beneficial use. A policy of the state may come in to affect the question. It is for the public interest that all our streams be improved as far as they can be. This rule has sometimes been applied to favor the larger mill-owner, but it should have regard also to small mill-owners, who are the great majority of those in such business, or who incline to go into it. These men of moderate capital, investing their means in mills upon our lesser streams, should be protected against such a use of the streams by mills disproportioned to their capacities as would practically deprive them of water and ruin their privileges. And, where the water is sufficient only for a few hours' use in a day, it is a reasonable demand of these lesser mills that they should be allowed water enough to run a part of every day, rather than it should be detained by any larger mill in such a way as to compel them to crowd into a single day or night all the work of a week. There would be no way in which the lesser mills could hold their own against the disproportionately large ones, with reservoirs of great capacity, but to enlarge their own reservoirs and ponds to an equal capacity; thus compelling all to enlarge their works in a manner not demanded by the capacity of the stream, and involving an unnecessary and perhaps ruinous expenditure. If a large mill-owner has made a reservoir which it requires several days to fill in the dry season, he has no more right, on that account, to detain the water for a week, to fill it, than he would have to detain it a month. His rights are not measured at all by the capacity of his reservoir, for he may be able to double or fourfold its capacity, and the law will not allow him to establish for himself the rule that shall decide his rights between himself and another. The question is not as to the capacity of the reservoir, but what is a fair use of the water between him and his neighbor below? Where the reservoir, as in the case at bar, is simply to store the water, and not to furnish the head and fall, he can as well use the water when it is a half or a quarter filled as the lower owner can use it when his smaller pond is wholly filled. A reservoir used to store surplus water, when the supply is abundant, for use at a time when it is deficient, is a great benefit to all the lower proprietors; but, if used to detain the water in the dry season, it may occasion great injury, as in this case.

* * *

But the general principle stated by us at the outset of the discussion, to the effect that, to justify a detention of the water by the upper proprietor long enough to make an advantageous use of it, his machinery, or so much of it as he operates, must be adapted to the fixed character of the stream (if it has any) as to deficiency of water during the dry seasons, apparently conflicts with the rule laid down in many cases, that the adaptation referred to must be to the usual quantity of water in the stream, or other equivalent expressions, by which we have no doubt was meant, as applicable to those cases, the medium average flow between a high and low stage of water. But in none of the cases where the rule has been applied, so far as we have examined them, did the seasons of great scarcity of water occur with such regularity, year after year, as in the case at bar. * * * "And during such dry seasons the amount of machinery to be driven at the defendant's mill has been and is greatly disproportionate to the diminished capacity of the stream; and it has been impossible for the defendant at such times to run all his machinery by water-power alone, except for a small fraction of the time." And the other fact found, that five days' detention of the water has enabled the defendant to run only five hours, shows still more forcibly the enormous disproportion of his machinery to the capacity of the stream during the dry season. * * * The reasoning of the court, however, in Drake v. Woolen Co., 99 Mass. 574, suggests the point that the rule to be adopted should be one to promote the largest possible utilization of water-power, which can only be accomplished by conceding to the mill-owner the right to erect machinery requiring the full average flow of the stream, with the incidental right to detain the water as may be necessary during the dry season, as otherwise the workmen must remain idle till the wet season returns and the scarcity is over. We find no fault with this rule applied to cases where the season of scarcity cannot be anticipated, but the reason of the rule makes it inapplicable to the case at bar, where it is manifest from the finding that, if water-power alone was used, the workmen could be employed only a small fraction of the time during the summer months. So if we concede to the defendant the right to detain the water, as claimed, for the propulsion of his entire machinery, the certain result would be that there could be no beneficial employment for men and machinery at the defendant's own mill, nor at the several mills of the plaintiffs. There can be no public policy in a rule thus applied.

Now, the defendant insists that any reasoning which is to determine his water-rights must leave out of the account the fact that he has steam-power which he can use with facility and without detriment, and this position we accept as substantially correct. At the same time the fact that steam-power must be used or the mill must stop, and that it always has been used, is a significant admission that his machinery has overburdened the water-power. It is found that his predecessors in the ownership of the mill, and who were carrying on the same business, so used the water in connection with their steam-power as not to injure the plaintiffs in the use of their mills. While the defendant has, of course, lost no rights to the water by the possession of steam-power, yet the fact that he is using such power, and can, by using the water in connection with it, get a reasonably advantageous use of the latter, without injury to the owners below, making his present mode of using it unnecessary, is a matter proper to be considered in determining whether he should be restrained from such injurious use.

If the principle we have been contending for is not sufficiently established to be accepted as controlling this case, still the fact of a regularly recurring deficiency of water is at least one important element in determining the question of reasonable use. The defendant knew the fact when he bought the property, and afterwards when, in 1881, he repaired and enlarged his reservoir, and when, with presumptive knowledge of the result to the plaintiffs, he changed the long-established mode of running the mill. And this suggests another element with which to test the reasonableness of the defendant's use of the water. The immemorial local custom upon the stream, down to the time of the defendant's interposition, to let the water flow to the plaintiffs' mills without any long or injurious detention, according to the authorities in this and other jurisdictions, has an important bearing upon the question. Again, there is still another element of great significance as it exists in this case, namely, the extent of benefit to the defendant by his detention as compared with the injury to the plaintiffs. * * * If we take the period of greatest detention, which has often occurred, we find that the three mills belonging severally to the three plaintiffs must each be idle five days to enable the defendant to enjoy the slight benefit of a five hours' use. * * *

NOTES

1. Suppose the defendant's mill and large pond had been on the stream *before* plaintiffs located their mills on the stream. Same result?

2. Is it clear that efficiency is promoted by this decision?

3. In Romey v. Landers, 392 N.W.2d 415 (S.D.1986), an upstream riparian constructed a series of earthen dams that cut off the flow of a prior downstream cattle rancher. Because of inadequate flow for irrigation and livestock watering, the rancher claimed that he suffered crop losses and was forced to sell some of his cattle. He also had to haul water to cattle that "could smell the impounded water, causing Romey to reinforce his fences." After the injured rancher petitioned the state Water Management Board, the Board issued an order requiring removal of all but two of the dams because they represented an unreasonable and wasteful use of water. On appeal, the court rejected the argument of the upper riparian who argued that a South Dakota statute that prohibited waste was void for vagueness.

> Although "waste" and "reasonable use" are not statutorily defined, the Legislature's general intent is capable of understanding and this general intent, coupled with the case law hereinbefore cited, sufficiently apprises riparian owners of forbidden water use and provides the Board with guidelines for enforcing these statutes.

392 N.W.2d at 419–20.

4. Under the reasonable use theory of riparian rights, of which Mason v. Hoyle is an oft-cited example, each riparian owner's right is correlative. It is protected from harm by other, unreasonable uses of water, but the use of the stream must be shared among other reasonable users. Eastern riparian cases seldom require a court to apportion the use of a stream among similar users. Often the court is not

convinced that a shortage exists. E.g., Ripka v. Wansing, 589 S.W.2d 333 (Mo.App.1979). As one would expect, what there is of the law of riparian apportionment comes from the West. In California, the courts developed a device for quantifying the water rights of competing riparians. In Half Moon Bay Land Co. v. Cowell, 160 P. 675, 678–79 (Cal.1916), Justice Shaw, the judicial architect of many important California water law doctrines, commented on an apportionment decree as follows:

> In apportioning the waters of a stream among the riparian owners, where there is not sufficient for the needs of all, many different facts are to be considered. In Harris v. Harrison, 93 Cal. 681, 29 Pac. 326, the court, in considering this question, said: "The length of the stream, the volume of water in it, the extent of each ownership along the banks, the character of the soil owned by each contestant, the area sought to be irrigated by each—all these, and many other considerations, must enter into the solution of the problem." See, also, Southern etc. Co. v. Wilshire, 144 Cal. 71, 77 Pac. 767. So far as we are aware, no court has ever undertaken to lay down a comprehensive rule on the subject. We are satisfied that the court may also consider the practicability of irrigation of the lands of the respective parties, the expense thereof, the comparative profit of the different uses which could be made of the water on the land, and that when the water is insufficient for all the land or for all of the uses to which it might be applied thereon, and there is enough only for that use which is most valuable and profitable, the shares may properly be limited to and measured by the quantity sufficient for that use, and the proportions fixed accordingly. The party taking, under such a decree, could, of course, put his share so fixed to another beneficial use if he so desired. The decree here does not, and it should not, prohibit him from doing so. The apportionment made appears to have awarded to each his reasonable share of the limited quantity of water flowing in the stream during the dry season of the excessively dry year taken as the basis upon which the apportionment was made. The fact that it was made with regard to the area of land capable of profitable irrigation does not of necessity make the apportionment inequitable. It was a reasonable division for a year of that character. No reason appears why it should not be equally fair and reasonable to divide the water in the same proportions in other years when there is more water.

Would an allocation of a specific amount of water to each riparian be superior to a percentage allocation? What is the effect of the failure to join a riparian owner as a party in litigation to apportion the water of a stream?

5. Do apportionment decrees quantify the parties' water rights in perpetuity, or are such decrees subject to being reopened?

In State v. Starley, 413 S.W.2d 451, 460–61, 464–66 (Tex.Civ.App. 1967), the court said:

In a great number of the western states where water adjudication has been a problem, it has been dealt with through constitutional provisions and statutory laws. These states have laws permitting certain administrative agencies or the courts, or both, to retain jurisdiction in water adjudication cases. In Texas we have a particular statute which permits this trial court to retain jurisdiction, but limits the court to the period of time pending appeal of the case. Tex.Rev.Civ.Stat.Ann. art. 7589b.

6. Recent scholarship recognizes that custom is the source of many property rights, although the "modern" positivist push for uniformity has obscured those origins. Hawaiian water law is a striking example of the interplay between custom and riparian rights. Prior to Hawaii's annexation by the United States, land was divided into *ahupua'as* and *ilis*.

An *ahupua'a* is a parcel of land, roughly wedge-shaped, extending from the highland to the ocean. Typically, the side boundaries ran down ridges, and the *ahupua'a* encompassed an entire watershed. Each *ahupua'a* was under the direction of a *konohiki,* or chief. Commoners lived on the *ahupua'as* and cultivated them, giving a portion of the crops to the *konohiki* and later to the King after the islands were unified under one sovereign. An *ili* is a smaller tract of land granted to a chief.

All Hawaiian land and water was held in common for the benefit of the people. After unification, land and water were under the ultimate control of the King. There were no individual land titles so westerners seeking land in the nineteenth century brought pressure to make land transferable. In 1848 the Great *Mahele* (division) took place. The King quitclaimed his interest in certain lands to the *konohikis,* and they in turn quitclaimed other lands to the King. This is the source of Hawaiian allodial land titles.

Water rights were based on the Hawaiian land tenure system. Traditionally there were two types of water rights: the appurtenant right and the *konohiki* right. The appurtenant right was based on the water requirements of taro farming. Taro is a root crop used to make a staple of the Hawaiian diet, *poi.* An owner of an *ahupua'a* had the right to use as much water from the watercourse of that *ahupua'a* as was needed for the cultivation of taro. Taro farming requires large diversions because the crop must be inundated with flowing water at regular intervals. However, it is not a highly consumptive use and much of the water returns to the watercourse. The *konohiki* right provided that rights in water not required to fulfill appurtenant rights (surplus waters) were controlled by the *konohiki.*

In Carter v. Territory, 24 Haw. 47 (1917), the territorial court superimposed the riparian doctrine over traditional Hawaiian allocation systems. At issue was the right to storm waters in a stream that flowed through two adjacent *ahupua'as.* The court held that the owner of the upstream *ahupua'a* had the right to use of storm water but not to diminish its quantity or quality. The court's language sounded like the "natural flow" approach to riparianism but in fact it dealt only with storm waters. It also said that water rights could be acquired by prescription. Early cases had held that appurtenant rights could be obtained by prescription.

The development of large water-consumptive sugar cane plantations led some Hawaiians to view water as a salable commodity. A line of cases appeared to hold that appurtenant and prescriptive rights were "owned" by the landowner and could be severed and put to use in other watersheds. Large sugar plantations were made possible by investments of millions of dollars in irrigation systems which transported water from one *ahupua'a* (and thus watershed) to another.

The practices on which many enterprises were built were thrown into question in McBryde Sugar Co. v. Robinson, 517 P.2d 26 (Haw. 1973), cert. denied 417 U.S. 976 (1974). For all surplus waters, the court adopted a version of the natural flow theory of riparian rights. Relying on ancient Hawaiian customary law, the court held that ancient appurtenant rights, which passed with the land at the Great *Mahele*, were merely usufructuary, not possessory rights. A series of unsuccessful constitutional challenges followed, see pages 376–80, infra, and in 1987 the state adopted a transferable permit system applicable to certain designated areas. Haw.Rev.Stat. § 174C–59 (1987).

HARRIS v. BROOKS

Supreme Court of Arkansas, 1955.
225 Ark. 436, 283 S.W.2d 129.

WARD, JUSTICE.

* * *

Appellant, Theo Mashburn, lessee of riparian landowners conducts a commercial boating and fishing enterprise. In this business he rents cabins, sells fishing bait and equipment, and rents boats to members of the general public who desire to use the lake for fishing and other recreational purposes. He and his lessors filed a complaint in chancery court on July 10, 1954 to enjoin appellees from pumping water from the lake to irrigate a rice crop, alleging that, as of that date, appellees had reduced the water level of the lake to such an extent as to make the lake unsuitable "for fishing, recreation, or other lawful purposes." After a lengthy hearing, the chancellor denied injunctive relief, and this appeal is prosecuted to reverse the chancellor's decision.

Factual Background. Horseshoe Lake, located about 3 miles south of Augusta, is approximately 3 miles long and 300 feet wide, and, as the name implies, resembles a horseshoe in shape. Appellees, John Brooks and John Brooks, Jr., are lessees of Ector Johnson who owns a large tract of land adjacent to the lake, including three-fourths of the lake bed.

For a number of years appellees have intermittently raised rice on Johnson's land and have each year, including 1954, irrigated the rice with water pumped from the lake. They pumped no more water in 1954 than they did in 1951 and 1952, no rice being raised in 1953. Approximately 190 acres were cultivated in rice in 1954.

The rest of the lake bed and the adjoining land is divided into four parts, each part owned by a different person or group of persons. One such part is owned by Ed Harris, Jesse Harris, Alice Lynch and Dora Balkin who are also appellants. In March 1954 Mashburn leased from the above named appellants a relatively small camp site on the bank of the lake and installed the business above mentioned at a cost of approximately $8,000, including boats, cabins, and fishing equipment. Mashburn began operating his business about the first of April, 1954, and fishing and boat rentals were satisfactory from that time until about July 1st or 4th when, he says, the fish quit biting and his income from that source and boat rentals was reduced to practically nothing.

Appellees began pumping water with an 8 inch intake on May 25, 1954 and continued pumping until this suit was filed on July 10, and then until about August 20th. They quit pumping at this time because it was discovered fish life was being endangered. The trial was had September 28, 1954, and the decree was rendered December 29, 1954.

The Testimony. Because of the disposition we hereafter make of this case, it would serve no useful purpose to set out the voluminous testimony in detail or attempt to evaluate all the conflicting portions thereof. The burden of appellants' testimony, given by residents who had observed the lake over a period of years and by those familiar with fish life and sea level calculations, was directed at establishing the *normal* or *medium* water level of the lake. The years 1952, 1953 and 1954 were unusually dry and the water levels in similar lakes in the same general area were unusually low in August and September of 1954. During August 1954 Horseshoe Lake was below "normal", but it is not entirely clear from the testimony that this was true on July 10 when the suit was filed. It also appears that during the stated period the water had receded from the bank where Mashburn's boats were usually docked, making it impossible for him to rent them to the public. There is strong testimony, disputed by appellees, that the *normal* level of the lake is 189.67 feet above sea level and that the water was below this level on July 10. Unquestionably the water was below normal when this suit was tried the latter part of September, 1954.

* * *

Issues Clarified. In refusing to issue the injunction the chancellor made no finding of facts, and did not state the ground upon which his decision rested. Appellants strongly insist that the chancellor was forced by the testimony to conclude first that the normal level of the lake was 189.67 feet above sea level and second that the water in the lake was at or below this level when the suit was filed on July 10th. This being true, appellants say, it was error for the chancellor to refuse to enjoin appellees from pumping water out of the lake. If it be conceded that the testimony does show and the chancellor should have found that the water in Horseshoe Lake was at or below the normal level when this suit was filed on July 10th, then appellants would have been entitled to an injunction provided this case was decided strictly under the uniform flow theory mentioned hereafter. However as explained later we are not bound by this theory in this state. * * *

Two Basic Theories. Generally speaking two separate and distinct theories or doctrines regarding the right to use water are recognized. One is commonly called the "Appropriation Doctrine" and the other is the "Riparian Doctrine".

Appropriation Doctrine. Since it is unnecessary to do so we make no attempt to discuss the varied implications of this doctrine. Generally speaking, under this doctrine, some governmental agency, acting under constitutional or legislative authority, apportions water to contesting claimants. It has never been adopted in this state, but has been in about 17 western states. This doctrine is inconsistent with the common law relative to water rights in force in this and many other states. One principal distinction between this doctrine and the riparian doctrine is that under the former the use is not limited to riparian landowners.

Riparian Doctrine. This doctrine, long in force in this and many other states, is based on the old common law which gave to the owners of land bordering on streams the right to use the water therefrom for certain purposes, and this right was considered an incident to the ownership of land. Originally it apparently accorded the landowner the right to have the water maintained at its normal level, subject to use for strictly domestic purposes. Later it became evident that this strict limitation placed on the use of water was unreasonable and unutilitarian. Consequently it was not long before the demand for a greater use of water caused a relaxation of the strict limitations placed on its use and this doctrine came to be divided into (a) the natural flow theory and (b) the reasonable use theory.

(a) *Natural Flow Theory.* Generally speaking again, under the natural flow theory, a riparian owner can take water for domestic purposes only, such as water for the family, live stock, and gardening, and he is entitled to have the water in the stream or lake upon which he borders kept at the normal level. There are some expressions in the opinions of this court indicating that we have recognized this theory, at least to a certain extent.

Reasonable Use Theory. This theory appears to be based on the necessity and desirability of deriving greater benefits from the use of our abundant supply of water. It recognizes that there is no sound reason for maintaining our lakes and streams at a normal level when the water can be beneficially used without causing unreasonable damage to other riparian owners. The progress of civilization, particularly in regard to manufacturing, irrigation, and recreation, has forced the realization that a strict adherence to the uninterrupted flow doctrine placed an unwarranted limitation on the use of water, and consequently the court developed what we now call the reasonable use theory. This theory is of course subject to different interpretations and limitations. In 56 Am.Jur., page 728, it is stated that "The rights of riparian proprietors on both navigable and unnavigable streams are to a great extent mutual, common, or correlative. The use of the stream or water by each proprietor is therefore limited to what is reasonable, having due regard for the rights of others above, below, or on the opposite shore. In general, the special rights of a riparian owner are such as are necessary for the use and enjoyment of his abutting property and the business lawfully conducted thereon, qualified only by the correlative rights of other riparian owners, and by certain rights of the public, and they are to be so exercised as not to injure others in the enjoyment of their rights." It has been stated that each riparian owner has an equal right to make a reasonable use of waters subject to the equal rights of other owners to make the reasonable use.

* * * We do not understand that the two theories will necessarily clash in every case, but where there is an inconsistency, and where vested rights may not prevent, it is our conclusion that the reasonable use theory should control.

In embracing the reasonable use theory we caution, however, that we are not necessarily adopting all the interpretations given it by the decisions of other states, and that our own interpretation will be developed in the future as occasions arise. Nor is it intended hereby that we will not in the future, under certain circumstances, possibly adhere to some phases of the uniform flow system. It is recognized that in some instances vested rights may have accrued to riparian landowners and we could not of course constitutionally negate those rights.

* * *

The result of our examination of the decisions of this court and other authorities relative to the use by riparian proprietors of water in non-navigable lakes and streams justifies the enunciation of the following general rules and principles:

(a) The right to use water for strictly domestic purposes—such as for household use—is superior to many other uses of water—such as for fishing, recreation and irrigation.

(b) Other than the use mentioned above, all other lawful uses of water are equal. Some of the lawful uses of water recognized by this state are: fishing, swimming, recreation, and irrigation.

(c) When one lawful use of water is destroyed by another lawful use the latter must yield, or it may be enjoined.

(d) When one lawful use of water interferes with or detracts from another lawful use, then a question arises as to whether, under all the facts and circumstances of that particular case, the interfering use shall be declared unreasonable and as such enjoined, or whether a reasonable and equitable adjustment should be made, having due regard to the reasonable rights of each.

* * *

We do not minimize the difficulties attendant upon an application of the reasonable use rule to any given set of facts and circumstances and particularly those present in this instance. It is obvious that there are no definite guide posts provided and that necessarily much must be left to judgment and discretion. The breadth and boundaries of this area of discretion are well stated in Restatement of the Law, Torts, § 852c in these words: "The determination in a particular case of the unreasonableness of a particular use is not and should not be an unreasoned, intuitive conclusion on the part of the court or jury. It is rather an evaluating of the conflicting interests of each of the contestants before the court in accordance with the standards of society, and a weighing of those, one against the other. The law accords equal protection to the interests of all the riparian proprietors in the use of water, and seeks to promote the greatest beneficial use of the water, and seeks to promote the greatest beneficial use by each with a minimum of harm to others. But when one riparian proprietor's use of the water harmfully invades another's interest in its use, there is an incompatibility of interest between the two parties to a greater or lesser extent depending on the extent of the invasion, and there is immediately a question whether such a use is legally permissible. It is axiomatic in the law that individuals in society must put up with a reasonable amount of annoyance and inconvenience resulting from the otherwise lawful activities of their neighbors in the use of their land. Hence it is only when one riparian proprietor's use of the water is unreasonable that another who is harmed by it can complain, even though the harm is intentional. Substantial intentional harm to another cannot be justified as reasonable unless the legal merit or utility of the activity which produces it outweighs the legal seriousness or gravity of the harm."

* * *

Our Conclusion. After careful consideration, an application of the rules above announced to the complicated fact situation set forth in this record leads us to conclude that the Chancellor should have issued an order enjoining appellees from pumping water out of Horseshoe Lake when the water level reaches 189.67 feet above sea level for as long as the material facts and circumstances are substantially the same as they appear in this record. * * * Our conclusion is based on the fact that we think the evidence shows this level happens to be the level below which appellants would be unreasonably interfered with. * * *

Reversed with direction to the trial court to enter a decree in conformity with this opinion.

McFADDIN, J., concurs.

NOTES

1. In *Harris,* Mashburn's fishing business apparently began in the spring of 1954, whereas Brooks had been growing rice for a "number of years" before that. Does the court attach any significance to Brooks' status as a prior user? Should it, and if so, how much significance? Priority of water use has traditionally carried weight with riparian courts, even those that purported to accept the "natural flow" theory. See, e.g., Bealey v. Shaw, 6 East. 208, 102 Eng.Rep. 1266 (K.B.1805) (using a "prior use" test to prevent newer mills from using water in a way that interfered with earlier mills).

2. What standard does the court in *Harris* employ in comparing the reasonableness of the two competing uses? Did Brooks' rice grow-

ing become less reasonable when the Mashburn fishing business started up? What would happen if another rice grower now began withdrawing water from the lake? Would Brooks and Mashburn be suing the newcomer? What is the relationship between the "normal" level of Horseshoe Lake and the "reasonable" level? Will they always be the same?

3. How do the results in *Harris* measure up to the criteria for sound resource allocation based on economics as discussed in Chapter 1, especially as set forth by Hirshleifer, DeHaven, and Milliman, page 22, supra?

4. Are nonconsumptive uses presumptively more "reasonable" than consumptive uses? In *Harris*, a consumptive use—the irrigation of rice—and a nonconsumptive use—commercial fishing and boating— are in conflict. Does the distinction between the two types of uses have an impact on the outcome? The court says that the irrigators "had merely been exercising their lawful rights as riparian owners." What are those rights, and why does their exercise not "disturb" the rights of other riparians on the lake? Compare Hoover v. Crane, 106 N.W.2d 563 (Mich.1960), page 91, infra, where the court approved a decree which allowed an irrigator to take "the total equivalent in pumpage of one-quarter inch of the content of Hutchins Lake to be used in any dry period in between the cessation of flow from the outlet and the date when such flow recommences." The littoral owners were unable to prove that the irrigator caused the decline in the water level. The court added that, in any event, it could not say "that use of the amount provided in the decree during the dry season is unreasonable in respect to other riparian owners."

In Taylor v. Tampa Coal Co., 46 So.2d 392 (Fla.1950), littoral recreational users succeeded in enjoining withdrawals from a twenty- six acre lake for citrus irrigation. The court quoted from 2 Farnham on Waters and Water Rights 1618 (1904) that "[t]he owner of land on the margin of a natural lake or pond has a right to have the natural level of the water maintained, so as to permit him to enjoy the advantages attendant upon riparian ownership, and to protect him from the disadvantage of having a strip of uncovered lake bottom left in front of his property," and concluded "it is plain that when the water of the lake here involved is at normal level the lake is too small in area and content to allow water to be pumped therefrom for irrigating purposes without consequent damage to other riparian owners."

Should courts consider possible future nonconsumptive uses of riparians in determining reasonableness of a consumptive use?

5. The respective rights of riparians to use the surface of a waterbody are considered at pages 432–47, infra.

6. Is there a riparian right to have a water level maintained even if the surface is not to be "used" in the ordinary sense?

The City of Los Angeles condemned rights in two streams that contributed 90 per cent of the inflow to Mono Lake, a closed mountain lake so permeated with alkaline compounds as to be unfit for domestic or irrigation use. Diversion of the streamflow into the city water system would cause the lake to dry up, leaving exposed salt flats. Condemnees were owners of resort properties around (and on an island in) the lake. The jury awarded damages which took into consideration the water-related values of the littoral land. Los Angeles appealed on the ground that the condemnees were making no beneficial use of the water of the lake and that under Art. XII § 3 of the California Constitution, only nominal damages for littoral rights were due. The Court of Appeals affirmed.

> For the reason that the existence of Mono Lake in its natural condition, with all of its attractive surroundings, is the vital thing that furnishes to the respondents' marginal land almost its entire value, and that the draining of the lake will nearly destroy the value of their properties and the incident littoral rights thereto, it seems clear that the lake is not being used by the respondents for an unreasonable or nonbeneficial purpose, but, upon the contrary, that their use of the lake in its natural condition is reasonably beneficial to their land, and the littoral rights thereof may therefore not be appropriated, even for a higher or more beneficial use for public welfare, without just compensation therefor.

City of Los Angeles v. Aitken, 52 P.2d 585 (Cal.1935). In recent years, litigation over diversions of water away from Mono Lake has raged. See pages 288–96, infra.

EVA MORREALE HANKS, THE LAW
OF WATER IN NEW JERSEY

22 Rutgers L.Rev. 621, 627–32 (1968).

The fundamental tenet of the riparian doctrine is that the owner of land bordering a watercourse has, because of that ownership, some rights or privileges in what nature has made to flow past his front door. Contrary to the Western system, however, these rights or privileges are not measured in quantitative terms. The amount the riparian may use depends in part on his purpose and in part on the amount other riparians are using, for all riparians have correlative rights. Still, each riparian has a "property right." But the nature of this property right defies precise definition, except for the emphasis which, since at least Blackstone's day, has been given to its temporary and usufructuary character: "There are some few things which, notwithstanding the general introduction and continuance of property, must still unavoidably remain in common, being such wherein nothing but an usufructuary property is capable of being had. * * * Water is a moveable, wandering thing, and must of necessity continue common by the law of nature; so that I can only have a temporary, transient, usufructuary property therein."

Blackstone has been paraphrased hundreds of times: the owner does not have a property right "in the water itself" but may only "use it" as it flows past his lands. It is difficult to imagine that the "pretty distinction" has ever played any real part in the practical solution of even a single private controversy. * * *

Beyond the general proposition that the landowner has a usufructuary right only, two distinct theories have developed relating to the manner in which the right—or privilege—may be exercised: the English rule of "natural flow" and the American rule of "reasonable use."

1. The English Rule of Natural Flow

Under the English rule, each landowner has the right to have the water flow past his lands undiminished in quantity and unimpaired in quality. In the famous language of Chancellor Kent: "Every proprietor of lands on the banks of a river, has naturally an equal right to the use of the water which flows in the stream adjacent to his lands, *as it was wont to run (currere solebat) without diminution or alteration.*" Strictly applied, the natural flow rule is almost completely unworkable. As Chancellor Kent observed: "Streams of water are intended for the use and comfort of man; and it would be unreasonable and contrary to the universal sense of mankind, to debar every riparian proprietor from the application of the water to domestic, agricultural, and manufacturing purposes. * * *"

The principles which eventually developed can very broadly be summarized as follows: The right of each riparian to the undiminished flow of the water is subject to certain unlimited uses by other riparians. These so-called natural uses are uses for domestic purposes, such as drinking, bathing, cooking, and washing. They are unlimited insofar as the owner may exhaust the source of supply altogether, and not merely diminish it, if that is necessary to satisfy his needs. Since each riparian is subject to a like right of all other riparians, his own right to the undiminished flow is far from assured, let alone absolute. For purposes not of domestic use, but for use *on or in connection with* the riparian land, all riparians have correlative rights. This rule obviously gives the courts an "elastic measuring rod" and frequently results in decisions not much different from those reached by courts applying the reasonable use doctrine. However, under the English rule no right exists at all to use water for purposes unconnected with the land or to use water on nonriparian land. It is irrelevant that the proposed use is an otherwise reasonable one. As a corollary of the English rule it follows that a transfer of a water right apart from the land is of dubious validity. In contrast, the American rule of reasonable use permits use unconnected with the land or on nonriparian land but subjects such use to criteria of reasonableness.

In applying the English rule, the courts have not hesitated to use the doctrine of *de minimis non curat lex,* primarily to prevent vexatious litigation. On the other hand, the English rule permits the riparian owner to maintain an action without proof of damages. The complainant, it is said, must have injunctive relief for the technical violation of his right. Otherwise, the defendant's admittedly noninjurious use might ripen into a prescriptive right. Of course, if it were not the case that noninjurious uses can ripen into prescriptive rights, injunctive relief, or for that matter any relief other than a declaratory judgment, would be unnecessary.

2. The American Rule of Reasonable Use

The American rule of reasonable use differs in two major respects from the English rule of natural flow. First, in order to maintain an action, it is essential for the complainant to show that he would suffer actual damages if the defendant continued his use. Noninjurious use of the water does not give rise to a cause of action. However, noninjurious use also cannot ripen into a prescriptive right. Second, the use of water on nonriparian land is not "necessarily unprivileged." Instead, its legality is evaluated by criteria of reasonableness, defined as early as 1883 in *Red River Roller Mills v. Wright:*

> In determining what is a reasonable use, regard must be had to the subject-matter of the use; the occasion and manner of its application; the object, extent, necessity, and duration of the use; the nature and size of the stream; the kind of business to which it is subservient; the importance and necessity of the use claimed by one party, and the extent of the injury to the other party; the state of improvement of the country in regard to mills and machinery, and the use of water as a propelling power; the general and established usages of the country in similar cases; and all the other and ever-varying circumstances of each particular case, bearing upon the question of the fitness and propriety of the use of the water under consideration.[35]

In the 85 years since then, not much that is helpful has been added to this general definition of so abstract a proposition as "reasonableness." The *Restatement of Torts* speaks, *inter alia,* of the social value of the proposed use as a factor in deciding reasonableness. Professor Powell, trying to impose some ordering principle, has categorized the problems in which the issue arises and in which certain standards have been developed. His main categories are reasonableness of purpose, of destination, of quantity, and of pollution.

The issue of reasonableness of purpose involves, as all questions of reasonableness do, the balancing of values and the search for reasonable alternatives. Typically, the purpose must be lawful and beneficial to the taker, and must be suitable to the stream. Though they do not always articulate it in their opinions, reasonable use courts weigh the relative social and economic values of the competing uses. The existence of economically reasonable alternative methods of use which would be less harmful will often be a deciding factor. One of the main problems of reasonableness of purpose is whether the withdrawal of water from the stream, with or without return of all or a part of the water to it, can ever be reasonable. This is closely intertwined with the issue of reasonableness of destination. Under the natural flow rule, the purpose for which the diversion is made may determine its legality. If it is for "natural uses," it is per se permissible; if it is for use on nonriparian land, it is per se impermissible. If the diversion is for use on or in connection with the riparian land, the notion that all riparians have correlative rights leads precisely to the sort of weighing and balancing that reasonable use courts do in all three cases. Since

35. Red River Roller Mills v. Wright, 30 Minn. 249, 253, 15 N.W. 167, 169 (1883).

climatic conditions in the Eastern states are roughly similar, it is not surprising that roughly similar results are reached under either theory in cases involving diversion for use in connection with riparian land. Diversion for purposes of irrigation is an important example. By contrast, diversion for purposes of sale may be permitted as a reasonable use under the American rule, whereas it is not permitted under the English rule.

Cases dealing with reasonableness of destination are influenced by a finding that the use is on riparian land. That finding, in turn, is influenced by the criteria respective jurisdictions bring to bear on defining riparian land, such as physical location, ownership of all or part of the stream bed, size of the watershed, and the history of the user's chain of title.

Professor Powell has pointed out that conflicts involving nonriparian diversions arise in three contexts: first, a nonriparian with no right makes such a diversion; second, a nonriparian claiming a right makes such a diversion; third, a riparian makes such a diversion. In jurisdictions adhering to the natural flow rule, judgment must be for the complainant riparian, irrespective of whether he has suffered actual damage, since the nonriparian use is per se impermissible. The rule of reasonable use would turn the answer to the first case on the plaintiff's ability to show actual damage; in most jurisdictions, such a showing would be sufficient for the third case as well. In other words, these (reasonable use) states consider inflicting actual damage on a riparian by way of making a nonriparian use to be *unreasonable as a matter of law*. In some reasonable use states, however, the plaintiff in the third case would have to show, in addition to actual damages, that the nonriparian use was *unreasonable as a matter of fact*. This approach carries a utilitarian philosophy of the use and allocation of water a considerable step further than is the case under the majority rule. The second case, diversion by a nonriparian claiming some right, will depend for its legality on the nature of the right claimed and the status of the complaining party. For example, a general rule in natural flow jurisdictions makes a nonriparian use per se impermissible. But a prescriptive right for such a use can be acquired, good against downstream riparians. Or, if the complaining riparian is the grantor (or his successor) of the defendant-grantee, the grant will be a valid defense, although it could not be relied upon against other riparians on the stream.

Factors such as the extent of the riparian land which fronts on the stream, the size of the stream, and the number and the kinds of users on the stream have played a part in cases dealing with the reasonableness of the quantity of a particular use. Similarly, reasonableness of pollution decisions have looked to stream volume and velocity, the character of the stream, and the extent of the damage inflicted. Here perhaps more than in other controversies, courts have paid substantial heed to the comparative public interest in the respective enterprises of plaintiff and defendant.

See also, Sheldon J. Plager, *Some Observations on the Law of Water Allocation as a Variable in Industrial Site Location,* 1968 Wis.L.Rev. 673.

NOTES

1. Pure natural flow decisions are historically rare and virtually absent from modern cases. One still encounters natural flow language in the occasional case. This characteristically occurs where an upstream riparian takes so much of the flow that it would interfere with most reasonable uses of downstream users. In Collens v. New Canaan Water Co., 234 A.2d 825 (Conn.1967), for instance, downstream riparians sued to enjoin defendant from diverting water from the Noroton River, thereby substantially diminishing the flow of the stream. The court granted the injunction and punitive damages because "The plaintiffs, as riparian owners along the Noroton River, are entitled to the natural flow of the water of the running stream through or along their land, in its accustomed channel, undiminished in quantity or unimpaired in quality." As the court pointed out, defendant had alternative supplies available and had failed to prove that the injunction would prevent it from meeting the demands of its customers. The court also indicated that defendant could condemn the rights if it needed them. See Dimmock v. New London, 245 A.2d 569 (Conn.1968), page 605, infra.

2. *Tyler v. Wilkinson,* page 51, supra, is generally cited for the introduction of riparian rights into American law. Was it a natural flow or reasonable use case? Courts after *Tyler* did sometimes hold that any diversion by an upper riparian was a violation of the lower's rights, but the natural flow theory was frequently challenged because it impeded industrial development. By the late nineteenth century the natural flow theory had been widely rejected and replaced by the reasonable use doctrine which required a showing of actual damages as a prerequisite to judicial protection of a riparian right and made protection of a use dependent on the reasonableness of the competing uses. E.g., Red River Roller Mills v. Wright, 15 N.W. 167 (Minn.1883). *Harris v. Brooks,* page 80, supra, is an example of modern acceptance of the reasonable use doctrine.

3. In an important study of the changes that the common law underwent in response to pressures for economic development, the Harvard University legal historian Morton Horwitz illustrates the switch from static legal doctrines, designed primarily to preserve an agrarian status quo, to doctrines that gave more weight to technological innovation in the evolution of water law. Morton Horwitz, The Transformation of American Law, 1780–1860 (1977).

In brief, Horwitz's thesis is that by the end of the eighteenth century American judges developed an instrumental conception of the common law and the application of this instrumental reasoning to water use conflicts can be found before Story's "classically transitional judicial opinion [in *Tyler*], filled with ambiguities sufficient to make any future legal developments possible." Id. at 39.

B. RIPARIANISM TODAY

1. Tort Doctrine

HOOVER v. CRANE

Supreme Court of Michigan, 1960.
362 Mich. 36, 106 N.W.2d 563.

This appeal represents a controversy between plaintiff cottage and resort owners on an inland Michigan lake and defendant, a farmer with a fruit orchard, who was using the lake water for irrigation. The chancellor who heard the matter ruled that defendant had a right to reasonable use of lake water. The decree defined such reasonable use in terms which were unsatisfactory to plaintiffs who have appealed.

The testimony taken before the chancellor pertained to the situation at Hutchins lake, in Allegan county, during the summer of 1958. Defendant is a fruit farmer who owns a 180–acre farm abutting on the lake. Hutchins lake has an area of 350 acres in a normal season. Seventy-five cottages and several farms, including defendant's, abut on it. Defendant's frontage is approximately ¼ mile, or about 10% of the frontage of the lake.

Hutchins lake is spring fed. It has no inlet but does have an outlet which drains south. Frequently in the summertime the water level falls so that the flow at the outlet ceases.

All witnesses agreed that the summer of 1958 was exceedingly dry and plaintiffs' witnesses testified that Hutchins lake's level was the lowest it had ever been in their memory. Early in August, defendant began irrigation of his 50–acre pear orchard by pumping water out of Hutchins lake. During that month the lake level fell 6 to 8 inches—the water line receded 50 to 60 feet and cottagers experienced severe difficulties with boating and swimming.

The testimony indicated that during August and September of 1958, defendant was taking water from the lake through a 5–inch pipe and pumping it through 4 lines and 120 sprinklers. The defendant testified that the pump used had a theoretical capacity of 500 to 600 gallons, but that the tractor used for the pump would not operate it at capacity. Defendant computed his total water usage in 1958 at an amount which would represent $^{45}/_{100}$ of an inch of a lake the size of Hutchins lake. Plaintiffs' testimony tended to dispute this figure and to establish much greater pumpage.

The tenor of plaintiffs' testimony was to attribute the 6– to 8–inch drop in the Hutchins lake level in that summer to defendant's irrigation activities. Defendant contended that the decrease was due to natural causes, that the irrigation was of great benefit to him and contributed only slightly to plaintiff's discomfiture. * * *

The circuit judge found it impossible to determine a normal lake level from the testimony, except that the normal summer level of the lake is lower than the level at which the lake ceases to drain into the outlet. He apparently felt that plaintiffs' problems were due much more to the abnormal weather conditions of the summer of 1958, than to defendant's irrigation activities.

* * *

Plaintiffs on appeal assert that any irrigation use when the lake level is below the outlet is unreasonable.

Michigan has adopted the reasonable-use rule in determining the conflicting rights of riparian owners to the use of lake water.

In 1874, Justice Cooley said:

"It is therefore not a diminution in the quantity of the water alone, or an alteration in its flow, or either or both of these circumstances combined with injury, that will give a right of action, if in view of all the circumstances, and having regard to equality of right in others, that which has been done and which causes the injury is not unreasonable. In other words, the injury that is incidental to a reasonable enjoyment of the common right can demand no redress." Dumont v. Kellogg, 29 Mich. 420, 425.

And in People v. Hulbert, 131 Mich. 156, at page 170, 91 N.W. 211, at page 217, 64 L.R.A. 265, the Court, quoting from Gehlen Bros. v. Knorr, 101 Iowa 700 (70 N.W. 757, 36 L.R.A. 697), said:

"No statement can be made as to what is such reasonable use which will, without variation or qualification, apply to the facts of every case. But in determining whether a use is reasonable we must consider what the use is for; its extent, duration, necessity, and its application; the nature and size of the stream, and the several uses to which it is put; the extent of the injury to the 1 proprietor and of the benefit to the other; and all other facts which may bear upon the reasonableness of the use. [Red River] Roller Mills v. Wright, 30 Minn. 249, 15 N.W. 167, 44 Am.Rep. 194, and cases cited."

See, also, Merkel v. Consumers Power Co., 220 Mich. 128, 189 N.W. 997.

The Michigan view is in general accord with the Restatement of the Law, Torts, vol. 4, §§ 851, 852, 853.

The first of these sections states the general principle thus:

"*§ 851. Intentional Harm by One Riparian Proprietor to Another.*

"Unless he has a special privilege, a riparian proprietor on a watercourse or lake who, in using the water therein, intentionally causes substantial harm to another riparian proprietor thereon through invasion of such other's interest in the use of water therein, is liable to the other in an action for damages if, but only if, the harmful use of water is unreasonable in respect to the other proprietor."

In Harris v. Brooks, 225 Ark. 436, 283 S.W.2d 129, 54 A.L.R.2d 1440, the Arkansas supreme court, faced with a somewhat similar problem to ours, restrained the use of water for irrigation when a lake level fell below the point which the court held to be the normal one. Appellants point to this case as authority.

The principal distinguishing feature between the Harris Case and the instant one is that in the present case the court was unable to determine the normal lake level with any certainty, and definitely rejected plaintiffs' implied contention that it corresponded to the level of the lake when the water was even with the outlet. Cf. Kennedy v. Niles Water Supply Co., 173 Mich. 474, 139 N.W. 241, 43 L.R.A.,N.S., 836.

We interpret the circuit judge's decree as affording defendant the total metered equivalent in pumpage of ¼ inch of the content of Hutchins lake to be used in any dry period in between the cessation of flow from the outlet and the date when such flow recommences. Where the decree also provides for the case to be kept open for future petitions based on changed conditions, it would seem to afford as much protection for plaintiffs as to the future as this record warrants.

Both resort use and agricultural use of the lake are entirely legitimate purposes. Neither serves to remove water from the watershed. There is, however, no doubt that the irrigation use does occasion some water loss due to increased evaporation and absorption. Indeed, extensive irrigation might constitute a threat to the very existence of the lake in which all riparian owners have a stake; and at some point the use of the water which causes loss must yield to the common good.

The question on this appeal is, of course, whether the chancellor's determination of this point was unreasonable as to plaintiffs. On this record, we cannot overrule the circuit judge's view that most of plaintiffs' 1958 plight was due to natural causes. Nor can we say, if this be the only irrigation use intended and the only water diversion sought, that use of the amount provided in the decree during the dry season is unreasonable in respect to other riparian owners.

Affirmed. Costs to appellee.

NOTE: THE RESTATEMENT AND RIGHTS AMONG RIPARIANS

As Hanks, page 86, supra, explains, the avenue to determining relative efficiency includes several considerations. Courts have differed on the importance of each. Rules have been developed that modify property concepts to account for conduct that seems "reasonable" in an era of economic growth. They are reflected in the Restatement (Second) of Torts, though it has not yet been embraced as containing perfectly any state's water law.

For historical reasons, water allocation rules have been assigned to the Restatement of Torts. Riparian water cases are usually after-the-fact claims for redress for a specific activity alleged to have caused harm rather than proceedings to allocate the risk of future shortages. Riparian cases are often resolved by the use of principles similar to the law of nuisance, and thus they have been seen as tort rather than property cases. The Restatement (Second) of Torts § 850 states:

A riparian proprietor is subject to liability for making an unreasonable use of the water of a watercourse or lake that causes harm to another riparian proprietor's reasonable use of water or his land.

Restatement (Second) of Torts § 850A describes the principles applicable in determining reasonableness:

The determination of the reasonableness of a use of water depends upon a consideration of the interests of the riparian proprietor making the use, of any riparian proprietor harmed by it and of society as a whole. Factors that affect the determination include the following:

(a) The purpose of the use,

(b) the suitability of the use to the watercourse or lake,

(c) the economic value of the use,

(d) the social value of the use,

(e) the extent and amount of the harm it causes,

(f) the practicality of avoiding the harm by adjusting the use or method of use of one proprietor or the other,

(g) the practicality of adjusting the quantity of water used by each proprietor,

(h) the protection for existing values of water uses, land, investments and enterprises, and

(i) the justice of requiring the user causing harm to bear the loss.

Comment a. *Determination of reasonable or unreasonable use.*

The reasonableness or unreasonableness of a use of water by a riparian proprietor must be determined by a court or jury from a number of points of view and upon the consideration of a number of factors. A conflict arising out of a claim of harm to one riparian proprietor caused by the water use of another proprietor involves an examination of the use or interest alleged to be harmed, the use causing the harm, the effect that the latter has upon the former and the effects upon society, the economy and the environment of making the uses and of resolving the conflict.

In a suit between two riparian users of water the reasonableness of both uses is in issue. The plaintiff, in order to show he has a right that has been violated, must establish that his use of the water is reasonable. (See § 850, Comment c.) This will normally call for the application of the first four factors stated in this Section. Clause (a) requires that the use be made for a beneficial purpose; Clause (b) that it be suited to the water source in question. Clauses (c) and (d) require the use to have both economic and social value. If the use serves no beneficial purpose and requires an inordinate amount of water, factors (a) and (b) are not met. If the product of the use has only slight or trifling economic value and the use has destructive or harmful side effects on other persons or the public, factors (b) and (c) are not met.

* * *

The defendant's use must in the first instance meet the same tests. If the plaintiff proves that his use is reasonable and has been harmed and that the defendant's use does not serve a beneficial purpose, is not suited to the source or has little or no economic or social value, he has established a prima facie case that the defendant's use is unreasonable. Most cases, however, are not so simple, since few uses of water are of such a sterile character. The typical case involves two riparians who are each making a beneficial use by suitable means and are each producing desirable values. The controversy arises because the two uses are inconsistent and both cannot be enjoyed, since one interferes with the other by reducing the availability of water in the source or the opportunities for its enjoyment.

In this case the courts must test the reasonableness of each use by considering the additional factors listed in this section. A major policy underlying the law of riparian rights is that of accommodating as many reasonable riparian uses of a stream or lake as possible. Clause (e) requires the court to find that the harm inflicted is substantial. If one water use causes no serious harm to another it cannot be said to be unreasonable, and accommodation can be reached by requiring the complaining proprietor to bear a minor inconvenience. Clause (f) directs an inquiry into the relative efficiency of the means of accomplishing the uses. If harm can be avoided by changing the practices, methods or facilities of one user or the other, the reasonableness of the uses may depend upon the determination of which party should make the change or bear the cost of making the change. Clause (g) directs attention to the possibility of finding a solution by adjusting the quantity of water used by each party. If one user takes more water than is necessary, reasonableness may be achieved by the elimination of waste. When a concurring cause of the harm is a drought or temporary water shortage, it is usually reasonable to require the water and the harm to be shared.

There will remain cases in which the defendant's use causes serious harm that cannot be avoided by these adjustments. These cases will arise when the demand for water exceeds the supply and there is not enough for both uses. The defendant's new use takes the plaintiff's water supply or makes the plaintiff's use and enjoyment of the water impossible in some other way. When this is the case, the controversy cannot be solved by a simple balancing of the interests of the parties or by determining the relative values of the uses and awarding the water to the user with the paramount interest or the better use. Often the two uses are essentially the same or are of equal utility. Even if one is more valuable than the other a transfer of a wealth-producing resource has taken place

and the court must decide whether the act or conduct of the
defendant in taking the water from the plaintiff is tortious.

Restatement (Second) of Torts § 850A, Comment a.

Clause (h) of Section 850A suggests a preference for uses in place
over new uses to provide a reasonable assurance of continuity to
existing investments. The late Professor Jacob Beuscher of the University of Wisconsin, a pioneering water law scholar, observed over thirty
years ago that "[t]here is actually much more protection given to the
prior user of water as against a subsequent water claimant than one
would have any reason to expect from a mere recitation of black-letter
riparianisms." Jacob H. Beuscher, *Appropriation Water Law Elements
in Riparian Doctrine States,* 10 Buffalo L.Rev. 448, 451–52 (1961). The
late Dean Frank J. Trelease was the Associate Reporter for the Water
Law Revisions. He proposed to restate protection of existing uses as
the law of riparian rights, but intense opposition ensued and § 850A(h)
was the resulting compromise. Despite the incorporation of prior
appropriation principles into the Restatement, there are significant
differences between the protections given to prior users under the
riparian doctrine and those afforded senior users under the appropriation doctrine, discussed in Chapter Three. For example, riparian
doctrine contemplates sharing in times of shortage while the appropriation system does not. And, riparian rights cannot be quantified in
advance of litigation.

Clause (i) deals with whether the person causing the harm should
bear the burden of the resulting loss. The Restatement (Second) of
Torts comments:

> The court must inquire whether imposing liability upon the innova-
> tor will discourage or deter desirable progress. Ordinarily it will
> not. If a shift from one water use to another can be characterized
> as progress, it should result in an overall increase of welfare. In
> economic terms, a desirable new use is one that produces benefits
> that exceed its costs, including as a cost the loss of the benefits of
> the old use. Quite generally, an increase in welfare is not regarded
> as desirable if it is achieved by the method of impoverishing one
> person to enrich another. A new use may have much social and
> economic value, but if it will cause substantial harm by taking the
> water supply from an existing use, even one with less value, it may
> nevertheless be characterized as unreasonable unless compensation
> is paid. The new user who produces greater wealth can ordinarily
> afford to compensate the person whose less productive use he
> displaces.

There is some debate—arguably along an east-west front—about
the impact of the Restatement of Torts (Second) on the solution of
riparian conflicts, especially inasmuch as few cases have explicitly
relied on it. In his treatise on water rights, one of the editors of this
casebook, Professor Tarlock, endorses the Restatement position:

> The Restatement of Torts (Second) is an important recodifica-
> tion of the doctrine of riparian rights. The Restatement (Second)
> attempts to promote the more efficient use of water by making

riparian rights a more complete property system. In many cases, doctrines that discourage efficient use are modified and replaced by advocates doctrines that encourage efficient use. Because the Restatement (Second) both attempts to restate the law of riparian rights in terms of what courts in fact do and is forward rather than backward looking, it has already had a substantial influence on modern decisions and is likely to have an even greater influence in the future.

Riparian law is not a complete system of property rights allocation, as is the law of prior appropriation. Most of the cases impose after the fact liability on one use for interfering with another. The courts try to do equity between the parties before the court and do not try to formulate general rules to guide future behavior. In short, the law of riparian rights follows a tort compared to property approach. Thus, it is not surprising that the American Law Institute assigned the law of riparian rights to the Restatement of Torts not to the Restatement of Property.

The water rights sections of the Restatement were extensively revised in the 1970s and a new approach to reasonableness was developed. The distinguished water law expert, Frank J. Trelease of the University of Wyoming, was made Associate Editor of the water rights chapter. He tried to substitute a prior appropriation rule for the common law balancing test, arguing that was, in fact, what courts did in the vast majority of riparian rights cases. His argument was unfortunately rejected by those who wanted to preserve judicial flexibility to trim or terminate inefficient or otherwise socially undesirable uses, but the core idea of protecting prior uses was retained in the new Restatement.

A. Dan Tarlock, Law of Water Rights and Resources § 3.14 (1989).

In another treatise, Professor Joseph W. Dellapenna, of the Villanova University School of Law, is sharply critical of the Restatement approach and of its philosophical origins:

> One must be careful in relying on the Restatement (Second) of Torts to resolve the uncertainties that abound in most states under riparian rights theory. Certain background points, while perhaps appearing to be mere curiosities, are significant in explaining why the Restatement (Second) substantially departs from established riparian rights law. Only time will tell whether these departures will be followed by state courts.[298] * * *
>
> When interference with riparian rights is analyzed as tortious interference with a land-connected right to use water, there is considerable, perhaps total, overlap with the doctrine of nuisance. The Restatement (Second) of Torts attempts to deal with this in two ways. First, the Restatement (Second) introduces the notion that interference with riparian rights covers "quantity disputes," while nuisance deals with "quality disputes" (pollution). There simply is

---

298. The only decision to date that considered the question followed the new Restatement. Pyle v. Gilbert, 245 Ga. 403, 265 S.E.2d 584 (1980).

no authority for this proposition. The traditional formulation of the natural flow theory addressed both quantity and quality disputes,[306] and courts continue to address both sorts of disputes under the reasonable use theory.

The second method adopted by the Restatement (Second) of Torts to distinguish the nuisance and riparian approaches is to introduce a conceptual difference between reasonableness in nuisance theory and reasonableness in riparian theory. The Restatement (Second) asserts that nuisance reasonableness is determined by balancing the competing parties' interests, whereas riparian rights reasonableness is determined abstractly, taking into account only the social and economic value of the plaintiff's activities. This method not only runs counter to statements made in virtually every reasonable use case outside of the western, dual-system states,[309] but it is not even supported by the black letter of the Restatement (Second) itself.[310]

The Associate Reporter for riparian rights, Professor Frank Trelease, was the source of these and other aberrant views in the Restatement (Second). Trelease undoubtedly was the foremost authority on water law in the United States at the time. Unfortunately, he had spent virtually his entire professional life working in a state that follows pure prior appropriation law, having been for many years Dean of the College of Law of the University of Wyoming.[311] As a result, Trelease wrote many articles demonstrating his hostility to riparian rights and his belief that riparian rights had failed as an effective body of law.

With such an attitude, Associate Reporter Trelease predictably stretched the traditional concepts of riparian rights more into the mold of his beloved prior appropriation law or otherwise changed the rules in ways which arguably make water more available for different kinds and places of use than was possible under traditional riparian law. To justify these new Restatement approaches, Trelease relied heavily on cases from "dual system" states where courts are already required to adjust their concepts of riparian rights to prior appropriation law or he indulged in some highly

---

306. "A riparian owner is entitled to the natural flow of the water * * * undiminished in quantity and unimpaired in quality." Dimmock v. City of New London, 157 Conn. 9, 14, 245 A.2d 569, 572 (1968).

309. See, e.g., Okaw Drainage Dist. v. National Distillers & Chem. Co., 882 F.2d 1241, 1246 (7th Cir.1989); Beaunit Corp. v. Alabama Power Co., 370 F.Supp. 1044, 1051 (N.D.Ala.1973); Harris v. Brooks, 225 Ark. 436, 445–46, 283 S.W.2d 129, 134–35 (1955); Lawrie v. Silsby, 76 Vt. 240, 252–53, 56 A. 1106, 1108–09 (1904).

310. "The determination of the reasonableness of a use of water depends upon a consideration of the interests of the riparian proprietor making the use, of any riparian proprietor harmed by it and of society as a whole. * * * " Restatement (Second) of Torts § 850A (1977).

311. After stepping down as dean at Wyoming, Trelease joined the faculty at McGeorge College of Law in Sacramento, California. California is the dual-system state from which some of Trelease's peculiar notions of riparian rights apparently derived. See, e.g., Joslin v. Marin Mun. Water Dist., 67 Cal.2d 132, 429 P.2d 889, 60 Cal.Rptr. 377 (1967) (reasonableness decided in the abstract rather than comparatively).

dubious readings of cases from pure riparian rights jurisdictions.[314] Thus, the Reporter's Notes for this part of the Restatement (Second) of Torts must be used with some caution.

Joseph W. Dellapenna, 1 Waters and Water Rights § 6.01(c) (1991 ed.).

In Joslin v. Marin Mun. Water Dist., 429 P.2d 889 (Cal.1967), cited by Prof. Dellapenna, a riparian in the rock and gravel business brought an inverse condemnation action after the defendant water district constructed an upstream dam that decreased the deposit of sand and gravel onto plaintiff's land. The value of the plaintiff's land was diminished by $250,000 when it became useless as a sand and gravel operation. The trial court's order granting defendant's motion for summary judgment was affirmed by the California Supreme Court because use of water to carry gravel was unreasonable "as a matter of law." It therefore found that there was not a compensable property interest "in the amassing of mere sand and gravel which for aught that appears subserves *no* public policy." Id. at 895 (emphasis in original). Can *Joslin* be reconciled with the principles of Clause (i) of the Restatement? With the Fifth and Fourteenth Amendments? Does the California Supreme Court's decision promote the efficient allocation of resources? Is it distributively fair? What social policy is served? Does a sand and gravel operation satisfy no social purpose? Suppose that the defendant upstream riparian had been another sand and gravel operator. Do you think the outcome would be different? Why? Compensation was required in a case similar to *Joslin,* Rose v. State, 246 N.E.2d 735 (N.Y.1969). A 1928 California constitutional amendment was intended to curtail the expansion of riparian rights in preference to greater use of appropriative rights. See pages 147–48, infra.

Brian E. Gray, "In Search of Bigfoot": The Common Law Origins of Article X, Section 2 of the California Constitution, 17 Hastings Const. L.Q. 225, 228, 230 (1989), argues that *Joslin* "is the cornerstone of modern California water law" because it holds that article X, section 2 "requires all water rights to be exercised in accordance with contemporary economic conditions and social values."

PYLE v. GILBERT

Supreme Court of Georgia, 1980.
245 Ga. 403, 265 S.E.2d 584.

HILL, JUSTICE.

This is a water rights case involving a non-navigable watercourse. It presents a confrontation between the past and the present. Plaintiffs are the owners of a 140–year–old water-powered gristmill. They

---

314. Trelease cited Harris v. Brooks, 225 Ark. 436, 283 S.W.2d 129 (1955), to support the proposition that in applying the reasonable use theory courts tend to protect from interference the use that was begun earlier in time. Not only does the opinion contain just the vaguest of dicta regarding undefined "vested rights" to support this citation, but the facts as given suggest that the use which began first was enjoined to protect the use which was begun later. The court does not clearly indicate which use it considered to have begun first, presumably because it thought the matter wholly irrelevant. See Restatement (Second) of Torts app. § 850A, reporter's note to comment k, at 30–31 (1977).

emphasize the natural flow theory. Defendants are upper riparians using water to irrigate their farms. They emphasize the reasonable use theory of water rights.

The plaintiffs, Willie and Arlene Gilbert, own property commonly known as Howard's Mill located on Kirkland's Creek, a non-navigable stream in Early County which goes into the Chattahoochee River. * * *

Until August 31, 1978, the Gilberts owned and operated a water-powered gristmill on their property. They also rented boats for profit and permitted fishing and swimming in the 40–acre pond. (On August 31, 1978, the mill was destroyed by fire.)

On July 7, 1978, the Gilberts filed a complaint against Sanford Hill, who is an owner of property that is upper riparian in relation to the Gilbert's property, alleging that since 1975 he has been diverting and using water from Kirkland's Creek for irrigation. * * *

The Gilberts characterized Hill's diversion of waters from Kirkland's Creek for irrigation as both a nuisance and a trespass and sought injunctive relief as well as actual and punitive damages and attorney fees.

The testimony at a hearing on July 18, 1978, revealed to plaintiffs that other upper riparian owners also had irrigated with water from the creek. The plaintiffs subsequently added four defendants: George Edgar Pyle, Jimmy Doster, Philip Buckhalter and Vinson Evans.[2] Following discovery, the trial court made an extensive examination of our water law and granted the plaintiffs' motions for summary judgment as to liability against all defendants, holding that the defendants' use of the water for irrigation constituted a diversion, a trespass, a nuisance and an unreasonable use as a matter of law, and enjoining any future use. The issue of damages was reserved for trial. The defendants appeal.

1. Over 100 years ago, when this court first considered riparian rights in Hendrick v. Cook, 4 Ga. 241 (1848), several bedrock principles were established. First, the court firmly rejected the doctrine of appropriation and instead applied riparian principles to the dispute. And in stating the principles of riparian rights, the court also adopted the doctrine of reasonable use. * * * The court also held that an injury to one's riparian rights gave rise to an action for damages for trespass even in the absence of proof of actual damage.

Subsequently, two statutes were enacted and codified in the Code of 1863. Section 2206 of the Code of 1863 appears today almost verbatim at Code § 85–1301: "Running water, while on land, belongs to the owner of the land, but he has *no right to divert it* from the usual channel, nor may he so use or adulterate it as to interfere with the enjoyment of it by the next owner." (Emphasis supplied.) (See also Code § 85–1305.) Section 2960 of the Code of 1863 now appears at Code

---

2. Vinson Evans owns non-riparian property which he admits having irrigated with the alleged permission of a riparian owner. The evidence does not show that he owns any riparian property. * * *

§ 105–1407: "The owner of land through which nonnavigable water-courses may flow is entitled to have the water in such streams come to his land in its natural and usual flow, subject only to such detention or diminution as may be caused by a *reasonable use* of it by other riparian proprietors; and the *diverting of the stream, wholly or in part,* from the same, or the obstructing thereof so as to impede its course or cause it to overflow or injure his land, or any right appurtenant thereto, or the pollution thereof so as to lessen its value to him, shall be a trespass upon his property." (Emphasis supplied.)

* * *

Thus it is clear that under both court decisions and statutes, Georgia's law of riparian rights is a natural flow theory modified by a reasonable use provision.

* * *

In this case, the trial court found that irrigation with modern equipment was a "diversion" which is entirely prohibited by Georgia law, Code §§ 85–1301, 105–1407, supra; i.e., the trial court found that irrigation with modern equipment constituted a trespass as a matter of law. We disagree. The use of water for agricultural purposes was recognized as a reasonable use along with domestic use in the first reported Georgia case on riparian rights.

* * * When our riparian rights statutes were enacted, irrigation apparently was practiced only moderately here and in other "humid" states. Thus the General Assembly would not have contemplated prohibiting the use of water for irrigation in enacting these laws. * * *

Rather we think the General Assembly intended to prohibit the diversion of water from a watercourse for other purposes, such as to drain one's own property or to create a new watercourse on the diverter's property. That this latter use would have been of some concern to the General Assembly is evidenced by the adoption of the natural flow theory, which recognizes that the mere presence of a watercourse on one's property generally enhances it.

* * *

In sum, we find that the right of the lower riparian to receive the natural flow of the water without diversion or diminution is subject to the right of the upper riparian to its reasonable use for agricultural purposes, including irrigation.

* * *

3. In its detailed analysis of Georgia water law, the trial court had to apply Hendrix v. Roberts Marble Co., 175 Ga. 389, 394, 165 S.E. 223, 226 (1932), to the effect that " * * * riparian rights are appurtenant only to lands which actually touch on the watercourse, or through which it flows, and that a riparian owner or proprietor can not himself lawfully use or convey to another the right to use water flowing along or through his property * * * " Thus *Hendrix* held water could only be

used on riparian lands.[9] Yet four years later, in reversing the denial of an injunction against the use of water on non-riparian land, the court did not rely heavily on *Hendrix,* supra. Instead the court (Russell, C.J., writing the opinion in both cases) based its decision more on general riparian water law principles than on the non-riparian use. *Robertson v. Arnold,* 182 Ga. 664, 671, 186 S.E. 806 (1936). To the extent that *Robertson v. Arnold* might reflect ambivalence as to the rule announced in *Hendrix,* that concern is well-founded.

A major study of Georgia water law concluded that "Another disadvantage of this doctrine is that it permits the use of stream water only in connection with riparian land." Institute of Law and Government, University of Georgia Law School, *A Study of the Riparian and Prior Appropriation Doctrines of Water Law* (1955), p. 104. Likewise, the American Law Institute now recommends allowing use of water by riparian owners on non-riparian land, Rest.Torts 2d § 855, as well as allowing non-riparian owners to acquire a right to use water from riparian owners. Id., § 856(2), (see also 7 Clark, Waters and Water Rights 71–72, § 614.1 (1976)). The Restatement relies on two principles: that riparian rights are property rights and as such could normally be transferred, and that water law should be utilitarian and allow the best use of the water. Id., Comment b. Also, the Institute considers the acquisition of water rights by condemnation a "grant of riparian right." Id., comment c.

Georgia recognizes the power to condemn riparian rights. * * * We agree with the American Law Institute that the right to use water on non-riparian land should be permitted and if that right can be acquired by condemnation, it can also be acquired by grant. Thus we find that the right to the reasonable use of water in a non-navigable watercourse on non-riparian land can be acquired by grant from a riparian owner. The contrary conclusion in *Hendrix v. Roberts Marble Co.,* supra, will not be followed.

Judgment reversed.

NOTES

1. The first Restatement of Torts dealt with nonriparian uses in § 855: "In determining what the law regards as the utility of a use of water (§ 853) or the gravity of the harm from an interference with a use of water (§ 854), the classification of the use as riparian or non-riparian is important." The drafters of the Restatement (Second) of Torts took an approach more typical of the prior appropriation doctrine by deemphasizing the locus of the use. In Tentative Draft No. 17 (1971), the following "Note to Council" appears.

> The Restatement of Torts, § 855, says that the classification of the use as riparian or non-riparian is "important" in determining reasonableness. It then states that "there is no reason in strict

---

9. It should be noted that the use of water in steam locomotives was a non-riparian use of that water unless the railroad right of way was considered riparian land wherever it went.

logic why an arbitrary distinction should be made." However, it goes on to note that "in a number of jurisdictions, it is definitely a policy of the law, where uses of the stream or lake are conflicting, to recognize riparian uses as preferred over non-riparian uses even though the latter are of considerable importance to those who benefit by them." It expounds the latter theory in three comments and five illustrations.

The Restatement 2d should take a positive stand on the split of authority on this question. The approach of the drafters of the Restatement 1st was ambivalent. They obviously seemed to prefer the rule stated in the recommendation made here, but they gave considerable aid and comfort to the more restrictive rule. The Restatement 2d should clearly prefer the rule most conducive to good use of water resources. The policy reasons for the suggested rule are given in the Comments.

The drafters proposed replacing the earlier language with a new § 855: "The reasonableness of a use of water by a riparian proprietor is not affected by the classification of the use as riparian or non-riparian." This was apparently too strong for the Institute. In § 855 as finally adopted, "affected" is replaced by "controlled." Restatement (Second) of Torts § 855.

Uses by nonriparians, as contrasted with nonriparian uses by riparian owners, remain disfavored in the Restatement (Second) of Torts. Section 856 states:

§ 856. Harm by Riparian Proprietor to Nonriparian—Effect of Grants, Permits and Public Rights

(1) Except as stated in Subsections (2), (3) and (4), a riparian proprietor is not subject to liability for making a use of the water of a watercourse or lake that causes harm to a use of water by a nonriparian.

(2) A riparian proprietor is subject to liability for making an unreasonable use of the water of a watercourse or a lake that causes harm to a reasonable use of water by a nonriparian who holds a grant from another riparian proprietor of the grantor's right to use the water.

(3) A riparian proprietor is subject to liability for making a use of the water of a watercourse or lake that causes harm to a nonriparian exercising a right created by governmental authority, permit or license to use public or private water.

(4) A riparian proprietor is subject to liability for making a use of public waters that interferes with the exercise of a public right to use the waters.

In sharp contrast is the liability of nonriparians under § 857: "Except as stated in Subsections (2), (3), and (4), a non-riparian is subject to liability for a use of the water of a watercourse or lake that interferes with the right of a riparian proprietor to use the water." As in § 856, the reference in § 857 to Subsection (2) refers to a nonriparian who holds a grant from a riparian, Subsection (3) to a nonriparian "exercising a right created by governmental authority, permit, or license to use public or private water," and Subsection (4) to a nonriparian exercising a public right. Public rights will be treated in Chapter Four infra.

2. Under the approach of the Restatement (Second) of Torts, what will be the treatment of defendant Evans in *Pyle v. Gilbert?*

2. Permit Systems

FRANK E. MALONEY, SHELDON J. PLAGER and FLETCHER
N. BALDWIN, WATER LAW AND ADMINISTRATION:
THE FLORIDA EXPERIENCE
172–73 (1968).

§ 60. Weaknesses of the Common Law Approach to Allocation of Water for Consumptive Use

In theory the standard of relative reasonableness under the reasonable use branch of the riparian system facilitates an adjustment of conflicts between uses in accordance with the demands of each user and the dictates of the general public interest.[1] It allows each riparian a certain amount of flexibility in commencing a new use or in expanding an existing one in the light of changing conditions of water use and supply.

Recently, however, criticism has been leveled at the riparian system and its restrictions on the use of stream water to riparian owners, along with its requirement that the water be used only on riparian land. Many critics feel better use may frequently be made at other places by riparian or nonriparian owners.[2]

The major criticism of the system relates to the element of uncertainty associated with the reasonable use of water for nondomestic purposes. Because the reasonableness of each use is determined by the needs of other riparians, unforeseen conditions arise when others commence or enlarge uses despite long nonuse of their rights. This uncertainty is increased in many states where a riparian neither making nor intending to make use of water can enjoin an existing use as unreasonable with regard to his right. In practice the court will occasionally regard the fact of priority of use as one element to be considered in assessing reasonableness.

Another criticism of the common law riparian system has concerned the lack of administrative controls in many jurisdictions where the extent of a riparian's right of reasonable use can be determined only by litigation. The critics maintain that this uncertainty results in a needless loss when industries utilizing water resources have their

---

1. "The advantages of this [reasonable use] theory are that it is entirely utilitarian and tends to promote the fullest beneficial use of water resources." Restatement of Torts at 345–46 (Ch. 41, topic 3, Scope Note) (1939).

2. See Fisher, *Western Experience & Eastern Appropriation Proposals,* in The Law of Water Allocation in the Eastern United States 75 (1958).

water use patterns upset by competing projects. Probably of greater concern is the waste of water going unused or devoted to less valuable uses because industries fearful of such losses refuse to come into a jurisdiction.

On occasion courts have apportioned streamflow between competing users to give the riparians a clear picture of their rights. The infrequency of such decisions may be accounted for in part by the fact that it would involve the court too closely in the supervision of those uses. Recognizing their lack of expertise and the inefficiency of a case-by-case approach, the courts have been reluctant to become involved. Also the numerous courts are structurally not as capable of uniformity in the application of the law as a single centralized agency.

As population growth and modern technological developments in both agriculture and industry have been making increasingly greater demands on eastern water supplies, the problem of maintaining stream-flows and ground water levels has assumed increasingly greater importance. Concern over the adequacy of existing laws to cope with emerging water resource problems has led many executive and legislative study committees to propose new methods to deal with the problems. The legislative creation of administrative authorities in a number of eastern states, with varying powers to grant permits authorizing the withdrawal of water from streams, has raised a number of interrelated legal and physical problems.

These uncertainties occasioned by the flexibility of the riparian system have sparked the recent movement for new water-rights legislation in many eastern states, including provisions for the establishment of permit systems to provide a means of regulation, through administrative agencies, of existing and future water uses.

GEORGE WILLIAM SHERK, EASTERN WATER LAW: TRENDS IN STATE LEGISLATION
9 Va. Envtl. L.J. 287 (1990).

A. Introduction

Over the past thirty years, several model water codes and proposed new state water laws have been drafted.[13] There have also been several analyses of the issues that state legislatures must consider and resolve in the enactment of any new state water laws.[14] The legislative issues, both substantive and procedural, presented in the proposed state water

---

13. See Model Water Use Act (National Conference of Commissioners on Uniform State Laws) in Suggested State Legislation Program for 1959, at 150–166 (Council of State Governments, 1958 & reprint 1972); F. Maloney, R. Ausness and J. Morris, [A Model Water Code with Commentary v–vi, 78 (1972)]; Trelease [*Alaska's New Water Use Act*, 2 Land & Water L.Rev. 1, 21–30 (1967)].

14. National Water Commission [Water Policies for the Future (1973)], at 227–315;

R. Ausness, *Water Rights Legislation in the East: A Program for Reform*, 24 Wm. & Mary L.Rev. 547 (1983)]; Trelease, [*The Model Water Code, The Wise Administrator and the Goddam Bureaucrat*, 14 Nat.Resources J. 207, 225–28 (1974)]; Trelease, [*New Water Legislation: Drafting for Development, Efficient Allocation and Environmental Protection*, 12 Land & Water L.Rev. 385, 404–16 (1977)].

laws and in the commentaries on the proposed legislation can be summarized as follows.

If a state chooses to convert the riparian system into a permit system, one of the most important substantive issues is the recognition of existing riparian water uses. The embodiment of a "water right" in a water use permit raises additional issues. For example, the duration of the permit is important. Permits of short duration may enhance state control over water, but they also discourage investment in water-related projects and facilities. Permits of unlimited duration provide the requisite degree of certainty to encourage investment, but they must be transferable to enable the permit system to respond to market forces.

The legislature may establish certain threshold use levels and provide exemptions from statutory requirements for water uses below the threshold levels. It may also wish to define allowable uses for state water resources and to establish preferences or priorities to control in the event of water shortages.

B. Permit and Registration Requirements

State responses to the uncertainties of the riparian system have fallen generally into two categories. For planning purposes, a state may need to determine only the number and quantity of existing uses. If this is the state's goal, then a registration system is sufficient. Registration of existing and future water uses will provide the state with needed information on the relationship between existing water supplies and both existing and proposed water uses.

A state wishing to exercise control over the uses of water within the state may require permits for those uses. In essence, a permitting system is a mechanism to quantify existing water uses and to vest the right of the water user to continue those uses.

The procedural aspects of a permitting system are relatively simple. States converting a riparian system into a permit system generally have required existing riparian water users to obtain a permit for their uses within a certain period of time. After the expiration of this registration period, all subsequent users must obtain a permit issued through the administrative structure that is established by the state to implement the state's water laws. Failure to register an existing use results in a presumption of abandonment or a similar penalty. Unused riparian water rights are thereby extinguished.[21]

---

21. It has been argued that restrictions on the use of riparian rights or the extinguishment of unused riparian rights constitute a taking of property without compensation. The issue was addressed by the Supreme Court of Florida in Village of Tequesta v. Jupiter Inlet Corp., 371 So.2d 663 (Fla.), cert. denied, 444 U.S. 965 (1979), which concluded that "the landowner does not have a constitutionally protected property right in the water beneath the property, requiring compensation for the taking of water when used for a public purpose," id. at 672, and, by comparison to zoning regulations, that "the right to the use of water may also be limited or regulated." Id. The Supreme Court of Texas reached a similar conclusion in In Re the Adjudication of the Water Rights of the Upper Guadalupe Segment of the Guadalupe River Basin, 642 S.W.2d 438, 444 (Tx.1982). See also Texaco, Inc. v. Short, 454 U.S. 516 (1981) (sustaining the constitutionality of

Nineteen eastern states [22] have enacted permitting or registration requirements applicable to the use of both surface and ground water. With certain exceptions, these requirements apply to all water uses above established threshold quantities.

* * *

C. Threshold Use Amounts

Those favoring an exemption from statutory requirements for users of small quantities of water argue that the benefits obtained by requiring such users to register their uses or to obtain a use permit are offset by the burden such requirements impose on the water user. Those opposing such exemptions cite the cumulative impact of such exemptions, and the uncertainty resulting from them, on the success of a state water management and allocation program.

All of the eastern states requiring permits or registration have established minimum use quantities to which the requirements apply. These quantity exemptions generally reflect one of two approaches. Either the requirements in general do not apply or, if the requirements do apply, the water user is exempted from certain procedural requirements.

An alternative approach, relating to water uses rather than to the quantity of water used, has been to exempt certain types of uses from statutory requirements. Such exemptions frequently include uses of water for domestic and livestock purposes. Both use exemptions and quantity exemptions have been provided by several states.

* * *

D. Allowable Use Definitions

At the common law, surface water was required to be put to a reasonable use. In the western states, beneficial use is generally required, with the waste of water being defined as the antithesis of beneficial use. If a state legislature addressed this issue, very careful legislative drafting is required to develop an allowable use definition that is neither too broad (including every possible use of water) nor too narrow (excluding water uses that may be of benefit to the state).

Eighteen eastern states [93] have defined or suggested allowable uses of both surface and ground water. These states have generally adopted a combination of three approaches. First, a specific definition of allowable uses is included in the statute. Second, a general policy

---

an Indiana statute which provided that a severed mineral interest would revert to the surface landowner after twenty years of nonuse).

22. Connecticut, Delaware, Florida, Georgia, Illinois, Indiana, Kentucky, Maine, Maryland, Mississippi, New Jersey, New York, North Carolina, Ohio, South Carolina, Tennessee, Virginia, West Virgi-

nia, and Wisconsin. In addition, Michigan, Ohio, Pennsylvania and Vermont have proposed legislation.

93. Connecticut, Delaware, Florida, Georgia, Illinois, Indiana, Kentucky, Maine, Maryland, Mississippi, New Hampshire, New York, North Carolina, Ohio, South Carolina, Tennessee, Virginia and Wisconsin.

statement is included regarding the uses to which the waters of the state may be put. Third, the legislature lists a series of factors to be considered (or impacts to be avoided) for a water use to be allowable. In essence, the focus of the issue is to determine the water uses that will be considered "legal" in a given state.

* * *

E. Preferences and Priorities

A major issue is how to resolve priority conflicts that exist whenever there is not enough water to meet conflicting demands. This is the essence of avoiding the "tragedy of the commons." There are two primary approaches to this issue. Those who favor the prior appropriations doctrine of the western states argue for temporal priority, that "first-in-time" should be "first-in-right." They argue that this results in greater efficiency in water use and is easier to administer than a system based on use preferences. Use of the prior appropriations doctrine would put the risk of water shortages on subsequent water users and would allow water users to respond to the free market in times of water shortage. This, it is argued, would result in the economic maximization of water use.[127]

The alternative to the prior appropriations doctrine is a series of preferences based on specific water uses or water use policies. These preferences could be determined either by the state legislatures or by the administrators of state water resources programs in response to specific water shortages. On first impression, use preferences appear to be an attractive alternative as such an approach would provide a state with the means to form a flexible response to specific situations. In practice, however, it may be both a legislative and an administrative nightmare. For this reason alone, it has been argued that the prior appropriations approach is superior to a system of use preferences established by statute or regulation.[128] With regard to the regulatory approach, Dean Trelease considered the likelihood of success of this approach in the event of a severe water shortage and concluded:

> I think the poor Bureaucrat, juggling equality, economic efficiency, public health and safety, protection of investment, and protection of workers' jobs and farmers' livelihoods, might at this point take to the bottle, either milk for his ulcer or whiskey to forget his troubles. I think he would think that there must be a better way to run this railroad, some way to get all those arguing, pleading people off his back.[129]

127. This assumes, of course, that the water use permit is transferable, of unlimited duration, that impacts on third parties can be ameliorated and that water uses are neither restricted nor appurtenant to riparian lands. See Trelease–1974, supra note [14], at 225–28; Trelease–1977, supra note [14], at 399–401, 411–16.

128. Trelease–1977, supra note [14], at 400.

129. Trelease–1974, supra note [14], at 217.

Despite the apparent advantages of the prior appropriations doctrine, the eastern states in general have adopted a regulatory approach based on use priorities.

* * *

F. *Area Of Use Or Diversion Restrictions*

It is clear that a state may not totally prohibit the export or diversion of water to another state without imposing an impermissible burden on interstate commerce under the rule established in *Sporhase v. Nebraska.*[167] What is unclear is the type of state-imposed restriction that will conform to constitutional requirements. The types of restrictions that may be imposed on intrastate water transfers is a closely-related issue as such restrictions may also raise constitutional issues.

This has emerged as an issue of great concern in the eastern states.[168] While these states are blessed with a generally abundant supply of water, that water is frequently unavailable in areas of greatest demand. States such as Virginia and Massachusetts, for example, have populations concentrated along their coasts while their most abundant fresh water resources lie inland.

Fifteen eastern states [169] have imposed area of use requirements, export restrictions or diversion restrictions. The legislation enacted in these states reflects one of two approaches. Either diversions are specifically restricted or approval of such diversions is required.

* * *

G. *Minimum Water Levels*

A state may wish to establish minimum stream flows, minimum lake levels or minimum ground water levels for a number of reasons. Establishment of such levels protects environmental, aesthetic and recreational values as well as wildlife habitat. This is of increasing importance in many of the eastern states as tourism and water-related recreation emerge as a major (if not *the* major) component of the state's economy. Furthermore, protection of water quality is easier given certain minimum water levels or flows as is protection of investments in facilities the construction of which assumed certain surface water or ground water levels.

---

167. 458 U.S. 941 (1982), [page 748, infra].

168. In fact, interbasin transfers may emerge as the single issue that motivates a State to abandon the riparian system. See, e.g., Putt, *An Analysis and Evaluation of Water Rights in Alabama in Perspective With Other States in the South Atlantic* *and Gulf Region,* 12 Cumb.L.Rev. 47, 97 (1981).

169. Connecticut, Florida, Georgia, Illinois, Indiana, Kentucky, Maine, Massachusetts, Michigan, New Jersey, New York, North Carolina, Ohio, South Carolina and Wisconsin. Similar legislation has been proposed in Florida and New Hampshire.

Sixteen eastern states [194] have considered the issue of minimum water levels or flows for both surface and ground water.

* * *

H. Water Conservation

The 1970's was the decade of energy. Great attention was focused on energy conservation and on the development of alternative sources of energy. The 1990's will be the decade of water. Like the "energy crisis" of the 1970's, great attention will be focused on water conservation. Unlike the 1970's, however, relatively little attention will be focused on alternative supplies for the simple reason that there are virtually no alternatives to the use of water.

Sixteen eastern [225] states have enacted legislation addressing the need to conserve both surface and ground water.

* * *

I. Conjunctive Use

The interdependence of atmospheric water, surface water and ground water in the hydrologic cycle is well known and increasingly well understood.[272] Unfortunately, in the management and allocation of state water resources, these interdependencies are rather consistently ignored. A conjunctive use approach recognizes the interrelationship of surface water and ground water and bases an allocation and management approach on that interrelationship.

Two states [Mississippi and Massachusetts] have adopted a conjunctive use approach.

NEKOOSA–EDWARDS PAPER CO. v. PUBLIC SERVICE COMMISSION

Supreme Court of Wisconsin, 1959.
8 Wis.2d 582, 99 N.W.2d 821.

Firkus, the owner of between 1,000 and 1,100 acres of potato land, of which 80 acres lie along Buena Vista creek, applied on March 23, 1957, for a permit to divert water therefrom at the rate of 800 gallons a minute (1.79 cubic feet a second [c.f.s.]) when needed between June 15th and August 15th each third year, starting in 1959, to irrigate a maximum of 65 acres. Okray, also a potato grower, owns 1,080 acres part of which is riparian to the creek. Okray sought a permit to divert 900 gallons of water per minute (2 c.f.s.) when needed between June

---

194. Connecticut, Florida, Illinois, Indiana, Maine, Massachusetts, Mississippi, Tennessee, New Hampshire, New Jersey, New York, Ohio, South Carolina, Virginia, West Virginia and Wisconsin. Similar legislation has been introduced in Mississippi.

225. Connecticut, Delaware, Florida, Illinois, Indiana, Kentucky, Maine, Massa-chusetts, New Hampshire, New Jersey, New York, North Carolina, Ohio, South Carolina, Virginia, and Wisconsin. Additional legislation has been proposed in Florida, Mississippi, Pennsylvania, South Carolina, West Virginia and Vermont.

272. See, e.g., A. Tarlock, [Law of Water Rights and Resources (1989)], § 4.03.

15th and August 15th each third year, starting in 1957, to irrigate a maximum of 140 acres.

Buena Vista creek is a navigable trout stream having its headwaters about 15 miles east of the Firkus and Okray properties. The sources of water for the creek are rainfall and water from a marsh in which the water is controlled by a system of drainage ditches and dams. The creek above the Firkus and Okray properties is 16 to 30 feet in width and is normally two to three feet deep at County Trunk F, some distance east of the point of taking. The creek flows westerly through Firkus' and Okray's lands in the town of Grant and continues some six or seven miles to where Four Mile creek joins it just above Lake Wazeecha, an artificial impoundment maintained by Wood County, a respondent, for public recreational purposes. The creek continues from Lake Wazeecha about two miles to Nepco Lake, another artificial impoundment which is maintained by the respondent, Nekoosa–Edwards Paper Company, to furnish a supply of pure water for paper making and to generate electric power. Nepco Lake is also used by the village of Port Edwards for part of its water supply. From Nepco Lake the creek flows into the Wisconsin River a short distance west. Frank R. Fey and Martin Kirchhoefer, respondents, are riparian owners below Firkus and Okray.

A hearing was held by the Public Service Commission on the applications which were opposed by the respondents who did not consent to the proposed diversion. The Public Service Commission found the water to be diverted from Buena Vista creek for irrigation purposes by the applicants would generally be at times when there is no surplus flow. The flow of the creek near the point of diversion has not been regularly gauged, but the probable average low flow is from 15 to 20 c.f.s. Other applications are pending before the Public Service Commission for permits to divert water from Buena Vista creek and Four Mile creek.

Since 1945, Okray and Firkus and others have been diverting water from Buena Vista creek without permits. The Public Service Commission found diversion by Firkus and Okray of 800 gallons a minute by each as needed during the period from June 15th to August 15th every third year would not injure public rights or the lower riparians who did not consent to the diversion. The commission concluded the lands of Firkus and Okray involved were riparian within the meaning of sec. 31.14, Stats., the applicants had met all the requirements for an irrigation permit, and it had jurisdiction to issue the permits. Orders were entered September 20, 1957, granting the permits.

Considerable technical evidence not pertinent to this opinion is contained in the rather voluminous record. However, it should be pointed out that a witness for the Wisconsin Conservation Department testified that damage would occur to fish and fish life in Buena Vista creek if the water therein went below a certain designated level, but he was unable to determine if such level would be reached while Firkus or Okray were pumping water from the stream under the permits. Several farmers who were riparian owners on the creek stated they had no objection to the granting of the permits. Witnesses for Nekoosa–Edwards testified to the point that the respondent would be injured by the diversion. The Port Edwards municipal water utility is dependent to some extent upon the supply of water from Nepco Lake, especially during the months from May to October when other sources of supply are inadequate. The testimony was to the effect the Nepco Lake water supply was necessary and vital for the public welfare. The respondent Wood County owns approximately the entire shore line of Lake Wazeecha, maintains a public park there with an investment of some $400,-000, and the lake is used by a large number of the public for recreational purposes including fishing, boating, and other water sports, and these facilities would be impaired by the taking of water. None of the respondents has consented to the diversion.

* * *

HALLOWS, JUSTICE.

The important question presented on these appeals which in our view of the cases makes it unnecessary to consider any others is: Does sec. 31.14, Stats., confer upon the Public Service Commission the jurisdiction to determine and regulate the common-law rights of all riparian owners to the use of nonsurplus water in a navigable stream? To determine this question requires a construction of sec. 31.14 which heretofore has not been construed. The primary source of construing the statute is the language of the statute itself. Sec. 31.14 is set forth in part in the footnote.[1]

Subsection (1) declares it to be lawful to temporarily divert surplus water of any stream to bring back or to maintain the normal level of a navigable lake or to maintain the natural flow of water in a navigable stream even though such lake or stream is not in the same water shed.

---

1. "31.14 *Diversion of surplus waters.* (1) It shall be lawful to temporarily divert the surplus water of any stream for the purpose of bringing back or maintaining the normal level of any navigable lake or for maintaining the normal flow of water in any navigable stream, regardless of whether such navigable lake or stream is located within the water shed of the stream from which the surplus water is diverted, and water other than surplus water may be diverted with the consent of riparian owners damaged thereby for the purpose of agriculture or irrigation but no water shall be so diverted to the injury of public rights in the stream or to the injury of any riparians located on the stream, unless such riparians shall consent thereto.

"(2) Surplus water as used in this section means any water of a stream which is not being beneficially used.

"(3) The public service commission may determine how much of the flowing water at any point in a stream is surplus water.

"(4) Before any water may be diverted for the purposes set forth in subsection (1), the applicant shall file an application with the public service commission setting forth * * * the name of the stream, the point in the same from which it is proposed to divert the surplus water, the name of the navigable lake or navigable stream or lands to which such water is to be diverted.

* * *

"(8) At the conclusion of the hearing if it shall appear that the water to be diverted is surplus water, or if not surplus water the riparians injured by such diversion have consented thereto, the commission shall so find and a permit for the diversion of such water shall issue. * * *

"(9) The quantity of water to be taken and the time or times when it may be taken shall be under the control of the commission, to the end that only surplus water be diverted from its natural channel, and that when any water in a stream ceases to be surplus water, the diversion of such water shall cease except that the commission may permit the diversion of other than surplus water with the consent of the riparian owners damaged thereby."

Nonsurplus water may be diverted with the consent of the riparian owners damaged thereby for the purpose of agriculture or irrigation. However, no water shall be so diverted to the injury of public rights or of any riparian owners unless such riparian shall consent thereto. The language of the statute seems clear. It makes a distinction between the diversion of surplus water and nonsurplus water and the purposes of such diversion and the conditions on which nonsurplus water may be diverted.

In subsection (2), surplus water is defined as any water of a stream which is not being beneficially used. Logically, nonsurplus water or water other than surplus water must be any water in a stream which is being beneficially used. The Public Service Commission is granted by subsection (3) the authority to determine how much of the flowing water at any point in a stream is surplus water. This is a logical provision since it is necessary in each case and from time to time to determine what water in any stream is surplus under the definition in subsection (2) as applied to the particular facts. Thus, to determine whether a riparian's consent is needed for diversion, the Public Service Commission must determine whether the proposed diversion is of surplus water or nonsurplus water. Subsection (8) provides that if the commission shall find either alternative a permit for diversion shall issue. Subsection (9) places control over the diversion in the Public Service Commission so that only surplus water shall be diverted and such diversion shall cease when the water in the stream ceases to be surplus water unless the riparian owners damaged by the diversion of nonsurplus water consent.

The commission contends it has the jurisdiction to determine whether the diversion of nonsurplus water will damage or injure riparian owners and if it finds no such injury the consent of such owners is not required. We find no authority in the statute for this position. The statute contemplates that a beneficial user is damaged or injured by the diversion of nonsurplus water and requires his consent. The commission having determined that the flow of water in a stream is not surplus water because it is being beneficially used by riparian owners, it follows that any diversion of such nonsurplus water as a matter of law would injure the riparian owners beneficially using such water and their consent must be obtained.

This is the only construction consistent with the rights of riparian owners in streams. The language of sec. 31.14, Stats., does not grant jurisdiction to the Public Service Commission to determine or adjust the rights of riparian owners injured because of a proposed diversion of nonsurplus water. The power of the Public Service Commission is limited to granting permits for the diversion of surplus water, and in the case of waters determined by it to be nonsurplus, only for agriculture and irrigation purposes when the riparian owners beneficially using such nonsurplus water have consented to such diversion. It is to be noted sec. 31.14 does not provide any standard for the determination of the relative rights of claimants to water, or for any consumptive use except agriculture and irrigation by consent of riparian owners for nonsurplus water.

* * *

The construction urged by the Public Service Commission creates a third class of cases not found in the language of the statute, namely, situations in which riparian owners are beneficially using nonsurplus water, and the commission finds are not substantially injured by the diversion of such water and therefore their consent is not required. This construction creates a permit system for the consumptive use of nonsurplus water for the purpose of agriculture and irrigation. This interpretation ignores subsections (2) and (3) and is based primarily upon inferences drawn from subsections (1), (8), and (9). No reasonable inference of legislative intent to simultaneously create a permit system for the consumptive use of water can be read into sec. 31.14, Stats., by ignoring subsections (2) and (3). In arriving at the intention of the legislature we must give all the words of the act their ordinary and accepted meaning and read the subsections together. State v. Resler, 1952, 262 Wis. 285, 55 N.W.2d 35.

* * *

The Public Service Commission is an administrative body created by the legislature and possesses neither legislative nor judicial functions. Sec. 31.14(8), Stats., requires it to exercise its delegated powers to conduct hearings and determine certain facts. When such facts are found the permits contemplated by the statute are to be issued. The Commission is not authorized to go further. * * *

The question on these appeals is not what are the rights of riparian owners or whether this section modified those rights or adopted the prior-use doctrine, but whether the commission has been given the jurisdiction to determine those rights.

* * *

Sec. 31.14, Stats., deals with only a small part of the conflicting interests in the water resources of Wisconsin. Rights of the public, sportsmen, consumptive users such as farmers and irrigators, and nonconsumptive users such as hydro-electric power companies—and the rights of manufacturers, municipalities, and those people interested in recreation, conservation, and the enjoyment of natural scenic beauty—all are a part of the water problem. Many efforts and studies have been made in recent years by the legislature and others to solve this problem.

* * *

Judgments affirmed.

NOTES

1. The Wisconsin court ruled that the Public Service Commission could determine whether water is "surplus" or "non-surplus," and allocate surplus water. How is "surplus" determined? How does the

allocation of such water differ from the allocation of water among riparians in absence of the statute? Notice the different procedures for determining new rights in surplus and non-surplus water. Suppose an upstream owner wants a right to a small amount of water but a downstream riparian hydroelectric plant uses and has a right to the full flow of the river for power generation. If it could be shown that the irrigation diversion was so small that it would not injure the power plant, could the irrigator obtain a water right?

The decision in the principal case interpreting Wis.Stat. § 30.18 effectively results in a requirement that irrigators who want permits must first get consent from downstream hydroelectric powerplant owners, "a dramatic grant of appropriative" rights which extend to the whole flow of the water. Jacob H. Beuscher, *Appropriation Water Law Elements in Riparian Doctrine States,* 10 Buffalo L.Rev. 448 (1961). Because of the statute's terms, the requirement only applies to agricultural irrigation uses.

The constitutionality of Wisconsin's permit system, the subject of *Nekoosa–Edwards Paper Co.,* was upheld in Omernik v. Wisconsin, 218 N.W.2d 734 (Wis.1974). The Supreme Court of Wisconsin held that § 30.18 does not constitute a taking without just compensation but was a "valid exercise of the police power." See also Omernick v. Department of Natural Resources, 238 N.W.2d 114 (Wis.1976), in which the court held that the legislature has "abrogated the common law riparian right of irrigation and has substituted the permit procedure under sec. 30.18." Thus, the riparian owner must obtain a permit before diverting water for irrigation purposes which requires the consent of all riparians injured by a diversion of non-surplus water. The taking question is discussed generally at pages 364–91, infra.

2. Permits for irrigation or agriculture may not be issued in Wisconsin if it appears that public rights will be injured. Wis.Stat. Ann. 31.18(1)(b). Conditions are also imposed on the permit that allow the permit to be amended or rescinded to protect public rights in the stream. See Harold W. Ellis, *et al.,* Water–Use Law and Administration in Wisconsin § 9.06 (1970). The Wisconsin Department of Natural Resources (as successor to the Public Service Commission) grants a permit if "the proposed dam is in the public interest, considering ecological, aesthetic, economic and recreational values * * *. The enjoyment of natural scenic beauty [is a] * * * public right to be considered along with other public rights * * *." Wis.Stat.Ann. 31.-06(3). The statute directs the department to weigh the recreational use and natural scenic beauty of the river in its natural state and in its altered state due to the dam, and "if it further appears that the economic need of electric power is less than the value of the recreational and scenic beauty advantage of such river in its natural state," the department shall deny the permit. Thus, the department weighs the public interests against the competing interests.

The Supreme Court of Wisconsin has indicated that the public right may have originated in use for navigation, that the right will not be "lost by failure of pecuniary profitable navigation," but that other uses may be developed, such as "sailing, rowing, canoeing, bathing, fishing, hunting, skating," or other public purposes. Nekoosa–Edwards Paper Co. v. Railroad Comm'n, 228 N.W. 144, 147 (Wis.1929).

3. A major effort at improving the common law riparian doctrine and providing a standardized framework is found in Frank E. Maloney, *et al.,* A Model Water Code (1972). The Code attempts to reflect the public's interest in water as a resource, with that interest defined to include wildlife preservation, maintenance of ecological balance, scenic beauty, navigation, recreation, and protection of municipal/public water supplies.

The Code is designed as a comprehensive approach to water management, and regulates uses of groundwater, surface water, and diffused surface water. Under its provisions, a state may reserve rights for minimum stream flows and lake levels, as well as regulate to preserve water quality. Use and quality considerations are both under one authority, called the State Water Resources Board. The Board is also given authority over the construction and regulation of wells and surface water works, weather modification operations, and negotiations on behalf of the state in federal and interstate water projects.

All uses other than those for individual domestic purposes are subject to permit. Permits are issued for a maximum of twenty years, except where a longer period is required to retire bonds issued by municipalities or other governmental bodies. In the latter event the maximum period is fifty years. In the event of competing permit applications for an inadequate supply of water, the application that "best serves the public interest" prevails.

The Code proposes the formulation of a state water use plan, based on water supply and demand information. One objective of the plan is to maximize "reasonable-beneficial use" of water, which is defined by the Code as "[t]he use of water in such a quantity as is necessary for economic and efficient utilization, for a purpose and in a manner which is both reasonable and consistent with the public interest."

4. For an assessment of the operation of existing permit systems see the following articles by Professor Robert H. Abrams: Charting The Course of Riparianism: An Instrumentalist Theory of Change, 35 Wayne L.Rev. 1381 (1989); Water Allocation By Comprehensive Permit Systems in the East: Considering A Move Away From Orthodoxy, 9 Va.Envtl.L.J. 255 (1990); and Replacing Riparianism in the Twenty–First Century, 36 Wayne L.Rev. 93 (1989).

LITTLE BLUE NATURAL RESOURCES DISTRICT v. LOWER PLATTE NORTH NATURAL RESOURCES DISTRICT

Supreme Court of Nebraska, 1980.
206 Neb. 535, 294 N.W.2d 598.

KRIVOSHA, CHIEF JUSTICE.

* * *

[The Little Blue Natural Resources District is a district formed under Nebraska law to perform multiple functions that historically were performed by several special districts. Neb.Rev.Stat. § 2–3203. The District planned an irrigation project to divert water from a point near the Platte River to District lands in another watershed which could not be irrigated with groundwater because there was no aquifer there.]

The Central Nebraska Public Power and Irrigation District, generally known as Tri–County, operates a supply canal south of the Platte River which transports water from a diversion dam on the Platte River east of North Platte, Nebraska, to a point near Overton, Nebraska, where the supply canal joins the Phelps County canal, a major irrigation canal operated by Tri–County. A wasteway located at this junction is used to return water to the river when it is not to be used for irrigation purposes. A gate located at the junction is used to send water in the supply canal into the Phelps County canal or into the wasteway.

The Little Blue project contemplates taking water at this structure, which would otherwise be returned through the wasteway to the river, and carrying it to the Campbell reservoir for storage for use during the following season. The plan contemplates the use of the Phelps County canal to a point near Axtell, Nebraska, where a new supply canal would be constructed which would connect with the Little Blue River southwest of Minden, Nebraska.

Since the Tri–County district would be using water for irrigation during the months of April through August, the Little Blue project would use the flow in the supply canal from September until January and would take only water which would otherwise be returned to the Platte River through the wasteway.

The director [of the Department of Water Resources] found there was unappropriated water in the Platte River sufficient to meet the demands of the proposed project, but that approval of the applications would result in water for irrigation purposes being taken from the Platte River and applied to land outside the basin of the Platte River, contrary to the rules announced by this court in Osterman v. Central Nebraska Public Power and Irrigation District, 131 Neb. 356, 268 N.W. 334 (1936). The director concluded that the *Osterman* case was controlling and, for that reason, the department was without authority to approve the applications. The applicant has appealed from the order denying the applications.

* * *

The *Osterman* case involved applications by the Central Nebraska Public Power and Irrigation District, generally known as Tri–County, to divert and store water from the Platte River for power purposes and to irrigate land in Gosper, Phelps, Kearney, and Adams Counties. Approximately 60 percent of the water to be used for irrigation purposes would have been transported out of the Platte River basin and applied to lands within the basin of the Blue River.

In the *Osterman* case, this court declared that, at common law, the right to use water was limited to the owners of riparian lands and, of necessity, there was "no right to transport waters beyond or over the divide or watershed that enclosed the source from which obtained."

* * *

The language of the Nebraska Constitution is clear and unambiguous with regard to the use of water. Neb. Const. art. XV, § 4, unequivocally provides: "The necessity of water for domestic use and for irrigation purposes in the State of Nebraska is hereby declared to be a natural want." * * *

Neb. Const. art. XV, § 5, provides: "The use of the water of every natural stream within the State of Nebraska is hereby dedicated to the people of the state for beneficial purposes, subject to the provisions of the following section." It is significant to note that the quoted section refers to the use of the water of *every* natural stream being dedicated to "the people." Nothing in art. XV, § 5, indicates or authorizes limiting the use of the water of every natural stream to *within a particular watershed basin* or dedicating its use to the people living *within a particular watershed basin.* Quite to the contrary, the clear and unambiguous language constitutionally mandates that the use of *every* stream, regardless of its location, be dedicated to *all* of the people of the state, regardless of their location, and not just to those who happen to live within the confines of a particular valley or watershed basin. Nowhere within the Constitution can such limiting words be found.

That fact is further made clear when one looks at Neb. Const. art. XV, § 6, which provides, in part: "The right to divert unappropriated waters of every natural stream for beneficial use shall *never be denied* except when such denial is demanded by the public interest." (Emphasis supplied).

* * *

The *Osterman* decision totally ignored the provisions of the Nebraska Constitution and relied solely upon the provisions of what is now Neb.Rev.Stat. § 46–265 (Reissue 1978), and what was formerly § 46–620 Comp.Stat.1929. It reads as follows:

> The owner or owners of any irrigation ditch or canal shall carefully maintain the embankments thereof so as to prevent waste therefrom, and shall return the unused water from such ditch or canal with as little waste thereof as possible to the stream from which such water was taken, *or to the Missouri River.*

(Emphasis supplied). The *Osterman* court concluded that the phrase "or to the Missouri River" had no application, was not a part of the statute, and should be ignored. The court, therefore, concluded that former § 46–620 prohibited transbasin diversion.

There is no basis, however, to conclude that the phrase "or to the Missouri River" has no meaning. All of the water of the State of Nebraska empties into the Missouri River and, therefore, it must be concluded that diversion may occur so long as the unused portion of the water is not in some manner unnecessarily impounded or wasted and is returned to its natural stream of origin or to the Missouri River.

The *Osterman* decision further concluded that former § 46–508, now § 46–206, which provides:

The water appropriated from a river or stream shall not be turned or permitted to run into the waters or channel of any other river or stream than that from which it is taken or appropriated, *unless such stream exceeds in width one hundred feet, in which event not more than seventy-five per cent of the regular flow shall be taken.*

(emphasis supplied), was superseded by the provisions of § 46–620 and should be disregarded.

* * * If transbasin diversion is prohibited entirely, as urged by appellees, then the last clause of § 46–206, permitting the diversion of up to 75 percent of the water from a stream more than 100 feet wide is meaningless.

When we then give both sections of the statute their plain meaning, we are left with no other conclusion but that, if a stream is more than 100 feet wide, up to 75 percent of the water not otherwise appropriated may be diverted so long as no waste is permitted, the unused portion is returned to its stream of origin or permitted to find its way back to the Missouri River, and the public interest does not otherwise require that such diversion be denied.

* * *

In Osterman, supra at 362, 268 N.W. at 337, we said:

It would be a sad commentary on our political organization, upon the department of roads and irrigation, and upon this reviewing court, if in rationing this necessity of life this beautiful valley should be left with a dry river bed and ruined farms, because of any mistaken theory that the protection of its natural fertility did not constitute a public interest within the policy of our laws.

We agree with that statement and believe that, under the provisions of our Constitution dealing with water, it is applicable to the entire state so long as the public interest does not otherwise demand. Would it not be a far sadder commentary if, in rationing this necessity of life, large areas of the state outside a particular valley were ruined while unappropriated water flowed into the Missouri River and on to other states.

When there is insufficient water to meet all needs, the Director of Water Resources may, under the law, limit the removal of water in accordance with statutorily established priorities similar to the restrictions imposed by the director and set out in Cozad Ditch Co. v. Central Nebraska Public Power & Irrigation Dist. [272 N.W. 560 (Neb.1937)]. Under our present Constitution and statutes, the determination of what constitutes a public interest sufficient to either limit or deny, as the situation may demand, the right to remove unappropriated waters from a stream must, in the first instance, be determined by the director. The Constitution tells us that the desire and need for water for domestic and irrigation purposes is a "natural want" of all our citizens

and we should not unnecessarily deny it to any who can obtain it
without doing harm to others.

* * *

Reversed and Remanded.

NOTES

1. After the principal case was decided, the Nebraska legislature
amended the transfer statute to enumerate the relevant factors to be
considered by the Director of the Department of Natural Resources in
determining the public interest:

(1) The economic, environmental, and other benefits of the
proposed interbasin transfer and use;

(2) Any adverse impacts of the proposed interbasin transfer
and use;

(3) Any current beneficial uses being made of the unappropriated water in the basin of origin;

(4) Any reasonably foreseeable future beneficial uses of the
water in the basin of origin;

(5) The economic, environmental, and other benefits of leaving
the water in the basin of origin for current or future beneficial
uses;

(6) Alternative sources of water supply available to the applicant; and

(7) Alternative sources of water available to the basin of origin
for future beneficial uses.

The application shall be deemed in the public interest if the
overall benefits to the state and the applicant's basin are greater
than or equal to the adverse impacts to the state and the basin of
origin.

Neb.Rev.Stat. § 46–289.

The statute was construed in Little Blue Natural Resources Dist. v.
Lower Platte North Natural Resources Dist., 317 N.W.2d 726 (Neb.
1982) which held that the director must consult with the Game and
Parks Commission to determine whether the proposed appropriations
would interfere with endangered species or their habitat. For a description of threats to one endangered species posed by proposed Nebraska water projects, and an analysis of the new transfer statute, see
Daniel C. Vaughn, Comment, *The Whooping Crane, the Platte River,
and Endangered Species Legislation,* 66 Neb.L.Rev. 175 (1987).

In a later case, In re Application of Hitchcock and Red Willow Irr.
Dists., et al., 410 N.W.2d 101 (Neb.1987), irrigation districts challenged
the Director of Water Resources' denial of an application to divert
water from the South Platte River for storage in Enders Reservoir.
The director's decision was based in part on the transbasin diversion
law, which appellants claimed to be unconstitutional. The director also
found that the project would harm endangered species habitat on the

South Platte River. Most significantly, however, the director found that no water was available for appropriation in the South Platte.

2. In *Osterman,* a nearly identical scheme for removing water from one basin to another was considered and rejected on the ground that interbasin diversions would be inconsistent with the common law. The court stated:

> "The common-law rules as to the rights and duties of riparian owners are in force in every part of the state, except as altered or modified by statute." Meng v. Coffee, 67 Neb. 500, 93 N.W. 713
> * * *

> The language of the above rule necessarily implies that the right to use water at common law is limited strictly to riparian lands. * * * This necessitates the further conclusion that at common law there was in general no right to transport waters beyond or over the divide or watershed that enclosed the source from which obtained.

268 N.W. 334, 338–39 (1936). In reversing the *Osterman* case based on state constitutional provisions, did the Nebraska court effectively hold the riparian doctrine unconstitutional? What is the effect of the *Little Blue* decision on the rights of riparians? See Regina M. Shields, Note, *Water Law—Transbasin Diversion in Nebraska,* 14 Creighton L.Rev. 887 (1980–81); Eric Pearson, *Constitutional Restraints on Water Diversions in Nebraska: The Little Blue Controversy,* 16 Creighton L.Rev. 695 (1982–83).

3. Water Quality Rights

SPRINGER v. JOSEPH SCHLITZ BREWING CO.

United States Court of Appeal, Fourth Circuit, 1975.
510 F.2d 468.

Before WINTER, BUTZNER, and WIDENER, CIRCUIT JUDGES.

BUTZNER, CIRCUIT JUDGE:

* * *

In North Carolina, a riparian landowner has a right to the agricultural, recreational, and scenic use and enjoyment of the stream bordering his land, subject, however, to the rights of upstream riparian owners to make reasonable use of the water without excessively diminishing its quality. Though he does not own the fish in the stream, the riparian owner's rights include the opportunity to catch them. Interference with riparian rights is an actionable tort, and a riparian owner may join several polluters as joint tort-feasors.

Nevertheless, an industry that uses a municipal sewage system to dispose of its waste is not liable to a riparian landowner for the

pollution caused by the city's failure to provide adequate treatment.
* * *

The Springers claim that their proof is sufficient to invoke exceptions to the general rule of immunity. Specifically, they contend that Schlitz should be held liable if it violated the city sewage ordinance, or if Schlitz knew, or should have known, of the inability of the city to adequately treat the brewery's wastes. Since no North Carolina court has considered these exceptions, we must determine the common law of the state by examining the rationale for the established rule, developments on this point in other states, and analogous areas of the state's common law.

* * *

II

In February 1970 the City of Winston–Salem enacted a comprehensive sewage ordinance to take effect in May. The ordinance requires every user of industrial sewers to have a discharge permit. Users may discharge only wastes containing 2500 ppm BOD or less,[3] and they are forbidden to release sewage containing a wide variety of dangerous or difficult-to-treat substances. The ordinance imposes surcharges for BOD pound loadings caused by a concentration above 300 ppm. * * *

Schlitz's effluent contained more than 2500 ppm BOD until April 1971. Beginning in May 1970, the city billed, and Schlitz paid, all BOD surcharges. The brewery and other industries, however, were allowed to operate in violation of the ordinance and without permits as long as they submitted schedules for compliance and conformed to them. It received its permit, one of the first issued to any industry, in May 1971.

The violation of a municipal sewage ordinance which is intended to protect downstream riparian owners can subject an industrial sewage source to private civil liability. * * * When an industry turns over the control of its sewage to the city, it can reasonably expect that the city will safeguard riparian property by effective treatment.[9] But it is not reasonable for an industry to expect a city to safely treat prohibited sewage. Consequently, the reason for granting immunity does not then apply.

* * *

3. Winston–Salem Code of Ordinances * * * § 23–1(2) defines B.O.D.:

"B.O.D. (denoting Biochemical Oxygen Demand) * * * is a measure of the polluting strength of wastes."

In other words, BOD is not a separate substance but a measure of the ability of decomposing sewage to remove dissolved oxygen from the water.

BOD has two important polluting effects, depending on the manner in which it decays. It first removes dissolved oxygen necessary for fish and other aquatic life from the stream, causing fish kills and other biological changes. Once the dissolved oxygen has been exhausted, the remaining BOD undergoes septic decomposition, which produces slime, scum, gas, and fecal odors.

9. A town is liable for pollution it causes by dumping inadequately treated sewage. Clinard v. Town of Kernersville, 215 N.C. 745, 3 S.E.2d 267 (1939); see Aycock, Introduction to Water Use Law in North Carolina, 46 N.C.L.Rev. 1, 11–13 (1967).

Schlitz's failure to obtain a permit until May 1971 does not afford the Springers a ground for recovery. The permit does not protect riparian owners. It is only an instrument of the city's enforcement program, and its absence does not pollute the stream. Moreover, the ordinance does not explicitly forbid the discharge of wastes containing more than 2500 ppm BOD. The ordinance is a criminal statute which must be construed in the defendant's favor in civil proceedings as well as in criminal ones. * * *

In contrast, the discharge of sewage prohibited by Section 23–2(2) is a crime, and under North Carolina law it is actionable if it proximately causes damage to riparian property. Section 23–2(2) states in part:

"(2) Except as hereinafter provided, it shall be unlawful for any person to discharge or cause to be discharged any of the following described materials, waters, liquids, or wastes into any public sanitary sewer:

* * *

"(g) Liquid wastes containing any toxic or poisonous substances in sufficient quantities to (i) interfere with the biological processes used in a sewage treatment plant, or (ii) which, in combination with other liquid wastes, upon passing through a sewage treatment plant will be harmful to persons, livestock, or aquatic life utilizing the receiving streams into which water from a sewage treatment plant is discharged."

In order to establish that Schlitz's violation of the ordinance was negligence, the Springers would have to prove that the brewery wastes had the characteristics forbidden by Section 23–2(2). Viewed in the light most favorable to them, the evidence showed that the brewery's wastes had a toxic or poisonous effect on bacteria that are essential to the sewage treatment process. The evidence also showed that after passing through the plant the wastes were harmful to aquatic life in the receiving stream. The jury should therefore be allowed to determine whether or not the discharge violated the ordinance. If it did, this was negligence, and the jury should then decide whether it proximately caused damage to the Springers' property.

Schlitz argues that its discharge of brewery wastes is not actionable because the city's officials did not require compliance with the ordinance until May 1971, except for the payment of surcharges. This contention lacks merit. * * *

* * * While it is true that the city's director of water and sewers believed that immediate, rigorous enforcement would be undesirable because it would "shut down just about every industry in Winston–Salem," there is no conflict between the public interest in keeping a factory open and the private right to recover damages for pollution. The two may be reconciled by requiring the source of pollution to pay damages while allowing it to operate. See Boomer v. Atlantic Cement Co., 26 N.Y.2d 219, 309 N.Y.S.2d 312, 257 N.E.2d 870 (1970). Since the plain language of the ordinance does not authorize city officials to

dispense with its requirements, their actions could not affect the Springers' rights. * * *

In addition, paying effluent surcharges did not relieve Schlitz from having to obey the rest of the ordinance. The city levies these charges "to cover some of the cost to the city of treating such wastes." They begin not at 2500 ppm but at 300 ppm, the approximate dividing line between domestic and industrial strength sewage. The charges are enumerated in the ordinance section which sets other fees, not in the one which describes prohibited uses. They are revenue measures rather than substitutes for civil liability.

III

As an alternative ground of recovery, the Springers argue that Schlitz should be held liable if it knew, or in the exercise of reasonable care should have known, that the city could not adequately treat the brewery's waste. The validity of this claim depends on an analysis of the underlying reasons for the general rule of immunity.

* * * The city, in the court's view, undertook to dispose of the residents' wastes in a nuisance free manner, and they in turn consented to such conditions as the city might put on the use of the sewers.

* * * The city controls the choice of methods that will be used to achieve the desired result, and the individual sewer user lacks authority to control the city's performance. * * * The liability of the user of a municipal sewer system therefore appears to be limited in the same way as the liability of an independent contractor's employer.

* * * Since the selection of the contractor is within the employer's control, "if it appears that the employer knew, or by the exercise of reasonable care might have ascertained that the contractor was not properly qualified to undertake the work, he may be held liable for the negligent acts of the contractor." Page v. Sloan, 12 N.C.App. 433, 183 S.E.2d 813, 817 (1971), aff'd, 281 N.C. 697, 190 S.E.2d 189 (1972).

The owner of a large industrial source of sewage, particularly one only planned or under construction, is similarly situated. A manufacturing company is in a position to know enough about its own operations to understand the nature of its wastes and the problems of treating them. If it has not yet selected a plant site, it may have a choice among cities and disposal systems. It may also be large enough to pre-treat or properly dispose of its own sewage. When the company represents a desirable source of jobs and tax revenues, the local authorities can be expected to provide it with technical information about the municipal sewers. In brief, a large industrial sewer user can make an informed decision whether to use a city sewer system to render its wastes nuisance free.

According to the Springers' evidence, Schlitz, which has more than a century of experience in brewing beer, considered several cities in the Southeast before selecting Winston–Salem for a brewery site. As part of its investigation, the company requested information about the city's sewage facilities, and its representatives toured the treatment plant. Had the company inquired, it would have learned that the plant was operating at or over its daily capacity of 18 million gallons of sewage containing 76,000 pounds of BOD. The city assured Schlitz that it would adequately treat its wastes after Schlitz advised the city to expect 15,000 pounds of BOD per day. Before the brewery had been open a year, however, it was discharging 56,000 pounds of BOD per day into a system which had previously reached its 76,000 pound capacity. Brewery wastes are known by sanitary engineers to be difficult to treat and to interfere with the treatment of other wastes because of their high concentration of BOD and fluctuating alkalinity.

These facts disclose that Schlitz knew the characteristics of its own sewage and that it exercised control over its selection of a site and of the sewage system which would dispose of its waste. The evidence also indicates that Schlitz could not rely on the city's acceptance of its sewage, because it had not furnished the city accurate information. Finally, the proof supports an inference that Schlitz knew, or in the exercise of reasonable care should have ascertained, that the city could not adequately treat its brewery wastes. The jury might reasonably have decided that Schlitz negligently selected the city of Winston–Salem to treat its sewage. Drawing upon North Carolina's common law principles governing the liability of an employer of an independent contractor, we conclude that Schlitz is not, as a matter of law, immune from liability. Accordingly, on remand, the district court should submit the issue of Schlitz's liability on the Springers' alternative theory.

IV

The record discloses that after the 1970 fish kills, Schlitz expended more than $1,300,000 for sewage treatment facilities, and it is now in compliance with the effluent quality standards of the city ordinance. The city has doubled the size of its treatment plant, and it can now properly treat the waste from the brewery. In view of this evidence, it is unlikely that an injunction is appropriate under North Carolina law.
* * *

WIDENER, CIRCUIT JUDGE (concurring and dissenting):

* * *

Since it is clear to me that the construction placed by the city on its own ordinances was the only reasonable one (a contrary construction would have shut down about every industry in Winston–Salem), and that Schlitz had complied with the ordinances as construed by the city authorities charged with their enforcement, I am of opinion liability should not be based upon a violation thereof.

NOTES

1. Could the Springers recover from Schlitz if there was no statute? If Schlitz was not actually in violation of the statute?

Violation of an applicable water quality standard is often asserted as a basis for nuisance or other tort liability. See generally Note, *Water Quality Standards in Private Nuisance Actions*, 79 Yale L.J. 102 (1969). Compliance with applicable standards has not historically been a defense to a nuisance action. Urie v. Franconia Paper Corp., 218 A.2d 360 (N.H.1966) and Varajabedian v. Madera, 572 P.2d 43 (Cal. 1977). Why? See Frank I. Michelman, *Pollution as a Tort: A Non-Accidental Perspective on Calabresi's Costs,* 80 Yale L.J. 647 (1971). State standards were not very strict until the passage of the federal Clean Water Act (CWA) in 1972. See pages 132–35, infra. Now they are, and compliance with nationally applicable National Pollutant Discharge Elimination System (NPDES) permit requirements of the Act raises a stronger claim to a defense. See Birchwood Lakes Colony Club v. Medford Lakes, 449 A.2d 472 (N.J.1982).

2. Could the city be held liable as well? See footnote 9. See also City of Columbus v. Myszka, 272 S.E.2d 302 (Ga.1980) (city liable for damages to plaintiff caused by sewage from a leaking, overloaded sewer that served a development, the construction of which was approved by the city); Moore v. Hampton Roads Sanitation Dist. Comm'n, 557 F.2d 1030 (4th Cir.1976).

3. In the absence of statute, municipalities that are often removed from a stream, and therefore nonriparians, may have no right to divert water for municipal uses. An analogous problem arises when the municipality seeks to use a stream to carry away wastes from nonriparian lands. How should a case involving the uses of a nonriparian city be analyzed? Should the city be treated any differently from a riparian operating a major factory that discharges waste into the stream?

4. If an upstream user located outside of the watershed of a stream discharges sewage into the stream and is sued by a downstream riparian, can the nonriparian defend on the ground that the discharge is reasonable because no "actual perceptible damage results" from it, or is the upstream use unreasonable as a matter of law? See Stanton v. Trustees of St. Joseph's College, 254 A.2d 597 (Me.1969). Compare Stearns v. State, 79 N.W.2d 241 (Wis.1956).

BOROUGH OF WESTVILLE v. WHITNEY HOME BUILDERS

Superior Court of New Jersey, 1956.
40 N.J.Super. 62, 122 A.2d 233.

[In connection with the development of a residential subdivision, defendant Whitney organized a sewerage company. The plans were approved by the State Board of Health. The treated sewage was discharged into a small natural stream which flowed for a mile into a pond in Westville's principal park. In time of drought, the flow was reduced to a trickle. Two plaintiffs brought suit, the local board of health and the borough as proprietor of the park. The evidence established that it was "highly improbable" that harmful bacteria would survive, and that the principal problem with the discharge was stench. The local health board's suit was dismissed on the ground that exclusive jurisdiction over public nuisance actions for discharge of sewage was in the state board, and no appeal was taken from that ruling. The trial court also dismissed the borough's private nuisance action based on its riparian rights, and the borough has appealed.]

CONFORD, J.A.D. * * *

IV.

We thus come to a consideration of the law governing the mutual rights and obligations of riparian owners, *inter sese*, in respect to the use of the water flow. It will be seen that this subject, in New Jersey as elsewhere in this country, is in a state of some doctrinal confusion. * * *

The natural flow theory, long held in England, contemplates that it is the right of every riparian proprietor to have the flow of water across his land maintained in its natural state, not sensibly diminished in quantity or impaired in quality. * * * Maloney, The Balance of Convenience Doctrine, 5 So.Car.L.Q. 159, 169 (1952).

The reasonable use doctrine does not concern itself with the impairment of the natural flow or quality of the water but allows full use of the watercourse in any way that is beneficial to the riparian owner provided only it does not unreasonably interfere with the beneficial uses of others, the court or jury being the arbiter as to what is unreasonable. * * *

An examination of the cases shows that while they sometimes repeat the rule in terms of natural flow and quality, expressions of criteria sounding in reasonable use are also to be found, sometimes in the same case, and that none of the decisions is inconsistent on its facts with the rationale of reasonable use.

* * *

An illuminating variant of the reasonable use doctrine is its expression in terms of "fair participation" between riparian owners. In Sandusky Portland Cement Co. v. Dixon Pure Ice Co., 221 F. 200, L.R.A. 1915E, 1210 (7th Cir.1915), certiorari denied 238 U.S. 630 (1915), a lower owner who manufactured ice from river water was held entitled to an injunction against the heating of the water by an upper proprietor to an extent which materially retarded the formation of ice. The court said (221 F., at page 204):

> "Complainant may not insist on such a use of the water by the defendant as will deprive the latter of any use thereof which may be necessary for its business purposes, provided complainant can by reasonable diligence and effort make the flowing water reasonably answer its own purposes. There must be a fair participation between them. * * * But where, as in the present case, it is shown by the evidence that defendant's use of the river water, while essential for its own purposes, entirely destroys the right of complainant thereto, there can be no claim by defendant that its use thereof is reasonable. In other words, the emergency of defendant's needs is not the measure of its rights in the water."

On principle, we conclude that the interests of a changing, complex and technologically mushrooming society call for the application of the "reasonable use" doctrine in this field; a rule which enables judicial arbitration, in the absence of controlling legislation, of the fair participation in common waters of those who have a right of property therein on the basis of what all of the attendant circumstances shows to be

reasonable. On analysis of the case authorities, we think the courts
have actually moved along that course, whatever the occasional ideolog-
ical conflict in expression. This, moreover, is the approach recently
taken by our Supreme Court in the closely cognate area of diversion of
surface waters. Armstrong v. Francis Corp., 20 N.J. 320 (1956). The
court there alluded to the consideration as to "whether the utility of
the possessor's use of his land outweighs the gravity of the harm which
results from his alteration of the flow of surface waters" (20 N.J., at
page 330). It further said (20 N.J., at page 330):

> "Social progress and the common wellbeing are in actuality
> better served by a just and right balancing of the competing
> interests according to the general principles of fairness and com-
> mon sense which attend the application of the rule of reason."

V.

It remains to apply the foregoing principles to the special problem
presented here. We have already taken notice of the plea of plaintiff
that the effluent flowing into the ditch and pond is "noisome" and
necessarily a pollutant because its origin in association with human
excreta and *secreta* engenders such revulsion in the average person as
assertedly must substantially impair the use of the pond as an important part of the public recreational and park area. The synthesis of the
evidence set out in II, supra, cannot help but lead to the fair conclusion
that the effluent is not reasonably to be regarded as a threat to health,
nor offensive, now or in fair prospect, to the senses of sight or smell.
No user of the park not knowing of the discharge of the effluent is ever
apt to suffer lessened enjoyment ascribable to its flow. Indeed the
contrary may be true in times of drought. As recognized by trial court
and counsel the question is substantially one of psychological impairment of the recreational function of the park.

We by no means make light of plaintiff's grievance. The problem
presented has impressed us as of considerable import. As conceded by
the trial court the people of Westville cannot be expected to be happy
over the continuous presence of sewage effluent in their park pond, no
matter how relatively pure. However, as will be more particularly
developed presently, it cannot be said that the discharge of treated
sewage effluent into a running stream is per se an unreasonable
riparian use in today's civilization. Under the reasonable use approach
we are called upon to counterweigh social uses and harms. And this
we must do in a realistic rather than a theoretical way, and on the
basis of the evidence of record, rather than on emotion or runaway
imagination.

* * *

These acts of legislation, and others (see, e.g., N.J.S.A. 58:12–2),
denote a public policy which recognizes the social importance of sewage
disposal plants and the necessity of fair and reasonable accommodation
to their functioning of the use of the waters of the State for other
purposes, even including that of human consumption, a use not involved in the present case. They tend to refute the idea that treated

sewage effluent, as claimed by plaintiff, is necessarily a polluting or contaminating agent.

Clearly inapposite is the body of law that the influx of raw sewage which pollutes a stream is an actionable invasion (in the absence of legislative authorization) of the rights of a lower riparian owner or that a sewage disposal or treatment plant which, because of malfunctioning, inefficiency, or otherwise, is in fact a nuisance or a source of pollution, may be enjoined, Harrisonville v. W.S. Dickey Clay Mfg. Co., 289 U.S. 334 (1933). Research discloses and counsel have cited no case wherein treated sewage effluent has been held *per se* an enjoinable water pollutant. The authorities are uniformly to the contrary.

* * *

On the basis of the entire case we cannot conclude that the denial of injunctive relief by the trial court was erroneous. We do not rest our conclusion on the premise, which plaintiff has properly been at pains to dissipate, that there is required a showing of any particular kind of damages or injury other than psychological where there has, indeed, been the invasion of a property right. Our conception is, rather, that a determination as to the existence of an actionable invasion of the unquestionable property right of a riparian owner in the flow of a water course depends upon a weighing of the reasonableness, under all the circumstances, of the use being made by the defendant and of the materiality of the harm, if any, found to be visited by such use upon the reasonable uses of the water by the complaining owner. For all of the reasons we have set out, we do not consider that the balance of uses and harms reflected by this record points to an injunction. We trust that what we have said will not be read in anywise to impugn the appropriateness of plaintiff's use of the ditch and pond for recreational and park purposes as a riparian owner. If defendants' future operation of the treatment plant is ever shown to be such, in fact, as unreasonably to affect the use and enjoyment by the people of Westville of their park and pond, nothing herein determined upon the basis of the present record will, of course, preclude appropriate relief.

Judgment affirmed.

NOTES

1. The court in *Westville* recognizes that under the riparian doctrine, landowners are entitled to have waters of waterbodies touching their lands unimpaired in quality as well as undiminished in quantity. Recall that riparian law from earliest times allowed for "natural uses" such as drinking and household uses. Does this then mean that a landowner can add pollutants to the water by washing in the stream? Does this entitle a riparian landowner to put household sewage into the stream?

2. The common law recognized causes of action in nuisance and trespass against pollution of drinking water by bathers when the bathers were owners of riparian property. Conflicts arose between riparian rights and the exercise of the police power to protect public

health.   In State v. Heller, 196 A. 337 (Conn.1937), for example, the
riparian property owner was convicted of violating a state statute by
bathing in a stream which traversed his property. The court found the
statute to be a legitimate exercise of the police power, and refused
claim for compensation for a taking of property, noting that most of the
riparian's rights remained intact, and that private rights must yield to
public needs.

In Newton v. Groesbeck, 299 S.W. 518 (Tex.Civ.App.1927), the
Texas Supreme Court found that a proposed development of a local
swimming hole into a public bathing resort was an unreasonable use in
light of a city's claim that the resort would interfere with the quality of
its water supply. But see City of Battle Creek v. Goguac Resort Ass'n,
148 N.W. 441 (Mich.1914) (right to operate a bathing resort upheld;
court suggested city purchase surrounding lands to prevent bathing in
the lake). Cf. Game & Fresh Water Fish Comm'n v. Lake Islands, 407
So.2d 189 (Fla.1981) (state regulation prohibiting use of motor boats
during duck hunting season was taking of island owners' riparian right
of access).

3.   In *Springer* the court held that a riparian landowner has a
cause of action for interference with riparian rights. *Westville* is based
on a nuisance theory. As a practical matter, why would a plaintiff
choose one theory over another? A trespass is an interference with the
exclusive possession of property while a nuisance is an interference with
the *use and enjoyment* of land. Is one cause of action more appropriate
to actions of a defendant that affect the quantity of flow of water than
to actions that affect the quality of the water? To establish nuisance a
plaintiff must prove that the defendant knew or should have known
that plaintiff's interests would be injured, that the defendant's conduct
was "unreasonable," and that the harm to plaintiff is substantial. The
Restatement (Second) of Torts § 826 calls for a balancing test. The
"intentional invasion of another's interest in the use and enjoyment of
land is unreasonable if (a) the gravity of the harm outweighs the utility
of the actor's conduct, or (b) the harm caused by the conduct is serious
and the financial burden of compensating * * * would not make continuation of the conduct not feasible."

4.   A further possible cause of action in the principal case was for
public nuisance. Under Restatement (Second) of Torts § 821B the
court must find the defendant's conduct is unreasonable considering:

  1.   whether the conduct involves a significant interference
  with the public health, the public safety, the public peace, the
  public comfort or the public convenience, or

  2.   whether the conduct is proscribed by a statute, ordinance,
  or administrative regulation, or

  3.   whether the conduct is of a continuing nature or has
  produced a permanent or long-lasting effect, and, as the actor
  knows or has reason to know, has a significant effect upon the
  public right.

Typically public nuisance actions must be brought by a public entity; however, a private citizen may bring a public nuisance action if the citizen has suffered injury different in kind, rather than degree. Some state statutes specifically allow private individuals or entities to sue to abate a public nuisance. E.g., Florida Wildlife Fed'n v. Department of Envtl. Reg., 390 So.2d 64 (Fla.1980).

In *Westville,* the local health agency was dismissed because public regulation was vested in the state health agency. When both a court and an administrative agency have concurrent jurisdiction, a court may postpone the exercise of jurisdiction until the agency has rendered a final decision. The doctrine of primary jurisdiction has been successfully used as a defense by dischargers to common law nuisance actions. Courts which have applied the doctrine have stressed the technical nature of the issues which require administrative expertise.

5. Suppose that a plaintiff is injured by several dischargers acting independently. Is each tortfeasor responsible only for the damages caused by that tortfeasor, so that the plaintiff must prove the damage attributable to each discharge? The leading case of Landers v. East Tex. Salt Water Disposal Co., 248 S.W.2d 731 (Tex.1952) holds that justice requires that a plaintiff be able to join independent tortfeasors and place the burden of apportioning the wrong on them.

The issue of joint and several liability is a major one under the federal Comprehensive Environmental Response, Compensation and Liability Act (CERCLA), also known as the Superfund Act. See discussion at pages 578–79, infra. Under the Act, parties with remote connections with a hazardous waste site are potentially responsible for damages. Joint and several liability has been adopted as the presumptive rule for all contributors to a "superfund" site. United States v. Gurley Refining Co., 788 F.Supp. 1473 (E.D.Ark.1992); B.F. Goodrich Co. v. Murtha, 958 F.2d 1192 (2d Cir.1992); United States v. A & N Cleaners & Launderers, Inc., 788 F.Supp. 1317 (S.D.N.Y.1992). Colorado v. ASARCO, Inc., 608 F.Supp. 1484 (D.Colo.1985), balances the imposition of joint and several liability by recognizing a federal common law right of contribution among defendants.

6. The problem of protecting municipal water supplies from pollution is not new. Until the mid-nineteenth century most cities obtained their water from local free-flowing rivers, small ponds or relatively shallow wells, and wastewater was dispersed in nearby dry well cesspools or privy vaults. Starting in the 1840s major cities built water supply systems to serve their growing populations, but they did not simultaneously build sanitary sewer systems. The result was an increase in urban pollution as many people installed "water closets." Modern sanitary sewers were built in England in the 1850s and for the next two decades sanitary engineers sought to convince the public that the benefits of lower morbidity and mortality rates outweighed the costs of system construction. By 1880, 103 out of 222 American cities used land disposal to treat wastewater, but many of these had to curtail the practice to protect their own sources of water supply. The battle for sanitary sewers was won, but choices of lower cost, inadequate

technology, and decisions to dump untreated or partially treated wastes into available rivers cancelled some of the anticipated benefits. These early decisions and directions continue to shape the law of pollution abatement and municipal sewage treatment policy.

The history of American sewerage development is traced in Joel A. Tarr, et al., *The Development and Impact of Urban Wastewater Technology: Changing Concepts of Water Quality Control, 1850–1930,* in Pollution and Reform in American Cities, 1870–1930 (Martin V. Melosi ed. 1980).

NOTE: FEDERAL WATER QUALITY REGULATION

Clean Water Act

In most states, water pollution laws exist separate from permit systems allowing water use. Their importance, however, has largely been eclipsed by a panoply of federal statutes passed since 1972. Today the nation's water quality is primarily controlled by an extensive federal statutory framework. The most comprehensive federal water pollution statute is the Clean Water Act, 33 U.S.C.A. §§ 1251–1387. The first Federal Water Pollution Control Act was adopted in 1948. It created a system of federal subsidies for state and local governments, but did not attempt any direct regulation. State regulation proved to be ineffective and uneven. In 1965, Congress enacted the Water Quality Act because state programs were failing to clean up the nation's waters. The Act required classification of all interstate receiving waters, reflecting an underlying belief that water pollution control depended on the capacity of streams to assimilate pollutants. The Act required the states to act or else the federal government would take over water quality enforcement. But the receiving water quality standards were essentially unenforceable because it was difficult to work backwards from a receiving water standard to the effluent limitation necessary to maintain the desired water quality level over time, especially where multiple discharges were involved. The definitive analysis of the legislation is N. William Hines, *Nor Any Drop To Drink: Public Regulation of Water Quality* (pts. 1–3), 52 Iowa L.Rev. 186, 432, 799 (1966–1967).

The continuing ineffectiveness of state programs after the 1965 Act aroused public concern. The 1899 Refuse Act had been revitalized first by the Supreme Court, United States v. Republic Steel Corp., 362 U.S. 482 (1960), then for a short period by the U.S. Army Corps of Engineers. Under that Act any person dumping any kind of refuse in navigable waters violated federal law. The Act was a clumsy mechanism for dealing with ordinary water pollution problems as it lacked specific standards. Furthermore, it did not apply to municipal sewage. Although the states had not done well at controlling pollution, the Refuse Act was not the answer.

Finally, Congress passed the Federal Water Pollution Control Act in 1972 (which has been called the Clean Water Act since 1977) and gave regulatory responsibility to the newly created Environmental Protection Agency (EPA). The goal of the Clean Water Act was to eliminate totally the discharge of pollutants by 1985 and to "restore and maintain the chemical, physical and biological integrity of the nation's waters * * *" It set an interim goal of swimmable, fishable waters by 1983. The Act attempted to achieve most of its purposes by the enforcement of two sets of standards. Effluent standards limit the concentrations of pollutants that may be discharged from a particular source. Water quality standards limit the concentration of pollutants in the stream. The basic difference between the 1965 Act and the 1972 Act is that the later Act controls water pollution principally by imposing absolute limits on the amounts of pollutants that can be discharged at their source. The receiving water quality standards that were the focus of the earlier Act were retained as a backup for the technology-forcing effluent limitations. Upon passage of the 1972 Act, there was finally a comprehensive national water pollution control system.

In the Clean Water Act, Congress attempted to promote cooperation between the federal government and the states. Absolute effluent standards were nationally determined, but applied according to state plans. Water quality control was left to the states under the threat of federal intervention if state action was shown to be inadequate. Thus, the Clean Water Act is enforced through an effluent permit system known as the National Pollutant Discharge Elimination System (NPDES). The law simply declares all discharge of pollutants from any "point sources" without a permit to be unlawful. The job of issuing NPDES permits is usually assigned to states adhering to federal standards, otherwise to the EPA. 33 U.S.C.A. § 1251(b).

To obtain an NPDES permit, the state or federal agency having jurisdiction over permitting must certify that the discharge will comply with uniform national effluent standards set by the EPA. EPA's power to set binding national effluent limitations that must be incorporated into federal or state individual NPDES permits was upheld in E.I. du Pont de Nemours & Co. v. Train, 430 U.S. 112 (1977). The standards are based on the level of pollution control technology that is available for several categories of industries and for publicly owned sewage treatment works. By 1977 all industrial point sources were required to meet effluent limitations requiring "application of the best practicable control technology currently available as defined by the [EPA] Administrator" (BPT). 33 U.S.C.A. § 1311(b)(1)(A). Use of the best available technology economically achievable (BAT) was required by March 31, 1989 for toxic pollutants and for "nonconventional" pollutants. 33 U.S.C.A. §§ 1311(b)(2)(A), (C), (D) & (F). "Conventional pollutants" (suspended solids, coliform bacteria, biological oxygen demand, and acidity) are subject to the best conventional control technology (BCT) by March 31, 1989. 33 U.S.C.A. § 1311(b)(2)(E). Application of the several statutory standards to particular pollutants is left to the Administrator through rulemaking.

The other water pollution control strategy incorporated in the Clean Water Act is the requirement that water quality standards be set and enforced by the states. These standards deal with the concentration of pollutants in particular stretches of a stream. State plans and standards for water quality maintenance and control must be submitted to the EPA Administrator. The Administrator determines whether the standards are consistent with the Act's goal for waters of the United States to become "fishable and swimmable." The states must identify "water quality-limited" segments of streams such as areas where discharges that may be consistent with effluent standards nevertheless result in overall water quality that is unacceptable. For these areas the state must set "total maximum daily loads" for each pollutant.

In its administration of the water quality controls under the Clean Water Act, the state may set effluent limitations that are more stringent than those imposed by the United States, Homestake Mining Co. v. Environmental Protection Agency, 477 F.Supp. 1279 (D.S.D.1979), and implement an antidegradation policy to protect high quality waters that constitute an outstanding national resource, 40 C.F.R. § 131.212. See generally Jeffrey M. Gaba, *Federal Supervision of State Water Quality Standards Under the Clean Water Act*, 36 Vand.L.Rev. 1167 (1983) and N. William Hines, *A Decade of Non–Degradation Policy in Congress and the Courts: The Erratic Pursuit of Clean Air and Clean Water*, 62 Iowa L.Rev. 643, 673–81 (1977). If a state does not adopt adequate water quality standards, the Administrator may adopt criteria and standards to override a state's standards and thereby change effluent limitations set in a point source discharge permit. Broad supervisory authority over water quality standards, including discretion in the Administrator to promulgate substitute standards, has been sustained by the courts. E.g., Mississippi Comm'n on Natural Resources v. Costle, 625 F.2d 1269 (5th Cir.1980).

The NPDES permitting process can raise issues that affect the allocation of rights to use quantities of water. In states which administer water resources through a permit system the permitting process can be used to control quality as well as quantity, but rarely is. Florida uses this approach. Water district administrators review permits under a statewide comprehensive plan for water use. No permit may be granted if the anticipated use will affect the quality of the water in any way. All discharges which "alter water quality" (including changes in taste, temperature, and turbidity) must be approved. If a violation occurs, the administrator may rescind the permit, order abatement of the use, and seek civil damages for injury to the resource. Florida's permit system (14 Fla.Stat.Annot. §§ 373.203–373.249) was adapted from a Model Water Code. See page 105 note 13, supra.

Courts have made it clear that technology-forcing effluent limitations apply even if the natural waste assimilative capacity of a stream can reduce the pollution. "Congress made the deliberate decision to rule out arguments based on receiving water capacity * * *." Weyerhaeuser Co. v. Costle, 590 F.2d 1011 (D.C.Cir.1978). However, § 301(g), 33 U.S.C.A. § 1311(g), allows what are in effect waivers based on receiving water characteristics for many pollutants including thermal discharges.

The NPDES is limited to regulation of point sources. A point source is defined as "any discernable, confined and discrete conveyance, including but not limited to any pipe, ditch, channel, tunnel, conduit, well, discrete fissure, container, rolling stock, concentrated animal feeding operation, or vessel or other floating craft, from which pollutants are or may be discharged. This term does not include return flows from irrigated agriculture." 33 U.S.C.A. § 1362(14). Diffused sources of water pollution such as runoff from city streets and seepage from mining operations are among the greatest threats to streams but do not fit the definition. Are discharges from a dam that change the quality of a stream discharges from a "point source"? See National Wildlife Fed'n v. Gorsuch, 693 F.2d 156 (D.C.Cir.1982).

The last sentence of the point source definition was added in 1977 after an administrative exemption for agricultural return flows was overturned as inconsistent with the definition. Natural Resources Defense Council v. Costle, 568 F.2d 1369 (D.C.Cir.1977). Because point sources are defined to exclude return flows from irrigated agriculture, major pollutant discharges remain unregulated unless states decide to do so. Thus, many agricultural chemicals and salts are put in streams with virtually no regulation. Although there has been speculation that Congress would act to regulate non-point source pollution from agricultural sources, it has not done so for political reasons. The 1987 Clean Water Act reauthorization provides a major program to assist states in the development of non-point source programs. Water Quality Act of 1987, Pub.L. No. 100–4, 101 Stat. 7 (codified in 33 U.S.C.A. §§ 1251–1387) (1992).

Other federal water pollution statutes deal primarily with controlling groundwater contamination. See Chapter Five, pages 576–89, infra.

Federal Pollution Statutes and the Common Law

Despite the apparent comprehensiveness of the statutory framework, common law remedies still have an important role to play. In *Theories of Water Pollution Litigation,* 1971 Wis.L.Rev. 738, Professor Peter Davis concludes that statutory coverage in some areas of water quality control is incomplete. He suggests that private use of common law actions such as nuisance and trespass may help fill these legislative gaps. The reasonable use standard applicable among riparian water users presumably includes considerations of water quality. Davis notes that many states have specifically preserved common law rights, either by statute or judicial decision. In the course of an opinion holding that neither the federal nor state Clean Water Acts preempted the riparian's right to be free from unreasonable diminutions in quality, the court in Biddix v. Henredon Furniture Inds., Inc., 331 S.E.2d 717, 724 (N.C.1985) said:

> We conclude that the Clean Water Act does not abrogate the common law civil actions for private nuisance and trespass to land for pollution of waters resulting from violation of a NPDES permit. First, the Clean Water Act, as amended, does not specifically abrogate these common law civil actions. Assuming for the purposes of this appeal that industrial discharges made under a NPDES permit would constitute a "reasonable use" of water in accordance with the common law, thereby effectively preventing a civil action founded in nuisance or trespass to land, plaintiff's

allegations in the case before us allege waste discharges in violation of defendant's NPDES permit.

Federal common law nuisance remedies have been held to be preempted by the Act, however. City of Milwaukee v. Illinois, 451 U.S. 304 (1981), discussed infra at page 856.

The Supreme Court has held that the Clean Water Act does not authorize an implied right of action for damages suffered as the result of an illegal discharge, Middlesex County Sewerage Auth. v. National Sea Clammers Ass'n, 453 U.S. 1 (1981).

In International Paper Co. v. Ouellette, 479 U.S. 481 (1987), page 862, infra, the Supreme Court held that an individual in one state who is injured by the discharge of pollution in another state may not apply the affected state's nuisance law to the point source in the source state. To do so would "subject the point source to the threat of legal and equitable penalties if the [source state's] permit standards were less stringent than those imposed by the affected state." Thus, the source would be subjected to another set of standards besides those set in the source state pursuant to the Clean Water Act. However, the Court determined that the injured individual was not without remedy in that a court sitting in the affected (or source) state could apply the source state's nuisance law. The decision effectively holds that the Clean Water Act preempts the affected state's nuisance law, to the extent that it seeks to impose liability on a point source in another state. The dissent responded that no language in the Clean Water Act requires such a result and that the majority failed to consider the conflict of law principles that determine which state's tort law should apply in interstate tort suits.

Recently, the United States Supreme Court overruled an appellate court decision allowing states more control over interstate water pollution. Arkansas v. Oklahoma, 112 S.Ct. 1046 (1992). The case disallows states affected by upstream discharges from blocking permits. Instead, states must ask the Environmental Protection Agency to disapprove federally (EPA) issued permits on the ground that they will have an undue impact on interstate waters. The courts will defer to the Environmental Protection Agency as to when a discharge complies with such standards.

4. Transfer and Loss of Riparian Rights

a. *Transfer of Riparian Rights*

When land with which riparian rights are associated is transferred, the riparian rights are presumed transferred as well, absent a reservation or severance in the granting instrument. Attempts to transfer riparian rights apart from the land, however, have generated controversy. The general rule is that riparian rights may be severed from the land, either by grant or reservation, and conveyed separately.

It is not clear whether a contract between a riparian owner-seller and a nonriparian owner-buyer is a covenant by the riparian not to sue for infringement of riparian rights or is a transfer of the riparian right itself, such right having been severed from the riparian land. The riparian owner who purports to transfer the full right to make use of the supply to a nonriparian thereafter has no right to complain of the nonriparian's use and, further, has no right to make use of the water supply over the objection of the transferee. Moreover, this set of legal relationships is binding on successors in interest to the transferor and it benefits successors in interest to the transferee. See Duckworth v. Watsonville Water and Light Co., 110 P. 927 (Cal.1910). Thus, if a seller owned the land on both sides of a stream from source to mouth, a sale of the right to use all the water of the stream to a purchaser in another watershed would extinguish any private claims of successors in interest to maintenance of the flow of the stream.

Other riparians not party to the transfer contract, however, remain unaffected by the transfer. Thus in State v. Apfelbacher, 167 N.W. 244 (Wis.1918), an upper riparian mill owner contracted to sell water to the state to maintain a fish hatchery. Under the contract the upper riparian agreed to maintain the level of the lake behind his dam at twelve inches above the average high water mark. In periods of low flow the state enforced this right by shutting off releases at the dam. A lower riparian mill operator suffered substantial injury from this detention of the flow and recovered judgment against the state on the theory that the state took only the rights of the vendor-riparian. "The condition of reasonable use attached to it [the water] before he conveyed it, and remained with it after such conveyance." Id. at 246.

The possible operation of a bargaining system is illustrated by Mason v. Hoyle, page 72, supra. If it had been worthwhile to do so, defendant could have bought from plaintiffs the right to alter the timing of the flow of the stream. This exchange would take place only if the value of the detention by the defendant exceeded the sum of the values to plaintiffs of a normal flow. The granting of an injunction in that case may raise problems of monopoly power in the plaintiffs, although defendant did have alternative sources of energy.

Interbasin and interstate transfers of water in riparian jurisdictions raise both legal and political questions. For a discussion of these issues, see Robert H. Abrams, *Interbasin Transfer in a Riparian Jurisdiction*, 24 Wm. & Mary L.Rev. 591 (1983).

Interesting questions have arisen as subdividers have attempted to convey riparian surface use rights to lot owners in the subdivision. A developer in 1907 platted a twelve-foot wide "walk" along the shore of Gun Lake for the benefit of all lot owners in the subdivision. An owner of a first-tier lot (separated from the lake only by the walk) got into a fight with owners of second-tier lots over the docking and anchorage of pleasure boats. Thies v. Howland, 380 N.W.2d 463 (Mich.1985), holds that the first-tier lot owners are riparians but that all other lot owners have only an easement to use the walk. The second-tier lot owners "are not riparian owners because they only possess an easement interest in the walk * * * the construction of docks and permanent anchorage of boats is not within the scope of the plattors' dedication of the walk." 380 N.W.2d at 469. See Thompson v. Enz, 154 N.W.2d 473

(Mich.1967), page 434, infra, involving asserted riparian surface use rights on Gun Lake by owners of subdivided lots.

Is transferability of riparian rights subject to a reasonableness standard, or is the standard only applicable to uses once the transfer has taken place?

BURKART v. FORT LAUDERDALE

Supreme Court of Florida, 1964.
168 So.2d 65.

Mason, Circuit Judge.

* * *

For the purposes of this review it is sufficient to relate that in 1921 the owner of certain property located on New River Sound, a navigable body of water in Broward County, recorded a subdivision plat of the land, which plat contained a dedication with pertinent portions as follows:

> "The *riparian rights* in and to the waters of New River and New River Sound opposite each lot or parcel of land fronting or abutting upon Ocean View Drive are *hereby reserved* to the New River Development Company, its successors, legal representatives or assigns, owners of said abutting lots or parcels of land. The streets, avenues and Ocean View Drive, shown hereon are hereby dedicated to the perpetual use of the public as thoroughfares, reserving to the New River Development Company * * * the reversion or reversions thereof, whenever discontinued by law." (Emphasis supplied).

Petitioners, through mesne conveyances from the subdivider, obtained various lots, with the reserved riparian rights, in the subdivision. These lots face east and abut the west side of Ocean View Drive, which runs along and borders upon New River Sound lying to the east of said Drive. This street runs generally in a north and south direction.

* * *

The majority opinion below held that the record in the case before the chancellor justified the chancellor's finding that there was no land lying east of the Ocean View Drive at the time of the recording of the plat, and that therefore there existed then no such land to which petitioners hold the absolute fee title as claimed by them, but that any land now so lying accumulated by accretion subsequent to the recording of the plat. With this holding we are in accord. * * *

The majority opinion conceded that the petitioners own the fee of Ocean View Drive but held that petitioners' ownership of the underlying fee does not vest them with riparian rights to the exclusion of the riparian rights accruing to the easement in the dedicated street, and that the riparian rights attached to the street's easement and accrued to the public and were not the property of the owner of the fee in the street, the petitioners herein. With this holding we cannot agree, for it overlooks, or does not give validity to, the riparian rights expressly reserved by the dedicator to itself and its assigns. In laying out the subdivision, including petitioners' lots, the dedicator specifically reserved to itself and to its assigns "the riparian rights in and to the waters of New River and New River Sound opposite each lot or parcel of land fronting or abutting upon Ocean View Drive." The dedicator, New River Development Company, constructed streets, pavements and sidewalks and sold lots according to the plat. Petitioners, plaintiffs below, in their complaint traced title to their lots back to New River Development Company and asserted title to the accreted tract lying opposite their lots between the Drive and the water, and claimed the right to fill the submerged lands so appurtenant to their lots so long as they did not obstruct the navigable channel. In their deraignment of title it appears that riparian rights were granted by a chain of conveyances culminating in the deed to the petitioners. The City in its answer claimed for itself the ownership of the street and of the increment between it and the water by reason of the dedication.

The petitioners undoubtedly own the fee to the street, but we agree with the chancellor and the District Court of Appeal that it would be inconsistent with the easement to permit petitioners to fill the submerged land. The plat, by placing the eastern boundary of the street contiguously along the water's edge, evinces an intent that the easement therein would continue to extend to the water's edge notwithstanding future accretion or erosion. We agree that it is correct to hold that the accretions attaching to the fee in the street became subject to the street easement and are a part of it. But, the fee interest remains in the petitioners, since accretions generally belong to the owner of the upland to which they attach. Ford v. Turner, Fla.App., 142 So.2d 335. Title to the accretions, *unless excepted* passes with the land to which they are appurtenant. American Mortgage Co. v. Lord, Fla.App., 132 So.2d 40.

The decree below goes further than merely to deny petitioners' right to fill these submerged lands or to appropriate to themselves full dominion over the accretions, for it denies petitioners all riparian privileges incident to the reservation of rights in the plat and, in effect, confers the totality of such rights upon the City. This cannot be, for such a holding is inconsistent with the petitioners' ownership of the fee and is consistent only with the City's ownership of it, which it does not have. The City owns neither the fee to the street nor to the accretions appurtenant to the street.

* * *

We conclude that because of the express reservation of riparian rights by the dedicator herein to itself and assigns, contained in the plat herein, these rights did not pass to the public as an incident to the street easement in Ocean View Drive. A contrary holding, in the words of Judge White in his able dissent below,

> "* * * unreasonably advances the servitude over the principal estate, materially prejudices the plaintiffs in the use and value of their property and is contrary to manifest intent."

The City's easement in the street and accretions thereto may be protected for the benefit of the general public without ascribing to it rights, privileges and properties over and beyond those reasonably incident to its prescribed use; which use is not limited solely to travel upon the street, but includes the general public's right to use the accreted property as a way of ingress and egress to the waters of New River Sound. The petitioners should be adjudged owners of the fee title in and to the subject land with such riparian rights and privileges as have been reserved in the dedication, and which do not burden the easement dedicated, all in accordance with the purpose of the dedication and in recognition of the riparian rights herein held to have been reserved to petitioners as successors in title to the dedicator.

NOTES

1. *Platted Streets.* The platted street problem, with particular reference to *Burkart* and earlier Florida cases, is discussed in depth in Frank E. Maloney, *et al.*, Water Law and Administration: The Florida Experience § 34 at 81 (1968). In discussing the severability of riparian rights from fee ownership of the upland, the authors note at § 34.3, page 96:

> In *Burkart* the dedicator had reserved the riparian rights. The District Court of Appeal took the position the reservation was invalid as against the dedication of the street easement, which carried the riparian rights with it. The Supreme Court disagreed, and held that the reservation was valid and that the riparian rights as such remained in the dedicator and its successors. This suggests that riparian rights were severable, to some extent at least, from the upland. The dedicator seemed to think so; he apparently made subsequent conveyances of the riparian rights to the purchasers of the upland tracts. This conclusion is further supported by the Supreme Court's view that once the original developer conveyed lots abutting on the platted waterfront street, he no longer owned any of the upland under the street—the conveyance carried the entire fee in the street with it. Any reserved riparian rights in the developer would at this point be totally separated from the upland ownership, at least as to such conveyed tracts.

2. Did the lot owners "win" as against the city's claim of title to the shore? If they cannot fill the land and the city can open the shore to the public, what rights do lot owners retain? To what extent can the lot owners use the shore if it might interfere with public uses? How extensive are the public rights that go with the street dedication?

Public access from a dedicated street may be limited. McCardel v. Smolen, 250 N.W.2d 496 (Mich.1976), reversed in part and remanded 273 N.W.2d 3 (Mich.1978) held that public access rights do not include lounging and picnicking because "[t]hose activities are in no way directly related to a true riparian use. * * * In that context, the only 'use' of the water is the enjoyment of its scenic presence." 250 N.W.2d at 499. Cf. Theis v. Howland, 380 N.W.2d 463 (Mich.1985) (access from private easement may be used to launch but not to anchor permanently boats or to construct a dock.)

3. The doctrine that riparian rights can be severed and retained by the grantor (or transferred to a third party) can have dramatic and frustrating consequences for those who purchase waterfront residential property. In Williams v. Skyline Development Corp., 288 A.2d 333 (Md.1972), the expectations of purchasers of bayfront lots with unobstructed bay views at the time of purchase were disappointed when they discovered that their grantors had retained the riparian rights to wharf out and fill so that their lots became lagoonfront rather than bayfront and faced similar condominiums rather than the bay. As one would expect, courts require a strong showing of intent to sever riparian rights because a subsequent exercise by their owner will deprive the riparian tract of considerable value and encourage fragmentation of interests in property.

NOTE: ACCRETION AND AVULSION

In their natural state, the shorelines of rivers and lakes are rarely fixed or permanent. Through the action of erosion, rock is dissolved and soil washed away. During the process of *accretion,* alluvion (composed of soil, sand, and other sediment) is deposited on the shore, gradually extending the banks into the bed of the waterway. *Reliction* occurs when water slowly recedes to expose land which was formerly submerged. A change in the course of a waterway, however, may be rapid, in which case the process of changing stream configuration is called *avulsion.* A storm or heavy flood may cause a sudden shift in the location of the banks of a waterway, as soil is carried off and deposited downstream. Each of these natural events alters the shape and location of the shoreline, and can have important and different consequences for the enjoyment of riparian rights.

Title to new land added by the process of accretion vests in the landowner whose property abuts the water.

> The question is well settled at common law, that the person whose land is bounded by a stream of water which changes its course gradually by alluvial formations, shall still hold by the same boundary, including the accumulated soil. * * * Every proprietor whose land is thus bounded is subject to loss by the same means which may add to his territory; and, as he is without remedy for his loss in this way, he cannot be held accountable for his gain.

Nebraska v. Iowa, 143 U.S. 359, 360–61 (1892). As the Court notes, one justification for this rule can be found in the principle of reciprocal compensation: those who may lose their land through erosion should keep any gains attributable to accretion. A further rationale is the important protection provided riparian rights by the common law rule. Vesting title to the new shoreland in the abutting owner assures that the necessary contact between riparian land and water will not be lost.

Although accretion and reliction are distinct physical processes, the law generally does not distinguish between them. A landowner whose property abuts relicted land is typically awarded title to the exposed soil. However, some jurisdictions recognize an exception for land created as a result of state-authorized drainage operations. Where riverbottom has been reclaimed as part of a governmental program to improve the waterway, title to the reclaimed land may vest in the state, as owner of the riverbed, as discussed below.

The law deals differently with title to land suddenly altered by avulsion. Because such events are considered "acts of God," affected landowners are expected to bear their own losses and others are not benefitted by the windfall. Boundaries do not shift with the river, but remain as described in their original location.

In most jurisdictions, changes are presumed to be by accretion. The resulting burden of proof may be difficult for those asserting avulsion to carry. The issue is how slowly a change must occur to be considered accretive. In Solomon v. Sioux City, 51 N.W.2d 472 (Iowa 1952), the court quieted title in the upland owner on the basis of accretion despite the city's claim that major alterations over a period of only three years should be characterized as avulsive. Contrast this result with the outcome in Nebraska v. Iowa, where the changes were annual.

When accretion adds land to the property of two adjacent landowners along a watercourse, how should ownership of the new land be divided? Some courts give each owner a share of the accreted land proportionate to the original ownership of the shoreline. Others base the allocation of title on the location of the beginning point of accretion. For example, in Burket v. Krimlofski, 91 N.W.2d 57 (Neb.1958), the court examined a series of photographs which documented a gradual transformation from island to peninsula. Because the alluvion had adhered to the island, rather than the mainland, the island's owner received title to all of the new land, while the mainland owner suffered the loss of his riparian status.

When states were established, waterways often formed the basis for political boundaries. Gradual changes in shorelines have not provoked major disputes. Rapid, avulsive changes, however, have created substantial disagreements over boundary locations. For example, the Missouri River, an extremely active waterway, formed the political boundary between Iowa and Nebraska. Every spring, heavy flooding altered the shorelines and changed the course of the river. Because these changes were considered to be avulsive, the two states were continually forced to relocate their boundaries. In Nebraska v. Iowa, 143 U.S. 359 (1892), the Supreme Court declined to treat these sudden changes in the Missouri as accretion, despite being urged to do so by both states. Today, many states, like Nebraska and Iowa, have located their boundaries by compacts. As a result, river changes, rapid or slow, have no effect on boundaries.

When accretion occurs as a result of artificial improvements to the waterway (such as the construction of dams or dikes), the rules governing vesting of title may be altered. An upland owner who benefits from the accretion, but had no part in its creation, will generally be allowed to claim title. A riparian cannot extend owned property by filling or purposely causing accretion.   Mein v. San Francisco Bay Conservation and Dev. Comm'n, 267 Cal.Rptr. 252 (Cal.App.1990); Seacoast Real Estate Co. v. American Timber Co., 113 A. 489 (N.J.1920).   This is the general rule, but in an original action to locate the boundary between South Carolina and Georgia at the mouth of the Savannah River, the Supreme Court awarded Georgia one mile of riverfront land connected to South Carolina as a result of the deposit of dredged spoil by the U.S. Army Corps of Engineers.   "The rapidity of some aspects of the dredging and other process led the Special Master to conclude that the changes in the Savannah River were primarily avulsive.   Although the question is close, on balance, we think this particular record * * * supports the recommendation * * *."   Georgia v. South Carolina, 497 U.S. 376, 404 (1990).

Governmental programs to stabilize soil and improve navigation are common.   When such projects result in accretion, title disputes may arise between the state, as owner of navigable riverbottoms, and the upland owners.   Until recently, many courts vested title in the riparian.   In addition to the usual preservation of access justification, courts have stressed that a contrary rule would jeopardize the marketability of riparian titles and would not adequately compensate riparians for erosion control programs "gone awry."   Board of Trustees of the Int'l Improvement Trust Fund v. Medeira Beach Nominee, Inc., 272 So.2d 209 (Fla.App.1973).   However, on the ground that the state should not lose land as a result of projects undertaken to promote the public interest, courts today tend to award ownership to the state.   A state may be forced to justify its need against an upland owner's beneficial use of the land, as in State Land Bd. v. Sause, 342 P.2d 803 (Or.1959), where the state's attempt to force the upland owner who constructed a log dump on a river bank to purchase the resulting accreted land failed because it could not demonstrate a beneficial use of its own.   Nevertheless, as public projects to improve waterways become more common, the trend appears to be toward state ownership of land created out of the riverbed.

b.　Prescription

PABST v. FINMAND

Supreme Court of California, 1922.
190 Cal. 124, 211 P. 11.

LENNON, J.   This action was instituted by the plaintiffs, Charlie Lee Pabst and the Priors, against H.H. Finmand and N.H. Finmand and the Cambrons, to quiet title to the waters of Eagle creek, in the county of Modoc, state of California.   Eagle creek, rising in the Warner Mountains, west of the lands of both plaintiffs and defendants, flows in a single channel until just before it reaches the land of the plaintiffs, Priors, and the defendant, N.H. Finmand.   There it forks and the north branch flows across the northwest corner of N.H. Finmand's lands and across the Prior lands.   The south branch flows across the south portion of N.H. Finmand's lands and thence onto and across the lands of plaintiff Pabst.

The lands of the other defendant, H.H. Finmand, are not riparian to the creek. They lie to the west of the lands of the plaintiffs Priors and to the northwest of the lands of the plaintiff Pabst and the defendant N.H. Finmand, and are irrigated by means of two ditches, the "Gee" and the "Grider" ditches, which run from the main channel of Eagle creek before it forks, northerly to the lands of H.H. Finmand.

* * *

The N.H. Finmand lands being riparian, whereas the H.H. Finmand lands are nonriparian, the rights arising from the use of water on these different tracts are necessarily based upon different principles, and for this reason these different tracts of lands will be considered separately.

As to the rights of the N.H. Finmand lands, it is conceded by counsel for defendants that the right to the amount of water awarded to the defendants by the judgment of the trial court must rest upon a prescriptive right alone. This is so for the reason that, as admitted by defendants, the right by appropriation is not supported by the evidence, and, while the trial court found that N.H. Finmand was a riparian owner, no judgment was given such defendant based upon his right as a riparian owner, and no attempt was made to apportion the waters among the plaintiffs and defendants as riparian owners.

The judgment for a prescriptive right was given in favor of the N.H. Finmand lands against both the Prior lands and the Pabst lands. The N.H. Finmand lands claimed this right, and it was adjudged to those lands upon the theory that said lands had gained it by adverse use of the water which was taken from the south fork of the creek. As to the Prior lands no right could be gained by prescription. This is so because the water used on the N.H. Finmand lands was taken from the south fork of the stream, which runs below and does not border the Prior lands, where as the water diverted for use on the Prior lands is taken from the north fork of the creek, which runs by a small portion of the northwest corner of the N.H. Finmand lands and on to the Prior lands. The Prior lands, therefore, are riparian only to the north fork of the stream. A right can be gained by prescription only by acts which operate as an invasion of the rights of the person against whom the right is sought and which afford a ground of action by such party against such claimant, and it is a rule of law so well settled by decisions in this and other states as to scarcely need any citation to support it that a lower use, since it interferes in no way with the flow above, constitutes no invasion of the upper riparian owner's right, and cannot, therefore, afford any basis for a prescriptive right.

As to the Pabst lands, the N.H. Finmand lands are the upper riparian lands, and the Pabst lands are lower riparian lands. It is the contention of defendants that the continuous use of a certain amount of water each year for the statutory period of time gave to them a prescriptive right to that certain quantity of water so used by them, and this in spite of the fact that the use of the water by the lower riparian owner was never in any manner interrupted or interfered with by such use, and in the absence of any indication or bringing of knowledge home to the lower riparian owner that the upper riparian owner was claiming such right, not as a riparian owner, but adversely to him. This contention cannot be maintained. In the absence of a showing that the upper owner is using the water under a claim of prescriptive right, the lower owner has the right to presume that such owner is only taking that to which he is entitled as a riparian owner by virtue of his riparian right. Such use was not hostile unless there was an actual clash between the rights of the respective owners. While there was sufficient water flowing down the stream to supply the wants of all parties, its use by one was not an invasion of the rights of the other.

A riparian owner is entitled to a reasonable amount of water for use on his riparian lands. What is a reasonable amount varies with the circumstances of each particular case and also varies from year to year, for the amount which might be reasonable in a season of plenty might be manifestly unreasonable in a season of drought. Nor is the question of reasonableness to be tested solely by the needs of the upper riparian proprietor. The rights of riparian proprietors are correlative, and the "reasonable" amount to which any one riparian owner is entitled is to be measured by comparison with the needs of the other riparian proprietors. The fact that there was always sufficient water coming down the creek for the Pabst lands with the exception of the two years prior to the trial is undisputed by any evidence offered by the defendants. And, so long as defendants left sufficient water in the stream for the use of the lower riparian proprietors, it cannot be said that they were using an unreasonable amount, and, so long as they were not using an "unreasonable" amount, the plaintiffs had no cause to complain, nor was any right of theirs invaded.

The adverse use must be such as to raise a presumption of a grant of an easement as the only hypothesis on which to account for the other party's failure to complain thereof. Lakeside Ditch Co. v. Crane, 80 Cal. 181, 22 Pac. 76. In the absence of any facts showing an actual knowledge by plaintiffs of the adverse nature of defendants' claim or of any facts sufficient to create a presumption of a knowledge of that claim, it cannot be said that a failure of plaintiffs to assert their rights by bringing an action against the defendants was such a submission as could be accounted for only on the hypothesis of a grant. Indeed, defendants have not shown such an unreasonable use of the water on their lands as to put plaintiffs on notice of their claim. We do not mean to hold that a right may not be gained by an upper riparian proprietor by prescription, but to do so it must be clearly shown either that actual notice of the adverse claim of such owner has been brought home to the other party, or that the circumstances are such, as, for instance, the use of all of the water of the creek, that such party must be presumed to have known of the adverse claim. In the instant case there was nothing to indicate to the lower riparian owners that the owners of the N.H. Finmand lands were exercising, or attempting to exercise, any more than their riparian rights, and, in the absence of such indication to plaintiffs that the owners of the N.H. Finmand lands were asserting a right hostile to the rights of the plaintiffs, no prescriptive title was acquired. Even if the upper riparian owner is using all the water of the stream, still, if the lower riparian owner is not then using any and has no desire to do so, such use by the upper riparian owner would not be adverse, and, if continued five years, would not gain him a prescriptive right.

* * *

It is the contention of plaintiffs that there was no invasion of plaintiffs' riparian rights by the nonriparian owners of the H.H. Finmand lands by the diversion by such nonriparian owners of water which the riparian owners did not need, and therefore no prescriptive right to the use of the water could be acquired in the absence of a showing of actual damage to the lands of the riparian owners caused by a deprivation of the water. As to a nonriparian owner the riparian owner is under no duty to share the waters of the creek, and the slightest use by such nonriparian owner diminishes to some extent the flow of the stream. Obviously, there is no question of reasonable use in the sense in which that term is applied to the rights of respective riparian owners, since a riparian owner, as against a nonriparian owner, is entitled to the full flow of the stream without the slightest diminution. The initial step in the diversion of the water by the nonriparian owner is therefore an invasion of the right of the lower riparian owner, and every subsequent diversion is a further invasion of that right. Against a person who seeks to divert water to nonriparian lands, the riparian owner is entitled to restrain any diversion, and he is not required to show any damage to his use. Although no damage to the present use of the riparian owner results from the diversion, yet damage to the future use may result, and an injunction will be granted to prevent the diversion from growing into a right by the lapse of the statutory period.

In the instant case the adverse use of the water on nonriparian lands was continued "openly and notoriously" for a period longer than five years, and, the slightest use by the owners of these lands being notice to all the lower riparian owners that a hostile right was being asserted, a prescriptive right was acquired by such adverse use by those lands.

* * *

Judgment reversed.

NOTES

1. Did N.H. Finmand have a prescriptive right as against Prior? Why? As against Pabst? Why? Under what circumstances might he have obtained prescriptive rights from Pabst? Did H.H. Finmand have prescriptive rights? Why? Can this case be reconciled with Stratton v. Mt. Hermon Boys' School, 103 N.E. 87 (Mass.1913), page 62, supra? What is the rationale for allowing prescription in a riparian jurisdiction when the plaintiff demonstrates no present harm?

2. A prescriptive right cannot be perfected without a showing of adversity. Ordinarily, a downstream riparian cannot adversely affect

an upper riparian's use. It is therefore said that "prescription does not flow upstream." In order to perfect a prescriptive right, a claimant must show adverse use over a specified period of time. The prescriptive period starts as soon as injury occurs to other users. At the time of *Pabst*, it was unclear whether California followed the reasonable use rule. See note 4, infra. How would a riparian demonstrate the necessary adversity in a reasonable use jurisdiction? Would the riparian have to show actual injury to other riparians in order to demonstrate a claim of right?

If injury is presumed, the prescriptive period begins as soon as the claimant initiates an impermissible use, regardless of the injury to the downstream riparian. In contrast, the modern American rule entitles each riparian to as much water as can be reasonably used, subject to being enjoined if the use unreasonably interferes with the rights of others. A prescriptor must show that use of the water caused actual injury to other riparians. This rule ensures that injured riparians will have notice of a prescriptor's hostile intent before the statutory period begins to run.

3. Once prescriptive rights have been recognized, courts must determine the quantity of water to which the claimant is entitled. Some jurisdictions treat a prescriptor like any other riparian, awarding only a proportionate share of the total flow of the waterbody. In times of shortage, each user's share is reduced in direct proportion to the decreased amount of water available in the stream. Other courts quantify the amount of water used during the prescriptive period, and award the claimant the right to use that quantity regardless of the amount of water available in the stream. This could put holders of prescriptive rights in a better position than other riparians in times of drought. A more practical approach is shown by Mally v. Weidensteiner, 153 P. 342 (Wash.1915). A nonriparian obtained a prescriptive right to 1.5 cfs. The court, however, limited the right to one-third of the water actually available at any time.

4. *Prescription in a Dual System.* In California, where the appropriation and riparian systems exist side-by-side, prescriptive rights have played a significant role. As *Pabst* illustrates, prior to 1928 any diversion for use outside the watershed in California created a prescriptive right against downstream riparians after five years of uninterrupted use. This rule operated without regard to the dates of the respective patents, and without the necessity of showing harm.

In 1928, the state adopted an amendment to then art. XIV, § 3 (now art. X, § 2) of the California Constitution:

> It is hereby declared that because of the conditions prevailing in this State the general welfare requires that the water resources of the State be put to beneficial use to the fullest extent of which they are capable, and that the waste or unreasonable use or unreasonable method of use of water be prevented, and that the conservation of such waters is to be exercised with a view to the reasonable and beneficial use thereof in the interest of the people and for the public welfare. The right to water or to the use or flow

of water in or from any natural stream or watercourse in this State is and shall be limited to such water as shall be reasonably required for the beneficial use to be serviced, and such right does not and shall not extend to the waste or unreasonable use or unreasonable method of use or unreasonable method of diversion of water. Riparian rights in a stream or water course attach to, but to no more than so much of the flow thereof as may be required or used consistently with this section, for the purposes for which such lands are, or may be made adaptable, in view of such reasonable and beneficial uses; provided, however, that nothing herein contained shall be construed as depriving any riparian owner of the reasonable use of water of the stream to which his land is riparian under reasonable methods of diversion and use, or of depriving any appropriator of water to which he is lawfully entitled. This section shall be self-executing, and the Legislature may also enact laws in the furtherance of the policy in this section contained.

After the 1928 amendment, the acquisition of riparian rights by prescription was much more difficult. The amendment was primarily designed to adjust the relationship between riparian and appropriative rights, by applying a rule of reasonableness to the exercise of all water rights. See Peabody v. Vallejo, 40 P.2d 486 (Cal.1935). Previously, the riparians had enjoyed a commanding advantage, based on the early-established principle " 'that the rights of the riparian owners to the use of the waters of the abutting stream were paramount to the rights of any other persons thereto; that such rights were parcel of the land and that any diminution of the stream against the will of the riparian owner by other persons was an actionable injury.' " Herminghaus v. Southern Cal. Edison Co., 252 P. 607, 613 (Cal.1927), quoting Chief Justice Lucien Shaw of the California Supreme Court, one of the architects of judicial water law reform in California.

The importance of the changing nature of the concept of reasonable beneficial use is underscored by Professor Harrison Dunning who notes that as a result of the recognition of the importance of instream values, "[t]he 'waste to the sea' so denigrated at the time of *Herminghaus* has now become legislative policy for parts of a number of * * * rivers." Harrison C. Dunning, *Article X, Section 2: From Maximum Water Development to Instream Flow Protection*, 17 Hastings Const.L.Q. 275, 278 (1989). See also Harrison C. Dunning, *Dam Fights and Water Policy in California: 1969–1989*, 24 J. of the West 14 (1990).

Chapter Three

PRIOR APPROPRIATION

Water law in the West, as in the East, is governed by statutes that grant rights to use water to private and public entities who satisfy certain conditions. A water user or a lawyer whose client seeks a water right for a particular use first confronts an administrative agency that requires an application to be completed and filed, usually followed by agency review, notice to existing water rights holders, and an opportunity for them to object. The agency ultimately decides how much water an applicant will have a right to use by applying rules and standards set in the statutes or administratively under them. The standards typically require determinations that sufficient water is available, that existing rights will not be harmed, and that the proposed use will be beneficial and not contrary to the public interest.

Each state has its distinct system for establishing water rights, approving changes in the use of water rights and administering water uses to be sure that uses are consistent with rights. The statutory systems of a few states are described at pages 237–44, infra.

Though procedures differ, western state water laws are all rooted in the appropriation doctrine. Thus, they all maintain respect for prior uses. Rights are given "priority" as of the date a "beneficial use" commenced, and prior rights are superior to those that commenced later. There is no sharing of shortages in dry years. Holders of the oldest rights are entitled to take the full amount of their rights regardless of the relatively greater social importance or productivity of newer uses. For example, the dewatering of high quality trout streams is a major issue in Montana and the state has adopted an experimental program to lease senior water rights to guarantee minimum stream flows during severe droughts. See Morris, When Rivers Run Dry Under the Big Sky: Balancing Agricultural and Recreational Claims to Scarce Water Resources in Montana and the West, 11 Stan.Envtl.L.J. 259 (1992). However, the Montana Supreme Court recently reaffirmed the right of irrigators to dewater a river by taking ⅔ of a drought-stressed flow, over the objections of an environmental group. Baker Ditch Co. v. District Ct. of the 18th J. Dist., 824 P.2d 260 (Mont.1992). Old rights endure as long as uses continue; they are extinguished only if they are not used.

The problems created by applying the simple but rigid principles of the appropriation doctrine in a modern society are exacerbated by the fact that most water in the West was allocated a long time ago to uses that seemed "beneficial" by the standards of that era, but which are less important in modern society. Water long ago allocated to placer mining or inefficient flood irrigation is now demanded by growing cities, industries, fishing streams, wetlands, and waterfalls.

149

A look at the rich and colorful history of the West provides an essential backdrop for understanding how the appropriation doctrine came to be accepted, why modern western water administration statutes and agencies were conceived, and for appreciating the current pressures for and impediments to change.

A. ROOTS AND EVOLUTION

Western water institutions were shaped by the arid climate and geography of the West. But economic expansion and social conditions of the nineteenth century were the most profound influences. See Terry L. Anderson and Donald J. Hill, *The Evolution of Property Rights: A Study of the American West* 18, J.L. & Econ. 163 (1975); Donald J. Pisani, *Enterprise and Equity: A Critique of Western Water Law in the Nineteenth Century* in Western Hist.Q. 15 (1987).

The origins of western water law lie in the conquest of the region by the early miners and pioneers. This conquest, which is responsible for so much of our national identity, has taken on the aura of a sacred myth that has important and continuing consequences for modern water lawyers. The history of western water law is first a history of mining and then of irrigation. It is a history of costly trial and error. Josiah Gregg's 1844 book, Commerce of the Prairies, the standard work on the Santa Fe trade, first expressed the naive idea that was to dominate the settlement of the West until the 1890s. "The extreme cultivation of the earth," he observed, "might contribute to the multiplication of showers, as it certainly does to fountains." Scientists, visionaries and land promoters reduced this observation to the dictum: "rain follows the plow." It took scientific studies, such as John Wesley Powell's Report on the Lands of the Arid Region of the United States, With a More Detailed Account of the Lands of Utah (1879) (essential reading for any serious student of water law), and the droughts of the 1880s to convince westerners that this dictum was false and that European and eastern agricultural practices must be modified in the West to adapt to the limiting condition of aridity.

Walter Prescott Webb's The Great Plains (1931) is the classic study of human effort to adapt to the limitations of the western climate and landscape. It was not until the battle for open range was lost by the cattle industry that irrigation emerged as a national agricultural strategy. After flirting with the occult and semi-occult of rainmaking, see W. Eugene Hollon, The Great American Desert Then and Now 141–80 (1966), western farmers eventually turned to dry farming (the retention of seasonable moisture by techniques such as deep plowing and vegetation cover) and to irrigation to cope with the imbalance between land and water in the West. They ultimately adopted techniques that had been used for centuries by Indians of the Southwest. Capping a life's study of western water law, the leading scholar, Wells A. Hutchins, summed up the conventional understanding in his treatise.

WELLS A. HUTCHINS, WATER RIGHTS LAWS
IN THE NINETEEN WESTERN STATES
159–75 (1971).

The prevailing Western doctrine of prior appropriation, as it is now recognized and applied throughout the 17 contiguous Western States and Alaska, is traceable chiefly to local customs and regulations developed spontaneously on public lands. The basic principles resulted from experience under varying conditions which, however, had an outstanding feature in common—inadequacy of water to supply completely the rapidly growing demands of industry and agriculture with use of the water control facilities then available. With considerable uniformity, these simple but effective principles became formalized into legal doctrine by decisions of courts and enactments of legislatures. Upon this foundation have been built the current complicated and voluminous water codes and case laws of the West.

As of the middle of the 19th century, the seeds of the appropriation doctrine are discernible in the status of three general movements of great historical and economic importance, which for the most part were probably unrelated—(1) Spanish settlements in parts of the Southwest, (2) the Mormon colonization of Utah, and (3) the California Gold Rush. Irrigation, although on the whole in its infancy, was being practiced in parts of the Southwest, chiefly under the Spanish-American community acequias and to a moderate extent by individuals in other scattered western areas. The Mormon irrigation agriculture development in Utah was getting under way. In California, the Gold Rush had started and mining ditches were being dug.

The early Utah and California water law situations have been the subject of much legal and historical literature, which facilitates appraisals of prevailing doctrine. In the southwestern areas, however, the situation with respect to appropriation of water is less clear and opinions concerning it differ.

Spanish Settlements in Parts of the Southwest

Irrigation in Arizona and New Mexico in aid of crop production is of prehistoric origin.

* * *

Opinions differ as to just how the appropriation doctrine came to the southwestern areas that had been occupied by the Spaniards and Mexicans. According to one school of thought, the Spanish settlers brought this doctrine from Europe with their civil law, which had been derived from the civil law of Rome. Thus, with respect to the Spanish, French, and Mexican penetration of what is now the American Southwest, it is said that:

> The extent to which this early western development has spread over and influenced the customs and laws of the subsequently created states may be debatable. But that such an influence existed, having as its background the old Roman water law, cannot be denied. How remarkably alike, in many vital respects, are the Roman laws concerning water and water rights and the doctrine of appropriation as interpreted and applied, for example, in Colorado.

* * *

Another view is that exclusive rights in the Spanish and Mexican settlements arose only by way of grants from the sovereign, or as the result of local custom * * * which would be prescription.

Apparently, exclusive rights to the use of water on nonriparian lands in the New World of Spain were obtainable and, in various instances, they doubtless were obtained from the sovereign. Perhaps some form of "appropriation" of water can be found in some of the local customs. But in view of the paucity of historical examples, establishment of the well-known principle of *priority of appropriation* under the Spanish-Mexican regime, in the form in which it is so widely applied in the West today, is lacking in satisfactory proof and therefore, to say the least, is questionable.

Mormon Colonization of Utah

The colonization of Utah began in 1847 when the Mormons, under the personal leadership of Brigham Young, entered the Great Salt Lake Valley.

* * *

In the year following the arrival of the first pioneers, this region was ceded to the United States by the Treaty of Guadalupe Hidalgo, which was proclaimed July 4, 1848. Without direction or interference from the United States Government, the Mormons improvised a temporary system of land titles, pending the acquisition of definitive Federal grants, and the roots of a permanent system of water titles.

* * *

During the earliest years, in the absence of political law, the Mormon Church approved the custom of diverting water by group effort and applying it to beneficial use, and supervised these operations. Early legislation made grants of water privileges, authorized the making of grants, and vested in the county courts control over appropriations of water. A statute passed in 1880 recognized accrued rights to water acquired by appropriation or adverse use, but did not contain a specific authorization to appropriate water. The principle of priority in time appears to have been recognized by custom before there was any general law on the subject.

California Gold Rush

Gold was discovered in the foothills of the Sierra Nevada, California, in January 1848. This development and the resulting mining industry had a profound influence upon the political and economic growth of California and on the development of water law throughout the West. As water was required in much of the gold mining processes, rights to the use of water were of fundamental importance. This mineral area was Mexican territory when gold was discovered but was ceded to the United States less than 6 months later by the Treaty of Guadalupe Hidalgo. There was no organized government there in the early years, nor much law except that made by the miners who helped themselves to the land, gold, and water under rules and regulations of their own making as they went along. In the words of the United States Supreme Court, speaking through Justice Field who had been Chief Justice of California, the miners "were emphatically the law-makers, as respects mining, upon the public lands in the State."

The rules and regulations of the miners were made by and for the individual camps and hence varied from one locality to another, but essentially the principles that they embodied were of marked uniformity. These principles related to the acquisition, holding, and forfeiture of individual mining claims, based upon priority of discovery and diligence in working them. And to the acquisition and exercise of rights to the needed water were applied comparable principles—posting and recording notice of intention to divert a specific quantity of water, actual diversion and application of water to beneficial use with reasonable diligence, continued exercise of the right, priority in time of initiating the appropriation, and forfeiture of priority for noncompliance with the rules—in other words, the doctrine of prior appropriation of water for beneficial use. These property rights in land and water were thus had, held, and enjoyed under local rules and were enforced by community action.

The California legislature took note of the miners' practices, but did not authorize appropriation of water until 1872. This was done in a short statute which essentially codified principles and practices that had been developed in the mining camps of the Sierra. In the meantime, these customs had been copied in mining areas of other States and Territories. Many water cases decided in the early years in several Western States involved relative rights to the use of water for mining purposes or for milling connected with mining. The miner's inch unit for measuring water in the mining camps is still used in some Western States, although its quantitative value varies from one area to another. The spreading influence of these mining customs is attested to by the considerable number of western jurisdictions in which early statutes authorizing appropriation of water contained the requirements of posting notice of appropriation, filing it for record, and diverting the water and putting it to beneficial use which were featured in the California statute of 1872. The present long, detailed "water codes," with their centralized administrative procedures, developed inevitably from these early brief declarations of a few basic principles.

There is no doubt that the major contribution to the arid region doctrine of appropriation as it is now recognized and applied throughout the West was made by these gold miners. But as to whether the mining water rights doctrine was actually made up out of whole cloth in the Gold Rush days, substantial doubt has been expressed. A writer who studied the scene on the ground a few decades after its height,[29] and another whose research was published in 1935,[30] concluded that the rules and regulations then established were strikingly characteristic of

29. Shinn, C. H., "Mining Camps, A Study in American Frontier Government," pp. 11–35 (1948, originally published in 1885).

30. Colby, William E., "The Freedom of the Miner and Its Influence on Water Law," published in "Legal Essays, in Tribute to Orrin Kipp McMurray," pp. 67–84 (1935).

much earlier mining enterprises in the Old World. The earlier writer compared the principle of "mining freedom" of the Germanic and Cornwall miners with that of the modern mining camps in California and other western jurisdictions. A half-century later, Professor Colby's well-documented article discussed the right of free mining and free use of flowing water for mining purposes as a part of the customs of Germanic miners in the Middle Ages, and the similarity of conditions under which the California and Germanic miners developed their rules, usages, and customs related to mining practices and uses of water for mining purposes. This principle of "free mining," with free use of water therefor, spread from the Germanic lands to various European countries and their colonies. In fact, Professor Colby's main thesis, with numerous examples, is the widespread existence of the doctrine of prior appropriation of water in the important mining regions of the world. Certain it is that the "Forty-niners" came to California from many countries. They may well have brought with them some knowledge of the old Germanic customs and applied this knowledge in their new environment.

Development of the Appropriation Doctrine

State and Local Laws and Customs

Possessory rights on the public domain. The appropriation doctrine developed chiefly on the public domain. For years the owner of these lands—the Federal Government—made no move either to assert or to grant away its water rights. The miners were trespassers, and so their claims to the use of water were not good as against the Government. However, in the absence of specific State or Federal legislation authorizing the appropriation of water, the customs established in the mining camps of recognizing rights to the use of water by appropriation—"first in time, first in right"—eventually became valid local law. This came about because of the policy of the courts to recognize miners' claims as possessory rights that were good among themselves and as against any other claimant but the Government.

An enlightening account of the events leading up to the establishment of the appropriative doctrine in California is contained in an opinion of the United States Supreme Court written in 1879 by Justice Field, who had been Chief Justice of the California Supreme Court during a part of this dynamic period.[31] Justice Field said that the discovery of gold was followed by an immense immigration into the State; that the gold-bearing lands, which belonged to the United States, were unsurveyed and not open to settlement; that the immigrants in vast numbers entered the Sierra Nevada with a love of order, system, and fair dealing. He continued:

> In every district which they occupied they framed certain rules for their government, by which the extent of ground they could severally hold for mining was designated, their possessory right to such ground secured and enforced, and contests between them either avoided or determined. These rules bore a marked similarity,

31. Jennison v. Kirk, 98 U.S. 453, 457–458 (1878).

varying in the several districts only according to the extent and character of the mines; distinct provisions being made for different kinds of mining, such as placer mining, quartz mining, and mining in drifts or tunnels. They all recognized discovery, followed by appropriation, as the foundation of the possessor's title, and development by working as the condition of its retention. And they were so framed as to secure to all comers, within practicable limits, absolute equality of right and privilege in working the mines. Nothing but such equality would have been tolerated by the miners, who were emphatically the law-makers, as respects mining, upon the public lands in the State. The first appropriator was everywhere held to have, within certain well-defined limits, a better right than others to the claims taken up; and in all controversies, except as against the government, he was regarded as the original owner, from whom title was to be traced. But the mines could not be worked without water. Without water the gold would remain forever buried in the earth or rock. To carry water to mining localities, when they were not on the banks of a stream or lake, became, therefore, an important and necessary business in carrying on mining. Here, also, the first appropriator of water to be conveyed to such localities for mining or other beneficial purposes, was recognized as having, to the extent of actual use, the better right. The doctrines of the common law respecting the rights of riparian owners were not considered as applicable, or only in a very limited degree, to the condition of miners in the mountains. The waters of rivers and lakes were consequently carried great distances in ditches and flumes, constructed with vast labor and enormous expenditures of money, along the sides of mountains and through cañons and ravines, to supply communities engaged in mining, as well as for agriculturists and ordinary consumption. Numerous regulations were adopted, or assumed to exist, from their obvious justness, for the security of these ditches and flumes, and the protection of rights to water, not only between different appropriators, but between them and the holders of mining claims. These regulations and customs were appealed to in controversies in the State courts, and received their sanction; and properties to the values of many millions rested upon them. * * * Until 1866, no legislation was had looking to a sale of the mineral lands. * * *

IRWIN V. PHILLIPS

Supreme Court of California, 1855.
5 Cal. 140.

HEYDENFELDT, J., delivered the opinion of the Court. MURRAY, C. J., concurred.

The several assignments of error will not be separately considered, because the whole merit of the case depends really on a single question, and upon that question the case must be decided. The proposition to be settled is whether the owner of a canal in the mineral region of this State, constructed for the purpose of supplying water to miners, has the right to divert the water of a stream from its natural channel, as against the claims of those who subsequent to the diversion take up lands along the banks of the stream, for the purpose of mining. It must be premised that it is admitted on all sides that the mining claims in controversy, and the lands through which the stream runs, and through which the canal passes, are a part of the public domain, to which there is no claim of private proprietorship, and that the miners have the right to dig for gold on the public lands was settled by this Court in the case of Hicks *et al. v.* Bell *et al.*, 3 Cal., 219.

It is insisted by the appellants that in this case the common law doctrine must be invoked, which prescribes that a water course must be allowed to flow in its natural channel. But upon an examination of the authorities which support that doctrine, it will be found to rest upon the fact of the individual rights of landed proprietors upon the stream, the principle being both at the civil and common law that the owner of lands on the banks of a water course, owns to the middle of the stream, and has the right in virtue of his proprietorship to the use of the water in its pure and natural condition. In this case the lands are the property either of the State or of the United States, and it is not necessary to decide to which they belong for the purposes of this case. It is certain that at the common law the diversion of water courses could only be complained of by riparian owners, who were deprived of the use, or those claiming directly under them. Can the appellants assert their present claim as tenants at will? To solve this question it must be kept in mind that their tenancy is of their own creation, their tenements of their own selection, and subsequent, in point of time to the diversion of the stream. They had the right to mine where they pleased throughout an extensive region, and they selected the bank of a stream from which the water had been already turned, for the purpose of supplying the mines at another point.

Courts are bound to take notice of the political and social condition of the country, which they judicially rule. In this State the larger part of the territory consists of mineral lands, nearly the whole of which are the property of the public. No right or intent of disposition of these lands has been shown either by the United States or the State governments, and with the exception of certain State regulations, very limited in their character, a system has been permitted to grow up by the voluntary action and assent of the population, whose free and unrestrained occupation of the mineral region has been tacitly assented to by the one government, and heartily encouraged by the expressed legislative policy of the other. If there are, as must be admitted, many things connected with this system, which are crude and undigested, and subject to fluctuation and dispute, there are still some which a universal sense of necessity and propriety have so firmly fixed as that they have come to be looked upon as having the force and effect of *res judicata*. Among these the most important are the rights of miners to be protected in the possession of their selected localities, and the rights of those who, by prior appropriation, have taken the waters from their natural beds, and by costly artificial works have conducted them for miles over mountains and ravines, to supply the necessities of gold diggers, and without which the most important interests of the mineral region would remain without development. So fully recognized have become these rights, that without any specific legislation conferring, or confirming them, they are alluded to and spoken of in various acts of the Legislature in the same manner as if they were rights which had been vested by the most distinct expression of the will of the law makers; as for instance, in the Revenue Act "canals and water races" are declared to be property subject to taxation, and this when there was none other in the State than such as were devoted to the use of mining. Section 2 of Article IX of the same Act, providing for the assessment of the property of companies and associations, among others mentions "dam or dams, canal or canals, or other works for mining purposes." This simply goes to prove what is the purpose of the argument, that however much the policy of the State, as indicated by her legislation, has conferred the privilege to work the mines, it has equally conferred the right to divert the streams from their natural channels, and as these two rights stand upon an equal footing, when they conflict, they must be decided by the fact of priority upon the maxim of equity, *qui prior est in tempore potior est in jure.* The miner, who selects a piece of ground to work, must take it as he finds it, subject to prior rights, which have an equal equity, on account of an equal recognition from the sovereign power. If it is upon a stream the waters of which have not been taken from their bed, they cannot be taken to his prejudice; but if they have been already diverted, and for as high, and legitimate a purpose as the one he seeks to accomplish, he has no right to complain, no right to interfere with the prior occupation of his neighbor, and must abide the disadvantages of his own selection.

It follows from this opinion that the judgment of the Court below was substantially correct, upon the merits of the case presented by the evidence, and it is therefore affirmed.

NOTES

1. In 1850 California adopted a statute that provided: "The common law of England, so far as it is not repugnant to or inconsistent with the constitution of the United States or the constitution or laws of this State, is the rule of decision in all the courts of this state." Stats. 1850, p. 219. Answering the argument that the case should have been decided by the common law of riparian rights, the court reasoned that riparian rights were not involved because there was only public, not private land, along the stream. Should a federal patent carry with it riparian rights? Did the federal government abandon all its water rights by not promptly asserting them and by enacting a federal mining law? In his great treatise, Samuel Wiel wrote of the miners:

They took possession of the public lands, mines, water and timber wherever they located, following out as between themselves the customs and rules of prior appropriation of all of these things prevailing in California, and not hearing from Congress one way or the other. Private rights to real estate all rested upon this rule of priority of occupation upon public land. "For a long period the general government stood silently by and allowed its citizens to occupy a great part of its public domain in California, and to locate and hold mining claims, water-rights, etc., according to such rules as could be made applicable to the peculiar situation; and when there were contests between hostile claimants, the courts were compelled to decide them without reference to the ownership of the government, as it was not urged or presented. In this way—from 1849 to 1866—a system had grown up under which the rights of locators on the public domain, as between themselves, were determined, which left out of view the paramount title of the government."

1 Samuel C. Wiel, Water Rights in the United States 88 (3d ed. 1911), quoting Cave v. Tyler, 65 P. 1089, 1095 (Cal.1901).

2.   In 1857 the California Supreme Court recognized the existence of riparian rights as between two claimants who located on and applied for patents to public lands. It acknowledged, however, the superior title of the federal government. Crandall v. Woods, 8 Cal. 136, 143 (1857): "One who locates upon public lands with a view of appropriating them to his own use, becomes the absolute owner thereof as against every one but the government, and is entitled to all the privileges and incidents which appertain to the soil, subject to the single exception of rights antecedently acquired." Is *Crandall* consistent with *Irwin*?

3.   Justice Field of the California Supreme Court affirmed the federal government's superior title in a major and controversial opinion that upheld the mining claim of a lessee of John C. Fremont against a miner who simply entered the land and began mining. Fremont, who was the leader of major western expeditions in the 1840s and the first Republican candidate for President, traced his claim as a riparian owner to a Mexican land grant. See Allen Nevins, Fremont, Pathmarker of the West (3d ed. 1955). Fremont's lessee, of course, characterized the entrant as a trespasser on the public domain, and the entrant argued that he was a licensee. Field rejected the license theory but laid the foundation for the ultimate recognition of title in those who entered and grabbed according to custom. "There is no license in the legal meaning of the term. * * * The most which can be said is, that the government has forborne to exercise its rights. * * * " Biddle Boggs v. Merced Mining Co., 14 Cal. 279, 374 (1859), affirmed 70 U.S. 304 (1865).

The logic of *Biddle Boggs* was followed by the Nevada Supreme Court, which held in 1872 that a subsequent federal patentee obtained riparian rights superior to a downstream prior appropriator who entered and diverted the stream while that land was part of the public domain. Vansickel v. Haines, 7 Nev. 249 (1872). A concurring justice observed that the rule that a federal patent carried with it riparian rights would disappoint expectations long considered by the public to be well founded. These decisions are important today because they illustrate that western water institutions were developed prior to the federal government's consistent assertion of any interest and thus the western states based their laws on the assumption that the United States permanently gave up whatever interests it might have had. See the interesting article, Charles W. McCurdy, *Stephen J. Field and*

Public Land Law Development in California, 1850–1866: A Case Study of Judicial Resource Allocation in Nineteenth-Century America, 10 Law & Soc.Rev. 235 (1976).

In § 9 of the 1866 Mining Act (quoted at page 169, infra), Congress confirmed rights to water on the public lands if they "are recognized and acknowledged by the local customs, laws, and decisions of courts." This was a sufficiently express statement to enable Justice Field, as a member of the United States Supreme Court, to enforce the customs of the miners in Jennison v. Kirk, 98 U.S. 453 (1878). Does the 1866 Act's recognition of private rights based on custom estop the government from ever asserting an interest in public domain water? Western states and the federal government have debated this question for more than a century and the debate forms an important theme in the development of western water law.

4. While prior appropriation became the law of all the Great Basin states, it apparently was not the early law of the first white irrigators in the West, the Mormons. Originally a theocracy, the early church and government were one, and an 1852 Utah Territorial statute (In 1850 Congress refused to admit the state of Deseret and created the territory of Utah) provided that "county courts shall * * * have control of all * * * water privileges * * * and exercise such powers as in their judgment shall * * * subserve the interests of settlement in the distribution of water for irrigation." Moses Lasky, *From Prior Appropriation to Economic Distribution of Water By the State—Via Irrigation Administration*, 1 Rocky Mtn.L.Rev. 161, 167 (1929). Mormon collectivism survived only until 1880, perhaps because of the increased secularization of state government and the general tendency toward individualism in the late nineteenth century. It may be, however, that the mutual water companies, discussed in Chapter Six at pages 597–99, infra, that abound in Utah are an offspring of the earlier community control of water.

Utah was not the only place that collective water distribution was tried by the settlers. Hutchins' assumption that the western states quickly and uniformly adopted prior appropriation is not accurate. Western history shows that the earliest irrigation developed around various quasi-utopian colony schemes, and these colonies were receptive to a variety of water allocation practices. Irrigation colonies in southern California and Colorado following the Mormon model were founded in the 1870s and early 1880s. In Colorado Nathan C. Meeker, the agricultural editor of Horace Greeley's enormously influential New York Tribune, founded a utopian irrigation colony in 1870 along the Cache la Poudre River. The settlement was named Greeley. The story of the Union Colony and other attempts to construct irrigation colonies before the triumph of prior appropriation in the late 1880s is well told in Robert G. Dunbar, Forging New Rights in Western Waters 9–85 (1983).

COFFIN v. LEFT HAND DITCH CO.

Supreme Court of Colorado, 1882.
6 Colo. 443.

HELM, J. Appellee, who was plaintiff below, claimed to be the owner of certain water by virtue of an appropriation thereof from the south fork of the St. Vrain creek. It appears that such water, after its diversion, is carried by means of a ditch to the James creek, and thence along the bed of the same to Left Hand creek, where it is again diverted by lateral ditches and used to irrigate lands adjacent to the last named stream. Appellants are the owners of lands lying on the margin and in the neighborhood of the St. Vrain below the mouth of said south fork thereof, and naturally irrigated therefrom.

In 1879 there was not a sufficient quantity of water in the St. Vrain to supply the ditch of appellee and also irrigate the said lands of appellant. A portion of appellee's dam was torn out, and its diversion of water thereby seriously interfered with by appellants. The action is brought for damages arising from the trespass, and for injunctive relief to prevent repetitions thereof in the future.

* * *

It is contended by counsel for appellants that the common law principles of riparian proprietorship prevailed in Colorado until 1876, and that the doctrine of priority of right to water by priority of appropriation thereof was first recognized and adopted in the constitution. But we think the latter doctrine has existed from the date of the earliest appropriations of water within the boundaries of the state. The climate is dry, and the soil, when moistened only by the usual rainfall, is arid and unproductive; except in a few favored sections, artificial irrigation for agriculture is an absolute necessity. Water in the various streams thus acquires a value unknown in moister climates. Instead of being a mere incident to the soil, it rises, when appropriated, to the dignity of a distinct usufructuary estate, or right of property. It has always been the policy of the national, as well as the territorial and state governments, to encourage the diversion and use of water in this country for agriculture; and vast expenditures of time and money have been made in reclaiming and fertilizing by irrigation portions of our unproductive territory. Houses have been built, and permanent improvements made; the soil has been cultivated, and thousands of acres have been rendered immensely valuable, with the understanding that appropriations of water would be protected. Deny the doctrine of priority or superiority of right by priority of appropriation, and a great part of the value of all this property is at once destroyed.

The right to water in this country, by priority of appropriation thereof, we think it is, and has always been, the duty of the national and state governments to protect. The right itself, and the obligation to protect it, existed prior to legislation on the subject of irrigation. It is entitled to protection as well after patent to a third party of the land over which the natural stream flows, as when such land is a part of the public domain; and it is immaterial whether or not it be mentioned in the patent and expressly excluded from the grant.

The act of congress protecting in patents such right in water appropriated, when recognized by local customs and laws, "was rather a voluntary recognition of a pre-existing right of possession, constituting a valid claim to its continued use, than the establishment of a new one." Broder v. Notoma W. & M. Co., 11 Otto, 274.

We conclude, then, that the common law doctrine giving the riparian owner a right to the flow of water in its natural channel upon and over his lands, even though he makes no beneficial use thereof, is inapplicable to Colorado. Imperative necessity, unknown to the countries which gave it birth, compels the recognition of another doctrine in conflict therewith. And we hold that, in the absence of express statutes to the contrary, the first appropriator of water from a natural stream for a beneficial purpose has, with the qualifications contained in the constitution, a prior right thereto, to the extent of such appropriation. See Schilling v. Rominger, 4 Col. 103.

The territorial legislature in 1864 expressly recognizes the doctrine. It says: "Nor shall the water of any stream be diverted from its original channel to the detriment of any miner, millmen or others along the line of said stream, *who may have a priority of right,* and there shall be at all times left sufficient water in said stream for the use of miners and agriculturists along said stream." Session Laws of 1864, p. 68, § 32.

The priority of right mentioned in this section is acquired by priority of appropriation, and the provision declares that appropriations of water shall be subordinate to the use thereof by prior appropriators. This provision remained in force until the adoption of the constitution; it was repealed in 1868, but the repealing act re-enacted it *verbatim.*

But the rights of appellee were acquired, in the first instance, under the acts of 1861 and 1862, and counsel for appellants urge, with no little skill and plausibility, that these statutes are in conflict with our conclusion that priority of right is acquired by priority of appropriation. The only provision, however, which can be construed as referring to this subject is § 4 on page 68, Session Laws of 1861. This section provides for the appointment of commissioners, in times of scarcity, to apportion the stream "in a just and equitable proportion," to the best interests of all parties, *"with a due regard to the legal rights of all."* What is meant by the concluding phrases of the foregoing statute? What are the legal rights for which the commissioners are enjoined to have a "due regard?" Why this additional limitation upon the powers of such commissioners?

It seems to us a reasonable inference that these phrases had reference to the rights acquired by priority of appropriation. This view is sustained by the universal respect shown at the time said statute was adopted, and subsequently by each person, for the prior appropriations of others, and the corresponding customs existing among settlers with reference thereto. This construction does not, in our judgment, detract from the force or effect of the statute. It was the duty of the commissioners under it to guard against extravagance and waste, and to so divide and distribute the water as most economically to supply all of the earlier appropriators thereof according to their respective appropriations and necessities, to the extent of the amount remaining in the stream.

It appears from the record that the patent under which appellant George W. Coffin holds title was issued prior to the act of congress of 1866, hereinbefore mentioned. That it contained no reservation or exception of vested water rights, and conveyed to Coffin through his grantor the absolute title in fee simple to his land, together with all incidents and appurtenances thereunto belonging; and it is claimed that therefore the doctrine of priority of right by appropriation cannot, at least, apply to him. We have already declared that water appropriated and diverted for a beneficial purpose is, in this country, not necessarily an appurtenance to the soil through which the stream supplying the same naturally flows. If appropriated by one prior to the patenting of such soil by another, it is a vested right entitled to protection, though not mentioned in the patent. But we are relieved from any extended consideration of this subject by the decision in Broder v. Notoma W. & M. Co., supra.

It is urged, however, that even if the doctrine of priority or superiority of right by priority of appropriation be conceded, appellee in this case is not benefited thereby. Appellants claim that they have a better right to the water because their lands lie along the margin and in the neighborhood of the St. Vrain. They assert that, as against them, appellee's diversion of said water to irrigate lands adjacent to Left Hand creek, though prior in time, is unlawful.

In the absence of legislation to the contrary, we think that the right to water acquired by priority of appropriation thereof is not in any way dependent upon the *locus* of its application to the beneficial use designed. And the disastrous consequences of our adoption of the rule contended for, forbid our giving such a construction to the statutes as will concede the same, if they will properly bear a more reasonable and equitable one.

The doctrine of priority of right by priority of appropriation for agriculture is evoked, as we have seen, by the imperative necessity for artificial irrigation of the soil. And it would be an ungenerous and inequitable rule that would deprive one of its benefit simply because he has, by large expenditure of time and money, carried the water from one stream over an intervening watershed and cultivated land in the valley of another. It might be utterly impossible, owing to the topography of the country, to get water upon his farm from the adjacent stream; or if possible, it might be impracticable on account of the distance from the point where the diversion must take place and the attendant expense; or the quantity of water in such stream might be entirely insufficient to supply his wants. It sometimes happens that the most fertile soil is found along the margin or in the neighborhood of the small rivulet, and sandy and barren land beside the larger stream. To apply the rule contended for would prevent the useful and profitable cultivation of the productive soil, and sanction the waste of water upon the more sterile lands. It would have enabled a party to locate upon a stream in 1875, and destroy the value of thousands of acres, and the improvements thereon, in adjoining valleys, possessed and cultivated for the preceding decade. Under the principle contended for, a party owning land ten miles from the stream, but in the valley thereof, might deprive a prior appropriator of the water diverted therefrom whose lands are within a thousand yards, but just beyond an intervening divide.

We cannot believe that any legislative body within the territory or state of Colorado ever *intended* these consequences to flow from a statute enacted. Yet two sections are relied upon by counsel as practically producing them. These sections are as follows:

"All persons who claim, own or hold a possessory right or title to any land or parcel of land within the boundary of Colorado territory, * * * when those claims are on the bank, margin or neighborhood of any stream of water, creek or river, shall be entitled to the use of the water of said stream, creek or river for the purposes of irrigation, and making said claims available to the full extent of the soil, for agricultural purposes." Session Laws 1861, p. 67, § 1.

"Nor shall the water of any stream be diverted from its original channel to the detriment of any miner, millmen or others along the line of said stream, and there shall be at all times left sufficient water in said stream for the use of miners and farmers along said stream." Latter part of § 13, p. 48, Session Laws 1862.

The two statutory provisions above quoted must, for the purpose of this discussion, be construed together. The phrase "along said stream," in the latter, is equally comprehensive, as to the extent of territory, with the expression "on the bank, margin or neighborhood," used in the former, and both include all lands in the immediate valley of the stream. The latter provision sanctions the diversion of water from one stream to irrigate lands adjacent to another, provided such diversion is not to the "detriment" of parties along the line of the stream from which the water is taken. If there is any conflict between the statutes in this respect, the latter, of course, must prevail. We think that the "use" and "detriment" spoken of are a use existing at the time of the diversion, and a detriment immediately resulting therefrom. We do not believe that the legislature intended to prohibit the diversion of water to the "detriment" of parties who might at some future period conclude to settle upon the stream; nor do we think that they were legislating with a view to preserving in such stream sufficient water for the "use" of settlers who might never come, and consequently never have use therefor.

But "detriment" at the time of diversion could only exist where the water diverted had been previously appropriated or used; if there had been no previous appropriation or use thereof, there could be no present injury or "*detriment.*"

Our conclusion above as to the intent of the legislature is supported by the fact that the succeeding assembly, in 1864, hastened to insert into the latter statute, without other change or amendment, the clause, "*who have a priority of right,*" in connection with the idea of "*detriment*" to adjacent owners. This amendment of the statute was simply the acknowledgment by the legislature of a doctrine already existing, under which rights had accrued that were entitled to protection. In the language of Mr. Justice Miller, above quoted, upon a different branch of the same subject, it "was rather a voluntary recognition of a pre-existing right constituting a valid claim, than the creation of a new one."

* * *

The judgment of the court below will be affirmed.

Affirmed.

NOTE: DEVELOPMENT OF THE "CALIFORNIA DOCTRINE"

Confronted with many of the same issues decided by the Colorado court in *Coffin*, the California Supreme Court took a different doctrinal turn because California (and other states) always recognized the federal government as the source of all water titles in which the U.S. retained an interest. After the bold stroke incorporating prior appropriation as the system of allocating water rights among miners on the public land, California recognized the common law of riparian rights as between landowners. Lux v. Haggin, 10 P. 674 (Cal.1886). The case is a colorful slice of California history and it is the spiritual foundation of the mixed, or hybrid, system of water law that prevails or once prevailed in the two tiers of states that bracket the arid, mountainous, "pure" prior appropriation states. The hybrid system states include or included the West Coast states—California, Oregon and Washington—and those along the one-hundredth meridian, an arid-humid line that bisects the country—North Dakota, South Dakota, Nebraska, Kansas, Oklahoma, and Texas.

Samuel C. Wiel, writing in 1936, described *Lux* and its impact as follows:

> In 1886 the Supreme Court of California was concerned with flooding for wild hay in one of its most noted cases, *Lux v. Haggin*. The principal plaintiff was the West's greatest "Cattle King", the late Henry Miller. The locality was the portion of the central valley of California comprising the south end of San Joaquin Valley.

> * * *

> This land was in what might be called the overflow basin of Kern River. Through it the river flowed in various channels or sloughs, the principal one being known as Buena Vista Slough, but in flood time the lands were entirely inundated, because the sloughs were inadequate to carry the water, which flowed over the land and finally drained into Tulare Lake.

> * * *

> As fast as land was acquired along the San Joaquin River, dams were thrown in the slough, levees were thrown up, and the water spread over large tracts for the production of grasses. The

economy and effectiveness of this method of wild irrigation were remarkable. * * * [Henry Miller] became the wizard of the west in making green grass grow. * * * In order to control the water he acquired land on both sides of the river for a distance of over a hundred and twenty miles. * * *

The Haggin interests, also very wealthy, were promoting an irrigation and land development to divert the water above Miller. Emphasizing the disproportionately little benefit that Miller's wild haying was getting as compared to the vast volume of water, they urged that Miller was not making the beneficial use required by a test based upon prior appropriation.

This was a test that, given up in England, appeared anew among the Forty Niners of California in their mining on the public domain. * * *

The trial court favored priority of appropriation and was reversed by the supreme court. The reversal sustained Miller, his land being private, in the common-law riparian right for flow of the water against the defendants, unlimited by use. The defendants persuaded the supreme court to grant a rehearing. Much public attention followed, and had its reflection in the length of the rehearing opinion, two hundred pages, bringing up in a heap most of what the books contained upon the subject of waters at that time. [The court] sustained Miller again. The first opinion of 1884, because it is shorter, is the better reading. It had been a concise embodiment that "Property rights are essentially the same and quite as secure here as elsewhere." An earlier period, also against much pressure, had ruled similarly in the analogous litigation over the once-famous Mariposa Grant of General Fremont. On that occasion Mr. Justice Field (subsequently of the United States Supreme Court) established as Chief Justice of California that free location of mines is confined to minerals on the vacant public domain and is barred from land that became private before the mining location is attempted. Numerous California cases had made like rulings about appropriating water, and *Lux v. Haggin* in 1886 was giving recognition to this legal history. It held, therefore, that questions of use were immaterial in the case.

Samuel C. Wiel, *Fifty Years of Water Law*, 50 Harv.L.Rev. 252, 256–59 (1936).

In limiting the appropriation doctrine to public lands still in federal ownership, the court in *Lux* held that "A grant of public land of the United States carries with it the common-law rights to an innavigable stream thereon, unless the waters are expressly or impliedly reserved by the terms of the patent, or of the statute granting the land, or unless they are reserved by the congressional legislation authorizing the patent. * * * *"

The court reconciled its earlier decisions and stated its view on the effect of federal legislation:

It has never been held by the supreme court of the United States, or by the supreme court of this state, that an appropriation of water on the public lands of the United States (made after the act of congress of July 26, 1866, or the amendatory act of 1870) gave to the appropriator the right to the water appropriated as against a grantee of riparian lands, under a grant made or issued prior to the act of 1866, except in a case where the water so subsequently appropriated was reserved by the terms of such grant. * * *

In the case at bar the grant of the lands to the state (containing no reservation of the waters of flowing streams, express or to be implied from its terms) was made nearly 30 years before the first appropriation of water by the defendant, which was *after* the act of congress of July, 1866, and the amendatory act of 1870.

In Osgood v. Water Co., 56 Cal. 571 [(1880)], it was held that where a person acquired a right, by appropriation, to water upon the public lands of the United States, *before* the issuance of a patent to another for lands through which the stream ran, the patentee's rights were, "by express statutory enactment, subject to the rights of the appropriator." The court cited the [1870] amendatory act of congress. * * *

[O]ne who acquired a title to riparian lands from the United States prior to the act of July 26, 1866, could not (in the absence of reservation in his grant) be deprived of his common-law rights to the flow of the stream by one who appropriated its waters after the passage of that act. * * *

The statutes passed long afterwards cannot affect rights acquired by the state by virtue of a [Swamp Land Act] grant made in 1850, [and later conveyed to Miller and Lux], nor can the subsequent policy of the United States (which is supposed to be indicated by a failure, by express laws, to prohibit the occupation of portions of its lands for mining, etc., and by the omission of the executive officers to attempt to remove miners and other occupants by force) be held to affect the rights acquired by the state through the grant of 1850. * * *

Lux v. Haggin, 10 P. at 724–30 (1886).

After *Lux*, when can a holder of a prior appropriative right prevail over a subsequent riparian? The *Lux* court distinguished *Coffin v. Left Hand Ditch Co.*, page 160, supra, based on the unequivocal incorporation of the prior appropriation doctrine by the Colorado Constitution of 1876. Article XV, § 5 provides:

The water of every natural stream, not heretofore appropriated, within the State of Colorado, is hereby declared to be property of the people of the State, subject to appropriation as hereinafter provided.

Coffin, however, involved rights that arose before the state constitution was adopted, and the Colorado court therefore never mentioned the provision.

Western states developed both appropriation and riparian systems on the assumption that both were sanctioned by the federal government. The western states also began to assume that the United States would assert no interest in allocating waters arising on the public domain. This assumption arose during what is called the "disposition era" of public land policy. Congress passed a variety of statutes to transfer land from public to private ownership. However, the disposition era came to an end before the federal government had disposed of all the public domain. In 1891, federal policy began to shift toward a policy of selective retention of public lands with the passage of legislation authorizing the presidential creation of forest reserves. In addition, the President made large-scale withdrawals of western lands from entry and the establishment of private rights. But the consequences of this shift for western water law were largely ignored. In his third edition, in 1911, Samuel Wiel observed that "[t]he future of Western law of waters will depend much on the course of the policy of conservation; at present that policy is in the ascendant, and demands a great change of the existing law." 1 Wiel at 166. Western states thought that their expectation of immunity from federal control was confirmed in the next case. Whether this is true continues to be the subject of considerable debate.

CALIFORNIA–OREGON POWER CO. v. BEAVER PORTLAND CEMENT CO.

Supreme Court of the United States, 1935.
295 U.S. 142, 55 S.Ct. 725, 79 L.Ed. 1356.

Mr. Justice Sutherland delivered the opinion of the Court.

* * *

Rogue River is a non-navigable stream, and in its course flows through and between lands of petitioner on the east bank of the river and lands of respondents upon the west bank, the thread of the stream being the boundary between the two. Petitioner's lands were acquired by a predecessor in interest in 1885 by patent from the United States under the Homestead Act of May 20, 1862. The lands were purchased by petitioner and conveyed to it in 1921. Petitioner is a public-service corporation engaged in manufacturing and supplying electrical current to its customers. The City of Gold Hill, a municipal corporation, owns the lands on the west side of the river, and the Beaver Portland Cement Company is in possession of them, together with certain adjudicated water rights and permits issued from the office of the state engineer, under a contract of sale from the city. The blasting complained of was all west of the thread of the stream, on respondents' property, and was for the double purpose of freeing the channel, incident to the use of the water rights adjudicated and permitted, and securing broken stone for a dam to be used in connection with a power plant which the cement company was about to build.

Neither petitioner nor any of its predecessors in interest has ever diverted the waters of the river for beneficial use on the real property or sought to make an actual appropriation thereof. The sole claim is based upon the common-law rights of a riparian proprietor, which petitioner says attached to the lands when the patent was issued to its first predecessor in title.

Petitioner insists that prior to the adoption of the Oregon Water Code of 1909, infra, the common-law rule that the riparian owner was entitled to the natural flow of the stream across or along the border of his land in its accustomed channel was recognized and in full force in the State of Oregon. Respondents contend to the contrary. Both cite many Oregon decisions and argue the matter at length. But an examination of the authorities leaves the question in doubt. In dealing with cases where the parties making conflicting claims were both riparian owners, the doctrine of the common law seems to have been recognized. Other cases appear to accept what is called a modified form of the common-law rule; and still other decisions apparently enforce the rule of appropriation. It is suggested by respondent that, prior to the adoption of the Water Code in 1909, the policy in respect of water rights was developing and the law on the subject of riparian rights was in a state of flux. There appears to be reason in the suggestion. But, in view of the conclusion to which we have come, it is unnecessary to pursue the inquiry further.

In 1909, the Water Code was adopted by the state legislature. Ore. Laws, 1909, Chap. 216. The act provides that all water within the state shall be subject to appropriation for beneficial use; but nothing therein is to be construed to take away or impair any vested right. In respect of a riparian proprietor, a vested right is defined "as an actual application of water to beneficial use prior to the passage of this act * * * to the extent of the actual application to beneficial use." * * *

First. The first question is of especial importance to the semi-arid states of California, Oregon and Washington, where climatic conditions in some sections so differ from those in others that the doctrine of the common law may be of advantage in one instance, and entirely unsuited to conditions in another. Probably, it was this diversity of conditions which gave rise to more or less confusion in the decisions—not only of Oregon, but of California—in respect of the subject. We have already spoken of the former; and one has only to compare the decision of the Supreme Court of California in Lux v. Haggin, 69 Cal. 255; 4 Pac. 919; 10 Pac. 674, with Modoc L. & L.S. Co. v. Booth, 102 Cal. 151; 36 Pac. 431, to realize that the rule with respect to the extent of the application of the common law of riparian rights is, likewise, far from being clear in the latter.

The question with which we are here primarily concerned is whether—in the light of pertinent history, of the conditions which existed in the arid and semi-arid land states, of the practice and attitude of the federal government, and of the congressional legislation prior to 1885—the homestead patent in question carried with it as part of the granted estate the common-law rights which attach to riparian proprietorship. If the answer be in the negative, it will be unnecessary to consider the second question decided by the court below.

For many years prior to the passage of the Act of July 26, 1866, c. 262, § 9, 14 Stat. 251, 253, the right to the use of waters for mining and other beneficial purposes in California and the arid region generally was fixed and regulated by local rules and customs. The first appropriator of water for a beneficial use was uniformly recognized as having the better right to the extent of his actual use. The common law with respect to riparian rights was not considered applicable, or, if so, only to a limited degree. Water was carried by means of ditches and flumes great distances for consumption by those engaged in mining and agriculture. Jennison v. Kirk, 98 U.S. 453, 457–458 [(1878)]. The rule generally recognized throughout the states and territories of the arid region was that the acquisition of water by prior appropriation for a beneficial use was entitled to protection; and the rule applied whether the water was diverted for manufacturing, irrigation, or mining purposes. The rule was evidenced not alone by legislation and judicial decision, but by local and customary law and usage as well. Basey v. Gallagher, 20 Wall. 670, 683–684; Atchison v. Peterson, 20 Wall. 507, 512–513.

This general policy was approved by the silent acquiescence of the federal government, until it received formal confirmation at the hands of Congress by the Act of 1866, supra. *Atchison* v. *Peterson*, supra. Section 9 of that act provides:

"That whenever, by priority of possession, rights to the use of water for mining, agricultural, manufacturing, or other purposes, have vested and accrued, and the same are recognized and acknowledged by the local customs, laws, and the decisions of courts, the possessors and owners of such vested rights shall be maintained and protected in the same; and the right of way for the construction of ditches and canals for the purposes aforesaid is hereby acknowledged and confirmed: * * * " This provision was "rather a voluntary *recognition of a pre-existing right of possession*, constituting a valid claim to its continued use, than the establishment of a new one." Broder v. Water Co., 101 U.S. 274, 276; United States v. Rio Grande Irrigation Co., 174 U.S. 690, 704–705. And in order to make it clear that the grantees of the United States would take their lands charged with the existing servitude, the Act of July 9, 1870, c. 235, § 17, 16 Stat. 217, 218, amending the Act of 1866, provided that—

" * * * all patents granted, or preëmption or homesteads allowed, shall be subject to any vested and accrued water rights, or rights to ditches and reservoirs used in connection with such water rights, as may have been acquired under or recognized by the ninth section of the act of which this act is amendatory."

The effect of these acts is not limited to rights acquired before 1866. They reach into the future as well, and approve and confirm the policy of appropriation for a beneficial use, as recognized by local rules and customs, and the legislation and judicial decisions of the arid-land states, as the test and measure of private rights in and to the non-navigable waters on the public domain.

If the acts of 1866 and 1870 did not constitute an entire abandonment of the common-law rule of running waters in so far as the public lands and subsequent grantees thereof were concerned, they foreshadowed the more positive declarations of the Desert Land Act of 1877, which it is contended did bring about that result. That act allows the entry and reclamation of desert lands within the states of California, Oregon, and Nevada (to which Colorado was later added), and the then territories of Washington, Idaho, Montana, Utah, Wyoming, Arizona, New Mexico, and Dakota, with a proviso to the effect that the right to the use of waters by the claimant shall depend upon *bona fide* prior appropriation, not to exceed the amount of waters actually appropriated and necessarily used for the purpose of irrigation and reclamation. Then follows the clause of the proviso with which we are here concerned:

" *   *   * all surplus water over and above such actual appropriation and use, together with the water of all lakes, rivers and other sources of water supply upon the public lands and not navigable, shall remain and be held free for the appropriation and use of the public for irrigation, mining and manufacturing purposes subject to existing rights." Ch. 107, 19 Stat. 377.

For the light which it will reflect upon the meaning and scope of that provision and its bearing upon the present question, it is well to pause at this point to consider the then-existing situation with respect to land and water rights in the states and territories named. These states and territories comprised the western third of the United States—a vast empire in extent, but still sparsely settled. From a line east of the Rocky Mountains almost to the Pacific Ocean, and from the Canadian border to the boundary of Mexico—an area greater than that of the original thirteen states—the lands capable of redemption, in the main, constituted a desert, impossible of agricultural use without artificial irrigation.

In the beginning, the task of reclaiming this area was left to the unaided efforts of the people who found their way by painful effort to its inhospitable solitudes. These western pioneers, emulating the spirit of so many others who had gone before them in similar ventures, faced the difficult problem of wresting a living and creating homes from the raw elements about them, and threw down the gage of battle to the forces of nature. With imperfect tools, they built dams, excavated canals, constructed ditches, plowed and cultivated the soil, and transformed dry and desolate lands into green fields and leafy orchards. In the success of that effort, the general government itself was greatly concerned—not only because, as owner, it was charged through Congress with the duty of disposing of the lands, but because the settlement and development of the country in which the lands lay was highly desirable.

To these ends, prior to the summer of 1877, Congress had passed the mining laws, the homestead and preëmption laws, and finally, the Desert Land Act. It had encouraged and assisted, by making large land grants to aid the building of the Pacific railroads and in many other ways, the redemption of this immense landed estate. That body thoroughly understood that an enforcement of the common-law rule, by greatly retarding if not forbidding the diversion of waters from their accustomed channels, would disastrously affect the policy of dividing the public domain into small holdings and effecting their distribution among innumerable settlers. In respect of the area embraced by the desert-land states, with the exception of a comparatively narrow strip along the Pacific seaboard, it had become evident to Congress, as it had to the inhabitants, that the future growth and well-being of the entire region depended upon a complete adherence to the rule of appropriation for a beneficial use as the exclusive criterion of the right to the use of water. The streams and other sources of supply from which this water must come were separated from one another by wide stretches of parched and barren land which never could be made to produce agricultural crops except by the transmission of water for long distances and its entire consumption in the processes of irrigation. Necessarily, that involved the complete subordination of the common-law doctrine of riparian rights to that of appropriation. And this substitution of the rule of appropriation for that of the common law was to have momentous consequences. It became the determining factor in the long struggle to expunge from our vocabulary the legend "Great American Desert," which was spread in large letters across the face of the old maps of the far west.*

In the light of the foregoing considerations, the Desert Land Act was passed, and in their light it must now be construed. By its terms, not only all surplus water over and above such as might be appropriated and used by the desert-land entrymen, but "the water of all lakes, rivers and other sources of water supply upon the public lands and not navigable" were to remain "free for the appropriation and use of the public for irrigation, mining and manufacturing purposes." If this language is to be given its natural meaning, and we see no reason why it should not, it effected a severance of all waters upon the public domain, not theretofore appropriated, from the land itself. From that premise, it follows that a patent issued thereafter for lands in a desert-land state or territory, under any of the land laws of the United States, carried with it, of its own force, no common law right to the water flowing through or bordering upon the lands conveyed. While this court thus far has not found it necessary to determine that precise question, its words, so far as they go, tend strongly to support the conclusion which we have suggested.

In United States v. Rio Grande Irrigation Co., 174 U.S. 690, the government sought to enjoin the irrigation company from constructing a dam across the Rio Grande in the Territory of New Mexico, and from appropriating the waters of that stream. The object of the company was to impound the waters and distribute the same for a variety of purposes. The company defended on the ground that the site of the

---

* Mr. Justice Sutherland immigrated with his parents to the Utah Territory in 1863 when he was 18 months old, his father having been converted to the Church of Jesus Christ of Latter-Day Saints. Sutherland practiced law in Utah from 1883 to 1905, when he was elected U.S. Senator. His account of the development of the West rests, therefore, on more than a cold record. [Eds. note.]

dam was within the arid region, and that it had fully complied with the water laws of the Territory of New Mexico in which the dam was located and the waters were to be used. The supreme court of the territory affirmed a decree dismissing the bill. This court reversed and remanded the case, with instructions to inquire whether the construction of the dam and appropriation of water would substantially diminish the navigability of the stream, and, if so, to enter a decree restraining the acts of the appellees to the extent of the threatened diminution. The opinion, dealing with the question of riparian rights, said that it was within the power of any state to change the common-law rule and permit the appropriation of the flowing waters for any purposes it deemed wise. Whether a territory had the same power the court did not then decide. Two limitations of state power were suggested: first, in the absence of any specific authority from Congress, that a state could not by its legislation destroy the right of the United States as the owner of lands bordering on a stream to the continued flow—so far, at least, as might be necessary for the beneficial use of the government property; and second, that its power was limited by that of the general government to secure the uninterrupted navigability of all navigable streams within the limits of the United States. With these exceptions, the court, however, thought (p. 706) that by the acts of 1866 and 1877 "Congress recognized and assented to the appropriation of water in contravention of the common law rule as to continuous flow," and that "the obvious purpose of Congress was to give its assent, so far as the public lands were concerned, to any system, although in contravention to the common law rule, which permitted the appropriation of those waters for legitimate industries." * * *

Only four of the desert-land states have spoken upon the matter, and their decisions are not in harmony. The Supreme Court of Oregon in Hough v. Porter, 51 Ore. 318; 95 Pac. 732; 98 Pac. 1083; 102 Pac. 728, held that the legal effect of the language already quoted from the Desert Land Act was to dedicate to the public all interest, riparian or otherwise, in the waters of the public domain, and to abrogate the common-law rule in respect of riparian rights as to all lands settled upon or entered after March 3, 1877. The supplemental opinion which deals with the subject beginning at p. 382 is well reasoned, and we think reaches the right conclusion. * * *

The Supreme Court of Washington in Still v. Palouse Irrigation & Power Co., 64 Wash. 606, 612; 117 Pac. 466, gave a more limited construction to the Desert Land Act, holding that thereby Congress recognized and assented to the appropriation of water in contravention to the common-law right of the riparian owner only in respect of desert lands granted under the act.

In San Joaquin & K. R. Canal Co. v. Worswick, 187 Cal. 674, 690; 203 Pac. 999, the Supreme Court of California followed the Washington court in holding that the language of the Desert Land Act applied only to desert-land entries.

To accept the view of the Washington and California courts would, in large measure, be to subvert the policy which Congress had in mind—namely, to further the disposition and settlement of the public domain. * * *

As the owner of the public domain, the government possessed the power to dispose of land and water thereon together, or to dispose of them separately. The fair construction of the provision now under review is that Congress intended to establish the rule that for the future the land should be patented separately; and that all non-navigable waters thereon should be reserved for the use of the public under the laws of the states and territories named. * * * The terms of the statute, thus construed, must be read into every patent thereafter issued, with the same force as though expressly incorporated therein, with the result that the grantee will take the legal title to the land conveyed, and such title, and only such title, to the flowing waters thereon as shall be fixed or acknowledged by the customs, laws, and judicial decisions of the state of their location. If it be conceded that in the absence of federal legislation the state would be powerless to affect the riparian rights of the United States or its grantees, still, the authority of Congress to vest such power in the state, and that it has done so by the legislation to which we have referred, cannot be doubted.

* * * There is nothing in the language of the [Desert Land Act], or in the circumstances leading up to or accompanying its adoption, that indicates an intention on the part of Congress to confine the appropriation of water in contravention of the common-law doctrine to desert-land entrymen.

Nothing we have said is meant to suggest that the act, as we construe it, has the effect of curtailing the power of the states affected to legislate in respect of waters and water rights as they deem wise in the public interest. What we hold is that following the act of 1877, if not before, all non-navigable waters then a part of the public domain became *publici juris*, subject to the plenary control of the designated states, including those since created out of the territories named, with the right in each to determine for itself to what extent the rule of appropriation or the common-law rule in respect of riparian rights should obtain. For since "Congress cannot enforce either rule upon any state," Kansas v. Colorado, 206 U.S. 46, 94, the full power of choice must remain with the state. The Desert Land Act does not bind or purport to bind the states to any policy. It simply recognizes and gives sanction, in so far as the United States and its future grantees are concerned, to the state and local doctrine of appropriation, and seeks to remove what otherwise might be an impediment to its full and success-ful operation.

NOTES

1. Does the decision in the principal case overrule *Lux v. Haggin?*

2. What was petitioner's theory? If the company claimed that its 1885 patent gave it riparian rights as a matter of federal law, the Court's holding that the 1877 Desert Land Act severed the land and water, so that no patent carried any federal water rights with it, is a complete answer. But suppose petitioner claimed not under federal

law but under state law. This theory would proceed as follows: The Desert Land Act granted authority to the states to adopt any system of water rights it chose. Until 1909, Oregon adhered to the riparian system. The 1909 Act purported to divest such rights and to make water rights dependent on an appropriation. But this statute cannot be constitutionally applied to property rights vesting prior to 1909, and petitioner's rights vested in 1885. Could the Supreme Court have avoided the question of the constitutional validity of the 1909 Act?

3. Suppose the Rogue River had been navigable. Would the result have been the same? Note that the 1877 Desert Land Act applies in terms only to "sources of water supply upon the public lands and not navigable." It is generally assumed that the rule of the *California Oregon Power Co.* case applies equally to navigable and non-navigable streams, except as Congress retains regulatory power over navigable streams. But there is no Supreme Court case so holding. If the Desert Land Act does not apply to navigable streams, what are the rights of users thereon? Note that the 1866 and 1870 Acts make no distinction between navigable and non-navigable streams.

4. Suppose petitioner's patent had been issued before 1866. Would the result have been the same? In other words, are the Acts of 1866, 1870, and 1877 declaratory of pre-existing law (see Farm Investment Co. v. Carpenter, 61 P. 258 (Wyo.1900)), or are they prospective only? This question, too, has not been answered by the Supreme Court.

5. In discussing United States v. Rio Grande Irrigation Co., the Court reiterated two limitations on state power to adopt a water law rights system of its own choosing: (1) the system remains subject to congressional power to regulate navigable streams as an incident of commerce; (2) the system, absent congressional permission, could not "destroy the right of the United States as the owner of lands bordering on a stream to the continued flow—so far, at least, as might be necessary for the beneficial use of the government property; * * *." Obviously congressional permission has been given to some degree, or else there could be no valid appropriative rights against the government. But note that the 1877 Act severs water from the "public lands." What happens when government land is withdrawn from entry and reserved for government use as National Parks, National Forests, military bases, Indian Reservations and the like? Such withdrawal raises the question of federal "reserved water rights," a subject considered in Chapter Seven.

6. While the Court at one point quotes with approval the statement in Kansas v. Colorado that "Congress cannot enforce either [the riparian or appropriation] rule upon any state" (a statement quoted out of context), it also seems to indicate that but for the 1866, 1870 and 1877 Acts, a federal patent would have carried with it federal common law riparian rights. There is some latter-day support for this proposition. In Hughes v. Washington, 389 U.S. 290 (1967), page 399, infra, the Court held that a successor in title to a federal patent had a federal common law right to accretions to beach land despite the state property rule that such accretions belong to the state.

7. In Andrus v. Charlestone Stone Products Co., Inc., 436 U.S. 604 (1978), the Supreme Court reversed a Ninth Circuit Court of Appeals decision holding that water could be a valuable mineral for purposes of location under the Mining Law of 1872. Reviewing the Acts of 1866, 1870, and 1872, the Court concluded that water was not "the type of valuable mineral that the 1872 Congress intended to make the basis of a valid claim." The Court also acknowledged that undesirable results would come of there being two parallel systems of acquiring water rights, a federal system of mining claims and state-created water rights as recognized and protected by the 1866 and 1870 mining laws.

8. Federal acquiescence to state water law has taken on the sacredness of the Passover story of the flight of the Israelites from Egypt, augmented by a Calvinist labor justification for state supremacy. The following case excerpt presents a current version of the conquest-of-the-West justification for state water law dominance. It is taken from a recent Colorado Supreme Court opinion that held that ground-water not tributary to a surface stream is subject to appropriation only if state law subjects it to that regime. In considering the court's analysis, ask: Does the Colorado Supreme Court merely restate *California Oregon Power* or does it extend it? Is the extension warranted by history or the logic of the Acts of 1866, 1870 and 1877?

COLORADO DEPARTMENT OF NATURAL RESOURCES v. SOUTHWESTERN COLORADO WATER CONSERVATION DIST.

Supreme Court of Colorado, 1983.
671 P.2d 1294.

LOHR, JUSTICE.

* * *

Colorado and the other western states derive their authority to develop a system of water law from the federal government, which once owned substantially all lands now within the boundaries of those states. In the latter half of the nineteenth century, the United States Congress enacted various public land laws for the purpose of encouraging settlement of the western frontier. These laws took many forms, but their common objective was to promote development of the agricultural and mineral resources of the west by granting public domain lands to those who should discover valuable minerals and to others who should settle the vast new country. Encouraged by these inducements, miners and other pioneers occupied parts of the arid lands west of the hundredth meridian of longitude before the formulation of federal law or policy concerning rights in water. Many of the mines and farms were remote from natural streams, and "the settlers in this new land quickly realized that the riparian doctrine of water rights that had served well in the humid regions of the East would not work in the arid lands of the West." California v. United States, 438 U.S. 645 (1978); see generally California Oregon Power Co. v. Beaver Portland Cement Co., 295 U.S. 142 (1935); United States v. City and County of Denver, 656 P.2d 1 (Colo.1982); Coffin v. Left Hand Ditch Co., 6 Colo. 443 (1882).

Spurred by the need to obtain water for domestic, irrigation and mining uses, the settlers did not await federal leadership, but instead developed their own laws, customs and judicial decisions recognizing priority of appropriation, linked to beneficial use of the water, as the basis for obtaining rights to this vital resource.

Prior to the enactment of the first mining laws in 1866, the federal government by silent acquiescence approved the rule—evidenced by local legislation, judicial decisions, and customary law and usage—"that the acquisition of water by prior appropriation for a beneficial use was entitled to protection. * * *" *California Oregon Power Co.*, 295 U.S. at 154. Then, in a series of acts providing for disposition of parts of the public domain, Congress accorded formal recognition to water rights acquired through local laws and customs and "rejected the alternative of a general federal water law." United States v. City and County of Denver, supra, 656 P.2d at 7.

The 1866 and 1870 Acts were not limited to confirmation of appropriative water rights acquired prior to 1866, but "[t]hey reach into the future as well, and approve and confirm the policy of appropriation for a beneficial use, as recognized by local rules and customs, and the legislation and judicial decisions of the arid-land states, as the test and measure of private rights in and to the non-navigable waters on the public domain." *California Oregon Power Co.*, 295 U.S. at 155. The Desert Land Act of 1877 made the application of the policy to future appropriations even more explicit. In construing the Desert Land Act of 1877 long after it had been implemented by the patenting of large areas of federal lands, the United States Supreme Court noted that "[a]s the owner of the public domain, the government possessed the power to dispose of land and water thereon together, or to dispose of them separately" and held that "[t]he fair construction of the provision [of the Desert Land Act of 1877] now under review is that Congress intended to establish the rule that for the future the land should be patented separately; and that all non-navigable waters thereon should be reserved for the use of the public under the laws of the states and territories named." California Oregon Power Co., 295 U.S. at 162. This rule extends to lands patented under the homestead and preemption laws as well as those disposed of under the Desert Land Act of 1877. *California Oregon Power Co.* Recently, the United States Supreme Court, in rejecting a claim that ground water is a "valuable mineral" locatable under the mining laws, again expressly recognized that the United States Congress established a "passive" water rights policy in the mining laws of 1866, 1870, and 1872 and by that legislation three times affirmed "the view that private water rights on federal lands were to be governed by state and local law and custom." Andrus v. Charlestone Stone Products Co., 436 U.S. 604, 614 (1978). Moreover, in *California v. United States,* supra, the United States Supreme Court noted that through the history of the relationship between the federal government and the states in the reclamation of the arid lands of the western states "runs the consistent thread of purposeful and continued deference to state water law by Congress." 438 U.S. at 653.

Additional congressional recognition of state law as the source of rights to obtain and use water is to be found in the legislative history of the adoption of the McCarran Amendment. In 1952 Congress enacted that amendment, codified at 43 U.S.C. § 666 (1976), providing for the joinder of the United States in judicial proceedings for adjudication or administration of water rights under state law. The Senate Report on the McCarran Amendment recognizes that "[i]n the arid Western States, for more than 80 years, the law has been that the water above and beneath the surface of the ground belongs to the public, and the right to the use thereof is to be acquired from the State in which it is found, which State is vested with the primary control thereof." S.Rep. No. 755, 82d Cong., 1st Sess. 3, 6 (1951).

The United States Supreme Court, in *California Oregon Power Co.*, made clear that each state affected by that decision is free to adopt such system for acquisition of water rights as it considers best. * * *

Recently, in *California v. United States*, supra, the United States Supreme Court reaffirmed that holding. * * *

The Congress of the United States authorized the admission of Colorado as a state of the Union in 1876. The Enabling Act provided for admission of this new state upon "an equal footing with the original states," §§ 1, 5; required disclaimer of "all right and title to unappropriated public lands" in Colorado, § 4, but made no mention of waters.

As the foregoing discussion reflects, federal statutes, as interpreted by the United States Supreme Court, recognize Colorado's authority to adopt its own system for the use of all waters within the state in accordance with the needs of its citizens, subject to the prohibitions against interference with federal reserved rights, with interstate commerce, and with the navigability of any navigable waters. * * *

B.   ELEMENTS OF APPROPRIATION

Prior appropriation assumes that water users will follow a series of steps leading to a perfected water right with priority over subsequently acquired rights. The requirements for establishing a water right were first defined by nineteenth century courts and incorporated in some state constitutions before states set up their statutory systems. They were commonly described as: (1) the demonstration of an *intent to appropriate* water, (2) the *diversion* of water from a watercourse, and (3) the application of the water to a *beneficial use*.

States have implemented these requirements by statute, and have added a host of regulatory provisions applicable to the acquisition, use, transfer, and loss of water rights. Regulations are designed to allow for fuller, more efficient uses of water, for better record keeping, and for more secure investments in water-using enterprises. All the appropriation states but Colorado have permit systems; Colorado uses a water court system to accomplish the same purposes.

With changing conditions and social values, the underlying principles of appropriation are often challenged. The principles have been offered as obstacles to changes that respond to new demands. Is a diversion always necessary? What uses are beneficial, and to what extent are the principles of beneficial use and waste interrelated? Can yesterday's acceptable beneficial use become tomorrow's wasteful practice and no longer support a water right? How can the "public interest" be accommodated within the appropriation system?

The suitability of the doctrine of prior appropriation for the modern West has been questioned by various commentators. Professor Wilkinson argues that most of the doctrine should be rejected because it promotes the destruction of watersheds. Charles F. Wilkinson, *Aldo Leopold and Western Water Law: Thinking Perpendicular to the Doctrine of Prior Appropriation,* 24 Land & Water L.Rev. 1 (1989). He has since pronounced the doctrine dead. "Prior * * * died this January 19th [1991] when his heart seized up after receiving a fax informing him that * * * the New Director of the Denver Water Board had recommended the water developers not file a law suit challenging EPA's rejection of the dam at Two Forks." Charles F. Wilkinson, *In Memoriam, Prior Appropriation 1848–1991,* 21 Envtl.L. v, xvi (1991). Compare John W. Leshy, *The Prior Appropriation Doctrine of Water Law in the West: An Emperor with Few Clothes,* 29 J.West 5 (July 1990) and A. Dan Tarlock, *New Water Transfer Restrictions: The West Returns to Riparianism,* 27 Water Resources Res. 987 (1991) which argue that appropriative water rights are being modified to reflect environmental and other public interest values. But see Gregory J. Hobbs, Jr., *The Reluctant Marriage: The Next Generation (A Response to Charles Wilkinson),* 21 Envtl.L. 1087 (1991).

1. Initiating an Appropriation: Intent and Diversion

SAND POINT WATER & LIGHT CO. v. PANHANDLE DEVELOPMENT CO.

Supreme Court of Idaho, 1905.
11 Idaho 405, 83 P. 347.

AILSHIE, J.

* * *

This action was commenced by the respondent corporation to restrain the appellant corporation from diverting and appropriating the waters of Sand creek and Switzer creek in Kootenai county, and to restrain and enjoin the defendants from interfering with or diverting the waters of those streams in any way or manner that would interfere with the rights and appropriation of the plaintiff. The case went to trial upon complaint and answer, and resulted in a judgment for the plaintiff, from which judgment and an order denying a motion for a new trial, the defendant has appealed.

* * *

On December 16, 1902, appellant's grantors located a water right on West Sand or Mill creek in Kootenai county, and the location notice thereof was posted and duly filed and recorded in the office of the county recorder of Kootenai county, and thereafter, in due time, was filed in the office of the State Engineer at Boise city. Within a few days thereafter the same parties duly and regularly made two additional locations on these streams. On the 14th day of January, 1903, and about 29 days after making the first location, work was commenced, which consisted in cutting out a trail up the canyon, and making a survey for flumes and ditches. Work was continuously prosecuted from that time until the date of the trial of this cause, with at least one man on the ground all the time engaged in building a road, and a flume and ditch through which to carry the waters of these streams, and the general work incident to the construction of the diverting work for carrying out the purposes for which the appropriation was being made.

* * *

The fact stands upon the record practically undisputed, that on the 29th day of September, 1903, the date on which respondent's grantor obtained his permit from the State Engineer to divert and appropriate the waters of these streams, the appellant was actively engaged in the construction of its diverting works, and had at that time expended from $700 to $800 in the prosecution of the work.

It should be observed that appellant's location and the prosecution of its work was made under the act of February 25, 1899 (Sess. Laws 1899, p. 380), while the respondent's right was initiated under act approved March 11, 1903 (Sess. Laws 1903, p. 223). By the latter act a permit is obtained from the State Engineer to divert and appropriate the waters of any of the public streams of the state, while under the act of 1899, notice was required to be posted and a copy thereof filed and recorded with the county recorder, and a duplicate thereof filed with the State Engineer. By section 6, p. 381, of the act of 1899, under which appellant initiated its right, it is provided: "Within sixty days after the notice is posted, the claimant must commence the excavation or construction of the works by which he intends to divert the water, and must prosecute the work diligently and uninterruptedly to completion, unless temporarily interrupted by snow, rain, or cold weather." Respondent claims that the appellant failed to show that it had prosecuted the construction of its diverting works with the diligence required by section 6, supra, and for that reason, if for none other, the judgment was properly entered against appellant. It seems to us, however, when we consider that this work was being prosecuted in a mountainous section of the state where there is a heavy snow fall and a long winter season with much rough and stormy weather which would interrupt and delay the character of work that was being carried on, that the amount and kind of work which is shown to have been done evidences good faith, reasonable diligence, and a purpose to complete the work and apply the waters to the beneficial use designated. Saying nothing of the record notice which the respondent had, the work upon the ground and its continued prosecution was ample actual notice to respondent, or any other subsequent claimant to these waters, as to the nature of the claim asserted by appellant.

It seems to us that the real difficulty in this case has arisen from a wrong construction and misapplication of the word appropriate as used in our statutes. Section 8 of the act of February 25, 1899, provides that where an appropriator has complied with the preceding sections in the posting and recording of notices and the commencement and prosecution of work, "the claimant's right to the use of water relates back to the time the notice was posted." Section 7 of the act provides that by a completion of the work "is meant conducting the waters to the place of intended use." A person desiring to appropriate the waters of a stream may do so either by actually diverting the water and applying it to a beneficial use, or he may pursue the statutory method by posting and recording his notice and commencing and prosecuting his work within the statutory time.

* * *

In other words, by pursuing the successive steps prescribed in the statute, and completing his diverting works, and applying the water to a beneficial purpose, the appropriation is completed.

* * *

It appears that the lower court proceeded on the theory that the appropriation, regardless of the posting of notice, dates from the actual diversion of the water, and its application to the use intended, and the court accordingly finds that "the plaintiff did on or before the 14th day of August, 1904, complete its water system and did actually appropriate the waters flowing in the said stream described in the complaint, and has ever since said date actually appropriated and used all the waters in said stream described in the complaint in supplying the inhabitants of the village of Sand Point with water for domestic uses and fire purposes." This theory is incorrect as applied to appellant, so long as appellant continued to prosecute its work with reasonable diligence. So long as it did so, it was entitled to have its appropriation relate back to the posting of its notice; and, in that event, appellant would be entitled to protection as a prior appropriator as against the respondent.

NOTES

1. What economic objective does the relation back doctrine serve? Does the decision in the principal case further this objective?

2. In *Sand Point*, intent was manifested by posting a location notice according to statute, and subsequently recording it. In the absence of such a statutory requirement, intent may be demonstrated in many ways, including having a surveyor mark out the proper location for ditches. In the case of a corporate appropriator, action by the board of directors approving a water development plan may suffice, provided it is accompanied by a physical manifestation such as some excavation or even placement of survey stakes. City of Aspen v. Colorado River Water Conservation Dist., 696 P.2d 758 (Colo. 1985) holds that such manifestations need not be on the land, but rather must only be sufficient to satisfy the purpose of affording adequate notice to all interested third parties. But compare Bar 70 Enterprises, Inc. v. Tosco Corp., 703 P.2d 1297 (Colo. 1985). The court held that a reconnaissance walk in the White River basin to look for reservoir and

diversion points for a planned (now dormant) oil shale project did not constitute the necessary concurrence of intent to appropriate water for a beneficial use and the performance of an overt act in furtherance of that intent. The 1976 reconnaissance did not manifest the requisite intent to appropriate because "Tosco did not conduct a survey of the reservoir or diversion sites, failed to set stakes or to locate monuments, and did not post signs or publish notices." Nor did the "field trip" demonstrate the taking of a substantial step toward application of the water to a beneficial use. "Tosco's crew did not conduct a field survey at all, but simply hiked along most of the route of the proposed pipeline * * *". Finally, the court held that the field crew's modest activities were not sufficient to put third parties on notice of the contemplated diversion. 703 P.2d at 1307–08. In the permit states, application for a permit to make an appropriation demonstrates the necessary intent. Colorado has not yet decided whether application for a conditional decree serves the same purpose. See City of Aspen v. Colorado River Water Conservation Dist., supra.

3. Should the priority date relate back to the date of physical work "on the ground," or the date at which a decision was made to proceed with the project, thus manifesting the requisite intent? In Elk–Rifle Water Co. v. Templeton, 484 P.2d 1211 (Colo.1971), the Colorado Supreme Court chose the latter of the two dates: "what is required is that at some point in time the two requirements—the open physical demonstration and the requisite intent to appropriate—co-exist, with the priority date to be set not earlier than the date on which both elements are present." For a recent discussion of the "first step" test, including consideration of what factors and actions qualify as manifestations of intent, see City of Thornton v. City of Fort Collins, 830 P.2d 915 (Colo.1992), page 206, infra.

4. Originally relation back of a priority was necessary to allow time for digging a ditch. In an era of multistage projects that require long lead times for planning, financing, and construction, relation back raises more difficult questions. Consequently, states have passed laws giving discretion to an official to prescribe a time within which certain work must be done and water applied to a beneficial use.

Permit granting authorities are normally given the discretion to condition permits on the application of the water to a beneficial use within a certain time period. Nev.Rev.Stat. § 533.380 (within ten years); N.M.Stat.Ann. § 72–5–6 (within nine years); Kans.Stat.Ann. § 82a–713 (within "reasonable" period of time). Opportunity is provided for extensions in circumstances involving excusable failure to apply the water to a beneficial use within the required time. Utah Code Ann. § 73–3–12 and Neb.Rev.Stat. § 46–238. See also Associated Enterprises, Inc. v. Toltec Watershed Improvement Dist., 578 P.2d 1359 (Wyo. 1978). Failure to meet the time limits or to procure an extension may result in cancellation of the permit. Idaho Code Ann. § 42–311 (permit may be cancelled after notice); S.Dak. Codified Laws Ann. § 46–5–25 (right under permit forfeited); Wyo.Stat. § 41–4–506 (state engineer may cancel permit upon default). See also Bailey v. State, 594 P.2d 734 (Nev.1979).

5. How far into the future ought *cities* be allowed to look in acquiring present water rights for anticipated future needs? Should they be treated differently from other appropriators?

In the principal case, Chief Justice Stone refers to Denver's needs as a "great city." This reference is similar to comments of the court in an earlier case that has been cited by the court when it countenances special treatment of growing cities. City and County of Denver v. Sheriff, 96 P.2d 836 (Colo.1939), page 346, infra, involved appropriations by Denver on the western slope of the continental divide. The court stated that flexibility was needed in amounts to be appropriated for future municipal uses: "it is not speculation but the highest prudence on the part of the city to obtain appropriations of water that will satisfy the needs resulting from a normal increase in population within a reasonable period of time." *Sheriff* seemed to allow municipalities to appropriate water beyond their immediate needs, thus treating them differently from other appropriators. Furthermore, the court held that Denver could lease water not needed for immediate use.

In Four Counties Water Users Ass'n v. Colorado River Water Conservation Dist., 414 P.2d 469 (Colo.1966), the court said that a court should not substitute its judgment as to future growth projections for that of the city itself. Second, the court held that the economic feasibility of completing a project is not a proper test to be used upon the application for a conditional decree: "If they have miscalculated and fail, the loss is theirs—if they succeed, it will be for the eternal benefit of the peoples of the state of Colorado."

Arizona requires a permit application for municipal uses to set forth "the population to be served and an *estimate of future population requirements.*" Ariz.Rev.Stat.Ann. § 45–152(B)(4) (emphasis added). The next section says that "[a]pplications for municipal uses may be approved to the exclusion of all subsequent appropriations if the estimated needs of the municipality so demand after consideration by and upon order of the director." Id., § 45–153(B). The California Water Code includes an article entitled "Preferred Priorities of Municipalities." Cal.Water Code §§ 1460–1464. The first section states: "The application for a permit by a municipality for the use of water for the municipality or the inhabitants thereof for domestic purposes shall be considered *first in right, irrespective of whether it is first in time.*" Id., § 1460 (emphasis added). The statute also requires an application for municipal water supply to "state the present population to be served, and *as near as may be, the future requirements of the city.*" Id., § 1464 (emphasis added). In Nevada, an application to appropriate water for municipal supply or for domestic use must state the approximate number of persons to be served and the approximate future requirements of that municipality. Nev.Rev.Stat.Ann. § 533.340. The state of Washington has an identical provision. Rev.Code Wash.Ann. § 90.03.-260. Oklahoma extends a municipality's right of eminent domain to include condemnation of land and water within and without its corporate limits to supply its contemplated future needs. Oregon's water laws put appropriations for hydroelectric power in the most prominent position, but also provide that the Water Resources Commission "may approve an application for a municipal water supply to the exclusion of all subsequent appropriations, if the exigencies of the case demand." Or.Rev.Stat.Ann. § 225.290 and § 537.190(2).

Colorado uses "conditional decrees" to ensure that large water projects will not lose priority to a subsequent appropriator during the typically lengthy development period before water can be put to beneficial use. The appropriator must make a showing of "reasonable diligence" to the water court every six years in order to perpetuate the conditionally decreed right. Colo.Rev.Stat. § 37–92–301(4). Failure to do so results in a cancellation of the water right. Once the water is actually put to beneficial use, the appropriator can receive an "absolute" decree dating back to the conditional decree.

CITY AND COUNTY OF DENVER v. NORTHERN COLORADO WATER CONSERVANCY DISTRICT

Supreme Court of Colorado, 1954.
130 Colo. 375, 276 P.2d 992.

[Denver appealed a decision of the District Court for Summit County awarding it a conditional decree in connection with the city's Blue River Project, which involved a proposed transmountain diversion from the Western Slope of the Rocky Mountains. Denver claimed 1600 c.f.s. with a priority date of March 21, 1914; the District Court awarded 788 c.f.s. as of June 24, 1946. On appeal, the Colorado Supreme Court addressed several issues, including Denver's need for the water, its intent to make an appropriation, and the doctrine of relation back. It then turned to Denver's demonstration of due diligence in the prosecution of the conditional decree.]

Stone, Chief Justice.

* * *

The Colorado River Water Conservation District and others protested the awarding of any decree whatever to Denver's Blue River project and here assign error to the decree awarded it on the ground that Denver now has an adequate water supply, and that a conditional decree should not be given for a larger quantity of water than it can reasonably expect to put to beneficial use. The uncontradicted evidence in the record discloses that Denver had adequate water supply at the time of the hearing without the Blue River water here sought. As to its further growth and consequent future need, there were divergent estimates, all necessarily without actual knowledge. We cannot hold that a city more than others is entitled to decree for water beyond its own needs. However, an appropriator has a reasonable time in which to effect his originally intended use as well as to complete his originally intended means of diversion, and when appropriations are sought by a growing city, regard should be given to its reasonably anticipated requirements. Van Tassel Real Estate & Livestock Co. v. City of Cheyenne, 49 Wyo. 333, 54 P.2d 906; City and County of Denver v. Sheriff, 105 Colo. 193, 96 P.2d 836. Particularly is this true in considering claims for conditional decrees. While the witnesses as to Denver's future water requirements were not in agreement, there was substantial evidence to support a finding of future need for water from the Blue River within a reasonable time. This is amply confirmed by the City's rapid subsequent growth.

* * *

In each of the plats filed by Denver as its Exhibits A, B and D, it is recited that work was commenced by survey on the 21st day of March, 1914. In its statement of claim, Denver asserts the same commencement date. However, from the evidence submitted, it appears without dispute that the 1914 date was based entirely on reconnaissance surveys made in that year by the Public Utilities Commission not followed by any construction, and in its briefs Denver now abandons that date and claims right to conditional decree to the Blue River project for 1200 second feet as of July 4, 1921, and 400 cubic feet as of October 19, 1927, the former being the date when it is contended that survey was begun on a project planned to divert 1200 second feet, but some two years before filing any plat thereof, and the latter date being the date of the filing of its plat Exhibit B, showing plan to divert 1600 second feet.

There is no evidence that any work, even of survey, on the Blue River project was begun on July 4, 1921, or at any time prior to the summer of 1922. The claim for the 1921 date is based solely on the fact that survey was started on that date on Denver's Williams Fork and Fraser River projects and the contention that those two projects and the Blue River project constitute in fact a single irrigation project, and consequently that in the determination of the date when the first step was taken, and also in the determination of reasonable diligence since such date, the three projects should be considered as a single project.

In determining the date "when the first step was taken," a survey made on the Fraser River or on the Williams Fork would of itself be no evidence of intent to appropriate water from the Blue River. Certainly such a survey in a far distant basin supplying water to another stream would constitute no notice to another appropriator of such intent. The filing of a plat of method of diversion from the Fraser or Williams Fork would be no evidence of intent to appropriate water from the Blue or notice of such intent. Therefore, there is nothing to support the contention that the priority should be dated as of July 4, 1921. At most, the priority for the Blue River project could date back only to the time when the first step was taken in construction of a project on the Blue River.

In determining reasonable diligence, also, we find no ground for holding, as urged by Denver, that the Blue River project, the Williams Fork project and Fraser River project are each units of a single project so that the construction work on those projects and the expenses incurred thereon can be considered as part of the construction of the Blue River project. Denver's claim for its Blue River project was made by survey, plat and filing entirely separate from those of its Fraser and Williams Fork projects. It seeks priority to water from an entirely separate stream, not even confluent with the Fraser River or Williams Fork except to the extent that each is ultimately a tributary of the Colorado River. It seeks water to be diverted from an entirely separate drainage basin. It was surveyed and planned after those projects. It directly affects other claimants who are protestants here but not directly affected by those projects. It is to be carried through an entirely separate conduit—the Fraser River being diverted through the Moffat Tunnel and the Williams Fork through the Jones Pass Tunnel, and the Blue, as now planned, to be carried in the Montezuma tunnel to be bored through the Continental Divide many miles to the south of the others. Its water rights are here sought to be adjudicated as entirely separate from the rights of those projects. It has even less relation to the Fraser River and Williams Fork projects than to Denver's South Platte water system with which it will share the same river channel and reservoirs. In fact, the only relation between the Blue River project and these other projects is that their several waters may ultimately rest in common filtration and concentration plants, and that by means of exchange they may be used cooperatively for supplying prior rights or filling storage reservoirs such as would be probable in the case of any other independent water right. The priority of appropriation which gives the better right under our Constitution is priority on a stream rather than on a project, and any diligence in construction to permit dating back of priority on the Blue River must be diligence relating to and promoting the Blue River appropriation. No such relation here appears. Therefore, diligence in the prosecution of the Fraser and Williams Fork projects cannot be imputed to the Blue River project. However, the fact that the City of Denver was engaged in the construction of these or other enterprises may properly be considered together with all other evidence as to existing facilities and ability of the city in determination of the issue of reasonable diligence.

* * * During the entire period from 1927 to 1946, substantially all the work done and all the money spent by Denver in connection with its Blue River project was for investigation and exploratory work or work in connection with Eastern Slope reservoirs which were not dependent on any one plan for diversion or even on Blue River water. This and similar evidence before the trial court presented substantial support to the contention of protestants that Denver had no fixed and definite plan and no definite point of diversion prior to the report and recommendation of said board in 1946, and supported the decree of the trial court consistent therewith.

As to the second question, that of diligence:

In summary, the evidence showed that the Exhibit A plan of 1923 has been abandoned without any construction whatever; that following the filing of the Exhibit B plan in 1927, no evidence of actual excavation work in connection with its proposed tunnel appeared until 1942, some fifteen years later, when a cut was made and a small exploratory tunnel was driven about 400 feet at a place then intended to be the west portal to ascertain the condition of the ground. The proposed location of the portal has since been changed and a part of the excavation has caved in. No other work was performed on the ground until July 1946 when work at the east portal of the tunnel was started. Denver's Chief Engineer testified that "That was the first actual construction work." It had been driven 2850 feet out of a total distance of approximately twenty-four miles in the period from 1946 to the date of hearing. In addition to the tunnel, Denver's plan of diversion as last approved at the time of the trial included the large Dillon Reservoir on the Blue River at the intake, plat of which was filed in 1942 but no construction begun before 1946.

As satisfying the requirement of reasonable diligence, Denver showed that after the filing of the plat in 1927, the tunnel line was staked in 1931–2, and triangulation survey monuments installed for geological studies. These surveys brought about an unfavorable report on the straight tunnel as platted and a recommendation that a dog-leg tunnel be constructed by way of Montezuma. But the new line was not staked and geologized until sometime in 1943, 1944 and 1945. Over a period from 1928 to 1948, Denver's witnesses testified that survey was made and rights of way acquired for the Two Forks Reservoir, but that reservoir is to be located on the South Platte River and, as shown in the application for right of way, was planned for regulation of that river, storage of its flood waters and power development. It has no essential connection with direct use diversion from the Blue River; even its construction would not indicate any plan for Blue River diversion or give another appropriator any notice of such plan. Between 1928 and 1932 surveys were made for power lines to carry the electrical energy proposed to be generated by the project. In 1932, right of way was granted for the twenty-three mile tunnel, but for a period of ten years no step was taken toward its construction. It appears that throughout the period from 1936 to 1941 efforts were made by the City to induce the United States Bureau of Reclamation to build the project, but without success. There was no evidence of any effort by Denver to finance the project itself prior to the year 1946, but only of efforts to induce the United States to do so.

To support its contention that this work was sufficient to satisfy the requirements of reasonable diligence, Denver cites Taussig v. Moffat Tunnel Co., 106 Colo. 384, 106 P.2d 363, wherein it was held that surveys, preparation of maps, acquiring of rights of way and options and obtaining a contract for the carriage of water through the Moffat Tunnel, drilling of test holes, clearing of timber along proposed ditch lines and other similar work was sufficient to satisfy the requirement of reasonable diligence in construction of a ditch leading to the Moffat Tunnel. However, there the party seeking diversion of the water was a private company of apparently limited resources. The dating back was apparently for a period of less than five years, and the decision of this court affirmed the finding of the trial court, holding that there was due diligence; while here, we are asked to hold that such expenditures on the part of a great city, without shown limitation upon its financial capacity, spread out over a period of nearly twenty years would require us to reverse the decision of the trial court and say that such expenditures were evidence of reasonable diligence as a matter of law.

Kinney, in his great work on irrigation, says: "Probably the best definition of the word diligence was given by Lewis, C. J., in rendering the opinion in an early Nevada case, Ophir Silver Min. Co. v. Carpenter, 4 Nev. 534. It is there defined as 'the steady application to business of any kind, constant effort to accomplish any undertaking.' 'It is the doing of an act or series of acts with all possible expedition, with no delay except such as may be incident to the work itself.' " Kinney on Irrigation and Water Rights, Vol. 2, § 735.

Our statute authorizing conditional decrees requires that each claimant shall offer proof in support of his claim and "if it shall appear that any claimant * * * has prosecuted his claims of appropriation and the financing and construction of his enterprise with reasonable diligence", 35 C.S.A. c. 90, § 195, the court shall enter decree determining the priority of right.

It is undisputed that during a period of about twenty years, Denver had not even begun the actual construction of its project and had made no effort whatever as appears from the record towards financing it, but only a laudable but fruitless attempt after nine years of inaction to induce the United States Reclamation Service to finance it for the joint use of Denver and the South Platte Water Users Association. Meanwhile others have worked diligently and long to put a part of this water to actual use. The record before us does not show such conclusive evidence of "steady application" to the business of constructing the project or of such "constant effort to accomplish" it as to require us to hold that the trial court erred in refusal to date back Denver's appropriation, to the loss of such prior users. On the contrary, in order to sustain Denver's claim, we should have to establish as a law of Colorado that a great city or a great corporation, by the filing of a plat of a water diversion plan and the fitful continuance of surveys and exploratory operations, could paralyze all development in a river basin for a period of nineteen years without excavating a single shovel full of dirt in actual construction and without taking any step towards bond issue or other financing plan of its own for carrying out its purpose; that for nineteen years no farmer could build a ditch to develop his farm and no other city or industry could construct a project for use of water in that area without facing loss of their water when and if the city or corporation which filed the plat should actually construct its project. This we cannot do.

* * *

Accordingly, the decree of the trial court herein is affirmed.   * * *

MOORE, JUSTICE (dissenting).

I agree generally with the views expressed by Mr. Chief Justice STONE in the opinion written by him, except for the disposition which he makes concerning the claim of the City and County of Denver. * * *

* * *

In fact, as we pointed out in the Taussig case, a conditional decree may be necessary to furnish that "reasonable assurance" essential to financing a private project. We see no reason why public funds are not entitled to equal assurance.

The question under discussion cannot be answered in terms applicable to all controversies. The facts must govern each individual case. The basis for examining the facts, under the law of Colorado as announced by our Court over the years, may well include the following:

(a) The appropriator's acts should evidence a fixed and definite intention to take a fixed amount of water for application to a beneficial use.

(b) A change in plan, which indicates a lack of fixed purpose or which shows only a general desire without a fixed determination to fulfill the desire, would not support an appropriation.

(c) Changes undertaken with the apparent intent to improve or make more efficient or less costly the whole work to be undertaken, should be regarded as the natural diligence of a prudent man rather than the want of constancy in the prosecution of the undertaking.

Within these three pertinent principles I think it is abundantly clear that, at least from and after the 19th day of October, 1927, the City and County of Denver made no change in its plan to develop the water right claimed, which would amount to a relinquishment of the plan and purpose then fixed upon to appropriate 1600 second feet of water.

* * *

It appears * * * that the test of the extent to which work on one part of a water system may properly relate to another for the purpose of determining due diligence, is whether the parts of the work relate to a single integrated purpose intimately enough that progress on one part has a direct bearing upon another part. What we are really considering is whether or not the work done is within the limits of what is reasonably to be considered as customary to an enterprise unified under single management * * *.

From an examination of the whole record it appears that Denver, with respect to its Blue River project has done what might reasonably have been expected of any city similarly situated. * * *

* * * [T]he majority opinion brushed off most pertinent and undisputed evidence, as well as facts concerning which our Court has judicial knowledge, concerning the desperate need, in the early years of the 1930 decade, for speedy increases in the water supply of the city, and the heavy demands upon the city for completion of developments of other related works for the diversion of water from streams tributary to the Colorado river. * * * Unmentioned is the fact, which every citizen then living well knows, that in 1929 the whole nation trembled and lay prostrate in depression; that the public treasuries were empty; that for years thereafter any attempt to finance such a large undertaking upon the local level would have been sheer folly; and that the only hope for resources sufficient to warrant a start at construction was to seek the financial backing of the United States. In those years all business, both public and private, looked only to Washington for rescue from total collapse.

At about the time when another approach to the financial problem might reasonably have been expected to succeed, World War II broke out and thereafter for several years the productive energies of all the people were concentrated on the war effort. Men and materials were not to be had for any development of this kind, which could possibly wait. Just as soon as the conflict ended and war demands relaxed, construction of the tunnel began, and, despite inadequate financing and disappointments, the city has gone forward with the work.   * * *

NOTES

1.   Are the policies supporting the relation back doctrine furthered by the decision in the principal case? What is the practical effect of limiting Denver's right to the tunnel's capacity? Are future water projects likely to be more or less costly? Efficient?

2.   Since the principal case, the concept of due diligence in connection with conditional decrees in Colorado has undergone a substantial evolution, commensurate, at least at first, with Justice Moore's dissent. In Metropolitan Suburban Water Users Ass'n v. Colorado River Water Conservation Dist., 365 P.2d 273 (Colo.1961), the court treated Metro's Homestake Project and its Eagle-Arkansas River Project as one "over-all integral plan" and granted a conditional right for the whole project relating back to the date the original surveys were begun, even though the evidence indicated that not all parts of the project had been worked on with equal diligence. In Colorado River Water Conservation Dist. v. Twin Lakes Reservoir and Canal Co., 506 P.2d 1226 (Colo.1973), the court again held that the priority belongs to the total project (citing *Metro*), and added that occasional changes that do not drastically alter or constitute abandonment of the overall plan are permissible. The same year, however, in Orchard Mesa Irr. Dist. v. City and County of Denver, 511 P.2d 25 (Colo.1973), the court indicated that stricter standards might be applied in future diligence cases. In cancelling a conditional decree where no steps had been taken for fifty years to apply the decreed water to a beneficial use, the court stated that a record showing only a hope to use the water, but no concrete action to finalize the intended appropriation, was insufficient to show diligence.

Orchard Mesa was cited with approval in Colorado River Water Conservation Dist. v. City and County of Denver, 640 P.2d 1139 (Colo. 1982), where conditional rights were cancelled when no on-site work or activity specifically related to individual parts of a general water development scheme were performed during the diligence period. Litigation and political activities designed to promote the overall project were held insufficient to constitute due diligence, in the absence of efforts to develop each conditionally decreed right individually.

3.   One purpose of placing statutory time limits on those who seek the benefit of the relation-back rule is to prevent speculation. In Colorado, where there is no definite time limit, conditional decrees have been used to reserve a priority date while the would-be appropriator shops for a specific beneficial use.

In Colorado River Water Conservation Dist. v. Vidler Tunnel Water Co., 594 P.2d 566 (Colo.1979), the trial court had awarded Vidler a conditional storage decree for 156,238 acre-feet of water for its proposed Sheephorn Reservoir on the mainstem of the Colorado River. Vidler planned to bring water, except for a portion it intended to use on its own lands, to the Eastern Slope for sale to various municipalities. The Colorado Supreme Court disallowed the conditional decree, because Vidler had not demonstrated an intent to put the water to a beneficial use. Noting that there was "no firm contractual commitment from any municipality to use any of the water," the court added:

> While Vidler's efforts possibly went beyond mere speculation, there was no sufficient evidence that it represented anyone committed to actual beneficial use of the water not intended for use on its own land. Indeed, there is not even evidence of firm sale arrangements. In essence, water rights are sought here on the assumption that growing population will produce a general need for more water in the future. But Vidler has no contract or agency relationship justifying its claim to represent those whose future needs are asserted.

Id. at 569. The conditional decree for water intended to be used on land owned by Vidler was approved, however. The legislative response to *Vidler* is Colo.Rev.Stat. § 37–92–305(9)(b):

> No claim for a conditional water right may be recognized or a decree therefor granted except to the extent that it is established that the waters can be and will be diverted, stored or otherwise captured, possessed and controlled and will be beneficially used and that the project can and will be completed with diligence and within a reasonable period of time.

The Colorado Supreme Court has applied this statute, known as the "can and will" requirement to defeat an application where the only way there would be sufficient unappropriated water was with an augmentation plan (providing existing water users with another source of supply) that the applicant had not yet concluded. Lionelle v. Southeastern Colorado Water Conservancy Dist., 676 P.2d 1162 (Colo.1984), and Southeastern Colorado Water Conservancy Dist. v. Florence, 688 P.2d 715 (Colo.1984).

What factors should a court consider when determining whether or not an applicant can and will perfect a water right? How can one be reasonably certain that the claimed waters will be diverted and applied to beneficial use and the project completed diligently within a reasonable period of time? Must financing be secure? How much assurance is necessary that federal permits will be granted? Is it necessary to have firm contracts for all of the water that will be developed? Enough water to make the project financially feasible?

4. For a discussion of conditional decrees, see Public Service Company of Colorado v. Board of Water Works of Pueblo, et al., 831 P.2d 470 (Colo.1992).

STATE ex rel. REYNOLDS v. MIRANDA

Supreme Court of New Mexico, 1972.
83 N.M. 443, 493 P.2d 409.

MONTOYA, JUSTICE.

Across the defendant's property from east to west runs a water course called the Abo Wash, which has its source in the mountains approximately 18 miles from the Rio Grande River into which it empties. Following certain rains, water would flow intermittently through the wash, across defendant's property, and into the Rio Grande River. In earlier times, farmers would turn their stock into the wash to graze upon the tall, thick grass which grew in the wash and, in the fall season, the farmers would cut and store the grass for winter use. Sometime after World War I, a natural arroyo was formed and water flowing into the wash was naturally diverted from the wash into the arroyo. As a consequence, irrigation of the grassland began to decline. From that time until the present, the wash has diminished as a source of pasture for stock.

In 1969, defendant filed a declaration of ownership of water rights, claiming perfection thereof prior to 1907, and filed two applications to change the point of diversion, seeking to drill two water wells to be used for irrigating lands belonging to defendant.

Defendant's claims evidently are based upon the fact that his predecessors had made beneficial use of the grasses grown in and near the wash and that this would be a sufficient appropriation to entitle him to water rights in the Rio Grande Underground Basin. This contention is bolstered by testimony of two witnesses who can recall defendant's predecessors using the grass from the wash prior to 1907. However, neither witness could recall any man-made diversion of the waters from the wash, nor could defendant offer evidence of man-made diversion.

* * *

In support of his contention that man-made diversion is not necessary to appropriate water rights, defendant relies upon Town of Genoa v. Westfall, 141 Colo. 533, 349 P.2d 370 (1960). There an injunction was sought to prohibit the town from diverting waters forming the source of certain springs located on plaintiff's property. The court found that the water being diverted into town wells was a tributary to the springs on plaintiff's land, and that plaintiff, by watering of cattle and domestic use, had appropriated the water for a beneficial use. Defendant in the instant case cites the following language from Town of Genoa v. Westfall, supra:

> "It is not necessary in every case for an appropriator of water to construct ditches or artificial ways through which the water might be taken from the stream in order that a valid appropriation be made. The only indispensable requirements are that the appropriator intends to use the waters for a beneficial purpose and actually applies them to that use."

We believe that defendant's reliance on the Westfall case is misplaced. The Colorado court has established the dual requirements that the appropriator intend to use the water, and that he actually apply it to a beneficial use in order for man-made diversion to be unnecessary to an appropriation of water. Even if man-made diversion were unnecessary, defendant would be required to show that his predecessors in interest intended to appropriate water for beneficial use. The mere cutting of the grasses would not be sufficient to manifest an intention to appropriate the water for beneficial use, nor can it be said that defendant's predecessors applied the waters to beneficial use by grazing cattle upon the grasses in the wash. These acts only manifested an intention to reap nature's bounty gratuitously provided by water flowing through the Abo Wash, not to appropriate the water itself. The lack of intention to appropriate the water in the wash is also buttressed by evidence in the record which shows that defendant and his predecessors in interest made no attempt to divert water from the arroyo into the wash when the waters flowing into the wash became diverted into the arroyo. The grazing on and harvesting of grasses does not constitute appropriation of the water in the Abo Wash.

* * *

We hold that man-made diversion, together with intent to apply water to beneficial use and actual application of the water to beneficial use, is necessary to claim water rights by appropriation in New Mexico for agricultural purposes.

The decision of the trial court is affirmed.

It is so ordered.

NOTES

1. If Miranda had immediately redirected waters back into the wash after the arroyo formed, would that have made a significant difference? Suppose Miranda and his predecessors in the principal case tossed rocks in the wash on his property to cause the runoff to spread out across the fields where he harvested grasses. Would that have satisfied the diversion requirement?

2. Town of Genoa v. Westfall, discussed in the principal case, involved stockwatering. Because no artificial means of diversion are usually involved, stockwatering has been one focus of the debate regarding the need for a diversion. Most states allow it to be the basis of an appropriation. In R.T. Nahas Co. v. Hulet, 674 P.2d 1036, 1043 (Idaho 1983), the court concluded that "we cannot justify imposing an economic burden, by requiring a diversion, which will not advance the interests of the public by promoting more efficient use of water, or reducing waste."

3. What policies are served by requiring appropriators to divert water? In light of the judicial and legislative recognition of a variety of acts short of diversion of water from the stream in order to demonstrate due diligence, does the diversion requirement have a purpose? One of the editors has suggested that the original function of the require-

ment—to give notice to subsequent appropriators—is better performed by modern permitting and recordation systems than by an actual diversion requirement. A. Dan Tarlock, Appropriation for Instream Flow Maintenance: A Progress Report on 'New' Public Western Water Rights, 1978 Utah L.Rev. 211.

NOTE: WATER STORAGE RIGHTS

In the arid West, storage of water is treated as an appropriation of water from a stream. While storage alone is not a beneficial use, storage for future use in irrigation or other beneficial purposes is considered a beneficial use.

Direct flow rights attach to water that is put to immediate beneficial use, and often are expressed in terms of the rate of flow, such as cubic feet per second, though they may also be defined by maximum volume in acre-feet. Storage rights, on the other hand, apply to water that is retained for later beneficial use, and are expressed in terms of storage volume, such as acre-feet. Storage rights may also be limited by the rate of flow and times in which water may be stored.

Storage rights, like direct flow rights, are given priorities and obtained through the same application or adjudication process. Some states require separate permits for storage and for application of water to a beneficial use. (E.g., Arizona, Nevada and Wyoming). In some states (e.g., Colorado) the developer of a storage facility may obtain conditional water rights fixing the priority at an early date, subject to a requirement of reasonably diligent completion of the project. Most states also regulate dam construction to ensure that a safe design is carried out. Most also consider fish and wildlife impacts and a variety of public interest factors. Federal regulatory statutes are usually implicated by on-stream storage facilities. See pages 728–29 infra.

Storage rights attach to on-channel and off-channel facilities. On-channel storage involves retaining streamflow behind a dam in a streambed. Off-channel storage involves a diversion through a canal or pipeline to a storage facility away from the stream. An offstream reservoir by definition involves diverting water from the stream. Utilizing structures to store water in onstream reservoirs is also considered a diversion, even though the water is merely detained, rather than actually diverted.

Storage and direct flow rights are integrated into a single administrative system so that rights to divert for direct use and rights to divert to storage are fully respected. A Colorado decision summarizes:

> The statute recognizes two classes of appropriations for irrigation, one for ditches diverting water to be used directly from the stream, and one for the storage of water, to be used subsequently. Holbrook Irr. Dist. v. Ft. Lyon Canal Co., 269 P. 574 (Colo.1928). To the amount that water when available is to be diverted directly to its use, a direct use decree must be sought. To the amount that it is to be held in a reservoir for later use, a storage decree must be sought. Where water is stored in a channel reservoir, a ditch headed in such reservoir has no right by virtue of direct use decree

to deplete such storage, but may properly take water from the reservoir by virtue of such decree only in the amount of the current inflow from sources subject to such direct use decree to the ditch. City & County of Denver v. Northern Colorado Water Conservancy Dist., 276 P.2d 992, 999 (Colo.1954). In City of Westminster v. Church, 445 P.2d 52 (Colo.1968), the city was allowed to change the use of its storage rights that had been used seasonally in agriculture by the previous owner to use for municipal supply. The Supreme Court said: "We hold that the trial court erred in ruling that the storage rights were limited to historical use. A reservoir right permits one filling of the reservoir per year. Change of use does not create a greater burden as to storage water." 445 P.2d at 58.

The *Westminster* holding was clarified in Southeastern Colorado Water Conservancy Dist. v. Fort Lyon Canal Co., 720 P.2d 133 (Colo. 1986), which rejected the broad assertion that the place of storage may be changed without considering historical return flow patterns. The court held that "diminished return flows, whether due to change in direct-flow or storage rights, must be considered when calculating the amount of injury to other appropriators." 720 P.2d at 146–47. Thus, although a purchaser of storage rights may use the full "paper decree" quantity (even if it was not used by the prior owner), the return flows may not be changed to injure other appropriators.

Under the one-fill rule, a reservoir may only be filled once a year. In other words, the reservoir appropriation to impound water is limited to the capacity of the reservoir, though the reservoir may be alternately filling and draining down throughout the year. The sum of all additions to the reservoir count against the single filling allowed under the rule.

Where the rule is applied strictly, as in Colorado, inefficiency may result. Larger reservoirs may be built because reservoirs may not be successively refilled during the year. Further, the one-filling restriction may limit creative means of obtaining water. For example, in Orchard City Irr. Dist. v. Whitten, 361 P.2d 130 (Colo.1961), a reservoir owner had decrees on two streams in the watershed, so that water from the second stream could make up for deficiencies in the first stream during dry years. The state engineer had approved rights equal to twice the storage capacity of the reservoir. This was disallowed by the court, however, as a "double filling." The court summarized Colorado precedent: "a reservoir is limited to one annual filling from whatever source the water may be derived." 361 P.2d at 137.

The inefficiency of the one-fill rule is compounded if carryover storage (water remaining in the reservoir from one year to another) is debited against the single filling. If it is not so debited, a reservoir can have a long term storage pool to protect against drought and an "active pool" that will be allowed to be filled and drawn down several times, with fillings cumulatively not to exceed the capacity of the reservoir.

Should the same rules apply to storage for hydroelectric power as for irrigation? A is a hydroelectric power generator located low on a stream and holding storage rights. For most of the year, A does not retain water in the reservoir for more than a few days, allowing it to flow through the turbines as necessary to generate power. Is A nevertheless considered to have "stored" the cumulative total of any waters held behind the dam in excess of natural flow, no matter how briefly, for purposes of the one-fill rule? There is surprisingly little law on this subject, probably because the operations of hydroelectric facilities are heavily regulated. See pages 709–28, infra; e.g., Idaho Power Co. v. Idaho, Dept. of Water Resources, 661 P.2d 741 (Idaho 1983).

2. The Evolving Doctrine of Beneficial Use

"Beneficial use" is said to be the basis, measure, and limit of an appropriative right. State constitutions, statutes, and judicial decisions throughout the western states recognize the concept. Is beneficial use the same as the reasonable use requirement applied in riparian states? (Chapter 2, pages 82–85.)

In the settlement of the West, the concept of beneficial use had both an allocative and a distributive function. The initially important societal uses that led to the doctrine were mining and agriculture. Of course, domestic uses have always been the most important to society but because they demanded so little water no legal doctrines were needed to protect them. State constitutions and statutes enshrined a utilitarian list of beneficial uses, indicating purposes to which water rights were properly allocated. But because the list was not complete or detailed, new and nontraditional uses of water sometimes required a legislative or judicial determination of whether they were "beneficial." In the mid-twentieth century, for example, recreation was added to the list (usually by statute), and this ultimately led to efforts by the western states to protect instream flows, a concept that challenged basic aspects of traditional appropriation doctrine. To the nineteenth century mind that created the doctrine, leaving water in place was simply not a use. Societal values had changed, however, and with them changed the interpretation of "beneficial use."

The distributive function of the beneficial use requirement was to promote widespread access to scarce supplies. Under the pure appropriation system as it was originally applied, the beneficial nature of a use was not dependent on the amount of water in the stream, nor were comparisons made with the uses of other appropriators. But a common theme running through the cases is that wasteful uses were not beneficial. This judgment can only be made in the context of surrounding use patterns. Theoretically, every water user operates under a threat that a water use can be challenged as wasteful and thereby held to be in excess of a decreed appropriative right. A successful challenge would result in more water being left in the stream for the benefit of junior appropriators. Such challenges have been rare, and success even rarer. A more seriously perceived threat is from non-use. Appropriators have operated under the specter of "use it or lose it," not "use it efficiently or lose it." Thus, far greater quantities of water than are needed to fulfill particular purposes have been diverted in the false hope of protecting rights to use quantities of water awarded in permits or decrees. In fact, however, recent cases indicate that water rights are not "protected" by wasteful overapplication.

The cases in the first subsection illustrate the response of courts to instream uses that were not traditionally considered to be "beneficial." The next subsection includes cases that deal with the anti-waste notions inherent in beneficial use.

a. Instream Flows

Cases involving stockwatering in the stream, irrigation by natural flooding, storage in on-stream reservoirs, and the like all ultimately involve traditional consumptive uses of water that are identifiable and quantifiable. But there is an increasing trend toward seeking legal protection for the maintenance of flows of water in the stream for fish, wildlife, recreation, and aesthetic purposes. Are the issues fundamentally different?

EMPIRE WATER & POWER CO. v. CASCADE TOWN CO.

United States Court of Appeals, Eighth Circuit, 1913.
205 Fed. 123.

[Cascade Town Company was the owner of a tourist resort located along Cascade Creek near the City of Colorado Springs. The creek descended into the resort rapidly from the mountains through a deep, beautiful canyon whose "floor and sides are covered with an exceptionally luxuriant growth of trees, shrubbery, and flowers. This exceptional vegetation is produced by the flow of Cascade creek through the cañon and the mist and spray from its falls." A hydroelectric power company proposed to make a diversion from Cascade Creek upstream from the defendant's property to generate electric power. Cascade sued for an injunction, which was granted by the trial court, and the power company appealed.]

Hook, Circuit Judge.

* * *

In this branch of the case the controversy was over the character of complainant's use, its relation to that proposed by defendants, and the extent of complainant's appropriation and application of the water. It is urged that a use for a summer resort is not a beneficial use for either domestic or agricultural purposes. Counsel say that the views and standards of the early settlers were reflected in the state Constitution, and that it should be construed accordingly; that they did not plan for rest and recreation, and that to them "domestic" had to do with sustenance for man and beast, and cleanliness; and that "agricultural" related to the raising of crops. We think such a view is too narrow. If the commerce clause of the federal Constitution had been construed in that way, much of the growth of this country would have been arrested. In framing Constitutions wisdom frequently requires the use of general terms, which should be held as progressively adaptable to natural development and as open to embrace new instances as they arise and come clearly within the spirit of the provisions. * * * Places such as that described here, favored by climatic conditions, improved by the work of man, and designed to promote health by affording rest and relaxation are assuredly beneficial. They are relatively as important as sanitariums or hospitals, and should not be dismissed by calling them mere resorts for idleness. They are a recognized feature of the times, are important in their influence upon health, and multitudes of people avail themselves of them from necessity. Cascade is well described as a place of this kind. With its railroad station, hotels, cottages, waterworks, park, roads, and trails and its 12,000 or 15,000 annual visitors, it is a summer city. That it is not an incorporated municipality, but is largely a private venture, is, we think, unimportant. Nor need the purpose to which the waters of the stream are devoted be a single one of those named in the classification in the Constitution. It need not be exclusively domestic nor exclusively agricultural. It may be and is both, like that of the ordinary city with its homes, business places, parks, and public grounds.

It is clear that complainant intended to appropriate the waters of the stream to its purpose. The intent was openly manifested by the extensive improvement of its property by buildings, roads, etc., in reliance, not only on the use of the water in the ditches that were constructed, but also on the continued natural falls and flow of the stream. At this point, however, we experience the most difficulty with complainant's case. The laws of Colorado are designed to prevent waste of a most valuable but limited natural resource, and to confine the use to needs. By rejecting the common-law rule they deny the right of the landowner to have the stream run in its natural way without diminution. He cannot hold to all the water for the scant vegetation which lines the banks but must make the most efficient use by applying it to his land. See Schodde v. Water Co., 224 U.S. 107, a case from Idaho, where a landowner claimed the whole current of a stream to raise part of the water to his land. The case before us is exceptional, but we think complainant is not entitled to a continuance of the falls solely for their scenic beauty. The state laws proceed upon more material lines. Complainant also relies upon the distribution by the falls of moisture for the trees and other vegetable growth on its lands, which it has extensively improved. As we have said, its intent to appropriate the waters has been shown by its expenditures and improvements beyond what is served by its ditches. Has there been that actual application which the law requires? Undoubtedly a landowner may rely upon an efficient application by nature, and need do no more than affirmatively to avail himself of it (Thomas v. Guiraud, 6 Colo. 530; Larimer, etc., Co. v. People, 8 Colo. 614, 9 Pac. 794); but the use in that way should not be unnecessarily or wastefully excessive. If all the water flowing over the falls, directly applied to the lands in the usual way of irrigation, would be required to produce the effect of the distributed mist and spray as now utilized, we think defendants would have no right to divert it for a manufacturing purpose. If nature accomplishes a result which is recognized and utilized, a change of process by man would seem unnecessary. But the trial court based its decision of this branch of the case largely upon the artistic value of the falls, and made no inquiry into the effectiveness of the use of the water in the way adopted as compared with the customary methods of irrigation. In all other respects the conclusions of the court were in accord with the views we have expressed. It may be that if the attention of the lawmakers had been directed to such natural objects of great beauty they would have sought to preserve them, but we think the dominant idea was utility, liberally and not narrowly regarded, and we are constrained to follow it.

* * *

The decree of the trial court is reversed and remanded for further proceedings in conformity with this opinion.

NOTES

1. What issues was the trial court to consider on remand?

2. The widespread benefits of recreation in the western states, economic benefits as well as public enjoyment, have cast the plausibility of instream flow rights in a new light. At the same time, a raised environmental consciousness augered for legal recognition of rights to maintain streamflows. The following case confronts the potential obstacles of a legal regime crafted in the nineteenth century to recognition of such instream rights.

IDAHO DEPARTMENT OF PARKS v. IDAHO DEPARTMENT OF WATER ADMINISTRATION

Supreme Court of Idaho, 1974.
96 Idaho 440, 530 P.2d 924.

SHEPARD, CHIEF JUSTICE.

This is an appeal and a cross-appeal from a judgment of the district court in an action wherein the Idaho Department of Parks, pursuant to statute, sought to appropriate in trust for the people of Idaho certain unappropriated waters of the Malad Canyon. * * *

In 1971 the Idaho Legislature enacted I.C. § 67–4307. In essence the statute directs the Department of Parks of the State of Idaho to appropriate in trust for the people of Idaho certain unappropriated natural waters of the Malad Canyon in Gooding County, Idaho. Additionally, it declares (1) that the preservation of the waters for scenic beauty and recreation uses is a beneficial use of water; (2) that the public use of those waters is of greater priority than any other use save domestic consumption, and (3) that the unappropriated state land located between the highwater marks on either bank of these waters is to be used and preserved in its present condition as a recreational site for the people of Idaho.

Pursuant to the statute the Idaho Department of Parks filed an application for a permit to appropriate the waters specified by the statute. The waters in question arise in part at least from springs in the canyon and are natural waters. There appears no argument but that there is unappropriated water available for appropriation.

That application was protested by the Idaho Water Users Association, Twin Falls Canal Company, and the North Side Canal Company under the provisions of I.C. § 42–203. Those parties are cross-appellants herein and are hereafter designated "Water Users." * * *

II.

The Water Users * * * assert error in the trial court's determination that the preservation of aesthetic values and recreational opportunities for the citizens of this state is a beneficial use in the sense that they will support an appropriative water right under the Idaho Constitution.

The foundation of the Water Users' argument is that the five uses specified in article 15, section 3 of the Constitution, i.e., domestic, agriculture, mining, manufacturing and power are exclusive and thus are the only uses that are cognizable beneficial uses under our Constitution. We reject that argument.

We find no support for the position of the Water Users in the discussions reported in II Idaho Constitutional Convention, Proceedings and Debate 1889 (1912), as pertaining to article 15, section 3. It appears that insofar as particular uses were mentioned in the debates, discussion was confined to the establishment of preferences for certain uses over others under certain circumstances. Such establishment of preferences appears to be a common feature of water law in the west. While it is well established in western water law that an appropriation of water must be made for a "beneficial use," nevertheless in Idaho at least the generic term "beneficial use" has never been judicially or statutorily defined. Our research does not disclose any case in which any court has attempted to define the term "beneficial use."

Consideration of the statute in question herein indicates clearly that the legislature has declared that "[t]he preservation of water in the area described for its scenic beauty and recreational purposes necessary and desirable for all citizens of the state * * * is hereby declared to be a beneficial use of such water." We note that numerous other western states have recognized through legislation that utilization of water for scenic or recreational purposes is a beneficial use. Such legislation in other states carries no binding effect on this court but, in the absence of persuasive case law to the contrary, it would appear to indicate that the use of water for providing recreational and aesthetic pleasure represents an emerging recognition in this and other states of social values and benefits from the use of water. The statute in question herein recognizes aesthetic and recreational values and benefits which will accrue to the people of the state in respect to the waters of Malad Canyon. We find no basis upon which to disturb that declaration of the legislature that in this instance those values and benefits constitute "beneficial uses." The decision of the district court upon this issue is affirmed.

* * *

We now reach the final issue as to whether there must be an actual physical diversion of the water in order to support an appropriation. * * *

The precise language of article 15, section 3, does not bear on this question but merely declares "[t]he right to divert and appropriate the unappropriated waters of any natural stream to beneficial use, shall never be denied * * *." * * *

We hold that our Constitution does not require actual physical diversion. We deem it clear that until the time of the enactment of the statute in question herein Idaho's statutory scheme regulating the appropriation of water has contemplated an actual physical diversion. * * *

In the statute before us, I.C. § 67–4307, the Idaho legislature has clearly stated a policy at odds with its previous general statutory scheme of water appropriation. I.C. § 67–4307 directs parks "to appropriate [not 'divert and appropriate'] the unappropriated natural spring flow" of the Malad Canyon and declares the "preservation of water in the area described for its scenic beauty and recreational purposes" is a beneficial use. Furthermore, the statute states that "license shall issue at any time upon proof of beneficial use to which said waters are now dedicated." We deem it clear that the legislature intended no physical diversion of water be required in the appropriation of the subject waters.

DONALDSON, J., concurs.

BAKES, JUSTICE (concurring specially):

I concur in the result reached by Chief Justice Shepard in his plurality opinion, although not necessarily everything stated therein. Additionally, I wish to address in a different manner the question of whether or not the preservation of the waters of Malad Canyon in a natural state is a beneficial use that may be appropriated without the means of a diversion. (Parts II and III of that opinion).

The first question to be considered is whether any uses other than the uses referred to in Article 15, § 3, of the Idaho Constitution—domestic, mining, agricultural and manufacturing—can be beneficial uses of water under the Idaho Constitution. * * *

The Idaho Constitution does not explicitly answer this question. * * *

* * * I think we should look to very practical considerations in attempting to construe it. Prior to the time that the Constitution was adopted there were a number of common uses of water which were neither domestic, mining, agricultural nor manufacturing. A community would store water in a tank for use in fighting fires. The operator of a livery stable or a stockyard would water the stock kept there. Logging operations used water both to transport logs and for storage in mill ponds. Communities would use water wagons to settle dust on their dirt streets. The railroad used water for its steam engines and other uses related to the operation of the railroad. All of these uses were undoubtedly considered beneficial, but none of them were domes-

tic, mining, agricultural or manufacturing. I do not believe that by adopting Article 15, § 3, of the Idaho Constitution that it was intended that uses such as these could no longer be considered beneficial uses. * * * I therefore conclude that uses other than those enumerated in Article 15, § 3, can be beneficial uses.

The next question is whether the use at issue in this case is beneficial. * * *

With the exception of those uses elevated to beneficial status by Article 15, § 3, of the Constitution, the concept of what is or is not a beneficial use must necessarily change with changing conditions. For example, if we were now presented with a question of whether or not using water to operate a public swimming pool, a fountain, or to flood a tract to provide ice for a skating rink were beneficial uses, a good argument could be presented that such uses, although not domestic, mining, agricultural or manufacturing uses, were nevertheless beneficial. But we cannot say that such uses will always be beneficial because conditions might so change that these uses would be an unjustifiable use of water needed for other purposes. The notion of beneficiality of use must include a requirement of reasonableness. With the exception of the uses implicitly declared to be beneficial by Article 15, § 3, there is always a possibility that other uses beneficial in one era will not be in another and *vice versa*. As stated in Tulare Irrig. Dist. v. Lindsay-Strathmore Irrig. Dist., 3 Cal.2d 489, 45 P.2d 972, 1007 (1935):

> "What is a beneficial use, of course, depends upon the facts and circumstances of each case. What may be a reasonable beneficial use, where water is present in excess of all needs, would not be a reasonable beneficial use in an area of great scarcity and great need. What is a beneficial use at one time may, because of changed conditions, become a waste of water at a later time."

What we have decided in this case is that the use now before us, although not specifically listed in Article 15, § 3, of the Constitution, is beneficial because, considering today's circumstances, the legislative classification is reasonable based on the record. I would restrict today's holding to the narrow proposition that the use before us is beneficial so long as, and only so long as, the circumstances of water use in the state have not changed to the extent that it is no longer reasonable to continue this use at the expense of more desirable uses for more urgent needs. * * *

Where an appropriative water right does not require a diversion to make it effective and beneficial, in the absence of a statute requiring a diversion there appears to be no practical reason why a diversion should be required. * * * If a beneficial use can be made of the water in its natural channel, Article 15, § 3, should not require the superfluous effort of construction of a diversion as a precondition for obtaining an appropriation. However, in an appropriation without a diversion, the right acquired is not to the stream flow as was the case under the riparian system, but to the use of a specific amount of water which is the subject of the right.   That amount must be a reasonable and efficient use of the water.

* * *

DONALDSON, J., concurs.

* * *

McQUADE, JUSTICE, (dissenting).

* * *

It is significant that the conjunctive was used when the Constitution was written, i.e., divert *and* appropriate rather than the disjunctive, i.e., divert *or* appropriate.   In the absence of any contrary evidence, we should presume that the framers of the Idaho Constitution chose the conjunctive deliberately and that they intended it be accorded its ordinary meaning.

McFADDEN, JUSTICE (dissenting).

* * *

In my view, the so-called "appropriation" authorized by I.C. § 67–4307 constitutes a denial of the constitutional right to appropriate the unappropriated waters of the Malad Canyon Springs.

I recognize that the state, acting in its proprietary capacity, may appropriate water without offending Article 15, section 3; but as in the case of private appropriators, the state's appropriative right depends upon the application of water to a "beneficial use."   In this case, however, the state agency is directed to hold unappropriated waters "in trust for the people of the state" for "scenic beauty and recreational purposes."   I.C. § 67–4307.   If the state were to hold unappropriated waters in trust for these purposes, it certainly would not be acting in a proprietary capacity; it would be doing nothing more than it already had a duty to do in its sovereign capacity.

* * * Under Article 15, section 3 of the Idaho Constitution, water held by the state in its sovereign capacity—even though being beneficially used by the general public—is subject to being appropriated for specific private (or proprietary) beneficial uses.   Thus, in-stream public use of unappropriated water for recreational purposes and for scenic beauty is subject to diminution by the exercise of the constitutional right to appropriate water for private (or proprietary) beneficial uses.
* * *

[A] reservation by the state of unappropriated waters is completely unauthorized by our Constitution.   Unlike the constitutions of some other western states, Idaho's Constitution does not provide that the right to appropriate "shall never be denied *except when such denial is demanded by the public interest.*" [1]   Our Constitution provides that the right to appropriate unappropriated waters "*shall never be denied,*

---

1. Neb.Const. art. XV, § 6; see also Wyo. Const. art. 8, § 3 ("No appropriation shall be denied except when such denial is demanded by the public interests").

except that the state may regulate and limit the use thereof *for power purposes.*" Art. 15, sec. 3, Idaho Const. (emphasis added).

The Idaho provision makes an exception only for power purposes—not for the demands of the public interest (and not for the purposes of recreation and scenic beauty). To allow the state to in effect reserve water from appropriation in furtherance of non-proprietary, non-power purposes—when the framers of the Constitution contemplated that private beneficial users could appropriate water being held by the state in its sovereign capacity—amounts to nothing less than a denial of the constitutional right to appropriate the "unappropriated waters" of any natural stream. "In other words, the state cannot by legislative act authorize its own agency to *monopolize or withdraw the very rights that section 3 of article 15 of the Constitution says 'shall never be denied' the people of the state.*" State Water Conservation Bd. v. Enking, 56 Idaho 722, 732, 58 P.2d 779, 783 (1936). The proper means to authorize such a withdrawal (or "appropriation") is to amend the Constitution to so provide.

It is beyond dispute that scenic beauty and recreation are both of vital importance to modern day life in Idaho. But this does not ipso facto mean the state has the right to promote these beneficial ends by withdrawing waters from appropriation, given the guarantee contained in the Idaho Constitution. I note, however, that the effect of a proposed appropriation upon scenic beauty and recreation can and should be considered in determining whether the use contemplated is "beneficial" within the meaning of the Constitution. Comment, *Water Appropriation for Recreation,* 1 Land & Water L.Rev. 209, 221 (1966). In other words, where the benefits of a proposed use are outweighed by the attendant detriment to scenic beauty and recreation, the use is not a "beneficial use," and the application for a permit to appropriate public waters for that use should be denied. As always, the question of beneficial use must be determined on a case by case basis, since the benefits of a particular proposed appropriation may outweigh the detriment to recreation and scenic beauty. Whether a use of water is "beneficial" is a question of fact to be resolved upon a consideration of the circumstances present in a particular case.

* * *

In conclusion, although I believe that recreation and scenic beauty can and should be taken into consideration on a case by case basis, they cannot be used as an excuse to deny all future appropriation of water for other purposes, at least until the Constitution is amended.

NOTES

1. Of what significance is it that the instream appropriation of water in the principal case was at the source of the river? By contrast, an instream appropriation of downstream water would interfere with subsequent private appropriation along the whole course of the river. Would this implicate the Idaho Constitution's provision that the "right to divert and appropriate the unappropriated waters * * * to beneficial

uses, shall never be denied"? Is there any difference analytically between a downstream appropriation by a municipality for domestic consumption, and downstream instream appropriation if there is unappropriated water available and both uses are beneficial?

2. After the Colorado Supreme Court, in Colorado River Water Conservation Dist. v. Rocky Mountain Power Co., 406 P.2d 798 (Colo. 1965), held an instream flow appropriation by the District for piscatorial purposes invalid for lack of an actual diversion, the legislature authorized the State Water Conservation Board to appropriate water for instream flows. The law (as amended) states:

> (3) Further recognizing the need to correlate the activities of mankind with some reasonable preservation of the natural environment, the Colorado water conservation board is hereby vested with the authority, on behalf of the people of the state of Colorado, to appropriate in a manner consistent with sections 5 and 6 of article XVI of the state constitution, such waters of natural streams and lakes as the board determines may be required to preserve the natural environment to a reasonable degree. * * * Prior to the initiation of any such appropriation or acquisition, the board shall request recommendations from the division of wildlife and the division of parks and outdoor recreation. The board also shall request recommendations from the United States Department of Agriculture and the United States Department of the Interior. * * *

Colo.Rev.Stat. § 37–92–102(3).

The bill also deleted reference to "diversion" in the definition of "appropriation" (Colo.Rev.Stat. § 37–92–102(3)) and changed the definition of beneficial use to include instream flows:

> "Beneficial use" is the use of that amount of water that is reasonable and appropriate under reasonably efficient practices to accomplish without waste the purpose for which the appropriation is lawfully made and, without limiting the generality of the foregoing, includes the impoundment of water for recreational purposes, including fishery or wildlife. For the benefit and enjoyment of present and future generations, "beneficial use" shall also include the appropriation by law of such minimum flows between specific points or levels for natural streams and lakes as are required to preserve the natural environment to a reasonable degree.

Given the standard in the statute how much discretion does the Board have in setting the amount of minimum flow? Could it appropriate all of the water flowing in a fishing stream used by a thousand fishermen and thereby preclude a 50,000 barrel-per-day oil shale plant? Could it acquire the rights to releases from a dam to maintain a constant flow beneficial to recreational boaters in a stream that seasonally experiences great fluctuations?

3. Other western states are enacting instream flow statutes and including instream flows in their water planning. The approaches differ widely.

Montana has authorized state and federal agencies to apply to the Board of Natural Resources and Conservation to reserve water for instream uses, and the state has reserved substantial amounts in the Yellowstone Basin. Mont. Code Ann. § 85–2–316. The scope of the power can be seen in a 1979 amendment that limited minimum flow reservations to 50% of the annual flow of gaged streams. The section was again modified in 1985 to restrict reservations to portions of five rivers, including the Yellowstone and Missouri. Oregon very early identified specific waterways for special protection, by withdrawing water from appropriation. Or. Rev. Stat. §§ 538.200; 538.270. Other states allow the designation of "scenic river areas," "wild rivers," or "free-flowing rivers." Okla. Stat. Ann. 82 §§ 1451–1458; Calif. Pub. Res. Code §§ 5093.50–5093.69. In addition to treating some waterways specifically, Oregon now allows the Water Resources Board to withdraw waters in all streams from appropriation. Or. Rev. Stat. § 536.410. Washington also allows administrative withdrawals of waters from appropriation for base flows. Wash.Rev. Code Ann. § 90.22.010.

Integration of instream flow rights as "appropriations" with priorities (rather than reserving or withdrawing water from appropriation) has not been widely accepted outside Colorado as yet. Montana formerly had a system of state appropriation of instream flows from 1947 until the law was amended in 1973 to provide for reservations of flows. This prevents any new appropriations of unappropriated water for instream flows. Wyoming has passed a law similar to Colorado's, allowing new appropriations and acquisition of existing rights by the State Division of Water Development, but it limits the quantities of flows to those necessary for fisheries. Wyo. Stat. § 41–3–1001. The statute permits appropriations for consumptive beneficial uses to the detriment of instream flow appropriations, however, in stream sections within a mile upstream of state boundaries or certain reservoirs. Utah has enacted a statute allowing existing appropriations to be transferred to the State Division of Wildlife Resources for instream flows with the same priorities as the established right. Utah Code Ann. § 73–3–3(11).

4. Most instream flow statutes limit appropriation of instream flows to state agencies. Should states allow the perfection of private instream flow rights? What problems might arise? See James Huffman, *Instream Water Use: Public and Private Alternatives* in Water Rights: Scarce Resource Allocation, Bureaucracy, and the Environment 249 (Terry L. Anderson ed. 1983) (arguing that a private market in instream flow rights is desirable).

5. The court in the principal case finds that the Idaho Constitution's preference provision is not an exhaustive list of beneficial uses. As the court indicates, most western states have such preferences in their water law. The practical effect of statutory or constitutional preferences is limited as Professor Davis explains:

> None of the western states [has] adopted a true preference: a right of preferred users to take water while inferior users have no privilege to do so in time of shortage regardless of temporal priority. Preferences adopted in prior appropriation states take

three forms: (1) giving the preferred user the power to condemn and pay for nonpreferred water rights, (2) giving the state the power to withdraw water from general appropriation and reserve it for preferred uses to be developed in the future, or (3) creating a rule for choosing between substantially simultaneous applications for water rights. Three western states have granted condemnation powers to preferred users by constitutional provision. Five others have created statutory preferences controlling simultaneous applications and three have granted condemnation powers.

None of these states agree on the content of the list of preferred uses or their order of preference. Generally, however, the preference order is: (1) domestic and municipal uses, (2) agricultural uses, and (3) manufacturing uses. This order of preference reflects the bias of economic thinking at the times the statutes were enacted. They may be out of step with current thought. Only an Oklahoma order of the 1920's, since repealed, seemed to be relatively modern, reflecting the need for cooling water and waste dilution flows.

Peter N. Davis, *Australian and American Water Allocation Systems Compared*, 9 B.C.Indus. & Com.L.Rev. 647, 695–96 (1968).

CITY OF THORNTON v. CITY OF FORT COLLINS
Supreme Court of Colorado, 1992.
830 P.2d 915.

JUSTICE MULLARKEY delivered the Opinion of the Court.

* * *

This case began when Fort Collins sought approval of conditional surface water rights along a segment of the Cache La Poudre River (Poudre River) which runs roughly from the northwest boundary diagonally toward the southeast boundary of Fort Collins. Fort Collins refers to that segment of the Poudre River as the Poudre River Recreation Corridor (Corridor). The Corridor is comprised of several parks, open space areas and trail systems. With the development of the Corridor, Fort Collins has enhanced the recreational opportunities and preserved the piscatory and wildlife resources of the Poudre River for the enjoyment of the residents of and visitors to Fort Collins. * * * The Nature Dam is a relatively new structure designed and built to divert the Poudre River back into its "historic" channel and away from a channel cut after heavy rains and flooding in 1983–84. Along the historic channel, Colorado State University (CSU) owns and maintains property slated for development as the Northern Colorado Nature Center. The Nature Center offers an interpretive trail system and picnic grounds for day use. Future plans include an arboretum and the relocation of the CSU raptor rehabilitation program to the Nature Center. Fort Collins and CSU cooperate with regard to the Nature Center and the continued development of the historic channel. Construction of the Nature Dam began after 1986 but was completed before trial to the water court. The Power Dam is an older structure on the Poudre River owned and maintained by Fort Collins. The Power Dam is so named because of its proximity to a retired municipal power plant which has received local historical designation. The old plant and the Power Dam are in the midst of numerous parks, a visual arts center and a community center, all integral to the Corridor. * * * Recently, Fort Collins renovated the Power Dam by strengthening the structure itself and by adding a boat chute and a fish ladder designed for recreational use and piscatorial preservation respectively. * * * The water court found that the water appropriation at the Nature Dam was a diversion and not a minimum stream flow and decreed Fort Collins a conditional Poudre River water right of 55 cfs with an appropriation date of February 18, 1986. However, the water court found that the water appropriation at the Power Dam was not a diversion, but a minimum stream flow, and thus did not decree a conditional Poudre River water right for the Power Dam.

Thornton appeals the water court's award of a conditional water right to Fort Collins for the Nature Dam, and Fort Collins cross-appeals the water court's denial of a decree for its claimed conditional water right for the Power Dam. * * * Thornton argues that because Fort Collins's claimed diversion at the Nature Dam is nothing more than a minimum stream flow right, the conditional decree cannot issue.

* * *

The water court held that the Nature Dam diverts Poudre River water from a more recent channel back into its historic channel. * * * A diversion in the conventional sense is not required. Under section 37–92–103(7), 15 C.R.S. (1990):

> "Diversion" or "divert" means removing water from its natural course or location, or controlling water in its natural course or location, by means of a ditch, canal, flume, reservoir, bypass, pipeline, conduit, well, pump, or other structure or device.

Thus, to effect a diversion under the statute, water either must be removed or it must be controlled. * * *

Controlling water within its natural course or location by some structure or device for a beneficial use thus may result in a valid appropriation. * * * This statute provides that water appropriated for municipal, recreational, piscatorial, fishery, and wildlife purposes is water put to beneficial uses. * * * The exclusive authority vested in the CWCB to appropriate minimum stream flows does not detract from the right to divert and to put to beneficial use unappropriated waters by removal or control. *See Colo.Const.*, Art. XVI, § 6.

* * * This is not an appropriation of a minimum stream flow, an appropriation given exclusively to the CWCB. A minimum stream flow does not require removal or control of water by some structure or device. A minimum stream flow between two points on a stream or river usually signifies the complete absence of a structure or device. Furthermore, that an appropriation of a minimum stream flow by the CWCB must put that stream flow to the beneficial use of the preservation of nature does not mean that the beneficial uses to which waters controlled by some structure or device may not also redound to the

preservation of piscatorial and other natural resources. Although controlling water within its natural course or location by some structure or device may effect a result which is similar to a minimum flow, that does not mean that the appropriation effected by the structure is invalid under the Act. When the application of water to beneficial use is effected by some structure or device, the resulting appropriation is by a diversion within the meaning of the Act.

The issue then is whether the appropriation of water effected by the Nature Dam is a removal or control of water for beneficial use within the meaning of the foregoing statutes. The water court found that the Nature Dam removes Poudre River water from its natural course or location and puts that water to a beneficial use. We agree. As on the issue of relation back of the 1988 amendments to the 1986 application, Thornton again argues that Fort Collins's persistent intent to appropriate minimum stream flows means that the appropriation at the Nature Dam is an invalid appropriation. To be sure, re-labeling what is otherwise a minimum stream flow without control by some structure or device as a diversion, that is, removal or control of water by some structure or device, does not transform the former into the latter from a legal point of view. However, it is clear that the Nature Dam is a structure which either removes water from its natural course or location or controls water within its natural course or location given that the Poudre's "historic" channel may be considered the River's natural course or location. The uses of the Poudre River water so controlled are recreational, piscatorial and wildlife uses, all valid under the Act.

The water court also found that Fort Collins does not claim a right to exercise dominion and control of the water after it leaves the point of the Nature Dam. Thornton argues that this means that Fort Collins has not appropriated the waters for the claimed beneficial uses because the water may be appropriated by others after leaving the Nature Dam thereby preventing its beneficial use by Fort Collins.

* * * Under the statutes, to control water within its natural course or location means that the appropriator exercises control over the water at least to the extent that the water continues to be put to beneficial use by the appropriator, in this instance by Fort Collins. Thus, Fort Collins may validly exercise dominion over the Poudre River water once it passes the Nature Dam and continues within that segment of the river in which such water is put to beneficial use. If and when the water passes downstream from that controlled segment of the Poudre it may be subject to further appropriation by others.

* * *

On cross-appeal Fort Collins argues that the water court erred in declining to award a conditional water right for the Power Dam.

* * *

The boat chute and the fish ladder were included in the reconstruction and renovation of the Power Dam in 1987. In general, boat chutes and fish ladders, when properly designed and constructed, are structures which concentrate the flow of water to serve their intended purposes. A chute or ladder therefore may qualify as a "structure or device" which controls water in its natural course or location under section 37–92–103(7). * * * That the chute and the ladder control and direct river water *only* at unspecified low flows in the river is not a defect since that is precisely what they are designed to do. We therefore reverse the water court's conclusion that the Power Dam does not effect a diversion within the meaning of the Act. * * * Whatever the appropriation date, we find that the Nature Dam may effect a valid appropriation. Finally, we hold that the Power Dam qualifies as a structure which controls water and thus also may effect a valid appropriation.

b. *Efficiency and Conservation*

Critics of the beneficial use doctrine have long observed that it does not effectively force users to adopt conservation practices. Extensive techniques for using water efficiently are available, such as drip irrigation to replace flood irrigation in agriculture and low flush toilets to reduce municipal use. A major premise of modern environmental laws is that polluters should be forced to adopt control technologies. An issue in beneficial use today is whether the concept can serve an analogous technology-forcing function.

There is an increasing tendency of courts and administrative agencies to insist that water be used in a manner that is "reasonable" or "efficient" relative to other uses. The right to use water simply does not extend to wasteful uses. Yet, historically courts have rarely restricted a nominally beneficial use—agriculture, mining, domestic— for the sake of another use that was more efficient or productive. Concepts of reasonableness (as applied under the riparian doctrine) were considered unnecessary because the allocation of one's right to use water was made based on priority of use. As streams become more fully appropriated and new, economically productive uses come into conflict with established uses that may be wasteful, junior users and states (confronted with demands that may force them to develop expensive new sources) are beginning to challenge whether particular uses or manners of using water are truly "beneficial." One of the most lively issues in contemporary water law is whether courts, administrative agencies and legislatures should impose stringent conservation duties on historic use patterns in order make water available for new uses or for wider distribution among similarly situated users. Should the resolution of such a conflict depend on whether judgments are made based on today's standards of efficiency or those that prevailed at the time the challenged appropriation was initiated?

The opinion in *Empire Water & Power Co.*, page 196 supra, observed that the trial court "made no inquiry into the effectiveness of the use of the water in the way adopted as compared with the customary methods of irrigation." The law of prior appropriation has consistently required diverters to make reasonably efficient diversions. The standard of reasonableness has changed over the years, but generally requires a method of diversion consistent with prevailing community practices. For example, overflow or natural flood irrigation has been held inefficient, inasmuch as it ties up the whole stream to supply an appropriator's right to a lesser amount of water. Warner Valley Stock Co. v. Lynch, 336 P.2d 884 (Or.1959). Other extreme agricultural practices have been curtailed in the name of beneficial use. In People ex rel. State Water Resources Control Bd. v. Forni, 126 Cal.Rptr. 851 (Cal.1976), the court found that pumping water directly from a river for frost protection of vineyards might not be a reasonable and beneficial use of water as required by article XIV, § 3 of the California Constitution. See also Fairfield Irr. Co. v. White, 416 P.2d 641 (Utah 1966) (irrigation of fields during non-growing season), and Tulare Irr. Dist. v. Lindsay-Strathmore Irr. Dist., 45 P.2d 972 (Cal.1935) (winter flooding of fields to control gophers).

If the profits to Cascade from tourism attributable to the falls exceeds Empire's profits from power generation, can it be said that use of the water for the waterfall is wasteful? Indeed, would not use of the water for power generation at the expense of the resort be economically wasteful under such circumstances? Suppose a court finds Cascade's use the more profitable use and therefore "beneficial." Can Cascade and Empire nevertheless allocate the water among themselves? On what terms? What problems might there be in such an allocation?

Who should decide whether a use is beneficial? In his concurring opinion in Idaho Dep't of Parks v. Idaho Dep't of Water Admin., page 198, supra, Justice Bakes suggested that in Idaho the courts have the ultimate authority to decide whether a use is beneficial if it is not one of the four uses (domestic, agricultural, mining and manufacturing) which were "elevated to beneficial status" by the state constitution. Does the court's role as "final arbiter of the construction of the Idaho Constitution" give it the power to reverse, modify or expand a legislative determination that "scenic and recreational uses" are a "beneficial use within the meaning of [the state] Constitution"? Justice Bakes cited Tulare Irr. Dist. v. Lindsay-Strathmore Irr. Dist., 45 P.2d 972 (Cal.1935), for the propositions that all uses not explicitly recognized as beneficial by the constitution are subject to a requirement of reasonableness and that reasonableness depends on conditions at any given time:

> What is a beneficial use, of course, depends upon the facts and circumstances of each case. What may be a reasonable beneficial use, where water is present in excess of all needs, would not be a reasonable beneficial use in an area of great scarcity and great need. What is a beneficial use at one time may, because of changed conditions, become a waste of water at a later time.

Id. at 1007.

Does this mean that any use of water is constantly subject to litigation for judicial determination of whether alleged changed conditions have rendered the use unreasonable and therefore nonbeneficial? Is the determination that beneficial use is a function of conditions at a given time consistent with the prior appropriation system?

STATE ex rel. CARY v. COCHRAN

Supreme Court of Nebraska, 1940.
138 Neb. 163, 292 N.W. 239.

CARTER, J.

* * *

The North Platte river is a nonnavigable stream which has its source in the mountains of Colorado and flows across a part of Wyoming and Nebraska to a point approximately 200 miles from the Wyoming-Nebraska line, where it joins the South Platte river to form the Platte river. The present case involves the administration of irrigation and power rights on the North Platte and Platte rivers from the Wyoming-Nebraska line to the headgate of the Kearney canal located 13 miles west of Kearney, Nebraska. * * *

The flow of the river even in the summer months is affected by the amount of snow falling in the mountains of Colorado within its drainage basin. The river passes through parts of Colorado and Wyoming, both of which states require irrigation water in excess of the available supply. Storage and control dams under the control of the federal government also exist along the river west of the point where the river enters Nebraska. Water rights, both senior and junior to existing rights and priorities in Nebraska, coupled with the uncertainty of their accurate administration, add to the indefiniteness of the amount of water that passes at any given time across the state line and under the control of the administrative officers of this state.

Losses from evaporation and transpiration are heavy, due to the wide and shallow character of the river. Changes of temperature and varying types of wind add to the uncertainty of the losses resulting from these changing conditions. Losses from percolation vary along the various sectors of the river. The evidence shows that the river valley from the Wyoming-Nebraska line to North Platte or thereabouts is underlaid with impervious formations which do not permit losses of subterranean waters into other watersheds. At some unknown point between North Platte and Gothenburg, the river cuts through the impervious formations and runs into the sheets of sand and gravel with which the territory is underlaid. Losses begin to occur at this point due to the percolation of river water through this sand and gravel formation, in a southeasterly direction into the basin of the Republican river. * * * Experts with experience on the river estimate that the loss in delivering water from North Platte to the headgate of the Kearney canal with a wet river bed amounts to three times the amount of delivery, and with a dry river bed that it is almost impossible to get water through without a flood or a large sustained flow. In other words, it requires approximately 700 second-feet of water at North Platte to deliver 162 second-feet at the headgate of the Kearney canal when the river bed is wet. The underlying sand and gravel beds thicken as the river moves east. With the bed of the river on the surface of these sand and gravel deposits, it requires a huge amount of water to recharge the river channel and surrounding water table after the river bed once becomes dry. Until the water table is built up to the surface of the river bed, the river channel will not support a continuous flow. It is also shown that the water table has been affected materially by pump irrigation. It was estimated that there are 500 irrigation pumps in Dawson county alone, which pump as much as 40,000 acre-feet of water in a single season. The evidence bears out the statement that the Platte river east of Gothenburg is a very inefficient carrier of water. In addition to the subterranean losses noted, the river spreads out, causing a broad surface of water and channel bed to be subjected to large evaporation losses. It is further established by early settlers along the river that it was not unusual for the river to go dry in July and August before irrigation was generally practiced along the river. That the river is generally considered a gaining stream, and can be so established by an examination of the statistical records of the mean flow for the calendar year, is borne out by the record. But it is just as clearly shown that the river is ordinarily a losing stream during the months of July and August, when the mean flow for that period is considered. These conditions and activities establish the cause of the huge losses of water between Gothenburg and the Kearney canal. They are important only as factors that must be considered by the officers of the state in distributing an insufficient supply of water to appropriators in the proper order of priority.

Appropriations of water are made throughout the length of the river. The priority dates of these appropriations have no relation whatever to their location on the stream. Hence, very early appropriations may be found at the upper and lower ends of the stream, while very late appropriations are likewise found at both ends. In times of water shortage, the later appropriators are the first to be deprived of water. The closing of canals in accordance with the inverse order of their priority dates necessarily requires certain canals to close their headgates all along the stream at the same time. Water moves down the stream at approximately 25 miles per day with the result that it requires approximately ten days to deliver water from the state line to the Kearney headgate under normal conditions. The resulting lag therefore becomes an important factor to be considered. During the lag period, conditions over which the administrator of the river has no control may change or disrupt all calculations. Excessive heat, continued drought, and unusual winds may greatly reduce estimated quantities of river-flow, or, on the other hand, low temperatures, rains and floods in the lower river basin may relieve immediate demands. These elements of uncertainty must be considered in protecting the rights of all on the stream. The position of relators at the lower end of the stream is in itself a recognized condition, and while they have the second oldest priority on the river, it is inescapable that their location subjects them to unfavorable conditions which are practically impossible to eliminate.

* * *

The use of water for irrigation in this state is a natural want. The inadequacy of supply to meet the demands of the public requires strict administration to prevent waste. It is therefore the policy of the law that junior appropriators may use available water within the limits of their own appropriations so long as the rights of senior appropriators are not injured or damaged. And so, in the instant case, junior appropriators may lawfully apply water to their lands within the limits of their adjudicated appropriations until the Kearney canal fails to receive its full appropriation of 162 second-feet. Until the senior appropriator is injured, there is the ever-present possibility of changed weather conditions, precipitation, or other sources of water supply which might alleviate the situation and supply the needs of the Kearney canal. To pursue any other rule would greatly add to the loss by waste of the public waters of this state. We conclude therefore that the use of water by a junior appropriator does not become adverse to or injure a senior appropriator until it results in a deprivation of his allotted amount, or some part thereof. This rule is supported, we think, by our decisions as well as the decisions of other states.

The real question to be decided, however, is the determination of the duty imposed upon the officers of the state in administering the waters of the stream when the available supply of water at the headgate of the Kearney canal is reduced to an amount less than the 162 second-feet to which the relators are entitled. The rights of relators to the use of this water as against all appropriators subsequent to September 10, 1882, cannot be questioned. It is the duty of the administrative officers of the state to recognize this right and to give force to relators' priority. This requires that junior appropriators be restrained from taking water from the stream so long as such water can be delivered in usable quantities at the headgate of the Kearney canal. If it appear that all the available water in the stream would be lost before its arrival at the headgate of the Kearney canal, it would, of course, be an unjustified waste of water to attempt delivery. Whether a definite quantity of water passing a given point on the stream would, if not diverted or interrupted in its course, reach the headgate of the Kearney canal in a usable quantity creates a very complicated question of fact. It therefore is the duty of the administrative officers of the state to determine from all available means, including the factors hereinbefore discussed, whether or not a usable quantity of water can be delivered at the headgate of the Kearney canal.   * * *

After determination that a given quantity of water passing a certain point on the river would not, even if uninterrupted, reach the headgate of the Kearney canal in usable quantities, the administrative officers of the state may lawfully permit junior appropriators to divert it for irrigation purposes. This results ofttimes in having junior appropriators receiving a head of water at a time when an appropriator farther downstream is getting none, though he is prior in time. Such situations are not therefore conclusive evidence of unlawful diversions.

Amici curiæ urge that the doctrine of reasonable use is in force in this state and that it should be applied to the case at bar. We recognize the principle that the public has an interest in the public waters of the state and it is the use thereof only that may be appropriated. Even though an adjudicated appropriation may be vested, it may be subjected to regulation and control by the state by virtue of its police power. It may likewise be circumscribed to the extent that a limited diversion for a specified purpose will not permit of an undue interference with the rights of other appropriators on the stream. But we cannot agree that the doctrine of reasonable use can be applied in a case where delivery of a usable quantity of water can be made, although the losses suffered in so doing are great. To permit the officers of the state the right to say whether prospective losses would or would not justify the delivery of usable quantities of water would clothe such officers with a discretion incompatible with the vested interests of the relators, and destroy the very purpose of the doctrine of appropriation existent in this state. When upstream appropriators applied for and received adjudicated priorities, they did so with the knowledge that there was an earlier appropriator at the lower end of the stream whose rights had to be recognized. When the relators applied for and received their adjudications, they are likewise presumed to have known that other appropriators would obtain inferior rights above them that would have to be recognized. Each is required to respect the vested rights of the others, even though some hardships may be thereby imposed. We therefore hold that the doctrine of reasonable use does not extend so far as to authorize the administrator of the waters of the stream to refrain from delivering a usable quantity of water to a senior appropriator because it might appear to him that excessive losses would result. The duty of the administrator, in administering the waters of the stream by virtue of the police power of the state, is to enforce existing priorities, not to determine, change or amend them. But in regulating the distribution of water it may become incidentally necessary for him to ascertain for that purpose only whether a prior appropriator is injured by a diversion above him. This finding of fact must be made, not to change existing priorities, but in order to determine whether or not a distribution of water may be made to a junior appropriator in accordance with existing priorities.

NOTES

1. The prohibition against the waste of water and the limitation of reasonable use on the exercise of an appropriative right would seem to be correlative doctrines; that is, water cannot be wasted because there is no right to use water in a nonbeneficial manner. Observe, however, that the loss between a flow of 700 cfs (second-feet) at North Platte and a flow of 162 second-feet at the Kearney Canal is nearly 77%. Even though the senior appropriators on the Kearney Canal make an efficient application of their 162 second-feet of water after it is received, can it be said that they have made a beneficial use of the 538 second-feet lost in transit? If the cost of building a pipeline from North Platte to the Kearney Canal is less than the value of 538 second-feet of water saved, can it be said that the 538 second-feet are being wasted? If the upstream junior appropriators installed a pipeline that would deliver 162 second-feet at Kearney, could they use the remaining 538 second-feet themselves? Assuming the answer is "yes," why did they not adopt such a scheme? Would it not have been economically feasible?

What if the value of 700 second-feet of water at and around North Platte is greater than 162 second-feet at the Kearney Canal? Has the 538 second-feet been wasted? What happened to the "lost" water? Might the answer to this question mitigate the criticism of the decision?

A careful analysis of the *Cary* case was made by a lawyer-economist (who was Secretary of Agriculture from 1989–92), Clayton K. Yeutter, *A Legal-Economic Critique of Nebraska Watercourse Law*, 44 Neb.L.Rev. 11, 39–43 (1965).

2. Seniors, faced with a shortage of water needed to satisfy their full water rights, generally may "call" upstream juniors, requiring them to forego diverting water until the seniors are fully satisfied. But if, as in *Cary*, there are conditions that will prevent water from reaching the seniors in a manner or at times that will enable it to be put to use, the juniors may continue to divert out of priority. In Colorado, this is known as the "futile call doctrine." Colo. Rev. Stat. § 37–92–502 states:

> "Each division engineer shall * * * order the total or partial discontinuance of any diversion in his division to the extent the water being diverted is required by persons entitled to use water under water rights having senior priorities, but no such discontinuance shall be ordered unless the diversion is causing or will cause material injury to such water rights having senior priorities. * * * In the event a discontinuance has been ordered pursuant to the foregoing, and nevertheless such does not cause water to become available to such senior priorities at the time and place of their need, then such discontinuance order shall be rescinded."

3. *Cary* and the futile call doctrine relate to natural conditions causing carriage losses. Should the analysis be different when losses occur in conveyances or systems that are constructed or controlled by appropriators?

STATE ex rel. CROWLEY v. DISTRICT COURT

Supreme Court of Montana, 1939.
108 Mont. 89, 88 P.2d 23.

JOHNSON, CHIEF JUSTICE.

* * *

The suit in question is for damages for alleged interference with plaintiff's use of irrigation water from the Madison River in 1935, 1936 and 1937.

* * *

[The plaintiff alleges] that the defendants impounded by their dams the entire natural flow of the river so that the water level at plaintiff's point of diversion was so low that he could not divert water into his ditches by his diversion dam, although the latter was suitable and efficient for the purpose and was a reasonably adequate means of diversion, and reasonably constructed and maintained to divert water from the river to plaintiff's land in spite of the fluctuations in flow incidental to the reasonable and lawful use of water by all persons lawfully entitled to use the same.

* * *

Defendants' contentions are that plaintiff has no cause of action merely because their acts so reduced the flow that he could not divert his appropriated water by his reasonably efficient diversion system; that he should have alleged that not enough was left to permit his diversion without leaving any water in the stream. In other words, they contend that plaintiff has no cause of action if there are 200 inches of water at his point of diversion, even though he cannot get the water into his ditches without a pump; that an appropriator's vested interest is only in the use of the quantum of water appropriated by him without reference to his means or manner of diversion, however reasonably efficient; that not reasonable efficiency but absolute efficiency is required. To this theory we cannot assent without doing violence to the entire principle of water rights by appropriation. If it is to be followed, there are few, if any, irrigation water rights in the state of Montana, however long established, which could not in effect be destroyed entirely by subsequent appropriations. One hundred per cent efficiency can be furnished by no system of diversion, and certainly by none financially available to the average water user. The law does not defeat its own end by requiring the impossible. The marginal character of many farming enterprises, and especially of the smaller ones, is well known, and if defendants' argument is followed, vested interests will be seriously affected and rights limited by the necessity of installing diversion systems by which the last drop may be taken from the stream.

There is no question that waste of our water resources must be minimized in the general interest, but it is equally manifest that there is a vanishing point at which the possible waste of water would be more than overcome by the waste incidental to the abandonment of reasonably efficient diversion systems and the establishment of diversion systems whose expense is neither warranted nor permitted by the benefit to be derived from the water.

It is well established that subsequent appropriators take with notice of the conditions existing at the time of their appropriations. In making their appropriation of storage or other water and their expenditures in connection therewith, defendants and their predecessors were chargeable with knowledge of the existing conditions, with reference not only to the amount of prior appropriations, but also to the existing diversion systems of prior appropriators. They cannot now argue that they are limited by the amount but not the means of prior appropriations, however reasonably efficient under the circumstances, or that so long as they leave the exact amount of plaintiff's appropriation in the river at his point of diversion, they have no further duty and that it is his worry and not theirs how or whether he can divert it upon his land. His right is to divert and use the water, not merely to have it left in the streambed; that is the essential difference between riparian and appropriation rights.

In Salt Lake City v. Gardner, 39 Utah 30, 114 P. 147, 152, appellants had appropriated water from Utah Lake by means of natural gravity flow, aided by a storage dam and pumping plant. The question was whether the respondents should be allowed to appropriate and divert water by means of a pumping plant, thus reducing or stopping the gravity flow and placing upon appellants an additional burden for installation and operation of pumps. The court said: "Counsel for respondents, however, insist that the prior appropriator acquires no right in his means of diversion, but obtains a prior right only to use the quantity of water appropriated and applied to a beneficial use by him. We cannot yield assent to this view. We think the original taker or appropriator from a stream or body of water also acquires the right to continue to use his method or means of diverting which he has installed. If this be not so, then prior appropriators, who have appropriated only in small quantities, and whose means of diversion from the stream are simple but sufficient for their purpose, could have their means made entirely ineffective by a subsequent appropriator of a large volume of water the diverting of which would so lower the stream that the water would no longer reach the point of diversion of the small appropriator. In this way it may well be that the cost to the small appropriator to make the water appropriated by him available for his purpose might under changed conditions be prohibitive if not ruinous. Upon the other hand, the cost of making the change might not be so great as to prevent the larger appropriator from supplying and paying for some means whereby the prior rights to the use of the water appropriated by the small user might be preserved, and the wants of the large appropriator could nevertheless be met and supplied. In this way, perhaps, very large quantities of water theretofore wasted, or used only to aid the original appropriator to obtain his meager supply, would be put to a useful and beneficial purpose without destroying the rights of any one. If it be held, therefore, that a subsequent appropriator of water need have no regard for the diverting means or methods of the prior appropriator, but may in fact or effect make prior appropriations of water unavailable with impunity, then there is in fact no such a right as a prior right, but all rights may, at any time, be invaded or destroyed by a subsequent appropriator by simply making the diverting means used by the prior appropriator useless. To permit such an invasion of a prior right would, in effect, amount to an indirect taking of a prior appropriator's water. This neither the legislative nor the judicial power can allow without permitting confiscation of property rights. * * * If all rights can be protected and preserved, a mere change in prior established means or methods of diversion, if possible, ought not to prevent the use of water which could otherwise not be beneficially applied. But, in our judgment, the risk of interfering with prior rights and the cost of any change in the prior appropriator's means or methods of diversion should be assumed and borne by the subsequent appropriator, and a court should in no case permit a subsequent appropriation unless all prior rights can by some feasible means be protected and maintained."

Defendants contend that the case of Schodde v. Twin Falls Land & Water Co., 224 U.S. 107, affirming 9 Cir., 161 F. 43, 88 C.C.A. 207, sustains their contention that a prior appropriator has no vested interest in his means of diversion. It cannot be so construed.

* * *

Obviously, of course, under the circumstances of that case, it was unreasonable to prevent the irrigation of 300,000 acres by an unusual and inefficient method of diverting water for 429 acres. The complaint there was not that the defendant had taken water out of the stream so as to interfere with the waterwheels; as a matter of fact, the defendant had confined more water there. What it had deprived plaintiff of was not the water, but the force of the water, which was no part of his appropriation. This can be made clear by an analogy. If, instead of building water wheels to utilize the force of the stream, he had constructed windmills to employ the force of the wind, it would have been entirely clear that his complaint was not of water right interference, but of something entirely different. If the conditions were such that he could have recovered for an obstruction to the flow of the wind to his windmills, it would still have been something entirely apart from and not appurtenant to his water right.

* * *

The rule in this connection is well stated as follows in Long on Irrigation, 2nd ed., 202, 203, sec. 116: "The irrigator may employ any means best suited to the existing physical conditions, and all the circumstances of the case, though undoubtedly he will be required to employ reasonably economical means, so as to prevent unnecessary waste.   * * *   As already stated, the means of diversion employed must not be unnecessarily wasteful, but when ditches and flumes are the usual and ordinary means of diverting water, parties who have made their appropriations by such means cannot be compelled to substitute iron pipes, though they will be required to prevent unnecessary waste by keeping their ditches and flumes in good repair."

* * *

Plaintiff alleges that he has diverted the water by means of a wing dam of brush, rocks and dirt, and proceeds to allege that the means of diversion was at the time in question "suitable and efficient for the diversion of water," and "a reasonably adequate means of diversion and reasonably constructed and maintained" for the purpose, notwithstanding the fluctuations incidental to the reasonable and lawful use of water by all those entitled, including defendants.   * * *   It follows that the demurrers should have been overruled.

NOTES

1.   The court discusses the United States Supreme Court's decision in Schodde v. Twin Falls Land & Water Co., 224 U.S. 107 (1912). The following excerpts from *Schodde,* quoting the Ninth Circuit opinion, 161 Fed. 43, present the factual setting and the essence of the decision:

Plaintiff is the owner of three tracts of land on the banks of Snake river, containing in the aggregate 429.96 acres. Two of these tracts, containing 263.96 acres, are on the south bank, and one tract of 160 acres is on the north bank. One of the tracts on the south bank is agricultural land, and the other is partly agricultural land and partly mining ground. The tract of land on the north bank is agricultural. In the year 1889 plaintiff's predecessors in interest, and in 1895 the plaintiff himself, appropriated certain quantities of water of the flow of Snake river for use on said lands. * * * The aggregate of water appropriated as alleged in the three counts is referred to in the briefs as 1,250 miner's inches. Soon after this water was appropriated the parties in interest erected water wheels in the river to lift the water to a sufficient height for distribution over the land. Nine of these wheels were erected opposite or near the tracts on the south side of the river, and two near the tract on the north side of the river. These wheels vary in height from 24 to 34 feet. The parties also constructed wing dams in the river adjoining or in front of the lands owned by them, for the purpose of confining the flow of the water of the river and raising it at such points above the natural flow of the river, so that the current would drive the water wheels and cause them to revolve and carry the water in buckets attached to the wheels to a height where it would be emptied into flumes and distributed over the lands by ditches and used thereon to irrigate and cultivate the agricultural land and work the mining ground. * * * In the year 1903, while plaintiff was using the appropriated water of the river upon the described premises, the defendant commenced the construction of a dam across Snake river at a point about nine miles westerly from and below the lands of the plaintiff. The work was prosecuted on said dam until its completion in March, 1905. This dam is so constructed as to impound all the water of Snake river flowing at said point, and to raise the water about forty feet in height. * * * It is alleged that by reason of this dam the waters of Snake river have been backed up from said dam and to and beyond plaintiff's premises and have destroyed the current in the river by means of which plaintiff's water wheels were driven and made to revolve and raise the water to the elevation required for distribution over plaintiff's lands * * *.

* * *

It is unquestioned that what he has actually diverted and used upon his land, he has appropriated, but can it be said that all the water he uses or needs to operate his wheels is an appropriation? As before suggested, there is neither statutory nor judicial authority that such a use is an appropriation. Such use also lacks one of the essential attributes of an appropriation; it is not reasonable.

* * *

The only way in which his wheels can be used for the purpose he intended them, is to preserve the river in the condition it was when he erected them. And with what result, it may be asked.

* * * Suppose from a stream of 1000 inches a party diverts and uses 100, and in some way uses the other 900 to divert his 100, could it be said that he had made such a reasonable use of the 900 as to constitute an appropriation of it? Or, suppose that when the entire 1000 inches are running, they so fill the channel that by a ditch he can draw off to his land his 100 inches, can he then object to those above him appropriating and using the other 900 inches, because it will so lower the stream that his ditch becomes useless? This would be such an unreasonable use of the 900 inches as will not be tolerated under the law of appropriation. In effect this is substantially the principle that plaintiff is asking to have established.

* * *

Did the court in *Crowley* satisfactorily distinguish *Schodde*?

2. What practical difference would it make in *Crowley* if the "reasonable efficiency" of an appropriator's means of diversion were determined based on present conditions instead of conditions at the time the diversion was made? In R. T. Nahas Co. v. Hulet, 674 P.2d 1036 (Idaho 1983), the junior appropriator argued that the senior appropriator's right should be reduced because the senior converted to a more efficient system of irrigation, sprinklers rather than flood irrigation and because the senior was growing alfalfa, which only required 3.5 acre-feet of water per acre. However, the senior proved to the court's satisfaction that 5 as opposed to 3.5 acre-feet per acre was reasonable and essential considering the soils, land, and climate.

3. Particularly egregious transportation losses through unlined, leaky ditches, have been categorized as inefficient means of diversion. Examples are Big Cottonwood Tanner Ditch Co. v. Shurtliff, 189 P. 587 (Utah 1919) (diversion of 323,000 gallons of water per day through an open ditch 807 feet long over porous and gravelly soil to supply a continuous flow of 20,000 gallons per day of pure and potable water for domestic and culinary purposes for a small family and a few head of stock); Erickson v. Queen Valley Ranch Co., 99 Cal.Rptr. 446 (Cal.1971) (loss of ⅝ths due to evapotranspiration and seepage in 2½-mile open ditch); City of Corpus Christi v. Pleasanton, 276 S.W.2d 798 (1955) (63–74% loss through evaporation, transpiration and seepage of water flowing from artesian wells down a natural streambed and through lakes for a distance of 118 miles); and Doherty v. Pratt, 124 P. 574 (Nev.1912) (loss of ⅔ of water conveyed by 3-mile open ditch through 300-acre swamp). The Idaho Supreme Court has said in dictum that an appropriator is not entitled to divert approximately double the amount needed to irrigate his crops in order to compensate for carriage losses which occur as the water is conducted from the stream or canal to the place of use. Reviewing a long line of previous cases the court stated, "However, the public policy against wasting water prohibits additional diversion to compensate for unreasonable loss. * * * Accordingly, waters appropriated will be measured for their sufficiency from the point of diversion, not at the place of use." Glenn Dale Ranches, Inc. v. Shaub, 494 P.2d 1029, 1032 (Idaho 1972). Cf. R. T. Nahas Co. v. Hulet,

674 P.2d 1036 (Idaho 1983) (the amount of water reasonably lost through evaporation from reservoir should be added to the amount of water plaintiffs could appropriate from the creek in order to fill the reservoir).

4. Much water "lost" through seepage from ditches and overflows from excess irrigation actually returns to the stream where it can be diverted and used by others. To the extent that return flows can be used by other appropriators, are "waste" figures overstated? Can you conceive of circumstances where excessive use or large quantities of such return flow seepage nonetheless would be "wasteful?"

5. In a case concerning one of the nation's first reclamation projects, the Newlands project in Nevada, the district judge awarded water duties of 3.5 and 4.5 acre-feet per acre per year respectively to bottomland and benchland farmers. The United States objected because landowner contracts with the Bureau of Reclamation limited the water duty to a maximum of 3 acre-feet. The Ninth Circuit Court of Appeals held that § 8 of the Reclamation Act, see pages 681–86, infra, required that beneficial use be determined by reference to state law. The court said that "beneficial use expresses a dynamic concept, which is variable according to conditions, and therefore over time. * * * The district court, in the absence of any earlier administrative or judicial determination of beneficial use, was correct to find beneficial use as of the present time as shown by the best available current information." United States v. Alpine Land & Reservoir Co., 697 F.2d 851, 855 (9th Cir. 1983), cert. denied 464 U.S. 863 (1983). Thus, the larger decreed rights prevailed over the contracts.

6. Consumptive use of irrigation water, which accounts for about 90% of the West's water use, can be reduced by techniques such as: installation of drip irrigation systems instead of flooding fields; gated pipes instead of open ditches; leveling of fields to reduce runoff; scientific scheduling and moisture sensing devices; and planting drought- and salt-resistant crops. For instance, installation of sprinkler systems instead of surface flooding can reduce waste from 47% to 29%. See generally, U.S. Office of Technology Assessment, Water Related Technologies for Sustainable Agriculture in U.S. Arid/Semiarid Lands (1983).

7. If the waste of water is unwise and conservation measures are truly efficient, why have not farmers and water distribution institutions already adopted such measures? One study points out that:

> Improvements to plug the leaks in [water delivery] systems will not come without significant investment and effort, however. The Soil Conservation Service (SCS) estimates that it will cost about $600 million a year just to repair, and replace as necessary, existing irrigation systems in the country. This would not improve their efficiency, but simply maintain the levels that now exist.

> Another $150 million a year would be needed to maintain irrigation water storage reservoirs. In addition, SCS predicts that it would take another $260 million per year in the 17 western states to get a 4 percent improvement in delivery systems and a 5

percent increase in on-farm efficiency. That total billion-dollar-per-year maintenance bill would amount to about $25 per acre per year, so farmers would no doubt still find it economical if they were faced with loss of their irrigation system.

R. Neil Sampson, Farmland or Wasteland: A Time to Choose 158–60 (1981).

8. Commentators observe that there are disincentives to conservation in western water law. George W. Pring and Karen A. Tomb, *License to Waste: Legal Barriers to Conservation and Efficient Use of Water in the West,* 25 Rocky Mtn.Min.L.Inst. 25–1 (1979). Reform suggestions include the modification of the beneficial use doctrine, the elimination of community custom as a defense, establishment of water banks, and other institutional changes.

9. Who can raise the question of excessive or wasteful use of water? Under what circumstances? In some states, the occasion arises only when an appropriator invokes administrative or judicial jurisdiction. Because nearly every other appropriator is potentially affected by a wasteful use, why shouldn't they all be able to commence an action? Is there a sufficient public interest in preventing waste that even non-appropriators should be able to raise the issue?

The California Constitution forbids the waste of water. Article X, § 2. In a case seeking to impose mandatory conservation duties on a water district, the California Supreme Court held that the State Water Resources Control Board, not the courts, should decide whether the district has a duty to reclaim wastewater before seeking additional freshwater supplies, citing the doctrine of primary jurisdiction. It also noted that "in administrative proceedings comprehensive adjudication considers the interests of other concerned persons who may not be parties to the court action." Environmental Defense Fund, Inc. v. East Bay Mun. Utility Dist., 572 P.2d 1128 (Cal.1977), vacated 439 U.S. 811 (1978), opinion on remand 605 P.2d 1 (1980). Later proceedings are considered in Stuart Somach, *The American River Decision: Balancing Instream Protection with Other Competing Beneficial Uses,* 1 Rivers 251 (1990).

A–B CATTLE COMPANY v. UNITED STATES

Supreme Court of Colorado, 1978.
196 Colo. 539, 589 P.2d 57.

GROVES, JUSTICE.

* * *

As a part of the Fryingpan-Arkansas Reclamation Project, the United States constructed Pueblo Dam across the Arkansas River a few miles west of Pueblo, creating Pueblo Reservoir. This inundated the headgate and first four miles of the Bessemer Ditch. In exchange for the water formerly transported from the headgate through the ditch, clear water is delivered from the dam into the ditch.

Prior to construction of the reservoir, the United States brought a condemnation proceeding in the United States District Court for the

District of Colorado against the Bessemer Co. for the taking of the headgate and the upper portion of the ditch.

* * *

The Bessemer Co. answered, alleging among other things, that the delivery of clear water instead of silty water would result in substantial damage to the individual stockholders. Subsequently, these shareholders brought the action in the Court of Claims, asking for damages of nearly $100,000,000, plus costs, disbursements and expenses, including reasonable attorney, appraisal and engineering fees. Thereafter, the United States District Court in the condemnation proceeding sustained the Government's motion to dismiss the action as to the silt issue without prejudice to determination of that question by the Court of Claims.

The Court of Claims in its statement of facts has given as the basis for the alleged damages the following:

> "The substitution of clear water from Pueblo Dam for the stream water with silt as diverted from the river has had certain adverse effects on the Bessemer Ditch system and the lands irrigated from the ditch. The silt in the water tended to seal the bed and banks of the ditch. Clear water leaks through the bottom and sides of the ditch in greater volume than silty water. More of the water passing the Bessemer Ditch gauging station about six miles below the original diversion point of the ditch seeps out of the bottom and sides of the ditch so that less of the diverted water reaches the points of delivery to Plaintiffs. There is an increase in the amount of aquatic vegetation growing in the ditch and the laterals. There has been an increase in erosion of the ditch and the laterals in places and sloughing off of material from the sides of the ditches into the bottom. There has been more seepage from the ditch into basements through the Pueblo reach of the ditch. When applied to land for irrigation, clear water does not spread as far as silty water."

[The Court of Claims certified to the Colorado Supreme Court the question of whether the holder of a water right has a right to receive water of the same quality, including the silt content thereof, as has historically been received under the right.]

I

* * *

This leads us to the fundamental question as to whether the original appropriations for the Bessemer Ditch were for silty water. In our view the appropriations were for water, and not for water containing silt. Silt is not a component of water. Rather, it is suspended sediment which comes principally from the banks and bottom of an onrushing stream and which settles to the bottom when there is no longer movement of the water. Thus, there is far more sediment being carried in the waters of the Arkansas River during the flood season of late spring, than in the early spring or fall.

* * *

We regard the storage of water, with consequent settling of silt to the bottom of the reservoir, as not constituting an unreasonable deterioration in quality.

II

There has not been cited any case holding that a senior appropriator has a vested right to the silt content of the water as of the time of his appropriation or at any other time.

* * *

The trend and philosophy of Colorado law are contrary to the result asked by the plaintiffs. The Arkansas River is overappropriated; water is scarce; and conservation of water and prevention of wastage is the order of the day. The plaintiffs have canals and laterals which leak and seep, thereby, so far as plaintiffs are concerned, wasting the water. They seek to continue their transport of water in leaky ditches by, in effect, calling upon the junior appropriators on the stream to pay for the portion of the leakage which silt will stop.

We said in Fellhauer v. People, 167 Colo. 320, 447 P.2d 986 (1968):

"For nearly a century the waters of the Arkansas River have been used and reused many times over as they proceed from elevations exceeding 12,000 feet to 3,375 feet at the state line. These uses, and similar uses on other rivers, have developed under article XVI, section 6 of the Colorado constitution which contains *inter alia* two provisions:

'The right to divert the unappropriated waters of any natural stream to beneficial uses shall never be denied. Priority of appropriation shall give the better right as between those using water for the same purpose;'

Under those provisions and the statutes enacted thereunder a great body of law has been established. In the six briefs, all ably written, sixty Colorado cases have been cited. These decisions are concerned primarily with the respective priorities of *vested rights* which have been established. It is implicit in these constitutional provisions that, along with *vested rights*, there shall be *maximum utilization* of the water of this state. As administration of water approaches its second century the curtain is opening upon the new drama of *maximum utilization* and how constitutionally that doctrine can be integrated into the law of *vested rights*. We have known for a long time that the doctrine was lurking in the backstage shadows as a result of the accepted, though oft violated, principle that the right to water does not give the right to waste it.

"*Colorado Springs v. Bender*, 148 Colo. 458, 366 P.2d 552, might be called the signal that the curtain was about to rise. There it was stated as follows:

'At his own point of diversion on a natural water course, each diverter must establish some reasonable means of effectuating his diversion. He is not entitled to command the whole or a substantial flow of the stream merely to facilitate his taking the fraction of the whole flow to which he is entitled. Schodde v. Twin Falls Land & Water Co., 224 U.S. 107.' "

Our answer in the negative to the question propounded by the Court of Claims is a part of the policy of this state that there should be maximum utilization of water and that the maximum utilization doctrine be integrated into the law of vested rights. Without the storage of water, the use thereof cannot be maximized.

It will be noted that in *Colorado Springs v. Bender*, supra, this court cited the United States Supreme Court in *Schodde v. Twin Falls Land & Water Co.*, supra. Schodde diverted his water from a shallow canyon and up to his fields by means of water-driven water wheels. Later, others built a dam which slowed the flow until it would not drive the water wheels. Schodde claimed damages against the defendant dam builder. The United States District Court dismissed the complaint on the ground that Schodde's claim to the right to have his water wheels turn was not a reasonable attribute of an appropriation. The Court of Appeals affirmed, as did the United States Supreme Court, stating, "extent of beneficial use was an inherent and necessary limitation upon the right to appropriate." See Empire Water and Power Co. v. Cascade Town Co., 205 F. 123 (8th Cir. 1913).

In using its leaky ditches the Bessemer Co. has not attempted to make maximum utilization of the water. As was indicated in 1909 in a case involving the Bessemer Co. and its main canal (Middelkamp v. Bessemer Irrigating Ditch Co., 46 Colo. 102, 103 P. 280), the time may not yet have arrived when all ditches can be required to be lined or placed in pipes. Even assuming that that proposition of 1909 still holds true, this does not change our view that the plaintiffs do not have the right to use silt content to help seal leaky ditches. To view it otherwise would run contra to a basic principle of western irrigation that conservation and maximum usage demand the storage of water in times of plenty for the use in times of drought.

III

* * *

The effect of granting any particular appropriator a constitutionally-protected property right in the concentration of silt present in the water at the time of the appropriation would seriously inhibit any subsequent upstream or downstream appropriation. Upstream diversions or impoundments will result in alteration of the silt concentration to downstream users if only due to the slowing impact on stream velocity. Applied in its extreme, an appropriator located on lower reaches of a stream with a very early appropriation date could put a call on the river for the receipt of its natural silt concentration, which would have the practical effect of halting all upstream use and commanding substantially the entire stream flow to satisfy its appropriation.

* * *

LEE, ERICKSON and CARRIGAN, JJ., dissent.

ERICKSON, JUSTICE, dissenting:

Since a change in water quality can affect the irrigative capacity and utility of a specific quantity of water appropriated, our courts have consistently recognized that appropriators are entitled to protection against detrimental changes in water quality. Larimer County Reservoir Co. v. People, 9 P. 794 (1885). The question of what constitutes a "diminution" in the quality of water must, therefore, be analyzed in terms of the use to which the water is put. An appropriator's expectations can just as easily be defeated by altering the quality of water as by changing the quantity. Thus, one aspect of an appropriation is the right to continue to receive water of the quality upon which the appropriator relied in making his appropriation. Because the defendants in this case altered the quality of the water which the plaintiffs receive, plaintiffs have been deprived of a quantity of water which they historically received and put to beneficial use.

* * * If a junior appropriator causes a reduction in the quantity of water delivered to a senior appropriator, the injury is obvious. Similarly, a change in the water's natural quality, which denies existing appropriators the full measure of their rights, whether by the addition of a pollutant or by the removal of a naturally-occurring element such as silt, also constitutes injury. The crucial consideration is that water rights which were appropriated for a specific purpose and which were limited in quantity to that amount necessary to achieve that purpose, are no longer sufficient to satisfy that purpose as a result of the change in water quality. The injury inflicted by the change in water quality under such circumstances lessens the value of the water rights and constitutes damage which is cognizable under Colorado Law.

NOTES

1. The dissenting opinion constituted the decision of the court until a rehearing. If it had remained the court's decision, what would the United States have had to pay in damages? The cost of lining all ditches? Could such a decision become precedent for limiting future appropriations on a stream where any lessening of flow would cause more silt to settle out and jeopardize "natural" ditch lining? Could a senior industrial user accustomed to using stagnant, algae-laden water for cooling demand that its "quality" be maintained because pure water would create more oxidation in the senior's facility?

The dissenting opinion recites "that appropriators are entitled to protection against detrimental changes in water quality." In fact, the right to water quality is enforced narrowly—not only in the strange factual setting of *A–B Cattle*. States tend to limit their control of water quality to regulatory programs implementing federal statutes. See summary of Clean Water Act, pages 132–35, supra. These regulations target almost exclusively discharges of pollutants into streams. As the following excerpt indicates, the manner of water use, as well as waste discharges, can seriously affect water quality, but water law is rarely used to achieve water quality goals.

DAVID H. GETCHES, LAWRENCE J. MACDONNELL & TERESA A. RICE, CONTROLLING WATER USE: THE UNFINISHED BUSINESS OF WATER QUALITY PROTECTION
91–120 (1991).

States generally do not limit water appropriations or uses to carry out their water quality protection policies

* * *

The need to regulate uses or new appropriations for legitimate water quality purposes becomes more apparent as other means of curbing the production or discharge of pollutants approach the limits of their economic feasibility. Restricting water uses is generally seen as a last resort, however, and the public's interest in water quality is often subordinated to maintaining the integrity of the appropriation system itself. The result has been a categorical resistance to regulating diversions, impoundments, and uses of water to protect water quality; at its extreme, it is manifested in explicit statutory prohibitions against water quality laws being applied in any way that impairs or inhibits the exercise of water rights.

Several states have proclaimed that water quality regulation will not affect water uses or water rights. The New Mexico Water Quality Act specifically denies the Water Quality Control Commission or any other entity power to take away or modify property rights in water.

Similarly, the Arizona Water Quality Control Act declares that the law shall not be interpreted to prevent the exercise of groundwater or surface water rights. Nevada law says that "Nothing in [the Water Pollution Control Law] shall be construed to amend, modify or supersede the [water allocation law] or any rule, regulation or order promulgated or issued thereunder by the state engineer." And Colorado's Water Quality Act states that it "shall not be construed, enforced, or applied so as to cause or result in material injury to water rights." Several other sections of the Colorado Act also limit regulatory authority if it conflicts with the exercise or establishment of water rights.

* * *

A reluctance to administer and enforce water quality laws alongside allocation laws can be explained partly by the usual division of authority between state agencies. Most western states assign responsibilities for water allocation and water quality to separate agencies. These separate agencies usually have different statutory missions and do not coordinate their decisions on specific issues, let alone their policies, with one another. Thus, water rights permits may be granted without regard to the effect of the depletion or manner of use on water quality. On the other hand, the pollution control agency may impose conditions on a pollutant discharge permit that are insensitive to water users' rights.

Nearly every western state has some form of water planning, and water quality concerns are expressed in several state water plans. The plans take many forms: some are processes for ongoing articulation of goals and policies; others primarily address water project development. Many plans contain simply a mention or cursory discussion of water quality issues. Only a few states, such as California and Kansas, actually implement water quality planning goals in the permitting process; permits must be consistent with the plan. Some states are beginning to adopt "planning" processes that are actually dynamic forums for articulating public policies related to all aspects of water use, including quality.

* * *

State efforts to integrate control of water use with water quality protection are in their infancy. * * * A review of western state water allocation and water quality laws and programs indicates four general ways in which states are seeking to address the relationship between water quality and water quantity:

* * *

1. States have several ways to integrate and coordinate water quality and water allocation responsibilities

* * *

Cooperative Mechanisms

* * *

The New Mexico State Engineer serves on the Water Quality Control Commission. Similarly, in North Dakota the head of the Water Commission sits on the State Water Pollution Control Board. This approach at least connects the individual with responsibility for water allocation decisions with the entity establishing water quality policy.

Oklahoma has established a Pollution Control Coordinating Board with the heads of a number of state agencies as members, including the Water Resources Board. Oregon has a State Water Management Group and a Governor's Watershed Enhancement Board in which the several water-related agency and commission heads participate. In Utah, the governor established a Water Development Coordinating Committee that includes the directors of the Division of Water Resources, Bureau of Water Pollution Control, Bureau of Public Water Supply, Division of Community Development, and the State Treasurer. The committee coordinates funding requests and actions on water resources, water pollution control, and drinking water projects, and makes recommendations to the legislature when the existing funding is inadequate for needed projects.

* * *

Single Agency Coordination

In Washington, the water allocation program and the water quality control program are in a single executive department under the same director. * * * When the water allocation section receives applications for water use permits that appear to have any potential impact on water quality, the water quality section is notified. * * * Fisheries and wildlife officials are notified if an application has a potential impact on these resources.

The Texas Water Commission reviews functions and policies for both water administration and water quality regulation. * * *

Formal Coordination and Planning

Kansas formally coordinates quality and allocation issues in the water planning process but relies on administrative methods to implement policy. The planning process is a dynamic system for exploring policy alternatives and selecting from among options one that becomes a mandate of every agency. The subject matter is wide-ranging to include all aspects of water quality, such as nonpoint sources, wetlands, instream flows, and other issues. Once policy has been set, the agencies coordinate their activities through a number of informal procedures.

* * *

Integrated Responsibility for Allocation and Quality

California is the only state that has merged water resource allocation functions with water pollution and water quality control in a single body. The State Water Resources Control Board issues permits to persons who want to initiate a new water use. * * *

One of the board's mandates in authorizing an appropriation is to coordinate the permitted use with regional water quality control plans. All permits require that a water user adhere to water quality plans even if change becomes necessary after the permit is granted. Thus, the board may limit existing water uses as well as newly permitted uses in order to impose water quality standards when it deems them necessary to fulfill planning objectives and to carry out the public interest. * * *

On balance, it appears that the fullest integration of state water quality and water allocation functions is the most effective and desirable. There are arguments against separating water quality matters and expertise from another agency charged primarily with regulating all other types of pollution (e.g., air, hazardous wastes) and concentrating them in a water agency. Separation arguably will fragment overall, multi-media pollution control efforts. Still, the most integrated and coordinated systems appear to work the best and states should study ways to improve their institutions in ways that will improve water quality and comport with water allocation systems.

* * *

2. The prior appropriation system offers many opportunities for protecting water quality

The prior appropriation doctrine recognizes the right to water quality protection to a limited degree. * * *

Protection of Existing Water Rights

* * *

A person whose property rights—including water rights—are harmed by another's pollution may sue in tort for nuisance or trespass.[152] Many early cases involved complaints by one water user of another's pollution. The courts recognized that appropriators have a right to water quality good enough to carry out the uses for which they made their appropriation. Typical cases involved downstream appropriators, often farmers, who successfully pursued remedies against upstream appropriators, often miners.[153] The rule that allows a downstream appropriator to protect beneficial uses from impairment by upstream pollution generally is applied if the downstream plaintiff is a senior appropriator. But it has also been applied to prevent a senior's upstream pollution to the detriment of a downstream user if the senior can prevent the harm to water quality at minimal expense and inconvenience.[154] * * * Pollution is restricted only if it can be shown to injure the water uses of another appropriator. People who do not hold water rights might want to protect water quality, but only those with appropriative rights can sue.

Appropriators also have difficulties enforcing their private remedies. They must prove causation, deal with multiple parties, and pay the costs of litigation; cost alone may deter them from taking action. When they do assert their rights, they may be inclined to accept a favorable settlement, and that will end the matter although the rights of other water rights holders continue to be affected.

The protection of water quality sufficient to meet the needs of future water appropriators or of recreational or other uses thus should not be left to the private remedies of individual appropriators. The inadequacies of traditional tort litigation to control pollution was one of the factors that led the federal government and the states to enact water pollution control legislation.

152. E.g., Springer v. Joseph Schlitz Brewing Co., 510 F.2d 468 (4th Cir.1975) [page 121, supra] (polluter liable to property owner for fish kills from pollutant discharges); Atlas Chemical Industries, Inc. v. Anderson, 514 S.W.2d 309 (Tex.Ct.App. 1974) (liability to property owners for polluting creek running through property); Cities Service Oil Co. v. Marritt, 332 P.2d 677 (Okla.1958) (nuisance liability for polluting well); Burr v. Eidemiller, Inc., 386 Pa. 416, 126 A.2d 403 (1956) (liability for contaminating water supply with releases of construction debris). These cases involve riparian water rights as well as appropriation rights.

153. E.g., Ravndal v. Northfork Placers, 60 Idaho 305, 91 P.2d 368 (1939); Cushman v. Highland Ditch Co., 33 P. 344 (Colo.App. 1893); Larimer County Reservoir Co. v. People ex rel. Luthe, 8 Colo. 614, 9 P. 794 (1886); State v. California Packing Co., 105 Utah 182, 141 P.2d 386 (1943); Humphries Tunnel and Mining Co. v. Frank, 105 P. 1093 (Colo.1909); Helena v. Rogan, 26 Mont. 452, 68 P. 798 (1902).

154. Suffolk Gold Mining & Milling Co. v. San Miguel Consol. Mining & Milling Co., 9 Colo.App. 407, 48 P. 828 (1897); appeal dismissed, 24 Colo. 468, 52 P. 1027 (1898). See also Wilmore v. Chain O'Mines, 44 P.2d 1024 (Colo.1934).

Considering Water Quality in the Allocation Process

* * *

In most states, water quality is included directly or indirectly in the considerations of state agencies that issue permits to appropriate water. Thus, state law may require agencies to consider water quality in finding that: the use will not impair existing rights; the use is beneficial; and the administrative decision is in the "public interest." In these cases, decisions to grant or deny a permit, or to impose conditions on uses, may be made on grounds of water quality.

Nonimpairment of existing rights

Existing water users do not have complete protection for their rights unless they are assured that new or changed uses will not interfere with their uses. Kansas law forbids the issuance of a surface or groundwater permit that will impair a use under an existing water right; impairment is defined to include the "unreasonable deterioration of the water quality at the water user's point of diversion beyond a reasonable economic limit." In Colorado, permits to appropriate groundwater within designated groundwater basins may not be issued if the proposed appropriation would "unreasonably impair existing water rights from the same source." Impairment of existing uses is defined to include "the unreasonable deterioration of water quality."

A change in a water right such as for a different purpose or place of use is always subject to a nonimpairment or "no injury" requirement. New Mexico decisions have dealt with water quality impairment to existing groundwater rights caused by a change in well location. These cases have established the authority of the state engineer to deny or condition proposed changes of rights if necessary to protect existing rights from water quality-related injury.

Colorado law promotes exchanges of water and the use of substitute supplies to maximize utilization of its water resources. It requires that exchanged or substituted water be of a quality (as well as quantity) that can "meet the requirements of use" to which the exchanged-for water has been put. * * *

Administrative examination of the water quality effects of new or changed uses can improve protection for existing rights. * * * States seem more inclined to condition or deny water permits or changes if existing water uses will be impaired than if there would be no immediate damage to water rights. Protection against impairment, however, does not fully carry out a policy of protecting water quality for future users or the public unless their interests coincide with those of existing users.

The beneficial use requirement

* * * Since the earliest western water rights decisions, the courts have recognized that there is no right to use water wastefully, i.e., nonbeneficially. The antiwaste principle embodied in the beneficial use requirement has been applied in a limited way, particularly in groundwater allocation. For example, an Oklahoma statute requires

the State Water Resources Board to find that waste will not occur before approving an application for a groundwater permit. * * * And, the Montana groundwater code prohibits the waste of groundwater and includes a requirement that all wells be constructed and maintained to prevent waste, contamination, or pollution of groundwater.

The beneficial use requirement is being applied more broadly to prohibit inefficient water use and could be expanded to prohibit undue water degradation. A policy of maximizing beneficial uses of water is inherent in the appropriation doctrine. Courts have interpreted that goal to require reasonably efficient means of diversion. The efficiency principle prevents appropriators from commanding more water than is reasonably necessary to satisfy their own appropriations; similarly, a polluter should not be able to use the stream to carry away so much waste that it limits other uses. The same principle would prevent depletions so great that pollutants become overly concentrated in the remaining water. Inefficient diversions and uses that result in a polluted stream should not be considered "beneficial uses," since both involve wasteful uses of the resource.

* * * For example, a water allocation agency could deny a right to irrigate a highly saline field, restrict the quantity of water applied to the field or require treatment of saline return flows. It also might deny the right to deplete or impound water that would degrade quality in the remaining stream to the extent of damaging other existing and future beneficial uses. Beneficial uses include recreation and fish and wildlife in most states. Adverse impacts on these uses thus can be considered in the determination that a proposed use will lead to maximum utilization.

The use of water law, specifically the doctrine of beneficial use, as a basis for enacting legislation, exercising police power regulation, and resolving cases in court to control pollution, has great untested potential. Efforts to maintain water quality can be based on the beneficial use doctrine in existing appropriation law, but stronger, more explicit statutes and regulations would bolster this approach.

Public interest review

Nearly all western states now consider the public interest in issuing a permit to use water. In a few states, statutes or case law expressly mention that water quality effects must be examined in determining the public interest. * * * Alaska law requires that "the effect on public health" be among the public interest considerations weighed in water decisions. A Montana statute requires a finding that the public interest, including water quality, be satisfied before a large appropriation is approved. Although some statutes fail to define the factors that are within the "public interest," water quality is probably the most logical and natural choice for inclusion. Accordingly, the Idaho Supreme Court has held that determinations under the Idaho public interest statute must include a consideration of water quality effects.

California water law requires that the State Water Resources Control Board reject an application for a permit to appropriate water found not to be in the public interest. A California Court of Appeal has said that this public interest provision extends to the consideration of water quality standards established under state and federal law.

* * *

Protecting Instream Flows to Safeguard Water Quality

* * *

If a certain quantity of water is required to remain in the stream, at some point existing appropriators may have to forego diverting water and new appropriators will be told that no water is available for appropriation. This may seem inconsistent with the prior appropriation doctrine, which allows diversions by anyone with a beneficial use. In fact, protection of a certain level of instream flows is essential to preserve the capacity of all appropriators to make beneficial uses of the water. If proper streamflows are maintained, appropriators can be assured that diversion and use of water by themselves and others will not adversely affect the quality of the water. * * *

Public Trust Considerations

Courts in a few western states have recognized that the state has a trust responsibility to all citizens in the allocation of state waters. Water is public property under several state constitutions, held and allocated by the state for the benefit of the people. Permits to use state waters must be consistent with the state's fiduciary responsibility for how water is used.

* * *

Professor Ralph Johnson has urged that the public trust doctrine be applied expansively to regulate water uses by prior appropriators in order to protect water quality. He argues that multiple dispersed sources of pollution individually are too insignificant to be controlled as nuisances or invasions of others' rights, although collectively they can profoundly degrade stream quality. Unless these sources are controlled, stream quality could become so degraded that the water would be useless for other appropriators and for the public.

* * *

3. Water management areas are sometimes used to protect water quality

Many western states have established special management areas to preserve and equitably allocate water supplies, usually groundwater. Typically, groundwater withdrawals exceed recharge in these areas. Management consists of limiting pumping to control depletions, although water quality protection may be an additional objective. Several states have authorized establishment of these areas specifically to respond to water quality problems.

* * *

4. States can consider the effects of water uses within existing water quality protection programs

* * *

Nonpoint Source Control

The largest remaining uncontrolled pollution of the nation's waters comes from nonpoint sources. Return flows from irrigated agriculture, which carry contaminants leached out of the soils and residues from fertilizer and pesticide applications into groundwater and surface water, are the primary source of water quality problems in agricultural areas of the West. Dams and other impoundments also affect water quality and are treated as nonpoint sources under the Clean Water Act.

Stronger control of nonpoint source pollution could be joined to the requirement under sections 208 and 303(e) of the Clean Water Act that the states develop water quality management plans. The plans are to identify nonpoint sources of pollution and management practices to reduce them. Section 303(d) of the Clean Water Act requires states to determine "total maximum daily loads" (TMDL) for all waters not achieving water quality standards, which are the total amounts of specified pollutants that can be discharged into that water without causing a violation of water quality standards. States may allocate the necessary load reductions among the pollutant sources, including nonpoint sources.

The attraction of this approach is that *all* sources of water quality impairment are identified and the states can devise strategies for sharing the burden of water quality improvement. If, for example, it is more cost effective for a point source discharger to help control pollution from nonpoint sources than to invest in further treatment of its effluent, the state could design such an approach. States have taken little action under sections 208 and 303, however, and there has been scant federal initiative or financial support for creating forceful nonpoint source programs under these provisions.

Congress amended the Clean Water Act in 1987, taking a more active approach to the issue. States now are required to assess nonpoint source problems and develop programs to remedy them. Generally the states have complied, but few state programs attempt to rigorously control nonpoint source pollution and none have yet proven their effectiveness.

States also are now required to identify the best management practices (BMPs) to reduce pollutant loadings from nonpoint sources identified in their assessment reports. Programs must be developed to implement the BMPs, including annual milestones, and sources of funding identified. These provisions have encouraged states to examine their nonpoint source problems, but they do not require performance. Thus, states are likely to emphasize voluntary actions such as demonstration projects and unlikely to pursue regulatory alternatives.

* * *

Section 401 Certification

Applicants for a federal license or permit to undertake an activity that will discharge pollutants are required under [section 401 of] the Clean Water Act to obtain a certification from the state that the discharge will meet state water quality requirements. This certification process allows states to ensure that activities requiring a dredge and fill permit under section 404 of the Clean Water Act, or hydroelectric facilities requiring a license from the Federal Energy Regulatory Commission (FERC), also comply with state water quality requirements, which can exceed federal standards.

States have limited experience to date in using the section 401 certification process to protect their water quality interests. * * *

Antidegradation

State water quality standards must conform with an "antidegradation" policy that assures that certain existing uses, and water quality necessary to protect them, will be maintained. Certain high quality waters that exceed standards necessary to protect existing uses also must be maintained unless it is determined through a public process that lowering the quality is necessary to accommodate important economic or social development.

* * *

States have not adequately addressed water quality impairment caused by water use

The picture that emerges from this review of approaches to water degradation caused by water use is that states have many opportunities to protect water quality within existing state laws and programs that accommodate water allocation systems but are only beginning to take advantage of them. Further, these crucial problems are being dealt with in a fragmented way. States have initiated several interesting individual efforts that are worthy components of a state program. But no state has developed a coherent and comprehensive program based on a well-considered state water quality protection policy. Unless states deal more decisively and comprehensively with water use-induced water quality problems, new and existing water uses that depend on maintaining high water quality remain threatened. * * *

C. THE STATUTORY OVERLAY

1. Overview

Appropriation, as originally developed by the courts, was essentially a rule of capture. A right was perfected by diverting a stream and putting it to use. At first, these were the only requirements for perfecting a water right, with some states also imposing minor procedural requirements such as posting a notice or filing a paper in a county courthouse.

Now, however, appropriation is controlled by complex state statutes. These statutes regulate every aspect of appropriation, laying out detailed conditions for new appropriations and changes of use and regulating the use and management of water. Today, one looks first to state statutes and the rules of administrative agencies and only secondarily to doctrines and concepts. A history of practical problems explains why states moved away from the apparent simplicity of the early prior appropriation law.

Early records were notoriously imprecise, and there was no single place one could look to determine rights claimed in a river that might run through several counties. In addition, most appropriators claimed rights to far more water than they actually needed or used. This was due in part to their own lack of knowledge and in part to the desire to assure that they would have plenty of water to meet any future needs. Poor records and paper over-appropriation made investments in expensive diversion and storage facilities risky.

What records were available were the result of judicial decisions in disputes that would arise among appropriators. The decree in a water rights adjudication might be helpful to a prospective appropriator but it was only conclusive as among those who actually were joined in the case. The first step in moving toward better water rights determinations was for states to allow general stream adjudications. All interested parties in a watershed would be joined in a lawsuit to decide their relative rights. Claims would be integrated with any piecemeal adjudications that had been made in the past and the priority dates and quantities of rights decided by the court.

General stream adjudications were improvements over the early free-for-all appropriation system but once judgments became final, they usually lacked any way to integrate new rights and there was no system for administering decreed rights. The actual opening and closing of headgates to divert or cut off the flow of water to individual appropriators was often not regulated by anyone but the water users themselves. This lack of supervision sometimes led to gunfire and other inappropriate forms of self-help. See Coffin v. Left Hand Ditch Co., page 160, supra.

Transfers of water rights provided another source of confusion. To the extent that changes in an appropriator's point of diversion were permitted without central coordination, a gap would arise between the record and actual locations of water rights on a given stream.

For these and other reasons, most of the western states began to exercise increasing administrative control over the acquisition and administration of water rights. Under the permit statutes adopted in all appropriation states but Colorado, a state administrative agency or official, such as the state engineer, is delegated the authority to administer the acquisition, transfer, and sometimes the loss of surface water rights. The agency has quasi-judicial functions. The same issues in Colorado are left to water courts that have administrative functions. Following, for comparison purposes, are brief descriptions of three states' permit systems, and Colorado's judicial approach. Wyoming represents the oldest and original model system. Montana's was enacted in 1973 and only recently implemented. California has a hybrid system of water rights; riparian and appropriative rights exist side-by-side.

For general discussions of the conditions which led to the enactment of legislation subjecting appropriation to a state permit process see Elwood Mead, Irrigation Institutions (1903), especially pages 60–87 and 147–59. See also Michael V. McIntire, *The Disparity Between State Water Rights Records and Actual Water Use Patterns—"I Wonder Where the Water Went?"*, 5 Land & Water L.Rev. 23 (1970).

2. State Variations

The Wyoming System

Before enacting a permit statute, Wyoming had a procedure under territorial law that required all water rights claimants to file statements in the proper district court in order to adjudicate water rights. Wyo.Laws 1886 Ch. 61, Irrigation Water Rights Act of 1886. In 1890, Wyoming passed a comprehensive water rights act immediately upon achieving statehood. The Act incorporated many of the ideas of Elwood Mead, reflecting his belief in centralized control of water. Mead, a young engineer and reformer lawyer while he was at Colorado Agricultural College, later Colorado State University, was the first territorial engineer, then the state engineer of Wyoming, and later the Commissioner of the Bureau of Reclamation. See James R. Kluger, Turning on the Water with a Shovel: The Career of Elwood Mead (1992).

Ironically, the "Wyoming" system of water rights administration is based on a system developed in Northern Colorado but rejected by the Colorado legislature twelve years earlier. The Wyoming Constitution embodied the ideal of state control espoused by Mead. The implementing legislation requires applicants to acquire a permit from a state agency, the Board of Control, to perfect a water right. An appropriator under this system does not have a choice between judicial and administrative acquisition of a right. The latter is exclusive and use of water without a permit is unlawful. Wyo.Stat. § 41–4–501.

The statute was attacked on the basis that it unconstitutionally delegated judicial functions to a non-judicial, administrative agency. Farm Investment Co. v. Carpenter, 61 P. 258 (Wyo.1900). The court upheld the statute stating:

> The statute nowhere attempts to divest the courts of any jurisdiction granted to them by the constitution to redress grievances and afford relief at law or in equity under the ordinary and well known rules of procedure. * * * The proceeding is one in which the claimant does not obtain redress for an injury, but secures evidence of title to a valuable right—a right to use a peculiar public commodity. * * * The board, it is true, acts judicially; but the power exercised is quasi-judicial only, and such as, under proper

circumstances, may appropriately be conferred upon executive officers or boards.

Under the Wyoming system, prior use without a state permit is subordinate to subsequent use with a permit because "[a] different decision would leave prevalent many of the acknowledged evils of the territorial system intended to be superseded by the system of state control contemplated in the Constitution and carried into effect by the law of 1890." Wyoming Hereford Ranch v. Hammond Packing Co., 236 P. 764 (Wyo.1925).

To obtain a permit to appropriate water, or to enlarge an existing right, one must apply to the state engineer who approves or rejects an application. The Wyoming Constitution provides that "no appropriation shall be denied except when such denial is demanded by the public interest." Wyo.Const. art. VIII, § 3. Implementing this mandate, the state engineer will approve an application to apply water to a beneficial use so long as the appropriation will not impair the value of existing rights or cause detriment to the public welfare. Wyo.Stat.Ann. § 41–4–503. If the proposed new use will lead to either type of harm the state engineer has a duty to reject the application. Though there is no express authority for the state engineer to impose conditions on the permit, the courts have held that such authority falls within the power to deny permits when it is in the public interest. Big Horn Power Co. v. State, 148 P. 1110 (Wyo.1915).

Once a permit has been issued, and any required work completed within the time set for construction (not to exceed five years), the applicant may submit proof that the appropriation has been perfected to the superintendent of the water division where the right is located. Final proof of appropriation must be made within five years of the time allowed for completion of the application of water to a beneficial use. Notice of permit issuance is given to the public who may contest any of the proposed determinations. All information on the appropriation is transmitted to the Board of Control, which issues a "Certificate of Appropriation" if it is satisfied that the appropriation has been perfected according to the terms of the permit and that no conflicts exist. The priority date of the perfected right dates from the filing of the permit application with the state engineer. Appeals are available to the board from the action of the state engineer or to the district court from the action of the board.

The Wyoming Act also provides a means for adjudicating all existing rights in a stream. Wyo.Stat. §§ 41–4–310 to 316. All general stream adjudications were complete by 1927 and parties were issued certificates evidencing recognized water rights. The validity of the adjudication procedure was upheld by the Wyoming Supreme Court. Anita Ditch Co. v. Turner, 389 P.2d 1018, 1021 (Wyo.1964). For a thorough review, see Mark Squillace, *One Hundred Years of Wyoming Water Law,* 26 Land & Water L.Rev. 93 (1991); Mark Squillace, *A Critical Look at Wyoming Water Law,* 24 Land & Water L.Rev. 309 (1989).

The Montana System

The Montana permit system has its roots in the Montana Water Use Act of 1973, 1973 Mont.Laws ch. 452, codified in various sections of Mont.Code Ann. title 85, passed after a new state constitution was adopted in 1972. Mont. Const. art. IX, § 3. Prior to that time, neither the state engineer, the State Water Conservation Board, nor their 1971 successor, the Department of Natural Resources and Conservation, were involved in the procedures for appropriating or adjudicating water rights. See Albert W. Stone, *The Long Count on Dempsey: No Final Decision On Water Right Adjudication,* 31 Mont.L.Rev. 1 (1965).

Under the Water Use Act, Mont.Code Ann. §§ 85–2–101 to 807, the Department of Natural Resources and Conservation was required to establish a centralized record system for existing rights and to initiate adjudications of water rights. The department selected specific areas or sources of water to begin proceedings to determine existing rights. The department did the on-site investigation to ascertain all of the persons who might have rights, as well as the quantity and priority of each. The task was enormous, because many of the rights were not of record, and may not have been in use for long periods, so that information was difficult to obtain. This proved to be inefficient and time consuming, and led to amendments to the Act, which divided the state into four large water divisions in an effort to expedite adjudications. The burden of gathering data on existing rights shifted to the users and claimants, who had to file their claims by April 30, 1982 or be conclusively presumed to have abandoned non-filed claims.

Each water division has a district judge designated as the water judge for that division, Mont.Code Ann. § 3–7–201. In practice, the water judge issues preliminary decrees within a division. In divisions where there are claims of federal or Indian reserved water rights, the judge will issue a "temporary preliminary decree." The purpose is to adjudicate only state water rights, with reserved rights to be inserted later as a result of pending negotiations on "compacts" with the United States and the tribes.

After issuance of a preliminary decree (or temporary preliminary decree), persons may file objections and obtain a hearing which can be complex and time consuming. After objections and hearings, the water judge may revise the preliminary decree, followed by further proceedings. Ultimately the judge issues a final decree that is appealable to the Montana Supreme Court. There may be multiple, legally-unrelated final decrees within a division.

As of October 9, 1992, 216,443 claims had been filed, 129,604 of which had been examined. Final decrees had been issued in 15,393 cases and another 81,875 claims had received preliminary or temporary preliminary decrees.

In a May, 1987 report, an engineering firm on contract with one of the large utilities involved in the adjudication process issued an evaluation critical of the accuracy of the adjudications in two sample sub-basins of the Clark Fork River drainage. The study reports that of the 70,000 claims decreed statewide by early 1986, only 20 had been verified by a field investigation. In one sub-basin, "[t]he Water Court decreed 9.5% more water volume than claimed and 171% more than calculated [by the department] in the verification process." The report concludes that there "is clearly an insufficient number of field investigations to ensure that the adjudication process is factually correct." Hydrometrics, Executive Summary of the Evaluation of the State of Montana Water Rights Adjudication Process for Sub–Basins 76K and 76E of the Clark Fork River Drainage, Montana (May 4, 1987).

The Montana courts have continually upheld the water adjudication process over constitutional challenges. The Montana Supreme Court held that the water court, not the Department of Natural Resources and Conservation, has the authority to promulgate rules for verification of water claims, although the supreme court determined that it would supervise the adoption of verification rules. Swift v. State, Dep't of Natural Resources & Conservation, 736 P.2d 117 (Mont. 1987). The supreme court upheld the constitutionality of requiring quantification of both flow rate and volume, McDonald v. Montana, 722 P.2d 598 (Mont.1986), and most recently the court upheld the constitutionality of barring claims which were filed late. In the Matter of Yellowstone River, 832 P.2d 1210 (Mont.1992).

To acquire a new right, as distinguished from adjudicating existing rights, application is made to the department, which must issue a permit if certain criteria are met as specified by statute. For applications of less than 4,000 acre-feet per year and less than 5.5 cfs, the principal limitations are that there be sufficient unappropriated water, that other appropriators will not be adversely affected, that the diversion will be properly constructed, and that the proposed use is beneficial. For applications in excess of that amount, the department is required by 1985 amendments to consider a broad range of economic and environmental factors, impacts and benefits to the state. Public interest factors in allocating waters are discussed further at page 263, infra. Private parties may not appropriate water if either: (1) water would be consumed in excess of 4,000 acre-feet per year and 5.5 cfs; or (2) water would be transported out of the basins of the Clark Fork, Kootenai, St. Mary, Little Missouri, Yellowstone, or Missouri rivers. Water in excess of such quantities or for export from these basins must be leased from the state. See John E. Thorson, et al., *Forging Public Rights in Montana's Waters,* 6 Pub.Land L.Rev. 1 (1985).

Once the appropriation has been made, the permittee receives a certificate of water right, but the certificate may not be issued for a right to a specific source until there has been a general adjudication of existing rights in that source. Because there have been very few final decrees, there are practically no final certificates of water rights. Objections to applications for water rights may be filed and a hearing will be held if the department either determines that an objection states a valid claim, or the department has imposed terms or conditions on the approval of the permit, and the applicant requests a hearing.

The priority date of a right obtained under the permit system is the filing date of the permit application. The permit system is the exclusive means of obtaining water rights; however, governmental entities may apply to the Board of Natural Resources and Conservation for a reservation of water for present or future use. Mont.Code Ann. § 85–1–316 (1985). These reservations can amount to half the flow of certain named rivers. See page 203, supra. Parties opposing decisions of the department may request a hearing before the Board of Natural Resources and Conservation. Both the distribution of water rights and the adjudication of disputes are within the district court's jurisdiction.

The California System

California's prior appropriation permit system is administered by the State Water Resources Control Board. Anyone wishing to appropriate surface water or water in "subterranean streams flowing in known and definite channels" must obtain a permit. Waters already appropriated or waters needed for useful and beneficial purposes on riparian lands are excepted. Cal.Water Code § 1201. Riparian rights are still recognized, but a 1928 constitutional amendment limited common law rights by imposing a requirement that all water rights not exceed an amount of water reasonably required for the purposes of the adjacent lands. Cal. Const. art. X, § 2; see pages 147–48, supra.

The permit application must provide information on the source, nature and amount of use, place of use and diversion, and time needed to construct the diversion structure and apply the water to beneficial use. The board must calculate the availability of unappropriated water and, if necessary, the amount that must remain in the source for other beneficial uses, including uses protected by water quality control plans. Notice must be given to the public. Any person, whether or not a water right holder, may protest the approval of an application, and the applicant has to file an answer to every protest.

The board conducts a field investigation to resolve protests. Formal hearings may be held or the parties may agree to a proceeding in lieu of a hearing. Before a permit is issued, each application is reviewed to determine whether an environmental impact report is needed pursuant to the California Environmental Quality Act. Most applications for water rights permits do not require impact reports.

Temporary permits are available to a party who has an urgent need to appropriate water if it is found that unappropriated water is available, the rights of downstream users are not injured, and the environment will not be unreasonably affected. Interim use permits are available to allow use by others of water already appropriated but not yet needed by a municipality. Before a permanent right to appropriate water is granted, the permittee must demonstrate "due diligence" in applying it to a beneficial use. Annual progress reports must be filed with the board or else permits may be revoked. The only exceptions are appropriations by municipalities and applications of the Department of Water Resources. Standard terms and conditions are included in permits, such as continuing authority by the board to prevent waste, unreasonable use, etc. This has become a powerful tool for conserving water. See IID–MWD transfer discussed at page 326, infra. In two situations, the board may reserve jurisdiction to change terms and conditions of a permit: if there was insufficient information to decide which conditions were needed, or if the permit is part of a large project and related applications are pending.

Once a permittee has completed construction of a diversion structure and applied the water to beneficial use, the board investigates to confirm completion and compliance. If all is in order, the board issues a license that may be subject to the terms and conditions included in the permit and others that may be required by statute. See pages 294–303, infra, on the Mono Lake litigation. A license is granted for so long as the water appropriated under it is used for a useful and beneficial purpose. Cal.Water Code § 1627. Licenses may be revoked for failure to use the water beneficially or reasonably, or for failure to comply with the terms and conditions imposed on the license.

California's permit system is not exclusive, so there are users with rights to surface waters who are not required to comply with the permitting process. Riparian owners, appropriators prior to 1914, users of spring waters originating and remaining on their land, and cities with pueblo rights * need not obtain water right permits. In principle, many should file statements of water diversion and use (see Cal.Water Code § 5105), but they often do not. The board's policy is to disregard prescriptive surface rights initiated subsequent to 1914 unless they are supported by a permit, a position sustained by the California Supreme Court. People v. Shirokow, 605 P.2d 859 (Cal.1980).

The hybrid system in which riparian rights coexist with rights by prior appropriation complicates administration of water rights. Superiority among rights depends largely upon the respective times of accrual of the rights, or date of priority. Generally, a riparian's date of priority is the date the lands first passed from public to private ownership.

California has adjudication procedures to determine and integrate all water rights claimed on a stream system, including those established by appropriation, riparian right, or any other basis. The statutory procedure, created in 1913, underwent a major revision in 1976 in an effort to shorten staff involvement time. Cal.Water Code § 2501.

An adjudication is initiated by petition to the board by a claimant on the stream system. Claimants are then notified, and an investigation and report follow. A decree ultimately establishes all rights to the use of water. This procedure does not include underground water supplies other than subterranean streams flowing through known and definite channels, but a specific exception was made by the legislature in 1971 for the Scott River stream system after it was discovered through investigation that withdrawal of the groundwater caused a reduction in surface flow.

When there is a suit over water rights on an unadjudicated stream, the courts may refer the suit to the board for a determination of

---

* A "pueblo right" is "The paramount right of an American city as successor of a Spanish or Mexican pueblo (municipality) to the use of water naturally occurring within the old pueblo limits for the use of the inhabitants of the city." Wells Aleck Hutchins, The California Law of Water Rights 256 (1956). See page 590, infra.

physical facts or an investigation of issues. Following this investigation and hearings, the court enters its decree.

The Colorado System

Colorado is the only prior appropriation state that does not have a permit system. Language in the state constitution is similar to many other western states' constitutions. It provides that "the right to divert the unappropriated waters of any natural stream shall never be denied." Colo. Const. art. XVI, § 6. This has been read so literally that some commentators and courts have argued that it means that appropriators may not be required to seek agency permission before claiming a water right. See John U. Carlson, *Report to Governor John A. Love on Certain Colorado Water Law Problems,* 50 Denver L.J. 293, 295 (1973). See also People ex rel. Park Reservoir Co. v. Hinderlider, 57 P.2d 894 (Colo.1936). Rather, appropriators make the claim first and then seek a "decreed" right in court. As a practical matter, however, an appropriation that has not been decreed has little value because it is junior to all decreed rights. Thus, it cannot be enforced until all decreed rights have been satisfied.

Prior to 1969, the adjudication of water rights was the responsibility of the district courts in some seventy water districts, roughly coterminous with county lines. The claimant sought an adjudication, with notice given to all parties. Following a court proceeding where the claims, along with minimal information provided by the state engineer, were considered, a decree was issued listing the rights in priority order. In the early days this system, with little participation by state agencies, resulted in many inflated paper decrees.

Substantial changes were made by the Water Right Determination and Administration Act of 1969, Colo.Rev.Stat. §§ 37–92–101 through – 602. Seven water divisions were created in the state, vastly simplifying the earlier administrative arrangements. Each division has a division engineer who reports to the state engineer. "Water matters" are considered in a water court in each division, with a water judge, referee, and a water clerk. Applicants for a conditional water right, absolute water right, or change in an existing water right (including transfer) file an application with the water clerk. Monthly resumes of the applications are published in the local media and sent to those potentially affected. An opportunity is provided to file statements of opposition to the applications. After consulting with the division and state engineers, the referee makes a ruling, approving, approving in part, or denying each application. Persons dissatisfied with the ruling may file a protest. A protest results in a hearing at which the water judge determines the issues de novo. Parties typically hire lawyers and engineers to represent them. Multiple party cases are not cheap in Colorado. The referee's rulings, including those against which no protest has been filed, are reviewed semi-annually by the water judge, who can confirm, modify, or reverse the ruling. Appeals go directly to the Colorado Supreme Court. Transfers and other changes in water rights are judged by standards designed to prevent injury to existing water rights, including those with later priorities than the right for which the change is sought. (Protection of "junior" appropriators is a major characteristic of the appropriation system, and is discussed at page 310, infra.)

Water rights can be lost through abandonment in Colorado. There is no statutory forfeiture provision, although non-use for a period of ten years creates a rebuttable presumption of abandonment. Colo.Rev. Stat. § 37–92–402. Division engineers compile and publish a tabulation of all water rights in their division every four years. The tabulation reflects all newly decreed conditional and absolute rights and abandonments. These tabulations may be protested in hearings before the water judge.

D. WATER AVAILABLE FOR APPROPRIATION

A prerequisite to obtaining a water right in a prior appropriation state is the availability of unappropriated water in a natural stream or lake. A water right is no guarantee that water will be available because rights may exist in flows that occur only occasionally. Administrative agencies must decide as a policy and technical matter how often water must be available in the stream to justify issuing rights in it. They must also determine how much impact or inconvenience of senior users will be allowed.

The sources of water from which appropriations may be made include natural watercourses; diffused water (runoff) is usually left to the control of landowners. The definition of watercourses establishes the extent of public control of waters. Some western states assert greater control by adopting a more inclusive definition. The tendency to consider water to be within natural watercourses, and thus under state regulation, is motivated in part by considerations of efficiency that can be enforced under the prior appropriation system. See pages 59–61, supra, discussing watercourses and diffused surface waters.

1. "Unappropriated Water"

Where the supply of water from a stream regularly exceeds the aggregate of all existing rights, a new appropriator has no trouble finding unappropriated water. But even if a stream is described as "over-appropriated" this does not necessarily mean that there is no water available for a new appropriation. "Over-appropriated" means only that there are users who perhaps are not satisfied in some average years, or who are not satisfied during a certain season of the year, usually the irrigation season. Some uses that appear to command water on paper may have been lost through abandonment or forfeitures not yet reflected in the records. Conditional rights may survive on paper, though in fact they will not ever be fully utilized and may be eventually cancelled for lack of diligent application to a beneficial use, thus "freeing up" now apparently appropriated water for the stream and for new appropriators. Do these possibilities suggest that appropriations should be liberally allowed, even when water "appears" to be in short supply?

When administrative agencies are charged with exercising discretion over new appropriations, they are confronted with a dilemma on over-appropriated streams: If a permit is granted, investments may be made on the expectation that water will continue to be available. If a permit is denied, important and valuable uses may be prevented or juniors may be forced to develop more costly alternative supplies. If a junior appropriator is willing to take a chance on making use of water that may in fact be available only every few years or that may be diverted away in the future by seniors with conditional rights, why not allow it? To do so seems consistent with the ideal of maximizing the beneficial use of streams. Are seniors prejudiced by allowing a stream to become over-appropriated? Are there public policy reasons for not doing so?

In determining what water is "unappropriated," should the water agency look behind the paper rights that exist on a stream and attempt to determine the amount of water that is actually being used, i.e., discount rights exceeding the quantity that can be used beneficially and those that are subject to abandonment or forfeiture?

Although the Colorado River in Texas appears fully appropriated on paper, some 1.6 million acre-feet of water flow to the Gulf of Mexico annually. Developers have attempted, unsuccessfully, to convince the state water commission and the state supreme court that they should discount existing paper water rights and find that water is available for appropriation. Lower Colorado River Auth. v. Texas Dept. of Water Resources, 689 S.W.2d 873 (Tex.1984). The court defended a restrictive interpretation of unappropriated water that counted all existing uncancelled permits and filings at their recorded levels, stating that the water agency should be more aggressive in pursuing actions to cancel rights that are subject to forfeiture.

Is the Texas court correct that the best way to protect senior rights is to consider all rights "on the books" as valid and unavailable for appropriation? Are factors other than senior rights protection and physical availability relevant?

The Colorado Supreme Court has held that even when a river is over-appropriated, a new appropriator will be allowed if no material injury will occur to senior users. Southeastern Colorado Water Conservancy Dist. v. Rich, 625 P.2d 977 (Colo.1981). What is a "material injury"? A later case held that the policy of encouraging maximum (or optimum) utilization of water resources allowed the state engineer to require senior appropriators to drill wells to fulfill their water rights in order to allow for junior appropriations, even though the senior rights were originally for surface diversions. Alamosa–La Jara Water Users Protection Ass'n v. Gould, 674 P.2d 914 (Colo.1983), page 281, infra. The court cautioned, however, that the state engineer must consider a variety of economic and environmental factors in deciding how much water was available for appropriation inasmuch as "the policy of maximum utilization does not require a single-minded endeavor to squeeze every drop of water from the valley's aquifer."

2. Reuse of Appropriated Water

Once water is diverted from a watercourse, and used, appropriators may be limited in their ability to reuse it. The extent of reuse may depend on the original source of the water and on whether the appropriator has relinquished control so that the water may be deemed to have returned to the watercourse. As with the definition of unappropriated water, whether to allow reuse entails technical and policy factors.

ESTATE OF PAUL STEED v. NEW ESCALANTE IRRIGATION CO.

Supreme Court of Utah, 1992.
846 P.2d 1223.

HOWE, ASSOCIATE CHIEF JUSTICE:

I. FACTS

This case involves the use of water in Alvey Wash, which is south of the town of Escalante in Garfield County. The wash is shaped like a horseshoe opening to the south, with one prong of the wash coming from the southwest and the other prong going to the southeast. Escalante is located immediately north of the bend in the horseshoe. The inside of the southwest prong is bordered by tall and impenetrable cliffs. The land inside the horseshoe slopes gently from the base of the east side of those cliffs across the middle of the horseshoe toward the east prong. A substantial part of that land has been irrigated for over one hundred years with water diverted from the Escalante River, which runs north of Escalante in a generally west to east direction, and with water taken from the southeast prong of the wash. The Escalante River is a tributary to the Colorado River. New Escalante's diversions are the last diversions from the Escalante River for irrigation in Utah. The unused water flows to Lake Powell on the Colorado River.

Alvey Wash is a natural watershed, with a drainage area of about 102 square miles. It empties into the Escalante River about 25 miles downstream from the irrigated lands of Steed and New Escalante's shareholders. However, the Escalante River does not naturally contribute any water to Alvey Wash. * * * New Escalante has historically delivered diverted water to the lands of its shareholders through open canals. The shareholders applied the water to their lands by flood-type irrigation. Some of their lands drain toward Alvey Wash, and consequently, runoff and seepage water reached the wash, where it commingled with the natural flow in the wash.

In 1982, New Escalante changed its irrigation system from flood irrigation to a pressurized sprinkler system of enclosed pipes. The open ditches and canals previously used were abandoned. The new system is much more efficient and has substantially diminished the runoff and seepage water which reaches Alvey Wash.

Steed owns a decreed water right in Alvey Wash from which it irrigates its lands. It contends that it had a vested right to receive the same amount of runoff and seepage flow to the wash. It characterizes itself as a downstream water user in the same river system affected by changes made by an upstream user. Steed sought an injunction, a replacement order, and money damages. The trial court held that because there was no natural contribution of water from the Escalante River to the wash, Steed had acquired no vested right, either by appropriation, by adverse use, or otherwise, to compel New Escalante to continue to let the same amount of water run off or seep from the lands of its shareholders into the wash.

II. VESTED RIGHT

Utah, along with the majority of western states, follows the appropriation doctrine: First in time, first in right for beneficial use is the basis of the acquisition of water rights. Gunnison Irrigation Co. v. Gunnison Highland Canal Co., 52 Utah 347, 174 P. 852 (1918).

In a long line of cases dating from 1912, this court has dealt with the rights of water users in runoff and seepage water from higher ground. In Garns v. Rollins, 41 Utah 260, 125 P. 867 (1912), waste or percolating water from the irrigation of the plaintiff's land ran into a ditch from which the defendant irrigated his adjoining land. The plaintiff brought an action to determine the title and the right to use the runoff irrigation water. The trial court held that the plaintiff was entitled to as much of that water as she could put to beneficial use. On appeal, we reversed and held that the plaintiff had the absolute right to all of the waste water which she could capture before it ran off her land. We stated: The law is well settled, in fact the authorities all agree, that one landowner receiving waste water which flows, seeps, or percolates from the land of another cannot acquire a prescriptive right to such water, nor any right (except by grant) to have the owner of the land from which he obtains the water continue the flow. 41 Utah at 272, 125 P. at 872. In Garns, we quoted approvingly the following statement from 1 Samuel C. Weil, Water Rights in the Western States 54 (3d ed. 1911): "Waste water soaking from the land of another after irrigation need not be continued, and may be intercepted and taken by such original irrigator, and conducted elsewhere, though parties theretofore using the waste are deprived thereof." Garns, 41 Utah at 273, 125 P. at 872. Seven years later, in Stookey v. Green, 53 Utah 311, 178 P. 586 (1919), we cited Garns for the holding that "the run-off, waste, and seepage from irrigation are not subject to appropriation as against the owner of the land irrigated who desires to recapture it and apply it on his own land." 53 Utah at 319, 178 P. at 589.

The question as to what rights one can acquire in water that wastes or seeps from the land of another arose again in Smithfield West Bench Irrigation Co. v. Union Central Life Insurance Co., 105 Utah 468, 142 P.2d 866 (1943). On the second appeal in that case, 113 Utah 356, 195 P.2d 249 (1948), this court gave a clear answer to that question: It is well established under the authorities cited in our previous opinion that waters diverted from a natural source, applied to irrigation and recaptured before they escape from the original appropriator's control, still belong to the original appropriator. If the original appropriator has a beneficial use for such waters he may again reuse them and no one can acquire a right superior to that of the original appropriator. 113 Utah at 363, 195 P.2d at 252–53.

Three years later, in Lasson v. Seely, 120 Utah 679, 238 P.2d 418 (1951), the plaintiff owned water rights in Panawats slough, which was fed in part by runoff irrigation water from the defendant's higher land. Once again, following the precedent set in earlier cases, this court wrote: We therefore do not agree with plaintiff's contention that defendant or others using irrigation waters as upper appropriators cannot utilize water more efficiently in the future than in the past, if such future use would diminish the quantity of surplus or waste water which has heretofore found its way into the slough through surface drainage or by percolation. The plaintiff cannot compel defendant or others to waste water nor to forego a water turn to build up the flow of Panawats slough * * *. The defendant is not precluded from changing the type or quantity of vegetation on his land, although by so doing less water may find its way into Panawats slough through percolation * * *. The decree of 1894 on which plaintiff relies, merely awarded the entire flow of Panawats slough to plaintiff's predecessor in title. It did not preclude more efficient use of the water by upper appropriators nor require upper appropriators to send any quantities of water into Panawats slough. The decree does not compel any upper appropriator to waste water nor to leave a surplus of water to drain into the slough. Nor could the decree direct the upper appropriators as to how they should utilize the water which they are entitled to use. 120 Utah at 689, 238 P.2d at 422–23.

One year later, in McNaughton v. Eaton, 121 Utah 394, 242 P.2d 570 (1952), this court addressed a dispute in which a natural wash was adjacent to irrigated land. Water accumulated in the wash from three sources: (1) natural waterways; (2) excess water diverted out of a nearby canal; and (3) waste water from irrigated lands on both sides of the wash. This court held that all three of these water sources were subject to reappropriation from the wash, but warned that the reappropriator acquired no rights as against the original appropriator to have the waste water continue to escape to the wash. We stated that the reappropriator of such water cannot require the first appropriator to continue to waste such water so that it will be available for use by the reappropriator. As long as the original appropriator has possession and control thereof, he may sell or transfer the right to the use of such waters to someone other than the reappropriator as long as he does so in good faith and they are beneficially used, or he may recapture and use them for further beneficial use if he does so before they get beyond his property and control. 121 Utah at 403–04, 242 P.2d at 574.

In two later cases, we again recognized and restated the rule that an upstream irrigator had the right to completely consume all the water it diverted by using it over and over again. However, in each case we carved out an exception to the general rule specific to the fact situation before the court. In East Bench Irrigation Co. v. Deseret Irrigation Co., 2 Utah 2d 170, 271 P.2d 449 (1954), we held that the rule did not apply when the runoff or waste water returned to the stream from which it was originally diverted. We quoted from Wells A.

Hutchins, Selected Problems in the Law of Water Rights in the West 362–68 (1942): Appropriations may generally be made of waste water which has been abandoned by the original appropriators, but with important qualifications. Generally, an independent right to the use of abandoned or waste water can be acquired only if the water has not yet returned to the stream from which it was diverted. If such water after abandonment has re-entered a portion of the stream system from which it was originally appropriated, as noted in greater detail below, it becomes a part of that watercourse in legal contemplation as well as physically, and from the standpoint of rights of use, it is just as much a part of the flow as is the water with which it is mingled; hence appropriative rights which before the mingling have attached to the waters of the stream attach with equal effect to the waste waters originally diverted from the stream and then abandoned into it, so that an independent appropriation cannot then be made of the waste waters as such * * *. 2 Utah 2d at 181 n. 6, 271 P.2d at 457 n. 6. In some of the cases relied upon by Steed, the runoff or waste water did return to the stream from which it was diverted.

* * *

Another exception was recognized in Stubbs v. Ercanbrack, 13 Utah 2d 45, 368 P.2d 461 (1962). Once again, we acknowledged the rule in Garns that "water rights could not be acquired in waste water so that the defendant would be obliged to continue to irrigate his higher ground to provide water to be collected in the plaintiffs' drains." 13 Utah 2d at 50, 368 P.2d at 464. However, we held that that rule did not apply because after the irrigation water had been used, it commingled with the water in the natural water table, thereby losing its identity as irrigation water. As such, it could no longer be considered owned by the defendant. Id.

Turning to the present case, we agree with the trial court that the determination of this case is controlled by the rule we adopted in Garns, which we have consistently followed for the past eighty years. The trial court properly concluded that the water reaching Alvey Wash by way of seepage and runoff water from irrigation by New Escalante's shareholders was subject to reappropriation in 1909 when Steed's predecessor filed his application to appropriate water in Alvey Wash. However, such reappropriation did not carry with it any vested right to require New Escalante to continue to divert water from the Escalante River or to convey the water through its irrigation system and to restrict its use of the same so that the flow to Alvey Wash would be maintained at its historic level. Neither of the exceptions which we recognized in East Bench or in Stubbs is applicable in the instant case. In East Bench, the water had returned to the stream from which it had been diverted. In Stubbs, there was no attempt by the upper water user to capture surplus or waste water before it went into the ground. There, the upper user let the excess water seep into the ground and then attempted to reuse it at the lower end of his land after it had commingled with natural water in the soil. No such fact situation is presented here.

Text writers on water law are in general agreement with our decisions in this area of the law. In the recent treatise Waters and Water Rights, it is stated that the only limitations which should compel an appropriator to continue wasting water are "(1) a finding that the amount released has been dedicated to the public and, therefore, the appropriator's water right has been modified to that extent; or (2) a cessation to purposefully harm the intervening user." 2 Robert E. Beck, et al., Waters and Water Rights § 13.04, at 150 (1991). That treatise further states that when water is applied to irrigation, there is an expectation that it is the water right holder's water and may be used by that owner to the fullest extent possible. Thus, the owner is allowed to "recapture" that water once it has been put to its ultimate use, whether in a sewage facility or on a field to irrigate a crop. The basic exception to allowing recapture is where the portion that would be subject to recapture has become return flow, that is, finds its way back to its source. At that point, if not before, it becomes tributary water and subject to the call of the stream. Id. at 152–53 (citations omitted).

III. BALANCE THE INTERESTS OF WATER USERS

Steed contends that regardless of whether it has a vested right, this court needs to balance the interests of upper and lower water users on the same river system. Steed asserts that New Escalante's change to the pressurized system has resulted in a 25 percent increase in efficiency and thus its shareholders now require about 25 percent less water to irrigate the same number of acres. Steed argues that allowing New Escalante to keep the excess water and expand the acreage watered by its shareholders ignores the loss of water to Steed. Steed concedes that increased efficiency in the use of water is desirable, but urges that out of the savings, losses caused to other users should be made up.

Moreover, Steed points out that there has actually been no increased efficiency. To the extent New Escalante now has water for more acreage, Steed has water for less acreage. Thus the basin as a whole has experienced no change. The technology employed by New Escalante has merely shifted water, giving the appearance of increasing efficiency without any real gain.

New Escalante counters that both the evidence and the trial court's findings are contrary to Steed's assertion that the change to the new system has resulted in substantial amounts of excess water. The evidence is to the effect that the pressurized sprinkler system is approximately 25 percent more efficient than flood-type irrigation. However, the new system does not make water. The system distributes an efficient application of the water, allowing the crops to consume more water. With a flood-type irrigation system, crops are somewhat over watered at the upper end and under watered at the lower end.

New Escalante's water right, with an 1875 priority, is for 40 cubic feet per second. The president of New Escalante testified that with the new system, the pipe capacity is 33 cubic feet per second (c.f.s.). The excess water is now stored in reservoirs and consumed in the late summer months when the flow of the Escalante River diminishes and New Escalante is unable to divert its entitlement of 40 c.f.s. He further testified that there is no water left at the end of the season. The trial court's finding on this matter is in accord with New Escalante. Moreover, New Escalante denied Steed's contention that an unauthorized expansion of acreage is being watered by its shareholders. Once again, neither the evidence nor the trial court's findings support Steed's contentions. At the time of trial, New Escalante had the decreed right to irrigate 2,712.28 acres. The evidence indicates that it operated within that limit.

We must therefore reject Steed's suggestions as to how the interests of the two users can be balanced. Unfortunately, both parties cannot "win." The law simply favors the first user by allowing it to capture seepage and runoff before it escapes from the land. When there is not enough water to satisfy the needs of all users, the user who depends upon another's seepage and runoff will suffer.

Underlying Utah's water law is a strong policy to promote conservation.

* * *

This can be done by encouraging the implementation of improvements in water systems to prevent seepage. In Big Cottonwood Tanner Ditch Co. v. Moyle, 109 Utah 213, 174 P.2d 148 (1946), we upheld the right of an irrigation company to cement and waterproof its ditches to prevent seepage even though it might harm trees, shrubs, and other plant life growing along the ditch banks on the servient property. We expressly rejected cases holding to the contrary because they were "decided in states where the need for water conservation does not exist or exists only to a limited degree * * *." 109 Utah at 235, 174 P.2d at 159.

In a concurring opinion in that case, Justice Wade wrote: I believe that from the earliest time when irrigation ditches and canals were constructed it was understood that they were at first makeshift in their construction and would be improved later. By nature the longer a ditch or canal stands without breaking, the more impervious it becomes to seeping waters. It has been a universal custom in this state for irrigation and canal companies to make necessary improvements in their systems to prevent loss of water by seepage, particularly in places where the ground is especially porous. The history of irrigation in this state has been one of continuous improvement of systems * * * 109 Utah at 244, 174 P.2d at 164. The Moyle case is an example of where, in the interest of conservation, an irrigation company was allowed to capture its seepage even though the seepage was serving a beneficial use in supporting the flora along the ditch banks.

In the instant case, New Escalante has expended more than two million dollars to convert its system to a pressurized, enclosed pipe and sprinkler system. The open canals from which water once seeped are no longer used. Sprinklers apply the water to the land so that nearly all the water is absorbed and little runs off. If the water conserved could not be used by New Escalante, there would be no incentive to make improvements. So long as New Escalante diverts only that volume of water to which it is entitled, it should be allowed to make the most efficient use of it.

* * *

V. CONCLUSION

Because Utah is an arid state, efficient and beneficial use of water should be encouraged.

In furtherance of that objective, an appropriator should be encouraged to apply water in the most efficient manner. Any technique which conserves water consumption and reduces waste is commendable. It is unfortunate that Steed lost some water which previously found its way to augment the water in Alvey Wash. However, absent a natural connection between the water in the wash and the water New Escalante diverted from the Escalante River, Steed acquired no vested right to compel New Escalante to allow the water applied to irrigation to run off their shareholders' lands.

Significant amounts of irrigation water can be lost through evaporation, seepage, or other means. We must encourage greater efficiency through water-saving techniques. As former Chief Justice Crockett so appropriately noted in Wayman v. Murray City Corp. some 23 years ago: "Because of the vital importance of water * * * both our statutory and decisional law have been fashioned in recognition of the desirability and of the necessity of insuring the highest possible development and of the most continuous beneficial use of all available water with as little waste as possible." 23 Utah 2d 97, 100, 458 P.2d 861, 863 (1969) (citations omitted).

Judgment affirmed.

NOTES

1. Is *Steed* an extension of the rule which allows for the recapture and reuse of water for the purpose of the original appropriation while it is still within the appropriator's land? In Cleaver v. Judd, 393 P.2d 193 (Or.1964), the court held that waste water could be salvaged and reused by the original appropriator even though a neighboring landowner who had been using the waste water for irrigation purposes would no longer be able to use it.

2. The general rule is that as soon as the water leaves the appropriator's land and is in or destined for a natural stream, it becomes subject to appropriation by others. See Fuss v. Franks, 610 P.2d 17 (Wyo.1980). In Ft. Morgan Reservoir & Irr. Co. v. McCune, 206 P. 393 (Colo.1922), a reservoir owner dug a trench in front of a dam to recapture water that was seeping out and began to put the water to use on the original land. The court held that as soon as water escapes from a ditch or reservoir and becomes percolating water that is destined for a natural stream, it is considered part of the stream and not subject to reuse by the original appropriator. Which rule encourages the greatest efficiency? Are there other policy considerations that are relevant?

3. In *Steed,* the Utah court allowed "saved" water to be applied to new fields. Compare this with Salt River Valley Water User's Ass'n v. Kovacovich, 411 P.2d 201 (Ariz.1966), where the court held that a farmer who required less water because of improved irrigation practices could not apply the saved water to new fields and produce new crops. Which rule makes more sense?

4. In Little Cottonwood Water Co. v. Kimball, 289 P. 116 (Utah 1930), applicant sought to appropriate water in a stream serving domestic uses. The state engineer granted the application, but upon appeal by contestants, the district court denied the application. Contestants' means of diversion required 15 cfs to provide a consumptive use of one cfs. Applicant proposed to save and appropriate to himself at least 10 cfs by building a closed pipeline system to replace open ditches. The Utah Supreme Court found that there may be "unappropriated water" under the circumstances, but that existing uses must be satisfied.

5. The California Water Code §§ 1010–11 provides that reclaimed waste water or water saved through conservation may be sold, leased, exchanged or otherwise transferred pursuant to the state's general transfer laws. Conservation is defined to include any "use of less water to accomplish the same purpose," and it includes reductions in use from land fallowing and crop rotation. The law also declares that failure to use all or part of one's water rights because of water conservation efforts cannot effect a forfeiture, and actually constitutes a beneficial use of water. At the Western Governor's Association October 30–31, 1985 Water Efficiency Workshop, it was noted that there was considerable support for legislation that gives the salvager clear title to salvaged water. However, some felt that to allow a "waster" of water to "profit" from his waste was akin to rewarding a "bum." Is it better to penalize or reward efficiency?

6. Just north of the Colorado River Delta is the fertile Imperial Valley of California. The Imperial Irrigation District (IID) is the single largest user of Colorado River water, diverting about 2.9 million acre-feet per year to produce crops that keep large parts of the country in fruits and vegetables all year. In 1984, the California State Water Resources Control Board found that a return flow loss of 38% from the IID to the Salton Sea (over a million acre-feet per year) was unreasonable and violated state constitutional and statutory prohibitions against waste. Imperial Irrig. Dist. v. State Water Resources Control Bd., 275 Cal.Rptr. 250 (Cal.App.1990), cert. denied __ U.S. __, 112 S.Ct. 171 (1991). The Metropolitan Water District of Southern California (MWD) saw these return flows as a potential source of water supply for the Los Angeles area and in 1989, after several years of negotiations spurred on by court decisions unfavorable to IID, IID and MWD signed a conservation agreement. According to the 1989 agreement, MWD will pay for structural and nonstructural conservation projects in the Imperial Valley that will conserve 106,100 acre-feet of water annually, which MWD will then have the right to use. The actual water right will stay with IID. MWD is expected to pay $97.8 million, plus $23 million in

indirect costs for the conserved water. For a more detailed explanation of the IID–MWD transfer, see pages 326–33, infra.

CITY AND COUNTY OF DENVER v. FULTON IRRIGATING DITCH CO.

Supreme Court of Colorado, 1972.
179 Colo. 47, 506 P.2d 144.

Mr. Justice Groves delivered the opinion of the Court.

This is an appeal from the decision in a declaratory judgment action by the plaintiffs, City and County of Denver (Denver) and the Adolph Coors Company (Coors). At issue are questions of Denver's rights in water obtained through transmountain diversions. These diversions are of water from the Colorado River basin, which naturally flows westerly from the west side of the Continental Divide to the Pacific Ocean. The waters are diverted to the South Platte River basin on the eastern side of the Continental Divide, the area in which Denver is located. The South Platte flows easterly, to the Missouri River. The defendant ditch companies divert water for irrigation purposes from the South Platte River downstream from the point of discharge of effluent from the plant of Metropolitan Sewage District No. 1 (Metro). Metro receives and processes Denver's sewage.

About half of Denver's water supply is Colorado River basin water. Approximately 100,000 acre feet annually—an average constant flow of about 137 cubic feet per second of time—of this water is placed in the South Platte River in the form of sewage effluent. The water is originally diverted from three Colorado River tributaries, the Fraser River, the Williams Fork River and the Blue River.

* * *

Denver sought a declaratory judgment as to two questions:

1. Whether Denver may make successive uses of the diverted transmountain water while its dominion over the water continues.

2. Whether Denver may make an exchange of water under agreement with Coors dated December 4, 1969.

We hold that Denver, in the absence of an agreement on its part not to do so, (1) may re-use, (2) may make a successive use of, and (3) after use may make disposition of imported water. Further, we affirm the trial court in its determination that, by reason of an agreement dated May 1, 1940 to which Denver is a party, Denver may not exchange water under the Coors agreement.

I.

The terms "re-use" and "successive use" have been used in the arguments with somewhat varying meanings. We add a third term, "right of disposition," and now define the three terms as used in this opinion.

"Re-use" means a subsequent use of imported water for the same purpose as the original use. For example, this could embrace the treatment of sewage resulting in potable water which is re-cycled into the regular water system.

"Successive use" means subsequent use by the water importer for a different purpose. This includes the practice of the City of Aurora and possibly other municipalities which treat sewage containing imported water for further use by the city for irrigation of public parks and facilities and for industrial uses.

"Right of disposition" means the right to sell, lease, exchange or otherwise dispose of effluent containing foreign water after distribution through Denver's water system and collection in its sewer system.

A statute adopted in 1969 apparently authorizes Denver to re-use, make successive uses, and after use to have the right of disposition of imported water, subject, of course, to its contractual obligations otherwise. This statute reads: "Whenever an appropriator has heretofore, or shall hereafter lawfully introduce foreign water into a stream system from an unconnected stream system, such appropriator may make a succession of uses of such water by exchange or otherwise to the extent that its volume can be distinguished from the volume of the streams into which it is introduced. Nothing in this section shall be construed to impair or diminish any water right which has become vested." 1969 Perm.Supp., C.R.S.1963, 148–2–6 [now Colo.Rev.Stat. § 37–82–106].

Even without the statute we think that Denver has the rights of re-use, successive use and disposition of foreign water, subject again to contrary contractual obligations.

Comrie v. Sweet, 75 Colo. 199, 225 P. 214 (1924) and Ripley v. Park Center Land and Water Co., 40 Colo. 129, 90 P. 75 (1907), involved developed water or allegedly developed water produced from mining operations. As the term was used in those opinions, "developed water" is that water which has been added to the supply of a natural stream and which never would have come into the stream had it not been for the efforts of the party producing it. In *Ripley* the water was judicially determined to be "developed water," and the sale of it by the developers to downstream users was validated as against holders of decrees in the stream. If these developers had instead made a completely consumptive use of the water, we believe this court would still have ruled that the holders of stream priorities could not complain. It follows that the developers without hindrance could use, re-use, make successive use of and dispose of the water. As far as the claims of defendants here are concerned, we see no distinction between the rights of owners of developed water from a mine and the rights of Denver as to its imported water.

* * *

In order to minimize the amount of water removed from Western Colorado, eastern slope importers should, to the maximum extent feasible, reuse and make successive uses of the foreign water.

* * *

The trial court determined that, absent negating circumstances, Denver had the right of re-use, successive use and disposition after use of foreign water. This, of course, we affirm. We do not agree, however, and reverse, the following determination of the trial court:

"It is the Court's ruling that pursuant to the evidence in this case [Denver's] dominion [over imported water] is lost at the customer tap delivery, but in any event the loss is final and complete at the point of delivery of Denver's sewage to the Denver Metropolitan Sewer intake line, and no question of loss of dominion at the point Denver's sewage is mixed with that of 15 other municipalities and governmental entities, processed on secondary treatment and delivered to Metro's outfall line to the South Platte River as treated effluent.

* * *

"[I]dentity of the water is lost, including dominion thereof, that such water has been abandoned with the result that no participant member in the Metro District would have any legal claim or right to any particular percentage of volume of the return sewage effluent, regardless of the source of the water, be it wells, South Platte River water or other transmountain water."

* * * Metro is merely an agent of Denver and other municipalities delivering sewage to it, and rights and responsibilities as between Denver and downstream irrigation users are the same as if Denver itself treated its sewage and returned it to the stream.

We hold that when Denver delivers water to a customer tap, it does not lose dominion over the water later returning to its sewer.

It was stipulated that Denver keeps records designed to disclose the amounts of various classes of water which it diverts, stores and distributes. * * *

There is no issue in this case as to quality of water. With the question of quality not involved, we accept Denver's argument that water is fungible or is to be treated the same as a fungible article. The particles of water do not have to be identified as coming from Western Colorado, but rather water, whether or not contained in effluent, can be divided volumetrically. A percentage of the effluent discharged by the Metro plant can be considered as imported water. Under the stipulated facts, we do not need to go into the processes of division of the water. We note with approval the stipulation that Denver will have the burden of demonstrating the identity of transmountain water.

* * *

NOTES

1. How can Colorado's restrictive rule on recapture and reuse of water stated in Fort Morgan Reservoir & Irr. Co. v. McCune, page 252, supra, be reconciled with the decision in the principal case? At what point do Denver's rights in the imported water cease? Can water be sold downstream in Nebraska? Are there any limits on how the

imported water is used? May it be used wastefully in the midst of a drought? Do those in the watershed of origin have a stake in how the water is used? For a review of Colorado law concerning the right to successive use and reuse, see Allison Maynard, *The Reuse Right in Colorado Water Law: A Theory of Dominion,* 68 Denv. U.L.Rev. 3 (1991).

2. Suppose Denver should conclude that a cheaper means of complying with pollution controls is to evaporate the effluent rather than treat and discharge it. Under *Fulton* could it do so? See Robert G. Berger, Comment, *Water Law—Cessation of Return Flow as a Means of Complying with Pollution Control Laws,* 12 Land & Water L.Rev. 431 (1977).

3. Can downstream appropriators ever acquire any continuing rights to developed water which the developer returns to the stream? The court in *Fulton Irr. Ditch Co.* avoided this question by finding that Denver had in mind, "possibly from its first transmountain diversion," reuse, successive use and disposition of the imported water. What of the situation where an importer uses its water, and then abandons the return flow to the stream for a number of years, only belatedly reusing it or changing the point of return to the detriment of downstream users? In a case factually similar to *Fulton,* appropriators were held not entitled to compensation when the city changed its point of sewage effluent return and bypassed their headgate, in part on the ground that the city could cease importing the water and eliminate the supply in any event. Thayer v. Rawlins, 594 P.2d 951 (Wyo.1979). New Mexico reached the same result under a law which classifies waste or drainage water as artificial surface water. N.M.Stat.Ann.1978 § 72–5–27; Reynolds v. Roswell, 654 P.2d 537 (N.M.1982). Suppose the developer never reuses the water. Is the water then available for appropriation? In Dodge v. Ellensburg Water Co., 729 P.2d 631 (Wash.1986), the water company diverted water from a creek fed by return flows from the transbasin diversions of upstream irrigation districts. A downstream water user objected to the diversion because the company had never perfected an appropriation, but the court refused to enjoin Ellensburg's use: "Foreign water, once abandoned by its developer, does not become part of the natural flow of the drainage area where it is discharged and may be used by the first person who takes it." Why?

SOUTHEASTERN COLORADO WATER CONSERVANCY DIST. v. SHELTON FARMS, INC.

Supreme Court of Colorado, 1974.
187 Colo. 181, 529 P.2d 1321.

MR. JUSTICE DAY delivered the opinion of the Court.

This is an appeal from two judgments and decrees awarding appellees Shelton Farms and Colorado–New Mexico Land Company ("the Company") water rights free from the call of any and all senior decreed water rights on the Arkansas River.

This case, so far as we are advised, is of first impression in the United States, dealing with whether the killing of water-using vegetation and the filling of a marshy area to prevent evaporation can produce a superior water right for the amount of water not transpired or evaporated. The Pueblo district court held it could, and granted both Shelton and the Company such a water right.

* * * We hold for the objectors, and reverse each judgment and decree.

I.

To comprehend the importance of this lawsuit, it is necessary to understand the Arkansas River and its tributaries.

In 1863 there were virtually no "water-loving" trees along the banks of the river. Their growth was prevented when the great roaming buffalo herds ate the saplings, and the native Indians used most of the timber. In the next 40 years both the buffalo and the Indians were decimated. Phreatophytes (water consuming plants) and cottonwood began to appear along the Arkansas. After the great Pueblo flood of 1921 the river bottom became thickly infested with tamarisk or salt cedar, a highly phreatophytic growth.

Since 1863 all surface flow of the river has been put to beneficial use, until today the Arkansas is greatly over-appropriated. There is not enough flow to satisfy decreed water rights. The phreatophytes have hindered the situation, for they have consumed large quantities of subsurface water which would otherwise have flowed in the stream and been available for decreed use.

In 1940, appellee Shelton bought 500 acres of land on the Arkansas River. Since then, he has cleared two land areas of phreatophytes, and filled in a third marshy area. Shelton claimed he had saved approximately 442 acre-feet of water per year, previously consumed by phreatophytes or lost to evaporation, which is now available for beneficial use. Shelton had 8 previously decreed wells. He asked for the right to augment his previous water rights with the salvaged water, to use during those times when pumping is curtailed by the State Engineer.

The objectors Southeastern Water Conservancy District, and others, moved to dismiss the augmentation application. The motion was denied and trial was held. The lower court awarded Shelton 181.72 acre-feet of water, free from the call of the river. The lower court analogized to the law of accretion, stating that the capture and use by another of water which ordinarily would be lost is not detrimental to prior holders. The decree contained a comprehensive series of safeguards to protect the prior vested interests. In an amendment to the decree, the trial court held that although 1971 Perm.Supp., C.R.S. 1963, 148–21–22 requires that later water rights adjudicated should be junior to prior decreed water rights, the provision did not apply in this case.

* * *

II.

* * * The issue can be stated very simply: May one who cuts down water-consuming vegetation obtain a decree for an equivalent amount of water for his own beneficial use free from the call of the river?

Appellees state that the Water Right Determination and Administration Act ("the Act"), 1969 Perm.Supp., C.R.S.1963, 148–21–1 et seq. [Colo.Rev.Stat. §§ 37–92–101 to 37–92–602 (1988, 1992 Cum.Sup.)] permits augmentation or substitution of water captured. Those are flexible terms. Thus, appellees feel that the source of water so provided—whether developed or salvaged—is immaterial, so long as prior vested rights are not injured. They insist that but for their actions the salvaged water would have been available to no one, so now they may receive a water right free from the call of prior appropriators, who are in no way harmed. Appellees conclude that their actions provide maximum utilization of water, protect vested rights, and encourage conservation and waste reduction in the water-scarce Arkansas River Valley.

* * *

The objectors assert that the lower court's resolution of the issue does violence to Colorado's firm appropriation doctrine of "first in time—first in right" on which the priority of previous decrees is bottomed. They point out that the existing case law in Colorado, which was not changed by statute, limits the doctrine of "free from call" to waters which are *truly developed and were never part of the river system*. They argue that appellees' claims were not for developed water, and thus must come under the mandates of the priority system. Furthermore, a priority date free from the call of the river will impinge the entire scheme of adjudication of water decrees as required by the Act.

There is no legal precedent squarely in point for either denying or approving these claims. The answer requires consideration of judicial precedent relating to "developed" and "salvaged" water, as well as consideration of the provisions of the Water Act. Also squarely before us is the equally serious question of whether the granting of such a unique water right will encourage denuding river banks everywhere of trees and shrubs which, like the vegetation destroyed in these cases, also consume the river water.

III.

We first consider existing case law. There is no question that one who merely clears out a channel, lines it with concrete or otherwise hastens the flow of water, without adding to the existing water, is not entitled to a decree therefor.

It is equally true and well established in Colorado that one who *adds* to an existing water supply is entitled to a decree affirming the use of such water. Strong evidence is required to prove the addition of the water. *Leadville Mine Development Co.*, supra. There are three important situations, analogous to this case, when these rare decrees have been granted. The first is when one physically transports water from another source, as when the Water Conservancy District transported water from the Frying Pan River basin to the Arkansas River. The second is when one properly captures and stores flood waters. The third is when one finds water within the system, *which would never have normally reached the river or its tributaries.* An example is trapped water artificially produced by draining a mine. *Ripley v. Park Center Land & Water Co.,* 40 Colo. 129, 90 P. 75 (1907). Another example is trapped water in an independent saucepantype formation composed of impervious shale which prevents the water from escaping. *Pikes Peak v. Kuiper,* 169 Colo. 309, 455 P.2d 882 (1969).

* * *

Thus, this case law draws a distinction between "developed" and "salvaged" water. Both terms are words of art. Developed implies *new* waters not previously part of the river system. These waters are free from the river call, and are not junior to prior decrees. Salvaged water implies waters in the river or its tributaries (including the aquifer) which ordinarily would go to waste, but somehow are made available for beneficial use. Salvaged waters are subject to call by prior appropriators. We cannot airily waive aside the traditional language of the river, and draw no distinctions between developed and salvaged water. To do so would be to wreak havoc with our water law. Those terms, and others, evolved specifically to tread softly in this state where water is so precious.

The roots of phreatophytes are like a pump. The trees, which did not have to go to court or seek any right, merely "sucked up" the water from prior appropriators. Appellees now take the water from the trees. Therefore, appellees also are continuing to take from the appropriators, but seek a court decree to approve it. They added nothing new; what was there was merely released and put to a different use. To grant appellees an unconditional water right therefor would be a windfall which cannot be allowed, for thirsty men cannot step into the shoes of a "water thief" (the phreatophytes). Senior appropriators were powerless to move on the land of others and destroy the "thief"—the trees and phreatophytes—before they took firm root. They are helpless now to move in and destroy them to fulfill their own decrees. The property (the water) must return from whence it comes—the river—and thereon down the line to those the river feeds in turn.

IV.

Each appellee decree was assigned an historical priority date. However, each decree was nevertheless to be free from the call of the river. In other words, despite a paper date the decree was to be outside the priority system, in derogation of the "first in time—first in right" water theory normally followed in Colorado.

* * *

Appellees would substitute the priority doctrine with a lack of injury doctrine. In *Fellhauer v. People,* supra, we spoke of the future of water law:

" * * * It is implicit * * * that, along with *vested rights,* there shall be *maximum utilization* of the water of this state. As administration of water approaches its second century the curtain is opening upon the new drama of *maximum utilization* and how constitutionally that doctrine can be integrated into the law of *vested rights.* We have known for a long time that the doctrine was lurking in the backstage shadows as a result of the accepted, though oft violated, principle that the right to water does not give the right to waste it." (Emphasis original.)

The Colorado legislature responded to the *Fellhauer* decision and its twin mandates of protecting vested rights and achieving maximum utilization by enacting various amendments to the 1963 Water Right Determination and Administration Act. 1969 Perm.Supp., C.R.S.1963, 148–21–2(1) [Colo.Rev.Stat. § 37–92–102] is a declaration of policy that all waters in Colorado have been

" * * * declared to be the property of the public, * * *. As incident thereto, it shall be the policy of this state to integrate the appropriation, use and administration of underground water tributary to a stream with the use of surface water, in such a way as to maximize the beneficial use of all of the waters of this state."

* * *

We do not read into the enactment of the post-*Fellhauer* amendments carte-blanche authority to substitute water consumption and raise it to a preferential right.

Beyond question, the Arkansas River is over-appropriated. Water promised has not been water delivered, for there is simply not enough to go around. Thus, the question is not whether prior appropriators are injured *today* by appellees' actions. The injury occurred *long ago,* when the water-consuming trees robbed consumers of water which would have naturally flowed for their use. The harm was real and enormous. The logical implication of the injury standard is that *until senior consumers have been saturated to fulfillment,* any displacement of water from the time and place of their need is harmful to them.

* * *

We arrive at the instant decision with reluctance, as we are loathe to stifle creativity in finding new water supplies, and do wish not to discourage maximized beneficial use of Colorado's water. But there are questions of policy to consider. If new waters can be had by appellees' method, without legislative supervision, there will be perhaps thousands of such super decrees on all the rivers of the state. S.E. Reynolds, State Engineer of New Mexico for many years, pointed out the dangers inherent in this procedure:

" * * * If one ignores the technical difficulty of determining the amount of water salvaged, this proposal, at first blush, might seem reasonable and in the interest of the best use of water and related land resources.

* * *

"On closer scrutiny, it appears that if the water supply of prior existing rights is lost to encroaching phreatophytes and then taken by individuals eradicating the plants the result would be chaos. The doctrine of prior appropriation as we know it would fall—the phreatophytes and then the individual salvaging water would have the best right. Furthermore, if individuals salvaging public water lost to encroaching phreatophytes were permitted to create new water rights where there is no new water, the price of salt cedar jungles would rise sharply. And we could expect to see a thriving, if clandestine, business in salt cedar seed and phreatophyte cultivation."

If these decrees were affirmed, the use of a power saw or a bulldozer would generate a better water right than the earliest ditch on the river. The planting and harvesting of trees to create water rights superior to the oldest decrees on the Arkansas would result in a harvest of pandemonium. Furthermore, one must be concerned that once all plant life disappears, the soil on the banks of the river will slip away, causing irreparable erosion.

* * *

We believe that in this situation unrestrained self-help to a previously untapped water supply would result in a barren wasteland. While we admire the industry and ingenuity of appellees, we cannot condone the removal of water on an *ad hoc,* farm by farm basis. The withdrawal of water must be orderly, and to be orderly it must come under the priority system.

V.

No one on any river would be adverse to a schematic and integrated system of developing this kind of water supply with control and balancing considerations. But to create such a scheme is the work of the legislature, through creation of appropriate district authorities with right of condemnation on a selective basis, not for the courts. Until such time as the legislature responds, actions such as appellees' should not be given court sanction.

Judgments reversed and cause remanded to the trial court with directions to vacate the decrees.

Mr. Justice Groves and Mr. Justice Kelley specially concur.

Mr. Justice Groves specially concurring:

* * *. It is earnestly to be hoped that the General Assembly can provide a solution so that this water, now being lost in such large quantities to the phreatophytes may be brought under reasonable control.

I wish to state, however, that, if the General Assembly does not act within a reasonable time in this area, I hope that the matter will be brought to this Court again. Then, in order to carry out the spirit of

Fellhauer v. People, 167 Colo. 320, 447 P.2d 986 (1968), and the legislative intent expressed in the 1971 amendments quoted in the opinion, I intend to urge the Court to reverse the opinion and permit persons in the position of the claimants here to take the water. They will not be taking water from holders of decreed rights, but rather from the robbers of the decreed rights—the phreatophytes.

Water lost is water wasted. The judiciary should not sit by forever and permit this to continue, even though its remedies cannot be as equitable as those that surely the legislature can fashion.

MR. JUSTICE KELLEY concurs in this opinion.

NOTES

1. Does the court destroy all incentive for the eradication of water-wasting vegetation? Under what circumstances will phreatophytes be removed? Who enjoys the benefits of their removal?

2. In the principal case Justice Day asserted that maximum utilization of water could only be accomplished by legislative action because of the necessity for long-range planning and ongoing regulation. Faced with the same problem, the Governor's Commission to Review California Water Rights Law proposed that salvagers be required to obtain a permit from the State Water Resources Control Board in order to appropriate salvaged water. The Commission would grant salvagers a right superior to all users along the stream in order to encourage salvage efforts. Governor's Commission to Review California Water Rights Law, Final Report 61 (1978). Presumably the Water Resources Control Board would balance the environmental effect of removing phreatophytes from streams against the production gains before granting the permit. But other problems remain. A proposal to grant salvagers the water they salvage assumes that the amount of water saved can be accurately measured. See Comment, *Phreatophyte Eradication as a Source of Water Rights in Colorado,* 43 U.Colo.L.Rev. 473 (1972).

E. PROTECTING THE PUBLIC INTEREST

1. Application for Rights

As we have seen, an applicant for a new water right must establish that unappropriated water is available and that vested rights will be unimpaired by the new appropriation. Can a state deny a permit when unappropriated water is available and vested rights will be unimpaired? Hutchins notes that "[i]n the 16 Western States in which control over appropriation of water is imposed by statute no person has an unqualified right to appropriate water." 1 Wells A. Hutchins, Water Rights Laws in the Nineteen Western States 403 (1971). Qualifications are usually expressed in statutes that allow a state water resources agency to deny applications that are not in the public interest.

The Utah Code provides, for example, that the state engineer is directed to reject or limit any application to appropriate unappropriated waters where the approval of the application would prove detrimental to the public welfare. Utah Code Ann. § 73–3–8. In Washington, the statute requires the supervisor to grant the permit only if "the appropriation thereof as proposed will not impair existing rights or be detrimental to the public welfare * * * " Wash.Rev.Code Ann. § 90.-03.290. If the proposed appropriation "threatens to prove detrimental to the public interest, having due regard to the highest feasible development of the use of the waters belonging to the public, it shall be the duty of the supervisor to reject such application and to refuse to issue the permit asked for." Id. The Nevada statute requires that "where * * * use or change [of use] threatens or proves detrimental to the public interest, the state engineer shall * * * refuse to issue the permit asked for." Nev.Rev.Stat. § 53. Wyoming grants the state engineer the power to consider whether the proposed use would "tend to impair the value of existing rights, or be otherwise detrimental to the public welfare." Wyo.Stat.Ann. § 41–4–503. Additionally, the state engineer may require the applicant to submit "such additional information as will enable him to properly guard the public interests," before he either approves or rejects the application. Wyo.Stat.Ann. § 41–4–505. These statutes do not confer unlimited discretion on state agencies to make "optimum" allocation decisions. They have a history.

Early case law provided a very limited interpretation of "public interest." The leading case is Young & Norton v. Hinderlider, 110 P. 1045 (N.M.1910). Hinderlider had applied for a permit to make an appropriation and construct a storage project. Over two months later, a competing applicant filed for a right to the waters of the same stream, and proposed to develop the water at a much lower cost. The territorial engineer found, among other things, "that it would not be to the best interests of the public to approve the [Hinderlider application], thereby forcing the protestants to pay more than double price for their water rights." Id. at 1047. On appeal, the court refused to limit the meaning of the term "contrary to public interest" to cases in which there was posed a menace to the public health or safety. Instead, it was held broad enough to prevent investors from making worthless investments in the state, thereby allowing the territorial engineer to evaluate the potential success of a proposed project, including economic feasibility. Id. at 1050.

Other courts have followed the *Young & Norton* broad definition of public interest. *Young & Norton* was applied in Tanner v. Bacon, 136 P.2d 957 (Utah 1943). The state engineer denied Tanner's 1925 application to appropriate 100 cfs of the Provo River for power purposes, finding that granting the application would be "detrimental to the public welfare," although unappropriated water was available. In 1922, the State Water Storage Commission had contracted with the Bureau of Reclamation for a study of a reservoir project that would import waters into the Provo River and store them for domestic and supplemental irrigation and industrial supply. In 1936, the Provo River Water Users' Association (a corporation created to act as intermediary between the Bureau of Reclamation and project users) contracted with the United States to construct a storage project. The Association filed for a right to divert and store up to 30,000 acre-feet annually. The trial court found that Tanner's proposed use conflicted with this later-proposed project which was "the more beneficial use of such waters for domestic, and irrigation purposes" and affirmed the state engineer's decision, but ordered the application reinstated subject to the rights of the Provo River Water Users' Association:

> The law which governed the right to make future appropriations when plaintiff filed his application is Sec. 48, Chap. 67, Laws of Utah for 1919 [as amended is now Utah Code Ann. § 73–3–8], which provides "Where there is no unappropriated water in the proposed source of supply, or where the proposed use will conflict with prior applications or existing rights, or where the approval of such application would in the opinion of the State Engineer *interfere with the more beneficial use for irrigation, domestic or culinary purposes, stock watering, power or mining development, manufacturing, or would prove detrimental to the public welfare,* it shall be the duty of the State Engineer to reject such application." (Italics added.) * * *

> These statutes may not vest the state with the proprietary ownership of the water but they clearly do enjoin upon the state the duty to control the appropriation of the public waters in a manner that will be for the best interests of the public.

* * *

> [T]he legislature intended that upon the filing of an application to appropriate water the State Engineer should determine from the facts and circumstances of each case whether the approval thereof would interfere with the more beneficial use of the water, for one of the purposes mentioned, whether the purpose proposed in the application was for one of the purposes mentioned or for some other purpose. This is the construction placed upon this provision by the District Court. It found that to store the flood waters of the Provo River to be later used for domestic, irrigation and other purposes was the more beneficial use which the approval of plaintiff's application, without making it subject to those rights, would interfere with. This decision not being arbitrary or capricious but based upon experience and well recognized principles must be sustained.

136 P.2d at 962.

"Public interest" may also be a factor in a court's determining which "use will be for the greatest public benefit" in a condemnation action. Mack v. Eldorado Water Dist., 354 P.2d 917, 918–19 (Wash. 1960).

SHOKAL v. DUNN

Supreme Court of Idaho, 1985.
109 Idaho 330, 707 P.2d 441.

BISTLINE, JUSTICE.

On December 21, 1978, respondent Trout Co. applied for a permit to appropriate 100 c.f.s. of waters from Billingsley Creek near Hagerman, Idaho. Numerous protests were filed by local residents, property owners, and Billingsley Creek water users. The Department of Water Resources (Water Resources) [issued a permit].

[On appeal, the district court] determined that Water Resources had failed to properly evaluate the question of "local public interest," holding that the applicant had the ultimate burden of proving that a proposed water use was in the local public interest under I.C. § 42–203A.

* * * The Director conditionally granted the application upon a subsequent showing by the applicant, Trout Co., that the project would meet certain requirements and restrictions set forth in the order. * * *

Subsequently, Trout Co. submitted a new set of drawings of the facility, and a document entitled "Contemplated Operational Criteria for the Trout Co. Fishraising Facility" (hereinafter "Operational Criteria"). * * *

The protestants filed * * * protests raising many factual issues regarding the "Operational Criteria." After reviewing the "Operational Criteria" and considering the objections raised by the protestants and other parties, Water Resources, without further hearing, issued its final order on July 21, 1982, granting the application for Permit No. 36–7834. Appeal was again taken to the district court, this time before the Honorable W.E. Smith. * * *

III. THE LOCAL PUBLIC INTEREST

[T]he only matters for the agency to consider on remand are those which relate generally to the local public interest. I.C. § 42–203A(5)(e). We turn first to the interpretation of this provision, a question of first impression before this Court.[2]

A. *Defining the Local Public Interest.*

Under I.C. § 42–203A(5)(e), if an applicant's appropriation of water "will conflict with the local public interest, where the local public interest is defined as the affairs of the people in the area directly affected by the proposed use," then the Director "may reject such application and refuse issuance of a permit therefor, or may partially

---

2. The requirement that Water Resources protect the public interest is related to the larger doctrine of the public trust, which Justice Huntley comprehensively discussed in Kootenai Environmental Alliance v. Panhandle Yacht Club, Inc., 105 Idaho 622, 671 P.2d 1085 (1983). The state holds all waters in trust for the benefit of the public, and "does not have the power to abdicate its role as trustee in favor of private parties." Id. at 625, 671 P.2d at 1088. Any grant to use the state's waters is "subject to the trust and to action by the State necessary to fulfill its trust responsibilities." Id. at 631, 671 P.2d at 1094. Trust interests include property val-

ues, "navigation, fish and wildlife habitat, aquatic life, recreation, aesthetic beauty and water quality." Id. at 632, 671 P.2d at 1095. Reviewing courts must "take a 'close look' at the action [of the legislature or of agencies such as Water Resources] to determine if it complies with the public trust doctrine and will not act merely as a rubber stamp for agency or legislative action." Id. at 629, 671 P.2d at 1092. Justice Huntley concluded, "The public trust at all times forms the outer boundaries of permissible government action with respect to public trust resources." Id. at 632, 671 P.2d at 1095.

approve and grant a permit for a smaller quantity of water than applied for, or may grant a permit upon conditions."

The Utah Supreme Court interpreted a similar provision [Utah Code Ann. § 100–8–1] to authorize the State Engineer "to reject or limit the priority of plaintiff's application [for a permit to appropriate water for a power project] in the interest of the public welfare." Tanner v. Bacon, 103 Utah 494, 136 P.2d 957, 964 (1943); see also People v. Shirokow, 26 Cal.3d 30, 162 Cal.Rptr. 30, 37, 605 P.2d 859, 866 (1980) (In the public interest, the Water Board may impose the condition that the applicant salvage the water required for his or her project.); East Bay Municipal Utility District v. Department of Public Works, 1 Cal.2d 476, 35 P.2d 1027, 1029 (1934) ("Where the facts justify the action, the water authority should be allowed to impose [on an application to appropriate water for a power project], in the public interest, the restrictions and conditions provided for in the act," or to reject the application "in its entirety."). Both the Utah and California Supreme Courts have upheld state water agencies which had granted appropriations subject to future appropriations for uses of greater importance—in effect prioritizing among uses according to the public interest. * * *

The Director of Water Resources has the same considerable flexibility and authority, which he has already implemented in earlier proceedings in this matter, to protect the public interest.

Indeed, I.C. § 42–203A places upon the Director the affirmative *duty* to assess and protect the public interest. In assessing the duty of the state water board imposed by California's "public interest" provision, the California Supreme Court declared, "If the board determines a particular use is not in furtherance of the greatest public benefit, on balance the public interest must prevail." *Skirokow,* supra, 162 Cal. Rptr. at 37, 605 P.2d at 866; accord, *Tanner,* supra, 136 P.2d at 962 (The State has "the *duty* to control the appropriation of the public waters in a manner that will be for the best interests of the public.") (emphasis added).

The authority and duty of the Director to protect the public interest spring naturally from the statute; the more difficult task for us is to define "the local public interest." Public interest provisions appear frequently in the statutes of the prior appropriation states of the West, but are explicated rarely. I.C. § 42–203A provides little guidance. Fortunately, however, the legislature did provide guidance in a related statute, I.C. § 42–1501. We also derive assistance from our sister states and from the academic community.

In I.C. § 42–1501 [providing for protection of instream flows,] the legislature declared it "in the public interest" that:

> The streams of this state and their environments be protected against loss of water supply to preserve the minimum stream flows required for the protection of fish and wildlife habitat, aquatic life, recreation, aesthetic beauty, transportation and navigation values, and water quality.

Not only is the term "public interest" common to both §§ 42–1501 and 42–203A, and the two sections common to the same title 42 (Irrigation and Drainage—Water Rights and Reclamation), but also the legislature approved the term "public interest" in both sections on the *same day*, March 29, 1978. Clearly, the legislature in § 42–203A must have intended the public interest on the local scale to include the public interest elements listed in § 42–1501: "fish and wildlife habitat, aquatic life, recreation, aesthetic beauty, transportation and navigation values, and water quality."

In so intending, the legislature was in good company. Unlike other state public interest statutes, the Alaska statute enumerates the elements of the public interest. The public interest elements of I.C. § 42–1501 are almost precisely duplicated within the Alaska statute, which is set out in the margin.[3] * * *

The Alaska statute contains other elements which common sense argues ought to be considered part of the local public interest. These include the proposed appropriation's benefit to the applicant, its economic effect, its effect "of loss of alternative uses of water that might be made within a reasonable time if not precluded or hindered by the proposed appropriation," its harm to others, its "effect upon access to navigable or public waters," and "the intent and ability of the applicant to complete the appropriation." Alaska Stat. § 46.5.080(b).

Several other public interest elements, though obvious, deserve specific mention. These are: assuring minimum stream flows, as specifically provided in I.C. § 42–1501, discouraging waste, and encouraging conservation. See *Shirokow,* supra, 162 Cal.Rptr. at 37, 605 P.2d at 866 (The California Supreme Court found water salvage to be sufficiently in the public interest to require it of a permittee.).

The above-mentioned elements of the public interest are not intended to be a comprehensive list. As observed long ago by the New Mexico Supreme Court, the "public interest" should be read broadly in order to "secure the greatest possible benefit from [the public waters] for the public." Young & Norton v. Hinderlider, 15 N.M. 666, 110 P. 1045, 1050 (N.M.1910) (Rejects considering only public health and safety; considers relative costs of two projects.). By using the general term "the local public interest," the legislature intended to include any locally important factor impacted by proposed appropriations.

---

3. Alaska Stat. § 46.15.080 provides:

(b) In determining the public interest, the commissioner shall consider

(1) the benefit to the applicant resulting from the proposed appropriation;

(2) the effect of the economic activity resulting from the proposed appropriation;

(3) the effect on fish and game resources and on public recreational opportunities;

(4) the effect on public health;

(5) the effect of loss of alternate uses of water that might be made within a reasonable time if not precluded or hindered by the proposed appropriation;

(6) harm to other persons resulting from the proposed appropriation;

(7) the intent and ability of the applicant to complete the appropriation; and

(8) the effect upon access to navigable or public waters.

See also Bank of Am. Nat. Trust & Sav. Assoc. v. State Water Resources Control Bd., 116 Cal.Rptr. 770, 771, 42 Cal.App.3d 198, 201 (1974) (If supported by the record, the state water board can condition a permit for a reservoir on providing for the public interest element of public access for recreation.).

Of course, not every appropriation will impact every one of the above elements. Nor will the elements have equal weight in every situation. The relevant elements and other relative weights will vary with local needs, circumstances, and interests. For example, in an area heavily dependent on recreation and tourism or specifically devoted to preservation in its natural state, Water Resources may give great consideration to the aesthetic and environmental ramifications of granting a permit which calls for substantial modification of the landscape or the stream.

Those applying for permits and those challenging the application bear the burden of demonstrating which elements of the public interest are impacted and to what degree. * * *

However, the burden of proof in all cases as to where the public interest lies * * * rests with the applicant:

[I]t is not [the] protestant's burden of proof to establish that the project is not in the local public interest. The burden of proof is upon the applicant to show that the project is either in the local public interest or that there are factors that overweigh the local public interest in favor of the project.

The determination of what elements of the public interest are impacted, and what the public interest requires, is committed to Water Resources' sound discretion.

* * *

The above elements of the public interest [including concerns with dewatering of streams and water quality], together with other elements and factors which Water Resources deems relevant, will be considered at the hearing on the amended application. Water Resources should accept relevant testimony and other evidence providing additional information on the public interest.

NOTES

1. For a history of the development of the public interest requirement in Idaho see Scott W. Reed, *The Public Trust Doctrine in Idaho,* 19 Envtl.L. 655 (1989).

2. In divining the public interest, administrative officials and courts have looked to various announcements of legislative intent in other contexts. The court in *Shokal* followed this approach. The Washington Supreme Court has interpreted the intent of public welfare considerations in an older statute in light of much more recent environmental legislation. It held that a State Environmental Policy Act, Wash.Rev.Code Ann. § 43.21C.030(2)(a–g) (like the counterpart National Environmental Policy Act, see page 747, infra), had become part of the mission of every agency to which it applied. Therefore, environmental values had to be considered as a part of the public welfare in a request for a permit to divert water from Loon Lake for domestic use when the withdrawn water was used near the lake and then returned to it from septic tanks. Stempel v. Dep't of Water Resources, 508 P.2d

166 (Wash.1973). The Washington Water Resources Act also expressed a concern for public health and preservation of natural resources. Provisions of Wash.Rev.Code Ann. § 90.54.010 referring to protection of water quality, though also passed subsequent to the permit law, were found to require evaluation of pollution reentry problems in applying the public welfare standard.

3. Montana law (see pages 239–41, supra) requires public interest review only in the case of large appropriations. The Montana Department of Natural Resources and Conservation must consider the following factors before approving appropriations of 4,000 acre-feet per year or greater and of 5.5 cfs or greater:

1. Other demands on the state water supply, including future beneficial uses, municipal water needs, irrigation needs, and minimum streamflows for aquatic life and the protection of existing water rights;

2. The benefits of the proposed water use to the applicant and the state;

3. Water quality;

4. The possible creation of saline seep; and

5. Other probable significant environmental effects identified through the environmental impact statement process.

Mont.Code Ann. § 85–2–311.

4. The administrator charged with determining the public interest has a difficult balancing task. How comfortable would you be as the Director of Water Resources after *Shokal* in deciding whether to grant a permit? Can the local public interest differ from the statewide public interest? Absent further legislative or judicial direction, the Director of the Department of Water Resources can exercise discretion to decide what is in the public interest. *Shokal* has been applied to deny and to condition permits to preserve environmental and recreational values. For instance, in 1990 the Director denied a permit to appropriate water from the Bear River for a small hydroelectric project. He based his denial on the possibility that downstream users would be adversely affected by evaporation losses and his finding that the project was not in the local public interest because the recreational use of a whitewater stretch of the river through a portion of the Bear River Canyon would be hampered, a wildlife habitat would be eliminated, and the applicant demonstrated insufficient financial resources.

5. The degree of judicial oversight of officials who determine what is in the "public interest" depends on the extent to which courts defer to the exercise of administrative discretion and the degree to which they are willing to evaluate evidence. Under usual administrative law principles, courts usually will not second-guess administrative officials. The Nebraska Supreme Court reviewed a decision by the Director of Water Resources finding an appropriation for an instream flow was in the "public interest." In re Application A–16642, 463 N.W.2d 591 (Neb.1990). In confirming the Director's finding the court stated:

[T]he several arguments of the complaining objectors are nothing more than attempts to entice this court into reweighing evidence. However, * * * when presented with an appeal from an order of the Director of Water Resources, this court does not reweigh evidence, its review is limited to a search for errors in the record.

Id. at 613.

A New Mexico trial court overturned the state engineer's approval of a proposed change of use of water from livestock watering and early season flood irrigating (for soil preparation) to a recreational lake for a new resort. The court found the change improper and disallowed it as contrary to the public interest, citing the importance of preserving the culture and traditions of Hispanic rural communities:

> 34. The Northern New Mexico region possesses significant history, tradition and culture of recognized value, not measurable in dollars and cents.
>
> 35. The relationship between the people and their land and water is central to the maintenance of that culture and tradition.
>
> 36. The imposition of a resort-oriented economy in the Ensenada area would erode and likely destroy a distinct local culture which is several hundred years old.

Ensenada Land and Water Association v. Sleeper, No. RA–84–53(C) (District Court, Rio Arriba County, New Mexico, June 2, 1985). Did the decision favor the public interest?

The case was reversed on appeal because the New Mexico transfer statute at the time did not allow such public interest considerations in transfers and the New Mexico Supreme Court refused to hear an appeal. Ensenada Land & Water Association v. Sleeper, 760 P.2d 787 (N.M.App.1988), cert. quashed 759 P.2d 200 (N.M.1988). The transfer never took place, however, because the developer went bankrupt. See *The Milagro Beanfield War Revisited in Ensenada Land & Water Association v. Sleeper: Public Welfare Defies Transfer of Water Rights,* 29 Nat. Resources J. 861 (1989). *Sleeper* has led to the suggestion that communities be given a veto over major water rights transfers similar to powers that communities exercise through zoning. See Charles T. DuMars & Michele Minnis, *New Mexico Water Law: Determining Public Welfare Values in Water Rights Allocation,* 31 Ariz.L.Rev. 817 (1989).

6. In absence of specific legislative standards, is there any limit on the factors an agency or a reviewing court should consider to be within the "public interest?" Professor Trelease has poignantly suggested in an aptly titled article that perceptions of the fine line between sound administrative judgment and apparent arbitrariness may depend on one's interest in a particular transaction:

> The Wise Administrator, as every one knows, is the man in a government office who protects "the public interests" (read *my* interests) from actions which would adversely affect those interests, when the public is (I am) otherwise unable to influence the course of those actions. The other fellow is as easy to spot; he is the man

in government who makes decisions for me that I would rather, and could better, make for myself.

Frank J. Trelease, *The Model Water Code, the Wise Administrator and the Goddam Bureaucrat,* 14 Nat. Resources J. 207, 209 (1974).

Familiar objections to broad administrative discretion in natural resources allocation include: standards may vary with incumbents in administrative positions; there is unpredictability as to how resources will be allocated; and costs and delays are built into the system. If the goal of water allocation is to maximize the benefits of water for society with a minimum of costs or harms, can it be achieved in a better way?

DAVID H. GETCHES, WATER PLANNING: UNTAPPED OPPORTUNITY FOR THE WESTERN STATES

9 J. Energy L. & Pol'y 1 (1988).

I.   INTRODUCTION

The western states face shifting and increasing resource demands that dictate, now more than ever, the implementation of workable, comprehensive state water planning.

* * *

Water planning, like planning for other resources, means articulating policy and applying that policy to specific facts and data. It was characterized by the National Water Commission as "the prelude to informed decisionmaking." To be effective, water planning must be a strategic effort that integrates policy with the best available resource information, providing guidance and assistance for future actions.

* * *

III.   THE FUNDAMENTALS OF WATER PLANNING

Water resource planning is widely misunderstood. It is often seen as a centralized, bureaucracy-dominated, inflexible blueprint for specific project development. The use of the terminology "state water plan" contributes to the confusion because it connotes a single, prescriptive document. If planning is to serve public needs, it must be a comprehensive, dynamic process, articulating policies and strategies relative to a state's particular water resources and needs. To be effective, the results of the process should be legally integrated into state decisions, giving "teeth" to the effort.

* * *

B.   *Comprehensive Process*

Water resources planning should include a wide range of subjects that affect or are affected by the use of water, including land use, pollution, wildlife, and recreation. A comprehensive planning process must consider all available sources of water, both surface and underground.

It is highly unusual for water planning to be integrated with land use planning, yet the two are inextricably connected. Land use plans and projections depend on the availability of water supplies. Similarly, water resources planning depends heavily upon plans made by state and local governments for future land use. The presence or absence of a water supply has not historically determined how growth will occur but the timing and cost of water supply may influence patterns of growth. If investments in land are to be reliable and a development pattern reasonably predictable, water needs should be anticipated based on land use plans, and the necessary infrastructure should be identified.

Water quality planning is traditionally divorced from water resource planning; most states divide the responsibilities for regulating water quality and allocating water resources between different agencies. Considerable water quality planning has been done in the United States. Congress required and funded water quality plans as a condition of local governments receiving major construction grants under the Clean Water Act, but this was carried out independent of any ongoing state water resources planning. Similarly, detailed plans for construction and operation of specific water projects have ignored water quality concerns. This is especially negligent in the case of irrigation projects, where there is a direct connection between application of water, which seeps and leaches through saline soils, and the pollution of surface and groundwater supplies by increased salinity levels.

* * *

Conjunctive management of groundwater and surface supplies has been urged for years, but the two sources are rarely considered together by water managers. Although some groundwater is hydrologically connected with surface streams, the two are treated as legally separate sources in some states. Even if this anomalous division of ground and surface water allocation is to continue, sound planning could lead to more rational decisions by the agencies or officials who implement the separate schemes.

* * *

States regularly plan for recreation, fish and wildlife management, flood protection, and instream flow needs. These state environmental and other resource plans should be integrated into water planning. Similarly, state economic development goals and plans need to be reflected in a water plan. Industrial expansion, development of new business, and satisfaction of municipal needs all may turn on sound water planning.

Comprehensive water planning requires states to consider how to manage existing supplies better, rather than simply to assume that future needs will be satisfied from newly developed sources. A key planning goal should be to identify optimum uses of a state's water resources and existing facilities, and to consider a variety of sources for those uses. A Western Governors Association report on water efficiency found that a tremendous amount of western water is wasted through inefficient use and management. It found that basin-wide co-operation, water conservation and efficiency, alternative physical solutions, and conjunctive use could satisfy much of the West's foreseeable future demand.

* * *

Legislative authorizations for planning and the actions of an entity carrying out planning responsibilities should be unambiguous about which aspects of the process are to be considered binding. Some parts of planning documents may be merely illustrations or examples of how the policy could be carried out. The identification of water development projects in the planning process is especially susceptible to the interpretation that it is prescriptive, as illustrated by the case of *Johnson Rancho County Water District v. State Water Rights Board,* 235 Cal.App.2d 863, 45 Cal.Rptr. 589 (3d Dist.1965).

In that case, the court considered the propriety of the state Water Rights Board's (predecessor to the state Water Resources Control Board) allowing development of a project at a point on a river that would preclude the future development of another project that was a specific feature of the California Water Plan. The California statutes provide that "it is the policy of the State that The California Water Plan * * * is accepted as the guide for the orderly and co-ordinated control, protection, conservation, development, and utilization of the water resources of the State." Interpreting this vague statement, the court pointed out that the statute also said that the declaration "does not constitute approval of specific projects * * * nor shall this declaration be construed as a prohibition of the development of the water resources of the State by any entity." Furthermore, the Code said that the Board is required only to "give consideration to * * * the California Water Plan * * *." Thus, the court rejected the contention that the Water Rights Board was legally powerless to grant a permit for a new project that would preclude building a project set out in the plan.

To avoid confusion and uncertainty about the effect and purposes of state water planning, state law should clearly specify the intended uses for the resulting plans and policies.

* * *

B. *Public Interest Determinations*

Courts and administrative agencies increasingly are being asked to make determinations of "the public interest" in their decisions concerning water rights allocation and transfers. Sixteen states have some form of public interest review.[139] These mandates create difficulties

---

139. Alaska Stat. §§ 46.15.040, –.080(a) (1984 & Supp.1986); Ariz.Rev.Stat.Ann. §§ 45–142, –143 (Supp.1986); Cal.Water Code §§ 1225, 2155 (West 1971 & Supp. 1987); Idaho Code §§ 42–201, –203A, –203C (Supp.1986); Kan.Stat. §§ 82a–705, –711 (1984); Mont.Code Ann. §§ 85–2–302, 311(2) (1985) (does not use typical "public interest" or "public welfare" phrasing but a permit can issue for larger appropriations only if the proposed use is "a reasonable use," which is defined in terms of typical public interest criteria); Neb.Rev. Stat. §§ 46–233, –234, –2,116 (1984); Nev. Rev.Stat. §§ 533.325, .370(3), 534.040(1) (1985); N.M.Stat.Ann. §§ 72–5–1, –6, –7,

and ambiguities for administrators because they typically lack legislative standards or guidance.

* * *

Even where there is no statutory requirement that administrators' decisions further the public interest, courts increasingly require agencies to consider a variety of environmental and economic factors as they administer water. In Colorado, where administrative agencies exercise virtually no discretion in allocating or administering water, the supreme court has been moving firmly toward demanding that decisions, rules, and regulations ensure optimum utilization of water.[148]

The courts almost certainly will continue in their attempts to inject newly asserted, widely held public values into determinations concerning water, notwithstanding the sparsity of legislative guidance. The absence or vagueness of legislative standards understandably frustrates judicial efforts [149] and, as the New Mexico case quoted above demonstrates, can produce surprising results.

Legislatures prefer to delegate broad discretion to administrative officials and agencies, rather than to catalogue detailed standards. The legislative process is not well suited to developing standards detailed enough to be applied meaningfully in multiple and diverse situations. The legislature can require a state agency to engage in a planning process and thereby to produce comprehensive standards and guidelines, along with a description of how they should be applied and balanced in various circumstances. Although it is unlikely that any comprehensive planning document would be durable enough for all situations, it almost inevitably would be better than the product of a legislative drafting process or, alternatively, ad hoc exercises by an administrative agency. A planning process can consider variables in advance and continue to adjust the approaches taken to reflect changing facts and changing policies. The legislature can oversee the process by making periodic revisions of the agency's articulated plans and policies so far as necessary to keep the agency within the fundamental tenets of state legislative policies.

NOTE: IMPACT ASSESSMENT

The environmental movement has led to modified water rights administration. Many states have enacted legislation paralleling the National Environmental Policy Act of 1969 (NEPA), see page 747, infra,

72–12–3, –3E (1985); N.D.Cent.Code §§ 61–04–02, 06 (1985); Or.Rev.Stat. §§ 537.130, –.170(4) (1985); S.D.Comp.Laws Ann. §§ 46–1–15, –2A–9, –5–10, –6–3 (1983); Tex.Water Code Ann. §§ 11.121, –134(3) (Vernon Supp.1987); Utah Code Ann. §§ 73–3–1, –8(1) (1980 & Supp.1986); Wash.Rev.Code Ann. §§ 90.03.250, –.290, –44.050, –44.060 (1962); Wyo.Stat. §§ 41–4–503, –3–930 to –932 (1977 & Supp.1986).

148. See Alamosa–La Jara Water Users Protection Ass'n v. Gould, 674 P.2d 914 (Colo.1983). The Colorado Supreme Court has found a "clear obligation [for the state engineer] to represent the public interest" in water rights determinations. Bar 70 Enterprises, Inc. v. Tosco Corp., 703 P.2d 1297, 1304 (Colo.1985); Wadsworth v. Kuiper, 193 Colo. 95, 562 P.2d 1114 (1977). See also *United Plainsmen,* supra note 77.

149. At least one court has expressed uneasiness about the difficulties involved in applying public interest standards without definite criteria. See Steamboaters v. Winchester Water Control Dist., 69 Or. 596, 688 P.2d 92 (1984).

and water permitting agencies have become increasingly involved with ecological considerations in the evaluation of water use applications. A few states have passed their own versions of NEPA and require consideration of environmental factors not just for major water development but also for water allocation.

In Washington, where the duties of the Department of Water Resources were transferred to a newly created Department of Ecology in 1970 (Wash.Rev.Code Ann. § 43.21A.060), the supreme court in Stempel v. Department of Water Resources, 508 P.2d 166 (Wash.1973), held that in determining whether an appropriation would "be to the detriment of the public welfare," the department was obligated "to consider the total environmental and ecological factors to the fullest." The court observed that the passage of recent legislation constituted "a legislative mandate of the ecological ethic" for the agency.

An ongoing example with a long history concerns the appropriation of water from the Owens River Valley in California for the City of Los Angeles. In the early 1970s the Los Angeles Department of Water and Power was once again looking to the Owens Valley for the solution to its water supply problems. The city had completed its first aqueduct from the valley to Los Angeles in 1913 and a second was operating by 1970. The system is largely gravity fed, so pumping costs are low. The Owens Valley supplied the city with 80% of its water—close to 4.6 million acre-feet of water flow each year through the Owens Valley Aqueduct to Los Angeles. In 1972, Los Angeles moved to increase its pumping of Owens Valley groundwater from 176.2 acre-feet per day (afd) to as much as 623.7 afd. The city told tenants on Los Angeles-owned land that their leases might not be renewed and warned that Lake Diaz, a small recreational lake, might be dried up. Owens Valley residents reacted bitterly to Los Angeles' announcement. "We are a colony of Los Angeles," one rancher said. "Less than two percent of our valley belongs to us. We pay rent to the Department of Water and Power even for our stores and churches. There is more Los Angeles land here than down there in the City." Some Owens Valley dwellers suspected that the city was deliberately trying to drive them from the valley so that it could continue its water exportation without objections.

The valley's residents responded in two ways. The first was violent, reminiscent of the 1920s. In the spring of 1976, Los Angeles locked the gates through which water flows into Lake Diaz. Angry Owens Valley dwellers took welding torches to the gates and forced them open. An explosion destroyed a section of the aqueduct in the fall of 1976, allowing more than 307 acre-feet of water to spill onto a dry riverbed. The day after the aqueduct explosion, a stick of dynamite tied to an arrow was fired into a Los Angeles fountain named for William Mulholland, the engineer who designed the Owens Valley aqueduct and pipeline system.

Inyo County, encompassing much of Owens Valley, reacted in a more restrained manner. It filed an action containing two charges against Los Angeles. First, the county claimed that the city's increased pumping threatened frail plants and wildlife and therefore violated California's Environmental Quality Act (CEQA), Cal.Pub.Res.Code §§ 21000–21176. See generally Daniel P. Selmi, *The Judicial Development of the California Environmental Quality Act,* 18 U.C.D.L.Rev. 197 (1984). The second challenge was that Los Angeles' action constituted a wasteful use of water in violation of California's constitution. In reply, the Los Angeles Department of Water and Power contended that its obligation, and the greater need, lay with Los Angeles. The state courts determined that because only 50% of the estimated cost of construction of the additional wells had actually been spent, the increased groundwater pumping was part of an "ongoing project." This ruling made the pumping subject to the CEQA even though the project was begun prior to the effective date of the Act. As a result, the city had to file an environmental impact report (EIR).

In a series of six reported decisions, the California Court of Appeals dealt with challenges to the adequacy of EIRs prepared by the city. Finally, the city and Inyo County settled the case with an agreement. The city agreed to pay the county about two million dollars a year for environmental impacts caused by continued groundwater pumping and an additional ten million dollars to re-establish a trout fishery in the Lower Owens River and to build recreational facilities. In exchange, Los Angeles was to have the right to take 200,000 acre-feet of water a year, down from 480,000 acre-feet a year which it was taking before the agreement.

When the parties jointly petitioned the court to accept the EIR prepared to support their settlement agreement, others contended that since there was no longer adversity between the city and the county that they should be permitted to challenge the EIR in order to carry out the purposes of CEQA. The court of appeals held, under the "public interest exception" to the mootness doctrine, that the court should scrutinize the EIR with the assistance of adversary amici curiae. County of Inyo v. Los Angeles, ___ Cal.Rptr. ___ (Cal.App.1993).

2. Existing Rights

Old water rights and uses create the greatest conflicts with public interest factors. They are the ones that were established when the technology of water diversion and use were primitive, water was plentiful (at least by western standards), and society's primary goal was to promote the opening of the West. Water was allocated and developed without regard for efficiency or environmental effects; it continues to be used in the same manner, protected by legal rights, aided by subsidized facilities.

The prior appropriation doctrine establishing those rights was developed to meet the demands for water in the 1800s; public interest considerations are being superimposed on it to meet demands. As Joseph Sax put it:

> The problem is really quite simple, it does not require mastery of obtuse legal doctrines to appreciate what is going on. The heart of the matter is that public values have changed, and the use of water

has reached some critical limits. One result is that we need to retrieve some water from traditional water users to sustain streams and lakes as natural systems and to protect water quality. Moreover, traditional sources of new supply—such as dams and transbasin transportation of water, on which conventional users depend—are being closed off for a variety of familiar reasons, including both federal reluctance to finance new projects, and environmental objections. Thus, we have a potential head-on conflict between existing water users and their existing and future demands, and future demands of what may broadly be called instream uses.

Joseph Sax, *Limits on Private Rights,* 19 Envtl.L. 973 (1989).

How "safe" are water rights acquired under prior appropriation? What channels are open to review and modify existing water rights through application of the "public interest?"

BONHAM v. MORGAN

Supreme Court of Utah, 1989.
788 P.2d 497.

PER CURIAM:

* * *

Plaintiff Stanley B. Bonham, who is not a water user, protested against a permanent change application filed under Utah Code Ann. § 73–3–3 (1980) in the office of the defendant state engineer (state engineer) in June of 1984 by defendants Salt Lake County Water Conservancy District and Draper Irrigation Company (applicants). Applicants sought to change the point of diversion, place, and nature of use of certain water rights in Bell Canyon, Dry Creek, Rocky Mouth Creek, and Big Willow Creek. At a subsequent hearing, Bonham produced evidence of substantial flooding and damage to plaintiffs' properties and adjacent public lands during 1983 and 1984. Bonham informed the state engineer that the flooding was the result of applicants' construction of a screw gate, pipeline, and diversion works after they obtained preliminary approval of their change application. According to Bonham, the flooding had occurred and would recur on a yearly basis whenever the applicants closed their screw gate, allowing the waters to be diverted down the hillside onto plaintiffs' properties and nearby property contemplated for use as a public park. Bonham objected that the proposed structures and improvements contemplated after final approval would detrimentally impact the public welfare.

The state engineer conducted on-site inspections but eventually issued his memorandum decision in which he concluded that he was without authority to address Bonham's claims in ruling on the permanent change application, as Bonham was not a water user, that the state engineer's authority was limited to investigating impairments of vested water rights, and that there was no evidence before him to indicate that the implementation of the change application would impair those rights. The state engineer then granted the permanent change application.   * * * In count one of their complaint, they claimed that the state engineer failed to review the plans and specifications of the improvements, failed to conduct an investigation as required by Utah Code Ann. § 73–3–8 (1985) to determine what damage the change application would have on private and public property, and failed to comply with section 73–3–3 (1980) by not considering the "duties" of the defendant applicants.   Plaintiffs alleged that the state engineer's disclaimer of any authority to consider, in connection with a permanent change application, any damages caused to plaintiffs as a result of his approval of the application, was contrary to the clear mandate of section 73–3–8, which requires an evaluation of the factors there set out, including any and all damage to public and private property and the impact the application will have on the public welfare. Plaintiffs also alleged that they had owned and occupied their approximately ten acres of property for twenty years and that for the approximately one hundred years since Draper Irrigation first constructed open ditches, flumes, pipelines, and other aqueducts to carry water from Bell Canyon Reservoir to its water treatment plant in Draper, Utah, plaintiffs' properties had remained undisturbed. Since the construction of the screw gates, in furtherance of the applied-for change, that was no longer the case. Virtual waterfalls cascaded down the hillside immediately east of plaintiffs' properties whenever applicants closed that gate and caused tremendous damage to plaintiffs' properties and the public area in the vicinity.

* * *

Utah Code Ann. § 73–3–3 (1980), at the time the state engineer rendered his decision, read in pertinent part:

* * *

No permanent change shall be made except on the approval of an application therefor by the state engineer * * *. *The procedure in the state engineer's office and rights and duties of the applicants with respect to applications for permanent changes of point of diversion, place or purpose of use shall be the same as provided in this title for applications to appropriate water;* but the state engineer may, in connection with applications for permanent change involving only a change in point of diversion of 660 feet or less, waive the necessity for publishing notice of such applications. No temporary change shall be made except upon an application filed in duplicate with the state engineer. . . .   The state engineer shall make an investigation and *if such temporary change does not impair any vested rights of others he shall make an order authorizing the change.*

(Emphasis added.)

Section 73–3–8 (1985), at the time the state engineer rendered his decision, read in pertinent part:

(1) It shall be the duty of the state engineer to approve an application if:

* * *

(e) the application was filed in good faith and not for purposes of speculation or monopoly. *If the state engineer, because of information in his possession obtained either by his own investigation or otherwise, has reason to believe that an application to appropriate water will interfere with its more beneficial use for irrigation, domestic or culinary, stock watering, power or mining development or manufacturing, or will unreasonably affect public recreation or the natural stream environment, or will prove detrimental to the public welfare, it is his duty to withhold his approval or rejection of the application until he has investigated the matter. If an application does not meet the requirements of this section, it shall be rejected.*

(Emphasis added.)

* * *

We agree with the position taken by plaintiffs * * * that both statutory purposes and a reasonable textual interpretation of water allocation statutes support the application of appropriation criteria to permanent change applications. The language critical to our determination was added to section 100–3–3, R.S.Utah 1933, in 1937. *See* L.1937, ch. 130, § 1. The amendment removed provisions addressing notice requirements and added for the first time language defining permanent and temporary changes. After setting out procedures relating to applications for permanent changes, the 1937 amendment continued:

The procedure in the state engineer's office *and the rights and duties of the applicant with respect to application for permanent changes* of point of diversion, place, or purpose of use *shall be the same as provided in this title for applications to appropriate water.*

(Emphasis added.)

* * * The only reasonable meaning to read into section 73–3–3 is that the state engineer must investigate and reject the application for either appropriation or permanent change of use or place of use if approval would interfere with more beneficial use, public recreation, the natural stream environment, or the public welfare. It is unreasonable to assume that the legislature would require the state engineer to investigate matters of public concern in water appropriations and yet restrict him from undertaking those duties in permanent change applications. Carried to its logical conclusion, such an interpretation would eviscerate the duties of the state engineer under section 73–3–8 and allow an applicant to accomplish in a two-step process what the statute proscribes in a one-step process. For all that an applicant would need to do to achieve a disapproved purpose under section 73–3–8 would be to appropriate for an approved purpose and then to file a change application under section 73–3–3.

* * *

NOTE

The New Mexico Supreme Court applied public interest review to a change in point of diversion but sustained the change where there was a lack of evidence showing that the change in point of diversion was the cause of deteriorating water quality. Stokes v. Morgan, 680 P.2d 335 (N.M.1984).

3. Limitations on the Exercise of Rights

ALAMOSA—LA JARA WATER USERS PROTECTION ASSOCIATION v. GOULD

Supreme Court of Colorado, 1983.
674 P.2d 914.

DUBOFSKY, JUSTICE.

This is an appeal from a judgment of the district court for Water Division 3 (water court) regarding rules promulgated by the Colorado State Engineer (proposed rules) limiting the use of surface and underground water in the San Luis Valley. Curtailment of water use in the valley is required by the terms of an interstate stipulation under which Colorado must meet its Rio Grande Compact (compact) obligation to deliver scheduled amounts of Rio Grande water at the Colorado–New Mexico border on an annual basis. The dispute over the proposed rules concerns the distribution of that curtailment: between Rio Grande and Conejos River water users, between Rio Grande mainstem and tributary users, and between well owners and surface diverters. The water court approved rules for administering separate obligations for deliveries from the Conejos River and the Rio Grande mainstem, and disapproved rules which phased out all wells in the San Luis Valley unless each well owner could demonstrate a lack of material injury to senior surface water users or provide a plan of augmentation to replace the water taken by a well. * * *

I.

The San Luis Valley in south-central Colorado extends approximately ninety miles from north to south and fifty miles from east to west at an elevation varying between 7,500 feet and 8,000 feet above sea level. The major mountain boundaries are the San Juan mountains to the west and the Sangre de Cristo mountains to the east. The Rio Grande mainstem rises in the San Juan mountains, flows southeasterly through the valley to Alamosa, and then runs south through a break in the San Luis hills, which border the valley on the south, into the state of New Mexico, then along the border between Texas and Mexico, emptying into the Gulf of Mexico. The Conejos River rises in the Conejos Mountains to the south-west and flows north-easterly along the southern edge of the valley, joining the Rio Grande mainstem at

Los Sauces. Despite its high altitude, short growing season, and average annual precipitation of only about 7.5 inches, the valley sustains a productive agricultural economy dependent upon irrigation water.

The upper 6000 feet of fill below the valley surface consists of unconsolidated clay, silt, sand, and gravel, and interbedded lava flows, containing an estimated two billion acre-feet of underground water. Some of the underground water is in an unconfined aquifer system at shallow depths. Beneath the unconfined aquifer are relatively impermeable beds of clay and basalt and beneath these confining layers are substantial quantities of water which comprise the confined aquifer. The confining clay layer generally does not exist around the valley's perimeter, and the confined aquifer system is recharged from surface flow to the underground water system at the edges of the valley. Because the recharge areas are higher in elevation than the floor of the valley, the confined aquifer is under artesian pressure, resulting in the free flow of water from some artesian wells and springs at natural breaks in the confining layer. In some places, where the confining layer is less thick and more transmissive, water from the confined aquifer will leak upward through the confining clay layers into the unconfined aquifer. The unconfined aquifer is directly connected with the surface streams in some places. To varying degrees, the surface streams, the unconfined aquifer, and the confined aquifer are hydraulically connected.[3]

* * *

Since before the turn of the century, valley water users have had to contend with out-of-state demands for Rio Grande water. * * * To avoid litigation, Colorado, New Mexico, and Texas began in 1923 to make efforts towards a negotiated apportionment of Rio Grande water. Negotiators from the three states signed a permanent compact in 1938. The compact subsequently was ratified by the legislature of each state and approved by the United States Congress in 1939. 53 Stat. 785 (1939). Codified at section 37–66–101, C.R.S., the compact obligates Colorado to deliver water in the Rio Grande at the New Mexico border based upon two schedules tying delivery obligations to levels of inflow, as measured at upstream gauges on the Rio Grande mainstem and the Conejos River, to which is added the flow of the Los Pinos and San Antonio rivers (tributaries of the Conejos) measured near Ortiz, New Mexico. The amount of required discharge varies according to natural supply. In low water years, small deliveries are required; in high water years, large deliveries are required. The compact fixes Colorado's overall obligation in the equitable interstate apportionment of the

---

3. North of the Rio Grande mainstem, a hydraulic divide provides the southern boundary of an area known as the Closed Basin. Four large mutual irrigation systems supply water from the mainstem to irrigate the agricultural land in the basin. Return water from irrigation and small streams within the basin flow toward the sump, the basin's lowest surface area, rather than returning to the mainstem, and consequently, most of the water is lost to evapotranspiration.

Rio Grande at a level intended to protect water use as it existed from 1928–1937 (the compact study period).

* * *

Between 1969 and 1975, the state engineer developed annual operating criteria to deliver water to the state line.

In 1975, the state engineer promulgated the proposed rules, publishing them in all counties of Water Division No. 3, which is generally coterminous with the San Luis Valley. * * * Numerous protests to the proposed rules were filed, requiring a hearing before a water judge under section 37–92–501(2)(h), C.R.S.

* * *

A lengthy trial ensued. * * *

II.

A.

The proposed rules are based on the premise that the separate delivery schedules provided for the Conejos and Rio Grande in Article III of the compact mandate separate administration of the rivers. This interpretation of the compact reflects administration of the rivers under the compact since 1968 when, as a result of the stipulation with New Mexico and Texas, the Colorado state engineer began to require curtailment of diversions in order to meet compact obligations.

As a result of separate administration of the rivers, senior water rights on the Conejos River have been curtailed at times when users with more recently acquired rights on the Rio Grande have continued to divert water. Moreover, although the Conejos system contributes only thirty percent of the inflow of water to the San Luis Valley, administration in accordance with the compact schedules requires the Conejos system to provide forty-five percent of Colorado's deliveries at the New Mexico state line. The Conejos District maintains that the Conejos River is a losing stream,[11] and that the state engineer has curtailed a large percentage of inflow at the headgates of the Conejos water users so that the stream will produce the amount required by the compact. In contrast the Rio Grande is a gaining stream, and its delivery obligation is satisfied to a large extent by return flows of water already diverted for irrigation. Since 1968, except for the severe drought years of 1972 and 1977, the state has curtailed diversions to some extent on the Conejos and its tributaries during the irrigation season. The effect of such curtailment in the Conejos area is to reduce the irrigation season by about one week at each end of the season, resulting in numerous hardships on farmers and ranchers in the area. Consequently, intense controversy has developed over whether administration according to the separate delivery schedules of Article III is required by the compact or permissible under state law.

* * *

11. A losing stream is one in which there are significant river losses other than for diversions below the inflow gauges.

We agree. The equitable apportionment of the waters of interstate streams may be accomplished either by the United States Supreme Court, Kansas v. Colorado, 206 U.S. 46 (1907), or by interstate compact, Colorado v. Kansas, 320 U.S. 383 (1943). Equitable apportionment, a federal doctrine, can determine times of delivery and sources of supply to satisfy that delivery without conflicting with state law, for state law applies only to the water which has not been committed to other states by the equitable apportionment. Hinderlider v. LaPlata River and Cherry Creek Ditch Co., 304 U.S. 92 (1938). In an equitable apportionment, strict adherence to prior appropriations may not always be possible. Colorado v. New Mexico, 459 U.S. 176 (1982); Nebraska v. Wyoming, 325 U.S. 589 (1945).

* * * The separate delivery rules, therefore, are not inconsistent with constitutional and statutory provisions for priority administration of water rights.

* * *

III.

The proposed underground water rules tie tributary underground water administration in the valley to regulation for compact requirements by integrating tributary underground water diversions into the priority system for surface streams. The rules are intended over a five-year period to curtail well diversions unless individual well owners prove that their wells do not cause injury to senior water rights or remedy such injury through plans for augmentation.

* * *

C.

The water court disapproved the well regulations because they did not contain a requirement that stream appropriators tap the enormous supply of water underlying the surface of the valley. * * * The state engineer asserts that the proposed rules properly place the burden of remedying the injury caused to senior appropriators on junior water users and that the water court's ruling is a misapplication of law. The state engineer relies upon the principle, codified in section 37–92–102, C.R.S., that the priority system governs water allocation and that junior water rights from whatever source are not entitled to divert water that otherwise would be available for use by senior water rights. See also sections 37–92–301(3) and 37–92–501, C.R.S. Under the prior appropriation doctrine, it is argued, the burden of integrating surface and groundwater rights falls upon junior water users, primarily through plans for augmentation under section 37–92–103(9), C.R.S. * * *

[T]he state policy of maximum utilization of water [was] first enunciated in *Fellhauer* [v. People, 167 Colo. 320], 447 P.2d [986 (1969)] at 994,

"It is implicit in these constitutional provisions [the two provisions are in Article XVI, Section 6 of the Colorado Constitution] that, along with *vested rights* there shall be *maximum utilization* of the water of this state. As administration of water approaches its second century the curtain is opening upon the new drama of *maximum utilization* and how constitutionally that doctrine can be integrated into the law of *vested rights.*" (Emphasis in original.)

The policy of maximum utilization was codified in the "Water Right Determination and Administration Act of 1969" where the General Assembly declared

"the policy of the state of Colorado that all waters originating in or flowing into this state, whether found on the surface or underground, have always been and are hereby declared to be the property of the public, dedicated to the use of the people of the state, subject to appropriation and use in accordance with law. As incident thereto, it is the policy of this state to integrate the appropriation, use, and administration of underground water tributary to a stream with the use of surface water in such a way as to maximize the beneficial use of all of the waters of this state.

(2) Recognizing that previous and existing laws have given inadequate attention to the development and use of underground waters of the state, that the use of underground waters as an independent source or in conjunction with surface waters is necessary to the present and future welfare of the people of this state, and that the future welfare of the state depends upon a sound and flexible integrated use of all waters of the state, it is hereby declared to be the further policy of the state of Colorado that in the determination of water rights, uses, and administration of water the following principles shall apply:

* * *

(b) The existing use of ground water, either independently or in conjunction with surface rights, shall be recognized to the fullest extent possible, subject to the preservation of other existing vested rights, but, at his own point of diversion on a natural water course, each diverter must establish some reasonable means of effectuating his diversion. He is not entitled to demand the whole flow of the stream merely to facilitate his taking the fraction of the whole flow to which he is entitled.

(c) The use of ground water may be considered as an alternate or supplemental source of supply for surface decrees entered prior to June 7, 1969, taking into consideration both previous usage and the necessity to protect the vested rights of others.

(d) No reduction of any lawful diversion because of the operation of the priority system shall be permitted unless such reduction would increase the amount of water available to and required by water rights having senior priorities."

Section 37–92–102(1) and (2), C.R.S.

The 1969 Act recognized in section 37–92–102(2)(b) that one method of achieving maximum utilization of water is to require that each diverter establish a reasonable means of effectuating his diversion. The section is based upon the holding in Colorado Springs v. Bender [148 Colo. 458, 366 P.2d 552 (1961), page 618, infra], a case involving senior wells which used tributary water to irrigate farm land and a junior well which supplied water for Colorado Springs. The plaintiffs, senior appropriators, sued to enjoin the defendant's diversion of water in violation of the plaintiffs' rights of prior appropriation, alleging that the defendant's pumping was lowering the water table below the intake of the plaintiffs' pumping facilities. * * * The *Bender* court then directed the trial court to consider whether adequate means for reaching a sufficient supply could be made available to the senior appropriators, and because senior appropriators cannot be required to improve their extraction facilities beyond their economic reach, whether an adequate means should be decreed at the expense of the junior appropriators. The court in *Bender* relied upon Schodde v. Twin Falls Land and Water Company, 224 U.S. 107 (1912), which requires a senior's method of diversion to be reasonable in order for it to be protected from injury caused by junior diversions * * *.[34]

Here, several witnesses testified that the water in storage in the valley's aquifers provides the support for the water above it to move to the streams. The well owners and the communities argue that it is not unreasonable to require surface diverters to deepen their headgates if the water from the stream is beneath their feet. The argument continues that the surface owners have lost nothing except a gravity flow source of supply which is cheaper and easier to divert, and that the loss only occurs at times when the surface stream is inadequate to fill the surface diverters' priorities. A reasonable means of diversion in this case, it is argued, is one that eliminates the need for supporting the surface stream, thereby freeing the underground water for maximum beneficial use.

The Conejos District recognizes the development of the maximum utilization of water under *Fellhauer* and the 1969 Act. However, Conejos argues that augmentation is one of the means provided to achieve maximum utilization under the 1969 Act, and that because the proposed rules require junior wells to augment, the rules are consistent with the policy of maximum utilization. Evaluation of different means of achieving maximum utilization, however, is a matter of policy, and therefore a task to be performed by the state engineer after full consideration of the available alternatives. * * *

The water court held that, under certain circumstances, surface stream appropriators may be required to withdraw underground water tributary to the stream in order to satisfy their surface appropriations. We affirm this legal conclusion and return the proposed well rules to the state engineer for consideration of whether the reasonable-means-

---

34. The state engineer attempts to distinguish the *Bender* and *Schodde* decisions on the basis that *Bender* concerned conflicts between underground water appropriations and *Schodde*, conflicts between surface appropriations. However, the 1969 Act integrated surface and underground water appropriations, thus allowing a conflict between a surface and underground water appropriation to be subject to the *Bender* doctrine as codified in the same act, section 37–92–102(2), C.R.S.

of-diversion doctrine provides, in this case, a method of achieving maximum utilization of water—a consideration which the state engineer erroneously believed was foreclosed. We note that the policy of maximum utilization does not require a single-minded endeavor to squeeze every drop of water from the valley's aquifers. Section 37–92–501(2)(e) makes clear that the objective of "maximum use" administration is "optimum use." [36] Optimum use can only be achieved with proper regard for all significant factors, including environmental and economic concerns. *See* section 37–92–102(3), C.R.S. (recognizing the need to correlate the activities of mankind with reasonable preservation of the natural environment); Harrison & Sandstrom, [*The Ground Water Surface Water Conflict and Recent Colorado Legislation,* 43 U.Colo.L.Rev. 1 (1971)], at 14–15 (An increase of well diversions at the expense of maintenance of a surface flow would increase the efficiency of irrigation at the expense of other environmental and economic values.). See also Trelease [*Conjunctive Use of Ground Water and Surface Water,* 27 Rocky Mtn.Min.L.Inst. 1853 (1982)], at 1866–1872 (Determination of what constitutes a reasonable means of diversion may be more a question of the proper allocation of the costs of more efficient diversion than of the quantity of water ultimately diverted.). The water court observed that the state engineer's reconsideration might take the form of requiring senior appropriators to drill new wells before requiring curtailment of junior rights and listed a number of suggestions for increasing utilization.[37] Similarly, the state engineer's reconsideration might result in assessment to junior appropriators of the cost of making those improvements to seniors' diversions which are necessitated by junior withdrawals. Selection among these and other possibilities, including retention of the scheme of the proposed rules, as a policy decision to be made by the state engineer, after consideration of all relevant factors.

We remand the rules to the water court for return to the state engineer.

---

36. Section 37–92–501(2)(e) states: "All rules and regulations shall have as their objective the optimum use of water consistent with preservation of the priority system of water rights."

37. Throughout the latter part of the trial, the parties' expert engineers met off the record in an attempt to agree upon a resolution of the water problems in the valley. At the conclusion of the water judge's opinion, he listed some of the engineers' suggestions as including:

(1) Elimination of the wasteful practice of subirrigation; (2) encouragement of improved irrigation efficiency, such as increased use of sprinklers; (3) prohibit the wasteful practice of allowing diverted water to collect in barrow pits, potholes and other areas, only to evaporate; (4) promote the Closed Basin Project; (5) construct new wells and use existing wells to deliver both confined and unconfined water to help satisfy Compact obligations; (6) construct new drains and rehabilitate existing drains to salvage water presently lost to non-beneficial evapotranspiration; (7) initiate channel rectification program to prevent the wasteful overflow losses on critical reaches on the river system in the valley; (8) a systematic augmentation plan for direct flow rights and wells from the confined and unconfined aquifers, pursuant to ongoing research to determine the effect of such augmentation upon senior priority rights; (9) development of reservoirs to store pre-Compact direct flow rights; (10) additional purchase of existing water rights and release of those waters to the streams.

NOTES

1. Unlike states with permit systems, Colorado initially allocates water without administrative intervention or public interest review. One claims rights to appropriate water for a use beneficial in light of the user's economic needs, and a water court only determines the priority of the new appropriation relative to all others. See pages 243–44, supra. Rights can be transferred in private transactions so long as the court finds that other appropriators will not be injured by a change in the place, manner, or time of the diversion or use of water.

Is the "public interest" ignored? Minimum streamflows "to protect the natural environment to a reasonable degree" are appropriated by a state agency, integrated in the resume of all appropriative rights, and enforced like any other rights. See pages 263–72, supra. Water quality is controlled by regulatory statutes. Water is otherwise unconstrained in moving to the uses having the highest economic values—and which therefore can pay the highest price for water. In light of the decision in *Alamosa–La Jara* may use of a new appropriation be challenged in water court by other water users or by the state engineer on the ground that it would not result in optimum utilization of water? Could existing appropriations be so challenged? If so, in what type of a proceeding?

2. The decision in *Alamosa–La Jara* was followed in R.J.A., Inc. v. Water Users Ass'n of Dist. No. 6, 690 P.2d 823, 828 (Colo.1984) ("[T]he general legislative policy of maximizing beneficial and integrated use of surface and subsurface water must be implemented with a sensitivity to the effect on other resources.")

3. On the subject of accommodating the public interest within the appropriation system, see Charles F. Wilkinson, *Western Water Law in Transition,* 56 Colo.L.Rev. 317 (1985).

4. Judicial Public Trust Review

NATIONAL AUDUBON SOCIETY v. SUPERIOR COURT OF ALPINE COUNTY

Supreme Court of California, 1983.
33 Cal.3d 419, 189 Cal.Rptr. 346, 658 P.2d 709,
cert. denied, 464 U.S. 977, 104 S.Ct. 413, 78 L.Ed.2d 351 (1983).

BROUSSARD, JUSTICE.

Mono Lake, the second largest lake in California, sits at the base of the Sierra Nevada escarpment near the eastern entrance to Yosemite National Park. The lake is saline; it contains no fish but supports a large population of brine shrimp which feed vast numbers of nesting and migratory birds. Islands in the lake protect a large breeding colony of California gulls, and the lake itself serves as a haven on the migration route for thousands of Northern Phalarope, Wilson's Phalarope, and Eared Greve. Towers and spires of tufa on the north and south shores are matters of geological interest and a tourist attraction.

Although Mono Lake receives some water from rain and snow on the lake surface, historically most of its supply came from snowmelt in the Sierra Nevada. Five freshwater streams—Mill, Lee Vining, Walker, Parker and Rush Creeks—arise near the crest of the range and carry the annual runoff to the west shore of the lake. In 1940, however, the Division of Water Resources, the predecessor to the present California Water Resources Board, granted the Department of Water and Power of the City of Los Angeles (hereafter DWP) a permit to appropriate virtually the entire flow of four of the five streams flowing into the lake. DWP promptly constructed facilities to divert about half the flow of these streams into DWP's Owens Valley aqueduct. In 1970 DWP completed a second diversion tunnel, and since that time has taken virtually the entire flow of these streams.

As a result of these diversions, the level of the lake has dropped; the surface area has diminished by one-third; one of the two principal islands in the lake has become a peninsula, exposing the gull rookery there to coyotes and other predators and causing the gulls to abandon the former island. The ultimate effect of continued diversions is a matter of intense dispute, but there seems little doubt that both the scenic beauty and the ecological values of Mono Lake are imperiled.

Plaintiffs filed suit in superior court to enjoin the DWP diversions on the theory that the shores, bed and waters of Mono Lake are protected by a public trust.

* * *

This case brings together for the first time two systems of legal thought: the appropriative water rights system which since the days of the gold rush has dominated California water law, and the public trust doctrine which, after evolving as a shield for the protection of tidelands, now extends its protective scope to navigable lakes. * * * They meet in a unique and dramatic setting which highlights the clash of values. Mono Lake is a scenic and ecological treasure of national significance, imperiled by continued diversions of water; yet, the need of Los Angeles for water is apparent, its reliance on rights granted by the board evident, the cost of curtailing diversions substantial.

* * *

1. *Background and history of the Mono Lake litigation.*

* * *

* * * The city applied to the Water Board in 1940 for permits to appropriate the waters of the four tributaries. At hearings before the board, various interested individuals protested that the city's proposed appropriations would lower the surface level of Mono Lake and thereby impair its commercial, recreational and scenic uses.

The board's primary authority to reject that application lay in a 1921 amendment to the Water Commission Act of 1913, which authorized the board to reject an application "when in its judgment the proposed appropriation would not best conserve the public interest." (Stats. 1921, ch. 329, § 1, p. 443, now codified as Wat.Code, § 1255.) [5]

---

5. In theory, the board could have rejected the city's application on the ground that the waters of the streams were already being put to beneficial use or that

The 1921 enactment, however, also "declared to be the established policy of this state that the use of water for domestic purposes is the highest use of water" (id., now codified as Wat.Code, § 1254), and directed the Water Board to be guided by this declaration of policy. Since DWP sought water for domestic use, the board concluded that it had to grant the application notwithstanding the harm to public trust uses of Mono Lake.

The board's decision states that "[i]t is indeed unfortunate that the City's proposed development will result in decreasing the aesthetic advantages of Mono Basin but *there is apparently nothing that this office can do to prevent it.* The use to which the City proposes to put the water under its Applications * * * is defined by the Water Commission Act as the highest to which water may be applied and to make available unappropriated water for this use the City has, by the condemnation proceedings described above, acquired the littoral and riparian rights on Mono Lake and its tributaries south of Mill Creek. This office therefore has *no alternative but to dismiss all protests based upon the possible lowering of the water level in Mono Lake and the effect that the diversion of water from these streams may have upon the aesthetic and recreational value of the Basin.*"

* * * By October of 1979, the lake had shrunk from its prediversion area of 85 square miles to an area of 60.3 square miles. Its surface level had dropped to 6,373 feet above sea level, 43 feet below the prediversion level.

* * *

2. *The Public Trust Doctrine in California.*

"By the law of nature these things are common to mankind—the air, running water, the sea and consequently the shores of the sea." (Institutes of Justinian 2.1.1.) From this origin in Roman law, the English common law evolved the concept of the public trust, under which the sovereign owns "all of its navigable waterways and the lands lying beneath them 'as trustee of a public trust for the benefit of the people.' " (Colberg, Inc. v. State of California ex rel. Dept. Pub. Works (1967) 67 Cal.2d 408, 416, 62 Cal.Rptr. 401, 432 P.2d 3.) The State of California acquired title as trustee to such lands and waterways upon its admission to the union (City of Berkeley v. Superior Court (1980) 26 Cal.3d 515, 521, 162 Cal.Rptr. 327, 606 P.2d 362 and cases there cited); from the earliest days (see Eldridge v. Cowell (1954) 4 Cal. 80, 87) its judicial decisions have recognized and enforced the trust obligation.

Three aspects of the public trust doctrine require consideration in this opinion: the purpose of the trust; the scope of the trust, particularly as it applies to the nonnavigable tributaries of a navigable lake; and the powers and duties of the state as trustee of the public trust. We discuss these questions in the order listed.

the DWP proposed an unreasonable use of water in violation of article X, section 2 of the California Constitution. It does not appear that the board considered either proposition.

(a) *The purpose of the public trust.*

The objective of the public trust has evolved in tandem with the changing public perception of the values and uses of waterways. As we observed in Marks v. Whitney, supra, 6 Cal.3d 251, 98 Cal.Rptr. 790, 491 P.2d 374, "[p]ublic trust easements [were] traditionally defined in terms of navigation, commerce and fisheries. They have been held to include the right to fish, hunt, bathe, swim, to use for boating and general recreation purposes the navigable waters of the state, and to use the bottom of the navigable waters for anchoring, standing, or other purposes." We went on, however, to hold that the traditional triad of uses—navigation, commerce and fishing—did not limit the public interest in the trust.

* * *

Mono Lake is a navigable waterway. (City of Los Angeles v. Aitken, 10 Cal.App.2d 460, 466, 52 P.2d 585 [(1935)].) It supports a small local industry which harvests brine shrimp for sale as fish food, which endeavor probably qualifies the lake as a "fishery" under the traditional public trust cases. The principal values plaintiffs seek to protect, however, are recreational and ecological—the scenic views of the lake and its shore, the purity of the air, and the use of the lake for nesting and feeding by birds. Under Marks v. Whitney, supra, 6 Cal.3d 251, 98 Cal.Rptr. 790, 491 P.2d 374, it is clear that protection of these values is among the purposes of the public trust.

(b) *The scope of the public trust.*

* * *

Mono Lake is, as we have said, a navigable waterway. The beds, shores and waters of the lake are without question protected by the public trust. The streams diverted by DWP, however, are not themselves navigable. Accordingly, we must address in this case a question not discussed in any recent public trust case—whether the public trust limits conduct affecting nonnavigable tributaries to navigable waterways.

* * *

"If the public trust doctrine applies to constrain *fills* which destroy navigation and other public trust uses in navigable waters, it should equally apply to constrain the extraction of water that destroys navigation and other public interests. Both actions result in the same damage to the public interest." (Johnson, Public Trust Protection for Stream Flows and Lake Levels (1980) 14 U.C.Davis L.Rev. 233, 257–258; see Dunning, The Significance of California's Public Trust Easement for California Water Rights Law (1980) 14 U.C. Davis L.Rev. 357, 359–360.)

We conclude that the public trust doctrine, as recognized and developed in California decisions, protects navigable waters from harm caused by diversion of nonnavigable tributaries.

(c) *Duties and powers of the state as trustee.*

* * * One consequence, of importance to this and many other cases, is that parties acquiring rights in trust property generally hold those rights subject to the trust, and can assert no vested right to use those rights in a manner harmful to the trust.

As we noted recently in City of Berkeley v. Superior Court, supra, 26 Cal.3d 515, 162 Cal.Rptr. 327, 606 P.2d 362, the decision of the United States Supreme Court in Illinois Central Railroad Company v. Illinois, supra, 146 U.S. 387 "remains the primary authority even today, almost nine decades after it was decided." (26 Cal.3d 521, 162 Cal.Rptr. 327, 606 P.2d 362.) The Illinois Legislature in 1886 had granted the railroad in fee simple 1,000 acres of submerged lands, virtually the entire Chicago waterfront. Four years later it sought to revoke that grant. The Supreme Court upheld the revocatory legislation. Its opinion explained that lands under navigable waters conveyed to private parties for wharves, docks, and other structures in furtherance of trust purposes could be granted free of the trust because the conveyance is consistent with the purpose of the trust. But the legislature, it held, did not have the power to convey the entire city waterfront free of trust.

* * *

[I]n our recent decision in City of Berkeley v. Superior Court, supra, 26 Cal.3d 515, 162 Cal.Rptr. 327, 606 P.2d 362, we considered whether deeds executed by the Board of Tidelands Commissioners pursuant to an 1870 act conferred title free of the trust. Applying the principles of earlier decisions, we held that the grantees' title was subject to the trust, both because the Legislature had not made clear its intention to authorize a conveyance free of the trust and because the 1870 act and the conveyances under it were not intended to further trust purposes.

Once again we rejected the claim that establishment of the public trust constituted a taking of property for which compensation was required: "We do not divest anyone of title to property; the consequence of our decision will be only that some landowners whose predecessors in interest acquired property under the 1870 act will, hold it subject to the public trust." (P. 532, 162 Cal.Rptr. 327, 606 P.2d 362.)

In summary, the foregoing cases amply demonstrate the continuing power of the state as administrator of the public trust, a power which extends to the revocation of previously granted rights or to the enforcement of the trust against lands long thought free of the trust. Except for those rare instances in which a grantee may acquire a right to use former trust property free of trust restrictions, the grantee holds subject to the trust, and while he may assert a vested right to the servient estate (the right of use subject to the trust) and to any improvements he erects, he can claim no vested right to bar recognition of the trust or state action to carry out its purposes.

* * *

3. *The California Water Rights System.*

* * *

Our recent decision in People v. Shirokow (1980) 26 Cal.3d 301, 162 Cal.Rptr. 30, 605 P.2d 859, described the early history of the appropriative water rights system in California. We explained that "California operates under the so-called dual system of water rights which recognizes both the appropriation and the riparian doctrines. * * *"

* * *

In 1926, however, a decision of this court led to a constitutional amendment which radically altered water law in California and led to an expansion of the powers of the board. In Herminghaus v. South California Edison Co. (1926) 200 Cal. 81, 252 P. 607, we held not only that riparian rights took priority over appropriations authorized by the Water Board, a point which had always been clear, but that as between the riparian and the appropriator, the former's use of water was not limited by the doctrine of reasonable use. That decision led to a constitutional amendment which abolished the right of a riparian to devote water to unreasonable uses, and established the doctrine of reasonable use as an overriding feature of California water law.

* * *

This amendment does more than merely overturn *Herminghaus*—it establishes state water policy. All uses of water, including public trust uses, must now conform to the standard of reasonable use.

* * *

The 1928 amendment itself did not expand the authority of the Water Board. The board remained, under controlling judicial decisions, a ministerial body with the limited task of determining priorities between claimants seeking to appropriate unclaimed water. More recent statutory and judicial developments, however, have greatly enhanced the power of the Water Board to oversee the reasonable use of water and, in the process, made clear its authority to weigh and protect public trust values.

* * *

4. *The relationship between the Public Trust Doctrine and the California Water Rights System.*

As we have seen, the public trust doctrine and the appropriative water rights system administered by the Water Board developed independently of each other. Each developed comprehensive rules and principles which, if applied to the full extent of their scope, would occupy the field of allocation of stream waters to the exclusion of any competing system of legal thought. * * *

* * * In our opinion, both the public trust doctrine and the water rights system embody important precepts which make the law more responsive to the diverse needs and interests involved in the planning and allocation of water resources. To embrace one system of thought and reject the other would lead to an unbalanced structure, one which would either decry as a breach of trust appropriations essential to the economic development of this state, or deny any duty to protect or even consider the values promoted by the public trust. Therefore, seeking an accommodation which will make use of the pertinent principles of both the public trust doctrine and the appropriative water rights system, and drawing upon the history of the public trust and the water rights system, the body of judicial precedent, and the views of expert commentators, we reach the following conclusions:

a. The state as sovereign retains continuing supervisory control over its navigable waters and the lands beneath those waters. This principle, fundamental to the concept of the public trust, applies to rights in flowing waters as well as to rights in tidelands and lakeshores; it prevents any party from acquiring a vested right to appropriate water in a manner harmful to the interests protected by the public trust.

b. As a matter of current and historical necessity, the Legislature, acting directly or through an authorized agency such as the Water Board, has the power to grant usufructuary licenses that will permit an appropriator to take water from flowing streams and use that water in a distant part of the state, even though this taking does not promote, and may unavoidably harm, the trust uses at the source stream. The population and economy of this state depend upon the appropriation of vast quantities of water for uses unrelated to in-stream trust values. California's Constitution, its statutes, decisions, and commentators all emphasize the need to make efficient use of California's limited water resources: all recognize, at least implicitly, that efficient use requires diverting water from in-stream uses. Now that the economy and population centers of this state have developed in reliance upon appropriated water, it would be disingenuous to hold that such appropriations are and have always been improper to the extent that they harm public trust uses, and can be justified only upon theories of reliance or estoppel.

c. The state has an affirmative duty to take the public trust into account in the planning and allocation of water resources, and to protect public trust uses whenever feasible. Just as the history of this state shows that appropriation may be necessary for efficient use of water despite unavoidable harm to public trust values, it demonstrates that an appropriative water rights system administered without consideration of the public trust may cause unnecessary and unjustified harm to trust interests. As a matter of practical necessity the state may have to approve appropriations despite foreseeable harm to public trust uses. In so doing, however, the state must bear in mind its duty as trustee to consider the effect of the taking on the public trust (see United Plainsmen v. N.D. State Water Con. Commission (N.D.1976) 247 N.W.2d 457, 462–463), and to preserve, so far as consistent with the public interest, the uses protected by the trust.

Once the state has approved an appropriation, the public trust imposes a duty of continuing supervision over the taking and use of the appropriated water. In exercising its sovereign power to allocate water resources in the public interest, the state is not confined by past allocation decisions which may be incorrect in light of current knowledge or inconsistent with current needs.

* * * In the case before us, the salient fact is that no responsible body has ever determined the impact of diverting the entire flow of the Mono Lake tributaries into the Los Angeles Acqueduct. This is not a case in which the Legislature, the Water Board, or any judicial body has determined that the needs of Los Angeles outweigh the needs of the Mono Basin, that the benefit gained is worth the price. Neither has any responsible body determined whether some lesser taking would better balance the diverse interests. Instead, DWP acquired rights to the entire flow in 1940 from a water board which believed it lacked both the power and the duty to protect the Mono Lake environment, and continues to exercise those rights in apparent disregard for the resulting damage to the scenery, ecology, and human uses of Mono Lake.

It is clear that some responsible body ought to reconsider the allocation of the waters of the Mono Basin. No vested rights bar such reconsideration. We recognize the substantial concerns voiced by Los Angeles—the city's need for water, its reliance upon the 1940 board decision, the cost both in terms of money and environmental impact of obtaining water elsewhere. Such concerns must enter into any allocation decision. We hold only that they do not preclude a reconsideration and reallocation which also takes into account the impact of water diversion on the Mono Lake environment.

* * *

This opinion is but one step in the eventual resolution of the Mono Lake controversy. We do not dictate any particular allocation of water. Our objective is to resolve a legal conundrum in which two competing systems of thought—the public trust doctrine and the appropriative water rights system—existed independently of each other, espousing principles which seemingly suggested opposite results. We hope by integrating these two doctrines to clear away the legal barriers which have so far prevented either the Water Board or the courts from taking a new and objective look at the water resources of the Mono Basin. The human and environmental uses of Mono Lake—uses protected by the public trust doctrine—deserve to be taken into account.

NOTES

1. Mono Lake inflows have been increased by judicial action and there is hope that minimum lake levels can be maintained through careful water management. Two related actions have resulted in the further protection of Mono Lake. California Trout, Inc. v. State Water Resources Control Bd., 255 Cal.Rptr. 184 (Cal.App.1989) held that California Fish and Game Code §§ 5937 and 5946 enacted in 1953, required that the State Water Resources Board condition Los Angeles Water and Power's post–1953 diversions from the tributaries of Mono

Lake to protect the pre-existing trout fishery. These diversions amount to 50,000 acre-feet, about one-half of Los Angeles' Mono Lake diversions. *California Trout II* held that a trial judge abused his discretion by deferring Los Angeles' compliance with *National Audubon* for two years pending the completion of field studies without any interim relief. California Trout, Inc. v. Superior Court, 266 Cal.Rptr. 788 (3d Dist. 1990).

In the public trust action, back in trial court in El Dorado County, the judge ruled that the lake level must be stabilized at 6,377 feet and that Los Angeles cannot divert any water from the four tributaries until the lake, at 6,375 and falling in the drought summer of 1991, rose two feet. The minimum level of 6,377 is close to the point where the basic stability of the Mono ecosystem, the maintenance of the brine shrimp population and the protection of the bird nesting islands from predators are all affected. The state legislature has appropriated $60 million for replacement supplies for the 50,000 acre-feet lost by the city.

2. *National Audubon* is a major expansion of the public trust concept. As the opinion notes, the trust was used historically only to protect a limited class of public rights in navigable waters. The historical origins of the public trust and its current significance are reviewed in detail in Chapter Four at pages 405–18, infra. The trust theory articulated in *National Audubon* has been evolving since the 1960s (before Congress enacted the current roster of environmental protection programs) in response to efforts by environmentalists to develop "common law" theories that would allow judges to force decision-makers to consider non-development as well as development values in making natural resource allocation choices that have adverse environmental impacts. The seminal article, cited by the court, is Joseph L. Sax, *The Public Trust Doctrine in Natural Resource Law: Effective Judicial Intervention,* 68 Mich.L.Rev. 471 (1970).

There is some precedential support for the court's expansion of the trust from submerged lands to consumptive water rights, but no previous case had applied the trust retroactively. United Plainsmen Ass'n v. North Dakota State Water Conservation Comm'n, 247 N.W.2d 457 (N.D.1976).

3. Some commentators have leveled articulate criticism at the public trust doctrine. E.g., Richard J. Lazarus, *Changing Conceptions of Property and Sovereignty in Natural Resources: Questioning the Public Trust Doctrine,* 71 Iowa L.Rev. 631 (1986). Allegations that the doctrine's application may be limited by the constitutional restraint on takings of private property without just compensation are considered at pages 364–91, infra.

4. California has gone farther than other states in integrating water quality concerns into the water allocation process. The pervasive authority of the state to review and modify decisions gives a new dimension to the public trust doctrine, dramatically bolsters powers of the State Water Resources Control Board, and sharply enhances the state's ability to regulate water quality. The following case upholds the Board's mandate in light of the public trust doctrine.

UNITED STATES v. STATE WATER RESOURCES CONTROL BOARD

California Court of Appeal, First District, 1986.
182 Cal.App.3d 82, 227 Cal.Rptr. 161.

RACANELLI, PRESIDING JUSTICE.

This appeal raises a number of novel and complex questions concerning the interrelationship of the law of water quality and the law of water rights. The coordinated cases arise out of efforts by the State Water Resources Control Board (the Board) to set new water quality standards for the Sacramento–San Joaquin Delta in order to take account of the combined effects upon the Delta of the state's two massive water projects: the Central Valley Project (CVP) and the State Water Project (SWP), operated by the U.S. Bureau of Reclamation (U.S. Bureau or Bureau) and the California Department of Water Resources (DWR), respectively.

The Sacramento–San Joaquin Delta serves as a conduit for the transfer of water by the statewide water projects. Both the CVP and the SWP divert water from the rivers that flow into the Delta and store the water in reservoirs. Quantities of this stored water are periodically released into the Delta. Pumps situated at the southern edge of the Delta eventually lift the water into canals for transport south to the farmers of the Central Valley and the municipalities of Southern California. Water which is neither stored nor exported south passes through the Delta where it is used by local farmers, industries and municipalities. The excess flows out into the San Francisco Bay.

The U.S. Bureau and the DWR hold a combined total of 34 permits for various units of the CVP and SWP to authorize diversion and use of the Delta's waters. These permits were issued by the Board and its predecessors over a period of years extending through 1970.

In 1976 the Board convened a hearing for two declared purposes: to formulate a water quality control plan for the Sacramento–San Joaquin Delta and to determine whether the water use permits held by the U.S. Bureau and the DWR should be amended to implement the plan. In August 1978, following an extensive evidentiary hearing over an 11–month period, the Board adopted the "Water Quality Control Plan for the Sacramento–San Joaquin Delta and Suisun Marsh" (hereafter sometimes called the Plan) and "Water Right Decision 1485" (hereafter sometimes called the Decision or D 1485).

In the Plan the Board established new water quality standards for salinity control and for protection of fish and wildlife in the Delta and Suisun Marsh. In D 1485 the Board modified the permits held by the U.S. Bureau and the DWR, compelling the operators of the projects to adhere to the water quality standards as set out in the Plan. In this appeal we are requested to review the validity of those actions: namely, the Board's establishment of water quality objectives in the Plan and its modification of the water use permits in the Decision.

* * *

The major factor affecting water quality in the Delta is saltwater intrusion. Delta lands, situated at or below sea level, are constantly subject to ocean tidal action. Salt water entering from San Francisco Bay extends well into the Delta, and intrusion of the saline tidal waters is checked only by the natural barrier formed by fresh water flowing out from the Delta.

But as fresh water was increasingly diverted from the Delta for agricultural, industrial and municipal development, salinity intrusion intensified, particularly during the dry summer months and in years of low precipitation and runoff into the river systems. One of the major purposes of the projects was containment of maximum salinity intrusion into the Delta. By storing waters during periods of heavy flow and releasing water during times of low flow, the freshwater barrier could be maintained at a constant level.

Water quality is controlled by both federal and state legislation. * * * [The court described the Federal Clean Water Act, page 132, supra.]

* * *

The federal statutes require each state to engage in "a continuing planning process" and to identify those waters within its boundaries for which discharge restrictions are inadequate to achieve the water quality standards. (33 U.S.C. § 1313(d)(1)(A), (e)(1).) * * *

A further aspect of each state's "continuing planning process" is the identification of so-called nonpoint source pollution. (33 U.S.C. §§ 1281, 1288.) *The Act expressly recognizes saltwater intrusion as a form of nonpoint source pollution.* (33 U.S.C. § 1288(b)(2)(I).) * * *

In California, the Porter–Cologne Water Quality Control Act (§ 13000 et seq.) establishes a comprehensive statewide program for water quality control administered by nine regional boards and coordinated by the State Board. The regional boards are primarily responsible for formulation and adoption of water quality control plans covering the state's sixteen planning basins (§ 13240) subject to the Board's review and approval (§ 13245). But the Board alone is responsible for setting statewide policy concerning water quality control (§§ 13140–13147).

* * *

In its *water quality* role of setting the level of water quality protection, the Board's task is not to protect water rights, but to protect "beneficial uses." The Board is obligated to adopt a water quality control plan consistent with the overall statewide interest in water quality (§ 13240) which will ensure "the reasonable protection of *beneficial uses*" (§ 13241, emphasis added). Its legislated mission is to protect the "quality of all the waters of the state * * * for use and enjoyment by the people of the state." (§ 13000, 1st para., emphasis added.)

The Board's attachment to the concept of protecting "rights" rather than "beneficial uses" apparently stems from the assumption that protection of beneficial uses will require maintenance of constant flow levels in the Delta even during water shortages, whereas protection of water rights will permit some variations in water flow depending upon availability since riparians are entitled only to the natural flow. But such a view overlooks the Board's statutory commitment to establish objectives assuring the "*reasonable* protection of beneficial uses." (§ 13241; emphasis added.) We think this statutory charge grants the Board broad discretion to establish reasonable standards consistent with overall statewide interest. The Board's obligation is to attain the highest reasonable water quality "*considering all demands being made and to be made on those waters* and the total values involved, beneficial and detrimental, economic and social, tangible and intangible." (§ 13000, emphasis added.)

* * *

In performing its dual role, including development of water quality objectives, the Board is directed to consider not only the availability of unappropriated water (§ 174) but also *all* competing demands for water in determining what is a reasonable level of water quality protection (§ 13000). In addition, the Board must consider "past, present, and probable future beneficial uses of water" (§ 13241, subd. (a)) as well as "[w]ater quality conditions that could reasonably be achieved through the coordinated control of *all* factors which affect water quality in the area" (§ 13241, subd. (c), emphasis added). Unfortunately, the Board neglected to do so.

In formulating the "without project" standards, the Board considered only the water use of the Delta parties (denominated "vested water rights") and the needs of the customers served by the projects (denominated "public interest"). No attention was given to water use by the upstream users.

* * *

We think the procedure followed—combining the water quality and water rights functions in a single proceeding—was unwise. The Legislature issued no mandate that the combined functions be performed in a single proceeding. The fundamental defect inherent in such a procedure is dramatically demonstrated: The Board set only such water quality objectives as could be enforced against the projects. In short, the Board compromised its important water quality role by defining its scope too narrowly in terms of enforceable water rights. In fact, however, the Board's water quality obligations are not so limited.

* * *

California, of course, has already combined both water resource functions within the exclusive jurisdiction of the Board. The stated purpose of this merger was to ensure that "consideration of water pollution and water quality" would become an integral part of the appropriative rights process. (§ 174.)

In the 1978 proceedings the Board, as noted, exercised its water rights authority as a means to implement the water quality standards for the Delta. In D 1485 the Board modified the appropriation permits held by the projects to require them to reduce their exports or release more water into the Delta to maintain the water quality standards contained in the Plan.

* * *

[The Bureau of Reclamation (but not the Department of Water Resources) challenged the power of the state to modify its state appropriative rights, but the court concluded: (1) the legislature reserved the power to condition both SWP and CVP permits; (2) the power was reasonably exercised to prevent the unreasonable use or waste of water because of changed circumstances, see Environmental Defense Fund, Inc. v. East Bay Mun. Util. Dist., 26 Cal.3d 183, 161 Cal.Rptr. 466, 605 P.2d 1 (1980). "Thus, * * * the Board's power to modify the permits pursuant to its reserved jurisdiction includes the authority to impose responsibility to maintain water quality on the projects equally." 227 Cal.Rptr. at 189; and (3) the salinity control conditions were consistent with the legislative directives for the CVP because river regulation includes stream flow maintenance, and thus the Board's conditions were permissible under California v. United States, 438 U.S. 645 (1978), page 715, infra.]

Enforcement of the standards, however, presents an entirely different issue. Succinctly stated, the question is whether the Board has authority to compel the projects to comply with such water quality standards. The purpose of the trial court's ruling, it seems apparent, was not to invalidate the standards themselves but rather to deny the Board's attempt to compel compliance by the projects to supply salinity control water free of charge. We think the court's ruling was incorrect.

Under its reserved jurisdiction to modify the permits (§ 1394), the Board was authorized to impose upon the projects water quality standards at whatever level of protection the Board found reasonable (§ 13241), whether "without project" or greater. By the very nature of the reserved jurisdiction, the Board was empowered to impose such terms and conditions upon the project permits as would in its judgment best serve "the public interest." (§§ 1253, 1257, 1258; Johnson Rancho County Water Dist. v. State Water Rights Board, supra, 235 Cal.App.2d 863, 45 Cal.Rptr. 589; Bank of America v. State Water Resources Control Bd., supra, 42 Cal.App.3d 198, 212, 116 Cal.Rptr. 770.) While the scope of that duty requires consideration of the public benefits derived from the projects (§ 1256), it also requires that water quality needs be taken into account. (§§ 1243.5, 1257, 1258, 13000.) Nothing in the statutory scheme limits the Board's supervisory authority over appropriation permits to provide a level of water quality protection which exceeds the quality afforded by water rights.

Further, as discussed before, the Board has the separate and additional power to take whatever steps are necessary to prevent unreasonable use or methods of diversion. (Cal. Const., art. X, § 2; §§ 275, 1050; Cal.Admin.Code, tit. 23, §§ 761, 764.11.) That independent basis of authority vests jurisdiction in the Board to compel compliance with the water quality standards insofar as the projects' diversions and exports adversely affect water quality. Such authority, we think, includes the power to impose related costs on the projects. (Cf. People ex rel. State Water Resources Control Bd. v. Forni, supra, 54 Cal.App.3d 743, 126 Cal.Rptr. 851 [the Board could require riparian owners to incur reasonable expenses to build water storage facilities].)

* * *

Although *Forni* dealt with riparian rights, the same reasoning applies to appropriative rights. The constitutional requirement of reasonable use applies "to all water rights enjoyed or asserted in this state, whether the same be grounded on the riparian right or * * * the appropriative right." (Peabody v. City of Vallejo, supra, 2 Cal.3d 351, 383, 40 P.2d 486; accord People ex rel. State Water Resources Control Bd. v. Forni, supra, 54 Cal.App.3d at p. 749, 126 Cal.Rptr. 851; see also Joslin v. Marin Mun. Water Dist., supra, 67 Cal.2d 132, 138, 60 Cal.Rptr. 377, 429 P.2d 889; Gin S. Chow v. City of Santa Barbara, supra, 217 Cal. 673, 703–705, 22 P.2d 5.)

However, we agree with the trial court that the Board failed to make necessary findings reflecting the balancing of interests between the domestic uses of the Canal and the domestic uses of the export recipients in determining the "public interest." We recognize that such findings need not be stated with the formality required in a judicial proceeding but must be adequate enough to permit a reviewing court " ' * * * to determine whether they are supported by sufficient evidence or a proper principle and to apprise the parties as to the reason for the administrative action in order that they may decide whether, and upon what grounds, additional proceedings should be initiated.' (Temescal Water Co. v. Department of Public Works, supra, 44 Cal.2d at p. 102 [280 P.2d 1].)" (Johnson Rancho County Water Dist. v. State Water Rights Board, supra, 235 Cal.App.2d 863, 874, 45 Cal.Rptr. 589; accord Bank of America v. State Water Resources Control Bd., supra, 42 Cal.App.3d at p. 208, 116 Cal.Rptr. 770.)

* * *

In addition to protecting consumptive uses of the Delta, the Board formulated revised standards of water quality to protect fish and wildlife, a function expressly authorized by state and federal law.

* * *

In the proceedings below the Bureau argued the Board had no authority to modify an appropriation permit once issued, and that the new standards for the protection of fish and wildlife will result in impairment of its vested appropriative rights. These arguments were, quite properly, rejected by the trial court. But the court nonetheless held the standards invalid by reason of the Board's failure to identify its *source* of authority. The court remanded the matter to the Board, presumably to ascertain whether a factual basis exists to support the revised standards. The court's ruling was erroneous.

The issue is now clearly controlled by National Audubon Society v. Superior Court, supra, 33 Cal.3d 419, 189 Cal.Rptr. 346, 658 P.2d 709, decided after the proceedings below. In that case the Supreme Court clarified the scope of the "public trust doctrine" and held that the state as trustee of the public trust retains supervisory control over the state's waters such that no party has a vested right to appropriate water in a manner harmful to the interests protected by the public trust.

* * *

This landmark decision directly refutes the Bureau's contentions and firmly establishes that the state, acting through the Board, has continuing jurisdiction over appropriation permits and is free to reexamine a previous allocation decision.   * * *

In the new light of *National Audubon,* the Board unquestionably possessed legal authority under the public trust doctrine to exercise supervision over appropriators in order to protect fish and wildlife. That important role was not conditioned on a recital of authority. It exists as a matter of law itself.

Finally, as already shown, the Board retained continuing jurisdiction (§ 1394) to impose new standards upon the projects in "the public interest." In acting upon appropriation permits, the Board was obliged to consider water quality for the protection of beneficial uses (§§ 174, 1243.5, 1257, 1258) which expressly includes "enhancement of fish and wildlife resources." (§ 1243.) Here, the Board found that the imposition of the modified without project standards was in the public interest, taking into account not only the needs of the fishery, but also the value of the projects.

NOTE

The Delta Water Rights controversy remains, along with the protection of Mono Lake, at the center of California water politics. The State Water Resources Control Board has proposed two major plans to implement the decision. The first crashed and the second is now in litigation. In 1988, the Board proposed a plan which called for increased spring flows, and thus, *inter alia,* decreased agricultural water use in the San Joaquin Valley, but this plan was withdrawn in 1989 after agricultural interests and Los Angeles strongly objected. Proposals drafted by economists for rural to urban water transfers and for aggressive urban and rural water conservation were rejected by these two most powerful constituencies in the California "water community." In May 1991, the Board issued a water quality control plan to establish salinity, temperature, and dissolved oxygen water quality standards under § 303(c)(2)(A) of the Clean Water Act, 33 U.S.C.A. § 1313(c)(2)(A). In 1987, the federal EPA declined to approve the State's previous plan, first proposed in 1978, because it afforded insufficient protection to striped bass. Since 1978, fish populations have declined precipitously. In January, 1993, the federal EPA Administrator for Region IX found that the State's Delta protection plan was inadequate and refused to approve the State's salinity and temperature water quality standards.

The Delta controversy has become further complicated by the listing of winter-run salmon and the Delta smelt, which inhabit or pass through the Delta, under the federal Endangered Species Act. Federal officials have suggested that Delta diversions may have to be reduced by as much as one-half of the dry year Central Valley Project and State Water Project supplies.

F. TRANSFERS

1. Background

Thornton had money but needed water. Farmers had water but needed cash.

So in 1986, the city of Thornton and the farmers of Larimer and Weld counties tried to solve each others' problem. In one of the biggest Colorado water deals ever, Thornton paid farmers $50.5 million for the rights to eight billion gallons of annual irrigation supplies.

Today the farmers are collecting interest off the money they made from the water sales.

But Thornton still hasn't seen a drop of water.

After spending six years on nasty court fights—and another $22.7 million on legal, engineering, real estate and other administrative fees—Thornton officials have learned that obtaining water from rural Colorado is no easy undertaking. In fact, some critics doubt the city [will ever] get enough water to make the project work financially.

As Front Range cities increasingly turn to rural Colorado for water, they're finding they must often do more than just write checks. They also face angry communities, prospective rural politicians and a state water court system that piles on delays and costs.

Soaked in Big Water Deal, The Denver Post, July 20, 1992, at 1.

LAWRENCE J. MACDONNELL, TRANSFERRING WATER USES IN THE WEST

43 Okla.L.Rev. 119 (1990).

An important option for supplying changing western water requirements is to transfer some existing uses of water to new uses. The economic attractiveness of this option is demonstrated by studies indicating a marked disparity in the value of water in many existing uses compared with water's value in alternative uses. And, in fact, water transfers are occurring in the western states. Economists and others have commented, however, that transfers are not occurring as widely as would be suggested by the apparent economic incentives. Some have suggested that the reasons for this less than economically desirable level of transfer activity can be found in legal barriers or impediments that either absolutely prevent transfers or make the transfers so difficult as to dissipate any economic incentives.

* * *

Water rights may be transferred in a variety of ways. There may be a simple transfer of ownership. For example, the sale of irrigated farmlands typically includes the sale of the associated water rights. Generally, the simple change in ownership of a water right does not require state review or approval. Transfers may also involve a change in the existing manner of use, either with or without a change in ownership. Changes such as the point of diversion, place of use, or type of use, normally do require state review.

Legal mechanisms available in the western states for transferring the use of water also are numerous. The traditional approach has been to go through a change-of-water-right proceeding seeking state approval for a proposed change of use of an existing appropriative water right. Commonly, the person with the new use purchases an existing water right for the purpose of making the change of use.

Instead of a permanent shift in ownership of the right, the transfer may be limited to the water itself. Short-term, seasonal leases of water are common throughout the West and typically occur on an informal basis. Longer leases and leases involving a change of water use may have to go through a change-of-use proceeding.

Water rights also may be exchanged in many western states. Normally, exchanges are voluntary arrangements between holders of water rights who find mutual advantages in trading water rights. In recent years, some states have recognized the potential value of allowing involuntary exchanges under certain circumstances.

* * *

The Origin of Water Transfer Principles

California courts, which were the first to recognize the right to appropriate water, also were the first to consider an appropriator's right to make changes.

The courts of other western states generally accepted California's water transfer principles. Several states enacted legislative provisions specifically authorizing changes in water rights. These provisions required that there be no injury to other water rights and usually established some kind of state review.

Transfers Reconsidered

This initial acceptance of water transfers began to falter as conditions changed and problems arose.   * * *

As the miners moved from claim to claim they took their water rights with them. When they decided that they had had enough of mining, often the only valuable asset they had was their water rights and the water conveyance systems they had built. Allowing changes and transfers of water rights under such circumstances made * * * sense.

As irrigated agriculture displaced mining as the dominant water use in the West, circumstances changed. Stability became important since patterns of water use in agriculture generally follow regular cycles. Farmers tended not to move the way miners did. And, in the arid West, farmers generally viewed water less as an asset to be bought and sold and more as an integral and permanent part of their lives. The agricultural community created mutual ditch and storage companies and irrigation districts to cooperatively develop the water supply. With the creation of the Bureau of Reclamation in 1902, major water storage and supply projects were built throughout the West with federal financial and technical support. Settlement and development of the West proceeded through the widespread irrigation of arid and semi-arid but cultivatable lands.

* * *

The major issues that arise in transfer cases are the validity of the original right (e.g., has it been abandoned?), the extent of the right— especially the quantity of water historically used, and whether the transfer will cause injury to other water rights. Each of these issues requires considerable technical and, perhaps, legal analysis. * * * Concerns about injury to other rights have been met by limiting the net depletion of the stream following the transfer to the quantity of water historically consumed in the original use. Additional terms and conditions may be added to the transfer approval if necessary to offset injury. * * *

The second type of concern reflected in these state statutes is the treatment of water as a commodity to be traded or sold. Many in the West, including Elwood Mead, have argued that water is a public resource, that its use is intended to serve the broadest possible public good, and that it should not be the basis for private profit except as results from direct beneficial use.[48] Thus, the Arizona Legislature limited those who could hold rights to irrigation water to those owning the lands on which the water was used.

Linked to this concern is the belief that water is an essential part of the community that it serves. Control and use of the resource should be governed by the collective community, not by individual users whose interests may differ from that of the community generally. This view is reflected most clearly in state statutes giving irrigation districts control over the allocation and use of water resources within their boundaries and limiting transfers of water to locations within the district. Protection provided to areas of origin in several states also recognizes this concern.

The Barriers Come Down But . . .

In recent years, water transfers have been viewed more favorably in the West. Shifting economic and demographic forces have increased the power of cities which need the water and reduced the relative value of water used for irrigation. Some environmentalists have seized on water transfers as a means of avoiding the need for construction of environmentally damaging dams. Conservatives are attracted to this market-oriented approach for allocating resources.

---

48. E. Mead, Irrigation Institutions 86–87 (1903). An eminent commentator from the eastern United States, Roscoe Pound, noted a trend in this direction in western water law in 1914. Pound, *The End of Law As Developed in Legal Rules and Doctrines*, 27 Harv.L.Rev. 195, 234 (1914).

In 1962, Arizona eliminated its strict appurtenancy requirement and explicitly allowed the transfer of water rights.[54] Wyoming enacted legislation in 1973 expressly authorizing changes in water rights.[55] In 1980, the California Legislature announced a general policy favoring voluntary water transfers.[56] In 1988, the Utah Legislature removed the restrictions against transfers of water outside conservancy district boundaries,[57] and in 1989, the Colorado Legislature allowed the leasing of water outside conservancy district boundaries.[58] Other western states have eliminated restrictions against transfers in recent years as well.[59]

While many of the absolute barriers to transfers are being removed, limitations beyond the traditional no "injurious consequence" rule are being instituted in their place. For example, the Arizona transfers legislation requires the approval of any irrigation district, agricultural improvement district or water users association affected by a transfer.[60] The Wyoming legislation makes transfers potentially subject to review concerning (1) economic losses to the community and the state related to the transfer, (2) the extent to which these economic losses would be offset by benefits from the new use, and (3) the availability of other sources of water.[61] The new California law requires that transfers not "unreasonably" affect either fish, wildlife, or other instream beneficial uses or the economy of the area from which the water is to be transferred.[62] In 1985, the New Mexico Legislature subjected water transfers to a requirement that the transfers not be detrimental to the public welfare.[63] And in 1989, the Utah Supreme Court ruled that water transfers in that state must pass a public interest review.[64]

In short, while there is more general acceptance of water transfers, there is also a trend towards providing protection for an increasingly broad set of interests. The effect of this trend is difficult to assess. Removing barriers at least makes transfers possible. On the other hand, the imposition of limitations and conditions adds to the cost and complexity of making a transfer. Apparently, the West is now entering a period in which additional obligations of transferors will be identified and defined. Increased definition will be required for presently open-ended public interest standards. The increasingly broad set of water-based values will have to be factored into the decision processes

54. Ariz.Rev.Stat. § 45–172 (1987).

55. Wyo.Stat. § 41–3–104 (1977). Curiously, the Wyoming legislature did not repeal the 1909 statute restricting water right changes.

56. Cal.Water Code § 109(a) (West Supp.1989).

57. Utah Code Ann. § 73–9–13(3) (Supp. 1989).

58. Colo.Rev.Stat. § 37–83–106 (1989).

59. See, e.g., Neb.Rev.Stat. § 46–289 (1984) (authorizing interbasin transfers of water); SB 178, 1989 S.D.Laws (amending S.D.Codified Laws Ann. § 46–5–34.1) (au-

thorizing transfer of irrigation rights to domestic uses on other lands).

60. Ariz.Rev.Stat.Ann. § 45–172(4), (5) (1987). Approval must be obtained if the water is to be transferred from lands within these entities or from the watersheds supplying water for their use.

61. Wyo.Stat. § 41–3–104(a) (1977).

62. Cal.Water Code § 386 (West Supp. 1989).

63. N.M.Stat.Ann. § 72–5–23 (1978).

64. Bonham v. Morgan, [788 P.2d 497 (Utah 1989)].

governing transfers of water uses. The decision processes themselves may well have to be changed to accommodate consideration of these matters.

* * *

NOTE

The transaction costs of water transfer were examined in a six-state study of transfers which Dr. MacDonnell directed. The study found:

> The case studies of transactions costs in Colorado and New Mexico suggest average costs in the range of $200 to $380 per acre-foot of water transferred. There appear to be significant scale economies so that the transfer of larger amounts of water results in lower per-acre-foot costs. The data also show that third party opposition to the transfer increased the acre-foot costs. The average transactions costs found in the Colorado sample of cases were considerably higher than those in New Mexico. This finding corresponds to the findings that the decision time in New Mexico is markedly less than in Colorado and that many fewer cases are protested in New Mexico than in Colorado. However, the average transactions costs in New Mexico appear to have increased dramatically from 1975 to 1987.

> Additional study is necessary to determine the effect of these costs on water rights transfer activity. The New Mexico data show that most applications incur relatively low transaction costs. * * *

Lawrence J. MacDonnell et al., The Water Transfer Process as a Management Option for Meeting Changing Water Demand, Vol. I, 68 (1990).

C. LEE, THE TRANSFER OF WATER RIGHTS IN CALIFORNIA

Governor's Commission to Review California Water Rights Law, Staff Paper No. 5
5–10 (1977).

1. *Water as a Marketable Resource*

    A. *Theory of Equimarginal Value*

Resources have value because they are scarce, in the sense that the quantity demanded exceeds the supply at zero price. Where scarcity exists, it is necessary to develop some method of resource allocation. Economists have commonly posited the economic efficiency objective as a criterion for optimal resource allocation. The theory of equimarginal value asserts that, as a necessary condition of economic efficiency, all users of a resource must derive equal value from the last unit of the resource each user has consumed.

The value of any unit of water is essentially measured by the maximum amount which the consumer would be willing to pay for that unit. The marginal value is the value of the last unit consumed. For any consumer, the marginal value will ordinarily decline or rise as the quantity of water consumed in any period increases or decreases.

Thus, if the marginal value to consumer "A" of one acre-foot of water is $20, and the marginal value to consumer "B" is $10, then both parties would be better off in terms of their own preferences if B sold A one acre-foot of water at some price between $10 and $20. Since B's consumption of water has decreased due to the sale, his marginal value for water will increase (perhaps to $11 an acre-foot). Similarly, since A's consumption has increased, his marginal value for water will decrease (perhaps to $19 an acre-foot). Economists have therefore concluded that the most efficient allocation of water resources requires the eventual equalization of the marginal values of all water consumers.

Water values will vary substantially depending upon the type of water use. The National Water Commission found a wide variation in values among the same uses and between different uses. The Commission therefore recommended the encouragement of water rights transfers in order to reduce such disparities in value.

B. *Problems in Application*

1. *The Theory of the Second Best*

As noted, one condition for the optimal allocation of a resource is the equalization of marginal values among the consumers of the resource. Some economists have argued that where the economy does not conform to *all* conditions for optimal resource allocation then a "second best" conformity may not necessarily increase total system efficiency. For example, where all goods and services are not priced at marginal cost, the introduction of marginal cost pricing in one sector of the economy might worsen the allocation of the resources. The obvious implication of the theory of the second best is that piecemeal efforts to achieve system efficiency may not be desirable.

Commentators on the theory of the second best have noted that the theory assumes an interdependent economic system. However economic optimization in some broad sector of the economy may be justified where the outputs and relative prices have negligible repercussion in the rest of the economy. The same argument would apply where a geographical area has tenuous economic links with the rest of the economy. Furthermore, where deviations from the conditions of optimal allocation are initially large in the free sectors of the economy and relatively small in the restrained sectors, then movement towards optimalization in the free sectors may still be desirable.

Finally, regardless of its impact on total system efficiency, the theory of the second best does not impair gains achieved by individual parties who seek to improve their position through private transfers. The reallocation of water so as to equalize marginal values will still increase the total value productivity of that water.

2. *Externalities, Spillover Effects and Third Party Effects*

An economic externality occurs where actions by one individual or a group of individuals affect outside parties because of a failure in markets. The market process fails because it does not cause the individual whose action results in an externality to adjust his behavior in accordance with the consequences. Thus, a private transaction imposes costs or benefits upon a third person who has not been party to the bargaining process.

For example, a paper mill that discharges untreated effluent into a river imposes costs that are not internalized in its transactions with paper purchasers. These wildlife, fishery and recreational losses are examples of negative externalities. On the other hand, the improvement by a private landowner of his property will commonly enhance the value of his neighbor's property. This increase in property value is an example of a positive externality.

It is also important to distinguish between technological externalities and pecuniary externalities. Most commentators agree that one should only consider the impact of technological externalities when evaluating the efficiency of any particular transfer. Technological externalities impose actual losses or gains on the productive capacity of society. The externality affects the actual, physical output or satisfaction that a third party producer or consumer can get from his physical inputs. For example, flooding agricultural land in order to operate a dam imposes actual, physical losses in the productive capacity of agriculture.

Pecuniary externalities, on the other hand, do not change the real productive capacity of society. Instead, the gains or losses suffered by the third parties occur through changes in prices. For example, the reservoir created by the new dam may increase recreational opportunities thereby reducing the existing gains of private recreation facility operators that service any neighboring reservoirs.

A discussion of water rights transfers requires consideration of externality theory because water rights transfers commonly affect third parties. A transfer by an upstream user outside of the watershed may reduce the return flow available to downstream users. Pumping by an overlying landowner for purposes of export to nonoverlying land may affect the availability of groundwater to adjacent landowners. Equalization of private marginal values through transfers would not, in such situations, meet the efficiency objective. The water transfer prices would not properly reflect the costs or the benefits imposed upon third parties. If external costs or benefits are created by these transfers, unadjusted prices would be too low or too high and the number of transfers would be too great or too small.

The sale of a water right is not as simple as the sale of a car or even a parcel of land. The operation of a free market in water rights is inhibited in several ways. Consider how economists would respond to each of the following:

(1) Junior water rights in return flow must be protected. This rule is applied in all western states; it is likely to continue to be applied for both constitutional and political reasons.

(2) Inadequacy of records and poor administration of water rights. Records of water rights are inadequate in two respects: some rights to use water do not appear of record and some claims that do appear are not legally enforceable because of abandonment or forfeiture. Moreover, administration of rights is sometimes inept; states often provide inadequate funds for professional water rights administration.

(3) Legal and institutional restrictions. Today, absolute legal prohibitions on transfers are few. Costly review procedures and restrictions remain. The Bureau of Reclamation, whose projects distribute about 20% of the water used in the West, mostly for irrigation, has several legal and policy restrictions that inhibit transfers. Increasingly, states impose restrictions on, or require review of, transactions to ensure that third parties are protected.

2. Junior Protection Entitlements

Since the earliest decisions under the appropriation doctrine, courts have allowed changes of use only if no injury will result to other users. E.g., McDonald v. Bear River and Auburn Water & Min. Co., 13 Cal. 220 (1896). Now most states embody the rule in statute. The Utah statute is exemplary; Utah Code Ann. § 73–3–3 (1986) provides:

(1) Any person entitled to the use of water may change the place of diversion or use and may use the water for other purposes than those for which it was originally appropriated, but no such change may be made if it impairs any vested right without just compensation. These changes may be permanent or temporary. Changes for an indefinite length of time with an intention to relinquish the original point of diversion, place, or purpose of use are defined as permanent changes. Temporary changes include and are limited to all changes for definitely fixed periods of not exceeding one year. Both permanent and temporary changes of point of diversion, place, or purpose of use of water including water involved in general adjudication or other suits, shall be made in the manner provided in this section.

* * *

(3) Applications for either permanent or temporary changes may not be rejected for the sole reason that the change would impair the vested rights of others, but if otherwise proper, they may be approved as to part of the water involved or upon the condition that conflicting rights are acquired.

(4) Any person holding an approved application for the appropriation of water may either permanently or temporarily change the point of diversion, place, or purpose of use, but no such change of an approved application may affect the priority of the original application; except that no change of point of diversion, place, or nature of use set forth in an approved application operates to enlarge the time within which the construction of work shall begin or be completed.

(5) Any person who changes or who attempts to change a point of diversion, place, or purpose of use, either permanently or temporarily, without first applying to the state engineer in the manner provided in this section, obtains no right and is guilty of a misdemeanor, each day of such unlawful change constituting a separate offense, separately punishable.

Protection of "rights of others" in cases and statutes dealing with transfers or changes of use benefits junior appropriators, since senior appropriators have a prior call on the stream in any event. Ordinarily, the portion of an irrigation right equivalent to the amount of water consumed in the irrigation process is transferable. The amount not consumed is relied on by junior appropriators and must be left in the stream.

Why should junior appropriators be protected? The answer lies in history, economic policy and common ideas of justice or good policy. Most direct flow rights were created in the nineteenth century. A farmer settled on land and diverted water from a nearby stream to irrigate it. The farmer did not know, and had no way of knowing, whether the water flowing in the river was return flow or original snow melt. The economic policy was to encourage investment. To promote this policy, rules were adopted that maintained the status quo—that gave legal security in the supply upon which the investment was predicated. Lastly, the long persistence of a state of affairs gives rise to expectations that it will continue in the future. While the law certainly does not always fulfill these expectations, it is not unusual for it to do so when investments have been made based on them.

A good ball-park figure for irrigation efficiency in the West is 50%. Thus, half of water diverted and turned onto the land is consumed by evapotranspiration, and the other half returns to the hydrologic cycle as return flow to a surface stream, as recharge to a groundwater aquifer or as evaporation. Over time, expectations arise that return flows from one user will supply another.

Suppose A Canal Co. obtained an appropriative right on Clear River in 1867 to divert 20 cfs of water during a growing season of 120 days. The annual diversion right would be approximately 4,800 acre feet. Thereafter, B Canal Co. knowing these facts, obtained a right for its downstream ditch to 10 cfs. Though B does not know it, 10 cfs return to the stream from A's diversion, and this return flow enters the stream above B's headgate. A proposes to sell its water right to Center City, which plans to move the point of diversion to an intake below B's canal. If A can move all 20 cfs, B will have no water supply when the flow of the river at A's old point of diversion is just 20 cfs. Center City could require the 20 cfs to bypass B's headgate, thus depriving B of the return flow from the old diversion. Such a transfer is not permitted; only A's consumptive use of 10 cfs may be transferred, leaving 10 cfs to substitute for the return flow. Our explanation of this rule is that B's expectations would be drastically upset if it lost the 10 cfs represented by return flow and that upsetting such expectations would not only strain the social fabric but would deter investment in partially developed streams. Hence courts and legislatures protect B.

GREEN v. CHAFFEE DITCH CO.

Supreme Court of Colorado, 1962.
150 Colo. 91, 371 P.2d 775.

MOORE, JUSTICE.

* * *

Lydia Hoffman Morrison and her brother Milton Coy Hoffman are the owners of seventy-two acres of land along the bank of the river. In the water adjudication of April 11, 1882, under priority No. 13, * * * approximately 16 c.f.s., is owned by Morrison and Hoffman. They entered into a contract to sell to the city of Fort Collins 8 c.f.s. of this water, and the city requests permission to change the point of diversion thirteen miles upstream. Numerous protests were filed to the requested change. These protests contain the assertion that Morrison and Hoffman did not own 16 c.f.s., and that if any such water rights had ever existed they had been abandoned.

The trial court entered findings which, in pertinent part, contain the following:

"That the land owned by said petitioners, Milton Coy Hoffman and Lydia Hoffman Morrison, irrigated by said water is seventy-two acres along the river bottom, the Cache La Poudre River dividing said land. That the top soil is a sandy loam and varies in thickness from about five feet to a few inches and is underlain with coarse gravel, which in some places comes to the surface. That because of the soil conditions and the proximity to the river, all water applied to said land, not consumed by plant life and evaporation, returns to the river within a very short time and again becomes a part of the river and available to other appropriators. That the amount of water necessarily consumed by plant life to produce a maximum crop, in addition to natural rainfall, is * * * one and one-fourth acre feet of water for each acre irrigated, thus requiring 90 acre feet of water each year for the proper irrigation of said land. That the efficiency of water on this particular land is 25%, requiring the application to this land of 360 acre feet of water during each irrigating season to produce maximum crops. That in addition to the 90 acre feet of water consumed on this land, five acre feet are lost by evaporation and seepage while the water is in transit from the headgate of the Coy Ditch to the Hoffman–Morrison farm, making a total consumptive use of 95 acre feet of water each year. That the only domestic use of this water has been a small amount for the watering of livestock. That the irrigating season on this land has been from April 15th to October 15th of each year.

"That the City of Fort Collins, during the period from April 15th and October 15th of each year has an average return flow through its sewage disposal plant, storm sewers and other sources of 50% of the water taken in at its intake pipeline.

"That for many years last past, and ever since the entry of the original adjudication Decree, the petitioners Milton Coy Hoffman and Lydia Hoffman Morrison and their predecessors in title and interest have never beneficially used at any one time more than eight cubic feet of water per second of time for the irrigation of the lands now owned by them. Any diversions by petitioners or others in excess of that amount were a subterfuge and not made in good faith.

"That any diversion of water from said priority from October 16th of any year to April 14th, inclusive, of the following year, except for livestock purposes, would injuriously affect the storage rights of protestants, or some one or more of them, as they have historically depended upon the filling of their storage decrees during said time."

* * *

The court decreed inter alia that:

"No diversion from Priority No. 13 awarded to the Coy Ditch can be transferred without injury to junior appropriators, except under the conditions herein set forth, and any transfer of water, heretofore beneficially used, must be upon condition that the land heretofore irrigated must be forever deprived of irrigation water from this Decree, and cannot be a transfer of water not needed or beneficially used.

"That there can be diverted from the headgate of the Coy Ditch to the headgate of the City of Fort Collins pipeline without injury to the protestants, that amount of water which, when the return flow from the City sewage plant and other sources is considered, permits the City to consumptively use 95 acre feet of water during the irrigating season. Therefore, under the foregoing findings, the City should be permitted to divert 190 acre feet of water during each irrigation season under the conditions that the City at no time shall divert more than eight cubic feet of water per second of time. * * * There is an abundance of evidence establishing the fact that at no time has an amount of water in excess of 8 c.f.s. been applied to beneficial use on the seventy-two acres of land involved. * * *"

Actually they had contracted to sell to the city all the water which they could lawfully have used at any time. Under the specific findings of the trial court that no more than 8 c.f.s. was ever applied to beneficial use, that volume of water was the full measure of the water right acquired.

* * * [Dismissing the petitioners' contentions, the court said that] Applicable and controlling rules concerning these contentions are to be found in the opinion of this court in Farmers Highline Canal and Reservoir Company, et al., v. City of Golden, et al., 129 Colo. 575, 272 P.(2d) 629. From that opinion we re-state basic concepts which require an affirmance of the judgment in the instant action. The case cited was one involving an application for change in the point of diversion of water. It was there held: * * *

(2) "It is recognized that water is a property right, subject to sale and conveyance, and that under proper conditions not only may the point of diversion be changed, but likewise the manner of use. It further is recognized that such change may be permitted, by proper court decree, only in such instances as it is specifically shown that the rights of other users from the same source are not injuriously affected by such change, and that the burden of proof thereof rests upon petitioner.

* * *

(4) "Equally well established, as we have repeatedly held, is the principle that junior appropriators have vested rights in the continuation of stream conditions as they existed at the time of their respective appropriations, and that subsequent to such appropriations they may successfully resist all proposed changes in points of diversion and use of water from that source which in any way materially injures or adversely affects their rights. * * *

(5) "All appropriations of water, and all decrees determining the respective rights of users, regardless of whether specific mention be made therein, are subject to all constitutional and statutory provisions and restrictions designed for the protection of junior appropriators from the same stream. * * * "

We think the following language contained in the opinion in the case cited is pertinent to the issues in the instant case:

"Petitioner contends, however, that it is entirely within the right of an appropriator of water to enlarge upon his use, and now that the City of Golden is the owner, it may enlarge upon the use to the extent of the entire decree. Counsel for petitioner here confuse two altogether different principles. This doctrine even on behalf of an original appropriator, may be applied only to the extent of use contemplated at the time of appropriation. It has no application whatever to a situation where a decree is sought for change of point of diversion or use. There the right is strictly limited to the extent of former actual usage. 'The right to change the point of diversion is, of course, nonetheless a qualified right because petitioner acquired it by purchase.' Fort Lyon Co. v. Rocky Ford Co., 79 Colo. 511, 515, 246 Pac. 781."

* * *

" * * * Where the entire amount fixed by the decree was reasonably required in the proper irrigation of the lands to which first applied, then the whole priority properly may be changed for similar usage; but where such irrigation did not require the entire volume of the decree, then only that portion may be changed which previously had been necessary for proper irrigation. It is not a question of whether the amount of water decreed was adequate, but whether it was excessive. The extent of needed use in original location is the criterion in considering change of point of diversion. This, of course, is premised upon the assumption that whatever of the decreed water was not properly used remained in the stream.

* * *

"Where it appears that the change sought to be made will result in depletion to the source of supply and result in injury to junior appropriators therefrom, the decree should contain such conditions as are proper to counteract the loss, and should be denied only in such instances as where it is impossible to impose reasonable conditions to effectuate this purpose."

We conclude that the trial court determined the issues in the instant case in a manner consistent with the foregoing principles, and find no error requiring a reversal of the judgment. There was no abuse of discretion in the assessment of costs.

The judgment accordingly is affirmed.

NOTES

1. Note that the court limits the amount of water that may be transferred to a maximum quantity (acre-feet) and rate of diversion (cubic feet per second). This is based on evidence of the amount of water needed for crops and is specified in terms of the quantity that may be consumed (190 acre-feet) and the quantity that may be diverted (190 acre-feet if there will be a 50% return flow). The rate at which the water could be taken (8 cfs) was based on evidence that this was the maximum historical rate of diversion. Water lawyers are generally familiar with these terms and calculations. A table of the equivalents is found in Appendix A at the end of the book.

Sophisticated formulae may be required to determine crop demand. For instance, the Blaney–Criddle formula is frequently used for calculating crop consumptive use requirements. Essentially, the formula considers such factors as mean monthly temperature, length of day, and available moisture to determine monthly consumptive water requirements. The formula is most useful where little or no data, except climatological, may be available. The authors of the formula explain it in Harry F. Blaney and Wayne D. Criddle, *Determining Water Requirements for Settling Water Disputes,* 4 Nat. Resources J. 29 (1964). Use of such formulae may require engineering and other expertise.

When a change of use issue reaches the courtroom, the parties typically hire their own experts to help them prove their contentions. In *Green,* for example, the court relied on expert testimony to find that although Hoffman and Morrison thought they had sold only half of their water right, they had, in fact, sold all the water to which they were entitled.

Where adversarial experts are permitted, they add considerably to the cost of a change of use or transfer. In Colorado, where no binding or presumptively correct determination of how much water may be transferred is made by a state agency or official, cases typically can involve multiple experts. Parties are obliged to hire them or risk loss of their rights. In one change of use case, the Colorado Supreme Court concluded: "The petitioners presented expert witnesses who testified that the junior appropriators would not be injured by the proposed change. The protestants produced no expert testimony. * * * The [protestants] did not meet their burden of going forward with the evidence." CF & I Steel Corp. v. Rooks, 495 P.2d 1134, 1136 (Colo.1972).

2. There are several methods of determining historical beneficial use. In Westminster v. Church, 445 P.2d 52 (Colo.1968), a change in point of diversion of a decreed right was limited to the amount historically diverted, despite a finding of nonabandonment of the same decreed right in connection with an earlier change in point of diversion. The court examined average annual diversions over a twenty-one year period to determine that the amount of water historically used was less than the "paper right." In diversions involving pumping, courts or agencies may examine electricity bills.

3. In Basin Electric Power Co-op. v. State Bd. of Control, 578 P.2d 557 (Wyo.1978), the court explained how the historical beneficial use requirement and the concept of abandonment, see pages 358–64, infra, both flow from the doctrine of beneficial use:

> We have previously said that the water right of an appropriator is limited to beneficial use, even though a larger amount has been adjudicated. The decreed amount of water may be prima facie evidence of an appropriator's entitlement, but such evidence may be rebutted by showing actual historic beneficial use. Beneficial use is not a concept which is considered only at the time an appropriation is obtained. The concept represents a continuing obligation which must be satisfied in order for the appropriation to remain viable. The state's abandonment statutes are recognition of this requirement. * * *

> In other words, the amount of water originally decreed or disclosed in a water permit is not necessarily the amount which may be transferred to a new place of use. In Colorado, at least, the amount which may be transferred is limited to the "Duty of Water," which is defined as the amount reasonably required for proper irrigation under the original appropriation. Contra, W.S. Ranch Company v. Kaiser Steel Corporation, 79 N.M. 65, 439 P.2d 714 (1968), where the change-in-use petitioner was allowed to transfer the entire amount of the decreed water right regardless of subsequent actual beneficial use.

> The key to understanding the application of beneficial-use concepts to a change-of-use proceeding is a recognition that the issues of nonuse and misuse are inextricably interwoven with the issues of change of use and change in the place of use. This is true even without the formal initiation of abandonment proceedings under the statutes. If an appropriator, either by misuse or failure to use, has effectively abandoned either all or part of his water right through noncompliance with the beneficial-use requirements

imposed by law, he could not effect a change of use or place of use for that amount of his appropriation which had been abandoned. 578 P.2d at 563–65.

4. The limitation that restricts transfers to historical consumptive use is essentially to protect juniors, though it may also be applied to carry out policy related to overall stream management. In Basin Electric Power Co-op. v. State Bd. of Control, supra, plaintiff had requested a change in type of use and point of diversion of water rights it had acquired from a former agricultural user. The land on which the water had been used straddled a geographical divide: water used on only 20% of the land returned to the Laramie River (from which it had been withdrawn). The rest of the irrigation was across the divide in a geologically closed basin, and return flows stayed there. Plaintiff, a power company, claimed a right to use all the water diverted by the former user which had not historically returned to the Laramie River. A Wyoming statute stated that a change would be allowed:

> provided that the quantity of water transferred by the granting of the petition shall not exceed the amount of water historically diverted under the existing use, nor increase the historic amount consumptively used under the existing use, nor decrease the historic amount of return flow, nor in any manner injure other lawful appropriators.

The plaintiff claimed that the prohibition of injury to other appropriators was the main purpose of the statute, and that it was therefore entitled to make a change in use so long as other appropriators were not injured. The court rejected that contention, and concluded that: "the statute forecloses anyone desiring to effect a change of use from transferring more water than has been historically consumptively used, regardless of the injury or lack thereof to other appropriators." The court found that the closed-basin return flows were not consumptive uses, and thus could not be transferred.

5. Are junior appropriator's rights impaired in any of the following cases? (a) An upstream senior hydroelectric power appropriator proposes to make a transbasin diversion at the power dam site; (b) A downstream senior irrigator is supplied by return flow from a junior and the senior wishes to move its point of diversion upstream, above the junior; (c) A senior irrigator with a diversion right of 20 cfs from May to September wishes to build a reservoir and store 20 cfs continuous flow from May to September.

6. An appropriator has a right to use 100 acre-feet of water per year to irrigate a particular field. For thirty years the appropriator has grown alfalfa in the field, which has only used 50 acre-feet per year. The appropriator decides to plant rice in the field instead. For proper irrigation the rice needs 100 acre-feet of water per year. Read the excerpt from *Farmers Highline Canal* quoted at pages 314–15. Does the "no injury" rule announced there prevent the original appropriator from "enlarging" on the use to the full extent of the decree if there is no change in the purpose (agriculture) or the place of use? If the purpose of the no injury rule is to protect expectations of juniors, does

this make sense? Would you recommend that your alfalfa-growing client, who anticipates future sales of water rights, switch to rice?

METROPOLITAN DENVER SEWAGE DIST. NO. 1 v. FARMERS RESERVOIR & IRR. CO.

Supreme Court of Colorado, 1972.
179 Colo. 36, 499 P.2d 1190.

GROVES, JUSTICE.

The defendants in error (plaintiffs) have decreed rights for irrigation purposes out of the South Platte River. In about 1937 Denver constructed a sewage treatment facility known as the Denver Northside Plant. Effluent from this plant was discharged into the South Platte River above the common headgate of the plaintiffs. Beginning in about 1966 the effluent from Denver's sewage was placed in the river downstream from this headgate. The plaintiffs brought before the court this declaratory judgment action asking, among other things, that it be adjudged that the plaintiffs are entitled to have the effluent placed in the river above their headgate. The trial court ruled in favor of the plaintiffs. We reverse. * * *

Nearly every decree for South Platte River water diverted downstream from Denver is dependent for its supply upon return flow of waste and seepage waters. See Comstock v. Ramsay, 55 Colo. 244, 133 P. 1107 (1913). The only inference to be drawn from the statement of facts is that, absent either effluent discharge above the headgate or change of the plaintiffs' point of diversion to a place below the plant, the plaintiffs' decrees will be substantially unfilled. * * *

The effluent with which we are concerned here is solely from water arising in the South Platte watershed, which has been acquired by Denver, and, after use within Denver, has been transported through Denver's sewer system to Metro's plant. * * *

We sense an underlying sentiment (or hope) by Denver that the plaintiffs may have the effluent involved to the extent of their decrees. Be that as it may, it is apparent that the parties are concerned primarily with the question of who shall bear the cost of transporting the water from the new place of discharge to the initial (common) section of the plaintiffs' ditch. Before proceeding further, we wish to emphasize that we are not expressing any opinion on the right of plaintiffs to the effluent. Rather, we are concerned with whether Denver, acting through Metro, may change its point of effluent discharge into the stream at the Metro plant with impunity as against the plaintiffs' objection.

In its oral announcement, the trial court stated in effect that the rules governing change of *point of return* (to the stream) are the same as those governing change of *point of diversion,* citing Brighton Ditch Co. v. Englewood, 124 Colo. 366, 237 P.2d 116 (1951), and Fort Collins Milling & Elevator Co. v. Larimer and Weld Irr. Co., 61 Colo. 45, 156 P. 140 (1916). An appropriator may not change his point of diversion except upon conditions which eliminate injury to other appropriators. See Farmers Highline Canal & Reservoir Co. v. Golden, 129 Colo. 575,

272 P.2d 629 (1954) and cases cited therein. The plaintiffs argue similarly that they are entitled to conditions on the stream as they have existed. * * * We cannot agree with the argument of the plaintiffs and the conclusion of the trial court. The cases cited by them and listed above are all change of point of diversion, and not change in point of return, cases. To us, they are not persuasive. Plaintiffs also cite Comstock, State Engineer v. Ramsay, 55 Colo. 244, 133 P. 1107 (1913), which involves the lack of right to intercept waste water which is proceeding toward the stream, and does not involve the right to change the point of return.

Changes of points of return of waste water are not governed by the same rules as changes of points of diversion. Conceivably, there may be instances (perhaps in the case of power water) in which a change of point of return may be enjoined, but this is not one of them. In Green Valley Ditch Co. v. Schneider, 50 Colo. 606, 115 P. 705 (1911) the Tegeler lateral carried waste water which plaintiff used. It was there held as follows:

"Plaintiff's rights were limited and only attached to the water discharged from the Tegeler lateral, whatever that happened to be, after the defendants and cross-complainants had supplied their own wants and necessities. This does not vest her with any control over the ditches or laterals of appellants, or the water flowing therein, nor does it obligate appellants to continue or maintain conditions so as to supply plaintiff's appropriation of waste water at any time or in any quantity, when acting in good faith."

We believe that it follows from this determination that there is no vested right in downstream appropriators to maintainance [sic] of the same point of return of irrigation waste water.[3]

At least in the absence of bad faith or of arbitrary or unreasonable conduct, the same rule should be applicable to sewage waste or the effluent therefrom of a municipality or sanitation district. Any question of arbitrary or unreasonable conduct here was removed by the agreed statement of facts. It was there stipulated that the Metro plant was placed at a location gravitationally below the Northside Plant and "was selected on the basis of economic feasibility and is a normal engineering selection. * * * " We hold, therefore, that the plaintiffs may not interfere with Denver's change of point of return.

It has not been argued that it may be against public policy for appropriators to prevent change of point of return of sewage effluent, i.e., the vitiation of the public health in a burgeoning urban area. We, of course, make no ruling in this respect, but think it well to suggest that possible public policy questions are worth expression.

We feel we should remark that the General Assembly may well wish to change, prospectively at least, the rule we here announce as to change of point of return.

* * *

3. This statement should not be construed as an expression concerning any right or lack of right to enlarge the use of irrigation water. See Fort Lyon Canal Co. v. Chew, 33 Colo. 392, 81 P. 37 (1905).

Under date of July 29, 1968, Denver, Metro and the plaintiffs entered into an agreement. This recited that Denver had constructed a pumping facility capable of delivering effluent from the Metro plant into the Burlington Ditch. The agreement provides among other things for the ultimate vesting of title to the pumping facility, for the payment of the cost of the facility, and for the payment of operational expenses connected therewith. The identity of the party or parties which obtain title and make payments, and rather complex arrangements relating thereto, are dependent upon the ultimate outcome of the instant case and of City and County of Denver etc. v. Fulton Irrigating Ditch Company, * * *.

KELLEY, J., did not participate.

ERICKSON, J., dissents.

NOTES

1. The decision in the principal case says that the no injury rule does not apply to changes in the point of return. Why? In fact, most "injuries" triggering application of the rule are the result of an appropriator's being deprived of return flow. Usually, the decrease in return flows is caused by a change in point of diversion or place of use. Is there any sound reason that a change in point of return unaccompanied by another such change of use should be exempt from the rule?

2. To apply the no injury rule in *Metro Denver* the court would have had to decide the extent of harm to the farmers deprived of Denver's returns. Presumably, a remedy would extend only to the amount of water Denver was obligated to return (i.e., any diversion right less amount it had a right to consume). This would have necessitated a determination of the amount of water Denver was entitled to consume. Presumably, that would mean the city's historical consumptive use. Suppose, however, that the city decided to recycle treated sewage indefinitely, giving it a 100% consumptive right without a "change of use" being involved. The result would have been the same as the court's actual decision. Should the court have decided that a municipal right is potentially 100% consumptive and therefore there is no cognizable injury when a municipal point of return is changed?

BOULDER v. BOULDER & LEFT HAND DITCH CO.

Supreme Court of Colorado, 1976.
192 Colo. 219, 557 P.2d 1182.

GROVES, JUSTICE.

Each of the parties is a decreed appropriator of water out of Boulder Creek. Left Hand and Farmers are mutual ditch companies. Their decrees are for irrigation and are prior to that of Boulder.

The ditch of Farmers (Farmers Ditch) has been used for more than 100 years for the irrigation of lands in the Boulder Creek watershed and the return flow from such irrigation proceeds to Boulder Creek.

The water decreed to the ditch of Left Hand (Left Hand Ditch) for almost 100 years has been used upon lands, the return flow of which returns largely to Dry Creek and South St. Vrain Creek.

The two mutual ditch companies have the same point of diversion out of Boulder Creek, being within the city limits of Boulder, and they utilize a common lateral for the first one and one-half miles from the point of diversion. Then, the ditch of each company proceeds from the lateral to the respective irrigated area served by each.

During the irrigation season, with the consent of Farmers, Left Hand is diverting and transporting in its ditch some of the water decreed to Farmers.[2] If this diversion were not made, the historic return flow therefrom would be used by appropriators out of Boulder Creek, upstream from its confluence with South St. Vrain Creek. Absent this return flow Boulder must permit the same portion of its decreed water to remain in Boulder Creek in order to satisfy the decree of these intervening appropriators.

There has been no decree permitting the change of place of use of the water involved. In the absence of such a decree, the plaintiff contends that it is entitled to injunctive relief whereby Left Hand would be prohibited from diverting the water from the watershed in which it has been historically used.

The fundamental basis for the dismissal of the complaint by the water judge was the rulings of this court in Metro Denver Sewage v. Farmers Reservoir, 179 Colo. 36, 499 P.2d 1190 (1972), and Tongue Creek v. Orchard City, 131 Colo. 177, 280 P.2d 426 (1955). For reasons which we will later elaborate, these cases are distinguishable.

It has been fundamental law in this state that junior appropriators have rights in return flow to the extent that they may not be injured by a change in the place of use of the irrigation water which provides that return flow. The basic principles were stated in Farmers Highline Canal v. Golden, 129 Colo. 575, 272 P.2d 629, 631 (1954).

* * *

The basic fallacy in the ground of decision used by the water judge is his statement, "there is no distinction * * * between waste water from irrigation and return flow water from irrigation. * * *" A typical example is that of the irrigator who turns water into individual furrows traversing his field. That portion which is not absorbed into the earth or transpires remains in the furrow at the end thereof, and is collected in a waste ditch. The contents of the waste ditch is waste water. When this waste water so collected runs in the waste ditch to the stream, the law is that one who appropriates the waste water from the stream cannot assert a right to have the irrigator continue to discharge the waste water into the stream. * * *

In *Metro Denver Sewage,* the real party in interest, Denver, was discharging at a certain place the effluent from its sewage after treatment into the same river from whence the water was diverted by Denver. Then Denver changed the point of discharge downstream,

2. While we have not noted mention of the fact in the complaint nor the decree, it appears from one of the briefs that Left Hand owns stock in Farmers and as a result is entitled to rights in the Farmers Ditch water represented by such stock. This portion of Farmers Ditch water, which Left Hand is taking out of the immediate watershed of Boulder Creek, is the subject of this action.

thereby preventing—or at least hindering—the user of the effluent, who had been diverting it from the stream below the old point of discharge and above the new. Thus, we were asked to determine whether we would follow the rule that one cannot change the point of diversion or place of use to the injury of a junior appropriator or the other rule that the junior appropriator has no right to the continuance—or the continuance of the place of discharge—of waste water. We elected to follow the irrigation waste water rule, saying, "in the absence of bad faith or of arbitrary or unreasonable conduct, the [waste water] rule should be applicable to sewage waste or the effluent therefrom of a municipality or sanitation district."

Return flow is not waste water. Rather, it is irrigation water seeping back to a stream after it has gone underground to perform its nutritional function. As already indicated, the law makes no distinction between change of point of diversion and change of place of use so far as the rights of junior appropriators are concerned. We made it clear in *Metro Denver Sewage* that the change of point of return of waste water or effluent is not governed by the same rules as changes of point of diversion and place of use.

We are here involved with the effect of a change of place of use because *return flow* results from *use* and not from water carried in the surface in ditches and wasted into the stream. Under the allegations of the complaint, therefore, this case should be treated as one of change of place of use and not under the rules of *Tongue Creek* and *Metro Denver Sewage*. We do not speculate as to the extent to which Boulder may prove its case, but do rule that it is entitled under the complaint to its day in court.

* * *

NOTES

1. On remand, how should the water court decide the amount of water that can be taken from Boulder Creek to Left Hand Ditch?

2. The court recited its decision in *Metro Denver*. Is the *Metro* rule necessarily involved?

3. The court goes to considerable lengths to distinguish the *Metro* case with its sweeping rule that juniors are not protected against a change in a senior's point of return. It contrives a distinction between irrigation waste (water returned to the stream in a ditch) and return flows (water that seeps back to the stream) and says that the former is not subject to the no injury rule while the latter is. *Metro* neither mentioned nor depended on the distinction. In fact, the ancient cases relied upon by the court for exempting return flows from the no injury rule, as well as the additional decisions cited in *Boulder,* make no such distinction. Furthermore, they are not even concerned with whether the no injury rule applies to waste (or return) water. They deal specifically with whether a water right can be perfected, and must be protected, when an alleged appropriator intercepts another's drainage as a source of water. The courts in those cases hold, unremarkably,

that the senior is not obliged to continue diverting and using water, thereby producing waste to supply the wastewater user.

Metro dealt with a situation where wastewater had been historically returned to a *stream* at a point below which others had made their appropriations. When the return was moved downstream of the others' diversion, they lost their supply. The old cases said that no one can count on another's continued diversion, use, and return of water to provide water to be appropriated from a drainage *ditch* or gully before it reenters a stream. But *Metro* said appropriators can no longer count on the stream as a source of a water right even if stream conditions are changed as the result to a change in point of return. *Boulder* softens the odd *Metro* rule, saying that seepage returns are protected from a change in point of return while returns by ditch are not. In Colorado, water that has seeped into the ground is considered to be in the "natural stream" from which appropriations can be made. See page 252, supra. Shouldn't junior appropriators be protected from being cut off from a source of supply that historically reaches the stream by a pipe or ditch as well as by seepage?

4. Does the decision in *Boulder* affect the rule that an irrigator may line an irrigation ditch to prevent seepage? Can an appropriator still decide not to irrigate a field in a particular year, or to abandon a water right altogether if the absence of return flows would deprive downstream appropriators of being able to fulfill their water rights? Can an appropriator consume or sell to others all "waste water"?

5. "Waste water" is a term of art and is different from "water which is being wasted." Baumgartner v. Stremel, 496 P.2d 705, 706 (Colo.1972). What is the difference?

6. A wide variety of "changes" in a water right may be subject to the no injury rule. Colorado has the most detailed list. Colo.Rev.Stat. § 37–92–103(5) defines "change of water right" as a change in the type, place, or time of use, a change in the point of diversion, a change from a fixed point of diversion, to alternate or supplemental points of diversion, a change from alternate or supplemental points of diversion to a fixed point of diversion, a change in the means of diversion, a change in the place of storage, a change from direct application to storage and subsequent application, a change from storage and subsequent application to direct application, a change from a fixed place of storage to alternate places of storage, a change from alternate places of storage to a fixed place of storage, or any combination of such changes. The term also includes changes of conditional water rights. The statute further provides that changes in water rights shall not "injuriously affect the owner of or persons entitled to use water under a vested water right or a decreed conditional water right." Colo.Rev.Stat. § 37–92–305(3). Note that a change in point of return (of "waste water" or "return flow") is not listed. Other states apply the no injury limitation to less sharply defined categories of change. See, e.g., Nev.Rev.Stat. § 533.-345; Or.Rev.Stat. § 540.520; Wyo.Stat. § 41–3–104.

7. Do the following effects constitute injury under the no injury rule: A diminution in quality? A loss of fishing opportunity? Limitations on future uses in an area of origin? Rendering an old, inefficient means of diversion useless? Cf. Roswell v. Reynolds, 522 P.2d 796 (N.M.1974) (change in point of diversion to a well disallowed absent showing by applicant that new wells would not increase salinity levels of others); Leavitt v. Lassen Irr. Co., 106 P. 404 (Cal.1909) (operator of public water system could not change to private use); Twin Lakes Reservoir & Canal Co. v. Aspen, 568 P.2d 45 (Colo.1977) (because transmountain diversions are necessarily 100% consumptive as to basin of origin, court need not inquire into consumption and return flow of the changed use).

8. Under real property law, an owner cannot prevent a change in the use of a neighbor's property that results in costs, inconvenience, or unpleasantness short of a nuisance. Absent regulations, building a bulky, architecturally unpleasing building that increases traffic and noise may be within the neighbor's right. Yet *any* inhibition on another's use of water rights is barred by the no injury rule. Why is this?

"THIRD PARTY IMPACTS AND OPPORTUNITIES," NATIONAL RESEARCH COUNCIL NATIONAL ACADEMY OF SCIENCE, WATER TRANSFERS IN THE WEST: EFFICIENCY, EQUITY, AND THE ENVIRONMENT.

38–39 (1992).

A water buyer and seller are the two primary parties in a water transfer, each of whom must be satisfied with the results of the negotiations for a transfer to be consummated. These primary parties negotiate in their own best interests and exercise control over whether a transfer will occur. Consequently, their interests are not typically a central concern of public policies governing water transfers. Instead, public policies must be concerned with the interests of so-called third parties, that is, those who stand to be affected by the transfer but are not represented in the negotiations and lack control over or input into the processes by which transfer proposals are evaluated and implemented.

The impacts of transfers and the parties affected are many, diverse, and potentially substantial. Third parties * * * can include

• other water rights holders;

• agriculture (including farmers and agricultural businesses in the area of origin);

• the environment (including instream flows, wetlands and other ecosystems, water quality, and other interests affected by environmental changes);

• urban interests;

• ethnic communities and Indian tribes;

• rural communities; and

• federal taxpayers.

The types of impacts felt by these parties are quite varied but can be broadly thought of as economic, social, and environmental. Economic effects include impacts on incomes, jobs, and business opportunities. Social impacts include changes in community structure, cohesiveness, and control over water resources, and such changes can occur in both rural and urban communities. Environmental effects are broad based, including effects not only on instream flow, wetlands, and fish and wildlife, but also on downstream water quality and on recreational opportunities that are dependent on streamflows, riparian habitats, and aesthetic qualities.

Because local governments in the area of origin are seldom the buyers or sellers in water transfer transactions, their interests and those of community residents frequently are of concern. Damage to the environmental and aesthetic amenities of natural and rural areas may be significant. For example, transfers that involve surface waters may decrease instream flows, leading to degradation of wetlands and water quality and to loss of riparian habitat. Such transfers also can result in increased sewage treatment costs to municipalities that rely on the depleted streams. Where surface water and ground water are closely linked, the export of ground water also can alter surface flows, with potential adverse effects on riparian vegetation and wetlands. Ground water transfers may lower the water levels in the aquifer, affecting other water users pumping from a common aquifer, drying up wetlands, and altering riparian vegetation and wildlife habitat. Negative effects tend to be most serious when transfers involve moving water from one watershed or region to another. In such instances, the benefits associated with that water are lost to the local area. Fiscal impacts include loss of property tax base and bonding capacity, tighter spending limitations, and reduced revenue sharing.

Water transfers from agricultural to other uses may lead to the retirement of irrigated land. Environmental consequences include soil erosion, blowing dust, and tumbleweeds, which arise after crop production ceases (Woodard, 1988). When farmland is retired from production, the loss of agricultural jobs and related businesses may inhibit future economic growth in the area of origin. When the tax base shrinks, causing local services to decline, the area of origin becomes less attractive to new businesses. Also, water and land resources needed for new local development may be unavailable as a result of major water transfers.

3. Water Salvage and Other Conservation Transfers

"CALIFORNIA'S IMPERIAL VALLEY: A 'WIN–WIN' TRANSFER?"
NATIONAL RESEARCH COUNCIL,
NATIONAL ACADEMY OF SCIENCE,
WATER TRANSFERS IN THE WEST:
EFFICIENCY, EQUITY, AND THE ENVIRONMENT

234–43 (1992).

In early 1989 the Imperial Irrigation District (IID) and the Metropolitan Water District (MWD) of Southern California signed a water conservation agreement. Two other irrigation districts, the Palo Verde Irrigation District and the Coachella Valley Water District, became part of the agreement in late 1989 (IID and MWD, 1989). In brief, MWD will pay for a program of water conservation for IID. In return, IID will reduce its call on the Colorado River by the amount conserved, and MWD will be entitled to divert this amount into its system at Parker Dam. Although MWD prefers not to characterize the agreement as a water transfer, it is otherwise almost universally viewed as the first major rural-to-urban transfer of irrigation water in California and will be a model for future transfers that try to accommodate urban demands and preservation of the state's productive agricultural economy. It is important to realize that the Imperial Irrigation District–Metropolitan Water District transfer was an "easy" case because no existing users were displaced and third party effects were minimal or indirect enough to be ignored. Still, it offers an important illustration of the potential of transfers.

THE SETTING

The Imperial Valley lies on the northern edge of the Sonoran Desert in southern California about 50 mi (80 km) west of the Colorado River (Figure 11.1). The area was originally called the Salton Sink and, for a while in the nineteenth century, the Valley of the Dead. It was renamed the Imperial Valley at the turn of the century by the irrigation pioneer and promoter George Chaffey as part of an effort to attract settlers to the harsh desert.

* * *

**Figure 11.1   Main waterways and features,
California's Imperial Valley**

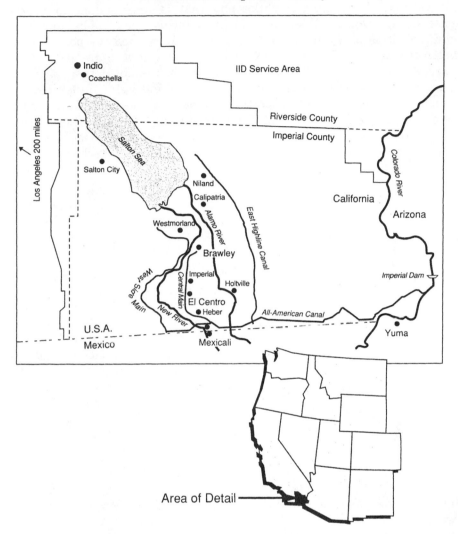

* * * It has been said that the Imperial Valley is one of nature's jokes—it contains hundreds of thousands of acres of flat fertile land formed by silt deposited in the ancient delta of the Colorado and the growing season is perpetual, but rainfall averages less than 3 in. (0.7 cm) per year. Ground water resources are minimal, so the valley, actually a geological sink, must rely on the Colorado River for its supply.

* * *

The history of the settlement and cultivation of the Imperial Valley is in large part the history of the regulation of the Colorado River and the growth of agribusiness in the state. As a 1991 appellate court opinion upholding the state's power to curb wasteful use practices in the valley observed, IID "has occupied a position of great strength, discretion and vested right in a geographical part of the country that is 'far western,' embracing a philosophy that is independent in every sense of the word. Recent trends in water-use philosophy and the administration of water law have severely undermined the positions of districts such as IID" (*Imperial Irrigation District v. State Water Resources Control Board*, 1991). That history has enabled the valley to chart its own destiny, but the valley is increasingly vulnerable to criticism that it uses a disproportionate share of southern California's water. Ninety-eight percent of Colorado River water deliveries to the IID go to irrigation, and the average use is more than 5 acre-feet (6 megaliters (ML)) per acre. A wide variety of irrigation techniques are used.

* * *

LEGAL BACKGROUND

* * *

The IID's water rights are subject to the requirement that the water be put to beneficial use. Western water rights are usufructuary—they are limited to the use of the water and cease if the water stops being put to a beneficial use. The prevailing assumption is that water that is not put to beneficial use is either forfeited or abandoned and is open to appropriation by others. Attacks on nonbeneficial or wasteful uses generally are brought by junior water rights holders against seniors. The IID has long been attacked for applying water in excess of crop needs, but its use was not seriously challenged until 1980. The most significant challenge to IID's water use was an ultimately unsuccessful effort by a valley activist to apply the excess land provisions of the Reclamation Act of 1902.

The geography of the valley makes excess use and the resulting drainage a serious problem. The U.S. Supreme Court Special Master, Simon Rifkind, noted in 1960 that much of California's water use was "wasted, as is apparent, for example, in the very large unused runoff each year into the Salton Sea." The IID has been sued by a number of landowners for damages caused by flooding. In 1980 a lawsuit filed by a Salton Sea farmer, who claimed that IID's tailwater drainage was raising the level of the Salton Sea and flooding his land, triggered a series of administrative and judicial orders requiring greater water conservation in the IID, although water salvage investigations had been under way since the mid–1960s. These state orders provided a strong incentive to negotiate a settlement.

In 1984, after a lengthy series of hearings in which a variety of interests (e.g., the California Department of Water Resources and the Environmental Defense Fund) presented substantial evidence on IID's water management practices and the potential for a conservation-induced water sale, the State Water Resources Control Board concluded that IID's use of water was unreasonable under California law and constituted waste. The next year the Bureau of Reclamation issued a report identifying measures that could conserve 354,000 acre-feet (436,-700 ML) per year.

THE 1989 WATER CONSERVATION AGREEMENTS

The 1989 Water Conservation Agreement obligates MWD to pay for both structural and nonstructural conservation projects designed to conserve 106,100 acre-feet (130,900 ML) annually, which it can then take for a period of 35 years. Total capital costs are estimated to be $97.8 million, plus $23 million in indirect costs. The program will be implemented over a 5–year period between 1990 and 1994; then the savings will be constant until MWD or another party agrees to an additional conservation program. The legal questions that initially created potential barriers were finessed. Section 6.5 of the agreement is replete with disclaimers that MWD shall not assert a right to the conserved waters, that the rights of the parties "except as specifically set forth in this agreement" to the use of the Colorado are not affected, and that the conserved water will at all times retain its third priority and has not been forfeited by IID. Likewise, the possibility of MWD's banking water in Lake Mead during wet years is acknowledged, but the irrigation districts reserve the right to challenge any future banking agreements.

Canal lining is the major conservation strategy being pursued, but IID will also build new regulating reservoirs and canal spill interceptors and will automate its delivery system. The agreement will be administered and monitored by a program coordinating committee composed of one IID, one MWD, and one neutral representative. The MWD must bear all capital construction costs, the "ongoing direct costs of the nonstructural projects of the program, and operation, maintenance and replacement costs of the structural projects of the program necessary to the keep the projects * * * in good operating condition during the terms of this agreement" (IID and MWD, 1989). In addition, MWD must bear $23 million in indirect costs such as lost hydroelectric revenues, "mitigation of adverse impacts on agriculture from increased salinity in the water," and environmental mitigation and litigation costs from any impact on water levels or water quality in the Salton Sea and the New and Alamo rivers (IID and MWD, 1989).

* * *

The IID and MWD Water Conservation Agreement is seen by both parties as a win-win agreement. The MWD, of course, increases its Colorado River supplies by 106,100 acre-feet (130,900 ML), and this additional margin of safety, about 20 percent of its anticipated dry year shortfall, will become important as Arizona takes more of its Colorado River entitlement and supplies become more scarce in both the Colorado basin and northern California. The IID obtains money in return for doing what it may well have become legally obligated to do in any event, while its irrigated acreage is unaffected by the agreement. This is the first such transaction and thus relatively straightforward to negotiate. Future attempts to reach such agreements may be more complicated.

* * *

"TYPES OF WATER TRANSFER OPPORTUNITIES," NATIONAL RESEARCH COUNCIL NATIONAL ACADEMY OF SCIENCE, WATER TRANSFERS IN THE WEST: EFFICIENCY, EQUITY, AND THE ENVIRONMENT.

30–34 (1992).

Several different types of transactions—including water leases, water banks, dry year option arrangements, and transfers of salvaged water—may be used to transfer water use from one party to another. Water rights may be sold or leased, and the transfer may be permanent or temporary.

Water Leases

A water lease occurs when a water rights owner and a new user negotiate an agreement to use a fixed quantity of water over a specific period of time, instead of purchasing a permanent right. Leases often occur during dry years, when some farmers or cities run low on water supplies in storage and need a temporary way to endure short-term drought. For example, junior rights irrigators with orchards and other high-value perennial crops sometimes lease water on a one-time basis for their late summer irrigations from neighboring seasonal crop growers who hold more senior rights. Orchard crop owners are willing to pay more for this water than it was worth to irrigate field crops because they face the danger of losing their long-term investment if their trees die.

Water lease prices in various areas of the West cover a broad range. For example, in 1988 the Bureau of Reclamation offered to lease water from its Green Mountain Reservoir in western Colorado at $6 per acre-foot ($4.85 per [megaliter] ML) for agricultural use, $10 per acre-foot ($8.10 per ML) for municipal use, and up to $80 per acre-foot ($65 per ML) for industrial use. In the same year, the bureau's central Arizona project office leased surplus water to Phoenix-area customers at prices ranging from $35 to $82 per acre-foot ($28.40 to $66.50 per ML). In another lease arrangement in the late 1980s, the Montana Fish, Wildlife and Parks Department paid $20,000 for a release of 10,000 acre-feet (12,335 ML) from Painted Rocks Reservoir into the Bitterroot River to preserve downstream fisheries.

Water Banks

Water banks are another transfer-related option. A water bank is a formal mechanism for pooling surplus water rights for rental to other users. In Idaho, for example, farmers with surplus entitlements from federal projects sell more than 100,000 acre-feet (123,400 ML) annually through water banks that are sanctioned by the state. Water bank leases generally result in changes in point of diversion of storage water or changes in place or purpose of use. Several tests must be met before reallocation through a water bank is approved, such as whether the lease would cause the use of water to be expanded beyond that authorized under the water right or whether it would conflict with the local public interest. Idaho water bank prices in the late 1980s ranged from $2.75 to $5.50 per acre-foot ($2.23 to $4.45 per ML) for one-time use of the water during the irrigation season. Part of the fees collected goes to the entity supplying the water to the rental pool; part goes to the water district to cover administrative costs. Prices are set by the water banks' governing boards and are actually well below the real market value of the water.

In 1991, California responded to a 5–year drought by establishing a water bank to facilitate market-like transfers of water. The arrangement provides for the state to buy water from voluntary sellers and distribute it at cost to urban and agricultural users with critical needs, urgent fish and wildlife protection needs, and carryover storage to guard against a sixth dry year.

Dry Year Option Arrangements

Many water users have enough water to meet their needs in most years but not in the driest years. As a result, users sometimes attempt to negotiate an option agreement with senior rights holders to use the senior water during dry years only. Dry year option arrangements allow the senior rights holders to continue to use the water (in most cases for farming) in normal years and give the option holder (often a municipal user) a cost-effective way to make its supply more reliable during dry years. For example, a dry year option agreement has been implemented by a Utah city and a nearby irrigator. The city paid the irrigator $25,000 for entering the option arrangement for a 25–year period; during those dry years in which the city takes water, it pays the farmer a set sum plus the quantity of hay the farmer might have grown. The farmer benefited from the cash payments and the guarantee of hay for his livestock; the city was assured more reliable supplies.

On a larger scale, the Metropolitan Water District (MWD) of southern California has proposed a dry year option arrangement to farmers in the Palo Verde Irrigation District. The MWD offered cash payments for each acre placed in the program and additional payments each time it asserts its option to transfer the water during dry years. The irrigators declined that offer, but negotiations continue. It is inevitable that more such agreements will be negotiated in the future. In northern California during the summer of 1988, the East Bay Municipal Utility District (EBMUD) offered irrigators a dry year option based on a payment for the water of $50 per acre-foot ($40.50 per ML). However, the irrigators felt the price was too low, and no agreement was reached.

Transfers of Salvaged Water

Transfers of salvaged water also occur. This is a variation of a water sale, in which a city or business that needs additional supplies finances irrigation improvements in exchange for rights to use the water that is conserved. In Wyoming, the city of Casper paid for upgrading irrigation systems in the Alcova Irrigation District in order to salvage several thousand acre-feet of water from the district for new municipal use. In California in 1989, after years of negotiations, MWD and the Imperial Irrigation District (IID) reached an agreement calling for MWD to pay for irrigation system improvements within IID in exchange for rights to use the water conserved. The IID is at the lower end of the river system, and there are no opportunities to reuse return flows, so the return flow is considered "wasted." In California, MWD has begun a closely watched pilot program with the Coachella Valley Water District to salvage Colorado River water imported to southern California via leaky canals. Through a multi-million dollar canal-lining project, MWD hopes to salvage up to 30,000 acre-feet (37,000 ML) annually for municipal use. Additional transfer arrangements involving water conservation are under serious consideration elsewhere in California.

Other Types of Exchanges

Water transfers also include exchanges in which one user trades some water or combination of water and money for another user's supply because the timing, guarantee of availability, or quality makes that supply more attractive to the first user. This type of exchange is relatively common in Colorado, where cities buy water rights in adjacent basins and exchange them for water that can be piped through existing conveyance systems.

California droughts have spurred exploration of water exchanges. To protect the quality of supplies for urban customers during the anticipated 1989 to 1990 drought, EBMUD, in the San Francisco region, wanted to trade low-quality water to local irrigators in exchange for an equivalent amount of their entitlement to higher-quality mountain runoff from the Mohelumne River, EBMUD's normal source of supply. Again, this proposal was rejected by local irrigators.

Another bank-like type of exchange that has occurred in California and could be used elsewhere involves trading surplus surface waters in wet years for accumulated ground water supplies during droughts. The MWD of Southern California has had a policy of storing imported water in ground water aquifers since 1931 (MWD, 1989). The MWD and other water users in California are recharging and stabilizing ground water aquifers by putting surplus surface water into the ground water in both adjudicated and unadjudicated basins. This activity could be extended to irrigation districts. Surplus surface water would be stored during wet years in exchange for use of local irrigation rights during droughts. During dry years, MWD would use the farmers' surface water rights for municipal use; the farmers would then pump the water that MWD has previously recharged into the ground water beneath their lands.

Several states have enacted legislation to encourage the sale of salvaged or conserved water. Oregon has enacted an innovative water conservation plan which splits the benefits of conservation between the saver and the state. If the state approves a conservation plan as feasible, effective, protective of junior rights and consistent with the public interest, the saver is entitled to the saved water, but the state may allocate 25% of the water to itself for instream flow maintenance and other environmental uses. Or.Rev.Stat. § 537.470. The argument that the legislation constitutes a taking is considered but rejected in Joseph L. Sax, *The Constitution, Property Rights and the Future of Water Law,* 61 Colo.L.Rev. 257 (1990).

NOTE ON BUREAU OF RECLAMATION TRANSFERS

Water stored and distributed by the Bureau of Reclamation is available for transfer from agriculture to urban and instream uses, but reclamation law is not structured to encourage or facilitate transfers. Federal reclamation law has created the expectation of eternally cheap water to be used on project lands. The original vision of the West as an Eden of family farms was never fulfilled and is fading. In many areas of the West—California, Colorado, Nevada and Texas, for example— federal reclamation projects have been identified as potential pools of water available for reallocation to urban and environmental uses. Some transfers of reclamation water have occurred, see R. Wahl, Markets for Federal Waters: Subsidies, Property Rights and the Bureau of Reclamation (1989), but there are major political and legal impediments to transfers. The two major legal impediments are the uncertainty over the transferability of reclamation rights and the possibility that the federal government will try to recapture a portion of value created by the subsidy. Federal reclamation law is at best neutral with respect to transfers because the congressional expectation was that reclamation law would create stable family farms. Bruce C. Driver, *The Effect of Federal Reclamation Law on Voluntary Transfers of Water,* 33 Rocky Mtn. Mineral L.Inst. 26–1, 26–7 (1987). However, there is no prohibition against transfers. The Supreme Court has held that under Section 8 the Bureau has legal title to the water as a trustee for the project beneficiaries, Ickes v. Fox, 300 U.S. 82 (1937), rehearing denied 300 U.S. 686 (1937), because the Bureau is "simply a carrier and distributor of water * * * with the right to receive the sums stipulated in the contracts as reimbursement for the cost of construction and annual charges for operation and maintenance of the works."

Section 8 provides that "[t]he right to the use of water acquired under the provision of this Act shall be appurtenant to the land irrigated, and beneficial use shall be the basis, the measure, and the limit of the right," but the courts have not developed a federal appurtenancy policy. A 1955 federal case refused to interpret the appurtenancy requirement to preclude a city's state law appropriation of storm and flood waters and unused return flows from the Rio Grande Project in Texas. The pervasive deference to state law "makes it very doubtful that the fact water rights in a reclamation project become 'appurtenant to the land irrigated,' renders such rights immune from state law * * *" El Paso County Water Improvement Dist. No. 1 v. City of El Paso, 133 F.Supp. 894 (W.D.Tex.1955), affirmed in part, reversed in part 243 F.2d 927 (5th Cir.1957), cert. denied 355 U.S. 820 (1957). More generally, this part of Section 8 may have been repealed by subsequent acts authorizing the use of water for non-irrigation purposes. E.g., Reclamation Projects Act of 1939, 43 U.S.C.A. § 390b. The Miscellaneous Water Supply Act of 1920, 43 U.S.C.A. § 521, allows the Bureau to supply water for non-irrigation purposes under limited conditions and appears to authorize surplus transfers to non-project uses when irrigation is not impaired.

For a useful examination of the problems and benefits of federal water transfers see Brian E. Gray, et al., *Transfers of Federal Reclamation Water: A Case Study of California's San Joaquin Valley*, 21 Envtl.L. 911 (1991). See generally, 2 Waters and Water Rights § 16.03 (Robert Beck ed. 1991).

4. Out of Priority Use

BOARD OF DIRECTORS OF WILDER IRRIGATION DIST. v. JORGENSEN

Supreme Court of Idaho, 1943.
64 Idaho 538, 136 P.2d 461.

HOLDEN, CHIEF JUSTICE.

* * * December 19, 1925, the Wilder Irrigation District was organized. * * *

It was found, in the course of time, the water supply provided under the terms of the contract between the United States and the District, dated April 6, 1926, was not sufficient for the proper irrigation and reclamation of the lands within the district. That led the district to take steps to obtain additional water and to that end, the district entered into another contract with the United States, dated January 13, 1941, also subject to later authorization by the electors of the district, for 33^{71}/$_{100}$ per cent of water to be stored in the Anderson Ranch Reservoir to be constructed by the United States. * * * Thereafter, a petition, in the usual form, was filed in the District Court of Canyon County praying that "each and all of the proceedings had and taken by the Board of Directors of Wilder Irrigation District, for and in connection with the special election * * * 'concerning the construction of Anderson Ranch Reservoir and related matters', between the United States of America and the Wilder Irrigation District * * * be examined, approved and confirmed by this Court, and that the legality and validity of said contract be determined and established by decree of this Court."

At the conclusion of the submission of proof by the District in support of its petition, it was stipulated by counsel for the respective parties that "the following [question] shall be submitted to the Court for its decision:

* * * Has the respondent District power to enter into a contract with the United States whereby the United States may, at some future time, substitute an equal amount of Payette and Salmon River water for District Boise River water?"

The right to substitute waters of one stream for those of another was presented to this Court in Agnes B. Reno et al. v. J.R. Richards et al., 32 Idaho 1, 178 P. 81, 82.

* * *

It thus appears in the Reno case the waters of Birch Creek had been decreed some 24 years before, and, therefore, that the waters of that stream had become appurtenant to the lands for the irrigation of which they had been decreed, just as it is contended by appellants the waters of Boise River have been decreed and become appurtenant to the lands of appellants' and, of course, other landowners in the respondent district. With substantially the same question presented as appellants contend is presented in the case at bar, this Court, in the Reno case, held that "in the absence of detriment to other users of waters from Birch creek, there is no doubt of [the divertors'] right to make a diversion from Birch creek, at their point of diversion, of the amount of [increased] water which they caused to flow therein for the use of other appropriators farther down the stream."

It follows from this holding the fact water has been decreed for the irrigation of lands and become appurtenant thereto does not, for that reason alone, as contended by appellants, prevent a substitution; and, further, that a decree and the appurtenancy of water to lands do not, in and of themselves, constitute a sufficient reason for denying a substitution or exchange of water.

* * *

It must be kept in mind the contest in the case at bar is between appellant landowners within respondent district and the district itself; that the sole purpose of the contract in question is to provide much-needed additional water for the irrigation of the irrigated lands within the boundaries of the district, including appellants' lands, in the manner and as expressly authorized by statute; that the additional supply of water contracted for from Anderson Ranch Reservoir does not depend upon a possible later substitution of water; that such additional supply is assured in any event; that the proposed contract will not have the effect of reducing the amount of water to which any landowner within the district is entitled; that no landowner is compelled to surrender any right whatsoever; that in the event an exchange of water is later made, such water would be emptied into the Boise River at a point above the diversion works of the respondent district; that in the event an exchange of water takes place as provided in the contract under consideration, then and in that case, a landowner within the district, for instance, instead of receiving as at present, under the 1926 contract, 100 inches of the waters of Boise River, would receive a like amount of the waters of Payette and Salmon Rivers, and that such landowner would also receive his share of the Anderson Ranch Reservoir storage water contracted for, which would not, under the circumstances above stated, operate to the detriment of any landowner.

* * *

We conclude the judgment must be affirmed, and it is so ordered, with costs to respondent.

NOTES

1. Colorado allows out-of-priority use or storage of water by juniors, and seniors are required to accept a substitute water supply:

(1) In every case in which the state engineer finds that water can be stored out of priority under circumstances such that the water so stored can be promptly made available to downstream senior storage appropriators in case they are unable to completely store their entire appropriative right due to insufficient water supply, the state engineer may permit such upstream storage out of priority * * *.

(2) Individuals and private or public entities, alone or in concert, may provide a substituted supply of water to one or more appropriators senior to them, * * * and to the extent that such substituted water is made available to meet the appropriative requirements of such senior, the right of such senior to draw water pursuant to his appropriation shall be deemed to be satisfied. The rights of such senior may be used for effectuating such substitution during the period while it is in operation, and the practice may be confirmed by court order as provided for determining water rights.

(3) Any substituted water shall be of a quality and continuity to meet the requirements of use to which the senior appropriation has normally been put. * * *

Colo.Rev.Stat. § 37–80–120.

2. There are other devices for managing water more efficiently by not adhering religiously to priorities, yet satisfying seniors' needs. Rotation is a practice whereby a schedule is devised, either through an agreement among water users or by court order, giving individual users the right to divert the entire flow of the stream, or that portion owned by the parties to the agreement, for a short period of time. Rotations can be between multiple owners of a single water right (e.g., users within a district), or between owners of independent diversions. Their purpose is to combat the inefficiencies that often result from continuous diversions of small amounts of water. All rotation plans are subject to the rights of other users on the stream. Many states have specific statutory authorizations for rotation plans. Nevada, for example, permits rotation among several users, or among different priorities of one user, to the end that each user will have an irrigation head of at least two cubic feet per second. Nev.Rev.Stat. § 533.075. Several states require that proposed rotation plans be submitted in advance to designated state officials. Or.Rev.Stat. § 540.150; Wash.Rev.Code Ann. § 90.03.390; Wyo.Stat.Ann. § 41–3–612. Rotation plans are sometimes imposed by court order, typically where there is not enough water to permit simultaneous use by all parties. What special circumstances would induce a court in an appropriation state to depart from the strict application of priorities and impose rotation among competing users? Compare Hufford v. Dye, 121 P. 400 (Cal.1912), with Cundy v. Weber, 300 N.W. 17 (S.D.1941). Is rotation a potential solution to the problems posed in *Crowley,* page 215, supra?

3. Exchange agreements have a purpose similar to that of rotations—increased efficiency in the use of water. They differ in that exchanges often involve water from two or more sources and do not normally involve the apportionment of water over a fixed time period. Exchange arrangements must avoid injury to other appropriators, both senior and junior to the parties to the exchange. See, e.g., Wyo.Stat. Ann. § 41–3–106(d). Some statutes authorizing exchanges require reductions in the exchanged rights to compensate for losses from seepage and evaporation. See Colo.Rev.Stat. §§ 37–83–101 to –105; N.M.Stat. Ann. § 72–5–26. Despite the existence of a valid exchange agreement, the parties are limited to the amount they can beneficially use at any

given time; in other words, a senior may not be able to transfer all of the "paper" rights, if some of these are deemed "surplus." Johnston v. Little Horse Creek Irr. Co., 79 P. 22 (Wyo.1904).

HARRISON C. DUNNING, THE "PHYSICAL" SOLUTION IN WESTERN WATER LAW
57 U.Colo.L.Rev. 445, 448, 458–61, 472–74, 477–78 (1986).

* * *

My objective in this article is to examine an approach to promoting optimal utilization while protecting established rights which I shall call the "physical solution." The term comes from twentieth-century California cases, but the practice, under one label or another, is found in several western states. In Utah and New Mexico, a comparable but narrower term is "right of replacement," while Colorado uses "substitute supply" and, more generally, the "plan for augmentation." In these states and others in the West, the idea is the same: in appropriate circumstances, a court or agency may (or, some say, *must*) compel a senior right holder to accept a substituted source of water or a modification of his means of diversion, distribution or use of water at a junior right holder's expense in order to benefit the junior and to achieve better overall utilization of the resource. As the pace of large-scale water development projects in the West slows, and as we are increasingly forced to look to mechanisms other than new water supply projects to balance supply and demand, the physical solution will likely become ever more important in western water law.

* * *

III. THE THEORY OF THE PHYSICAL SOLUTION

* * * The courts which have approved physical solutions have done so on two different bases. The earliest was to ground the concept on principles of equity appropriate to the granting of injunctive relief. But in this century the courts have more often derived the basis for the physical solution from the practical necessities of the arid West. * * *

A. *Equity as a Basis for Physical Solutions*

An early example of physical-solution doctrine rooted in equity is *Montecito Valley Water Company v. City of Santa Barbara.*[66] There the water company, an appropriator, diverted flow from a creek in order to sell water to the inhabitants of Montecito. Subsequently Santa Barbara and others put tunnels in lands adjacent to the creek in order to collect water for delivery to other service areas. This water was percolating groundwater, a part of which was tributary to the stream.

On the assumption that the tributary water belonged to the water company, the court in *Montecito Valley* noted that an injunction against those operating the tunnels might be appropriate. It then stated, however, the conventional proposition that injunctive relief should be granted only if no other relief was adequate. In light of several factors present, the court observed that if the junior could make

---

66. 144 Cal. 578, 77 P. 1113 (1904).

good to the senior the amount of water diverted from the stream, then "the judgment, in common equity, should provide accordingly."

* * *

B. Necessity and the Policy of Optimal Utilization

Another judicial approach to the physical solution doctrine has been to refer to the necessity in the arid West of promoting the optimal utilization of water. An early decision from Utah is illustrative.[73] Salt Lake City and others, senior appropriators from Utah Lake, protested an application to appropriate water from the lake. The protest was overruled by the state engineer, and the seniors brought suit. Their complaint alleged in part that further diversion from the shallow lake would interfere with the pumps which assisted in their diversions.

In affirming the overruling of the protests, the Supreme Court of Utah relied on Utah authority which permits an appropriator by condemnation to acquire a right to the use of the ditches or means of diversion of a prior water user.[74] It reasoned that, given this authority, "the right to apply to a beneficial use water which cannot be so applied without in some way affecting prior rights, where such rights may nevertheless be protected and maintained, cannot well be questioned."[75] The applicant could appropriate, but he would either have to cause water to flow to the seniors' pumping plant "as now constructed" or to pay any additional pumping costs his diversion imposed on them.[76]

In linking physical solutions to statutorily granted authority for a private person to condemn property needed for the impoundment, distribution or drainage of water, the Utah court clearly was grounding itself ultimately on the necessities of the West. * * *

V. SOME PHYSICAL SOLUTION ISSUES

A. Hydrological and Legal Uncertainty

Physical solutions are one way a system of water law can respond to the inflexibility which is possible when rules are laid down to protect established property rights in water. Physical solutions are designed to provide an acceptable combination of security for seniors and opportunity for juniors. However, they must themselves be designed to be flexible. It would be ironic and unfortunate if a tool designed to accommodate change became itself a barrier to change.

* * *

* * * [I]t should be accepted that the essence of the plan is a continuing obligation on the part of the junior to protect the senior if the junior wishes to continue to have favorable access to water. The form of that protection should be able to change over time. It should

---

73. Salt Lake City v. Gardner, 39 Utah 30, 114 P. 147 (1911).

74. Nash v. Clark, 27 Utah 158, 75 P. 371 (1904), aff'd, 198 U.S. 361 (1905). That decision refers to several statutory provi-

sions in Utah on this type of condemnation.

75. Salt Lake City v. Gardner, 39 Utah 30, 45, 114 P. 147, 152.

76. Id. at 48, 114 P. at 153.

be permissible to substitute new sources of replacement water for old sources, or it should be possible to give the senior less replacement water, if he can enjoy equivalent benefits because of improvements in the way the water is distributed and used.

To require seniors to rely upon performance of a continuing obligation on the part of juniors obviously exposes the seniors to some degree of risk. The seniors must then look first to the juniors for their water, not to the source. As pointed out long ago by a Utah judge objecting to a physical solution,[155] the situation is one ripe for litigation. And as a practical matter seniors are entitled * * * to wonder how successful they would be, in the event of augmentation plan defaults, in eliminating injurious pumping by thousands of junior wells. To the extent that physical solutions allow new water development to take place, they obviously increase the pressure on a limited resource. They consequently increase the possible difficulties of the earliest resource users, who seek to protect their favored positions.

* * *

B. Complexity of Administration

* * *

In practice, tremendous uncertainty often exists as to just how upstream use affects the downstream availability of water. Decisions may turn on computer modeling more than anything else in many situations, and the "physical solution" or "plan for augmentation" may be nothing more than a name lawyers use for an agreed-to state of uncertainty. In such circumstances some of the assumptions made by the computer modelers are bound to prove inaccurate and some seniors are likely to be injured. When this happens, it is unlikely anyone will try to put Humpty-Dumpty together again and restore to the injured seniors their original priority. Prior appropriation in those cases will likely be replaced with a system much more akin to equitable apportionment.

C. The Need for an Adequate Statutory Foundation

Physical solution doctrine in the West is rooted in conventional equitable concepts and in notions of necessity drawn from the region's arid condition. Courts have alluded to or developed ideas about physical solutions in a number of cases, and, as explained above, a few states have given some statutory expression to the idea. But no state has provided a fully adequate statutory foundation for physical solutions. Until each western state does so, it is unlikely that the large potential contribution of physical solutions will be fully realized.

An adequate physical solution statute would apply to all users of water, whether they be appropriators, riparians, holders of contractual rights to water or something else. If the objective is to increase

---

155. "What the plaintiffs need, and they are entitled to, is not a lawsuit, but the use of the waters appropriated by them more than a quarter of a century ago." Salt Lake City v. Gardner, 39 Utah 30, 59, 114 P. 147, 157 (1911) (Straup, J., dissenting). The same point was made in Board of Directors of Wilder Irr. Dist. v. Jorgensen, 64 Idaho 538, 136 P.2d 461, 475 (1943) (Givens, J., dissenting).

efficiency and reduce waste in the use of the West's limited developed water supply, neither the basis of the senior entitlement nor that of the junior seeking to improve or initiate a use matters. What does matter is that the senior have reasonable security in obtaining needed water and that the junior be allowed to be innovative in taking care of his own needs while protecting the senior against unreasonable injury.

CACHE LaPOUDRE WATER USERS ASSOCIATION v. GLACIER VIEW MEADOWS

Supreme Court of Colorado, 1976.
191 Colo. 53, 550 P.2d 288.

GROVES, JUSTICE.

The applicant Glacier View Meadows, a limited partnership, is a developer of residential lots in the mountains northwest of Fort Collins, Colorado. It filed with the water court two applications for approval of a plan of augmentation. The plans would provide future owners of presently unimproved lots with domestic water from wells to be drilled in the future. * * *

The objector, North Poudre Irrigation Company, is a ditch and reservoir company. The objector, Cache LaPoudre Water Users Association, is a nonprofit protective association, whose members own substantial reservoir and direct flow decrees on the Cache LaPoudre River.

* * *

The applicant owns 75 "preferred shares" of the Mountain and Plains Irrigation Company, which entitle applicant to both reservoir and direct flow water. Applicant acquired these 75 shares from Ideal Cement Company, Dreher Pickle Company and City of Fort Collins, which historically had made year-around use of their water. Under the plan some of applicant's reservoir rights will be used to replace consumptively used water from proposed wells. The water from the wells will be exclusively devoted to in-house, residential domestic use. Under the two applications which are the subject of the court's decree, there will be a maximum of 1892 single-family residential units. In some cases, one well will furnish water for more than one unit.

The reservoirs containing replacement water and the points of discharge of water therefrom into the stream, as well as all of the residential units and the points of return flow therefrom into the stream, lie above the points of diversion of any water of the objectors.

* * *

Of the 1892 units, at ultimate development 105 units are expected to use an evapotranspiration system of sewage disposal. The consumptive use for these 105 units will be 100% of the water diverted from wells. This 100% will be replaced entirely by reservoir water plus enough to account for evaporative losses during transportation in the stream.

The remaining 1787 units, when ultimately developed, will have septic-soil absorption sewage systems. From these latter diversions there will be a consumptive use of not more than 10% and at least 90% will constitute return flow to the stream. Replacement water for the 10%, plus an amount sufficient to embrace transportation losses, will be replenished by the aforementioned releases from the reservoirs.

The rate of flow permitted and claimed for each well will be four gallons per minute for each dwelling unit to be served by any well. The plan is predicated upon the assumption that each dwelling unit will be occupied by 3.5 persons 365 days a year, and that each person will require 80 gallons of well water per day. The entire consumptive use of well water (including those units having 100% consumptive use) will not exceed 89 acre feet per year. 55 of applicant's 75 shares will be devoted to replacement of this consumptively used water. 55 shares represent an amount of 94.71 acre feet per year. After deducting 5% for transportation losses, 89.97 feet remain for replacement.

* * *

As mentioned earlier, the applicant acquired the 75 shares from Ideal Cement Company, Dreher Pickle Company and the City of Fort Collins. Historically, only 25% of the water used by these three returned to the stream. The plan allocates the water from 20 of the 75 shares of stock for use in the stream in lieu of the 25% return flow which no longer exists.

The return flow from these three sources was obtained for each month of the year, being an annual aggregate of 31.29 acre feet. The decree fixes the discharges of reservoir water into the stream, representing this return flow plus transportation losses and other factors, on a daily basis for each month, thereby assuring more than the historic return flow from the three sources. Using a factor of 30 days per month, we convert the monthly figures into an aggregate annual amount of 34.2 acre feet per year. The decree fixes a maximum for this purpose of 34.44. Within this limitation the Division Engineer may use his discretion in "aggregating" the releases for more efficient administration.

We find no mention of the subject in the record or the briefs, but assume that the replacement of return flow from the three sources just discussed is based upon the ultra-conservative view that the matter is treated as if the water represented by the 75 shares had been transported out of the water shed with no return flow or that such water was entirely consumptively used if devoted for some other purposes in the water shed.

* * *

It is contemplated by the plan that, so long as its provisions are followed, there will be no injury to the holders of prior rights. However, if there is a call by a right superior to the association's priority rights, that call must be met. The water court concluded that the only thing that will upset the plan will be an extended period of drought. If such a drought causes insufficient water to be available for replacement, the well water users will be obliged to acquire additional water by lease or otherwise, or else to reduce their consumptive use, to the end that water consumptively used under the plan will not exceed that available for replacement.

The principal argument of the objectors is that, except during flood stages, the Cache LaPoudre River is over-appropriated. With this we agree. Hall v. Kuiper, 181 Colo. 130, 510 P.2d 329 (1973). The argument continues that, unless there is 100% replacement of the water taken from the wells, senior water rights will be injured and there will be a violation of the Water Right Determination and Administration Act of 1969 (section 37–92–101 et seq., C.R.S.1973, hereinafter called the "Act"), and the rules and regulations of the State Engineer's office.

Further, it is argued, the reservoir water held in storage in the Cache LaPoudre Basin has been used historically so that, after use (presumably irrigation), 50% returns to the stream. The result is that the reservoir water, used under the plan for replacement of well water consumptively used, is 100% consumptively used with none thereof returning to the stream; and the result is that injury results to senior rights.

* * *

The objectors' assertion that there must be 100% replacement of withdrawn well water brings us to the major subject of the case: Is this plan of augmentation valid?

* * *

Except as specifically noted, we find that the plan of augmentation has been formulated and approved consonant with, and in furtherance of, the purpose and intent of our recent statutes; and that the plan is valid.

We hold here, and in the companion opinion announced contemporaneously with this one, Kelly Ranch v. Southeastern Colorado Water Conservancy District, Colo., 550 P.2d 297 (1976), that under the plans for augmentation involved water is available for appropriation when the diversion thereof does not injure holders of vested rights.

Objectors cite Southeastern Colorado Water Conservancy District v. Shelton Farms, 187 Colo. 181, 529 P.2d 1321 (1974), in which this court ruled that one, who cuts down water-consuming vegetation (phreatophytes) along the Arkansas River, does not have a right to a decree for an equivalent amount of water to that consumed by the vegetation, free of the call of the river. * * * Shelton Farms involved a factual situation which makes it distinguishable from this and Kelly Ranch, supra. * * *

There, the senior rights had adjusted to the loss of the water caused by the growth of phreatophytes; and, once returned to the river, the water would still belong to the senior users in satisfaction of their decrees. In the instant case, the water to be used in replacement never was that of the senior users. Here, there is not displacement "from the time and place of their need." Under the findings here, the stream will be the same, irrespective of the well diversions.

Under the circumstances of this case, there is no significant difference between the prior appropriation doctrine, and the lack of injury doctrine. Here, where senior users can show no injury by the diversion of water, they cannot preclude the beneficial use of water by another. *Fellhauer*, supra, was cited as authority in *Shelton Farms*. It is likewise authority here. As was there said, "As administration of water approaches its second century the curtain is opening upon the new drama of *maximum utilization* and how constitutionally that doctrine can be integrated into the law of *vested rights.*"

We rule that, in a matter such as this one, water is available for appropriation if the taking thereof does not cause injury. Therefore, the argument of the objectors, to the effect that water withdrawn from the wells must be replaced 100%, falls.

* * *

The next argument of the objectors is that the applicant's reservoir water historically has been used so that 50% thereof has returned to the stream. The argument continues that, since applicant's reservoir water is being used to replace water which has been 100% consumptively used, the usual 50% is not being permitted to return to the stream. If the applicant has answered this, its response is oblique, to say the least. The plain and simple answer is that the reservoir water which the applicant acquired historically had been used in such a way that only 25% of that water returned to the stream after use. As has been already set forth, the applicant is returning all of this 25% flow, plus transportation losses, directly to the stream. The reservoir water used for replacement of well water consumptively used is in addition to the replacement of the 25%. It is clear that there has been no infringement upon the historic return flow to the stream.

NOTES

1. When plans for augmentation involve changes in type and place of use, the timing of water use, as in the principal case, may change significantly. This makes administration of the plan a matter of critical importance in protecting vested rights. In *Glacier View Meadows*, the trial court on remand approved the plan and granted considerable discretion to the state engineer in managing the release of replacement water into the stream. It noted that well diversions would be limited by restrictive covenants and the terms of the individual well permits, and that the groundwater withdrawals assumed by the plan for augmentation were higher than those projected by the evidence, thus assuring a margin of safety. The water court also commented that:

> Inherent in the hydrological and geological analysis upon which the plan for augmentation herein is founded, is a degree of uncertainty, but the uncertainty is no greater than that inherent in the administration of water rights generally and is not of great significance. The assumptions upon which the plan is based allow more than adequate latitude. If the plan for augmentation is operated in accordance with the detailed conditions herein, it will have the

effect of replacing water in the stream at the times and places and in the amounts of the depletions caused by the development's use of water. As a result, the underground water to be diverted by the development wells, which would otherwise be considered as appropriated and unavailable for use, will now be available for appropriation without adversely affecting vested water rights or decreed conditional water rights on the South Platte River or its tributaries.

In re Application of Glacier View Meadows for Water Rights in Larimer County, Nos. W–7438 and W–7629 (Colo.Dist.Ct., Water Div. No. 1, Oct. 6, 1976).

2. The plan for augmentation was introduced into Colorado water law by the Water Right Determination and Administration Act of 1969. The Act defines a plan:

"Plan for augmentation" means a detailed program to increase the supply of water available for beneficial use in a division or portion thereof by the development of new or alternate means or points of diversion, by a pooling of water resources, by water exchange projects, by providing substitute supplies of water, by the development of new sources of water, or by any other appropriate means. "Plan for augmentation" does not include the salvage of tributary waters by the eradication of phreatophytes, nor does it include the use of tributary water collected from land surfaces which have been made impermeable, thereby increasing the runoff but not adding to the existing supply of tributary water.

Colo.Rev.Stat. § 37–92–103(9).

Compare the definition offered by a leading Colorado water lawyer: "Plans for augmentation, a word of art for using a little surface water to divert a larger amount of ground water, became a classic Colorado compromise which both accommodated and restrained the use of wells and surface rights through traditional court proceedings." D. Monte Pascoe, *Plans and Studies: The Recent Quest for a Utopia in the Utilization of Colorado's Water Resources,* 55 U.Colo.L.Rev. 391, 399 (1984).

Plans for augmentation have become an increasingly important means of facilitating development where supplies are fully appropriated. Prior to 1977, preliminary plans could be approved by the state engineer but now a plan is submitted to a referee and then reviewed by the water court. Colo.Rev.Stat. § 37–92–301. The state engineer's office is limited to administering the court-approved plans, although it is directed to "exercise the broadest latitude possible in the administration of waters under their jurisdiction to encourage and develop augmentation plans * * * to allow continuance of existing uses and to assure maximum utilization of the waters of this state." Colo.Rev.Stat. § 37–92–501.5.

3. A plan for augmentation is based on the same principles as a conventional water rights transfer, in that the proponent of a plan has the burden of establishing that vested or conditional rights will not be

injured as a result of the plan. Thus, the court will limit augmentation sources to the former duty of water and historical use and will protect juniors' rights to a continuation of stream conditions. Weibert v. Rothe Bros., Inc., 618 P.2d 1367 (Colo.1980).

As in the principal case, plans for augmentation often involve well drilling, and will be further discussed in that context in Chapter Five. Groundwater is not a necessary ingredient of a plan, however, nor does a valid plan require the introduction of new water into the system. See Kelly Ranch v. Southeastern Colo. Water Conservancy Dist., 550 P.2d 297 (Colo.1976). But if no new water is introduced, as it was in *Glacier View Meadows* where tributary groundwater was to be used, can the plan truly result in "no injury" to existing users if more water is actually consumed from a stream that is fully appropriated?

4. What are the risks of drainage basin alteration with which the court was concerned? Unanticipated loss of use of runoff by senior appropriators? General ecosystem disruption?

5. Transbasin Diversion

The possessory origin of the law of appropriation of water has its strongest survival in the rule that the right is independent of ownership or possession of any land, and independent of the manner, means, place or purpose of use or of point of diversion * * * [A]s the authorities generally stand today, the water may be taken from and over and be used on distant lands owned entirely by the government or (with their permission) by other private parties, as was and is frequently the case with canal companies. This is a distinguishing feature of the law of appropriation.

1 Samuel C. Wiel, Water Rights in the Western United States § 281 (3d ed. 1911).

Early prior appropriation cases consistently followed this principle to allow water to be put to a productive use on arid lands far from a watercourse. As Coffin v. Left Hand Ditch Co., page 160, supra, illustrates, the need for interbasin use of water permeates the history of the West. The first homesteads on the public domain were generally along river bottoms and thus proximity to water coincided in many cases with seniority of use. But there were many early reasons to move water away from streams and even to other watersheds. Mines could only be located where minerals were found. Some early settlements were on streams that proved inadequate for all the potential uses. Often, extensive arable lands were found away from narrow river valleys. All these reasons sent settlers to distant sources. Canals and tunnels were dug through forbidding terrain, often as cooperative efforts because of the capital requirements. Transbasin diversions increased in scale as the federal government promoted reclamation and urban areas grew in places such as the Front Range of Colorado and Southern California where water is in short supply. The results vein the West today.

Although transbasin diversions have been vital to the growth of the West, concerns for the protection of areas of origin have moved courts and legislatures to modify pure appropriation law in some respects. Early restrictions in some areas demanded that surplus waters be returned to the stream of origin.   Later, as laws were passed to facilitate the financing of large diversions, legislatures imposed conditions on interbasin transfers.   The idea behind area of origin protection is that these areas need special protection to prevent one area's future from being sacrificed for another's benefit.   This became especially apparent after the one person-one vote principle of Baker v. Carr, 369 U.S. 186 (1962), attenuated the political power of rural areas.

The fate of the Owens Valley, on the eastern slope of California's Sierra Nevada Mountains is a classic example of the changes in economy, ecology and lifestyle of an area of origin that can occur from the massive export of water.   A visionary engineer, William Mulholland, and wealthy speculators in Los Angeles outmaneuvered the Bureau of Reclamation and local farmers to dewater the valley for the benefit of greater Los Angeles; and agricultural and other options have been limited for over seventy years.   The full Owens Valley story is told in William L. Kahrl, Water and Power (1982).

How should areas of origin be protected?   Colorado requires the construction of water storage facilities for the water-rich but sparsely populated western slope when water is diverted by conservancy districts to the populous Front Range.   Is it enough that individual water rights holders are compensated for their rights?   Does the answer change when an importing area seeks adequate supplies to meet highly speculative growth projections?

CITY AND COUNTY OF DENVER v. SHERIFF

Supreme Court of Colorado, 1939.
105 Colo. 193, 96 P.2d 836.

OTTO BOCK, JUSTICE.

* * *

In 1918, when Denver acquired its water system, the population was between 150,000 and 200,000.   The population served by the system at this time is approximately 350,000.   The city has not been unmindful of its obligation to seek further water sources for its growing needs.   As early as 1914 its Public Utilities Commission made investigation through employed engineers.   After the city acquired the Denver Union Water Company, and in 1921, it caused a location survey to be made for projects of Western Slope water, and particularly the Fraser river and Williams Fork diversion projects, these latter being involved in the instant case, and which the trial court decreed as of July 4, 1921, as the appropriation date.   The filing of the map for these projects with the state engineer occurred January 28, 1922.   The claims as filed seek water for irrigation as well as for domestic and other purposes.   To bring water over the divide so that it may be applied to a beneficial use by the city, engineering and financial problems always have been a serious concern.   Several futile attempts were made until the successful culmination in the organization of the Moffat Tunnel District in 1922, which provides two tunnels, one for rail transportation and a similar one for irrigation purposes. The tunnel commission continued work on the water tunnel until January 2, 1929, when it was turned over to the city by lease, under the terms of which provision was made that it be finished by the lessee and placed in operation to bring water to Denver. The expense of the construction of the water tunnel is estimated at $5,000,000. At the time of the trial it had a usable capacity of 600 second feet * * *. When completed and lined its capacity will be 1280 cubic feet per second. In addition to the completion of the water tunnel by the city to a capacity of 600 second feet, it constructed various gathering ditches, conduits, diversion works, tunnels and pipe-lines necessary to bring the water to Denver at an expense of approximately $12,000,000. It is hoped that by this development about 74,000 acre-feet of water will be made available at a cost of approximately $160 per acre-foot, which it is asserted is a considerably higher sum than farmers could afford to expend for water for the irrigation of agricultural land.

* * *

The assignments of error raise but two questions, namely:

First, that the trial court, in giving the city its priorities from the Western Slope streams, made such priorities subject to unlawful and burdensome restrictive conditions; and,

Second, that the trial court denied the city any priorities whatever for general irrigation purposes.

In each of the three divisions of the decree we find the paragraph of which the city complains, as follows: "Any waters decreed herein, whether decreed therefor, to be for direct flow or for storage, and whether the said decree be absolute or conditional, be diverted, taken and used as supplemental to the decreed water rights now belonging to claimant, which said decrees are from the waters of the natural streams of the State of Colorado and that the said claimant be required to satisfy its needs for waters from said existing decrees owned by it before it shall be held to require or need waters herein decreed or shall be entitled to take the same. That the waters herein decreed shall be held by the said claimant as a water supply supplemental to its present supply of water available under water decrees which the said claimant now holds and to be used only to the extent necessary to fill the needs and requirements of the claimant for municipal purposes, after it has made full and economical use of the waters available to it under water decrees now owned by it."

* * *

It will be noted that the restrictions relate to "water decrees now owned by it," being the Eastern Slope water rights, and "any waters decreed herein" being the Western Slope water rights.

We shall first discuss these restrictive conditions to the decrees of the city as they relate to its Eastern Slope water rights. These appropriations are all based upon unconditional and absolute decrees. That they take on the attribute of property rights cannot be questioned.

Counsel for defendants in error do not question this. This carries with it the right, under certain circumstances, to lease, sell and convey title.

* * *

The trial court's purpose in these restrictive conditions is disclosed in the record, wherein it is stated: "In making this right a supplemental right to the rights already owned by Denver, we are guarding against the City of Denver going into the business of selling water or disposing of a part or all of her present water rights and substituting the water acquired or to be acquired in this proceeding for her present water supply."

In part, the express purpose is to prevent any sale, lease or alienation of the Eastern Slope water. This would operate to prevent the city from leasing Eastern Slope water to farmers, which, under certain circumstances, we have said it had a right to do. Denver v. Brown, 56 Colo. 216, 233, 138 P. 44. If the city, for some legitimate reason, desired to abandon or sell any of its Eastern Slope water, it would, by so doing, and under these restrictions, jeopardize its water rights on the Western Slope. The furnishing of an adequate supply of water to 350,000 people requires managerial judgment and involves an ever-changing problem. To so freeze and straight-jacket the city's Eastern Slope water rights, by the restrictions involved here, would be an arbitrary invasion of vested property rights of the city.

* * *

It is not speculation but the highest prudence on the part of the city to obtain appropriations of water that will satisfy the needs resulting from a normal increase in population within a reasonable period of time. * * *

Concerning these restrictions as applied to the 335 cubic feet of Western Slope water awarded the city as an absolute appropriation, such restrictions are a novelty in a water adjudication decree. True, no one has a property right in, or the right to sell or lease, water which has not first been legally appropriated. The system operated by the city embraces reservoirs of considerable magnitude. Much of the appropriated water, when it reaches these reservoirs located on the Eastern Slope, cannot be returned to the public stream from which it was diverted. This statement also applies to water stored in the city's water system. The possession of the water is different in character from that which is used solely for agricultural purposes.

We do not here controvert the general rule recited by counsel for defendants in error as announced in Ft. Lyon Canal Co. v. Chew, 33 Colo. 392, 81 P. 37, 41, as follows: "The general rule is that, when an appropriator has no present need of water for irrigating his lands, he must not divert it from the natural stream, but it is his duty to let it flow in the natural channel, to be enjoyed by other appropriators as their numerical priorities entitle them. If a senior appropriator who has not such need for his own land may disregard the usual rule, and pass over one or more appropriators who are junior to him, and confer upon other appropriators, who are junior to those ignored, his senior rights, it is his duty to show the facts that justify the departure."

It will be noted that we there referred to "need of water for irrigating his lands." Our problem here relates to the need of water for municipal purposes. This difference has received legislative recognition in the enactment of chapter 172, p. 811, S.L.1931 (section 398, ch. 163, '35 C.S.A.), which is as follows: "In the event any municipal appropriator of water having a population in excess of two hundred thousand (200,000) people shall hereafter lease water not needed by it for immediate use, no rights shall become vested to a continued leasing or to a continuance of the conditions concerning any return water arising therefrom, so as to defeat or impair the right to terminate the leases, or change the place of use; provided, however, that any leasing shall not injuriously affect rights, theretofore vested in other appropriators; provided, further, that nothing herein contained shall authorize an appropriator to recapture water for a second use after it has once been used by it."

* * * That such water must first be applied to a beneficial use by the city before it has any property right in it is not disputed. All we now say is that the factors which enter into a determination of a beneficial use here, which is based upon a normal need, are more flexible than those relating to the use of water on agricultural land. The construction of a great distribution system necessarily involves a large financial investment. That such investment may be entitled to a return derived from a leasing of water not necessary to the city for immediate use, has heretofore received our implied approval.

When the court found that the city had diverted and applied to a beneficial use 335 cubic feet, that appropriation ripened into a property right, without any restrictions except those which the Constitution and the laws of this state impose.

* * *

We come now to the second question—a denial by the trial court to the city of any priorities to the Western Slope waters for general irrigation purposes. The decrees provide that the water "is being and will be used for all municipal uses, including domestic use, fire protection, street sprinkling, watering of parks, lawns and grounds, mechanical uses and every other type of municipal use, and for maintaining adequate storage reserves."

* * *

It is, therefore, conceded that in so far as the 335 cubic feet of water per second of time absolutely decreed herein is concerned, it may be used for irrigation purposes within the area served by the Denver Municipal Water System.

* * *

One of the problems in the case before us is whether the water not needed for immediate use, as distinguished from a normal need, under all the circumstances, could be leased temporarily to consumers for agricultural purposes outside of the city area.

* * *

No relation of carrier and consumer is involved in this case. In our opinion, there is no basis upon which the trial court could have made a finding of a beneficial use for irrigation outside of the area served by the Denver Municipal Water System. The need of water to satisfy beneficial use, contended for by the city, necessarily must apply to the system area. This, however, as we have heretofore stated, does not prohibit the city from leasing the water not needed for immediate use * * *. It, therefore, was not error for the trial court to deny the city an appropriation based on beneficial use for irrigation purposes outside of the Denver Municipal Water System area.

NOTES

1. The court held in *Sheriff* that it was improper to impose conditions on the use of water for the protection of western slope water users. Courts and administrative agencies often consider the public interest in exercising their authority to allocate water. How then did the district court err? The supreme court seems very concerned with supporting a public policy that assures Denver's ability to grow. It is impressed with the economic value of water in Denver. Does the supreme court actually substitute its judgment for that of the trial court?

2. Denver is allowed to establish its beneficial use of water by leasing it out to eastern slope farmers at prices below what it costs to develop and import the water. Is this sound policy? Does it sanction speculation? Is speculation bad? What complaint might western slope farmers have about Denver's scheme?

COLORADO RIVER WATER CONSERVATION DIST. v. MUNICIPAL SUBDISTRICT, NORTHERN COLORADO WATER CONSERVANCY DIST.

Supreme Court of Colorado, 1979.
198 Colo. 352, 610 P.2d 81.

Erickson, Justice.

The appellant, the Colorado River Water Conservation District (the River District), appeals from a conditional decree entered by the District Court, Water Division No. 5, which granted to the appellee, the Municipal Subdistrict, Northern Colorado Water Conservancy District (the Subdistrict) the conditional rights to the use of water to be exported from the natural basin of the Colorado River. In reaching its decision, the water court determined that the appellee was in compliance with the provisions of section 37–45–118(1)(b)(IV), C.R.S.1973 (hereafter subparagraph IV),[1] which specifies certain requirements for trans-

---

1. The subparagraph in issue provides: "(IV) However, any works or facilities   planned and designed for the exportation of water from the natural basin of the

basin exportation of water by water conservancy districts and subdistricts thereof.

* * *

A. *Timing of Plan Submission*

The trial court determined that a plan in compliance with subparagraph IV need not be demonstrated at the time a claim for conditional water rights is decreed. Under the procedures set forth by the trial court, an applicant's obligation to demonstrate such a plan arises at a later stage in the appropriation process, at which time a "reasonable diligence" hearing is held to determine compliance with subparagraph IV.

We believe that the trial court's interpretation ignores the language and purpose of the statute, and therefore is erroneous. Subparagraph IV is a clear limitation upon the general powers of the water conservancy districts and subdistricts. It begins with the word "however" and conditions the grant of power to "take by appropriation * * * water * * * water rights * * * and sources of water supply * * *." The intent of the General Assembly was to protect not only present appropriations but "in addition thereto prospective uses of water" within the natural basin of the Colorado River. The mechanism for accomplishing this is the submission of project plans detailing the design, construction and operation of facilities aimed at achieving these stated goals. To allow the required plan to be submitted at a later hearing would subvert the legislative intent of subparagraph IV, which is to obtain a definition and description of the plan in advance of the conditional decree during the early stages of the decree process. In addition, such a procedure would result in substantial expenditures of public funds between the time of the conditional decree and the hearing on reasonable diligence without assurance that the plan would protect the present and future appropriators within the natural basin of the Colorado River.

* * *

We * * * hold that in order to obtain a conditional decree a conservancy district or subdistrict must first comply with the statute "which gave it existence and which imposed conditions upon it before it could obtain such sought-for appropriation."

B. *Adequacy of the Subdistrict's Plan*

The following plan was submitted by the Municipal Subdistrict:

Colorado river and its tributaries in Colorado, by any district created under this article, shall be subject to the provisions of the Colorado river compact and the 'Boulder Canyon Project Act.' Any such works or facilities shall be designed, constructed and operated in such manner that the present appropriations of water, and in addition thereto prospective uses of water for irrigation and other beneficial consumptive use purposes, including consumptive uses for domestic, mining, and industrial purposes, within the natural basin of the Colorado river in the state of Colorado, from which water is exported, will not be impaired nor increased in cost at the expense of the water users within the natural basin. The facilities and other means for the accomplishment of said purpose shall be incorporated in and made a part of any project plans for the exportation of water from said natural basin in Colorado."

1) The Windy Gap Water System will divert water from the upper drainage area of the Colorado River at Windy Gap and transport it back upstream to Granby Reservoir.

2) The existing facilities of the Colorado–Big Thompson Project will be used to transport the water from Granby Reservoir to the points of delivery for ultimate use on the Eastern Slope.

3) All diversions will be made strictly under the priority system, thus protecting all conditional and absolute water rights senior in priority to the Windy Gap Water System decrees.

4) Future uses of water in the natural basin of the Colorado River will be protected by:

i) bypassing 75 cubic feet per second of water or the run of the river, whichever is less, at all times at the Windy Gap Diversion Dam, and

ii) complete compliance by the Municipal Subdistrict with all of the terms and provisions of Senate Document 80 (which [describes facilities of the Colorado–Big Thompson federal reclamation project, analyzes prospective water uses, and] contains a finding that operation under its terms will not harm present or prospective uses of waters on the Western Slope) in the design, construction and operation of the Windy Gap Water System.

The water court determined that a plan in compliance with subparagraph IV need only be in "broad conceptual form" at the time of initiation of a conditional decree and accordingly declared the Subdistrict's plan to be adequate.

We hold that the plan did not comply with the statute which required that "[t]he facilities and other means for accomplishment of said purpose shall be incorporated in and made a part of any project plans for the exportation of water from said natural basin in Colorado." Section 37–45–118(1)(b)(IV), C.R.S.1973.

The plan required by subparagraph IV must be at least as detailed as that necessary to document the elements of an appropriation.

* * *

The requirement that a plan need only be in broad conceptual form impermissibly weakens these common law mandates. The purpose of demanding physical acts manifesting intent is to put others on notice as to the demand an appropriation will make upon the available water supply. Consistent with this theme, subparagraph IV was enacted to put in-basin users on notice as to the supply remaining after a proposed appropriation. As noted, the provision appears as a limitation on the otherwise general power to appropriate and must therefore be considered in a determination of whether the intent to appropriate exists in sufficiently specific form. The specificity mandated by subparagraph IV, then, is nothing short of a physical demonstration that any project works or facilities will be "designed, constructed and operated in such a manner that the present appropriations of water, and in addition thereto prospective uses of water * * * within the natural basin of the

Colorado river * * * will not be impaired nor increased in cost at the expense of the water users within the natural basin."

* * *

Accordingly, we reverse and remand for further proceedings consistent with the directions contained in this opinion.

NOTES

1. The court insists not only that adequate compensatory storage facilities ultimately be built, but that they be planned in detail and demonstrated as adequate even before a conditional decree can be issued to divert water over the Continental Divide. Is this an overly technical reading of the statute? Are there practical reasons for the requirement?

2. Following the decision in the principal case, a settlement agreement was reached among the parties and many other interests. The Subdistrict agreed to pay up to $10 million for a western slope compensatory storage reservoir known as the Azure Reservoir. Other concessions were made, including the grant of storage space to a western slope water district in an existing western slope reservoir owned by the Northern Colorado Conservancy District and the Subdistrict agreed to subordinate its rights to in-basin rights. Payments were also made to upgrade water treatment facilities and to study salinity problems. Does this type of agreement satisfy the requirements of "a physical demonstration that any project works will not impair or increase the cost of water in the basin?"

It is interesting that five years later the Subdistrict and the Colorado River Water Conservation District agreed that the Azure Project should not be pursued further. Instead, the Subdistrict agreed to pay $10.2 million to the district so that it could build a storage project of its choosing. The water court approved.

3. The compensatory storage requirement read into the conservancy district law in the principal case does not apply to transbasin diversions by Denver or other municipalities. Should it? Why have such protective legislation at all? If future western slope water uses are socially important, why not let the future users buy out senior users on the eastern slope?

4. If it is shown that there are projections for the western slope to grow from its present size (about 100,000 population) to over a million, should any exports be allowed under the statute?

5. The concept of compensatory storage embodied in the Colorado Conservancy District Act is based on an accord reached a few years before the Act was passed. The agreement was necessary to reconcile eastern and western slope interests that were to be affected by the Colorado–Big Thompson (CBT) Project. The Project was planned to take water from the upper reaches of the Colorado River and transport it across the Rocky Mountains to the northern Front Range. Negotiations resulted in a resolution that included several principles for transmountain diversion projects. One was that an "essential part" of such projects should be the "construction of a compensatory reservoir

on the western slope of sufficient capacity to hold an amount of water equal to the amount to be annually diverted * * *" This and other principles were included in "Senate Document 80" mentioned in the principal case, which in turn was incorporated by reference in the CBT authorizing legislation. Accordingly, the 152,000 acre-foot Green Mountain Reservoir was built on the western slope as part of the CBT. The Bureau of Reclamation is still searching for purchasers of Green Mountain water; some fifty years after the reservoir's construction, the water remains virtually unused except for electric power generation.

6. The National Water Commission's 1973 Report was critical of compensatory storage schemes in that they may cause "economic waste because the area of origin may not be prepared to use the compensatory storage for many years." National Water Commission, Water Policies For the Future 324 (1973). Given that future water demand projections will be uncertain (see State and National Water Use Trends To The Year 2000, A Report Prepared For the Congressional Research Service of the Library of Congress for the Committee on Environment and Public Works U.S. Senate, S. 96–12 (1980)), how should determinations about location, capacity and use of compensatory storage projects be made?

NOTE: AREA OF ORIGIN PROTECTION

Area of origin protection statutes represent political responses to the effects of larger transbasin diversions and are a departure from the original prior appropriation doctrine, which placed no limits on where water could be used. Colorado's "compensatory storage" statute is only one means of protecting the basin of origin.

There are two main approaches. The first is to allocate future local rights so as to preempt exports. This method involves "informed guessing" in order to determine what the future demand will be. These guesses will invariably be wrong. Thus, the area may end up with too little water (at least from its perspective) and no chance of acquiring more because all the existing supplies are under long-term contracts. Or, the area may end up with more water than it needs and be reluctant to release this excess water for use elsewhere.

The second approach is to grant the area of origin a priority right to appropriate whatever water may become necessary for development when it is required. This allows water to be used in another basin until the basin of origin "needs" the water, at which point the basin of origin can recapture its water and invalidate transfer contracts. This method can lead to unsettling results for the holder of water contracts because there would be no guarantee of delivery. In addition, as a practical matter, it may be difficult for an area of origin to interrupt long-standing water deliveries in the importing area.

California's area of origin laws give the exporting area absolute priority to make future use of water over that of the importing area. One statute leaves for the county of origin all the water it may need for future development. Cal. Water Code §§ 10505–05.5.[1]

Who makes the determination of when, and to what extent, water is "necessary for the development of the county"? The California statute provides that it shall be the Water Resources Control Board. This board is a quasi-judicial body set up to regulate water rights, water pollution and water quality control, whose five members are appointed by the Governor. The board is not subject to the California Administrative Procedure Act. Should a genuine dispute develop between, say, the Metropolitan Water District of Southern California (the main recipient of State Water Project water) and Butte County (north of Sacramento on the Feather River) as to the amount of water that has become "necessary for the development of [Butte County]," do you think that both the parties would accept the determination of the Water Resources Control Board as final? In view of the substantial interests involved, it is more likely that the losing party in the board's decision will press for legislative relief. What is the effect of the reapportionment cases on a political solution? Once water from the area of origin has been committed to use in another area, albeit temporarily, what is the effect on investments and plans for growth in the area of origin as opposed to the importing area? If the restrictions were put into the contracts on the calculated assumption that a situation requiring their use would never arise, why put them in at all?

Under the county of origin statute, only those counties in which the water "originates" are protected. This wording is construed to mean that counties are protected only to the extent that water actually originates, in the form of rain or snow, within their boundaries. This interpretation raises difficult problems for the foothill counties. In California, these counties usually receive minimal rainfall but have abundant water in the rivers that are fed by mountain runoff and snow melt. Thus, most of the water "originates" in mountainous counties which are usually too rugged for much development. The foothill counties, whose potential for development is often much greater, receive little protection for the abundant water presently flowing into them. This problem became urgent when the state decided to construct the massive Central Valley Project. To solve it, the legislature enacted the Watershed Protection Act as an integral part of the Central Valley Act of 1933, California Water Code §§ 11460–63.[2]

1. § 10505. **Restrictions on release or assignment**

No priority under this part shall be released nor assignment made of any application that will, in the judgment of the board, deprive the county in which the water covered by the application originates of any such water necessary for the development of the county.

§ 10505.5. **Territorial Restrictions on Use**

Every application heretofore or hereafter made and filed pursuant to Section 10500, and held by the State Water Resources Control Board, shall be amended to provide, and any permit hereafter used pursuant to such application, and any license issued pursuant to such a permit, shall provide, that the application, permit, or license shall not authorize the use of any water outside of the county of origin which is necessary for the development of the county.

2. § 11460. **Prior right to watershed water**

In the construction and operation by the department of any project under the provisions of this part a watershed or area wherein water originates, or an area immediately adjacent thereto which can conveniently be supplied with water therefrom,

The main idea of the Watershed Protection Act was to extend source area water priorities to the entire watershed area and not limit them to the areas of precipitation. This obviously grants some relief to the foothill areas, as these are almost always included in "the region or area which contributes to the supply of the stream in question." 25 Ops.Cal.Atty.Gen. 8, 19 (1955). The proviso that the "article shall not be so construed as to create any new property rights * * * " precludes the board from assigning water rights to an area based on a determination of its potential need. All that is granted is a priority to water users in the area so that when they require more water, they can "recapture" the water from any other non-watershed user. The statute ran into some unusual difficulties. It was enacted in 1933 and was meant to apply to the state's Central Valley Project (CVP). The Depression was, however, well underway and the state was unable to finance the project. The federal government took over the CVP in 1935 and by 1940 was deeply involved in the water business in California. It was nevertheless assumed that the county of origin and watershed protection acts were still effective since § 8 of the Reclamation law purported on its face to apply state (rather than federal) law. We examine the validity of this assumption and the present status of the protection statutes in connection with California v. United States, page 715, infra.

Problem: A stream flows through two mountain counties before entering the Central Valley. There are two private diverters, 1 and 2, that use the water within the watershed and a diversion, 3, by the State of California to supply a project that is subject to area of origin restrictions. The three diverters use all the available supply during low flow periods. A fourth diverter petitions the State Water Resources Control Board for a diversion to supply a second home development within the watershed of the stream. What are the respective priorities among the four diverters? See Ronald B. Robie & Russell R.

shall not be deprived by the department directly or indirectly of the prior right to all of the water reasonably required to adequately supply the beneficial needs of the watershed, area, or any of the inhabitants or property owners therein.

§ 11461. **Purchase of watershed water rights**

In no other way than by purchase or otherwise as provided in this part shall water rights of a watershed, area, or the inhabitants be impaired or curtailed by the department, but the provisions of this article shall be strictly limited to the acts and proceedings of the department, as such, and shall not apply to any persons or state agencies.

§ 11462. **Creation of new property rights**

The provisions of this article shall not be so construed as to create any new property rights other than against the department

as provided in this part or to require the department to furnish to any person without adequate compensation therefor any water made available by the construction of any works by the department.

§ 11463. **Exchange of watershed water**

In the construction and operation by the department of any project under the provisions of this part, no exchange of the water of any watershed or area for the water of any other watershed or area may be made by the department unless the water requirements of the watershed or area in which the exchange is made are first and at all times met and satisfied to the extent that the requirements would have been met were the exchange not made, and no right to the use of water shall be gained or lost by reason of any such exchange.

Kletzing, *Area of Origin Statutes—The California Experience*, 15 Idaho L.Rev. 419, 435–36 (1979).

For a discussion of other area of origin protection approaches, see Gary D. Weatherford, *Legal Aspects of Interregional Water Diversion*, 15 UCLA L.Rev. 1299, 1313 (1968); Lawrence J. MacDonnell & Charles W. Howe, *Area-of-Origin Protection in Transbasin Water Diversions: An Evaluation of Alternative Approaches*, 57 U.Colo.L.Rev. 527 (1986).

"WATER TRANSFERS BETWEEN BASINS SHOULD BE EVALUATED TO DETERMINE AND ACCOUNT FOR THE SPECIAL IMPACTS ON INTERESTS IN THE AREAS OF ORIGIN." NATIONAL RESEARCH COUNCIL, NATIONAL ACADEMY OF SCIENCES, WATER TRANSFERS IN THE WEST: EFFICIENCY, EQUITY, AND THE ENVIRONMENT

257–59 (1992).

Water is not merely a commodity in the normal sense of the word but rather a resource held in common for all citizens, and this should be recognized in the processes used to evaluate water transfers. The interests of communities, local governments, individuals, and the environment in the areas from which water is proposed to be exported are not now adequately represented in the laws and policies of many western states. Communities hold strong values that support maintaining water within its natural watershed. For some, water is the basis of present and future economic vitality and environmental amenities; these values often are augmented by water-related social and cultural concerns and traditions. * * * [T]he threat to cultural values is illustrated dramatically in the case of the acequias of northern New Mexico.

State laws and policies often fail to recognize that when water is removed from its natural watershed a variety of economic, social, and environmental harms can occur. Prior appropriation law has never limited the use of water to the watershed in which it originates, and the committee does not recommend that water be constrained to its watershed of origin. However, states do need to ensure that the special problems caused the public by transbasin export are fully addressed before such transfers are permitted. Although basin-of-origin interests should not have veto power over transfers, their interests should be represented in the evaluation process, to the extent that those interests are important to society.

State tax laws often provide incentives for transfers because local taxing jurisdictions cannot impose taxes or in lieu payments, and these incentives could be revised to address the equities of reallocation. Municipalities and certain quasi-public water utilities that purchase or lease water supplies or build and operate works to use water supplies from outside their service areas ordinarily pay no property taxes to local governments in areas of origin because of intergovernmental immunity from taxation. In addition, western states usually provide by law that private entities may be taxed on the value of water facilities only by the county where the water is used. The inability to tax facilities that dewater areas of origin compounds the disadvantages to the communities in these areas. For instance, states could revise their tax laws to make exporting entities bear a larger portion of the costs of mitigating the third party effects of transfers. Exporters could be subject to local property or other taxes. States might consider developing a transaction tax for water rights transfers. This transaction tax would be analogous to a severance tax and would be used to mitigate adverse environmental effects caused by transfers (interbasin as well as others). Setting the level of such a tax would require careful analysis so that desirable transfers are not discouraged but adequate revenues for mitigation are collected.

RECOMMENDATIONS:

• States and tribal governments should develop specific policies to guide water transfer approval processes regarding the community and environmental consequences of transferring water from one basin to another, because such transfers may have serious long-term consequences.

• Water transfer processes should formally recognize interests within basins of origin that are of statewide and regional importance, and these interests should be weighed when transbasin exports are being considered.

• Although each state or tribe should select the approach that suits its needs best, area-of-origin protection generally would include impact assessment, opportunities for all affected interests to be heard, regulatory mechanisms to help avoid adverse effects, compensation (e.g., financial payments or mitigation), and authority to deny a proposed transfer or water use involving a transbasin export if the effects are judged unacceptable.

• States should revise laws that now exempt water facilities from taxation by the county of origin either because the exporter is a public entity or because of provisions that make such facilities taxable only in the county where the water is used. Mechanisms to compensate communities for transfer-related losses of tax base, such as an annual payment in lieu of taxes, may be needed.

G. LOSS

1. Abandonment and Forfeiture

JENKINS v. STATE, DEPARTMENT OF WATER RESOURCES
Supreme Court of Idaho, 1982.
103 Idaho 384, 647 P.2d 1256.

SHEPARD, JUSTICE.

* * *

Jenkins is the owner of 280 acres of land near the town of Kilgore in Clark County, Idaho. Appurtenant to that property are two separate water rights, one for 2.4 cfs of water from Cottonwood Creek, and the second for 3.2 cfs of water from Ching Creek. Those water rights were adjudicated by decree of federal court in 1930. Both creeks flow southerly in a generally parallel direction from the mountains of Targhee National Forest. Ching Creek is the more easterly and the Jenkins property is located further east of Ching Creek. There are a series of channels approximately 2 miles in length running easterly from Cottonwood Creek to Ching Creek that are the principal subject of this dispute. It is contended by appellant Jenkins that the water representing his Cottonwood right flows from Cottonwood Creek through channels into Ching Creek from whence it is diverted by him together with the water representing his Ching Creek right.

In 1978, Jenkins filed an application with the Department of Water Resources, seeking to transfer the point of diversion for his Ching Creek water right to the location of a recently built headgate. At that time an examination of the records indicated that the decreed point of diversion for Jenkins' Cottonwood right was not located on any stream. Jenkins filed an amended application to transfer the point of diversion of the Cottonwood right and locate that point of diversion on Cottonwood Creek.

Several water users on both Ching and Cottonwood Creeks protested these proposed transfers, and the district water master recommended that the Department deny the transfer of the Cottonwood right. A hearing was held thereon at which all parties were represented by counsel. Thereafter the director of the Department issued an order granting the transfer of the point of diversion of the Ching Creek right but denying the transfer of the point of diversion of the Cottonwood Creek right. The director found that no water had been diverted from Cottonwood Creek for use on Jenkin's land for the previous 18 years. He also found that waters of both Ching and Cottonwood Creeks were overappropriated. He concluded that to allow a resumption of use of the Cottonwood right would represent an enlargement of the use over the prior 18 years, that the water users would be injured thereby, and that I.C. § 42–222 authorized denial of an application in such circumstances. The director relied upon that portion of I.C. § 42–222 which provides for the forfeiture of a water right not used for five years.

From that decision of the director, Jenkins appealed to the district court. * * *

The trial court found that water from Cottonwood Creek only flowed to Ching Creek irregularly during the spring run off and that any such contribution was not the result of a physical diversion. The court also found that Jenkins took only 3.2 cfs of water from Ching Creek which was the amount he was entitled to under his Ching Creek right, and therefore he received no water in excess of his Ching Creek right, which could be construed as Cottonwood right water. * * *

[W]e conclude that the director of the Department of Water Resources has jurisdiction to determine the question of abandonment and forfeiture and such is required as a preliminary step to performance of his statutory duty in determining whether or not the proposed transfer would injure other water rights. While ordinarily abandonment and forfeiture are to be determined in a separate proceeding, it is clear that when a water right is sought to be transferred and protestors allege that it has been abandoned or forfeited, and that to allow resumption of that right would cause some injury, a determination of abandonment or forfeiture is necessary for the performance of his powers of determining injury. The director is statutorily required to examine all evidence of whether the proposed transfer will injure other water rights or constitute an enlargement of the original right, and evidence which demonstrates that the right sought to be transferred has been abandoned or forfeited, is probative as to whether that transfer would injure other water rights. If a water right has indeed been lost through abandonment or forfeiture, the right to use that water reverts to the state and is subject to further appropriation. * * *

Hence a person making a subsequent appropriation will be injured by resumption of the abandoned or forfeited water right. If a senior right has been abandoned or forfeited, the priority of the original appropriator is lost, and the junior appropriators move up the ladder of priority. If a senior right which had been forfeited or abandoned were allowed to be reinstated through a transfer proceeding, clearly injury would result to otherwise junior appropriators. Priority in time is an essential part of western water law and to diminish one's priority works an undeniable injury to that water right holder.

* * *

We note initially that care must be taken in this type of proceeding to distinguish between abandonment and forfeiture. Each is a related concept but each carries with it distinctive requirements. * * * However, this Court has recently reaffirmed that those terms relate to different legal concepts * * *. Sears v. Berryman, 101 Idaho 843, 623 P.2d 455 (1981); Gilbert v. Smith, 97 Idaho 735, 552 P.2d 1220 (1976). As stated in *Sears v. Berryman,* supra:

> "Abandonment is a common law doctrine involving the occurrence of (1) an intent to abandon and (2) an actual relinquishment or surrender of the water right. Forfeiture, on the other hand, is predicated upon the statutory declaration that all rights to use water are lost where the appropriator fails to make beneficial use of the water for a continuous five year period. I.C. § 42–222(2)."

101 Idaho at 847, 623 P.2d at 459.

Intent to abandon must be proved by clear and convincing evidence of unequivocal acts, and mere non-use of a water right, standing alone, is not sufficient for a *per se* abandonment. *Sears v. Berryman,* supra; *Gilbert v. Smith,* supra. Intent to abandon is a question of fact to be decided by the trier of fact. *Sears v. Berryman,* supra. As in *Sears,* there was no finding by the trial court, nor by the director of the Department, that Jenkins intended to abandon his Cottonwood water right. The record shows only non-use, disclosing no intent to abandon, and hence Jenkins did not lose his water right by common law abandonment.

We then proceed to a determination of whether the findings are sufficient to support a determination of a statutory forfeiture. * * *

Statutory forfeiture is based upon the legislative declaration in I.C. § 42–222(2) that water rights may be lost if they are not applied to a beneficial use for a period of five continuous years. Gilbert v. Smith, 97 Idaho 735, 738, 552 P.2d 1220, 1223 (1976). Certain defenses to forfeiture have been recognized. Extension of the five year period may be made upon a showing of good cause, providing the application for extension is made within the first five-year period. I.C. § 42–222(2). Also wrongful interference with a water right or failure to use the water because of circumstances over which the water right holder has no control have been recognized as defenses. Further, if use of the water right is resumed after the five year period, but before any third parties make a claim in the water, then the courts will decline to declare a forfeiture. Here Jenkins has raised none of these defenses, and the record is devoid of any evidence to indicate that any of the established defenses would be applicable even if argued. The entire case was tried and appealed on Jenkins' theory that he had used the Cottonwood water the entire time.

Forfeitures are not favored, and clear and convincing proof is required to support a forfeiture.

There is substantial, albeit conflicting, evidence indicating that Jenkins failed to use Cottonwood Creek water for a beneficial use between 1961 and 1979, a period of 18 years. The water master testified that he had delivered water from the two creeks for those 18 years, but has not delivered nor been requested to deliver to Jenkins the 2.4 cfs water out of Cottonwood Creek. The trial court found that the channels from Cottonwood Creek to Ching Creek do not carry a regular flow of water except during the spring runoff. Those facts are supported by clear and convincing evidence, and support the conclusion of statutory forfeiture.

* * *

Accordingly, we affirm the order of the district court, which in turn affirmed the decision of the Director of the Department of Water Resources which denied the application for the transfer of the point of diversion of Jenkins' Cottonwood water right. Costs to respondents.

NOTES

1. Abandonment is a common law concept that requires proof of intent to relinquish dominion and control over a property interest and the proponent of abandonment bears the burden of proving the requisite state of mind. Given the high value of water rights, instances where the owner of such rights consciously intends to abandon them are rare. Courts say that intent and the act of relinquishment of dominion and control are separate jural acts. In Edgemont Imp. Co. v. N.S. Tubbs Sheep Co., 115 N.W. 1130 (S.D.1908), the court said "[i]t is

well settled that mere non-use of water does not amount to abandonment, nor is mere lapse of time alone sufficient to establish abandonment. In all cases abandonment is a question of intention." See also Gilbert v. Smith, 552 P.2d 1220 (Idaho 1976), where it was held that fifty-three years of non-use did not constitute abandonment per se. Nevertheless, mere non-use of water or mere lapse of time may create a presumption of intent to abandon the water right. As a practical matter non-use is the best evidence of intent. In Cundy v. Weber, 300 N.W. 17 (S.D.1941), the court, faced with a forty-seven year period of non-use, held that a prima facie showing of intent to abandon may be made by evidence of failure to apply the water to a beneficial use for an unreasonable period of time.

2. Statutes in some states create a rebuttable presumption of abandonment after a certain period of time. Colo.Rev.Stat. § 37–92–402(11) (ten years); Mont.Code Ann. § 85–2–404 (ten years).

What reasons are sufficient to rebut a presumption of intent to abandon? Colorado has held that economic, financial or legal obstacles may be sufficient, Hallenbeck v. Granby Ditch & Reservoir Co., 420 P.2d 419 (Colo.1966), but economic infeasibility is not an excuse, CF & I Steel Corp. v. Purgatoire River Water Conservancy Dist., 515 P.2d 456 (Colo.1973).

The Colorado Supreme Court is moving, albeit uneasily, toward firmer use of abandonment to make more water available for appropriation. It has held that small water rights transfers on paper did not overcome the presumption of abandonment when there was a 29 year period of non-use of hydroelectric rights. City and County of Denver v. Snake River Water Dist., 788 P.2d 772 (Colo.1990). The dissent cited the court's earlier decision in People ex rel. Danielson v. City of Thornton, 775 P.2d 11, 19 (Colo.1989) (actual good faith attempts to sell a water right are strongly indicative of an absence of intent to abandon).

3. Forfeiture is the statutory termination of water rights if they are not used for a given period. E.g., Nev.Rev.Stat. § 533.060 (failure to put water to beneficial use for five successive years results in forfeiture); N.M.Stat.Ann. § 72–5–28 (non-use for a period of four years, followed by a one year notice period, results in reversion to the public); Wyo.Stat.Ann. § 41–3–401 (failure to put water to beneficial use for which it was appropriated for five successive years works a forfeiture of the right); and Or.Rev.Stat. § 540.610(1) (five successive years of non-use of all or part of a water right establishes a rebuttable presumption of forfeiture). See Rencken v. Young, 711 P.2d 954 (Or. 1985).

Although forfeiture statutes often appear straightforward enough, attempts to apply them have revealed the influence of the common law on defenses to temper the harsh consequences. What happens, for instance, where water is put to a beneficial use during one year in a five-year statutory forfeiture period? See Rocky Ford Irr. Co. v. Kents Lake Reservoir Co., 140 P.2d 638 (Utah 1943). What if water is not used at all for the statutory period, but the appropriator resumes the use before any steps are taken to declare a forfeiture? Compare

Bausch v. Myers, 541 P.2d 817 (Or.1975), with Sturgeon v. Brooks, 281 P.2d 675 (Wyo.1955), and Application of Boyer, 248 P.2d 540 (Idaho 1952).

4. Periods of non-use may be excused from the operation of a forfeiture statute for a variety of reasons. Exemptions range from not penalizing an appropriator for non-use during a period of drought to allowing non-use while the holder of the right is on active duty with the armed forces (N.M.Stat.Ann. § 72–5–28(E)). Exemptions raise the question whether the running of the statute is merely suspended for the period of the statutorily excused non-use, or whether the end of the period of excused non-use marks the beginning of a new limitations period. The New Mexico statute addresses this problem. N.M.Stat. Ann. § 75–5–28(D). The statute also allows a one-year grace period during which forfeiture can be avoided by recommencing the use.

Are forfeiture statutes constitutional? The Supreme Court of Nevada had held that they are, even as applied to rights perfected before the state changed applicable law from abandonment to forfeiture. Eureka v. Office of State Engineer of Nev., 826 P.2d 948, 950–51 (Nev.1992). Does the allowance of a defense for circumstances similar to those that rebut intent to abandon solve any constitutional problems with terminating a right for a relatively brief period of non-use? See Sheep Mountain Cattle Co. v. State, Dept. of Ecology, 726 P.2d 55 (Wash.1986) (water right holder entitled to notice and hearing prior to forfeiture). Would a law holding that the failure to use a surface estate for five years results in an escheat to the state be constitutional?

5. An appropriator has rights to 40 cfs and for twenty years raises corn, regularly using 30 cfs. Will the other 10 cfs be held abandoned or forfeited? How will the issue arise?

6. In what kind of proceedings can the issue of forfeiture be raised? Note that in *Jenkins,* the proceeding was for a change in the point of diversion. Jurisdiction over water transfers and related actions may be split between administrative agencies and courts. If the courts have concurrent jurisdiction with administrative agencies, who should make the initial factual determinations? The Wyoming Supreme Court has applied the doctrine of primary jurisdiction. In cases where the issue of abandonment is "intertwined with other issues" the court proposed that the Board of Control adopt rules permitting a trial court to certify the abandonment issue to the board for initial determination. Under the doctrine of primary jurisdiction, when the issue returns to the court with an administrative record judicial review is circumscribed by the usual limited standards of review provided by state administrative procedure acts. Having said all this, the court concluded by observing that the doctrine of primary jurisdiction is flexible and its application will depend on whether its purpose— allocating the power to make initial determinations of fact and law to the better decider—will be "aided * * * in the particular litigation." Kearney Lake, Land & Reservoir Co. v. Lake Desmet Reservoir Co., 487 P.2d 324 (Wyo.1971).

2. Prescription

Many western states have applied the assertion of public ownership to make a state permit the exclusive method of acquiring a water right. Thus, prescriptive rights both as against the state and among private parties are barred on the same principle of sovereign immunity that precludes gaining rights to government land by adverse possession. See A. Dan Tarlock, Law of Water Rights and Resources § 5.18[4] (1988). Several states' statutes specifically prohibit the acquisition of water rights by prescription or adverse possession, including Alaska, Idaho, Nevada, Kansas, and Utah. Utah's law (Utah Code Ann. § 73–3–1) was passed after the state supreme court held that water rights could be established by prescription. Hammond v. Johnson, 66 P.2d 894 (Utah 1937). In Idaho, although prescriptive claims are barred by statute, the courts continue to entertain adverse possession claims. Boise–Kuna Irrigation Dist. v. Gross, 801 P.2d 1291 (Idaho 1990). The issue was extensively debated in California until the supreme court held that the state's permit system was the exclusive means of acquiring a post–1914 appropriative right as against the state, but left open the question of whether prescriptive rights would be recognized among private users. People v. Shirokow, 605 P.2d 859 (Cal.1980).

Independent of theoretical sovereign immunity principles, what practical objections are there to the recognition of prescriptive rights against state-created prior appropriation rights? See Coryell v. Robinson, 194 P.2d 342 (Colo.1948), holding that under a prior appropriation system everyone has a right to assume that persons using water do so pursuant to the priority system. See also, Campbell v. Wyoming Dev. Co., 100 P.2d 124 (Wyo.1940).

H. PROPERTY RIGHTS AND CONSTITUTIONAL TAKINGS

Water rights are a form of property but "water rights" do not amount to ownership of the liquid itself (though it is possible to own a container of water as personalty). A property right in water is usufructuary in that it only entitles the owner to the *right to use* the water.

The right to use water under both riparian and prior appropriation systems has been dramatically redefined in the past century. All property is necessarily defined by government action; property exists only to the extent that it is legally protected by government. The amount of water that rights holders can use has been changed through legislative, administrative, and judicial decisions. Similarly, the manner of use has been limited and methods of perfecting rights have been changed. Some states have switched systems, going from riparian rights to prior appropriation.

The Fifth Amendment to the federal constitution, as applied through the Fourteenth Amendment, says that state governments cannot take private property for a public use without just compensation. Is the modification of water rights to meet the changing needs and perceptions of society a "taking" requiring compensation? How much can rights be changed before it constitutes a taking?

1. Changing to Statutory Systems

Over the years, most riparian and appropriation states have modified their water administration by changing to a permit system. See pages 235–44, supra. For riparians, such a change may result in the loss or diminishment of common law rights available to owners of streamside land. Under the common law, riparian land owners typically are entitled to all the water they can reasonably use solely by reason of their location. If a riparian's needs change, or a new use arises, the riparian may increase the quantity used, subject to being challenged by other users arguing the use is unreasonable. Under the typical permit system, both the quantity of water and the uses to which the water may be put are dictated by the terms of the permit. Changes may not be made without the approval of the permitting authority. If the use is inefficient or unreasonable, it may not be allowed.

In many states, permit holders will lose their rights if the water is not used diligently. Permit holders may forfeit their permits if they fail to put water to use within a specific period of time, usually two or three years. As permits expire, they are not automatically renewed, but instead are subjected to the same scrutiny as new applications. This requirement detracts from the value of both appropriative and riparian rights. Holders of expired permits must justify the reasonableness and efficiency of their water use on the same basis as new applicants. This ensures that the permitting process remains responsive to changing needs by aiding the entry of new uses into the system, and encouraging the application of economically efficient technology.

Obviously, riparian landowners suffer significant limitations on their common law rights under such statutory systems. Expectations may be disappointed and the apparent value of a riparian's estate may be diluted. Surprisingly, there have been few suits directly challenging the constitutionality of these statutes. Richard Ausness explains that this is probably because most state regulations are neither comprehensive nor severely restrictive. Richard C. Ausness, *Water Use Permits in a Riparian State: Problems and Proposals,* 66 Ky.L.J. 191, 240–42 (1977).

IN RE WATERS OF LONG VALLEY CREEK STREAM SYSTEM

Supreme Court of California, 1979.
25 Cal.3d 339, 158 Cal.Rptr. 350, 599 P.2d 656.

Mosk, Justice.

The significant problem in this case is the extent to which the State Water Resources Control Board (Board) has the power to define and otherwise limit prospective riparian rights when, pursuant to the statutory adjudication procedure set forth in Water Code section 2500 et seq., it determines all claimed rights to the use of water in a stream system. * * *

The action arises out of a statutory proceeding to adjudicate the rights of all claimants to the waters of the Long Valley Creek Stream System (stream system) in Lassen, Sierra and Plumas Counties. * * *

Because of the limited water supply, there has been prolific litigation among the various water claimants in the area since at least 1883. In the interest of resolving the conflicts that have fostered such litigation, nine claimants filed a petition in 1966 with the Board for statutory adjudication of all water rights in the stream system. (Wat.Code, § 2525.) The staff of the Board conducted a preliminary investigation and recommended in favor of the petition, which the Board subsequently granted. Thereafter the Board prepared and published a notice of the proceedings (Id., §§ 2526, 2527), and all persons claiming a right to the waters of the stream system notified the Board of their intention to file a claim. (Id., § 2528.) As required by Water Code section 2550, the Board then conducted an extensive investigation; it published a report containing the results of this investigation for the principal purpose of assisting water users in filing their claims of right.

After filing its report, the Board advised persons who notified it of their intention to file a claim that the claim and proof in support of it must be formally presented. It heard 234 claims and proofs, and 42 contests thereto, concerning the rights of the stream system. After consideration of these claims, proofs and contests, it "entered of record in its office an order determining and establishing the several rights to the water of the stream system." (Id., § 2700.)

Donald Ramelli (Ramelli), as a party aggrieved or dissatisfied with the order of determination, filed a notice of exceptions in the superior court pursuant to Water Code section 2757. Ramelli owns land upon which Balls Creek originates. For the past approximately 60 years he and his predecessors have irrigated 89 acres of this land, but before the Board he claimed prospective riparian rights in the creek for an additional 2,884 acres. The order of determination nevertheless awarded him various amounts of water for only the 89 acres as to which he was currently exercising his riparian rights; it extinguished entirely his claim as a riparian landowner to the future use of water with respect to the remaining 2,884 acres.

The trial court denied Ramelli's exceptions and entered a decree consistent with the Board's order of determination. Ramelli appealed from the decree, and we reverse.

* * *

In this case the Board entirely extinguished Ramelli's riparian claim to the future use of water. Such extinction raises a substantial constitutional issue as a result of our holding in Tulare Dist. v. Lindsay–Strathmore Dist. (1935) supra, 3 Cal.2d 489, 531, 45 P.2d 972, that section 11 of the Water Commission Act violated article X, section 2 (formerly art. XIV, § 3); the section, as stated above, provided in essence for the complete extinction of riparian rights that remained unused for 10 consecutive years. We consequently decline to construe the statutory adjudication procedure as authorizing the Board to extinguish altogether future riparian rights. * * *

A.

Article X, section 2, acknowledges that in California a riparian landowner has historically possessed a common law right to the future use of water in a stream system. The provision does so by declaring that "The right to water or to the use or flow of water in or from any natural stream or water course in this State is and shall be limited to such water as shall be *reasonably required for the beneficial use to be served * * *"* and that "Riparian rights in a stream or water course attach to, but to no more than so much of the flow thereof as may be required or used consistently with this section, for the purposes for which such lands are, *or may be made adaptable,* in view of such reasonable and beneficial uses * * *." (Cal.Const., art. X, § 2, italics added.)

As the above language also discloses, however, riparian rights are limited by the concept of reasonable and beneficial use. Moreover, they must not be exercised in a manner that is inconsistent with constitutional policy provisions that are to govern interpretations of water rights in California. In light of these policies and of the constitutional intent to limit unduly expansive interpretations of water rights that would contravene them, it becomes clear that article X, section 2, enables the Legislature to exercise broad authority in defining and otherwise limiting future riparian rights, and to delegate this authority to the Board.

* * * This authorization discloses that the framers of article X, section 2, recognized that the promotion of its salutary policies would require granting the Legislature broad flexibility in determining the appropriate means for protecting scarce state water resources.[6]

6. The importance of broad legislative authority for the conservation and regulation of scarce water resources has also been recognized by courts in other states. For example, in Belle Fourche Irrigation District v. Smiley (1970) 84 S.D. 701, 176 N.W.2d 239, the South Dakota Supreme Court upheld a statute that recognized riparian rights as vested only "to the extent of the existing beneficial use"; the court reasoned that the statute was an appropriate exercise of the state's power to provide for the "maximum utilization of the water resources of the state." (Id., at p. 245.) In State v. Knapp (1949) 167 Kan. 546, 207 P.2d 440, the Kansas Supreme Court sustained a statute that inter alia (1) limited vested riparian rights to those uses actually instituted at the time the legislation was enacted or within three years prior thereto, and (2) required approval from the state for the commencement of any further uses. (See also Brown v. Chase (1923) 125 Wash. 542, 217 P. 23, 26 [water of nonnavigable stream subject to appropriation when riparian cannot use it beneficially, "either directly or prospectively, within a reason-able time"]; In re Hood River, 114 Or. 112, (1924) 227 P. 1065, 1084 ["state may change its common-law rule as to every stream within its dominion, and permit the appropriation of the flowing water for such purposes as it deems wise"]; c.f. Baeth v. Hoisveen (N.Dak.1968) 157 N.W.2d 728, 732 [no absolute ownership of groundwater that has not actually been diverted and applied to a beneficial use]; Knight v. Grimes (1964) 80 S.D. 517, 127 N.W.2d 708, 711 [right to take and use percolating groundwater does not constitute actual ownership prior to withdrawal]; Williams v. City of Wichita (1962) 190 Kan. 317, 374 P.2d 578, 589, app. dism. (1963) 375 U.S. 7 [legislature may change principles of common law and abrogate decisions made thereunder when in its opinion it is necessary to the public interest]; Baumann v. Smrha (1956) 145 F.Supp. 617, 624, affd. 352 U.S. 863 [state has power "to modify or reject the doctrine of riparian rights because unsuited to the conditions in the state and to put into force the doctrine of prior appropriation and application to beneficial use or reasonable use"].)

Our conclusion that article X, section 2, does not preclude legislative or administrative determinations with respect to the nature of future riparian rights becomes even more readily apparent upon examination of the history of the provision. Article X, section 2, was adopted by amendment in 1928. It was a direct response to the decision by this court in Herminghaus v. Southern California Edison Co. (1926) 200 Cal. 81, 252 P. 607, which held that a downstream riparian's right against an inferior upstream appropriator permits him to command the entire flow of the stream to flood his pastureland.

* * *

We next examine whether such a broad grant of authority to the Board is consistent with the constitutional holding of Tulare Dist. v. Lindsay–Strathmore Dist., supra, 3 Cal.2d 489, 45 P.2d 972. Ramelli argues that a riparian's prospective right cannot be defined or otherwise limited in a statutory proceeding because of our holding in Tulare that section 11 of the Water Commission Act—which declared that 10 years' nonuse, without an intervening use, constituted an abandonment of a riparian right—was "incongruous and in violation of the spirit of the constitutional provision * * *" (Id. at p. 531, 45 P.2d at p. 989.) Ramelli's expansive reading of the limits *Tulare* places on legislative authority is unsupportable in light of the amendment's grant of authority to the Legislature to enact laws in the furtherance of the constitutionally expressed state water policy. Moreover, *Tulare* is distinguishable from the issue before us in that the statute therein treated the right as automatically abandoned as a result of 10 years' nonuse, without consideration of other needs and uses of the water in the stream system. The statute therefore was inconsistent with the mandate of the amendment to promote the reasonable beneficial use of state waters.

It is well established that what is a reasonable use of water varies with the facts and circumstances of the particular case. And it appears self-evident that the reasonableness of a riparian use cannot be determined without considering the effect of such use on all the needs of those in the stream system, nor can it be made "in vacuo isolated from state-wide considerations of transcendent importance." (Joslin v. Marin Muni. Water Dist. (1967) 67 Cal.2d 132, 140, 60 Cal.Rptr. 377, 382, 429 P.2d 889, 894). * * * The Legislature has enacted a comprehensive administrative scheme for the final determination of *all* rights in a stream system. (Wat.Code, § 2500 et seq.) The statutory adjudication procedure involves a complex balancing of both public and private interests, with the final decree assuring certainty to the existing economy and reasonable predictability to the uses of water in a stream system. In so doing, it falls within the amendment's specific grant of authority to the Legislature. (Cal.Const., art. X, § 2.) That the statutory adjudication procedure promotes the policies of the amendment is reflected in a recent report of the Governor's Commission To Review California Water Rights Law. (Final Rep. (Dec.1978).) This document identifies uncertainty as one of the major problems in contemporary

California water rights law, and it discloses that riparian rights are a principal source of this uncertainty.

Uncertainty concerning the rights of water users has pernicious effects. Initially, it inhibits long range planning and investment for the development and use of waters in a stream system.

* * * And, as the Board engineer observed, the inconclusive fragmentary definition of water rights resulting from that litigation was "the prime reason for the proposed adjudication." The principal cause of this untoward effect appears to be that a private suit for determining title to water binds only those who are parties to the suit; such suits are inadequate, however, because shortages in supply or new appropriations or riparian uses have the potential for bringing all water users on the stream in conflict. * * *

Finally, uncertainty impairs the state's administration of water rights. * * *

B.

A more difficult question is whether the Board may constitutionally extinguish a riparian landowner's unexercised claim to the use of water. * * *

* * * In light of *Tulare's* holding that section 11 of the Water Commission Act was unconstitutional, however, we are reluctant to conclude that the Board may altogether extinguish a riparian's future claim when it has not been established that the imposition of other less drastic limitations on the claim would be less effective in promoting the most reasonable and beneficial use of the stream system. Because no such showing has been made in this case, it is clear that the Board's decision to extinguish Ramelli's future riparian claim raises a serious constitutional issue. Thus, since the Legislature has not clearly expressed an intention that the statute should be construed otherwise, we interpret it as not authorizing the Board in these circumstances to extinguish altogether Ramelli's claim to the future use of waters in the Long Valley stream system.

* * *

Thus, the Board is authorized to decide that an unexercised riparian claim loses its priority with respect to all rights currently being exercised. Moreover, to the extent that an unexercised riparian right may also create uncertainty with respect to permits of appropriation that the Board may grant after the statutory adjudication procedure is final, and may thereby continue to conflict with the public interest in reasonable and beneficial use of state waters, the Board may also determine that the future riparian right shall have a lower priority than any uses of water it authorizes before the riparian in fact attempts to exercise his right. In other words, while we interpret the Water Code as not authorizing the Board to extinguish altogether a future riparian right, the Board may make determinations as to the scope, nature and priority of the right that it deems reasonably necessary to the promotion of the state's interest in fostering the most reasonable and beneficial use of its scarce water resources.

* * *

The judgment is reversed for further proceedings consistent with this opinion.

BIRD, C.J., and TOBRINER and NEWMAN, JJ., concur.

RICHARDSON, JUSTICE, concurring and dissenting.

* * * [T]he applicable cases expressly *deny* authority to limit or fix prospective riparian uses "until the need for such use arises," because at all times such uses remain "paramount to any right of the appropriator." (*Tulare,* supra, 3 Cal.2d at p. 525, 45 P.2d at p. 986.) Although a *presently exercised* riparian use must be "reasonable and beneficial" under the constitutional provision, no limitation or quantification of a reasonable *future* use is possible in light of the difficulty in predicting future needs.

* * *

CLARK, J., concurs.

MANUEL, JUSTICE, concurring and dissenting.

* * * I agree that although the subject provisions of the Water Code should not be interpreted to permit the Board to altogether extinguish the presently unused portion of a riparian right, they may be interpreted in a manner consistent with the relevant constitutional provision (Cal.Const., art. X, § 2; formerly art. XIV, § 3) to permit the Board to undertake a present quantification of the right in order to bring about certainty and thereby promote the efficient and beneficial use of the water resources of this state. I do not agree, however, that in the course of such a determination the Board has the power to fix such a right at the level of its present use and "determine that the future riparian right shall have a lower priority than any uses of water [the Board] authorizes before the riparian in fact attempts to exercise his right." In my view the exercise of such a power would be plainly inconsistent with the provisions of article X, section 2, of our state Constitution; the considerations which have led the majority to interpret the relevant Water Code provisions to preclude the extinguishment of the unused portion of a riparian right also demand that the same provisions be read to preclude the procedure here approved. I conclude, in short, that in permitting the Board to assign less than riparian status to the unused portion of a riparian right, the majority has essentially approved the extinguishment of that portion of the right—and thereby has reached a result inconsistent with its fundamental holding and the clear command of the Constitution.

* * *

Hearing denied; CLARK, RICHARDSON and MANUEL, JJ., dissenting.

NOTES

1. If there are already more claims to water than there is water in Balls Creek, is it any consolation to Ramelli that the court refused "to

extinguish altogether future riparian rights" while making them subject to all existing uses? Does the decision leave Ramelli, as a riparian landowner, with any advantage over nonriparians who may have a future use for water?

2. Was the court's resolution necessary to carry out the purposes of the California constitutional provision and the statutory adjudication procedure? What do you think of Justice Manuel's suggestion that unused riparian rights be quantified? Is the overriding policy to eliminate uncertainty or to eliminate the riparian doctrine?

3. In Fox River Paper Co. v. Railroad Comm'n of Wisconsin, 274 U.S. 651 (1927) the Court held that a state can redefine property rights so as to deprive a riparian of a reservoir site.

2. Conversion From Riparian to Appropriation Systems

The three Pacific Coast states and the six states divided by the 100th meridian were first settled in their more humid regions. They applied riparian law on private lands, and only later moved—in varying degrees—toward an appropriation system. This has created so-called dual or hybrid systems of water rights. States that have switched to prior appropriation have tried to make the new system the exclusive one, but there are constitutional barriers to a quick transition. When a state shifts from the common law to a property rights system that places substantial limits on the use of a resource, holders of common law rights may argue that the new property rights regime is an unconstitutional taking of property without due process of law. The issue, however, is not a hard one for courts because common law rights are seldom totally eliminated, and holders of unexercised rights may still perfect rights under the new system. Many of the cases raising such a challenge are cited in note 6 of In re Waters of Long Valley Creek Stream System, page 367, supra.

Wasserburger v. Coffee, 141 N.W.2d 738 (Neb.1966), illustrates the relatively simple change from the riparian system based in common law to an appropriation system like those developed in other states. In *Wasserburger* the Nebraska Supreme Court faced several issues: (1) *when* common law riparian rights had been modified by legislative adoption of the prior appropriation doctrine; (2) *what* land patented prior to the legislative modification retained its riparian status; and (3) *how* to resolve the conflicts between riparian and appropriative claims. The court held that the appropriation system was not adopted by the legislature until the Irrigation Act of 1895 expressly dedicated the use of unappropriated water of every stream to the people subject to appropriation for beneficial use. Removing land from the public domain and putting it in private ownership prior to the 1895 Act could, therefore, make a riparian water right superior to an appropriative right. Any land later severed from the riparian tract, however, lost its riparian status. See discussion of the unity of title rule, pages 68–70, supra. Finally, the court held that riparian rights would be protected even against appropriations prior in time when an appropriator intentionally caused substantial harm to a riparian proprietor or the harmful appropriation was "unreasonable." The reasonableness of an appropriation turns on the social value of the respective uses, the extent of the harm, the practicality of allowing both the riparian and the appropriative uses, and the time the respective uses were initiated.

The principal problem of moving from riparianism to appropriation is, of course, what to do with unused riparian rights. The Oregon statute mentioned in *California Oregon Power Co.,* page 167, supra, simply extinguished them, raising a substantive due process question that the Supreme Court ducked. Lower courts have often had to confront the question. Kansas, for example, was not a Desert Land Act state, but the legislature moved from a riparian system to an exclusive appropriation system in which "vested right" was defined as the right to continue to use water "having actually been applied to any beneficial use" when the statute was enacted or within the three years before enactment. All waters were then declared to be subject to appropriation as provided in the statute, but "vested rights" were excepted from the appropriation regime. Kan.Stat.Ann. § 82a–701, 703. In Williams v. Wichita, 374 P.2d 578 (Kan.1962), appeal dismissed 375 U.S. 7 (1963), the constitutionality of the statute was raised. An overlying owner who claimed common law rights to the future use of groundwater sued to enjoin the city from pumping from the aquifer under a statutory appropriation permit. The court sustained the statute and entered judgment for the city. See also, F. Arthur Stone & Sons v. Gibson, 630 P.2d 1164 (Kan.1981).

South Dakota has ended up in the same place, although the path was more tortuous. The South Dakota court originally adopted the riparian rule and invalidated a broad appropriation statute enacted in 1907 as an unconstitutional taking of riparian property rights. St. Germain Irr. Co. v. Hawthorn Ditch Co., 143 N.W. 124 (S.D.1913). Later, however, the court backtracked to some extent by holding that the Desert Land Act severed land and water and that federal patents issued after 1877 carried no water rights with them. Cook v. Evans, 185 N.W. 262 (S.D.1921), and Haaser v. Englebrecht, 186 N.W. 572 (S.D.1922). Although Mr. Justice Sutherland cited these cases in *California Oregon Power Co.,* the South Dakota court refused the compliment, taking advantage of the opportunity provided by that case to declare its previous decisions wrong, and holding that in South Dakota the Desert Land Act did not sever land and water and therefore riparian rights attached to all land grants, Platt v. Rapid City, 291 N.W. 600 (S.D.1940). Then in 1955, the legislature sought to abolish unused riparian rights, invoking the Kansas technique of defining vested rights to include only rights to water in actual use. 1955 S.D.Sess. Laws Ch. 430; S.D. Codified Laws Ann. §§ 46–1–1 to –9. The statute was held constitutional in Knight v. Grimes, 127 N.W.2d 708 (S.D.1964). North Dakota reached a similar result in Baeth v. Hoisveen, 157 N.W.2d 728 (N.D.1968). A 1970 South Dakota case, Belle Fourche Irr. Dist. v. Smiley, 176 N.W.2d 239 (S.D.1970), sustained the statute again, but held that when an appeal is taken from a water resources commission finding on the quantity of a riparian's vested right, the commission must present evidence to the trial court to sustain the commission determination.

The problem of dual rights is especially complex in Texas. Vested riparian rights are recognized for lands granted before July 1, 1895, the date of the enactment of the Irrigation Act of 1895. In brief, riparians were entitled to the ordinary flow of the stream and appropriators to the flood waters. Motl v. Boyd, 286 S.W. 458 (Tex.1926). The 1967 Water Rights Adjudication Act (Tex. Water Code Ann. § 11.303(b)) limited riparian rights to the water actually put to a beneficial use between 1963–1967. An intermediate court of appeals held that the Act was an unconstitutional taking in Schero v. Texas Dep't of Water Resources, 630 S.W.2d 516 (Tex.Ct.App.1982), but the Texas Supreme Court followed the precedents discussed above and held that the Act was constitutional. In re Adjudication of the Water Rights of the Upper Guadalupe Segment of the Guadalupe River Basin, 642 S.W.2d 438 (Tex.1982); In re Adjudication of the Water Rights in the Llano River Watershed of the Colorado River Basin, 642 S.W.2d 446 (Tex. 1982). In *Upper Guadalupe* the Texas Supreme Court cited Texaco, Inc. v. Short, 454 U.S. 516 (1982) which held that the Indiana Dormant Mineral Act, which revests mineral interests unused for twenty years in the surface estate if the interest has not been otherwise maintained, was neither a taking nor a violation of Texaco's right to procedural due process.

Washington switched from the California dual system to an exclusive prior appropriation system in 1917. Existing riparian rights were preserved, Wash.Rev.Code Ann. § 90.03.010, and a 1923 decision, Brown v. Chase, 217 P. 23 (Wash.1923), stated that unexercised rights put to a beneficial use within a reasonable period after 1917 were also preserved. The state supreme court has held that all rights must have been put to use by 1932, the year suggested by the state, because fifteen years is a constitutionally sufficient period of notice for riparians to adjust to the new requirements for the perfection of a water right. Matter of Deadman Creek Drainage Basin in Spokane County, 694 P.2d 1071 (Wash.1985).

3. Controls and Limits on Use of Existing Rights

What happens to water rights holders when the state, through its administrative, legislative, or judicial branch, decides to require a more efficient use of water by holders of existing rights?

ENTERPRISE IRR. DIST. v. WILLIS

Supreme Court of Nebraska, 1939.
135 Neb. 827, 284 N.W. 326.

CARTER, JUSTICE.

The record discloses that in the year 1889 the Enterprise Ditch Company made an appropriation of water from the North Platte river, in accordance with the law of appropriation then in existence, in an amount in excess of 138.90 second-feet, subject only to the common-law rule that no more water could be diverted and appropriated than could be applied to a beneficial use. * * * The irrigation law of 1895 limited for the first time the quantity of water that could be appropriated to a specific amount; the statute stating "that no allotment for irrigation shall exceed one cubic foot per second for each 70 acres of land for which said appropriation shall be made." Laws 1895, c. 69, § 20. The same act also provided: "Nothing in this act contained shall be so construed as to interfere with or impair the rights to water appropriated and acquired prior to the passage of this act." Laws 1895, c. 69, § 49. In 1911, the legislature placed a further limitation upon the quantity of water that could be appropriated, the statute providing, "that no allotment for irrigation shall exceed one cubic foot per second of time for each seventy acres of land nor *three acre-feet in the aggregate during one calendar year for each acre of land for which such appropriation shall be made."* Laws 1911, c. 153, § 19. (Italics ours). These same limitations appear in the irrigation law contained in the civil administrative code law of 1919. Laws 1919, c. 190, p. 837. The 1919 law also provided: "Nothing in this article contained shall be so construed as to interfere with or impair the rights to water appropriated and acquired prior to the fourth day of April, 1895." Laws 1919, p. 832. * * * It is the contention of the defendants that the limitation of three acre-feet in the aggregate during one calendar year for each acre of land for which the appropriation shall have been made * * * applies to plaintiff's appropriation and, that amount having been exceeded at the time this suit was commenced, the plaintiff was not entitled to any more water and defendants should not be enjoined from closing the headgates of plaintiff's canal. Plaintiff contends that its appropriation is a right vested as of March 28, 1889, and that the statute in question has no retroactive force and, if such retroactive construction be placed upon it, it is violative of the due process clauses of the Constitution of Nebraska (article 1, § 3) and the Fourteenth Amendment to the Constitution of the United States, U.S.C.A. Defendants contend that the statute is a proper exercise of the police power of the state and is not inhibited by either the state or federal Constitutions.

* * * It is a principle of the common law that one may not divert more water, even under a valid appropriation, than he can put to a beneficial use. While many elements must be considered in determining whether water has been put to beneficial use, one is that it shall not exceed the least amount of water that experience indicates is necessary in the exercise of good husbandry for the production of crops. The extent to which landowners need and are entitled to have the benefit of irrigation water under a vested appropriation ordinarily depends upon aridity, rainfall, location, soil porosity, adaptability to particular forms of production and the use to which the irrigable lands are put. In other words, the duty of water may be defined as such a quantity of water necessary, when economically conducted and applied to the land without unnecessary loss, as will result in the successful growing of crops. 2 Kinney, Irrigation and Water Rights (2d Ed.) secs. 902 and 903.

Many persons engaged in farming within the plaintiff district testified that the water used by them had been used in the usual and ordinary way to produce crops, that there had been no waste or misapplication of the irrigation water, and that, at the time the closing of the headgate was threatened, their crops were in need of water.

They also testified that a failure to obtain water would have resulted in a material decrease in the crop returns from their lands.

* * * It must be borne in mind that the quantity of water that can be diverted under a vested water right for irrigation purposes is an element of importance equal to that of its priority in determining its value. While such a right may be regulated and supervised by the state and its administrative officers for the purpose of protecting all adjudicated rights of appropriators having an interest in the waters of the stream, yet a law of this character cannot operate to divest rights already vested at the time it was enacted. While vested water rights may be interfered with within reasonable limits under the police power of the state to secure a proper regulation and supervision of them for the public good, any interference that limits the quantity of water or changes the date of its priority to the material injury of its holder is more than regulation and supervision and extends into the field generally referred to as a deprivation of a vested right.

In a similar situation the legislature of California declared that the term "useful or beneficial purposes" shall not be construed to mean the use in any one year of more than two and one-half acre-feet of water per acre in the irrigation of uncultivated areas of land not devoted to cultivated crops. It was contended that the act of the legislature was justified as a proper exercise of the police power of the state. In holding to the contrary, the supreme court of that state said: "* * * To concede that the state Legislature has the right arbitrarily to fix as to [unadulterated lands] the amount of water which the riparian proprietor may take and use thereon would be to concede an equal power to make a like arbitrary fixation in respect to cultivated areas also, entirely regardless of the foregoing elements which are necessarily the determining factors in such fixation. To concede this would be to concede to the legislative department of the state government the arbitrary power to destroy vested rights in private property of every kind and character." Herminghaus v. Southern California Edison Co., 200 Cal. 81, 252 P. 607, 622. We are of the opinion that the principle of law set forth in the foregoing case is correct and that it has particular application to the facts in the case at bar. The evidence, as we view it, shows that the plaintiff district has diverted more than three acre-feet of water for every irrigable acre in its district. It further shows that the water used has been applied to a beneficial use without waste. It is not disputed that additional water was required when the injunction was threatened and that plaintiff's appropriation, without the limitations complained of, was sufficient to provide it without infringing upon the rights of prior appropriators. The evidence of the expert witnesses tendered by the defendants was not sufficient to overcome the undisputed evidence offered by the plaintiff. * * * We fully realize the difficulty of regulating and supervising the holder of an appropriation such as the plaintiff possesses. However, the difficulty must be overcome by regulation and control over the district by virtue of a proper exercise of the police power of the state. The difficulties of the situation cannot be advanced as a justification for violating vested property rights.

NOTES

1. To what extent does *Willis* curb the ability of legislatures to limit use of water under existing rights by passing "duty of water" statutes like the one at issue in that case? Is the decision inconsistent with the *Alamosa–La Jara* case, page 281, supra, in which the court held that the state engineer could require senior users to drill wells to get water they historically had taken from the stream in order to allow for fuller use of water by juniors?

2. If the administrative and legislative branches of state governments are controlled by takings law (i.e., the Fifth and Fourteenth Amendments), what controls are placed on the judiciary? Professor Barton Thompson writes that the United States Supreme Court has never held that a judicial redefinition of property is a taking. Barton Thompson, *Judicial Takings*, 76 Va.L.Rev. 1449 (1990). Is the judiciary exempt from takings law? Should it be?

ROBINSON v. ARIYOSHI

United States Court of Appeals, Ninth Circuit, 1985.
753 F.2d 1468, remanded for further proceedings, 477 U.S. 902, 106 S.Ct. 3269,
91 L.Ed.2d 560 (1986), opinion vacated, 887 F.2d 215 (9th Cir.1989).

GOODWIN, CIRCUIT JUDGE.

The district court, in an action brought under 42 U.S.C. § 1983 challenging an alleged threat to divest plaintiffs' irrigation water rights, enjoined the named state officials from taking any action to enforce a recent decree of the state courts that appeared to be adverse to the property rights of the plaintiffs. * * *

Background

In 1889 the predecessors in title of the plaintiffs, Gay and Robinson, owned substantial land grants within the ahupuaa of Hanapepe, a local designation of land extending from the top of the central mountain mass of the Island of Kauai to the sea and roughly encompassing the drainage of the Hanapepe River. At the mauka, or upper part of the ahupuaa, the annual rainfall ranges from four to five hundred inches. At lower elevations rainfall averages as little as twenty-three inches and in many parts of the ahupuaa most types of agriculture are not possible without irrigation.

In the early days of the development of sugar cane fields on Kauai, the owners and lessees of the privately-owned lands built dams, flumes and ditches in order to distribute the abundant rainfall from the wettest portions of their lands to fertile but dry neighboring land areas. As the years went by and more lands were brought into production, the irrigation works became fairly elaborate. * * *

In the 1920's the territorial government's increasing interest in water for the development of dry lands at lower elevations, some of which were owned or controlled by the Territory of Hawaii, produced litigation which in 1931 resulted in a decree of the Territorial Court. The Territorial Court held that Gay and Robinson were the owners of "normal surplus" water flowing from their Ilis of Koula and Manuahi into the Hanapepe River, and confirmed their right to divert that water for use outside the Hanapepe drainage. *Territory v. Gay,* 31 Hawaii 376, 387–88 (1930), *aff'd,* 52 F.2d 356 (9th Cir.), *cert. denied,* 284 U.S. 677, 52 S.Ct. 131, 76 L.Ed. 572 (1931) *(Territory I).* * * * The Hawaiian Statehood Act, confirmed existing statutory law of the territory and approved the new state's constitution. Gay and Robinson claim that the state constitution includes protection of their court-decreed and vested right to divert and use water from their mauka lands drained by the Koula and Manuahi branches of the Hanapepe. The state officials, however, argue as if the matter were open for a fresh decision, that the private use outside the ahupuaa of a large volume of Hanapepe water by Gay and Robinson and their associates is both undesirable and contrary to state law.

In 1959 the McBryde Sugar Company commenced in the new state court an action against a number of defendants, among whom Gay and Robinson were named. * * * The Hawaii state trial court in 1968 declared in a 65–page decision the rights of the parties including "other" small holders whose "ancient" and "appurtenant" rights were acknowledged by the principal parties in the controversy. * * *

The Supreme Court of Hawaii in 1973 *sua sponte* overruled all territorial cases to the contrary and adopted the English common law doctrine of riparian rights. *McBryde Sugar Co. v. Robinson, et al.,* 54 Hawaii 174, 504 P.2d 1330, 1344 (1973). In this decision, which we will refer to as *McBryde I,* the court also held *sua sponte* that there was no such legal category as "normal daily surplus water" and declared that the state, as sovereign, owned and had the exclusive right to control the flow of the Hanapepe River. *McBryde I* further announced that because the flow of the Hanapepe was the sovereign property of the State of Hawaii, McBryde's claim of a prescriptive right to divert water could not be sustained against the state.

The parties adversely affected by the holding in *McBryde I* petitioned for rehearing and the state supreme court allowed a rehearing on the limited issue of the proper construction of Hawaii Rev.Stat. § 7–1 (a century-old territorial statute dealing largely with drinking water and rights of way on roads over private lands) and the meaning of the word "appurtenant". The parties attempted to enlarge the scope of the rehearing to include state and federal constitutional claims but their attempt was summarily rejected. *See Robinson v. Ariyoshi,* 441 F.Supp. 559, 564 (D.Hawaii 1977) *(Robinson I).* Rehearing was denied in *McBryde Sugar Co. v. Robinson,* 55 Hawaii 260, 517 P.2d 26 (1973) *(McBryde II).* In due course the Supreme Court of the United States denied review, *McBryde Sugar Co. v. Hawaii,* 417 U.S. 962, 94 S.Ct. 3164, 41 L.Ed.2d 1135 (1974) *(McBryde III),* and in 1974 this litigation began in the United States District Court for the District of Hawaii. * * *

* * *

The state conceded at oral argument that the Fourteenth Amendment would require it to pay just compensation if it attempted to take vested property rights. The substantive question, therefore, is whether the state can declare, by court decision, that the water rights in this case have not vested. The short answer is no.

The district court's opinion in *Robinson I* makes clear that considerable property interests were at stake.

In summary form, the interests affected by *McBryde I* and *II* include:

(1) The water rights which as private property had been bought, sold and leased freely, and which had been the subject of state and local taxation as well as condemnation for ditch rights-of-way;

(2) The expenditures by G & R and, [its successors] of almost one million dollars in building an extensive water transportation system for irrigation of their sugar lands, lands now potentially destined to become pasture; and

(3) The interests of McBryde Sugar Company, which stands, if its rights are vested, in the same position as Gay and Robinson.

On April 28, 1930, the Supreme Court of the Territory of Hawaii, in litigation between substantially the same parties that are here today, except for the McBryde Sugar Company, held that the common law doctrine of riparian rights was not in force in Hawaii with reference to surplus waters of the normal flow of a stream. The same court further held that the owner (konohiki) of the land (ili) could use the water collected on his ili as he saw fit, subject to the rights of downstream owners to drinking water and other domestic uses that the parties in all this litigation have agreed have not been in controversy. * * * When that case reached this court, we affirmed in an opinion which stated that the definition of property rights and water rights in light of the feudal history of land tenure in the islands was best left to the local courts. Territory of Hawaii v. Gay, 52 F.2d 356, 359 (9th Cir.1931) (*Territory II*). The water law, at least between the territorial government and the Gay and Robinson interests, thereafter remained settled until statehood.

Relying upon the decrees in *Territory I and II*, Gay and Robinson proceeded with further development of their plantations. By the time this litigation reached the district court, in *Robinson I*, improvements costing many millions of dollars had been constructed on the affected lands. By any reasonable interpretation of the word "vested," Gay and Robinson's rights to the continued use of their water and related engineering works had become vested.

The *Robinson I* court found that McBryde Sugar Company also relied upon the law set forth in *Territory II*, and developed water rights that became vested.

* * *

The parties concede that the State of Hawaii has the sovereign power to change its laws from time to time as its legislature may see fit, and may, by changing its laws, radically change the definitions of property rights and the manner in which property rights can be controlled or transferred.

The state may also change its laws by judicial decision as well as by legislative action. Insofar as judicial changes in the law operate prospectively to affect property rights vesting after the law is changed, no specific federal question is presented by the state's choice of implement in changing state law. *See Hughes v. Washington,* 389 U.S. 290, 295, 88 S.Ct. 438, 441, 19 L.Ed.2d 530 (1967) (Stewart, J. concurring) [infra, page 399]. * * * We assume, therefore, for the purposes of this case, that the Supreme Court of Hawaii was acting well within its judicial power under the state constitution when it overruled earlier cases and declared for the first time, after more than a century of a different law, that the common law doctrine of riparian ownership was the law of Hawaii. This declaration of a change in the water law of Hawaii may be effective with respect to real property rights created in Hawaii after the *McBryde I* decision became final. New law, however, cannot divest rights that were vested before the court announced the new law. *See Hughes,* 389 U.S. at 295–98, 88 S.Ct. at 441–43. * * * There is no constitutional barrier to the state's exercise of its power of eminent domain to condemn and take vested property rights for public purposes. *See Hawaii Housing Authority v. Midkiff,* [467 U.S. 229], 104 S.Ct. 2321, 2330, 81 L.Ed.2d 186 (1984). ("Redistribution of fees simple [can be] a rational exercise of the eminent domain power.") The state has the power to take over the water works constructed by Gay and Robinson and their associates upon exercising the powers of eminent domain in a manner compatible with the Fourteenth Amendment. *See Pennsylvania Coal Co. v. Mahon,* 260 U.S. 393, 415, 43 S.Ct. 158, 160, 67 L.Ed. 322 (1922). * * * In light of the above authorities, the plaintiffs in this case, having acquired through judicial process a *de jure* vested right to divert water from their lands within the Hanapepe watershed to their own or related lands outside the watershed * * * cannot now be divested of this right without just compensation.

It has been clear since *Territory I* that the downstream rights of small owners to domestic water and "ancient" rights to water for taro cultivation on lands that were wet lands before the litigation commenced have never been contested by Gay and Robinson. These rights were specifically left open by the trial court in the first territorial litigation arising out of the earliest diversions of water. The rights of the small holders that were declared in *McBryde I* and *II* were not disturbed in the district court in the case at bar but were left to be sorted out by the state courts consistent with the recognition of any rights that vested before 1973. * * * The state must bring condemnation proceedings before it can interfere with vested water rights and the enjoyment of the improvements made in reliance thereon.

The judgment of the district court is affirmed in all respects insofar as it declares the rights of the parties.

NOTE

Shortly after the principal case was decided, Hawaii adopted a comprehensive water law that modified the born-again riparianism resulting in *McBryde*. The 1987 statute established a permit system under which existing uses, as well as new uses, must receive a permit if they are in designated water management areas established by a Commission on Water Resource Management. Once an area is designated, holders of common law appurtenant rights are entitled to a permit as a matter of right. Permits are transferable. The legislation grants jurisdiction to the Commission to resolve water disputes whether or not they arise in a water management area. Hawaii Rev.Stat. ch. 174C (Supp.1991).

For a review of the Hawaii water code see Douglas W. MacDougal, *Testing the Current: The Water Code and the Regulation of Hawaii's Water Resources,* 10 Hawaii L.Rev. 205 (1988).

LUCAS v. SOUTH CAROLINA COASTAL COUNCIL

United States Supreme Court, 1992.
___ U.S. ___, 112 S.Ct. 2886, 120 L.Ed.2d 798.

JUSTICE SCALIA delivered the opinion of the Court.

In 1986, petitioner David H. Lucas paid $975,000 for two residential lots on the Isle of Palms in Charleston County, South Carolina, on which he intended to build single-family homes. In 1988, however, the South Carolina Legislature enacted the Beachfront Management Act, S.C.Code § 48–39–250 et seq. (Supp.1990) (Act), which had the direct effect of barring petitioner from erecting any permanent habitable structures on his two parcels. * * *

* * * In its original form, the South Carolina Act required owners of coastal zone land that qualified as a "critical area" (defined in the legislation to include beaches and immediately adjacent sand dunes) to obtain a permit from the newly created South Carolina Coastal Council (respondent here) prior to committing the land to a "use other than the use the critical area was devoted to on [September 28, 1977]." § 48–39–130(A). * * * No portion of the lots, which were located approximately 300 feet from the beach, qualified as a "critical area" under the 1977 Act; accordingly, at the time Lucas acquired these parcels, he was not legally obliged to obtain a permit from the Council in advance of any development activity. * * * Under that 1988 legislation, the Council was directed to establish a "baseline" connecting the landward-most "point[s] of erosion * * * during the past forty years" in the region of the Isle of Palms that includes Lucas's lots. * * * In action not challenged here, the Council fixed this baseline landward of Lucas's parcels. That was significant, for under the Act construction of occupiable improvements was flatly prohibited seaward of a line drawn 20 feet landward of, and parallel to, the baseline. * * * The Act provided no exceptions.

Lucas promptly filed suit in the South Carolina Court of Common Pleas, contending that the Beachfront Management Act's construction bar effected a taking of his property without just compensation.

* * *

Prior to Justice Holmes' exposition in Pennsylvania Coal Co. v. Mahon, 260 U.S. 393, 43 S.Ct. 158, 67 L.Ed. 322 (1922), it was generally thought that the Takings Clause reached only a "direct appropriation" of property, *Legal Tender Cases,* 12 Wall. 457, 551, 20 L.Ed. 287 (1871), or the functional equivalent of a "practical ouster of [the owner's] possession." * * * Justice Holmes recognized in *Mahon,* however, that if the protection against physical appropriations of private property was to be meaningfully enforced, the government's power to redefine the range of interests included in the ownership of property was necessarily constrained by constitutional limits. * * * If, instead, the uses of private property were subject to unbridled, uncompensated qualification under the police power, "the natural tendency of human nature [would be] to extend the qualification more and more until at last private property disappear[ed]." * * * These considerations gave birth in that case to the oft-cited maxim that, "while property may be regulated to a certain extent, if regulation goes too far it will be recognized as a taking."

* * * As we have said on numerous occasions, the Fifth Amendment is violated when land-use regulation "does not substantially advance legitimate state interests *or denies an owner economically viable use of his land.*" * * * The trial court found Lucas's two beachfront lots to have been rendered valueless by respondent's enforcement of the coastal-zone construction ban. Under Lucas's theory of the case, which rested upon our "no economically viable use" statements, that finding entitled him to compensation. Lucas believed it unnecessary to take issue with either the purposes behind the Beachfront Management Act, or the means chosen by the South Carolina Legislature to effectuate those purposes. The South Carolina Supreme Court, however, thought otherwise. In its view, the Beachfront Management Act was no ordinary enactment, but involved an exercise of South Carolina's "police powers" to mitigate the harm to the public interest that petitioner's use of his land might occasion. * * * By neglecting to dispute the findings enumerated in the Act or otherwise to challenge the legislature's purposes, petitioner "concede[d] that the beach/dune area of South Carolina's shores is an extremely valuable public resource; that the erection of new construction, *inter alia,* contributes to the erosion and destruction of this public resource; and that discouraging new construction in close proximity to the beach/dune area is necessary to prevent a great public harm." * * * In the court's view, these concessions brought petitioner's challenge within a long line of this Court's cases sustaining against Due Process and Takings Clause challenges the State's use of its "police powers" to enjoin a property owner from activities akin to public nuisances. See Mugler v. Kansas, 123 U.S. 623, 8 S.Ct. 273, 31 L.Ed. 205 (1887) (law prohibiting manufacture of alcoholic beverages). * * * For a number of reasons, however, we think the South Carolina Supreme Court was too quick to conclude that that principle decides the present case. The "harmful or noxious uses" principle was the Court's early attempt to describe in theoretical terms why government may, consistent with the Takings Clause, affect property values by regulation without incurring an obligation to compensate—a reality we nowadays acknowledge explicitly with respect to the full scope of the State's police power.

* * * Where the State seeks to sustain regulation that deprives land of all economically beneficial use, we think it may resist compensation only if the logically antecedent inquiry into the nature of the owner's estate shows that the proscribed use interests were not part of his title to begin with. This accords, we think, with our "takings" jurisprudence, which has traditionally been guided by the understandings of our citizens regarding the content of, and the State's power over, the "bundle of rights" that they acquire when they obtain title to property. It seems to us that the property owner necessarily expects the uses of his property to be restricted, from time to time, by various measures newly enacted by the State in legitimate exercise of its police powers; "[a]s long recognized, some values are enjoyed under an implied limitation and must yield to the police power." Pennsylvania Coal Co. v. Mahon, 260 U.S., at 413, 43 S.Ct., at 159. And in the case of personal property, by reason of the State's traditionally high degree of control over commercial dealings, he ought to be aware of the possibility that new regulation might even render his property economically worthless (at least if the property's only economically productive use is sale or manufacture for sale). * * * In the case of land, however, we think the notion pressed by the Council that title is somehow held subject to the "implied limitation" that the State may subsequently eliminate all economically valuable use is inconsistent with the historical compact recorded in the Takings Clause that has become part of our constitutional culture.

* * * We believe similar treatment must be accorded confiscatory regulations, i.e., regulations that prohibit all economically beneficial use of land: Any limitation so severe cannot be newly legislated or decreed (without compensation), but must inhere in the title itself, in the restrictions that background principles of the State's law of property and nuisance already place upon land ownership. A law or decree with such an effect must, in other words, do no more than duplicate the result that could have been achieved in the courts—by adjacent landowners (or other uniquely affected persons) under the State's law of private nuisance, or by the State under its complementary power to abate nuisances that affect the public generally, or otherwise. On this analysis, the owner of a lake bed, for example, would not be entitled to compensation when he is denied the requisite permit to engage in a landfilling operation that would have the effect of flooding others' land. Nor the corporate owner of a nuclear generating plant, when it is directed to remove all improvements from its land upon discovery that the plant sits astride an earthquake fault. Such regulatory action may well have the effect of eliminating the land's only economically productive use, but it does not proscribe a productive use that was previously

permissible under relevant property and nuisance principles. The use of these properties for what are now expressly prohibited purposes was *always* unlawful, and (subject to other constitutional limitations) it was open to the State at any point to make the implication of those background principles of nuisance and property law explicit. * * * In light of our traditional resort to "existing rules or understandings that stem from an independent source such as state law" to define the range of interests that qualify for protection as "property" under the Fifth (and Fourteenth) amendments this recognition that the Takings Clause does not require compensation when an owner is barred from putting land to a use that is proscribed by those "existing rules or understandings" is surely unexceptional. When, however, a regulation that declares "off-limits" all economically productive or beneficial uses of land goes beyond what the relevant background principles would dictate, compensation must be paid to sustain it.

The "total taking" inquiry we require today will ordinarily entail (as the application of state nuisance law ordinarily entails) analysis of, among other things, the degree of harm to public lands and resources, or adjacent private property, posed by the claimant's proposed activities, see, e.g., Restatement (Second) of Torts §§ 826, 827, the social value of the claimant's activities and their suitability to the locality in question, see, e.g., id., §§ 828(a) and (b), 831, and the relative ease with which the alleged harm can be avoided through measures taken by the claimant and the government (or adjacent private landowners) alike, see, e.g., id., §§ 827(e), 828(c), 830. The fact that a particular use has long been engaged in by similarly situated owners ordinarily imports a lack of any common-law prohibition (though changed circumstances or new knowledge may make what was previously permissible no longer so), see Restatement (Second) of Torts, supra, § 827, comment *g.* So also does the fact that other landowners, similarly situated, are permitted to continue the use denied to the claimant.

* * * South Carolina must identify background principles of nuisance and property law that prohibit the uses he now intends in the circumstances in which the property is presently found.

* * *

The judgment is reversed and the cause remanded for proceedings not inconsistent with this opinion.

So ordered.

* * *

Justice Blackmun, dissenting.

Today the Court launches a missile to kill a mouse.

* * *

If the state legislature is correct that the prohibition on building in front of the setback line prevents serious harm, then, under this Court's prior cases, the Act is constitutional. "Long ago it was recognized that all property in this country is held under the implied obligation that the owner's use of it shall not be injurious to the community, and the Takings Clause did not transform that principle to one that requires compensation whenever the State asserts its power to enforce it." Keystone Bituminous Coal Assn. v. DeBenedictis, 480 U.S. 470, 491–492, 107 S.Ct. 1232, 1245, 94 L.Ed.2d 472 (1987). * * *

* * * In determining what is a nuisance at common law, state courts make exactly the decision that the Court finds so troubling when made by the South Carolina General Assembly today: they determine whether the use is harmful. Common-law public and private nuisance law is simply a determination whether a particular use causes harm. * * * There is nothing magical in the reasoning of judges long dead. They determined a harm in the same way as state judges and legislatures do today. If judges in the 18th and 19th centuries can distinguish a harm from a benefit, why not judges in the 20th century, and if judges can, why not legislators? * * *

* * * Nothing in the discussions in Congress concerning the Takings Clause indicates that the Clause was limited by the common-law nuisance doctrine. Common law courts themselves rejected such an understanding. They regularly recognized that it is "for the legislature to interpose, and by positive enactment to prohibit a use of property which would be injurious to the public." [Commonwealth v. Tewksbury, 11 Metc., at 57 (Mass.1846)] * * * Commonwealth v. Parks, 155 Mass. 531, 532, 30 N.E. 174 (1892) (Holmes, J.) ("[T]he legislature may change the common law as to nuisances, and may move the line either way, so as to make things nuisances which were not so, or to make things lawful which were nuisances").

In short, I find no clear and accepted "historical compact" or "understanding of our citizens" justifying the Court's new taking doctrine. Instead, the Court seems to treat history as a grab-bag of principles, to be adopted where they support the Court's theory, and ignored where they do not. If the Court decided that the early common law provides the background principles for interpreting the Taking Clause, then regulation, as opposed to physical confiscation, would not be compensable. If the Court decided that the law of a later period provides the background principles, then regulation might be compensable, but the Court would have to confront the fact that legislatures regularly determined which uses were prohibited, independent of the common law, and independent of whether the uses were lawful when the owner purchased. What makes the Court's analysis unworkable is its attempt to package the law of two incompatible eras and peddle it as historical fact.

* * *

JOSEPH L. SAX, "THE CONSTITUTION, PROPERTY RIGHTS AND THE FUTURE OF WATER LAW"
61 U.Colo.L.Rev. 257 (1990).

* * *

What exactly is the problem? At its crudest the claim would be that whatever uses an appropriator has been making, and that have been recognized as lawful in the past, must as a matter of property right be permitted to continue or be compensated as a taking. If successful, such demands would deny a state effective authority to mandate more efficient use of existing supplies. The notion seems to be that to declare an existing use wasteful, or non-beneficial, is a sort of prohibited *ex post facto* law that impairs a vested right.

* * *

A second property dispute arises from the demand that existing appropriators give up some water in order to restore instream flows. Here the claim is that an appropriator with a recognized right to abstract and use a given quantum of water from a stream cannot be required to divert less, or to make discharges from storage, in order to produce desired stream conditions. The appropriator would say that the right to abstract water from a stream is the very essence of his property right in water and that to diminish that right because the state wants increased instream flows is the most blatant sort of taking without compensation.

* * *

I. WATER RIGHTS AS CONSTITUTIONALLY PROTECTED PROPERTY

* * *

The following is a brief statement of the constitutional situation. The regulatory authority of the state under the aegis of the police power is very broad. Even the Court's most conservative and property-oriented Justices accept the capaciousness of the police power. The reason, no doubt, is reluctance to second-guess legislatures about the need for regulation, and a recognition that we live in a regulatory state. Significant changes in takings doctrine would put the court at odds with the modern legislative style of governance. Short of regulation that is forbidden by some other constitutional provision, * * * or is seen as not serving a public function at all, it is difficult to imagine subjects that might garner legislative majorities whose purpose would be viewed today as beyond the police power. Certainly legislation that constrains uses of property to achieve environmental protection goals is firmly within the police power,[12] as is legislation that constrains property use in order to conserve scarce natural resources by requiring more efficient use.[13] The same is true of legislation to promote efficient administration.[14] Those three categories cover just about all the regulatory proposals that are likely to be made as to western water law.

---

12. E.g., United States v. Riverside Bayview Homes, 474 U.S. 121 (1985) (wetlands); Hodel v. Virginia Surface Mining and Reclamation Ass'n, 452 U.S. 264 (1981) (strip mining); Agins v. City of Tiburon, 447 U.S. 255 (1980) (open space).

13. E.g., State v. Dexter, 32 Wash.2d 551, 202 P.2d 906 (1949), aff'd per curiam, 338 U.S. 863 (1949) (requiring those engaged in commercial logging operations to leave a certain number of trees standing for reseeding and restocking purposes). For a reference to the history of efforts at sustained-yield forestry see Sibley, *An America That Did Not Happen,* High Country News, Dec. 22, 1986, at 8.

14. E.g., Texaco v. Short, 454 U.S. 516 (1982), where the Court upheld (unanimously on the takings issue) a state statute providing that mineral interests unused for many years lapsed unless the owner filed a

The question then is under what circumstances compensation is due even for a valid exercise of the police power? There are essentially only two grounds on which it is possible to win a takings case today. The first is where there is a "physical invasion," that is, where government physically appropriates to itself some part of an owner's property, as in the recent *Nollan,*[15] *Loretto,*[16] and *Kaiser Aetna*[17] cases. The second is where the effect of the regulation, though its purpose is valid under the police power, is so greatly to diminish the value of the property that it is no longer economically viable. As to this latter test—the so-called diminution of value standard—the Supreme Court has been extremely deferential to regulators. Even diminutions approaching 90% of value have been sustained without compensation. That has been the Court's unvarying position for many decades.

Under these standards, the only new water law regulation that would *prima facie* raise a taking problem is a release requirement: requiring existing appropriators to make releases in order to augment instream flows for public purposes such as ecosystem protection and public recreation. If the appropriator's property right were an unqualified one, such a requirement might well be viewed as a "physical invasion," and would thus be compensable. But, * * * original limitations on the property that can be acquired in water undermines this facially appealing claim for compensation.

Otherwise, the regulations most likely to be challenged are those that require existing uses to be cut back as wasteful. There is no property right to waste water, and that would seem to end the matter. But several claims may nonetheless be anticipated against such regulation. First, that it would be retroactive; conduct previously considered legal would be made illegal. Second, insofar as such regulation is sought to be justified under the preexisting waste doctrine, it may be urged that the doctrine has been unused or loosely construed for a long time and should not be tightened up now. Or it may be urged that definitions of waste should not change over time.

The first of these issues is easily answered. There is no constitutional bar to retroactive regulatory legislation. The U.S. Supreme Court has recently and explicitly sustained retroactive legislation

statement of claim in the county recorder's office.

15. Nollan v. California Coastal Comm'n, 483 U.S. 825 (1987) (state's demand for dedication of right-of-way to allow public to walk across homeowner's oceanfront land as a condition for grant of building permit to enlarge beachfront home held an unconstitutional taking because no causal nexus was found between the public harm created by the home enlargement and the public benefit of walking across beach).

16. Loretto v. Teleprompter Manhattan CATV Corp., 458 U.S. 419 (1982) (governmentally required, virtually uncompensated installation of cable television wiring by landlords to benefit tenants held an uncon-

stitutional taking of landlord's property). For reasons not germane to this discussion, I view *Loretto* as wrongly decided. Be that as it may, it nonetheless demonstrates that physical invasion is the event that primarily triggers a demand for compensation by the Supreme Court. Even physical invasion is not a guarantee of compensation, however. Pruneyard Shopping Center v. Robins, 447 U.S. 74 (1980).

17. Kaiser Aetna v. United States, 444 U.S. 164 (1979) (governmentally required public boating access to privately created marina excavated from non-navigable pond, now (but not formerly) connected to ocean, held an unconstitutional taking of marina developer's property).

against taking challenges. The issue no longer presents a substantial federal question. Nonetheless, a notion seems to have been advanced in some circles that what might be called the "non-conforming use" rule in land zoning states a constitutional proposition. The claim is that a use that is already being made and that was lawful when initiated cannot be regulated away without compensation, even though similarly situated new uses may be regulated. The short answer is that there has never been a non-conforming use rule in federal constitutional property law. Valid preexisting uses have been subject to rezoning and owners have been required to change their use to conform to the new law.

Although the non-conforming use rule may be a prudent one for certain relatively low priority public purposes (such as removing highway billboards or clearing commercial uses out of residential neighborhoods), it would fundamentally subvert the regulatory process if it were implemented as a constitutional principle. New fire and safety laws could hardly await a whole new generation of buildings, and for that reason required retrofitting of devices like fire sprinklers, or removal of hazards like asbestos, raise no constitutional taking problem.

The notion that a standard once set (such as a waste rule in water law) cannot be subsequently revised is just another version of the "non-conforming use" argument. Indeed, if the argument were correct that standards cannot be upgraded, all of our environmental statutes would be unconstitutional. We could not require industries to retrofit new air and water pollution control equipment to meet new, tighter standards so long as they had been in compliance with the standards that were in effect when their facility was built. Although the Supreme Court has never in so many words sustained the constitutionality of new pollution standards applied to existing facilities, betting on the constitutionality of such laws as against taking claims is as safe a wager as the law has to offer. * * * [T]here are two differences in water doctrine that put holders of water rights in a weaker position than other property owners subject to retrospective regulation. First, there has always been a law saying in effect that water could not be wasted, or could only be used beneficially. While owners of most property have a right to make inefficient uses if they so choose, this is not true of owners of water rights.

Second, new laws defining existing uses as wasteful are more prospective, and less retroactive, than a number of other laws whose constitutionality has been sustained by the Supreme Court. In the leading retroactive regulation cases, property owners were required to make supplemental payments to compensate for conduct wholly in the past which was legal when engaged in. In the water situation, imposition of waste laws would only change the uses that can be made in the future. No reparation would be required for past wasteful uses.

II. THE TRADITION OF CHANGE IN WATER LAW

* * *

Far from being a modern invention of goal-oriented judges, change is the unchanging chronicle of water jurisprudence. When the question was getting timber to market in places which lacked highways or railroads but not rivers, those rivers suitable for floating logs to market magically became navigable. When the needs of commerce required it, navigability was extended from tidal waters (which had been its historic limit) to nontidal waters suitable for waterborne navigation. New needs have always generated new doctrines and, thereby, new property rights.

Water, as a necessary and common medium for community development at every stage of society, has been held subject to the perceived societal necessities of the time and circumstances. In that sense water's capacity for full privatization has always been limited. The very terminology of water law reveals that limitation: terms such as "beneficial," "non-wasteful," "navigation servitude," and "public trust" all import an irreducible public claim on waters as a public resource, and not merely as a private commodity. In the following section I address those doctrines that limit full privatization of water. A discussion of these doctrines will show why, in demanding releases to meet instream flow needs, a state is only asserting a right it has always had and never granted away.

III. A TRADITION OF PUBLIC SERVITUDES

A. *The Public Trust and Its Predecessors*

There is a tradition that recognizes a pre-existing right of the State in the flow of its rivers. Private diversions, at least those in tidal or navigable waters and affected tributaries, have always been subject to a servitude and a trust in favor of the public. Only California courts have thus far fully explored the implications of this tradition for the imposition of release requirements on existing appropriators. They have resolved the question strongly in favor of the public, first in the Mono Lake case,[38] then in the intermediate appellate decision in the Delta water case,[39] and most recently in a carefully crafted Superior Court decision, *Environmental Defense Fund v. East Bay Municipal Utility District.*[40]

* * *

B. *Appropriators as Polluters*

Where releases are required to protect downstream water quality, appropriators may be seen as in no better position than conventional polluters. The water rights and uses of industrial and municipal polluters are subject to all controls necessary to restore desired water quality even if such controls prohibit or limit uses that have been lawfully made for many decades. For example, it seems unquestionable that both the intake and discharge of water by industrialists may be

---

38. National Audubon Soc'y v. Superior Court, 33 Cal.3d 419, 658 P.2d 709, 189 Cal.Rptr. 346, cert. denied, 464 U.S. 977 (1983). [p. 288, supra].

39. United States v. State Water Resources Control Bd., 182 Cal.App.3d 82, 227 Cal.Rptr. 161 (1986). [p. 297, supra].

40. No. 425955 (Alameda County Sup. Ct., Nov. 27, 1989).

extensively regulated where their uses pollute the water body into which they discharge.

The situation of the industrial water user/polluter puts in perspective the appropriator's claim that it has a right to dewater a river and destroy it as a natural system—and that if the state wants now to restore the river, the public should pay. Prior to federal water quality legislation, the shoreline oil refinery or power plant that discharged heated or tainted water back into the source was permitted to destroy the river as a sustaining natural system. Now the public is reclaiming rivers from industrial polluters in order to restore their natural functioning and the public is not paying.

In at least some circumstances the situations of irrigators and industrial polluters seem indistinguishable. The following illustration suggests the similarity. Mineralized return flows from irrigation appropriators contaminated California's Kesterson refuge with selenium, killing birds that roosted there. One way to control the contamination is to reduce the total amount of water flowing through irrigation systems. Reductions in amounts of water diverted and passed over the irrigated lands would decrease the mineral content of the water and reduce the concentration of the contaminated water downstream. Assuming that the reduced-diversion approach is part of the best and most economical strategy for dealing with the contamination issue, and that such a requirement would not deprive the irrigators of all economic viability, would such a release requirement be viewed as a physical invasion (government seizure) of the water, or as a legitimate noncompensable regulation?

No legally or factually significant difference is apparent between the Kesterson-type hypothetical case and a conventional case of industrial pollution. Both involve a physical discharge of water that has been contaminated. Though the issue has not been authoritatively litigated, the operating premise has been that the pollution model applies, so that the government can require releases without incurring an obligation to compensate.

* * *

NOTES

1. Is Professor Sax's analysis consistent with the Supreme Court's latest word on takings in *Lucas?* What is included in the "bundle of rights" which a water right holder acquires? How does the doctrine of beneficial use inform the issue? How far can a water right be reduced before it has "no economically beneficial use?"

2. Some people have suggested that any reduction of a water right is a complete taking. David Hallford, *Environmental Regulations as Water Rights Takings*, 6 Nat.Res. & Envt. 13, Summer 1991. By contrast, Professor Sax argues that the use of all property is necessarily limited to "uses compatible with the community's dependence on the property as a resource." Joseph L. Sax, *Property Rights and the Economy of Nature: Understanding Lucas v. South Carolina Coastal Commission, 45 Stan.L.Rev. 1433 (1993)*.

3.   Is the recognition of the state's public trust powers over water equivalent to a recognition of the state's police powers? See Anthony B. Manzanetti, Note, *The Fifth Amendment as a Limitation on the Public Trust Doctrine in Water Law,* 15 Pac.L.J. 1291 (1984); Harrison C. Dunning, *The Public Trust Doctrine and Western Water Law: Discord or Harmony,* 30 Rocky Mtn.Min.L.Inst. 17–1 (1984). An assistant attorney general who represented the State of California in National Audubon Society v. Superior Court, page 288, supra, argued that "the public trust doctrine provides the conceptual basis of the water right laws [and] under the water right laws, the state has the right to balance environmental values and economic needs, and also to re-examine and if necessary modify existing rights to reflect changing public needs." Roderick E. Walston, *The Public Trust Doctrine: Implications for State Water Rights Administration,* Speech Delivered Before American Bar Association Natural Resources Section, January 8, 1985. Did the California Supreme Court adopt this argument? If not, how does the court's trust-based duty differ from the state's theory of the power to modify vested water rights? Is the court's opinion a complete answer to Los Angeles' inevitable claim that any modification of vested rights is a taking without due process of law?

The prior appropriation doctrine was established to protect and define water rights. When states modify existing rights by effectively applying or redefining "beneficial use" under one or more of the methods of "public interest" review discussed at pages 263–303, supra, how secure are those rights? What remedy, if any, does the holder of a modified right have?

Consider the following answer to the taking argument in the special context of water rights:

> Although some commentators have pointed to the fifth amendment's prohibition against the taking of private property without the payment of just compensation as a potential "limitation on the public trust doctrine," these arguments are dependent on the acceptance of the premise that recipients of water rights from the states had no notice of the retention of sovereign ownership interests by the states and the accompanying public trust obligations. That such a premise is untenable is evident when one recalls that the usufructuary principle of western water law is a universally recognized "expression of the state's trust responsibilities to its citizens in the water rights context." Moreover, given the constitutional and statutory declarations of state or public ownership of water resources upon which western water law was founded, the "no notice" premise of the takings argument is, at best, a strained appeal to equity for it also ignores the numerous judicial affirmations of the public nature of state inland water resources and the common understanding, prevalent throughout the West, that the inland water resources of a state "belong" to all the people of the state. Thus, the acquisition of water rights by a state under the public trust doctrine would, like federal reserved rights acquired by the federal government, not require the payment of just compensation for the infringement of privately-held water rights.

Peter A. Fahmy, Comment, *The Public Trust Doctrine as a Source of State Reserved Water Rights,* 63 Denver U.L.Rev. 585, 600–01 (1986). For a discussion stating that modification of existing water rights through "public interest" is a taking, see John Herbson, *Waist Deep in the Big Muddy: Property Rights, Public Values and Instream Waters,* 25 Land & Water L.Rev. 549 (1991).

4. Would the following regulatory actions result in a compensable taking:

a.) A senior water rights holder "calls" an upstream junior, demanding that the junior forgo diverting water because the senior needs to satisfy earlier priority uses. The state engineer refuses to enforce the senior right against the junior because the senior could invest in a well to pump groundwater that would draw the same amount of water from the same basic source. The result is to render a costly surface diversion works worthless and to require the senior to make a large expenditure for the well. See Alamosa–La Jara Water Users Protection Ass'n v. Gould, 674 P.2d 914 (Colo.1983), page 281, supra.

b.) A farmer, who has been using a water right to irrigate the same fields for many years, is ordered to cease using the water. The fields contain highly saline soils and the return flows pollute the stream beyond legislatively adopted water quality standards.

c.) A farmer sells a senior water right to a chemical company, but the change of use is refused because the chemical company's return flow will pollute the stream.

d.) The legislature passes a law requiring minimum streamflows in all streams valuable as public fisheries. The owner of a hydroelectric dam is required by law to bypass half the water historically used to generate power in order to protect fish populations in the river.

e.) The law referred to in d results in an order to remove the dam entirely to avoid total destruction of the fishery.

f.) A new water quality law requires limitation of water uses that significantly diminish water quality. A senior irrigator of hay meadows has long diverted much of the flow of a creek just above a natural salt seep. The diminished flow is inadequate to dilute the salty water and the stream is rendered useless for fifty miles below that point. The senior user is ordered to cease the diversion. This incidentally allows dozens of junior agricultural and municipal uses to flourish in the fifty mile stretch and for fish life to be reestablished.

g.) Would it make any difference in f if the pollutant discharges needing dilution were from a municipal sewage treatment plant (operating in compliance with all federal and state pollution laws)?

h.) Would it make any difference in f if the primary purpose of the law was not to improve water quality but to expand beneficial uses (agriculture, municipal, fish and wildlife, recreation)?

Chapter Four

RIGHTS TO SURFACE USE
OF WATERBODIES

Property rights in water are incomplete in that they have a dimension of non-exclusivity greater than property rights in land or personal property. All water rights—riparian or appropriative—are, of necessity, correlative; the use of water must be shared among a class of private and public claimants. Water rights are further incomplete because the use of certain streams and lakes considered to be "public" must be shared by accommodating uses of the general public as well as other water right holders or landowners. The public-private distinction can be traced to Roman law and perhaps earlier. See Eugene F. Ware, Roman Water Law (1905, reprinted 1985).

Everyone who has ever waited for a boat to pass under a drawbridge has seen an example of the oldest recognized public right, navigation. Public rights historically concentrated on navigation and fishing. Public waters have sometimes been defined as navigable waters, but this is an illusive concept. See Kaiser Aetna v. United States, 444 U.S. 164 (1979), pages 678–79, 702–03, infra. Heavy judicial reliance on the concept of "navigability" for a variety of purposes led the district judge in that case to cite an earlier edition of this casebook for the proposition that "a navigable river is any river with enough water in it to float a Supreme Court opinion." United States v. Kaiser Aetna, 408 F.Supp. 42, 49 (D.Hawaii 1976). Today, public rights include non-commercial recreational uses and in many states the classes of public waters have been expanded to all watercourses capable of supporting recreational activity. Furthermore, the environmental movement has had an important impact on public rights and their relationship with private rights.

The exercise of public rights diminishes the exclusivity of water rights and, to an extent, rights in associated real property. Thus, the use of the beds underlying public waters and, in some cases, the use of and access to shorelines have been limited. Because legislative and judicial regulation was initially aimed at preventing navigation obstructions, the exercise of public rights did not traditionally interfere with the consumptive use of water. This is becoming less true today because the scope of public rights is expanding. Public rights, encompassing a wider range of recreation and even ecological integrity of water systems, imposes new and substantial constraints on the use of watercourses and related lands. This chapter explores the sources and scope of rights to use the surface of waterways and the submerged lands beneath them, including rights among private landowners and traditional public rights.

Section A of this chapter considers the public interest in the bed and banks of "navigable" waters and how it drives concepts of underlying land ownership. If a body of water is navigable, the bed and banks passed to the ownership of the state upon statehood. Navigability for determining the ownership of the bed and banks is called "navigability for title" and has been defined through a long history of case law. The title to the bed and banks was transferred to the states for the benefit of the public and is burdened by what is called the "public trust." The public trust limits the ability of states to transfer these lands into private ownership, protecting the public's right to use navigable waterways. The rights to use submerged land of private landowners who succeed to title are also limited by the public trust.

Section B considers the allocation of rights to surface use among private owners of the bed and banks of waterways. They constitute a special class whose rights as among one another are often in dispute. Finally section C deals with the public's right to use the surface of navigable waterways, and covers the expansion of public rights to use the surface of waters through state legislation and common law. This includes uses beyond those under the public trust and covers non-navigable waters. State law also determines public rights of access to beaches and shorelines.

A. THE PUBLIC TRUST IN NAVIGABLE WATERS

1. Ownership of Beds

As between the federal government and the states, title to the beds underlying navigable waters is vested in the states:

> For when the Revolution took place, the people of each state became themselves sovereign; and in that character hold the absolute right to all their navigable waters and soil under them for their own common use, subject only to rights surrendered by the Constitution to the general government.

Martin v. Waddell's Lessee, 41 U.S. (16 Pet.) 367, 410 (1842).

Ancient Origins of Public Ownership. Martin v. Waddell was a conflict between two patentees, both claiming exclusive rights to cultivate oysters in the tidelands of Raritan Bay, New Jersey. One claimed under the patent from the King of England to the Duke of York establishing a colony in New Jersey. His theory was that: (1) The Crown owned the tidelands and held them in trust for the public for certain purposes; (2) the Crown could grant title to tidelands subject to the trust; (3) the patent to the Duke of York conveyed the tidelands in question together with an exclusive right of fishery; and (4) the conveyance was consistent with the public trust because fishing rights are not part of the public trust. This theory was adopted by Mr. Justice Thompson, dissenting, but the Court (by Chief Justice Taney) held to the contrary:

> And in deciding a question like this, we must not look merely to the strict technical meaning of the words of the letters patent. The laws and institutions of England, the history of the times, the

object of the charter, the contemporaneous construction given to it, and the usages under it, for the century and more which has since elapsed, are all entitled to consideration and weight. It is not a deed conveying private property to be interpreted by the rules applicable to cases of that description. It was an instrument upon which was to be founded the institutions of a great political community; and in that light it should be regarded and construed.

Taking this rule for our guide, we can entertain no doubt as to the true construction of these letters patent. The object in view appears upon the face of them. They were made for the purpose of enabling the Duke of York to establish a colony upon the newly discovered continent, to be governed, as nearly as circumstances would permit, according to the laws and usages of England; and in which the duke, his heirs and assigns, were to stand in the place of the king, and administer the government according to the principles of the British constitution. And the people who were to plant this colony, and to form the political body over which he was to rule, were subjects of Great Britain, accustomed to be governed according to its usages and laws.

It is said by Hale in his Treatise de Jure Maris, Harg. Law Tracts, 11, when speaking of the navigable waters, and the sea on the coasts within the jurisdiction of the British crown, "that although the king is the owner of this great coast, and, as a consequent of his propriety, hath the primary right of fishing in the sea and creeks, and arms thereof, yet the common people of England have regularly a liberty of fishing in the sea, or creeks, or arms thereof, as a public common of piscary, and may not, without injury to their right, be restrained of it, unless in such places, creeks, or navigable rivers, where either the king or some particular subject hath gained a propriety exclusive of that common liberty."

The principle here stated by Hale, as to "the public common of piscary" belonging to the common people of England, is not questioned by any English writer upon that subject. The point upon which different opinions have been expressed, is whether since Magna Charta, "either the king or any particular subject can gain a propriety exclusive of the common liberty." For, undoubtedly rights of fishery, exclusive of the common liberty, are at this day held and enjoyed by private individuals under ancient grants. But the existence of a doubt as to the right of the king to make such a grant after Magna Charta, would of itself show how fixed has been the policy of that government on this subject for the last six hundred years; and how carefully it has preserved this common right for the benefit of the public.

41 U.S. at 411–12.

Under English common law, the Crown owned only the beds of waters which were: (1) below the high-water mark, (2) navigable, and (3) affected by the ebb and flow of the tide. Title to non-tidal beds was prima facie in the owner of the shore to the thread of the stream, *usque ad filum aquae*. In 1851 the Supreme Court held that admiralty jurisdiction extended to non-tidal waters. The Genesee Chief, 53 U.S. (12 How.) 443 (1851). In Barney v. Keokuk, 94 U.S. (4 Otto) 324 (1876), The Genesee Chief was applied to hold that the states owned the beds to non-tidal navigable waters.

Navigability for title. A body of case law has developed to define "navigability." Issues in older cases related to congressional power under the Commerce Clause, though whether a stream is navigable has little to do with congressional power today. Other cases deal with "the navigation servitude," which allows the federal government to impact or destroy the value of land in aid of navigation. Both of these concerns with navigation are discussed in Chapter 7.

"Navigability for title" refers to lakes or rivers that became state property at statehood. There have been frequent title conflicts between states and the United States, and among the grantees of these sovereigns, over which sovereign could grant land ownership in the beds to private parties. The issue may arise when lands along a river were patented by the federal government to a homesteader or other private party. The question is whether the title includes the bed of the abutting river. Some cases have dealt with who (which sovereign or its grantees) can reap income from, say, oil wells drilled in a riverbed.

The navigability for title cases also inform the issue of public use rights because states are limited in their conveyances of lands beneath navigable waters. They cannot defeat public uses. Navigable waterways are subject to a public trust, and private rights in any such lands that are conveyed may be commensurately limited. In defining rights of public use and access, states have placed limits on owners of private lands underlying or abutting waterways, some of which waterways meet the federal definition of navigable for title and some of which do not. These state laws sometimes refer to "navigability" but may have a different definition in regulations enacted under the state's police power. Only those state regulations that interfere with federally protected public uses or some other constitutional restraint are prohibited.

Navigability for title purposes has been dealt with in three major U.S. Supreme Court cases: United States v. Oregon, 295 U.S. 1 (1935), United States v. Utah, 283 U.S. 64 (1931), and United States v. Holt State Bank, 270 U.S. 49 (1926). Summarizing these cases, Johnson and Austin conclude:

> (2) Such navigability is determined by the natural and ordinary condition of the water at that time, not whether it could be made navigable by artificial improvements. However, the fact that rapids, rocks, or other obstructions make navigation difficult will not destroy title navigability so long as the waters were usable for a significant portion of the time.

> (3) Navigability in intrastate commerce is all that is required, not usability in interstate commerce.

> (4) The waters must be usable by the "customary modes of trade or travel on water." This may include waters usable for

commercial log floating. This includes waters as little as three or four feet deep that are geographically located so they have been, or can be used by canoes and rowboats for commercial trade and travel (fur traders' canoes). This does not include waters which are difficult to access because of surrounding mud flats or the like, *and* which are geographically isolated from habitation and transportation routes, *and* which have never been and are not likely to be used for commercial trade or travel. This probably does not include waters that are geographically isolated from habitation and transportation routes and which have never been and are not likely to be used for commercial trade or travel, even though these waters are deep enough and large enough to float commercial type vessels, and are not physically inaccessible because of mud flats or the like.

Ralph W. Johnson and Russell A. Austin Jr., *Recreational Rights and Titles to Beds on Western Lakes and Streams*, 7 Nat. Resources J. 1, 24–25 (1967).

The meaning of the standard "or are susceptible of being used, in their ordinary condition, as highways for commerce" announced in The Daniel Ball, was litigated in Utah v. United States, 403 U.S. 9 (1971). The Court held that the Great Salt Lake was navigable at the time Utah entered the Union.

Although the evidence is not extensive, we think it is sufficient to sustain the findings. There were, for example, nine boats used from time to time to haul cattle and sheep from the mainland to one of the islands or from one of the islands to the mainland. * * *.

There was, in addition to the boats used by ranchers, one boat used by an outsider who carried sheep to an island for the owners of the sheep. It is said that one sheep boat for hire does not make an artery for commerce; but one sheep boat for hire is in keeping with the theme of actual navigability of the waters of the lake in earlier years.

There was, in addition, a boat known as the *City of Corinne* which was launched in May 1871 for the purpose of carrying passengers and freight; but its life in that capacity apparently lasted less than a year. In 1872 it was converted into an excursion boat which apparently plied the waters of the lake until 1881. There are other boats that hauled sheep to and from an island in the lake and also hauled ore, and salt, and cedar posts. Still another boat was used to carry salt from various salt works around the lake to a railroad connection.

The United States says the trade conducted by these various vessels was sporadic and their careers were short. It is true that most of the traffic which we have mentioned took place in the 1880's, while Utah became a State in 1896. Moreover, it is said that the level of the lake had so changed by 1896 that navigation was not practical. The Master's Report effectively refutes that contention. It says that on January 4, 1896, the lake was 30.2 feet deep. He finds that on that date "the Lake was physically capable of being used in its ordinary condition as a highway for floating

and affording passage to water craft in the manner over which
trade and travel was or might be conducted in the customary
modes of travel on water at that time."

403 U.S. at 11–12.

Federal-State Conflicts over Ownership.   States admitted to the
Union subsequent to the original thirteen succeeded to the same rights
as the original states on the theory that the lands acquired by the
United States from the colonies or from foreign governments were held
in trust for the new states in order that they might be admitted on an
equal footing with the original states.   Pollard v. Hagan, 44 U.S. (3
How.) 212 (1845).   *Pollard* was a conflict between federal and state
patentees to tidelands under Mobile Bay, Alabama, a state carved out
of lands ceded to the federal government by the original states and by
Spain.   The Supreme Court rejected the argument that the federal
government rather than states succeeded to full sovereignty partly on
the theory that deeds of cession from the original states imposed the
trust in favor of future states.   (It also thought that any attempt to
assume sovereignty would have been unconstitutional "because the
United States has no constitutional capacity to exercise municipal
jurisdiction, sovereignty, or eminent domain, within the limits of a
state or elsewhere, except in cases where it is expressly granted."   44
U.S. at 223.   This limit on federal legislative power was not accepted in
later cases.)

The extent of the trust for future states was thrown into some
doubt in Knight v. United States Land Ass'n., 142 U.S. 161 (1891).   The
federal government confirmed a title to tidelands based on the claim of
the city of San Francisco as successor to the rights of the Mexican
pueblo as against a state patentee.   The Court upheld the pueblo grant
because the Treaty of Guadalupe Hildago required the United States to
protect property rights which had been created by its predecessor, the
Mexican government.   *Knight* seems inconsistent with the constitutional theory of *Pollard* for it suggested in dictum that, besides treaty
obligations, federal lands might be "subject to trusts which would
require their disposition in some other way."   Thus, after *Knight*
federal patentees had another opening to argue that their grants
included tidelands.

In 1894 the Supreme Court reasserted *Pollard* and sought to
harmonize it with federal public domain disposition policy.   Shively v.
Bowlby, 152 U.S. 1 (1894) contains a virtual treatise on the question of
title to beds underlying navigable waters:

> By the Constitution, as is now well settled, the United States,
> having rightfully acquired the Territories, and being the only
> government which can impose laws upon them, have the entire
> dominion and sovereignty, national and municipal, Federal and
> state, over all the Territories, so long as they remain in a territori-
> al condition.

> We cannot doubt, therefore, that Congress has the power to
> make grants of lands below high water mark of navigable waters in
> any Territory of the United States, whenever it becomes necessary

to do so in order to perform international obligations, or to effect the improvement of such lands for the promotion and convenience of commerce with foreign nations and among the several States, or to carry out other public purposes appropriate to the objects for which the United States hold the Territory.

* * *

The Congress of the United States, in disposing of the public lands, has constantly acted upon the theory that those lands, whether in the interior, or on the coast, above high water mark, may be taken up by actual occupants, in order to encourage the settlement of the country; but that the navigable waters and the soils under them, whether within or above the ebb and flow of the tide, shall be and remain public highways; and, being chiefly valuable for the public purposes of commerce, navigation and fishery, and for the improvements necessary to secure and promote those purposes, shall not be granted away during the period of territorial government; but, unless in case of some international duty or public exigency, shall be held by the United States in trust for the future States, and shall vest in the several States, when organized and admitted into the Union, with all the powers and prerogatives appertaining to the older States in regard to such waters and soils within their respective jurisdictions; in short, shall not be disposed of piecemeal to individuals as private property, but shall be held as a whole for the purpose of being ultimately administered and dealt with for the public benefit by the State, after it shall have become a completely organized community. 152 U.S. at 48–50.

Once title has been allocated to the states, they are free to decide whether the bed shall pass out of state ownership into private hands or shall be retained by the state. The public interest has not always been served by these transfers. Sometimes they have been made advisedly (as when California deeded lands in San Francisco Bay into private ownership). Sometimes private title has been obtained by fraud (as where the surveyor describes a lake bed as dry land). And sometimes title has been obtained by legal error (as where the state regards a water body as non-navigable and hence recognizes title as tracing to the federal patentee of land adjoining the bed).

A common legal error has occurred with lakes. Some states have adopted the rule that a lake that has been meandered (shorelines surveyed and mapped) by U.S. Government surveyors is navigable and, correlatively, a lake that has not been meandered is non-navigable. State courts decided bed titles on the basis of these rules, but the U.S. Supreme Court has indicated that meander lines marking the shores as shown by surveyors do not decide titles to beds of water bodies but were only run to determine the quantity of upland to be sold and the price to be collected. Hardin v. Jordan, 140 U.S. 371 (1891). Once it is authoritatively decided that the bed of the lake or stream is in private ownership it becomes necessary to determine how the bed is shared among riparian owners and what rights the riparians and members of the public have to use the overlying waters. With respect to rivers, the property line is the center of the stream, sometimes determined as a line midway between the banks of the river at ordinary height but sometimes determined as the thread of the main channel of the stream. As to lakes and ponds, various means of apportioning the lake bed have been devised, e.g., on the basis of lake frontage and by extending property lines from the shore to the center of the lake. See 1 Patton on Titles §§ 132–33 (1957). Ownership lines do not necessarily determine the limits of uses that may be made on the surface by riparians themselves. Limits on the extent of any private rights that may exist in water bodies for the benefit of the public are determined, first, by whether the waterway is navigable for title. Second, one must look to state law. State law can extend public rights to use both navigable and non-navigable waterways, but may not defeat certain public rights in navigable waters.

The next case shows the overriding importance of federal law in determining what federal patentees receive from their grants.

HUGHES v. WASHINGTON

Supreme Court of the United States, 1967.
389 U.S. 290, 88 S.Ct. 438, 19 L.Ed.2d 530.

MR. JUSTICE BLACK delivered the opinion of the Court.

The question for decision is whether federal or state law controls the ownership of land, called accretion, gradually deposited by the ocean on adjoining upland property conveyed by the United States prior to statehood. The circumstances that give rise to the question are these. Prior to 1889 all land in what is now the State of Washington was owned by the United States, except land that had been conveyed to private parties. At that time owners of property bordering the ocean, such as the predecessor in title of Mrs. Stella Hughes, the petitioner here, had under the common law a right to include within their lands any accretion gradually built up by the ocean.[1] Washington became a State in 1889, and Article 17 of the State's new constitution, as interpreted by its Supreme Court, denied the owners of ocean-front property in the State any further rights in accretion that might in the future be formed between their property and the ocean. This is a suit brought by Mrs. Hughes, the successor in title to the original federal grantee, against the State of Washington as owner of the tidelands to determine whether the right to future accretions which existed under federal law in 1889 was abolished by that provision of the Washington Constitution. The trial court upheld Mrs. Hughes' contention that the right to accretions remained subject to federal law, and that she was the owner of the accreted lands. The State Supreme Court reversed, holding that state law controlled and that the State owned these lands. 67 Wash.2d 799, 410 P.2d 20 (1966). We granted certiorari. 385 U.S. 1000 (1967). We hold that this question is governed by federal, not

1. Jones v. Johnston, 18 How. 150   23 Wall. 46 (1874).
(1856); County of St. Clair v. Lovingston,

state, law and that under federal law Mrs. Hughes, who traces her title to a federal grant prior to statehood, is the owner of these accretions.

While the issue appears never to have been squarely presented to this Court before, we think the path to decision is indicated by our holding in Borax, Ltd. v. Los Angeles, 296 U.S. 10 (1935). In that case we dealt with the rights of a California property owner who held under a federal patent, and in that instance, unlike the present case, the patent was issued after statehood. We held that

> "[t]he question as to the extent of this federal grant, that is, as to the limit of the land conveyed, or the boundary between the upland and the tideland, is necessarily a federal question. It is a question which concerns the validity and effect of an act done by the United States; it involves the ascertainment of the essential basis of a right asserted under federal law." 296 U.S., at 22.

No subsequent case in this Court has cast doubt on the principle announced in *Borax*. See also United States v. Oregon, 295 U.S. 1, 27–28 (1935). The State argues, and the court below held, however, that the *Borax* case should not be applied here because that case involved no question as to accretions. While this is true, the case did involve the question as to what rights were conveyed by the federal grant and decided that the extent of ownership under the federal grant is governed by federal law. This is as true whether doubt as to any boundary is based on a broad question as to the general definition of the shoreline or on a particularized problem relating to the ownership of accretion. See United States v. Washington, 294 F.2d 830, 832 (C.A. 9th Cir. 1961), cert. denied, 369 U.S. 817 (1962). We therefore find no significant difference between *Borax* and the present case.

Recognizing the difficulty of distinguishing *Borax*, respondent urges us to reconsider it. *Borax* itself, as well as *United States v. Oregon*, supra, and many other cases, makes clear that a dispute over title to lands owned by the Federal Government is governed by federal law, although of course the Federal Government may, if it desires, choose to select a state rule as the federal rule. *Borax* holds that there has been no such choice in this area, and we have no difficulty in concluding that *Borax* was correctly decided. The rule deals with waters that lap both the lands of the State and the boundaries of the international sea. This relationship, at this particular point of the marginal sea, is too close to the vital interest of the Nation in its own boundaries to allow it to be governed by any law but the "supreme Law of the Land."

This brings us to the question of what the federal rule is. The State has not attempted to argue that federal law gives it title to these accretions, and it seems clear to us that it could not. A long and unbroken line of decisions of this Court establishes that the grantee of land bounded by a body of navigable water acquires a right to any natural and gradual accretion formed along the shore. In Jones v. Johnston, 18 How. 150 (1856), a dispute between two parties owning land along Lake Michigan over the ownership of soil that had gradually been deposited along the shore, this Court held that "[l]and gained from the sea either by alluvion or dereliction, if the same be by little and little, by small and imperceptible degrees, belongs to the owner of the land adjoining." 18 How., at 156. The Court has repeatedly reaffirmed this rule, County of St. Clair v. Lovingston, 23 Wall. 46 (1874); Jefferis v. East Omaha Land Co., 134 U.S. 178 (1890), and the soundness of the principle is scarcely open to question. Any other rule would leave riparian owners continually in danger of losing the access to water which is often the most valuable feature of their property, and continually vulnerable to harassing litigation challenging the location of the original water lines. While it is true that these riparian rights are to some extent insecure in any event, since they are subject to considerable control by the neighboring owner of the tideland,[3] this is insufficient reason to leave these valuable rights at the mercy of natural phenomena which may in no way affect the interests of the tideland owner. See Stevens v. Arnold, 262 U.S. 266, 269–270 (1923). We therefore hold that petitioner is entitled to the accretion that has been gradually formed along her property by the ocean.

The judgment below is reversed, and the case is remanded to the Supreme Court of Washington for further proceedings not inconsistent with this opinion.

Reversed and remanded.

MR. JUSTICE MARSHALL took no part in the consideration or decision of this case.

MR. JUSTICE STEWART, concurring.

I fully agree that the extent of the 1866 federal grant to which Mrs. Hughes traces her ownership was originally measurable by federal common law, and that under the applicable federal rule her predecessor in title acquired the right to all accretions gradually built up by the sea. For me, however, that does not end the matter. For the Supreme Court of Washington decided in 1966, in the case now before us, that Washington terminated the right to oceanfront accretions when it became a State in 1889. The State concedes that the federal grant in question conferred such a right prior to 1889. But the State purports to have reserved all post-1889 accretions for the public domain. Mrs. Hughes is entitled to the beach she claims in this case only if the State failed in its effort to abolish all private rights to seashore accretions.

Surely it must be conceded as a general proposition that the law of real property is, under our Constitution, left to the individual States to develop and administer. And surely Washington or any other State is free to make changes, either legislative or judicial, in its general rules of real property law, including the rules governing the property rights of riparian owners. Nor are riparian owners who derive their title from the United States somehow immune from the changing impact of

3. It has been held that a State may, without paying compensation, deprive a riparian owner of his common-law right to utilize the flowing water, St. Anthony Falls Water Power Co. v. Water Comm'rs, 168 U.S. 349 (1897), or to build a wharf over the water, Shively v. Bowlby, 152 U.S. 1 (1894). It has also been held that the State may fill its tidelands and thus block the riparian owner's natural access to the water. Port of Seattle v. Oregon & W.R. Co., 255 U.S. 56 (1921).

these general state rules. *Joy* v. *St. Louis*, 201 U.S. 332, 342. For if they were, then the property law of a State like Washington, carved entirely out of federal territory, would be forever frozen into the mold it occupied on the date of the State's admission to the Union. It follows that Mrs. Hughes cannot claim immunity from changes in the property law of Washington simply because her title derives from a federal grant. Like any other property owner, however, Mrs. Hughes may insist, quite apart from the federal origin of her title, that the State not take her land without just compensation. *Chicago, B. & Q.R. Co.* v. *Chicago*, 166 U.S. 226, 236–241.

* * *

We cannot resolve the federal question whether there has been such a taking without first making a determination of our own as to who owned the seashore accretions between 1889 and 1966. To the extent that the decision of the Supreme Court of Washington on that issue arguably conforms to reasonable expectations, we must of course accept it as conclusive. But to the extent that it constitutes a sudden change in state law, unpredictable in terms of the relevant precedents, no such deference would be appropriate. For a State cannot be permitted to defeat the constitutional prohibition against taking property without due process of law by the simple device of asserting retroactively that the property it has taken never existed at all. Whether the decision here worked an unpredictable change in state law thus inevitably presents a federal question for the determination of this Court. * * *

* * * I can only conclude, as did the dissenting judge below, that the state court's most recent construction of Article 17 effected an unforeseeable change in Washington property law as expounded by the State Supreme Court.

There can be little doubt about the impact of that change upon Mrs. Hughes: The beach she had every reason to regard as hers was declared by the state court to be in the public domain. Of course the court did not conceive of this action as a taking. As is so often the case when a State exercises its power to make law, or to regulate, or to pursue a public project, pre-existing property interests were impaired here without any calculated decision to deprive anyone of what he once owned. But the Constitution measures a taking of property not by what a State says, or by what it intends, but by what it *does*. Although the State in this case made no attempt to take the accreted lands by eminent domain, it achieved the same result by effecting a retroactive transformation of private into public property—without paying for the privilege of doing so. Because the Due Process Clause of the Fourteenth Amendment forbids such confiscation by a State, no less through its courts than through its legislature, and no less when a taking is unintended than when it is deliberate, I join in reversing the judgment.

NOTES

1. If the federal government has expressly reserved the bed of a navigable watercourse prior to statehood, can a subsequently created state claim ownership?

When the United States issued oil and gas leases on certain lands under Utah Lake, the state of Utah sued to assert its ownership of the lake bed. The 150 square mile lake is navigable and the state's title was asserted based on the equal footing doctrine, in that other states have received title to the beds of navigable waterways. The United States invoked an 1888 statute that had been used to set aside the lake as a future federal reservoir site. Utah became a state in 1896. The United States Supreme Court rejected this theory and said that the test is whether "Congress * * * clearly express[ed] an intention to defeat Utah's claim to the lake bed under the equal footing doctrine." Utah Division of State Lands v. United States, 482 U.S. 193 (1987). Several years before, the Supreme Court refused to review the ruling of the Ninth Circuit Court of Appeals that oil deposits under the bed of a navigable lake in the Kenai National Moose Range were federal property because the lands and waters of the 2 million acre range had been withdrawn by executive order prior to Alaska statehood. United States v. Alaska, 423 F.2d 764 (9th Cir.1970), cert. denied 400 U.S. 967 (1970). Thus, until 1987 it was generally assumed that pre-statehood withdrawals were effective to preserve federal title to the beds of navigable waters without specific congressional action.

2. *Hughes* involved ocean property, but the opinion suggests that all post-statehood title disputes to beds underlying navigable waters might be decided by federal rather than state rules. This dictum became the rule in Bonelli Cattle Co. v. Arizona, 414 U.S. 313 (1973). The dispute in *Bonelli* was whether the state or a private party whose title was based on a federal patent held title to land that reemerged after completion of a federal rechanneling project. The court said the federal test applied and added:

> The equal-footing doctrine was never intended to provide a State with a windfall of thousands of acres of dry land exposed when the main thread of a navigable stream is changed. It would be at odds with the fundamental purpose of the original grant to the States to afford a State title to land from which a navigable stream had receded unless the land was exposed as part of a navigational or related public project of which it was a necessary and integral part * * *.

> The advance of the Colorado's waters divested the title of the upland owners in favor of the State in order to guarantee full public enjoyment of the watercourse. But, when the water receded from the land, there was no longer a public benefit to be protected; consequently, the State, as sovereign, has no need for title. That the cause of the recession was artificial, or that the rate was perceptible, should be of no effect.

414 U.S. at 322–24. Four years later the court reversed *Bonelli* in Oregon ex rel. State Land Bd. v. Corvallis Sand & Gravel Co., 429 U.S. 363 (1977). The state of Oregon claimed title to the bed of a navigable channel which became the main channel of Willamette River after a major flood. Mr. Justice Rehnquist explained why state law alone should govern post-statehood title disputes:

Our error, as we now see it, was to view the equal-footing doctrine enunciated in *Pollard's Lessee v. Hagan* as a basis upon which federal common law could supersede state law in the determination of land titles. Precisely the contrary is true; in *Pollard's Lessee* itself the equal-footing doctrine resulted in the State's acquisition of title notwithstanding the efforts of the Federal Government to dispose of the lands in question in another way.

The equal-footing doctrine did not, therefore, provide a basis for federal law to supersede the State's application of its own law in deciding title to the Bonelli land, and state law should have been applied unless there were present some other principle of federal law requiring state law to be displaced. * * *

429 U.S. at 371–72. What is the status of *Hughes* and *Borax* after *Corvallis Sand & Gravel*? Justice Rehnquist explained that federal law was applied in *Borax* to determine boundaries between uplands and tidelands at the time of statehood. He continued, saying:

> * * * This same principle would require that determination of the initial boundary between a riverbed, which the State acquired under the equal-footing doctrine, and riparian fast lands likewise be decided as a matter of federal law rather than state law. But that determination is solely for the purpose of fixing the boundaries of the riverbed acquired by the State at the time of its admission to the Union; thereafter the role of the equal-footing doctrine is ended, and the land is subject to the laws of the State. The expressions in *Bonelli* suggesting a more expansive role for the equal-footing doctrine are contrary to the line of cases following *Pollard's Lessee*.[6]

429 U.S. at 376–77.

3. The federal government's power to reserve the beds underlying navigable waters must be exercised under before-statehood circumstances that clearly demonstrate an intention to defeat state ownership. In Montana v. United States, 450 U.S. 544 (1981), the Crow Tribe asserted the right to regulate fishing by non-Indians in the Big Horn River. The United States claimed that it had conveyed title to the river's bed. The state argued that the United States had held the bed in trust, and that upon statehood it passed to Montana. The United States relied on Shively v. Bowlby, 152 U.S. 1 (1894), pages 397–98,

---

6. *Amici* Utah and New Mexico also urge us to reconsider our decision in *Hughes v. Washington*, 389 U.S. 290 (1967). They advance the same reasons for such reconsideration as they do with respect to *Bonelli*. But *Hughes* was not cited by the Oregon courts below, and in *Bonelli* we expressly declined to rely upon it as a basis for our decision there, see 414 U.S., at 321 n. 11. We therefore have no occasion to address the issue. We are aware of the fact that *Hughes* gave to *Borax* the same sort of expansive construction as did *Bonelli*, but we are likewise aware that *Hughes* dealt with ocean-front property, a fact which the Court thought sufficiently different from the usual situation so as to justify a "federal common law" rule of riparian proprietorship:

> "The rule deals with waters that lap both the lands of the State and the boundaries of the international sea. This relationship, at this particular point of the marginal sea, is too close to the vital interest of the Nation in its own boundaries to allow it to be governed by any law but the 'supreme Law of the Land.'" 389 U.S. at 293.

supra, but the court held that there is a presumption against any conveyance or retention of title to the bed by the United States, citing United States v. Holt State Bank, 270 U.S. 49 (1926):

> The Crow treaties in this case, like the Chippewa treaties in *Holt State Bank*, fail to overcome the established presumption that the beds of navigable waters remain in trust for future States and pass to the new States when they assume sovereignty. The 1851 treaty did not by its terms formally convey any land to the Indians at all, but instead chiefly represented a covenant among several tribes which recognized specific boundaries for their respective territories. Treaty of Fort Laramie, 1851, [11 Stat. 749] Art. 5. It referred to hunting and fishing only insofar as it said that the Crow Indians "do not surrender the privilege of hunting, fishing, or passing over any of the tracts of country heretofore described," a statement that had no bearing on ownership of the riverbed. * * * The treaty in no way expressly referred to the riverbed, Packer v. Bird, 137 U.S., at 672, nor was an intention to convey the riverbed expressed in "clear and especial words," Martin v. Waddell, 16 Pet., at 411 [41 U.S., at 349] or "definitely declared or otherwise made very plain," United States v. Holt State Bank, 270 U.S., at 55, Rather, as in *Holt*, "[t]he effect of what was done was to reserve in a general way for the continued occupation of the Indians what remained of their aboriginal territory." Id. at 58.

> Though Article 2 gave the Crow Indians the sole right to use and occupy the reserved land, and implicitly, the power to exclude others from it, the respondents' reliance on that provision simply begs the question of the precise extent of the conveyed lands to which this exclusivity attaches. The mere fact that the bed of a navigable water lies within the boundaries described in the treaty does not make the riverbed part of the conveyed land, especially when there is no express reference to the riverbed that might overcome the presumption against its conveyance.

450 U.S. at 553–54. Justices Blackmun, Brennan and Marshall dissented on the ground that the purpose of the reservation indicated an intent to grant the tribe title to that portion of the bed that was totally encompassed by the reservation. See Choctaw Nation v. Oklahoma, 397 U.S. 620 (1970).

2. Public Interest in Submerged Lands

Rights to enjoy water-related land resources are shared between private owners and the public to a greater extent than rights in other lands. Private activities that conflict with navigation are usually prohibited or restricted.

The public trust doctrine was articulated by the courts as a way to prevent private control of waters needed for public purposes, primarily navigation. Regardless of who owns or controls submerged lands, any state actions or private uses that conflict with public rights such as navigation may be prohibited. The public trust has been urged by environmentalists as a common law theory to protect a variety of public uses and even as a ground to prevent the filling of wetlands. See Marks v. Whitney, 491 P.2d 374 (Cal.1971), page 414, infra.

The notion that submerged lands are subject to a public trust implies that owners (whether public or private) must use such lands consistent with historically important public purposes. Invariably, this constrains development and can depress the economic value of submerged lands and adjacent uplands. The argument (made in Illinois Central Railroad v. Illinois, 146 U.S. 387 (1892), page 409, infra) that the beds underlying navigable waters are subject to a public trust was consistent with an historic use of waterways for commerce that has constitutional roots. The assertion of the public trust is based on a broader tradition of recognizing rights of public use of waters as well as in constitutional doctrine. See Note, *The Public Trust in Tidal Areas: A Sometime Submerged Traditional Doctrine,* 79 Yale L.J. 762 (1970).

CHARLES F. WILKINSON,
THE HEADWATERS OF THE PUBLIC TRUST:
SOME THOUGHTS ON THE SOURCE
AND SCOPE OF THE TRADITIONAL DOCTRINE

19 Envtl.Law 425, 428–31 (1989).

* * * Public values in water can be traced back * * * to the Roman *Institutes of Justinian* and the Magna Carta—often cited as historical antecedents for the public trust—and to medieval Spain and France. But these ideas extended far beyond Europe. In the Orient, recognition of public uses of water existed well before the birth of Christ. African nations held similar traditions: "from time immemorial the people of Nigeria have enjoyed the right to fish the sea, with its creeks and arms and navigable rivers within the tides." In Moslem countries, "the fundamentals of Islamic water law purport to ensure to all members of the Moslem community the availability of water." Spanish and Mexican laws and institutions in the New World evinced a powerful tradition that large portions of the water supply must be dedicated to the community good.

This general and nearly universal notion—the reluctance to allow our great watercourses to be subject to wholesale private acquisition—goes back even further on this continent, for most American Indian cultures wholly denied the possibility of ownership of land, air, and water. * * *

The English, whose common law is the most direct source of our public trust doctrine, saw ownership differently than did American Indian people and generally favored private ownership of natural resources. But the British made an exception for navigable waterways. The common law distinguished between the *jus privatum,* which the Crown could transfer to individuals in fee ownership, and the *jus publicum,* which the Crown held in trust for the public. The most important areas of these public rights were the coasts and those stretches of rivers affected by the ebb and flow of the tide.

* * *

Public values in water certainly existed in America at the time of its founding. Indeed, it is hard to overstate the importance of the major watercourses during the formative years of the United States. To the early settlers, the rivers furnished paths of exploration and avenues for the fur trade and log floats. Due to the density of the forests and the difficulty of road construction, the watercourses provided transportation routes, and their shores afforded logical areas for settlement. Fishing was significant, both for commercial and subsistence purposes. The Revolutionary War and the War of 1812 demonstrated the military necessity of controlling the natural highways.

* * *

In an even larger sense, water was a unifying factor for the Nation. Rivers and lakes facilitated trade, allowed immigration to new areas, and established communication lines among the states. The need for one central governing body to oversee water traffic was a key impetus for Congress' primacy under the commerce clause of the Constitution.[53] Chief Justice Marshall explained the significance of the clause and of navigation to the nation as a whole in Gibbons v. Ogden,[54] by saying that "[t]he power over commerce, including navigation, was one of the primary objects for which the people of America adopted their government, and must have been contemplated in forming it." *Gibbons v. Ogden,* one of the first Supreme Court commerce clause decisions, involved a monopoly of the steamboats in New York State; the conflict between steamboat monopolies and free watercourses was of great concern nationally. Marshall, upholding a federal license granted outside of the New York scheme and justifying the need for federal regulation of the waterways, wrote that "deep streams * * * pass through the interior of almost every State in the Union, and furnish the means of exercising this right [to regulate commerce]. If Congress has the power to regulate it, that power must be exercised whenever the subject exists."

Thus, the ribbons of waterways tied the early nation together— economically, politically, and symbolically.

* * *

Since all new states took title to the beds and banks of navigable watercourses at statehood as a matter of implication, and since the public trust applies to the same bodies of water, it is logical to view the trust as an implied condition of statehood—a key adjunct of Congress' general purpose of keeping those watercourses "forever free." Congressional power to impose such a condition, in implementing the commerce authority, is beyond question.[134] This analysis, of course, would mean

---

53. "The Congress shall have Power * * * To regulate Commerce with foreign Nations, and among the several States, and with the Indian Tribes." U.S. Const. art. I, § 8, cl. 3. Other constitutional provisions indicating the framers' overriding concern with free navigation include the tonnage duty clause of U.S. Const. art. I, § 10, cl. 3; the import-export clause, U.S. Const. art. I, § 10, cl. 2; the ports and vessels clause, U.S. Const. art. I, § 9, cl. 6; and the admiralty clause, U.S. Const. art. III, § 2, cl. 1.

54. 22 U.S. (9 Wheat.) 1 (1824).

134. See Pollard's Lessee v. Hagan, 44 U.S. (3 How.) 212, 229–30 (1844), where the Court upheld Congress' power to include

that the public trust doctrine is not constitutionally mandated. Rather, it is accomplished by preemption, with congressional policy being effected through the statehood acts and the many statutes governing navigation. The approach would be attractive to modern courts because preemption, rather than recognition of constitutional standards, is the preferred method of analysis in constitutional adjudication.

Nevertheless, in the context of the law involving watercourses navigable for title, with its special traditions and heavy overlay of constitutional doctrine, locating the public trust doctrine in the Constitution itself is perhaps more persuasive. The navigation servitude, a limit on state authority on exactly the same watercourses, is an implied component of the commerce clause. The navigation servitude and the public trust doctrine are parallel doctrines, both affording complementary protections to major watercourses—the Court has recently, and correctly, described the public trust as a "servitude." [138] Similarly, the Court has found that the extraordinary implied land transfer to the states upon admission is guaranteed to the states under the Constitution by the equal footing doctrine. It follows that the trust, a "servitude" or "easement" on the underlying land title, is also imposed by the same source, the Constitution. For more than 150 years, the Supreme Court has consistently given a constitutional cast to state and federal prerogatives and obligations with regard to waters navigable for title, due ultimately to the key role of these watercourses in the country's commerce and society and in the formation of the national government. Thus, although the other federal alternatives mentioned above have characteristics that cut in their favor, the fairest and most principled conclusion is that the public trust doctrine is rooted in the commerce clause and became binding on new states at statehood.

* * *

Molly Selvin, *The Public Trust Doctrine in American Law and Economic Policy, 1789–1920,* 6 Wis.L.Rev. 1403 (1980) is a careful study of the nineteenth and early twentieth century antecedents of the modern use of the public trust doctrine that illustrates how the courts

the "common highways, and forever free" condition in a statehood act under the commerce power. In determining the validity of such a condition in the statehood act of Alabama, the Court stated:

[a]s the provision of what is called the compact [that all navigable waters within the said State shall forever remain public highways, free to the citizens] between the United States and the state of Alabama does not, by the above reasoning [from Gibbons v. Ogden, 22 U.S. (9 Wheat.) at 196], exceed the power thereby conceded to Congress over the original states on the same subject * * *.

This supposed compact is, therefore, nothing more than a regulation of commerce, to that extent, among the several States * * *.

Id. at 230. See also United States v. Riverside Bayview Homes, Inc., 474 U.S. 121 (1985); Heart of Atlanta Motel, Inc. v. United States, 379 U.S. 241 (1964); Katzenbach v. McClung, 379 U.S. 294 (1964).

138. See Summa Corp. v. California ex rel. State Lands Comm'n, 466 U.S. 198, 206 (1984). * * *

used the vague concept to assert the power to control the use of navigable waters for public purposes important to the times.

ILLINOIS CENTRAL RAILROAD v. ILLINOIS

Supreme Court of the United States, 1892.
146 U.S. 387, 13 S.Ct. 110, 36 L.Ed. 1018.

[The facts of the case grew out of the complex history of federal, state and local land grants to railroads. To encourage the Illinois Central, the City of Chicago made a number of concessions, allowing the railroad to extend its lines for better access to its station. In 1869 the legislature gave it fee title to the submerged bed of Lake Michigan east of its tracks to the breakwater for a distance of one mile in return for a yearly rental calculated from the gross earnings the land conveyed. The court noted in its opinion that the original purpose of the 1869 act was to convey the state lands to the City of Chicago to allow it to enlarge its harbor but "during the passage of the act its purport was changed." In 1873 the legislature had a change of mind and repealed the act of 1869. The state brought a quiet title action and won. In affirming, the Supreme Court addressed the state's power to enact the 1869 and 1873 legislation:]

The question, therefore, to be considered is whether the legislature was competent to thus deprive the State of its ownership of the submerged lands in the harbor of Chicago, and of the consequent control of its waters; or, in other words, whether the railroad corporation can hold the lands and control the waters by the grant, against any future exercise of power over them by the State.

That the State holds the title to the lands under the navigable waters of Lake Michigan, within its limits, in the same manner that the State holds title to soils under tide water, by the common law, we have already shown, and that title necessarily carries with it control over the waters above them whenever the lands are subjected to use. But it is a title different in character from that which the State holds in lands intended for sale. It is different from the title which the United States hold in the public lands which are open to preemption and sale. It is a title held in trust for the people of the State that they may enjoy the navigation of the waters, carry on commerce over them, and have liberty of fishing therein freed from the obstruction or interference of private parties. The interest of the people in the navigation of the waters and in commerce over them may be improved in many instances by the erection of wharves, docks and piers therein, for which purpose the State may grant parcels of the submerged lands; and, so long as their disposition is made for such purpose, no valid objections can be made to the grants. It is grants of parcels of lands under navigable waters, that may afford foundation for wharves, piers, docks and other structures in aid of commerce, and grants of parcels which, being occupied, do not substantially impair the public interest in the lands and waters remaining, that are chiefly considered and sustained in the adjudged cases as a valid exercise of legislative power consistently with the trust to the public upon which such lands are held by the State. But that is a very different doctrine from the one which would sanction the abdication of the general control of the State over lands under the navigable waters of an entire harbor or bay, or of a sea or lake. Such abdication is not consistent with the exercise of that trust which requires the government of the State to preserve such waters for the use of the public. The trust devolving upon the State for the public, and which can only be discharged by the management and control of property in which the public has an interest, cannot be relinquished by a transfer of the property. The control of the State for the purposes of the trust can never be lost, except as to such parcels as are used in promoting the interests of the public therein, or can be disposed of without any substantial impairment of the public interest in the lands and waters remaining. It is only by observing the distinction between a grant of such parcels for the improvement of the public interest, or which when occupied do not substantially impair the public interest in the lands and waters remaining, and a grant of the whole property in which the public is interested, that the language of the adjudged cases can be reconciled. General language sometimes found in opinions of the courts, expressive of absolute ownership and control by the State of lands under navigable waters, irrespective of any trust as to their use and disposition, must be read and construed with reference to the special facts of the particular cases. A grant of all the lands under the navigable waters of a State has never been adjudged to be within the legislative power; and any attempted grant of the kind would be held, if not absolutely void on its face, as subject to revocation. The State can no more abdicate its trust over property in which the whole people are interested, like navigable waters and soils under them, so as to leave them entirely under the use and control of private parties, except in the instance of parcels mentioned for the improvement of the navigation and use of the waters, or when parcels can be disposed of without impairment of the public interest in what remains, than it can abdicate its police powers in the administration of government and the preservation of the peace. In the administration of government the use of such powers may for a limited period be delegated to a municipality or other body, but there always remains with the State the right to revoke those powers and exercise them in a more direct manner, and one more conformable to its wishes. So with trusts connected with public property, or property of a special character, like lands under navigable waters, they cannot be placed entirely beyond the direction and control of the State.

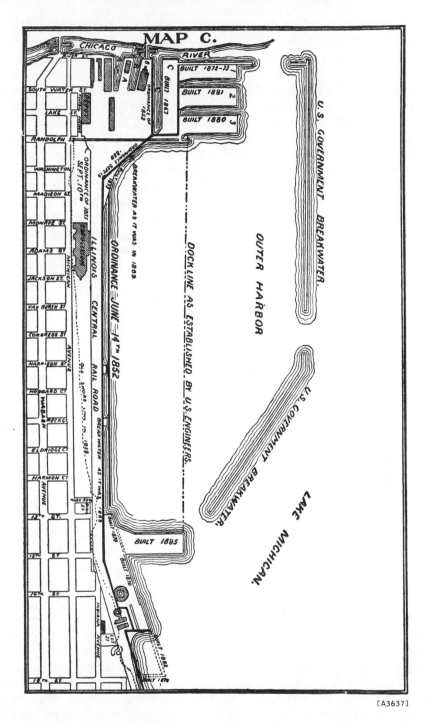

[A3637]

The harbor of Chicago is of immense value to the people of the State of Illinois in the facilities it affords to its vast and constantly increasing commerce; and the idea that its legislature can deprive the State of control over its bed and waters and place the same in the hands of a private corporation created for a different purpose, one limited to transportation of passengers and freight between distant points and the city, is a proposition that cannot be defended.

The area of the submerged lands proposed to be ceded by the act in question to the railroad company embraces something more than a thousand acres, being, as stated by counsel, more than three times the area of the outer harbor, and not only including all of that harbor but embracing adjoining submerged lands which will, in all probability, be hereafter included in the harbor. It is as large as that embraced by all the merchandise docks along the Thames at London; is much larger than that included in the famous docks and basins at Liverpool; is twice that of the port of Marseilles, and nearly if not quite equal to the pier area along the water front of the city of New York. And the arrivals and clearings of vessels at the port exceed in number those of New York, and are equal to those of New York and Boston combined. Chicago has nearly twenty-five per cent of the lake carrying trade as compared with the arrivals and clearings of all the leading ports of our great inland seas. In the year ending June 30, 1886, the joint arrivals and clearances of vessels at that port amounted to twenty-two thousand and ninety-six, with a tonnage of over seven millions; and in 1890 the tonnage of the vessels reached nearly nine millions. As stated by counsel, since the passage of the Lake Front Act, in 1869, the population of the city has increased nearly a million souls, and the increase of commerce has kept pace with it. It is hardly conceivable that the legislature can divest the State of the control and management of this harbor and vest it absolutely in a private corporation. Surely an act of the legislature transferring the title to its submerged lands and the power claimed by the railroad company, to a foreign State or nation would be repudiated, without hesitation, as a gross perversion of the trust over the property under which it is held. So would a similar transfer to a corporation of another State. It would not be listened to that the control and management of the harbor of that great city—a subject of concern to the whole people of the State—should thus be placed elsewhere than in the State itself. All the objections which can be urged to such attempted transfer may be urged to a transfer to a private corporation like the railroad company in this case.

Any grant of the kind is necessarily revocable, and the exercise of the trust by which the property was held by the State can be resumed at any time. Undoubtedly there may be expenses incurred in improvements made under such a grant which the State ought to pay; but, be that as it may, the power to resume the trust whenever the State judges best is, we think, incontrovertible. The position advanced by the railroad company in support of its claim to the ownership of the submerged lands and the right to the erection of wharves, piers and docks at its pleasure, or for its business in the harbor of Chicago, would place every harbor in the country at the mercy of a majority of the legislature of the State in which the harbor is situated.

We cannot, it is true, cite any authority where a grant of this kind has been held invalid, for we believe that no instance exists where the harbor of a great city and its commerce have been allowed to pass into the control of any private corporation. But the decisions are numerous which declare that such property is held by the State, by virtue of its sovereignty, in trust for the public. * * *

NOTES

1. The Illinois Legislature transferred 194.6 acres of land beneath Lake Michigan to United States Steel for $19,460.00 after a legislative finding that the grant would not impair the public interest. A public park was located north of the proposed mill. The Illinois Supreme Court invalidated the grant. The court found that prior cases have never upheld a grant where "the primary purpose was to benefit a private interest." Because the transferred trust lands were "adjacent to waters presently in important public use [which] would be irretrievably removed from the use of the people of Illinois * * * " the court held that "to preserve meaning and vitality in the public trust doctrine, when a grant of submerged land beneath waters of Lake Michigan is proposed under the circumstances here, the public interest to be served cannot be only incidental and remote. The claimed benefit here to the public through additional employment and economic improvement is too indirect, intangible and elusive to satisfy the requirement of a public purpose." People ex rel. Scott v. Chicago Park Dist., 360 N.E.2d 773, 780–81 (Ill.1976). Accord: Lake Michigan Federation v. United States Army Corps of Engineers, 742 F.Supp. 441 (N.D.Ill.1990) (invalidating state legislation conveying 18.5 acres of Lake Michigan bed to private university for a landfill). Cf. Lane v. Redondo Beach, 122 Cal.Rptr. 189 (Cal.Ct.App.1975).

2. The doctrine of *Illinois Central* has been offered as the basis for a general theory of public rights in natural resources requiring the assertion of state police power to ensure the protection of public rights. Joseph Sax, *The Public Trust Doctrine in Natural Resources Law: Effective Judicial Intervention,* 68 Mich. L. Rev. 471 (1970). Sax argues that the question is

> has the government granted to some private interest the authority to make resource-use decisions which may subordinate broad public resource uses to that private interest? In the extreme case, that question raises the problem of *Illinois Central,* and a court might appropriately interpose a flat legal prohibition on the ground that the state has divested itself of its general regulatory power over a matter of great public importance.

Id. at 562.

Does *Illinois Central* impose a "flat legal prohibition"?

3. Courts have not been enthusiastic about extending the trust to other resources such as public lands, e.g., Sierra Club v. Andrus, 487 F.Supp. 443 (D.D.C. 1980), affirmed 659 F.2d 203 (D.C. Cir. 1981) (national parks). See Steven M. Jawetz, Comment, *The Public Trust Totem in Public Land Law—Ineffective—and Undesirable—Judicial Intervention,* 10 Ecology L.Q. 455 (1982). What is the future role of the doctrine in light of the rapid expansion of environmental regulation and the Supreme Court's seemingly continued willingness to allow the use of the police power to restrict the use of private property? See

Richard J. Lazarus, *Changing Conceptions of Property and Sovereignty in Natural Resources: Questioning the Public Trust Doctrine,* 71 Iowa L.Rev. 631 (1986); Charles F. Wilkinson, *The Headwaters of the Public Trust: Some Thoughts on the Source and Scope of the Traditional Doctrine,* 19 Envtl. L. 425 (1989).

MARKS v. WHITNEY

Supreme Court of California, 1971.
6 Cal.3d 251, 98 Cal.Rptr. 790, 491 P.2d 374.

[Marks was a tidelands patentee whose lands adjoined almost the entire shoreline of Whitney's upland property. Marks asserted the right to fill all the tidelands he owned and Whitney objected. The trial court held that Whitney had obtained a prescriptive easement of access to public waters which enabled him to locate a seven-foot wide wharf across Marks' tidelands.]

This land was patented *as tidelands* to Marks' predecessor in title. The patent of May 15, 1874, recites that it was issued by the Governor of California "by virtue of authority in me vested" pursuant to "Statutes enacted from time to time" for the "Sale and Conveyance of the *Tide Lands belonging to the State by virtue of her sovereignty.*" (Emphasis added.)

The governing statute was the act of March 28, 1868, entitled "An Act to provide for the management and sale of the lands belonging to the State." By its terms it repealed all other laws relating to the sale of swamp and overflowed, salt-marsh and tidelands. These laws, including the Act of March 28, 1868, were codified in former Political Code sections 3440–3493½. They were explicitly and expansively considered by this court entirely separate from the restrictions contained in Article 15, sections two and three, of the State Constitution (enacted in 1879)—In Forestier v. Johnson (1912) 164 Cal. 24, 127 P. 156 and People v. California Fish Co., 166 Cal. 576, 589–598, 138 P. 79. Prior to the issuance of this patent it was held that a patent to tidelands conveyed no title; or a voidable title (Taylor v. Underhill (1871) 40 Cal. 471). It was not until 1913 that this court decided in People v. California Fish Co., supra, 166 Cal. 576, 596, 138 P. 79, 87, that "The only practicable theory is to hold that all tideland is included, but that the public right was not intended to be divested or affected by a sale of tidelands under these general laws relating alike both to swamp land and tidelands. Our opinion is that * * * the buyer of land under these statutes receives the title to the soil, the *jus privatum*, subject to the public right of navigation, and in subordination to the right of the state to take possession and use and improve it for that purpose, as it may deem necessary. In this way the public right will be preserved, and the private right of the purchaser will be given as full effect as the public interests will permit."

* * *

Public trust easements are traditionally defined in terms of navigation, commerce and fisheries. They have been held to include the right to fish, hunt, bathe, swim, to use for boating and general recreation purposes the navigable waters of the state, and to use the bottom of the navigable waters for anchoring, standing, or other purposes. The public has the same rights in and to tidelands.

The public uses to which tidelands are subject are sufficiently flexible to encompass changing public needs. In administering the trust the state is not burdened with an outmoded classification favoring one mode of utilization over another (Colberg, Inc. v. State, 67 Cal.2d 408, 421–422, 62 Cal.Rptr. 401, 432 P.2d 3.) There is a growing public recognition that one of the most important public uses of the tidelands—a use encompassed within the tidelands trust—is the preservation of those lands in their natural state, so that they may serve as ecological units for scientific study, as open space, and as environments which provide food and habitat for birds and marine life, and which favorably affect the scenery and climate of the area. It is not necessary to here define precisely all the public uses which encumber tidelands.

*   *   *

The power of the state to control, regulate and utilize its navigable waterways and the lands lying beneath them, when acting within the terms of the trust, is absolute (People v. California Fish Co., supra, 166 Cal. p. 597, 138 P. 79), except as limited by the paramount supervisory power of the federal government over navigable waters (Colberg, Inc. v. State, supra, 67 Cal.2d 416–422, 62 Cal.Rptr. 401, 432 P.2d 3). We are not here presented with any action by the state or the federal government modifying, terminating, altering or relinquishing the *jus publicum* in these tidelands or in the navigable waters covering them. Neither sovereignty is a party to this action. This court takes judicial notice, however, that there has been no official act of either sovereignty to modify or extinguish the public trust servitude upon Marks' tidelands. The State Attorney General, as amicus curiae, has advised this court that no such action or determination has been made by the state.

We are confronted with the issue, however, whether the trial court may restrain or bar a private party, namely, Whitney, "from claiming or asserting any estate, right, title, interest in or claim or lien upon" the tidelands quieted in Marks. The injunction so made, without any limitation expressing the public servitude, is broad enough to prohibit Whitney from asserting or in any way exercising public trust uses in these tidelands and the navigable waters covering them in his capacity as a member of the public. This is beyond the jurisdiction of the court. It is within the province of the trier of fact to determine whether any particular use made or asserted by Whitney in or over these tidelands would constitute an infringement either upon the *jus privatum* of Marks or upon the *jus publicum* of the people. It is also within the province of the trier of fact to determine whether any particular use to which Marks wishes to devote his tidelands constitutes an unlawful infringement upon the *jus publicum* therein. It is a political question, within the wisdom and power of the Legislature, acting within the scope of its duties as trustee, to determine whether public trust uses should be modified or extinguished (see City of Long Beach v. Mansell, 3 Cal.3d at p. 482, fn. 17, 91 Cal.Rptr. 23, 476 P.2d 423), and to take the necessary steps to free them from such burden. In the absence of state or federal action the court may not bar members of the public from lawfully asserting or exercising public trust rights on this privately owned tidelands.

There is absolutely no merit in Marks' contention that as the owner of the *jus privatum* under this patent he may fill and develop his property, whether for navigational purposes or not; nor in his contention that his past and present plan for development of these tidelands as a marina have caused the extinguishment of the public easement. Reclamation with or without prior authorization from the state does not *ipso facto* terminate the public trust nor render the issue moot.

* * *

A proper judgment for a patentee of tidelands was determined by this court in People v. California Fish Co., supra, 166 Cal. at pp. 598–599, 138 P. at p. 88, to be that he owns "the soil, subject to the easement of the public for the public uses of navigation and commerce, and to the right of the state, as administrator and controller of these public uses and the public trust therefor, to enter upon and possess the same for the preservation and advancement of the public uses, and to make such changes and improvements as may be deemed advisable for those purposes."

NOTES

1. Can the state terminate the trust and convey the lands free from the trust? *Marks* seems to suggest that the decision to terminate the trust is unreviewable but *Illinois Central* holds the opposite. Though no court has ever held that trust lands are *per se* inalienable, few courts hold that legislative grants or use decisions are unreviewable. The Wisconsin Supreme Court said: "The trust reposed in the state is not a passive trust. * * * [T]he trust, being both active and administrative, requires the law-making body to act in all cases where action is necessary, not only to preserve the trust, but to promote it." City of Milwaukee v. State, 214 N.W. 820, 830 (Wis.1927).

2. The *Marks* dictum about the expanded purpose of the public trust in light of modern societal tastes was carried forward in City of Berkeley v. Superior Court of Alameda Cty., 606 P.2d 362 (Cal.1980). In a 4–3 decision, the court held that two acts of the California legislature passed in 1868 and 1870 did not convey fee simple title to tidelands and that some of the tidelands remained subject to the public trust. The two statutes allowed some 88 square miles of San Francisco Bay to be conveyed and filled, and in 1915 the California Supreme Court held that these acts conveyed fee simple interests freed from the trust. Knudson v. Kearney, 152 P. 541 (Cal.1915). Writing for the majority, Justice Mosk, the author of *Marks*, reasoned that *Knudson* was wrong. Either the two acts were not intended to promote navigation and thus grants made pursuant to them were not free of the public trust or, in the alternative, even if the purpose was navigation improvement, "*Illinois Central* holds that a state may not grant to private persons tidelands as vast in area as the board was authorized to sell by

the 1870 act." 606 P.2d at 371. To balance longstanding reliance on *Knudson* with the court's modern perception of the scope of the trust, the court held that tidal lands in private ownership remained subject to the public trust unless they had already been filled, in which case they were held in absolute title free of the trust.

Two other important public trust opinions authored by Justice Mosk include State v. Superior Court of Lake County (*Lyon*), 625 P.2d 239 (Cal.1981), and State v. Superior Court of Placer County (*Fogerty*), 625 P.2d 256 (Cal.1981). *Lyon* holds that the trust extends to non-tidal waters conveyed to private parties. Under California law, riparian and littoral owners own to the low water mark of bodies of water navigable in 1850 (at statehood) but the submerged land between the high and low water marks remains subject to the public trust. Thus, the state could deny a permit to fill the foreshore for ecological reasons or to preserve public recreational opportunities. *Fogerty* was a Civil Rights Act § 1983 suit to prevent the state from asserting its public trust claims to the foreshore, but the supreme court held that the state cannot be estopped from asserting these claims for public policy reasons.

Justice Mosk continued his theory of the public trust in City of Los Angeles v. Venice Penninsula Properties, 644 P.2d 792 (Cal.1982), holding that the trust applied to tidelands ceded by Mexico under the Treaty of Guadalupe Hidalgo, but the Supreme Court did not agree. "We hold that California cannot at this late date assert its public trust easement over petitioner's property, when petitioner's predecessors-in-interest had their interest confirmed without any mention of such an easement in proceedings taken pursuant to the Act of 1851." Summa Corp. v. California ex rel. State Lands Comm'n, 466 U.S. 198, 209 (1984).

3. In Kootenai Envtl. Alliance v. Panhandle Yacht Club, Inc., 671 P.2d 1085 (Idaho 1983), a public interest group challenged the state's grant of a permit for a ten-year lease of five surface acres to a private club to build a marina for 112 sailboats in Lake Coeur d'Alene, a navigable lake. The group charged that such a grant was contrary to the public trust. The court held that the Department of Lands properly determined that the yacht club's use "did not violate the public trust, at this time." The grant remained subject to the public trust, however, so that the state could later determine that the "conveyance is no longer compatible with the public trust * * *." As attorney for the yacht club, what advice would you give to your client about the future security of its lease? See City of Redondo Beach v. Taxpayers, 352 P.2d 170 (Cal.1960) (small boat harbor consistent with state tideland grant for a harbor to improve commerce and navigation).

4. In California the legislature has granted much of the state's tide and submerged lands to cities, counties and special districts. The initial grants were for harbor purposes and were made in anticipation of reaping benefits from the opening of the Panama Canal. When a tide and submerged lands grantee has desired to use the lands for non-harbor purposes it has generally obtained special legislation amending

the grant. How would you resolve the following challenges? Grant amendments allowed the lease of trust lands for "the construction, maintenance and organization of nonprofit benevolent and charitable institutions * * * for the promotion of the moral and social welfare of seamen, naval officers and enlisted men and other persons engaged in and about the harbor and commerce, fishery and navigation [*sic*]." People v. Long Beach, 338 P.2d 177 (Cal.1959). What about a grant amendment permitting a convention center with exhibition and banquet halls to be used in part to promote a port but also by organizations not connected with the port? Cf. Haggerty v. Oakland, 326 P.2d 957 (Cal.1958). What about a grant amendment allowing a park and parkway along the edge of a harbor? See Los Angeles Athletic Club v. Long Beach, 17 P.2d 1061 (Cal.1932). What about a shopping center, a golf course, or a junior college?

3. Private Use of Submerged Lands

At common law a wharf placed in navigable waters was a purpresture (unlawful inclosure of public property). If injury to the public right of navigation was shown, it was also a public nuisance. The difference was that if only a purpresture was proved, the court could decide if it would be more beneficial to the public to abate it or let it remain. But, if a public nuisance existed, the court could not balance and the wharf had to be removed. See Joseph Kinnicut Angell, A Treatise On The Right Of Property In Tidewaters And In The Soil And Shores Thereof 196–206 (2d ed. 1847). Colonial ordinances "early allowed the owners of lands bounding on tide waters greater rights and privileges in the shore below high water mark, than they had in England." Shively v. Bowlby, 152 U.S. 1, 18 (1892). A 1661 Massachusetts ordinance permitted a riparian to wharf out 100 rods from the high water mark. Gradually the eastern and midwestern states came to recognize the right by statute or custom and usage. Modern cases typically are consistent with such rights. E.g., Johnson v. Bryant, 350 So.2d 433 (Ala. 1977) (a dock erected pursuant to the common law right to wharf out and authorized by the Corps of Engineers "does not constitute a nuisance per se"). In the Pacific coast states, however, the right has always been entirely statutory as the courts have consistently held that any wharf which is not authorized by the legislature is a purpresture.

In California, the state may allow the riparian to wharf out upon the payment of fees or may eject the wharfing out riparian as a trespasser. If the state elects not to bring suit, another riparian claiming injury from the wharf can only obtain relief upon proof that the wharf is a public nuisance that causes special damage. Woods v. Johnson, 50 Cal.Rptr. 515 (Cal.Ct.App.1966).

How can the public right to use the surface of the water overlying state-owned beds be reconciled with the riparian's easement to wharf out? Capune v. Robbins, 160 S.E.2d 881 (N.C.1968) offers one answer. Plaintiff was attempting to go from Coney Island, New York, to Florida via surfboard. Defendant owned a fishing pier built into the Atlantic Ocean and it was his policy to keep surfboarders away from it. He failed to realize the epic nature of the plaintiff's trip and when plaintiff passed under the pier, defendant yelled at him not to go under the pier and as plaintiff was trying to turn his board struck him on the head with a pop bottle. Plaintiff recovered damages in tort and on appeal defendant argued that plaintiff had no legal right to travel under the pier. While it is hard to believe that defendant's force was reasonable even if plaintiff was a trespasser, the court chose in part to rest plaintiff's recovery on his right as a member of the public to use navigable waters for recreational purposes.

On non-navigable lakes surrounded by private lands riparian owners also seek to build docks and fill in privately-owned submerged lands. Though the waterbody is not technically navigable it may support boat traffic and a variety of recreational uses of the surface that are within the correlative rights of other riparian owners, if not the public. The nature of those rights is discussed at pages 432–47, infra. Conflicts in this setting are essentially disputes among riparians whose competing property rights have equal status, though states may extend public rights in ways that bring them into conflict with private rights.

WILBOUR v. GALLAGHER

Supreme Court of Washington, 1969.
77 Wash.2d 306, 462 P.2d 232.

HILL, J. * * *

Lake Chelan is a glacial gorge in Chelan County, approximately 55 miles in length, and with a width, generally speaking, of from 1 to 2 miles. Its navigability is conceded. Prior to 1927, it lay in its natural state with the level of its waters at 1,079 feet above sea level. By 1891 the land involved in this action had passed into private ownership being included in the "Plat of the Town of Lake Park." The platter dedicated and quitclaimed all streets and alleys therein to the use of the public forever. All of the platted property subsequently became a part of the town of Lakeside, and is now a part of the town of Chelan. The date of incorporation of Lakeside does not appear from the record, but on May 2, 1927, by ordinance No. 24, the town vacated certain specifically described streets and alleys. * * *

It should be noted that the public is the beneficiary of the grant in perpetuity of " * * * the right of access * * * over the lands included within the boundaries of those portions of the vacated streets and alleys hereinafter described, to Lake Chelan, at all stages of water * * * "

The Chelan Electric Company constructed a dam, pursuant to a permit by the Federal Power Commission, which permitted the annual raising of the level of the lake to 1,100 feet above sea level, with the requirement that it reach that level by June 15 each year. Thereafter in May of each year the dam was closed and the waters gradually rose to the 1,100 foot level, presumably by June 15th. They were maintained at that level until September when the dam was opened and the waters gradually subsided to the natural 1,079 foot level.

We come now to a consideration of the right claimed by the defendants, Norman G. Gallagher and Ruth I. Gallagher, his wife, to fill their land below the 1,100 foot level to a height 5 feet above that level, and thus prevent its being submerged and making it available for use at all times. (Certain fills have now been completed.)

The claimed right is challenged by the plaintiffs (Charles S. Wilbour and Harriet G. Wilbour, his wife; and Chester L. Green and Ruby Green, his wife) who brought a class action on behalf of themselves and the public asking that the fills be removed, and asking for damages to their own properties caused by the fills.

To assist in an understanding of the situation, we have prepared a drawing, which appears [below]. It is not drawn to scale, neither is it an exhibit in the case and it has been prepared for illustrative purposes only. It is based primarily on exhibit 5, a large drawing by Mr. Gallagher showing the fills he has made. It shows also the approximate water line of Lake Chelan at both the 1,079 and 1,100 foot levels. The lots, blocks, streets and alleys are as shown in the plat of Lake Park, and State Highway 97 has been superimposed. Unfortunately, the block numbers, other than 2 and 3, were omitted, and they will be supplied in our narrative explanation of the drawing.

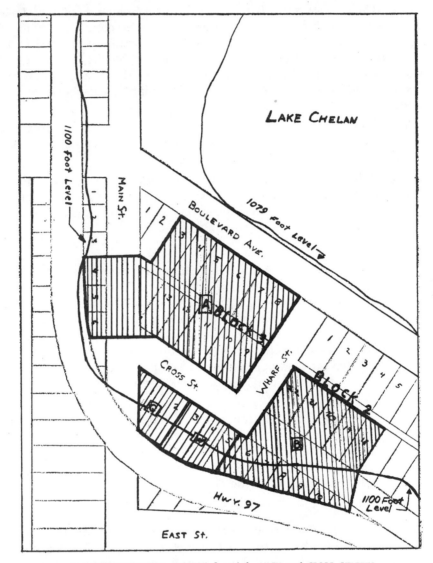

A - GALLAGHER FILL, BLOCKS 3 and 6, MAIN and CROSS STREETS
B - GALLAGHER FILL, BLOCKS 2 and 4, CROSS STREET
G - GREEN PROPERTY
W - WILBOUR PROPERTY

LA 306]

The shaded area has been divided into 4 lettered segments. G and W are the properties owned by the plaintiffs (the Greens and the Wilbours), improved with their respective homes, and lying partially above and below the 1,100 foot level (all of block 4, plat of Lake Park). A and B represent the two fills made by the defendants (the Gallaghers), both fills have access to Highway 97, and are now being used as trailer courts. A includes block 3, plat of Lake Park (except lots 1 and 2), including the alley in that block extending from vacated Wharf Street to vacated Main Street; a portion of block 6, plat of Lake Park, between the highway and vacated Main Street; also portions of vacated

Main and Cross [10] Streets. B includes a part of block 4, plat of Lake Park between the highway and vacated Cross Street; lots 18 to 22 inclusive, block 2, plat of Lake Park; and the portion of vacated Cross Street lying between the indicated portions of blocks 4 and 2. A portion of the intersection of vacated Cross and Wharf Streets also has been blockaded by a construction of the defendants, not shown on the drawing.

The trial court found that for 35 years prior to the trial (July and September 1965) and except for the filling by the defendants, commenced in 1961, the waters of Lake Chelan:

> covered the lands of Defendants in Blocks 2 and 3, Lake Park, including the streets and alleys in and adjacent to said Blocks 2 and 3, for a period each year from late spring through September, to a depth of three feet to fifteen feet.

And that for the same period:

> the general public, including Plaintiffs and their respective predecessors in interest, have used the waters covering the portions of Blocks 2 and 3, Plat of Lake Park, now owned by the Defendants, as well as the water covering portions of the streets and alleys adjacent thereto, for fishing, boating, swimming and for general recreational use and that said use was open adverse, notorious and uninterrupted for said period, during the period of each year when water covers the said portions of Block 2 and 3 and the adjacent streets and alleys.

The trial court ultimately concluded (based upon estoppel) that the defendants should not be compelled to remove their fills, but awarded the plaintiffs damages, finding that the value of the Wilbour property had been lessened $8,500, and the value of the Green property had been lessened $11,000 by reason of the fills established by the defendants.

* * *

This lessening of value was predicated principally on the loss of view, but also on inability to use the water over the filled land for navigation, fishing, swimming, boating and general recreational uses; and because, in consequence of the defendants' fill, "algae has become an increasing problem, which has created an unsightly situation on Plaintiffs' beaches."

From this judgment the defendants appealed, urging that they were simply making their own property usable and that any damages sustained by the plaintiffs were damnum absque injuria.

The plaintiffs have cross-appealed urging that the defendants' fills should have been abated.

The importance of this litigation transcends the consideration it has received from the public authorities. If every owner of property

10. The portion of vacated Cross Street included in A is quite small and is right at the intersection of vacated Main with Cross Streets. The unfilled portion of Cross Street, now a shallow moat at high water, affords the Greens their only access by water to the lake.

between the 1,079 foot and the 1,100 foot level around Lake Chelan has the right the defendants claim, the public's right in the navigable waters of that lake above the 1,079 foot level would be practically nil.

The property owners could make any use, not prohibited by law, of their properties—from fills for trailer parks close to the highways to high-rise apartments close to the lake.

Unless the laws applicable to the use of navigable waters apply to this annual artificial extension of the water of Lake Chelan, to preserve the status quo, it would seem that everybody is on his own.

The plaintiffs have made an excellent case on the basis of prescriptive rights. The filling of the vacated streets and alleys by the defendants cannot be sustained on any basis, since they had acquired no title to them and, in any event, the public had the right of access over the lands included within the boundaries of the vacated streets and alleys to Lake Chelan at all stages of water. Further, the obvious purpose of the contemporaneous vacation and the grant to the public of the right of access was to enable the Chelan Electric Company to acquire the right to submerge the streets and alleys and yet to preserve to the public the right of access over them to the lake "at all stages of water."

However, it is unnecessary to rely on prescriptive rights, or on the rights of the public to use the land within the vacated streets and alleys for access to the lake. We prefer to rest our decision on the proposition that the fills made by the defendants constitute an obstruction to navigation.

While this is a matter of first impression and no exactly comparable case has been found, our holding represents the logical extension of established law in somewhat comparable situations.

There was no private ownership of the land under Lake Chelan in its natural state, and no right to obstruct navigation.

It is well settled that if the level of the lake had been raised to the 1,100 foot level and had been maintained constantly at that level for the prescriptive period, the 1,100 foot level would be considered the natural level of the lake with the submerged lands being converted into part of the lake bed and to state ownership. The public would have the right to use all of the water of the lake up to the 1,100 foot level.

We have here, however, not only the raising of the lake level by artificial means, but the distinctive features that the level does not remain constant and that the owners of the land between the 1,079 and the 1,100 foot level can occupy their property during most of the year.[11]

11. Title to the defendants' property below the 1,100 foot level is deraigned through deeds which make it subject "to the perpetual right to raise the waters of Lake Chelan, Washington to the elevation of eleven hundred (1100) feet above mean sea level, and to perpetually inundate and overflow [said property] to said elevation of eleven hundred (1100) feet above mean sea level." We do not inquire as to who can now enforce this right; or whether property owners whose title is subject to similar flowage and inundation rights have any cause for complaint, if other property owners fill their land so that it cannot be overflowed. We merely call attention to this reserved right to indicate that the defendants must have purchased their

We find a somewhat comparable situation in those navigable lakes which have a natural or seasonal fluctuation in extent, and have a recognized high water line and low water line. However, in those cases the problems involved usually hinge on the rights accorded riparian owners (whose titles go to the low water mark) in the areas between the high and low water marks.

The law is quite clear that where the level of a navigable body of water fluctuates due to natural causes so that a riparian owner's property is submerged part of the year, the public has the right to use all the waters of the navigable lake or stream whether it be at the high water line, the low water line, or in between. In such situations the riparian owners whose lands are periodically submerged are said to have the right to prevent any trespass on their land between the high and the low marks when not submerged. However, title between those lines is qualified by the public right of navigation and the state may prevent any use of it that interferes with that right. When the land is submerged, the owner has only a qualified fee subject to the right of the public to use the water over the lands consistent with navigational rights, primary and corollary.

Thus, in the situation of a naturally varying water level, the respective rights of the public and of the owners of the periodically submerged lands are dependent upon the level of the water. As the level rises, the rights of the public to use the water increase since the area of water increases; correspondingly, the rights of the landowners decrease since they cannot use their property in such a manner as to interfere with the expanded public rights. As the level and the area of the water decreases, the rights of the public decrease and the rights of the landowners increase as the waters drain off their land, again giving them the right to exclusive possession until their lands are again submerged.

When the circumstance of an artificial raising of navigable waters to a temporary higher level is synthesized with the law dealing with navigable waters having a naturally fluctuating level, the logically resulting rule for the protection of the public interest is that, where the waters of a navigable body are periodically raised and lowered by artificial means, the artificial fluctuation should be considered the same as a natural fluctuation with the rights of the public being the same in both situations, i.e., the public has the right to go where the navigable waters go, even though the navigable waters lie over privately owned lands.

* * *

Following the reasoning of these cases we hold that when the level of Lake Chelan is raised to the 1,100 foot mark (or such level as submerges the defendants' land), that land is subjected to the rights of navigation, together with its incidental rights of fishing, boating, swimming, water skiing, and other related recreational purposes generally

property with full knowledge of it, and that there can be no limitations as to when   the right may be exercised.

regarded as corollary to the right of navigation and the use of public waters. When the level of the lake is lowered so that the defendants' land is no longer submerged, then they are entitled to keep trespassers off their land, and may do with the land as they wish consistent with the right of navigation when it is submerged.

It follows that the defendants' fills, insofar as they obstruct the submergence of the land by navigable waters at or below the 1,100 foot level, must be removed. The court cannot authorize or approve an obstruction to navigation.

* * *

FINLEY, ROSELLINI, HAMILTON, HALE, and McGOVERN, JJ., concur.

NEILL, J. (dissenting in part). * * *

The majority opinion reaches the conclusion that the fill on defendants' lots is to be removed on the basis that this fill constitutes an obstruction to navigation. Analogizing from the rule that the public has the right to the use of navigable water at both high levels and low levels, subject to the right of littoral owners to reasonably obstruct them with "aids to navigation" such as docks, wharfs, etc., the majority holds that fluctuations of water levels which are artificially created are no different than fluctuations created by nature.

The difficulty, as I view it, is that under the majority's holding there is a taking of defendants' property right for public use without just compensation. Defendants (through their antecedents in the chain of title) have a full fee title diminished *only* by the right of the power company to periodically inundate their lands to a specific elevation. I see no reason in law or equity for preventing such an owner from protecting his land against such inundation by raising the grade of the land.

The periodic flooding involved here is entirely different from a natural raising and lowering of the lake level by reason of rains, seasonal runoff, and drought. In the latter instance, the littoral owner's rights to the foreshore lands between high and low water, whatever these rights may be, are subject to the public's navigation rights. Here, the defendants' lots, *all of which lie above natural high water*, are not subject to public navigation rights unless there has been a voluntary conveyance, eminent domain proceedings, estoppel, or loss through prescription. Unless precluded by one of the aforementioned reasons, defendants have the right to use their lots, including the right to change the grade thereof, in order to make any lawful use thereof. Accordingly, I do not agree that the fill on defendants' lots is unlawful. They should not be required to remove it.

* * *

HUNTER, C. J., and DONWORTH, J. PRO TEM., concur with NEILL, J.

NOTES

1. What implications does *Wilbour* hold for patentees of tide- and shoreland grants? Are those who have filled in a better "equity"

position than those who have not done so? Harris v. Hylebos Indus., 505 P.2d 457 (Wash.1973) holds that a state tideland patentee in the Tacoma harbor can fill his property and cut off an upland owner's access to navigable waters and thus reaffirms Port of Seattle v. Oregon & Wash. R.R., 255 U.S. 56 (1920). The various state tideland disposition acts were reviewed and the court concluded "[t]hus it is apparent that the legislature has regarded the filling and improving of * * * tidelands, particularly in commercial harbors, as an aid to navigation, rather than an obstruction." 505 P.2d at 462. *Wilbour* was distinguished because coastal and bay tidelands as opposed to recreational lake bottoms "have never been classified by the state as navigable waters, but rather have been treated as land. * * * In that case, there was no evidence that the legislature or other governing body intended that the lands in question be reclaimed. The legislative intent regarding the use of tidelands in harbors of cities is manifestly that the navigable portions of such harbors, behind the harbor lines, shall consist of commercial waterways, and that the filling and reclaiming of the tidelands which have been sold to private parties shall be encouraged." 505 P.2d at 466. The court also suggested that appropriate governmental bodies could authorize filling in lakes subject to the *Wilbour* rule.

2. Why did the Gallaghers not argue that they had a right to fill as an incident to their common law riparian rights to wharf out? See pages 432–47, supra; Bloom v. Water Resources Comm'n, 254 A.2d 884 (Conn.1969). The reason may have been a common assumption in Washington that there are no riparian rights in watercourses navigable for title under the federal test. See Port of Seattle v. Oregon & Wash. R.R., 255 U.S. 56, 64 (1921). Only if the legislature authorizes encroachments into navigable waters are they not considered purprestures.

Professor Johnson has synthesized the Washington judicial decisions, concluding that "the court has effectively restricted private riparian rights on navigable waters where those rights are in conflict with the constitutional power of the State to control such waters. The constitution [Wash.Const. art. 17, § 1 (1889)] does not purport to eliminate riparian rights as between individuals, and the court has not so construed it." Ralph W. Johnson, *Riparian and Public Rights To Lakes and Streams*, 35 Wash.L.Rev. 580, 604–05 (1960).

3. Lake Chelan in Wilbour v. Gallagher had been enlarged by private effort and its navigability was held to extend to increased surface area. Does the public have any right to use a wholly artificial but navigable lake? When a plaintiff and defendant each took title to portions of an artificial but navigable lake bottom with a deed containing a restrictive covenant limiting surface use of the lake to homeowners' association members, defendant's apartment tenants asserted a right to use the surface. The Florida Supreme Court held that the restriction applied. Silver Blue Lake Apts. v. Silver Blue Lake Home Owners Association, 245 So.2d 609 (Fla. 1971). The dissenting chief justice set forth some conditions under which privately-owned, artificial lakes might be open to public use:

Where, for example, there is acquiescence in the use of the water-body by persons not members of the designated exclusive group, principles of dedication or abandonment may operate to create public rights therein. Also, for example, where an artificial water-body was not specifically developed originally pursuant to a given plan or design to exclusively limit the public use thereof and where, as suggested by certain evidence in the instant case, the scheme for limiting the use of the waterbody was advanced by developers subsequent to the actual creation of the man-made lake and subsequent to its use by members of the public for recreation, there may be a weakening of those policy considerations which favor private ownership of the waterbody to the extent that recognition of public rights therein may be warranted by virtue of countervailing considerations, including the anticipated increased pressure in this state for the availability of more water sources for public recreational purposes.

245 So.2d at 618. What difficulties do you see with the chief justice's proposal? See James N. Corbridge, *Surface Rights in Artificial Waters*, 24 Nat. Resources J. 887, 908–09 (1984).

Compare Kaiser Aetna v. United States, 444 U.S. 164 (1979), discussed at page 702–03, infra. A private developer deepened a pond adjacent to the ocean and converted it into a marina with a channel. When the Army Corps of Engineers asserted a right of public access to the pond, the Supreme Court held that it was not "navigable" such that access could be obtained without compensation to the owner. The Court said, however, that the Corps had sufficient regulatory power over the pond to prevent activities interfering with navigation. See also, Vaughn v. Vermilion, 444 U.S. 206 (1979) (no right of public use of manmade canals that connect the Gulf of Mexico with an inland waterway).

4. Once a water body is determined navigable, a state may legislate the extent of public uses to which the water body is subject. The federal navigability for title test classifies the water body, but it may then be opened to the public for uses beyond traditional notions of what constitutes navigation.

The Wisconsin Water Power Act requires a finding by the State Public Service Commission, before granting a permit for a hydroelectric project, that "the proposed dam will not materially obstruct existing navigation or violate other public rights." In applying the statute the Wisconsin Supreme Court held that "other public rights" include boating and other recreational uses. Accordingly, the court held that the Public Service Commission must find whether public rights for recreational enjoyment of the Namekagon River "in its present natural condition outweigh the benefits to the public which would result in the construction of the dam." Muench v. Public Serv. Comm'n, 53 N.W.2d 514 (Wis.1952).

Wetlands are threatened by extensive drainage and filling to increase the lands available for agriculture and for development. A growing awareness of the importance of wetlands has led to state legislation and judicial pronouncements.

In the eastern coastal states, regulation is generally limited to the dredging and filling of coastal wetlands. Conn.Gen.Ann. §§ 22a–28 to 22a–15; Ga.Code Ann. §§ 43–2401 to 43–2413; 38 Me.Rev.Stat.Ann. §§ 471–476, 478; Md.Nat.Res.Code Ann. §§ 9–201, 9–202, 9–301 to 9–310; Mass.Gen.Laws Ann. ch. 131 § 40A (Wetlands Protection Act); Miss.Code Ann. §§ 49–27–1 to 49–27–69; N.H.Rev.Stat.Ann. 483–A:1 to 6; N.J.Stat.Ann. 13:9–A–1 to 10; N.Y.Envir.Conserv.Law §§ 25–0101 to 25–0602; N.Car.Gen.Stat. § 113–229; R.I.Gen.Laws 1978, § 11–46.1–1 (dredge & fill penalty), §§ 2–1–13 to 2–1–25, 49–27–1 to 49–27–69; Va.Code Ann.1978, §§ 62.1–13.1 to 62.1–13.20. In the Midwest and in Washington development in the bed of the water body as well as related shoreland development is regulated. Mich.Comp. Laws Ann. §§ 281–631 to 281–644; Minn.Stat.Ann. § 105–485; 10 Vt.Stat.Ann. §§ 1421 to 1426; Wash.Rev.Code Ann. ch. 90.58; Wis.Stat.Ann. §§ 59.971, 144.26.

California and Washington have gone farther and passed comprehensive coastal zone management statutes which control all forms of development along the coastal band (and on inland waterways in Washington). Cal.Gov.Code §§ 66601 to 66661, and Wash.Rev.Code Ann. ch. 90.58. A similar statute exists in Maine, 38 Me.Rev.Stat. §§ 471–476, 478. For an insightful case study of the formulation and administration of a shoreland zoning scheme see Bryden, *The Impact of Variances: A Study of Statewide Zoning*, 61 Minn.L.Rev. 769 (1977). Wisconsin was the first state to regulate shoreland development.

5. Private owners may have their rights to fill or develop submerged lands limited because of the effects on other property owners or upon the public. Where limitations on property owners are for the general public benefit, not simply to adjust the rights of competing users, questions of constitutionality arise. How far can a private property owner be limited in the use of property before it becomes a "taking" by the government for a public use, which requires compensation under the United States Constitution?

JUST v. MARINETTE COUNTY

Supreme Court of Wisconsin, 1972.
56 Wis.2d 7, 201 N.W.2d 761.

HALLOWS, C.J. Marinette county's shoreland zoning ordinance * * * follows a model ordinance published by the Wisconsin Department of Resource Development in July of 1967. * * *

* * * The state shoreland program is unique. All county shoreland zoning ordinances must be approved by the department of natural resources prior to their becoming effective. If a county does not enact a shoreland zoning ordinance which complies with the state's standards, the department of natural resources may enact such an ordinance for the county.

* * * The [Marinette County] ordinance provides for permitted uses and conditional uses. One of the conditional uses requiring a

permit under sec. 3.42(4) is the filling, drainage or dredging of wetlands according to the provisions of sec. 5.0 of the ordinance. "Wetlands" are defined in sec. 2.29 as "[a]reas where ground water is at or near the surface much of the year or where any segment of plant cover is deemed an aquatic according to N. C. Fassett's 'Manual of Aquatic Plants.'" Sec. 5.42(2) of the ordinance requires a conditional use permit for any filling or grading "Of any area which is within three hundred feet horizontal distance of a navigable water and which has surface drainage toward the water and on which there is: (a) Filling of more than five hundred square feet of any wetland which is contiguous to the water * * * (d) Filling or grading of more than 2,000 square feet on slopes of twelve percent or less."

* * *

The land owned by the Justs is designated as swamps or marshes on the United States Geological Survey Map and is located within 1,000 feet of the normal high-water elevation of the lake. Thus, the property is included in a conservancy district and, by sec. 2.29 of the ordinance, classified as "wetlands." Consequently, in order to place more than 500 square feet of fill on this property, the Justs were required to obtain a conditional use permit from the zoning administrator of the county and pay a fee of $20 or incur a forfeiture of $10 to $200 for each day of violation.

In February and March of 1968, six months after the ordinance became effective, Ronald Just, without securing a conditional use permit, hauled 1,040 square yards of sand onto this property and filled an area approximately 20 feet wide commencing at the southwest corner and extending almost 600 feet north to the northwest corner near the shoreline, then easterly along the shoreline almost to the lot line. * * *

The real issue is whether the conservancy district provisions and the wetlands-filling restrictions are unconstitutional because they amount to a constructive taking of the Justs' land without compensation. Marinette county and the state of Wisconsin argue the restrictions of the conservancy district and wetlands provisions constitute a proper exercise of the police power of the state and do not so severely limit the use or depreciate the value of the land as to constitute a taking without compensation.

To state the issue in more meaningful terms, it is a conflict between the public interest in stopping the despoliation of natural resources, which our citizens until recently have taken as inevitable and for granted, and an owner's asserted right to use his property as he wishes. The protection of public rights may be accomplished by the exercise of the police power unless the damage to the property owner is too great and amounts to a confiscation. The securing or taking of a benefit not presently enjoyed by the public for its use is obtained by the government through its power of eminent domain. The distinction between the exercise of the police power and condemnation has been said to be a matter of degree of damage to the property owner. In the valid exercise of the police power reasonably restricting the use of property, the damage suffered by the owner is said to be incidental. However, where the restriction is so great the landowner ought not to bear such a burden for the public good, the restriction has been held to be a constructive taking even though the actual use or forbidden use has not been transferred to the government so as to be a taking in the traditional sense.   * * *

Many years ago, Professor Freund stated in his work on *The Police Power*, sec. 511, at 546, 547, " * * * it may be said that the state takes property by eminent domain because it is useful to the public, and under the police power because it is harmful.   * * *   From this results the difference between the power of eminent domain and the police power, that the former recognizes a right to compensation, while the latter on principle does not." Thus the necessity for monetary compensation for loss suffered to an owner by police power restriction arises when restrictions are placed on property in order to create a public benefit rather than to prevent a public harm.

This case causes us to re-examine the concepts of public benefit in contrast to public harm and the scope of an owner's right to use of his property. In the instant case we have a restriction on the use of a citizens' property, not to secure a benefit for the public, but to prevent a harm from the change in the natural character of the citizens' property. We start with the premise that lakes and rivers in their natural state are unpolluted and the pollution which now exists is man made. The state of Wisconsin under the trust doctrine has a duty to eradicate the present pollution and to prevent further pollution in its navigable waters. This is not, in a legal sense, a gain or a securing of a benefit by the maintaining of the natural *status quo* of the environment. What makes this case different from most condemnation or police power zoning cases is the interrelationship of the wetlands, the swamps and the natural environment of shorelands to the purity of the water and to such natural resources as navigation, fishing, and scenic beauty. Swamps and wetlands were once considered wasteland, undesirable, and not picturesque. But as the people became more sophisticated, an appreciation was acquired that swamps and wetlands serve a vital role in nature, are part of the balance of nature and are essential to the purity of the water in our lakes and streams. Swamps and wetlands are a necessary part of the ecological creation and now, even to the uninitiated, possess their own beauty in nature.

* * *

Wisconsin has long held that laws and regulations to prevent pollution and to protect the waters of this state from degradation are valid police-power enactments. The active public trust duty of the state of Wisconsin in respect to navigable waters requires the state not only to promote navigation but also to protect and preserve those waters for fishing, recreation, and scenic beauty. *Muench v. Public Service Comm.* (1952), 261 Wis. 492, 53 N.W.2d 514, 55 N.W.2d 40. To further this duty, the legislature may delegate authority to local units of the government, which the state did by requiring counties to pass shoreland zoning ordinances.

* * *

It seems to us that filling a swamp not otherwise commercially usable is not in and of itself an existing use, which is prevented, but rather is the preparation for some future use which is not indigenous to a swamp. Too much stress is laid on the right of an owner to change commercially valueless land when that change does damage to the rights of the public. It is observed that a use of special permits is a means of control and accomplishing the purpose of the zoning ordinance as distinguished from the old concept of providing for variances. The special permit technique is now common practice and has met with judicial approval, and we think it is of some significance in considering whether or not a particular zoning ordinance is reasonable.

* * *

The Justs argue their property has been severely depreciated in value. But this depreciation of value is not based on the use of the land in its natural state but on what the land would be worth if it could be filled and used for the location of a dwelling. While loss of value is to be considered in determining whether a restriction is a constructive taking, value based upon changing the character of the land at the expense of harm to public rights is not an essential factor or controlling.

We are not unmindful of the warning in *Pennsylvania Coal Co. v. Mahon* (1922), 260 U.S. 393, 416:

> " * * * We are in danger of forgetting that a strong public desire to improve the public condition is not enough to warrant achieving the desire by a shorter cut than the constitutional way of paying for the change."

This observation refers to the improvement of the public condition, the securing of a benefit not presently enjoyed and to which the public is not entitled. The shoreland zoning ordinance preserves nature, the environment, and natural resources as they were created and to which the people have a present right. The ordinance does not create or improve the public condition but only preserves nature from the despoilage and harm resulting from the unrestricted activities of humans.

NOTES

1. See discussion of takings generally at pages 364–91, supra. Is *Just* consistent with the Supreme Court's *Lucas* decision, page 380, supra?

2. National regulation of the use of wetlands is under the program established in § 404 of the Clean Water Act. 33 U.S.C.A. § 1344. The statute restricts the "dredging and filling" of waters of the United States. The Act surely has a more pervasive effect in terms of the numbers of activities and the types of wetland areas that it regulates than any state laws. Section 404 is discussed at pages 728-36, infra. The Supreme Court has held that where the United States exercises its legislative authority to protect the navigable capacity of streams, it is an exercise of federal regulatory authority and not a compensable taking. United States v. Rio Grande Dam & Irrigation Co., 174 U.S. 690 (1899). In United States v. Riverside Bayview Homes, Inc., 474 U.S. 121 (1985), page 729, infra, the Supreme Court upheld a Corps determination that 80 acres adjacent to a body of navigable water were "wetlands" requiring a § 404 permit. Questions of constitutionality also have arisen under the Clean Water Act § 404 program, however. Florida Rock Indus., Inc. v. United States, 21 Cl.Ct. 161 (1990), held that the denial of a § 404 permit for limestone mining in a large inland wetlands area that is part of the Florida Everglades was a taking. The court rejected the Corps of Engineer's claim that limestone mining was a nuisance and therefore an exception to the Fifth Amendment's requirement of just compensation.

B. RIGHTS TO SURFACE USE AMONG RIPARIANS

Owners of land abutting a waterway ordinarily have rights to use the surface of the water. If they own the bed of the waterway, they may have rights to fill in the submerged lands or construct improvements on it. These rights of riparian owners are, of course, qualified in navigable waters by dominant public uses. Many private riparian owners own the shores and some, as successors to the state, may own the beds as well. The determination of ownership of the bed itself may depend on whether a waterbody is navigable for title. In a navigable stream or lake "property" is effectively burdened with an easement for public use.

Property owners, whether on a navigable or non-navigable waterway, also have rights vis a vis one another—riparian rights—that may allow them to use the surface and submerged lands in ways that others cannot. For instance, the right to wharf out can belong only to a riparian. With these rights go certain reciprocal obligations. A riparian with lakefront property has a right to use the entire surface of the lake, but may own only a portion of the bed. On the other hand, the lakefront owner must allow use by other riparians of the owned portion.

Most reported cases dealing with the respective rights of riparians to use water surfaces and submerged lands tend to involve non-navigable waterways. Issues concerning surface use by riparians arise largely on non-navigable waterways because on navigable waters riparian surface rights are generally synonymous with public rights. Because rights to use submerged lands under navigable waters may be more restricted in favor of public uses, plaintiffs, riparian or not, generally assert public rights.

That the principles governing these cases are called "riparian" is misleading. They are applicable in states that follow prior appropriation laws to allocate water rights as well as in states where water allocation disputes are resolved according to riparian doctrine. The cardinal principle of riparian water law, reasonable use, does control most conflicts among surface users, however. The application of this principle in disputes among users of water for irrigation, water power, and other purposes are covered in Chapter 2, pages 82–95, supra.

To succeed in asserting riparian rights to use the surface of a waterway or the submerged lands, the owner must show that the use is truly a "riparian" use and that it is reasonable. The issues were joined in Bach v. Sarich, 445 P.2d 648 (Wash.1968). Defendants owned the bed of a non-navigable lake and proposed to build an apartment house that would project into the lake approximately 130 feet. The court enjoined the construction of the apartment:

> Mere proximity of the apartment to the water does not render it a riparian use. With respect to a structure, such a use must be so intimately associated with the water that apart from the water its utility would be seriously impaired. This is not the case with defendants' prospective use. The utility of the apartment is in no way dependent upon the waters of Bitter Lake, and its utility as an apartment would be in no way impaired apart from this lake. This is evidenced by the fact that apartments Nos. 2, 3 and 4 are entirely on upland property.
>
> Nor may defendants justify the presence of their apartment by the commercial zoning classification imposed by the city of Seattle or by the issuance of a building permit.
>
> All riparian owners along the shore of a natural, non-navigable lake share in common the right to use the entire surface of the lake for boating, swimming, fishing, and other similar riparian rights so long as there is no unreasonable interference with the exercise of these rights by other respective owners. These rights are vested property rights, and may not be taken or damaged for public or private use without just compensation.

The court's order resulted in the substantial work completed on the project being demolished. Specific relief is sometimes specific.

Similar principles were applied, resulting in approval of a defendant's challenged project, in the following cases: Harris v. Brooks, 283

S.W.2d 129 (Ark.1955), page 80, supra; Burt v. Munger, 23 N.W.2d 117 (Mich.1946); Flynn v. Beisel, 102 N.W.2d 284 (Minn.1960); State Game & Fish Comm'n v. Louis Fritz Co., 193 So. 9 (Miss.1940); Duval v. Thomas, 114 So.2d 791 (Fla.1959); and Improved Realty Corp. v. Sowers, 78 S.E.2d 588 (Va.1953).

The common law has not dealt comfortably with these matters. This has led to legislative responses. Professor Ralph W. Johnson argued after *Bach* that state zoning would be a more appropriate device for reconciling the conflicts among recreational preferences. Ralph W. Johnson & G. Richard Morry, *Filling and Building on Small Lakes— Time for Judicial and Legislative Controls,* 45 Wash.L.Rev. 27 (1970). Washington now has a special statutory scheme for shoreline management. Shoreline Management Act of 1971, Wash.Rev.Code §§ 90.58.-020–90.58.930. In brief, developments along the shore require a permit from the appropriate local government authority consistent with Shoreline Management Act guidelines for local plans promulgated by the state Department of Ecology as well as the state master program.

THOMPSON v. ENZ

Supreme Court of Michigan, 1967.
379 Mich. 667, 154 N.W.2d 473.

[A land development corporation purchased a riparian parcel of land on a lake which was used primarily for recreational purposes. The corporation subdivided the parcel into lots only 16 of which abutted directly on the lake. The back lots would have access to the lake by a canal dug by the corporation. Other riparians on the lake sued to enjoin the proposed subdivision and the digging of the canal on the grounds that it would constitute an interference with their riparian rights. The riparian owners were unable to prove that the level of the lake would be lowered or that the quality of the water would be impaired.]

T.M. KAVANAGH, J.

* * *

This case concerns certain property rights in and around Gun lake, which is situated partly in Barry county and partly in Allegan county. The parties agree that this lake has approximately 2,680 acres of surface area and approximately 30 miles of shoreline.

The defendant corporation is a contract purchaser of a riparian parcel of land having approximately 1,415 feet of frontage on said lake, and the individual defendants are the sole stockholders of the corporation.

* * *

The following questions are raised on appeal:

1. May a right of access to Gun lake be created by dredging an artificial canal from the lake through lots having frontage on Gun lake to back lots having no frontage thereon, and may ownership of such lots carry with it riparian rights?

2. Does the development by defendants of their property which partially fronts on Gun lake by the construction of a canal connecting back lots to the lake and granting rights of access to the lake constitute an illegal invasion of the rights of the plaintiffs and an infringement of their riparian rights in and to the surface of Gun lake and in and to the subaqueous land thereunder?

"Riparian land" is defined as a parcel of land which includes therein a part of or is bounded by a natural water course.

* * *

A "riparian proprietor" is a person who is in possession of riparian lands or who owns an estate therein.

* * *

Land abutting on an artificial water course has no riparian rights.

* * *

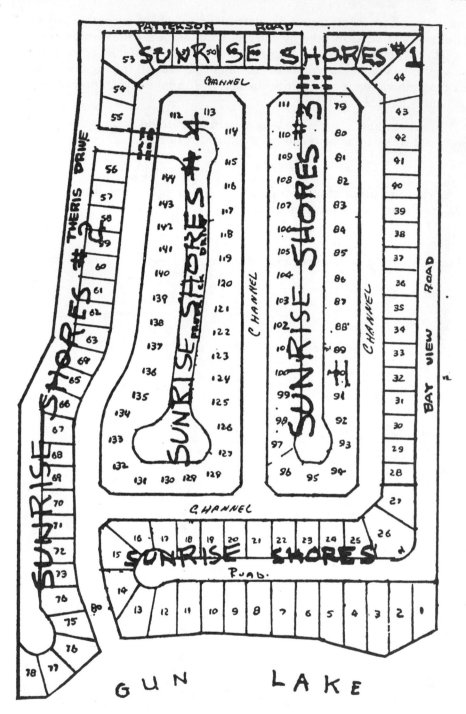

[A3630]

We, therefore, conclude that parcels of land to be subdivided from the main tract of land bordering on Gun lake have no riparian rights as: (1) they neither include therein a part of nor are they bounded by

Gun lake, and (2) the canal itself would be an artificial water course giving rise to no riparian rights.

The remaining question for decision is whether or not riparian rights may be conveyed to a grantee or reserved by the grantor in a conveyance which divides a tract of land with riparian rights into more than one parcel, of which parcels only one would remain bounded by the water course.

In the case of *Harvey Realty Co. v. Borough of Wallingford,* supra, Justice Hinman, writing for the Court, stated (111 Conn. 352, 358, 359):

"It is clear that the grantees or contractees, from the plaintiff, of lots separated from and not bordering on Pine lake can have, of their own right, no riparian privileges in its waters. *And any attempted transfer of the right made by a riparian to a non-riparian proprietor is invalid.*" (Citing text and cases.) (Emphasis supplied.)

* * *

We hold that what is meant by this "reservation" of riparian rights is merely the reservation of a right-of-way for access to the water course. * * * This, however, cannot and does not give rise to riparian rights.

* * *

We hold that riparian rights are not alienable, severable, divisible, or assignable apart from the land which includes therein, or is bounded, by a natural water course.

While riparian rights may not be conveyed or reserved—nor do they exist by virtue of being bounded by an artificial water course—easements, licenses and the like for a right-of-way for access to a water course do exist and ofttimes are granted to nonriparian owners.

We will, therefore, treat the proposal here as though easements for rights-of-way for access are given to the back lot purchasers. We must then consider what right, if any, the owners of the back lots have to use these rights-of-way. In so doing, attention must be given to the use of riparian rights by the defendants and the remaining proprietors on Gun lake.

Riparian uses are divided generally into two classes. The first of these is for natural purposes. These uses encompass all those absolutely necessary for the existence of the riparian proprietor and his family, such as to quench thirst and for household purposes. Without these uses both man and beast would perish. Users for natural purposes enjoy a preferred nonproratable position with respect to all other users rather than a correlative one.

The second of these is a use for artificial purposes. Artificial uses are those which merely increase one's comfort and prosperity and do not rank as essential to his existence, such as commercial profit and recreation. Users for artificial purposes occupy a correlative status with the other riparians in exercise of their riparian rights for artificial purposes. Use for an artificial purpose must be (a) only for the benefit of the riparian land and (b) reasonable in light of the correlative rights of the other proprietors. It is clear in the case before us that the use made of the property by the defendants is for a strictly artificial purpose and must meet the test of reasonableness.

* * *

The trial court made no finding of fact as to the reasonableness of the use. This record is insufficient for us to make a determination as to reasonableness. Therefore, we remand to the trial court for such determination. The trial court should keep in mind the following factors in determining whether the use would be reasonable:

First, attention should be given to the water course and its attributes, including its size, character and natural state. In determining the reasonableness of the use in the case at bar, it should be considered that Gun lake is not a large lake, that it is used primarily for recreational purposes, and that the defendants are changing its natural state by expanding the lake frontage of their property from an actual 1,415 feet to a total, inclusive of the canals, of 12,415 feet, being an increase in frontage of approximately 800 per cent.

Second, the trial court should examine the use itself as to its type, extent, necessity, effect on the quantity, quality, and level of the water, and the purposes of the users. Factors in this particular case that should be considered include: (a) that this use would permanently add approximately one family without riparian rights to each 18 acres of surface area (or 137 families); (b) the possibility that the level of the lake may be reduced by withdrawing trust waters into over 2 miles of the proposed canals, as is alleged by the attorney general in his motion to intervene; (c) the possibility that pollution may result; (d) that there is nothing in the record showing any necessity for this use; and (e) the fact that it appears that the purpose of the defendants herein is merely commercial exploitation.

Third, it is necessary to examine the proposed artificial use in relation to the consequential effects, including the benefits obtained and the detriment suffered, on the correlative rights and interests of other riparian proprietors and also on the interests of the State, including fishing, navigation, and conservation. An additional fact to be considered by the trial court in this litigation is whether the benefit to the defendant subdividers would amount merely to a rich financial harvest, while the remaining proprietors—who now possess a tranquil retreat from everyday living—would be forced to endure the annoyances which would come from an enormous increase in lake users.

Undoubtedly, at the new hearing, the attorney general of the State of Michigan will intervene under his statutory general powers of intervention for the purpose of protecting the rights of the public.

If, after considering all of these factors and any additional testimony the parties may desire to present, the trial court (as chancellor) concludes the use is unreasonable, that court should retain jurisdiction of the matter for the purpose of granting such further necessary or proper relief as may be necessary to protect the rights and interests of plaintiffs, the public, and riparian owners of property abutting this lake.

The judgment of the Court of Appeals is reversed and the case is remanded to the circuit court for a determination, pursuant to this opinion, of the reasonableness of the proposed use.

Plaintiffs shall have costs.

BLACK, SOURIS, and ADAMS, JJ., concurred with T.M. KAVANAGH, J.

———

On remand the trial judge held that the defendant's proposed use was unreasonable. While the Supreme Court approved the trial court's findings, it decided to vacate the judgment because plaintiffs waited until defendant had completed most of the excavation required for construction of the canals before seeking an injunction and therefore the plaintiffs were estopped from obtaining equitable relief. Thompson v. Enz, 385 Mich. 103, 188 N.W.2d 579 (1971). Justice Brennan, in a separate opinion, argued that the trial court's decision should be reversed, not just vacated:

> We do not believe that a great deal of analysis needs to be addressed to the trial court's findings and opinion. The trial court found "that the lake's tolerance level may have been reached." He concedes that any further development of the undeveloped shoreline may "start the lake down the road toward becoming a nuisance lake." The trial judge then says: "In any event, nothing can be done to stop this if done in single tier construction." We cannot but ponder why the circuit judge arrived at this conclusion. Was the circuit judge recognizing a Fourteenth Amendment protected property right to build cottages in a single tier along the undeveloped shoreline? In this conclusion, we would certainly concur. But if the defendants' right to use their property in any lawful manner and to exercise their riparian rights in the same fashion as the other riparian owners is a right of property protected by the Fourteenth Amendment to the Federal Constitution, we fail to see why it would be arbitrarily limited to a single tier development of lake front cottages.

> In the trial of this case, exhibits were introduced which depict the numerous existing canal developments on Gun Lake. The trial court found that the existing canal developments represent 6.4 miles of canal frontage and that the defendants' proposed development would add 2.3 miles of canal frontage to the lake. Our computation of the actual lake frontage of all the existing canal developments taken together is approximately 4,800 feet. Thus the ratio of canal frontage to lake frontage of the defendants' development is approximately the same as the ratio of all the previous canal developments taken in combination. Even the most cursory review of the exhibits discloses that many of the previous canal developments show canal frontage to lake frontage ratios substantially greater than that sought by the defendants.

All of which is pointed out merely as a means of emphasizing the plain and obvious truth of this case, and the gross injustice of the result arrived at in the trial court. These defendants do not propose to exercise any rights or inaugurate any uses which are in the slightest fashion more detrimental to the lake than the existing uses of other lake owners. In fact all necessary permits were obtained, fees paid and approval granted to proceed with this development. The trial court would brand these defendants' use as the "straw that broke the camel's back," and in the name of preserving to these plaintiffs a quasi-monopoly to use a lake which belongs to the people of Michigan, our Court would approve the arbitrary, unlawful and unconstitutional confiscation of the defendants' property without payment of compensation therefor. The defendants have excavated canals on their own property. That excavation was lawful and, in fact, authorized when undertaken. It is lawful today.

385 Mich. at 122–24, 188 N.W.2d at 587–88 (1971).

NOTES

1. Under the court's test, must each activity (e.g., the canal construction, the decision to subdivide and convey lots, the particular uses of the surface by each new canal lot owner) be judged by the reasonable use standard? Are they to be judged and balanced against all existing uses as each decision is made or use commenced, or should the decisionmaker attempt to project future uses?

2. The trial judge's tipping point analysis modifies the traditional doctrine that equity will not enjoin an activity without proof of imminent irreparable injury. This doctrine requires a plaintiff to show that it is highly probable that injury will occur in the foreseeable future in cases where the evidence can establish, at best, that there is a risk of future injury.

The history of the doctrine of imminent irreparable injury is developed and criticized in Charles L. Hellerich, Note, *Imminent Irreparable Injury: A Need for Reform,* 45 So.Cal.L.Rev. 1025 (1972). The author recommends that in determining the appropriateness of injunctive relief the courts should consider: (1) the probability of the anticipated harm both to complainant and society if injunctive relief is denied, (2) the magnitude and nature of the anticipated harm, (3) the burden on the defendant and society if the injunction is granted, (4) an allowance of a margin-of-safety, and (5) available alternatives to the activity. "In setting a margin-of-safety, the court should take into consideration: (1) the availability of definitive knowledge as to the effects, especially long-term, of the proposed action; (2) the magnitude and nature of the anticipated harm; (3) the cumulative effect of many users; and (4) the potential synergistic effects." Id. at 1057.

Two usual justifications for the imminent irreparable harm requirement are (1) it is not certain that the harm will in fact materialize and thus the controversy is not yet ripe for adjudication and (2) the problem may be solved by the development of new technologies.

Compare Bass River Ass'n v. Mayor of Bass River Township, 573 F.Supp. 205 (D.N.J.1983), aff'd 743 F.2d 159 (3d Cir.1984) (town could prohibit floating marina to prevent "gray water" pollution). See generally, Richard W. Bartke & Susan H. Patton, *Water Based Recreational Developments in Michigan—Problems of Developers,* 25 Wayne L.Rev. 1005 (1979).

3.   Michigan's legislative response to *Thompson* was The Inland Lakes and Streams Act of 1972, Mich.Comp.Laws § 281.951, et seq. The statutory requirement of a permit does not eliminate the common law remedy recognized in *Thompson.* In addition to such direct regulation three other types of statutes can have a significant although indirect impact on riparian development activities. These are (1) state environmental policy acts which superimpose an environmental impact statement requirement on existing permit or regulatory approval procedures, (2) critical areas legislation which requires new local or state approval for activities in a designated area, and (3) legislation which gives the public standing to sue to protect environmental rights.

An example of the third type of legislation, the Michigan Environmental Protection Act (MEPA), Mich.Comp.Laws Ann. §§ 691.1201–1207, was applied in Opal Lake Ass'n v. Michaywe Ltd. Partnership, 209 N.W.2d 478 (Mich.Ct.App.1973). The Act eliminates standing barriers for public interest plaintiffs who lack an Hofeldian interest in the litigation. It allows governmental entities and "any person * * * or other legal entity" to sue to enjoin a public or private entity whose act "has, or is likely to pollute, impair or destroy the air, water or other natural resources or the public trust therein." Id., §§ 691.1202(1), 691.1203(1). This Act, which has been copied in several other states, offers opportunities to challenge allegedly environmentally harmful activities, and to supplement legislation such as the Inland Lakes and Stream Act with added environmental standards. See e.g., Attorney General v. Balkema, 477 N.W.2d 100 (Mich.1991) (filling of shallow lake without a permit violated MEPA because the lake was home to black terns and the system acted as a nutrient trap). In *Opal Lake* the court enjoined a proposed lakeshore development, addressing the question of uncertain harm as follows:

> Here there seems to be little argument that should a significant number of the proposed 2,250 individual lot owners and their guests in Michaywe decide to use the Opal Lake access site at the same time a nuisance to *everyone* will result. Here also plans have been nearly fully developed for the access site. One hundred twenty-five purchasers had already at the time of this suit bought land in the Michaywe project on the apparent representation that they would have access to the Swim'n Sun Club. It seems patently unreasonable to ignore such facts and their probable effects until the clear waters of Opal Lake are muddied, the noise around the Swim'n Sun Club is deafening, and the other private shore owners on Opal Lake have put up "For Sale" signs on their property simply because in some distinguishable past nuisance cases the courts refused to enjoin anticipated harm. We do not believe the unrestricted use of the Michaywe beachfront by hundreds, if not

thousands, of non-riparian landowners is so "anticipatory" as to negate the possibility of giving injunctive relief.

209 N.W.2d at 483. The court also cited language in MEPA establishing a right of action "to prevent pollution" and describing the burden of proof in terms of proving the defendant is likely to pollute.

4. Are the owners of the back lots in *Thompson* now riparian to the lake? Wisconsin permits such canals to be dug pursuant to a permit issued by the Department of Natural Resources, but the department must find that "the project will not injure public rights or interest, including fish and game habitat, that the project conforms to the requirement of laws for platting of land and for sanitation and that no material injury to the rights of any riparian owners on any body of water affected will result * * *." Wis.Stat. § 30.19(4) (1973). The predecessor to the department, the Wisconsin Public Service Commission, denied two permits in 1965 because the area riparian to the lake would be increased without a compensating increase in the area of the lake itself, and the enlargement would unduly increase residential waterway use of the lake. C. Richard Glesner, Note, *Riparian Water Law—Lakeshore Developments,* 1966 Wis.L.Rev. 172, 188–89.

5. Suppose that a riparian owner puts in a parking lot and boat ramp, charges for admission, and allows "guests," members of the public, to use the lake. Do these licensees have riparian rights? Are there any limitations on the licensor's exercise of littoral rights? Does it matter if the licensor is a government agency and the other riparian owners are private parties? In Botton v. State, 420 P.2d 352 (Wash. 1966), the state purchased a lot on Phantom Lake near Seattle for a fishing access site. The shoreline of the lake had been privately owned, and the other littoral owners sued the state complaining that thefts, noise, littering, safety hazards and generally unacceptable social behavior impaired their right to use the lake for recreational purposes. The court held that all littoral owners are subject to the reasonable use standard. Members of the public may be admitted by littoral owners, but the state's failure to control the public's use of the lake was found to be an unreasonable interference with the rights of the other littoral owners. Professor Ralph Johnson of the University of Washington School of Law reports that after *Botton* the Department of Game closed the lake to the public; the department was unable to come to an agreement with the littoral owners to limit public access and it lacked the funds to provide a full-time employee to police the area.

Would it matter if public access was being provided by a riparian before other riparians decided to exercise their surface rights, thereby coming into conflict with the members of the public? In *Thompson,* Judge Brennan noted in a separate opinion that the state maintained a public park on the shore of Gun Lake. How should that fact be weighed in the court's test?

PUBLIX SUPER MARKETS v. PEARSON

District Court of Appeal of Florida, 1975.
315 So.2d 98.

PER CURIAM.

* * * The appellees filed a complaint seeking, inter alia, to prohibit the appellant from reclaiming and filling approximately ten acres of water-filled phosphate pits located on its lands situate in Polk County. After hearing and based upon the pleadings filed and consideration of the stipulation agreed to by the parties, which resolved all factual issues, and the exhibits submitted by the respective parties, the circuit judge found that such reclamation would be an unreasonable use of the appellant's lands and that it would significantly impair the use and enjoyment of the entire surface water of the phosphate pits into which appellees' residential property extends. The circuit judge enjoined appellant from proceeding with its proposed reclamation and development of the phosphate pits and, at the same hearing, denied appellant's motion to dismiss the appellees' complaint. This interlocutory appeal is filed from that order.

The parties agreed that the sole question for the trial court was whether the phosphate pits, or water bodies, comprising approximately 47 acres, resulting from phosphate mining operations prior to the year 1960, and commonly called phosphate pits, are subject to the same riparian rights as natural, nonnavigable lakes.

The trial court's decision was based upon the principle of law enunciated in the case of Duval v. Thomas, Fla.1959, 114 So.2d 791, which established the proprietary rights of riparian owners in and to nonnavigable, natural lakes. In its conclusions of law, the trial court in the instant case found:

> * * * The facts, circumstances and respective positions of the parties in the case sub judice are poles apart from those in Duval. However, the legal principles of rights to use of the water in a nonnavigable water body are the same.

Under the factual situation presented in the case before us, we have been unable to find any authority in Florida law to support the trial court's decision in extending the application of the principles of Duval, supra, to artificial water bodies formed as a result of surface mining operations long since discontinued. The facts agreed upon by the parties disclose that appellant owns portions of five water-filled, finger-like phosphate pits which are joined along the northerly extension of the elongated pits to form a hand-shaped water body. We point out that the eminent trial judge found from examination of one of appellees' exhibits that it does not appear that the western most pit is so connected.

This unnamed artificial water body, around which no planned development has been made, encompasses, as stated, 47 acres and was formed as a result of surface mining operations prior to 1960. Appellant proposes to develop a shopping center by filling ten acres of the two westerly pits by excavation of the spoil banks dividing the fingers by installation of impervious steel plates along its northern boundary. Appellant's plans include construction of a drainage lake to retain runoff from the shopping center parking lot. Although the appellant owns a portion of the eastern most pit, into which the appellees' property extends, no filling will occur at that place. As a consequence of the proposed construction, the southern most portion of the four westerly pits will be dredged and filled, thereby cutting off appellees' use of and access to said portions of the existing water body.

The property of the appellees, upon which they have built homes of substantial value, borders on and extends into the eastern most and largest pit. The parties have stipulated that appellant's reclamation will not disturb the waters or the ecology or the use and enjoyment of the water of the remaining pits, except to cut off access to and use of the surface waters of the westerly pits for fishing and boating.

Our research of the law applicable discloses that there is little or no case law in Florida or other jurisdictions which is helpful in arriving at a proper answer to the question presented to us relating to the problems concerning the rights of parties in artificial water bodies. As a general proposition, it has been held that riparian rights do not ordinarily attach to artificial water bodies or streams, although in Silver Blue Lake Apartments, Inc. v. Silver Blue Lake Home Owners Association, Inc., Fla.1971, 245 So.2d 609, the Supreme Court of Florida did prohibit the unreasonable use of an artificial lake by tenants of an abutting land owner. In Silver Blue Lake the artificial water body was originally created by limerock excavations and was subsequently named Silver Blue Lake. We believe that the Silver Blue Lake case is distinguishable from the instant case for the reason that in the cited case the water body was specifically incorporated into the subdivision and the deeds of conveyance to the property owner fronting the water contained deed restrictions allowing said owners to use the lake. Consequently, we do not regard that case as conclusive authority for applying the Duval supra, principle of riparian rights to these particular surface pits.

The Supreme Court of Florida in Duval, supra, adopted the civil law rule defining littoral rights in nonnavigable, natural lakes, which doctrine permits reasonable use of the entire water body by each individual owning a part of the water bed and denies to any one owner the right to fill or otherwise exclude other persons who also own part of the lake bed. As we construe Duval, the principle pronounced therein is applicable only to nonnavigable, natural lakes and does not expressly extend to artificial lakes and, *a fortiori*, cannot reasonably be interpreted to extend to water-filled phosphate pits that are the result of phosphate mining operations.

We mention that there are other legal distinctions which have been made between natural and artificial geological conditions. Artificial water bodies have been differentiated from natural bodies or lakes for tort law purposes. See, Allen v. William P. McDonald Corp., Fla.1949, 42 So.2d 706. Statutory mandates have made a distinction between artificial pits or holes which may create safety hazards and natural depressions in the earth. Dutton Phosphate Co. v. Priest, 1914, 67 Fla. 370, 65 So. 282.

The Wisconsin Supreme Court in Mayer v. Grueber, 1965, 29 Wis.2d 168, 138 N.W.2d 197, was faced with the problem of determining relative rights to a water-filled gravel pit. After a comprehensive examination of authorities on riparian ownership, that court concluded:

> The right to use an artificial lake as well as the right to the bed of the lake are incidents of ownership that are vested exclusively in the owner of the fee upon which the lake is located. If he is to be divested of these rights, it can only be by deed or the eventual acquisition of these rights by prescription or adverse possession.
> * * *

[138 N.W.2d, page 205].

We reiterate that the phosphate pits here are not encircled by a subdivision, nor have they been dedicated to recreational use by means of deed restriction as in Silver Blue Lake Apartments, supra. The water body has also never been denoted by a name or designation other than phosphate pits. Since the origins of the pits date only to 1957, no prescriptive rights have so far been acquired between the parties, or the other owners of the pit bed.

Therefore, it is our opinion that appellees have no greater rights to the waters of the phosphate pits than an owner of land whose dominion over the fee is confined within his legal boundaries. Consequently, we find that these water-filled phosphate pits, resulting from phosphate mining operations prior to 1960, are not subject to the same riparian rights as natural, nonnavigable lakes as defined in Duval v. Thomas, supra.

For the foregoing reasons, we conclude that the order of the circuit court granting the motion for a temporary injunction is hereby reversed with directions to the trial court to enter an order dissolving the temporary injunction and granting appellant's motion to dismiss with prejudice.

Reversed and remanded.

HOBSON, ACTING C.J., and BOARDMAN and SCHEB, JJ., concur.

NOTES

1. In Mayer v. Grueber, quoted with approval in the principal case, the water was adjacent to the land of the person claiming riparian rights who owned no bottom land under the artificial watercourse. What significance, if any, should ownership of the bottom have on the allocation of surface rights in such artificial watercourses?

If an artificial expansion of a non-navigable waterbody floods a portion of an existing riparian's land, may the riparian use the entire surface of the artificially expanded waterbody? Though common use of the entire surface was impliedly rejected as applied to wholly artificial waterbodies in Mayer v. Grueber there seems to be no valid reason for not allowing such use in a jurisdiction which follows the common use approach for natural waterbodies. See Custis Fishing & Hunting Club, Inc. v. Johnson, 200 S.E.2d 542 (Va.1973). In Anderson v. Bell, 433

So.2d 1202 (Fla.1983), a small, nonnavigable lake was expanded by plaintiff's dam so that it covered portions of defendant's previously dry land. Plaintiff sought to enjoin defendants from fishing and boating on the surface area lying above plaintiff's property. After reviewing *Publix Supermarkets,* and *Duval* and *Silver Blue Lake Apartments* which were cited in it, the Florida Supreme Court held that "an owner of lands that lie contiguous to or beneath a portion of a man-made lake has no right to the beneficial use of the entire lake merely by virtue of the fact of ownership of the land." 433 So.2d at 1207.

2. Does the public acquire rights when non-navigable, private waters become navigable due to artificial expansion? In Ten Eyck v. Warwick, 75 Hun. 562, 27 N.Y.S. 536 (1894) the court expressed the majority rule that public rights to the surface are not thereby created. Where the expansion is characterized instead as the flooding of private land by navigable waters, the result differs. See People v. Kraemer, 164 N.Y.S.2d 423 (Police Ct., Village of Lloyd Harbor, Suffolk Co. 1957), where the court concluded that in such circumstances, the private landowner (whose lands were flooded) should be required to accept the public right of navigation where he allowed the condition to continue. 164 N.Y.S.2d at 432. Some courts have limited the scope of public rights on artificially expanded waters to those enjoyed on the waterbody in its natural state. Tapoco, Inc. v. Peterson, 373 S.W.2d 605 (Tenn.1963); Wilbour v. Gallagher, page 419, supra. Cf. Dycus v. Sillers, 557 So.2d 486 (Miss.1990) (fishing hole connected to public waters by chute or drain created by Corps of Engineers dredging is a private waterbody, and the public does not acquire a right to surface use).

3. If A purchases a littoral tract on a lake formed by the construction of a private or state-licensed dam, what rights does A acquire to the maintenance of the water level, absent an express easement? Suppose the dam owner has acquired by prescription a flowage easement which permits the flooding of A's land. See Pahl v. Long Meadow Gun Club, 233 N.W. 836 (Minn.1930). Can A subsequently assert a reciprocal negative easement against lowering the lake level based on A's recreational use of the lake for the prescriptive period? In Kiwanis Club Found., Inc. v. Yost, 139 N.W.2d 359, 361 (Neb.1966) the court rejected this argument:

> Construction and maintenance of a dam over a long period of time may well tend to lead persons owning property above the dam to believe that a permanent and valuable right has been acquired, or is naturally present. The very fact that a man-made dam is obviously present, however, is sufficient to charge them with notice that the water level is artificial as distinguished from natural, and that its level may be lowered or returned to the natural state at any time * * *.

> We hold that where a dam has been built for the private convenience and advantage of the owner, he is not required to maintain and operate it for the benefit of an upper riparian owner who obtains advantages from its existence; and that the construc-

tion and maintenance of such a dam does not create any reciprocal rights in upstream riparian proprietors based on prescription, dedication and estoppel.

4. A riparian might also want to prevent artificial lake levels from rising. In Natural Soda Products Co. v. Los Angeles, 143 P.2d 12 (Cal.1943), cert. denied 321 U.S. 793 (1944), the defendant city, from 1919 to 1937, diverted virtually all the flow of the Owens River, which supplied Owens Lake, a waterbody with no outlet. When the lake dried up, brines containing valuable chemicals collected on the exposed bottom. Plaintiff, a chemical company, built a plant to process the brines. In 1937 the defendant opened its diversion dam and water flowed into Owens Lake, flooding the lake to a depth of three to four feet and inundating plaintiff's plant. In a subsequent suit for damages, plaintiff was awarded over $153,000 in the trial court. What result on appeal? (Damages upheld, as plaintiff had made substantial expenditures in reliance on city's diversions).

5. Despite the hostility of the courts to the concept of riparian rights in artificial watercourses, even such wholly artificial structures as manmade canals and ditches may be treated as natural if they have been in place for a substantial period of time. Bollinger v. Henry, 375 S.W.2d 161 (Mo.1964) allowed the owner of lands alongside a century-old millrace to exercise consumptive riparian rights. Ramada Inns, Inc. v. Salt River Valley Water Users Ass'n, 523 P.2d 496 (Ariz.1974) refused to apply the common law rule of strict liability for flooding caused to another's property with water by an artificial impoundment (Rylands v. Fletcher, L.R. 3 H.L. 330 (1868)). There, the ninety year-old Arizona Canal had been surrounded by expansion of metropolitan Phoenix. The subsequent locators had the same "duty" to avoid losses as would anyone locating next to a natural stream subject to flooding. For a review of the problems of artificial watercourses, see James N. Corbridge, *Surface Rights in Artificial Watercourses,* 24 Nat. Resources J. 887 (1984).

6. Several midwestern states and the state of Washington have lake level maintenance statutes. They are designed to perform two functions. First, they establish a level through a statutory procedure or an administrative or judicial proceeding that quantifies the littoral owner's common law right. Second, and related to this, the statute provides some protection for littoral owners from property damage caused by dams or other structures which cause the alteration of the lake. The methods of administration vary.

C. EXPANDING PUBLIC RIGHTS TO SURFACE USE

We have seen that the public has rights to use the surface of bodies of water that fit the federal test of navigability at the time of statehood. But in waters where there is no such public trust interest, and even in such waters where the public wants to assert rights going beyond those protected by the public trust, any right to use the surface is necessarily a result of state law. The growing economic and social importance of recreational uses of water has led to the recognition of public rights to use the surface of waterbodies for boating, fishing, hunting and other recreational purposes under several legal theories.

One means of deeming the waterbodies open to public access is the adoption of a more liberal state test of navigability. In the nineteenth century the lumber industry in the east and midwest was encouraged by the adoption of the "saw log" test of navigability. The saw log test laid the basis for extending the definition of navigability to those waters capable of supporting noncommercial recreational activities. As an early Minnesota case, Lamprey v. State, 53 N.W. 1139, 1143 (Minn. 1893), observed, "The division of waters into navigable and nonnavigable is but a way of dividing them into public and private waters, a classification which, in some form, every civilized nation has recognized; the line of division being largely determined by its conditions and habits." * Shortly thereafter, Wisconsin adopted an expanded concept of navigability based in part on the Northwest Ordinance's guarantee of free highways and carrying places for the Mississippi, Saint Lawrence and rivers in between. Diana Shooting Club v. Husting, 145 N.W. 816 (Wis.1914). The theory is that the public rights recognized by the ordinance were not superseded by admission to statehood. See Elder v. Delcour, 269 S.W.2d 17 (Mo.1954); Coleman v. Schaeffer, 126 N.E.2d 444 (Ohio 1955).

More recently, courts have expanded state definitions of navigability in a manner that directly recognizes the public importance of recreational uses. Others have anchored such rights on constitutional and statutory declarations that describe the nature of public and private legal interests in water and waterbodies. Still some courts have resorted to little more than ipsi dixit to expand public rights. E.g., Curry v. Hill, 460 P.2d 933 (Okl. 1969).

The expansion of public rights to non-navigable waters is an extension beyond both the English and the federal common law. In many instances it requires a change in the common law of the state itself. The effect of the expansion is, of course, to redistribute resources from private ownership and control to public ownership, that is, to make the resource a common good. Does this reallocation diminish the market value of the riparian land? Would the reallocation amount to a taking without just compensation?

ARKANSAS v. McILROY

Supreme Court of Arkansas, 1980.
268 Ark. 227, 595 S.W.2d 659, cert. denied
449 U.S. 843, 101 S.Ct. 124, 66 L.Ed.2d 51.

HICKMAN, JUSTICE.

W. L. McIlroy and his late brother's estate, owners of 230 acres in Franklin County, sought a chancery court declaration that their rights as riparian landowners on the Mulberry River were, because the stream was not a navigable river, superior to the rights of the public.

---

* *Lamprey* erroneously assumed that a state could determine the definition of navigability for *title*. The court subsequently corrected this mistake, State v. Adams, 89 N.W.2d 661 (Minn.1957).

McIlroy joined as defendants the Ozark Society, a conservationist group, and two companies that rent canoes for use on the Mulberry and other Ozark Mountain streams. The State of Arkansas, intervening, claimed the Mulberry was a navigable stream and the stream bed the property of the state, not the McIlroys.

* * *

The Mulberry River, located in northwest Arkansas, heads up in the Ozark Mountains and flows in a westerly direction for about 70 miles until it joins the Arkansas River. It could best be described as an intermediate stream, smaller than the Arkansas River, the lower White and Little Red Rivers and other deep, wide rivers that have been used commercially since their discovery. But neither is it like the many small creeks and branches in Arkansas that cannot be regularly floated with canoes or flatbottomed boats for any substantial period of time during the year. The Mulberry is somewhere in between. It is a stream that for about 50 or 55 miles of its length can be floated by canoe or flatbottomed boat for at least six months of the year. Parts of it are floatable for longer periods of time. The Mulberry is a typical rock-bottomed Ozark Mountain stream, flowing with relatively clear water and populated by a variety of fish. Smallmouth bass favor such a stream and populate the Mulberry.

For most of its distance it is a series of long flat holes of water interrupted by narrower shoals. These shoals attract the canoeists. McIlroy describes the stream as following a tortuous course; canoeists find it an exciting stream testing the skill of an experienced canoeist. Watergraps, affairs of wire or boards erected across the stream to hold cattle, have at times been erected but, according to W. L. McIlroy, they go down with the first rise of water. It is not a stream easily possessed. In recent years, the Mulberry has claimed the lives of several canoeists.

Annually, since 1967, the Ozark Society has sponsored for its members one or more float trips on the Mulberry River. These trips take them through McIlroy's property, which is located about 23 miles up the river from where the Mulberry enters the Arkansas. McIlroy said he had a confrontation with Ozark Society members in 1975 when about 600 people put in at a low water bridge on his property. The bridge, near Cass, serves a county road, and is undisputably a public bridge. Canoeists and fishermen have regularly used it as an access place to the river.

* * *

The evidence by testimony and exhibits demonstrates conclusively that the Mulberry had been used by the public for recreational purposes for many years. It has long been used for fishing and swimming and is today also popular among canoeists.

Seven witnesses from the locality testified. All testified they had fished or swum in the Mulberry at this locality and had never sought permission nor thought they needed it. * * *

Several state and federal officials testified. Richard Davies, Director of Arkansas State Parks and Tourism, said his agency, along with the Arkansas Game and Fish Commission, published, in 1978, a pamphlet, "The Float Streams of Arkansas," listing 14 of Arkansas' most popular fishing and canoeing streams. The Mulberry was touted as Arkansas' finest white water float stream and as an excellent habitat for smallmouth bass. Davies said he considered the water open to the public. George Purvis of the Arkansas Game and Fish Commission said the Mulberry was included in the pamphlet because it was one of the top five or six streams in the state for both floaters and fishermen. He also considered it open to the public. William E. Keith, an employee of the Game and Fish Commission, said fish were stocked on the Mulberry periodically from 1952 through 1977, sometimes at the low water bridge at Cass.

Nineteen canoeists testified and three others' testimony was offered by stipulation. All had floated the Mulberry, most several times; some numerous times. None had ever sought permission nor thought they needed it. No one's right to canoe was challenged until McIlroy challenged some of them in 1978.   * * *

The facts presented prove that the Mulberry River at the point in question is capable of recreational use and has been used extensively for recreational purposes. We must now decide whether such a stream is navigable.

Determining the navigability of a stream is essentially a matter of deciding if it is public or private property. Navigation in fact is the standard modern test of navigability, and, as embroidered by the federal courts, controls when navigation must be defined for federal purposes—maritime jurisdiction, regulation under the Commerce Clause, and title disputes between the state and federal governments. Otherwise, the states may adopt their own definitions of navigability.

* * *

Arkansas has adopted the standard definition of navigability. * * * Therefore, a river is legally navigable if actually navigable and actually navigable if commercially valuable.

However, in the case of *Barboro v. Boyle*, 119 Ark. 377, 178 S.W. 378 (1915), this Court foresaw, no doubt, that things would change in the future and that recreation would become an important interest of the people of Arkansas. The language in the *Barboro* case is almost prophetic. While adhering to the standard definition of navigability, with its dependence upon a commercial criterion, the Court went on to say:

> * * * Pleasure resorts might even be built upon the banks of the lake and the water might be needed for municipal purposes. *Moreover, the waters of the lake might be used to a much greater extent for boating, for pleasure, for bathing, fishing and hunting than they are now used.* [Emphasis added.] *Id.* at 382–383, 178 S.W. at 380.

Since that time no case presented to us has involved the public's right to use a stream which has a recreational value, but lacks commercial adaptability in the traditional sense. Our definition of navigability is, therefore, a remnant of the steamboat era.

However, many other states have been presented with this same problem. Back in 1870, the Massachusetts Supreme Court found a stream navigable that could only be used for pleasure. The stream was about two feet deep at low water. The court stated:

> If water is navigable for pleasure boating, it must be regarded as navigable water though no craft has ever been upon it for the purpose of trade or agriculture. *Attorney General v. Woods*, 108 Mass. 436, 440 (1870).

In Ohio, the court recently was faced with this problem and decided to change its definition of navigation. The Ohio court said:

> We hold that the modern utilization of our water by our citizens requires that our courts, in their judicial interpretation of the navigability of such waters, consider their recreational use as well as the more traditional criteria of commercial use. *State ex rel. v. Newport Concrete Co.*, 44 Ohio App.2d 121, 127, 336 N.E.2d 453, 457, 73 Ohio Ops.2d 124 (1975).

Applying a "public trust" to the Little Miami River, the Ohio court found that the State of Ohio " * * * holds these waters in trust for those Ohioans who wish to use the stream for all legitimate uses, be they commercial, transportational, or recreational." *State ex rel. v. Newport Concrete Co., supra.*

Michigan reached a similar conclusion in 1974. Navigability in Michigan was significantly affected by whether logs had been, or could be, floated down a stream. That "floatable test" had been used by the Michigan court until it was confronted with the same problem that we have. Michigan readily admitted that its definition needed to be changed:

> We therefore hold that members of the public have the right to navigate and to exercise the incidents of navigation in a lawful manner at any point below high water mark on waters of this state which are capable of being navigated by oar or motor propelled small craft. *Kelley, ex. rel. MacMullan v. Hallden*, 51 Mich.App. 176, 214 N.W.2d 856, 864 (1974).

For examples of other states that have adopted similar definitions of navigation, see: *People v. Mack*, 19 Cal.App.3d 1040, 97 Cal.Rptr. 448 (1971); *Lamprey v. State*, 52 Minn. 181, 53 N.W. 1139 (1893); *Luscher v. Reynolds*, 153 Or. 625, 56 P.2d 1158 (1936).*

* * *

McIlroy and others testified that the reason they brought the lawsuit was because their privacy was being interrupted by the people who trespassed on their property, littered the stream and generally

---

* Other states that have adopted the pleasure boat test of navigability include: Idaho (Southern Idaho Fish & Game Ass'n v. Picabo Livestock, Inc., 528 P.2d 1295 (Idaho 1974)); and New York (People v. Kraemer, 164 N.Y.S.2d 423 (N.Y. Police Ct. 1957)).—Eds.

destroyed their property. We are equally disturbed with that small percentage of the public that abuses public privileges and has no respect for the property of others. Their conduct is a shame on us all. It is not disputed that riparian landowners on a navigable stream have a right to prohibit the public from crossing their property to reach such a stream. * * *

Reversed.

FOGLEMAN, C. J., concurs in part and dissents in part.

I cannot join in the court's new definition of navigability, even though I concur in the reversal of the decree in this case. My disagreement is based upon the court's departure from two overriding and interrelated legal principles, i.e., the effect of a rule of property and the vesting of property rights.

* * *

Where persons have acquired property rights upon the faith and credit of prior judicial decisions, those decisions and the rights acquired thereunder should not be disturbed. At least one owner, Al Weiderkehr, acquired property on the Mulberry thinking that the waters were private, and he was justified in doing so under our prior decisions.

A settled legal principle governing the ownership and devolution of property is a rule of property. Decisions of the highest court of a state when they relate to and settle some principle of local law directly applicable to title are rules of property. A rule of property so established should not be disturbed.

The test of navigability is the means of determining the property rights of riparian owners. As such it is a rule of property. To repudiate this rule of property by judicial decision will have the effect of invalidating titles that were acquired in reliance upon the rule and such a change, if desirable, should be brought about by legislation, which operates only prospectively and cannot upset titles already vested. * * *

Even a legislative enactment cannot destroy vested rights which riparian owners have in a nonnavigable stream. * * *

The adoption of a so-called modern test changes a rule of property and apparently divests titles that have been vested under the prior test. In Arkansas, unlike communist states, it is the right of private property, not the rights of the public, that rises above constitutional sanction. Art. 2, § 22, Constitution of Arkansas. This is one of the fundamental distinctions between our system and the communistic form of government and its focus is directed to public rights asserted in streams. * * * I submit that, insofar as titles vested under the test of navigability applied up until this very date, the change of the test is a violation of due process of law under both the state and federal constitutions, as well as of Art. 2, §§ 22 and 23 of the Arkansas constitution. Judicial submission to public clamor is not in keeping with constitutional government.

* * *

Acquisition by prescription, or adverse possession, cannot be based upon hunting and fishing (or presumably swimming) upon the stream. This question was put to rest in *State ex rel. Thompson v. Parker*, 132 Ark. 316, 200 S.W. 1014, where we said:

> * * * The act of hunting and fishing on the unenclosed lands of another is not an act of possession. It does not denote any purpose to hold the same adversely, and thereby exclude the owner from dominion over his property, and it does not have any such effect.
> * * *

> * * * On the other hand, any use of the water of a nonnavigable stream for boating purposes by one other than the owner is an infringement of the rights of the owner.

> * * * I think that it was shown by a clear preponderance of the evidence that the owners of the McIlroy lands should be presumed to have known that a passageway on the Mulberry River was being used by the public adversely to them and under a claim of right.

Since I cannot agree to the taking and appropriating by judicial fiat of vested property rights of riparian owners on streams which are nonnavigable under the test applied in Arkansas for a century, I must dissent from the majority opinion, but I would reverse the decree on the ground that a prescriptive easement has been acquired by adverse use.

NOTES

1. Michigan was included among the states adopting the pleasure boat test, citing a court of appeals case. The Michigan Supreme Court later applied a more rigorous version of the test in Bott v. Michigan Dept. of Natural Resources, 327 N.W.2d 838 (Mich.1982). In *Bott* landowners owned almost all of the land around two small, spring-fed lakes and the shallow creeks connecting the lakes to somewhat larger lakes. Littoral owners on the larger lakes, joined by the state, sought to establish a right of access through the connecting creeks from the larger to the smaller lakes. Although the creeks were too shallow even to float logs, the Michigan Supreme Court decided to swim against modern precedent and held that the littoral owners on the two small lakes had exclusive use of them. It found that the small creeks connecting several small lakes were "not of sufficient width and depth to be used for recreation." Therefore, the lakes themselves could be used exclusively by the property owners surrounding them. The court expressed dissatisfaction with the pleasure boat test, suggesting that it is not, indeed, the law of Michigan: "Adoption of recreational-boating test would subject many formerly private inland waters to what are in essence recreational easements."

327 N.W.2d at 850.

2. What is the practical effect of a state's adopting the prescription rule urged by Chief Justice Fogleman instead of the pleasure boat test of navigability? Prescriptive rights of recreational boaters had been recognized in Arkansas before *McIlroy*. Buffalo River Conservation & Recreation Council v. National Park Serv., 558 F.2d 1342 (8th

Cir. 1977). Pursuant to the Buffalo National River Act, 86 Stat. 44 (1972), the Park Service acquired several parcels along the Buffalo River in Arkansas. Its congressional appropriation of funds was exhausted, resulting in a checkerboard pattern of acquired and nonacquired land. The Service posted a map showing acquired land at its headquarters and posted "no trespassing" signs on some private lands. Nevertheless, those floating the river "trespassed upon the land of private owners, left gates open, left debris, annoyed owners by requests to use their phones and bathroom facilities." A suit by the nonacquired landowners against the Park Service on a taking theory was dismissed. The Eighth Circuit held that the property owners could fence off their shorelands but could not obstruct the bed of the river because the public had acquired a prescriptive easement of flotation.

3. A has title to land on a navigable river protected by a levee; the levee breaks and floods the tract. No effort is made to reclaim the land for 9 years and during that time many pleasure boats use the newly formed waterbody. The evidence shows that there is no water over seven or eight feet deep in the area. Does the public have a right to use the water for recreational purposes? Can A later reclaim the land and thus deprive the public of the use of the area for recreation? See Bohn v. Albertson, 238 P.2d 128 (Cal.1951). See also People v. Summer School of Painting at Saugatuck, Inc., 307 N.W.2d 87 (Mich. 1981) (lake completely surrounded by private land and accessible from a river through a swamp traversed by several people in small boats); and Michigan Conference Ass'n of Seventh-Day Adventists v. Commission of Natural Resources, 245 N.W.2d 412 (Mich.1976) (lake completely surrounded by private land and untouched by any public road; accessible by canoe from outlet creek).

4. See generally Paige A. Parker, Note, *Fishing From the Bank: Public Recreational Rights Along Idaho's Rivers and Lakes*, 21 Idaho L.Rev. 275 (1985), and Richard S. Eximoto & Jean E. Rice, Comment, *Constitutional Right to Fish: A New Theory of Access to the Waterfront*, 16 U.C.D.L.Rev. 661 (1983).

MONTANA COALITION FOR STREAM ACCESS, INC. v. CURRAN
Supreme Court of Montana, 1984.
210 Mont. 38, 682 P.2d 163.

The Dearborn River is approximately sixty-six miles long and originates along the east slope of the Continental Divide in west-central Montana. The river flows generally in a southeasterly direction from its source near Scapegoat Mountain, approximately thirty miles southwest of Augusta, Montana, to the Missouri River.

The first twenty miles of the Dearborn is through mountains and canyon terrain, roughly twelve miles of which is within the Scapegoat Wilderness. After it leaves the Wilderness area, the river emerges onto rolling plains and continues its flow for about twenty-nine miles, where it again enters a moderately timbered region. It then extends another seventeen miles and enters the Missouri River near Craig, Montana.

The Coalition is a nonprofit Montana corporation formed to promote public access to Montana's rivers. Individual members of the

Coalition use the stretch of the Dearborn running through Curran's property for recreational pursuits such as floating and fishing. Some members of the Coalition who have floated or attempted to float the Dearborn have experienced interference and harassment from Curran or his agents.

* * *

Curran claims title to the banks and streambed of a portion of the Dearborn River and claims to have the right, as an owner of private property, to restrict its use.

* * *

The first issue to be addressed is whether the District Court erred in its application of the federal test of navigability for title purposes.

Curran maintains that the District Court erred by misconstruing the law to be applied in determining the navigability of the Dearborn at the time Montana was admitted to the Union.

The United States Supreme Court has held, and all parties agree, that federal law controls the issue of navigability for title purposes. *Brewer-Elliott Oil and Gas Company v. United States* (1922), 260 U.S. 77.

* * *

Navigability in fact under federal law can be determined by the log-floating test. *The Montello*, supra; *Sierra Pacific Power Co. v. Federal Energy Regulatory Commission* (9th Cir.1982), 681 F.2d 1134, cert. denied, 460 U.S. 1082 (1983); *State of Oregon v. Riverfront Protection Association* (9th Cir.1982), 672 F.2d 792. In *Riverfront Protection Association*, supra, the McKenzie River was declared navigable despite the fact that log drives could only be conducted during April, May and early June.

The evidence in this case, supplied by the affidavits of two competent historians, demonstrates that the Dearborn River was used in 1887, two years before Montana statehood, to float approximately 100,000 railroad ties. Furthermore, in 1888 and 1889, one or two log drives per year were floated down the Dearborn. One drive in 1888 contained 700,000 board feet. Clearly, the Dearborn satisfied the log-floating test for navigability under the federal test of navigability for title purposes.

Since the Dearborn was navigable under the log-floating test at the time of statehood in 1889, title to the riverbed was owned by the federal government prior to statehood and was transferred to the State of Montana upon admission to the Union.

* * *

Of further importance to the issue of navigability for title is the Public Trust Doctrine. The theory underlying this doctrine can be traced from Roman Law through Magna Carta to present day decisions.

The Public Trust Doctrine was first clearly defined in *Illinois Central Railroad v. Illinois* (1892), 146 U.S. 387[, page 409, supra]. In this case the United States Supreme Court was called upon to determine whether the State of Illinois had the right to convey, by legislative grant, a portion of Chicago's harbor on Lake Michigan to the Illinois Central Railroad.

"That the State holds the title to the lands under the navigable waters of Lake Michigan, within its limits, in the same manner that the State holds title to soils under tide water, by the common law, we have already shown, and that title necessarily carries with it control over the waters above them whenever the lands are subjected to use. * * * It is a title held in trust for the people of the State that they may enjoy the navigation of the waters, carry on commerce over them, and have liberty of fishing therein freed from the obstruction or interference of private parties. * * * The trust devolving upon the State for the public, and which can only be discharged by the management and control of property in which the public has an interest, cannot be relinquished by a transfer of the property. The control of the State for the purposes of the trust can never be lost, except as to such parcels as are used in promoting the interests of the public therein, or can be disposed of without any substantial impairment of the public interest in the lands and waters remaining. * * * *The State can no more abdicate its trust over property in which the whole people are interested, like navigable waters and soils under them, so as to leave them entirely under the use and control of private parties, except in the instance of parcels mentioned for the improvement of the navigation and use of the waters, or when parcels can be disposed of without impairment of the public interest in what remains, than it can abdicate its police powers in the administration of government and the preservation of the peace.*" (Emphasis added.) Illinois Central, 146 U.S. at 452–453.

In summary, the "equal-footing" doctrine as set forth in *Pollard's Lessee*, which held that the federal government retained title to navigable waters so that all states entering the Union subsequent to the original thirteen would enter on an "equal footing" and the Public Trust Doctrine, which provides that states hold title to navigable waterways in trust for the public benefit and use are two important doctrines to be considered in determining a navigability-for-title question. In this matter, the log-floating test was properly applied and the State found to hold title to the riverbed of the Dearborn. In this matter, where title to the bed of the Dearborn rests with the State, the test of navigability for *use* and not for title, is a test to be determined under state law and not federal law.

* * *

The third issue is whether the District Court erred in determining that recreational use and fishing make a stream navigable. We find no error.

The concept of determining navigability based upon public recreational use is not new. * * *

 * * * *Lamprey v. State* (Metcalf) (1893), 52 Minn. 181, 53 N.W. 1139, 1143.

Since 1893, the concept expressed in *Lamprey* has been followed and the idea of navigability for public recreational use has spread to numerous other jurisdictions. According to Albert W. Stone, a professor of Law at the University of Montana and an acknowledged expert in the field of Water Law, there is a tendency in adjudicated cases from other jurisdictions to abandon the tool of defining "navigability" and simply directing the inquiry to whether the water is susceptible to public use. Under this concept, the question of title to the underlying streambed is irrelevant. A. W. Stone, *Montana Water Law for the 1980's* (1981). Thus, the issue becomes one of use, not title.

Navigability for use is a matter governed by state law. It is a separate concept from the federal question of determining navigability for title purposes.

" * * * The Propeller Genesee Chief [The Propeller Genesee Chief v. Fitzhugh, (1851) 53 U.S. (12 How.) 443], Gibbons v. Ogden [(1824) 22 U.S. (9 Wheat.) 1], and the Daniel Ball [(1870) 77 U.S. (10 Wall.) 557] established the basic test for public waters for the purposes of our federal system. But the problems of federalism are not the same as the problems which may arise entirely within a state; the federal test for land-title and federal jurisdiction does not have to be the test for state determinations of the waters that are public for various state purposes." 1 Waters and Water Rights (Clark Ed.) pgs. 212–213, (1967). (Footnotes omitted.)*

In 1961, the Wyoming Supreme Court supported public use of waters suitable therefor without regard to title or navigability. The Court held:

"Irrespective of the ownership of the bed or channel of waters, and irrespective of their navigability, the public has the right to use public waters of this State for floating usable craft and that use may not be interfered with or curtailed by any landowner. It is also the right of the public while so lawfully floating in the State's waters to lawfully hunt or fish or do any and all other things which are not otherwise made unlawful." *Day v. Armstrong* (Wyo.1961), 362 P.2d 137, 147.

In essence, the Wyoming court held that public recreational use of waters was limited only by the susceptibility of the waters for that purpose.

The Constitution of Montana provides:

"All surface, underground, flood, and atmospheric waters within the boundaries of the state are the property of the state for the use of its people and are subject to appropriation for beneficial uses as provided by law."

Thus, Curran has no right to control the use of the surface waters of the Dearborn to the exclusion of the public except to the extent of his prior appropriation of part of the water for irrigation purposes, which is not at issue here. Curran has no right of ownership to the riverbed or surface waters because their ownership was held by the federal government prior to statehood in trust for the people. Upon statehood, title was transferred to the State, burdened by this public trust.

In essence, the question is whether the waters owned by the State under the Constitution are susceptible to recreational use by the public. The capability of use of the waters for recreational purposes determines their availability for recreational use by the public. Streambed ownership by a private party is irrelevant. If the waters are owned by the State and held in trust for the people by the State, no private party may bar the use of those waters by the people. The Constitution and the public trust doctrine do not permit a private party to interfere with the public's right to recreational use of the surface of the State's waters.

Curran has also raised questions regarding ex post facto laws, violation of the contract clause, and irrevocable rights and privileges. However, since Curran has no title to the streambed or right to exclude the public from use of the surface waters of the Dearborn for recreational purposes, these matters are not germane to this case.

* * *

We add the cautionary note that nothing herein contained in this opinion shall be construed as granting the public the right to enter upon or cross over private property to reach the State-owned waters hereby held available for recreational purposes.

NOTES

1. The recognition of public rights in *Curran* could have been sustained based on the fact that the Dearborn River was determined to be navigable for title by the federal test, and hence "burdened by this public trust." The decision, however, was independently grounded on the recreational capability of the river. A month after *Curran*, the Montana Supreme Court decided Montana Coalition for Stream Access, Inc. v. Hildreth, 684 P.2d 1088 (Mont.1984).

We held in *Curran*, supra, that the question of title to the underlying streambed is immaterial in determining navigability for recreational use of State-owned waters. This holding applies equally to the case now before us.

* * *

Since title to the underlying bed is not at issue and is immaterial to the determination of the public's right of use, the District Court did not err in failing to make findings of fact and conclusions of law relative to the ownership of the streambed.

684 P.2d at 1092. The sole issue in determining the availability of waterbodies for public recreational use was said to be "the capability of

use of the waters for recreational purposes * * *." 684 P.2d at 1091. The court expressly declined to adopt the pleasure boat test of navigability saying that it was "unnecessary and improper to determine a specific test under which to find navigability for recreational use." Id.

For a useful analysis of the cases see John E. Thorson, et al., *Forging Public Rights in Montana's Waters*, 6 Pub. Land L.Rev. 1 (1985).

2. Montana responded to *Curran* and *Hildreth* by passing legislation that creates two classes of waters. Class I waters are those owned by the state under the federal navigability for title test or those that are or have been capable of supporting commercial uses such as log floating or fur skin transportation. Class II waters are all other waters. Class II waters capable of no or limited recreational use may be identified and recreational use limited to the actual capacity. All surface waters "capable of recreational use" are subject to public use. The legislation also limits landowner liability to acts of wilful or wanton misconduct and bars the acquisition of prescriptive easements by the recreational use of surface streams. Mont. Code Ann. §§ 23–2–311 to –322. The use of both Class I and II waters is subject to further state regulation. Provisions of the statute allowing camping, big game hunting, and duck blind construction between the high water marks of privately owned streambeds were held unconstitutional in Galt v. Montana, 731 P.2d 912 (Mont.1987) because the public's right to make recreational use of privately owned streambeds does not include such activities. The court said that the public's right is "only to such use as is necessary to utilization of the water itself." The court also struck down a provision that required landowners to pay the cost of establishing portage routes around artificial barriers, in that the benefit of such routes is to the public, not the landowner, and thus the states should pay the expense.

3. Both Montana cases noted that the public has no right to trespass across private property to get to waters open for recreational use. It did hold that "[t]he public has the right to use the waters and the bed and banks up to the ordinary high water mark," regardless of land ownership. In cases of obstructions, "the public is allowed to portage around such barriers in the least intrusive manner possible, avoiding damage to the adjacent owner's property and his rights." Montana Coalition for Stream Access, Inc. v. Hildreth, 684 P.2d 1088, 1091 (Mont.1984). Most decisions recognizing public recreational rights show some concern for landowners, but the respective rights of the public and landowners are far from clear as yet.

What protection exists for landowners who are fearful that a flotilla of pleasure boaters will bring large numbers of fishermen, campers and picnickers wading on the beds and walking along the banks? It is clear that the landowner is now prohibited from erecting barriers across the stream to prevent the public from exercising its easement. Equally clear is that absent established custom, discussed infra, most courts would not hold that the state could grant its licensees immunity from trespass if they gained access to the water by walking across private lands. These and other more permanent privileges such as mooring boats must be acquired by prescription. See Shellow v. Hagen, 101 N.W.2d 694 (Wis.1960). But does it then follow that the recreationist must remain inside the boat to avoid a trespass suit? Some courts define the public easement as a "right of flotage" and recognize that some right to disembark is a necessary incident of full enjoyment.

To determine the scope of an easement for the purpose of deciding if it is overburdened, courts start by asking if the present use is a substantial increase in the use of the servient estate contemplated by the parties at the time of grant. However, its utility in the case of public recreational rights is limited because: (1) The servitude is imposed by courts and legislatures rather than by a voluntary conveyance. While this is true for easements by necessity also, the courts insist that the necessity exist at the time that the unified tract was severed, thus limiting the easement to the extent necessary to serve the landlocked tract at that time. (2) The servitude is explicitly perceived as elastic for it is imposed to accommodate new public demands with the present capacity of the water to support them. The cases dealing with these problems are few and the answers inconsistent. The narrowest servitude is illustrated in Wyoming which relied on saw log cases to confine the right to "disembark and pull, push or carry over shoals, riffles and rapids." Day v. Armstrong, 362 P.2d 137 (Wyo. 1961). Michigan, one of the original saw log states, apparently permits fisherman to wade on the bed so long as there is no trespassing on uplands. Rushton ex rel. Hoffmaster v. Taggart, 11 N.W.2d 193 (Mich. 1943). Missouri permits wading and walking on the bed and use of the channel for recreation. Elder v. Delcour, 269 S.W.2d 17 (Mo.1954).

As mentioned on page 448, supra, some states carved out of the Northwest Ordinance apply that ordinance as a source of public rights. The ordinance speaks not only of navigable waters, but also provides that "the carrying places between the same, shall be common highways * * *." See Lundberg v. University of Notre Dame, 282 N.W. 70 (Wis.1938), motion for rehearing overruled 285 N.W. 839 (Wis.1939), noted 1939 Wis.L.Rev. 547, for a case rejecting application of the ordinance to a dispute involving a portage to a lake used for recreational purposes.

PEOPLE v. EMMERT

Supreme Court of Colorado, 1979.
198 Colo. 137, 597 P.2d 1025.

Lee, Justice.

The defendants-appellants were convicted of third-degree criminal trespass in violation of section 18–4–504, C.R.S. 1973.

* * * The record shows that on July 3, 1976, the defendants entered the Colorado River from public land for a float-trip downstream. The Colorado River flows westerly and bisects the ranch of the Ritschard Cattle Company. As it passes through the Ritschard ranch,

it varies in depth from twelve inches to several feet. The rafts on which the defendants floated were designed to draw five to six inches of water, and had leg-holes through which the occupants could extend their legs into the water below the rafts. This enabled the defendants as they floated down the river to touch the bed of the river from time to time to control the rafts, avoid rocks and overhangs, and to stay in the main channel of the river. They touched the riverbed as it crossed the Ritschard ranch. The defendants did not, however, leave their rafts or encroach upon the shoreline or the banks of the river or islands owned by the Ritschard Cattle Company.

* * *

Upon being notified that a party of floaters was approaching, Con Ritschard and his foreman extended a single strand of barbed wire across the river at the location of the Ritschard private bridge. The strand of barbed wire was from eight to ten inches above the surface of the water and was placed in this position specifically to impede the defendants. Ritschard and his foreman remained on the bridge to tell defendants they were trespassing on private property. Defendants Taylor and Wilson were stopped at the bridge and told they were trespassing. They denied this and floated their rafts under the barbed wire and remained under the bridge for a period of time until defendant Emmert, and others in the rafting party, caught up with them. Shortly, a deputy sheriff arrived and placed the defendants under arrest, and they were subsequently charged with third-degree criminal trespass.

The parties stipulated that the river is non-navigable and had not historically been used for commercial or trade purposes of any kind. However, the river had been used in the past by recreational floaters using rafts, tubes, kayaks and flat-bottom boats, despite the express objection of the Ritschards. At the time of this incident, the river had been posted with no-trespassing signs.

Also, it was agreed that substantially all of the Ritschard ranch land was deeded land with no exclusion of the bed of the river, and that the area where the defendants were stopped was such an area, with the land on both sides of the river owned by the Ritschard ranch.

I.

The third-degree criminal trespass statute, section 18–4–504, C.R.S. 1973, provides:

"A person commits the crime of third degree criminal trespass if he unlawfully enters or remains in or upon premises. Third degree criminal trespass is a class 1 petty offense."

Defendants do not argue that they did not intentionally float on the river over the Ritschard ranch property without the owner's consent. Their contention is that they did so lawfully as a matter of right under the authority of section 5, Article XVI of the Colorado Constitution. Thus, if the defendants' interpretation is incorrect, it follows that they committed the offense of third-degree criminal trespass.

II.

It is the general rule of property law recognized in Colorado that the land underlying non-navigable streams is the subject of private ownership and is vested in the proprietors of the adjoining lands. More v. Johnson, 193 Colo. 489, 568 P.2d 437 (1977); Hartman v. Tresise, 36 Colo. 146, 84 P. 685 (1906); Hanlon v. Hobson, 24 Colo. 284, 51 P. 433 (1897). It is clear, therefore, that since the section of the Colorado River here involved is non-navigable the title to the stream bed is owned by the riparian landowner, the Ritschard Cattle Company. Defendants do not dispute the ownership by the Ritschard Cattle Company of the riverbed in question.

The common law rule holds that he who owns the surface of the ground has the exclusive right to everything which is above it (*"cujus est solum, ejus est usque ad coelum"*). This fundamental rule of property law has been recognized not only judicially but also by our General Assembly when in 1937 it enacted what is now codified as section 41–1–107, C.R.S. 1973:

> "The ownership of space above the lands and waters of this state is declared to be vested in the several owners of the surface beneath, subject to the right of flight of aircraft."

Applying this rule, which was implicitly adopted by the court in *Hartman*, supra, the ownership of the bed of a non-navigable stream vests in the owner the exclusive right of control of everything above the stream bed, subject only to constitutional and statutory limitations, restrictions and regulations. Thus, in *Hartman*, supra, ownership of the stream bed was held to include the exclusive right of fishery in the waters flowing over it. It follows that whoever "breaks the close"— intrudes upon the space above the surface of the land—without the permission of the owner, whether it be for fishing or for other recreational purposes, such as floating, as in this case, commits a trespass. See *Restatement (Second) of Torts* § 159.

We have not been cited to any Colorado decisions interpreting constitutional or statutory provisions which may have modified the common law rule of property law upon which we predicate this decision. And we do not feel constrained to follow the trend away from the coupling of bed title with the right of public recreational use of surface waters as urged by defendants. We recognize the various rationales employed by courts to allow public recreational use of water overlying privately owned beds, i.e., (1) practical considerations employed in water rich states such as Florida, Minnesota and Washington; (2) a public easement in recreation as an incident of navigation; (3) the creation of a public trust based on usability, thereby establishing only a limited private usufructuary right; and (4) state constitutional basis for state ownership. We consider the common law rule of more force and effect, especially given its longstanding recognition in this state. As noted in Smith v. People, 120 Colo. 39, 206 P.2d 826 (1949): "If a change in long established judicial precedent is desirable, it is a legislative and not a judicial function to make any needed change." We specifically note that it is within the competence of the General Assembly to modify rules of common law within constitutional parameters.

III.

The defendants claim that section 5 of Article XVI of the Colorado Constitution establishes the public right to recreational use of all waters in the state. We do not agree with this interpretation. We note that Article XVI is entitled "Mining and Irrigation." Section 5, under the heading "Irrigation," reads:

> "The water of every natural stream, not heretofore appropriated, within the state of Colorado, is hereby declared to be the property of the public, and the same is dedicated to the use of the people of the state, subject to appropriation as hereinafter provided."

This provision of the Colorado Constitution, upon which the defendants so heavily rely, simply and firmly establishes the right of appropriation in this state. In this regard, we agree with the decision in *Hartman*, supra, where this court rejected an argument similar to defendants' here, that a person had a right under section 5 of Article XVI to fish in a non-navigable stream bounded by private property without the consent of the owner. In rejecting this contention, the court stated:

> " * * * The section of the Constitution relied upon declares the unappropriated waters of our natural streams to be the property of the public, and dedicates the same to the use of the people of the state, subject to appropriation, as in that instrument provided; and the following section provides that the right to divert the same to beneficial uses shall never be denied. It is this right of appropriation which the general government has recognized and confirmed, and subject to which its grants of public lands in the arid states since 1866 have been made. * * * "

The defendants attempt to distinguish *Hartman*, supra, on the grounds that the main thrust of the decision was to hold unconstitutional, as taking of private property without just compensation, that part of Colo.Sess. Laws, 1903, ch. 112, section 7 at 233, which provided: "That the public shall have the right to fish in any stream in this state, stocked at public expense, subject to actions in trespass for any damage done property along the bank of any such stream." The defendants fail to recognize, however, that their misplaced reliance on the constitutional provision was squarely rejected by the language of *Hartman*, supra. We here reaffirm, therefore, that section 5, Article XVI of the Colorado Constitution was primarily intended to preserve the historical appropriation system of water rights upon which the irrigation economy in Colorado was founded, rather than to assure public access to waters for purposes other than appropriation.

Defendants also urge as a better resolution of this controversy that we follow the Wyoming decision in Day v. Armstrong, 362 P.2d 137 (Wyo.1961). We decline to do so. There, under similar facts to those presented in this case, the Wyoming supreme court declared that the public has the right to the recreational use of the surface waters of non-navigable streams bounded by private property.

This conclusion, the Wyoming court declared, was "based solely upon Wyoming's Constitutional declaration that all waters within its boundaries belong to the State * * *."[1] Significantly, unlike Colorado's counterpart constitutional provision, the Wyoming provision does not mention appropriation. As such, it has been regarded as a stronger statement of the public's right to recreational use of all surface waters. See Joseph L. Sax, Water Law, 354 (1965).[2]

The interest at issue here, a riparian bed owner's exclusive use of water overlying his land, is distinguished from the right of appropriation. Constitutional provisions historically concerned with appropriation, therefore, should not be applied to subvert a riparian bed owner's common law right to the exclusive surface use of waters bounded by his lands. Without permission, the public cannot use such waters for recreation. If the increasing demand for recreational space on the waters of this state is to be accommodated, the legislative process is the proper method to achieve this end.

* * *

Finally, we note that in 1977, after the incident here in controversy had occurred, the legislature clarified the meaning of the word "premises" by the enactment of section 18–4–504.5, which provides:

"As used in sections 18–4–503 and 18–4–504, 'premises' means real property, buildings, and other improvements thereon, and the stream banks and beds of any non-navigable fresh water streams flowing through such real property."

We hold that the public has no right to the use of waters overlying private lands for recreational purposes without the consent of the owner.

Accordingly, the judgment is affirmed.

GROVES and CARRIGAN, JJ., dissent.

GROVES, JUSTICE, dissenting:

I respectfully dissent.

The majority opinion narrowly construes *Colo. Const.* Art. XVI, § 5. * * * The provision establishes that the waters of the state are the property of the public and are dedicated to the use of the people of the state. The clause "subject to appropriation as hereinafter provided"

---

1. Article 8 of the Wyoming constitution is entitled "Irrigation and Water Rights." Section 1 thereof, entitled "Water is state property," reads: "The water of all natural streams, springs, lakes or other collections of still water, within the boundaries of the state, are hereby declared to be the property of the state."

2. A possible explanation for the Wyoming supreme court's result is that the allocation and use of water in Wyoming is centrally controlled by the state through an administrative permit system whereby a permit may be denied if determined to be detrimental to the public welfare. This approach contrasts Colorado's minimal state control over appropriation of water. See Colo. Const. Art. XVI, Sec. 6, which provides that "[t]he right to divert the unappropriated waters of any natural stream to beneficial uses shall never be denied."

functions as a caveat establishing that appropriation for a beneficial use is superior to other uses. The clause in itself does not limit other uses.

At the beginning of this century, Justice Bailey in a dissenting opinion, set forth the same interpretation of the constitutional provision:

> "This makes the waters of every natural stream public. They are dedicated to the use of the people, to be used by them in such manner as they see fit, subject only to one condition; that of the right of appropriation for beneficial purposes. Until the waters are appropriated and diverted from the stream, they belong to the public.
>
> "No stronger words could have been used by the people than are used in this declaration. It is idle to say that the waters of the streams are dedicated to the public for the purpose of appropriation, because those are not the words of the Constitution. It is a grant made subject to that right.
>
> * * * " Dissenting opinion Hartman v. Tresise, 36 Colo. 146, 84 P. 685 (1906).

The constitutional language in no way supports any intent to provide for exclusive private use of public waters. * * *

Hartman concerned the constitutionality of a statute which purported to give the public the right to fish in any stream in the state, subject to actions for trespass for damages done to the privately owned banks of a stream. The facts of the case are not explained clearly. Nonetheless, it appears that the defendant entered the plaintiff's land to fish in a natural stream flowing there. Both the statute and the defendant's conduct concerned trespass to land. The majority in *Hartman* held only that the defendant had no right to fish in a stream whose beds and banks were privately owned and that the legislative attempt to create public easements on private land to facilitate access to streams constituted a taking of private property without compensation.

* * *

No determination as to the rights to use of streams in the absence of a trespass to land was necessary. Consequently, the statements to the effect that *Colo.Const.* Art. XVI, § 6 only provides for a right of appropriation are merely *dicta*, not precedent. * * *

* * *

In sum, the constitutional language clearly dictates a result opposite to that reached by the majority. Even if the constitutional provision were deemed ambiguous, contemporary concerns with the availability of natural resources for recreation argues for a broad interpretation of the public's rights in the waters of the state, rather than reliance upon inapplicable case law and common law made irrelevant by the express adoption of a scheme of appropriation.

CARRIGAN, J., joins in this dissent.

CARRIGAN, JUSTICE, dissenting:

* * * Although it is clear that the defendants touched their feet to the stream bed owned by the Ritschards, it is unclear why that contact alone is insufficient to uphold the trespass convictions. If the majority believes that such "foot-dragging" is an inadequate basis for supporting the trespass convictions, it should say so and say why. But if the touching was a trespass, that violation was ripe for a decision and should have been the only basis for a decision. All of the majority's assertions about landowners' rights to water in adjoining streams, therefore, are assertions that amount to dicta. The majority has decided a major constitutional issue of far-ranging implications but, in so doing, has decided an issue that was not ripe for consideration.

The majority reaches deep into the common law of feudal England for the principle it today imposes on modern Colorado. The principle is of such antiquity that the majority has to express it in Latin: "Cujus est solum, ejus est usque ad coelum." [1]

A long "leap of faith" would be necessary to assume that that ancient rule had been imported into Colorado's early common law. And an even longer leap would be required to conclude that it was intended to govern the controversy at hand. But even if those leaps were made, it would seem obvious that the people of Colorado, in adopting the state constitution, repealed those principles and set forth the rule that unappropriated waters of Colorado's natural streams belong to all the people. *Colo.Const.*, Art. XVI, section 5.

Indeed, if "cujus est solum, ejus est usque ad coelum," is the law in Colorado, the majority opinion creates some serious problems for Colorado. If a landowner, for instance, has the right to all of the air flowing above his or her land, he or she also has the exclusive right to exclude others from trespassing in the airspace. Violators who infringe that airspace may be prosecuted for criminal trespass (as in this case), sued for damages or both. Anyone who floats a balloon, pilots a hang glider, flies a kite or shoots fireworks through another's airspace, therefore, is subject either to criminal prosecution, civil suit or both. Similarly and presumably, so are the owners and operators of industrial, utility and other plants which spew smoke or pollutants into the airstream and over the property of others.

* * *

The majority opinion dramatically alters the law of Colorado as it has been perceived by the many boaters, rafters and tubers who for years have sought rest, recreation and relaxation on our beautiful streams and rivers. As our population grows, so grows the need for surcease from the cares and concerns of city dwelling. Those who in our state constitution dedicated our natural streams "to the use of the people of the state * * * " were not elitists. *Colo.Const.*, Art. XVI,

---

1. He who owns the surface of the   thing which is above it.
ground has the exclusive right to every-

section 5. They did not reserve the enjoyment of these great natural resources to the few. Nor did they exclude from such pleasures all but the few who owned land on stream banks. If the recreational use of streams was not among those uses for which streams were reserved to the public, it is impossible to conceive what uses were contemplated and reserved by the constitution.

* * *

Ironically the majority opinion, while implying that the General Assembly is competent to change the rule adopted today, has complicated the prospects of having the rule changed in the future. The Court has painted the state into a corner, and its brushwork assures that any effort to alter the rule will be difficult and expensive. The Court, by creating a vested property right in stream water (with the concomitant right to exclude all others from that water), has created a valuable property interest. And the General Assembly, therefore, cannot give the public recreational access to rivers without taking away from landowners their newly recognized property interests and paying them "just compensation." *U.S.Const.*, Amendment V; *Colo.Const.*, Art. II, section 15.

It is difficult to imagine a more stark contrast than the disparity between the result which the majority reaches and the language and spirit of Article XIV, section 5, ("The water of every natural stream, not heretofore appropriated, within the State of Colorado, is hereby declared to be the property of the *public*, and the same is dedicated to the use of the *People* of the State, subject to appropriation as hereinafter provided." (Emphasis added.)).

Eleven states west of the Mississippi River have recognized the right of public or non-owners' use of waters in river beds which are privately owned. Such rights are flourishing in California, Idaho, Iowa, Minnesota, Missouri, New Mexico, Oregon, South Dakota, Texas, Washington, and Wyoming. See Ralph W. Johnson and Russell A. Austin, Jr., *Recreational Rights and Titles to Beds on Western Lakes and Streams*, 7 Nat. Resources J. 38–40 (1967). See also Joseph B. Gaudet, Note, *Water Recreation—Public Use of "Private Waters,"* 52 Cal. L. Rev. 171 (1964).

NOTES

1. The decision in *Emmert* placed Colorado in a small minority of states that reject the expanded theory of public rights in water that traverses private lands. Was the court constrained by the language of the state constitution? Is the different result supported by the difference in Colorado's constitutional provision regarding rights to water from the provision in the Montana Constitution that was relied upon in *Curran* or in the Wyoming Constitution, which was construed in Day v. Armstrong? "Peculiar" Kansas chose to join the minority. State ex rel. Meek v. Hays, 785 P.2d 1356 (Kan.1990) adopted the narrow federal test for title as the state test of navigability for recreational use, citing the fact that in 1986 the legislature "killed" two bills which would have

allowed public use of streams that are non-navigable under the federal test.

2.   The court defers to the legislature to take any action needed to accommodate the demand for recreational uses.   Justice Carrigan in dissent perceives constraints (legal and economic) on the legislature after *Emmert*.   What can a future legislature do?   See Liza La Belle Scott, Note, *The Public Trust Doctrine—A Tool for Expanding Recreational Rafting Rights in Colorado*, 57 U.Colo.L.Rev. 625 (1986).

3.   Prior to the decision in *Emmert*, but after the facts occurred, the state's criminal trespass law was amended to clarify the meaning of "premises," as noted at page 464, supra.   The Attorney General opined that:

> The legislative definition of "premises" in section 18–4–504.5 * * * was restricted to real property and does not include either the waters of streams or the airspace above private property.   * * * The statute then would repeal "ad coelum" in the criminal trespass context, and would reverse the *Emmert* result in the situation * * * where persons float over private property but do not touch the river bed or banks.

> * * *

> An examination of the legislative history of section 18–4–504.5 reveals quite clearly that the intent of the legislature was to protect riparian landowners from trespasses to the privately owned banks and beds of streams, while insuring that those who float or boat upon those streams without intruding on real property would not be liable for a criminal trespass.   * * *

> * * *   Because section 18–4–504.5 speaks to criminal trespass and does not address civil remedies, it cannot be viewed as authorizing the owners of stream banks and beds to prohibit or otherwise control the use for floating of waters passing over their lands.

> * * *

Op.Colo. Att'y Gen. File No. ONR8303042/KW (1983).

Without a remedy in criminal trespass, what recourse does an objecting property owner have to boaters and sportsmen floating through their property?   Although, as the Attorney General concludes, the amendment does not "authorize" civil remedies, are such remedies precluded?   Is self-help appropriate?   Could the problem be solved with barbed wire?

4.   *Emmert* found that the framers of Colorado's Constitution were primarily concerned with preserving the ability of the citizens to appropriate water.   Is it realistic to expect conflicts between the public's use of water for recreation and the exercise of water rights established by prior appropriation?

A has an 1895 appropriation on Trout Paradise River.   In 1993 the river is declared suitable for recreational use and thus open to public use.   During the 1994 summer irrigation season A makes a call on the river that is rejected by the water master on the ground that the diversion will interfere with the use of the water for paramount public fishing and flotation rights. Can the state withhold the water?

In Ritter v. Standal, 566 P.2d 769 (Idaho 1977) defendant constructed a fish farm in an estuary of the Snake River which blocked both a private riparian's and the public's access to the river. Idaho Code § 36–907 declared the river navigable for fishing. The court held that Southern Idaho Fish and Game Ass'n v. Picabo Livestock, Inc., 528 P.2d 1295 (Idaho.1974), extended the public use rights to recreation, and that the reach of the river had long been used for these purposes. Defendant was ordered to remove the fish farm and restore the estuary because the farm was a public and private nuisance obstructing free passage of a navigable estuary. Of special interest is the court's rejection of defendant's argument that his state water license allowed him to maintain the farm to the detriment of public rights.

If there is state constitutional preference for appropriative water rights, how should such cases be resolved?

NOTE: DEDICATION

If water is not navigable for purposes of imposing a public servitude under a state definition of "navigability" or an application of the public trust doctrine for recreational uses, it still might be open to the public through the common law doctrine of dedication. The leading Supreme Court decision, City of Cincinnati v. White's Lessees, 31 U.S. (6 Pet.) 431 (1832), suggested that a dedication was both a contract and an estoppel in pais. The contract analogy dominates the formal elements, for although dedication need not be manifested by any formal act, an intent on the part of the owner to devote land to a public use must be proven, see 4 Tiffany, Real Property § 1101 (3rd ed. 1939), and the land must also be accepted by the public in order for the dedication to be perfected. However, many courts which hold that the property is open to public use remain faithful to the contract analogy in theory by either inferring an intent to dedicate from public use or simply holding that the owner is estopped to deny the public's use. See 4 Tiffany at page 362. The modern consensus is that intent has become a fiction and that the basis of the doctrine is a mixture of estoppel and prescription. The irrelevance of the owner's intent is illustrated by the modern tendency to apply principles of prescription in deciding whether there has been an intent to dedicate. Strictly speaking, prescription is not an appropriate common law theory because it is based on a presumed lost grant and the public cannot take by grant, see Nature Conservancy v. Machipongo Club, Inc., 419 F.Supp. 390 (E.D. Va. 1976), but the result may be the same in states which have abandoned the fiction of the lost grant. State ex rel. Haman v. Fox, 594 P.2d 1093 (Idaho 1979).

In Bartlett v. Stalker Lake Sportsmen's Club, 168 N.W.2d 356 (Minn.1969), the owner of a littoral tract on a bog granted the public a perpetual easement for a road over his land to guarantee them a right to hunt on the lake. The open water was "150 acres; with the bog, the total area is about 500 acres. The maximum depth of the water is approximately 4 feet, but the average depth is 1½ feet. There are no fish in the lake and it is unsuitable for swimming or boating but is extremely well suited to duck hunting." Later all tracts were purchased by a hunting club which tried to enjoin use of the surface of the lake by members of the general public reaching it by the county road. The court concluded that the two elements of a common law dedication, the intent to devote property to a public use and its acceptance by the public, were satisfied. Evidence showed that members of the public "accepted" the dedication by hunting on the bog and even building a catwalk and a dock on the lake and by the county building an access road.

What if the state stocks a lake with fish at public expense and then argues that the water has been dedicated to the public? This argument has been consistently rejected by the courts on a variety of grounds. At common law, fishing rights were a *profit a prendre* and thus could be transferred only by grant. What if the state enacts a statute granting members of the public the right to fish in stocked streams and grants them a right of access over private lands so long as they compensate the owner for any actual damage which results from their trespass? See Hartman v. Tresise, 84 P. 685 (Colo.1906) (holding the statute unconstitutional).

New York provides funds for the state and municipalities to acquire fee titles and easements along the shores of streams and lakes to provide public camping and fishing sites. New York Conservation Law §§ 1–0702–0715 (1967).

Statutory enactments in some states may be a basis for expanding the dedication doctrine. Consider, for example, Ind.Code Ann. § 13–2–11.1–2 which provides:

> The natural resources and the natural scenic beauty of Indiana are declared to be a public right, and the public of Indiana is hereby declared to have a vested right in the preservation, protection and enjoyment of all the public fresh water lakes of Indiana in their present state, and the use of such waters for recreational purposes.

Section 13–2–11.1–1 defines as public "all lakes which have been used by the public with the acquiescence of any or all riparian owners * * *." If a riparian permits a non-riparian family to enjoy a swim in the lake, is it now public? If so, would the statute be constitutional? See Graham Waite, *Public Rights in Indiana Waters*, 37 Ind.L.J. 467, 481–83 (1962).

Under the Minnesota lake level statute, Minn.Stat.Ann. § 110.34, a public action may be brought to declare that a flowage easement to maintain the water level in an artificial lake created by a dam has been dedicated to the state if the dam has been maintained for at least 15 years primarily for public purposes like navigation, fishing and hunting, and the lake has been continuously used for those purposes. Minn.Stat.Ann. § 110.31. This statute has been interpreted to mean that the common law elements of dedication—intent to dedicate and acceptance by the public—must be shown but that if the specified conditions are met, a dedication is presumed. See State by Burnquist v. Fischer, 71 N.W.2d 161, 164–65 (Minn.1955).

GION v. SANTA CRUZ

Supreme Court of California, 1970.
2 Cal.3d 29, 84 Cal.Rptr. 162, 465 P.2d 50.

PER CURIAM.

We consider these two cases together because both raise the question of determining when an implied dedication of land has been made.

* * *

In Dietz v. King, plaintiffs, as representatives of the public, asked the court to enjoin defendants from interfering with the public's use of Navarro Beach in Mendocino County and an unimproved dirt road, called the Navarro Beach Road, leading to that beach. The beach is a small sandy peninsula jutting into the Pacific Ocean. It is surrounded by cliffs at the south and east, and is bounded by the Navarro River and the Navarro Beach Road (the only convenient access to the beach by land) on the north. The Navarro Beach Road branches from a county road that parallels State Highway One. The road runs in a southwesterly direction along the Navarro River for 1,500 feet and then turns for the final 1,500 feet due south to the beach. The road first crosses for a short distance land owned by the Carlyles, who maintain a residence adjacent to the road. It then crosses land owned by Mae Crider and Jack W. Sparkman, proprietors of an ancient structure called the Navarro-by-the-Sea Hotel, and, for the final 2,200 feet, land now owned by defendants.

The public has used the beach and the road for at least 100 years. Five cottages were built on the high ground of the ocean beach about 100 years ago. A small cemetery plot containing the remains of shipwrecked sailors and natives of the area existed there. Elderly witnesses testified that persons traveled over the road during the closing years of the last century. They came in substantial numbers to camp, picnic, collect and cut driftwood for fuel, and fish for abalone, crabs, and finned fish. Others came to the beach to decorate the graves, which had wooden crosses upon them. Indians, in groups of 50 to 75 came from as far away as Ukiah during the summer months. They camped on the beach for weeks at a time, drying kelp and catching and drying abalone and other fish. In decreasing numbers they continued to use the road and the beach until about 1950.

In more recent years the public use of Navarro Beach has expanded. The trial court found on substantial evidence that "For many years members of the public have used and enjoyed the said beach for various kinds of recreational activities, including picnicking, hiking, swimming, fishing, skin diving, camping, driftwood collecting, firewood collecting, and related activities." At times as many as 100 persons have been on the beach. They have come in automobiles, trucks, campers, and trailers. The beach has been used for commercial fishing, and during good weather a school for retarded children has brought its students to the beach once every week or two.

None of the previous owners of the King property ever objected to public use of Navarro Beach Road. * * *

In 1960, a year after the Kings acquired the land, they placed a large timber across the road at the entrance to their land. Within two hours it was removed by persons wishing to use the beach. Mr. King occasionally put up No Trespassing signs, but they were always removed by the time he returned to the land, and the public continued to use the beach until August 1966. During that month, Mr. King had another large log placed across the road at the entrance to his property. That barrier was, however, also quickly removed. He then sent in a caterpillar crew to permanently block the road. That operation was stopped by the issuance of a temporary restraining order.

The various owners of the Navarro-by-the-Sea property have at times placed an unlocked chain across the Navarro Beach Road on that property. One witness said she saw a chain between 1911 and 1920. Another witness said the chain was put up to discourage cows from straying and eating poisonous weeds. The chain was occasionally hooked to an upright spike, but was never locked in place and could be easily removed. Its purpose apparently was to restrict cows, not people, from the beach. In fact, the chain was almost always unhooked and lying on the ground.

From about 1949 on, a proprietor of the Navarro-by-the-Sea Hotel maintained a sign at the posts saying, "Private Road—Admission 50¢— please pay at hotel." With moderate success, the proprietor collected tolls for a relatively short period of time. Some years later another proprietor resumed the practice. Most persons ignored the sign, however, and went to the beach without paying. The hotel operators never applied any sanctions to those who declined to pay. In a recorded instrument the present owners of the Navarro-by-the-Sea property acknowledged that "for over one hundred years there has existed a public easement and right of way" in the road as it crosses their property. The Carlyles and the previous owners of the first stretch of the Navarro Beach Road never objected to its use over their property and do not now object.

The Mendocino county superior court ruled in favor of defendants, concluding that there had been no dedication of the beach or the road and in particular that widespread public use does not lead to an implied dedication.

In our most recent discussion of common-law dedication, Union Transp. Co. v. Sacramento County (1954) 42 Cal.2d 235, 240–241, 267 P.2d 10, we noted that a common-law dedication of property to the public can be proved either by showing acquiescence of the owner in use of the land under circumstances that negate the idea that the use is under a license or by establishing open and continuous use by the public for the prescriptive period. When dedication by acquiescence for a period of less than five years is claimed, the owner's actual consent to the dedication must be proved. The owner's intent is the crucial factor.

(42 Cal.2d at p. 241, 267 P.2d 10, quoting from Schwerdtle v. County of Placer (1895) 108 Cal. 589, 593, 41 P. 448.) When, on the other hand, a litigant seeks to prove dedication by adverse use, the inquiry shifts from the intent and activities of the owner to those of the public. The question then is whether the public has used the land "for a period of more than five years with full knowledge of the owner, without asking or receiving permission to do so and without objection being made by any one." (42 Cal.2d at p. 240, 267 P.2d at p. 13, quoting from Hare v. Craig (1929) 206 Cal. 753, 757, 276 P. 336.) As other cases have stated, the question is whether the public has engaged in "long-continued adverse use" of the land sufficient to raise the "conclusive and undisputable presumption of knowledge and acquiescence, while at the same time it negatives the idea of a mere license."

In both cases at issue here, the litigants representing the public contend that the second test has been met. Although there is evidence in both cases from which it might be inferred that owners preceding the present fee owners acquiesced in the public use of the land, that argument has not been pressed before this court. We therefore turn to the issue of dedication by adverse use.

Three problems of interpretation have concerned the lower courts with respect to proof of dedication by adverse use: (1) When is a public use deemed to be adverse? (2) Must a litigant representing the public prove that the owner did not grant a license to the public? (3) Is there any difference between dedication of shoreline property and other property?

In determining the adverse use necessary to raise a conclusive presumption of dedication, analogies from the law of adverse possession and easement by prescriptive rights can be misleading. An adverse possessor or a person gaining a personal easement by prescription is acting to gain a property right in himself and the test in those situations is whether the person acted as if he actually claimed a personal legal right in the property. Such a personal claim of right need not be shown to establish a dedication because it is a public right that is being claimed. What must be shown is that persons used the property believing the public had a right to such use. This public use may not be "adverse" to the interests of the owner in the sense that the word is used in adverse possession cases. If a trial court finds that the public has used land without objection or interference for more than five years, it need not make a separate finding of "adversity" to support a decision of implied dedication.

Litigants, therefore, seeking to show that land has been dedicated to the public, need only produce evidence that persons have used the land as they would have used public land. If the land involved is a beach or shoreline area, they should show that the land was used as if it were a public recreation area. If a road is involved, the litigants must show that it was used as if it were a public road. Evidence that the users looked to a governmental agency for maintenance of the land is significant in establishing an implied dedication to the public.

Litigants seeking to establish dedication to the public must also show that various groups of persons have used the land. If only a limited and definable number of persons have used the land, those persons may be able to claim a personal easement but not dedication to the public. An owner may well tolerate use by some persons but object vigorously to use by others. If the fee owner proves that use of the land fluctuated seasonally, on the other hand, such a showing does not negate evidence of adverse user. "[T]he thing of significance is that whoever wanted to use [the land] did so * * * when they wished to do so without asking permission and without protest from the land owners." (Seaway Company v. Attorney General (Tex.Civ.App., supra), 375 S.W.2d 923, 936.)

The second problem that has concerned lower courts is whether there is a presumption that use by the public is under a license by the fee owner, a presumption that must be overcome by the public with evidence to the contrary.   * * *

No reason appears for distinguishing proof of implied dedication by invoking a presumption of permissive use. The question whether public use of privately owned lands is under a license of the owner is ordinarily one of fact. We will not presume that owners of property today knowingly permit the general public to use their lands and grant a license to the public to do so. For a fee owner to negate a finding of intent to dedicate based on uninterrupted public use for more than five years, therefore, he must either affirmatively prove that he has granted the public a license to use his property or demonstrate that he has made a bona fide attempt to prevent public use. Whether an owner's efforts to halt public use are adequate in a particular case will turn on the means the owner uses in relation to the character of the property and the extent of public use. Although "No Trespassing" signs may be sufficient when only an occasional hiker traverses an isolated property, the same action cannot reasonably be expected to halt a continuous influx of beach users to an attractive seashore property. If the fee owner proves that he has made more than minimal and ineffectual efforts to exclude the public, then the trier of fact must decide whether the owner's activities have been adequate. If the owner has not attempted to halt public use in any significant way, however, it will be held as a matter of law that he intended to dedicate the property or an easement therein to the public, and evidence that the public used the property for the prescriptive period is sufficient to establish dedication.

A final question that has concerned lower courts is whether the rules governing shoreline property differ from those governing other types of property, particularly roads.   * * *

Even if we were reluctant to apply the rules of common-law dedication to open recreational areas, we must observe the strong policy expressed in the constitution and statutes of this state of encouraging public use of shoreline recreational areas.

Among the statutory provisions favoring public ownership of shoreline areas is Civil Code, section 830. That section states that absent specific language to the contrary, private ownership of uplands ends at the high-water mark. The decisions of this court have interpreted this provision to create a presumption in favor of public ownership of land between high and low tide.

There is also a clearly enunciated public policy in the California Constitution in favor of allowing the public access to shoreline areas:

"No individual, partnership, or corporation, claiming or possessing the frontage or tidal lands of a harbor, bay, inlet, estuary, or other navigable water in this State, shall be permitted to exclude the right of way to such water whenever it is required for any public purpose, nor to destroy or obstruct the free navigation of such water. * * * " (Art. XV, § 2.)

Recreational purposes are among the "public purposes" mentioned by this constitutional provision. Although article XV section 2 may be limited to some extent by the United States Constitution it clearly indicates that we should encourage public use of shoreline areas whenever that can be done consistently with the federal constitution.

* * *

We conclude that there was an implied dedication of property rights in both cases. In both cases the public used the land "for a period of more than five years with full knowledge of the owner, without asking or receiving permission to do so and without objection being made by any one." (Union Transp. Co. v. Sacramento County, supra, 42 Cal.2d 235, 240, 267 P.2d 10, 13 quoting from Hare v. Craig, supra, 206 Cal. 753, 757, 276 P. 336.) In both cases the public used the land in public ways, as if the land was owned by a government, as if the land were a public park.

* * *

NOTES

1. *Gion* applies the law of dedication to find access to waters that were open to the public at common law. The access issue arises whenever waters are open to public use, whether because they are navigable or because statutes or court decisions declare them open.

At common law, public rights to use coastal waters are confined to the sea and foreshore (the land covered and uncovered by the regular cycles of the tide), and the foreshore and sea must be reached without trespassing on private property. Federal and state regulatory jurisdiction has been extended over waters which were considered non-navigable at common law and similarly public rights have been extended to smaller and smaller water bodies. It was probably inevitable that the expansion of public rights to use the surface of waters would spill over to the assertion of public rights to use dry shoreland areas. There are 59,157 miles of coastline—including Alaska and the Great Lakes—in the United States. Of these, 21,724 are suitable for public recreation, but only 1209 miles were open to the public in 1976. Joseph F. Lefargue, *Practical Legal Remedies to the Public Beach Shortage,* 5

Envtl Affairs 447, 448 (1976). Pressure for expanded public rights to usable dry sand beaches thus exists.

Because purchase of beach front property by the state is not always financially feasible, there has been considerable pressure to impress dry sand areas with public rights. Public rights can be recognized in one of three ways. First, the definition of the boundary line between public and private ownership can be changed to extend it landward. Second, private property can be impressed with a public easement or other public access rights. Third, the state can purchase or condemn more beachfront land.

The states have limited flexibility to move public boundary lines landward. To determine the boundary between public and private land, most coastal states use the mean high tide line or a variant of this standard, although Delaware, Massachusetts, Maine, New Hampshire and Virginia use the low waterline. See James F. Maloney, *The Ordinary High Water Mark: Attempts at Settling an Unsettled Boundary Line*, 13 Land & Water L.Rev. 465 (1978) for a discussion of the standards used to map these lines. Can a low water mark state shift to the mean high tide line, and therefore expand the amount of submerged land subject to public use? See State v. Ashmore, 224 S.E.2d 334 (Ga.1976), cert. denied, 429 U.S. 830 (1976).

Washington has declared that portion of foreshore lying between the vegetation line and the mean high tide line to be public highway. Wash.Rev.Code Ann. §§ 79.16.130–.170. In Hughes v. Washington, 410 P.2d 20 (Wash.1966), the Washington state supreme court declared the vegetation line to be the mean high tide line arguably reaffirming a 1901 precedent. Shelton Logging Co. v. Gosser, 66 P. 151 (Wash.1901) interpreting Shively v. Bowlby, 152 U.S. 1 (1894). The United States Supreme Court did not rule on this issue in *Hughes*, page 399, supra. See Ralph W. Johnson, Craighton Goepple, David Jansen & Rachael Paschal, *The Public Trust Doctrine and Coastal Zone Management in Washington State*, 67 Wash.L.Rev. 521 (1992).

2. Coastal shoreline access in California is provided for under the California Coastal Act of 1976. Cal.Pub.Res.Code §§ 30210–30213 require that new coastal zone developments provide public access to the ocean unless it would interfere with public safety, military security or a fragile coastal area, if adequate access exists nearby, or if agriculture would be threatened.

The California Coastal Commission's practice of requiring subdivision exactions for public beach access under the act was challenged by developers on the theory that such exactions must be directly or indirectly related to the demand for beach use caused by the subdivision. This standard supports school and park exactions, but can landowners successfully assert that since the beneficiaries of beach access exactions are more likely to be the public at large, they are thus invalid? Several California cases held that the justification for the required dedication is not the need created by the particular project but that the Commission may consider the cumulative impact of many small projects that collectively create a need for access.

The U.S. Supreme Court imposed the requirement that public benefits be specifically related to the project being permitted under the California Coastal Act. In Nollan v. California Coastal Comm'n, 483 U.S. 825 (1987), a beach lot owner applied for a coastal development permit to demolish a small bungalow and replace it with a house three times as large. The Coastal Commission approved the application with a condition requiring the Nollans to provide lateral access to the public along their beach frontage. There was no way for the public to reach tidelands and the sea at high tide directly in front of the house except by trespassing or by boat. The Supreme Court reversed a state court of appeals decision sustaining the condition. Writing for a 5–4 majority, Justice Scalia concluded that the condition was an unjustified imposition of an easement and thus was a taking. The Commission argued that the condition was reasonably related to the public need for maximum access to and along the coast as stated in the Coastal Act. It said the house would interfere with visual access and create a psychological barrier to beach use. Justice Scalia said: "there is nothing to it. It is quite impossible to understand how a requirement that people already on the public beaches be able to walk across the Nollans' property reduces any obstacles to viewing the beach created by the new house." 483 U.S. at 838. The dissenters disputed the majority's holding that the condition was insufficiently tailored to address the precise public benefit caused by the new construction, contending that it was too narrow a standard in that only a showing of a rational purpose was necessary. Further, Justice Brennan cited evidence in the record to support the Commission's conclusion that the Nollans' development would burden the public's ability to exercise their public rights to traverse the shoreline.

3. Access to the dry sand beach (above the high tide line) was secured in State ex rel. Thornton v. Hay, 462 P.2d 671 (Or.1969) based on custom. The court applied Blackstone's requirements for recognizing a customary right, which are that it must be ancient, continuously exercised, peaceably asserted, reasonable, certain, obligatory on all owners, and not contrary to other laws. Custom is an especially strong basis for access in Hawaii where traditional native subsistence food-gathering and ceremonial uses are protected by the state constitution, Hawaii Const. art. XII, § 7, and statute, Hawaii Rev.Stat. § 1–1. Kalipi v. Hawaiian Trust Co., Ltd., 656 P.2d 745 (Hawaii 1982) (traditional food gathering); Hatton v. Piopio, 6 Haw. 334 (1882) (fishing); Hawaii County v. Sotomura, 517 P.2d 57 (Hawaii 1973) (beach use).

4. Other courts have implied a public right of access across private land to exercise rights guaranteed by the public trust doctrine. Thus, it has been held that the privately-owned dry sand area adjoining a municipal beach was subject to reasonably necessary public access and use for related recreation. Matthews v. Bay Head Improvement Ass'n, 471 A.2d 355 (N.J.1984).

Chapter Five

GROUNDWATER MANAGEMENT

Our need for water—for good, cool mountain water—was very great indeed. Many of the folks had heard of "Water Witches" who could locate underground streams by means of a forked stick, so when one came to town and persuaded the Bishop and several other leading brethren to go with him to run some tests, all were pleased when the forked stick would turn and point downward at the same approximate point in the wash, indicating that there had to be an underground stream along that line * * *. The salesman talked of a gushing stream of clear, cool mountain water from the snows that fell around the Noon Peak. * * * At last they struck mud! Such an excitement as went through the town! When the first buckets of muddy water came out, the workers told themselves that they just hadn't hit the main stream yet. But another day's work convinced them all: the water was brackish like slough water—totally unfit to drink!

Juanita Brooks, Quicksand and Cactus: A Memoir of the Southern Mormon Frontier 8–9 (1982).

This comic but sad tale illustrates the most important problem in groundwater law: Initial allocation was based on myths rather than geohydrology. Even in the pre-enlightened seventeenth century, scientists did not think that groundwater was derived from rainfall because the supply was assumed to be insufficient and the ground to be too impervious. Ironically, a French lawyer, Pierre Perrault, was the first person to posit a clear understanding of the hydrologic cycle. His studies of the Seine River drainage basin, published in 1674, confirmed that rainfall was the sole source of surface and subsurface flows. David Keith Todd, Groundwater Hydrology 2–3 (1959). Unfortunately for the development of the law, groundwater was early subdivided into three arbitrary and unscientific categories: artesian, percolating and underground watercourses. Leading water attorney Raphael J. Moses attributes the tripartite division to Clesson S. Kinney as reflected in volume two of his treatise, Law of Irrigation and Water Rights 2095 (2d ed. 1912). Raphael J. Moses, The Law of Groundwater—Does Modern Buried Treasure Create a New Breed of Pirates?, 11 Rocky Mtn.Min. L.Inst. 277 (1966).

The lack of understanding of the nature of groundwater resources has been an impediment to sound policymaking. Different rules have attached to different classes of water, not necessarily based on hydrologic effects of their withdrawal on surface or other groundwater sources. As a result, it has been difficult for courts and legislatures to develop efficient and fair allocation rules and to coordinate surface and groundwater rights.

Some water users dependent on surface supplies have found them depleted by groundwater pumpers, but have lacked the kind of legal protection they would have if someone interfered with their above-ground diversions. For instance, a water user sunk a well in a small island in the middle of the Platte River that would diminish the water available to users whose surface diversions were downstream. Senior users alleged that the pumper interfered with their rights. But the Nebraska Supreme Court held that the state's prior appropriation law did not extend to "groundwater." Metropolitan Utils. Dist. of Omaha v. Merritt Beach Co., 140 N.W.2d 626 (Neb.1966).

Some groundwater resources are essentially nonrenewable in time frames that are within the reach of water managers and policymakers. Many important groundwater deposits may be replaced only over extended periods, refilling perhaps only in geologic time. Pumping from them is essentially mining a finite resource. Most states lack adequate laws to deal wisely with nonrenewable groundwater. If pumpers are allowed to take groundwater out of an aquifer based solely on priority (a rule that may be reasonable for a surface source or with hydrologically connected groundwater), a non-renewable aquifer may be depleted by the first few users or it may be physically destroyed if pumping occurs far faster than recharge. If overlying landowners are considered the "owners" of groundwater, they can develop it at rates that may hurt others, perhaps setting off a race among landowners to deplete the aquifer. Neither the rule of priority nor the rule of ownership considers the needs of society. Generally, groundwater laws have not required pumpers to compare the present benefits of extraction to the benefits of deferred extraction in order to minimize the overall costs of production and maximize the value of the resource in the future. Many state laws do not even discern whether groundwater sources are essentially renewable or nonrenewable, let alone determine a safe yield that has both scientific validity and economic rationality, based on the length of time it will take to deplete the resource.

Another physical reality that has been ignored in groundwater management has been the connection between contamination of groundwater and how or when groundwater is pumped. At one extreme, there are some states that allocate rights to use groundwater without regard to whether the water is safe to use and without limitations that will protect an aquifer from contamination. Thus, pumpers may pierce more than one aquifer and allow polluted water from one to migrate through the well shaft into a pure source. And pumping rates may be set without regard to rates of natural recharge so that water is withdrawn so fast that salt water from a nearby sea or a contamination plume from a pollution source is drawn into, and destroys, a good source. Thus legal and administrative dichotomies between groundwater allocation and protection of groundwater quality also create obstacles to sound resource management.

The basic choices to be made in groundwater management are: (1) What protection is to be afforded to competing pumpers? and (2) What is the allowable rate of extraction? The former issue has received the most attention, and consequently, has often determined the answer to the latter. Groundwater allocation, then, has been approached largely as a tort issue among holders, or prospective holders, of property rights. In humid regions, like the eastern United States, the common law has dealt principally with the conflicts that have arisen between two neighbors. However, as some groundwater sources have begun to prove unreliable, we are beginning to challenge the assumption that judicial allocation among individuals is adequate to determine access and the scope of use of the resource.

The Report of the National Water Commission, Water Policies for the Future (1973) at 232 summarized the major modern management problems:

> (1) integrating management of surface water and groundwater, (2) depletion of groundwater aquifers at rates exceeding recharge (often referred to as the "mining" of groundwater), and (3) impairment of groundwater quality. Lesser, though important, problems are also considered: accelerating collection of groundwater data together with fuller and more meaningful interpretation of it.

The public importance of how these issues are addressed is tremendous. Over 23% of all freshwater supplies in the United States comes from groundwater. Agricultural irrigation uses almost 70% of all groundwater produced. Remarkably, in recent years about a quarter of all the groundwater withdrawals for western agriculture were overdrafts (i.e., in excess of annual precipitation and natural recharge). James Wilson, Groundwater: A Non-Technical Guide 32 (1982). The rate of growth in the quantities of groundwater used for irrigation began to decline in 1975, reflecting the higher costs of pumping due to rising electric rates and fuel prices and the lowered groundwater levels in some places. Municipal and industrial uses of groundwater, however, have increased 15% since 1975. Conservation Foundation, America's Water: Current Trends and Emerging Issues 5–10 (1984). Increasingly, agricultural uses come into conflict with growing municipal demands for groundwater as deep, high capacity wells draw down aquifers and render wells of farmers and small domestic users inadequate. As southeastern and midwestern farmers invest in supplemental irrigation equipment, heavier pumping occurs and conflicts among them intensify. J.W. Looney, *Modification of Arkansas Water Law: Issues and Alternatives*, 38 Ark.L.Rev. 221 (1984). Resource managers consequently have begun to cope with the question of pumping rates as an issue in which there is a broad public interest.

What institutions should be created to allocate groundwater basins efficiently and fairly? Economists usually answer by suggesting a property rights regime. One argument is that well-defined, enforceable and transferable property rights will tend to allocate basins efficiently because market prices will emerge and make owners aware of the costs of wasting water:

Definition and enforcement are necessary to give individuals the incentive to use water efficiently. In order for an exchange to take place, traders must have some idea of what rights are included. Less will be paid for rights that are not well defined and enforced, and in the extreme no trade will occur. * * *

The transferability of property rights ensures that individuals will take into account the opportunity costs of their actions. As long as individuals are free to buy and sell water rights, market prices will emerge, making owners aware of the cost of wasting water. If rights are not transferable, however, the fact that water has more valuable alternative uses will make little difference; the owner will not be able to sell the rights and capitalize on these higher valued uses.

Terry L. Anderson, Oscar R. Burt & David T. Fractor, *Privatizing Groundwater Basins: A Model and Its Application,* in Water Rights: Scarce Resource Allocation, Bureaucracy, and the Environment 223, 227 (Terry L. Anderson ed. 1983).

While the argument for addressing groundwater management by allocation of transferable property rights seems compelling, it may not work as well in practice as in theory. Successful resource management may depend on the initial distribution of property rights, the interrelationship between laws allocating surface and groundwater, and the institutional ability to consolidate or coordinate the management of groundwater throughout all or part of an aquifer. Unless rights are carefully defined, the creation of private rights to use groundwater may lead—as it did at great cost in oil and gas—to a race to develop shallow, high pressure wells first. If the basis for allocating rights in groundwater is to assign rights to overlying landowners, the result may be to allow a few to monopolize an otherwise public resource and, unless controls are placed on the manner and rates of pumping, to rapid depletion of a resource that could be used by the larger community in the future in conjunction with surface water resources.

The doctrine of prior appropriation has some conservation features: it assigns rights that must be respected by others. But, it is not as well-suited to groundwater allocation as it is to surface water allocation. If the rights of the senior are absolutely protected from any interference, as are surface rights, many aquifers would be limited to a single pumper. For this reason, most states allow some junior interference with senior pumpers in contrast to the administration of surface priorities. The standard is the familiar "reasonableness" limitation.

Recognition of the special nature of groundwater has led many states to the conclusion that it should be managed as a common resource. Rights can be defined to maximize the use of available resources over time. This may mean greater governmental control over groundwater management than is the case with surface water. Increasingly, water managers are recognizing the advantages in integrating plans for surface water development with groundwater management plans.

The problem of groundwater quality is becoming more important with the realization that a contaminated aquifer may be tantamount to a depleted aquifer.   Federal laws now ban most land disposal of hazardous wastes, regulate deep-well injection of such wastes, and provide for cleaning up existing disposal sites.   Control of non-hazardous wastes is largely left to the states.   There is a limited tradition of state laws to protect groundwater quality.   An exception is New York which has long required permits to drill wells on Long Island to minimize the effects of salt water intrusion.   17½ N.Y.Envtl.Conserv.L. § 15–1527.

The introductory materials in this chapter are designed to provide a basic understanding of groundwater hydrology and the economic and legal barriers to the creation of efficient allocation regimes.   We then turn to an examination of various regimes for allocating groundwater rights.   Consider whether: (1) The property rights in groundwater that the courts have recognized result in the efficient allocation of the resource.   (2) The administrative allocation regime is superior to a property rights regime.

The public's interest in maintaining a reliable supply of groundwater has influenced modern allocation schemes.   Whatever fundamental principles may guide the allocation of property rights and determine the respective rights of competing users, there are broader concerns with the long-term security and quality of groundwater supplies.   Section B describes the methods that have been used to allocate rights in groundwater to individuals and to resolve claims among them.   Section C explores schemes for regulating production of groundwater to ensure that public concerns with its protection and use are satisfied, consistent with the rights allocated to individuals.

A. INTRODUCTION TO THE GEOLOGY AND ECONOMICS OF GROUNDWATER

HAROLD E. THOMAS, UNDERGROUND SOURCES OF OUR WATER

in United States Department of Agriculture,
THE YEARBOOK OF AGRICULTURE 63–77 (1955).

The selection of ground water as a supply, rather than the surface-water sources, has generally been on the basis of one or more of the following advantages:

1.   Ground water may be reached within a few hundred feet of the place where it is to be used, and on the same property, whereas surface water may require pipelines and rights-of-way over stretches of several miles.

2.   Ground water may be available for use in areas where the water in streams and lakes has already been appropriated by other users.

3.   Yield from wells and springs generally fluctuates less than streamflow in alternating wet and dry periods.

4.   Ground water is more uniform in temperature and soluble mineral load than surface water, and is generally free of turbidity and bacterial pollution.

The development of water from surface sources has been a necessity in many places where ground water can be obtained only at excessive depth below the surface or where it cannot be obtained in sufficient quantity at any depth, where the ground water is deemed to be fully appropriated, or where it is of a quality that makes it unsuitable for the use intended. Even where good-quality ground water is available it may be at a disadvantage as an alternate to surface water in that its use generally requires expenditure of energy for pumping, whereas the surface water may produce energy besides supplying water for other uses.

The controversial features of ground water are numerous. Many disputes as to the effect of one well on another or on a spring have been decided in the courts. Many others undoubtedly have avoided the courts only because of the high cost and the apparent hopelessness of obtaining proof in support of individual opinions. Many of the controversies reflect the general lack of understanding and uncertainty in the public mind regarding ground water.

* * *

The water beneath the land surface is not all ground water. A man with his feet on the ground might assume that by picking up a handful of moist earth he obtains some ground water, or that in pouring a bucketful of water upon absorbent land he increases the ground-water resources by that amount. Those assumptions are incorrect.

Figure 1. Ground-water Zones and Belts

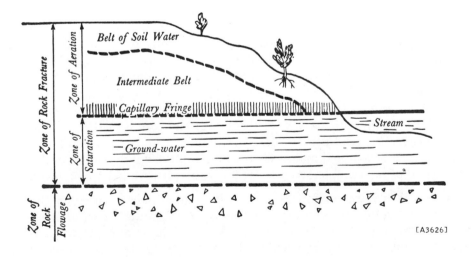

[A3626]

Figure 2. Seepage

Ground Water to Stream

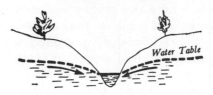

Water Table

Stream to Ground Water

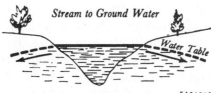

Water Table

[A3627]

Ground water is only the part of the subterranean water that occurs where all pores in the containing rock materials are saturated. The "zone of saturation" may extend up to the land surface in some places, notably in seep areas and in some stream channels, lakes, and marshes. At all other places, above the ground-water zone, "a zone of aeration" exists that may range in thickness from a few inches to hundreds of feet. Some water is in the zone of aeration at all times, held there by molecular attraction—in particular, soils may hold significant volumes of water against the downward pull of gravity. Wells cannot extract any of this water; they must be drilled through the zone of aeration and obtain their supplies from ground water.

The normal field of operations of the ground-water hydrologist is delimited only approximately by such a definition of ground water. Thus the top of the zone of saturation cannot readily be identified from the land surface. The hydrologist therefore measures the water levels in shallow wells. From the measurements he constructs a map of the "water table," which is thus a phreatic surface—that is, pertaining to a well—where the water is at atmospheric pressure. The water table may coincide approximately with the top of the zone of saturation in coarse gravel but is likely to be several inches or even several feet below it in finer grained materials, because capillary rise results in the saturation of a zone above the water table (the capillary fringe).

Often it is hard to identify or classify subterranean water on the basis of the definition above. There may be saturated flow, at least temporarily, in parts of the soil zone. A well driller may encounter a saturated zone and then continue on down into dry materials, obviously in the zone of aeration. Or he may find saturated materials that yield no water to his well, so that there is no water table. And he may drill through materials that yield no water, and then encounter a stratum from which water rises in the well to a level high in the zone of aeration, and the water may even overflow. All these are typical of the wide range in conditions of occurrence of ground water. They reflect the great variations in porosity and permeability of the solid components of the earth's crust.

* * *

The porosity of loose rock materials varies with the arrangement, shape, and degree of assortment of the particles. The size of grain is not a determining factor, because, if other conditions are the same, a material will have the same porosity whether it consists of large or small grains. Silt or clay, consisting entirely of minute particles, may have a porosity as great as coarse gravel, although the pores are less easily seen. In some consolidated rocks the original porosity has been reduced by compaction or by deposition of cement in the pore spaces. In others it has been increased by development of fractures or by the dissolving of some of the rock material.

* * *

Rock materials of high porosity can yield copious quantities of water, but not necessarily. One saturated rock may yield most of the water in its pores to wells or springs. Another, of equal porosity but smaller pores, may retain practically all its water and yield negligible amounts to wells. The difference then is in the proportion of the contained water that is held by molecular attraction and the proportion that can be moved by gravity. The rock that permits water to move through it by gravity is far more permeable than the one that holds water by molecular attraction.

Molecular attraction becomes more and more significant with declining size of pore because of the larger surface area of solid material to which water can adhere. In a cubic foot of well sorted gravel whose particles are a quarter of an inch in diameter, the combined surface area of the grains is about 200 square feet, or about the floor space of an average living room. In a well sorted sediment of rounded, clay-size grains 0.001 millimeter in diameter, the porosity may be equal to that of the gravel, but the surface area of the grains in a cubic foot may exceed a million square feet, or about 23 acres, and the molecular attraction for water is correspondingly greater.

* * *

The rate of movement of water beneath the surface depends a great deal on the permeability of the rock material, which is its capacity for transmitting water. In permeable materials, gravity is the force that moves water downward from the land surface to the zone where all pores are saturated, thence laterally toward lower elevations, and ultimately to the oceans or to places where the water is discharged at the land surface by springs or seeps, or by evaporation or transpiration.

In the development of ground water by means of wells, a hole is drilled into the zone of saturation. Water that drains from the saturated rock materials into the well is called gravity ground water. As that water is pumped out, other water moves toward the well. The rate at which water moves toward the well, and therefore the rate at which water can be withdrawn from the well, depends largely on the permeability of the materials from which the water is drawn.

* * * The term "aquifer" is sometimes used to designate individual water-bearing beds, perhaps only a few feet thick, and sometimes to designate thick series of beds of varying permeability, where the individual beds are more or less interconnected hydraulically.

The term "ground-water reservoir" also has rather flexible usage. Commonly it is used interchangeably with aquifer. More broadly it may represent the water-bearing materials in an extensive area, as for example the San Joaquin Valley ground-water reservoir in California, which supplies water equal to about a quarter of all the water pumped from wells in the United States.

* * *

Great variations in permeability of rock materials have been chiefly responsible for the considerable variation in occurrence of water in the ground-water reservoirs of the continent. In some areas the ground-water reservoir and the materials above it are all relatively permeable, although some variation is almost inevitable. Wells dug or drilled in those areas commonly penetrate first some dry strata, then materials that are increasingly moist (the capillary fringe), and then materials from which water enters the well—thus they have gone through the zone of aeration and reached the zone of saturation. The water table rises as water enters the ground-water reservoir; it falls as water drains away to lower parts of the reservoir or as it is discharged by wells or other means. That water is unconfined.

* * *

Impermeable material may be present at various depths below the land surface, whether as hardpan within the soil zone, or clay or other tight material at greater depth. Such material may be poorly permeable and thus retard downward percolation, so that there is an accumulation of water and temporary saturation of material immediately above it. Or it may be so impermeable as to prevent downward percolation, so that a ground-water reservoir is permanently maintained above the impermeable zone. Such bodies of ground water within the zone of aeration are perched. Many are of very small extent and may disappear in a short time after rains. Some perched groundwater reservoirs yield water to wells and springs and are thus of economic value, but they are of very minor importance in the Nation's overall water economy.

Many deep wells penetrate far into the zone of saturation, and go through rock materials that range widely in their permeability. Water may rise markedly above the top of the aquifer whence it comes, and may even overflow at the surface. Such water is confined beneath less permeable material. It is not necessary that the confining bed be impermeable, but only that it be less permeable than the aquifer. Thus the Dakota sandstone in North Dakota and South Dakota is a famous artesian aquifer in which water is confined beneath dense shale. At the base of the Wasatch Range in Utah there are beds of loose sand more permeable than the Dakota sandstone; nevertheless, that sand constitutes the confining bed above coarse gravel. In both instances water moves far more easily through the aquifer tapped by wells than through the overlying beds. If the water in the aquifer is under sufficient pressure to rise above the zone of saturation, it is artesian, and the aquifer is then an artesian reservoir.

* * * For artesian aquifers, as well as for other ground-water reservoirs, there must be some area in which the soil or other surficial material and any underlying unsaturated material are sufficiently permeable to permit water to enter the aquifer. Such areas are the recharge areas for ground-water reservoirs—the areas in which replenishment occurs.

* * *

The amount of storage in a ground-water reservoir is no indication of the capabilities of the reservoir for sustained yield of water to the wells and springs. The limit of perennial yield is set by the average annual recharge to the reservoir, just as the useful yield of a surface reservoir is set by the inflow to it. Some small ground-water reservoirs along streams are capable of a large sustained yield because they are readily recharged from the stream. Others, notably in desert areas, may be far larger and hold vast quantities of water in storage, but yet have very low capabilities for perennial yield because of meager recharge. As an example, the ground-water reservoir under a 6,700-square-mile area in the Southern High Plains of Texas is estimated to hold more than 5 times as much water as Lake Mead (formed by Hoover Dam), but its annual recharge is less than 0.5 percent of the annual inflow to Lake Mead.

Characteristically there is natural movement of water through ground-water reservoirs, but that movement is at snail's pace. Whereas stream velocities are commonly quoted in terms of feet per second, ground-water velocities are measured in feet per day or even feet per year. The ground water moves from recharge areas to areas of natural discharge, and through the years the average natural discharge from the reservoir is equivalent to the average recharge. Wells intercept some of the water along its route, and if their yield is sustained year after year, it is because the water drawn by them is replaced by increased recharge, or is diverted from its course toward ultimate natural discharge.

As a rule, water will not remain under a piece of property until the owner is ready to use it: Eventually it will be discharged from the ground-water reservoir whether he takes it out or not. In other words, conservation of ground water is not necessarily achieved by not using it.

The velocity of ground-water movement is an important factor determining the sustained yield of wells, for that yield is limited to the quantity of water that moves to the well from the places where the water entered the ground. Wells remote from a source of replenishment cannot yield water perennially at rates greater than the rate at which water moves through the aquifer, even though the quantity available at the source is many times as great.

Artesian supplies in particular are limited by this factor of transmissivity of the aquifer, and many of the Nation's problems of "failing water supplies" stem from this limitation. The problems are analogous to those of a town that has an adequate overall water supply but has distribution lines too small to carry the water needed in some parts of the town.

Some guides may be offered for the effective development of underground storage for perennial use. The sustained yield of a groundwater reservoir (using the term to describe an underground unit of the hydrologic cycle, with its areas of recharge and discharge) cannot be greater than the average recharge, whether that recharge occurs by natural or artificial means, or both. Generally the quantity recovered from the entire reservoir for use will be appreciably less than that inflow, because of the practical limitations of the recovery techniques. In any part of the reservoir—even at any particular well—a further limitation is imposed by the rate at which water can be transmitted through the aquifer. This limitation applies least to wells within the recharge area, where they can reap the benefit of any inflow in short order. The limitations are an oversimplification of a complex problem and are only the hydrologic limitations. In many regions economic, social, or legal factors limit the yield of ground-water reservoirs to a rate far below their hydrologic capabilities.

* * *

Three types of ground-water areas may be identified:

1. Watercourses, consisting of a channel occupied by a perennial stream, together with the enclosing and underlying alluvial material saturated with water that comes from the stream, from infiltration at the surface, or from adjacent water-bearing materials.

2. Loose water-bearing materials, chiefly gravel and sand, including the productive aquifers of the Coastal Plains, Great Plains, glacial drift and outwash, and western valleys. Buried glacial valleys not now occupied by perennial streams are included in this group. The areas shown include known and potential areas of well development as well as the recharge areas.

3. Consolidated water-bearing rocks, of which limestone, basalt, and sandstone are the most important. The areas include the recharge localities, which generally coincide with the areas of outcropping of the permeable rocks, as well as areas where the rocks are buried beneath less permeable materials but yield usable water to wells.

* * *

Recharge to practically all ground-water reservoirs—whether large or small, important or negligible—moves downward from the surface. The amount of recharge depends partly on the permeability of the soil or mantle rock and partly on the available water from precipitation or streams or other sources. Many of the best recharge areas are underlain by materials so permeable that they would not be classed as soils at all, because water moves down through them so rapidly that they support little vegetation: The talus on mountain slopes, the bouldery beds of streams at the mouths of canyons, barren lavas, sand dunes, and areas of outcrop of cavernous limestone.

In most ground-water reservoirs only a part—and perhaps a very small part—of the infiltration in the recharge area becomes ground water. Near the land surface water may be pulled upward by solar energy—evaporation or transpiration—and returned to the atmosphere. In desert basins most of the water from the scant precipitation is dissipated in this way, and the ground-water reservoirs may be recharged only a few times a century, during exceptional "wet" years.

* * *

The serious problems of ground-water shortage occur in areas where water is pumped out faster than the entire ground-water reservoir is replenished. Under those conditions the reservoir is being emptied of water that may have taken decades or centuries to accumulate, and there is no possibility of a continuous perennial supply unless present conditions are changed. Even more serious is the condition where salty or otherwise unusable water flows into a ground-water reservoir as the good water is pumped out, for those reservoirs may be ruined before they are emptied. Most of the excessively pumped reservoirs are in the arid regions, where precipitation is generally inadequate for the needs of man. Some have an area of a hundred square miles or less; others may embrace several counties or extend across State or international boundaries. Users of ground water generally are aware that they are using more than the perennial supply and that the supply will be exhausted unless action is taken. Corrective measures already applied in some areas include prevention of waste, a pro rata reduction of pumping from all wells, prohibition of further development, reclaiming of used water, artificial ground-water replenishment by surplus stream water, and importation of water from other areas.

Pumping from closely spaced wells has caused significant declines of water level in parts of nearly every State, chiefly in municipal or industrial areas that use large quantities of ground water. The water levels have reached approximate equilibrium in some of those areas, indicating that the pumped water is now being replaced by the water transmitted through the aquifer. In other areas the water levels are still declining each year. Concentrated draft has induced an inflow of ocean water or other unusable water to some wells.

The watercourse problems result from the pumping wells along rivers, where the ground water is so closely related to the water in the stream that pumping from wells depletes the stream-flow. Diversions from the stream for various purposes may increase the amount of ground water at one place and reduce it at another. The intimate relation between surface and ground water is also shown at some river cities where protection from floods requires not only protection from a rise in the river but also protection from the simultaneous rise of ground-water levels under the city.

———

Hydrology has advanced considerably as a science, but the law has not kept pace. Artificial distinctions between "watercourses" and groundwater are notorious. For instance, many cases are concerned with the factual question of whether groundwater is in an underground stream or is percolating underground water because entirely different bodies of law apply to the "different kinds" of water. An underground stream has been defined as waters that flow underground within "reasonably ascertainable boundaries" or as "a constant stream in a known and well-defined natural channel." Hayes v. Adams, 218 P. 933 (Or.1923). Underground waters not meeting the narrow definition of an underground stream are said to be percolating waters. Underground streams generally are subject to the law of surface streams; percolating waters are subject to groundwater law. In fact, however, "percolating" waters may be destined for a stream and closely related as an hydrologic matter. Factual determination of whether waters are percolating is often difficult, making the burden of proof onerous. Furthermore, it may be based on factors other than whether the use of water from the source at issue affects the use of another. In Commonwealth Dep't of Highways v. Sebastian, 345 S.W.2d 46, 47 (Ky. 1961), the following evidence was held sufficient to create a jury issue as to the existence of an underground flowing stream:

> The evidence for the Sebastians was that the course of an underground stream running from a hill on their neighbor's land across the highway right of way and to the springs was identifiable and marked by a line of green grass which grew on the surface even in dry weather. In Hale v. McLea, 53 Cal. 578 [(1879)], it was held that the presence of a line of bushes usually found nowhere except over watercourses could be sufficient to establish the existence of an underground stream flowing in a known and defined channel. And in Maricopa Cty. Mun. Water Conservation Dist. No. 1 v. Southwest Cotton Co., 4 P.2d 369 [(Ariz.1931)], it was said that surface indications such as trees, shrubs, bushes and grasses growing along a defined course are the simplest and surest proofs of the existence of an underground stream as distinguished from percolating water.

Are these sound policy reasons or a scientific basis for distinguishing the legal treatment of percolating waters and so-called underground streams?

Texas has made a creative use of the law of underground streams to get state control of pumping from the Edwards Aquifer which extends between San Antonio and Austin. Withdrawals have long exceeded the 450,000 acre-foot per year safe yield recommended by numerous studies since the 1960s. The Texas Water Commission regulates only withdrawals of water from streams. The state's adherence to the absolute ownership rule, see pages 494–99, infra, allowed unregulated withdrawals from the aquifer. Efforts to induce the major users, especially farmers and the city of San Antonio, voluntarily to limit their pumping were unsuccessful. A special district, seeking to protect spring flows, joined with the Sierra Club, seeking to protect the fountaindarter and other endangered species, in a suit against the Texas Water Commission. In 1992, the Commission declared an emergency, and classified the aquifer as an underground river subject to its jurisdiction. Texas Administrative Code §§ 298.01–298.7. The district court then ordered the Commission to prepare a plan to maintain water levels in the aquifer. Sierra Club v. Lujan, ___ F.Supp. ___ (W.D.Tex. 1993). The legislature then enacted a law limiting aquifer withdrawals.

Some states have long recognized that where surface water and subsurface water are connected, they should be administered in an integrated fashion. This requires a sophisticated level of proof, but has been well within the competence of engineers for many years. Similarly, engineering studies are needed to establish the nature and extent of the effects of pumping from one well to another and the effects of contamination from landfills and other sources or aquifers.

The administration of groundwater rights and resolution of disputes involving aquifers, where causes and effects of water uses must be proved, increasingly depend on the use of advanced computer simulation models. Groundwater models were initially developed to determine the relationship between flow and pressure rates, but the federal and state focus on contamination has stimulated the development of much more sophisticated models. Groundwater models are either deterministic or stochastic. The former indicate cause and effect relationships while the latter indicate only probability ranges. Models are further subdivided between hydrogeologic framework and process models. Framework models depict the aquifer, often in three dimensions, and process models describe flow, transport, and chemical characteristics in the aquifer. Conjunctive use models now exist to describe surface and groundwater interaction. Models are relevant evidence in water rights and pollution cases, and it is easy to find an expert to challenge the selection and application of a model. After a model has been selected, it must be verified (by proof that the computer code used performs the necessary numerical calculations correctly), validated (by proof that the model successfully "analogues" the real system) and calibrated (adjusted to the known information about the system) before it can be used. Inevitable disagreements among experts are resolved by the usual rules of evidence and judicial review of the record. Models used by regulatory agencies are subject to challenge as arbitrary and capricious. State of Ohio v. Environmental Protection Agency, 784 F.2d 224 (6th Cir.1989). Courts have generally deferred to the agency's expertise, e.g. State of California ex rel. State of California Air Resources Board v. Environmental Protection Agency, 774 F.2d 1437 (9th Cir.1985), but it is possible to challenge successfully the lack of validation studies or a significant discrepancy between the model's assumptions and the hydrogeology of the aquifer. A similar reasonableness standard applies to models used in water rights litigation.

B. INDIVIDUAL RIGHTS IN GROUNDWATER

JACK HIRSHLEIFER, JAMES C. DE HAVEN AND JEROME
W. MILLIMAN, WATER SUPPLY: ECONOMICS,
TECHNOLOGY, AND POLICY

59–64 (1960).

1. Common-Pool Problems

The common-pool problem in the exploitation of water resources, in the narrow sense, occurs when a number of overlying property-owners are engaged in competitive pumping of water from a common underlying aquifer. In the wider sense, all cases where users draw competitively on a "fugitive" supply—that is, where the commodity is no one's property until and unless captured for use, wildlife being the classical example—are common-pool problems. Since rights in percolating ground water can normally be obtained only by actual "capture" of the water, pumpers are induced to withdraw at a rate greater than would otherwise be rational for fear that the withdrawals of others will lower water levels in the wells. Or, to look at the matter in another way, each individual considers in his decisions only the effect of his pumping upon the water level in his well—which may be negligible if there are many pumpers, since all are drawing upon a common pool—and does not consider the fact that his pumping will adversely affect all those interested in the pool.

* * *

Three solutions—that is, methods for assuring that the decisions made will meet the criteria of allocative efficiency—have been proposed for common-pool problems. They are (1) centralized decision-making; (2) assignment of pro rata production rights or quotas; and (3) imposition of "use" taxes.

There are several difficulties in the application of the solution via centralized management to water-resource problems. In the first place, the very concept of a "pool" in the sense of a quantum of a resource effectively localized applies only roughly to water. There will be ground, surface, and atmospheric interconnection between "pools," and only in certain circumstances can the problems of a single area be isolated from others—unless, indeed, the area is made very large, in which case we face both the administrative and political difficulties involved in centralized administration of a resource subject to highly variable local conditions. In California, for example, the natural water supplies of the southern regions largely originate in the snow pack of the Sierras; centralized management of the pool of resources would require a bureaucratic determination of the optimal pattern of consumptive and non-consumptive uses among all the competing ends in widely separated geographical areas which could be served by the use of the resource. Even in limited geographical areas, a highly varied pattern of use may exist which is hardly amenable to centralized government of the resource. Some users may pump water for irrigation, others may impound and divert for municipal supply while still others may want sufficient river flow for navigation or saline-water repulsion. * * *

The advantages of * * * an assignment include its simplicity and directness. A point of great practical importance is that the goal of the assignment is not the difficult and subtle matter of optimal use but an "equitable" apportionment of rights among claimants (some may, indeed, question that the latter is much easier than the former, but in many cases no doubt it is). Under such an apportionment the complicated questions of best use are left up to the successful claimants themselves, though perhaps with some restrictions. Another advantage is that in a certain sense the assignment of quotas does get really to the heart of the problem—the common nature of the resource—by replacing commonality of rights with specificity of shares.

There are, however, difficulties as well. First there is the matter of "equitable" apportionment. Assignment of quotas has not prevented waste in the case of petroleum because apportionment has typically been based on "well potential," so that an incentive to drill unnecessary wells remains. Where historical use is the basis, an incentive is created to initiate use excessively early in order to establish a history of use before final apportionment takes place. Ideally speaking, rights to all water should be assigned once and for all, but this rarely occurs.

A second difficulty turns on the question of efficiency. A single user might, for example, concentrate all his withdrawals on a few wells near the more productive lands, whereas an "equitable" apportionment might give a distribution of quotas whose exploitation through a great many wells leads to some social waste. It might be argued that, in such circumstances, quotas will be bought and sold until they end up in the most efficient distribution. Aside from the fact that certain limitations on transfer of such rights may exist, the process may not work perfectly. Thus there may be a gain in efficiency if both B and C sell their quotas to A, but it may be in the separate interest of each to hold out until the other sells, because, if C ceases pumping, B may be able to capture part of the gain in the form of locally increased water pressure or level, and vice versa. This is analogous to, if not so serious as, the problem of achieving rationality along a river, where intervening users may be in a position to reap a similar unearned benefit. The difficulty rests ultimately on the fact that the quotas really are not perfectly exchangeable between any two uses; the pool, while indeed common, has stream or serial-use aspects.

The third and most serious difficulty turns upon the question of how to achieve rationality in the use of the resource over time. Quotas are normally thought of as being assigned to exhaust the "safe yield" of the common water pool, that is to say, the amount which on the average equals the recharge rate so as to keep water levels constant. But why should water levels be kept constant? To take a ridiculous case, suppose petroleum quotas were similarly based on safe yield—which is, of course, zero. To use more than the safe yield means the water supplied in past years is being "mined," but this is sometimes undoubtedly rational and may even be in the normal case. In the high plains of Texas an extreme instance of this situation exists wherein the accumulation of water over past ages has been immense, but the annual recharge is very small indeed. One other consideration is that steady improvement in the technology of pumping has taken place in the past and may be reasonably projected to the future, so that larger and larger pumping lifts may not always represent increased economic cost of pumping.

The third or "use-tax" solution to the common-pool problem is in some ways logically the neatest, but it has been applied in practice in only one case to the authors' knowledge—in Orange County, California. The economic theory of the solution is based on the following considerations. Each pumper, in deciding how much to withdraw, compares the marginal cost of pumping with the marginal value in use to him of the water. This will usually be the value of the marginal product, the water being normally used as an intermediate good in the production of goods and services for the market. But his withdrawals will tend to lower the water levels for everyone using the common pool—a consideration which he will ignore or at least not consider fully, because the impact on himself will be partial and may be negligible. (In certain cases, "spillover" costs of pumping may show themselves most conspicuously in the form of salt-water intrusion under someone else's lands.) The use-tax solution would require a payment which would be added to the cost of pumping so that, ideally, the individual would consider the marginal *social* cost in his decision on how much to pump rather than merely the marginal private cost. The payment, of course, would represent the loss of productivity on lands owned by others.

Early systems for allocating rights to use groundwater were based on the ownership of the overlying land. The "absolute ownership" doctrine, sometimes called the English rule, allowed landowners an unlimited right to withdraw water from beneath their property. See Acton v. Blundell, 12 Mees and W. 324, 152 Eng.Rep. 1223 (1843). The doctrine was based on the ancient concept that a landowner's interest extends to the center of the earth. This was adopted as the law in many states in the nineteenth century, but was short-lived in most places. Carried to its logical conclusion, the absolute ownership doctrine allowed even malicious pumping aimed at draining the aquifer under neighboring land. E.g., Huber v. Merkel, 94 N.W. 354 (Wis. 1903). Virtually all states now make malicious injury actionable. Thus, there are remedies in most of the United States for groundwater pumping causing land subsidence or other injury.

As groundwater hydrology became a more precise science, and as the effects of groundwater use on others became more apparent, American states rejected the absolute ownership doctrine in favor of rules allowing "reasonable use" or establishing correlative rights that allow all pumpers to share with one another. Even those states that still declare themselves to embrace absolute ownership actually have tempered the doctrine with concepts designed to protect uses of groundwater by other pumpers and to protect the public's interest in conserving the resource.

Most states once followed a rule of reasonable use, correlative rights, prior appropriation, or some combination of these doctrines to determine limits on pumpers. Most of these rules were first applied by courts in tort suits by one pumper seeking damages or an injunction against another. Now the usual mechanism is to issue permits based on certain conditions developed to allocate the available water fairly and to accomplish public purposes such as prolonging aquifer life and preventing contamination. The rules for determining rights remain viable in private lawsuits among pumpers.

1. Rights of Landowners

Notions of land ownership remain important in applying modern liability rules and in issuing permits. The extent of overlying land owned by a pumper may determine rights to groundwater. Some systems limit uses of groundwater to uses on or connected with the overlying land. Some allocate rights to pumpers in proportion to the relative amounts of land owned by them. Tying water rights to land ownership causes obvious problems for municipalities seeking to use groundwater as their source of supply.

HIGDAY v. NICKOLAUS

Kansas City Court of Appeals, Missouri, 1971.
469 S.W.2d 859.

SHANGLER, PRESIDING JUDGE.

* * * Appellants are the several owners of some 6000 acres of farm land overlying an alluvial water basin in Boone County known as the McBaine Bottom. These lands (projected on Exhibit "A" appended hereto) extend from Huntsdale at the north to Easley at the south; they are bordered by a line of limestone bluffs on the east and are enclosed by a sweeping bend of the Missouri River on the west. Underlying this entire plain are strata of porous rock, gravel and soil through which water, without apparent or definite channel, filtrates, oozes and percolates as it falls. This water (much of which has originated far upstream within the Missouri River Valley) has been trapped by an underlying stratum of impervious limestone so that the saturated soil has become a huge aquifer or underground reservoir.

Appellants have devoted the overlying lands to agricultural use with excellent resultant yields. They attribute the fertility of the soil to the continuing presence of a high subterranean water level which has unfailingly and directly supplied the moisture needs of the crops whatever the vagaries of the weather. Appellants also use the underground water for personal consumption, for their livestock, and in the near future will require it for the surface irrigation of their crops.

Respondent City of Columbia is a burgeoning municipality of 50,000 inhabitants which has been, since 1948, in quest of a source of water to replenish a dwindling supply. Following the advice of consulting engineers, it settled on a plan for the withdrawal of water by shallow wells from beneath the McBaine Bottom where appellants' farms are located and thence to transport the water to the City some twelve miles away for sale to customers within and without the City. In December of 1966, the electorate approved a revenue bond issue for the development of a municipal water supply by such a system of shallow wells in the McBaine Bottom. Further scientific analysis and measurement of the basin's water resources followed. With the aid of a test well, it was determined that the underground percolating water table, when undisturbed, rises to an average of ten feet below the soil surface. These waters move laterally through the McBaine alluvium at the rate of two feet per day and in so doing displace 10.5 million gallons of water daily.

Respondent City, by threat of condemnation, has acquired from some of these appellants five well sites totalling 17.25 acres. The City now threatens to extract the groundwater at the rate of 11.5 million gallons daily for purposes wholly unrelated to any beneficial use of the overlying land, but instead, intends to transport the water to its corporate boundaries some miles away for purposes of sale. The mining of the water as contemplated will reduce the water table throughout the basin from the present average of ten feet to a new subsurface average of twenty feet. Appellants complain that this reduction of the water table will divert percolating waters normally available and enjoyed by appellants for their crops, livestock and their personal use and will eventually turn their land into an arid and sterile surface.

On the basis of these pleaded allegations, plaintiffs sought (1) a judicial declaration that defendant City is without right to extract the percolating waters for sale away from the premises or for other use not related with any beneficial ownership or enjoyment of the land from which they are taken when to do so will deprive them, the owners of the adjacent land, of the reasonable use of the underground water for the beneficial use of their own land, and (2) that defendant City be enjoined from undertaking to do so.

* * * Respondent [City] maintains that since Springfield Waterworks Co. v. Jenkins, 62 Mo.App. 74, was decided by the St. Louis Court of Appeals in 1895, Missouri has recognized the common law rule that a landowner has absolute ownership to the waters under his land and, therefore, may without liability withdraw any quantity of water for any purpose even though the result is to drain all water from beneath his neighbors' lands. Therefore, contends respondent, since the threatened damage plaintiffs plead describes a consequence of the rightful use by respondent of its land, it is *damnum absque injuria* and not actionable. * * *

* * * At an early day, the courts expressed dissatisfaction with the English common law rule and began applying what has come to be known variously, as the rule of "reasonable use", or of "correlative rights", or the "American rule." By the turn of the century, a steady trend of decisions was discernible away from the English rule to a rule of reasonable use. The trend continues.

Generally, the rule of reasonable use is an expression of the maxim that one must so use his own property as not to injure another—that each landowner is restricted to a reasonable exercise of his own rights and a reasonable use of his own property, in view of the similar rights of others.

As it applies to percolating groundwater, the rule of reasonable use recognizes that the overlying owner has a proprietary interest in the water under his lands, but his incidents of ownership are restricted. It recognizes that the nature of the property right is usufructuary rather than absolute as under the English rule. Under the rule of reasonable use, the overlying owner may use the subjacent groundwater freely, and without liability to an adjoining owner, but only if his use is for purposes incident to the beneficial enjoyment of the land from which the water was taken. * * *

The principal difficulty in the application of the reasonable use doctrine is in determining what constitutes a reasonable use. What is a reasonable use must depend to a great extent upon many factors, such as the persons involved, their relative positions, the nature of their uses, the comparative value of their uses, the climatic conditions, and all facts and circumstances pertinent to the issues. However, the modern decisions agree that under the rule of reasonable use *an overlying owner, including a municipality, may not withdraw percolating water and transport it for sale or other use away from the land from which it was taken if the result is to impair the supply of an adjoining landowner to his injury.* Such a use is unreasonable because nonbeneficial and "is not for a 'lawful purpose within the general rule concerning percolating waters, but constitutes an actionable wrong for which damages are recoverable' ".

The "reasonable use" rule as developed in the law of ground waters must be distinguished from the "correlative rights" rule. In 1902, the California Supreme Court repudiated the English common law rule in favor of the distinctive correlative rights doctrine which is based on the theory of proportionate sharing of withdrawals among landowners overlying a common basin.[9] Under the doctrine, overlying owners have no proprietary interest in the water under their soil. California remains the only important correlative rights state; Utah has abandoned it, and only Nebraska also applies it to some extent. The administration of such a system of rights has proved extremely difficult in times of water shortage and has tendered towards an "equalitarian rigidity" which does not take into account the relative value of the competing uses. However suitable this doctrine may be for California—the prime consumer of ground water in the country—or any other state which may follow it, the reasonable use rule offers a more flexible legal standard for the just determination of beneficial uses of ground water, particularly under the climatic conditions of Missouri.

* * * The premise that the owner of the soil owns all that lies beneath the surface so that he may use the percolating water in any way he chooses without liability to an adjoining owner fails to recognize

9. Katz v. Walkinshaw, 141 Cal. 116, 74 P. 766 (1903).

that the supply of groundwater is limited, and that the first inherent limitation on water rights is the availability of the supply. Another postulate of the common law doctrine ascribes to percolating waters a movement so "secret, changeable and uncontrollable", that no attempt to subject them to fixed legal rules could be successfully made. Chatfield v. Wilson, 28 Vt. 49, 53 (1855); Frazier v. Brown, 12 Ohio St. 294 (1961). Modern knowledge and techniques have discredited this premise also. The movement, supply, rate of evaporation and many other physical characteristics of groundwater are now readily determinable. In fact, respondent City's decision to turn to the McBaine Bottom as the source of its water supply was made only after careful scientific analysis confirmed that this land was particularly adaptable for water production. * * * The City cannot be permitted to escape liability by appeals to a doctrine which assumes that the very information the City has acted upon was not available to it.

Recently, in Bollinger v. Henry, supra, 375 S.W.2d l.c. 166[9, 10] (1964) the Supreme Court of Missouri applied the rule of reasonable use to determine the rights of riparian owners. Subterranean streams are governed by the rules applying to natural watercourses on the surface, so the rule of reasonable use is now applicable to them also. We believe the same rule should apply to subterranean percolating waters. It is that legal standard, in absence of a statutory expression of a priority of uses, by which existing water resources may be allocated most equitably and beneficially among competing users, private and public. The application of such a uniform legal standard would also give recognition to the established interrelationship between surface and groundwater and would, therefore, bring into one classification all waters over the use of which controversy may arise.

Under the rule of reasonable use as we have stated it, the fundamental measure of the overlying owner's right to use the groundwater is whether it is for purposes incident to the beneficial enjoyment of the land from which it was taken. Thus, a private owner may not withdraw groundwater for purposes of sale if the adjoining landowner is thereby deprived of water necessary for the beneficial enjoyment of his land. Here, the municipality has acquired miniscule plots of earth and by the use of powerful pumps intends to draw into wells on its own land for merchandising groundwater stored in plaintiffs' land, thereby depriving plaintiffs of the beneficial use of the normal water table to their immediate injury and to the eventual impoverishment of their lands. * * *

NOTES

1. Do you agree with the following analysis of the opinion? "[I]n effect, it appears that the court did not apply the reasonable use doctrine, but rather the doctrine of correlative rights." Rhonda Churchill Thomas, Note, *Water Law—Groundwater Rights in Missouri—A Need for Clarification*, 37 Mo.L.Rev. 357, 362 (1972). Which rule would a city prefer? If on retrial the court decides to award only damages to the plaintiffs, do they have a right to damages for loss of

the natural high water table? Does Higday's application of the rule of reasonable use restrict the use of groundwater to overlying land? Does it mean that municipalities can be enjoined from developing a well field unless they purchase the overlying rights of surrounding owners? What is the rationale for restricting the place groundwater is used to overlying land as opposed to basing the right to withdraw groundwater on owning overlying land?

Higday was followed in City of Blue Springs v. Central Dev. Ass'n, 831 S.W.2d 655 (Mo.App.W.D.1992), which held that a landowner may transfer the right to use underlying water but may not sever title to the water. Under *Higday,* "water is not severable from the land through or under which it flows." Thus, the water could not be valued separately when the overlying land was condemned.

In many states municipalities are given the power of eminent domain over water and, as a result, injured overlying owners are confined to damage remedies. See Richard S. Harnsberger, *Eminent Domain and Water Law,* 48 Neb.L.Rev. 325, 366–77 (1969).

2. The absolute ownership and American reasonable use rules were initially adopted because the courts thought that the lack of scientific knowledge about groundwater movement made it unfair to impose liability on a pumper for damage to other overlying landowners which could not be reasonably foreseen. E.g., Wheatley v. Baugh, 25 Pa. 528, 64 Am.Dec. 721 (1855). Developments in hydrology have led to vigorous attacks on these rules as *Higday* illustrates. After a survey of the cases, Professor Peter N. Davis suggests that Wheatley v. Baugh may still be good policy, at least as to small wells, and proposes that groundwater rights should not be based on the premise that all movement is measurable but should be determined by the size of the pumper's well. Peter N. Davis, *Wells and Streams: Relationship at Law,* 37 Mo.L.Rev. 189, 236–37 (1972). See Prather v. Eisenmann, 261 N.W.2d 766 (Neb.1978), discussed at page 511, infra, for an example of the application of the distinction suggested by Professor Davis.

3. A major difference between the English and American applications of the absolute ownership rule is that the English rule allows withdrawals for bona fide property improvements as well as for malicious injuries to adjoining property owners. American courts have generally enjoined malicious pumping. E.g., Gagnon v. French Lick Springs Hotel Co., 72 N.E. 849 (Ind.1904).

4. Vermont reaffirmed the absolute ownership rule in 1973, Drinkwine v. State, 300 A.2d 616 (Vt.1973), but in 1985 the legislature expressly abolished the common law doctrine of absolute ownership of groundwater, and provided a cause of action for unreasonable harm caused by withdrawals, diversions or pollution, effectively adopting a correlative rights rule. 10 Vt.Stat.Ann. § 1410.

5. One semi-arid state, Oklahoma, has enacted legislation allowing overlying owners to receive fixed allocations based on "that percentage of the total annual yield of the basin or subbasin * * * which is equal to the percentage of the land overlying the fresh groundwater basin or subbasin which he owns or leases." Okla. Stat. Ann. tit. 82,

§ 1020.9. The determination of the maximum annual yield is an adjudicative decision. Texas County Irrigation and Water Resources Association v. Oklahoma Water Resources Board, 803 P.2d 1119 (Okl. 1990).

6. The Restatement (Second) of Torts, § 858 states:

(1) A proprietor of land or his grantee who withdraws ground water from the land and uses it for a beneficial purpose is not subject to liability for interference with the use of water by another, unless

(a) the withdrawal of ground water unreasonably causes harm to a proprietor of neighboring land through lowering the water table or reducing artesian pressure,

(b) the withdrawal of ground water exceeds the proprietor's reasonable share of the annual supply or total store of ground water.

The Restatement rule is increasingly being adopted by the courts to award dewatered landowners damages against large-scale pumpers. Wisconsin was the first state to apply § 858. State v. Michels Pipeline Constr., Inc., 217 N.W.2d 339 (Wis.1974), overruled Huber v. Merkel, 94 N.W. 354 (Wis.1903), which had applied the English rule to its logical limit and allowed malicious pumping. Since *Michels Pipeline*, Michigan and Ohio have adopted § 858. Maerz v. United States Steel Corp., 323 N.W.2d 524 (Mich.App.1982); Cline v. American Aggregates Corp., 474 N.E.2d 324 (Ohio 1984). See generally Richard P. Fahey, and Stephanie Denbow-Hubbard, *Groundwater Law in Ohio Past and Future: A Proposed Legislative Solution to Past Problems and Future Needs*, 14 Cap.U.L.Rev. 43 (1984). Only Indiana has specifically rejected § 858, Wiggins v. Brazil Coal & Clay Corp., 440 N.E.2d 495 (Ind. App. 1982), vacated 452 N.E.2d 958 (Ind. 1983).

The Restatement rule in subsection (b) limits the rights of a landowner to a reasonable share of the "annual supply or total store of ground water." This stops short of asserting a public interest in the resource, but nevertheless indicates some limitation besides the immediate effect of pumping on other users. See John S. Lowe, et al., *Beyond Section 858: A Proposed Groundwater Liability and Management System for the Eastern United States*, 8 Ecology L.Q. 131 (1979).

7. *Subsidence.* In Finley v. Teeter Stone, Inc., 248 A.2d 106 (Md.1968), plaintiff farmer alleged that from thirty-five to fifty-seven acres of his land were injured as a result of subsidence. Defendant conceded that his pumping to drain a quarry on neighboring land caused the subsidence, but escaped liability on the ground that he was a groundwater user making a reasonable use of his land that was not negligent. See also Adams v. Lang, 553 So.2d 89 (Ala.1989) (extraction of groundwater for catfish pond causing artesian wells on adjoining land to be dewatered was reasonable use). After an extensive review of the same result as *Finley*. Langbrook Properties, Ltd. v. Surrey County Council, 3 All E.R. 1424 (Ch.1969).

Plaintiffs in *Finley* relied upon Gamer v. Town of Milton, 195 N.E.2d 65 (Mass.1964). In that case, a town drained a small pond to recover underlying gravel, causing land under some nearby homes to subside. The court imposed liability because of the failure to take reasonable precautions to protect plaintiff's adjacent land. Why is *Gamer* a "negligence" question which imposes the costs on the pumper and *Finley* a "water rights" question? Should liability for withdrawals which cause subsidence depend on the manner in which the court characterizes the problem? The Florida Supreme Court held a defendant liable for excavations for a yacht basin which interrupted underground waters feeding plaintiff's spring. The court cited Restatement of Torts, § 849 and §§ 822–840 for the proposition that "In the absence * * * of surface indications, an interference with subterranean water is, of course, unintentional and damnum absque injuria unless the conduct resulting therein is negligent, reckless or ultrahazardous." Labruzzo v. Atlantic Dredging & Const. Co., 54 So.2d 673, 676 (Fla. 1951).

In a Texas case, an industrial pumper withdrew massive amounts of groundwater with the knowledge that it would damage appellant landowners. It negligently placed its wells, concentrating the land subsidence, and pumped too much water from these wells in too short a time, compounding the damage. Texas had been a leading absolute ownership state, but the court recognized a narrow exception to the general principle of non-liability for damage by negligence in pumping where the negligence was a proximate cause of the subsidence of another's land. Friendswood Dev. Co. v. Smith–Southwest Indus., Inc., 576 S.W.2d 21 (Tex. 1978). The court held that the new liability rule applied only prospectively because the common law rule was an established rule of property law. Texas has since enacted legislation to control subsidence. It includes a fee of 1.2 cents per thousand gallons pumped which was upheld in Beckendorff v. Harris–Galveston Coastal Subsidence Dist., 558 S.W.2d 75 (Tex. Civ. App. 1977).

Some Texas water lawyers read *Friendswood* as the forerunner of the abandonment of the absolute ownership rule, but the courts continue to adhere to the rule. City of Sherman v. Public Util. Comm'n of Texas, 643 S.W.2d 681 (Tex.1983); Denis v. Kickapoo Land Co., 771 S.W.2d 235 (Tex.App.—Austin 1989). Planners and commentators continue to argue that, independent of short-run concerns of individual pumpers, more stringent conservation measures are needed, especially in the High Plains (Ogallala) Aquifer where it is estimated that irrigated acreage could shrink from a present 5.9 to 2.9 million acres by the year 2030. Texas groundwater law changed dramatically with the declaration that the Edwards Aquifer is an underground stream. See pages 490–91, supra. Texas groundwater law and recent legislative changes are further discussed at page 538, infra.

2. Prior Users' Rights

The issue in groundwater appropriation suits is not usually a claim of priority to an absolute amount of water but of a right to a given pressure level. The consequence of losing pressure may be to increase the depth from which water must be pumped (pump lift), requiring the drilling of a deeper well or installation of a more powerful pump. It may mean conversion of an artesian well whose water once flowed readily above ground to a well requiring expensive drilling and pumps. Groundwater withdrawals may also affect the supply or the accessibility of water available to surface water appropriators because the two sources are hydrologically connected. Only a few states clearly recognize the connection and administer such waters as coming from a single source, notwithstanding scientific evidence. A few states like Colorado apply prior appropriation principles to the use of groundwater that is connected with surface water; priority determines rights among pumpers as well as between pumpers and surface users.

The "right" to static pressure was addressed by the Utah Supreme Court in 1959. The court held that "[p]rior appropriators of * * * underground water who have beneficially used it through the natural flow of springs or artesian wells were entitled to have the subsequent appropriators restrained from drawing the water out of and lowering the static head pressure of this underground basin unless they replaced the quality and quantity of the water by pumping or other means to the prior appropriator at the sole cost of the subsequent appropriators." Current Creek Irr. Co. v. Andrews, 344 P.2d 528 (Utah 1959). Justice Crockett vigorously dissented:

> * * * I doubt the wisdom of seeking solutions to problems such as the instant ones in such a generality as a rule that a prior user has the absolute right not only to the water, but to have preserved to him the pressure and the means of diversion under all circumstances. Such a rule may seem easy for the court to apply to rid itself of immediate problems, but it is far from easy in practical operation. More important, it does not serve the fundamental purpose of our water law of providing for the fullest conservation and the highest development of water by making it available to all users in the most convenient and economical way. The rule is impractical because in some instances it would produce these bad effects: (1) it would compel wasteful exposures at and near the surface and/or wasteful drainage from the basin; (2) the foregoing would result because in some instances it would be too expensive for later users to pay the cost of lifting their own water and also to bear the expense of maintaining pressure for all prior appropriators; and (3) the problem of administering the allocation of the costs of doing so would be insuperable.

Id. at 504.

ALBUQUERQUE v. REYNOLDS

Supreme Court of New Mexico, 1962.
71 N.M. 428, 379 P.2d 73.

GEO. L. REESE, JR., DISTRICT JUDGE.

The city of Albuquerque filed with the state engineer four separate applications for permits to appropriate underground waters from the Rio Grande Underground Water Basin. Under each application it was proposed that a well be drilled to a depth of 1200 feet at a described location on the mesa, some six or seven miles east of the Rio Grande River within the exterior boundaries of the basin, and that 1500 acre feet of water per annum be pumped and used for municipal water supply. * * *

After due notice by publication, a hearing was held by the state engineer and substantial and adequate testimony and evidence was received to show that the underground waters sought to be appropriated constitute a part of the base flow of the Rio Grande River; that all of the waters flowing in said river have been fully appropriated; and that the granting of the applications would impair the existing rights of the prior appropriators of river water.

* * * [T]he state engineer issued his findings and order in which he found that the granting of the applications would impair existing rights to the use of the waters of the Rio Grande and that the city had refused to take the steps required by him to offset the adverse effect upon the rights of such users. The applications were accordingly denied.

* * *

The applications in question were filed pursuant to § 75–11–1, et seq., N.M.S.A., 1953 Comp. These statutes provide for application by one desiring to appropriate public unappropriated water for beneficial use and, upon the filing of an application, a notice is published by which all interested persons are advised of the amount of water sought to be appropriated, its source, the point of diversion, and the beneficial use to which it is to be put. Any interested person is afforded an opportunity to file a protest to the granting of the application and, if one or more protests are filed, a hearing is held after which the statute, § 75–11–3, supra, as it existed when these applications were filed, provided in pertinent part:

> "* * * the state engineer shall, if he finds that there are in such underground * * * reservoir * * * unappropriated waters, or that the proposed appropriation would not impair existing water *rights from such source*, grant the said application and issue a permit to the applicant to appropriate all or a part of the waters applied for subject to the rights of all prior appropriators from said source." (Emphasis added)

It is apparent that under this statute there are only two questions to be determined: (1) Whether there are unappropriated waters; and (2) whether the taking of such waters will impair existing water rights from such source.

* * *

The city next argues in support of its position that the statute, § 75–11–3, supra, as it existed at the time of the filing of its applications and prior to amendment in 1959, by its own terms required the state engineer to approve an application to appropriate underground water where there is unappropriated water in the basin, unless the approval would result in impairment of existing rights to take water directly from the basin, itself.

This statute is quoted supra with emphasis supplied by us to point up the emphasis on certain language which the city relies upon. To state the matter simply, the city argues that the engineer, in acting on an application to appropriate underground water, must protect none other than appropriators taking directly from the underground basin itself—that "existing water rights from such source" means appropriators having existing wells in the basin, as distinguished from and to the exclusion of appropriators from streams fed by waters from the same basin or source. Such a construction of the statute could not constitutionally deprive the prior stream appropriators of their right to protect their vested water rights by appropriate actions in court, but it would lend legislative sanction to a wrongful act on the part of a subsequent appropriator. It would, practically speaking, result in a use of state power to impose an unconscionable burden of time and expense of litigation on prior stream appropriators. We are not forced to such a construction and, in fact, are not called upon to strain the English language to say that the statute directs disapproval of an application to appropriate underground water in all cases where the granting would result in impairment of "existing water rights from such source," including existing rights in streams which substantially derive water from such source. The statute makes no exception as to "existing water rights from such source" and we will make none.

In Templeton v. Pecos Valley Artesian Conservancy Dist., [65 N.M. 59, 332 P.2d 465 (1958)] we were not faced with the argument made here as to the meaning in the statute of the phrase "existing water rights from such source," but we did there hold that a prior appropriator of stream water had the right to follow the stream water to its underground source and the right to drill wells and take the underground water necessary to fill his prior stream right, regardless of detriment to other underground water appropriators whose rights were subsequent in time to the stream right. This case, and what we have announced supra, effectively disposes of the broad proposition advanced by the city that the state engineer has no direction or authority from the legislature to protect prior appropriators of stream water from impairment at the hands of subsequent appropriators of underground water in basins, the waters of which constitute a part of the base flow of a surface stream.

Having found legislative authority in the state engineer to deny the city's applications on the ground that their granting would result in impairment of the rights of Rio Grande River appropriators, we next consider the argument that the state engineer exceeded his power and jurisdiction by establishing and promulgating rules and regulations requiring the retirement of surface water rights as a condition to new appropriations of underground water from the Rio Grande Underground Water Basin. We have already referred to the fact that no attack is made here, nor has one been made elsewhere in these proceedings, on the reasonableness of the regulations promulgated by the state engineer. If we assume, as we must, from the findings made by the state engineer and also by the district court that the underground waters in questions cannot be taken without impairment to the rights of the river appropriators, even though there are unappropriated underground waters in the basin, then it would seem to follow that some method should be devised, if possible, whereby the available unappropriated water can be put to beneficial use. Because of the interrelationship between the two waters, as discussed in the findings of the state engineer from which we have extracted quotations supra, it would seem that a method has been devised to serve this purpose. Having the statutory power and duty to prohibit the taking, by denying the applications in toto if necessary to protect existing rights, the state engineer has reasonably exercised his power by imposing suitable conditions so as to permit such taking as will not result in impairment. This power to impose suitable conditions is inherent in the broader power to prohibit and may also be expressly covered by that portion of § 75–11–3, supra, which provides that, under the conditions set out, the state engineer shall grant the said application and issue a permit to the applicant to appropriate "all or a part of the waters applied for." Furthermore, no quarrel is made here with the physical fact stated by the state engineer, that:

> "The relationships derived from Darcy's law show that the effects of ground-water withdrawals on a nearby stream arise gradually and that if the well is some distance from the stream many years elapse before the effects of the withdrawal are fully reflected in the stream-flows. The relationships show, however, that ultimately the annual stream-flow is reduced by an amount equal to the annual ground-water appropriation. The relationships also show that once a ground-water appropriation is made, and continued for a period of time, the effects on surface water flows are not terminated at the time that the ground-water appropriation is terminated but continue, gradually diminishing, for many years after the ground-water appropriation is ended."

The conditions imposed by the state engineer provide for measuring the pumped water and the return flow to the stream, and take into account the accretion to the stream flow which would result therefrom and, in his decision, the state engineer referred to calculations and charts, introduced as exhibits in the hearing before him, showing that under the applications of the city and with a return flow of 40% from the city's works, as at present, the water taken from the basin would, over a 75-year period, be extracted about one-half from underground storage and one-half from surface flows.

We feel constrained to hold that the state engineer adopted the only known plan to avoid impairment to existing rights and that his requirement, that surface rights be retired to the extent necessary to protect prior stream appropriators as a condition of the granting of an application to appropriate from the basin, is within the lawful power and authority of the state engineer.

NOTES

1. The *Templeton* doctrine, allowing an appropriator to "follow the source" of water in which rights are held, was followed in Langenegger v. Carlsbad Irr. Dist., 483 P.2d 297 (N.M.1971). The state engineer approved an application for a change of diversion point that allowed appropriators, whose direct flow right from the Pecos River had been diminished by heavy pumping of groundwater from the Roswell Basin, to drill wells to enable them to fulfill their water rights. The supreme court recognized that, unlike *Templeton*, where the trial court found that the source of the new wells was the same as the source of the direct flow rights, the artesian aquifer in which the wells would be drilled was only one of two aquifers through which the base flow of the river came. It held that the appropriators were entitled to rely on any sources which feed the main stream above their points of diversion, all the way back to the farthest limits of the watershed. 483 P.2d at 300.

The *Templeton* doctrine was found not applicable, however, in Brantley v. Carlsbad Irr. Dist., 587 P.2d 427, 429 (N.M.1978). The evidence established either that the water sought to be recaptured did not come from the surface flow of the river or that the area in which the appropriator sought to drill was separated from the area of the loss by an impermeable geologic formation. "In either case the 'Templeton Doctrine' does not apply since Brantley seeks to drill *below* his point of diversion into waters which are not a source of his surface right."

2. Surface rights holders may find it more convenient, reliable, and efficient to pump some of their water from the ground. They may face the Catch-22 situation of having their surface rights cancelled for non-use, however. To avoid this, in 1983 Nebraska enacted legislation to authorize the issuance of permits for the use of incidental underground water storage to holders of perfected surface appropriations. Neb.Rev.Stat. § 46–226.01 (Reissue 1984). The statute was upheld against a takings challenge. Central Nebraska Public Power Co. and Irrigation District v. Abrahamson, 413 N.W.2d 290 (Neb.1987) (incidental storage did not harm overlying landowners because no profitable or claimed use of land was foreclosed).

3. Under Arizona law, "percolating water" is not appropriable but belongs to the landowner. A spring surfaced in a dry creek bed on land in Arizona owned by the Colliers. They named it "Miracle Spring," dammed the waters flowing from it, and sought a permit to appropriate the water. Because the spring water was percolating water belonging to them, and from which they could have freely pumped until it broke through the surface, the Colliers argued that it is a new appropriable source. Ranchers with vested surface water rights to waters of the creek where it flows on the surface at lower elevations, contended that they had already appropriated the waters flowing from Miracle Spring. Experts testified that the spring's waters contributed to the flow of the creek. The court held:

Arizona water law has developed into a bifurcated system in which percolating groundwater is regulated under a set of laws completely distinct from the laws regulating surface water. While this bifurcation provides a workable legal system, it often ignores the scientific reality that groundwater and surface water are often connected. The Colliers also ask us to ignore this reality. Our legislature, however, has tied the approval of new appropriations to their *effect* on existing appropriations. Thus, we are able to look beyond the legal fiction and see that the water the Colliers seek to appropriate is water which has historically fed an appropriated stream. We therefore hold that because the Colliers are seeking to appropriate water which has in the past contributed to Kirkland Creek in an unappropriable form and which now would flow naturally in an appropriable form into the creek above the point where the prior appropriators divert their water, their application to appropriate water was correctly denied on the ground that the appropriation would interfere with prior vested rights.

Collier v. Arizona Dep't of Water Resources, 722 P.2d 363, 366 (Ariz. App. 1986).

4. What rights, if any, were created in groundwater underlying western lands that passed from the public domain to private individuals by federal patents? Was such water part of the real estate transferred? Was it severed from the land and made subject to appropriation under state law? State ex rel. Bliss v. Dority, 225 P.2d 1007 (N.M.1950), rejected a landowner's claim that a statute declaring underground water "to belong to the public and to be subject to appropriation for beneficial use" was an unconstitutional taking of property without due process of law. Relying on the foundation case of Yeo v. Tweedy, 286 P. 970 (N.M.1929), the court held that no appurtenant groundwater rights passed with a federal patent under the Desert Land Act of 1877.

5. In many western states geothermal resources—steam or hot water coming from beneath the earth's surface—are classified as minerals and developed by rules analogous to oil and gas law. But in some states geothermal resources are classified as water and an appropriation must be perfected. If, as is often the case, there is no physical interconnection between a geothermal reservoir and an aquifer dedicated to beneficial use, it can be argued that the geothermal reservoir is developed water and thus not subject to prior and junior rights. See Owen Olpin and A. Dan Tarlock, *Water That Is Not Water*, 13 Land and Water L.Rev. 391 (1978), and Owen Olpin, A. Dan Tarlock and Carl F. Austin, *Geothermal Development and Western Water Law*, 1979 Utah L.Rev. 773.

WAYMAN v. MURRAY CITY CORP.

Supreme Court of Utah, 1969.
23 Utah 2d 97, 458 P.2d 861.

CROCKETT, CHIEF JUSTICE.

In contest here are rights to water, as to amounts and pressure, in an underground water basin, known as the Murray Artesian Basin. It underlies an area in and adjacent to Murray City, lying between the Wasatch Mountains on the east and the Jordan River on the west. Plaintiffs are five families who own residences along Vine Street in

Murray. Each has one or more smart wells (1½ to 3 inches in diameter) of varying depths. Each owns established rights to take water by means of their wells approved by the State Engineer. The right of the defendant Murray City derives from its acquisition of seven old wells known as the Baker Wells with rights to use 750 gallons per minute (1.67 c.f.s.) of water from the same underground basin. The rights under some of these wells are prior in time to some of the plaintiffs' wells and later than others. For a period of several years the Baker Wells had not furnished the permitted 750 gallons per minute; and by 1959 the flow had diminished to around 220 gallons per minute. Because of this, Murray City made plans to improve its wells. Pursuant to written permission obtained from the State Engineer on April 10, 1961, it caused a new 16-inch well to be drilled to a depth of 496 feet. It produced an excellent flow, of some variation, up to 1100 gallons per minute. The exact potential of the well is immaterial here because Murray City only contends for its right to draw the 750 gallons of water per minute to which its ownership is not challenged. The Baker Wells were permanently plugged and sealed and the new well was put into continuous operation in May of 1964; and in that month, the change of diversion from the old wells to the new well was approved by the State Engineer, Wayne D. Criddle, by Change Application A–3887.

Plaintiffs brought this suit in the district court against Murray City and the State Engineer to overturn the latter's decision on the ground that the new well had diminished the flow in their own wells and thus deprived them of their entitled water. * * *

Because of the vital importance of water in this arid region both our statutory and decisional law have been fashioned in recognition of the desirability and of the necessity of insuring the highest possible development and of the most continuous beneficial use of all available water with as little waste as possible.[1] * * *

* * * [T]his is not a situation where a party (Murray City) has initiated a *new* withdrawal in a basin which adversely affects the flow of wells prior in time and right.[3] What the City has done is to create a more efficient means of taking the 750 gallons of water per minute from this basin it acquired by its purchase of the Baker Wells. There thus arises the foundational question as to whether a water user, whose well for some reason or another is not producing the water to which he is entitled, may improve his method of taking his entitlement of water from the basin. That in most circumstances this question should be answered in the affirmative is clearly indicated by Sec. 73–3–3, U.C.A. 1953, which provides that:

1. Title 73, U.C.A.1953, especially Section 73–1–1: "All waters in this state, whether above or under the ground are hereby declared to be the property of the public." And Sec. 73–1–3: "Beneficial use shall be the basis, the measure and the limit of all rights to the use of water in this state," * * *.

3. Thus in that respect different from the case of Current Creek Irr. Co. v. Andrews, 9 Utah 2d 324, 344 P.2d 528 (1959).

Any person entitled to the use of water *may change the place of diversion* or use and may use the water for other purposes than those for which it was originally appropriated, * * *.

* * * Nevertheless, there are other considerations to be reckoned with. The quoted statute, Sec. 73–3–3, further provides: "But no such change shall be made if it impairs any vested right without just compensation." The trial court, upon the trial de novo procedure allowed under Secs. 73–3–14 and 15, found that the new well did adversely affect the flow in the plaintiffs' wells. Inasmuch as there is other substantial evidence in the record to support this finding, under traditional rules of review it cannot be disturbed.

It was in implementation of its finding that the trial court, as authorized under Sec. 73–3–23, provided that Murray City "must at his sole cost *permanently* replace to the plaintiffs water in amount and quality equal to the level of their prior use." This imposes upon Murray City a sweeping and pervasive responsibility. It seems tantamount to requiring it to insure to the plaintiffs a continuous supply of 100% of their allotted flow henceforward, i.e., we assume, forever. * * * From what we have been able to learn about underground water it seems obvious that any decree so "set in concrete" could prove to be highly inequitable and inconsistent with the objectives of our water law as set forth herein. In order to harmonize with those objectives and to have a realistic application to the rights to the use of water any such decree should be understood as relating to the then existing conditions as shown by the evidence in the particular case, and also should be understood as being subject to change if it is shown that there is any substantial change in such conditions.

* * *

If the water table in such an underground basin must be maintained at a sufficiently high level to sustain pressure in the wells in the higher areas, there may be water above and near the surface in the lower areas, forming ponds, marshes, and swamps. This results in wasteful losses from surface evaporation and from consumption by water-loving plants, tules, reeds and rushes, indigenous to such areas, which are of little or no value. There is often further loss by unproductive drainage from the basin. * * *

From the considerations relating to underground water law hereinabove discussed there has come to be recognized what may be referred to as the "rule of reasonableness" in the allocation of rights in the use of underground water. This involves an analysis of the total situation: the quantity of water available, the average annual recharge in the basin, the existing rights and their priorities. All users are required where necessary to employ reasonable and efficient means in taking their own waters in relation to others to the end that wastage of water is avoided and that the greatest amount of available water is put to beneficial use.

Our neighboring state of Colorado, which has water problems similar to our own, in the case of City of Colorado Springs v. Bender[6] has stated:

> At his own point of diversion on a natural water course, each diverter must establish some reasonable means of effectuating his diversion. He is not entitled to command the whole or a substantial flow of the stream merely to facilitate his taking the fraction of the whole flow to which he is entitled. Schodde v. Twin Falls Land & Water Co., 224 U.S. 107, 119. This principle applied to diversion of underflow or underground water means that *priority of appropriation does not give a right to an inefficient means of diversion*, such as a well which reaches to such a shallow depth into the available water supply that a shortage would occur to such senior even though diversion by others did not deplete the stream below where there would be an adequate supply for the senior's lawful demand.

* * *

That an efficient and practical allocation and regulation of underground waters requires a recognition of this principle is further indicated by the fact that several of our western neighbors have in substance codified such a rule.

We perceive nothing in our statutory law inconsistent with this "rule of reasonableness" just discussed, nor which compels a conclusion that owners of rights to use underground water have any absolute right to pressure. * * *

It is further evident from our statutes on this subject that the legislature, in an awareness of the complexities involved in the regulation and use of underground water, has recognized that it is essential to have the benefit of the expertise of the State Engineer and his staff who are professionally qualified to make such determinations. * * *

* * * What is desirable is the best possible adjustment of the rights of these parties in relationship to each other, and without undue or unreasonable burden upon either, and at the same time serve the desideratum of our water law of putting and keeping to the beneficial use the greatest possible amount of available water. Because it is our judgment that the decree of the district court does not achieve that objective, and because of the importance of the rights, not only of the parties here in contention, but of the policy considerations underlying this proceeding, we feel impelled to remand this case for further proceedings and settlement of rights in conformity with the principles we have set forth in this opinion. * * *

NOTES

1. Who must bear a loss of pressure under an application of the reasonable use rule? The Restatement of Torts (Second) § 858A imposes liability only if the "withdrawal of groundwater unreasonably causes harm * * * through lowering of the water table or reducing artesian

---

6. 148 Colo. 458, 366 P.2d 552, 555 (1961).

pressure." § 858A(1)(a). In Prather v. Eisenmann, 261 N.W.2d 766 (Neb.1978), plaintiff proved that the cone of influence of defendant's high capacity irrigation wells caused plaintiff's artesian pressure to drop. An award of $5,346.58, the costs of deepening the well, was approved. The supreme court held the matter was controlled by Nebraska's domestic preference statute, Neb.Rev.Stat. § 46–613, not the Restatement rule. *Prather* stated that no domestic user could obtain relief against another domestic user for the loss of artesian pressure so long as water was available at deeper levels. Is the loss of artesian pressure caused by a high capacity agricultural, municipal, or industrial well, per se unreasonable? See Stephen S. Gealy, Comment, *Protection Unlimited: A Preferred User's Right to Means of Groundwater Diversion in Nebraska*, 62 Neb.L.Rev. 270 (1983), for a good discussion of *Prather*.

Under the Oregon groundwater appropriation act, a permit application may be rejected if the state engineer finds that a well may unduly interfere with existing wells or substantially interfere with surface rights. Or. Rev. Stat. § 537.620(3).

2. The California rule of correlative rights has been adopted by several other states, at least in dicta. In Woodsum v. Pemberton, 412 A.2d 1064 (N.J.Super.1980), a homeowner whose well pressure declined sued the city for causing the decline, but the court held that the plaintiff's use was not reasonable because the well could have been deepened at a cost of between $750.00–$1,700.00: "[I]f his use is to be described as 'reasonable,' he must dig his well to a depth which anticipates the lowering of the water table by virtue of other proper users." 412 A.2d at 1076. The court balanced the plaintiff's need for the original pressure level against the public's need for the water. Was it correct to do so? The case was affirmed but on different grounds. All issues were then moot because plaintiff recovered the cost of deepening the well from a settlement with one defendant.

3. The decision in the principal case relies on Colorado Springs v. Bender, 366 P.2d 552 (Colo.1961). In that case, Bender, who had a small (55 head) cattle operation, sought to prevent the city of Colorado Springs from rendering his shallow, hand-dug well useless. The city had been granted an easement to place its well on the land of Bender's neighbor, a corn farmer. Because the aquifer sloped away from Bender's land, lowering the water table took it out of his reach. The state supreme court instructed the trial court as follows:

> Following such additional evidence as the litigants may desire to present, the following things must be done:
>
> (1) The rate of flow of senior and junior appropriators whose rights are involved, together with the dates of priority of each appropriation, must be determined.
>
> (2) The elevation of water in the aquifer at which each junior appropriator must cease to divert water in order to meet the demands of a senior appropriator must be fixed.

(3) In determining the facts mentioned [under (2)] the conditions surrounding the diversion by the senior appropriator must be examined as to whether he has created a means of diversion from the aquifer which is reasonably adequate for the use to which he has historically put the water of his appropriation. If adequate means for reaching a sufficient supply can be made available to the senior, whose present facilities for diversion fail when water table is lowered by acts of the junior appropriators, provision for such adequate means should be decreed at the expense of the junior appropriators, it being unreasonable to require the senior to supply such means out of his own financial resources.

* * * The court must determine what, if anything, the plaintiffs [seniors] should be required to do to make more efficient the facilities at their point of diversion, due regard being given to the purposes for which the appropriation had been made, and the "economic reach" of plaintiffs. The plaintiffs * * * cannot be required to improve their extraction facilities beyond their economic reach, upon a consideration of all the factors involved.

After *Bender,* the state engineer attempted to decide which wells met the "economic reach" rule announced in *Bender* and which did not. In one case, however, he shut down thirty-six wells in the Arkansas Valley without formulating any guidelines. The supreme court held that the action was arbitrary. Fellhauer v. People, 447 P.2d 986 (Colo.1968). Subsequent legislation and administrative regulations established standards. Fellhauer has had a broader impact, however, for in dictum the supreme court gave its blessing to new approaches to regulating uses under both ground and surface water rights that extends beyond simple considerations of their relative priorities:

These uses, and similar uses on other rivers, have developed under article XVI, section 6 of the Colorado constitution which contains *inter alia* two provisions:

"The right to divert the unappropriated waters of any natural stream to beneficial uses shall never be denied. Priority of appropriation shall give the better right as between those using the water for the same purpose;"

* * * It is implicit in these constitutional provisions that, along with *vested rights*, there shall be *maximum utilization* of the water of this state. As administration of water approaches its second century the curtain is opening upon the new drama of *maximum utilization* and how constitutionally that doctrine can be integrated into the law of *vested rights*. We have known for a long time that the doctrine was lurking in the backstage shadows as a result of the accepted, though oft violated, principle that the right to water does not give the right to waste it.

447 P.2d at 994. Colorado Springs v. Bender might be called the signal that the curtain was about to rise.

4. In Colorado there has been a complete integration of administration of groundwater and surface water rights that are connected.

The state has consistently held that all groundwater is presumed to be tributary to a natural stream. Safranek v. Limon, 228 P.2d 975 (Colo.1951). As such, tributary groundwater is integrated into the administration of surface water priorities. Colo. Rev. Stat. § 37–92–102. It is defined as "that water in the unconsolidated alluvial aquifer of sand, gravel, and other sedimentary material * * * which can influence the rate or direction of movement of water in that alluvial aquifer or natural stream." Colo. Rev. Stat. § 37–92–103(11).

Integrated administration requires sophisticated determinations of when and to what extent junior pumpers must be limited to satisfy the "call" of senior surface users (and vice versa). Groundwater travels more slowly than surface water so that a cessation in pumping may take a long time to have an effect on stream flows. To implement integrated administration, the state engineer developed a zone plan along the South Platte River. Wells in Zone A were estimated to affect the river in 10 days, in Zone B in 10–30 days, and in Zone C from 30–75 days. In response to the challenges of junior pumpers arguing that shutting down wells under the zone plan will not cause any water to reach the stream in time of need, the Colorado Supreme Court wrote:

> Three of the findings are related: (1) shutting down of wells will not cause water to reach the stream to satisfy any call in time of need; (2) the regulation promotes and encourages futile calls; and (3) waste results from shutting off of wells. Several witnesses on behalf of the plaintiff testified that by the time water reached the point of diversion of a person making a call the person might no longer need the water by reason of an intervening storm. We are not favorably impressed with this argument because the same thing is true with respect to calls upon inferior surface diversions, albeit to a lesser extent of time. As an illustration, if a ditch near Sterling, Colorado, having senior priority, should make a call under which the ditches with inferior priorities in the upper reaches of the Platte River in the South Park area would have to cease diversion, it is common knowledge that it would take 10 to 14 days for the water to flow from South Park to Sterling. We can see no logical distinction between the result of an intervening storm in the case of a call on surface right and the case of a call on a well.
>
> We found no evidence in the record to support the finding that the regulations promote and encourage futile calls.

Kuiper v. Well Owners Conservation Ass'n, 490 P.2d 268, 280 (Colo. 1971).

5. In Colorado, a junior may be allowed to pump from the tributary aquifer of an overappropriated stream on the condition that senior rights are protected under a plan of augmentation by which some replacement water is added to the stream, discussed at page 344, supra. Colo.Rev.Stat. § 37–92–301(2). Colorado Supreme Court decisions have strongly endorsed the use of such plans. See pages 340–43, supra.

6. In Kuiper v. Well Owners Conservation Ass'n, supra, the court rejected an interpretation of state law requiring senior appropriators,

using ground and surface water conjunctively, to satisfy their surface decrees with well water prior to making a call on the river.

This limited interpretation was rejected, however, in Alamosa–La Jara Water Users Protection Ass'n v. Gould, 674 P.2d 914 (Colo. 1983), page 281, supra. The court reviewed the 1969 Act, *Fellhauer* and *Bender*:

> We believe that *Well Owners* construed the 1969 Act too narrowly. The prior appropriation doctrine is not a legal barrier to the concurrent consideration by the state engineer of the various methods of implementing the state policy of maximum utilization set out in the 1969 Act. See Baker v. Ore-Ida Foods, Inc., 95 Idaho 575, 513 P.2d 627 (1973). Therefore, to the degree *Well Owners* precludes consideration of a reasonable-means-of-diversion requirement as a method of maximizing utilization of integrated underground and surface waters, we overrule *Well Owners*.

674 P.2d at 934–35. The court further found that the maximum, or optimum, utilization policy of state water law requires the state engineer to make policy judgments in administering groundwater rights that may affect surface rights based on environmental and economic concerns and not simply the respective individual rights of pumpers.

7. What rule should a court or administrator formulate to allocate the cost of lower static pressure levels between senior and junior appropriators? Economics provides one set of criteria in the definition of efficiency. Applied to water the resource is efficiently allocated and social welfare maximized when it is consumed to the point that demand equals marginal cost. Marginal cost in the case of groundwater has both an internal (the cost borne by the pumper) and an external (the costs imposed on all other units) component. Demand is a function of the value of the marginal product—the increase in the amount of output by the application of water multiplied by the price of the product.

Consider the outcome in *Wayman* and the economic reach rule of Colorado Springs v. Bender. Under what circumstances should the court enjoin a junior pumper or impose damages? Suppose that A has a well from which 10 cfs is pumped to irrigate barley. A usually makes $10,000 a year on the barley. B then drills a well to produce 50 cfs needed for a business that will enjoy a $1 million a year profit. What remedy lies if: (1) B's well makes it impossible for A to produce water, causing A to go out of business? (2) B's well makes it necessary for A to construct a new well at a cost of $10,000? (3) B's well lowers the water table so that A must pay $1000 more a year for electricity to run the pump?

C. GROUNDWATER ALLOCATION AND THE PUBLIC INTEREST

As the cases illustrate, absolute principles upon which the rights of competing users may be based—land ownership or priority—do not automatically resolve disputes. Whatever theoretical basis a state adopts for its rules of liability among pumpers or for a groundwater allocation scheme, the law must address the interests of landowners and non-landowners (often municipalities), and senior users and junior users in judgments about how much a pumper can extract and at what rate. The groundwater resource is so broadly important to society that modern courts simply will not settle for a wooden allocation of rights solely to overlying landowners or to the first pumper without regard to the equities of later pumpers or public concerns. Thus, decisionmakers have resorted to rules like "reasonable use" and "correlative rights." These approaches consider factors other than the interests of the pumpers themselves. In addition, administrators have been given authority to regulate pumping rates to provide for public and private benefits from the aquifer over the long term.

Most states have enacted extensive statutory schemes to allocate groundwater resources. Although the purpose was originally to provide certainty and predictability among individual users, considerably greater interests are now apparent. In particular, it is important to avoid depleting groundwater too fast.

There are physical and economic reasons not to pump out all the groundwater that is available from an aquifer. The physical danger is that the underground formation bearing the water may collapse or compress, reducing the capacity of the aquifer to refill. Furthermore, it may be unwise to take out too much water because the result may be shortages in future years. Thus, water managers have talked of "safe yield"—a term that may refer to the amount of water that can be removed without danger to the aquifer or may refer to the amount that can be removed without jeopardizing the reliability of future supplies for a particular period. The latter usually relates to an average rate of annual recharge.

Essentially nonrenewable groundwater sources, sometimes called non-tributary aquifers, demand different considerations. Because any use of them amounts to "mining" the resource, decisions must be made about how long the aquifer should last. The depletable resource effectively is then amortized over the desired life by allowing pumping at a particular rate. The objective of nonrenewable resource management is the same as it is for any stock resource: an optimum intertemporal allocation. Harold Hotelling, *The Economics of Exhaustible Resource*, 39 J.Pol.Econ. 137 (1931).

Problems of overdraft have rarely been foreseen. More typically, a state will superimpose "critical area legislation" or other regulatory measures on its system of groundwater rights after land begins subsiding, wells begin drying up, or salt water begins to intrude. Many states are beginning to appreciate the desirability of preventing such harm and therefore are taking a more active role in determining pumping rates. They are guided not only by the relative interests of today's pumpers as expressed in a property rights system, but also by concerns for the sustainability of the resource for future users.

In some states it has been necessary to limit sharply the exercise of pre-existing rights to use groundwater in order to place necessary limits on aquifer life. Thus, pumping rates have been curtailed to prevent or regulate mining. Some states, like Arizona, have enacted sweeping new laws designed to protect depleting aquifers. This has caused some landowners to challenge groundwater pumping regulation as a deprivation of property without due process of law.

There seems to be little question that states have the regulatory power to limit groundwater pumping among similarly situated users. The rationale of public regulation of groundwater pumping was established by the Supreme Court in a case upholding a New York statute which forbade the drilling of wells over natural mineral springs for the purpose of extracting carbonic gas to be sold as a separate commodity where a large portion of the waters from which the gas was extracted were permitted to run to waste.

> Thus these pumping operations generally result in an unreasonable and wasteful depletion of the common supply and in a corresponding injury to others equally entitled to resort to it. It is to correct this evil that the statute was adopted. * * * It does not take from any surface owner the right to tap from the underlying rock and to draw from a common supply, but, consistently with the continued exercise of that right, so regulates its exercise as reasonable to conserve the interests of all who supply it.

Lindsley v. National Carbonic Gas Co., 220 U.S. 61, 77 (1911). Can this rationale extend to a reallocation among different classes of users? How far can a legislature go in making "public welfare" judgments about the allocation of a resource in which individual rights have been established?

Another important interest of the public is in preventing groundwater contamination. In the past, this has rarely been considered in allocating rights to pump groundwater; however, suits have arisen over contamination of a plaintiff's groundwater source allegedly caused by the defendants activity on the land. The tremendous difficulties of proof and the general public interest in preventing such problems make regulatory schemes more appropriate than litigation for controlling groundwater contamination.

There is an important, but as yet virtually unexplored relationship between groundwater quality and quantity. For example, to prevent the migration of contaminated plumes, it may be necessary to maintain existing fresh water barriers. Rapid pumping in an area could create cones of depression that accelerate the migration of contaminated plumes.

Virtually no states integrate groundwater quality concerns with their systems for allocating rights to pump groundwater. Most of the attention to groundwater contamination has come from the federal government. The resulting laws rarely mesh with state allocation laws, and they almost never are administered as a part of the same system.

U.S. NATIONAL WATER COMMISSION, WATER POLICIES FOR THE FUTURE
238–39 (1973).

Ground Water Mining

Ground water mining occurs when withdrawals are made from an aquifer at rates in excess of net recharge. The problem becomes serious when this practice continues on a sustained basis over time: ground water tables decline, making the pumping of water more and more expensive; compaction may occur in the aquifer, adversely affecting storage capacity and transmissivity; and quality may be threatened by salt water intrusion. Ground water mining may occur in aquifer systems having ample recharge as well as those having negligible recharge. In recharge aquifers, mining results from withdrawals substantially in excess of net recharge. In aquifers with little or no recharge, virtually any withdrawal constitutes mining and sustained withdrawals will, in due course, exhaust the supply or lower water tables below economic pump lifts. A prime example of ground water mining in an aquifer system with negligible recharge is found in the Ogallala Formation in the High Plains of Texas, an area that also has limited surface water resources.

* * *

Mining ground water is not inherently wrong. It is wrong, however, when the water is mined out without taking account of the future value of the water and the storage capacity of the reservoir. If a ground water aquifer were entirely unrelated to other aquifers and to surface water bodies, and if it were entirely owned by one person or organization, society could leave the decision to mine or not to mine to the owner. Presumably, the owner would seek to balance benefits from present production against anticipated benefits from future production in such a way as to maximize economic return from the resource over time as in the case of any other type of mining. The owner's self-interest would ordinarily coincide with society's interest. But ground water reservoirs are often associated with surface supplies and with other aquifers and are rarely in a single ownership. Accordingly, ground water reservoirs often suffer from the mismanagement associated with other "common pool" resources, namely, excessive use leading to premature exhaustion.

U.S. GEOLOGICAL SURVEY, NATIONAL WATER SUMMARY, 1983: HYDROLOGIC EVENTS AND ISSUES
36–40 (1984).

A great deal of use has been made of the terms "overdevelopment" and "safe yield" with regard to ground-water development. As it is often used, "safe yield" seems to refer to the pumpage that can be sustained at equilibrium, without continued withdrawal from storage. However, sustained withdrawal from storage or, as it is often termed, "ground-water mining," is no more "unsafe" than the mining of any other mineral resource, provided it is recognized and planned. Neither should pumpage at equilibrium necessarily be considered "safe," unless the attendant impacts, such as reduced streamflow or degradation of water quality, are deemed acceptable. The expression "safe yield" can, in fact, only be defined in terms of specific impacts of pumpage. The consequences of pumpage must be assessed for each level of development, and "safe yield" must be taken as the maximum pumpage for which the consequences are considered acceptable. The term "overdevelopment" then implies pumpage beyond that maximum.

* * *

Pumpage has increased steadily over the last three decades * * *. The total pumpage of ground water in 1980 represented about 20 percent of the total withdrawal of fresh and saline water in the United States. The largest single use of ground water is for irrigation, which accounted for slightly more than 60 bgd in 1980. It is important to note, however, that although irrigation represents the largest withdrawal, roughly half of the population of the country relies on ground water for domestic supply. Some of the factors responsible for the continued increase in ground-water use include significant expansion of irrigation in the humid East as well as in the West, particularly through the increased use of center-pivot systems; water-supply requirements of growing urban areas, particularly in the South and Southwest; water demands associated with energy production; a desire to establish drought-resistant supplies; objections to the construction of surface reservoirs; and objections to export of water from one area to another.

1. Administrative Regulation

BAKER v. ORE–IDA FOODS, INC.

Supreme Court of Idaho, 1973.
95 Idaho 575, 513 P.2d 627.

[The Idaho Groundwater Act, I.C. § 42–226 provides that "while the doctrine of 'first in time is first in right' is recognized, a reasonable exercise of this right shall not block full economic development of underground water resources, but early appropriators * * * shall be protected only in the maintenance of reasonable groundwater pumping levels as may be established by the director of the department of water resources * * * ". This case focuses on an aquifer with an average recharge rate of 5,500 acre feet per year where water had been withdrawn "far in excess of safe annual recharge causing a 20 foot per year drop in the aquifer's water level." Pursuant to I.C. § 42–226, the trial court found that the entire average rate of recharge could be pumped by four senior wells and enjoined pumping from all the wells (eight of which were owned by Ore-Ida) and turned the decree over to the Idaho Department of Water Administration (IDWA) for further administration.]

The instant case requires construction of the Ground Water Act against the backdrop of the uneven development of our common law concerning ground water. Idaho has vacillated on the question of the appropriability of ground water. * * *

In 1963 amendments to the Ground Water Act, I.C. § 42–229 (S.L.1963, ch. 216, § 1, p. 624), altered the traditional assumption that ground water in Idaho could be appropriated by either the constitutional method or the permit method. We construed that amendment in State ex rel. Tappan v. Smith, 92 Idaho 451, 456, 444 P.2d 412, 417 (1968). * * *

Smith says the state may regulate appropriations of ground water without violating our constitutionally mandated prior appropriation system.

We turn now to problems concerning the maintenance of water table levels. * * *

In * * * Noh v. Stoner, 53 Idaho 651, 657, 26 P.2d 1112, 1114 (1933) the Court upheld an injunction forbidding a junior well owner from interfering with a senior's appropriation of ground water. The Court stated:

> "If subsequent appropriators desire to engage in such a contest [a race for the bottom of the aquifer] the financial burden must rest on them and with no injury to the prior appropriators or loss of their water. Otherwise, if the users [seniors] go below the appellants [juniors] and respondents were to go below them appellants would in turn, according to their theory, be deprived of their water with no redress."

Noh suggests that a senior appropriator of ground water is forever protected from any interference with his *method* of diversion. Under *Noh* the only way that a junior can draw on the same aquifer is to hold the senior harmless for any loss incurred as a result of the junior's pumping. If the costs of reimbursing the senior became excessive, junior appropriators could not afford to pump from the aquifer. See Colorado Springs v. Bender, 148 Colo. 458, 366 P.2d 552 (1961). *Noh* was inconsistent with the full economic development of our ground water resources.

Apparently our Ground Water Act was intended to eliminate the harsh doctrine of *Noh*.

* * *

Where the clear implication of a legislative act is to change the common law rule we recognize the modification because the legislature has the power to abrogate the common law. We hold *Noh* to be inconsistent with the constitutionally enunciated policy of optimum development of water resources in the public interest. *Noh* is further inconsistent with the Ground Water Act.

* * *

The Idaho Ground Water Act, I.C. § 42–237a(g) provides in pertinent part:

> " * * * *Water in a well shall not be deemed available to fill a water right therein* if withdrawal therefrom of the amount called for by such right would affect, contrary to the declared policy of this act, the present or future use of any prior surface or ground water right or *result in the withdrawing the ground water supply at a rate*

beyond the reasonably anticipated average rate of future natural recharge." (Emphasis supplied)

We now hold that Idaho's Ground Water Act forbids "mining" of an aquifer. The evidence herein clearly shows that the pumping by all parties was steadily drawing down the water in the aquifer at the rate of 20 ft. per year. Since our statute explicitly forbids such pumping, the district court did not err in enjoining pumping beyond the "reasonably anticipated average rate of future natural recharge."

Perhaps dispositive of this case is the Act's prohibition of ground water "mining." The trial court found that the four senior appropriators would exhaust the aquifer's entire annual recharge. If the junior appropriators were permitted to continue pumping in the amount of their asserted rights they would mine the aquifer. Even so, appellants argue that "under the facts presented, the court of equity should have decreed that each of the parties had a proportional interest in the water resource." Appellants argue that our Act's phrases "reasonable pumping levels" and "full economic development" command a decree granting each of the appropriators, regardless of seniority, a proportionate amount of the aquifer's water.

We reiterate our holding that Idaho's Ground Water Act clearly prohibits the withdrawal of ground water beyond the average rate of future recharge. I.C. § 42–237a(g). In this regard Idaho differs from those of other less fortunate states because we have not yet had to develop legislation regarding withdrawals from non-rechargeable aquifers.

Idaho's Ground Water Act seeks to promote "full economic development" of our ground water resources. I.C. § 42–226. Other western states have enacted analogous ground water legislation enunciating the same policy. We hold that the Ground Water Act is consistent with the constitutionally enunciated policy of promoting optimum development of water resources in the public interest. Idaho Const. art. 15, § 7. Full economic development of Idaho's ground water resources can and will benefit all of our citizens.

* * *

A senior appropriator is only entitled to be protected to the extent of the "reasonable ground water pumping levels" as established by the IDWA. I.C. § 42–226. A senior appropriator is not absolutely protected in either his historic water level or his historic means of diversion. Our Ground Water Act contemplates that in some situations senior appropriators may have to accept some modification of their rights in order to achieve the goal of full economic development.

In the enactment of the Ground Water Act, the Idaho legislature decided, as a matter of public policy, that it may sometimes be necessary to modify private property rights in ground water in order to promote full economic development of the resource. The legislature has said that when private property rights clash with the public interest regarding our limited ground water supplies, in some instances at least, the private interests must recognize that the ultimate goal is the promotion of the welfare of all our citizens. We conclude that our legislature attempted to protect historic water rights while at the same time promoting full development of ground water. Priority rights in ground water are and will be protected insofar as they comply with reasonable pumping levels. Put otherwise, although a senior may have a prior right to ground water, if his means of appropriation demands an unreasonable pumping level his historic means of appropriation will not be protected.

Because of the need for highly technical expertise to accurately measure complex ground water data the legislature has delegated to the IDWA the function of ascertaining reasonable pumping levels. Implicit in this delegation is the recognition that reasonable pumping levels can be modified to conform to changing circumstances. We note that the findings of the IDWA are vested with a presumption of correctness. Idaho's Administrative Procedure Act, I.C. § 67–5215 sets out standards for judicial review of such agency action.

In the case at bar it is apparent under our Ground Water Act that the senior appropriators may enjoin pumping by the junior appropriators to the extent that the additional pumping of the juniors' wells will exceed the "reasonably anticipated average rate of future recharge." The seniors may also enjoin such pumping to the extent that pumping by the juniors may force seniors to go below the "reasonable pumping levels" set by the IDWA.

A necessary concomitant of this statutory matrix is that the senior appropriators are not entitled to relief if the junior appropriators, by pumping from their wells, force seniors to lower their pumps from historic levels to reasonable pumping levels. It should also be noted that those reasonable pumping levels are subject to later modification by the IDWA.

* * *

DONALDSON, C. J., and McQUADE, McFADDEN, and BAKES, JJ., concur.

NOTES

1. The director of water resources, pursuant to the statutory mandate, undertook to calculate the amounts of water that the four senior appropriators had historically pumped. Using a formula based on power company records, the director found that the four senior appropriators had pumped from 28% to 38% less water than they were entitled to under the decrees. Each senior pumper was allowed to pump the amount of water necessary in a dry year so long as the water user did not pump five times his annual historical water use in any consecutive five-year period. The unused water was distributed to the next senior pumper. Procedural problems prevented the supreme court from reaching the issue of whether any excess water allowed under the decree was "water in the bank" for the four seniors to be carried over to future years or was available for redistribution to the juniors. *Briggs v. Golden Valley Land & Cattle Co.*, 546 P.2d 382 (Idaho 1976).

2. Historically, entry into a groundwater basin by new pumpers has been relatively easy, but several western states are tightening

access. For example, the Nevada Supreme Court has ruled that the state engineer may deny an application because a basin is overappropriated when the amount of outstanding rights, not simply the amount of water being pumped, exceeds the estimated perennial yield. Office of the State Engineer v. Morris, 819 P.2d 203 (Nev.1991). The decision's significance is underscored by pending groundwater applications of the Las Vegas Valley Water District. Las Vegas obtains 85% of its water from its 300,000 acre-feet share of the Colorado River. This remnant allocation seemed sufficient in 1928, but it is not adequate for a desert urban area approaching a million people. As part of a $2 billion plan to locate and import 250,000 additional acre-feet, the district has filed for 145 groundwater diversions in rural areas north of the city that extend to the town of Ely. Las Vegas' response is typical supply-side management. See Chapter 7, pages 670–71 for a discussion of demand management approaches to water scarcity.

MATHERS v. TEXACO, INC.

Supreme Court of New Mexico, 1966.
77 N.M. 239, 421 P.2d 771.

LaFel E. Oman, Judge, Court of Appeals.

The applicant-appellant, Texaco, Inc., hereinafter referred to as Texaco, filed applications with the State Engineer for permits to appropriate 700-acre feet of water per year from the Lea County Underground Water Basin. Upon the hearing of the applications and the protests thereto, the respondent-appellant, the State Engineer, hereinafter referred to as the State Engineer, made and entered findings and an order that the applications should be granted for the appropriation by Texaco of 350-acre feet per year for the purpose of water flooding 1,360 acres of oil-bearing formation in a producing oil field. By this water flooding operation, which has been approved by the New Mexico Oil Conservation Commission, it is contemplated that slightly in excess of one million barrels of oil will be recovered.

The protestants-appellees, hereinafter referred to as protestants, who had acquired prior rights to appropriate waters from the Lea County Underground Water Basin, appealed to the district court of Lea County from the findings and order of the State Engineer * * *.

There is no question concerning the following facts:

(1) The use of the water for the proposed flooding of the oil field is a reasonable and beneficial use;

(2) The fresh water in the Lea County Underground Water Basin is found in the Ogalalla formation which varies in thickness from a thin edge to something over 200 feet;

(3) The waters in the basin are replenished only by surface precipitation, which is very limited, and which is just about equalled by a natural discharge from the basin. Thus, for all practical purposes, no recharge takes place, and the pumping of any water from the basin depletes the stock or supply to that extent, and in effect amounts to a mining operation;

(4) In 1952 the State Engineer made a determination of the amount of water in each township in the basin, the amount of water that had been appropriated in each township, and the amount of water that would be drawn from the stock or supply in each township into the surrounding townships, when the waters in the surrounding townships were fully appropriated.

In determining what constitutes full appropriation in each township, and thus in the basin as a whole, he calculated the amount of water that could be withdrawn from each township and still leave one-third of the water in storage at the end of forty years. At that time it was contemplated that some of the remaining water could be economically withdrawn for domestic, and perhaps some other uses, but that it would no longer be economically feasible to withdraw the water for agricultural and most other purposes.

On the basis of this method of administration and operation established in 1952, there remains and is available for appropriation by Texaco the 350-acre feet per year which the State Engineer granted;

(5) The appropriation of the water by Texaco will unquestionably lower the water table in the wells of the protestants, and will result in an increase in pumping costs and in shortening the time during which the protestants can economically pump water from their wells.

* * *

The administration of a non-rechargeable basin, if the waters therein are to be applied to a beneficial use, requires giving to the stock or supply of water a time dimension, or, to state it otherwise, requires the fixing of a rate of withdrawal which will result in a determination of the economic life of the basin at a selected time.

The very nature of the finite stock of water in a non-rechargeable basin compels a modification of the traditional concept of appropriable supply under the appropriation doctrine. Each appropriation from a limited supply of non-replaceable water of necessity reduces the supply in quantity and shortens the time of use to something less than perpetuity. Each appropriator, subsequent to the initial appropriation, reduces in amount, and in time of use, the supply of water available to all prior appropriators, with the consequent decline of the water table, higher pumping costs, and lower yields.

This leads us directly to the main issue on this appeal, and that is whether or not the rights of prior appropriators are impaired, because a subsequent appropriator, by withdrawing waters from a non-rechargeable basin, causes a decline in the water level, higher pumping costs, and lower pumping yields. It was the view of the trial court that the taking of any water from the basin, which could never be replaced, amounted to an impairment of existing rights. He expressed his view in his Finding of Fact No. 11 in the following language:

"The undisputed evidence in the case supports the premise that the taking of any water from the basin depletes the basin to the extent of the amount of water taken, and this can never be replaced. The undisputed evidence clearly shows impairment to existing rights would result from the granting of the Texaco applications."

Protestants take the position that an application for a permit to withdraw waters from an underground basin must be denied if the evidence establishes that such withdrawal will cause a decline in the water table, because prior appropriators will, of necessity:

" * * * be damaged and their rights impaired by the lowering of the water table through the shortening of the useful life of the wells, the additional lift costs and the decline in the ability to produce in proportion to a square, making it necessary to drill more wells to produce the same amount of water. * * * "

If the position of protestants be correct, then Texaco, as stated in its brief in chief,

" * * * shot itself out of the saddle with its own undisputed evidence that the Lea County basin is a *non-rechargeable* basin, that the taking of any water from it constitutes a *mining* operation, and that its appropriation for what the court found was a reasonable and beneficial use could 'never be replaced'."

In fact, if the position of protestants be correct, then each and all of the many permits to withdraw waters from this basin issued by the State Engineer, subsequent to the initial permit, have been issued wrongfully and unlawfully, because each withdrawal, to some degree, has caused a lowering of the water level, and thus an impairment of the rights of the initial appropriator.

* * *

The only premise upon which the position of protestants can be logically supported is that "existing rights" embraces the element of perpetuity. As above stated, the beneficial use by the public of the waters in a closed or non-rechargeable basin requires giving to the use of such waters a time limitation. In the case of the Lea County Underground Water Basin, that time limitation was fixed by the State Engineer in 1952 at forty years, after having first made extensive studies and calculations. There is nothing before us to prompt a feeling that this method of administration and operation does not secure to the public the maximum beneficial use of the waters in this basin.

The rights of the protestants to appropriate water from this basin are subject to this time limitation, just as are the rights of all other appropriators. A lowering of the water level in the wells of protestants, together with the resulting increase in pumping costs and the lowering of pumping yields, does not constitute an impairment of the rights of protestants as a matter of law. These are inevitable results of the beneficial use by the public of these waters.

Section 75–11–3, N.M.S.A.1953, provides in part that:

" * * * the state engineer shall, if he finds that there are in such underground stream, channel, artesian basin, reservoir or lake, unappropriated waters, or that the proposed appropriation would not impair existing water rights from such source, grant the said application and issue a permit to the applicant to appropriate all or a part of the waters applied for subject to the rights of all prior appropriators from said source. * * * "

The State Engineer found that there were unappropriated waters, and that the appropriation granted would not impair existing rights. As above stated, on the basis of the method of administration and operation established in 1952, there were available for appropriation by Texaco the 350-acre feet of water per year.

* * *

The judgment of the trial court overruling and reversing the findings and order of the State Engineer is hereby reversed.

It is so ordered.

MOISE and COMPTON, JJ., concur.

NOTES

1. Does *Mathers* hold that a senior appropriator is entitled to no protection of the ability to maintain pump lift? The New Mexico Supreme Court held in City of Roswell v. Reynolds, 522 P.2d 796 (N.M.1974), that the state engineer could impose certain conditions on the city as junior pumper to protect seniors. Although *Mathers* denies seniors absolute protection against any lowering of pressure in their wells, the court (in *Roswell*) said that "it does not follow that the lowering of the water table may never in itself constitute an impairment of existing rights."

2. The court's decision in *Mathers* prompts two questions: (1) Why should any groundwater mining be allowed (in contrast to *Baker* which disallowed mining)? (2) If mining is allowed, on what legal basis could the state engineer place limits on appropriations so long as there is unappropriated water? What considerations might lead an administrator to choose a forty year aquifer life? Consider the language of the respective statutes and the different physical situations in each case.

3. New Mexico has a long tradition of strong groundwater administration. In 1890 a large artesian aquifer was discovered in the Pecos Valley near Roswell. Farmers immediately drilled wells that flowed day and night. Just as the flaring of natural gas led to pressure for conservation legislation, uncapped artesian wells ultimately led to legislation to prevent waste. After the Wichita Federal Land Bank indicated that it would not lend in the valley because of waste, civic leaders in Roswell came to the conclusion that an administrative system employing elements of prior appropriation should be applied to limit pumping. Robert G. Dunbar, *Forging New Rights in Western Waters* 162–72 (1983). Legislation was passed in 1927 allowing the state engineer to designate basins within the state that would be subject to appropriation. The state supreme court declared the legislation unconstitutional because of technical defects in its passage, though it saw no impediment to limiting landowners' rights in favor of appropriators. Yeo v. Tweedy, 286 P. 970 (N.M.1929).

2. Permit Systems

Minnesota has the most extensive regulation of agricultural groundwater withdrawals in the midwestern United States. All major agricultural withdrawals require a state permit. The state has five priorities or, more accurately, preferences. The first is for domestic use "excluding industrial and commercial uses of municipal water supply," the second is for any use that requires less than 10,000 gallons per day, the third is for agricultural irrigation in excess of 10,000 gallons per day and the use of water for food processing, the fourth is for power production and the fifth is for all other uses in excess of 10,000 gallons per day. Minn. Stat. Ann. § 105.41. The statute specifies two classes of agricultural use permits. Class A permits are required for areas in which adequate groundwater data exist. Class B permits are for all other areas and require the applicant to submit extensive data as a precondition to a permit. Class A or Class B permits may be issued only where the commissioner of natural resources "determines that proposed soil and water conservation measures are adequate based on recommendations of the soil and water conservation districts and that water supply is available for the proposed use without reducing water levels beyond the reach of vicinity wells constructed in accordance with the water well construction code * * * ." Minn. Stat. Ann. § 105.416. What allocation rule has Minnesota adopted? The constitutionality of the statute was upheld in Crookston Cattle Co. v. Minnesota Dep't of Natural Resources, 300 N.W.2d 769 (Minn. 1980).

Due to Florida's geology, 92% of its residents consume groundwater from its extensive aquifers, and it is not surprising that Florida has recently experimented with sophisticated conservation legislation. The aquifers have a high rate of recharge, but over-rapid pumping causes salt water intrusion or other contamination. In response to these problems, the Florida Water Resources Act of 1972, Fla. Stat. Ann. § 373.013 et seq. (based on a model code drafted by the late Frank E. Maloney), creates a permit system for groundwater withdrawals and creates districts with the taxing authority to undertake recharge programs. Id. at § 373.106. The Florida Supreme Court sustained the permit authority against a challenge that it was an unconstitutional taking of property and held that regulation was necessary to protect the correlative rights of aquifer users. Village of Tequesta v. Jupiter Inlet Corp., 371 So.2d 663 (Fla.1979), cert. denied 444 U.S. 965 (1979). The districts must set minimum groundwater levels beyond which further withdrawals would be significantly harmful to the water resources of the area, § 373.042, and may issue twenty-year renewable permits for reasonable beneficial uses. §§ 373.219–223.

The criteria for the issuance of permits are set forth in the following sections:

373.223　Conditions for a permit

(1) To obtain a permit pursuant to the provisions of this chapter, the applicant must establish that the proposed use of water:

(a) Is a reasonable-beneficial use as defined in § 373.019(4); and

(b) Will not interfere with any presently existing legal use of water; and

(c) Is consistent with the public interest.

(2) The governing board or the department may authorize the holder of a use permit to transport and use ground or surface water beyond overlying land across county boundaries, or outside the watershed from which it is taken if the governing board or department determines that such transport and use is consistent with the public interest, and no local government shall adopt or enforce any law, ordinance, rule, regulation, or order to the contrary.

(3) The governing board or the department by regulation may reserve from use by permit applicants water in such locations and quantities, and for such seasons of the year, as in its judgment may be required for the protection of fish and wildlife or the public health and safety. Such reservations shall be subject to periodic review and revision in the light of changed conditions. However, all presently existing legal uses of water shall be protected so long as such use is not contrary to the public interest.

373.233 Competing applications

(1) If two or more applications which otherwise comply with the provisions of this part are pending for a quantity of water that is inadequate for both or all, or which for any other reason are in conflict, the governing board or the department shall have the right to approve or modify the application which best serves the public interest.

(2) In the event that two or more competing applications qualify equally under the provisions of subsection (1), the governing board or the department shall give preference to a renewal application over an initial application.

Rule 17–40 Fla. Admin. Code, adopted in lieu of a state plan, sets out seventeen factors including "other relevant factors" that are to be considered in deciding what is a reasonable beneficial use. Florida's water management law is breaking new ground in the coordination of water supplies and land development. The power of a city to use zoning to preserve an adequate drinking water supply and general aquifer ecosystem stability was upheld in Moviematic Indus. Corp. v. Board of Cty. Comm'rs of Metropolitan Dade Cty., 349 So.2d 667 (Fla. App. 1977).

Proponents of prior appropriation argue that courts will almost inevitably protect prior users regardless of the state's allocation rule. Florida law supports this thesis. The drafters of the Florida code were hostile to the "wasteful" doctrine of prior appropriation and rejected it. However, under the permit system, an applicant must prove that a proposed withdrawal is a reasonable and beneficial use of water and that it will not interfere with existing uses. The intent was that priority would be a non-determinative factor in water allocation. Frank E. Maloney, et al., A Model Water Code With Commentary 159–

60 (1972). Nevertheless, Harloff v. City of Sarasota, 575 So.2d 1324, 1328 (Fla.App.1991), holds that permittees enjoy "superiority" over subsequent applicants. The court protected municipal well field pressure levels from a 1.7 foot drop in the water table by substantially reducing an 8,500–acre agricultural user's application.

Indiana requires persons who want to begin or increase pumping more than 100,000 gallons per day to obtain a permit subject to the following conditions:

> (c) In granting or refusing a permit, the department shall consider the effect the withdrawal of additional ground water from the restricted use area will have on future supplies in the area, what use is to be made of the water, how it will affect present users of ground water in the area, whether the future natural replenishment is likely to become more or less, whether future demands for ground water are likely to be greater or less, and how the withdrawal of additional ground waters will affect the health and best interests of the public.

> (d) In granting a permit, the department may impose such conditions or stipulations as may be necessary to conserve the ground waters of the area and prevent their waste, exhaustion, or impairment.

> (e) In regard to withdrawing and using water taken from the ground in the restricted area referred to in this chapter, the department may require such water to be returned to the ground through wells, pits, or spreading grounds and if this condition is imposed by the department, the water shall be returned under such rules as the department may adopt subject to the approval of the water pollution control board in order to avoid pollution of underground water.

Ind. Code Ann. § 13–2–2–5. Further, the agency director can declare groundwater emergencies whenever there is a substantial lowering of groundwater levels so that wells fail to produce their normal supplies of water. In such emergencies, the director can restrict large pumpers if their pumping is reasonably believed to have caused other wells to fail, and no replacement of natural withdrawals could exceed natural recharge capabilities.

What are the limits of a state's legitimate interests in groundwater regulation? It is now clear that the state may not restrict interstate commerce in groundwater (and other water resources). Sporhase v. Nebraska ex rel. Douglas, 458 U.S. 941 (1982), page 748, infra. Constitutionally valid state groundwater regulation that affects interstate commerce must be based on health and welfare considerations, not economic protectionism. The Supreme Court also suggested that Congress has the power to preempt state groundwater regulation should it choose: "Groundwater overdraft is a national problem and Congress has the power to deal with it on that scale." 458 U.S. at 954.

A particular type of permit statute, considered in the following subsection, identifies areas of particular public concern and targets them for special management.

3. Special Groundwater Management Districts

FUNDINGSLAND v. COLORADO GROUND WATER COMMISSION

Supreme Court of Colorado, 1970.
171 Colo. 487, 468 P.2d 835.

PRINGLE, JUSTICE.

On September 2, 1966, Mr. Fundingsland (hereinafter referred to as the plaintiff) filed an application with the Colorado Ground Water Commission (hereinafter referred to as the commission) for a permit to drill a well on certain property located in the Northern High Plains Designated Ground Water Basin in Kit Carson County. No objections to the application were filed. On February 27, 1967, the plaintiff's application was denied by the commission on the basis that there was over appropriation in the area where the well was to be drilled. The plaintiff objected to the ruling of the commission, and a hearing was held before the commission on December 12, 1967. As the result of the hearing the commission sustained its previous denial of the plaintiff's application. * * *

The plaintiff appealed the decision of the commission to the district court, and a trial de novo was held with expert testimony being presented by both the plaintiff and the commission. * * * Under [the Ground Water Management Act, page 532, infra] the commission is empowered to deny an application if it finds that the proposed appropriation will unreasonably impair existing water rights from the same source, or will create unreasonable waste. * * *

[T]he trial court determined that a so-called three mile test provided a reasonable basis for assessing the effect of a proposed use on other users in the district. The three mile test was developed for use in the Northern High Plains. It is partly based on policy and partly based on fact and theory. Using that test, a circle with a three mile radius is drawn around the proposed well site. A rate of pumping is determined which would result in a 40% depletion of the available ground water in that area over a period of 25 years. If that rate of pumping is being exceeded by the existing wells within the circle, then the application for a permit to drill a new well may be denied.

The three mile test takes into account all of the considerations specified in the statute. The factors involved in the three mile test were explained to the court by Mr. Erker, senior engineer in the ground water section of the State Engineer's office. He testified that the three mile circle represents the area over which a well, located at the center, would have an effect if permitted to pump intermittently for 25 years. Intermittent pumping, he explained, meant approximately 100 days per year. Other factors which are considered are the saturated thickness of the aquifer within the three mile circle, the number of wells located within the circle, and the yield of those wells. Multiplying the number of wells within the circle times the yield of those wells gives the total, present appropriation within the three mile circle.

Mr. Romero, an assistant water resource engineer for the State of Colorado Division of Water Resources, testified that the modified Theiss equation was used in determining what the draw down effect on the water in the aquifer would be within the three mile circle. He further testified that in determining the balance of water in the aquifer, he considered the fact that there was only intermittent pumping, the amount of recharge to the aquifer due to precipitation and ground water inflow from outlying areas, recharge due to excess irrigation, and possibly recharge from some other source such as leakage from ditches or rivers.

There does not seem to be any contention that the 40% depletion figure is unreasonable or irrational. The assumption in the three mile test is that a 40% depletion of the aquifer within that area would constitute lowering of the water balance beyond reasonable economic limits of withdrawal or use for irrigation.

Likewise, the selection of 25 years as the period during which the 40% depletion is to be allowed is not contested. Mr. Leslie, a farm and ranch loan representative for Northwestern Mutual Life Insurance Company, testified that 25 years was a reasonable, average period in which a loan for the construction of well facilities would have to be repaid.

The testimony and other evidence in the record before the district court support the reasonableness of the three mile test and establish that the three mile test takes into account the factors specified by the statute. If the three mile test was a proper method for the court to use in determining the effect of plaintiff's proposed use on the ground water supply in the district, then the decision of the district court must be upheld.

* * *

The plaintiff calls our attention to Article XVI, Section 6 of the Colorado Constitution which provides: "The right to divert the unappropriated waters of any natural stream to beneficial uses shall never be denied." We find, however, that the record clearly supports the finding that there is no unappropriated water within the three mile circle surrounding the plaintiff's proposed well site.

Ground water existing in designated underground water basins is made subject to the doctrine of prior appropriation by 1965 Perm.Supp., C.R.S.1963, 148–18–1 [now codified at Colo. Rev. Stat. § 37–90–102]. The statute further provides:

" * * * While the doctrine of prior appropriation is recognized, such doctrine should be modified to permit the full economic development of designated ground water resources. Prior appropriations of ground water should be protected and reasonable ground water pumping levels maintained, but not to include the maintenance of historical water levels. * * * "

Underground water basins require management that is different from the management of surface streams and underground waters tributary to such streams. In the case of the latter waters, seasonal regulation of diversion by junior appropriators can effectively protect the interests of more senior appropriators and no long range harm can come of over appropriations since the streams are subject to seasonal recharge. The underground water dealt with by 148–18–1 is not subject to the same ready replenishment enjoyed by surface streams and tributary ground water. It is possible for water to be withdrawn from the aquifer in a rate in excess of the annual recharge creating what is called a mining condition. Unless the rate of pumping is regulated, mining must ultimately result in lowering the water balance below a level from which water may be economically withdrawn. Due to the slow rate at which underground waters flow through and into the aquifer, it may be many years before a reasonable water level may be restored to a mined aquifer.

It is clear that the policies of protecting senior appropriators and maintaining reasonable ground water pumping levels set forth by the underground water act require management which takes into account the long range effects of intermittent pumping in the aquifer. In this case all of the experts testifying before the commission and the district court were in agreement that a mining condition exists in the Northern High Plains Designated Ground Water Basin. The commission has determined that proper use of the ground water resource requires that the mining be allowed to continue. However, the maximum allowable rate of depletion, at least when considering applications for permits to drill new wells, has been set at 40% depletion in 25 years. We have pointed out that the depletion rate in the area which would be affected by the plaintiff's proposed well is in excess of the rate allowed by the commission and approved by the district court.

If the plaintiff were permitted to proceed on his theory of "unappropriated water" and pump water from his proposed well until such time as it was no longer economically feasible to withdraw water from the aquifer, then no subsequent regulation of his pumping could protect senior appropriators, and all pumping from the basin within the area of influence of the plaintiff's well would have to cease until a reasonable pumping level was restored through the slow process of recharge. This is not the concept of appropriation contained in the statute, and not the one this Court will follow.

When, as in this case, water is being mined from the ground water basin, and a proposed appropriation would result in unreasonable harm to senior appropriators, then a determination that there is no water available for appropriation is justified.

* * *

NOTE

In drawing the mining circle, Colorado has excluded land in Nebraska thus reducing the volume which determines if there is a sufficient Colorado water supply for new entrants. Thompson v. Colorado

Groundwater Comm'n, 575 P.2d 372 (Colo.1978) upheld the exclusion of 24% of the circle on the ground that the rule was a reasonable means of protecting senior appropriators against injury, fostering the full economic development of resources and conserving designated groundwater resources:

> Expert testimony supported the commission's position that overappropriation of the aquifer at the state line, with the intent to stabilize or reverse the aquifer flow to the benefit of Colorado, would seriously injure vested Colorado rights far west of the state line and could ignite a destructive aquifer depletion race with Nebraska, an adjoining state. Evidence that a portion of Colorado's ground water naturally flows into adjoining states, when considered in the context of the commission's overall ground water policy, does not establish a breach of statutory duty by the commission in its determination.

Groundwater pumping in Colorado is intense along the Nebraska border. Nebraska has a procedure to designate critical areas, but regulation remains in the hands of local districts and pumping has not yet been curtailed. See generally J. David Aiken and Raymond J. Supalla, *Ground Water Mining and Western Water Rights Law: The Nebraska Experience*, 24 S.D.L.Rev. 607 (1979).

NOTE: STATUTORY CONTROL OF GROUNDWATER IN COLORADO

As discussed above, groundwater in Colorado is presumed to be tributary to a natural stream. Safranek v. Limon, 228 P.2d 975 (Colo.1951). Tributary groundwater is administered as part of the state's prior appropriation system. See pages 511–12, supra. But if the "rate or direction of movement of water" in a natural stream will not be affected, the water is "non-tributary" and outside the appropriation system. As such, it may be in a "designated basin" under the Ground water Management Act as in Fundingsland, or it may be administered under a statutory scheme for "non-tributary, non-designated" groundwater.

Tributary or Non-Tributary? A one-hundred year limit on the effects necessary to establish tributariness has been embraced by the state supreme court. Where effects are felt within forty years, groundwater was held to be tributary. Hall v. Kuiper, 510 P.2d 329 (Colo. 1973). It is not necessary that groundwater actually reach the stream in 100 years, only that streamflow be affected. District 10 Water Users Ass'n v. Barnett, 599 P.2d 894 (Colo.1979) (groundwater would reach stream in 171 years but pumping would affect stream in forty years). What about effects felt in fifty years? ninety years?

The Ground water Management Act. For many years, non-tributary groundwater was not within any regulatory scheme in Colorado. Accordingly, in 1963 the supreme court refused to uphold an adjudication of priorities among non-tributary groundwater pumpers. It found that the deep aquifers there in question were outside the scope of the presumption of tributariness and hence were outside the appropriation system. Whitten v. Coit, 385 P.2d 131 (Colo.1963). The court in *Whitten* alluded to the reasonable use rule as controlling rights among competing users, but in absence of statute there was no administrative or regulatory system to control mining. Legislation passed in 1957 dealt only with well drilling.

In 1965 Colorado enacted the Ground Water Management Act. Colo. Rev. Stat. §§ 37–90–102 et seq. The Act subjected designated groundwater basins to principles of prior appropriation "modified to permit the full economic development of designated ground water resources." Rights to pump groundwater are determined administratively after a quasi-judicial proceeding. The constitutionality of this proceeding was upheld in Larrick v. North Kiowa Bijou Management Dist., 510 P.2d 323 (Colo.1973). The manner of acquiring rights to use groundwater in designated basins is specified:

> (1) Any person desiring to appropriate ground water for a beneficial use in a designated ground water basin shall make application to the commission in a form to be prescribed by the commission. * * *

> (3) After the expiration of the time for filing objections, if no such objections have been filed, the commission shall, if it finds that the proposed appropriation will not unreasonably impair existing water rights from the same source, and will not create unreasonable waste, grant the said application, and the state engineer shall issue a conditional permit to the applicant to appropriate all or a part of the waters applied for subject to such reasonable conditions and limitations as the commission may specify.

> * * *

> (5) In ascertaining whether a proposed use will create unreasonable waste or unreasonably affect the rights of other appropriators, the commission shall take into consideration the area and geologic conditions, the average annual yield and recharge rate of the appropriate water supply, the priority and quantity of existing claims of all persons to use the water, the proposed method of use, and all other matters appropriate to such questions. With regard to whether a proposed use will impair uses under existing water rights, impairment shall include the unreasonable lowering of the water level, or the unreasonable deterioration of water quality, beyond reasonable economic limits of withdrawal or use.

Colo. Rev. Stat. § 37–90–107.

The Ground Water Management Act created a two-level system of administrative regulation. The Ground Water Commission is authorized to create "designated groundwater basins." No finding of overdraft need be made. Groundwater management districts may be formed "to regulate the use, control, and conservation" of groundwater in the district. The statutory powers of the Commission must be exercised in consultation with districts in areas where they have been formed. Those powers include:

(a) To supervise and control the exercise and administration of all rights acquired to the use of designated ground water. In the exercise of this power it may, by summary order, prohibit or limit withdrawal of water from any well during any period that it determines that such withdrawal of water from said well would cause unreasonable injury to prior appropriators; except that nothing in this article shall be construed as entitling any prior designated ground water appropriator to the maintenance of the historic water level or any other level below which water still can be economically extracted when the total economic pattern of the particular designated ground water basin is considered; and further except that no such order shall take effect until six months after its entry.

(b) To establish a reasonable ground water pumping level in an area having a common designated ground water supply. Water in wells shall not be deemed available to fill the water right therefor if withdrawal therefrom of the amount called for by such right would, contrary to the declared policy of this article, unreasonably affect any prior water right, or result in withdrawing the ground water supply at a rate materially in excess of the reasonably anticipated average rate of future recharge.

* * *

(e) To order the total or partial discontinuance of any diversion within a ground water basin to the extent the water being diverted is not necessary for application to a beneficial use;

* * *

Colo. Rev. Stat. § 37–90–111.

Where a groundwater management district has been formed, the district board promulgates rules and regulations that set the essential limits on groundwater withdrawals such as allowable depletion rates. The need to obtain permission from the district to divert designated groundwater was demonstrated in State ex rel. Danielson v. Vickroy, 627 P.2d 752 (Colo. 1981). Vickroy applied to the water court to change the point of diversion for a 1922 appropriation from a surface source to a well. The North Kiowa-Bijou Groundwater Management District objected because Vickroy proposed to take designated groundwater. The state and the District filed suit in another district court which enjoined the change of diversion point, and the injunction was sustained on appeal. As a matter of statutory policy "any relief sought which involves the taking of ground water in a designated ground water basin must be sought first through administrative and judicial channels, as appropriate, prescribed for resolution of questions arising under the Management Act. * * * Only if such proceedings result in a determination that a water matter is at issue can the jurisdiction of the water court be invoked." Id. at 760.

The power of the Ground Water Commission to coordinate ground and surface rights within a designated basin was reaffirmed in Pioneer Irr. Dist. v. Danielson, 658 P.2d 842 (Colo. 1983).

The Ground Water Management Act has been applied only in the eastern plains of Colorado. Primarily deep, non-tributary agricultural wells in the Ogallala Aquifer are affected. Eight groundwater basins have been designated under the Act and thirteen groundwater management districts have been formed. An amendment to the law prevents designation of groundwater in the Denver Basin, leaving tremendous non-tributary groundwater reserves outside the Act.

Non–Tributary, Non–Designated Groundwater. In anticipation of an energy boom creating new demands for water, several parties asserted rights to acquire rights to over 20 million acre-feet of deep, non-tributary groundwater. The sources were outside designated groundwater basins and at the time statutory law addressed such "non-tributary, non-designated" groundwater only by requiring a well permit. Language in the permit statute allowed such groundwater to be pumped at a rate that would not deplete the water that underlies the land owned by the applicant in less than 100 years. The dearth of statutory treatment left room for applicants to argue that this groundwater was subject to prior appropriation. Others in the case argued that it was the property of the overlying landowners. Some water court judges (who have jurisdiction over surface water appropriation) had assumed jurisdiction to adjudicate rights to non-tributary, non-designated groundwater, but had recognized control by the overlying landowner. Under either theory, vast stores of groundwater would be claimed by a few interests who hoped to market the water to the energy industry. The cases were consolidated in a huge case that the supreme court assigned to a water judge.

Reviewing the lower court's determination of many issues, the Colorado Supreme Court concluded that only the well permit process applied to rights in non-tributary groundwater:

> We believe that, given the state's plenary control over development of water law, the traditional property concept of fee ownership is of limited usefulness as applied to nontributary ground water and serves to mislead rather than to advance understanding in considering public and private rights to utilization of this unique resource. * * * Nontributary ground water is not subject to appropriation under *Colo. Const.* Art. XVI, §§ 5 and 6, or to adjudication or administration under the 1969 Act. The modified doctrine of prior appropriation provided for in the 1965 Act applies to nontributary ground water, and rights to such water in designated ground water basins must be obtained through the procedures established in that Act. Rights to nontributary ground water not located in a designated basin may be obtained only through application for a well permit from the state engineer under section 37–90–137 of the 1965 Act.

State of Colorado, Dept. of Natural Resources v. Southwestern Colorado Water Conservation Dist., 671 P.2d 1294, 1316 (Colo.1983) (The *Huston* case).

After the so-called *Huston* case, in 1984, the General Assembly addressed the issue of how to allocate non-tributary groundwater. First, it clarified the definition of non-tributary groundwater as "that ground water, located outside the boundaries of any designated ground water basins * * * the withdrawal of which will not, within one hundred years, deplete the flow of any natural stream * * * at an annual rate greater than one tenth of one percent of the annual rate of withdrawal." Colo. Rev. Stat. § 37–90–103(10.5). The most significant legislative pronouncement, contrary to the recommendations of a blue-ribbon commission appointed by the Governor, was that rights in non-tributary groundwater are to be allocated according to overlying land-ownership. Colo. Rev. Stat. § 37–90–137(4)(b)(II).

Well permitting provisions were also expanded in the 1984 Colorado legislation. The clause prohibiting harm to vested rights was retained, but the amendment deemed that injury does not occur as the result of lowering hydrostatic pressure or water levels. Colo. Rev. Stat. § 37–90–137(4)(b)(II). Water courts were given authority to adjudicate rights in non-tributary groundwater, though the state engineer is authorized to make rules and regulations pertaining to permitting. Colo. Rev. Stat. § 37–90–139(a) and (b).

Special rules under detailed statutory specifications apply to the copious Denver Basin aquifers. Colo. Rev. Stat. § 37–90–137(9)(c). All groundwater in the four Denver Basin aquifers is declared non-tributary although they in fact contribute about 50,000 acre-feet of water per year to the South Platte River. Any wells that will withdraw groundwater that is not non-tributary require a plan for augmentation. Normally an augmentation plan replenishes water to avoid all injury to senior rights holders. See page 344, supra. But the requirement of protecting seniors from all injurious depletions caused by withdrawals of Denver Basin water applies only within one mile of a stream. Beyond one mile a pumper need only replace a flat 4% of the amount annually pumped from the well back to the affected stream, regardless of actual losses. By regulation, the state engineer draws an outside boundary for the 4% "not non-tributary" replenishment zone, beyond which the rules may require up to 2% replenishment for non-tributary groundwater pumping. This recognizes that nearly all water pumped in the basin is partially tributary. The state engineer's rules consist largely of maps that enable a well permit applicant to determine the applicable replacement duty: 2%, 4%, or the amount of actual effects on seniors.

NOTE: LOCAL DISTRICT CONTROL OF GROUNDWATER

Some states have opted for special management of groundwater by districts, but have vested primary authority in local agencies rather than with a state administrative official or boards. Agricultural users in states such as Kansas, Nebraska and Texas have opposed statewide management, and the courts have refused to develop allocation rules. To conserve groundwater, therefore, these states rely on local management initiatives.

Kansas, which applies the law of prior appropriation to groundwater, authorized the creation of local districts with the power to adopt local management programs, subject to state approval. Kan. Stat. Ann.

§§ 82a–1020 to 82a–1035.　Several such districts have been created in western and south-central Kansas.　Well-spacing requirements to protect existing pumpers have generally been applied, and some districts have adopted safe yield policies resulting in pumping limitations.　Professor John Peck of the University of Kansas has described the safe yield program in the Equus Beds Groundwater Management District (GMD), northwest of Wichita:

> The safe yield policy is found in the statement that "a balance will be maintained between recharge to the Equus Beds and total groundwater withdrawals (discharge) from the Equus Beds."　To accomplish safe yield, the GMD bases its recommendation for approval or denial of an application permit on a two-mile radius formula as follows:　(1) a circle with a radius of two miles is drawn around the proposed well, and within the circle all of the existing wells as shown on prior applications for permits, certificates of appropriation, or vested rights are totalled as to annual quantity;　(2) that annual quantity is added to the quantity of water requested in the application;　(3) if the total quantity found by the addition in (2) is less than 4025 acre-feet, approval of the application will be recommended, if it meets other criteria;　if the total is greater than 4025 acre-feet, denial of the application will be recommended, unless it is the quantity of the proposed well that puts the total over 4025 acre-feet, in which case the GMD may recommend a quantity that would make the withdrawals equal 4025 acre-feet.
>
> The 4025 acre-feet is the average amount of recharge within an average two mile radius circle in the GMD.　This amount is calculated by assuming that out of an average rainfall of thirty inches, twenty percent or six inches returns to the aquifer as recharge.

John C. Peck, *Kansas Groundwater Management Districts*, 29 U.Kan. L.Rev. 51, 75–76 (1980).

A number of other states apply Kansas's circle method for assessing the potential impacts of a well.　Professor Peck points out that circle size can have a substantial effect on pumping entitlements:　"[A]n applicant might be denied a permit if his requested amount were totalled with existing amounts in a small radius circle because the combined total might exceed the allowable figure.　Yet he might be granted a permit if his requested amount were added to existing amounts in a larger circle, even though the density of existing wells were the same in both circles."　Id. at 86.

In 1975 Nebraska, which applies a combination of correlative rights and appropriative rights to groundwater, authorized Natural Resources Districts to establish groundwater "control areas."　Neb. Rev. Stat. §§ 46–656 to 46–674.　Control areas may be approved by the State Department of Water Resources after a finding that:　(1) the use of groundwater has caused, or is likely to cause, supplies to be inadequate to meet present or reasonably foreseeable future needs;　or (2) there is a risk of quality degradation due to groundwater mining.　Establishment of a control area is a strong step in Nebraska, and the Director of the

Department has refused to designate control areas where the effect on pumping has merely been a seasonal reduction of artesian pressure, not amounting to groundwater mining. J. David Aiken, *Nebraska Ground Water Law and Administration*, 59 Neb.L.Rev. 917, 960–66 (1980). Within designated control areas, well-spacing restrictions, pumping rotations, quantity allocations, transfer restrictions, and well-drilling moratoria may be imposed. Once a control area is established, a state permit is required for new wells, but a permit application can only be denied if approval would violate a condition imposed by a Natural Resources District. Nebraska, unlike Colorado (see pages 532–36, supra), has not yet chosen to coordinate ground and surface rights and thus rights of surface appropriators are not a consideration.

Until recent years, Texas regulated groundwater use only through voluntarily created local water districts, despite years of warnings about the need to conserve water in the High Plains and other parts of the state. Both the state supreme court and the legislature long refused to modify the absolute ownership rule in any significant way. In 1985, however, Texas voters approved a water resources development and conservation package that included some modest indirect controls on groundwater usage. Groundwater districts may be enlarged and the state may now designate "critical areas" after a study and hearing process. Districts are formed by special or general legislation. District powers are expanded to include the purchase and sale of either surface or groundwater. More records on well drilling and use of groundwater are now required. To curb excessive pumping, the districts rely on education programs to induce irrigators to use more efficient cropping and irrigation methods. See also the recent decision of the Texas Water Commission to treat the Edwards Aquifer as an underground stream in order to squeeze it under the Commission's regulatory jurisdiction, pages 490–91, supra.

4. Legislative Redefinition of Rights

TOWN OF CHINO VALLEY v. CITY OF PRESCOTT
Supreme Court of Arizona, 1981.
131 Ariz. 78, 638 P.2d 1324.
Appeal dismissed, 457 U.S. 1101, 102 S.Ct. 2897, 73 L.Ed.2d 1310 (1982).

STRUCKMEYER, CHIEF JUSTICE.

* * *

The Town of Chino Valley lies approximately fifteen miles north of the City of Prescott in Yavapai County, Arizona. Prescott owns 164 acres of land in the Chino Valley. In 1948, it drilled wells on some of its Chino Valley property and began transporting groundwater through a seventeen-mile pipeline to its municipal customers. In 1962, pursuant to a petition by Chino Valley residents and A.R.S. § 45–301 et seq., the State Land Department established the Granite Creek Critical Groundwater Area. On September 20, 1970, the Town was incorporated. It was within the Granite Creek Critical Groundwater Area and it owned lands and was withdrawing groundwater from the same underground basin as Prescott. Prescott, itself, was not within the Granite Creek Critical Groundwater Area.

This action was filed on August 21, 1972, seeking to enjoin the pumping of groundwater by Prescott. It did not seek damages for the unlawful pumping or transportation of groundwaters. The lawsuit proceeded at a desultory pace until the order of dismissal on November 3, 1980. Meanwhile, in 1977 the Legislature amended the Arizona Groundwater Code. The Town in 1978 brought an original action in this Court which challenged the constitutionality of the prohibitions against injunctive relief contained in the 1977 amendments. That challenge was rejected. Town of Chino Valley v. State Land Department, 119 Ariz. 243, 580 P.2d 740 (1978).

Thereafter, in June of 1980, the Legislature enacted the Groundwater Management Act, herein called the Act or the 1980 Act.* It repealed the 1977 amendments and abolished critical groundwater areas, substituting geographic units of groundwater management called Active Management Areas and Irrigation Non-Expansion Areas. Certain areas which had been declared critical groundwater areas under former laws were included in the Active Management Areas. By A.R.S. § 45–411(A)(3), the Prescott Active Management Area was established. It includes the Little Chino and Upper Agua Fria Sub-basins.

---

* The 1980 Act provided for the establishment of Active Management Areas which are geographical areas where groundwater supplies are imperiled. A.R.S. §§ 45–411 to 45–637. Active Management Areas encompass a whole groundwater basin or basins. A.R.S. § 45–412(B). Groundwater basins are areas designated as enclosing a relatively hydrologically distinct body or related bodies of groundwater. A.R.S. § 45–402(10). Groundwater sub-basins are areas designated so to enclose a smaller hydrologically distinct body of groundwater found within a groundwater basin. A.R.S. § 45–402(25).

The 1980 Act provides limitations on use of groundwater in Active Management Areas. In general the Act restricts new uses of water drawn from Active Management Areas. The Act sets up a system of determining grandfathered rights to use groundwater in Active Management Areas, A.R.S. §§ 45–461 to 45–482, defining certain usages of groundwater previously being made and allowing these usages to continue. A.R.S. § 45–462. The Act also establishes the rights of cities, towns, private water companies and irrigation districts in Active Management Areas to withdraw as much groundwater as is needed from within their service areas to serve their customers although restrictions are provided on extensions of service areas and the types of service that may be provided by these entities. A.R.S. § 45–491. The Act also specifies a few other new uses of groundwater that may be made in Active Management Areas. It allows limited new withdrawals for domestic purposes. A.R.S. § 45–454. It also sets up a system for obtaining permits to withdraw new amounts of water for certain specific purposes. A.R.S. §§ 45–511 to 45–528.

Provided withdrawal is permitted under any of the provisions of the Act, transportation of groundwater within the same sub-basin may be made without payment of damages. A.R.S. § 45–541. Transportation of groundwater between sub-basins or away from Active Management Areas is also authorized if the groundwater is allowed to be withdrawn under the Act's provisions, but damages must be paid for any injury caused. A.R.S. §§ 45–542, 45–543. Rules for determining damage are set out in A.R.S. § 45–545. The transportation rules apply whether in or outside of Active Management Areas, A.R.S. § 45–544, although the restrictions on new uses of groundwater do not apply outside of Active Management Areas. A.R.S. § 45–453.

The Act provides for conservation for all uses of groundwater in Active Management Areas. A.R.S. §§ 45–561 to 45–579. The Act ends with provisions governing the drilling and registering of wells for withdrawing groundwater, A.R.S. §§ 45–591 to 45–604, and financial and enforcement provisions to carry out the legislation, A.R.S. §§ 45–611 to 45–615, 45–631 to 45–637.

Both the Town of Chino Valley and Prescott are within the Little Chino Sub-basin of the Prescott Active Management Area.

By A.R.S. § 45–541(A) of the 1980 Act, transportation of groundwater is allowed within a sub-basin of an Active Management Area. Prescott, being within the Little Chino Sub-basin from which it was drawing water, moved for dismissal of the Town's complaint for injunctive relief. The Superior Court granted Prescott's motion, but ordered that the Town have twenty days in which to file an amended complaint specifying any damages. The Town's appeal from that portion of the trial court's order dismissing appellants' claim for injunctive relief is based upon the asserted unconstitutionality of the Act of 1980 since the Act, by permitting the transportation of groundwater, legitimatizes the prospective withdrawal of groundwater from the Little Chino Sub-basin by Prescott. Appellants' principal attack is that the Act takes property without due process of law and without just compensation. The Act is also challenged on the grounds that it is a legislative encroachment on judicial powers and that it violates art. 4, part 2, § 13 of the Arizona Constitution in that there are provisions in the Act of 1980 which were not included in the title of the Act.

By the Constitution of Arizona, art. 17, § 1, effective at statehood in 1912, it was provided that the common law doctrine of riparian water rights "shall not obtain or be of any force or effect in the State." Thereafter, in 1919, the Arizona Legislature provided that the water of all sources falling in streams, canyons, ravines, natural channels or definite underground channels belonged to the public and were subject to appropriation for beneficial use. Waters percolating beneath the soil were not included among those subject to appropriation. Appellants rely on the cases of Howard v. Perrin, 8 Ariz. 347, 76 P. 460 (1904), and Maricopa County Water Conservation District No. 1 v. Southwest Cotton Co., 39 Ariz. 65, 4 P.2d 369 (1931), for their basic proposition that they own the water percolating beneath their lands under the doctrine of reasonable use.

The Territorial Supreme Court, in *Howard v. Perrin*, commented:

"Throughout the Pacific Coast, where the doctrine of appropriation obtains, the decisions are uniform to the effect that waters percolating generally through the soil beneath the surface are the property of the owner of the soil * * *." 8 Ariz. at 353, 76 P. at 462.

Howard v. Perrin was a case in which Howard's grantor went upon unsurveyed lands and sank a well, developing a flow of water which he conducted to some water troughs and a reservoir. About six years later, Howard posted a notice that he had appropriated water from a definite underground channel pursuant to the Laws of 1893, Act 86. The issue was whether the waters which Howard claimed to have appropriated were in a definite underground channel or, as the court said: "constituted a running stream flowing in natural channels between well-defined banks * * *." 8 Ariz. at 353, 76 P. at 462. It was held that Howard, having alleged an appropriable subterranean stream, had the burden of proof to establish that fact by competent evidence. The court said it failed "to find sufficient evidence in the testimony of the witnesses * * * to establish the existence of 'a subterranean stream with well-defined channels or banks,' * * *." Id. at 354, 76 P. at 463. Palpably the statement that waters percolating through the soil beneath the surface are the property of the owner of the soil is dictum.

Maricopa County Water Conservation District No. 1 v. Southwest Cotton Co., 39 Ariz. 65, 4 P.2d 369 (1931), was also a case in which it was determined that the proof did not establish an underground stream so as to permit appropriation of water. The court cited to *Howard v. Perrin*, saying:

> "[A]nd therein we held that waters percolating generally through the soil are the property of the owner * * *.
>
> * * * Whether such statement was, strictly speaking, *dicta* or not, it has been accepted as the law of this jurisdiction for so long, and so many rights have been based on it, that only the clearest showing that the rule declared was error would justify us in departing from it." Id. at 82–83, 4 P.2d at 375–76.

The Town of Chino Valley relies on the two foregoing cited cases, but there are others in which the statement first made in *Howard v. Perrin* was repeated, although there was at no time, according to the way we read the cases, an arguable issue as to the precise nature of the right which the owner of the overlying lands had to the waters beneath.

Dictum thrice repeated is still dictum. It is a court's statement on a question not necessarily involved in the case and, hence, is without force of adjudication. It is not controlling as precedent. We therefore hold that the statement first made in *Howard v. Perrin* and reiterated under circumstances where the exact nature of the overlying owner's rights to the water beneath his property were not in question is not precedent for the decision in this case.

In 1952, in Bristor v. Cheatham, 73 Ariz. 228, 240 P.2d 185, a majority of this Court held that waters percolating beneath the surface of the land were subject to appropriation. On rehearing, however, one new judge having been elected and one judge having changed his position, it was held that groundwater was not subject to appropriation. The majority said:

> "[M]any and large investments have been made in the development of ground waters. Under these circumstances the court's announcement of the rule becomes a rule of property * * *." 75 Ariz. 227, 231, 255 P.2d 173, 175 (1953).

In 1970, in Jarvis v. State Land Department, 106 Ariz. 506, 479 P.2d 169, we said:

> "The right to exhaust the common supply by transporting water for use off the lands from which they are pumped is a rule of law controlled by the doctrine of reasonable use and protected by the constitution of the state as a right in property." 106 Ariz. at 509–10, 479 P.2d at 172–73.

The statements in *Bristor* and *Jarvis* do not mean that rights to the use of groundwaters cannot be modified prospectively by the Legislature. They only mean that courts will adhere to an announced rule to protect rights acquired under it and that if any change in the law is necessary, it should be made by the Legislature. The doctrine of rule of property has no operation as against subsequent legislation.

We therefore hold that since the Act of 1980 is prospective in application, it is not a legislative encroachment on judicial powers.

Appellants urge that the 1980 Act denies them due process of law and just compensation. The question therefore is, what are a landowner's rights in the water percolating under his lands?

In our recent case of Town of Chino Valley v. State Land Dept., 119 Ariz. 243, 580 P.2d 704 (1978), we said:

> "Under the doctrine of reasonable use property owners have the right to capture and use the underground water beneath their land for a beneficial purpose on that land * * *." Id. at 248, 580 P.2d at 709.

This statement we think is supported by the better reasoned decisions in this country. In the absolute sense, there can be no ownership in seeping and percolating waters until they are reduced to actual possession and control by the person claiming them because of their migratory character. Like wild animals free to roam as they please, they are the property of no one.

In Knight v. Grimes, 80 S.D. 517, 127 N.W.2d 708, 711 (1964), the court noted that South Dakota is largely a semi-arid state and that the legislature was fully justified in finding the public welfare required the maximum protection and utilization of its water supply. It said:

> "The notion that this right to take and use percolating water constitutes an actual ownership of the water prior to withdrawal has been demonstrated to be legally fallacious."

In the recent case of Village of Tequesta v. Jupiter Inlet Corp., 371 So.2d 663, 666–67 (Fla.), cert. denied, 444 U.S. 965 (1979), it was held:

* * *

> "The right of the owner to ground water underlying his land is to the usufruct of the water and not to the water itself."

We therefore hold that there is no right of ownership of groundwater in Arizona prior to its capture and withdrawal from the common supply and that the right of the owner of the overlying land is simply to the usufruct of the water.

This brings us to conclude that appellants' position that the 1980 Act violates the Fifth and Fourteenth Amendments to the Constitution of the United States and art. 2, § 17 of the Constitution of the State of Arizona as a taking of private property without due process of law and just compensation cannot be sustained.

The Legislature, in Ch. 2 of the 1980 Act, A.R.S. § 45–401, declared:

"A. The legislature finds that the people of Arizona are dependent in whole or in part upon groundwater basins for their water supply and that in many basins and sub-basins withdrawal of groundwater is greatly in excess of the safe annual yield and that this is threatening to destroy the economy of certain areas of this state and is threatening to do substantial injury to the general economy and welfare of this state and its citizens. The legislature further finds that it is in the best interest of the general economy and welfare of this state and its citizens that the legislature evoke its police power to prescribe which uses of groundwater are most beneficial and economically effective.

B. It is therefore declared to be the public policy of this state that in the interest of protecting and stabilizing the general economy and welfare of this state and its citizens it is necessary to conserve, protect and allocate the use of groundwater resources of the state and to provide a framework for the comprehensive management and regulation of the withdrawal, transportation, use, conservation and conveyance of rights to use the groundwater in this state."

We do not doubt but that the overdraft of groundwater in this state is a serious problem which has no chance of correcting itself, and that it is necessary for comprehensive legislation to both limit groundwater use and allocate its use among competing interests.

More than twenty-five years ago, this Court decided that the Legislature might choose between competing interests where the supply of groundwater was limited. In Southwest Engineering Co. v. Ernst, 79 Ariz. 403, 291 P.2d 764 (1955), we said in holding constitutional the groundwater act of 1948:

* * * held that there was a preponderant public interest in the preservation of lands then in cultivation as against lands potentially reclaimable "and that where as here the choice is unavoidable because a supply of water is not available for both, we cannot say that the exercise of such choice, controlled by considerations of social policy which are not unreasonable, involves a denial of due process." Id. at 410, 291 P.2d at 769. The Legislature in the Act of 1980 again recognized that the supply of groundwater is limited and again exercised a choice for the preservation and use of groundwater.

Legislation which denies or restricts rights to use property necessarily results in a diminution of that property's value. Yet the United States Supreme Court has on numerous occasions upheld under the state's police power regulations of land use which have virtually destroyed private interests. Most recently, in Agins v. City of Tiburon, 447 U.S. 255 (1980), it was held that a zoning ordinance restricting the use of a five-acre tract of land to single family residences would not effect a taking of property without compensation. The city ordinance was found to further the legitimate state interest of protecting the residents of the city from the ill effects of urbanization. Id. at 262. In the present case, appellants may make such use of their property as they choose, except that their lands may not be irrigated if they were not legally irrigated in the last five years. The 1980 Act furthers legitimate state interests.

Legislatures of various states have from time to time abolished the prevailing uses of groundwater and substituted other plans for its use. State courts have uniformly rejected the idea that groundwater percolating through the soil may not be limited and regulated and must be acquired by eminent domain.

"Like zoning legislation, legislation which limits or regulates the right to use underlying water is permissible. * * * Where regulation operates to arbitrate between competing public and private land uses, however, as does the water priority statute in this case, such legislation is upheld even where the value of the property declines significantly as a result." Crookston Cattle Co. v. Minnesota Department of Natural Resources, 300 N.W.2d at 774 (citation omitted).

We hold that the Act of 1980 does not deny appellants due process of law and does not require that they be paid compensation for any possible diminution of their rights which they may have had under the doctrine of reasonable use.

NOTES

1. The 1980 Act has also been upheld in federal court. Cherry v. Steiner, 543 F.Supp. 1270 (D. Ariz. 1982), affirmed 716 F.2d 687 (9th Cir. 1983). See generally Michael J. Kelly, *Management of Groundwater Through Mandatory Conservation*, 61 Denver L.J. 1 (1983). Does the non-ownership rationale of *Chino* mean that if a landowner's land is condemned for a well field, no recovery for the loss of groundwater use may be had? See Sorensen v. Lower Niobrara Natural Resources Dist., 376 N.W.2d 539 (Neb.1985).

2. Is the *Chino Valley* court saying the reasonable use doctrine has always applied in Arizona? Or does its dismissal, as *dictum*, of statements in *Howard v. Perrin* and its progeny indicate that landowners never had the unqualified right to pump, even for use on their own lands? What rule now applies outside the AMAs or INEAs established by the 1980 Groundwater Management Act?

3. Is the court's statement that "dictum thrice repeated is still dictum" *dictum*? The plaintiffs, including the town of Chino Valley and neighboring farmers, were already pumping groundwater. Therefore, how is the question of what rights a landowner who is not now pumping has in underlying groundwater relevant to the issue before the court in *Chino Valley*? To put the question another way, is the court really being accurate when it says "[w]e therefore hold that there is no right of ownership of groundwater prior to its capture and withdrawal from the common supply. * * * "?

4. Does the state now have a relatively free hand to devise management plans which stringently regulate existing uses to bring water supply and demand into balance? What constitutional (as op-

posed to statutory or political) limits on this power remain? See discussion of takings law at pages 364–91, supra.

5. No arid state is more dependent on declining groundwater supplies than Arizona. Prior to 1980, Arizona was a classic example of non-management. Arizona's agricultural use of groundwater, especially for cotton production, was long considered economically irrational. The 1980 Groundwater Management Act purported to limit the rate of extraction, and was clearly intended to shift groundwater from agricultural to municipal and industrial uses. Thus, Arizona became the first state to begin making the hard choices required to shift water systematically from lower-valued agriculture to higher-valued non-agricultural uses. The following note expands on the history and description of the Act found in *Chino Valley*.

NOTE: THE ARIZONA GROUNDWATER MANAGEMENT ACT

Background

In the 1970s Arizona used about 4.8 million acre-feet per year of groundwater and 1 million acre-feet per year of surface water. Alternative Futures: Phase II Arizona State Water Plan 3 (Arizona State Water Comm'n 1977). The annual rate of recharge was only 2.6 million acre-feet, leaving a yearly overdraft of 2.2 million acre-feet. The state's ultimate strategy for controlling groundwater overdraft was premised on a federal bailout, the Central Arizona Project (CAP), first proposed more than a half-century ago to import new water from the Colorado River. The United States Bureau of Reclamation took the position that the project would not prevent severe water shortages among Arizona water users unless a law was passed that would prevent expansion of groundwater uses from outstripping the supply of new water from the project. When the CAP was finally authorized by Congress in 1968, it included the stipulation that no CAP water would be delivered to any area that, in the judgment of the Secretary of the Interior, did not have in place adequate measures to control expansion of irrigation from aquifers in the CAP service area. 43 U.S.C.A. § 1524(c).

At the state level, legislation adopted in 1948 limited irrigation wells in certain designated "critical areas" serving lands cultivated for five years prior to 1948. That legislation was upheld against a constitutional challenge. Southwest Engineering Co. v. Ernst, 291 P.2d 764 (Ariz.1955).

The delay in securing the CAP created great pressures on expanding cities, but it took a series of judicial decisions restricting urban and industrial uses of water to produce an adequate legislative response. Although the state supreme court in 1952 had declared that all groundwater was public and open to appropriation, Bristor v. Cheatham, 240 P.2d 185 (Ariz.1952), the decision was short-lived. On rehearing, the court reversed itself and readopted the common law rule, adding a reasonable use limitation. Bristor v. Cheatham, 255 P.2d 173 (Ariz. 1953).

Sixteen years later, the Arizona Supreme Court confronted the conflict between the reasonable use rule's preference for agriculture (by favoring use on the overlying land) and the municipal needs of Arizona's fast-growing cities. In Jarvis v. State Land Dep't, City of Tucson (Jarvis I), 456 P.2d 385 (Ariz.1969), it held for the farmers, enjoining Tucson's pumping and transportation of groundwater from a farming area. Tucson refused to comply, and eighteen months later the court relented in Jarvis v. State Land Dep't, 479 P.2d 169 (Ariz.1970). Citing a provision in the surface water code that put municipal use higher than agricultural use when there were conflicting applications to appropriate, the court allowed Tucson to pump and transport if it purchased and retired the farmland from which it was pumping. In Jarvis v. State Land Dep't, 550 P.2d 227 (Ariz.1976), the court further clarified its earlier decisions by allowing Tucson to pump and transport only as much groundwater as the farmer who had previously owned the land had consumed ("that quantity which, were the lands in cultivation, would not return to the water table") 550 P.2d at 229.

Almost immediately after this decision, however, the court heightened the controversy with another decision, Farmers Invest. Co. v. Bettwy (FICO), 558 P.2d 14 (Ariz.1976), which grew out of a fight between a group of pecan farmers, the city of Tucson, and a mining company. The court was forced to resolve an issue that had seldom been addressed by the common law: what constitutes "overlying land" in the context of reasonable use? The court favored the farmers and held unreasonable the use of water for a mine and the city, both outside a designated critical area where the water was pumped. This narrow definition of overlying land "created a storm of protest from the strong Arizona mining lobby," heightened the fears of cities such as Tucson that they would be unable to obtain adequate new supplies, and led directly to the formation of a Groundwater Management Commission in 1977. John L. Kyl, The 1980 Arizona Groundwater Management Act: From Inception to Current Constitutional Challenge, 53 U.Colo.L.Rev. 471, 476 (1982).

The cities and the mining industry forged a strong coalition that captured control of the issue from the farmers. They rejected a farmer-backed plan to buy out agricultural lands. (As you study the Act, however, ask how much farmers really lost.) The compromises that led to the legislation were not easy. All groups finally rejected specific pro rata pumping cutbacks and the retirement of agricultural lands (though a purchase and retirement program may begin, if necessary, after the year 2006) in favor of granting the Director of Water Resources broad authority to mandate conservation and more efficient use.

The final impetus for agricultural and mining and urban interests to cut a deal came from Secretary of the Interior Cecil Andrus. To carry out the now almost forgotten limitation in the CAP authorizing legislation, and in furtherance of the Carter Administration's goal of promoting water conservation, he announced the federal CAP position: no state groundwater management legislation, no CAP. Secretary Andrus' condition for removing the CAP from the list spurred the creation of a negotiating group (popularly known as the "rump group") chaired by Governor Bruce Babbitt which included representatives of all major water interests. The group was largely responsible for the actual compromises that led to the Act. One key decision the group made was to support state management under a single administrative official, rather than local management. This was done because:

> The negotiators thought that by making the director [of water resources] a political appointee, at least some recourse against him would be available. The Governor realized that some vagueness in the standards and a powerful director were necessary for the Act to be completed. As part of his strategy to reach a consensus, he frequently deferred consideration of difficult issues or suggested that their resolution be delegated to the director. This strategy worked in part because of intense pressure on the group to reach agreement.

Desmond D. Connall, Jr., *A History of the Arizona Groundwater Management Act*, 1982 Ariz.St.L.J. 313, 334.

The *Chino Valley* decision relates the enactment of the Groundwater Management Act in June, 1980, to an existing dispute. Footnote 22 of that case summarizes the major provisions of the Act. The following is an expanded description of how the Act works.

Active Management Areas

The Groundwater Management Act created the Department of Water Resources to administer the Act. The Act created two classes of areas in which new uses were severely restricted. The first is an Active Management Area (AMA) which covers a basin or subbasin. Four AMAs were created: Phoenix, Tucson, Prescott, and Pinal (southeast of Phoenix). These areas cover 80% of the state's population, and 69% of the overdraft. New AMAs may be designated by the Department of Water Resources or by voter initiative in the proposed area. Ariz. Rev. Stat. Ann. § 45–411–417. The second type of area is an Irrigation Non-Expansion Area (INEA) which includes the two prior Critical Groundwater Areas not included in the AMAs.

Management goals are specified for the four AMAs. § 45–562. For Phoenix, Tucson and Prescott the goal is no withdrawals in excess of safe annual yield by the year 2025. § 45–562(A). "Safe annual yield" is defined as a "groundwater management goal which attempts to achieve and thereafter maintain a long-term balance between the annual amount of groundwater withdrawn * * * and the annual amount of natural and artificial groundwater recharge" in an AMA. For the Pinal AMA, the goal is the preservation of agriculture as long as this is feasible and "consistent with the necessity to preserve future water supplies for non-irrigation uses." § 45–562(B). The Director is to prepare a forty-five year management plan that consists of four ten-year plans with a final five-year period to achieve conservation, and more direct roll-back strategies to meet these goals. § 45–565. Pump taxes of up to $5.00 an acre-foot are also authorized.

The management goals are implemented over a forty-five year period through a series of four management plans adopted serially in later AMAs. Each plan must screw down limitations on water use tighter than the previous period to make steady progress toward gradual achievement of safe yield. The first planning cycle, for example, sets water "duties" for conservation, calculated to determine the quantity of water reasonably required to irrigate crops historically grown on pre-1975 acreages. Water duty is a conservation standard that represents a compromise between a pro rata reduction schedule and compensated land retirement. The theory is that farmers are entitled to a gradual phase-in of conservation practices. Philip R. Higdon & Terence W. Thompson, *The 1980 Arizona Groundwater Management Code*, 1980 Ariz.St.L.J. 621, 639–40. The 1990–2000 plans for the Phoenix, Tucson and Prescott AMAs must establish irrigation water duties that reflect "prudent long-term farm management practices within areas of similar farming conditions, considering the time required to amortize conservation investments and farming costs." Industrial users must use "the latest commercially available conservation technology consistent with reasonable economic return," and municipal users must make "additional reasonable reductions in per capita use" over those required in the first management period. § 45–565(2).

Because of "the politics of mutual accommodation," some observers have concluded that the plans adopted for the Tucson AMA are not nearly as stringent for most people as expected. Per capita usage must be reduced by only 3% for most consumers. Some can actually increase their usage. William E. Martin & Helen M. Ingram, Planning and Growth in the Southwest 19–20 (1985). Domestic wells, defined as "withdrawals of groundwater for domestic purposes including the non-commercial irrigation of not more than one acre of land from wells having a pump with a maximum capacity of not more than thirty-five gallons per minute," are exempt as are decreed appropriative rights. However, exempt wells are regulated and must be drilled according to construction standards. § 45–594.

Regulation of Uses

The Act makes almost all groundwater use in an AMA dependent on a statutory category or a state permit. The Act regulates the state's three major uses: (1) agricultural, (2) municipal, and (3) industrial, primarily mining. There are three classes of grandfathered rights, agricultural, non-agricultural, and agricultural to be converted to non-agricultural. Existing uses are vested but conversions and transfers are regulated, and even grandfathered rights must comply with the management plan's conservation requirements. As you review the sections delineating vested rights, ask who benefits from the rights recognized.

(a) Municipal Use

Municipal use in an AMA is limited to the service area of a municipality or public utility, which is generally defined as the area actually being served with water. § 45–402(26).

Agricultural interests succeeded in imposing four restrictions on service area expansion. A public or private entity may not expand "primarily" to: (1) include a well field in the service area; (2) deliver "disproportionately large amounts of water to an industrial or any other large water user" unless the expansion of service is consistent with an AMA plan; (3) gerrymander to extinguish the right to convey a grandfathered irrigation right to a non-irrigation use; or (4) for the purpose of withdrawing water for irrigation. § 45–493. This is a very controversial provision, and because of its lack of precision and its lack of an explicit enforcement mechanism, it has already spawned contentious but inconclusive litigation. See, e.g., Contaro Water Users' Ass'n v. Steiner, 714 P.2d 836 (Ariz.App.1985).

Although the major limitation on municipal use will probably be the conservation measures in the ten-year AMA plans, the Act also integrates land use controls and water rights. Subdivided lands within an AMA may only be sold or leased after the developer has an "assured water supply." To get a certificate of assured water supply, a person must demonstrate that there is sufficient ground or surface water to supply the needs of the subdivision for 100 years, that the projected water use is consistent with the AMA management plan, and that the service entity has the financial capacity to construct an adequate delivery and treatment system. § 45–576. If the developer plans to supply the project with CAP water, the demonstration of assured supply must still be made, but the Director of the Department of Water Resources has the discretion to conclude that a CAP contract meets the requirement. § 45–576(g).

(b) Industrial Use

The main objective of Arizona's industrial users in supporting the Act was to secure a reversal of the *FICO* decision, page 546, supra, that virtually prohibited the extraction of groundwater for mining. This goal was attained. Seven classes of industrial permits are authorized. They are: (1) mine dewatering, (2) mineral extraction and metallurgical processing, (3) general industrial use, (4) poor-quality groundwater use, (5) temporary permits, (6) drainage water permits, and (7) hydrologic testing permits. § 45–512. Industrial users must, however, also comply with conservation requirements in the management plan.

The constraints that new industrial users face are illustrated by the following excerpt from James W. Johnson, *The 1980 Arizona Groundwater Management Act and Trends in Western States Groundwater Administration and Management: A Minerals Industry Perspective*, 26 Rocky Mtn.Min.L.Inst. 1031, 1055 (1980):

> During all management periods, all industrial users shall be required to use the "latest commercially available conservation technology consistent with reasonable economic return." [87]

No new industrial uses will be permitted except on conditions designed to require maximum conservation. Industrial users may not pump groundwater unless they have first purchased available

---

87. §§ 45–564.A.2; 45–565.A.2; 45–566.A.2; 45–567.A.2; 45–568.A.

Central Arizona Project water, which may be several times more expensive than pumping groundwater. The Director may also require industrial users to use alternative supplies such as sewage effluent, even though the cost may exceed what the user would otherwise pay to pump groundwater by up to 25%. Industrial users, other than mines, will also be required to purchase and retire irrigated land, if it is available at a reasonable price, and to show that their uses are consistent with the management plan.

(c) Agricultural Use

The Act creates certain grandfathered rights relevant to farmers in AMAs. Grandfathered irrigation rights are quantified by the Director of Water Resources based on the maximum acreage in the AMA that a farmer had irrigated in any one of the five years preceding the designation of the AMA ("water duty acres") and a water duty set for the particular farm unit.

Conversion of agricultural to municipal uses: A number of features of the Act are designed to facilitate the purchase and conversion of agricultural land to municipal uses. For example, Type 1 non-irrigation rights are for the benefit of lands retired from irrigation. They are appurtenant to the land and are vested in landowners for non-irrigation uses according to a development plan associated with the retired agricultural land. If a farmer in an AMA sells a water right, the land must be sold at the same time. If the rights are sold for an irrigation use, the entire grandfathered quantity may be sold (though the right remains subject to the conservation requirements). If the rights are sold for a non-irrigation use, e.g., to a city, the farmer may only transfer a maximum of three acre-feet per acre. The legislature set the figure as the typical consumptive use (pumping minus recharge) for agricultural irrigation. If, however, the land is within the service area of a city, town or private water company, the farmer may not transfer the water rights at all—they simply disappear without compensation. The rationale is that the farmer's land has appreciated tremendously in value by being enveloped by urbanization, and cities resisted topping off this "windfall" with another increment of value representing the water right.

(d) Transportation

The Act also cured the immediate problem that led to its enactment—the judicial restriction on cities and mines transporting groundwater. Higdon and Thompson describe the possible restrictions on transportation:

> The regulation of the transportation of groundwater is a function of the point of withdrawal, the point of use, and the type of right. Basically, the transportation rules of the 1980 Code reflect an implicit legislative finding that the intra-sub-basin transportation of groundwater does not cause a legal injury, even though some harm may actually result. Thus, the 1980 Code broadens the concept of "reasonable use," which at common law did not include

the harmful withdrawal of groundwater for transportation off the land.

The Code's provisions regarding transportation of groundwater originating from points of withdrawal outside of AMAs are relatively straightforward. If the point of use is within the same sub-basin as the point of withdrawal or within the same basin, if there are no sub-basins within the basin, then groundwater may be transported without payment of damages. On the other hand, if the point of use is located in a sub-basin other than that of the point of withdrawal, or is outside the basin of the point of withdrawal, then groundwater may be transported "subject to payment of damages."

If the point of withdrawal is located within an AMA, the rules become somewhat more complicated. If the point of withdrawal is within an AMA and the point of use is within the same sub-basin of the AMA as that of the point of withdrawal, generally the transportation may be made without payment of damages. There are, however, certain limitations upon such transportation which are peculiar to the type of right pursuant to which the groundwater is withdrawn. If the transported water is withdrawn pursuant to a grandfathered or permitted right, the point of use is restricted by sections 45–472 and 45–473 of the Arizona Revised Statutes. If the entity withdrawing the water is a city, town, private water company, or irrigation district, the place of withdrawal and the place of use must be within the entity's service area; however, a city or town may transport water to other places of use if such transportation is pursuant to a delivery contract authorized by section 45–492(C).

Where the point of withdrawal is within an AMA and the point of use is in a sub-basin of the AMA (other than the sub-basin of the point of withdrawal, or is outside the AMA of the point of withdrawal), the rules become most complicated. Generally, groundwater withdrawn pursuant to an irrigation grandfathered right or a type-1 non-irrigation grandfathered right may be transported between sub-basins or away from an AMA without the payment of damages if two limitations are met. The place of use must be in conformance with special rules set forth in section 45–472 for irrigation grandfathered rights or section 45–473 for type-1 non-irrigation grandfathered rights.[320] If the water is withdrawn from retired irrigated land, the amount transported cannot exceed three acre-feet per acre per year; any transportation in excess of that amount will be subject to payment of damages.[321] An inter-sub-basin transfer from an AMA sub-basin may also be made pursuant to a type-2 irrigation grandfathered right or a permitted right subject to the payment of damages.[322] A city, town, private water company, or irrigation district may, subject to the payment

---

320. Id. (to be codified at Ariz.Rev.Stat. Ann. § 45–542(A), (B)).

321. Id. (to be codified at Ariz.Rev.Stat. Ann. § 45–542(C)).

322. Id. at A–672 (to be codified at Ariz. Rev.Stat.Ann. § 45–543(A)(1), (4)).

of damages, transport groundwater between sub-basins, so long as both the point of withdrawal and the point of use are within the entity's service area.[323] A special rule applies to cities or towns which transport groundwater pursuant to a delivery contract authorized by section 45–492(C). They may make such inter-sub-basin transfers *without* the payment of damages, so long as the withdrawal is pursuant to a type-1 non-irrigation grandfathered right and the point of use is in a sub-basin of the same AMA.[324]

Higdon & Thompson, supra at 662. See also, Mary Doyle, *The Transportation Provisions of Arizona's 1980 Groundwater Management Act: A Proposed Definition of Compensable Injury*, 25 Ariz.L.Rev. 655 (1983).

The right to initiate new uses depends on the site of the use. Outside AMAs and Irrigation Non-Expansion Areas (INEAs), the reasonable use rule apparently continues to apply. Within INEAs (see §§ 45–431 to 45–439) agricultural use of water is limited to acreage for which a vested right exists. Inside AMAs, the groundwater code contains an absolute prohibition on putting new agricultural land into irrigation with ground or surface water. § 45–452(A), (G). On the other hand, an ambiguous and as yet untested provision counsels that nothing in the Act shall be "construed to affect decreed or appropriative water rights." § 45–451(B). Within a designated service area included in an AMA, cities, towns and private water companies may withdraw and transport sufficient water for non-irrigation uses to supply their service needs. Other non-irrigation groundwater uses can be initiated by obtaining a groundwater withdrawal permit. § 45–512.

Since new wells are hard to drill, the Code creates considerable incentives for new users to purchase existing grandfathered irrigation or non-irrigation rights. See §§ 45–473 to 45–475.

The relatively unfettered ability of a city within an AMA to transport groundwater from outside an AMA, described by Higdon and Thompson, became a source of intense controversy in the mid–1980s as suburbs began purchasing "water ranches" in rural counties in order to meet the 100–year assured water supply requirement, page 549, supra. The legislature tempered this trend in 1991 by prohibiting future direct or indirect transfers of water from an area outside of one of the original AMAs into that AMA unless specifically authorized. Ariz.Rev.Stat. § 45–551(B). Cities that purchased land in groundwater basins outside of an original AMA before 1988 may transfer water from the purchased land (§ 45–552(A)). However, the Department of Water Resources sets annual transportation allotments generally limited to 3 acre-feet per acre per year for the historically irrigated land owned by the city in the basin. § 45–552(B).

The legislation also prohibits transfers unless the transferee makes "voluntary" payments to the counties of origin. § 45–556(E). In addition, the state may levy a sliding scale of transportation fees, although credits are allowed for voluntary payments. §§ 45–556(A)–(E). Market discipline has also lessened the fear of dewatered rural areas. In late

323. Id. (to be codified at Ariz.Rev.Stat. Ann. § 45–543(B)).

324. Id.

1992, Scottsdale, which purchased a ranch in northwest Arizona in 1984 for $11.7 million, announced that it planned to sell or trade the ranch, which lost $1.1 million in 1992 and from which no water was ever exported. An Indian water rights settlement eliminated Scottsdale's need for the reserved source of water supply by providing for marketing some of the tribe's water to the city.

Politics and Economics*

Putting aside for the moment questions about the Act's constitutionality, possible amendments, and the vigor with which it will be enforced, will the Act work to achieve the long-term safe yield goals for the Phoenix, Tucson and Prescott AMAs? Where will most of the reduction in current pumping required to meet the goals come from? Retirement of agricultural land and conversion to urban uses? Reduction in existing uses pursuant to the limits on transfer of grandfathered rights? Conservation requirements imposed by the Director in management programs?

What role will simple economics play? That is, agricultural pumping is much more vulnerable than municipal or industrial pumping to declining water tables and well yields, and increased pumping costs. Without any regulation, we might well expect many farms to go out of business eventually anyway; in that sense, the problem would solve itself without government intervention.

The answers to the above questions are, of course, sheer speculation, but asking them is one way to focus attention on the effect of the act as a whole. Another way is to approach it in interest-group terms. The three key interests responsible for the delicate, complex and perhaps fragile compromises achieved were the cities, the mines and power producers and the farmers. What did each lose, and what did each obtain in the legislation?

Is the Code really an effort to save water so more people can move here? Is it largely an effort by cities and housing developers to take farmers' water rights without paying for them?

The Arizona Water Commission informally estimated that the groundwater overdraft in central Arizona could be largely solved immediately by the purchase and permanent retirement of a few hundred thousand acres of agricultural land in key areas (saving a few million acre-feet of water) at a cost of several hundred million dollars. Such a solution was never seriously considered as a central part of the Act. Why not? Who would oppose it? A program of state purchase and retirement of grandfathered rights is allowed, after January 1, 2006, § 45–566(a)(6), and implicitly is forbidden before then.

The Central Arizona Project, by comparison, will cost over $2 billion for a firm supply of about one million acre-feet, but then that's mostly federal money. Still, it seems more than faintly questionable to operate the CAP, involving pumping Colorado River water 1800 feet

* This section was prepared by Professor   College of Law, 1987.
John D. Leshy, Arizona State University

uphill, in order to ease demands on groundwater pumping now at a depth of 200–500 feet or so.

A purchase and retirement program, coupled with a ban on new wells or pumping, would allow much future population growth and husband the area's water resources for the longer term, at a much reduced cost of bureaucratic administration, with attendant red tape and regulation, not to mention the demands for lawyers' time and judicial involvement.

Another simple solution, perhaps best used in combination with a purchase and retirement program, would have been to impose a tax (perhaps on the consumption of electricity used to drive the pumps), and use the proceeds to purchase and retire farmland. The solution would work like this: The overdraft is now 2.5 million acre-feet. Assuming the average farmer uses 5 acre-feet per acre (and ignoring recharge of groundwater) to eliminate the overdraft about 450,000 acres should be taken out of production. Taking recharge into account would increase the acreage needed to be retired, because a proportion of water used percolates to groundwater. If 33 percent of the water applied goes to recharge, then something like 600,000 acres would have to be retired. At a price of $2300 per acre, this would mean a total cost of, say, $1.4 billion. If the program were to take 20 years to complete, about $70 million per year would be needed, say $80 million with administrative costs and overruns. About 4.8 million acre-feet is pumped now each year, so a pump tax of $15 per acre-foot (or a lower initial amount gradually increased over time) would go a long way toward solving the problem and provide ample incentive for conservation by all remaining users as well.

Are there any constitutional objections to such a tax? If the immediate effect of such a large tax is to drive a lot of farmers out of business, does that make it unconstitutional? Is the power to tax, as John Marshall said, the power to destroy? Although there is provision in the Act for a groundwater withdrawal fee (see Article 11) it is modest. (One dollar per acre-foot maximum until 1988; three dollars per acre-foot maximum between 1988 and 2006; five dollars per acre-foot maximum thereafter.)

What political factors implicitly guided the drafters to reject these solutions in favor of the highly complex one they adopted? Is the 1980 Act a reflection of the opposite of Occam's Razor (the simplest solution is the best); namely, that the political process in a democracy tends to allocate previously unregulated uses of finite resources by something-for-everybody solutions which inevitably require complex regulation and bureaucratic controls? (Call that Leshy's First Law.*) Consider, for example, Congress' initial response to the oil embargo—a mind-numbing array of regulations controlling the price and allocation of oil and gas supplies.

* And reflect upon this bit of wisdom from Albert Einstein: "Make everything as simple as possible, but not more so."

Note that the Code was not an issue upon which political ideology controlled; i.e., legislators and the state's establishment did not take stands along party lines. Isn't it ironic that—despite the prevailing free-market, anti-regulation attitude apparently shared by most Arizonans (at least that's what I gather from reading the *Arizona Republic*)—the political process ignored a more market-oriented solution? Can one be a Reagan/Milton Friedman devotee and still support this Groundwater Code? For many Arizonans the answer seems to be a yes. Why?

What follows is McNulty and Woodard on contrasting legal and economic perspectives. (Their description is applicable to water issues Westwide, not just in Arizona):

> An interesting aspect of water resource policy in Arizona is that issues can be categorized as either price or allocation issues: that is, "who pays for the water" versus "who gets the water." For example, CAP financing issues including the amount of money collected from property tax surcharges in Pima, Pinal and Maricopa Counties, from Hoover Dam power surcharges, and from various classes of users are not tightly linked to issues of how much CAP water any given entity can or will contract to receive. Water pricing and allocation issues often are disparate in Arizona because water resources are subject primarily to legal and political decisions. If water were subject to the same kinds of economic forces ruling other market goods, then questions of who pays for water, at what prices and how much water is received by whom would be inextricably linked through supply and demand equilibria. But though we rely on the market system to efficiently allocate most other natural resources, the allocation of water in this state is based instead upon a complex and shifting tangle of federal, state and local statutes, court decisions and administrative regulations.

> How water came to be allocated by such a Byzantine process is a long and convoluted tale, closely tied to historical patterns of economic development and political "muscle." Suffice to say that what has evolved over time is a uniquely complex allocation system which leaves resource economists enormously frustrated and keeps water lawyers extremely busy.

* * *

The Economic Perspective

> A basic tenet of economics is that an efficient allocation of resources results from free market pricing. (There are caveats for public goods, for products with significant externalities and for those declining cost industries which, in the absence of regulation, tend to result in monopolies, but none of these necessarily apply to water.) Two main benefits are assumed to flow from market pricing: resources go to the "highest bidder," that potential user willing to pay the highest price, thus assuring that they are put to their highest-valued use; and supply is kept in line with demand, thereby eliminating long-term shortages or surpluses.

By contrast, the system of laws and regulations under which water is allocated in Arizona does not assure either highest-valued use or long-run equilibrium between supply and demand. As a result, future shortages of water for certain uses in specific areas of the state are forecast, and many current water consumers are viewed as "wasteful" by others.

Despite the apparent benefits of market pricing for water, resource economists who have proposed major overhauls of Arizona's water allocation system have been largely ignored. They have tended to overlook or underestimate concerns regarding costs associated with the uncertainty of new property rights arrangements and the fairness of redistributing resources without adequately compensating the losers. Indeed, it can be shown that many of the economists' "solutions" to Arizona's water resources problems would require constitutional amendments, restructuring or eliminating industries, and perhaps calling out the National Guard to preserve the peace. It is far more difficult to efficiently reallocate existing resources than efficiently allocate new resources. Anything more than incremental changes results in nearly everyone's "ox being gored" and, the 1980 Groundwater Management Act being a heroic exception, such major changes will be extremely rare events.

The Legal Perspective

In contrast to resource economists, attorneys and judges are more concerned with protecting established property rights and promoting equity than with searching for ways to increase economic efficiency. The legal system contributes to societal welfare by legitimizing and securing existing property allocations.

Legal scholars generally are condescending toward economists who, because of their training in what *could* be, do not consider seriously enough the historical evolution of water rights in the West.

* * *

Arizona has taken a first small step toward a market in water in the creation of Type 2 non-irrigation grandfathered rights, a water right that is severable from the land. The state will be following the progress of that market with intense interest.

Unquestionably, the security of water supplies is more significant for agriculture than it is for other sectors. Industrial users can afford to pay more for water and explore more options for importation or treatment than can agricultural users for whom water is an essential but necessarily cheap input to production. As central Arizona becomes more urban and less agricultural in character, the Legislature may allow some continued drift toward efficiency at the expense of security. But since there is not growth without water, the politically potent trio of cities, farms and industries will cling tenaciously to whatever advantages they enjoy under the existing legal system.

McNulty & Woodard, *Arizona Water Issues: Contrasting Economic and Legal Perspectives*, Ariz.Rev., 2–4 (Fall, 1984).

The Future

Arizona continues to expand its management of groundwater and to adopt more stringent conservation requirements, although controversy over the effectiveness of existing efforts continues. Demand for CAP water is far short of the assumptions on which the project was constructed and "there is substantial doubt about whether agricultural users will be able to afford to use their CAP allocations." Katherine Jacobs & Robert Glennon, Arizona Groundwater Management Act: Recent Issues and Future Prospects 17, in Natural Resources Law Center (University of Colorado Law School, June 15–17, 1992). In addition to the transportation restrictions discussed above, the legislature has enacted a groundwater storage program primarily to allow the storage of CAP water, Ariz.Rev.Stat. §§ 45–808 to 45–809, and created a groundwater replenishment district for the Phoenix and Tucson AMAs. Ariz.Rev.Stat. § 45–611.

Recent evidence indicates that safe annual yield may not be achieved in the Phoenix and Tucson AMAs because population continues to expand, but there is no consensus about what, if any, new management strategies should be adopted. The State Auditor has suggested that existing reserves will carry the state for 500 years, while other observers argue that agricultural land retirement will be necessary to achieve safe yield. Failing that, the state will be unable to continue promoting unrestricted urban growth. Robert Glennon, *"Because That's Where the Water Is": Retiring Current Water Uses To Achieve the Safe–Yield Objective of the Arizona Groundwater Management Act,* 33 Ariz.L.Rev. 89 (1991). See also William Parsons & Douglas Matthews, *The Californiazation of Arizona Water Politics,* 30 Nat. Resources J. 341 (1990). The relationship between growth control, and urban water supply pricing is further discussed in Chapter 6, pages 615–17, infra.

Under the Act, water duties for irrigated agriculture, which still consumes 80% of the state's water but contributes 1% of its total income, were set at historic use. Irrigators can obtain a credit for use below the conservation target which they can use in the year immediately following the accrual or can sell to other irrigators. As of 1992, farmers had accumulated approximately 3,000,000 acre-feet of credits. A former director of the Department of Water Resources has argued that "conservation requirements for farmers are meaningless." Kathleen Ferris, *The Arizona Groundwater Management Code: The First Ten Years, in Arizona's Water Law: Overview and Current Topics* 129, 149 (State Bar of Arizona, 1990).

5. California: Basinwide Adjudication; Institutional Response

It is appropriate to speak of a water industry in California, since many of the pumpers, especially in Southern California, are large municipal suppliers or industries such as oil companies. The issue in the several basinwide adjudications has not been simply how to allocate scarce resource among competing users over time, but the more complex question of how to balance the use of groundwater and use of water imported from the Colorado River and from Northern California rivers. The problem is, of course, cost, as sufficient water to meet existing demands has always been available. For example, in 1945 when the West Basin adjudication commenced, Metropolitan Water District was potentially able to take 1,212,000 acre-feet of Colorado River water but was selling only 32,000 acre-feet and looking for customers. Because of transportation costs, the price of Colorado River water was higher than that of local supplies, and pumpers desired to maximize their use of the cheaper groundwater. However, the California experience supports the economists' hypothesis that institutional settlements of common pool resource controversies will follow once property rights have been made definite. See William Blomquist, Dividing the Waters: Governing Groundwater in Southern California (1992).

California followed the rule of absolute ownership until 1903 when the common law was rejected in favor of the correlative rights rule. Katz v. Walkinshaw, 70 P. 663 (Cal.1902), 74 P. 766 (Cal.1903). Correlative rights allocates a "fair and just portion" of the common pool to overlying owners. These rights are analogous to riparian rights, for they can be asserted at any time provided the use is reasonable and beneficial under Cal. Const. art. 10, § 2, and subsequent rights are entitled to equal dignity with existing rights. Burr v. Maclay Rancho Water Co., 98 P. 260 (Cal.1908).

Appropriative rights in the basin may also be perfected provided that two conditions are met. First, water must be available in excess of safe annual yield. Second, the water must not be needed by the overlying owners. If the basin is in overdraft and there is insufficient water to satisfy the uses of the overlying owners, the available supply is restricted to overlying owners based on each user's reasonable need. See Tehachapi-Cummings Cty. Water Dist. v. Armstrong, 122 Cal.Rptr. 918 (1975). What constitutes overlying use has never been clearly defined. Some cases have equated it with use of land within the groundwater basin rather than the parcel of land beneath which the water is actually pumped. It seems clear, however, that municipalities cannot claim overlying rights to supply customers throughout the basin from which water is pumped. City of San Bernardino v. Riverside, 198 P. 784 (Cal.1921). Because most groundwater users in Southern California are cities and industries, the distinction favoring overlying users was less important, at least between 1949 and 1975.

PASADENA v. ALHAMBRA
Supreme Court of California, 1949.
33 Cal.2d 908, 207 P.2d 17.

GIBSON, CHIEF JUDGE.

* * *

The Raymond Basin Area, a field of ground water located at the northwest end of San Gabriel Valley, includes the city of Sierra Madre, almost all of the city of Pasadena, and portions of South Pasadena, San Marino, and Arcadia. The field of ground water contains alluvium consisting of sands, gravels and other porous materials through which water percolates. The northern side is formed by the San Gabriel range of mountains which rise back of the valley to a general elevation of from 5,000 to 6,000 feet. The area comprises 40 square miles and is separated from the rest of the valley along its southern boundary by the Raymond Fault, sometimes known as Raymond Dike, a natural fault in the bedrock constituting a "Barrier in the alluvium * * * which greatly impedes the sub-surface movement of water from the area, although it does not entirely stop it, thus creating a vast underground storage reservoir." * * *

Natural underground formations divide the area into two practically separate units. * * *

Our concern is with the Western Unit where the principal ground water movement is from north and west of Monk Hill to the south and east and across Raymond Fault. The water in this unit is replenished by rainfall, by return water arising from the use of water in the unit, and by the runoff and underflow from the San Gabriel Mountains to the north and from the San Rafael hills to the west. Appellant's wells, from which it obtains all its production, are in the southeastern part of this unit, and the underlying water constitutes one ground water body which is a common source of all parties taking water therefrom. The water pumped from the ground in the Western Unit has exceeded the safe yield thereof in every year since 1913–14 (commencing October 1) except during the years 1934–35 and 1936–37. The safe yield of the unit was found to be 18,000 acre feet per year, but the average annual draft was 24,000 acre feet, resulting in an average annual overdraft of 6,000 feet.

With respect to the water rights acquired by the various parties it was stipulated by all of them, including appellant, that "all of the water taken by each of the parties to this stipulation and agreement, at the time it was taken, was taken openly, notoriously and under a claim of right, which claim of right was continuously and uninterruptedly asserted by it to be and was adverse to any and all claims of each and all of the other parties joining herein."

The findings set forth in terms of acre feet per year "the highest continuous production of water for beneficial use in any five (5) year period prior to the filing of the complaint by each of the parties in each of said units, as to which there has been no cessation of use by it during any subsequent continuous five (5) year period." This was designated, for convenience, the "present unadjusted right" of each party, and the court concluded that each party owned "by prescription" the right to take a certain specified amount of water, and that the rights of the parties were of equal priority. The total of the unadjusted rights for the Western Unit was found to be 25,608 acre feet per year, and water pumped by nonparties to the action was 340 acre feet per year. The court also found that a continued draft in these amounts will result in an unreasonable depletion and the eventual destruction of the ground water as a source of supply.   * * * The amount of water limited to each party, designated the "decreed right," was set out in the findings, and this allocation gave each party about two-thirds of the amount it had been pumping.

The court enjoined all pumping in excess of the decreed right and appointed a "Water Master" to enforce the provisions of the judgment. It reserved jurisdiction to modify the judgment or make such further orders as might be necessary for adequate enforcement or for protection of the waters in the Raymond Basin Area from contamination.

* * *

The question of who shall bear the burden of curtailing the overdraft, and in what proportion, depends upon the legal nature and status of the particular water right held by each party.   Rights in water in an underground basin, so far as pertinent here, are classified as overlying, appropriate, and prescriptive.   Generally speaking, an overlying right, analogous to that of a riparian owner in a surface stream, is the right of the owner of the land to take water from the ground underneath for use on his land within the basin or watershed; the right is based on ownership of the land and is appurtenant thereto.   The right of an appropriator depends upon an actual taking of water.   The term "appropriation" is said by some authorities to be properly used only with reference to the taking of water from a surface stream on public land for nonriparian purposes.   The California courts, however, use the term to refer to any taking of water for other than riparian or overlying uses.   Where a taking is wrongful, it may ripen into a prescriptive right.

Although the law at one time was otherwise, it is now clear that an overlying owner or any other person having a legal right to surface or ground water may take only such amount as he reasonably needs for beneficial purposes.   (Katz v. Walkinshaw, 141 Cal. 116 [70 P. 663, 74 P. 766, 99 Am.St.Rep. 35, 64 L.R.A. 236]; Peabody v. City of Vallejo, 2 Cal.2d 351 [40 P.2d 486]; Cal. Const., art. XIV, § 3.)   Public interest requires that there be the greatest number of beneficial uses which the supply can yield, and water may be appropriated for beneficial uses subject to the rights of those who have a lawful priority.   Any water not needed for the reasonable beneficial uses of those having prior rights is excess or surplus water.   In California surplus water may rightfully be appropriated on privately owned land for nonoverlying uses, such as devotion to a public use or exportation beyond the basin or watershed.

It is the policy of the state to foster the beneficial use of water and discourage waste, and when there is a surplus, whether of surface or ground water, the holder of prior rights may not enjoin its appropriation.   Proper overlying use, however, is paramount, and the right of an appropriator, being limited to the amount of the surplus, must yield to that of the overlying owner in the event of a shortage, unless the appropriator has gained prescriptive rights through the taking of nonsurplus waters.

As between overlying owners, the rights, like those of riparians, are correlative and are referred to as belonging to all in common; each may use only his reasonable share when water is insufficient to meet the needs of all. As between appropriators, however, the one first in time is the first in right, and a prior appropriator is entitled to all the water he needs, up to the amount that he has taken in the past, before a subsequent appropriator may take any.

Prescriptive rights are not acquired by the taking of surplus or excess water, since no injunction may issue against the taking and the appropriator may take the surplus without giving compensation; however, both overlying owners and appropriators are entitled to the protection of the courts against any substantial infringement of their rights in water which they reasonably and beneficially need. (Peabody v. City of Vallejo, 2 Cal.2d 351, 368–369, 374 [40 P.2d 486].) Accordingly, an appropriative taking of water which is not surplus is wrongful and may ripen into a prescriptive right where the use is actual, open and notorious, hostile and adverse to the original owner, continuous and uninterrupted for the statutory period of five years, and under claim of right. To perfect a claim based upon prescription there must, of course, be conduct which constitutes an actual invasion of the former owner's rights so as to entitle him to bring an action. Appropriative and prescriptive rights to ground water, as well as the rights of an overlying owner, are subject to loss by adverse user. This is in accord with the rule announced in cases dealing with water in a surface stream.

* * *

It follows from the foregoing that, if no prescriptive rights had been acquired, the rights of the overlying owners would be paramount, and the rights of the appropriators would depend on priority of acquisition under the rule that the first appropriator in time is the first in right. The latest in time of the appropriations would then be the first to be curtailed in limiting total production of the area to the safe yield. If such were the case, the overdraft could be eliminated simply by enjoining a part of the latest appropriations, since the record shows that there is ample water to satisfy the needs of all the overlying users and most of the appropriators, and appellant's appropriative rights would depend primarily upon evidence of priority in time of acquisition.

The principal dispute between appellant and respondents, however, concerns whether any water rights in the Western Unit have become prescriptive and, if so, to what extent. Respondents assert that the rights of all the parties, including both overlying users and appropriators, have become mutually prescriptive against all the other parties and, accordingly, that all rights are of equal standing, with none prior or paramount. Appellant, on the other hand, contends that in reality no prescriptive rights have been acquired, and that there has been no actionable invasion or injury of the right of any party using water because each party has been able to take all the water it needed and no party has in any manner prevented a taking of water by any other party. It would follow, under appellant's theory, that not even an overlying owner could have obtained an injunction against a subsequent taking.

* * *

The record shows that there has been an actual adverse user of water in the Western Unit. There was an invasion, to some extent at least, of the rights of both overlying owners and appropriators commencing in the year 1913–1914, when the overdraft first occurred. Each taking of water in excess of the safe yield, whether by subsequent appropriators or by increased use by prior appropriators, was wrongful and was an injury to the then existing owners of water rights, because the overdraft, from its very beginning, operated progressively to reduce the total available supply. Although no owner was immediately prevented from taking the water he needed, the report demonstrates that a continuation of the overdraft would eventually result in such a depletion of the supply stored in the underground basin that it would become inadequate. The injury thus did not involve an immediate disability to obtain water, but, rather, it consisted of the continual lowering of the level and gradual reducing of the total amount of stored water, the accumulated effect of which, after a period of years, would be to render the supply insufficient to meet the needs of the rightful owners.

The proper time to act in preserving the supply is when the overdraft commences, and the aid of the courts would come too late and be entirely inadequate if, as appellant seems to suggest, those who possess water rights could not commence legal proceedings until the supply was so greatly depleted that it actually became difficult or impossible to obtain water. Where the quantity withdrawn exceeds the average annual amount contributed by rainfall, it is manifest that the underground store will be gradually depleted and eventually exhausted, and, accordingly, in order to prevent such a catastrophe, it has been held proper to limit the total use by all consumers to an amount equal, as near as may be, to the average supply and to enjoin takings in such quantities or in such a manner as would destroy or endanger the underground source of water. There is, therefore, no merit to the contention that the owners of water rights were not injured by the additional appropriations made after all surplus waters were taken, and they clearly were entitled to obtain injunctive relief to terminate all takings in excess of the surplus as soon as it became apparent from the lowering of the well levels that the underground basin would be depleted if the excessive pumping were continued.

The lowering of the water table resulting from the overdraft was plainly observable in the wells of the parties * * *.

This evidence is clearly sufficient to justify charging appellant with notice that there was a deficiency rather than a surplus and that the appropriations causing the overdraft were invasions of the rights of overlying owners and prior appropriators. The elements of prescription being present in the record, the statute of limitations ran against the original lawful holders of water rights to whatever extent their rights were invaded.

It must next be determined whether the rights of all of the prior owners were invaded and whether all or only a part of the right of any particular owner was damaged. It has been established that the rights of appropriators as well as of overlying owners will be protected by the courts and that an invasion of either type of right will start the running of the statute. Where, as here, subsequent appropriators reduce the available supply and their acts, if continued, will render it impossible for the holder of a prior right to pump in the future, there is an enjoinable invasion. In this respect there is no difference between an overlying owner and an appropriator. Although neither may prevent a taking of surplus waters, either may institute legal proceedings to safeguard the supply once a surplus ceases to exist and may enjoin any additional user beyond the point of safe yield.

Cases are cited for the proposition that an appropriator's rights are not invaded if he continues to receive the quantity of water to which he is entitled. These cases, however, do not deal with the problem of gradual depletion of water stored in a basin or lake, but, rather, with surface streams or ditches in which water flows but is not retained for future use. The type of injury there considered would immediately deprive the owner of water, and the language in the opinions does not apply to an invasion of rights in a stored supply of water to be used only in future years.

Neither the overlying owners nor the appropriators took steps to obtain the aid of the courts to protect their rights until the present action was instituted, many years after the commencement of the overdraft, and at first glance it would seem to follow that the parties who wrongfully appropriated water for a period of five years would acquire prior prescriptive rights to the full amount so taken. The running of the statute, however, can effectively be interrupted by self help on the part of the lawful owner of the property right involved. Unlike the situation with respect to a surface stream where a wrongful taking by an appropriator has the immediate effect of preventing the riparian owner from receiving water in the amount taken by the wrongdoer, the owners of water rights in the present case were not immediately prevented from taking water, and they in fact continued to pump whatever they needed. As we have seen, the Raymond Basin Area is similar to a large lake or reservoir, and water would be available until exhaustion of the supply. The owners were injured only with respect to their rights to continue to pump at some future date. The invasion was thus only a partial one, since it did not completely oust the original owners of water rights, and for the entire period both the original owners and the wrongdoers continued to pump all the water they needed.

The pumping by each group, however, actually interfered with the other group in that it produced an overdraft which would operate to make it impossible for all to continue at the same rate in the future. If the original owners of water rights had been ousted completely or had failed to pump for a five-year period, then there would have been no interference whatsoever on the part of the owners with the use by the wrongdoers, and the wrongdoers would have perfected prior prescriptive rights to the full amount which they pumped. As we have seen, however, such was not the case, and, although the pumping of each party to this action continued without interruption, it necessarily interfered with the future possibility of pumping by each of the other parties by lowering the water level. The original owners by their own acts, although not by judicial assistance, thus retained or acquired a right to continue to take some water in the future. The wrongdoers also acquired prescriptive rights to continue to take water, but their rights were limited to the extent that the original owners retained or acquired rights by their pumping.

[Affirmed.]

NOTES

1. Determining the relationship between correlative and appropriative rights plagues California courts. Wright v. Goleta Water Dist., 219 Cal.Rptr. 740 (Cal.Ct.App.1985) held that California law protects the unexercised correlative rights of overlying landowners, and that they are superior to appropriative rights. The court recognized the unusual correlative rights of overlying landowners in an overdrafted coastal groundwater basin and refused to subordinate them to present beneficial uses of a district. Although the court indicated that it would be logical to extend the principles of In re Long Valley Creek Stream System, 599 P.2d 656 (Cal.1979), page 365, supra, to groundwater adjudications, it found that the legislature had created a comprehensive adjudication system for surface waters only.

2. California relies on the courts to adjudicate groundwater controversies, but judicial allocation has been supplemented by statutes designed for Southern California. The 1955 Ground Water Recordation Act requires that pumpers in four Southern California counties file notices with the State Water Resources Board of the quantity of water extracted unless the amount was less than twenty-five acre-feet per year. Cal. Water Code §§ 4999–5008.

3. A serious problem in coastal groundwater basins is salt water intrusion. Prevention of salt water intrusion has been a major motivation in several post-*Pasadena* adjudications in Southern California. Voluntary settlements have been approved by the courts and one unreported, but widely cited, trial court decision has held that the prescriptive period beings to run when salt water intrusion threatens the quality of the basin. In San Luis Rey Water Conservation Dist. v. Carlsbad Mun. Water Dist. (San Diego County Superior Court No. 184855, Aug. 3, 1959). Commonly recognized methods of controlling salt water intrusion are:

   (1) reduction of pumping or rearrangement of pumping patterns;

   (2) recharge of the basin (ordinarily with imported water) to raise the groundwater level above sea level;

   (3) creation of a coastal fresh water ridge through injection wells and spreading basins;

   (4) construction of an artificial subsurface physical barrier;

(5) creation of a pumping trough along the coast.

The State Water Resources Board may file suit "to restrict pumping, or to impose physical solutions, or both, to the extent necessary to prevent destruction of or irreparable injury to the quality of [ground] water." Cal. Water Code §§ 2100–2102.

4. California has resisted the conjunctive management of groundwater basins by the state or super-regional agencies. However, through the widespread use of adjudications based on the doctrine of mutual prescription followed by the creation of special districts pursuant to state enabling legislation, a high level of management has been functionally achieved for the objectives of cutting back pumping to safe annual yield levels and preventing salt water intrusion. The Los Angeles coastal basins were the first to institute litigation after Pasadena v. Alhambra. First, the West Basin, located on the Pacific Ocean, instituted litigation and then the Central Basin, located adjacent to the West Basin and in effect upstream, followed suit.

The West Basin litigation in Los Angeles has produced the most sophisticated institutional responses to salt water intrusion. Yet after 16 years of litigation, reportedly costing $5 million, resulting in reductions on pumping, salt water intrusion continued to be a problem in the Basin. In 1955 the legislature passed the Water Replenishment District Act, Cal.Water Code §§ 60000–65000. As a result the Central and West Basin Replenishment District was formed.

Under the enabling legislation a replenishment district may determine the amount of annual overdraft and assess pumpers for the costs of purchasing imported water. If the basin has been adjudicated, assessments may be levied only against those who extract in excess of their declared rights. The district may also levy ad valorem taxes not in excess of $.20 per $100.00 of assessed valuation. As a result of the Act the Central and West Basin Replenishment District was formed in 1959 after lengthy negotiations with the state and with the major water service organizations in the Los Angeles area. Basically, the district agreed that pumping levies rather than ad valorem taxes would be used to purchase replenishment water from the Metropolitan Water Department of Southern California (MWD); the imported water would be spread to recharge the basin and prevent salt water intrusion by the Los Angeles County Flood Control District. See Carl Fossette and Ruth Fossette, The Story of Water Development in Los Angeles County (1986); Blomquist, page 573, infra.

The Central Basin benefited from the West Basin's pumping reductions and spreading operations. An adjudication of rights was necessary to assess the pumpers an appropriate amount in order to finance the spreading operations under the Central and West Basin Replenishment District.

LOS ANGELES v. SAN FERNANDO
Supreme Court of California, 1975.
14 Cal.3d 199, 123 Cal.Rptr. 1, 537 P.2d 1250.

[In 1955 the City of Los Angeles brought an action against numerous private and public defendants to quiet its title to groundwater in the Upper Los Angeles River Area (ULARA) and enjoin all pumpers from extracting water other than in subordination to the plaintiff's prior rights. Los Angeles pumped from the basin, then spread imported water from the Owens Valley, using the area underlying the river as a reservoir, and subsequently extracted it for delivery to customers within and without the Area. The various pumpers extracted groundwater from four subareas of the ULARA. It was stipulated that 42.5 percent of the basin's supply was derived from imported water and the rest from rain and snow within the watershed. Los Angeles claimed: (1) a right to all the native water on the grounds that the city was the successor of the Pueblo of Los Angeles and this gave it a paramount right to all groundwaters it needed to supply all the original and annexed areas of the Pueblo and (2) a right to all imported water and return flows therefrom on the grounds that Los Angeles controlled the imported water and thus had not abandoned it by spreading. The defendants denied the existence of a Pueblo right, argued that all had pumping rights that had to be determined by the doctrine of mutual prescription, and contended that Los Angeles had abandoned their imported water and thus it went into the mutual prescription pool.

Pueblo rights are primarily important in California, New Mexico and Texas. The theory is that Spanish law gave the Pueblos a paramount claim to supply their needs. The supreme court conceded that prior cases may have misinterpreted Spanish law but held that this was irrelevant because (1) the rights had been consistently recognized by the courts, (2) had been declared a rule of property, and (3) there had been substantial reliance on the part of the City of Los Angeles, because the city had imported Owens Valley water relying on the Pueblo right to retain priority to its native supply "once this surplus was exhausted." 527 P.2d at 1283, 1284–85. The right was further limited by the standard that Pueblo rights only attach to "waters * * * required for satisfying its municipal needs and those of its inhabitants." See also pages 776–77, infra.

On the issue of the rights of the various parties to imported water Chief Justice Wright wrote as follows:]

GROUND SUPPLIES ATTRIBUTABLE TO IMPORTED WATER

Return Flow Derived From Delivered Imported Water: San Fernando Basin

* * * Apart from the relatively small quantities of imported water spread by plaintiff for direct recharge of the basin, this ground water consisted of a return flow attributable to *delivered* imported water reaching the ground as waste, seepage, or spillage, or by similar means in the course of use. Most of this delivered water had been imported by plaintiff from Owens Valley and Mono basin; the remainder was Colorado River water purchased by plaintiff and by defendants Glendale and Burbank from the Metropolitan Water District.

Ground water is extracted from San Fernando basin by plaintiff, defendants Glendale and Burbank, and seven private defendants. Plaintiff claims a prior right to the ground water attributable to the return flow from its Owens imports and from the delivered water it purchases from MWD. Plaintiff asserts that defendants Glendale and Burbank are entitled to such return water in the basin derived from their MWD purchases. Those defendants, on the other hand, deny any special rights in return water as such and are joined by the seven private defendant claimants of San Fernando basin ground water in opposing plaintiff's claim to priority in return waters.

In City of Los Angeles v. City of Glendale, 23 Cal.2d 68, 142 P.2d 289, this court affirmed a judgment which declared that plaintiff had prior rights, as against defendants Glendale and Burbank, to "return waters" beneath the San Fernando Valley. These return waters were described as those which were imported by plaintiff and "sold to the farmers of the San Fernando Valley, and which settle after use beneath the surface and join the mass of water below, as anticipated when sold." It was held that plaintiff had a prior right to the water when it was imported and that "[t]he use by others of this water as it flowed to the subterranean basin does not cut off plaintiff's rights."

This holding had a dual basis. One basis for the holding was the trial court's finding that before commencing the importation of Owens water, plaintiff had formed an intention to recapture the return waters used for irrigation in the San Fernando Valley whenever such return waters were needed for its municipal purposes and the use of its inhabitants, and that the Los Angeles Aqueduct had been planned and located to facilitate the availability and recapture of such return waters. Under these circumstances, plaintiff retained its prior right to the return waters wherever they might appear.

The other basis for the *Glendale* holding, found in the reasoning of Stevens v. Oakdale Irr. Dist. (1939) 13 Cal.2d 343, 90 P.2d 58, did not depend on the existence of an intent to recapture return waters *before* importation began. In *Stevens*, water brought from the Stanislaus River into the defendant district's irrigation system reached Lone Tree Creek as seepage, waste and spill from irrigation uses. Lone Tree Creek was in a different watershed from the Stanislaus. After an owner of land traversed by Lone Tree Creek downstream from the district's territory had commenced irrigating with the water, the district for the first time manifested an intention to recapture the water from the creek within its own boundaries for irrigation uses, thereby cutting off the lower user's supply. The district's right to do so was upheld. Even though the district had abandoned the particular quantities of water it had allowed to flow downstream, it retained the right to recapture a subsequent flow as long as it did so within its own irrigation works or on its own land. Applying *Stevens*, the *Glendale* court pointed out that the return waters claimed by plaintiff had "reappeared in the basin of the San Fernando Valley, used by plaintiff for the storage of other imported waters [through spreading] and containing natural waters to which plaintiff had a prior [pueblo] right. Once within the basin en route to plaintiff's diversion works, it was in effect within plaintiff's reservoir." (23 Cal.2d at pp. 77–78, 142 P.2d at p. 295.)

The adjudication in *Glendale* of plaintiff's prior right to return waters derived from delivered Owens water is binding in the present case on defendants Glendale and Burbank.

* * * The recapture right, however, does not necessarily attach to the corpus of water physically traceable to particular deliveries but is a right to take from the commingled supply an amount equivalent to the augmentation contributed by the return. * * *

Defendants Glendale and Burbank each delivers imported MWD water to users within its territory in the San Fernando basin and each has been extracting ground water in the same territory before and during the importation. Accordingly, each has rights to recapture water attributable to the return flow from such deliveries for the same reasons that plaintiff has such a right. These multiple rights necessitate apportionment of the ground water derived from return flow into the amounts attributable to the import deliveries of each defendant and plaintiff. The record in this case, including the referee's report, demonstrates that such apportionment can be made within reasonable limits of accuracy.

Defendants contend that if any party is given rights to a return flow derived from delivered *imported* water, it is "obvious" and "axiomatic" that the same rights should be given to the return flow from delivered water derived from all other sources, including native water extracted from local wells. This argument misconceives the reason for the prior right to return flow from imports. Even though all deliveries produce a return flow, only deliveries derived from imported water add to the ground supply. The purpose of giving the right to recapture returns from delivered imported water priority over overlying rights and rights based on appropriations of the native ground supply is to credit the importer with the fruits of his expenditures and endeavors in bringing into the basin water that would not otherwise be there. Returns from deliveries of extracted native water do not add to the ground supply but only lessen the diminution occasioned by the extractions.

* * *

OVERDRAFT AND PRESCRIPTION

Relationship of Pasadena Decision to Equitable Ground Basin Management

As stated above, the trial court's judgment awarded "mutually prescriptive rights" and "restricted pumping" quotas to the parties purportedly pursuant to the decision in City of Pasadena v. City of Alhambra, supra, 33 Cal.2d 908, 207 P.2d 17. * * *

In the present case, none of the defendants now before us commenced their uses of ground water from the basins of the ULARA after the years in which the trial court found overdraft to have commenced. To the contrary, the amount that each defendant was using at the beginning of overdraft was substantial in relation to such defendant's later use, and there is a notable correlation between the relative levels of usage at the time of overdraft and the restricted pumping quotas allocated in the decree based on awards of prescriptive rights.

Thus, the mutual prescription doctrine was not needed or applied in the present case for the purpose achieved in *Pasadena*—that of avoiding complete elimination of appropriative rights stemming from uses of recent years in favor of those based on earlier uses. Instead, the effect of the trial court's judgment in the present case was to eliminate plaintiff's priorities based not on the timing of its appropriations but on its importation of Owens water and on its pueblo right. * * *

Effect of Civil Code Section 1007 on Prescriptive Claims Against Cities

The trial court awarded prescriptive water rights against plaintiff to both city and private party defendants in the San Fernando and Sylmar basins. Plaintiff asserts that any prescription of its water rights by defendants was precluded by the 1935 amendment to section 1007 of the Civil Code which provided until 1968 that "no possession by any person, firm or corporation no matter how long continued of any * * * water right * * * or other property * * * dedicated to or owned by any * * * city * * * shall ever ripen into any title, interest or right against such * * * city."

Defendants argue that City of Pasadena v. City of Alhambra, supra, 33 Cal.2d 908, 207 P.2d 17, decided that the acquisition of water rights against cities by prescription was not barred by the 1935 amendment to Civil Code section 1007, which had been in effect for two years when the complaint in that action was filed. But this court did not reach the issue in that case. * * *

We are of the opinion that the 1935 amendment to section 1007 was intended to enlarge the classes of property exempt from prescription by *any* party rather than to immunize such enlarged classes of property from prescription by private parties only. * * *

We construe the word "person," in the 1935 amendment's provision that "no possession by any person, firm or corporation" shall ripen into prescriptive title against certain public entities, to include governmental agencies. This construction does not infringe on their sovereign powers. Such agencies are thereby deprived of nothing except the power to take away the property rights of their fellow public entities through adverse possession. Those other entities are thus protected against prescriptive invasion of their property rights from public as well as private sources. The result is not a diminution of sovereign powers but only the elimination of prescription as a means of transferring property from one arm of the government to another.

Commencement of Overdraft

A ground basin is in a state of surplus when the amount of water being extracted from it is less than the maximum that could be withdrawn without adverse effects on the basin's long term supply. While this state of surplus exists, none of the extractions from the basin for beneficial use constitutes such an invasion of any water right as will entitle the owner of the right to injunctive, as distinct from declaratory, relief. Overdraft commences whenever extractions increase, or the withdrawable maximum decreases, or both, to the point where the surplus ends. Thus on the commencement of overdraft there is no surplus available for the acquisition or enlargement of appropriative rights. Instead, appropriations of water in excess of surplus then invade senior basin rights, creating the element of adversity against those rights prerequisite to their owners' becoming entitled to an injunction and thus to the running of any prescriptive period against them.

* * *

* * * According to plaintiff, overdraft commenced in the ULARA only when (1) total extractions exceeded safe yield and (2) the available water storage capacity of the basin was sufficient to permit cycling of the safe yield throughout the 29-year base period of wet and dry years without causing a waste of water in the wet years. The referee's report as well as other evidence showed that when ground basin levels were relatively high, and storage space correspondingly diminished, waste occurred. Ground basin levels tended to vary in accordance with wide fluctuations in precipitation. Thus if a rising level of extractions were halted at the point of the safe yield based on the 29-year average, ensuing heightening of ground water levels during years of higher-than-average precipitation would cause waste. Since this waste would constitute a loss of basin water in addition to the safe yield extractions, it would eventually create enough additional storage space to stop further similar waste, but the wasted water itself would be lost to any beneficial use. On the other hand, a withdrawal of water from the basin over and above its safe yield in the amount necessary to create the storage space sufficient to prevent the waste would result in a net addition to the beneficially used supply.

We agree with plaintiff that if a ground basin's lack of storage space will cause a limitation of extractions to safe yield to result in a probable waste of water, the amount of water which if withdrawn would create the storage space necessary to avoid the waste and not adversely affect the basin's safe yield is a temporary surplus available for appropriation to beneficial use. Accordingly, overdraft occurs only if extractions from the basin exceed its safe yield plus any such temporary surplus.

* * *

Notice of Adversity as Prerequisite to Commencement of Prescriptive Period

* * *

The fact that one party's taking of water from a basin is open, notorious, and under claim of right does not invade any other party's water rights in the basin so as to entitle the other party to injunctive relief or start the running of any prescriptive period against the other party's rights so long as the taking is only from a surplus of basin water, that is, so long as there is not an overdraft on the basin supply. The commencement of overdraft provides the element of adversity which makes the first party's taking an invasion constituting a basis for injunctive relief to the other party. But if the other party is not on *notice* that the overdraft exists, such adverse taking does not cause the commencement of the prescriptive period.

* * *

Effect of Surplus on Running of Prescriptive Period

* * * Prescriptive rights in the basin were awarded to plaintiff, defendant City of San Fernando and two private defendants based on the "highest continuous annual production of water for beneficial use in any five (5) year period *subsequent to the commencement of overdraft and prior to the filing of the complaint* by each of the parties from the Sylmar basin as to which there has been no cessation of use by it during any subsequent continuous five (5) year period." (Italics added.) From this formula it appears that the award of prescriptive rights may have been based on extractions of water during a continuous five-year period which included years of surplus.

Years of surplus should not be included in the prescriptive period because the taking of surplus water cannot invade the basin water rights of others.

* * *

Appropriate Relief in San Fernando Basin

* * *

The trial court limited the parties' total extractions from the San Fernando basin to an annual 90,680 acre feet, which it found to be the 1964–1965 safe yield, reserving jurisdiction to redetermine the safe yield from time to time in accordance with changed hydrologic conditions. This finding established the basin's available supply for purposes of injunctive relief, the finding being supported by substantial evidence and there being no claim of any temporary surplus over and above the safe yield in 1964–1965.

Undoubtedly injunctive relief is called for in view of the undisputed overdraft prior to rendition of the present judgment. Although by far the largest share of the basin's supply must be allocated to plaintiff, the injunction should restrict plaintiff's as well as defendants' extractions. Plaintiff asserts a need for the entire safe yield of the basin and has demonstrated such need by appropriating substantially more than that amount in 1964–1965. Notwithstanding plaintiff's larger interest the defendant cities have a sufficient interest in maintaining the basin supply to warrant the restriction on plaintiff, stemming from their right to recapture the return flow attributable to their imports, which will probably increase as a result of (1) the defendants' substitution of imported water for the ground supply relinquished in deference to plaintiff's prior rights and (2) the overall expansion of their total water needs. The exercise of the return flow right would become more difficult and eventually impossible if the basin levels were continually lowered by an excess of extractions over safe yield.

On remand, the basin's safe yield should be apportioned between amounts attributable to (1) native waters produced by precipitation within the ULARA and (2) water imported from outside the ULARA. The latter amount should in turn be apportioned among the respective quantities derived from imports by plaintiff, defendant Glendale and defendant Burbank. Plaintiff should be awarded an unadjusted pumping right to the portion of the safe yield derived from native waters and from its own imports, and defendants Glendale and Burbank should each be awarded an unadjusted pumping right to the portion of the safe yield attributable to its own imports.

The new judgment should provide for adjustments in each party's pumping right to be administered by the watermaster under supervision of the court. Plaintiff's pumping right should be adjusted to take into account (1) the separate judgments entered under stipulation between plaintiff and defendants who are not parties to this appeal and (2) the imported water spread by plaintiff. The defendants' pumping rights should be adjusted to reflect return flow from their imports in excess of those for the safe yield year. * * *

Plaintiff seeks injunctive relief against extractions by the private defendants from the San Fernando basin. As already stated, these defendants' rights to the basin ground water are all subordinate to plaintiff's pueblo right and plaintiff's right to the return flow derived from its delivered imported water as well as to such return flow rights of defendants Glendale and Burbank. Accordingly, plaintiff is entitled to have the private defendants' extractions enjoined insofar as they would constitute an overdraft on the basin supply.

Some of the private defendants asserted at the trial, however, that a part or all of their respective uses of the basin water did not diminish the supply available to plaintiff. Certain defendants declared, for example, that their uses were nonconsumptive in that substantially all the extracted water was returned underground after use. Other defendants claimed that geological factors such as underground faults would prevent the water they extracted from ever reaching plaintiff's wells even if it were left in the ground. The trial court did not rule on these contentions in view of its award of prescriptive rights to these defendants based on the historic gross amounts of their extractions. On remand these contentions should be considered in the formulation of any injunctive relief. Plaintiff is not entitled to such relief against extractions which have no immediate or long-range effects on its available supply. If extractions which affect plaintiff's rights nevertheless preserve water for beneficial use that would otherwise go to waste, the trial court should endeavor to arrive at a physical solution which would avoid such waste.

WILLIAM BLOMQUIST, DIVIDING THE WATERS
146–50 (1992).

[The Central and West Basin Water Replenishment District provided a means for pursuing the adjudication of groundwater rights in the Central Basin.]

A settlement committee was appointed by the CBWA to draft an interim agreement for the reduction of pumping. The settlement committee worked with the replenishment district's attorney and engineers to develop a formula for calculating the prescriptive rights acquired in the basin. The committee met every month, and presented a draft of an interim agreement to the Central Basin Water Association on May 3, 1962, just four months after the filing of the complaint. Included as Exhibit A were the engineer's verifications of pumping records to date, which already had accounted for 93 percent of the production from the basin. Meetings with water producers began immediately thereafter to explain the interim agreement and encourage them to sign.

Those who signed the interim agreement would be required after October 31, 1962, to reduce their groundwater production to an "agreed pumping allocation" that was 80 percent of their "assumed relative right." The agreement listed the parties' assumed relative rights, based on their groundwater production and imports of water (which under the Water Code were preserved as rights for producers who had substituted imported water for groundwater). The interim agreement would be presented to the court when parties representing 75 percent of the assumed relative rights had signed.

* * *

Like the West Basin judgment, the Central Basin judgment avoided a statement of the basin's safe yield. A Department of Water Resources estimate of the 1957 safe yield was 137,300 acre-feet. Reducing pumping to that amount would have required a 50 percent cut, rather than the 20 percent decrease the parties negotiated. Central Basin water users chose instead to attempt to restore a balance to the basin by relying on a combination of a 20 percent reduction in groundwater extractions, a guaranteed minimum inflow from the Upper Area, and the artificial replenishment program.

The Central Basin negotiators placed some provisions in their stipulation that differed from those in West Basin. Exchange pool water prices were calculated by a different formula, which made prices significantly higher in Central Basin. As a result, an active market in water right leases emerged in Central Basin, since lease prices negotiated between lessor and lessee were usually lower than exchange pool prices. Watermaster service costs, too, were allocated differently in Central Basin. In the Raymond and West basins, watermaster service costs are apportioned among the parties according to their groundwater rights, which means, for some parties, issuing invoices and collecting payments that are so small the cost of billing them exceeds the amount collected. In Central Basin, a minimum charge of $5.00 is assessed every party; any remaining watermaster service costs are apportioned among parties according to their agreed pumping allocation. If the total cost of watermaster service works out to less than $5.00 per party, each party is assessed that lesser amount equally.

DEBORAH A. de LAMBERT, COMMENT, DISTRICT MANAGEMENT FOR CALIFORNIA GROUNDWATER

11 Ecology L.Q. 373, 391–93 (1984).

Orange County Water District—A Case Study

The Orange County Water District (OCWD) is often cited as a model for effective groundwater management in California. Created by a special district act, the OCWD has not needed to resort to adjudication to determine each pumper's rights in the basin. As a result, it has been able to take a more flexible and comprehensive approach to groundwater management.

The OCWD possesses the broad powers necessary for effective groundwater management. The district's express purposes are the protection, conservation, and management of the groundwater supply. Since all pumpers must register with the OCWD, the district is able to monitor the amount of groundwater pumped each year. Further, it is specifically authorized to levy four different types of assessments: *ad valorem* taxes on all property owners, replenishment assessments (pump taxes) on all water pumped when the basin is overdrafted, supplemental replenishment assessments on production of groundwater for all but irrigation purposes, and basin equity assessments. Because of its broad powers, the OCWD is able to carry out all programs and operations it deems necessary to protect the quality and supply of groundwater. Moreover, the OCWD's jurisdiction corresponds roughly to the Orange County groundwater basin.

One of OCWD's most effective management tools has been its extensive replenishment program. Supplemental water supplies are purchased for basin recharge operations and for direct use by consumers. During the 1980–81 water year, over one-half of the total water consumed in the OCWD was imported; most was used directly rather than for replenishment. The efficacy of this program is illustrated by the fact that the accumulated overdraft in the Orange County basin has declined from 700,000 acre-feet in 1956 to 120,634 acre-feet in 1980–81.

The OCWD's replenishment program depends in large part on the district's basin equity assessments and pump taxes, which serve to equalize water costs among users. In 1980–81 the district spent $1,994,-445, raised by pump taxes, to purchase supplemental water. Because imported water is more expensive than groundwater for non-irrigation users, incentives are necessary to encourage pumpers to use supplemental water in lieu of pumping. The basin equity assessments provide this incentive by taxing the consumers of groundwater in order to subsidize the users of imported water.

Other factors besides the OCWD's activities have reduced the rate of overdraft in the Orange County basin. Changing trends in land use have allowed population growth without increasing the demand for water because urban uses require much less water than agricultural uses. Changes in agricultural practices may also have contributed to the declining overdraft. Drip and low-flow irrigation, currently used in Orange County, are more efficient than flood irrigation. Additionally, farmers have shifted from irrigated crops, such as deciduous fruits and nuts, to non-irrigated crops, such as pasture. Nonetheless, total groundwater extractions in Orange County actually increased by fifty percent between 1956 and 1981.

Thus, the OCWD's management of Orange County's groundwater has produced significant results. The groundwater level rose from 12 feet below sea level in the 1950's to 17 feet above sea level in 1971. The question remains whether this type of management would work on a statewide basis.

NOTES

1. Conjunctive use stimulated by basinwide adjudications has not occurred in California's other major area of overdraft, the southern San Joaquin Valley. Large pumpers have resisted direct limitations on groundwater use. However, a study of water use in the area concludes that significant conjunctive use, if not management, has occurred in the area. Surface supplies from federal reservoirs and the state water project have been allocated to influence indirectly, and at a very uneven rate of success, the rate of groundwater use. The authors' major conclusion is that:

> private and local district groundwater decisionmaking are closely linked with surface water availability and allocation. Surface water quantity, quality, availability, and price are the most important variables in the local groundwater equation. They determine pumping rates and provide the major impetus for undertaking management programs. Groundwater management, therefore, is not direct control over pumping control; rather, it involves the conjunctive use, both planned and unplanned, of surface water and groundwater supplies.

Barbara T. Andrews and Sally K. Fairfax, *Groundwater and Intergovernmental Relations in the Southern San Joaquin Valley of California: What Are All These Cooks Doing To The Broth?*, 55 U.Colo.L.Rev. 145, 200–01 (1984).

2. There is increasing acceptance of the use of pumping charges to induce conservation. The federal government has the authority under the Reclamation Act of 1902 to impose charges for the use of groundwater which results from spreading surface water distributed to the project. 43 U.S.C.A. § 485(h). Cf. Flint v. United States, 906 F.2d 471 (9th Cir.1990) (maximum charges for operation and maintenance costs are committed to agency discretion by law). In 1987, the Texas legislature authorized the creation of a special district to conserve the Edwards Aquifer which is the sole source of supply for San Antonio.

Texas Water Code Ann. §§ 52.151–52.173. The Act allows the imposition of user charges but not taxes. A group of large pumpers challenged the imposition of fees arguing that they were in fact taxes because they were primarily designed to raise revenue as opposed to regulating the use of water. They contended that the fees would not discourage use as the additional cost would be passed on to the utility's customers. The court of appeals upheld the fee. Creedmoor Maha Water Supply Corp. v. Barton Springs—Edwards Aquifer Conservation Dist., 784 S.W.2d 79 (Tex.Ct.App.1989).

6. Prevention and Clean–Up of Contamination

Protection of the public's interest in groundwater is nowhere greater than it is with preserving the quality of underground waters for present and future uses.

Controlling groundwater quality entirely separately from regulation and allocation of rights to use groundwater is curious in light of the substantial connection between the two subjects. Although the use of a polluted supply can endanger public health, authorities deciding whether to allow pumping often look only to the quantity of water available, not the quality. The need for integrated management of quality and quantity seems obvious. Excessive groundwater pumping may lead to salt water intrusion and contamination of an aquifer. An improperly drilled well can allow a good, clean aquifer to be contaminated by polluted waters migrating from a second aquifer.

Various theories of tort law, including negligence, nuisance, trespass, and strict liability have been asserted in groundwater pollution cases, as they have been in cases of surface water pollution. Theories of ownership and rights based on prior use often are the basis for a plaintiff's claim for relief against a polluter. Peter N. Davis, *Groundwater Pollution: Case Law Theories for Relief*, 39 Mo.L.Rev. 117 (1974). See discussion of common law remedies for water pollution at pages 121–32, supra. Leaking landfills located near public drinking water supplies are likely to be classified as nuisances, see, e.g., Wood v. Picillo, 443 A.2d 1244 (R.I.1982), even if the landfill is in compliance with federal and state regulations. Neal v. Darby, 318 S.E.2d 18 (S.C.1984). Similarly, the New Mexico Supreme Court has held that the state Oil Conservation Commission's approval of a salt water disposal well does not immunize the disposer for common law liability if the water encroaches on adjoining land. Snyder Ranches, Inc. v. Oil Conservation Comm'n, 798 P.2d 587 (N.M.1990).

Some recent cases apply the strict liability rule of Rylands v. Fletcher, S.C.L.R. 3 H.L. 330 (1868), to groundwater pollution cases. See, e.g., Branch v. Western Petroleum, Inc., 657 P.2d 267 (Utah 1982) (contamination of household well from oil well chemical wastes). What is the difference between nuisance and strict liability? See State Dept. of Envtl. Protection v. Ventron Corp., 468 A.2d 150 (N.J.1983).

The following descriptions of federal statutory programs do not purport to alter the several principles for determining rights to use groundwater described in this chapter. The effect of regulation, however, is to impose a further dimension of control upon the use of the resource in order to protect the public's interest in it.

Federal statutes focus on the protection of public drinking water supplies and on the prevention of groundwater contamination from specific sources. Most pollutants are introduced into groundwater from wastes that have been disposed of in landfills, that percolate from above the ground, or that are injected into the aquifer directly. The Clean Water Act, 33 U.S.C.A. §§ 1251–1376, controls primarily surface water pollution. Although there are sections of the Act that direct the Environmental Protection Agency (EPA) to cooperate with federal and state agencies to develop programs to control groundwater contamination, the operative provisions of the Act do not directly deal with groundwater. The Act is implemented through a permitting system that is described at pages 132–35, supra. Permits are required for discharges of pollutants from "point sources" like pipes, but not for pollution from seepage, runoff and other diffused sources. Even deep-well injections are not regulated as "point sources" under the Clean Water Act. Exxon Corp. v. Train, 554 F.2d 1310 (5th Cir. 1977). Courts have suggested that discharges into groundwater connected to surface waters may be point source discharges, e.g., McClellen Ecological Seepage Situation v. Weinberger, 707 F.Supp. 1182 (E.D.Cal.1988) and Inland Steel v. EPA, 901 F.2d 1419 (7th Cir.1990).

The Safe Drinking Water Act, 42 U.S.C.A. §§ 300f et seq., provides special protection for groundwater quality. The EPA sets end-of-the-pipe standards for public drinking water systems, determines standards for state underground waste injection control (UIC) programs, and designates "sole source aquifers." After designation of an aquifer as a drinking water source, no federal funds or other financial assistance may be used for activities that the EPA determines may contaminate the aquifer through a recharge zone so as to create a public health hazard. 42 U.S.C.A. § 300h–3(e). See generally James T.B. Tripp and Adam B. Jaffe, *Preventing Groundwater Pollution: Toward a Coordinated Strategy to Protect Critical Recharge Zones*, 3 Harv.Envtl.L.Rev. 1 (1979); Linda A. Malone, *The Necessary Interrelationship Between Land Use and Preservation of Groundwater Resources,* 9 UCLA J.Envtl.L. & Pol'y 1 (1990). The 1986 Safe Drinking Water Act Amendments, Pub. L. No. 99–339, 42 U.S.C.A. §§ 300f–300j.11, require the states to prepare wellhead protection programs to protect areas surrounding wells used for public water systems from contaminants that may have adverse health effects. EPA, however, cannot impose a program if the state fails to submit one. Wellhead protection programs do not require the states to allocate or regulate the use of ground and surface waters so as to protect drinking water sources. 42 U.S.C.A. § 300h–7(j). The amendments also provide grants to enable states and local governments to prepare comprehensive management plans for designated sole source aquifers.

Most federal and state efforts under the UIC provisions of the Act so far have focused on the regulation of Class II wells, those for the production of oil, gas or geothermal resources. States have expanded the jurisdiction of their oil and gas conservation agencies to identify vulnerable groundwater areas and to regulate the disposal of fluids, usually salt water, produced or used in connection with mineral extraction. To allow uranium mining, EPA exempted 3,000 acres of the Chadron aquifer not currently used for drinking water. This exemption was upheld in Western Nebraska Resources Council v. EPA, 943 F.2d 867 (8th Cir.1991), but the court noted that any migration that injured wells outside of the carefully drawn exempt area would be a violation of the permit. Some states have gone beyond the Safe Drinking Water Act and have required permits for the direct or indirect discharge of contaminants into groundwater, e.g., N.M. Stat. Ann. § 74–6–5 (with an exemption for discharges from irrigated agriculture). See generally Roger K. Ferland, *The Protection of Groundwater Quality in the Western States—Regulatory Alternatives and the Mining Industry*, 29 Rocky Mtn.Min.L.Inst. 899 (1983).

Two federal statutes protect groundwater from contamination by releases of hazardous substances. The Resource Conservation and Recovery Act of 1976, 42 U.S.C.A. §§ 6901–6987 (RCRA), sets up a "cradle-to-grave" system to track wastes from their generation, through transportation, to treatment, storage or disposal. RCRA originally was not technology-forcing, and allowed the disposal of wastes (as opposed to their chemical alteration) so long as a facility complied with EPA regulations. In 1984, Congress intervened and prohibited the land disposal of hazardous wastes unless the EPA Administrator determines that prohibition is not necessary for public health protection. 42 U.S.C.A. § 6924(d). Before issuing a permit, EPA must determine that land disposal will be protective of human health as long as the waste remains hazardous. Deep well injection of hazardous wastes is also extensively regulated under RCRA. Wastes must be pre-treated to reduce toxicity. See Chemical Waste Management, Inc. v. EPA, 976 F.2d 2 (D.C.Cir.1992) (dilution is not an acceptable pre-injection treatment).

The Comprehensive Environmental Response, Compensation, and Liability Act of 1980, 42 U.S.C.A. §§ 9601–9657 (CERCLA or "Superfund"), is not a regulatory statute but an act that allows federal, state and local governments to bring suit against parties responsible for the unsafe disposal of hazardous wastes. Most of the damage caused by such disposal is to groundwater. The statute imposes liability on current and past owners or operators, generators who arranged for wastes to be taken to the site, and transporters. 42 U.S.C.A. § 9607(a). Liability has been held to be strict (United States v. Northeastern Pharmaceutical & Chem. Co., 579 F.Supp. 823 (W.D. Mo. 1984)), retroactive (United States v. Shell Oil Co., 605 F.Supp. 1064 (D. Colo. 1985)), and joint and several.

Several courts have recognized that private parties have a right of action for response (clean-up) costs incurred as the direct result of a release or threatened release. E.g., Wickland Oil Terminals v. Asarco, Inc., 792 F.2d 887 (9th Cir. 1986).

The prima facie case for a Superfund action is a release from a facility. 42 U.S.C.A. § 9607. Proof of a release requires a showing that a substance has begun to contaminate the soil or water in and around a site. See State of New York v. Shore Realty Corp., 759 F.2d 1032 (2d Cir. 1985). "Facility" has been broadly defined. See, e.g., State of New York v. General Elec. Co., 592 F.Supp. 291 (N.D.N.Y. 1984).

CERCLA allows three basic actions to clean up a hazardous waste site: (1) removal; (2) remedial action; and (3) abatement of an imminent hazard. A removal action may either be a short-term emergency response or a longer term planned removal. Remedial actions are long-term remedies that are designed to produce a permanent clean-up such as the restoration of an aquifer. CERCLA initially contained no technology-forcing standards so there were no statutory standards to determine the appropriate clean-up level. Decisions are made solely on a site-by-site basis. Congress imposed clean-up standards in the 1986 Superfund Amendment and Reauthorization Act. In brief, wastes may be transferred offsite only to a facility that complies with RCRA, other relevant federal laws, and all applicable state requirements. Federal and state offsite clean–ups must obtain legally applicable or relevant appropriate standards and criteria unless the EPA waives compliance.

It is generally conceded that it is too costly to clean up all hazardous waste sites. A preliminary assessment of the implementation of Superfund reveals that enormous sums of money may be spent to achieve solutions that are not permanent and often merely transfer the risks from one community to another. Office of Technology Assessment, Superfund Strategy (1985). The 1986 Superfund Reauthorization Amendments address this problem by requiring that the President (through EPA) select, to the maximum extent practicable, remedies that utilize permanent solutions and alternative treatment or resource recovery technologies that will result in a permanent and significant decrease in the toxicity, mobility or volume of a hazardous substance or contaminant. Superfund Amendments and Reauthorization Act of 1986, Pub. L. No. 99–499, 1986 U.S. Code Cong. & Admin. News (100 Stat.) 1672.

ATTORNEY GENERAL v. THOMAS SOLVENT CO.

Court of Appeals of Michigan, 1985.
146 Mich.App. 55, 380 N.W.2d 53.

T. M. BURNS, PRESIDING JUDGE.

Defendant Thomas Solvent Company (hereinafter defendant) appeals by leave granted from an order of the trial court granting a preliminary injunction to abate a public nuisance pursuant to GCR 1963, 782, now MCR 3.601.

In September, 1981, public health officials discovered that the water drawn from 10 to 30 wells which supply water to the City of Battle Creek were contaminated with toxic organic chemicals. Similar contaminants were also found in even higher concentrations in approximately 80 nearby private residential water supply wells. The 30 wells which supply the City of Battle Creek with its water are located in the Verona Well Field which is located just north of the defendant's facility. The private residential wells which are contaminated are located approximately 800 feet northwest of defendant's facilities.

Defendant is engaged in the business of selling industrial solvents and other chemicals and transporting liquid waste to recycling and disposal facilities. Defendant maintains two facilities in the Battle Creek area, the Raymond Road Facility and the Emmett Street Facility. Both of these facilities are located in Emmett Township, Calhoun County, and are a short distance from the Verona Well Field and the contaminated private wells.

At these two facilities, defendant stores a number of industrial solvents in 55-gallon drums. Defendant also has a number of underground tanks on these facilities in which defendant stores such solvents as xylene, toluene, trichloroethylene, perchloroethylene, and 1–1–1 trichloroethane, among others. Defendant uses hoses to transfer these chemicals in the underground tanks to other underground tanks and to trucks.

From 1981 through 1982, a number of soil and water samples were taken from the Verona Well Field area and defendant's facilities sites. Tests were performed with these samples by several federal, state and private agencies, including the United States Environmental Protection Agency (EPA), Michigan Department of Natural Resources (DNR), Michigan Department of Public Health and a Chicago-based technical assistance team known as Ecology and Environment Incorporated. From these tests, officials discovered the existence of a high level of toxic contaminants in the wells and on defendant's property. Accordingly, the EPA designated the Battle Creek Verona Well Field as a "superfund" site on its national priority list under 42 U.S.C. § 9601 et seq.

Because of the strong correlation between the types of contaminants found in the soil at both the Raymond Facility and the Emmett Street Facility, and the types of solvents and chemicals discovered in the wells downstream from defendant's site, it was determined by plaintiffs that defendant was at least partially responsible for the groundwater pollution. Therefore, on January 12, 1984, plaintiffs filed the instant complaint against defendant seeking a preliminary injunction, damages, and penalties. Plaintiffs' complaint alleged that defendant had violated § 6(a) and § 7 of the water resources commission act, M.C.L. § 323.1 et seq.; M.S.A. § 3.521 et seq., Thomas J. Anderson, Gordon Rockwell Environmental Protection Act, M.C.L. § 691.1201 et seq.; M.S.A. § 14.528(201) et seq., and had unlawfully committed a common-law public nuisance.

The trial court held hearings pursuant to GCR 1963, 782, in February, March and April, 1984. On May 2, 1984, the trial court issued a preliminary injunction after finding that an immediate threat of potentially irreparable harm to the public health existed at the defendant's two Battle Creek facilities and that immediate correction was necessary to remove the contaminants from the ground water, stop encroachment of the contaminants onto unpolluted land, and halt the hydrological movement of the contaminated water beneath the two facilities owned by defendant. The order required defendant to install two ground water purge wells and two monitoring wells and to treat all purged ground water with a granular activated carbon filtration system. The order also contained requirements as to the operation of the purge well and treatment system, including the requirements that defendant engage in frequent water sampling and testing procedures. Finally, the order specifically allowed either party to petition the court to modify the purge well and treatment system as necessary.

We note that, while the trial court proceedings were pending, defendant filed a petition under Chapter 11 of the Bankruptcy Code in the United States Bankruptcy Court for the Western District of Michigan. After a hearing, the bankruptcy court determined that the entry of the circuit court's preliminary injunction did not violate the automatic stay provision of the Bankruptcy Code. Subsequently, however, the bankruptcy court issued a preliminary injunction, enjoining all further proceedings to enforce the circuit court's preliminary injunction. While the bankruptcy court's injunction may make this appeal moot, defendant does not provide us with a copy of the bankruptcy court's order. The parties also do not argue that this appeal is moot. Since the validity of the bankruptcy court's injunction is seriously in question, we will consider the merits of this case.

* * *

Contrary to defendant's assertions, the trial court carefully considered the defendant's ability to pay for the clean-up. We specifically note that the trial court did not order the most costly clean-up procedures requested by plaintiff, but instead ordered more conservative measures.

We do not feel that the trial court abused its discretion. Plaintiff's experts testified that the ground water contaminated by defendant's facilities contained extremely high levels of pollutants such as 53,000 parts per billion of TCE, 78,000 parts per billion of PCE, 8,300 parts per billion of dichloroethane, and 1,700 parts per billion of carbon tetrachloride. According to the experts, the presence of these contaminants establish the existence of an emergency situation which had to be stopped immediately to prevent nearby areas from becoming contaminated. These experts also testified that exposure to these chemicals posed substantial risks to individuals including the significant increased risk of developing cancer, detrimental effects on the liver and kidneys, muscular uncoordination, the development of fluid in the lungs, and intoxicating effects such as problems with balance and behavior changes. Some of these chemicals were also flammable. It is clear that the record supports the trial court's finding that defendant's financial harm was outweighed by the public's health risk.   * * *

* * * There was ample evidence that the toxic substances which contaminated the wells in question flow through the ground water from the defendant's facilities. Defendant's claim that a finding of nuisance was unsupported by the evidence is merely speculation. While there were two other suspected sources contributing to the wells' contamina-

tion, there was a well-defined plume of contaminants leaving defendant's property. * * *

Defendant next argues that the circuit court lacked jurisdiction in this matter. First defendant claims that the passage of the Comprehensive Environmental Response, Compensation and Liability Act (CERCLA), 42 U.S.C. § 9601 et seq., directly preempted state law governing the abatement of public nuisances and, therefore, according to defendant, the circuit court in this matter did not have jurisdiction to hear the case. In the alternative, defendant argues that, even if CERCLA did not expressly preempt state law, application of the primary jurisdiction doctrine necessitates a conclusion that the circuit court was required to defer jurisdiction to the EPA.

With regard to its preemption argument, defendant relies primarily upon 42 U.S.C. § 9614(a), which states that nothing in the statute shall be construed as to preempt any state from imposing any "additional liability" or requirement with respect to the release of hazardous substances within that state. We however do not read isolated portions of statutes out of context. A plain reading of § 9614 shows that, instead of preempting state law, that statute provides that states may supplement any liability or requirements that may be imposed under CERCLA. Section 9614 does not state that the individual states are precluded from duplicating liability imposed under CERCLA. Defendant's reliance upon that provision is therefore misplaced. Moreover, § 9606(a) expressly provides that jurisdiction over pollution abatement actions is vested in both the states and local governments and in the President of the United States and his delegates. Both state and federal governments therefore have concurrent jurisdictions over pollution abatement cases. CERCLA was primarily enacted to fill gaps left by earlier federal legislation in dealing with abandoned dump sites and was intended to provide funds for state hazardous waste programs. Jones v. Inmont Corp., 584 F.Supp. 1425, 1428 (S.D.Ohio 1984). It is clear that CERCLA was intended only to supplement hazardous waste programs and not to preempt state programs.

Defendant also claims that, since the EPA is better equipped to handle this case, the trial court should have deferred jurisdiction to the EPA. During the bankruptcy proceeding, an EPA agent testified that, as a result of the circuit court's preliminary injunction, there is no longer an emergency situation regarding the possible contamination of groundwater surrounding defendant's facilities. Since the agency which defendant now claims should control this action admits that the circuit court's actions were proper, we decline to apply the doctrine of primary jurisdiction to this case. In light of the resources of the EPA and the demands on that agency, we do not feel that it would be proper to transfer sole jurisdiction of this matter to the EPA. The circuit court had jurisdiction and properly issued the preliminary injunction.

Affirmed.

NOTES

1. States and local governments not only have remedies under CERCLA to recover damages for clean-up costs and to obtain equitable relief, but may recover "damages for injury to, destruction of, or loss of natural resources." 42 U.S.C.A. § 9607(a)(4)(C). Natural resources are broadly defined to include "land, wildlife, biota, air, water, ground water, drinking water supplies, and other such resources * * *" 42 U.S.C.A. § 9601(16). How much is an aquifer worth?

2. Other federal statutes directly or indirectly control groundwater quality. For instance, the Nuclear Waste Policy Act designates Yucca Mountain, Nevada as the sole area to be evaluated as a repository for radioactive waste. 42 U.S.C.A. § 10131(b)(1). See Esmeralda County v. Dep't of Energy, 925 F.2d 1216 (9th Cir.1991) (Department of Defense acted arbitrarily in refusing to identify Inyo County, California as a potentially affected unit of government in the evaluation even though it shares an aquifer with Yucca Mountain).

UTAH v. KENNECOTT CORP.

U.S. District Court, District of Utah, 1992.
801 F.Supp. 553.

This matter is before the court on the joint motion of plaintiff, the State of Utah, and defendant, Kennecott Corporation, for approval of a proposed Consent Decree relating to a negotiated monetary settlement for damages to the State's interest in ground waters in an area within Salt Lake County, Utah. The proposed Consent Decree would settle the State's claim for natural resources damage under Section 107 of the Comprehensive Environmental Response Compensation and Liability Act (CERCLA), 42 U.S.C. 9601, et seq.

I. BACKGROUND FACTS

A. Kennecott's Five-year Hydrogeologic Study

In 1983, Kennecott undertook a five-year hydrogeologic study to assess surface and ground water conditions in a 216 square mile area affected by mining and milling operations in the Bingham Mining District. Officials of the State of Utah and Salt Lake County were consulted and informally participated in the study through advisory groups. On October 4, 1983, Kennecott submitted ground water monitoring data to the State which indicated significant ground water contamination from the Kennecott operations.

* * *

B. State Claim And Lawsuit For Natural Resources Damage

On July 31, 1986, the State filed a Notice of Claim for Natural Resource Damages under section 107 of CERCLA in the amount of $129 million dollars. The damage figure was based upon present and anticipated injury to 59,406—109,215 acre feet of ground water in the affected area over a ten to twenty year period.

* * *

D. Kennecott Offer Of Settlement

In August 1990, Kennecott presented an offer of settlement to the State which envisioned exchange of water rights valued at about $2 million dollars for the natural resource damage, plus providing about $100 million worth of remediation work. The Kennecott proposal involved:

- Kennecott undertaking remedial actions aimed at curtailing potential sources of groundwater pollution;

- Kennecott undertaking actions to remediate the heavy metals plume;

- Kennecott assigning water rights to the State as replacement for ground water containing elevated levels of sulfates and heavy metals;

- The State dismissing the lawsuit with prejudice.

The remedial action proposed by Kennecott involved drilling very deep wells below the low pH or heavy metals plume (area of contamination characterized by low pH materials or heavy metals) and pumping the contaminated water down through the uncontaminated soil, attenuating the metals and raising the pH.

E. State's Evaluation Of The Kennecott Offer

The State looked to its own staff at the Utah Department of Environmental Health, environmental health personnel at Salt Lake City—County, and experts it hired to evaluate the Kennecott offer. The principal expert concerning natural resources damages was RCG/Hagler, Bailly, Inc. of Boulder, Colorado, which organization supplied a substantial "Preliminary Assessment of Natural Resource Damages Associated with Kennecott Mining Operations in the Great Salt Lake Valley" dated December 20, 1990. ("Hagler report"). * * *

The Hagler report was never finalized, but it set forth much information and a proposed course of action which would have identified more fully damages suffered and to be suffered by the State as a result of the contamination, as well as alternatives for remediation. The report stressed that the heavy metals plume where there is much contamination presents a dynamic and spreading problem rather than a static situation. As to the potential quantity of ground water which may be regarded as damaged, the report states:

> To estimate total groundwater damages, the above range of values ($283/AF to $1429/AF) was multiplied by the annual yield represented by the plume. Kennecott's estimate of 8,000 AF as a safe annual yield relies on an overly limited interpretation of the plume (delineating the plume at 1000 mg/l of sulfates, rather than the 400 to 500 mg/l range that the U.S. EPA has stated it intends to propose for health-based drinking water standards). With a larger plume so defined, and with more appropriate interpretations of the concept of safe annual yield, *the impacted yield may be as high as 100,000 AF/year.* (emphasis added.)

Estimated damages to the State were set forth in the Hagler report using three approaches—restoration, replacement and loss of value. Estimated damages values based on these methods alone, apart from other damage considerations noted in the report, ranged from $2.3 million to $216 million, depending upon the quantity of ground water contamination and the method of valuation. It was also noted in the Hagler report that one "appreciable negative attribute" of the proposed settlement was that it "use[d] dismissal with prejudice to preclude future claims for natural resource damages other than those associated with groundwater plume remediation," and that it did not cover other damages, including "potential losses of intrinsic values."

* * *

After due consideration and review from September 1990 to March 1991, the State rejected the Kennecott settlement proposal.

F. Negotiations And Agreement For Separate Settlement Of Natural Resources Damage Claim

In rejecting the Kennecott proposal, the State determined that remedial action issues should be analyzed in greater detail and pursued with the approval and cooperation of the Environmental Protection Agency (EPA). Mr. Alkema testified at the hearing that ultimate remediation "probably would and will cost in excess of several hundred million dollars." Negotiations involving EPA, the Utah Department of Environmental Quality [DEQ] and Kennecott began in February 1991 to establish a "framework for the parties to negotiate a legally enforceable consent decree." This resulted in an Agreement in Principle which was executed on about April 1, 1992. The agreement covers all Kennecott property located in and around the Oquirrh mountains, excluding active mining operations in Barneys Canyon, and calls for Kennecott to pay response costs which will be incurred by EPA and DEQ in cleaning up the contamination at or from Kennecott's property. *The natural resource damage claim in the case at bar will not be affected by the future clean up consent decree.*

* * *

During the period March to July 1991 the State and Kennecott negotiated settlement of the State's natural resource damage claim apart from remediation. Coincidentally during this same time frame, on April 5, 1991, the Utah State Engineer released the "Salt Lake Valley Interim Ground–Water Management Plan" (Interim Plan) which identified nine water quality zones in the Salt Lake Valley, and set out the maximum annual withdrawals from each zone. * * * The Interim Plan identified area eight as having a maximum withdrawal rate of 13,000 acre feet per year. Thereafter, the State and Kennecott determined that area eight of the Interim Plan embraced the apparent area in which Kennecott's operations have caused underground water contamination. Accordingly, this area was adopted as the appropriate area within which damages should be calculated, and was designated as the "Mining Impact Area" (MIA).

* * *

G.   Proposed Consent Decree

On or about July 31, 1991 a proposed Consent Decree was tendered to the court which envisioned settlement of the State's natural resource damage claim for $11.7 million. Kennecott and the State assume in the Consent Decree that the safe annual yield of underground waters within the entire MIA has been permanently lost because of contamination and that the estimated 13,000 acre feet safe annual yield must be permanently replaced. Another assumption is that the sulfate plume and the heavy metals or low pH plume will continue to be confined within the MIA. For purposes of settlement, it was also agreed that the waters lost should be valued at the same market value as waters of drinking water quality. In exchange for $11.7 million, the proposed Consent Decree provides that the State releases and covenants not to sue Kennecott as follows:

> 1) regarding *damages for injury to, destruction of, or loss of surface water or groundwater* in the Mining Impact Area under federal law, State law, or common law including the cost of assessing such injury, destruction or loss; and 2) for administrative or injunctive relief or *response costs in connection with any groundwater plume remediation* (as that term is commonly understood, not as defined by statute or regulation) in the Mining Impact Area under CERC-LA, the State Hazardous Substances Mitigation Act (Utah Code Ann. Section 19–6–301 et seq.), or under common law. The term "groundwater remediation" does not include remediation or control of sources that have contributed, or may contribute, to contamination of surface or groundwater. (emphasis added.)

* * *

[The Salt Lake City Water Conservancy District (SLCWCD)] was granted permissive intervention to participate in discovery and to present evidence at the hearing.

H.   Evidentiary Hearing

A week-long evidentiary hearing was held from March 23, 1992 to March 30, 1992, and on May 15, 1992, at which various exhibits and extensive testimony were presented to the court by the State, Kennecott and the SLCWCD.

* * *

It appears to the court that the area of contamination is not now nor in the future will continue to be neatly contained within water area eight which was identified in the Utah State Engineer's Interim Ground–Water Management Plan and adopted by the State and Kennecott as the Mining Impact Area. There is no physical barrier to prevent the contaminated waters from spreading or moving. Because of the dynamic nature of the plumes in question, it is likely that the area of contamination will shift, spread out and continue to grow larger.

2. Determination Regarding The Infeasibility Of Restoration

The State and Kennecott presented evidence that it would be onerous and extremely costly to pump and treat the heavy metals within the low pH plume. Mr. Alkema testified on behalf of the State that pumping the ground water and cleaning it would be unworkable.

* * *

SLCWCD presented expert testimony to the effect that reverse osmosis would be feasible to remediate a portion of the plume.

* * *

The State ultimately may be proven correct in having concluded that it would be infeasible to restore the contaminated waters. However, such finding may well be in error because the State failed to require completion of studies which were begun, and failed to identify and fully discuss possible alternatives for plume remediation and restoration.

* * *

It appears to the court that while substantial source remediation has occurred, much more needs to be done. Yet, there is no specific requirement for such set forth in the proposed Consent Decree.

* * *

5. Measure Of Damages

Mr. Alkema testified that the State evaluated the following methods of damage assessment: loss of value, cost of treatment, and replacement. * * * With regard to the loss of value method, Mr. Alkema characterized it as "a market value method" that "looks at the value of the resource strictly as a sale of water rights versus what that overall impact may be to the public." As to the cost of treatment method, Mr. Alkema said that it involved the cost of "pumping water from the mining impact area and treating it and then using it as a drinking water supply." * * *

Mr. Alkema testified that the cost of replacement method of damage involves "purchasing water rights for water of comparable quality that would have been there." * * *

It is clear that the loss of value or loss of use method of evaluation was regarded by the State as strictly a market value method of computing damages. In this regard, neither Kennecott nor the State presented evidence of damages suffered by the State for loss of use other than estimated market value of the 13,000 acre feet. No amounts were presented as to existence and option values or damages. Existence value is derived from the satisfaction of simply knowing that a natural resource exists, even if no use occurs. Option value is the value associated with an individual's desire to preserve the option to use the natural resource, even if it is not currently being used.

* * *

It appears to the court that the State prematurely utilized the "loss of value" measure of damages since it had not developed sufficient facts to justify its conclusion that the contaminated plumes could not be remediated. In any event, it appears that the loss of value method was not correctly applied. In this regard, the State purported to utilize the loss of value method in determining damages to its ground water resources, but it actually utilized a strictly market value approach, based upon water quantity measured by safe annual yield. Other use and non-use values apart from market value, including option and existence values, were regarded as inapplicable. Failure to take into account damages such as loss of the aquifer apart from market value of the quantity of water the State determined to be contaminated resulted in an inadequate assessment of damages under the loss of use method.

* * *

II. LEGAL ANALYSIS

* * *

The court has determined from a preponderance of the evidence at the hearing that the settlement contained within the proposed Consent decree is deficient in at least three major respects. *First,* lack of sufficient foundation for the State's determination that its ground water natural resource cannot be restored. *Second,* failure to require substantial protection of State natural resources from further contamination. *Third,* failure to apply the proper measure of damages, which resulted in failure adequately to take into account the extent of the damages the State has suffered and will suffer as a result of the contamination. Failure to develop sufficient factual foundation to support the State's determination that contaminated ground waters cannot be restored requires that the proposed Consent Decree be rejected for failure to demonstrate that the remedial purposes CERCLA was intended to achieve cannot be achieved. Failure to mandate containment and management of the contaminated waters, and failure to require further source control does not comport with the CERCLA requirement to "*protect* and restore."

* * * The State simply failed to assess the non-consumptive use values of the aquifer, i.e., option and existence values.[29]

It appears to the court that significant additional possible damages such as loss of the aquifer are not provided for in the proposed Consent Decree, even assuming that loss of value ultimately is determined to be the proper standard. Moreover, the State failed to calculate into the settlement the costs of preventing the plumes from spreading and contaminating the remaining unspoiled portion of the aquifer, by pumping water or other methods. In addition, the State did not require

---

29. Although the aquifer is unlike most other natural resources such as lakes, eagles or seals which have more obvious existence and option values, its existence value should have been considered in the settlement given the fact that people who live in a desert most likely would assign substantial value in just knowing that an aquifer exists. The Hagler Report notes that there is "water scarcity in the valley." There was conflicting testimony at the hearing on this matter, but if true, this would certainly enhance existence value.

that the settlement include the cost of further source control which would at least lessen contamination from continuing on a daily basis. Apparently, the State clings to the possibility of future plume remediation to be ordered by EPA. That possibility is not a justifiable reason for the State to fail to adequately study possible alternatives or to fail to require a covenant to "protect and restore" State owned natural resources. In this regard, the settlement as proposed does not "capture fully all aspects of the loss." *Ohio,* 880 F.2d at 463.

This court concludes that inadequate consideration of damages requires that the proposed Consent Decree be rejected for failure to demonstrate to the court the existence of substantive fairness under CERCLA.

NOTES

1. In deciding between diminution in value and restoration as the measure of damages, what assumptions about the future value of the aquifer should be made? Traditionally, economists have assumed a constant value for crops grown with groundwater and thus have put a high discount rate on the future value. The benefits of an immediate clean-up therefore are generally small compared to the costs. However, if the value of crops grown from the aquifer is expected to increase, the equation changes dramatically, easily offsetting the discount rate. A recent study showed that the growth in value of specialty crops supports the conclusion that the expense of cleaning up groundwater salinity immediately was justified even if the most unfavorable discount rate set by some economists is used. Michael Howitt, *Putting a Price on Ground Water Quality,* in Proceedings, Changing Practices in Ground Water Management—the Pros and Cons of Regulation, Report No. 77 (University of California Water Resources Center) September, 1992, at 31.

2. As the principal case indicates, public resources may have non-market values such as non-use, existence, or option values. Economists are attempting to value the demand for these resources by new techniques such as contingent valuation. See Ronald C. Cummings, et al., Valuing Environmental Goods: An Assessment of the Contingent Valuation Method (1986). Contingent valuation asks selected people how much they would be willing to pay for an improvement in the quality of a specific resource. Contingent valuation has not been fully accepted by economists, and the outcome of this debate may influence the use of surveys in litigation. For an argument that contingent valuation is too flawed for use in natural resource damage assessments see Note, *"Ask a Silly Question * * *": Contingent Valuation of Natural Resource Damages,* 105 Harv.L.Rev.1981 (1992). Even if contingent valuation is a legitimate indicator of economic value, can it be applied to all natural resources? For example, does a contaminated aquifer have the same non-use values as the Grand Canyon?

Chapter Six

WATER DISTRIBUTION ORGANIZATIONS

For many purposes water service and supply organizations should be, and are, treated like other competitors for available water supplies. The acquisition, exercise and transfer of water rights by these entities are governed by general rules of water law in the relevant jurisdiction. In addition, there are special laws applicable to them. As the entities charged with allocating water resources among the ultimate users, they are the primary water managers. Most lawyers who practice water law are concerned with the affairs of water distribution organizations because in the West, about half the water is controlled by special districts.

The necessity of water for the support of life, its scarcity in many areas of the country, and the economic and engineering uncertainties of moving water from where it originates and naturally collects to where it is needed have all contributed to the formation of a water "industry." The industry is comprised of a variety of private and public water distribution organizations, to provide users with a dependable supply of water. The industry has been shaped by responses to particular demands or opportunities to expand water supplies. It has not necessarily evolved in a way that reflects society's changing needs and values.

There is a pervasive confusion of roles, as water distribution organizations are characterized variously as public and private entities, depending on the issue or occasion. The corporate or public nature of these entities raises a host of legal problems. There is a constant tension between the public purpose in furnishing a reliable water supply and other purposes, such as protecting the public from unfair or excessive economic burdens and managing growth.

In the settlement of the humid eastern United States, water was primarily needed for domestic purposes, for waterborne transportation, and, with the arrival of industry, for driving mills. These needs could be satisfied through individual enterprise. Rural dwellers dug wells, and industry located alongside streams and rivers. With the development of large towns and cities, however, the urban population soon required organized municipal water distribution facilities.

The Pueblo Indians of the Southwest had established community ditches five to six hundred years before the first Spanish colonists. Long before the Europeans discovered the New World, irrigation systems of the Anasazi, ancestors of today's New Mexico Pueblo Indians, along the Upper Rio Grande Valley were irrigating substantial areas of desert land. In southern Arizona's Salt River Valley, the Hohokam began using irrigation canals by 700 A.D. They constructed more than

125 miles of canals, allowing them to irrigate over 100,000 acres. The Indians lined the bottoms of many of their ditches, canals and aqueducts with hardened clay, thereby reducing seepage.

When the Spanish began to settle in the Southwest in the late 1500s, they were impressed with the canal systems of the Tewa Pueblos in New Mexico. The Spaniards promoted systems of community ditches, known as *acequias*, to support their missions and pueblo lands. These irrigation systems were improved in the following two centuries to include sandstone dams, stone aqueducts and clay pipes. One such sandstone structure, Mission Dam at Santa Barbara, California, is still standing. So important was irrigation to the development of Southwest communities that the *acequias* were usually completed before houses, churches and town buildings. Institutions were created for the administration of these ditches and canals. A superintendent was appointed to supervise the construction and maintenance of the ditches, to distribute the water among the users, and to arbitrate disputes. The irrigators provided labor according to their land holdings. A case evidencing the continuing existence of pueblo water rights is Cartwright v. Public Serv. Co. of New Mexico, 343 P.2d 654 (N.M.1958). See also pages 565–66, supra, and 776–77, infra. *Acequia* systems remain important in some communities, especially in northern New Mexico. For interesting discussions of the development of early irrigation practices, see Michael C. Meyer, Water in the Hispanic Southwest: A Social and Legal History, 1550–1850 (1984) and Robert G. Dunbar, Forging New Rights in Western Waters (1983).

The Mormons, beginning in the late 1840s, also perfected irrigation techniques in the State of Deseret, later the Utah Territory. Community sites were selected by Brigham Young so that water from the nearby mountains could be used efficiently. Mormon towns were characteristically platted in acre-square blocks; ditches with laterals were dug alongside the streets and can still be seen in small Utah towns. Farming land was adjacent to the town, with separate canals dug to irrigate this land. Within a decade, Mormon settlements were found throughout the entire Utah Territory, southern Idaho, northern Arizona and western Wyoming. Like the Spanish settlers in the Southwest, the Mormons developed community-based institutions governing water use. Brigham Young declared all water the property of the people, allocated land to settlers and ordered the construction of community dams and ditches. The administration of water was in the hands of local church leaders who distributed the water to those who built projects in proportion to the labor contributed. Leonard J. Arrington, Great Basin Kingdom: Economic History of the Latter-Day Saints, 1830–1900, 52–53 (1958). In the early days of settlement, the Church allocated the settlers' land to them and appointed watermasters to distribute the water. Formal prior appropriation came to Utah only after the theocracy gave way to a civil state, but the early church cooperative control over water evolved into the farmer-owned mutual irrigation companies characteristic of Utah today. The watermaster's duties were similar to those of the superintendent in Southwest communities.

Many of the pioneers in the West—early miners and farmers—relied on individual diversion works. Later, it became necessary for them to follow the example of the Indians and the Spanish colonists. When mining and irrigation projects moved away from the few flowing streams, it became obvious that more ambitious cooperative enterprises would be required. Mutual ditch or water companies were formed, with individual users sharing the costs of building and maintaining headgates and ditches. Finally, under the impetus of state statutes and the national reclamation movement, quasi-public conservancy and other special water districts evolved. In some cases, their activities included the generation of electricity and the provision of municipal and industrial (M & I) water, in addition to supplying the needs of irrigators.

The resulting welter of sometimes conflicting water supply institutions is exemplified in the following excerpt from Joe S. Bain, et al., Northern California's Water Industry (1966), at 76–79:

At present, general enabling statutes in California provide for the formation of fourteen classes of local public districts which have, or may have, the supplying of water for use as a primary function; in addition, special statutes providing for the formation of specific districts have created in effect two main classes of local districts similarly engaged in water supply. Added to these are numerous municipal water departments, and, outside the public realm, there are a great many private water suppliers in the form of individual proprietorships, mutual water companies, and privately owned public utility companies. This listing omits, moreover, ten more classes of "water" districts, provided for by general statutes, which are not engaged at all, or are only incidentally engaged, in supplying water, and three similar types of district that have been created individually by special statutes—none of which are considered in the following discussion.[41]

Classifying agency types according to the water service they provide is difficult and may be misleading because each of most types has some members which provide only one specific kind of service, and others which provide only one different kind of service, and, perhaps, still others which provide two or more types of service. Thus, if an agency type is classified as supplying both irrigation water and urban water, this may be taken to mean that the category includes some agencies which specialize in one sort of water service and some in another, or that all or most agencies in the category provide two or more sorts of service, or both. With this brief caveat, we offer the following classification of types of

---

41. The districts so omitted from discussion here include the following provided for as classes by general statutes: county drainage districts, levee districts, protection districts, reclamation districts, recreation and park districts, resort districts, soil conservation districts, storm drain maintenance districts, storm water districts, and water replenishment districts. Special enactments have created individually numerous county flood control districts, and a few county storm drainage districts and conservation districts, which we also will not discuss. (See California Department of Water Resources, *General Comparison of California Water District Acts* (1958); and California *Water Code* (1963), divs. 11–20.)

local water agencies in California according to the nature of predominant water service offered; there is no distinction of agency types according to whether or not they generate electric power:

A. *Types of agencies predominantly or entirely engaged in supplying irrigation water*
   1) Irrigation districts
   2) California water districts

B. *Types of agencies engaged to significant degree in supplying both irrigation water and urban water*
   3) Individual proprietorships
   4) Mutual water companies
   5) Privately owned public utilities
   6) Water storage districts
   7) Water conservation districts
   8) Water storage and conservation districts
   9) County water districts
   10) Flood control and water conservation districts
   11) County flood control and water conservation districts
   12) County water authorities
   13) County water agencies

C. *Types of agencies predominantly or entirely engaged in supplying urban water*
   14) Municipal water departments
   15) County waterworks districts
   16) Public utility districts
   17) Community service districts
   18) Municipal water districts
   19) Municipal utility districts
   20) Metropolitan water districts.

The nomenclature used in giving a title to a type of local public agency is sometimes an accurate indication of the general kind of service it predominantly supplies (for example, municipal water department, irrigation district, municipal utility district); sometimes an ambiguous indication of agency service (California water district, county water district, public utility district); and sometimes misleading (county flood control and water conservation district—often significantly involved in wholesaling or re-wholesaling water for consumptive use and, to some extent, in capturing water for use).

A. PRIVATE COMPANIES

The law of water service and distribution organizations is fundamentally different in its application to public utilities as compared to private entities. Either by statute or common law, public utilities are legal monopolies authorized to provide a public service. Generally, in return for an exclusive service area, public utilities must serve all those persons within the service area who can afford the service, charging reasonable rates applied in a non-discriminatory manner. A. J. Gustin Priest, Principles of Public Utility Regulations 227–326 (1969). Most municipal water distribution organizations are now public. In many states, investor-owned water distribution systems have been replaced by public entities, usually municipal water supply systems or special districts. See Nelson Manfred Blake, Water For the Cities (1956). Municipal water supply systems are often exempt from state public utility regulation. See Ann J. Gellis, *Water Supply in the Northeast: A Study in Regulatory Failure*, 12 Ecology L.Q. 429 (1985). Still, municipal water distribution may be subject to judicial controls based on traditional public utility principles. The next case illustrates the difference that public utility status might make to a water service organization.

THAYER v. CALIFORNIA DEVELOPMENT CO.

Supreme Court of California, 1912.
164 Cal. 117, 128 P. 21.

PER CURIAM. This is a proceeding in mandamus, instituted in the superior court of Imperial county on December 20, 1910, to compel the California Development Company, a corporation, through its receiver, to deliver to plaintiff C. E. Thayer, the wife of her co-plaintiff, W. A. Thayer, out of its central main in Imperial valley, water to irrigate her lands, upon the theory that the water therein is appropriated and held by it for sale, rental, and distribution generally to the members of that farming neighborhood. Defendants and intervener joined issue on that question. The trial court found with plaintiffs and entered judgment accordingly. These are appeals from such judgment by defendant Holabird, the receiver, and by the intervener.

The California Development Company was organized under the laws of the state of New Jersey for the purpose, among others, of acquiring, holding, constructing, and maintaining headings, dams, ditches, etc., for collecting, storing, and conducting water and irrigating land; supplying and distributing water to and irrigating and cultivating the land of itself and of others; and of selling or letting such water or the right to use the same. On December 15, 1895, it caused to be posted at a point on the Colorado river in this state, distant 1,600 feet north of the point where the international boundary line between the United States and Mexico crosses said river, a notice of appropriation claiming for itself and others 10,000 cubic feet flow per second of the waters of said river at that point. The notice further stated that it claimed the right to said water for the purpose of "developing power and for the irrigation of land in San Diego county, state of California, and in Lower California, Republic of Mexico." It was also stated in said notice that "we purpose carrying the water from the above-described point of diversion through a canal which will run in a southwesterly direction through Lower California, Republic of Mexico, and thence into that portion of San Diego county, state of California, lying to the east of the San Jacinto mountains and known as the 'New River Country.' Said canal will be 200 feet in width, and will carry a depth of 10 feet of water. Its length will be 50 miles, more or less." The detour into Mexico was rendered necessary by topographical conditions. The portion of San Diego county referred to was what is now known as the

Imperial valley, and all of the same is now contained in the subsequently created county known as Imperial county.

* * *

The plan adopted by the Development Company for its disposition of the water for irrigating such lands was substantially as follows: The company mapped out districts of territory in Imperial valley as units of irrigation, each of which was to be occupied by a mutual water company formed under the laws of this state. These companies were to be organized by the Development Company, each of said companies to have a capital stock divided into as many shares as there were approximately acres of land in the district described in its articles of incorporation, which the Development Company believed could be reasonably irrigated. The purpose of each said company was to be to procure water for the irrigation of said tract and distribute the same upon land owned by its stockholder only within said general tract, at the rate of not to exceed four acre feet per annum per acre for such share of stock owned by each stockholder, and for its stockholders only. Each share of stock was to be located upon lands at the rate of one share per acre for each acre of land owned by stockholders, where the same could be served by the ditches of the company. The Development Company was to furnish to each of said mutual companies the requisite water for its purposes at a fixed charge per acre foot.

* * *

There are between 15,000 and 30,000 acres of land within the district of Imperial Water Company No. 1 in excess of the number of shares of the capital stock provided in its articles of incorporation. Plaintiff C. E. Thayer owns 40 acres of such land which is in condition for cultivation and irrigation, and which she desires to irrigate and plant, but upon which no water stock has been located. This land is under the flow of the canal of the Development Company, and constitutes a part of the lands for irrigation of which the said waters were appropriated. By reason of the fact that all of the stock of said Imperial Water Company No. 1 has been disposed of to others who have located it upon other land, she is unable to procure stock to locate thereon, and Imperial Water Company No. 1 has no water except such as it has procured for its stockholders. On October 18, 1910, she demanded of the defendant receiver that he deliver to her water for the irrigation of such land, namely, 100 miner's inches for 24 hours, tendering him $20 therefor, which, as we understand, is at the rate of 50 cents for each acre foot, which it is claimed was the rate fixed and charged by said Development Company to the other consumers of water. The board of supervisors of Imperial county has never fixed the rates at which the Development Company shall sell, etc., water in such county. The receiver refused to comply with the demand of Mrs. Thayer.

* * *

The claim of the plaintiff is, and of necessity must be, that the California Development Company is, either directly or indirectly through auxiliary companies, engaged in supplying water for public use; that the water controlled by it is dedicated to such use; that the land of plaintiff C. E. Thayer is a part of the lands to which such water is dedicated; and therefore that she is entitled to a portion of the water for the irrigation thereof on payment of the lawfully established rate therefor. See Fellows v. Los Angeles, 151 Cal. 58, 90 Pac. 137. The controlling question in the case, therefore, is whether or not the water here involved is devoted to public use.

Under the law of this state as established at the beginning, the water right which a person gains by diversion from a stream for a beneficial use is a private right—a right subject to ownership and disposition by him, as in the case of other private property. All the decisions recognize it as such. Many of them refer to it in terms which can have no other meaning than that the right is private property.

* * *

In the case of the use of water in villages, towns, and cities, the right to the use usually extends to every inhabitant within the range of the distributing system or who can get access thereto. In the case of water for irrigation, the class is necessarily more select, and does not include the general public within the area served. But this is so because it is not every inhabitant that can make that use of the water. Only those occupying land can do so. And for this reason it is held that, while there may be a public use for the benefit of landowners, the use of water for irrigation is not public unless the water is available, as of right, upon equal terms, to all landowners of the class and within the area to be benefited who can get water from the ditches to their lands. If the dispenser of water has the right to say who shall have it, and upon what terms, selling to one and refusing to sell to another at will, it is not devoted to public use.

* * *

Under the doctrines thus established, it is evident that the California Development Company has not dedicated to public use the water which it diverts from the Colorado river, and that it has not offered it for sale, rental, or distribution in such a manner as to constitute a public use thereof. In its notice of appropriation, it declared that it claimed the water for itself and others. It did not claim it for use by the public, nor designate the "others" to whom it was to be furnished. The notice stated that the water was claimed for the purpose of developing power, and for the irrigation of lands in the "New River Country," situated in what was then San Diego county, but it did not say that it was to be used upon all said lands, nor generally upon the lands in said country. Upon each of these essential elements of a public use, the most that can be said is that the notice is silent. There never was any declaration by that company that the water was to be devoted to public use, or that it was to be offered generally for sale in California, or to all landowners in the New River Country, or in any district or part thereof, or even to all landowners along the lines of its ditches or the ditches of its auxiliary companies. No such offer or declaration has ever been made, nor has it ever been the custom or practice of the company or of its auxiliary companies to sell water in that way. The method adopted by it for the disposition of the water, and its conduct in distributing the same, have been wholly inconsistent with the idea that the water was held out for general sale or distribution, and it has been consistent only with the theory that the intention was to retain control of the water to the extent, at least, of choosing for itself the persons and corporations to whom it should be sold or delivered, and the terms and conditions on which such sales or deliveries should be made. It has, in fact, retained such control, and it has not disposed of the water otherwise than according to this plan. For this purpose it laid out seven separate districts in the New River Country, with distinct boundaries. In each of these it organized a private water corporation. The purpose of each corporation, as expressed in its articles, was to procure water for the irrigation of such lands situated within the exterior limits of the district as should belong to its stockholders, and to no other persons. Each share of the stock was to be located upon certain designated lands—one share being allotted to each acre—and the water was to be apportioned ratably among the stockholders according to the number of shares owned. The stock was not free, but was to be sold at a fixed price. To these corporations, and to no other persons, the Development Company sold the water it diverted, receiving therefor certain shares of stock of said corporations, with the right to sell the same and have them located on lands in the district by the purchasers, and with an agreement by each auxiliary company to pay thereafter an annual charge of 50 cents per acre foot for the water delivered to it. There were other restrictions which it is not necessary to mention. The Development Company sold the stock of these auxiliary companies to the landowners within the respective districts, and the same has been located by the respective companies upon particular tracts of land therein. No water has ever been sold or distributed, or offered for sale or distribution, in any other way, or to any other persons, except small quantities furnished by special agreement to a power company and to the city of Imperial. No right in any other person to demand or receive water upon any terms or at all has ever been recognized, allowed, or conceded either by the Development Company or any of the auxiliary companies. It appears, therefore, that the Development Company has always, either directly or through the auxiliary companies, selected the persons to whom it would sell and distribute the water and fixed its own prices. A use thus restricted, limited, and controlled by the owner is in no proper sense, according to the foregoing authorities, a public use.

NOTE: MUTUAL IRRIGATION COMPANIES

"The mutual irrigation companies grew out of neighborhood or community construction of ditches. After ditches were constructed it was necessary to determine the quantity of water to which each farmer was entitled and to create an institutional structure for the upkeep of the project and the division of water among the users." Robert G. Dunbar, Forging New Rights in Western Waters 28 (1983). Mormon community control of ditches in Utah is usually cited as the origin of the mutual irrigation company, but similar early cooperative efforts among farmers were reported in Arizona and Colorado.

Mutual ditch or water companies are nonprofit entities and are under the control of local water users. Consequently, they have been exempted from regulation as public utilities in some states. They should be distinguished from commercial irrigation enterprises, sometimes called "carrier ditch" companies. The latter are organized to distribute irrigation water for the profit of investors, who provide the capital and retain ownership of the works, and who are normally *not* local users. Beset by regulation as public utilities, and plagued by financial reverses, the commercial irrigation companies have virtually passed from the water scene. Mutual ditch companies and water companies, in contrast, have continuing importance.

Mutual water companies were often formed by land speculators as part of their schemes to develop and market lands. Many mutual ditch companies were created to sponsor and operate projects begun around the turn of the century under the Carey Act of 1894, 43 U.S.C.A. §§ 641–644, though most such projects were operated by irrigation districts, discussed at pages 617–63, infra. In many cases mutuals were reorganized into irrigation districts. The Act, named after its proponent, Senator Joseph M. Carey of Wyoming, authorized grants of millions of acres of land to each of the eleven westernmost states and territories for reclamation, with the expectation that private enterprises would finance irrigation projects on these lands. Carey Act projects were organized and operated as described in Valier Co. v. State, 215 P.2d 966, 968 (Mont.1950), cert. denied 340 U.S. 827 (1950):

> The Federal Government grants arid lands to the state, upon condition that the state will provide for the reclamation of the lands so granted. The state, to accomplish this condition, enters a contract with a construction company, wherein the construction company agrees to construct an irrigation system on the lands in question and to procure actual settlement of those lands by actual settlers. When the construction of the irrigation system has reached a point where there is an adequate supply of water available for the land, the state requests and the Federal Government patents to it the lands so concerned. The construction company sells shares of water stock in an operating company to the settlers; the state sells the Carey Act lands so reclaimed only to those persons who shall have bought shares of water stock from the construction company. The settler, thus armed with this contract of purchase of water stock goes to the Carey Land Board which represents the state and applies for a patent to the Carey Act lands. The water stock is issued to the settler, a patent is granted to him by the state and under the provisions of the Acts and the contracts, the water stock then becomes appurtenant to the lands.

> It is provided under the Carey Land Act and state legislation concurrent with the Act, that after the construction company has completed the building of the irrigation system and it has been

accepted as satisfactory by the state with whom the contract was made, and after the construction company has sold a certain percentage (in this case 90%) of the water stock to the settlers and has been paid in full for such 90% of the water stock, it must then turn the ownership of the system over to an operating company, the medium through which the settlers are to control the irrigation system.

The operating company is composed of the owners of Carey Act land to which the water stock so sold is appurtenant; thus, the holder and owner of the share of water stock has two distinct rights as a result of his ownership; he has the right to a specified amount of water per acre and he also has a proportionate ownership of the entire irrigation system.

Mutual ditch companies, sometimes called water users associations, were often used to contract with the Secretary of the Interior for repayment of project costs and operations of projects constructed under the Reclamation Act of 1902. See pages 622–23, infra.

Only a few original Carey Act projects, such as the Twin Falls South Side Project in Idaho, still operate today. Many of the projects suffered from miscalculated project costs, overestimated water supplies, and a shortage of settlers to buy into the operating companies. The Act was amended several times in an effort to ensure greater project stability and success, but economic and legal problems continued, and only one-eighth of the land applied for under the Act actually was patented to settlers.

B. MUNICIPAL SERVICE

"Until very recently, the universal objective of land use and related water use has been to protect public health and support economic growth and its resultant opportunities for landowners, job seekers, and people from throughout the world who seek a better life." Jerome B. Gilbert, *Water Supply and Land Use Planning: Respecting the Boundaries,* 1 Land Use Forum 338, 340 (1992). The historic policy that water should not be a barrier to urban growth was driven by three economic and legal factors. See Robert A. Gottlieb, A Thirst For Growth (1991). First, the distributive politics of water made supply augmentation the cheapest policy for urban water suppliers as well as for irrigators. Second, the politics of local governments forced communities to compete with one another for property tax revenues. Third, the endless extension of water service was supported by public utility law. The basic premise of utility service law is that service must be made available to all who can afford it. Water rates were based on average rather than marginal cost. Over the last two decades, municipalities in rapidly growing areas have changed their water distribution financing, but this has not altered the notion that a city should obtain supplies adequate to accommodate the maximum future growth.

The end of the Reclamation Era has now forced urban water suppliers to focus on water transfers and demand management (conservation) to meet new service demands, and a few in the water community have even begun to question the assumption that the local governments in arid and drought-prone areas should continue to support unlimited growth. This section examines the existing and emerging relationship between water service and urban growth.

THORNTON v. FARMERS RESERVOIR & IRRIGATION CO.

Supreme Court of Colorado, 1978.
194 Colo. 526, 575 P.2d 382.

GROVES, JUSTICE.

The City of Thornton ("Thornton"), a home rule municipality, on November 14, 1973 brought a proceeding in eminent domain against The Farmers Reservoir and Irrigation Company ("Farmers"). The property sought to be condemned may be described generally as the water and water rights, ditches and ditch rights of the Standley Lake Division of Farmers.

Farmers is a mutual ditch company * * *. The Standley Lake Division is one of four divisions of Farmers' extensive water distribution system. * * *

On June 29, 1975 the Water Rights Condemnation Act was adopted, to become effective on July 1, 1975. Sections 38–6–201 through 216, C.R.S.1973 (1976 Supp.). This legislation is here referred to as the 1975 Act. With notable exceptions, the 1975 Act contains the same provisions as sections 38–6–101 through 118, C.R.S.1973 (Eminent Domain Proceedings by Cities and Towns).

We now consider some of these exceptions. The 1975 Act provides that, in its petition for condemnation filed in the district court, the municipality shall pray for the appointment of three commissioners "to determine the issue of the necessity of exercising eminent domain as proposed in the petition." The 1975 Act further states that no municipality shall be allowed to condemn water rights for any anticipated or future needs in excess of 15 years. The 1975 Act further specifies that the municipality shall prepare a "community growth development plan" and a detailed statement concerning the proposed condemnation of water rights and the effect of the taking of the same. The plan and statement are to be presented to the commissioners.

Throughout these proceedings Thornton has maintained the position that it derives its authority to condemn from the Colorado Constitution and it is attempting to follow the procedures of the general eminent domain statute, sections 38–1–101 et seq., C.R.S.1973. It has consistently taken the position that the action was not brought under the 1975 Act for the reason that it regards provisions of that act to be unconstitutional as applied to it.

After the Standley Lake Division stockholders were brought into the action, six motions to dismiss and two motions for summary judgment were filed. Most of these contained the ground, among others, that Thornton had failed to comply with the provisions of the 1975 Act. The district court granted all of these motions in a single order of dismissal. * * *

From this order of October 6, 1976 a timely appeal was taken to the Colorado Court of Appeals. We accepted jurisdiction of the case from the court of appeals. * * *

I. CONSTITUTIONALITY AS APPLIED TO THORNTON

A. *Commission to Determine Necessity.*

The 1975 Act contains the following provisions relating to the commission:

> The municipality's petition for condemnation of a water right "shall pray for the appointment of three disinterested commissioners appointed by the court * * * to determine the issue of the necessity of exercising eminent domain as proposed in the petition and, if the condemnation is to be allowed, to appraise the award of damages." Section 38–6–202(1), C.R.S.1973 (1976 Supp.).

> Prior to any hearing of condemnation the municipality shall prepare and update a community growth development plan and a detailed statement describing: (1) the water rights to be required and their present uses; (2) the effects from the change of the use of the water to the proposed use, including economic and environmental effects; (3) unavoidable adverse and irreversible effects from the taking; and (4) alternative sources of water supply that might be acquired. These statements shall be presented to the commission. Section 203.

> It is the duty of the commissioners to "[e]xamine and assess the growth development plan and statement provided by the municipality * * * obtain necessary information pursuant to powers granted * * * and make a determination as to the necessity of exercising the power of eminent domain for the proposed purposes." The commissioner shall provide "one of the following recommendations to the court, based upon their findings: (I) There exists no need and necessity for condemnation as proposed." Section 207(1).

> The commissioners shall, after hearing, certify the proper compensation to be made to the owners of property to be taken but, if "the commissioners find there exists no need and necessity for the condemnation proposed, they shall make no finding as to the value of the condemned property." Section 207(3) and (4).

> After filing of the report of the commissioners, written objections may be made thereto. "Any party interested in said proceeding may introduce such evidence as may tend to establish the right of the matter. The burden of proof to change any finding, award, or assessment of said commissioners shall be upon the person objecting thereto. * * * The court, for good cause shown, may modify, alter, change, annul, or confirm the report of the commissioners, or any part thereof, or may order a new appraisement and assessment as to any of the property affected in the proceeding by the same commissioners or by other commissioners appointed by the court." Section 210.

The provisions of the 1975 Act relating to the appointment, action and effect of a commission to determine the issue of necessity of exercising eminent domain are unconstitutional as applied to Thornton as a home rule municipality. These provisions are in conflict with the express grant of eminent domain powers to home rule cities by Colo. Const. Art. XX, Sec. 1.

The 1975 Act does not state specifically the effect of a finding by the commission that there exists no need or necessity for condemnation as proposed. It is to be implied from the Act, however, that such a finding of the commission prevents the proposed condemnation; or, with the burden of proof upon a person objecting thereto, such finding is subject to judicial review.

* * *

Colo. Const. Art. XX, Sec. 1 provides in part that a home rule municipality:

"shall have the power, within or without its territorial limits, to construct, *condemn and purchase*, purchase, acquire, lease, add to, maintain, conduct and operate, *water works*, light plants, power plants, transportation systems, heating plants, and any other public utilities or works or ways local in use and extent, in whole or in part, *and everything required therefore* * * * and * * * the same or any part thereof may be purchased by said city and county which may enforce such purchase by proceedings at law as in taking land for public use by right of eminent domain." (emphasis added.)

By the adoption of Article XX, and particularly the above quoted provisions thereof, the people of Colorado intended to, and in effect did, delegate to home rule municipalities full power to exercise the right of eminent domain in the effectuation of any lawful, public and municipal purpose, including particularly the acquisition of water rights. * * *

The determination of necessity is an essential part of the power of eminent domain and, once necessity is determined by legislative act, no further finding or adjudication is required. * * *

B. *The Fifteen-Year Limitation.*

The 1975 Act provides that: "No municipality shall be allowed to condemn water rights, as provided in section 38–6–207, for any anticipated or future needs in excess of fifteen years * * *." Section 38–6–202(2), C.R.S.1973 (1976 Supp.). This must be considered as one of the new provisions in the 1975 Act, as to which Thornton's failure of compliance caused the district court to dismiss the action. Section 38–6–207, referred to in the last quoted provision of the statute, relates to the duties of the commissioners, including their duty to make a determination as to necessity and their power to find that no need and necessity exists for the proposed condemnation. It is obvious that the General Assembly, in adopting the so-called 15-year provision and referring to section 38–6–207, intended the 15-year limitation to be binding upon the commissioners in their determination of necessity.

This 15-year provision, as applied to home rule municipalities, is unconstitutional for the same reasons set forth earlier in this opinion. As already emphasized, the only review of a home rule municipality's finding of necessity results from fraud or bad faith. Under certain circumstances anticipating future needs for a period less than 15 years might be in bad faith and, under other circumstances, anticipating them for a period more than fifteen years might not be in bad faith.

C. *Furnishing of Irrigation Water by Farmers a Public Use.*

While no authority is cited therefor, it is argued that the service of irrigation water by a mutual ditch company to its shareholders is a public use. Our research has not developed any authority for this proposition. Assuming, however, that such service is a public use, it is argued that under the authority of Beth Medrosh Hagodol v. City of Aurora, 126 Colo. 267, 248 P.2d 732 (1952), a municipality may not condemn property dedicated to a public use for another public use. *Beth Medrosh Hagodol* recognizes that Colo. Const. Art. XX grants to home rule municipalities ample power to acquire by condemnation property already devoted to a public use.

D. *Thornton's Sale to Users Outside Its Municipal Boundaries.*

It is argued that the sale by a municipality of water to users outside its boundaries is not a public use and that a home rule municipality does not have constitutional power to condemn water for such a purpose. Section 31–15–708(d), C.R.S.1973 (1977 Repl.Vol.) provides that the governing body of each municipality has the power to "supply water from its water system to consumers outside the municipal limits of the municipality and to collect such charges upon such conditions and limitations as said municipality may impose by ordinance." We view this as a legislative pronouncement that such use of water is a public use, and we are bound by it. The right of a home rule municipality under the Colorado Constitution to supply water users outside the city limits was upheld in Colorado Open Space Council, Inc. v. Denver, 190 Colo. 122, 543 P.2d 1258 (1975).

We wish to make it clear, however, that we do *not* hold that a home rule city may condemn water for its needs which cannot reasonably be anticipated.

* * *

ERICKSON and CARRIGAN, JJ., dissent.

I.

Applicability of the Water Rights Condemnation Act of 1975

* * *

A municipality's election to exercise eminent domain powers to condemn water rights is a matter of statewide concern, subject to statutory regulation by the General Assembly. Expanding water requirements of growing municipal populations are causing much of Colorado's scarce water, previously devoted to agricultural use, to be acquired for municipal use. Municipal condemnation of water rights necessarily has a tremendous impact upon the economies of agricultural areas and disrupts farm operations which are far distant from the condemning city. Therefore, I cannot accept the majority's conclusion that this area of statewide concern cannot be regulated on a statewide basis by the Water Rights Condemnation Act of 1975.

* * *

NOTES

1. Notwithstanding the court's strong support for municipal condemnation powers and its understanding of the pressures to shift water from agriculture to satisfy the needs of growing municipalities, there is relatively little condemnation activity in Colorado or elsewhere in the West. Most transfers are made in negotiated transactions. Why do you think this is the case?

2. Usually, a municipality must look to sources outside its boundaries for the acquisition of water supplies. This raises the question of municipal authority to act beyond the city limits. In the absence of statutory authorization, many early cases implied such authority. See, for instance, Hall v. Calhoun, 79 S.E. 533 (Ga.1913). The problem is now addressed by statute in most states. A useful discussion of the issues is John C. Feirich, Note, *Municipal Power Arising from the Ownership of Extraterritorial Property*, 1957 Ill.L.Forum 99. A Colorado statute limiting municipal condemnation of land to property located within five miles of the city limits was held to be inapplicable to Denver under the constitutional grant of condemnation powers in the provision discussed in *Thornton*. Denver v. Board of Comm'rs of Arapahoe County, 156 P.2d 101 (Colo.1945).

3. Is condemnation of water by a municipality always for a "public use"? Courts have generally held that if the primary purpose of the condemnation is to supply water, incidental benefits are permissible, or that incidental private benefits will be disregarded where it is difficult to segregate the private from the public uses. See Richard S. Harnsberger, *Eminent Domain in Water Law*, 48 Neb.L.Rev. 325, 366–69 (1969). Condemnation of water rights to serve users located outside a city's boundaries was upheld in *Thornton*. But the Nebraska Supreme Court has held that condemnation of water rights by a municipality for use by a single industry outside the municipal boundaries is not a public use, although the city would, of course, benefit from the revenues. Burger v. Beatrice, 147 N.W.2d 784 (Neb.1967). See also City of Aurora v. Commerce Group Corp., 694 P.2d 382 (Colo. App. 1984) (city cannot condemn stream outside its boundaries for fishing purposes).

4. Are the considerations relating to condemnation of water rights in a riparian jurisdiction different from those that apply to condemnation of rights in a prior appropriation state?

DIMMOCK v. NEW LONDON

Supreme Court of Connecticut, 1968.
157 Conn. 9, 245 A.2d 569.

HOUSE, J. The plaintiffs, who are riparian owners along the course of Harris Brook and one of its source streams known as Fraser Brook, in Salem, instituted this action to enjoin the defendant from diverting water from a branch of Fraser Brook and to recover damages for the diversion already made.

The finding, with the addition of such admitted and undisputed facts as the plaintiffs are entitled to have included, establishes the following facts material to the issues on this appeal: The defendant, the city of New London, owns a large tract of land east of route 85 and south of Forsythe Road in Salem. On this land there is a reservoir known as Fairy Lake, which is a part of the defendant's water system. North of Fairy Lake and also on the defendant's land is Bond Pond, which was created in 1916 or 1918 by a previous owner, who built a concrete dam across the course of a branch of Fraser Brook and thus impounded the waters of that brook to create the pond. Although they are not far apart, Fairy Lake and Bond Pond lie in separate and distinct watersheds. The natural flow of water out of Fairy Lake is to the south. The flow of the branch of Fraser Brook dammed to create Bond Pond is in a general westerly direction into a branch of Harris Brook, this flow being across the lands of the plaintiffs.

As the result of a severe six-year drought, the supply of water in the defendant's reservoirs had been seriously depleted, and as of December 29, 1965, water in storage in the defendant's reservoirs was but 18.8 percent of capacity. Restrictions on the use of water by consumers on the defendant's water supply system were imposed, and the defendant made a lease arrangement to take water for its system from a pond known as Beckwith Pond, commencing pumping operations to obtain water from this source in February, 1966. In February or March, 1966, the defendant also caused a canal to be excavated between Bond Pond and Fairy Lake. The canal is 400 feet in length with a width at its base of six feet. For approximately 200 feet on the center line of the canal, the excavation was made through ledge, the maximum cut of the ledge being approximately ten feet on the center line. The canal slopes on a 1 percent grade from Bond Pond to Fairy Lake. On March 18, 1966, the defendant installed stop logs to a height of 2.3 feet on the dam which had created Bond Pond, the stop logs being about the same height as the invert of the canal, and they were maintained at this height from that date to the time of trial on October 11, 1966. As a result, slightly more than half the water from Bond Pond goes over the dam and in its natural course continues in streams over the plaintiffs' lands, and slightly less than half is diverted from that natural watershed and instead flows south through the canal to Fairy Lake and into the defendant's water system. Readings taken a week after the defendant installed the stop logs at Bond Pond showed that, of a total flow in the brook course of 994,500 gallons per day, 439,000 gallons were diverted by the defendant through its canal. Readings taken on nine days between April 4 and June 2, 1966, showed 185,000 gallons per day flowing over the dam into the lower part of the brook course and 155,000 gallons per day being diverted into the defendant's canal. During the summer of 1966, there was little or no flow in any of the brooks of the area, and as of August 31, 1966, precipitation for the calendar year to that date was 30.65 percent below normal.

Between June 23, 1966, and October 6, 1966, there was no flow of water out of Bond Pond into either the canal or the brook. As a result of its 2,000,000 gallons per day temporary pumping operation at Beckwith Pond and to a very small extent as a result of its springtime diversion from Bond Pond, the defendant was able to increase its water supply in storage from 18.8 percent of reservoir capacity on December 29, 1965, to 52.6 percent of capacity on August 31, 1966. In the late spring or early summer of 1966, it removed the restrictions which it had imposed on the use of water by its customers, and between January 1, 1966, and the date of trial on October 11, 1966, it approved the sale of water to sixty additional residential properties in Waterford and the sale of 50,000 gallons per day to an atomic power site.

On the foregoing facts, the trial court concluded that the defendant's use of the water from Bond Pond was a public use; that the measures taken by the city were not unreasonable; that its action was necessary and appropriate to protect the communities served by the water supply of the defendant's reservoirs and ponds; that to grant an injunction would adversely affect the interest of the public; and that no damages were proven by the plaintiffs. It rendered judgment for the defendant, and it is from that judgment that the plaintiffs have appealed.

So far as actual damage sustained by the plaintiffs is concerned, the conclusion of the trial court cannot be successfully attacked. Each of the plaintiffs testified to the manner in which his property was adversely affected by the defendant's diversion of water from Bond Pond. The weight and degree of credibility to be given to this testimony, however, was for the trial court to determine. Despite their testimony, the court, as the trier of fact, could find that the plaintiffs failed to sustain their burden of proof as to any actual damage to their property or, under the circumstances, that any actual damage they did sustain as a result of lack of water in the stream crossing their properties was due, not to any diversion of water by the defendant, but rather to the severe drought which dried up all the streams in the area. The lack of such proof, however, is not decisive where, as in this case, the gravamen of the plaintiffs' complaint is the defendant's infringement of their riparian rights. The facts found by the trial court clearly establish that the defendant did divert and appropriate to its own use a portion of the natural flow of a branch of Fraser Brook which would otherwise, in its natural course, have flowed through the properties of the plaintiffs.

A riparian owner is entitled to the natural flow of the water of the running stream through or along his land, in its accustomed channel, undiminished in quantity and unimpaired in quality. As we noted in Stamford Extract Mfg. Co. v. Stamford Rolling Mills Co., 101 Conn. 310, 320, 125 A. 623, this is an ancient common-law right which a riparian owner can protect without reference to any beneficial use of the water actually made by him. * * *

The defendant did not seek to invoke such powers of eminent domain as it has. See "An Act to Provide the City of New London with a Supply of Pure and Wholesome Water," approved July 5, 1871 (7 Spec. Laws 157), as amended by No. 75 of the 1901 Special Laws (13 Spec. Laws 646). The trial court was not called upon to determine the extent and applicability of these powers, and neither are we.

That the defendant's use of the diverted water was a public use and that its action in making the diversion was necessary and appropriate to protect the communities served by the water supply of the defendant's reservoirs and ponds were factors relevant to the question whether a court of equity would enjoin any future diversion, but they did not make the completed diversion any the less wrongful as to the plaintiffs whose rights were infringed by it.

The conclusion must be that the defendant's diversion of the water from Bond Pond constituted a wrongful infringement of the riparian rights of the plaintiffs for which they are, at the least, entitled to nominal damages.

This determination brings us to the remaining issue on appeal: Did the court err in refusing to enjoin the defendant from any future diversion of the waters of a branch of Fraser Brook? The granting of relief by way of injunction lies in the sound discretion of the court. That discretion, however, is not an unlimited one. As we said in the *Adams* case, supra [138 Conn. 205, 83 A.2d 177]: "It is well within a court's discretion to deny an injunction against the infringement of riparian rights if to grant it would adversely affect the interest of the public." Because of the drought conditions which the court found to exist at the time of the trial of the present case, it could reasonably and logically conclude, as did the court in the *Adams* case, supra, 219, that relief to the plaintiffs by way of such an injunction as requested would at that time seriously and adversely affect the public interest. The concluding portion of the opinion in the *Adams* case is, however, also particularly pertinent (p. 219): "Except for one consideration, therefore, the denial of the plaintiffs' prayer for that injunction was correct. That consideration is this: The plaintiffs do have property rights to the accustomed flow of * * * [Fraser Brook]. In the emergency of a drought the public interest may require the court to refuse to protect those rights by way of injunction. However, the riparian owners ought not to be deprived permanently of those rights without compensation. If the judgment of the trial court stands in its present form, there is nothing to prevent the defendant from continuing indefinitely to * * * [take] water from the * * * [brook] as the most economical way of getting [a portion of] its required supply. * * * The result would be that the plaintiffs would for many years continue to be deprived of their rights without any compensation except that which they might recover by a multiplicity of actions. It is obviously not doing equity to leave them in such a position. Under the circumstances of this case, equity demanded that the defendant be allowed a reasonable time within which to make adequate compensation to the plaintiffs for the permanent taking of their water rights if it intends to acquire them, and, if that compensation is not made within such reasonable time, the defendant should be enjoined from further diversion of the waters of the stream. Harding v. Stamford Water Co., 41 Conn. 87, 95. Although the granting or withholding of an injunction lies in the discretion of a trial court, when the only reasonable conclusion is that a plaintiff is, in equity, entitled to an injunction in a given form, it is competent for us to order such an injunction even though the trial court has refused it. Hammerberg v. Leinert, 132 Conn. 596, 604, 46 A.2d 420. The trial court was in error in unconditionally denying the injunction against the diversion of the waters of the stream."

There is error, the judgment is set aside and the case is remanded with direction (a) to award to the plaintiffs damages in a nominal amount for the infringement by the defendant of their riparian rights and (b) to hear the parties and fix a reasonable time for the defendant to acquire the water rights of the plaintiffs by voluntary negotiation or, if the defendant has the power of eminent domain in the circumstances and elects to exercise it, by condemnation and then to render a judgment which shall direct that, unless compensation is made within that reasonable time, the defendant shall be enjoined from further diversion of the waters from the branch of Fraser Brook as prayed.

In this opinion the other judges concurred.

NOTES

1. Does the order of the court put plaintiff in a monopoly position? What factors will establish the bargaining range for the price to be paid for plaintiff's water rights? Is plaintiff alone among riparians on Harris and Fraser Brooks in the right to receive compensation? Or will New London be required to pay riparian landowners all the way downstream from Bond Pond to salt water?

2. Suppose the trial court had found that one half the water in Bond Pond had originated as precipitation on New London's land. Would the diversion have been justified under these circumstances? New London contended that with 10,000 workers, carrying 10,000 buckets, all of the runoff could have been carried to Fairy Lake and that transporting it by more efficient means should make the water the property of the defendant. How would you answer this contention? See Paul M. Ginsberg, Note, *Ownership of Diffused Surface Waters in the West*, 20 Stan.L.Rev. 1205 (1968).

3. When a city in a riparian jurisdiction seeks to acquire water rights, it is generally assumed that it must condemn riparian land and compensate any landowners who are injured by the diversion. This is normally accomplished by public or private corporations authorized to condemn water rights to secure public water supplies. See Wibert L. Ziegler, *Acquisition and Protection of Water Supplies by Municipalities*, 57 Mich.L.Rev. 349 (1959). When challenged, a city can use the preference for domestic uses to establish that the condemnation is for a public use or purpose and to urge that it is immune from injunctive relief. But can a city owning riparian land also claim that it is a riparian and invoke the domestic use preference to avoid damage payments to injured riparians? The usual answer is no, although there

is contrary authority. Compare City of Canton v. Shock, 63 N.E. 600 (Ohio 1902), with Pernell v. City of Henderson, 16 S.E.2d 449 (N.C.1941). For a collection of cases, see 2 Julius L. Sockman, Nichols' The Law of Eminent Domain § 5.39 (rev. 3d ed. 1990). The argument for the city is that it stands in its corporate capacity as a single proprietor. How would you articulate the case for compensation of injured riparians?

4. An adequate water supply is necessary for urban growth; until recently most water providers encouraged urban development by the extension of the necessary services, and supplied water at rates that many considered artificially low. See the classic discussion in Jack Hirschleifer et al., Water Supply, Economics, Technology, and Policy 87–113 (1960). In recent years advocates of infrastructure planning have argued that water service should be subordinated to community growth control policies and that water should be distributed through marginal cost-based tariffs.

5. The legal issues involved in the implementation of infrastructure planning will vary from jurisdiction to jurisdiction, but the overriding issue is the characterization of the provider's function. If the provider is characterized as a public utility, then the denial of service in a growing area may be inconsistent with its duty of nondiscriminatory service. If the function is characterized as governmental, the discretion to adopt a service policy is greater. A utility has some duty to render unprofitable service as long as the system as a whole earns a fair rate of return, e.g., Ridley Township v. Pennsylvania Pub. Util. Comm'n, 94 A.2d 168 (Pa.Super.Ct.1953). See generally, Barbara A. Ramsey Note, *Control of the Timing and Location of Government Utility Extensions*, 26 Stan.L.Rev. 945 (1974). The following case and notes illustrate some of the problems of coordinating water service with land use policies.

ROBINSON v. BOULDER

Supreme Court of Colorado, 1976.
190 Colo. 357, 547 P.2d 228.

DAY, JUSTICE.

This is an appeal brought by appellant, City of Boulder (Boulder), seeking reversal of a trial court order mandating its extension of water and sewer service to appellees. We affirm.

Appellees (landowners) sought to subdivide approximately 79 acres of land in the Gunbarrel Hill area northeast of Boulder and outside of its city limits. The landowners proposed a residential development in conformity with its county rural residential (RR) zoning.

As a condition precedent to considering the question of development, the county required the landowners to secure water and sewer services; they were referred to the city for that purpose.

Boulder operates a water and sewer utility system. In the mid 1960's it defined an area beyond its corporate limits, including the subject property, for which it intended to be the only water and sewer servicing agency. The record reflects that this was accomplished in order to gain indirect control over the development of property located within the service area. Boulder contracted with and provided water and sewer service to the Boulder Valley Water and Sanitation District (the district), which is located within the service area. The subject property is immediately adjacent to the district. The contract between Boulder and the district vests in the former almost total control over water and sewer service within district boundaries. The latter functions in merely a nominal administrative capacity. For example, Boulder retains control over all engineering and construction aspects of the service as well as decision-making power over the district's authority to expand its boundaries. Pursuant to a city ordinance, the district cannot increase its service area without the approval of city council.

The landowners applied to the district for inclusion, and the application was accepted; however, Boulder disapproved the action on the grounds that the landowners' proposal was inconsistent with the Boulder Valley Comprehensive Plan and various aspects of the city's interim growth policy. The trial court found that:

> " * * * The City seeks to effect its growth rate regulation goals in the Gunbarrel Hill area by using its water and sewer utility as the means to accomplish its goals. * * * "

The decision was *not* based on Boulder's incapacity to supply the service or the property's remote location from existing facilities or any economic considerations.

* * *

I.

On appeal Boulder argues that its service program in Gunbarrel is not a public utility under the test which we enunciated in City of Englewood v. Denver, 123 Colo. 290, 229 P.2d 667 (1951):

> " * * * to fall into the class of public utility, a business or enterprise must be impressed with a public interest and that those engaged in the conduct thereof must hold themselves out as serving or ready to serve all members of the public, who may require it, to the extent of their capacity. The nature of the service must be such that all members of the public have an enforceable right to demand it. * * * "

Boulder contends that it has never held itself out as being ready to serve all members of the public to the extent of its capacity. The trial court made findings to the contrary and the record amply supports them. * * *

Boulder relies on *City of Englewood*, supra, to support its position that it is not operating as a public utility within the area in question; that reliance is misplaced. The determination that Denver did not operate as a public utility in supplying Englewood with water was premised on an entirely different factual background. Denver's supplying of water to Englewood users was wholly incidental to the operation of its water system which was established for the purpose of supplying Denver inhabitants. Denver did not "stake out" a territory in Englewood and seek to become the sole supplier of water in the territory. Here, by agreements with other suppliers to the effect that the latter would not service the Gunbarrel area and by opposing other methods or sources of supply, Boulder has secured a monopoly over area water and sewer utilities. Further, as the trial court pointed out:

" * * * The City of Boulder had dedicated its water and sewer service to public use to benefit both the inhabitants of Boulder and the residents of the Gunbarrel Hill area in the interest of controlling the growth of the area and to provide living qualities which the City deems desirable. * * * "

II.

Boulder argues that even if its program satisfies the tests of a public utility in the Gunbarrel area that it may use public policy considerations in administering its service program. It contends that the rules which apply to private utilities should not apply to a governmental utility authorized to implement governmental objectives, one of which is the adoption of a master plan of development.

Section 31–23–106(1), C.R.S.1973, in relevant part, states:

"*Master plan.* (1) It is the duty of the municipal planning commission to make and adopt a master plan for the physical development of the municipality, including any areas outside of its boundaries, *subject to the approval of the legislative or governing body having jurisdiction thereof*, which in the commission's judgment, bear relation to the planning of such municipality. Such plan, with the accompanying maps, plats, charts, and descriptive matter, shall show the commission's recommendations for the development of said territory including, among other things:

* * *

"(b) The general location and extent of *public utilities* and terminals, whether publicly or privately owned or operated, *for water*, light, *sanitation*, transportation, communication, power, and other purposes;

"(c) The removal, relocation, widening, narrowing, vacating, abandonment, change of use, or extension of any of the ways, grounds, open spaces, buildings, property, *utility*, or terminals referred to in paragraphs (a) and (b) of this subsection (1); * * * " (Emphasis added.)

To this end, the city of Boulder and Boulder County jointly developed and adopted the Boulder Valley Comprehensive Plan, one of the purposes of which is to provide a basis for the discretionary land use decisions which it must make. Boulder also cites section 31–23–109, C.R.S.1973, which states in relevant part:

"*Legal status of official plan.* When the municipal planning commission has adopted the master plan of the municipality or of one or more major sections or districts thereof, no street, square, park or other public way, ground or open space, or public building or structure, or *publicly* or privately *owned public utility* shall be constructed or authorized in the municipality or in such planned section and district until the location, character, and extent thereof has been submitted for approval by the commission. In case of disapproval, the commission shall communicate its reasons to the council, which has the power to overrule such disapproval by a recorded vote of not less than two-thirds of its entire membership. If the public way, ground space, building, structure, or utility is one the authorization or financing of which does not, under the law or charter provisions governing the same, fall within the province of the municipal council, then the submission to the planning commission shall be by the board, commission, or body having jurisdiction, and the planning commission's disapproval may be overruled by said board, commission, or body by a vote of not less than two-thirds of its membership. The failure of the commission to act within sixty days from and after the date of official submission to it shall be deemed approval." (Emphasis added.)

Boulder argues that its decision to deny the extension of services to the landowners in this case was based on the proposed development's noncompliance with growth projections outlined in the comprehensive plan. In the event of an alleged conflict between Boulder's public utility and land use planning duties we are asked to rule that the latter are paramount.

A municipality is without jurisdiction over territory outside its municipal limits in the absence of legislation. We find nothing in the above-cited statutes which indicates a legislative intent to broaden a city's authority in a case such as the one before us. In our view, sections 31–23–106(1) and 31–23–109 place ultimate governmental authority in matters pertaining to land use in unincorporated areas in the county. In effect, a city is given only an advisory role.

The record reflects that the proposed development would comply with county zoning regulations; and the county planning staff has indicated that it conforms with their interpretation of the comprehensive plan, though final consideration was put off pending a determination of whether the area would have adequate water and sewer facilities.

* * *

In conclusion, we hold that inasmuch as Boulder is the sole and exclusive provider of water and sewer services in the area surrounding the subject property, it is a public utility. As such, it holds itself out as ready and able to serve those in the territory who require the service. There is no utility related reason, such as insufficient water, preventing it from extending these services to the landowners. Unless such reasons exist, Boulder cannot refuse to serve the people in the subject area.

Judgment affirmed.

NOTES

1. Compare City of Colorado Springs v. Kitty Hawk Dev. Co., 392 P.2d 467 (Colo.1964), cert. denied 379 U.S. 647 (1965), where the court said "It is now well established in this state that a city is under no obligation to sell or furnish water or sewer services to anyone outside its corporate limits, but, if it elects to do so, it acts in a proprietary capacity, and the relationship entered into between a city as a supplier and such users is purely contractual." 392 P.2d at 471. What factors cause a municipality to cross the line from contractor to public utility? Should a city's power to subordinate utility service to land use planning goals turn on whether the city is acting as a public utility?

Robinson is criticized in Stuart L. Deutsch, *Capital Improvement Controls As Land Use Control Devices*, 9 Envtl.L. 61, 66–67 (1978). The case has not been followed in some states. Dateline Builders, Inc. v. Santa Rosa, 194 Cal.Rptr. 258 (1983) and Tisei v. Town of Ogunquit, 491 A.2d 564 (Me. 1985). *Dateline Builders* rejected *Robinson* and the rule that the city was subject to the public utility duty of equal service:

> Builders' contention that denial of the certificate could not be used as a planning device overlooks a fundamental distinction between such a decision as an improper initial use of the police power, and as here, a necessary and proper exercise of the power once the planning decision had been made.

194 Cal.Rptr. at 266.

2. May a municipality expand its sphere of influence by conditioning its willingness to supply water to outsiders on an agreement to comply with other municipal requirements, such as annexation, building codes, or land use regulations? See Brookens v. Yakima, 550 P.2d 30 (Wash.Ct.App.1976), where the city, having provided water to a portion of plaintiffs' land, refused to increase deliveries to plaintiffs' remaining acreage when a proposed mobile home park failed to comply with the city's general plan. A related issue involves a municipality's refusal to provide a building permit unless an adequate water supply is available for the proposed development. See Associated Home Builders of Greater Eastbay, Inc. v. Livermore, 557 P.2d 473 (Cal.1976).

3. Cities generally are not required to sell their water outside the city boundaries, but often have excess water that they wish to sell to outsiders. May they? The usual answer is yes, subject to the dangers of acquiring public utility status as illustrated in *Robinson*. Many states have authorized outside sales by statute. See, for instance, Utah Code Ann. § 10–8–14.

4. The Supreme Court's decisions broadening the opportunities for finding municipal liability for antitrust violations (Lafayette v. Louisiana Power & Light Co., 435 U.S. 389 (1978), and Community Communications Co. v. Boulder, 455 U.S. 40 (1982)), excited challenges to city and county coordination of water and sewer service with land use policies. E.g., Unity Ventures v. Lake County, 631 F.Supp. 181 (N.D.Ill.1986), affirmed 841 F.2d 770 (7th Cir.1988). cert. denied 488 U.S. 891 (1988) (judgment n.o.v. overturning $28.5 million judgment for developer de-

nied sewer service because the development conflicted with a city-county sphere of influence agreement). Then, in Town of Hallie v. Eau Claire, 471 U.S. 34 (1985), a unanimous Court ruled that a Wisconsin statute simply authorizing the defendant city to provide sewage services and to determine the areas to be served was adequate to confer immunity from the antitrust laws. The decision has plainly enlarged the class of statutes that will immunize a municipality. In addition, the recent decision in Fisher v. Berkeley, 475 U.S. 260 (1986), indicates that municipalities that are not immune may be able to avail themselves of defenses that would not be available to private defendants. Finally, the Local Government Antitrust Act of 1984, 15 U.S.C.A. §§ 15(a)–(c), has eliminated the threat of treble damage liability prospectively.

5. A longstanding source of controversy has been the rates charged by municipalities when they choose to supply water beyond their boundaries. Can the rates for outsiders be higher than those charged residents? See Joseph L. Sax, *Municipal Water Supply for Nonresidents: Recent Developments and a Suggestion for the Future*, 5 Nat. Resources J. 54 (1965). The historical answer was that because cities had no duty to supply water to outsiders, they could condition the services on their own terms, including discriminatory rate setting. E.g., Zepp v. Mayor & Council of Athens, 348 S.E.2d 673 (Ga.App.1986) (sale of water to non-residents subject to U.C.C. but rate not unconscionable because city has unrestricted authority to set price.) In the past thirty years there has been a substantial movement away from the "no-duty" rule in favor of a rule of reasonableness, requiring that cities which choose to serve outsiders do so on reasonable and nondiscriminatory terms. The leading case is City of Texarkana v. Wiggins, 246 S.W.2d 622 (Tex.1952). Although the reasonableness rule rejects differential rates that are based solely on the "outsider" status of the customer, there may be other, valid reasons, for a higher charge to outsiders, including a higher cost of service in a given case. City attorneys commonly attempt to justify differential rates by introducing evidence of factors supporting their reasonableness. This leaves the customer with the burden of showing that the rates are in fact unreasonable. A review of the case law indicates that this has proven difficult to do. See City of Pompano Beach v. Oltman, 389 So.2d 283 (Fla.Dist.Ct.App.1980). In his article, Professor Sax observes that nonresident customers are disadvantaged by the need to adduce evidence of discrimination from complex economic data, and suggests "imposing upon the defendant cities a duty of compiling and producing the cost data for each item which is utilized in determining the rates." 5 Nat. Resources J. at 60. Would this approach shift the burden of proof to the defendant city?

6. Regulation of rates and requirements that services be provided on an equitable basis are generally imposed under state utility regulation schemes. Typically municipal water service agencies are exempt from such laws.

In Board of County Comm'rs of Arapahoe County v. Denver Board of Water Comm'rs, 718 P.2d 235 (Colo. 1986), the municipal water service agency for the City and County of Denver was sued by neighboring counties seeking to have water supplied by Denver to their citizens and to have reasonable rates charged for the service. Denver had supplied water to users outside its boundaries for many years under distributors' contracts for prices higher than the cost of service, and greater than rates charged within the city and county. The state supreme court had held in *Englewood*, which was relied upon by the court in *Robinson* for the test of public utility status, that the Denver Water Department was not a public utility. The counties argued that the proliferation of extraterritorial service arrangements since *Englewood* was decided amounted to a change of circumstances. The supreme court held that the test for determining public utility status was no longer the *Englewood* test, and instead referred to the definitions in the "comprehensive scheme for regulation of public utilities by the [Public Utilities Commission]." The regulatory scheme, based on language in a 1954 constitutional amendment (three years after *Englewood*), broadly defined "public utility" to include "every * * * water corporation, person, municipality operating for the purpose of supplying the public * * *." The court held that Denver "clearly fits this definition of a 'public utility.' " While the court found no constitutional barrier to the regulation of municipalities as public utilities by the Public Utility Commission (PUC), it found that the public policy of the state expressed in the statutes is "that municipal utilities have total authority over the provision of water service to users inside and outside municipal boundaries." 718 P.2d at 245. It noted that *Robinson* did not hold that the City of Boulder was a public utility subject to PUC regulation, but rather only held that a municipality could be found "to be a public utility under some common law test and to [be subject to] a court-supervised remedy" even in light of the state regulatory structure. It did caution that, to the extent that *Robinson* or *Englewood* is contrary to the legislative intent to permit "a municipality's governing body to retain sole control over extraterritorial water service without interference from any source * * * those opinions no longer represent Colorado law." 718 P.2d at 246.

Does this change the effect of *Robinson* in any way? See Thompson v. Salt Lake City Corp., 724 P.2d 958 (Utah 1986).

LOCKARY v. KAYFETZ

United States Court of Appeals, Ninth Circuit, 1990.
917 F.2d 1150.

[The Bolinas Community Public Utility District (BCPUD), public provider of water in Bolinas, California, had enacted a moratorium on new water hookups in response, it claimed, to a water shortage. It therefore refused to supply water to the owners of undeveloped land within its service area. The owners thereupon sued in federal district court, where summary judgment was granted in favor of the district. On appeal, the owners asserted that the denial of water constituted a regulatory taking of their land and violated their constitutional rights to substantive and procedural due process and equal protection.]

BCPUD's failure to grant water hookups does not constitute a taking of the Gilberts', Lockarys' and Macey's interest in their land if it: 1) substantially advances a legitimate state interest; and 2) does not deny them economically viable use of his land. Nollan v. California Coastal Comm'n, 483 U.S. 825, 834, 107 S.Ct. 3141, 3146, 97 L.Ed.2d 677 (1987). Here, there is a tenable claim that BCPUD's failure to grant water hookups to the Gilberts, Lockarys and Macey may deny them all economically viable use of their land.

A regulation which destroys a major portion of the land's value denies a property owner of all economically viable use of his land. See Moore v. City of Costa Mesa, 886 F.2d 260, 263 (9th Cir.1989). Whether a regulation denies landowners all economically viable use of their land requires consideration of the existence of other permissible uses of that land, Agins v. City of Tiburon, 447 U.S. 255, 262, 100 S.Ct. 2138, 2142, 65 L.Ed.2d 106 (1980), and the economic impact of the regulation and the extent to which it interferes with the landowners' reasonable investment backed expectations. Williamson County Regional Planning Comm'n v. Hamilton Bank, 473 U.S. 172, 191, 105 S.Ct. 3108, 3118, 87 L.Ed.2d 126 (1985). Also included within this inquiry is the consideration whether the regulation caused the loss of economic viability. If the loss is caused by something other than the government regulation, it does not constitute a taking.

The Gilberts, Lockarys and Macey have submitted evidence that Marin County conditions the grant of building permits on first securing water hookups from BCPUD for their residentially zoned land. Construing the evidence in the light most favorable to the Gilberts, Lockarys and Macey, BCPUD's refusal to grant them a water hookup prohibits them from building anything on their land. Additionally, they raise a genuine issue of material fact concerning whether a shortage of water caused a loss in the economic viability of their properties, as opposed to the arbitrary denial of water to their properties by BCPUD.

Withholding available water from land zoned exclusively for residential use might interfere with the landowners' reasonable investment-backed expectations by preventing all practical use of that land. That the Gilberts, Lockarys and Macey can still walk on, or ride a bike on, or look at their land does not, at this preliminary stage of the case, reassure us to the contrary. In this context, assuming the Gilberts, Lockarys and Macey can show that sufficient water was available, then BCPUD's water moratorium may indeed constitute more than a mere reduction in property value.

However, the determination of what constitutes an economically viable use of land requires a case-by-case factual analysis of the particular circumstances presented. Resolution by plenary hearing rather than by summary judgment is particularly important for claims of regulatory taking. Because appellants have raised triable issues of fact surrounding their as applied takings claim, we reverse and remand.

NOTE

Water suppliers and planners in arid, drought-prone areas are beginning a fundamental reevaluation of the role of water pricing and urban growth policies in water conservation. See Andrew Cohen,

Water Supply and Land Use Planning: Making the Connection, 1 Land Use Forum 341 (1992). If water supply and urban growth are linked, there will be many challenges to the linkage, using the public utility law arguments relied on in *Robinson.* However, there may be a trend toward allowing the linkage:

> * * * The assumption that the duty to serve required the acquisition of supplies stretching into the unforseeable future must be modified to reflect development opportunities to be allocated by water providers. * * *

> The starting point for the development of a new water service policy is the recognition that the duty to serve has never been absolute. Courts have long recognized municipal discretion to refuse to extend water services, [see Moore v. City Council of Harrodsburg, 105 S.W. 926 (Ky.1907)] and courts have allowed cities to adjust growth rates to supply availability through moratoria. * * *

> Service moratoria are, of course, premised on the assumption that the capacity defect will be cured within a reasonable period of time. However, recent water service and development exaction cases reveal a broader skepticism of the merits of unlimited growth. The public utility theory of strict service duties is being replaced by one which allows cities to subordinate utility service to growth management objectives. In contrast to older cases, recent cases have accepted the argument that utility extensions must be subordinated to land use policies if cities are to be permitted to implement rational growth management policies. [See *Dateline Builders,* 194 Cal.Rptr. 258].

A. Dan Tarlock, *Western Water Law, Global Warming, and Growth Limitations,* 24 Loy.L.A.L.Rev. 979, 1010–11 (1991). See also Dennis J. Herman, *Sometimes There's Nothing Left to Give: The Justification for Denying Water Service to New Consumers to Control Growth,* 44 Stan. L.Rev. 429 (1992).

Lockary illustrates the potential constitutional challenges that linkage schemes raise, but courts have not recognized a fundamental right to water service. See Magnuson v. City of Hickory Hills, 933 F.2d 562 (7th Cir.1991) (city may constitutionally discontinue service because there is no fundamental right to continued municipal service, but discontinuance must bear a substantial relationship to public health, safety, and welfare).

C. SPECIAL WATER DISTRICTS

JOHN D. LESHY, SPECIAL WATER DISTRICTS—THE
HISTORICAL BACKGROUND, *IN* SPECIAL WATER
DISTRICTS: CHALLENGE FOR THE FUTURE

11–27 (James N. Corbridge, Jr., ed. 1983).

I. Introduction

* * *

Special governmental districts today fulfill a dizzying array of purposes, including transportation, housing, education, soil conservation, recreation and, more recently, such specialized functions as mosquito and weather control and industrial development. In the last two decades in particular, districts have proliferated rather dramatically. Though the number of school districts has declined, the number of other districts grew by nearly 50% in just fifteen years, so that as of 1977, there were almost 26,000 such entities in the United States. Because of the relative obscurity in which this proliferation has taken place, and which shrouds the operation of such entities, special districts have aptly been described as the "new Dark Continent of American government," or "phantom governments."

Special water districts remain among the most important of these districts, particularly in the west. Of the nearly 1000 special districts nationwide engaged in 1977 in supplying water for various uses, more than 95% are in the seventeen western states (not including Alaska and Hawaii), and about 40% are in California, Arizona, New Mexico, Utah and Colorado.

The vast bulk of developed water supply in the west is still used for agricultural irrigation. The most recent Census of Agriculture data shows that organizations of all types delivered in 1969 about 68 million acre feet (MAF) in the seventeen western states for all purposes, about 93% of which went to farms and ranches for irrigation. Almost half of this water was delivered by special water districts. Table I shows the various types of entities delivering water for irrigation purposes in 1969, and also shows the percentage of total acreage irrigated by type of entity.

Table I.

Organization	Percentage of all organizations	Percentage of all acreage irrigated by organization
Unincorporated mutuals	53.7	10.8
Incorporated mutuals	32.6	34.3
All districts (irrigation and other)	9.1	47.1
Bureau of Reclamation constructed and operated [a]	.7	1.8
Bureau of Indian Affairs	.7	2.9
State and local governments	.5	.2
Commercial companies	2.7	2.9
	100.0	100.0

[a] Most Bureau of Reclamation (BR) projects are turned over to some other type of irrigation organization once construction is completed. Acreage serviced by BR-constructed and user-operated projects accounted for nearly 27 percent of the acreage irrigated by other organizations.

Table II gives historical perspective, showing the steady growth since 1890 in both the number of, and acres served by, special water districts. * * *

II. Historical Development—The Early Years

By definition, special water districts have been legislatively classified as governmental entities; more precisely, as political subdivisions of state governments. Historically, the primary reason to give these entities governmental status was to overcome difficulties private enterprise had in raising money to build more ambitious water supply projects.

Table II.

Population and Acres Irrigated (by Irrigation Districts and the Bureau of Reclamation) 17 Western States, 1890–1970

Year	Population	Total Acres Irrigated	By Special (No.)	District (Acres)	By Bureau of Reclamation
1890	8,322,503	3,631,559	NA	NA	—
1900	11,187,961	7,542,782	NA	NA	—
1920	19,943,531	NA	NA	1,822,887	1,254,569
1930	24,749,633	14,085,967	363	3,452,275	1,485,028
1940	27,036,281	17,243,396	441	3,807,967	3,284,474
1950	34,009,255	24,270,566	483	4,962,413	682,413
1960	43,995,031	30,738,117	558	6,920,527	710,904
1970	52,504,548	34,785,717	687	9,689,181	363,320

In passing, it should be noted that special water supply districts had some precursors; most notably, special districts formed to build levees and drain wetlands to render them suitable for agricultural cultivation. Such districts, usually called "reclamation" districts, predated irrigation districts by a number of years, and their constitutionality was upheld by the United States Supreme Court in 1884. [Hagar v. Reclamation Dist. No. 108, 111 U.S. 701 (1884).] For obvious reasons, draining wetlands was never important in much of the west as a source of land for cultivation, and reclamation districts have not had a great deal of influence over western water supplies.

In general, early private irrigation enterprises encountered two interrelated problems: a difficulty in raising the often large amounts of up-front capital to construct water supply and delivery works, and the lack of a mechanism to compel prospective beneficiaries to participate. Over-optimism, bad planning and the inevitable time lag between initiating project construction and reaping the rewards of the new more stable water supply came to severely hamper the enthusiasm of private investors. Moreover, potential beneficiaries were often satisfied with their existing water supply or otherwise balked at participating, rendering the feasibility of many projects dubious. The early history of private water supply ventures was thus littered with failures.

To overcome these problems, project proponents turned first to state legislatures. The most prominent and successful early statute, though not quite the pioneering one, was California's Wright Act, adopted in 1887. The principal mechanism adopted to provide construction capital was the compulsory property assessment levied against all property in the district determined to benefit, directly or indirectly, from the proposed works. Other financial benefits provided by the Wright Act included the authority to issue bonds, and exemption from state and local taxes for district property.

In the original Wright Act, control was placed in the hands of local residents qualified to vote in general state elections on a one-person one-vote basis. While districts were vested with an array of powers, the basic function was limited to providing water supply for agricultural irrigation. Though the Wright Act allowed districts to levy financial "assessments" rather than taxes against lands within the district deemed to benefit from proposed projects, functionally the effect was the same. The distinction was maintained solely to avoid problems with typical state constitutional provisions requiring taxes to be equal and uniform. Assessments were levied against individual parcels of property on the basis of the value of the property taking into account the benefits received from the district. Interestingly, while the water supply function was exclusively agricultural, the district could include and assess against town lots on the idea that, though they received no water, they benefited from the agricultural economy facilitated by the district.

This compulsory taxation feature was, as might be expected, controversial. Landowners satisfied with their water supplies protested this tax, rallied opposition to such "communism and confiscation," and instituted litigation challenging the Wright Act which eventually made its way to the United States Supreme Court. There the protestors were soundly rebuffed. Following its prevailing practice of giving substantial deference to state legislatures concerning the organization and structure of state political subdivisions, the Court found the Act constitutional in all respects in 1896 [Fallbrook Irr. Dist. v. Bradley, 164 U.S. 112 (1896), page 625, infra]. In its opinion, the Court took judicial notice of the aridity of most western states and what was then generally understood as the public importance of promoting irrigation. It deferred to the legislature and the district in setting the level of financial assessments, noting the difficulty of measuring with any precision the benefits the district would provide, and expressly acknowledging that these benefits may be indirect as well as direct.

The nearly blank check which the Court found the federal constitution had handed to the state legislatures cleared away any lingering doubts about the federal constitutionality of special water district legislation (though questions of state constitutionality remained and are occasionally still litigated.) Within twenty-one years of the Court's decision, all seventeen western states had followed California's lead. All these acts, with some variations reflecting local conditions, were based on the Wright Act.

III.   Refinement and Modification

* * * Like any system of taxation, the special district assessment poses the chronic difficulty of fashioning an equitable and effective scheme for taxing district landowners to pay for district functions.

Hand-in-hand with experiments and modifications in assessment practices came similar adjustments in political control of the districts' management and policies. Though the Wright Act followed the one resident-one vote principle, other states restricted voter eligibility to landowners or just to owners of agricultural land, and some parceled out votes on the basis of acreage of land owned or amount of water received. The trend has generally been toward acreage-based voting, which has of course tended to concentrate district control in the hands of agricultural interests and more particularly larger landowners.

Still another problem area which received some state legislative attention was the lack of state supervision over district activities. The Wright Act, for example, had for the most part simply prescribed how these districts would be created and structured and what their general functions would be, leaving their actual operation almost completely in the hands of the district governing board and electors. The failure rate of the early districts prompted many state legislatures to initiate or increase supervision of district activities by one or another arm of state government. State agencies were, for example, given responsibility to investigate the sufficiency of a proposed district's water supply, and perhaps even allocate it to particular parcels. State courts were sometimes given responsibility to approve proceedings leading to district bond issuance and, in at least one case, to regulate district activity much as a public utility commission regulates public utilities. California (eventually followed by a majority of other western states) took a more direct route, by creating a special state agency to approve districts' proposals for issuing bonds after investigating their feasibility against the district's financial position. State legislatures also acted directly to place statutory ceilings on district indebtedness and to require landowner approval of bond issues. All these measures increasing state supervision of district activities were aimed at improving investor confidence in district bonds, an increasingly important source of district capital. (At the same time it created a special agency to pass on district bond proposals prior to issuance, for example, the California legislature also designated these bonds as legal investments for trust, insurance, banking and state school funds.)

Another modification state legislatures often made in second-generation irrigation districts was to enlarge their functions to embrace purposes other than agricultural irrigation. Some of these were so closely related to the core irrigation purpose or so insignificant as not to change markedly the district or its financial position; e.g., flood control, drainage, and supplying water for fire protection. Two others in particular, however, had a lasting impact on many irrigation districts: authority to deliver water for general purposes other than agricultural irrigation, and authority to generate and sell electric power.

The broadening of districts' authority over water delivery has become increasingly important as the west has grown in population, especially in metropolitan areas, and farmlands have been converted into residential and industrial areas. Moreover, such urbanization has created substantial stress on the management of these districts, and in some areas created substantial tensions between rural and urban interests—a tension exacerbated by the typical voting schemes which invest rural interests with political control of district policies.

Giving some districts the authority to generate and sell electricity (and concomitantly, to use the revenues to meet district financial obligations such as bond payments) has had similar far-reaching effects. Some have aggressively exercised this authority, to such an extent that power now far outstrips water as a source of revenue. (Districts' authority is typically not limited to generating electricity with falling water; i.e., hydropower, but instead covers power generated from any source whatsoever.) Coupled again with the voting mechanisms by which rural landowners are vested with political control, this has allowed power producing districts to subsidize agricultural irrigation with power revenues. Moreover, as groundwater has become more important as a source of water supply for districts in many areas, district power production can be used to drive the pumps necessary to retrieve the water.

IV. The Federal Government Steps In

Though the Reclamation Act of 1902 marked the entry of the federal government into the business of directly financing western agricultural development, it did not have any immediate influence on the formation or functioning of special water districts. The initial act, which actually contemplated a modest federal role (the federal government financing and constructing the projects and the beneficiaries repaying the outlay in full, though without interest, within 10 years), was bottomed on the premise that the federal government would deal directly with individual landowners. Despite the fact that the Wright Act had been in existence for a decade and a half and had already been adopted in seven other states, in other words, Congress expected the federal government to make the necessary repayment arrangements directly with individual water users or their (private) associations. In part this organizational approach reflected the program's original design—to further settlement of the federal lands in the west with small yeoman farmers in Jefferson's vision of an agrarian ideal. Because Congress thought federal lands would be homesteaded, cultivated, and obtained mostly by reclamation beneficiaries, and it limited the amount of land on which any beneficiary could receive reclamation water to 160 acres, it seemed to make sense to Congress for the federal government to deal directly with individual beneficiaries.

* * * Congress between 1911 and 1926 largely substituted special governmental districts for individuals and water users associations as the contact point (and contracting entity) between farmers and the federal government.

In 1926, in fact, Congress recognized special water districts as the exclusive form of local participation in new federal reclamation projects. Though it retreated a bit from that rigid view in 1939, it is still common for Congress, in authorizing construction of a particular reclamation project, to require the formation of a special water district under state law to contract with the federal government for project water delivery and payment of the designated charges.

During this same period the federal Bureau of Reclamation sent emissaries around the west urging the formation of special governmental water districts and their substitution as the contracting entity for existing as well as new reclamation projects. * * *

* * *

A final federal policy, whose importance perhaps surpasses all those mentioned above, is found not in federal reclamation law but in the Internal Revenue Code. It bestows tax-exempt status on special water district property, revenues and the interest paid on district bonds. This exemption is one of long standing, not limited to special water districts but applying to any "political subdivision" of a state. It gives states the unusual power to create exemptions from federal taxation without any further action or approval by the federal government.

* * * The Department of the Treasury estimates that the interest rate spread between taxable and tax-exempt bonds averages 30–35%. Such tax-exempt financing is, moreover, functionally more expensive to the federal government than a direct interest subsidy of 30–35% because part of the revenue loss to the federal treasury accrues to the benefit of bond purchasers, who are often high income lenders seeking shelter from income taxes.

* * *

Given the substantial financial advantage governmental status affords to water supply entities, it is not surprising that, according to Wells Hutchins, whose surveys of special water districts across the west are the most extensive available, "the chief object in forming many irrigation districts has been to issue (tax exempt) bonds." * * *

* * * These districts typically have authority to levy taxes on real and personal property within the district as well as the more traditional "assessments." The procedures for formation and selection of governing officers vary widely, as do their management authorities, and may or may not be analogous to the more traditional irrigation districts.

Even more recently, special water districts have been created to oversee withdrawal of groundwater where the rate of extraction exceeds recharge or aquifer contamination is a problem. * * *

While the proliferating complexity of modern special water districts defies easy description or categorization, a few issues of policy and law are present in most of them, and bear brief mention here.

The first is the relationship between the special water district and the actual water users within it (as well as any other special water districts which may exist covering the same area) in the matter of legal rights to allocate and use water. Generally, state laws governing appropriation and use of water apply to districts of all kinds like they do to private entities, but this has scarcely answered the numerous difficult questions which have arisen from the earliest days of special water districts. The district statutes are often quite opaque on water rights matters, and in this legislative vacuum state courts have fashioned a number of approaches: Some regard the district as holding formal title to the water right while the actual users have a beneficial or equitable ownership interest in it. Others have deemed the actual users to hold legal and equitable title, with the district holding title only to the project's physical works and acting as trustee in delivering the water. One state views the district and actual users to hold the water right in common. Numerous variations on these approaches are found from district type to district type, or where a district was formed after a water supply had already been developed, or where a federal reclamation project is involved.

The matter can be crucial. First and most obviously, it affects the apportionment of water supplies among numerous potential recipients in a district, a question of utmost importance when water is in short supply, as in a drought. It also has a great deal of influence over the district's financial arrangements with its water users and, ultimately, over its ability to act as a water manager, promoting efficient and discouraging inefficient uses of project water. Functionally, the various approaches adopted by the states range from regarding districts as mere deliverers of water to satisfy already established water rights, to giving districts substantial power to allocate and distribute water to actual users according to the district's own determination of equity and efficiency.

When a federal reclamation project is involved, some additional wrinkles are present. Though the applicable statutes are far from clear, and judicial interpretations not wholly reconcilable with each other, recently the Supreme Court has characterized the federal government's ownership interest in reclamation water rights as "mere title" and "at most nominal," with the beneficial interest found in the owners of land within the project to which the water is applied. Thus it appears, as a lower court has held, that the federal government has little management control over the water it makes available (at mostly federal expense), and may not reduce the amount of water supplied to project beneficiaries in order to promote more efficient use or help satisfy other needs, even where the applicable contract with the local beneficiaries reserves this right to the federal government.

The matter of promoting more efficient use is one of growing importance in the west as more demands are placed on existing water supplies and large new supplies seem out of reach. Another aspect of this problem concerns the role of these districts in transferring water from one place or type of use to another, because such transfers are often the best or even the only way of improving efficiency in water use. Here too the power of districts to effect, prevent or otherwise influence transfers of water uses is both murky and variegated. It appears that some kinds of districts possess considerable power in this regard (even, as in Arizona, to the extent of possessing an absolute veto over applications to transfer any water rights within all watersheds— whether or not within the district itself—in which the district possesses water rights). Others, however, may have little or no authority over transfers, approval of which seems to remain in the hands of the state water rights agency.

Another generic issue concerns district governance; more specifically, the procedures for selecting district governing boards. As districts assume new functions and cover wider geographic areas, and as the areas in which they are found undergo substantial demographic, economic and cultural change, the matter of control becomes increasingly important and, concomitantly, controversial. Here too district laws reflect substantial variation: one resident or one landowner—one vote, one acre—one vote or even voting based on assessed valuation of the property owned. Furthermore, corporations and other entities are sometimes excluded from the franchise even if they own property within or are served by the district.

* * *

A third generic issue is closely related to the previous ones; namely, the appropriate degree of control which should be exercised by the states over district activities. All western states have traditionally administered their water laws on a statewide basis; moreover, many of these states have moved in the direction of adopting state-wide plans to govern the allocation and use of water. Further, as has been described, the trend has been to provide more state oversight of special water district activities. In the abstract, the issue is whether special water districts should be regulated much as other non-governmental water users in the state are regulated, or whether instead their existing governmental stature should be built upon to allow them to play a more directly managerial and regulatory role in implementing state water policy.

Existing state laws generally manifest a schizophrenic approach to this issue. To some extent districts are treated much as private entities would be, but in other areas they are given special treatment because of their cloak of government authority. Perhaps the most prominent example of the latter is their exemption from statewide regulation in carrying out such "natural monopoly" functions as delivering water or generating and selling electric power—regulation to which ordinary business entities exercising similar monopoly power have traditionally been subject. The Advisory Commission on Intergovernmental Relations has recommended, in this connection, that pricing policies of all special districts be made subject to review and approval by state regulatory agencies if they are not otherwise reviewed by the governing body of a unit of general government.

1.　Formation

FALLBROOK IRRIGATION DISTRICT v. BRADLEY

Supreme Court of the United States, 1896.
164 U.S. 112, 17 S.Ct. 56, 41 L.Ed. 369.

Mr. Justice Peckham, after stating the case, delivered the opinion of the court.

The decision of this case involves the validity of the irrigation act enacted by the legislature of the State of California [the Wright Act] * * *. The principal act, passed in 1887, has been amended once or twice by subsequent legislation, but in its main features it remains as first enacted. The title of the act indicates its purpose. It is admitted by all that very large tracts of land in California are in fact "arid lands," which require artificial irrigation in order to produce anything of value. * * *

* * * It was stated by counsel that something over thirty irrigation districts had been organized in California under the act in question, and that a total bonded indebtedness of more than $16,000,000 had been authorized by the various districts under the provisions of the act, and that more than $8,000,000 of the bonds had been sold and the money used for the acquisition of property and water rights and for the construction of works necessary for the irrigation of the lands contained in the various districts.

* * * All these moneys, if the act be valid, must eventually be repaid from assessments levied upon the lands embraced within the respective districts, while the annually recurring interest upon these moneys is also to be paid in the same way. Taking the California act as a model, it was also stated and not contradicted that several of the other States which contain portions of the arid belt (seven or eight of them) had passed irrigation acts, and that proceedings under them were generally awaiting the result of this litigation. The future prosperity of these States, it was claimed, depended upon the validity of this act as furnishing the only means practicable for obtaining artificial irrigation, without the aid of which millions and millions of acres would be condemned to lie idle and worthless, which otherwise would furnish enormous quantities of agricultural products and increase the material wealth and prosperity of that whole section of country. On the other hand, it has been asserted, with equal earnestness, that the whole scheme of the act will, if carried out to the end, result in the practical confiscation of lands like those belonging to the appellees herein for the benefit of those owning different kinds of land upon which the assessments for the water would be comparatively light, and the benefits resulting from its use far in excess of those otherwise situated. Such results, it is said, are nothing more than taking by legislation the property of one person or class of persons and giving it to another, which is an arbitrary act of pure spoliation, from which the citizen is protected, if not by any state constitution at least by the Federal instrument, under which we live and the provisions of which we are all bound to obey.

* * *

The form in which the question comes before the court in this case is by appeal from a decree of the United States Circuit Court for the Southern District of California, perpetually enjoining the collector of the irrigation district from executing a deed conveying the land of the plaintiff, Maria King Bradley, under a sale made of such land pursuant to the provisions of the act under consideration. The grounds upon which relief was sought were that the act was in violation of the Federal Constitution * * *.

* * *

The assertion that it does is based upon that part of the Fourteenth Amendment to the Constitution, which reads as follows: "Nor shall any State deprive any person of life, liberty or property without due process of law, nor deny to any person within its jurisdiction the equal protection of the laws."

* * *

Is this assessment, for the non-payment of which the land of the plaintiff was to be sold, levied for a public purpose? The question has, in substance, been answered in the affirmative by the people of California, and by the legislative and judicial branches of the state government. The people of the State adopted a constitution which contains this provision:

"*Water and Water Rights*—SEC. 1. The use of all water now appropriated or that may hereafter be appropriated, for sale, rental or distribution, is hereby declared to be a public use and subject to the regulation and control of the State in the manner to be prescribed by law." Constitution of California, ART. 14.

The latter part of § 12 of the act now under consideration, as amended in March, 1891, reads as follows:

"The use of all water required for the irrigation of the lands of any district formed under the provisions of this act, together with the rights of way for canals and ditches, sites for reservoirs, and all other property required in fully carrying out the provisions of this act, is hereby declared to be a public use, subject to the regulation and control of the State, in the manner prescribed by law."

The Supreme Court of California has held in a number of cases that the irrigation act is in accordance with the state constitution, and that it does not deprive the landowners of any property without due process of law; that the use of the water for irrigating purposes under the provisions of the act as a public use, and the corporations organized by virtue of the act for the purpose of irrigation are public municipal corporations organized for the promotion of the prosperity and welfare of the people.

* * *

Viewing the subject for ourselves and in the light of these considerations we have very little difficulty in coming to the same conclusion reached by the courts of California.

The use must be regarded as a public use, or else it would seem to follow that no general scheme of irrigation can be formed or carried into effect. In general, the water to be used must be carried for some distance and over or through private property which cannot be taken *in invitum* if the use to which it is to be put be not public, and if there be no power to take property by condemnation it may be impossible to acquire it at all. The use for which private property is to be taken must be a public one, whether the taking be by the exercise of the right of eminent domain or by that of taxation. A private company or corporation without the power to acquire the land *in invitum* would be of no real benefit, and at any rate the cost of the undertaking would be so greatly enhanced by the knowledge that the land must be acquired by purchase, that it would be practically impossible to build the works or obtain the water. Individual enterprise would be equally ineffectual; no one owner would find it possible to construct and maintain water works and canals any better than private corporations or companies, and unless they had the power of eminent domain they could accomplish nothing. If that power could be conferred upon them it could only be upon the ground that the property they took was to be taken for a public purpose.

While the consideration that the work of irrigation must be abandoned if the use of the water may not be held to be or constitute a public use is not to be regarded as conclusive in favor of such use, yet that fact is in this case a most important consideration. Millions of acres of land otherwise cultivable must be left in their present arid and worthless condition, and an effectual obstacle will therefore remain in the way of the advance of a large portion of the State in material wealth and prosperity. To irrigate and thus to bring into possible cultivation these large masses of otherwise worthless lands would seem to be a public purpose and a matter of public interest, not confined to the landowners, or even to any one section of the State. The fact that the use of the water is limited to the landowner is not therefore a fatal objection to this legislation. It is not essential that the entire community or even any considerable portion thereof should directly enjoy or participate in an improvement in order to constitute a public use. All landowners in the district have the right to a proportionate share of the water, and no one landowner is favored above his fellow in his right to the use of the water. It is not necessary, in order that the use should be public, that every resident in the district should have the right to the use of the water. * * *

Second. The second objection urged by the appellees herein is that the operations of this act need not be and are not limited to arid, unproductive lands but include within its possibilities all lands, no matter how fertile or productive, so long as they are susceptible "in their natural state" of one mode of irrigation from a common source, etc. * * *

As an evidence of what can be done under the act it is alleged in the complaint in this suit that the plaintiff is the owner of forty acres of land in the district, and that it is worth $5000, and that it is subject to beneficial use without the necessity of water for irrigation, and that it has been used beneficially for the past several years for purposes other than cultivation with irrigation. These allegations are admitted by the answer of the defendants, who nevertheless assert that if a sufficient supply of water is obtained for the irrigation of the plaintiff's land, the same can be beneficially used for many purposes other than that for which it can be used without the water for irrigating the same.

What is the limit of the power of the legislature in regard to providing for irrigation? Is it bounded by the absolutely worthless condition of the land without the artificial irrigation? Is it confined to land which cannot otherwise be made to yield the smallest particle of a return for the labor bestowed upon it? If not absolutely worthless and incapable of growing any valuable thing without the water, how valuable may the land be and to what beneficial use and to what extent may it be put before it reaches the point at which the legislature has no power to provide for its improvement by that means? The general power of the legislature over the subject of providing for the irrigation of certain kinds of lands must be admitted and assumed. The further questions of limitation, as above propounded, are somewhat legislative in their nature, although subject to the scrutiny and judgment of the courts to the extent that it must appear that the use intended is a public use as that expression has been defined relatively to this kind of legislation.

The legislature by this act has not itself named any irrigation district, and, of course, has not decided as to the nature and quality of any specific lands which have been included in any such district. It has given a general statement as to what conditions must exist in order to permit the inclusion of any land within a district. The land which can properly be so included is, as we think, sufficiently limited in its character by the provisions of the act. It must be susceptible of one mode of irrigation, from a common source and by the same system of works, and it must be of such a character that it will be benefited by irrigation by the system to be adopted. * * *

* * * If land which can, to a certain extent, be beneficially used without artificial irrigation, may yet be so much improved by it that it will be thereby and for its original use substantially benefited, and, in addition to the former use, though not in exclusion of it, if it can then be put to other and more remunerative uses, we think it erroneous to say that the furnishing of artificial irrigation to that kind of land cannot be, in a legal sense, a public improvement, or the use of the water a public use.

* * *

Fourth. The fourth objection and also the objection above alluded to as the final one, may be discussed together, as they practically cover the same principle. It is insisted that the basis of the assessment upon the lands benefited, for the cost of the construction of the works, is not in accordance with and in proportion to the benefits conferred by the improvement, and, therefore, there is a violation of the constitutional amendment referred to, and a taking of the property of the citizen without due process of law.

* * * The way of arriving at the amount may be in some instances inequitable and unequal, but that is far from rising to the level of a constitutional problem and far from a case of taking property without due process of law.

* * *

An objection is also urged that it is delegating to others a legislative right, that of the incorporating of public corporations, inasmuch as the act vests in the supervisors and the people the right to say whether such a corporation shall be created, and it is said that the legislature cannot so delegate its power, and that any act performed by such a corporation by means of which the property of the citizen is taken from him, either by the right of eminent domain or by assessment, results in taking such property without due process of law.

We do not think there is any validity to the argument. The legislature delegates no power. It enacts conditions upon the performance of which the corporation shall be regarded as organized with the powers mentioned and described in the act.

After careful scrutiny of the objections to this act we are compelled to the conclusion that no one of such objections is well taken. The judgment appealed from herein is therefore

Reversed and the cause remanded to the Circuit Court of the United States for the Southern District of California for further proceedings not inconsistent with this opinion.

Mr. Chief Justice Fuller and Mr. Justice Field dissented.

NOTES

1. *Fallbrook* is significant because it upheld the constitutionality of the Wright Act, ch. 34, 1887 Cal.Stat. 29, an early attempt by California to enable local farmers to organize irrigation districts. Ten years after its passage, it was superseded by the Wright-Bridgeford Act, ch. 189, 1897 Cal.Stat. 254, which continued the theme of the original Act, and became the model for irrigation district statutes in all of the seventeen western states. The Wright Act was an attempt to undo the results of Lux v. Haggin, 10 P. 674 (Cal.1886), page 164, supra. For a discussion of the Act, see Donald Worster, Rivers of Empire 108–09 (1985).

2. When an irrigation district was formed under the Wright Act, its board of directors was empowered to manage the general affairs of the district, including the acquisition of property, water rights, and irrigation system. The board could also call elections regarding the issuance of bonds and, most importantly, levy assessments to repay bond obligations and to support general expenditures. Although hearings were provided to exclude land which, although within district boundaries, was not irrigable from the common source, the Act enabled districts to include, and assess, recalcitrant landowners whose lands *could* be benefited. This feature of irrigation districts is in sharp contrast to the mutual irrigation company, in which membership was completely voluntary.

By allowing the district to incur indebtedness for which all of the potentially benefited landowners in the district were liable, the Act was intended to add financial stability to local irrigation enterprises. Nevertheless, many districts suffered financial failure. Wells Hutchins has suggested that among the reasons for this were inadequate water supplies, inclusion within districts of non-productive lands, engineering difficulties, and exploitation by speculators more concerned with profits than with sound economics. See Wells A. Hutchins, *Irrigation Districts, Their Organization, Operation and Financing*, in U.S. Dep't of Agriculture, Tech. Bull. No. 254 (1931). Amendments to the Wright-Bridgeford Act, and to the irrigation district statutes of other states, have attempted to remedy some of the perceived deficiencies. Representation in district elections has been a particular bone of contention, discussed in Ball v. James, 451 U.S. 355 (1981), page 651, infra, and the notes following it.

Irrigation districts are creatures of state law. As populations have increased in formerly agricultural areas, posing new problems for districts, many state statutes have been modified to expand district powers beyond irrigation, to include drainage, flood control, and the generation of electric power. Some irrigation districts have evolved into more complex water distribution entities. A useful discussion of the history and future of irrigation districts is Comment, *Desert Survival: The Evolving Western Irrigation District*, 1982 Ariz.St.L.J. 377.

3. The development of irrigation districts was encouraged by federal reclamation law. See pages 622–23, supra. The original Reclamation Act of 1902, Pub. L. No. 161, 32 Stat. 288, contemplated that the Bureau of Reclamation, in seeking repayment of reclamation project costs to the federal government, would deal directly with private users or irrigation companies. The 1911 Warren Act, 43 U.S.C.A. §§ 523–525, permitted an irrigation district to contract for project water. General authority for the Secretary of the Interior to contract directly with irrigation districts for repayment was forthcoming in 1922, 43 U.S.C.A. § 511. Thereafter, the Bureau encouraged both the formation of such districts and the passage of state laws enabling them to contract with the United States in regard to reclamation projects.

4. Assessments levied by irrigation districts can be either general or for specialized purposes. They are used to cover current expenses including maintenance costs, to repay obligations to the federal government arising in connection with reclamation projects, and to retire the bonded indebtedness incurred by the districts themselves. Several methods are available to determine assessment amounts, including ad valorem taxation of property, uniform rates per acre, and assessments related to the level of benefits received. What are the advantages and disadvantages of each of these approaches? Timothy De Young, *Special Water Districts: Their Role in Western Water Use*, in Western Water: Expanding Uses/Finite Supplies, Seventh Annual Summer Program, Natural Resources Law Center, University of Colorado School of Law (1986) argues that assessment based on land ownership permits the costs of water distribution to be spread over a large population base, with the result that agricultural users, especially those with large landholdings, are subsidized, and offers the following example:

> New Mexico's Middle Rio Grande Conservancy District provides flood control and irrigation services to a rapidly urbanizing area which includes Albuquerque, the state's largest city. The

proportion of irrigable acreage has declined from about 46% in 1930 when the district was formed, to about 21% in 1980. A continuing source of controversy is the district's levy assessment policies. "A" lands, irrigable parcels of one acre or larger, are charged a fixed per acre fee irrespective of assessed valuation or amount of water consumed. (No water tolls are assessed.) "B" lands, non-irrigated lands benefitted by district drainage and flood control services, are assessed an ad valorem levy that is collected by the counties in the district. For a number of years, the district kept "A" land charges extremely low so that "B" land levies provided most of the district's revenues. In response to complaints in the late 1970s, the district adopted a $7^5/_{25}$ cost apportionment policy for "B" and "A" lands. Requiring further pricing revisions has been proposed but not adopted in each session of the State Legislature during the 1980s.

5. Under what circumstances should land be excluded from an irrigation district and therefore from district assessments? When irrigation districts are being formed, landowners with a dependable supply of irrigation water (and resulting high land values) had little incentive to contribute to the development of the district's water supply; hence the mandatory inclusion of lands "susceptible" of being irrigated from a common source of supply, or "benefited" by the district's projects. What if land with vested rights is excluded from a district, but the district includes the headgate for the canal that serves the excluded land? The general rule is that the district must continue to supply water to the excluded land. Matter of the Establishment and Organization of the Ward Irr. Dist., 701 P.2d 721 (Mont.1985).

On the other hand, some parcels of land within district boundaries may not be suitable for farming. What if land is already devoted to a non-agricultural use? What if a parcel has been irrigated, but would be more valuable for an alternate use, such as manufacturing or real estate development? The issues are addressed in In re Reno Press Brick Co., 73 P.2d 503 (Nev.1937).

The standards for exclusion may depend on the type of district being formed, as the landowner in Atchison, Topeka and Santa Fe Ry. Co. v. Kings Cty. Water Dist., 302 P.2d 1, 4–5 (Cal.1956) found out. The railway argued that it made only incidental agricultural use of its right of way for haying by tenant farmers which it undertook only as an alternative to weed abatement. But the court held that:

> * * * [I]t is not the present, immediate use of the land which is the criterion for exclusion under the statute. The determining factor is whether any substantial and direct benefit accrues to the land itself, as distinguished from the particular use which a landowner may choose to make of the land. The record shows that shortly after its formation, the Kings County Water District obtained a court decree settling various disputes affecting the district's underground water supplies and pumping therefrom; that the district engages in studies and research as to the water needs of lands therein and possible future sources of supply; and that

successful agricultural development of land in the district is dependent on the supplementary underground waters for purposes of irrigation.

The question of the standards for exclusion from a district was sharply presented in Wilson v. Hidden Valley Mun. Water Dist., 63 Cal.Rptr. 889 (Cal.Ct.App.1967). A small water district was formed north of Los Angeles for the express purpose of preserving the valley's agricultural economy and to prevent the area from being included in the Metropolitan Water District of Southern California. A landowner who did not wish to be preserved petitioned to be excluded.

[T]he Legislature has the rightful power also by general law to authorize the formation of a district such as is proposed here without any hearing preliminary to the election as to whether the land included will be benefited. This type of district has been termed a *quasi*-municipal district. It is formed for the purpose of supplying general municipal needs, although these needs may be specific in their delineated character; the creation of this type of district is not for the purpose of making a specific and narrowly limited improvement, but is comparable to the organization of a city; whatever assessments are made are, like taxes, general in nature and based on the valuation of the several parcels of land within the district. * * *

Petitioners finally claim that even if the action was quasi-legislative the District is not entitled to the limitation upon judicial review, which the application of this rule affords it. Their argument is essentially that the District is an illegal one, fraudulent in nature and organized in abuse of the power delegated by the Legislature to form and maintain local water districts, since the District's sole raison d'etre is to serve as an illegal regulator of land use or as an illegal zoning agency. These damning conclusions stem from the fact that the District does not provide and has not provided water for use within the District. We agree that a district of this type is normally formed and maintained for the purpose of bettering either the water supply or the water service, or both, within its boundaries and that this district has not done so and has no present plans for doing so. But in our view a water district may properly be formed and maintained for largely negative purposes as well as for positive purposes. This district was quite evidently formed and has been maintained to prevent the importation of Metropolitan Water District water into Hidden Valley and the subdivision and urbanization of that Valley which the great majority of people within the Valley feel would then inevitably occur. * * * By the exercise of their right of political self-determination, they thereby, as an incident thereto, regulate the kind of land use that can prevail within the Valley.

* * *

According to the statutory law applicable to these proceedings, the actions of the board of directors of the District upon these two petitions were governed solely by its quasi-legislative discretion as to what the directors thought was in the best interests of the District. In this situation judicial review by ordinary mandamus is limited to an examination of the proceedings before the board to determine whether its action has been arbitrary, capricious or entirely lacking in evidentiary support, or whether it has failed to follow the procedure and give the notice required by law.

63 Cal.Rptr. at 898.

The State of Utah has codified its criteria for exclusion of lands from a special district. The provision allows either an individual landowner, or the governing body of any city, town or county with land inside the boundaries of a water conservancy district, to petition the board of directors of the district for exclusion of certain specified lands. Utah Code Ann. § 17A–2–1438 (1992). With respect to a city, town or county, a petition for exclusion may be filed with the district's board of directors upon a request filed with the appropriate governing body, signed by 5% of the qualified electors residing within the boundaries of the land proposed for exclusion. § 17A–2–1438(2)(a). Alternatively, a petition for exclusion may be filed with the board upon majority approval of a referendum conducted at a general or special election among residents of the land proposed for exclusion. § 17A–2– 1438(2)(b). Upon filing of a petition, the district's board of directors will hold a hearing to consider the petition and all relevant comments and information. § 17A–2–1451(3). The board may approve the petition if acceptable water supplies and delivery capability have been secured by the area proposed for exclusion, or if the district itself will not serve the area in the foreseeable future. § 17A–2–1452(1). The board has wide discretion, though, to deny the petition if it determines that exclusion would not be in the "best interest" of the district. § 17A–2–1452(2). In addition, even if the board does approve the petition, it may include in its order any reasonable terms and conditions, including assessments and taxes. §§ 17A–2–1452(4)–(6).

6. In many cases, landowners actively seek benefit from the district's power of taxation. In other cases, special districts have been opposed because they pose too great a threat to existing social and political institutions. A special irrigation district can superimpose new influences upon existing formal and informal allocations of political power that are based on control of water. An economist and a political scientist describe the defeat of a proposed federal irrigation project in Taos County, New Mexico, after Hispanic farmers became concerned about how the local repayment obligation might effect existing water use patterns.

F. LEE BROWN AND HELEN M. INGRAM, WATER AND POVERTY IN THE SOUTHWEST

60–61 (1987).

Journalist-novelist John Nichols (author of *Milagro Beanfield War*) chronicled these events:

Originally, I'm sure almost 100 percent of Taos County was in favor of Indian Camp Dam. The government was going to pay 96.5% of the construction costs of the 16 million dollar dam which was going to be built, so the government claimed, solely for the benefit of the small irrigators in the Taos Valley. And even though Taos is a relatively wet area, bisected by some half dozen rivers which often run pretty strong from ample snowmelt, nobody in his right mind, in a semi-arid state, would think to knock access to more water, or at least access to a guaranteed supply.

* .* * (People) began to get uneasy when they realized they would be paying off the other 3.5% construction costs over fifty years, and would also be responsible for maintenance costs which, if the dam didn't break or something untoward didn't happen, would be about $34,000 a year. * * * Then people learned that the only way the government could build the Indian Camp Dam was by imposing a conservancy district on the most irrigable portions of the Taos Valley. And when they figured out that conservancy districts are one of the more powerful political subdivisions of the state, with enormous planning and taxing and foreclosure powers, and when it began to be clear who would control the Taos conservancy district, the fourteen major ditch systems in the area which would fall within the conservancy borders, and which up until then had been represented on a local council working with state and federal agencies to implement the Indian Camp Dam, pulled out of the pro-dam council, banded into an organization called the Tres Rios Association, and prepared to fight the dam and the conservancy district tooth and nail.

The account by Nichols indicates that as more information was obtained about the project and the conservancy district, opposition began to appear. As Hispanic owners of small plots received more information about project design, they began to understand its implications. The opposition to the conservancy district arose on several counts.

1. The proposed conservancy district lien would have been on all lands for 50 years. Although the district's assessments would not be large, failure to pay would probably result in foreclosure. The idea of an agency having this power was intimidating to Hispanic owners of small plots of land.

2. The fees to be assessed by the conservancy district seemed relatively small, but, for Hispanic owners of small plots, these fees were significant. People owning farms of ten acres or less were not commercially oriented and might not have money to pay fees. The possible benefits of more water seemed small compared to the fees.

3. The conservancy district would supplant existing acequias in the watershed, and this change would imply altering Hispanic traditions in dealing with water. Change in an institution with a history of two hundred years was an important event.

4. There were major concerns about who would have authority in the conservancy district. At that time New Mexico law provided that conservancy district board members would be appointed by district judges for six-year terms. Hispanic owners of small plots felt this

procedure was undemocratic, and they feared that appointed directors would represent mainly Anglo owners of large land tracts in the watershed.

Although not a complete list, these concerns of Hispanic farmers in the Taos area do indicate the major points of dispute. Underlying all of these issues was the question of whether Hispanic concerns had been adequately incorporated into project conception and design. Was the initial Hispanic participation effective or only nominal with inadequate information about the implications of the project? Eventually the proposed conservancy district was declared illegal by the New Mexico Supreme Court on technical grounds, and the project was abandoned. In view of this outcome, and the depth of the highly emotional controversy that preceded it, the evidence implies that Hispanic participation, at least at the grassroots level, was not effective. The promise of more water hid the true social and economic costs, particularly to the small farmers. However favorable the financial terms in a national context, they were not acceptable.

2. Allocation of Water Within and Without a District

FORT LYON CANAL CO. v. CATLIN CANAL CO.

Supreme Court of Colorado, 1982.
642 P.2d 501.

LOHR, JUSTICE.

I.

Catlin owns a canal having a headgate on the Arkansas River. The water diverted through the canal historically has been used to irrigate agricultural land in Otero County. A history of the State's efforts to change the point of diversion of water to which it is entitled as a stockholder in Catlin is necessary to an understanding of the dispute now before us.

The State acquired 2,097.58 shares of the capital stock of Catlin, constituting 11.2% of that stock, and in 1973 filed an application in the water court for a change of water right, No. W–4025, seeking to change the nature and place of use of its water from domestic and irrigation purposes in Otero County to storage in the John Martin Reservoir in Bent County for fish propagation, wildlife development, and all other recreational uses. Statements of opposition were filed by Catlin and others. The objectors moved for summary judgment. The water court determined that the chain of title to the water rights upon which the Catlin stock rights are based includes deeds limiting the use of the water to irrigating and domestic purposes on land in Otero County. Concluding that these limitations on the place and character of use were enforceable against the State as equitable servitudes, and that similar restrictions in Catlin's articles of incorporation and bylaws also were binding upon the State, the water court ruled that the requested change of water right was impermissible, granted summary judgment for the objectors, and dismissed the State's application on March 9, 1977.

After dismissal of Case No. W–4025 the State entered into a water exchange agreement with Ft. Lyon whereby the point of diversion for the State's Catlin water rights would be changed to the headgate of the Ft. Lyon Canal which is also located on the Arkansas River, 25 miles downstream from the Catlin Canal headgate. The water would be used for irrigation purposes on lands previously irrigated by use of the Ft. Lyon Canal in Otero County. In exchange, Ft. Lyon would make other water rights available to support diversions for storage in John Martin Reservoir.

In pursuance of this water exchange agreement, the State and Ft. Lyon applied to the water court in case No. 79CW27 for the necessary change in point of diversion of the State's Catlin water rights. Again, Catlin and others filed statements of opposition. Catlin moved to dismiss the application based on failure of the State to request Catlin's board of directors to approve the desired change. After an evidentiary hearing on that motion, the water court found that a Catlin bylaw required that any stockholder desiring to change the place to which water is to be delivered must make a written request to the Catlin directors to approve the change. It concluded that the bylaw applies to applicants for transfer both within and without the Catlin Canal system, and that compliance with the bylaw is a condition precedent to application to the water court for approval of the requested change of point of diversion. * * *

In this appeal the State and Ft. Lyon urge reversal of the trial court's judgment on the bases that (1) the Catlin bylaw should be construed as applicable to only those changes of points of delivery not involving a transfer of water out of the Catlin Canal system, and (2) the water court's exclusive jurisdiction over an application for a change of water right is impermissibly infringed by a mutual ditch company bylaw purporting to require director approval before a change may be accomplished. We find these arguments unpersuasive.

II.

We first address the contention that, by its own terms, the disputed bylaw applies only to changes of points of delivery within the Catlin Canal system. The challenged bylaw reads as follows:

Section 2: (as amended 12/4/61) Each holder of corporate stock shall be entitled to receive from the company's canal, water for domestic and irrigation purposes in the following amount: The proportion of the total water available to and deliverable by the company under the priorities of the company (or purchased or otherwise obtained by the company) which each stockholder's shares of stock bears to the total number of shares of stock issued and outstanding. *Each stockholder desiring to change the place to which any water he may be entitled shall be delivered, shall make written request therefor to the directors. If, in the opinion of the [directors], such transfer may be made without injury to the canal, the company or other stockholders, such water shall be then delivered to such place or places as requested.* Provided that in such case all other stockholders who are entitled to delivery of water at either the place or to which delivery is changed shall be notified in writing of such change. (Emphasis added.)

The trial court concluded that this bylaw applies to a transfer of a water right out of the Catlin Canal system as well as a change in the place of delivery within the system. We agree.

The bylaw applies to a change of "the place to which any water [to which a stockholder] may be entitled shall be delivered." Historically, water diverted on the basis of water rights evidenced by the State's Catlin stock has been delivered through the Catlin Canal and applied to croplands lying under the canal. The State requests that the water to which it is entitled be allowed to bypass the headgate of the Catlin Canal so that it can be taken from the Arkansas River downstream through the headgate of the Ft. Lyon Canal. The fact that delivery to the new point of diversion will not be accomplished through the Catlin Canal cannot be permitted to obscure the essential fact that a change in the place of delivery of the water is requested. The challenged bylaw makes no distinction between in-system and out-of-system changes in place of delivery. Based upon the plain meaning of the words used in the bylaw, the contemplated change constitutes a change of place of delivery of the State's water, and so is governed by the bylaw requirements.

The bylaw construction which we adopt is also consistent with the purpose of the requirement of director approval. The directors are to evaluate a requested change of place of delivery to determine whether it "may be made without injury to the canal, the company or other stockholders." Although the record does not supply the details of the operational interdependency of the various features of the Catlin Ditch system, any alteration of the delivery point for one stockholder's water can be expected to have impact upon the ability of the Catlin Canal system to supply water to the other stockholders. See generally, Model Land and Irrigation Co. v. Madsen, 87 Colo. 166, 285 P. 1100 (1930).

* * *

III.

We next consider the contention of Ft. Lyon and the State that if the bylaw provision requires director approval of the requested change in point of diversion it impermissibly infringes upon the exclusive jurisdiction of the water judge. We do not agree.

* * * There is no question but that to effect the desired change of water right the State must obtain a decree from the water judge. But this does not dispose of the issue before this court. We must determine, in addition, whether a mutual ditch company bylaw purporting to further condition or limit the right to a change in point of diversion can be given effect consistent with allowing full scope to the jurisdiction of the water court.

The concept that the rights incident to water right ownership can be modified by private agreement is not novel. We have previously given effect to a mutual ditch company bylaw in a situation very similar to the one we face today. In *Model Land and Irrigation Co. v. Madsen,* supra, a mutual ditch company bylaw required board of directors' approval as a condition to a change in the place of use of a stockholder's water. A mutual ditch company brought suit to restrain a change in place of use by the stockholder in the face of the directors' disapproval of the requested transfer. The trial court dismissed the complaint and we reversed. After concluding that valid bylaws are binding on the stockholders, we held:

> The by-law in question is not against public policy or unreasonable. We have held that a contract between a ditch company and a landowner restricting the use of water to certain land is not unreasonable and against public policy. Wright v. Platte Valley Irrigation Co., 27 Colo. 322, 61 Pac. 603. A similar construction should be given to the by-law, for "By-laws enter into the contract between the corporation and its stockholders or members." 1 Fletcher, Cyc. Corporations, § 501.

87 Colo. at 168, 285 P. at 1101; see also Jacobucci v. District Court, 189 Colo. 380, 541 P.2d 667 (1975).

The change at issue in *Model* would have resulted in the removal of water from the canal many miles above the original irrigated tract. We concluded that the board of directors did not act arbitrarily in deciding that the transfer would injuriously affect the corporation and its stockholders:

> If permitted to [remove the water many miles higher on the canal], the volume of water flowing down the canal to the Model tract miles below would be diminished, thus increasing the loss by evaporation. Witnesses testified that the loss by evaporation and seepage would be greater if the water should be distributed in small amounts throughout the length of the canal, instead of being carried in a concentrated volume for use upon land in the Model tract, and also that the change would increase the cost of operation.

87 Colo. at 169, 285 P. at 1101–02.

Under these circumstances we held that the board of directors properly exercised the discretion given to it by the bylaws in refusing to permit the transfer and that the court was not justified in overriding the action of the board.

* * *

Although the Water Right Act provides protection against a change of water right that would injuriously affect other vested water rights or decreed conditional water rights, section 37–92–305(3), C.R.S.1973, this is not inconsistent with or frustrated by private agreements contractually limiting an owner's right to a change of water right so long as those limitations are reasonable. As the *Model* opinion recognized, severe adverse effects can result from a reduction in the volume of water flowing through a canal system. We are reluctant to deny force and effect to private agreements protecting against these adverse effects where those agreements supplement rather than frustrate the purposes of the Water Right Act.

* * *

Based on *Model,* * * * we hold that, under the circumstances present in this case, a mutual ditch company bylaw imposing reasonable limitations, additional to those contained in section 37–92–305, C.R.S.1973, upon the right of a stockholder to obtain a change in the point of diversion can be enforced.

* * *

We now direct our attention to the bylaw at issue here to determine whether it is reasonable. Considered in light of the purposes of mutual ditch companies, we conclude that it is.

A mutual ditch company is a cooperative venture typically created to finance the construction and maintenance of extensive ditch systems and to administer delivery of water through those ditches to its stockholders. See generally, Jacobucci v. District Court, supra, 189 Colo. at 385–86, 541 P.2d at 670–71; Moses, *Irrigation Corporations,* 32 R.M.L.Rev. 527 (1960). Because of the large capital requirements of such a project, the economies of scale resulting from a cooperative venture were essential to securing an adequate irrigation supply for development of the arid west. Id. The importance of such organizations, at least in earlier times, is further evidenced by the special statute enacted to facilitate the formation of mutual ditch companies. See section 7–42–101 et seq., C.R.S.1973 (1981 Supp.) which has its roots in G.L. § 274 et seq. (1877). The board of directors of a mutual ditch company can be expected to be especially familiar with the ditch system and the probable effects of a transfer of some part of the canal system's water supply to a point outside the mutual ditch network. We perceive no public policy that would be offended by permitting the stockholders, by voluntary agreement in the form of a bylaw, to require that anyone seeking to change a point of diversion to a place outside the system first submit an application to the board of directors for evaluation of the effect of the change on the rights of others dependent on the ditch for delivery of their water. Indeed, the process may promote dispute resolution, and the information so developed may prove useful in the later water court proceeding, facilitating a just and reasonable decree by the court.

Furthermore, we find nothing unreasonable in the bylaw criteria which the board is to apply. The directors were charged with evaluating the requested change to determine if it will cause injury to the canal, the company or other stockholders. The questions of injury are central to the fair and effective operation of what is inherently an interdependent undertaking for the delivery of water to a number of stockholders. We find no reason in public policy to deny the directors, pursuant to bylaw authorization, the right to review a proposed change of place of delivery to assure that it does not create the injury upon which the bylaw focuses.

NOTES

1. The state continued to press forward in its attempts to provide a permanent pool of water in John Martin Reservoir on the Arkansas River by exchanging the water rights represented by its share of Catlin stock with the Fort Lyon Canal Company. In a further proceeding, In the Matter of the Application for Water Rights of the Fort Lyon Canal Company, 762 P.2d 1375 (Colo.1988), the Colorado Supreme Court reiterated the position it adopted in the principal case, and sustained a water court decision that the Catlin board of directors had not acted arbitrarily or capriciously or abused its discretion in turning down the state's application for a change of water right.

2. In East–Jordan Irrigation Co. v. Utah State Engineer (pending before the Utah Supreme Court), the district court held that a shareholder in a mutual irrigation company may file an application for a change in the point of diversion, or place or kind of use, without the company's permission, as long as the rights of other shareholders are not impaired. (Rocky Mountain Mineral Law Foundation, Water Law Newsletter, no. 1, p. 11, 1992).

3. When water distribution organizations organized primarily to supply irrigation water are faced with the transition from farmland to residential development, problems often arise. In Nueces County Water Control and Improvement Dist. No. 3 v. Texas Water Rights Comm'n, 481 S.W.2d 930 (Tex.Civ.App.1972), a conservation and reclamation district had been converting water from irrigation to municipal use over a period of several decades. The Texas Water Rights Commission sought to cancel a converted right on the ground that such a conversion could not be made without Commission approval, and therefore converted irrigation rights were lost. A trial court opinion sustaining the Commission's order was overturned on appeal.

When cities grow at the perimeter and create urban sprawl, they often come into direct conflict with neighboring rural water distribution organizations, both for water and for customers. A companion case, Nueces County Water C. & I. Dist. No. 3 v. Texas Water Rights Comm'n, 481 S.W.2d 924 (Texas Civ.App. 1972), decided the same day, reveals that the City of Corpus Christi had sued the improvement district over the right to scarce water in the Nueces River.

Urbanization also brings rural irrigation water suppliers into such unfamiliar areas as sewage disposal and the production and sale of electric power. State legislatures sometimes have been slow to modify district enabling legislation to reflect these changing roles, thus increasing the difficulty of districts in meeting current needs.

More than 83% of the residents of the western United States live in cities. This urbanization has exacerbated the conflict between cities and rural irrigation water suppliers. In recognition of the need for representation of urban water interests, a Western Urban Water Coalition (WUWC) was formed in 1992. Members of the WUWC include Denver, Las Vegas, Reno, Portland, Salt Lake City, and Seattle water suppliers, and the California Urban Water Agencies. The WUWC is expected to play a pivotal role in water politics and assist western metropolitan areas in finding new approaches to obtaining water supplies. The new alliance shatters the historic coalition between urban and agricultural users that was powerful in moving Congress to appropriate funds for major water projects.

4. A further problem of urbanization is illustrated by Abbott v. West Extension Irr. Dist., 822 P.2d 747 (Or.App.1991). Plaintiff's four-year-old child fell into defendant's 26-mile long, unfenced irrigation canal and drowned. Although the jury's finding of non-negligence was upheld on appeal, irrigation ditches winding through heavily populated residential areas provide fertile opportunity for litigation.

5. Who owns the water rights held by a mutual ditch company? The company itself? The shareholders? Does the answer depend on the purposes for which ownership is being determined? In Jacobucci v. District Court In and For Jefferson County, 541 P.2d 667 (Colo.1975), a municipality sought to condemn water rights held by the Farmers Reservoir and Irrigation Company. The rights in question were used to irrigate 15,000 acres of land farmed by 271 shareholders of the ditch company. Emphasizing that "the shares of stock owned by Farmers' shareholders represent a definite and specific water right, as well as a corresponding interest in the ditch, canal, reservoir, and other works by which the water is utilized," the court held that the shareholders were indispensable parties to the condemnation proceedings, and must be joined. The court cited Wadsworth Ditch Co. v. Brown, 88 P. 1060 (Colo.1907), in which it was held that the right of a mutual ditch company shareholder to change the point of diversion of use from within to without the area served by the ditch was a property right. Exercise of the right is subject, however, to the company's bylaws providing for assessments of shareholders and the company's right to withdraw the individual shareholder's appropriation through the ditch headgate for others to use when the shareholder has no immediate use for the water.

6. What protection exists for landholders within a water distribution organization to receive water in times of shortage? A mutual ditch company's rights to establish classes of shares based on the priority of different shareholders' appropriations for the purpose of water distribution schedules and to assess those with earlier priorities higher maintenance expenses have been upheld, Robinson v. Booth-Orchard Grove Ditch Co., 31 P.2d 487 (1934), but such a pro rata allocation have been held not to be a conclusive adjudication of priorities among shareholders. Brose v. Bd. of Directors of Nampa and Meridian Irr. Dist., 132 P. 799 (Idaho 1913). Otherwise, the rule is that among shareholders of the same class there is no priority. Sanderson v. Salmon River Canal Co., 200 P. 341 (Idaho 1921). Suppose a shareholder-landowner argues that its water rights are being jeopardized by sales of stock to new irrigators or other users. See Laramie Rivers Co. v. Watson, 241 P.2d 1080 (Wyo.1952).

7. The court in Swasey v. Rocky Point Ditch Co., 617 P.2d 375 (Utah 1980) characterized stock certificates in a mutual ditch company and described the company's relationship to shareholders as follows:

> The board of directors of a mutual water company, as a matter of law, owes the duty to distribute to each stockholder his proper proportion of the water available for distribution among the stockholders. A mutual irrigation company has a duty to use reasonable care and diligence in maintaining its canal and keeping it supplied with water, and of regulating and dividing its use among the shareholders in accordance with their interests. The company is liable and must respond in damages to a shareholder injured by its neglect or failure to discharge such duty.
>
> * * * However, defendant does not have the duty to extend its canal and thereafter maintain it to plaintiffs' property as they contend. There is neither a provision in the articles of incorporation nor has there been established by custom, a duty to deliver the water to the property of a shareholder.
>
> * * * Plaintiffs' position is particularly untenable, since they failed to establish by the evidence either a shortage of water or resulting damages from loss thereof. * * *

617 P.2d at 379.

8. Duyck v. Tualatin Valley Irr. Dist., 723 P.2d 1043 (Or.App.1986) affirmed 728 P.2d 531 (Or.1986) held an exculpatory clause was reasonable that excused district liability "for failure to deliver water during the irrigation season when such failure occurs from a deficiency of water or from other causes beyond the control of the district. * * * " The case also explores the possibility of a negligence action based on a district's failure to warn that promised water will not arrive on schedule.

9. A shareholder may wish to transfer the use of water to other lands held by the shareholder, to the lands of other shareholders or to non-shareholders outside of the company service area. Each shareholder is considered to be the beneficial owner of a water right. Great Western Sugar Co. v. Jackson Lake Reservoir and Irr. Co., 681 P.2d 484 (Colo. 1984). Thus, shareholders have a duty not to injure the rights of other shareholders. For example, In re Application for Water Rights of Certain Shareholders in the Las Animas Consol. Canal Co., 688 P.2d 1102 (Colo. 1984), approved the sale of the water rights of two mutual ditch companies to a power plant on the condition that no junior rights would be injured, and the water court reserved jurisdiction to consider the question of injury for five years. The court assumed that water under junior priorities was distributed to the shareholders on the basis of their pro rata ownership interests because there was insufficient evidence of actual consumption by each shareholder. The presumption that water is used on the basis of legal entitlements

> permits applicants who can demonstrate gross patterns of historic use of water rights to seek beneficial changes in such patterns of use which otherwise would be prohibited not because of demonstra-

ble injury to the legal rights of others but because of the practical problem of the unavailability of reliable records. A shareholder asserting that historic use differed from use based on legal ownership may, of course, attempt to rebut the presumption. 688 P.2d at 1107–08. Stock may be made appurtenant to the land in order to protect the company from having to make uneconomical water deliveries. Thus shares may pass only with the transfer of the land, or the shares may be made severable. See John H. Davidson, *Distribution and Storage Organizations,* in 3 Water and Water Rights §§ 26.02(e)–(e)(2) (Robert E. Beck ed.)

10. Suppose one canal company wants to use another company's canal to transport water to its shareholders or customers? "Virtually all of the western states have enacted statutes providing that an individual may acquire the right to enlarge or to use an existing canal in common with the owners thereof, upon the payment of proper compensation." Canyon View Irr. Co. v. Twin Falls Canal Co., 619 P.2d 122, 127 (Idaho 1980).

11. Federal reclamation projects, designed in the main to provide irrigation water, are a significant potential source for transfers to municipal and other uses. Who owns project water, and what are the impediments to transfers? The Supreme Court, in Ickes v. Fox, 300 U.S. 82 (1937), held that the irrigator was the owner of the water right, and characterized the government as "simply a carrier and distributor of the water, with the right to receive the sums stipulated in the contracts as reimbursement for the cost of construction and annual charges for operation of the works." Id. at 95. That case, however, involved a situation where the repayments had been completed. What of the case, likely to exist under today's lengthy repayment periods, where reimbursement is continuing? Professor Tarlock presumptively identifies the Bureau of Reclamation as the holder of legal title "as a trustee for the project beneficiaries." A. Dan Tarlock, Law of Water Rights and Resources § 5.17[6][6] (1992). Whatever the state of title, proposed transfers must run the gamut of state law—deferred to by Section 8 of the Reclamation Act, 43 U.S.C.A. § 372—including state no-injury rules, Bureau of Reclamation contract provisions, approval of the Secretary of the Interior, and whatever anti-transfer protections cover the special districts that customarily hold project water rights.

NOTE: SPECIAL DISTRICTS AND WATER EFFICIENCY

Water districts are in a position to play a major role in promoting the efficient allocation of water resources. But there are legal and political impediments to the promotion of efficiency. Districts have been criticized as providing undue subsidies to agriculture. Their ability to spread costs among all taxpayers insulates the districts from the cost of developing or using water. Many charge very little or nothing for water usage. If anything is charged for the water used, it is generally a flat rate or a rate based on the average cost of developing water.

The "energy crisis" of the late 1970s stimulated intense interest in resource use conservation, especially in electric utility rates. Environmentalists and welfare economists argued that average cost rates often created incentives to use more electricity because rates declined with increased usage. The suggested remedy was to base rates on the marginal costs of power generation. The theory was that costs would rise with use and thus there would be incentives to conserve. The same criticism is made of water prices: "The use of taxpayer revenues, fee assessments, and historical average cost pricing procedures sends water price signals to users which are far below the marginal costs of new supply projects. In some cases, particularly in agriculture, no water price signal is sent at all." Zach Willey, *Least Cost Alternatives For Satisfying Water Demand: An Alternative Analysis*, in Western Water: Expanding Uses/Finite Supplies, Seventh Annual Summer Program, Natural Resources Law Center, University of Colorado School of Law (1986). As in the case of electric power, marginal, variable cost pricing, is suggested as the proper standard for water rates. The assumption is that this will result in higher prices and more efficient use of water. See generally Steve H. Hanke, *Demand For Water Under Dynamic Conditions*, 6 Water Resources Research 1253 (1970); Robert A. Young, *Price Elasticity of Demand For Municipal Water: A Case Study of Tucson, Arizona*, 9 Water Resources Research 1068 (1973); and Zamora, et al., *Pricing Urban Water: Theory and Practice in Three Southwestern Cities*, 1 Sw.Rev. Mgmt. Econ. 89 (1981). Theoretical marginal cost pricing may be too costly to implement, but rate structures can be modified to reflect different use patterns and thus send better signals to users.

There are some important examples of districts where water has been freely marketed among users in the service area. By allowing agricultural, municipal and industrial water users to buy and sell rights to use water annually, greater economic efficiency is achieved. The following excerpt is illustrative:

WATER MARKETS IN THE NORTHERN COLORADO WATER CONSERVANCY DISTRICT

The federal Colorado—Big Thompson Project (C–BT) was started in 1937 and completed in 1957 to bring supplemental irrigation water from the western side of the Rocky Mountains to Northeastern Colorado. The Northern Colorado Water Conservancy District (NCWCD) was established to contract with the federal government for purchase of the water, repayment of project costs, and distribution of the water to final users. C–BT has provided an historical average of 2.83×10^8 m^3 (230,000 acre-feet) or about 17% of the total water supply of the region. While this supply is primarily for supplemental irrigation, towns and a growing number of industries use C–BT as a raw water supply. This supply represents the easily tradable margin needed to provide flexibility in allocation.

The area encompassed by NCWCD included areas of quite different natural water supplies in relation to the amount of arable land. As a result, potential users did not want a mandatory, uniform assignment of water to the land. These sentiments led, in 1957, to a system in which water was to be delivered to the owners of NCWCD shares, a share representing a freely transferable contract between the District and the holder entitling the holder to $\frac{1}{310},000$th of the water available to NCWCD (this has averaged approximately 863.8m³ (0.7 acre-feet) of water per year). The transferable nature of the allotments stimulated the creation of a market in which they could be traded.

Much of the water needed for urban and nonagricultural industrial growth has been provided by the sale of NCWCD allotments from agriculture. These nonagricultural users often "rent" excess water back to irrigation on a short-term (annual) basis. In the early years many irrigators gave away their allotments because they did not want to pay the $1.50 annual charge. Allotment prices increased from $30 in 1960 to $291 in 1973. This trend accelerated sharply in 1974 with average prices reaching a peak of $2161 in 1980. Since 1980, prices have fallen back to about $900, partly because of the completion of a premature water supply project that will bring 5.92×10^7 m³ (48,000 acre-feet) of water to towns in the region.

Rentals are transfers of water among users for one season only without transferring the allotment titles. The NCWCD office facilitates communications among prospective buyers and sellers, so that rentals are easily effected in response to relatively small discrepancies in water values among users. About 30% of the C–BT water is involved in rental transactions each year, with towns being big renters of water to agriculture.

Third-party and instream flow problems have not been solved in NCWCD, but they have been evaded. The complexities and high transaction costs imposed on most water transfers by possible third-party intervention have been evaded because the District has retained title to all return flows. This is permitted under Colorado Law for waters newly imported to a basin. Third-party effects still occur and leave open the possibility that some sales are economically inefficient. Instream flow values have not been protected in spite of evidence that they are quite high in the region.

While the NCWCD market arrangements ignore return flow effects, they allow greater flexibility than alternative water distribution mechanisms. Transaction costs are certainly lower than for transfers under state laws, which frequently involve court trials. Flexibility is greater than under some Bureau of Reclamation contracts that prohibit water transfers from specific land parcels. Security of tenure is greater than that found under administrative procedures, such as those found in the Southeastern Colorado Water Conservancy District, where water is reallocated annually by the Board of Directors. The possibility of easily and advantageously replicating these NCWCD market structures in other project areas warrants serious consideration.

Charles W. Howe, et al., *Innovative Approaches to Water Allocation: The Potential for Water Markets*, 22 Water Resources Research 439, 443–44 (1986).

It is difficult to provide incentives for public entities to function efficiently, when the economic returns seem attenuated and the idea of "selling out" an important resource is politically unpopular. See Dwight R. Lee, *Political Provision Of Water: An Economic/Public Choice Perspective, in* Special Water Districts: Challenge For the Future 51 (James N. Corbridge, Jr., ed. 1983). If transfers within districts can promote more efficient water use, the opportunities for efficiency are multiplied when transfers outside the district are considered. So are the difficulties multiplied. Typically, district bylaws, state laws and provisions in federal reclamation contracts provide for water to be supplied to a specific service area defined by district boundaries. For them to be changed usually requires political action. This may be difficult because out-of-district transfers are often politically unpalatable, though they may be economically rewarding. Political opposition also rises to proposals to transfer agricultural water to municipal uses.

There have been some advantageous transactions in which water conserved in a district was transferred to a municipality. When the city of Casper, Wyoming needed an additional water supply it negotiated an agreement with the Alcova Irrigation District under which the city is paying to rehabilitate and line portions of the district's 59 miles of canals and 160 miles of laterals in order to reduce seepage. This will enable the district to reduce the amount of water it diverts from the North Platte River, but still deliver the same quantity of water for crop irrigation. Casper will have the benefit of some 7000 acre-feet a year of saved water.

The role of districts in facilitating agricultural to municipal transfers is significant. The most notable example is the Metropolitan Water District—Imperial Irrigation District agreement, discussed at pages 326–30, supra, and 899–903, infra.

The Western Governors Association (WGA) accepted a report in July, 1986 calling for greater efficiency in water use and finding that "local special water districts are central to the implementation of policies to enhance western water use; however, they usually operate outside the effective scope of state water policy." The report went on to say that

> [S]ubsidies and rolled-in pricing generally obscure the marginal cost implications of consumption by the districts, not to mention to individual users within districts. Additionally, Reclamation law together with state law creating them, discourage the lease or sale of water from districts, even if it is "surplus" to their needs, to users outside their boundaries. The unavailability of district water to those outside their boundaries forces those seeking incremental water supplies to look elsewhere, often at an increased cost. These arrangements should be reevaluated with the goal of protecting the rights of district members, enhancing the welfare of the surrounding economy, and creating incentives for districts to play their part in efficient water policy.

Bruce C. Driver, Western Water: Tuning the System, Report to the Western Governors Association 38–39 (1986). The WGA Report accordingly made the following recommendations concerning special districts:

States could authorize special water districts to transfer water to users outside of their boundaries, by sale, sale and leaseback, lease with an option to use in wet years, and a wide array of other arrangements. (In many instances state authorization of transfers outside of district boundaries would not be sufficient to enable such transfers due to restrictions contained in Reclamation law and district contracts with the Bureau of Reclamation. This is another area where states and the Bureau will need to work together to effect change.) California has also taken this step by authorizing special districts to transfer water that is "surplus" to their needs. "Surplus" has been defined broadly to include conserved water.

Special districts could be encouraged to permit the development of markets for water rights, shares or contracts within their boundaries perhaps using some of the auction and other procedures implemented by the Northern Colorado Water Conservancy District. Means of encouragement include conditioning state financial assistance for new projects on the allowance of markets or inclusion in the charters of new districts of requirements to encourage intra-district markets.

* * *

Provisions of western state law that constrain the mobility of water by requiring transferees to purchase land with water or that give special districts veto power over the transfer of water that is not used within their boundaries could be eliminated.

In 1988, the Department of the Interior, as part of its self-declared transition from a construction to a management agency, adopted the following policy to encourage federal water transfers.

DEPARTMENT OF THE INTERIOR

PRINCIPLES GOVERNING VOLUNTARY WATER TRANSACTIONS THAT INVOLVE OR AFFECT FACILITIES OWNED OR OPERATED BY THE DEPARTMENT OF THE INTERIOR

Transactions that involve water rights and supplies are occurring pursuant to State law with increasing frequency in the Nation, particularly in the Western United States. Such transactions include direct sale of water rights; lease of water rights; dry-year options on water rights; sale of land with associated water rights; and conservation investments with subsequent assignment of conserved water.

The Federal Government, as owner of a significant portion of the Nation's water storage and conveyance facilities, can assist State, Tribal, and local authorities in meeting local or regional water needs by improving or facilitating the improvement of management practices with respect to existing water supplies. Exchanges in type, location or priority of use that are accomplished according to State law can allow water to be used more efficiently to meet changing water demands, and also can protect and enhance the Federal investment in existing facilities. In addition, water exchanges can serve to improve many local and Indian reservation economies.

DOI's interest in voluntary water transactions proposed by others derives from an expectation that, to an increasing degree, DOI will be asked to approve, facilitate, or otherwise accommodate such transactions that involve or affect facilities owned or operated by its agencies. The DOI also wishes to be responsive to the July 7, 1987, resolution of the Western Governors' Association, which was reaffirmed at the Association's July 12, 1988, meeting, that the DOI "develop and issue a policy to facilitate water transfers which involve water and/or facilities provided by the Bureau of Reclamation."

The following principles are intended to afford maximum flexibility to State, Tribal, and local entities to arrive at mutually agreeable solutions to their water resource problems and demands. At the same time, these principles are intended to be clear as to the legal, contractual, and regulatory concerns that DOI must consider in its evaluation of proposed transactions.

For the purpose of this statement of principles, all proposed transactions must be between willing parties to the transaction and must be in accordance with applicable State and Federal law. Presentation of a proposal by one party, seeking Federal support or action against other parties, will not be considered in the absence of substantial support for the proposal among affected non-Federal parties.

VOLUNTARY WATER TRANSACTION PRINCIPLES

1. Primacy in water allocation and management decisions rests principally with the States. Voluntary water transactions under this policy must be in accordance with applicable State and Federal laws.

2. The Department of the Interior (DOI) will become involved in facilitating a proposed voluntary water transaction only when it can be accomplished without diminution of service to those parties otherwise being served by such Federal resources, and when:
   (a) there is an existing Federal contractual or other legal obligation associated with the water supply; or
   (b) there is an existing water right held by the Federal government that may be affected by the transaction; or
   (c) it is proposed to use Federally-owned storage or conveyance capacity to facilitate the transaction; or
   (d) the proposed transaction will affect Federal project operations; and
   (e) the appropriate State, Tribal, or other non-Federal political authorities or subdivisions request DOI's active involvement.

3. DOI will participate in or approve transactions when there are no adverse third-party consequences, or when such third-party conse-

quences will be heard and adjudicated in appropriate State forums, or when such consequences will be mitigated to the satisfaction of the affected parties.

4. As a general rule, DOI's role will be to facilitate transactions that are in accordance with applicable State and Federal law and proposed by others. In doing so, DOI will consider the positions of the affected State, Tribal, and local authorities. DOI will not suggest a specific transaction except when it is part of an Indian water rights settlement, a solution to a water rights controversy, or when it may provide a dependable water supply the provision of which otherwise would involve the expenditure of Federal funds. Such a suggestion would not be carried out without the concurrence of all affected non-Federal parties.

5. The fact that the transaction may involve the use of water supplies developed by Federal water resource projects shall not be considered during evaluation of a proposed transaction.

6. One of DOI's objectives will be to ensure that the Federal government is in an acceptable financial, operational, and contractual position following accomplishment of a transaction under this policy. Unless required explicitly by existing law, contracts, or regulations, DOI will refrain from burdening the transaction with additional costs, fees or charges, except for those costs actually incurred by DOI in performance of its functions in a particular transaction.

7. DOI will consider, in cooperation with appropriate State, Tribal and local authorities, necessary measures that may be required to mitigate any adverse environmental effects that may arise as a result of the proposed transaction.

How much encouragement will be given by this cautious policy to the transfer of project waters? As a recent study by the National Research Council observed, "[m]ore transactions probably will be facilitated than would have been without the principles, criteria, and guidance, but the DOI policy by no means provides clear sailing for western water transfers involving federal facilities or federal water rights." Water Transfers in the West, Efficiency, Equity, and the Environment (National Research Council, National Academy of Sciences, 1992). For a general discussion of the transfer of project water rights, see Bruce C. Driver, *The Effect of Reclamation Law on Voluntary Transfers of Water*, 33 Rocky Mtn.Min.L.Inst. 26–1 (1987) and Brian Gray, et al., *Transfers of Federal Reclamation Water: A Case Study of California's San Joaquin Valley*, 21 Envtl.L. 911 (1991).

Some of the promise of transfers is being realized by districts in California. The official state policy is now to "facilitate the voluntary transfer of water and water rights where consistent with the public welfare of the place of export and the place of import." Cal.Water Code § 109(a). To accomplish this goal, the Department of Water Resources (DWR), the State Water Resources Control Board (SWRCB), and all other appropriate state agencies are directed to provide technical assistance on water conservation measures which will make additional water available for transfer. § 109(b). In addition, DWR is directed to establish "an ongoing program to facilitate the voluntary exchange or transfer of water" which has already been developed, diverted, or which has been conserved. Cal.Water Code § 480. This legislation reduces the barriers to the free marketing of waters in California.

In 1992, Congress further encouraged water transfers in California through passage of the Central Valley Project Improvement Act, Pub.L. No. 102–575, §§ 3401–3412 (1992). The Central Valley Project (CVP), operated by the Bureau of Reclamation, controls about 20% of the state's water and operates federal reclamation projects located within, or diverting water from or to, the watershed of the Sacramento and San Joaquin rivers. See pages 684–85, infra. The Act specifies that one of its goals is to assist California urban areas by authorizing all individuals or districts who receive CVP water to transfer all or a portion of the water to a number of designated users, agencies or, organizations, for any beneficial use. All transfers are subject to approval by the Secretary of the Interior, and the water subject to any transfer is limited to water that would have otherwise been consumptively used or irretrievably lost to beneficial use during the transfer period. For a discussion of California water banking, see pages 330–31, supra.

3. Political Accountability

BALL v. JAMES

Supreme Court of the United States, 1981.
451 U.S. 355, 101 S.Ct. 1811, 68 L.Ed.2d 150.

JUSTICE STEWART delivered the opinion of the Court.

This appeal concerns the constitutionality of the system for electing the directors of a large water reclamation district in Arizona, a system which, in essence, limits voting eligibility to landowners and apportions voting power according to the amount of land a voter owns. The case requires us to consider whether the peculiarly narrow function of this local governmental body and the special relationship of one class of citizens to that body releases it from the strict demands of the one-person, one-vote principle of the Equal Protection Clause of the Fourteenth Amendment.

I

The public entity at issue here is the Salt River Project Agricultural Improvement and Power District, which stores and delivers untreated water to the owners of land comprising 236,000 acres in central Arizona. The District, formed as a governmental entity in 1937, subsidizes its water operations by selling electricity, and has become the supplier of electric power for hundreds of thousands of people in an area including a large part of metropolitan Phoenix. Nevertheless, the history of the District began in the efforts of Arizona farmers in the 19th century to irrigate the arid lands of the Salt River Valley, and, as the parties have stipulated, the primary purposes of the District have always been the storage, delivery, and conservation of water.

* * * [T]he legislature allowed the district to limit voting for its directors to voters, otherwise regularly qualified under state law, who own land within the district, and to apportion voting power among those landowners according to the number of acres owned. * * *

II

This lawsuit was brought by a class of registered voters who live within the geographic boundaries of the District, and who own either no land or less than an acre of land within the District. The complaint alleged that the District enjoys such governmental powers as the power to condemn land, to sell tax-exempt bonds, and to levy taxes on real property. It also alleged that because the District sells electricity to virtually half the population of Arizona, and because, through its water operations, it can exercise significant influence on flood control and environmental management within its boundaries, the District's policies and actions have a substantial effect on all people who live within the District, regardless of property ownership. Seeking declaratory and injunctive relief, the appellees claimed that the acreage-based scheme for electing directors of the District violates the Equal Protection Clause of the Fourteenth Amendment.

* * *

III

Reynolds v. Sims [377 U.S. 533 (1964)], held that the Equal Protection Clause requires adherence to the principle of one-person, one-vote in elections of state legislators. Avery v. Midland County, 390 U.S. 474, extended the *Reynolds* rule to the election of officials of a county government, holding that the elected officials exercised "general governmental powers over the entire geographic area served by the body." 390 U.S., at 485. The Court, however, reserved any decision on the application of *Reynolds* to "a special-purpose unit of government assigned the performance of functions affecting definable groups of constituents more than other constituents." 390 U.S., at 483–484. In Hadley v. Junior College District, 397 U.S. 50, the Court extended *Reynolds* to the election of trustees of a community college district because those trustees "exercised general governmental powers" and "perform[ed] important governmental functions" that had significant effect on all citizens residing within the district. 397 U.S., at 53–54. But in that case the Court stated: "It is of course possible that there might be some case in which a State elects certain functionaries whose duties are so far removed from normal governmental activities and so disproportionately affect different groups that a popular election in compliance with *Reynolds* * * * might not be required. * * * " Id., at 56.[6]

The Court found such a case in *Salyer*. The Tulare Lake Basin Water Storage District involved there encompassed 193,000 acres, 85%

6. The Court held that the Junior College District in *Hadley* did not fall within this exception because "[e]ducation has traditionally been a vital governmental function, and these * * * are governmental officials in every relevant sense of that term." 397 U.S., at 56.

of which were farmed by one or another of four corporations. Salyer Land Co. v. Tulare Lake Basin Water Storage District, 410 U.S., at 723. Under California law, public water districts could acquire, store, conserve, and distribute water, and though the Tulare Lake Basin Water Storage District had never chosen to do so, could generate and sell any form of power it saw fit to support its water operations. The costs of the project were assessed against each landowner according to the water benefits the landowner received. At issue in the case was the constitutionality of the scheme for electing the directors of the district, under which only landowners could vote, and voting power was apportioned according to the assessed valuation of the voting landowner's property. The Court recognized that the Tulare Lake Basin Water Storage District did exercise "some typical governmental powers," including the power to hire and fire workers, contract for construction of projects, condemn private property, and issue general obligation bonds. Nevertheless, the Court concluded that the district had "relatively limited authority," because "its primary purpose, indeed the reason for its existence, is to provide for the acquisition, storage, and distribution of water for farming in the Tulare Lake Basin." Id., at 728 (footnote omitted). The Court also noted that the financial burdens of the district could not but fall on the landowners, in proportion to the benefits they received from the district, and that the district's actions therefore disproportionately affected the voting landowners.[7] The *Salyer* Court thus held that the strictures of *Reynolds* did not apply to the Tulare District, and proceeded to inquire simply whether the statutory voting scheme based on land valuation at least bore some relevancy to the statute's objectives.[8] The Court concluded that the California Legislature could have reasonably assumed that without voting power apportioned according to the value of their land, the landowners might not have been willing to subject their lands to the lien of the very assessments which made the creation of the district possible.

As noted by the Court of Appeals, the services currently provided by the Salt River District are more diverse and affect far more people than those of the Tulare Lake Basin Water Storage District. Whereas the Tulare District included an area entirely devoted to agriculture and populated by only 77 persons, the Salt River District includes almost half the population of the State, including large parts of Phoenix and other cities. Moreover, the Salt River District, unlike the Tulare District, has exercised its statutory power to generate and sell electric power, and has become one of the largest suppliers of such power in the State. Further, whereas all the water delivered by the Tulare District

---

7. On the same day it decided *Salyer*, the Court upheld a similar scheme in Wyoming, under which the voters in a referendum on the creation of a water district had to be landowners, and in which the decision to create the district required the votes of landowners representing a majority of the acreage of the lands within the proposed district. *Associated Enterprises, Inc. v. Toltec Watershed Improvement Dist.*, 410 U.S. 743 (*per curiam*).

8. In *Kramer* v. *Union Free School District No. 15*, 395 U.S. 621, 627, the Court stated that the exclusion of otherwise qualified voters from a particular election must be justified by some compelling state interest. But in considering whether the voting scheme for the Tulare Lake Basin Water Storage District bore some relevancy to the purpose for which the scheme was adopted, *Salyer* imposed no such requirement.

went for agriculture, roughly 40% of the water delivered by the Salt River District goes to urban areas or is used for nonagricultural purposes in farming areas. Finally whereas all operating costs of the Tulare District were born[e] by the voting landowners through assessments apportioned according to land value, most of the capital and operating costs of the Salt River District have been met through the revenues generated by the selling of electric power. Nevertheless, a careful examination of the Salt River District reveals that, under the principles of the *Avery, Hadley*, and *Salyer* cases, these distinctions do not amount to a constitutional difference.

First, the District simply does not exercise the sort of governmental powers that invoke the strict demands of *Reynolds*. The District cannot impose ad valorem property taxes or sales taxes. It cannot enact any laws governing the conduct of citizens, nor does it administer such normal functions of government as the maintenance of streets, the operation of schools, or sanitation, health, or welfare services.

Second, though they were characterized broadly by the Court of Appeals, even the District's water functions, which constitute the primary and originating purpose of the District, are relatively narrow. The District and Association do not own, sell, or buy water, nor do they control the use of any water they have delivered. The District simply stores water behind its dams, conserves it from loss, and delivers it through project canals. * * * As repeatedly recognized by the Arizona courts, though the state legislature has allowed water districts to become nominal public entities in order to obtain inexpensive bond financing, the districts remain essentially business enterprises, created by and chiefly benefiting a specific group of landowners. As in *Salyer*, the nominal public character of such an entity cannot transform it into the type of governmental body for which the Fourteenth Amendment demands a one-person, one-vote system of election.

Finally, neither the existence nor size of the District's power business affects the legality of its property-based voting scheme. As this Court has noted in a different context, the provision of electricity is not a traditional element of governmental sovereignty, *Jackson v. Metropolitan Edison Co.*, 419 U.S. 345, 353, and so is not in itself the sort of general or important governmental function that would make the government provider subject to the doctrine of the *Reynolds* case. In any event, since the electric power functions were stipulated to be incidental to the water functions which are the District's primary purpose, they cannot change the character of that enterprise. * * *

The appellees claim, and the Court of Appeals agreed, that the sheer size of the power operations and the great number of people they affect serve to transform the District into an entity of general governmental power. But no matter how great the number of nonvoting residents buying electricity from the District, the relationship between them and the District's power operations is essentially that between consumers and a business enterprise from which they buy. * * *

The functions of the Salt River District are therefore of the narrow, special sort which justifies a departure from the popular-election requirement of the *Reynolds* case. And as in *Salyer*, an aspect of that limited purpose is the disproportionate relationship the District's functions bear to the specific class of people whom the system makes eligible to vote. * * *

As in the *Salyer* case, we conclude that the voting scheme for the District is constitutional because it bears a reasonable relationship to its statutory objectives. Here, according to the stipulation of the parties, the subscriptions of land which made the Association and then the District possible might well have never occurred had not the subscribing landowners been assured a special voice in the conduct of the District's business. Therefore, as in *Salyer*, the State could rationally limit the vote to landowners. Moreover, Arizona could rationally make the weight of their vote dependent upon the number of acres they own, since that number reasonably reflects the relative risks they incurred as landowners and the distribution of the benefits and the burdens of the District's water operations.

The judgment of the Court of Appeals is reversed, and the case is remanded for further proceedings consistent with this opinion.

It is so ordered.

* * *

Justice White, with whom Justice Brennan, Justice Marshall, and Justice Blackmun join, dissenting.

In concluding that the District's "one-acre, one-vote" scheme is constitutional, the Court misapplies the limited exception recognized in Salyer Land Co. v. Tulare Lake Basin Water Storage District, 410 U.S. 719 (1973), on the strained logic that the provision of water and electricity to several hundred thousand citizens is a "peculiarly narrow function." Because the Court misreads our prior cases and its opinion is conceptually unsound, I dissent.

* * *

An analysis of the two relevant factors required by *Salyer* demonstrates that the Salt River District possesses significant governmental authority and has a sufficiently wide effect on nonvoters to require application of the strict scrutiny mandated by *Kramer*.

II

The District involved here clearly exercises substantial governmental powers. The District is a municipal corporation organized under the laws of Arizona and is not, in any sense of the word, a private corporation. * * * The District's bonds are tax exempt, and its property is not subject to state or local property taxation. * * * The District also has the power of eminent domain, a matter of some import. * * *

The District here also has authority to allocate water within its service area. It has veto power over all transfers of surface water from one place or type of use to another, and this power extends to any "watershed or drainage area which supplies or contributes water for the irrigation of lands within [the] district. * * * " Ariz. Rev. Stat. Ann. § 45–172.5 (Supp. 1980–1981).

* * * The authority and power of the District are sufficient to require application of the strict scrutiny required by our cases. This is not a single-purpose water irrigation district, but a large and vital municipal corporation exercising a broad range of initiatives across a spectrum of operations. Moreover, by the nature of the state law, it is presently exercising that authority without direct regulation by state authorities charged with supervising privately owned corporations involved in the same business. The functions and purposes of the Salt River District represent important governmental responsibilities that distinguish this case from *Salyer*.

* * *

NOTES

1. *Ball* has been followed in other cases involving water districts. E.g., Stelzel v. South Indian River Water Control Dist., 486 So.2d 65 (Fla.Dist.Ct.App.1986) (one vote per acre in district that exercised road construction and maintenance functions and aquatic weed abatement authority).

2. State constitutional provisions may impose stricter requirements for voting than the United States Constitution. The Washington Supreme Court has struck down a law limiting the right to vote for irrigation district board members to owners of agricultural land. Foster v. Sunnyside Valley Irr. Dist., 687 P.2d 841 (Wash.1984). The limitation was found to be inconsistent with the state constitution's guarantee of "free and equal" elections. The court specifically found that a Ball v. James analysis, focusing on the primary purpose of special districts in allowing only landowners to vote, was inconsistent with the state constitution. The court did hold that a district exercising largely non-governmental powers, as determined by the *Ball* test, could apportion votes among the affected class based on the different relative impacts of the district's activities on some members rather than being bound to a one-person, one-vote requirement. The scheme in question in *Foster* gave owners of one to ten acres of agricultural land one vote, and owners of additional agricultural land an additional vote. Because owners of non-agricultural land were completely denied suffrage, the scheme was inadequate. The court said it will subject any apportionment scheme to strict scrutiny to ensure that votes are apportioned according to the level of the district's impact on definable classes of voters.

3. A related issue is whether directors of irrigation and other water districts should be elected or appointed, and if appointed, by whom. In Choudhry v. Free, 552 P.2d 438 (Cal.1976), the California Supreme Court struck down a statute requiring candidates for the board of directors of the Imperial Irrigation District to be landowners within the district. The court held that the requirement violated the constitutional rights of the candidates and the voters.

Under Colorado law, members of conservancy district boards are appointed by the local district court judge. The board must reflect a balance among beneficial water users in the district. This approach (along with a variety of broad powers given to districts) was upheld in People ex rel. Rogers v. Letford, 79 P.2d 274 (Colo.1938). In districts organized after 1945, election of board members was originally available on petition of 15% of the "qualified taxpaying electors" of a water conservancy district. Colo. Rev. Stat. § 37–45–114. After the statute was amended in 1985, an election may be triggered by a petition of 15% of the "registered electors" of the district. Colo. Rev. Stat. § 37–45–114.

Appointment of board members is often criticized on the ground that it tends to perpetuate control of district affairs in the hands of agricultural interests, when the district's problems may be increasingly urban in nature. What are the advantages and disadvantages of appointed as opposed to elected boards?

Special districts were developed outside of the English heritage of local governments that only recognized cities and counties. Often districts were created to avoid state constitutional debt limitations that had been adopted in an attempt to curb the excesses of public "speculation" in improvements that occurred in the nineteenth century. In the twentieth century, some state legislatures have struggled to gain control of these districts, many of which are very powerful. In addition to franchise controls, states have attempted to increase the accountability of special districts through the centralization and integration of district powers into state water planning and management generally. A useful analysis of this effort is Timothy De Young, *Discretion Versus Accountability: The Case of Special Water Districts*, in Special Water Districts: Challenge For The Future 31 (James N. Corbridge, Jr., ed. 1983).

4. Courts have had difficulty deciding whether irrigation districts are private or public. The problem is typified by the following language from Maricopa County Mun. Water Conservation Dist. No. 1 v. La Prade, 40 P.2d 94, 99 (Ariz.1935):

What, then, is the nature of an irrigation district under our laws? That it is a public, instead of a private, corporation established by the Legislature for a public use cannot be questioned, for otherwise it could not exercise the right of taxation, and compel unwilling landholders within its limits to subject their lands to such taxation. Fallbrook Irr. Dist. v. Bradley, 164 U.S. 112; In re Madera Irr. Dist., 92 Cal. 296, 28 P. 272, 675.

But is it also a political subdivision of the state? The decisions on this point, even in the same jurisdictions, are in hopeless conflict.   * * *

We think the true rule and the reasons therefor are well set forth in Day v. Buckeye Water, etc., Dist. [28 Ariz. 466, 237 P. 636] * * * "[I]rrigation districts and similar public corporations, while in some senses subdivisions of the state, are in a very different class. Their function is purely business and economic, and not political and governmental. They are formed in each case by the direct act of those whose business and property will be affected, and for the express purpose of engaging in some form of business, and not of government. The power of incurring obligations of any nature is ultimately left in the hands of those whose property is affected thereby."

Districts of the kind involved in this proceeding therefore belong to that class of organizations, once rare but becoming more and more common, established for the pecuniary profit of the inhabitants of a certain territorial subdivision of the state, but having no political or governmental purposes or functions. In some respects these organizations are municipal in their nature, for they exercise the taxing power, the greatest attribute of sovereignty, and can compel the inclusion of unwilling landholders within their bounds. In other ways they resemble private corporations, for they are liable for the torts of their servants in the same manner and to the same extent, and indeed generally have the same rights and responsibilities. Probably the best definition we can give then is to say that they are corporations having a public purpose, which may be vested with so much of the attributes of sovereignty as are necessary to carry out that purpose, and which are subject only to such constitutional limitations and responsibilities as are appropriate thereto.

TIMOTHY DE YOUNG, SOME THOUGHTS ON GOVERNING SPECIAL DISTRICTS

OCCASIONAL PAPERS SERIES, NATIONAL RESOURCES LAW
CENTER, UNIVERSITY OF COLORADO SCHOOL OF LAW
(1991).

I grew up at the southern edge of the Los Angeles urban sprawl in Orange County, California. * * * Most of southern Orange County had been held in large tracts since Spanish colonial times. Mission Viejo, Laguna Niguel, and the O'Neil and Irvine Ranches covered thousands of acres. Eventually, as is the custom in California, these ranches were subdivided and became suburban communities. While my story should be familiar, the use of irrigation districts, technically California Water Districts, as vehicles for south Orange County's development, however, is a largely untold story.

The Irvine, Los Alisos, Moulton Niguel Water Districts, for example, were formed and governed in the 1950s by large ranch corporations. Their control over district policy was assured by a weighted voting system for the selection of boards of directors, usually one vote * * * for each $100 of assessed property value. Much like a closely held corporation, the weighted voting system assured control by vested interests.

Of course, building sewage treatment plants and municipal water delivery systems was an expensive proposition, but one which the districts readily assumed. * * * Tax free general obligation or revenue bonds encumbered the districts with long-term debt. District policy often was to defer repayment of the debt as long as possible so that the developers would never shoulder the burden of repayment. * * *

In northern New Mexico, near my new home, acequias or community ditch associations are the dominant agencies of irrigation. Stanley Crawford's *Mayordomo* (UNM Press, 1988) weaves a rich tapestry of life on a community ditch and should be read by anyone interested in irrigation communities. * * *

Throughout Crawford's book, one is struck both by the lack of participation by those served by the ditch and the endless hours of thankless work required of Crawford as mayordomo. * * * In New Mexico's acequias, we see both how traditional local irrigation districts used to work and how they now struggle to continue. They fiercely guard their autonomy, distrust the state but are willing to accept their benefits, and apathy by most farmers is the rule, rather than the exception.

TWO TYPES OF IRRIGATION DISTRICTS

Irrigation districts in New Mexico and California perhaps represent two ends of the irrigation district continuum. Despite their differences, both represent a community of interests. In Crawford's words, the acequia is "bound together—by a narrow channel of water that flows through everyone's backyard." * * * In the Orange County water districts, the community of interest was much smaller and less diverse, limited to surprisingly few developers. Eventually, the community became larger and more diverse through urbanization.

Second, all districts seem to share a parochial perspective to some extent. Rather than be overwhelmed by the multitude of district types, district powers, and district styles, let's consider two primary types of irrigation districts. The most predominant type of district might be called special interest or captured districts.

Merrill Goodall, a long time observer of California special districts, calls special interest districts the "preferred public appendages of private interests." Or to paraphrase Justice Stewart in his landmark decision, Ball v. James, 451 U.S. 355 (1981), special purpose districts, created to benefit a specific group of landowners, are nominal public entities formed in order to obtain inexpensive bond financing to accomplish private purposes.

The incredible diversity in special district enabling legislation simply may reflect the diversity of special interest needs. Conservancy districts and California Water Districts are early examples of successful efforts by special interests to modify the Wright Act electoral and financial provisions. More recently, special interests have literally designed the scope and extent of their powers as well as the opportunities for subsidy by forming districts through special legislation. California's Metropolitan Water District and New Mexico's Albuquerque Metropolitan Arroyo and Flood Control Authority ("AMAFCA") are cases in point, but there are examples in each of the western states. In short, a narrow band of economic interest groups formed and dominated special interest districts.

In contrast to special interest districts, some districts represent a community of diverse interests. Community districts include many, but are by no means limited to, mutual ditch and water companies, acequias and California's Municipal Utility Districts. In general, community districts are found in relatively stable rural areas where the need to cooperate led to the formation of some form of collaborative enterprise. Unlike special interest districts, community districts are more governmental in the sense that they represent a diverse array of interests. In many areas, community districts were the first form of government, but their number, and more importantly their vitality, is declining rapidly.

INSTITUTIONAL DECAY

After formation and over time, special interests and community districts, like all things, change. Crawford's book is also about institutional decay. * * *

These second generation institutions are not governed, they are managed. Maintenance replaces construction and administration replaces capture. * * *

In special interest districts, democratic election procedures uniformly have failed to elect good directors, although they may be a fairly effective means to remove bad ones. * * * In effect, popular election of board directors is a *de facto* appointment system. The only real difference between elections and appointive systems is that in the former, appointers become qualified by their voluntary decision to vote whereas in the latter, other criteria are used.

DEBUNKING DEMOCRACY

Any discussion of democratic institutions and irrigation districts should at least mention Chief Justice Rehnquist's controversial opinion in Salyer Land Company v. Tulare Lake Basin Water Storage District, 410 U.S. 719 (1974) and the subsequent extension in Ball v. James, supra. Although I severely criticized and disagreed with the *Ball* decision shortly after its announcement, I now see that for perhaps the wrong motives, Justice Rehnquist and the majority were probably right in certain respects. In particular, I admire their courage in rejecting the blind application of our most cherished democratic formula for government: one person, one vote.

The folly of the *Ball* and *Salyer* decisions was the Court's approval of weighted voting, an equally inappropriate method of selection. Weighted voting systems are premised on the corporate principle that control should be allocated in direct proportion to shares or investment. If special interest districts in fact are "essentially business enterprises," then corporate methods of selection may be appropriate. To the extent that districts must represent a diverse community of interests, weighted voting assures unequal representation skewed in favor of wealth and privilege. If one views districts as vehicles for public subsidies, such as subsidies to agriculture in the form of low cost irrigation water, then a weighted voting system similarly assures that the subsidy will be allocated in direct proportion to the wealth of the recipient. * * *

Finally and perhaps most obviously, weighted voting discourages participation as a direct function to the distribution of votes; the more votes controlled by any individual, the less incentive for other voters to participate. * * *

The Ninth Circuit Court of Appeals recently revisited the Salt River Project Agricultural Improvement and Power District in *Gorenc v. Salt River Project Agr. Imp. & Power*, 869 F.2d 503 (1989). In certain respects, the decision is remarkable. An employee of this irrigation district had filed a civil rights suit alleging that the district had terminated his employment under "color of state law." The Court of Appeals held that the district, although designated as a political subdivision under the Arizona Constitution, was not a "state actor." Therefore, civil rights protections are inapplicable to special districts. In explaining the decision, the court noted that the district is "owned and operated by private individual landowners—it is not operated for the benefit of the general public but for the benefit of the private landowners in the district—it only serves a governmental function when it engages in 'the reclamation and irrigation of arid lands, the drainage of water logged lands, and the production of electricity for these purposes.' "

The court conceded that the district could levy property taxes, sell tax-exempt bonds, and exercise eminent domain, and was immune from taxation on the sale of electricity. However, the court quoted *Ball* to the effect that the district could not enact any general laws governing a person's conduct, provide general governmental services such as schools, street maintenance, or sanitation, impose *ad valorem* property taxes or sales taxes, and unlike public entities, its employees are allowed to strike under their labor contract. Moreover, the district was not immune from banking laws, exempt from the city's power of eminent domain, or immune from tort liability in the maintenance of its irrigation canals. Overall, this decision solidifies the *Ball* decision, a decision that in effect allows districts to be chameleons. They affect public colors when it is advantageous to do so, but resort to private camouflage when needed.

Along the same lines, an Arizona Court of Appeals recently held that irrigation district elections are not general elections and thus are not subject to state constitution residency requirements. *Porterfield v. Van Boening*, 744 P.2d 468 (1987). In this case, Porterfield, a losing candidate for an irrigation district election, brought a suit challenging the district's practice of allowing foreign corporations to vote as landowners in the district. Van Boening in fact would have lost if only residents of Arizona were allowed to vote. The court disallowed Porterfield's challenge on the basis that the voting franchise in irrigation district elections is by its nature based on landownership (read special interest) and is not based on traditional notions underlying a one-person, one-vote principle (read community of diverse interests). Accord *People ex rel. Cheyenne Soil Erosion Dist. v. Parker*, 118 Colo. 13, 192 P.2d 417 (1948); but see *Foster v. Sunnyside Valley Irr. Dist.*, 687 P.2d 841 (Wash.1984) (constitutionally qualified electors significantly affected by district decisions must be given an opportunity to vote).

Because special interest districts legally are not governments, there apparently are no constitutional requirements for democratic elections. Are there other compelling reasons for requiring one-person, one-vote systems? I think not.

Advocates of democracy seem to confuse process with outcome. Those who would elect and require democratic elections across the board may argue that there is some inherent value to the democratic process and to this argument, I have no response. But if democracy is being advocated because it produces real advantages in terms of outcomes, then I need to be persuaded. A common argument made for popular elections is that elections provide a mechanism for accountability. The electorate will turn out to oust the rascals or when they are very displeased with district directions, to defeat certain proposals such as bond referenda. This sounds good in theory, but I wonder how often it happens in practice. * * *

If it is true that most special districts have entered the age of management and maintenance, then the most important function of the directors is to act as a personnel committee for hiring a competent manager. Whether called mayordomo, manager, or chief executive officer, a well governed district must be administratively well managed. * * *

A MODEST PROPOSAL

Given the problems of apathy and the resultant failure of democratic processes on the one hand and the inherent problems of weighted voting on the other, then what is the solution? While it is laudable to try to increase the political awareness of the electorate, it may not be realistic. Moreover, increased public involvement often increases the difficulties of management both in terms of making essentially administrative decisions and achieving management continuity. After several years of study and thought, I am convinced that some form of appointment works best. Of course, appointive systems are used widely, but little research has documented their relative costs and benefits. However, the rationale for such systems is clear.

Both special interest and community districts increasingly are being called on to be responsive members of the intergovernmental community. Efforts to control nonpoint source water pollution, increase recreational opportunities, and preserve open space are three areas where districts can play a pivotal role. Because state governments are principally responsible for natural resources management, an elected official at the state level such as the governor or his designee should be allowed to appoint at least some of the directors of each irrigation district. In light of a long tradition of local autonomy in water resources management and the practical need for local knowledge, some of the directors should also be appointed by elected local government officials. Appointment by elected officials probably is required constitutionally and practically, makes appointment somewhat more palatable to true democrats and others afflicted with technocracy phobias. Florida has adopted such a system and perhaps can provide a model for the western states.

Perhaps a majority or popular vote should be required to form either a community or special interest district, but after formation, then appointment or approval voting should be used. In community districts that serve diverse constituents and provide a range of service, community interest may be sufficient to allow for popular elections. But in most cases, districts are one of several governments in an area. Appointed directors enhance the chances for intergovernmental cooperation, whereas elected directors tend to be accountable only to the narrow band of constituents or special interests that they represent.

Chapter Seven

FEDERAL ALLOCATION AND CONTROL OF WATER RESOURCES

A. PLANNING AND DEVELOPMENT OF WATER RESOURCES

This section examines the role of the federal government in directly developing or authorizing the development of water. Since the passage of the Reclamation Act of 1902, huge federal water resources programs have been devoted to promoting the settlement of the arid West. The goal of the Bureau of Reclamation, created under the Act, was to conserve and distribute water in the West, primarily for agricultural irrigation of otherwise dry and unproductive lands. However, other regions of the country also have demanded federal intervention in water resource development. Throughout the nineteenth century, federal water resources policy was concentrated on the protection and the promotion of navigation by the building of canals and locks and the dredging and improving of harbors and inland waterways, principally in the East and Southeast. See Beatrice H. Holmes, A History of Federal Water Resources Programs, 1800–1960 (Dept. of Agriculture Misc.Pub. 1233, Wash.D.C.1972). The leading history of the triumph of multiple purpose development is Samuel P. Hays, Conservation and the Gospel of Efficiency; The Progressive Conservation Movement 1890–1920 (1959).

In the twentieth century the authority of the chief navigation protection agency, the United States Army Corps of Engineers, was expanded to include controlling floods, enhancing recreation, supplying municipal water, and finally, to protecting the environmental quality of water. This opened the arid West to greater water development possibilities under the auspices of the Corps.

JOHN R. MATHER, WATER RESOURCES: DISTRIBUTION, USE, AND MANAGEMENT

294–305 (1984).

* * *

A History of Federal Water Resources Legislation

Promoting commerce and transportation has long been one of the major concerns of the Federal government (witness the present emphasis on our interstate highway system). In the early 1800s, this interest was expressed in the government's desire to promote river improvements and canal developments to aid in inland transportation. It was clearly stated that navigable waters would be treated as public highways and would be maintained free for the use of all. The westward movement of the nation after the Louisiana Purchase resulted in the Senate asking Secretary of the Treasury Albert Gallatin to prepare a national plan for the development of roads and canals. The Gallatin Report of 1808 called for a nationwide system of canals and other river improvements that could be justified on the basis of the economic development of the West, national defense, and political unity.

While the Gallatin Report, and its later revision by Secretary of War Calhoun in 1819, suggested that Congress had the power to spend money on river improvements because of its concern for national defense and the general welfare, the famous *Gibbons v. Ogden* decision by the Supreme Court in 1824 acknowledged that the power of Congress to regulate interstate commerce also included the power to regulate navigation within each of the states insofar as that navigation was connected with commerce.

* * *

As farmers moved into drier and drier areas, the need for irrigation became obvious. The Desert Land Act of 1877 authorized sale of 640–acre parcels of land in certain arid states and territories provided the purchasers would irrigate them within 3 years. Various land speculation scandals severely limited the implementation of this Act.

The period from 1900 to 1920, under the administrations of Roosevelt, Taft, and Wilson, marked a most significant and what might be called progressive period in Federal water resources programs and developments. The principles directing the water resources development during this period were (a) conservation of national resources for the use of present and future generations; (b) elimination of control and/or exploitation of the resources by monopolies; (c) elimination of "giveaways" of resources to special interests; (d) encouragement of individual, independent groups such as the family farm.

* * *

A number of agencies were established to coordinate planning and development of water resources. For example, the Reclamation Act of 1902 established, among other things, the Reclamation Fund with money made available from the sale of public lands * * *. The Secretary of the Interior was authorized to use the fund to plan and construct irrigation works in those states.   * * *

The Federal Power Commission was started as a Cabinet-level committee of the Departments of War, Interior, and Agriculture to license non-Federal development of water power on navigable streams and to sell surplus government power when in the public interest.

* * *

During the 1920s (until 1933) under Republican administrations, the general trend was to deemphasize the antimonopolistic policies of the previous two decades and to eliminate, as much as possible, government competition with private enterprise. For a while, work was stopped on the nearly completed Wilson Dam near Muscle Shoals while a private purchaser was sought. Hoover, as Secretary of Commerce, recommended national planning of public works as well as multi-purpose planning by the various governmental drainage basin commissions. But the matter of public vs. private control of power continued to be one of the most sensitive political issues in the nation for years.

In 1925, Congress asked the Corps of Engineers and the Federal Power Commission to prepare a list (with cost estimates) of navigable streams and their tributaries which might be surveyed for possible power development. * * * And in 1928, following a most severe flood on the Mississippi River, the Corps was authorized to do what was necessary for flood control (including the construction of reservoirs on tributaries); the Federal government would cover the entire cost of the project in view of the fact that there had been large local expenditures for flood control previously. The Bureau of Reclamation meanwhile acquired control over all regional multi-purpose planning in the basin of the Colorado River.

* * *

The depression of the 1930s and the new administration under Franklin Roosevelt resulted in the formulation of many construction plans in the form of public works projects in order to stimulate the economy. Multi-purpose water resource development with public power programs was promoted to provide regional economic growth and to benefit the largest numbers of people. Planning the development of "national" resources, which included both human and natural resources, became a key to the programs proposed. Roosevelt enlarged the role of the Executive in the proposing of legislation and Congress accepted its role to consider and modify the programs initiated in the Executive Branch.

A number of new water planning agencies were established to push new concepts of regional resources development. One cornerstone of this concept was the creation of the Tennessee Valley Authority in 1933, an agency authorized to exercise all Federal functions of development and management of water and land resources within a large geographic region. As such, it had the power to plan, build, and operate dam and reservoir projects for navigation, flood control, and power. Even more uniquely, it had to obtain only the approval of the House and Senate Appropriations Committees before undertaking any proposed work. The TVA could also make and sell electric power from thermally-driven generators, build transmission lines, direct soil conservation, recreation development, and fish and wildlife improvements.

* * *

By 1953, the TVA had completed 20 multi-purpose dams on the Tennessee River and its major tributaries. Although this activity greatly reduced the heights of major floods, it still had not eliminated damaging floods on smaller streams in the area. In the mid–1950s, the TVA, therefore, began a program of land-use planning at the local level to try to help local communities mitigate flood damage where they could not completely prevent floods. By 1959, some 21 communities had begun floodplain planning studies while 9 communities had adopted programs of floodplain regulation. The apparent success of the program led the agency to recommend its use across the nation and the 1960 Flood Control Act permitted the Corps of Engineers to begin a similar program.

* * *

Current Federal water laws and programs are quite involved and complex. More than 40 Federal agencies have some water programs or statutory responsibilities and the programs keep changing. * * *

———

A wide repertoire of federal water development possibilities has allowed regional political combinations to capture major federal programs for all parts of the country. The demand for cheap public power led to the establishment of federal authorities, such as the Tennessee Valley Authority and the Bonneville Power Authority, to construct reservoirs for hydroelectric power generation. Flood control structures are, of course, useful in all regions of the country. Promotion of water resources development for a variety of purposes created powerful development constituencies and united political parties and factions around particular development projects. During most of this century water resources development has been equated with progress. The widespread national distribution of federal monies also minimized interregional political checks.

Even those who appreciate the value of the many existing water projects now ask whether it makes sense for the federal government to build more large projects. There is little doubt that such projects as Hoover Dam enriched not only the Southwest but the nation by providing flood protection, a supply of water for growing cities and productive farms, and copious cheap power for homes and industries. But the damming and diversion of western rivers permanently changed the landscape of the West. See, e.g., W. Eugene Hollon, The Great American Desert Then and Now (1966). We are just now beginning to ask whether the effort was worth the price. For a clear "no" answer see Donald Worster, Rivers of Empire: Water, Aridity, and the Growth of the American West (1985). Soaring federal deficits since 1981 have necessitated rethinking all large federal expenditures. But even in the brighter economic times of the sixties and seventies the climate began to change for water development projects.

A concern about the need for more comprehensive planning, rather than simple political logrolling, led to passage of the Water Resources and Planning Act in 1965, 42 U.S.C.A. §§ 1962 to 1962d–18. The Act encouraged state, local and regional water resources planning. However, many projects had already been authorized simply because they were feasible from an engineering standpoint and the proponent states had enough political clout to move them through Congress. The belated concern for water resources planning also prompted Congress to establish the National Water Commission in 1968. The Commission was directed to study future water requirements and alternative means of meeting them,

> giving consideration * * * to conservation and more efficient use of existing supplies, increased usability by reduction of pollution, innovations to encourage the highest economic use of water, inter-basin transfers, and technological advances * * * [and to] consider economic and social consequences of water resource development on regional economic growth, on institutional arrangements, and on esthetic values affecting the quality of life of the American People.

Pub.L. No. 90–515, § 3(a), 82 Stat. 868 (1968).

The resulting report of the National Water Commission has become a cornerstone for national decision-making about water resources. See U.S. National Water Commission, Water Policies For the Future—Final Report to the President and to the Congress of the United States (1973). As the authorizing language suggested, the federal focus was to change from responding to requests for funds to build water projects to considering a variety of broad public concerns about the use of water resources.

A barrage of water-related environmental legislation followed passage of the Water Resources and Planning Act and the National Water Commission Act. A few days after acting to establish the Commission, Congress passed the Wild and Scenic Rivers Act, 16 U.S.C.A. §§ 1271–1287. The next year the National Environmental Policy Act was passed. 42 U.S.C.A. §§ 4321–4370. Far-reaching legislation to impose national controls on water pollution were included in the Federal Water Pollution Control Act Amendments of 1972 (the Clean Water Act). 33 U.S.C.A. §§ 1251–1376. In 1973 the Endangered Species Act became law. 16 U.S.C.A. §§ 1531–1543. Planning and management mandates were imposed on the public lands (including the associated waters) in 1976 by the Federal Land Policy and Management Act, 43 U.S.C.A. §§ 1701–1782 and the National Forest Management Act, 16 U.S.C.A. §§ 1600–1614.

In 1977 a newly-elected President Carter targeted thirty-three water projects for elimination from the federal budget. Henceforth, he announced, all projects would be reviewed in light of environmental factors and benefit-cost ratios. The trend of federal policy away from narrow, structural responses to water issues was supported by strong public sentiment for wise resources protection and use. Still, the tradition of federal water development runs deep, and the Carter "hit list" rocked the West and water development interests throughout the nation. To have the government change the rules of federal financial assistance dashed expectations for construction projects that could assist local economies. Many westerners had resented federal controls on water use and development as being intrusive and unnecessary. As federal assistance receded, westerners viewed the controls as intolerable.

Although the "hit list" was modified after it created a political maelstrom, and a few of the targeted projects were built, the Carter policy eventually became conventional wisdom. Most of the economic and environmental tests for water projects have remained. The Reagan and Bush Administrations also have insisted that states and other non-federal entities bear a portion of the initial costs of constructing water projects funded by the Bureau of Reclamation or the Corps of Engineers. New Corps projects are subject to specific non-federal cost-sharing requirements under 1986 and later legislation. See Water Resources Development Act of 1986, Pub.L. No. 99–662, as amended 1990, Pub.L. No. 101–640.

Few large projects will be financed by the federal programs in the future. The government continues to have a role in operating existing projects. The largest project in the nation, the Central Arizona Project, is now complete. The Central Utah Project is under construction, but appropriations to fund its completion have been made subject to new conditions that enable the fulfillment of broad environmental purposes. In the future it is likely that only a few, mostly small projects will be built. The future mission of federal water development agencies has not been determined, however. The Bureau of Reclamation has announced that it has a new mission that includes improving water use efficiency but its functions have not yet changed greatly. Change is surely afoot. The Reclamation Projects Authorization and Adjustment Act of 1992 changes the purposes and operations of the Central Valley Project to shift water from agriculture to urban uses, to facilitate marketing of water, to promote greater water use efficiency, and to fulfill major environmental goals. The Act may provide a model for reforming much of the present Reclamation system.

The United States has become involved in even more water project developments through its licensing authority under the Federal Power Act than through its direct development activities. Concerned with promoting the most effective and efficient use of the nation's waterways for power generation, Congress passed the Federal Power Act, 16 U.S.C.A. §§ 791a–828c. It requires a license to be obtained from the Federal Energy Regulatory Commission (FERC), formerly Federal Power Commission, before a hydroelectric dam is built on any navigable river. Licensing depends on determinations of the public interest and of compliance with a host of federal regulatory statutes that are applied by the Commission. The original intent of the Act was to ensure rational use of resources in the interest of conservation, in the sense of full and efficient development. Today, it implements policies on conservation that impact broader concerns for environmental protection as part of the "public interest." FERC's judgments often bring it into conflict with the water policy judgments of state legislatures and agencies. Through the authority of the Federal Power Act, FERC allows public and private entities to develop water for production of electric power in ways that do not always conform to state law. Hence, even when the federal government is not itself the developer, federal anointment can allow projects to proceed by invoking federal preemption.

There are several themes that run through this section:

Federal power. Federal involvement in water resources, the scope of federal constitutional authority, and much of the law of federal water resources development is a history of the expansion of federal power.

Regional politics. Federal water resources investment has always raised questions about regional equity in the distribution of national wealth. Federal funding of water resources projects has long been criticized by economists as an inefficient allocation of national resources. E.g., Otto Eckstein, Water Resources Development (1958) and John V. Krutilla & Otto Eckstein, Multiple Purpose River Development (1958). Furthermore, development has rarely followed principles of river basinwide planning, although the wisdom of that approach has been perceived since at least the New Deal era. For a concise history of this idea and its limitations see James L. Wescoat, Jr., Integrated Water Development: Water Use and Conservation Practice in Western Colorado 7–21 (1984). Regional political alliances have historically resisted efforts to apply rational criteria to water resources development proposals, although Congress has attempted to legislate the river basin idea over the years. The longstanding partnership among large water users, the states and the Bureau of Reclamation is the subject of a fast-paced history of the post-World War II Bureau. Marc Reisner, Cadillac Desert: The American West and Its Disappearing Water (1986). Rational allocation takes on more urgency as the era of large-scale federal water resources development draws to an end.

Federalism. Assertions of federal control over water resources are inevitably resisted as intrusions on state sovereignty. The issue that arose early in the history of federal water development was whether state law, and hence policy, is preempted by the assertion of federal regulatory or spending authority. Because the federal government first deferred to the states to set water policy and then began to assert a federal interest in water allocation, federalism issues are especially intense in water law.

Trend toward improved management. There is a growing appreciation of new uses of water and of non-structural management options. Historically, "water conservation" meant storing water for consumptive use, power generation, and flood control; it meant constructing dams and other facilities. A national environmental consciousness has produced a greater recognition of the value of instream uses and more efficient use practices. The repercussions of this apparent fundamental shift in national thinking about natural resources is reflected, for example, in pollution control and species diversity protection programs discussed in the subsection on environmental control. See generally, A. Dan Tarlock, *The Changing Meaning of Water Conservation in the West,* 66 Neb.L.Rev. 145 (1987).

The rejection of large-scale structural responses to water demands is related to the growing appreciation of instream uses and a greater willingness to employ decentralized solutions to produce or free up supplies. For instance, water can be reallocated from existing federal water projects by market transfers of water as an alternative to building more projects to create new supplies. For years economists have urged the application of marginal cost pricing, and this idea— which has taken root in other areas such as public utility rate structure and air pollution emission trading—is having a profound influence on the debate about future water resources policy.

The future federal role in managing its existing projects more efficiently, in keeping with public values, and in encouraging states and others to do so through technical and financial assistance has not yet been defined. Revolutionary changes in the purposes and operations of California's Central Valley Project were enacted by Congress in 1992, however, and may be a bellwether of reform and redefinition for reclamation projects throughout the West.

1. The Reach of Congressional Power

Under the United States Constitution, the federal government's authority is limited to the exercise of powers expressly delegated it, and powers necessary and proper in carrying out those enumerated powers. The federal government has been active in the planning, construction, and operation of flood control, hydroelectric, and irrigation projects since the turn of the century. Federal involvement in water planning and development can find its justification in many of the powers enumerated in the Constitution. Dams and power plants have been justified under the war power as necessary for national defense. The Newlands Act of 1902, creating the Bureau of Reclamation, was premised on the Property Clause, art. IV, sec. 2, granting Congress the power to control the use of federal public lands.

The most extensive power in practice and as construed by Congress, and the one most often relied on in the exercise of federal jurisdiction over water planning and development, is the commerce power. In the exercise of its power to promote and regulate interstate commerce under article I, sec. 8, cl. 3, the federal government is involved in navigation, flood control, watershed development, power production, and environmental protection. It is not surprising that any of these subjects could be regulated or promoted. A wide array of subject matter can be included under the rubric of "interstate commerce" based on the Supreme Court's finding of even the most attenuated theoretical connection with commercial intercourse that concerns more than one state. See generally Laurence H. Tribe, American Constitutional Law §§ 5.4–5.8 (2d ed. 1988). Rather the question has been whether, in the case of a particular law or project, the geographic impact is so limited that it lies outside Congress's commerce power. In the early cases, the Court focused on whether a waterway was navigable as an indicator that it was surely within the realm of interstate commerce.

UNITED STATES v. APPALACHIAN ELEC. POWER CO.

Supreme Court of the United States, 1940.
311 U.S. 377, 61 S.Ct. 291, 85 L.Ed. 243.

MR. JUSTICE REED delivered the opinion of the Court.

This case involves the scope of the federal commerce power in relation to conditions in licenses, required by the Federal Power Commission, for the construction of hydroelectric dams in navigable rivers of the United States. To reach this issue requires, preliminarily, a decision as to the navigability of the New River, a water-course flowing through Virginia and West Virginia. The district court and the circuit court of appeals have both held that the New River is not navigable, and that the United States cannot enjoin the respondent from constructing and putting into operation a hydroelectric dam situated in the river just above Radford, Virginia.

Sections 9 and 10 of the Rivers and Harbors Act of 1899 make it unlawful to construct a dam in any navigable water of the United States without the consent of Congress. By the Federal Water Power Act of 1920, however, Congress created a Federal Power Commission with authority to license the construction of such dams upon specified conditions. Section 23 of that Act provided that persons intending to construct a dam in a nonnavigable stream may file a declaration of intention with the Commission. If after investigation the Commission finds that the interests of interstate or foreign commerce will not be affected, permission shall be granted for the construction. Otherwise construction cannot go forward without a license.

* * *

[The respondent argued before the FPC that no license was necessary because the stream was not navigable and therefore the 1920 Act did not apply. In the alternative, respondent argued that if the stream were navigable, the conditions imposed on licenses by the Act were invalid because they related to regulation of electric power companies, not to navigation. Respondent offered to take a "minor-part" license—one without regulatory condition—but the FPC denied such a license and forbade construction of the dam without a "full-condition" license, which respondent declined to take. Thereafter, respondent commenced its project, precipitating the litigation.]

* * *

Navigability. The power of the United States over its waters which are capable of use as interstate highways arises from the commerce clause of the Constitution. "The Congress shall have Power * * * To regulate Commerce * * * among the several States." It was held early in our history that the power to regulate commerce necessarily included power over navigation. To make its control effective the Congress may keep the "navigable waters of the United States" open and free and provide by sanctions against any interference with the country's water assets. It may legislate to forbid or license dams in the waters; its power over improvements for navigation in rivers is "absolute."

The states possess control of the waters within their borders, "subject to the acknowledged jurisdiction of the United States under the Constitution in regard to commerce and the navigation of the waters of rivers." It is this subordinate local control that, even as to navigable rivers, creates between the respective governments a contrariety of interests relating to the regulation and protection of waters through licenses, the operation of structures and the acquisition of projects at the end of the license term. But there is no doubt that the United States possesses the power to control the erection of structures in navigable waters.

The navigability of the New River is, of course, a factual question but to call it a fact cannot obscure the diverse elements that enter into the application of the legal tests as to navigability. We are dealing here with the sovereign powers of the Union, the Nation's right that its waterways be utilized for the interests of the commerce of the whole country. It is obvious that the uses to which the streams may be put vary from the carriage of ocean liners to the floating out of logs; that the density of traffic varies equally widely from the busy harbors of the seacoast to the sparsely settled regions of the Western mountains. The tests as to navigability must take these variations into consideration.

Both lower courts based their investigation primarily upon the generally accepted definition of The Daniel Ball.[21] In so doing they were in accord with the rulings of this Court on the basic concept of navigability. Each application of this test, however, is apt to uncover variations and refinements which require further elaboration.

In the lower courts and here, the Government urges that the phrase "susceptible of being used, in their ordinary condition," in the *Daniel Ball* definition, should not be construed as eliminating the possibility of determining navigability in the light of the effect of reasonable improvements.   * * *

To appraise the evidence of navigability on the natural condition only of the waterway is erroneous. Its availability for navigation must also be considered. "Natural and ordinary condition" refers to volume of water, the gradients and the regularity of the flow. A waterway, otherwise suitable for navigation, is not barred from that classification merely because artificial aids must make the highway suitable for use before commercial navigation may be undertaken. Congress has recognized this in § 3 of the Water Power Act by defining "navigable waters" as those "which either in their natural or improved condition" are used or suitable for use. The district court is quite right in saying there are obvious limits to such improvements as affecting navigability. These limits are necessarily a matter of degree. There must be a balance between cost and need at a time when the improvement would be useful. When once found to be navigable, a waterway remains so.

---

21. 10 Wall. 557, 563:

" * * * Those rivers must be regarded as public navigable rivers in law which are navigable in fact. And they are navigable in fact when they are used, or are susceptible of being used, in their ordinary condition, as highways for commerce, over which trade and travel are or may be conducted in the customary modes of trade and travel on water. And they constitute navigable waters of the United States within the meaning of the acts of Congress, in contradistinction from the navigable waters of the States, when they form in their ordinary condition by themselves, or by uniting with other waters, a continued highway over which commerce is or may be carried on with other States or foreign countries in the customary modes in which such commerce is conducted by water."

This is no more indefinite than a rule of navigability in fact as adopted below based upon "useful interstate commerce" or "general and common usefulness for purposes of trade and commerce" if these are interpreted as barring improvements. Nor is it necessary that the improvements should be actually completed or even authorized. The power of Congress over commerce is not to be hampered because of the necessity for reasonable improvements to make an interstate waterway available for traffic.

Of course there are difficulties in applying these views. Improvements that may be entirely reasonable in a thickly populated, highly developed, industrial region may have been entirely too costly for the same region in the days of the pioneers. The changes in engineering practices or the coming of new industries with varying classes of freight may affect the type of the improvement. Although navigability to fix ownership of the river bed [29] or riparian [30] rights is determined as the cases just cited in the notes show, as of the formation of the Union in the original states or the admission to statehood of those formed later, navigability, for the purpose of the regulation of commerce, may later arise. An analogy is found in admiralty jurisdiction, which may be extended over places formerly nonnavigable. There has never been doubt that the navigability referred to in the cases was navigability despite the obstruction of falls, rapids, sand bars, carries or shifting currents. The plenary federal power over commerce must be able to develop with the needs of that commerce which is the reason for its existence. It cannot properly be said that the federal power over navigation is enlarged by the improvements to the waterways. It is merely that improvements make applicable to certain waterways the existing power over commerce.[35] In determining the navigable character of the New River it is proper to consider the feasibility of interstate use after reasonable improvements which might be made.

Nor is it necessary for navigability that the use should be continuous. The character of the region, its products and the difficulties or dangers of the navigation influence the regularity and extent of the use. Small traffic compared to the available commerce of the region is sufficient * * *. With these legal tests in mind we proceed to examine the facts to see whether the 111–mile reach of this river from Allisonia to Hinton, across the Virginia–West Virginia state line, has "capability of use by the public for the purposes of transportation and commerce."

Physical Characteristics. * * *

We come then to a consideration of the crucial stretch from Radford to below Wiley's Falls where junction is made with the interstate reach from Wiley's Falls to Hinton. * * *

29. Shively v. Bowlby, 152 U.S. 1, 18 and 26; United States v. Utah, 283 U.S. 64, 75.

30. Oklahoma v. Texas, 258 U.S. 574; United States v. Oregon, 295 U.S. 1, 14.

35. Illustrative of this natural growth is United States v. Cress, 243 U.S. 316, involving riparian proprietors' rights where improvements raise the river level so that uplands are newly and permanently subjected to the servitude of public use for navigation. Compensation was decreed for the taking with a declaration that the waterways in question, as artificially improved, remained navigable waters of the United States (243 U.S. pages 325 and 326). Cf. Arizona v. California, 283 U.S. 423.

Use of the River from Radford to Wiley's Falls. Navigation on the Radford–Wiley's Falls stretch was not large. Undoubtedly the difficulties restricted it and with the coming of the Norfolk & Western and the Chesapeake & Ohio railroads in the 80s, such use as there had been practically ceased, except for small public ferries going from one bank to the other. Well authenticated instances of boating along this stretch, however, exist. * * *

In 1861 the Virginia General Assembly appropriated $30,000 to improve the New River to accommodate transportation of military stores by bateaux from Central depot [Radford] to the mouth of the Greenbrier. While there is no direct proof that this particular appropriation was spent, reports of the War Department engineers make it clear that the Confederate government effected some improvements on the river. * * *

From the end of the Civil War to the coming of the railroads, the evidence of elderly residents familiar with events along the banks of the river between Radford and Wiley's Falls leaves no doubt that at least sporadic transportation took place in and throughout this stretch. * * *

In addition to the testimony of use in the days before railways and good roads, there was a demonstration of the possibility of navigation by a government survey boat with an outboard motor, 16 feet long, five feet wide, drawing $2\frac{1}{2}$ to 3 feet, loaded with a crew of five and its survey equipment. * * * Going upstream it was not necessary to pull or push the boat more than a mile and a quarter and not more than a few hundred feet on the return trip.

Use of a stream long abandoned by water commerce is difficult to prove by abundant evidence. Fourteen authenticated instances of use in a century and a half by explorers and trappers, coupled with general historical references to the river as a water route for the early fur traders and their supplies in pirogues and Durham or flat-bottomed craft similar to the keelboats of the New, sufficed upon that phase in the case of the DesPlaines. Nor is lack of commercial traffic a bar to a conclusion of navigability where personal or private use by boats demonstrates the availability of the streams for the simpler types of commercial navigation.

The evidence of actual use of the Radford–Wiley's Falls section for commerce and for private convenience, when taken in connection with its physical condition, makes it quite plain that by reasonable improvement the reach would be navigable for the type of boats employed on the less obstructed sections. * * *

Effect of Improvability. Respondent denied the practicability of artificial means to bring about the navigability of the New River and the effectiveness of any improvement to make the river a navigable water of the United States. The Government supported its allegation of improvability by pointing out that the use of the section for through navigation and local boating on favorable stretches of the Radford–Wiley's Falls reach showed the feasibility of such use and that little was needed in the way of improvements to make the section a thoroughfare for the typical, light commercial traffic of the area. Keelboats, eight feet wide, drawing two feet, were the usual equipment. In the 1872 report of the Chief of Engineers, Major Craighill in charge of New River reports that to get "good sluice navigation of 2 feet at all times" for 54 miles up from the mouth of the Greenbrier River, near Hinton, would cost $30,000 and for 128 miles, Greenbrier to the lead mines (above Allisonia), would cost $100,000. * * *

* * * By 1912 the region's need for use of the river had so diminished that the army engineers advised against undertaking improvements again, and even referred to the cost as "prohibitive". From the use of the Radford–Wiley's Falls stretch and the evidence as to its ready improvability at a low cost for easier keelboat use, we conclude that this section of the New River is navigable. It follows from this, together with the undisputed commercial use of the two stretches above Radford and Hinton, that the New River from Allisonia, Virginia, to Hinton, West Virginia, is a navigable water of the United States.

License Provisions. The determination that the New River is navigable eliminates from this case issues which may arise only where the river involved is nonnavigable. But even accepting the navigability of the New River, the respondent urges that certain provisions of the license, which seek to control affairs of the licensee, are unconnected with navigation and are beyond the power of the Commission, indeed beyond the constitutional power of Congress to authorize. * * * There is no contention that the provisions of the license are not authorized by the statute. In the note below [65] the chief statutory conditions for a license are epitomized. The license offered the respondent on May 5, 1931, embodied these statutory requirements and we assume it to be in conformity with the existing administration of the Power Act. We

65. Section 4(a) of the Act allows the Commission to regulate the licensee's accounts.

Section 6 limits licenses to 50 years.

Section 8 requires Commission approval for voluntary transfers of licenses or rights granted thereunder.

Section 10(a), as amended in 1935, requires that the project be best adapted to a comprehensive plan for improving or developing the waterway for the use or benefit of interstate or foreign commerce, for the improvement and utilization of water-power development, and for other beneficial public uses, including recreational purposes. Under § 10(c) the licensee must maintain the project adequately for navigation and for efficient power operation, must maintain depreciation reserves adequate for renewals and replacements, and must conform to the Commission's regulations for the protection of life, health and property; (d) out of surplus earned after the first 20 years above a specified reasonable rate of return, the licensee must maintain amortization reserves to be applied in reduction of net investment; (e)

the licensee must pay the United States reasonable annual charges for administering the Act, and during the first 20 years the United States is to expropriate excessive profits until the state prevents such profits; (f) the licensee may be ordered to reimburse those by whose construction work it is benefited.

By § 11, for projects in navigable waters of the United States the Commission may require the licensee to construct locks, etc., and to furnish the United States free of cost (a) lands and rights-of-way to improve navigation facilities, and (b) power for operating such facilities.

Section 14 gives the United States the right, upon expiration of a license, to take over and operate the project by paying the licensee's "net investment" as defined, not to exceed fair value of the property taken. However, the right of the United States or any state or municipality to condemn the project at any time is expressly reserved.

Section 19 allows state regulation of service and rates; if none exists, the Commission may exercise such jurisdiction.

shall pass upon the validity of only those provisions of the license called to our attention by the respondent as being unrelated to the purposes of navigation. These are the conditions derived from §§ 10a, 10c, 10d, 10e and 14. * * *

The respondent's objections to the statutory and license provisions, as applied to navigable streams, are based on the contentions (1) that the United States' control of the waters is limited to control for purposes of navigation, (2) that certain license provisions take its property without due process, and (3) that the claimed right to acquire this project and to regulate its financing, records and affairs, is an invasion of the rights of the states, contrary to the Tenth Amendment.

Forty-one states join as *amici* in support of the respondent's arguments. * * *

The respondent is a riparian owner with a valid state license to use the natural resources of the state for its enterprise. Consequently it has as complete a right to the use of the riparian lands, the water, and the river bed as can be obtained under state law. The state and respondent, alike, however, hold the waters and the lands under them subject to the power of Congress to control the waters for the purpose of commerce. The power flows from the grant to regulate, i.e., to "prescribe the rule by which commerce is to be governed." This includes the protection of navigable waters in capacity as well as use. This power of Congress to regulate commerce is so unfettered that its judgment as to whether a structure is or is not a hindrance is conclusive. Its determination is legislative in character. The Federal Government has domination over the water power inherent in the flowing stream. It is liable to no one for its use or non-use. The flow of a navigable stream is in no sense private property; "that the running water in a great navigable stream is capable of private ownership is inconceivable." Exclusion of riparian owners from its benefits without compensation is entirely within the Government's discretion.

Possessing this plenary power to exclude structures from navigable waters and dominion over flowage and its product, energy, the United States may make the erection or maintenance of a structure in a navigable water dependent upon a license. This power is exercised through § 9 of the Rivers and Harbors Act of 1899 prohibiting construction without Congressional consent and through § 4(e) of the present Power Act.

It is quite true that the criticized provisions summarized above are not essential to or even concerned with navigation as such. Respondent asserts that the right of the United States to the use of the waters is limited to navigation. * * *

In our view, it cannot properly be said that the constitutional power of the United States over its waters is limited to control for navigation. By navigation respondent means no more than operation of boats and improvement of the waterway itself. In truth the authority of the United States is the regulation of commerce on its waters. Navigability in the sense just stated, is but a part of this whole. Flood protection, watershed development, recovery of the cost of improvements through utilization of power are likewise parts of commerce control. As respondent soundly argues, the United States cannot by calling a project of its own "a multiple purpose dam" give to itself additional powers, but equally truly the respondent cannot, by seeking to use a navigable waterway for power generation alone, avoid the authority of the Government over the stream. That authority is as broad as the needs of commerce. Water power development from dams in navigable streams is from the public's standpoint a by-product of the general use of the rivers for commerce. To this general power, the respondent must submit its single purpose of electrical production. The fact that the Commission is willing to give a license for a power dam only is of no significance in appraising the type of conditions allowable. It may well be that this portion of the river is not needed for navigation at this time. Or that the dam proposed may function satisfactorily with others, contemplated or intended. It may fit in as a part of the river development. The point is that navigable waters are subject to national planning and control in the broad regulation of commerce granted the Federal Government. The license conditions to which objection is made have an obvious relationship to the exercise of the commerce power. Even if there were no such relationship the plenary power of Congress over navigable waters would empower it to deny the privilege of constructing an obstruction in those waters. It may likewise grant the privilege on terms. It is no objection to the terms and to the exertion of the power that "its exercise is attended by the same incidents which attend the exercise of the police power of the states." The Congressional authority under the commerce clause is complete unless limited by the Fifth Amendment. * * *

Reversed.

NOTES

1. Many years after the decision in the principal case, the Court, per Justice Rehnquist, wrote in Kaiser Aetna v. United States, 444 U.S. 164 (1979):

Reference to the navigability of a waterway adds little if anything to the breadth of Congress' regulatory power over interstate commerce. It has long been settled that Congress has extensive authority over this Nation's waters under the Commerce Clause. Early in our history this Court held that the power to regulate commerce necessarily includes power over navigation. *Gibbons v. Ogden,* 9 Wheat. 1, 189 (1824). * * * The pervasive nature of Congress' regulatory authority over national waters was more fully described in *United States v. Appalachian Power Co.:* [quoting from the last paragraph of the opinion as edited].

Appalachian Power Co. indicates that congressional authority over the waters of this Nation does not depend on a stream's "navigability." And, as demonstrated by this Court's decisions in NLRB v. Jones & Laughlin Steel Corp., 301 U.S. 1 (1937), United States v. Darby, 312 U.S. 100 (1941), and Wickard v. Filburn, 317 U.S. 111 (1942), a wide spectrum of economic activities "affect" interstate commerce and thus are susceptible of congressional regulation under the Commerce Clause irrespective of whether navigation, or, indeed, water, is involved. The cases that discuss Congress' paramount authority to regulate waters used in interstate commerce are consequently best understood when viewed in terms of more traditional Commerce Clause analysis than by reference to whether the stream in fact is capable of supporting navigation or may be characterized as "navigable water of the United States."

If congressional power did not depend on navigability at the time of *Appalachian Power,* why did the Court spend so much time discussing whether the New River was navigable?

2. Nearly ten years before *Appalachian Power,* Justice Brandeis had used the navigation power to sustain Congressional authorization of Hoover Dam, a multipurpose project designed principally to provide municipal and irrigation water and electric energy. Recitals in the Colorado River Compact had declared the river no longer to be navigable and Arizona, opposing the dam, said that the facilities and the diversion of water would destroy navigable capacity even if it were navigable. He seemed reluctant to venture into any other manifestations of Congress's commerce power, choosing instead to defer to Congress's declaration of "navigation purposes" in the first Arizona v. California, 283 U.S. 423 (1931). Apparently less certain of Congress's commerce power beyond navigation, he wrote:

> The bill further alleges that the "recital in said act that the purpose thereof is the improvement of navigation" "is a mere subterfuge and false pretense." It quotes a passage in Art. IV of the [Colorado River] compact, to which the Act is subject, which declares that "inasmuch as the Colorado River has ceased to be navigable for commerce and the reservation of its waters for navigation would seriously limit the development of its basin, the use of its waters for purposes of navigation shall be subservient to the uses of such waters for domestic, agricultural, and power purposes;" and alleges that "even if said river were navigable, the diversion, sale and delivery of water therefrom as authorized in said act, would not improve, but would destroy its navigable capacity."

> Into the motives which induced members of Congress to enact the Boulder Canyon Project Act, this Court may not enquire. The Act declares that the authority to construct the dam and reservoir is conferred, among other things, for the purpose of "improving navigation and regulating the flow of the river." As the river is navigable and the means which the Act provides are not unrelated to the control of navigation, * * * the erection and maintenance of such dam and reservoir are clearly within the powers conferred upon Congress. Whether the particular structures proposed are reasonably necessary, is not for this Court to determine. And the fact that purposes other than navigation will also be served could not invalidate the exercise of the authority conferred, even if those

other purposes would not alone have justified an exercise of Congressional power.

It is urged that the Court is not bound by the recital of purposes in the Act; that we should determine the purpose from its probable effect; and that the effect of the project will be to take out of the river, now non-navigable through lack of water, the last half of its remaining average flow. * * * This Court may not assume that Congress had no purpose to aid navigation, and that its real intention was that the stored water shall be so used as to defeat the declared primary purpose.

3.   Where the United States conceded the non-navigability of a stream, could it legislate a water development program?

In Kansas v. Colorado, 206 U.S. 46 (1907), page 833, infra, Kansas brought suit in the original jurisdiction of the Supreme Court to enjoin Colorado from making diversions from the Arkansas River. The United States petitioned to intervene, asserting its interest in reclamation under the 1902 Act and urging the Court to adopt the rule of prior appropriation to secure water for use in its projects. The Court addressed the issue as follows:

The primary question is, of course, of national control. * * * [I]f in the present case the National Government was asserting, as against either Kansas or Colorado, that the appropriation for the purposes of irrigation of the waters of the Arkansas was affecting the navigability of the stream, it would become our duty to determine the truth of the charge. But the Government makes no such contention. On the contrary, it distinctly asserts that the Arkansas River is not now and never was practically navigable beyond Fort Gibson in the Indian Territory, and nowhere claims that any appropriation of the waters by Kansas or Colorado affects its navigability.

It rests its petition of intervention upon its alleged duty of legislating for the reclamation of arid lands; alleges that in or near the Arkansas River, as it runs through Kansas and Colorado, are large tracts of those lands; that the National Government is itself the owner of many thousands of acres; that it has the right to make such legislative provision as in its judgment is needful for the reclamation of all these lands and for that purpose to appropriate the accessible waters.

* * * That involves the question whether the reclamation of arid lands is one of the powers granted to the General Government. * * *

Turning to the enumeration of the powers granted to Congress by the eighth section of the first article of the Constitution, it is enough to say that no one of them by any implication refers to the reclamation of arid lands. * * *

We must look beyond section 8 for Congressional authority over arid lands, and it is said to be found in the second paragraph of section 3 of Article IV, reading: "The Congress shall have power to dispose of and make all needful rules and regulations respecting the territory or other property belonging to the United States; and nothing in this Constitution shall be so construed as to prejudice any claims of the United States, or of any particular State."

This very matter of the reclamation of arid lands illustrates this: At the time of the adoption of the Constitution, within the known and conceded limits of the United States there were no large tracts of arid land, and nothing which called for any further action than that which might be taken by the legislature of the state in which any particular tract of land was to be found; and the Constitution, therefore, makes no provision for a national control of the arid regions or their reclamation. But, as our national territory has been enlarged, we have within our borders extensive tracts of arid lands which ought to be reclaimed, and it may well be that no power is adequate for their reclamation other than that of the national government. But, if no such power has been granted, none can be exercised.

It does not follow from this that the national government is entirely powerless in respect to this matter. These arid lands are largely within the territories, and over them, by virtue of the second paragraph of § 3 of article 4, heretofore quoted, or by virtue of the power vested in the national government to acquire territory by treaties, Congress has full power of legislation, subject to no restrictions other than those expressly named in the Constitution, and therefore, it may legislate in respect to all arid lands within their limits. As to those lands within the limits of the states, at least of the Western states, the national government is the most considerable owner and has power to dispose of and make all needful rules and regulations respecting its property. We do not mean that its legislation can override state laws in respect to the general subject of reclamation. * * *

206 U.S. at 85–92.

In a later case, the U.S. Supreme Court rejected the navigation power as enabling a federal reclamation project. Absent the presence of public lands, it cited the spending power as the basis of Congress's action. United States v. Gerlach Live Stock Co., 339 U.S. 725 (1950), page 705, infra. The Supreme Court has held that congressional authorization of a hydroelectric dam in the National Defense Act of 1916 was a proper exercise of constitutional authority under the defense power. Ashwander v. Tennessee Valley Auth., 297 U.S. 288 (1936). Because uses of waterways implicate national and international commerce, the United States has far-reaching interests in how waterways are used.

NOTE: THE RECLAMATION ACT AND RECLAMATION POLICY

John Wesley Powell, after an historic voyage down the Colorado River, recommended in his 1879 Report on the Lands of the Arid Region of the United States that there be a coordinated, communal effort to develop irrigation throughout the West as a means of settling the region. He also criticized the homestead laws because the maximum authorized entries were too small for the successful settlement of the arid West. The Preemption Act and Homestead Law allowed a farmer to acquire title to only 320 acres. The Desert Land Act of 1877 had expanded the maximum amount to 640 acres if the land was irrigated but, as Wallace Stegner observed, "the Desert Land Act of 1877, linked as it was to the rectangular surveys, and making no allowance for the problems of bringing water to claims, served only to delude the hopeful and to encourage fraud by large land owners, principally cattlemen." Editor's Introduction, John Wesley Powell, Report on the Lands of the Arid Region of the United States, With a More Detailed Account of the Lands of Utah (Belknap Press of Harvard University Press 1962). Powell spent the rest of his life after his 1879 report fighting for land and water laws adapted to aridity.

Powell's irrigation survey work laid the groundwork for the Newlands Act of 1902, creating the Bureau of Reclamation, in the year of his death. A series of national irrigation congresses had been held beginning in 1891, which helped promote government participation in the development of irrigation. A concerted political effort growing out of these congresses led to the 1902 Act.

It was the federal government's second attempt to promote an irrigation program. The first was the 1894 Carey Act. Under that Act, the western states received millions of acres of federal lands that were to be sold for the benefit of reclamation programs conducted by the states. The states, however, did not in most instances establish any viable irrigation programs. This convinced many that only a national program could suffice.

Under the leadership of then Congressman Newlands of Nevada, a national water development program was pushed and ultimately succeeded in Congress. The Act created a reclamation fund from the sale of public lands to finance federal irrigation projects. Farmers were required to repay project costs in ten interest-free installments. The funds repaid in this way were then available for other projects. Sixteen western states were to be the beneficiaries. Texas was added in 1906. Although it was a national program, as opposed to the state programs envisioned under the Carey Act, congressional intent to defer to state prior appropriation laws was clear. Thus, federal funding was not to mean an invasion of the state's control over the allocation and distribution of water. As President Theodore Roosevelt stated: "Irrigation works should be built by the National Government * * * the distribution of the water, the diversion of the streams among irrigators, should be left to the settlers themselves, in conformity with State laws and without interference with those laws or with vested rights." Attempts to reflect this intention in the Act resulted in language, chiefly in § 8, that has been a frequent subject of litigation as most of the cases in this subsection demonstrate.

The Reclamation Act was designed to promote settlement of the public lands by independent farmers. Thus, the Act included provisions that were designed to deter speculation. Reclamation water was not to be used on more than 160 acres in a single ownership and water users were required to be bona fide residents on or near the land. These provisions were intended to prevent project benefits from being diverted by large, wealthy interests and absentee landlords. Thus, section 5 of the Act (43 U.S.C.A. § 381) prohibited the sale of reclamation water for more than 160 acres in single ownership (320 acres for a husband and wife).

Congress was determined to curb speculation and to prevent monopolization of public land. This effort to avoid the mistakes of the homestead laws failed, however. Generally speaking, the acreage limitations did not work. Speculators tried a variety of devices to subvert the limitations. In some cases lands were put in the names of individuals in a speculator's family or company to evade the 160–acre limitation. Leasing allowed a single operator to control a large area. In other cases, excess lands were held out of production, then later sold to settlers who were eligible to hold them as nonexcess lands, with substantial profits being reaped by the speculators because land that they had bought unirrigated would be eligible for irrigation in the buyer's hands.

In 1926 Congress passed the Omnibus Adjustment Act and attempted to clamp down on speculation. 43 U.S.C.A. § 423e. Section 46 of the Act provided that owners must enter into a "recordable contract" with the Secretary of Interior agreeing to sell the excess land. The terms of the contracts, which are specified by the Secretary, usually give the Secretary a power of attorney to sell the lands if the owner fails to do so within ten years. Several individual projects were specifically exempted from the acreage requirements (e.g., San Luis Valley Project, Colorado–Big Thompson Project). After an epic litigation, the Supreme Court found implied exemptions under the Boulder Canyon Project Act. See Bryant v. Yellen, 447 U.S. 352 (1980).

The excess land law was controversial in many parts of the West, but nowhere more so than in the Central and Imperial Valleys of California where large land holdings had been assembled prior to the construction of the projects. The fight over the enforcement of the "excess land" law in California is a rich history involving almost every major political figure in the state from the 1930s on. It is either a history of the triumph of "special interests" or a case study in the futility of economically irrational limitations on resource use. The first view was vigorously advocated by an economist from the University of California, Berkeley, Paul Taylor. Professor Taylor's studies and polemics against state and federal attitudes toward the excess land law are essential reading for anyone who wishes to understand the history of the issue. The writings are collected in Paul Taylor, Essays on Land, Water and the Law in California (1979).

The residency requirement, also in § 5, was rarely enforced. The Department of the Interior took the position for about fifty years that this requirement was superseded by the recordable contract provisions of the 1926 Act.

The Reclamation Reform Act of 1982, Pub.L. No. 97–293, 96 Stat. 1261, repealed the residency requirement and raised the acreage limitation in § 4 from 160 (320 for husband and wife) to 960 acres. Because acreage limitations had regularly been avoided by leasing lands and other technical legal devices, an overall, combined ownership and acreage leasing limit of 2,080 acres was imposed. The Act provided that when lands are leased in excess of the overall ownership and leasing limitations, recipients of irrigation water must pay the "full cost" of irrigation water, a factor that includes many costs such as full amortization of construction costs and unpaid operation and maintenance obligations for which other irrigation users are not liable. Districts were required to amend their contracts with the Bureau of Reclamation to conform with the law in order to enjoy the larger acreage limitations. Individuals in districts that did not do so would be subject to the old law and, under a "hammer clause" in the Reclamation Reform Act, they were required to pay the full cost rate for water delivered to more than 160 acres beginning April, 1987. The Secretary's implementing regulations, however, allow a number of management arrangements (other than leasing, which is directly prohibited by the Act) for treating large acreages as separately held, enabling some operations to skirt the acreage limitation. 43 C.F.R. part 426.

Reclamation has been a costly and controversial experiment for the federal government. "The federal projects were elaborate ones, projects that private enterprise would not undertake. The earlier, simpler works that cost not more than $15 or $20 per acre of land [served] had already been built by private enterprise. The federal projects cost from $43 to $163 an acre, averaging $85 an acre. Land so costly did not produce return enough to repay the investment." Frederick Merk, History of the Westward Movement 511 (1978). In the Great Depression of the 1930s, reclamation projects became part of the Roosevelt Administration's effort to restore the economy through government investment in public works projects. The Boulder Canyon Project Act to benefit the Imperial Valley marked the federal government's entry into large-scale reclamation projects. In the 1930s the government started the Columbia Basin Project—the largest federally-financed irrigation enterprise ever—that led to other projects in Washington, Idaho, Oregon, Montana, and in Canada, and bailed out California's state-sponsored Central Valley Project.

The role of the Reclamation program in California's Central Valley is especially interesting. In 1922, California voters rejected an initiative to create a state water development agency, after private power companies campaigned vigorously against passage. Local water agencies and utilities were able to preempt most of the lower dam sites on the Central Valley rivers. See Joe S. Bain, *Water Resource Development in California,* in Thomas H. Campbell & Robert O. Sylvester, Water Resources Management and Public Policy 14–18 (1968). But the state continued to study the potential for large-scale, higher dams to allow agriculture to expand in the Valley. The legislature finally authorized the sale of $170 million in revenue bonds in 1933 to finance the Central Valley plan, and voters narrowly approved the Act in a referendum. California could not sell the bonds during the depression, so between 1935–1937 the federal government stepped in and converted the state project to a federal one. The Reclamation Act's small-farmer provision led to major fights in the Central Valley. The enforcement (or non-enforcement) of the acreage limitation against large private and corporate landowners provoked a decade-long "Battle Royal" in California. The perspective of the Valley landowners is colorfully stated in Senator Sheridan Downey's book, They Would Rob the Valley (1947), where "they" refers to the Bureau of Reclamation.

The latest chapter in the history of the Central Valley was written when President George Bush signed Pub.L. No. 102–575, the Reclamation Projects Authorization and Adjustment Act of 1992. Title XXXIV of this legislation constitutes the Central Valley Project Improvement Act of 1992, which mandated the first major reallocation of Central Valley Project (CVP) water since the federal government assumed control of the project from the state. The Central Valley is stressed by two major demands. Along with the Imperial Valley southeast of Los Angeles, CVP water is the most likely source of new water for urban Southern California. In addition, the shift of political power to urban areas, which have strongly supported environmental protection along with the legal mandates of federal and state water quality laws and the Endangered Species Act, requires that the environmental costs of irrigation now be addressed. The CVP Improvement Act responded to these pressures by authorizing for the first time large-scale transfers of reclamation project water out of the CVP. The Act also addressed the problem of restoring depleted river flows for fisheries maintenance and water quality enhancement by allocating to the Secretary of the Interior 800,000 acre-feet of CVP water to be used for these purposes. To some, the Act was but another salvo in the ongoing California water wars. Agricultural interests feared increasing federal encroachment on the state's water supply and accused the Congress of gambling with the future of California's farms. Environmentalists were cautiously optimistic, but argued that the bill did not go far enough to protect an environment that had been systematically abused for decades.

The federal investment in completed project facilities since the inception of the Reclamation program totalled $9.9 billion as of 1990. The Bureau provided irrigation water for 9.3 million acres—some 19% of the nation's total irrigated acreage. Reclamation projects generated hydroelectricity worth $648 million in 1990.

Reclamation projects have been lyrically defended as the realization of the Jeffersonian dream in the West, but others have questioned the wisdom of reliance on these "soft" benefits. A debate over the efficiency of large-scale reclamation projects arose in the late 1930s when economists began to probe the relationship between irrigation subsidies and federal crop surplus policy. A renewed debate today fuels efforts to reform the Reclamation program.

In 1987, the Bureau of Reclamation issued a short report concluding that its mission should change. The *Assessment '87* report stated that

The Bureau's primary role as the developer of large federally financed agricultural projects is drawing to a close * * *. The Bureau of Reclamation must change from an agency based on federally supported construction to one based on resource management.

To that end, the Department of the Interior in 1988 issued a set of principles to guide the Bureau in review and approval of voluntary water transfers involving Bureau facilities. See pages 648–51, supra.

In some senses, the change in direction for the Bureau predated the 1987 report. President Carter had issued an executive order calling for consideration of conservation in all proposals for new supplies. The Reagan Administration introduced policies requiring states to share an unspecified portion of the initial costs of any project to be funded by the federal government. The recognition that states could no longer rely on the federal government to finance water projects led to calls for state financing programs and policies well before the Bureau released its 1987 report. See Rodney T. Smith, Troubled Waters: Financing Water in the West (1984).

RICHARD W. WAHL, MARKETS FOR FEDERAL WATER: SUBSIDIES, PROPERTY RIGHTS, AND THE BUREAU OF RECLAMATION

27–46 (1989).

Bureau of Reclamation publications frequently claim that the costs of the reimbursable functions of reclamation projects will be repaid to the United States:

It has long been the philosophy of the Nation that all reclamation project costs for the purpose of irrigation, power, and municipal and industrial water supply should be repaid in full. (U.S. Department of the Interior, Bureau of Reclamation, 1972, p. ix)

In reality, the situation is far different. * * *

Irrigation subsidies in Reclamation law take two forms: interest-free repayment and the basing of irrigators' repayment on the bureau's estimate of their "ability to pay." Revenues from federal hydropower are used to "repay" costs beyond the irrigators' "ability to pay." However, repayment by hydropower embodies a substantial subsidy as well, both because it is interest-free and because it occurs after forty or fifty years of irrigation repayment. If federal borrowing costs 4 percent annually, then repayment forty years later interest-free returns to the United States only 20.8 percent of the true cost of the loan. At a borrowing cost of 7 percent, only 6.7 percent is returned * * *.

The Gradual Enlargement of Irrigation Subsidies

* * *

The Reclamation Act of 1902 did not specifically exclude interest from the charges to be recovered for irrigation, but this has become standard bureau practice. The act stated that "charges shall be determined with a view of returning to the reclamation fund the estimated cost of construction of the project." The bureau's administrative interpretation not to charge interest was based on the fact that the act did not specifically mention interest charges and on the implicit approval of Congress, which did not object to bureau practice over the years. * * * [I]nterest-free repayment over ten years at the federal long-term borrowing rates of 1902 would have provided a subsidy of 14 percent of project construction costs. However, settlers had difficulty meeting repayment even under these terms. As a result, in 1914 Congress passed the Reclamation Extension Act (38 Stat. 686), which stretched the repayment period to twenty years. * * *

[T]his provision increased the interest subsidy to 42 percent of construction costs. The 1914 act also provided for a graduated repayment schedule. For new projects, a settler was to pay 5 percent of the construction charges for each of the first five years and 7 percent annually starting in the sixth year until all costs were repaid. Relief was also provided for settlers on existing projects. Repayment was extended to twenty years from the date of the act on a graduated scale based on the remaining construction charges: 2 percent for the first four years, 4 percent for the next two years, and 6 percent for the next fourteen years. However, the act levied a 1 percent penalty on all payments more than three months late and provided that no water should be delivered to lands for which payments were more than one year in arrears. * * *

Still, repayment continued to be a problem. In 1921, "in view of the financial stringency and the low price of agricultural products," the Secretary of the Interior was authorized to continue water deliveries to settlers for that year even if the settlers were more than one year behind in repayment (42 Stat. 4). Similar legislative deferrals were granted in 1922 (42 Stat. 489) and 1923 (42 Stat. 1324): upon a showing of hardship, both capital and operation and maintenance charges could be deferred for the two-year period. * * * Then, in 1926 the secretary was given the authority to defer repayment of operation and maintenance charges for another five years and to defer the repayment of construction charges on whatever schedule he found necessary (44 Stat. 479). In either case, the amount deferred carried an interest charge of 6 percent. * * * [A]ll told this legislation would have allowed qualifying settlers to defer operation and maintenance charges from 1922 through 1931 and to defer capital charges for at least as long, provided interest charges were added to the amount deferred.

* * *

The Omnibus Adjustment Act of 1926 (44 Stat. 636) allowed the Secretary of the Interior to double the interest-free repayment period for irrigation construction costs to forty years, which * * * increased the subsidy to more than 50 percent of costs given the 4 percent rate of government borrowing prevailing at the time. * * *

Since 1939, inflation has raised the level of the interest subsidy for newly constructed projects (or new construction in established projects). * * *

In summary, various pieces of general reclamation legislation have lengthened the interest-free repayment period for irrigation, thereby increasing the value of the interest subsidy. The effect of the interest subsidy in the Reclamation Act of 1902 was to forgive about 14 percent of construction costs, but by 1939 this level had reached 50 percent. In addition, the gradual rise in nominal interest rates has greatly increased the value of the subsidy since 1960, reaching levels as high as 95 percent. The various deferrals granted by additional reclamation legislation also resulted in extensions of the repayment period, thereby further increasing the effective subsidy. * * *

Estimates of the Interest and "Ability-to-Pay" Subsidies

In addition to the interest subsidy * * * the Reclamation Project Act of 1939 provided an additional subsidy: irrigation costs above the irrigators' estimated "ability to pay" could be shifted to other project beneficiaries, such as consumers of the project's hydroelectric power. * * * Various estimates have been made of the combined effect of the interest and "ability-to-pay" factors on the subsidy to irrigation. * * * [One] study, based on the repayment of capital costs only, was conducted for a sample of reclamation projects by the Department of the Interior in its draft environmental impact statement on acreage limitation (U.S. Department of the Interior, Bureau of Reclamation, 1981). This study focused on eighteen representative irrigation projects. * * * [T]he absolute value of the construction cost subsidy ranges from a low of $58 per acre on the Moon Lake Project in Utah to a high of $1,787 per acre on the Wellton–Mohawk Irrigation District in Arizona (both in 1978 dollars). In percentage terms, from 56.9 percent to 96.7 percent of the full irrigation construction costs are subsidized. On twelve of the eighteen projects, the subsidy exceeds 80 percent of construction costs. * * *

This brief history of the evolution of the reclamation subsidy is revealing. What began as a proposal for modest federal assistance in settling the arid West, providing a revolving fund to which costs would be repaid within ten years, evolved into a program that provided major subsidies to irrigation water users—sometimes more than 90 percent of construction costs. Several factors led to enlargement of the subsidy. (1) Congress did an inadequate job in specifying a program that would be viable. (2) The Bureau of Reclamation developed projects in locations where soil conditions were not conducive to long-term irrigation. (3) The hardships that settlers had to endure, whether from inexperience, drought, or poor project design, undoubtedly aroused the sympathies of members of Congress as well as Bureau of Reclamation personnel administering the program. (4) Once federal dollars had been committed to specific irrigation projects, the federal government was vulnerable to arguments that additional financial concessions were necessary to make continued farming viable on project lands. (5) Inflation considerably enhanced the value of interest-free repayment.

(6) Once the precedent of the interest subsidy had been established, there was little inclination on the part of Congress to modify it.

* * *

Conclusions: Effects of the Irrigation Subsidy

* * * The provision of federal subsidies increases the amount of land that will yield sufficient private returns in comparison with private costs. The provision of subsidies merely changes the quantity of arid land on which farming can be economical, but farming on the most marginal lands may be just as difficult.

Therefore, the principal effects of the irrigation subsidy have been locational. In general, it can be said that federal water subsidies have resulted in more irrigation development in the western states at the expense of bringing additional land into production in the Midwest and South. For example, cotton grown on reclamation projects in California with subsidized water competes with privately developed cotton grown in the South. Of course, this locational effect was one of the principal goals of establishing the original Reclamation Act—that is, to encourage the settlement of the arid West through the provision of water to lands that could be homesteaded.

From the standpoint of national economic development, these extensive water subsidies have led to inefficient use of land and water resources as well as capital, labor, and materials. Since the 1950s, reclamation projects have been subject to benefit-cost analyses. In principle, if projects were designed and constructed so that incremental benefits were greater than costs, then there would be no distortions of resource use. As has been shown, however, many projects have been located where benefits fail to exceed costs * * *. Consequently, dams have been placed where the rivers, in the absence of the irrigation subsidy, would have been left in their natural state. Furthermore, low-cost water has provided little incentive for careful use of the resource. This means that water has been diverted to uses other than those that would produce the greatest economic benefits and has, for the most part, continued to be used for the original purposes.

Significant amounts of hydropower on reclamation projects are dedicated to the pumping of irrigation project water supply. Hydropower is provided at a very low charge because of the interest-free subsidy for irrigation pumping. This means that reliable and relatively inexpensive hydropower has been diverted from other productive uses to provide for irrigation. In some cases, the Bureau of Reclamation has found it necessary to participate in the construction of thermal power plants to provide necessary power for project pumping. In general, in the absence of the irrigation subsidy, many of the natural and human resources dedicated to these water diversions and power plants would have been devoted to other, more productive uses.

PETERSON v. UNITED STATES DEPT. OF INTERIOR

United States Court of Appeals, Ninth Circuit, 1990.
899 F.2d 799.

Before NORRIS, NOONAN and LEAVY, CIRCUIT JUDGES.

WILLIAM A. NORRIS, CIRCUIT JUDGE:

In these consolidated cases, we are asked by various public water agencies in California's Central and Solano Valleys (the "Water Districts") to declare unconstitutional a provision of the Reclamation Reform Act of 1982 which interferes, they argue, with their contractual right to receive subsidized water from federal reclamation projects for distribution to agricultural users in their districts. This appeal raises important questions of Congress's ability to reshape federal water policy and to decide who shall receive federally subsidized water from the government's reclamation projects in the western states.

I

Each of the Water Districts entered into a long-term contract in the past 30 years with the Department of the Interior, Bureau of Reclamation ("the Bureau") to receive water from two vast systems of federally-owned and operated reservoirs, dams and canals: the Central Valley Reclamation Project and the Solano Project. Under these contracts the federal government agreed to provide water to the Water Districts at a fixed rate for the contract period. Although each District was charged a different rate for the water it received, all of the contract rates represent a significant government subsidy. In exchange, the Water Districts agreed to distribute the water to eligible lands within their jurisdictions. The only express eligibility requirement contained in the contracts was that no water could be provided to any farm in excess of 160 acres whether owned by a natural person or a corporation. Because the contracts did not expressly prohibit the Water Districts from providing water to farms of more than 160 acres if the land was leased rather than owned, the Water Districts have for many years delivered subsidized water to farms consisting of thousands of acres of leased land, as well as to small farms complying with the acreage limitation.

The Reclamation Reform Act of 1982, 43 U.S.C. §§ 373(a); 390aa–390zz–1; 422e; 425b; 485h; 502 (1982 & West Supp.1989) ("the RRA") amended federal reclamation law in three important ways: (1) it increased the acreage limitation from 160 to 960 acres;[3] (2) it closed the "leasing loophole" by making the acreage limitation expressly applicable to holdings that were leased as well as owned; see 43 U.S.C. §§ 390dd, 390ee, and (3) it raised the price of reclamation water to a level that reduced, but did not eliminate, the federal subsidy. See 43 U.S.C. § 390hh.

The provision of the RRA in dispute in this litigation is section 203(b), also known as the "hammer clause." The hammer clause puts water districts to an election. They are permitted to amend their contracts to conform to the requirements of the RRA, which means a 960–acre limitation applicable to all lands, whether owned or leased,

---

3. The RRA made one exception to the new 960–acre limitation: Large business entities, defined as those benefiting more than twenty-five persons, could not receive reclamation water at subsidized rates for any land owned or leased in excess of 320 acres. 43 U.S.C. § 390ee(a)(2) & (3).

and an increased, but still subsidized, price. If Water Districts choose not to so amend their contracts, they are permitted to deliver water to leased lands in excess of 160 acres provided they pay the government's "full cost" of delivering the water. 43 U.S.C. § 390cc(b).

In these cases, the Water Districts claim that application of section 203(b) to their existing water contracts violates the due process clause and the taking clause of the fifth amendment. The district court granted the government's motion for summary judgment on both claims, and the Water Districts now appeal. We affirm the district court's decision that neither the due process nor the taking clause prevents Congress from limiting the volume of subsidized water that the Water Districts can deliver to leased lands under their pre-existing contracts with the Bureau of Reclamation.

II

The starting place for understanding the 1982 amendments to the federal water reclamation law is nearly one hundred years ago when the federal government initially became involved in developing irrigation systems for the western states. The opening of the West to farming through the harnessing of its waters provides not only fascinating history but also necessary background to the constitutional questions raised by these cases.

The final westward migration of the late 1800s resulted in an enormous demand by the settlers for irrigation systems. The western states, however, lacked the means to finance the enormous systems of dams, reservoirs, and canals needed to regulate and distribute water from the western rivers and snow melt. See California v. United States, 438 U.S. 645, 663, 98 S.Ct. 2985, 2995, 57 L.Ed.2d 1018 (1978). Responding to the pressing demand for federal assistance in funding water reclamation projects, Congress passed the Reclamation Act of 1902, ch. 1093, 32 Stat. 388 (codified as amended at 43 U.S.C. §§ 371– 600e (1982)).

With the Reclamation Act of 1902, Congress committed itself to the task of constructing and operating dams, reservoirs, and canals for the reclamation of the arid lands in 17 western states. California, 438 U.S. at 650, 98 S.Ct. at 2988. The projects were to be built on federal land and the actual construction and operation were to be in the hands of the Secretary of the Interior. Id. at 664, 98 S.Ct. at 2995. * * *

III

The first step in both due process and taking analyses is to determine whether there is a property right that is protected by the Constitution. See, e.g., Bowen v. Public Agencies Opposed to Social Security Entrapment ("Public Agencies"), 477 U.S. 41, 54–55, 106 S.Ct. 2390, 2397–98, 91 L.Ed.2d 35 (1986); F.H.A. v. The Darlington, Inc., 358 U.S. 84, 91 (1958). In *Public Agencies,* a taking case, the Court held that the contractual right at issue "did not rise to the level of 'property'" and "[could] not be viewed as conferring any sort of 'vested right.'" 477 U.S. at 55, 106 S.Ct. at 2398. Without a property right, there could be no "taking within the meaning of the Fifth Amendment." Id. at 55–56, 106 S.Ct. at 2398.

The Water Districts maintain that as a result of the water contracts they have a constitutionally protected property interest in the delivery of subsidized water to leased tracts of any size. They claim that the hammer clause, section 203(b), violates this right by restricting the size of the leased tracts that can receive subsidized water.

* * *

* * * The Water Districts' argument in support of this right proceeds along two tracks. First, the Water Districts contend that because Congress did not include in the Act an express provision reserving to Congress the right to amend the reclamation law's eligibility requirements, Congress's right to amend the water service contracts is limited. Second, the Water Districts argue that absent an express reservation of the right to amend the contracts in the controlling legislation itself, we look only to the language of the contracts themselves. The Water Districts claim that their contracts must be interpreted (1) as giving them an implied right to deliver subsidized water to leased tracts of any size, and (2) as including an express waiver by Congress of its right to amend the contracts without the Water Districts' consent.

We consider first the Water Districts' argument that Congress was required to reserve expressly the right to amend the reclamation law in the body of the statute itself. Although it is true that there is no express provision in the statutory scheme retaining Congress's ability to amend, alter or repeal the provisions of the Reclamation Act, this silence cannot be construed as a waiver of any of Congress's powers. The sovereign's power to enact subsequent legislation affecting its own contractual arrangements endures, albeit with some limitations, unless "surrendered in unmistakable terms." *Public Agencies,* 477 U.S. at 52, 106 S.Ct. at 2397.

* * *

We now address the Water Districts' argument that the contract language itself gives the Water Districts a vested right to deliver subsidized water to leased tracts of any size and contains an express waiver of Congress's power to amend the reclamation law in any way that interferes with that right. The specific contractual provisions that form the basis of the Water Districts' claim vary slightly in each contract. The following portions of the Lower Tule River Irrigation District water service contract, however, are exemplary of those provisions:

* * *

Article 18(a). No water made available pursuant to this contract shall be furnished to any excess lands as defined in Article 20 hereof unless the owners thereof shall have executed valid recordable contracts in form prescribed by the United States * * *.

Article 20(a). As used herein the term 'excess land' means that part of the irrigable land within the District in excess of one hundred and sixty (160) acres held in the beneficial ownership of any private individual, whether a natural person or a corporation.

Article 21. In the event that the Congress of the United States repeals the so-called excess-land provisions of the Federal reclamation laws, Articles 18, 19, and 20 of this contract will no longer be of any force or effect, and, in the event that the Congress amends the excess-land provisions or other provisions of the Federal reclamation laws the United States agrees, at the option of the District, to negotiate amendments of appropriate articles of this contract, all consistently with the provision of such repeal or amendment.

The Water Districts claim that because Article 18(a) contains only one express restriction on the type of land that can receive project water, and that restriction applies only to land in excess of 160 acres held "in common ownership," their contracts with the Bureau give them an implied right to deliver water to farms of any size, as long as the farms are leased instead of owned. Thus, while acknowledging that they are expressly forbidden from delivering project water to forty acres of a 200 acre family-owned farm, the Water Districts contend that Articles 18(a) and 20(a), when read together, give them an implied right to deliver subsidized water to lands leased by large corporations that consist of hundreds of thousands of acres. As further support for their claim to an implied right to the water, the Water Districts point to Article 21's statement that "the United States agrees, at the option of the District, to negotiate amendments of appropriate articles of this contract," which the Water Districts construe as an express relinquishment by the United States of its ability to interfere with this implied right.

We read the contracts differently. The Water Districts concede, as they must, that the contracts do not expressly authorize the delivery of water to leased tracts. Instead, the Water Districts proceed on the theory that it is *implicit* in the terms of their contract that they can provide reclamation water without limit to leased tracts and that Congress will not interfere with this implied right. On this basis, they claim to have a vested contractual right to continue to deliver subsidized water to leaseholds of any size, a right allegedly impaired by section 203(b). We take a different view. As the Supreme Court has stated when reviewing a similar claim to a vested right based on an implied contractual provision, the Water Districts' claim "lies in the periphery where vested rights do not attach." *Darlington,* 358 U.S. at 90, 79 S.Ct. at 146.

The Supreme Court considered and rejected a similar due process claim to an implied contractual right against the government in *Darlington,* and its analysis controls. *Darlington* involved another federal subsidy, a mortgage insurance program embodied in the 1942 National Housing Act, 56 Stat. 303, 12 U.S.C. § 1743, as amended by § 10 of the Veterans' Emergency Housing Act of 1946, 60 Stat. 207, 214, and the regulations issued thereunder. Congress enacted the program with the aim of making housing more accessible to veterans and their families. A corporation, which had entered into a federal contract to obtain mortgage insurance, rented apartments to transients, a use not *expressly* prohibited by the contract, controlling statute, or regulations promulgated thereunder. * * *

To determine whether a right to rent to transients could fairly be *implied* in the contracts, the Court turned to the legislation that had authorized the contracts. Review of the controlling statute, the National Housing Act, convinced the Court that the "legislation [was] passed to aid veterans and their families, not * * * to promote the hotel or motel business." Id. at 87, 79 S.Ct. at 144 (footnote omitted). * * * The Court rejected the argument advanced by the dissent that Darlington's contract gave it a vested right to make rentals to any persons and in any manner that was not expressly prohibited by the statute or contract. Id. at 95, 79 S.Ct. at 147 (Harlan, J., dissenting). Instead, the Court concluded that "[t]hose who do business in the regulated field cannot object if the legislative scheme is buttressed by subsequent amendments to achieve the legislative end." Id. at 91, 79 S.Ct. at 146. By passing legislation barring rentals to transients, Congress was simply making explicit the policy underlying the legislation, thus "doing no more than protecting the regulatory system which it had designed." Id.

* * *

As in *Darlington*, the implied right asserted here clearly violates the spirit, if not the letter, of the reclamation laws which authorized such contracts. The reclamation projects were funded by the federal government with the express intent that the subsidized water be used to promote the development of family-owned farms.

* * *

In sum, the fact that the reclamation laws had as their *end* the dismantling of large landholdings in the West and the redistribution of that land to families, effectively undercuts the Water Districts' argument that they were given an implied right to deliver the water to farms regardless of size, as long as the land was not actually *owned* by the operator of the farm. To find a vested contract right with these facts, we believe, would seriously impair Congress's sovereign power to pass laws for the public welfare. Were we to accept the Water Districts' argument, parties that enter into contracts with the government pursuant to such legislation could claim vested rights to engage in all conduct not expressly forbidden in the contracts. We do not believe that Congress must exhaustively proscribe conduct in a regulated field to prevent parties from claiming an "implied vested right" to engage in conduct found by later Congresses to be harmful to the public welfare.

* * *

There is still an additional reason for not finding an implied vested right in the Water Districts' contracts. The contracts contain no language that can be construed as a "surrender[ ] in unmistakable terms" of the sovereign's ability to regulate the quantity of subsidized water that may be provided to leased farm lands. *Public Agencies,* 477 U.S. at 52, 106 S.Ct. at 2397. Article 21, which the Water Districts claim is a clear waiver of the federal government's sovereign power, cannot be so interpreted, especially if we follow the Supreme Court's dictate that governmental contracts "should be construed, if possible, to avoid foreclosing exercise of sovereign authority." Id. at 52–53, 106 S.Ct. at 2397.

Article 21 has two primary clauses. The first states that if Congress were to repeal the excess land provisions of the federal reclamation law, then the contracts would be modified automatically to eliminate related provisions in the contract. The second clause of Article 21 provides that if Congress *amends* the excess land provisions or any other aspect of the reclamation law, the contracts will be modified "consistently with the provisions of such * * * amendment," and "at the option of the District."

The Water Districts argue that these two clauses of Article 21 make the contracts inviolable, absent a negotiated amendment between the parties. They claim that the two clauses "expressly deprive the United States of the power to make subsequent amendments of the law applicable to the contracts." We read Article 21 differently.

* * *

As we read Article 21, the Water Districts have a choice between renegotiating their contracts to bring them into conformity with the new law or withdrawing from the reclamation program. In other words, the Water Districts have the option of continuing to receive reclamation water but only under the terms of the new law. Thus, they can continue to receive and deliver water to holdings up to 160 acres, whether owned or leased, at the low price specified in their preexisting contracts, but they cannot continue to deliver water at the old price to holdings in excess of 160 acres.

* * *

In sum, because the Water Districts have no vested property right to buy reclamation water for delivery to leased lands, the restrictions imposed by section 203(b) do "not effect a taking within the meaning of the Fifth Amendment." *Public Agencies,* 477 U.S. at 56, 106 S.Ct. at 2398. For the same reason, the Water Districts' due process claim also must fail. See *Darlington,* 358 U.S. at 91, 79 S.Ct. at 146 ("The Constitution is concerned with practical, substantial rights, not with those that are unclear and gain hold by subtle and involved reasoning."). In the absence of a vested property right, the Water Districts can prevail on their due process claim only if they establish that section 203(b) is arbitrary and irrational. This they have failed to do.

We agree with the district court that section 203(b) of the Reclamation Reform Act is rationally related to a legitimate governmental purpose. The provisions of the Act, and its legislative history, clearly demonstrate that Congress's primary concerns were not with the federal budget, but rather, with the promotion of small farming operations, equitable distribution of water under modern farming conditions, and water conservation.

To these ends, Congress increased the size of farms that could receive reclamation water to 960 acres (whether leased or owned) and raised the price of reclamation water to reflect more accurately its true cost to the government. Section 203(b) authorized the Water Districts to amend their contracts to take advantage of the 960–acre limitation, albeit at a potentially higher, but still subsidized, rate than that provided in their contracts. The Water Districts were not required to amend their contracts because any water district that wanted to maintain the 160–acre limitation and lower contract price was left free to do so. Section 203(b), the so-called hammer clause, simply provided that those who elected to continue under the original contracts could no longer continue to deliver subsidized water to leased tracts of any size. Section 203(b) requires the Water Districts to choose between continuing under previous federal water policy, but without the "leasing loophole" tolerated by the Department of the Interior, or conforming with the new 960–acre limitation of the RRA. In our opinion, section 203(b) is a reasonable way for Congress to further its federal reclamation policy of promoting small farming operations, equitable distribution of water, and water conservation.

The summary judgment in favor of the government and the Natural Resources Defense Council is

Affirmed.

2. Navigation Servitude

UNITED STATES v. RANDS
Supreme Court of the United States, 1967.
389 U.S. 121, 88 S.Ct. 265, 19 L.Ed.2d 329.

MR. JUSTICE WHITE delivered the opinion of the Court.

In this case the Court is asked to decide whether the compensation which the United States is constitutionally required to pay when it condemns riparian land includes the land's value as a port site. Respondents owned land along the Columbia River in the State of Oregon. They leased the land to the State with an option to purchase, it apparently being contemplated that the State would use the land as an industrial park, part of which would function as a port. The option was never exercised, for the land was taken by the United States in connection with the John Day Lock and Dam Project, authorized by Congress as part of a comprehensive plan for the development of the Columbia River. Pursuant to statute the United States then conveyed the land to the State of Oregon at a price considerably less than the option price at which respondents had hoped to sell. In the condemnation action, the trial judge determined that the compensable value of the land taken was limited to its value for sand, gravel, and agricultural purposes and that its special value as a port site could not be considered. The ultimate award was about one-fifth the claimed value of the land if used as a port. The Court of Appeals for the Ninth Circuit reversed, apparently holding that the Government had taken from respondents a compensable right of access to navigable waters and concluding that "port site value should be compensable under the Fifth Amendment." 367 F.2d 186, 191 (1966). We granted certiorari, 386 U.S. 989, because of a seeming conflict between the decision below and United States v. Twin City Power Co., 350 U.S. 222 (1956). We reverse the judgment of the Court of Appeals because the principles underlying *Twin City* govern this case and the Court of Appeals erred in failing to follow them.

The Commerce Clause confers a unique position upon the Government in connection with navigable waters. "The power to regulate commerce comprehends the control for that purpose, and to the extent necessary, of all the navigable waters of the United States * * *. For this purpose they are the public property of the nation, and subject to all the requisite legislation by Congress." Gilman v. Philadelphia, 3 Wall. 713, 724–725 (1866). This power to regulate navigation confers upon the United States a "dominant servitude," FPC v. Niagara Mohawk Power Corp., 347 U.S. 239, 249 (1954), which extends to the entire stream and the stream bed below ordinary high-water mark. The proper exercise of this power is not an invasion of any private property rights in the stream or the lands underlying it, for the damage sustained does not result from taking property from riparian owners within the meaning of the Fifth Amendment but from the lawful exercise of a power to which the interests of riparian owners have always been subject. Thus, without being constitutionally obligated to pay compensation, the United States may change the course of a navigable stream, or otherwise impair or destroy a riparian owner's access to navigable waters, even though the market value of the riparian owner's land is substantially diminished.

The navigational servitude of the United States does not extend beyond the high-water mark. Consequently, when fast lands are taken by the Government, just compensation must be paid. But "just as the navigational privilege permits the Government to reduce the value of riparian lands by denying the riparian owner access to the stream without compensation for his loss, * * * it also permits the Government to disregard the value arising from this same fact of riparian location in compensating the owner when fast lands are appropriated." United States v. Virginia Elec. & Power Co., 365 U.S. 624, 629 (1961). Specifically, the Court has held that the Government is not required to give compensation for "water power" when it takes the riparian lands of a private power company using the stream to generate power. United States v. Chandler–Dunbar Water Power Co., 229 U.S. 53, 73–74 (1913). Nor must it compensate the company for the value of its uplands as a power plant site. Id., at 76. Such value does not "inhere in these parcels as upland," but depends on use of the water to which the company has no right as against the United States: "The Government had dominion over the water power of the rapids and falls and cannot be required to pay any hypothetical additional value to a riparian owner who had no right to appropriate the current to his own commercial use." Ibid.

All this was made unmistakably clear in United States v. Twin City Power Co., 350 U.S. 222 (1956). The United States condemned a promising site for a hydroelectric power plant and was held to be under no obligation to pay for any special value which the fast lands had for power generating purposes. The value of the land attributable to its location on the stream was "due to the flow of the stream; and if the United States were required to pay the judgments below, it would be compensating the landowner for the increment of value added to the fast lands if the flow of the stream were taken into account." 350 U.S., at 226.

We are asked to distinguish between the value of land as a power site and its value as a port site. In the power cases, the stream is used as a source of power to generate electricity. In this case, for the property to have value as a port, vessels must be able to arrive and depart by water, meanwhile using the waterside facilities of the port. In both cases, special value arises from access to, and use of navigable waters. With regard to the constitutional duty to compensate a riparian owner, no distinction can be drawn. It is irrelevant that the licensing authority presently being exercised over hydroelectric projects may be different from, or even more stringent than, the licensing of port sites. We are dealing with the constitutional power of Congress completely to regulate navigable streams to the total exclusion of private power companies or port owners. As was true in *Twin City,* if the owner of the fast lands can demand port site value as part of his compensation, "he gets the value of a right that the Government in the exercise of its dominant servitude can grant or withhold as it chooses. * * * To require the United States to pay for this * * * value would be to create private claims in the public domain." 350 U.S., at 228.

Respondents and the Court of Appeals alike have found *Twin City* inconsistent with the holding in United States v. River Rouge Improvement Co., 269 U.S. 411 (1926). In that case, the Government took waterfront property to widen and improve the navigable channel of the Rouge River. By reason of the improvements, other portions of the riparian owner's property became more valuable because they were afforded direct access to the stream for the building of docks and other purposes related to navigation. Pursuant to § 6 of the Rivers and Harbors Act of 1918, the compensation award for the part of the property taken by the Government was reduced by the value of the special and direct benefits to the remainder of the land. The argument here seems to be that if the enhancement in value flowing from a riparian location is real enough to reduce the award for another part of the same owner's property, consistency demands that these same values be recognized in the award when any riparian property is taken by the Government. There is no inconsistency. *Twin City* and its predecessors do not deny that access to navigable waters may enhance the market value of riparian property. And, in *River Rouge,* it was recognized that state law may give the riparian owner valuable rights of access to navigable waters good against other riparian owners or against the State itself.   But under *Twin City* and like cases, these rights and values are not assertable against the superior rights of the United States, are not property within the meaning of the Fifth Amendment, and need not be paid for when appropriated by the United States.   Thus, when only part of the property is taken and the market value of the remainder is enhanced by reason of the improvement to navigable waters, reducing the award by the amount of the increase in value simply applies in another context the principle that special values arising from access to a navigable stream are allocable to the public, and not to private interest.   Otherwise the private owner would receive a windfall to which he is not entitled.

Our attention is also directed to Monongahela Navigation Co. v. United States, 148 U.S. 312 (1893), where it was held that the Government had to pay the going-concern value of a toll lock and dam built at the implied invitation of the Government, and to the portion of the opinion in *Chandler–Dunbar* approving an award requiring the Government to pay for the value of fast lands as a site for a canal and lock to bypass the falls and rapids of the river.   *Monongahela* is not in point, however, for the Court has since read it as resting "primarily upon the doctrine of estoppel.   * * *"   Omnia Commercial Co., Inc. v. United States, 261 U.S. 502, 513–514 (1923).   The portion of *Chandler–Dunbar* relied on by respondents was duly noted and dealt with in *Twin City* itself, 350 U.S. 222, 226 (1956).   That aspect of the decision has been confined to its special facts, and, in any event, if it is at all inconsistent with *Twin City,* it is only the latter which survives.

Finally, respondents urge that the Government's position subverts the policy of the Submerged Lands Act, which confirmed and vested in the States title to the lands beneath navigable waters within their boundaries and to natural resources within such lands and waters, together with the right and power to manage, develop, and use such lands and natural resources.   However, reliance on that Act is misplaced, for it expressly recognized that the United States retained "all its navigational servitude and rights in and powers of regulation and control of said lands and navigable waters for the constitutional purposes of commerce, navigation, national defense, and international affairs, all of which shall be paramount to, but shall not be deemed to include, proprietary rights of ownership * * *."   Nothing in the Act was to be construed "as the release or relinquishment of any rights of the United States arising under the constitutional authority of Congress to regulate or improve navigation, or to provide for flood control, or the production of power."   The Act left congressional power over commerce and the dominant navigational servitude of the United States precisely where it found them.

For the foregoing reasons, the judgment of the Court of Appeals is reversed and the case remanded with direction to reinstate the judgment of the District Court.

Reversed and remanded.

MR. JUSTICE MARSHALL took no part in the consideration or decision of this case.

NOTES

1.   Suppose the United States had condemned Rands' land for a highway.   Would the measure of compensation be the same?

2.   Prior to *Rands*, the two most important cases on the "navigation servitude" were *Chandler–Dunbar* and *Twin City*, both relied on in *Rands*.

In *Chandler–Dunbar*, the owner of the dam site had erected a dam with the revocable permission of the Secretary of War and was producing and selling water power.   Congress chose to destroy the water power value in order to promote navigation.   In denying recovery of the water power values of the condemned dam site, the Court seemed to state that since Congress could forbid the placing of a dam in a navigable stream, no property interest in water power could be obtained and hence no compensation was due.

However, the Court did uphold the landowner's claim for compensation for "lock and canal" values of fast land.   While the facts are not clear, it appears that the land was uniquely suited for development for water transportation as traffic increased on the lake.   How can this award be reconciled with the denial of water power values?

Twin City concerned the claim of a dam site owner who planned to develop a hydroelectric power project on a navigable river.   Congress authorized a public power project that pre-empted claimant's site.   In short, the United States took claimant's hydroelectric power site for its own hydroelectric project.   Ruling first that Congress authorized the project at least in part for incidental navigation benefits and that if "the interests of navigation are served, it is constitutionally irrelevant that other purposes may also be advanced," the Court held in a 5–4 decision that *Chandler–Dunbar* controlled the decision: "To require the United States to pay for this water power value would be to create private claims in the public domain."

The dissenting judges relied heavily on the "lock and canal" award in *Chandler–Dunbar*, but the majority dismissed it in a footnote, stating that perhaps the *Chandler–Dunbar* Court had sustained the award because the "lock and canal" values were consistent with the navigation improvement planned by the United States.   In any event, the "lock and canal" values of *Chandler–Dunbar* seem to afford little ground for argument in the light of the 8–0 decision (and the comment on *Chandler–Dunbar*) in *Rands*.

For a full discussion see Eva H. Morreale, *Federal Power in Western Waters: The Navigation Power and the Rule of No Compensation*, 3 Nat. Resources J. 1 (1963).

3.   When a benefit-cost evaluation of a federal project is undertaken, what value should be assigned to a privately owned dam site to be acquired for the project: fair market value or cost to the United States under the servitude?

4.   A certain amount of confusion exists about the effect of the navigation servitude on non-navigable streams.   In United States v.

Kansas City Life Ins. Co., 339 U.S. 799 (1950), the Court (5 to 4) granted compensation to a landowner whose farm was ruined by saturation of the subsoil when the United States raised the level of the Mississippi River to the mean high-water mark and thereby backed water up the non-navigable tributary on which the farm lay. Then in United States v. Grand River Dam Auth., 363 U.S. 229 (1960), the Court held that the United States owed no compensation for water power values in a dam site condemned on a non-navigable tributary as part of the Arkansas River flood control and navigation project.

Suppose the United States condemns a vacation home on a non-navigable river for a post office. If vacation homes fronting on the river bring higher prices than homes away from the stream must the United States pay the higher value?

5. Section 10(c) of the Federal Power Act, 16 U.S.C.A. § 803(c) provides in part:

> Each licensee hereunder shall be liable for all damages occasioned to the property of others by the construction, maintenance, or operation of the project works or of the works appurtenant or accessory thereto, constructed under the license, and in no event shall the United States be liable therefor.

Seattle, holding a Federal Power Act license, and proceeding under federal eminent domain power conferred by the Act, claimed that as a federal licensee it enjoyed the same navigation servitude that the federal government would have had if it were constructing the project, and thus that it was not liable for power site values of land it condemned. In Public Util. Dist. No. 1 v. Seattle, 382 F.2d 666 (9th Cir.1967), cert. dismissed 396 U.S. 803 (1969), the Court of Appeals rejected the contention, resting its judgment on two not clearly distinguishable grounds: (1) that the servitude is a privilege held exclusively by the government and is not delegable; (2) in the alternative, if the power is delegable, the United States has not done so, for § 10(c) expressly requires payment for state-created water values taken by licensees. There was one dissent. After certiorari was applied for in the Supreme Court, that Court invited the Solicitor General to file an *amicus* brief (391 U.S. 962) but thereafter the petition was dismissed (396 U.S. 803 (1969)) under Rule 60 (voluntary settlement by the parties), leaving the legal question unresolved.

6. The River and Harbors Act of 1970, § 111, 33 U.S.C.A. § 595(a), altered the compensation requirements of *Rands*. It states that:

> * * * compensation to be paid for real property taken by the United States above the normal high water mark of navigable waters of the United States shall be the fair market value of such real property based upon all uses to which such real property may reasonably be put, including its highest and best use, any of which uses may be dependent upon access to or utilization of such navigable waters.

How much of the no-compensation rule of *Rands* survives under the law? How would *Twin City* and *Chandler–Dunbar* be decided today?

Does the new law offer any protection to those losing their permits for wharfs or artificial landfills, whose uses and facilities are below the normal high water mark? Consider the following illustration of how the now-modified rule of *Rands* works: A landowner owns a twenty-acre tract consisting of two adjacent ten-acre parcels, one on the shore of a navigable stream, one immediately upland of it. The upland parcel is worth $2,000 an acre. The waterfront parcel is worth $4,500 an acre, the difference being attributable to its waterfront location. The United States condemns the waterfront parcel which is to be inundated as part of a federal lock and dam project. The upland parcel will become attractive waterfront property (worth $4,500 an acre). The landowner will receive nothing under the *Rands* rule, but is entitled to $20,000 compensation under the rule as modified by the 1970 amendment (because the amendment left intact the rule that the increased value of new waterfront land must be subtracted from the award).

7. Kuapa Pond is a shallow 523–acre lagoon on Oahu, Hawaii, separated from a Pacific Ocean bay by a barrier beach. The pond had historically been used as a fishpond, and under Hawaiian land law was the private property of the landowner, the Bishop Estate. Bishop leased 6,000 acres, including the pond, to Kaiser Aetna in 1961 for a marina subdivision. Kaiser Aetna dredged the pond and opened an eight-foot-deep channel to the bay. In 1972 a dispute arose between Kaiser and the U.S. Army Corps of Engineers. The Corps argued that further filling in the marina required a § 10 permit and that as a result of the improvements the pond was now subject to a public navigation easement, despite the fact that in 1961 the Corps had informed Kaiser that no permit was needed for dredging the pond and subsequently acquiesced to the dredging of the channel. In a 6–3 decision, the Supreme Court held that Kuapa Pond was now navigable and subject to the Corps' regulatory jurisdiction, but further held that the imposition of a navigation easement on behalf of members of the public would constitute a taking and could not be characterized as an exercise of the navigation servitude. Kaiser Aetna v. United States, 444 U.S. 164 (1979).

Writing for the majority, Justice Rehnquist distinguished the servitude cases:

> There is no denying that the strict logic of the more recent cases limiting the Government's liability to pay damages for riparian access, if carried to its ultimate conclusion, might completely swallow up any private claim for "just compensation" under the Fifth Amendment even in a situation as different from the riparian condemnation cases as this one. But, as Mr. Justice Holmes observed in a very different context, the life of the law has not been logic, it has been experience. The navigational servitude, which exists by virtue of the Commerce Clause in navigable streams, gives rise to an authority in the Government to assure that such streams retain their capacity to serve as continuous highways for the purpose of navigation in interstate commerce. Thus, when the Government acquires fast lands to improve navigation, it is not required under the Eminent Domain Clause to compensate land-

owners for certain elements of damage attributable to riparian location, such as the land's value as a hydroelectric site, *Twin City Power Co.,* supra, or a port site, United States v. Rands, supra. But none of these cases ever doubted that when the Government wished to acquire fast lands, it was required by the Eminent Domain Clause of the Fifth Amendment to condemn and pay fair value for that interest. * * *

Here, the Government's attempt to create a public right of access to the improved pond goes so far beyond ordinary regulation or improvement for navigation as to amount to a taking under the logic of Pennsylvania Coal Co. v. Mahon, 260 U.S. 393 (1922). More than one factor contributes to this result. It is clear that prior to its improvement, Kuapa Pond was incapable of being used as a continuous highway for the purpose of navigation in interstate commerce. Its maximum depth at high tide was a mere two feet, it was separated from the adjacent bay and ocean by a natural barrier beach, and its principal commercial value was limited to fishing. It consequently is not the sort of "great navigable stream" that this Court has previously recognized as being "[incapable] of private ownership." See, e.g., United States v. Chandler–Dunbar Co., 229 U.S., at 69; United States v. Twin City Power Co., 350 U.S., supra, at 228. And, as previously noted, Kuapa Pond has always been considered to be private property under Hawaiian law. Thus, the interest of petitioners in the now dredged marina is strikingly similar to that of owners of fast land adjacent to navigable water.

Id. at 177–79.

Justice Blackmun dissented and argued that the navigation servitude was coextensive with navigable waters of the United States and that, on balance, Kaiser Aetna was not entitled to compensation for the imposition of the servitude: the government had a substantial interest in maintaining free highways of navigability and "[w]hatever expectation petitioners may have had in control over the pond for use as a fishery was surrendered in exchange for the advantage of access when they cut a channel into the bay." Id. at 190–91. In a companion case, the Court applied the *Kaiser Aetna* reasoning to deny applicability of the navigation servitude to a system of man-made canals in Louisiana that connect the Gulf of Mexico with an inland waterway. Vaughn v. Vermilion Corp., 444 U.S. 206 (1979).

Kaiser Aetna is apparently limited to shallow navigable waters. The Court has since held that the navigation servitude precludes the recovery of damages by an Indian tribe for damages to sand and gravel deposits caused by a navigation improvement project. United States v. Cherokee Nation of Oklahoma, 480 U.S. 700 (1987). The court of appeals had applied a balancing test to award compensation, but the Court held that no balancing was required "where, as here, the interference with in-stream interests results from the exercise of the Government's power to regulate navigational uses 'of the deep streams which penetrate our country in every direction.'" 480 U.S. at 703. The

Court also rejected the argument that tribal ownership of title to the bed was an exception to the rule that *"all "* riparian owners are subject to the servitude.

8.   Is there a state navigation servitude? Colberg, Inc. v. State ex rel. Dept. of Public Works, 432 P.2d 3 (Cal.1967), cert. denied 390 U.S. 949 (1968), holds that the state does not have to compensate shipyard owners whose access to a deep water ship channel was substantially impaired by the construction of two freeway bridges across the channel. The California Supreme Court said that the state servitude was subject to the same limitation as the federal. The servitude does not apply to the actual physical invasion or encroachment upon fast lands. *Colberg* recognized that the states are split on the issue of whether private rights impaired as the result of projects in aid of navigation are compensable. Commonwealth, Dept. of Highways v. Thomas, 427 S.W.2d 213 (Ky.1967), is an example of a case allowing compensation on very similar facts to *Colberg*.

Alaska has rejected *Colberg* and followed *Commonwealth Dept. of Highways v. Thomas* because "a declaration that littoral access could be taken for any public purpose without compensation will immediately devalue property * * * and limit the development of many isolated communities where only means of access is by water." Wernberg v. State, 516 P.2d 1191, 1201 (Alaska 1973), rehearing denied 519 P.2d 801 (Alaska 1974). However, improvements that only render access more expensive and difficult are not compensable. Classen v. State, Dept. of Highways, 621 P.2d 15 (Alaska 1980). See also St. Lawrence Shores v. State, 302 N.Y.S.2d 606 (1969) (no compensation); Marine Air Ways, Inc. v. State, 116 N.Y.S.2d 778 (1952) (no compensation).

PROBLEMS

1.   Power company acquired a flowage easement allowing lands to be inundated by reservoir pool created by development of the company's hydroelectric power plant. Thereafter, the United States acquired the land, subject to the flowage easement for use in a navigation project. The power company disclaimed any water power values for the easement but claimed that the servient land had value for agricultural, timber and grazing uses and therefore the dominant easement had value unconnected with riparian uses. The Court sustained the power company's contention by a 6–3 vote. What is the argument for the United States? See United States v. Virginia Elec. & Power Co., 365 U.S. 624 (1961).

2.   The United States condemned claimants' land as part of a wilderness area in which all mechanical devices and permanent structures were to be prohibited. Claimant seeks compensation for three thirty-five-ton motorized houseboats, built by him on his land and used by paying guests for fishing trips on the adjacent lake. The boats cannot be removed from the landlocked lake without being completely dismantled. Claimants' land with the boats treated as fixtures is worth $149,000; without the boats as part of the realty, the land is valued at $64,000. The government argues that under *Rands*, it has the right to exclude all persons from navigable waters and that the consequent loss

of use of the boats on the navigable lake is not compensable and therefore the land cannot be valued as if the boats were affixed to it. What result? See United States v. 967,905 Acres of Land, 305 F.Supp. 83 (D.Minn.1969), reversed 447 F.2d 764 (8th Cir.1971), cert. denied 405 U.S. 974 (1972).

UNITED STATES v. GERLACH LIVE STOCK CO.

Supreme Court of the United States, 1950.
339 U.S. 725, 70 S.Ct. 955, 94 L.Ed.2d 1231, 20 A.L.R.2d 633.

MR. JUSTICE JACKSON delivered the opinion of the Court.

We are asked to relieve the United States from six awards by the Court of Claims as just compensation for deprivation of riparian rights along the San Joaquin River in California caused by construction of Friant Dam, and its dependent irrigation system, as part of the Central Valley Project.

This is a gigantic undertaking to redistribute the principal freshwater resources of California.   *   *   *

Such a project inevitably unsettles many advantages long enjoyed in reliance upon the natural order, and it is with deprivation of such benefits that we are here concerned.

*   *   *

Uncontrolled grass lands involved in the claims are parts of a large riparian area which benefits from the natural seasonal overflow of the stream. Each year, with predictable regularity, the stream swells and submerges and saturates these low-lying lands. They are moistened and enriched by these inundations so that forage and pasturage thrive, as otherwise they can not. The high stage of the river, while fluctuating in height and variable in arrival, is not a flood in the sense of an abnormal and sudden deluge. The river rises and falls in rhythm with the cycle of seasons, expansion being normal for its time as curtailment is for others, and both are repeated with considerable constancy over the years. It should be noted, however, that claimants' benefit comes only from the very crest of this seasonal stage, which crest must be elevated and borne to their lands on the base of a full river, none of which can be utilized for irrigation above and little of it below them. Their claim of right is, in other words, to enjoy natural, seasonal fluctuation unhindered, which presupposes a peak flow largely unutilized.

The project puts an end to all this. Except at rare intervals, there will be no spill over Friant Dam, the bed of the San Joaquin along claimants' lands will be parched, and their grass lands will be barren. Unlike the supply utilized for nearby crop and "controlled" lands, the vanishing San Joaquin inundation cannot be replaced with Sacramento water. Claimants have been severally awarded compensation for this taking of their annual inundations, on the theory that, as part of the natural flow, its continuance is a right annexed to their riparian property. 111 Ct.Cl. 1, 89, 76 F.Supp. 87, 99. The principal issues are common to the six cases in which we granted certiorari.

I. NAVIGATION OR RECLAMATION PROJECT?

The Solicitor General contends that this overall project, and each part of it, has been authorized by Congress, under the commerce power, as a measure for control of navigation. Claimants on the other hand urge that although improvement of navigation was one objective of the Central Valley undertaking as a whole, nevertheless construction of the Friant Dam and the consequent taking of San Joaquin water rights had no purpose or effect except for irrigation and reclamation. This, it is claimed, was not only the actual, but the avowed purpose of Congress. On these conflicting assumptions the parties predicate contrary conclusions as to the right to compensation.

In the Rivers and Harbors Act of August 26, 1937, § 2, 50 Stat. 844, 850, and again in the Rivers and Harbors Act of October 17, 1940, 54 Stat. 1198, 1199–1200, Congress said that "the entire Central Valley project * * * is * * * declared to be for the purposes of improving navigation, regulating the flow of the San Joaquin River and the Sacramento River, controlling floods, providing for storage and for the delivery of the stored waters thereof * * *." The 1937 Act also provided that "the said dam and reservoirs shall be used, first, for river regulation, improvement of navigation, and flood control * * *."

We cannot disagree with claimants' contention that in undertaking these Friant projects and implementing the work as carried forward by the Reclamation Bureau, Congress proceeded on the basis of full recognition of water rights having valid existence under state law. By its command that the provisions of the reclamation law should govern the construction, operation, and maintenance of the several construction projects, Congress directed the Secretary of the Interior to proceed in conformity with state laws, giving full recognition to every right vested under those laws.[8]

* * *

It is not to be doubted that the totality of a plan so comprehensive has some legitimate relation to control of inland navigation or that particular components may be described without pretense as navigation and flood control projects. This made it appropriate that Congress should justify making this undertaking a national burden by general reference to its power over commerce and navigation.

The Government contends that the overall declaration of purpose is applicable to Friant Dam and related irrigation facilities as an integral

---

8. The Reclamation Act of 1902, 32 Stat. 388, as amended, 43 U.S.C.A. § 371 et seq., to which Congress adverted, applies only to the seventeen Western States. Section 8 provides:

"That nothing in this Act shall be construed as affecting or intended to affect or to in any way interfere with the laws of any State or Territory relating to the control, appropriation, use, or distribution of water used in irrigation, or any vested right acquired thereunder, and the Secre-

tary of the Interior, in carrying out the provisions of this Act, shall proceed in conformity with such laws, and nothing herein shall in any way affect any right of any State or of the Federal Government or of any landowner, appropriator, or user of water in, to, or from any interstate stream or the waters thereof: * * *"

To the extent that it is applicable this clearly leaves it to the State to say what rights of an appropriator or riparian owner may subsist along with any federal right.

part of "what Congress quite properly treated as a unit." Adverting to United States v. Willow River Co., 324 U.S. 499; United States v. Commodore Park, 324 U.S. 386; United States v. Appalachian Power Co., 311 U.S. 377; United States v. Chandler–Dunbar Co., 229 U.S. 53, the Government relies on the rule that it does not have to compensate for destruction of riparian interests over which at the point of conflict it has a superior navigation easement the exercise of which occasions the damage.   And irrespective of divisibility of the entire Central Valley undertaking, the Government contends that Friant Dam involves a measure of flood control, an end which is sensibly related to control of navigation.

* * *

Since we do not agree that Congress intended to invoke its navigation servitude as to each and every one of this group of coordinated projects, we do not reach constitutional or other issues thus posed. Similarly, we need not ponder whether, by virtue of a highly fictional navigation purpose, the Government could destroy the flow of a navigable stream and carry away its waters for sale to private interests without compensation to those deprived of them.   We have never held that or anything like it, and we need not here pass on any question of constitutional power; for we do not find that Congress has attempted to take or authorize the taking, without compensation, of any rights valid under state law.

On the contrary, Congress' general direction of purpose we think was intended to help meet any objection to its constitutional power to undertake this big bundle of big projects.   The custom of invoking the navigation power in authorizing improvements appears to have had its origin when the power of the Central Government to make internal improvements was contested and in doubt.   It was not until 1936 that this Court in United States v. Butler, 297 U.S. 1, declared for the first time, and without dissent on this point, that in conferring power upon Congress to tax "to pay the Debts and provide for the common Defence and general Welfare of the United States," the Constitution delegates a power separate and distinct from those later enumerated, and one not restricted by them, and that Congress has a substantive power to tax and appropriate for the general welfare, limited only by the requirement that it shall be exercised for the common benefit as distinguished from some mere local purpose.   * * *

Thus the power of Congress to promote the general welfare through large-scale projects for reclamation, irrigation, or other internal improvement, is now as clear and ample as its power to accomplish the same results indirectly through resort to strained interpretation of the power over navigation.   * * *

Even if we assume, with the Government, that Friant Dam in fact bears some relation to control of navigation, we think nevertheless that Congress realistically elected to treat it as a reclamation project.   It was so conceived and authorized by the President and it was so represented to Congress.   Whether Congress could have chosen to take claimants' rights by the exercise of its dominant navigation servitude is immaterial. By directing the Secretary to proceed under the Reclamation Act of 1902, Congress elected not "to in any way interfere with the laws of any State * * * relating to the control, appropriation, use or distribution of water used in irrigation, or any vested right acquired thereunder." 32 Stat. 388, 390.

We cannot twist these words into an election on the part of Congress under its navigation power to take such water rights without compensation. * * *

We conclude that, whether required to do so or not, Congress elected to recognize any state-created rights and to take them under its power of eminent domain.

* * *

[The Court went on to hold that under California law claimants owned compensable property rights in the seasonal flood waters of the San Joaquin.]

MR. JUSTICE DOUGLAS, concurring in part and dissenting in part.

I think it is clear under our decisions that respondents are not entitled to compensation as a matter of constitutional right. For we have repeatedly held that there are no private property rights in the waters of a navigable river. * * * That is true whether the rights of riparian owners or the rights of appropriators are involved. As the *Appalachian Power* case makes plain (311 U.S. 424, 427), the existence of property rights in the waters of a navigable stream are not dependent upon whether the United States is changing the flow of the river in aid of navigation or for some other purpose.

* * *

[Mr. Justice Douglas then reviews the legislative history and administrative practice under the Reclamation Act and concludes:]

I conclude that Congress by § 8 of the Reclamation Act agreed to pay (though not required to do so by the Constitution) for water rights acquired under state law in navigable as well as nonnavigable streams. As the Court holds, respondents under California law have a water right. Section 8 therefore recognizes it as the basis for payment in connection with this federal project.

QUESTIONS

1. The Senate approves a treaty allocating water in the Colorado River to Mexico. In order to honor the treaty commitment, prior appropriators are denied water. Under the majority opinion, is compensation due? Under Justice Douglas's opinion? What if the river were non-navigable?

2. Congress authorizes the construction of a nuclear power plant using water from a navigable river for cooling purposes. Riparian owners claim damages from thermal pollution. The government contends that riparians have no rights in navigable waters as against the government. Is the contention valid? Suppose the statute authorizing

the project invokes only the power to spend for the public welfare. Would this affect the answer?

3. Federal Preemption of State Laws

Strictly speaking, there can be no federal-state conflicts over water management; either the federal government has the constitutional power to act or it does not. If it does, the supremacy clause of the Constitution (Art. VI, cl. 2) overrides all state opposition. Disputes between the federal government and the states over water management related to federal reclamation projects are nonetheless grave. The issues are: To what extent did Congress exercise federal power? To what extent did Congress intend to preempt the field and oust state power? To what extent did Congress explicitly provide for continuing, coordinate or subordinate power in the states? The issues require a close look at the particular statutes authorizing the project.

FIRST IOWA HYDRO–ELECTRIC COOPERATIVE v. FEDERAL POWER COMMISSION

United States Supreme Court, 1946.
328 U.S. 152, 66 S.Ct. 906, 90 L.Ed. 1143.

Mr. Justice Burton delivered the opinion of the Court.

This case illustrates the integration of federal and state jurisdictions in licensing water power projects under the Federal Power Act. The petitioner is the First Iowa Hydro–Electric Cooperative, a cooperative association organized under the laws of Iowa with power to generate, distribute and sell electric energy. On January 29, 1940, pursuant to § 23(b) of the Federal Power Act, it filed with the Federal Power Commission a declaration of intention to construct and operate a dam, reservoir and hydro-electric power plant on the Cedar River, near Moscow, Iowa.

On April 2, 1941, it also filed with the Commission an application for a license, under the Federal Power Act, to construct an enlarged project essentially like the one it now wishes to build.   * * *

On January 29, 1944, after extended hearings, the Commission rendered an opinion including the following statements:

> "As first presented, the plans of the applicant for developing the water resources of the Cedar River were neither desirable nor adequate, but many important changes in design have been made. [The opinion here quoted in a footnote § 10(a) of the Federal Power Act.] The applicant has also agreed to certain modifications proposed by the Chief of Engineers of the War Department. The present plans call for a practical and reasonably adequate development to utilize the head and water available, create a large storage reservoir, and make available for recreational purposes a considerable area now unsuitable for such use, all at a cost which does not appear to be unreasonable.

> "Further changes in design may be desirable, but they are minor in character and can be effected if the applicant is able to

meet the other requirements of the act." *Re First Iowa Hydro–Electric Cooperative,* 52 PUR(NS) 82, 84.

We believe that the Commission would have been justified in proceeding further at that time with its consideration of the petitioner's application upon all the material facts. Such consideration would have included evidence submitted by the petitioner pursuant to § 9(b) of the Federal Power Act [6] as to the petitioner's compliance with the requirements of the laws of Iowa with respect to the petitioner's property rights to make its proposed use of the affected river beds and banks and to divert and use river water for the proposed power purposes, as well as the petitioner's right, within the State of Iowa, to engage in the business of developing, transmitting, and distributing power, and in any other business necessary to effect the purposes of the license.   * * *

The findings made by the Commission on June 3, 1941, in response to the petitioner's declaration of intention are not in question. For the purposes of this application it is settled that the project will affect the navigability of the Cedar, Iowa and Mississippi Rivers, each of which has been determined to be a part of the navigable waters of the United States; will affect the interests of interstate commerce; will flood certain public lands of the United States; and will require for its construction a license from the Commission. The project is clearly within the jurisdiction of the Commission under the Federal Power Act. The question at issue is the need, if any, for the presentation of satisfactory evidence of the petitioner's compliance with the terms of Chapter 363 of the Code of Iowa. This question is put in issue by the petition for review of the order of the Commission which dismissed the application solely on the ground of the failure of the petitioner to present such evidence. The laws of Iowa which that State contends are applicable and require a permit from its Executive Council to effect the purposes of the federal license are all in §§ 7767–7796.1 of the Code of Iowa, 1939, constituting Chapter 363, entitled "Mill Dams and Races." Section 7767 of that chapter is alleged to require the issuance of a permit by the Executive Council of the State and is the one on which the Commission's order must depend. It provides:

> "7767 Prohibition—permit. No dam shall be constructed, maintained, or operated in this state in any navigable or meandered stream for any purpose, or in any other stream for manufacturing or power purposes, nor shall any water be taken from such streams for industrial purposes, unless a permit has been granted by the executive council to the person, firm, corporation, or municipality constructing, maintaining, or operating the same."

6. "SEC. 9. That each applicant for a license hereunder shall submit to the commission—

* * *

"(b) Satisfactory evidence that the applicant has complied with the requirements of the laws of the State or States within which the proposed project is to be located with respect to bed and banks and to the appropriation, diversion, and use of water for power purposes and with respect to the right to engage in the business of developing, transmitting, and distributing power, and in any other business necessary to effect the purposes of a license under this Act." 41 Stat. 1068, 16 U.S.C. § 802(b).

To require the petitioner to secure the actual grant to it of a state permit under § 7767 as a condition precedent to securing a federal license for the same project under the Federal Power Act would vest in the Executive Council of Iowa a veto power over the federal project. Such a veto power easily could destroy the effectiveness of the Federal Act. It would subordinate to the control of the State the "comprehensive" planning which the Act provides shall depend upon the judgment of the Federal Power Commission or other representatives of the Federal Government. * * * For example, § 7776 of the State Code requires that "the method of construction, operation, maintenance, and equipment of any and all dams in such waters shall be subject to the approval of the Executive Council." This would subject to state control the very requirements of the project that Congress has placed in the discretion of the Federal Power Commission. A still greater difficulty is illustrated by § 7771. This states the requirements for a state permit as follows:

"7771 When permit granted. If it shall appear to the council that the construction, operation, or maintenance of the dam will not materially obstruct existing navigation, or materially affect other public rights, will not endanger life or public health, and *any water taken from the stream in connection with the project is returned thereto at the nearest practicable place* without being materially diminished in quantity or polluted or rendered deleterious to fish life, it shall grant the permit, upon such terms and conditions as it may prescribe." (Italics supplied.)

This strikes at the heart of the present project. The feature of the project which especially commended it to the Federal Power Commission was its diversion of substantially all of the waters of the Cedar River near Moscow, to the Mississippi River near Muscatine. Such a diversion long has been recognized as an engineering possibility and as constituting the largest power development foreseeable on either the Cedar or Iowa Rivers. It is this diversion that makes possible the increase in the head of water for power development from a maximum of 35 feet to an average of 101 feet, the increase in the capacity of the plant from 15,000 kw. to 50,000 kw. and its output from 47,000,000 kwh. to 200,000,000 kwh. per year. It is this diversion that led the Federal Power Commission, on January 29, 1944, to make its favorable appraisal of the enlarged project in contrast to its unfavorable appraisal, and to the State's rejection, of the smaller project. It is this feature that brings this project squarely under the Federal Power Act and at the same time gives the project its greatest economic justification.

If a state permit is not required, there is no justification for requiring the petitioner, as a condition of securing its federal permit, to present evidence of the petitioner's compliance with the requirements of the State Code for a state permit. Compliance with state requirements that are in conflict with federal requirements may well block the federal license. * * *

In the Federal Power Act there is a separation of those subjects which remain under the jurisdiction of the States from those subjects which the Constitution delegates to the United States and over which Congress vests the Federal Power Commission with authority to act. To the extent of this separation, the Act establishes a dual system of control. The duality of control consists merely of the division of the common enterprise between two cooperating agencies of government, each with final authority in its own jurisdiction. The duality does not require two agencies to share in the final decision of the same issue. Where the Federal Government supersedes the state government there is no suggestion that the two agencies both shall have final authority. In fact a contrary policy is indicated in §§ 4(e), 10(a), (b) and (c), and 23(b). * * *

The Act leaves to the States their traditional jurisdiction subject to the admittedly superior right of the Federal Government, through Congress, to regulate interstate and foreign commerce, administer the public lands and reservations of the United States and, in certain cases, exercise authority under the treaties of the United States. These sources of constitutional authority are all applied in the Federal Power Act to the development of 'the navigable waters of the United States.

* * *

Sections 27 and 9 are especially significant in this regard. Section 27 expressly "saves" certain state laws relating to property rights as to the use of water, so that these are not superseded by the terms of the Federal Power Act. It provides:

"SEC. 27. That nothing herein contained shall be construed as affecting or intending to affect or in any way to interfere with the laws of the respective States relating to the control, appropriation, use, or distribution of water used in irrigation or for municipal or other uses, or any vested right acquired therein." 41 Stat. 1077, 16 U.S.C. § 821.

Section 27 thus evidences the recognition by Congress of the need for an express "saving" clause in the Federal Power Act if the usual rules of supersedure are to be overcome. Sections 27 and 9(b) were both included in the original Federal Water Power Act of 1920 in their present form. The directness and clarity of § 27 as a "saving" clause and its location near the end of the Act emphasizes the distinction between its purpose and that of § 9(b) which is included in § 9, in the early part of the Act, which deals with the marshalling of information for the consideration of a new federal license. In view of the use by Congress of such an adequate "saving" clause in § 27, its failure to use similar language in § 9(b) is persuasive that § 9(b) should not be given the same effect as is given to § 27.

The effect of § 27, in protecting state laws from supersedure, is limited to laws as to the control, appropriation, use or distribution of water in irrigation or for municipal or other uses of the same nature. It therefore has primary, if not exclusive, reference to such proprietary rights. The phrase "any vested right acquired therein" further emphasizes the application of the section to property rights. * * *

Section 9(b) does not resemble § 27. It must be read with § 9(a) and (c). The entire section is devoted to securing adequate information for the Commission as to pending applications for licenses. Where § 9(a) calls for engineering and financial information, § 9(b) calls for legal information. This makes § 9(b) a natural place in which to describe the evidence which the Commission shall require in order to pass upon applications for federal licenses. This makes it a correspondingly unnatural place to establish by implication such a substantive policy as that contained in § 27 and which, in accordance with the contentions of the State of Iowa, would enable Chapter 363 of the Code of Iowa, 1939, to remain in effect although in conflict with the requirements of the Federal Power Act. There is nothing in the express language of § 9(b) that requires such a conclusion.

It does not itself require compliance with any state laws. Its reference to state laws is by way of suggestion to the Federal Power Commission of subjects as to which the Commission may wish some proof submitted to it of the applicant's progress. The evidence required is described merely as that which shall be "satisfactory" to the Commission. The need for compliance with applicable state laws, if any, arises not from this federal statute but from the effectiveness of the state statutes themselves.

When this application has been remanded to the Commission, that Commission will not act as a substitute for the local authorities having jurisdiction over such questions as the sufficiency of the legal title of the applicant to its riparian rights, or as to the validity of its local franchises, if any, relating to proposed intrastate public utility service. Section 9(b) says that the Commission may wish to have "satisfactory evidence" of the progress made by the applicant toward meeting local requirements but it does not say that the Commission is to assume responsibility for the legal sufficiency of the steps taken. The references made in § 9(b) to beds and banks of streams, to proprietary rights to divert or use water, or to legal rights to engage locally in the business of developing, transmitting and distributing power neither add anything to nor detract anything from the force of the local laws, if any, on those subjects. In so far as those laws have not been superseded by the Federal Power Act, they remain as applicable and effective as they were before its passage. The State of Iowa, however, has sought to sustain the applicability and validity of Chapter 363 of the Code of Iowa in this connection, on the ground that the Federal Power Act, by the implications of § 9(b), has recognized this chapter of Iowa law as part of a system of dual control of power project permits, cumbersome and complicated though it be. If it had been the wish of Congress to make the applicant obtain consent of state as well as federal authorities to each project, the simple thing would have been to so provide. * * *

[T]he Federal Power Act * * * was the outgrowth of a widely supported effort of the conservationists to secure enactment of a complete scheme of national regulation which would promote the comprehensive development of the water resources of the Nation, in so far as it was within the reach of the federal power to do so, instead of the piecemeal, restrictive, negative approach of the River and Harbor Acts and other federal laws previously enacted.

* * *

The detailed provisions of the Act providing for the federal plan of regulation leave no room or need for conflicting state controls. The contention of the State of Iowa is comparable to that which was presented on behalf of 41 States and rejected by this Court in United States v. Appalachian Power Co., 311 U.S. 377. * * *

Reversed.

MR. JUSTICE JACKSON took no part in the consideration or decision of this case.

MR. JUSTICE FRANKFURTER, dissenting.

* * *

With due respect, I have not been able to discover an adequate answer to the position of the Federal Power Commission, thus summarized in the Solicitor–General's brief:

"Unless Section 9(b) is to be given no effect whatever, some evidence of compliance with at least some state laws is a prerequisite to the issuance of a federal license, and the view of the court below, that there is no occasion, in this case, to anticipate conflicts between state and federal authority and the consequent invalidity of the state law, is not an unreasonable one. 'To predetermine, even in the limited field of water power, the rights of different sovereignties, pregnant with future controversies, is beyond the judicial function.' United States v. Appalachian Electric Power Co., 311 U.S. 377, 423. Here petitioner, since the modification of its plans, has given the State Executive Council and the Iowa courts no opportunity to express their views on its proposed project with reference to matters which may be peculiarly of local concern; without such an expression, it is difficult to assess the propriety of what is only an anticipated exercise of the State's power."

Accordingly, I think that the judgment should be affirmed.

NOTES

1. With a Federal Energy Regulatory Commission (FERC) license goes some of the United States' preemptive power. Should courts presume that Congress did not intend to bestow its ability to override state law upon non-federal entities in absence of a clear legislative statement to that effect? In City of Tacoma v. Taxpayers of Tacoma, 357 U.S. 320 (1958), the Supreme Court held that a FERC license effectively delegated condemnation authority to a licensee city so that the city could condemn state property contrary to state law. The state property, a fish hatchery, was located where it would be flooded by waters impounded behind the city's proposed dam.

2. The tension between state water rights and FERC's regulatory authority became more acute when Congress decided to promote small-

scale hydroelectric development. In an early effort to legislate a national energy policy, Congress enacted the Public Utility Regulatory Policies Act of 1978 (PURPA). PURPA, along with the Energy Security Act of 1980, attempted to stimulate the increased development of alternative renewable energy sources. PURPA's main stimulus for low-head hydroelectric facilities was to create a market for their power. Public utilities were not historically enthusiastic about purchasing small amounts of alternative energy, but Congress mandated enthusiasm. Utilities must purchase the output from qualifying facilities at "a rate that exceeds the incremental cost to the electric utility of alternative electric energy." To carry out PURPA's goal of promoting secure, renewable alternative energy sources, FERC defined incremental cost as full avoided cost.

Activity related to licensing small hydroelectric projects accounted for much of the increase in FERC business, which grew from 76 preliminary applications in 1979 to 1856 in 1981. The growth in FERC activity increased the opportunity for FERC to argue that it can preempt state and federal environmental laws and state water laws.

3. Short of prohibiting a project, how far may a state go in imposing conditions on FERC applicants? At what point are conditions effectively prohibitions?

CALIFORNIA v. UNITED STATES

Supreme Court of the United States, 1978.
438 U.S. 645, 98 S.Ct. 2985, 57 L.Ed.2d 1018.

MR. JUSTICE REHNQUIST delivered the opinion of the Court.

* * *

I

Principles of comity and federalism, which the District Court and the Court of Appeals referred to and which have received considerable attention in our decisions, are as a legal matter based on the Constitution of the United States, statutes enacted by Congress, and judge-made law. But the situations invoking the application of these principles have contributed importantly to their formation. Just as it has been truly said that the life of the law is not logic but experience, see O. Holmes, The Common Law 1 (1881), so may it be said that the life of the law is not political philosophy but experience.

* * *

In order to correctly ascertain the meaning of the Reclamation Act of 1902, we must recognize the obvious truth that the history of irrigation and reclamation before that date was much fresher in the minds of those then in Congress than it is to us today. "[T]he afternoon of July 23, 1847, was the true date of the beginning of modern irrigation. It was on that afternoon that the first band of Mormon pioneers built a small dam across City Creek near the present site of the Mormon Temple and diverted sufficient water to saturate some five acres of exceedingly dry land. Before the day was over they had planted potatoes to preserve the seed." [1] During the subsequent half century, irrigation expanded throughout the arid States of the West, supported usually by private enterprise or the local community. By the turn of the century, however, most of the land which could be profitably irrigated by such small scale projects had been put to use. Pressure mounted on the Federal Government to provide the funding for the massive projects that would be needed to complete the reclamation culminating in the Reclamation Act of 1902.

* * *

If the term "cooperative federalism" had been in vogue in 1902, the Reclamation Act of that year would surely have qualified as a leading example of it. In that Act, Congress set forth on a massive program to construct and operate dams, reservoirs, and canals for the reclamation of the arid lands in 17 western States. Reflective of the "cooperative federalism" which the Act embodied is § 8, whose exact meaning and scope are the critical inquiries in this case:

> "*[N]othing in this Act shall be construed as affecting or intended to affect or to in any way interfere with the laws of any States or Territory relating to the control, appropriation, use or distribution of water used in irrigation,* or any vested rights acquired thereunder, *and the Secretary of the Interior, in carrying out the provisions of this Act, shall proceed in conformity with such laws,* and nothing herein shall in any way affect any right of any State or of the Federal Government or of any landowner, appropriator, or user of water in, to or from any interstate stream or the waters thereof: *Provided,* that the right to the use of water acquired under the provisions of this Act shall be appurtenant to the land irrigated, and beneficial use shall be the basis, the measure, and the limit of the right." [43 U.S.C.A. § 383] (emphasis added).

* * *

The New Melones Dam, which this litigation concerns, is part of the California Central Valley Project, the largest reclamation project yet authorized under the 1902 Act. The Dam, which will impound 2.4 million acre-feet of water of California's Stanislaus River, has the multiple purposes of flood control, irrigation, municipal use, industrial use, power, recreation, water quality control and the protection of fish

---

1. A. Golze, Reclamation in the United States 6 (1961). The author was at the time of publication the Chief Engineer of the California Department of Water Re- sources and had been formerly Assistant Commissioner of the United States Bureau of Reclamation.

and wildlife. The waters of the Stanislaus River that will be impounded behind the New Melones Dam arise and flow solely in California.

The United States Bureau of Reclamation, as it has with every other federal reclamation project, applied for a permit from the appropriate state agency, here the California State Water Resources Control Board, to appropriate the water that would be impounded by the Dam and later used for reclamation. After lengthy hearings, the State Board found that unappropriated water was available for the New Melones Project during certain times of the year. Although it therefore approved the Bureau's applications, the State Board attached 25 conditions to the permits. California State Water Resources Control Board, Decision 1422 (April 14, 1973). The most important conditions prohibit full impoundment until the Bureau is able to show firm commitments, or at least a specific plan, for the use of the water.[8] The State Board concluded that without such a specific plan of beneficial use the Bureau had failed to meet the California statutory requirements for appropriation.

* * *

II

The history of the relationship between the Federal Government and the States in the reclamation of the arid lands of the western States is both long and involved, but through it runs the consistent thread of purposeful and continued deference to state water law by Congress.

[The Court discusses several Supreme Court decisions, the Acts of 1866, 1870 and 1877, the decision in *California Oregon Power Co.,* page 167, supra, and proceeds with an analysis of the several legislative acts that led to the enactment of the comprehensive Reclamation Act.]

III

* * *

From the legislative history of the Reclamation Act of 1902, it is clear that state law was expected to control in two important respects. First, and of controlling importance to this case, the Secretary would have to appropriate, purchase, or condemn necessary water rights in strict conformity with state law. * * *

---

8. Other conditions prohibit collection of water during periods of the year when unappropriated water is unavailable; require that a preference be given to water users in the water basin in which the New Melones Project is located; require storage releases to be made so as to maintain maximum and minimum chemical concentrations in the San Joaquin River and protect fish and wildlife; require the United States to provide means for the release of excess waters and to clear vegetation and structures from the reservoir sites; require the filing of additional reports and studies; and provide for access to the project site by the State Board and the public. Still other conditions reserve jurisdiction to the Board to impose further conditions on the appropriations if necessary to protect the "beneficial use" of the water involved. The United States did not challenge any of the conditions under state law, but instead filed the federal declaratory action that is now before us.

Second, once the waters were released from the dam, their distribution to individual landowners would again be controlled by state law.
* * *

A principal motivating factor behind Congress' decision to defer to state law was thus the legal confusion that would arise if federal water law and state water law reigned side by side in the same locality. Congress also intended to "follow the well-established precedent in national legislation of recognizing local and state law relative to the appropriation and distribution of water." 35 Cong.Rec. 6678–6679 (Cong. Mondell). * * *

Both sponsors of and opponents to the Reclamation Act also expressed constitutional doubts as to Congress' power to override the States' regulation of waters within their borders. * * *

IV

For almost half a century, this congressionally mandated division between federal and state authority worked smoothly. No project was constructed without the approval of the Secretary of the Interior, and the United States through this official preserved its authority to determine how federal funds should be expended. But state laws relating to water rights were observed in accordance with the congressional directive contained in § 8 of the Act of 1902. In 1958, however, the first of two cases was decided by this Court in which private land owners or municipal corporations contended that state water law had the effect of overriding specific congressional directives to the Secretary of the Interior as to the operation of federal reclamation projects. In Ivanhoe Irrigation District v. McCracken, 357 U.S. 275 (1958), the Supreme Court of California decided that California law forbade the 160–acre limitation on irrigation water deliveries expressly written into § 5 of the Reclamation Act of 1902, and that therefore, under § 8 of the Reclamation Act, the Secretary was required to deliver reclamation water without regard to the acreage limitation. Both the State of California and the United States appealed from this judgment, and this Court reversed it, saying:

> "Section 5 is a specific and mandatory prerequisite laid down by the Congress as binding in the operation of reclamation projects, providing that '[n]o right to the use of water * * * shall be sold for a tract exceeding one hundred and sixty acres to any one landowner. * * *' Without passing generally on the coverage of § 8 in the delicate area of federal-state relations in the irrigation field, we do not believe that the Congress intended § 8 to override the repeatedly reaffirmed national policy of § 5." Id., at 291–292.

Five years later, in City of Fresno v. California, 372 U.S. 627 (1963), this Court affirmed a decision of the United States Court of Appeals for the Ninth Circuit holding that § 8 did not require the Secretary of the Interior to ignore explicit congressional provisions preferring irrigation use over domestic and municipal use.[24]

---

24. "Section 9(c) of the Reclamation Project Act of 1939 * * * provides: 'No contract relating to municipal water supply or miscellaneous purposes * * * shall

Petitioner does not ask us to overrule these holdings, nor are we presently inclined to do so. Petitioner instead asks us to hold that a State may impose any condition on the "control, appropriation, use or distribution of water" through a federal reclamation project that is not inconsistent with clear congressional directives respecting the project. Petitioner concedes, and the government relies upon, dicta, in our cases that may point to a contrary conclusion. Thus, in *Ivanhoe,* the Court went beyond the actual facts of that case and stated:

> "As we read § 8, it merely requires the United States to comply with state law when, in the construction and operation of a reclamation project, it becomes necessary for it to acquire water rights or vested interests therein. * * * We read nothing in § 8 that compels the United States to deliver water on conditions imposed by the State." 357 U.S. 275, at 281–292.

Like dictum was repeated in *City of Fresno,* 372 U.S., at 630, and in this Court's opinion in Arizona v. California, 373 U.S. 546 (1963), where the Court also said:

> "The argument that § 8 of the Reclamation Act requires the United States in the delivery of water to follow priorities laid down by state law has already been disposed of by this Court in *Ivanhoe Irr. Dist. v. McCracken,* * * * and reaffirmed in *City of Fresno v. California* * * *. Since § 8 of the Reclamation Act did not subject the Secretary to state law in disposing of water in [*Ivanhoe*], we cannot, consistently with *Ivanhoe,* hold that the Secretary must be bound by state law in disposing of water under the Project Act." Id., at 586–587.

While we are not convinced that the above language is diametrically inconsistent with the position of petitioner, or that it squarely supports the United States, it undoubtedly goes further than was necessary to decide the cases presented to the Court. *Ivanhoe* and *City of Fresno* involved conflicts between § 8, requiring the Secretary to follow state law as to water rights, and other provisions of Reclamation Acts that placed specific limitations on how the water was to be distributed. Here the United States contends that it may ignore state law even if no explicit congressional directive conflicts with the conditions imposed by the California State Water Control Board.

be made unless, in the judgment of the Secretary [of the Interior], it will not impair the efficiency of the project for irrigation purposes.' * * * It therefore appears clear that Fresno has no preferential rights to contract for project water, but may receive it only if, in the Secretary's judgment, irrigation will not be adversely affected." 372 U.S., at 630–631.

The Court also concluded in a separate portion of its opinion "§ 8 does not mean that state law may operate to prevent the United States from exercising the power of eminent domain to acquire the water rights of others. * * * Rather, the effect of § 8 in such a case is to leave to state law the definition of the property interests, if any, for which compensation must be made." 372 U.S., at 630. Because no provision of California law was actually inconsistent with the exercise by the United States of its power of eminent domain, this statement was dictum. It also might have been apparent from examination of the congressional authorization of the Central Valley Project that Congress intended the Secretary to have the power to condemn any necessary water rights. We disavow this dictum, however, to the extent that it implies that state law does not control even where not inconsistent with such expressions of congressional intent.

In *Arizona v. California,* the States had asked the Court to rule that state law would control in the distribution of water from the Boulder Canyon Project, a massive multistate reclamation project on the Colorado River. After reviewing the legislative history of the Boulder Canyon Project Act, 43 U.S.C.A. § 617 et seq., the Court concluded that because of the unique size and multistate scope of the Project, Congress did not intend the States to interfere with the Secretary's power to determine with whom and on what terms water contracts would be made. While the Court in rejecting the States' claim repeated the language from *Ivanhoe* and *City of Fresno* as to the scope of § 8, there was no need for it to reaffirm such language except as it related to the singular legislative history of the Boulder Canyon Project Act.

But because there is at least tension between the above quoted dictum and what we conceive to be the correct reading of § 8 of the Reclamation Act of 1902, we disavow the dictum to the extent that it would prevent petitioner from imposing conditions on the permits granted to the United States which are not inconsistent with congressional provisions authorizing the project in question. Section 8 cannot be read to require the Secretary to comply with state law only when it becomes necessary to purchase or condemn vested water rights. That section does, of course, provide for the protection of vested water rights, but it also requires the Secretary to comply with state law in the "control, appropriation, use, or distribution of water." Nor, as the United States contends, does § 8 merely require the Secretary of the Interior to file a notice with the State of its intent to appropriate but to thereafter ignore the substantive provision of state law. The legislative history of the Reclamation Act of 1902 makes it abundantly clear that Congress intended to defer to the substance, as well as the form, of state water law. The Government's interpretation would trivialize the broad language and purpose of § 8.

* * *

* * * Assuming, *arguendo,* that the United States is still free to challenge the consistency of the conditions, resolution of their consistency may well require additional factfinding. We therefore reverse the judgment of the Court of Appeals and remand for further proceedings consistent with this opinion.

Reversed and remanded.

Mr. Justice White, with whom Mr. Justice Brennan and Mr. Justice Marshall join, dissenting.

* * *

The majority reads *Ivanhoe* as holding that § 5 and similar explicit statutory directives are exceptions to § 8's otherwise controlling mandate that state law must govern both the acquisition and distribution of reclamation water. This misinterprets that opinion. It is plain enough that in response to the argument that § 8 subjected the § 5 contract provisions to the strictures of state law, the Court squarely rejected the submission on the ground that § 8 dealt only with the acquisition of water rights and required the United States to respect the water rights that were vested under state law. That the Court might have saved the § 5 provision on a different and narrower ground more acceptable to the present Court majority does not render the ground actually employed any less of a holding of the Court or transform it into the discardable dictum the majority considers it to be.

It is also beyond doubt that both *Fresno* and *Arizona* considered *Ivanhoe* to contain a holding that § 8 was limited to water-right acquisition and did not reach the distribution of reclamation water. But whatever the proper characterization of the Court's pronouncement in *Ivanhoe* might be, *Fresno* itself held that in distributing project water the United States, despite state law and § 8, not only was not bound by the municipal preference laws of California, which were contrary to a specific federal statute, but also could export water from the watershed without regard to the county- and watershed-of-origin statutes. The Court held the latter even though no provision of federal law forbade the federal officers from complying with the preferences assertedly established by those state laws.

Much the same is true of *Arizona*, where the Court heard two arguments totaling over 22 hours and considered voluminous briefs that dealt with a variety of subjects, including the important issue of the impact of § 8 on the Secretary's freedom to contract for the distribution of water. In its opinion, the Court not only dealt with both *Ivanhoe* and *Fresno* as considered holdings that § 8 did not bear on distribution rights, but also expressly disagreed with its Special Master and squarely rejected claims that the Secretary could not contract for the sale of water except in compliance with the priorities established by state law. Nor, as suggested by the majority, is there anything in the *Arizona* case to suggest that the Court arrived at its conclusion by factors peculiar to the statutes authorizing the project. The particular terms of the Secretary's contracts were not authorized or directed by any federal statute. The Court's holding that he was free to proceed as he did was squarely premised on the proposition that § 8 did not control the distribution of the project water.

The short of the matter is that no case in this Court, until this one, has construed § 8 as the present majority insists that it be construed. All of the relevant cases are to the contrary.

* * *

Only the revisionary zeal of the present majority can explain its misreading of our cases and its evident willingness to disregard them. Congress has not disturbed these cases, and until it does, I would respect them. * * * *All* of the relevant cases are contrary to today's holding, and in none of them was the Court on a frolic of its own. * * *

Even less explicable is the majority's insistence on reaching out to overturn the holding of this Court in *Fresno*, which reflected the decision in *Dugan* [v. Rank, 372 U.S. 609 (1963)] and was in turn grounded on a similar approach in *Ivanhoe*, that state law may not restrict the power of the United States to condemn water rights. The issue was squarely presented and decided in both *Dugan* and *Fresno*. In both cases it was claimed—and state attorney's general's opinions supported the claim—that some of the rights at issue were not condemnable under state law and that § 8 therefore forbade their taking by the Federal Government. In both cases, the claim was rejected by this Court, just as it was in the Court of Appeals. Without briefing and argument, the majority now discards these holdings in a footnote. See n. 24.

Section 7 of the Reclamation Act, now 43 U.S.C.A. § 421, authorizes the Secretary to acquire any rights or property by purchase or condemnation under judicial process, and the Attorney General is directed to institute suit at the request of the Secretary. Also, as Mr. Justice Jackson explained for the Court in *Gerlach*, 339 U.S., at 735 n. 8, when the Central Valley Project was authorized in 1937, the Secretary of Interior was "authorized to acquire 'by proceedings in eminent domain, or otherwise, all lands, rights-of-way, water rights, and other property necessary for said purposes * * *.' 50 Stat. 844, 850." Furthermore, § 10 of the Reclamation Act, now 43 U.S.C.A. § 373, authorizes the Secretary to perform any and all acts necessary to carry out the Act. * * * Never has there been a suggestion in our cases that Congress, by adopting § 8, intended to permit a State to disentitle the Government to acquire the property necessary or appropriate to carry out an otherwise constitutionally permissible and statutorily authorized undertaking. *Gerlach, Ivanhoe, Dugan* and *Fresno* are to the contrary.

The Court's "disavowal" of our prior cases and of the Government's power to condemn state water rights, all without briefing and argument, is a gratuitous effort that I do not care to join and from which I dissent.

* * *

NOTES

1. On remand, the district court upheld state conditions that prohibited the impoundment of surplus waters until the Bureau of Reclamation had potential contract buyers and limited the use of water for consumptive purposes to four counties. The state's restrictions on the impoundment of water for hydroelectric generation to save a portion of the Stanislaus for white water rafting were, however, found inconsistent with the purposes of the project. United States v. California, 509 F.Supp. 867 (E.D.Cal.1981). The state fared better in the Ninth Circuit Court of Appeals, which held that, before impounding water behind the dam, the United States must demonstrate a clear need for that water to fulfill project purposes where the storage would flood out fish, wildlife, and recreation uses above the dam. United States v. State of California, 694 F.2d 1171 (9th Cir.1982). Because of extreme winter flooding, the New Melones Reservoir filled by 1983 and the white waters of the Stanislaus River were virtually destroyed in spite of the Ninth Circuit's opinion. With many environmental concerns mooted by intervening events, on March 8, 1983 the California

State Water Resources Control Board issued Order WR 83–3 amending the federal government's permit, allowing it to fill the reservoir and generate full capacity hydroelectric power. The litigation is the subject of a case study that places the decisions in the broader context of state and federal water resources development. Barbara T. Andrews & Marie Sansone, Who Runs the Rivers? Dams and Decisions in the New West (1983). See also Amy K. Kelley, *Developments in Water and Environmental Law: Staging a Comeback—Section 8 of the Reclamation Act,* 18 U.C.Davis L.Rev. 97 (1984).

2. In City of Fresno v. California, 372 U.S. 627 (1963), the Supreme Court held that California's statutory preferences for domestic uses and for uses in the area of origin could not be applied to limit the operation of Friant Dam, which is part of the federally supported Central Valley Project. The Court found that the command of § 8 of the Reclamation Act was overridden where observing state law would conflict with § 9(c) which gives specific preference to irrigation uses. See South Delta Water Agency v. United States Department of Interior, 767 F.2d 531 (9th Cir.1985).

What are the standards for determining if federal law preempts state law? Should a "clear" statement of congressional intent be required? Does this standard give insufficient weight to federal interests implicit in legislation authorizing a project? Do reclamation cases call for a different standard of preemption?

CALIFORNIA v. FEDERAL ENERGY REGULATORY COMMISSION

Supreme Court of the United States, 1990.
495 U.S. 490, 110 S.Ct. 2024, 109 L.Ed.2d 474.

JUSTICE O'CONNOR delivered the opinion of the Court.

* * *

I

The Rock Creek hydroelectric project lies near the confluence of the South Fork American River and one of the river's tributaries, Rock Creek. Rock Creek runs through federally managed land located within California. The project draws water from Rock Creek to drive its generators and then releases the water near the confluence of the stream and river, slightly less than one mile from where it is drawn. The state and federal requirements at issue govern the "minimum flow rate" of water that must remain in the bypassed section of the stream and that thus remains unavailable to drive the generators.

In 1983, pursuant to the Federal Power Act (FPA), the Federal Energy Regulatory Commission (FERC) issued a license authorizing the operation of the Rock Creek project. Section 4(e) of the FPA empowers FERC to issue licenses for projects "necessary or convenient * * * for the development, transmission, and utilization of power across, along, from, or in any of the streams * * * over which Congress has jurisdiction." 16 U.S.C. § 797(e) (1982 ed.). Section 10(a) of the Act also authorizes FERC to issue licenses subject to the conditions that FERC deems best suited for power development and other public uses of the waters. 16 U.S.C. § 802(b) (1982 ed.). Congress' subsequent amendments to those provisions expressly direct that FERC consider a project's effect on fish and wildlife as well as "power and development purposes." Electric Consumers Protection Act of 1986, Pub.L. 99–495, 100 Stat. 1243, 16 U.S.C. §§ 797(e), 803(a). FERC issued the 1983 license and set minimum flow rates after considering the project's economic feasibility and environmental consequences. * * *

The licensee had also applied for state water permits, and in 1984 the State Water Resources Control Board (WRCB) issued a permit that conformed to FERC's interim minimum flow requirements but reserved the right to set different permanent minimum flow rates. When the WRCB in 1987 considered a draft order requiring permanent minimum flow rates of 60 cfs from March through June and 30 cfs during the remainder of the year, the licensee petitioned FERC for a declaration that FERC possessed exclusive jurisdiction to determine the project's minimum flow requirements. *Rock Creek Limited Partnership,* 38 FERC ¶ 61,240, p. 61,772 (1987). The licensee, by then respondent Rock Creek Limited Partnership, also claimed that the higher minimum flow rates sought by the WRCB would render the project economically infeasible.

In March 1987, FERC issued an order directing the licensee to comply with the minimum flow requirements of the federal permit. In that order, FERC concluded that the task of setting minimum flows rested within its exclusive jurisdiction. The Commission reasoned that setting minimum flow requirements was integral to its planning and licensing process under FPA § 10(a); giving effect to competing state requirements "would interfere with the Commission's balancing of competing considerations in licensing" and would vest in States a veto power over federal projects inconsistent with the FPA, as interpreted in First Iowa Hydro–Electric Cooperative v. FPC, 328 U.S. 152, 66 S.Ct. 906, 90 L.Ed. 1143 (1946). FERC also directed an administrative law judge to hold a hearing to determine the appropriate permanent minimum flow rates for the project. After considering proposals and arguments of the licensee, the CDFG, and FERC staff, the administrative law judge set the minimum flow rate for the project at 20 cfs during the entire year. *Rock Creek Limited Partnership,* 41 FERC ¶ 63,019 (1987). Four days after FERC's declaratory order, the WRCB issued an order directing the licensee to comply with the higher minimum flow requirements contained in its draft order. The WRCB also intervened to seek a rehearing of FERC's order. FERC denied the rehearing request, concluded that the State sought to impose conflicting license requirements, and reaffirmed its conclusion that the FPA, as interpreted in *First Iowa,* provided FERC with exclusive jurisdiction to determine minimum flow rates. *Rock Creek Limited Partnership,* 41 FERC ¶ 61,198 (1987).

The Court of Appeals for the Ninth Circuit affirmed FERC's order denying rehearing. California ex rel. State Water Resources Board v. FERC, 877 F.2d 743 (1989). That court, too, concluded that *First Iowa* governed the case; that FPA § 27 as construed in *First Iowa* did not preserve California's right to regulate minimum flow rates; and that the FPA preempted WCRB's minimum flow rate requirements.   Ibid. We granted certiorari, 493 U.S. 991 (1989), and we now affirm.

II

In the Federal Power Act of 1935, 49 Stat. 803, 863, Congress clearly intended a broad federal role in the development and licensing of hydroelectric power.   That broad delegation of power to the predecessor of FERC, however, hardly determines the extent to which Congress intended to have the Federal Government exercise exclusive powers, or intended to pre-empt concurrent state regulation of matters affecting federally licensed hydroelectric projects.   The parties' dispute regarding the latter issue turns principally on the meaning of § 27 of the FPA, which provides the clearest indication of how Congress intended to allocate the regulatory authority of the States and the Federal Government.   That section provides:

> "Nothing contained in this chapter shall be construed as affecting or intending to affect or in any way to interfere with the laws of the respective States relating to the control, appropriation, use, or distribution of water used in irrigation or for municipal or other uses, or any vested right acquired therein."   16 U.S.C. § 821 (1982 ed.).

Were this a case of first impression, petitioner's argument based on the statute's language could be said to present a close question.

* * *

But the meaning of § 27 and the pre-emptive effect of the FPA are not matters of first impression.   Forty-four years ago, this Court in *First Iowa* construed the section and provided the understanding of the FPA that has since guided the allocation of state and federal regulatory authority over hydroelectric projects.

* * *

We decline at this late date to revisit and disturb the understanding of § 27 set forth in *First Iowa.*   As petitioner prudently concedes, *First Iowa*'s interpretation of § 27 does not encompass the California regulation at issue: California's minimum stream flow requirements neither reflect nor establish "proprietary rights" or "rights of the same nature as those relating to the use of water in irrigation or for municipal purposes."

Instead, petitioner requests that we repudiate *First Iowa*'s interpretation of § 27 and the FPA.   This argument misconceives the deference this Court must accord to long-standing and well-entrenched decisions, especially those interpreting statutes that underlie complex regulatory regimes.   * * * There has been no sufficient intervening change in the law, or indication that *First Iowa* has proved unworkable or has fostered confusion and inconsistency in the law, that warrants our departure from established precedent.

* * *

* * * By directing FERC to consider the recommendations of state wildlife and other regulatory agencies while providing FERC with final authority to establish license conditions (including those with terms inconsistent with the States' recommendations), Congress has amended the FPA to elaborate and reaffirm *First Iowa*'s understanding that the FPA establishes a broad and paramount federal regulatory role.

Petitioner also argues that we should disregard *First Iowa*'s discussion of § 27 because it was merely dictum. It is true that our immediate concern in *First Iowa* was the interpretation of § 9(b) of the FPA, which governs submission to the federal licensing agency of evidence of compliance with state law. The Court determined that § 9(b) did not require licensees to obtain a state permit or to demonstrate compliance with the state law prerequisites to obtaining such a permit. * * * Only the Court's narrow reading of § 27 allowed it to sustain this interpretation of § 9(b). Had § 27 been given the broader meaning that Iowa sought, it would have "saved" the state requirements at issue, made the state permit one that could be issued, and supported the interpretation of § 9(b) as requiring evidence of compliance with those state requirements, rather than compliance only with those requirements consistent with the federal license.

* * *

Petitioner also argues that our decision in California v. United States, 438 U.S. 645, 98 S.Ct. 2985, 57 L.Ed.2d 1018 (1978), construing § 8 of the Reclamation Act of 1902, requires that we abandon *First Iowa* 's interpretation of § 27 and the FPA. Petitioner reasons that § 8 is similar to and served as a model for FPA § 27, that this Court in *California v. United States* interpreted § 8 in a manner inconsistent with *First Iowa* 's reading of § 27, and that that reading of § 8, subsequent to *First Iowa,* in some manner overrules or repudiates *First Iowa* 's understanding of § 27. *California v. United States* is cast in broad terms and embodies a conception of the States' regulatory powers in some tension with that set forth in *First Iowa,* but that decision bears quite indirectly, at best, upon interpretation of the FPA. The Court in *California v. United States* interpreted the Reclamation Act of 1902; it did not advert to or purport to interpret the FPA, and held simply that § 8 requires the Secretary of the Interior to comply with state laws, not inconsistent with congressional directives, governing use of water employed in federal reclamation projects. *California v. United States,* supra. Also, as in *First Iowa,* the Court in *California v. United States* examined the purpose, structure, and legislative history of the entire statute before it and employed those sources to construe the statute's savings clause. See id., at 649–651, 653–670, 674–675, 98 S.Ct., at 2988–2989, 2990–2998, 3000–3001. Those sources indicate, of course, that the FPA envisioned a considerably broader and more active federal oversight role in hydropower development than did the Reclamation Act.

* * * Although *California v. United States* and *First Iowa* accord different effect to laws relating to water uses, this difference stems in part from the different roles assumed by the federal actor in each case,

as reflected in § 8's explicit directive to the Secretary. The Secretary in executing a particular reclamation project is in a position analogous to a licensee under the FPA, and need not comply with state laws conflicting with congressional directives respecting particular reclamation projects, see id., at 672–674, 98 S.Ct., at 2999–3001; similarly, a federal licensee under the FPA need not comply with state requirements that conflict with the federal license provisions established pursuant to the FPA's directives. An additional textual difference is that § 8 refers only to "water used in irrigation" and contains no counterpart to § 27's reference to "other uses," the provision essential to petitioner's argument. Laws controlling water used in irrigation relate to proprietary rights, as the *First Iowa* Court indicated, 328 U.S., at 176, and n. 20, 66 S.Ct., at 917, and n. 20, and § 8 does not indicate the appropriate treatment of laws relating to other water uses that do not implicate proprietary rights.

* * *

Adhering to *First Iowa*'s interpretation of § 27, we conclude that the California requirements for minimum in-stream flows cannot be given effect and allowed to supplement the federal flow requirements. A state measure is "pre-empted to the extent it actually conflicts with federal law, that is, when it is impossible to comply with both state and federal law, or where the state law stands as an obstacle to the accomplishment of the full purposes and objectives of Congress." Silkwood v. Kerr–McGee Corp., 464 U.S. 238, 248, 104 S.Ct. 615, 621, 78 L.Ed.2d 443 (1984) (citations omitted). As Congress directed in FPA § 10(a), FERC set the conditions of the license, including the minimum stream flow, after considering which requirements would best protect wildlife and ensure that the project would be economically feasible, and thus further power development. Allowing California to impose significantly higher minimum stream flow requirements would disturb and conflict with the balance embodied in that considered federal agency determination. FERC has indicated that the California requirements interfere with its comprehensive planning authority, and we agree that allowing California to impose the challenged requirements would be contrary to congressional intent regarding the Commission's licensing authority and would "constitute a veto of the project that was approved and licensed by FERC." 877 F.2d, at 749; cf. *First Iowa*, supra, at 164–165, 66 S.Ct., at 911–912.

For the foregoing reasons, the decision of the Court of Appeals for the Ninth Circuit is

Affirmed.

NOTES

1. How much of United States v. California is left after California v. FERC? For the view that Congress should overrule the preemptive power of FERC affirmed by California v. FERC see Michael C. Blumm, Federalism, Hydroelectric Licensing and the Future of Minimum Streamflows After California v. Federal Energy Regulatory Commission, 21 Envtl.L. 113 (1991).

2. The Ninth Circuit Court of Appeals has interpreted California v. FERC as limiting state authority over FERC licensed projects to "allocating proprietary rights in water." Otherwise, "federal laws have occupied the field, preventing state regulation." Sayles Hydro Assoc. v. Maughan, 985 F.2d 451 (9th Cir. 1993). The Federal Power Act, howev-

er, is not the only federal law that affects hydropower development. Section 401 of the Clean Water Act requires that a state certify that a federal project or license will not cause any violation of the state's water quality standards. Thus, the Washington Supreme Court upheld a state-imposed condition on the certification, and hence on the FERC license, that a proposed hydroelectric project must maintain minimum streamflows. State, Department of Ecology v. PUD No. 1 of Jefferson County, 849 P.2d 646 (Wash.1993).

4. Federal Regulation of Water

A tradition of federal deference to states in the allocation and management of water would suggest restraint in the exercise of federal powers that conflict with state water rights. In fact, Congress has passed several environmental protection laws that often require, or give federal agencies the authority to require, water management practices that may conflict with state-created rights.

Conflicts with state water allocation and control occur when federal law effectively requires that water be used in a particular manner or amount. The effects may be felt when a water user attempts to put the water to use such as when a reservoir or other project is constructed. But there are instances where simply changing the quantity or timing of one's use may conflict with a federal environmental protection law.

One of the federal government's earliest ventures into the regulation of activities relating to water was in the Rivers and Harbors Act mentioned in *Appalachian Power*, pages 671, 677, supra. The Act, passed in 1899, restated some earlier laws, the purpose of which was to prevent obstructions to navigation. The Act today states that:

> The creation of any obstruction not affirmatively authorized by Congress, to the navigable capacity of any of the waters of the United States is prohibited; and it shall not be lawful to build [any structure in any port,] navigable river, or other water of the United States * * * except on plans [authorized by the Corps of Engineers]; and it shall not be lawful to excavate or fill, or in any manner to alter or modify the course, location, condition, or capacity of, any port * * * or of the channel of any navigable water of the United States, unless the work has been [authorized by the Corps of Engineers].

33 U.S.C.A. § 403. Under it the Corps has long required permits for bridges, dams, dikes, causeways, and obstructions in navigable waters. The Corps' permitting authority under § 10 of the Act for any activity or structure that would obstruct navigation, and § 9 of the Act which requires permission for "any bridge, dam, dike, or causeway over or in" navigable water of the United States was and is a powerful means of regulating water development and water related activities within states.

For many years the 1899 Act was narrowly applied by the Corps to protect the navigable capacity of waterways. The exercise of the Corps' authority was limited to situations in which a waterway met tests of navigability as set forth in The Daniel Ball, 77 U.S. (10 Wall.) 557 (1870), quoted at page 673, n. 21, supra. Harbor lines were designated and no obstructions were permitted seaward of the harbor line, but riparians could fill (but not dredge) almost as a matter of right landward of the line.

The Act was invigorated as a precursor of the substantial federal role in environmental protection. In 1968, the Corps promulgated regulations that allowed it to consider environmental factors in its permit decisions in response to growing criticisms that the former policy was destroying too many wetlands. The regulations were challenged when the Corps denied a permit to dredge and fill in Boca Ciega Bay, Florida after finding that fish and wildlife would be harmed, but that the project would not adversely affect navigation. The Corps' authority to deny dredge and fill permits "for factually substantial ecological reasons even though the project would not interfere with navigation, flood control, or the production of power" was upheld in Zabel v. Tabb, 430 F.2d 199 (5th Cir.1970), cert. denied 401 U.S. 910 (1971). It would be hard to read the 1899 Act as a delegation of this broad power, so the court chose to rest its decision primarily on the Fish and Wildlife Coordination Act, 16 U.S.C.A. §§ 661–666c, which mandated the Secretary "to weigh the effect a dredge and fill permit will have on conservation."

A provision of the Clean Water Act regulating dredge and fill operations more extensively than the 1899 Act later opened the door to direct conflicts between state water rights and federal regulatory "uses" of water. To protect waters from interference by dredge and fill operations, § 404 of the Act requires anyone who wants to put any fill material in waters of the United States to get a permit from the Army Corps of Engineers. Denial or conditioning of one's ability to fill wetlands can limit land uses, draining and filling of lands needed for agriculture, and construction, including construction of facilities needed to store or divert waters to which one is entitled under state water rights.

Although the Corps' regulatory activities under the Rivers and Harbors Act expanded beyond what was necessary to protect navigability, its authority under the Rivers and Harbors Act nevertheless is narrower than under § 404. The Corps' rules now define the "navigable waters of the United States" covered by the Rivers and Harbors Act as "those waters of the United States that are subject to the ebb and flow of the tides and/or are presently used, have been used in the past, or may be susceptible for use to transport interstate or foreign commerce." 33 C.F.R. § 323.2(b) (1986). Section 404 of the Clean Water Act, 33 U.S.C.A. § 1344, however, has a much more extensive application than the Rivers and Harbors Act. See Minnehaha Creek Watershed Dist. v. Hoffman, 597 F.2d 617 (8th Cir.1979) (a 25–acre lake with an outlet flowing into the Mississippi River is not navigable under the Rivers and Harbors Act of 1899, but a § 404 permit is required for the construction of a dam).

UNITED STATES v. RIVERSIDE BAYVIEW HOMES, INC.

Supreme Court of the United States, 1985.
474 U.S. 121, 106 S.Ct. 455, 88 L.Ed.2d 419.

JUSTICE WHITE delivered the opinion of the Court.

* * *

I

The relevant provisions of the Clean Water Act originated in the Federal Water Pollution Control Act Amendments of 1972, 86 Stat. 816, and have remained essentially unchanged since that time. Under §§ 301 and 502 of the Act, 33 U.S.C. §§ 1311 and 1362, any discharge of dredged or fill materials into "navigable waters"—defined as the "waters of the United States"—is forbidden unless authorized by a permit issued by the Corps of Engineers pursuant to § 404, 33 U.S.C. § 1344. After initially construing the Act to cover only waters navigable in fact, in 1975 the Corps issued interim final regulations redefining "the waters of the United States" to include not only actually navigable waters but also tributaries of such waters, interstate waters and their tributaries, and nonnavigable intrastate waters whose use or misuse could affect interstate commerce. * * * More importantly for present purposes, the Corps construed the Act to cover all "freshwater wetlands" that were adjacent to other covered waters. A "freshwater wetland" was defined as an area that is "periodically inundated" and is "normally characterized by the prevalence of vegetation that requires saturated soil conditions for growth and reproduction." In 1977, the Corps refined its definition of wetlands by eliminating the reference to periodic inundation and making other minor changes. The 1977 definition reads as follows:

> "The term 'wetlands' means those areas that are inundated or saturated by surface or ground water at a frequency and duration sufficient to support, and that under normal circumstances do support, a prevalence of vegetation typically adapted for life in saturated soil conditions. Wetlands generally include swamps, marshes, bogs and similar areas." 33 CFR § 323.2(c) (1978).

In 1982, the 1977 regulations were replaced by substantively identical regulations that remain in force today. See 33 CFR § 323.2 (1985).

Respondent Riverside Bayview Homes, Inc. (hereafter respondent), owns 80 acres of low-lying, marshy land near the shores of Lake St. Clair in Macomb County, Michigan. In 1976, respondent began to place fill materials on its property as part of its preparations for construction of a housing development. The Corps of Engineers, believing that the property was an "adjacent wetland" under the 1975 regulation defining "waters of the United States," filed suit in the United States District Court for the Eastern District of Michigan, seeking to enjoin respondent from filling the property without the permission of the Corps. * * * [T]he question whether the regulation at issue requires respondent to obtain a permit before filling its property is an easy one. * * * The plain language of the regulation refutes the Court of Appeals' conclusion that inundation or "frequent flooding" by the adjacent body of water is a *sine qua non* of a wetland under the regulation. Indeed, the regulation could hardly state more clearly that saturation by either surface or ground water is sufficient to bring an area within the category of wetlands, provided that the saturation is sufficient to and does support wetland vegetation.

* * *

Without the nonexistent requirement of frequent flooding, the regulatory definition of adjacent wetlands covers the property here. * * *

An agency's construction of a statute it is charged with enforcing is entitled to deference if it is reasonable and not in conflict with the expressed intent of Congress.   Chemical Manufacturers Assn. v. Natural Resources Defense Council, Inc., 470 U.S. 116, 125 (1985);   Chevron U.S.A. Inc. v. Natural Resources Defense Council, Inc., 467 U.S. 837, 842–845 (1984).   Accordingly, our review is limited to the question whether it is reasonable, in light of the language, policies, and legislative history of the Act for the Corps to exercise jurisdiction over wetlands adjacent to but not regularly flooded by rivers, streams, and other hydrographic features more conventionally identifiable as "waters."

* * * Section 404 originated as part of the Federal Water Pollution Control Act Amendments of 1972, which constituted a comprehensive legislative attempt "to restore and maintain the chemical, physical, and biological integrity of the Nation's waters."   CWA § 101, 33 U.S.C. § 1251.   This objective incorporated a broad, systemic view of the goal of maintaining and improving water quality: as the House Report on the legislation put it, "the word 'integrity' * * * refers to a condition in which the natural structure and function of ecosystems [are] maintained."   H.R.Rep. No. 92–911, p. 76 (1972).   Protection of aquatic ecosystems, Congress recognized, demanded broad federal authority to control pollution, for "[w]ater moves in hydrologic cycles and it is essential that discharge of pollutants be controlled at the source."   S.Rep. No. 92–414, p. 77 (1972).

In keeping with these views, Congress chose to define the waters covered by the Act broadly.   Although the Act prohibits discharges into "navigable waters," see CWA §§ 301(a), 404(a), 502(12), 33 U.S.C. §§ 1311(a), 1344(a), 1362(12), the Act's definition of "navigable waters" as "the waters of the United States" makes it clear that the term "navigable" as used in the Act is of limited import.   In adopting this definition of "navigable waters," Congress evidently intended to repudiate limits that had been placed on federal regulation by earlier water pollution control statutes and to exercise its powers under the Commerce Clause to regulate at least some waters that would not be deemed "navigable" under the classical understanding of that term.

Of course, it is one thing to recognize that Congress intended to allow regulation of waters that might not satisfy traditional tests of navigability;   it is another to assert that Congress intended to abandon traditional notions of "waters" and include in that term "wetlands" as well.   Nonetheless, the evident breadth of congressional concern for protection of water quality and aquatic ecosystems suggests that it is reasonable for the Corps to interpret the term "waters" to encompass wetlands adjacent to waters as more conventionally defined.   Following the lead of the Environmental Protection Agency, see 38 Fed.Reg. 10834 (1973), the Corps has determined that wetlands adjacent to navigable waters do as a general matter play a key role in protecting and enhancing water quality:

"The regulation of activities that cause water pollution cannot rely on * * * artificial lines * * * but must focus on all waters that together form the entire aquatic system. Water moves in hydrologic cycles, and the pollution of this part of the aquatic system, regardless of whether it is above or below an ordinary high water mark, or mean high tide line, will affect the water quality of the other waters within that aquatic system.

"For this reason, the landward limit of Federal jurisdiction under Section 404 must include any adjacent wetlands that form the border of or are in reasonable proximity to other waters of the United States, as these wetlands are part of this aquatic system." 42 Fed.Reg. 37128 (1977).

We cannot say that the Corps' conclusion that adjacent wetlands are inseparably bound up with the "waters" of the United States—based as it is on the Corps' and EPA's technical expertise—is unreasonable. In view of the breadth of federal regulatory authority contemplated by the Act itself and the inherent difficulties of defining precise bounds to regulable waters, the Corps' ecological judgment about the relationship between waters and their adjacent wetlands provides an adequate basis for a legal judgment that adjacent wetlands may be defined as waters under the Act.

* * * In short, the Corps has concluded that wetlands adjacent to lakes, rivers, streams, and other bodies of water may function as integral parts of the aquatic environment even when the moisture creating the wetlands does not find its source in the adjacent bodies of water. Again, we cannot say that the Corps' judgment on these matters is unreasonable, and we therefore conclude that a definition of "waters of the United States" encompassing all wetlands adjacent to other bodies of water over which the Corps has jurisdiction is a permissible interpretation of the Act. Because respondent's property is part of a wetland that actually abuts on a navigable waterway, respondent was required to have a permit in this case.

Following promulgation of the Corps' interim final regulations in 1975, the Corps' assertion of authority under § 404 over waters not actually navigable engendered some congressional opposition. The controversy came to a head during Congress' consideration of the Clean Water Act of 1977, a major piece of legislation aimed at achieving "interim improvements within the existing framework" of the Clean Water Act. H.R.Rep. No. 95–139, pp. 1–2 (1977). In the end, however, * * * Congress acquiesced in the administrative construction.

* * *

The significance of Congress' treatment of the Corps' § 404 jurisdiction in its consideration of the Clean Water Act of 1977 is twofold. First, the scope of the Corps' asserted jurisdiction over wetlands was specifically brought to Congress' attention, and Congress rejected measures designed to curb the Corps' jurisdiction in large part because of its concern that protection of wetlands would be unduly hampered by a narrowed definition of "navigable waters." * * *

Second, it is notable that even those who would have restricted the reach of the Corps' jurisdiction would have done so not by removing wetlands altogether from the definition of "waters of the United States," but only by restricting the scope of "navigable waters" under § 404 to waters navigable in fact *and their adjacent wetlands.* * * *

We are thus persuaded that the language, policies, and history of the Clean Water Act compel a finding that the Corps has acted reasonably in interpreting the Act to require permits for the discharge of fill material into wetlands adjacent to the "waters of the United States." The regulation in which the Corps has embodied this interpretation by its terms includes the wetlands on respondent's property within the class of waters that may not be filled without a permit; and, as we have seen, there is no reason to interpret the regulation more narrowly than its terms would indicate. Accordingly, the judgment of the Court of Appeals is

Reversed.

NOTES

1. The Corps' far-reaching regulation under § 404 is traceable to a change in policy that followed the decision in Natural Resources Defense Council v. Callaway, 392 F.Supp. 685 (D.D.C.1975). After the decision holding that Congress had exercised the power to the full extent of the Commerce Clause, the Corps adopted new regulations and policies to exert its jurisdiction.

In one surprising decision, later vacated on rehearing, the Seventh Circuit Court of Appeals held that the Clean Water Act does not give the EPA jurisdiction to regulate section 404 dredge and fill operations on some isolated intrastate wetlands for a housing development. Hoffman Homes, Inc. v. Administrator, Environmental Protection Agency, 961 F.2d 1310 (7th Cir.1992), vacated 975 F.2d 1554 (7th Cir.1992). The court said that for Congress to give EPA power to regulate wetlands under the Act, it would have to ground that power in the Commerce Clause, and that in order for EPA to regulate the dredge and fill operation it would have to show that the operation would affect interstate commerce. In response to EPA's argument that migrating birds might possibly use the area and thereby affect commerce, the court wrote, "The birds obviously do not engage in commerce. Until they are watched, photographed, shot at or otherwise impacted by people who do (or, we suppose, have the potential to) engage in interstate commerce, migratory birds do not ignite the Commerce Clause. The idea that the *potential* presence of migratory birds itself affects commerce is even more far-fetched." 961 F.2d at 1320.

The decision generated much controversy in the environmental community. A lawyer for the National Wildlife Federation called the legal reasoning "appalling," and one for the Natural Resources Defense Council said the case was "flat wrongly decided." In a rather unusual decision, the court vacated its opinion upon rehearing, and appointed its own senior staff attorney to mediate a settlement between the EPA (which had imposed a $50,000 administrative fine) and Hoffman Homes. 975 F.2d at 1554.

2. The § 404 program is controversial because it affects water resource development projects and land use decisions that have traditionally been subject only to local and state regulation. In United States v. Byrd, 609 F.2d 1204 (7th Cir.1979), a landfill in a small inland lake was held to require a § 404 permit. See also United States v. Robinson, 570 F.Supp. 1157 (M.D.Fla.1983). The extent of wetland areas subject to § 404 is explored in Avoyelles Sportsmen's League v. Marsh, 715 F.2d 897 (5th Cir.1983).

The activities covered under § 404 range from common "dredge and fill" operations to a variety of other activities that do not readily come to mind at the mention of that term. For instance, constructing a dam, drainage ditch, levee, or any type of structure within a wetland requires a permit. Further, clearing wetland vegetation and even mosquito control activity within a wetland are regulated. The Corps' power under § 404 can be a major constraint on the construction of water storage and diversion projects. Virtually every such project involves wetlands and is subject to a permit requirement. There are, however, exceptions that were enacted in 1977 in reaction to the revised regulations that followed Natural Resources Defense Council v. Callaway. The Act now exempts: "normal farming, silviculture, and ranching activities," maintenance of existing structures, maintenance of farm and stock ponds, irrigation ditches and drainage ditches, temporary sedimentation ponds on construction sites, maintenance of forest, farm or temporary mining roads, and activities regulated by statewide programs under § 208(b)(4) of the Clean Water Act to control sedimentation runoff through best management practices. The exemptions do not include "[a]ny discharge of dredged or fill materials into the navigable waters incidental to any activity having as its purpose bringing an area of the navigable waters into use to which it was not previously subject, where the flow or circulation of navigable waters may be impaired or the reach of such waters be reduced * * *." 33 U.S.C.A. § 1344(f)(2).

3. Once the Corps of Engineers has jurisdiction over an activity pursuant to the broad language of § 404, its decision to issue a permit incorporates a variety of considerations. The Corps makes a far-ranging public interest review. Under the Corps' regulations, it engages in a balancing process in which "[t]he benefits which reasonably may be expected to accrue from the proposal must be balanced against its reasonably foreseeable detriments." 33 C.F.R. § 320.4(a). The Corps is directed to consider

[a]ll factors which may be relevant to the proposal, including the cumulative effects thereof. Among those are conservation, economics, aesthetics, general environmental concerns, wetlands, cultural values, fish and wildlife values, flood hazards, floodplain values, land use, navigation, shore erosion and accretion, recreation, water supply and conservation, water quality, energy needs, safety, food and fiber production, mineral needs, considerations of property ownership, and, in general, the needs and welfare of the people.

Can the Corps properly consider such concerns, many of which are traditionally state concerns, private concerns, or specifically committed to private decision making by state law and policy? At what point has the Corps by regulation exceeded the purposes of a permit system for dredging and filling in navigable waters? Under the regulation is it not possible for the federal government acting through the Corps of Engineers to take complete control over all, or virtually all, of a state's water development policy and planning? Did Congress intend preemption this broad?

The denial of a Section 404 permit may constitute a taking if the denial virtually "wipes out" the value of the property. Florida Rock Industries, Inc. v. United States, 21 Cl.Ct. 161 (1990) (95% drop in value.) See page 432, supra. Jan G. Laitos, *Water Rights, Clean Water Act, Section 404 Permitting, And The Taking Clause,* 60 U.Colo.L.Rev. 901, 917 (1989) argues that water right holders will most likely not succeed with takings challenges "if the affected water right still has 'fair market value' after the permit denial or conditioning."

In weighing the public interest factors, the Corps has tempered their effect by deferring to state judgments on many of the public interest factors where there are no "overriding national factors of public interest * * *." 33 C.F.R. § 320.4(j)(4). Presumably the existence of a state wetlands protection program would be influential in the Corps' decision to defer to the state. Generally speaking, state programs to regulate wetlands are much more limited in their reach than the federal law under § 404. However, some of the programs are more specific and demanding in imposing regulatory requirements on activities in wetlands. See page 431, supra. States have a veto over a § 404 (or Rivers and Harbors Act § 10) permit. See 33 U.S.C.A. § 1341; 33 C.F.R. §§ 320.3(a), 325.2(b)(i). The veto is based largely on compliance with state water quality requirements but also extends to other substantive requirements.

4. A Corps decision to grant a § 404 permit may be reviewed and the activity prohibited by the Environmental Protection Agency (EPA). This was done in 1990 in the case of the Two Forks Dam in Colorado. In that case, the state had no program to review water development except in the context of water rights. Although millions of dollars were spent to review the impacts of the project in the process of preparing the Corps' environmental impact statement (under the National Environmental Policy Act), the EPA found that it would have "unacceptable and avoidable" environmental effects.

Bersani v. Robichaud, 850 F.2d 36 (2d Cir.1988), cert. denied 489 U.S. 1089 (1989), upheld an EPA permit veto where alternative sites were available for development of a proposed shopping center.

5. The Corps of Engineers consults with the U.S. Fish and Wildlife Service on all § 404 permit applications. The Endangered Species Act, 16 U.S.C.A. §§ 1531–1543 (ESA), places limits on all actions that may be taken by federal officials. The ESA authorizes the Secretary of the Interior to list endangered or threatened species and to designate critical habitats of these species. Once a species is listed, § 7 of the Act

imposes consultation duties between United States Fish and Wildlife Service and any federal agency planning to take an action that is likely to jeopardize the species.

Federal duties under the ESA may be triggered by the review of a proposal for federal action or for federal approval of private action pursuant to § 404 of the Clean Water Act. The consultation process may result in a biological opinion showing no jeopardy to threatened or endangered species and thus the project may proceed. If the opinion finds that the action is likely to jeopardize a protected species, the Fish and Wildlife Service must suggest "reasonable and prudent alternatives" to the proposed action. A reasonable and prudent alternative is one that would not violate the Act.

RIVERSIDE IRRIGATION DIST. v. ANDREWS

United States Court of Appeals, Tenth Circuit, 1985.
758 F.2d 508.

McKay, Circuit Judge.

* * *

Plaintiffs seek to build a dam and reservoir on Wildcat Creek, a tributary of the South Platte River. Because construction of the dam involves depositing dredge and fill material in a navigable waterway, the plaintiffs are required to obtain a permit from the Corps of Engineers under Section 404 of the Clean Water Act, 33 U.S.C. § 1344.
* * *

A nationwide permit is one covering a category of activities occurring throughout the country that involve discharges of dredge or fill material that will cause only minimal adverse effects on the environment when performed separately and that will have only minimal cumulative effects. Such a permit is automatic in that if one qualifies, no application is needed before beginning the discharge activity. The Corps has the authority and duty, however, to ensure that parties seeking to proceed under a nationwide permit meet the requirements for such action. One condition of a nationwide permit is that the discharge not destroy a threatened or endangered species as identified under the Endangered Species Act, or destroy or adversely modify the critical habitat of such species. 33 C.F.R. § 330.4(b)(2). The regulations thus are consistent with the Corps' obligation, under the Endangered Species Act, to ensure that "any action authorized, funded, or carried out by such agency * * * is not likely to jeopardize the continued existence of any endangered species or threatened species or result in the destruction or adverse modification of habitat of such species which is determined by the Secretary * * * to be critical." 16 U.S.C. § 1536(a)(2).

No one claims that the fill itself will endanger or destroy the habitat of an endangered species or adversely affect the aquatic environment. However, the fill that the Corps is authorizing is required to build the earthen dam. The dam will result in the impoundment of water in a reservoir, facilitating the use of the water in Wildcat Creek.

The increased consumptive use will allegedly deplete the stream flow, and it is this depletion that the Corps found would adversely affect the habitat of the whooping crane.

The Endangered Species Act does not, by its terms, enlarge the jurisdiction of the Corps of Engineers under the Clean Water Act. However, it imposes on agencies a mandatory obligation to consider the environmental impacts of the projects that they authorize or fund. As the Supreme Court stated in TVA v. Hill, 437 U.S. 153, 173 (1978):

> One would be hard pressed to find a statutory provision whose terms were any plainer than those of § 7 of the Endangered Species Act. Its very words affirmatively command all federal agencies "to *insure* that actions *authorized, funded or carried out* by them do not jeopardize the continued existence" of an endangered species or "result in the destruction or adverse modification of habitat of such species." 16 U.S.C. § 1536. This language admits of no exception.

(emphasis in original). The question in this case is how broadly the Corps is authorized to look under the Clean Water Act in determining the environmental impact of the discharge that it is authorizing.

Plaintiffs claim that the Corps is authorized to consider only the direct, on-site effects of the discharge, particularly the effects on water quality, and that the Corps exceeded its authority by considering downstream effects of changes in water quantity. However, both the statute and the regulations authorize the Corps to consider downstream effects of changes in water quantity as well as on-site changes in water quality in determining whether a proposed discharge qualifies for a nationwide permit. The statute explicitly requires that a permit be obtained for any discharge "incidental to any activity having as its purpose bringing an area of navigable waters into a use to which it was not previously subject, where the flow or circulation of navigable waters may be impaired or the reach of such waters reduced." 33 U.S.C. § 1344(f)(2). The guidelines for determining compliance with section 404(b)(1), developed by the Secretary of the Army and the Environmental Protection Agency, require the permitting authority to consider factors related to water quantity, including the effects of the discharge on water velocity, current patterns, water circulation, and normal water fluctuations. 40 C.F.R. §§ 230.23, 230.24. Thus, the statute focuses not merely on water quality, but rather on all of the effects on the "aquatic environment" caused by replacing water with fill material. 33 U.S.C. § 1344(f)(1)(E). Minnehaha Creek Watershed District v. Hoffman, 597 F.2d 617, 627 (8th Cir.1979).

Plaintiffs argue that, even if the Corps can consider effects of changes in water quantity, it can do so only when the change is a direct effect of the discharge. In the present case, the depletion of water is an indirect effect of the discharge, in that it results from the increased consumptive use of water facilitated by the discharge. However, the Corps is required, under both the Clean Water Act and the Endangered Species Act, to consider the environmental impact of the discharge that it is authorizing. To require it to ignore the indirect effects that result from its actions would be to require it to wear blinders that Congress has not chosen to impose. The fact that the reduction in water does not result "from direct federal action does not lessen the appellee's duty under § 7 [of the Endangered Species Act]." National Wildlife Federation v. Coleman, 529 F.2d 359, 374 (5th Cir.1976). The relevant consideration is the total impact of the discharge on the crane. In *National Wildlife Federation,* the Fifth Circuit held that the federal agency was required to consider both the direct and the indirect impacts of proposed highway construction, including the residential and commercial development that would develop around the highway interchanges. Similarly, in this case, the Corps was required to consider all effects, direct and indirect, of the discharge for which authorization was sought.

* * * The reduction of water flows resulting from the increased consumptive use *is* an effect, albeit indirect, of the discharge to be authorized by the Corps. The discharge thus may "destroy or adversely modify" the critical habitat of an endangered species, and the Corps correctly found that the proposed project did not meet the requirements for a nationwide permit.

Plaintiffs claim that the Corps cannot deny them a nationwide permit because the denial impairs the state's right to allocate water within its jurisdiction, in violation of section 101(g) of the Act (the "Wallop Amendment").[3] Even if denial of a nationwide permit is considered an impairment of the state's authority to allocate water, a question that we do not decide, the Corps acted within its authority. As discussed above, the statute and regulations expressly require the Corps to consider changes in water quantity in granting nationwide permits. Section 101(g), which is only a general policy statement, "cannot nullify a clear and specific grant of jurisdiction, even if the particular grant seems inconsistent with the broadly stated purpose." Connecticut Light and Power Co. v. Federal Power Commission, 324 U.S. 515 (1945). Thus, the Corps did not exceed its authority in denying a nationwide permit based on its determination that the depletion in water flow resulting from increased consumptive use of water would adversely affect the critical habitat of the whooping crane.

The Wallop Amendment does, however, indicate "that Congress did not want to interfere any more than necessary with state water management." National Wildlife Federation v. Gorsuch, 693 F.2d 156, 178 (D.C.Cir.1982). A fair reading of the statute as a whole makes clear that, where both the state's interest in allocating water and the federal government's interest in protecting the environment are implicated, Congress intended an accommodation. Such accommodations are best reached in the individual permit process.

3. The Wallop Amendment provides that:

It is the policy of Congress that the authority of each State to allocate water within its jurisdiction shall not be superseded, abrogated or otherwise impaired by this Act. It is the further policy of Congress that nothing in this Act shall be construed to supersede or abrogate rights to quantities of water which have been established by any State.

33 U.S.C. § 1251(g) (1982).

* * * Plaintiffs are entitled to proceed under a nationwide permit only if they can show that they meet the conditions for such a permit. Thus, plaintiffs must show "that the discharge *will not* destroy a threatened or endangered species as identified in the Endangered Species Act or destroy or adversely modify the critical habitat of such species." 33 C.F.R. § 330.4(b)(2). The record supports the Corps' finding that the discharge may adversely modify the critical habitat of the whooping crane. Thus, plaintiffs did not meet their burden of showing, as a matter of fact, that the discharge will not have such an adverse impact. The Corps acted within its authority in requiring the plaintiffs to proceed under the individual permit procedure.

Affirmed.

NOTES

1. Section 3 of the Endangered Species Act (ESA) mandates that the Department of Interior "conserve" endangered species. It has been held that this provision requires the Secretary to operate a federal reservoir so that species preservation is preferred to all other uses until the numbers and condition are restored to a satisfactory level. Carson–Truckee Water Conservancy Dist. v. Clark, 741 F.2d 257 (9th Cir.1984), cert. denied 470 U.S. 1083 (1985). Conflicts between the ESA and state water law are discussed in A. Dan Tarlock, *Western Water Rights and the [Endangered Species] Act*, in The Endangered Species Act and Lessons for the Future 167 (Kathryn A. Kohm ed. 1991); see also Mellissa K. Estes, *The Effect of the Federal Endangered Species Act on State Water Rights*, 22 Envtl.L. 1027 (1992).

Section 9 of the Act prohibits taking endangered species. "Taking" means to "harass, harm, pursue, hunt, shoot, wound, kill, trap, capture, or collect." Palila v. Hawaii Department of Land & Natural Resources, 649 F.Supp. 1070 (D.Haw.1986), affirmed 852 F.2d 1106 (9th Cir.1988). See Robert D. Thornton, *Searching for Consensus and Predictability: Habitat Conservation Planning under the Endangered Species Act of 1973*, 21 Envtl.L. 605, 608–14 (1991), for a discussion of the role of the courts in shaping the current definition of Section 9 "takings." The Department of Interior has tried to limit the definition of takings to habitat modification activities that actually kill or injure an individual species, but the courts have defined a taking to include habitat modifications such as irrigation intakes that put a species at risk. United States v. Glenn–Colusa Irrigation District, 788 F.Supp. 1126 (E.D.Cal. 1992) (district's withdrawals of water from Sacramento River were the proximate cause of death of listed winter run salmon); Department of Fish & Game v. Anderson–Cottonwood Irrigation District, 11 Cal. Rptr.2d 222 (Cal.Ct.App.1992) (California Endangered Species Act prohibits irrigation withdrawals without proper fish screens because taking not limited to hunting or fishing); and Sierra Club v. Lyng, 694 F.Supp. 1260 (E.D.Tex.1988) (destruction of Red-cockaded woodpecker habitat by clear cutting national forest).

2. The Fish and Wildlife Service has in some instances allowed water developments that would jeopardize an endangered species if the

developer agreed to pay depletion charges that are dedicated to conservation and recovery measures. See Lawrence J. MacDonnell, *The Endangered Species Act and Water Development Within the South Platte Basin* 32–38 (Colorado Water Resources Research Institute, Research Report No. 137, 1985). Do you think that payment of money can satisfy the requirement that the Secretary take no action that is "likely to jeopardize the continued existence of any endangered or threatened species or result in the destruction or adverse modification of [critical] habitat"? Is the payment of money a "reasonable and prudent alternative"?

In the early 1980s, water development on the Colorado River in much of Colorado, Utah and Wyoming appeared to be stalled by the Secretary's proposal that ambitious minimum flows be maintained to avoid jeopardy to endangered fish species (squawfish, humpback chub, bonytail chub). In 1987, after three years of negotiations, representatives of the Fish and Wildlife Service, the three states, the Bureau of Reclamation, water developers and environmentalists recommended a multi-faceted recovery plan for the fish that they had developed by consensus based on considerable technical advice. The plan includes measures such as acquisition of instream flows within the state water rights system, releases from federal reservoirs, creation of better habitat, curtailing of planting of exotic (non-native) fish such as bass, construction of passage facilities, artificial propagation, and creation of a fund to support continued recovery efforts from federal and state contributions and one-time payments from new water projects. A committee representing the state and federal agencies is to oversee the plan's implementation. A similar effort is being made to deal with the whooping crane habitat issue described in the *Riverside* case. The advantage of such approaches is that they ensure compliance with federal law by means that minimize intrusions on state water law systems.

3. The federal Clean Water Act, 33 U.S.C.A. §§ 1251–1376, discussed at pages 132–36, supra, created a national water pollution control program that dictates limits on how water can be used within the states. The Act prohibits discharges of pollutants from point sources into the waters of the United States without a National Pollutant Discharge Elimination System (NPDES) permit, the terms and conditions of which are set by federal standards. The Wallop Amendment, § 101(3), discussed in the principal case at page 738 n. 3, supra, disclaims congressional intent to interfere with the state's authority to allocate water or to abrogate state-created rights to quantities of water. There is, nevertheless, a potential for conflict. Suppose that diversion of water results in less dilution of pollutants so that water quality standards under the Act will be violated. It is also possible that sewage treatment methods required to comply with the NPDES permit conditions will result in greater consumption of water by municipal users.

One state court has ruled that water rights may be regulated as necessary to achieve federal (and state) water quality standards. The court upheld requirements that direct diversions of water be reduced or that releases be made from storage in order to maintain sufficient flows to maintain water quality by preventing salt water "intrusion" into the Sacramento–San Joaquin Delta. United States v. State Water Resources Control Board, 227 Cal.Rptr. 161 (Cal.Ct.App.1986). The decision, however, was made by a state court in the context of a state water law system that required water quality considerations in water allocation. It is interesting that the decision arose out of the state board's amendment of water use permits held by the United States Bureau of Reclamation and the State Department of Water Resources.

Neither the federal Environmental Protection Agency nor the federal courts have viewed the Clean Water Act's pollution discharge permitting process as a way to expand federal control over state management of water resources. The United States Court of Appeals for the District of Columbia has ruled that discharges from a nonfederal dam that may change the chemical and temperature composition of a stream are, nevertheless, not discharges of pollutants. Thus, the court declined to order the EPA to issue NPDES permits for such discharges. National Wildlife Federation v. Gorsuch, 693 F.2d 156 (D.C.Cir.1982). The court found that, while the discharges might qualify as pollutants under the Act's definition, regulation would be contrary to Congress's intent not "to interfere any more than necessary with state water management, of which dams are an important component." Where federal activities are involved or where federal statutes are more directive, however, the potential interference with state water allocation and control is great.

The extent of federal power under the Act is illustrated by Quivira Mining Co. v. United States Environmental Protection Agency, 765 F.2d 126 (10th Cir.1985), which holds that a uranium mine must obtain a discharge permit under the CWA's National Pollutant Discharge Elimination System (NPDES) for a pond that might overflow into two arroyos that ultimately connect to navigable waters, but that flowed only during period of heavy rainfall and were part of an "underground [where else?] aquifer." There would seem to be no constitutional barriers to the extension of federal regulatory jurisdiction to all watercourses and related land areas, but there are statutory limits to federal jurisdiction. The Clean Water Act has been construed to exclude aquifers unconnected to surface streams from United States Environmental Protection Agency (EPA) and state permit jurisdiction. Exxon Corp. v. Train, 554 F.2d 1310 (5th Cir.1977). There is contrary authority and the EPA's decision to follow *Exxon* has been much criticized. See J. Stephen Dycus, *Development of a National Groundwater Protection Policy,* 11 B.C.Envtl.Aff.L.Rev. 211, 238–48 (1984), and Adam B. Jaffe & James T.B. Tripp, *Preventing Groundwater Pollution: Towards a Coordinated Strategy to Protect Critical Recharge Zones,* 3 Harv.Envtl. L.Rev. 1 (1979).

A. DAN TARLOCK, THE ENDANGERED SPECIES ACT AND WESTERN WATER RIGHTS
20 Land & Water L.Rev. 1, 12, 17, 26, 29, 30 (1985).

The Endangered Species Act effectively creates de facto regulatory water rights. That is, the federal government now has a new basis to claim that specific but undetermined amounts of water either be released from a reservoir or not be impounded. * * *

The existence of regulatory rights under the Endangered Species Act and section 404 of the Clean Water Act raises the following issue: whether private expectations that the ground-rules under which state water rights are acquired will not be changed are equally as strong when the federal government exercises its constitutional power retroactively to regulate in the public interest. A tentative answer is no. What seems to be emerging out of recent water adjudications is that state-created water rights are not different from any other property rights despite the vast energy dissipated by western water lawyers to will a contrary result. Thus, state water rights are not immune from the retroactive application of state police power or of federal constitutional authority.

* * *

The characterization of permit conditions as "regulatory property rights" is a conceptual analysis: neither Congress nor the courts have adopted it. As permit conditions are imposed, however, the issue of how these "regulatory property rights" should be applied will arise.

The solution which best serves the needs of the federal government and the states is to assign water rights to the project operator. The result is that except in extraordinary cases, the project operator, as a water rights holder, should be subject to state procedural law. The project operator's water rights would also appear in the state record system, notifying subsequent appropriators of the federal government's claims.

State substantive doctrines may operate to frustrate federal water rights claimed under the Endangered Species Act. When conflicts between state law and federal objectives arise, however, state law should be presumptively preempted. * * *

Unlike section 404 of the Clean Water Act, the Endangered Species Act should impose a duty on new and existing federal or private project operators to supply sufficient water to protect the endangered species. Senior water rights holders should not have to suffer uncompensated reallocation, but project beneficiaries and other rights holders may expect to see water allocation patterns that differ from those provided under state law.

* * *

The integration into western water law of the values represented by the Endangered Species Act and section 404 of the Clean Water Act will not be easy. The first step is to recognize that it is legitimate for the federal government to claim water rights under these acts. These Acts represent a federal decision to add to the list of "beneficial" uses served by our water resources. The issue is not whether such rights can be claimed, but under what circumstances and in what manner they can be asserted.

* * *

Courts could start the process of accommodating federal and state interests by adopting a rule requiring the federal government to determine that non-flow release protection strategies are unlikely to preserve the species as compared to flow release strategies. This inquiry will reinforce the federal government's duty to seek mitigation strategies that include active management programs.

* * *

The federal government should be entitled to the minimum amount of water deemed necessary to prevent the species' habitat from a further risk of deterioration. This determination must be based on the best available evidence. Judicial ground rules for species protection should provide sufficient incentives for all interested parties to strike some creative bargains rather than requiring parties to resort to the courts to solve future protection claims.

NATIONAL WILDLIFE FEDERATION v. FEDERAL ENERGY REGULATORY COMMISSION

United States Court of Appeals, Ninth Circuit, 1986.
801 F.2d 1505.

JAMES R. BROWNING, CHIEF JUDGE:

I

The Director of the Office of Electric Power Regulation of the Federal Energy Regulatory Commission ("Commission") issued seven preliminary permits to develop license applications for hydroelectric power projects along the Salmon River, flowing in a 420 mile-long arc through central Idaho. The Nez Perce Tribe ("Tribe"), and the National Wildlife Federation and Idaho Wildlife Federation (jointly referred to as "the Federation"), appealed to the Commission. * * *

The question presented is whether the Commission's decisions not to develop a comprehensive plan, not to require permittees to study cumulative impacts, not to impose uniform study guidelines on permittees, and not to collect baseline environmental data, were arbitrary, capricious, not in accordance with law, or unsupported by the record.

Congress' commitment to coordinated study and comprehensive planning along an entire river system before hydroelectric projects are authorized is a central feature of the Federal Power Act. * * *

The Federal Power Act requires that a comprehensive plan for river basin development be available before licensing.[6]

* * *

If the needed information can be collected by permittees in the absence of a comprehensive plan, it may not be necessary to develop such a plan before preliminary permits are issued. If, on the other

---

6. 16 U.S.C. § 803 states in relevant part: "All *licenses* issued under this subchapter shall be on the following conditions: (a) That the project adopted * * * shall be such as in the judgment of the Commission will be best adapted to a comprehensive plan. * * *" (Emphasis added.)

hand, the necessary information cannot be obtained unless a comprehensive plan is first developed, the Commission would abuse its discretion if it issued a preliminary permit without first developing a comprehensive plan. * * *

In short, the issue before the Commission was whether the ecological system in the Salmon River Basin was so complex and the proposed power projects so numerous that the Commission should have taken any of the following steps requested by petitioners before issuing the preliminary permits: (1) prepared a comprehensive plan; (2) required permittees to conduct studies to provide data by which cumulative impacts of proposed projects could be assessed; (3) collected baseline environmental data and furnished it to permittees; (4) included uniform study criteria and guidelines in the permit articles. * * *

Anticipating the large number of permit applications for hydroelectric development in what all concede is an ecologically sensitive area, the Federation sought to intervene in some of the early applications for permits and requested the Commission to prepare a comprehensive plan for the Salmon River Basin, to require permittees to conduct studies designed to produce information from which the Commission could assess the likely cumulative impacts of proposed hydropower development, to require uniform study guidelines as a condition of the permit articles, and to collect baseline environmental data.

* * *

The Federation, the Tribe, developers, state and federal agencies, and other interested parties participated in the hearings and presented extensive evidence. The Commission also received written comments. The United States National Marine Fisheries Service submitted a draft comprehensive development plan.

All of the evidence received at the hearings supported the need for development of a comprehensive plan before issuing preliminary permits, and for requiring permittees to study cumulative impacts. * * *

No evidence was received suggesting comprehensive planning should be deferred or cumulative impacts need not be studied.

Despite these extensive hearings on the question of whether to develop a comprehensive plan, require studies of cumulative impacts, impose uniform study guidelines, and collect baseline environmental data, the Commission did not address those issues at all. Instead the Director of the Commission's Office of Electric Power Regulations simply began issuing standard permits, including the seven challenged here.

In rejecting petitioners' appeal from the Director's action, the Commission gave three reasons for denying petitioners' requests: (1) its usual experience had been that standard permits issued before development of a comprehensive plan were satisfactory; (2) permittees might be put to unnecessary expense and effort if required to conduct cumulative impact studies; and (3) cumulative studies undertaken at the permit stage might be useless if many projects were abandoned before licensing.

The Commission's decision is not supported by any evidence in the record, let alone "substantial evidence," as required by 16 U.S.C. § 825l(b). We are unable to determine on the present record whether the Commission's decision is "arbitrary, capricious, an abuse of discretion, or otherwise not in accordance with law." 5 U.S.C. § 706(2)(A) (1982).

* * *

The situation is not unlike that before the Supreme Court in Udall v. FPC, 387 U.S. 428 (1967). In *Udall,* the Federal Power Commission granted a license to build hydroelectric power projects without conducting "an exploration of all issues relevant to the 'public interest,' " id. at 450. Without deciding whether or not the license should have been granted, the Court vacated the Commission's decision, and remanded to the Commission with instructions to provide "an exploration of these neglected phases of the cases, as well as the other points raised by the Secretary." Id.

We do not hold the Commission must develop a comprehensive plan before issuing permits, must require permittees to collect data useful for studying cumulative impacts, must develop uniform study guidelines, or must collect baseline environmental data. We do hold the Commission's decision to reject these options is not sustainable on the present record.

* * *

The statute requires the Commission to measure proposed projects against a comprehensive plan. If the Commission had first prepared a comprehensive plan for hydropower development in the Salmon River Basin, establishing the optimal number, type, size and location of hydropower projects in the basin, cumulative impacts could be studied on the assumption that all projects detailed in the comprehensive plan eventually would be brought on line. Alternatively, permittees could have been required to conduct cumulative impact studies and prepare reports based on several development assumptions.

* * *

III

The Federation contends the Commission breached the Northwest Power Act. The Northwest Power Act was adopted to "protect, mitigate and enhance the fish and wildlife, including related spawning grounds and habitat, of the Columbia River and its tributaries," 16 U.S.C. § 839(6), and to aid the development of hydroelectric power in the Columbia River Basin. Id. at § 839(1). The Federation argues the Commission violated the statute by ignoring the Fish and Wildlife Program promulgated by the Northwest Power Planning Council,[19] and

---

19. The Council is an interstate compact organization created by the Northwest Power Act, 16 U.S.C. § 839b, and is charged with developing a conservation and energy plan for the Pacific Northwest, see 16 U.S.C. § 839b(d)(1), and a fish and wildlife conservation program for the Columbia River and its tributaries. See id. at § 839b(h)(1)(A).

by denying fish and wildlife "equitable treatment," as required by the Act.

* * *

[T]he Commission failed to consider the Council's Program at all—a clear violation of the Northwest Power Act's express requirement that the Council's Program be "tak[en] into account at each relevant stage." 16 U.S.C. § 839b(h)(11)(A)(ii).

* * *

The Commission also maintains it is not required to consider the Council's Program because the Northwest Power Act imposes no new substantive requirements on federal agencies. But the Act specifically requires the Commission to take the Council's program into account "to the fullest degree practicable," 16 U.S.C. § 839b(h)(11)(A)(ii), and we have already rejected the argument that the Act does not impose new substantive requirements on the Commission and other federal agencies. Confederated Tribes & Bands of the Yakima Indian Nation v. FERC, 746 F.2d 466, 473 (9th Cir.1984) (as amended).

* * *

IV

* * *

We do not reach petitioners' NEPA claims. If the Commission adopts petitioners' position and requires permit studies geared to a comprehensive plan, the NEPA claim will become moot. If, on the other hand, the Commission rejects petitioners' claim with a statement of reasons based upon the record, and also takes the Council's Program into account to the fullest extent practicable, the Commission's decision may constitute a satisfactory Environmental Assessment, even assuming the decision to defer comprehensive planning is governed by NEPA.

NOTES

1. The Federal Power Act specifically requires the Commission to consider effects on fish and wildlife. The decision in the principal case relied on Udall v. Federal Power Commission, 387 U.S. 428 (1967). In *Udall* the Supreme Court found a requirement to consider the effects of a project on anadromous fish implicit in the provision of the Act that says that the Commission must find that licensed projects are "best adapted to a comprehensive plan for navigation, water power, and for other beneficial public uses, including recreational purposes." The authority of the Commission to impose conditions on FERC licenses to protect fish and wildlife gives it the ability to impose minimum flow requirements contrary to state law as shown in California v. FERC, 495 U.S. 490 (1990), page 723, supra. Further, the Fish and Wildlife Coordination Act, 16 U.S.C.A. §§ 661–666c, requires that federal agencies give "equal consideration" to wildlife conservation when undertaking or authorizing water development projects. The latter Act is basically toothless, but it can be used to require mitigation measures as

a condition of a project permit. Requirements of environmental considerations in FERC licensing were strengthened in the Electric Consumers Protection Act of 1986, Pub.L. No. 99–495, § 3, 100 Stat. 1243, 16 U.S.C.A. §§ 797(e), 803(a), which amended the Federal Power Act to require that:

> in deciding whether to issue any license * * * the Commission, in addition to the power and development purposes for which licenses are issued, shall give equal consideration to the purposes of energy conservation, the protection, mitigation of damage to, and enhancement of, fish and wildlife (including related spawning grounds and habitat), the protection of recreational opportunities, and the preservation of other aspects of environmental quality.

Furthermore, § 10(a) of the Act was amended to specify that comprehensive planning incorporate such environmental considerations and that the state and Indian tribal recommendations for conditions be included in licenses. Conditions requiring mitigation of effects to fish and wildlife also must be included in licenses. Prior to the new Act, it was held in The Steamboaters v. FERC, 759 F.2d 1382 (9th Cir.1985), that FERC was not required to impose conditions proposed by the National Marine Fisheries Service of the Department of Commerce. The Commission now must adopt the recommendations of state and federal fish and wildlife agencies unless it publishes findings that to follow those recommendations would be inconsistent with the purposes of the Act.

How should the Commission implement the vague mandate to give "equal consideration" to environmental factors? Can the Commission insulate itself from attack on the ground that it did not follow the requirement of "equal consideration"?

2. The National Environmental Policy Act (NEPA), 42 U.S.C.A. §§ 4331–4344, requires federal agencies to prepare an environmental impact statement concerning the environmental effects of any proposed projects that constitute "major Federal actions significantly affecting the quality of the human environment." The principal case indicates that data developed under the comprehensive planning mandate of § 10(a) may satisfy the EIS requirement.

Initially, courts heard a number of challenges to inadequate environmental impact statements, but these challenges are harder to make today. NEPA's duties are procedural not substantive, and agencies have learned how to prepare an adequate EIS. The Act can also be applied to the operation of on-going projects. For example, in 1989, the Secretary of the Interior agreed to prepare an EIS for the operation of Glen Canyon Dam on the Colorado River. The EIS process provides a vehicle for the agency and other interested parties to examine ways to mitigate the tension between historic operating patterns and those that accommodate new values such as environmental protection and recreation enhancement.

3. FERC cannot license any facility on or directly affecting a component of the Wild and Scenic Rivers system. Swanson Mining Corp. v. FERC, 790 F.2d 96 (D.C.Cir.1986), holds that § 7 of the Wild

and Scenic Rivers Act, 16 U.S.C.A. § 1278, meant what it said when it prohibited development on designated rivers that would interfere with their free-flowing condition. An applicant wanted to develop a project near the bank of the South Fork of the Trinity River in California, a state-administered component of the system, that used water from a tributary of the river. It argued that the project would not impair the values of the river that led to its inclusion in the system, but the court refused to allow FERC to exempt itself from the Wild and Scenic River Act on a case-by-case basis.

4. Suppose FERC imposes conditions on a license that require the maintenance of certain minimum instream flows below a proposed facility for a certain stretch of the river. If the state does not allow private entities like the licensee to hold instream flow rights (or does not recognize such rights as a beneficial use), how can the flows be assured? Could an appropriator take water just below the facility and thereby defeat the minimum flow condition? Can the state agency issue permits for others to use water attributable to the flows? Or has FERC, by its minimum flow condition, made an allocation of water rights below the dam?

5. On the Northwest Power Planning Act see Michael C. Blumm, *NEPA Meets the Northwest Power Act (and prevails)*, 25 Nat. Resources J. 1005 (1985); *The Northwest's Hydroelectric Heritage: Prologue to the Pacific Northwest's Energy Planning and Conservation Act*, 58 Wash. L.Rev. 175 (1983); Roger D. Mellem, *Darkness to Dawn? Generating and Conserving Electricity in the Pacific Northwest: A Primer on the Northwest Power Planning and Conservation Act*, 58 Wash.L.Rev. 245 (1983); Henry M. Jackson, *The Pacific Northwest Electric Power Planning and Conservation Act—Solution for a Regional Dilemma*, 4 U. Puget Sound L.Rev. 7 (1980).

B.   FEDERAL LIMITS ON STATE EXPORT RESTRICTIONS

Interstate disputes may arise when interests in one state attempt to export water to another state. States have tried various means to prevent exports. The United States Supreme Court has ruled that states ordinarily may not prevent exports of water from within their boundaries for purely economic or political reasons. Unless the restriction on export is found to be for the health or welfare of state citizens, it will be deemed an impermissible interference with interstate commerce. At what point are state interests in controlling exports sufficiently substantial for export restrictions to be constitutional?

SPORHASE v. NEBRASKA ex rel. DOUGLAS

United States Supreme Court, 1982.
458 U.S. 941, 102 S.Ct. 3456, 73 L.Ed.2d 1254.

JUSTICE STEVENS delivered the opinion of the Court.

Appellants challenge the constitutionality of a Nebraska statutory restriction on the withdrawal of ground water from any well within Nebraska intended for use in an adjoining State. The challenge presents three questions under the Commerce Clause: (1) whether ground water is an article of commerce and therefore subject to Congressional regulation; (2) whether the Nebraska restriction on the interstate transfer of ground water imposes an impermissible burden on commerce; and (3) whether Congress has granted the States permission to engage in ground water regulation that otherwise would be impermissible.

Appellants jointly own contiguous tracts of land in Chase County, Nebraska, and Phillips County, Colorado. A well physically located on the Nebraska tract pumps ground water for irrigation of both the Nebraska tract and the Colorado tract. Previous owners of the land registered the well with the State of Nebraska in 1971, but neither they nor the present owners applied for the permit required by § 46–613.01 of the Nebraska Revised Statutes. That section provides:

> "Any person, firm, city, village, municipal corporation or any other entity intending to withdraw ground water from any well or pit located in the State of Nebraska and transport it for use in an adjoining state shall apply to the Department of Water Resources for a permit to do so. If the Director of Water Resources finds that the withdrawal of the ground water requested is reasonable, is not contrary to the conservation and use of ground water, and is not otherwise detrimental to the public welfare, he shall grant the permit if the state in which the water is to be used grants reciprocal rights to withdraw and transport ground water from that state for use in the State of Nebraska."

Appellee brought this action to enjoin appellants from transferring the water across the border without a permit. * * *

I

In holding that ground water is not an article of commerce, the Nebraska Supreme Court and appellee cite as controlling precedent Hudson County Water Co. v. McCarter, 209 U.S. 349 (1908). In that case a New Jersey statute prohibited the interstate transfer of any surface water located within the State. The Hudson County Water Company nevertheless contracted with New York City to supply one of its boroughs with water from the Passaic River in New Jersey. The state attorney general sought from the New Jersey courts an injunction against fulfillment of the contract. Over the water company's objections that the statute impaired the obligation of contract, took property without just compensation, interfered with interstate commerce, denied New York citizens the privileges afforded New Jersey citizens, and denied New York citizens the equal protection of the laws, the injunction was granted. This Court, in an opinion by Justice Holmes, affirmed.

Most of the Court's opinion addresses the just compensation claim. Justice Holmes refused to ground the Court's holding, as did the New Jersey state courts, on "the more or less attenuated residuum of title that the State may be said to possess." Id., at 355. For the statute was justified as a regulatory measure that, on balance, did not amount to a taking of property that required just compensation. Putting aside the "problems of irrigation," the State's interest in preserving its waters was well within its police power. That interest was not dependent on any demonstration that the State's water resources were inadequate for present or future use. The State "finds itself in possession of what all admit to be a great public good, and what it has it may keep and give no one a reason for its will." Id., at 357.

Having disposed of the just compensation claim, Justice Holmes turned very briefly to the other constitutional challenges. In one paragraph, he rejected the Contract Clause claim. In the remaining paragraph of the opinion, he rejected all the other defenses. His treatment of the Commerce Clause challenge consists of three sentences: "A man cannot acquire a right to property by his desire to use it in commerce among the States. Neither can he enlarge his otherwise limited and qualified right to the same end. The case is covered in this respect by Geer v. Connecticut, 161 U.S. 519 [(1896)]." 209 U.S., at 357.

While appellee relies upon Hudscn County, appellants rest on our summary affirmance of a three-judge District Court judgment in City of Altus v. Carr, 255 F.Supp. 828 (WD Tex.), summarily aff'd, 385 U.S. 35 (1966). The city of Altus is located near the southern border of Oklahoma. Large population increases rendered inadequate its source of municipal water. It consequently obtained from the owners of land in an adjoining Texas county the contractual right to pump the ground water underlying that land and to transport it across the border. The Texas Legislature thereafter enacted a statute that forbade the interstate exportation of ground water without the approval of that body.[7] The city filed suit in Federal District Court, claiming that the statute violated the Commerce Clause.

The city relied upon West v. Kansas Natural Gas Co., 221 U.S. 229 (1911), which invalidated an Oklahoma statute that prevented the interstate transfer of natural gas produced within the State,[8] and Pennsylvania v. West Virginia, 262 U.S. 553 (1923), which invalidated a West Virginia statute that accorded a preference to the citizens of that State in the purchase of natural gas produced therein. The Texas Attorney General defended the statute on two grounds. First, he asserted that its purpose was to conserve and protect the State's water resources by regulating the withdrawal of ground water. The District Court rejected that defense because similar conservation claims had met defeat in West v. Kansas Natural Gas Co., supra, and Pennsylvania v. West Virginia, supra. Second, the State argued that the statute regulated ground water and that ground water is not an article of commerce, citing Geer v. Connecticut, 161 U.S. 519 (1896), and Hudson County Water Co. v. McCarter, 209 U.S. 349 (1908). The court rejected this argument since the statute directly regulated the interstate trans-

---

7. The District Court quoted the statute: " 'No one shall withdraw water from any underground source in this State for use in any other state by drilling a well in Texas and transporting the water outside the boundaries of the State unless the same be specifically authorized by an Act of the Texas Legislature and thereafter as approved by it.' " 255 F.Supp., at 830.

8. Justice Holmes, the author of the Court's opinion in Hudson County, noted his dissent.

portation of water that had been pumped from the ground, and under Texas law such water was an article of commerce. The court then had little difficulty in concluding that the statute imposed an impermissible burden on interstate commerce.[11]

In summarily affirming the district court in *City of Altus*, we did not necessarily adopt the court's reasoning. Our affirmance indicates only our agreement with the result reached by the district court. That result is not necessarily inconsistent with the Nebraska Supreme Court's holding in this case. For Texas law differs significantly from Nebraska law regarding the rights of a surface owner to ground water that he has withdrawn. According to the district court in *City of Altus*, the "rule in Texas was that an owner of land could use all of the percolating water he could capture from the wells on his land for whatever beneficial purposes he needed it, on or off the land, and could likewise sell it to others for use on or off the land and outside the basin where produced, just as he could sell any other species of property." Since ground water, once withdrawn, may be freely bought and sold in States that follow this rule, in those States ground water is appropriately regarded as an article of commerce. In Nebraska the surface owner has no comparable interest in ground water. As explained by the Nebraska Supreme Court, " 'the owner of land is entitled to appropriate subterranean waters found under his land, but he cannot extract and appropriate them in excess of a reasonable and beneficial use upon the land which he owns, especially if such use is injurious to others who have substantial rights to the waters, and if the natural underground supply is insufficient for all owners, each is entitled to a reasonable proportion of the whole.' " 305 N.W.2d at 617 (quoting Olson v. City of Wahoo, 248 N.W. 304, 308 (Neb.1933)).

City of Altus, however, is inconsistent with *Hudson County*. For in the latter case the Court found *Geer v. Connecticut*, supra, to be controlling on the Commerce Clause issue. *Geer*, which sustained a Connecticut ban on the interstate transportation of game birds captured in that State, was premised on the theory that the State owned its wild animals and therefore was free to qualify any ownership interest it might recognize in the persons who capture them. One such restriction is a prohibition against interstate transfer of the captured animals. This theory of public ownership was advanced as a defense in *City of Altus*. The State argued that it owned all subterranean water and therefore could recognize ownership in the surface owner who withdraws the water, but restrict that ownership to use of the water

---

11. "Considering the statute in question only with regard to whether it regulates the transportation and use of water after it has been withdrawn from a well and becomes personal property, such statute constitutes an unreasonable burden upon and interference with interstate commerce. Moreover, on the facts of this case it appear[s] to us that [the Texas statute] does not have for its purpose, nor does it operate to conserve water resources of the State of Texas except in the sense that it does so for her own benefit to the detri- ment of her sister States as in the case of West v. Kansas Natural Gas Co. In the name of conservation, the statute seeks to prohibit interstate shipments of water while indulging in the substantial discrimination of permitting the unrestricted intrastate production and transportation of water between points within the State, no matter how distant; for example, from Wilbarger County to El Paso County, Texas. Obviously, the statute had little relation to the cause of conservation." 255 F.Supp., at 839–840.

within the State. That theory, upon which the Commerce Clause issue in *Hudson County* was decided, was rejected by the district court in *City of Altus*. In expressly overruling *Geer* three years ago, this Court traced the demise of the public ownership theory and definitively recast it as " 'but a fiction expressive in legal shorthand of the importance to its people that a State have power to preserve and regulate the exploitation of an important resource.' " Hughes v. Oklahoma, 441 U.S. 322, 334 (1979) (quoting Toomer v. Witsell, 334 U.S. 385, 402 (1948)). In *Hughes* the Court found the State's interests insufficient to sustain a ban on the interstate transfer of natural minnows seined from waters within the State.

* * * Appellee, and the *amici curiae* that are vitally interested in conserving and preserving scarce water resources in the arid Western States, have convincingly demonstrated the desirability of state and local management of ground water. But the States' interests clearly have an interstate dimension. Although water is indeed essential for human survival, studies indicate that over 80% of our water supplies is used for agricultural purposes. The agricultural markets supplied by irrigated farms are worldwide. They provide the archetypical example of commerce among the several States for which the Framers of our Constitution intended to authorize federal regulation. The multistate character of the Ogallala aquifer—underlying appellants' tracts of land in Colorado and Nebraska, as well as parts of Texas, New Mexico, Oklahoma, and Kansas—confirms the view that there is a significant federal interest in conservation as well as in fair allocation of this diminishing resource. Cf. Arizona v. California, 373 U.S. 546 (1963).

The Western States' interests, and their asserted superior competence, in conserving and preserving scarce water resources are not irrelevant in the Commerce Clause inquiry. Nor is appellee's claim to public ownership without significance. Like Congress' deference to state water law, these factors inform the determination whether the burdens on commerce imposed by state ground water regulation are reasonable or unreasonable. But appellee's claim that Nebraska ground water is not an article of commerce goes too far: it would not only exempt Nebraska ground water regulation from burden-on-commerce analysis, it also would curtail the affirmative power of Congress to implement its own policies concerning such regulation. If Congress chooses to legislate in this area under its commerce power, its regulation need not be more limited in Nebraska than in Texas and States with similar property laws. Ground water overdraft is a national problem and Congress has the power to deal with it on that scale.

II

Our conclusion that water is an article of commerce raises, but does not answer, the question whether the Nebraska statute is unconstitutional. For the existence of unexercised federal regulatory power does not foreclose state regulation of its water resources, of the uses of water within the State, or indeed, of interstate commerce in water. Determining the validity of state statutes affecting interstate commerce requires a more careful inquiry:

"Where the statute regulates evenhandedly to effectuate a legitimate local public interest, and its effects on interstate commerce are only incidental, it will be upheld unless the burden imposed on such commerce is clearly excessive in relation to the putative local benefits. If a legitimate local purpose is found, then the question becomes one of degree. And the extent of the burden that will be tolerated will of course depend on the nature of the local interest involved, and on whether it could be promoted as well with a lesser impact on interstate activities." Pike v. Bruce Church, Inc., 397 U.S. 137, 142 (1970) (citation omitted).

The only purpose that appellee advances for § 46–613.01 is to conserve and preserve diminishing sources of ground water. The purpose is unquestionably legitimate and highly important, and the other aspects of Nebraska's ground water regulation demonstrate that it is genuine. Appellants' land in Nebraska is located within the boundaries of the Upper Republican Ground Water Control Area, which was designated as such by the Director of the Nebraska Department of Water Resources based upon a determination "that there is an inadequate ground water supply to meet present or reasonably foreseeable needs for beneficial use of such water supply." Neb.Rev.Stat. § 46–658(1). Pursuant to § 46–666(1), the Upper Republican Natural Resources District has promulgated special rules and regulations governing ground water withdrawal and use.

* * *

The State's interest in conservation and preservation of ground water is advanced by the first three conditions in § 46–613.01 for the withdrawal of water for an interstate transfer. Those requirements are "that the withdrawal of the ground water requested is reasonable, is not contrary to the conservation and use of ground water, and is not otherwise detrimental to the public welfare." Although Commerce Clause concerns are implicated by the fact that § 46–613.01 applies to interstate transfers but not to intrastate transfers, there are legitimate reasons for the special treatment accorded requests to transport ground water across state lines. Obviously, a State that imposes severe withdrawal and use restrictions on its own citizens is not discriminating against interstate commerce when it seeks to prevent the uncontrolled transfer of water out of the State. An exemption for interstate transfers would be inconsistent with the ideal of evenhandedness in regulation. At least in the area in which appellants' Nebraska tract is located, the first three standards of § 46–613.01 may well be no more strict in application than the limitations upon intrastate transfers imposed by the Upper Republican Natural Resources District.

Moreover, in the absence of a contrary view expressed by Congress, we are reluctant to condemn as unreasonable measures taken by a State to conserve and preserve for its own citizens this vital resource in times of severe shortage. Our reluctance stems from the "confluence of [several] realities." Hicklin v. Orbeck, 437 U.S. 518, 534 (1978). First, a State's power to regulate the use of water in times and places of shortage for the purpose of protecting the health of its citizens—and not simply the health of its economy—is at the core of its police power. For Commerce Clause purposes, we have long recognized a difference between economic protectionism, on the one hand, and health and safety regulation, on the other. Second, the legal expectation that under certain circumstances each State may restrict water within its borders has been fostered over the years not only by our equitable apportionment decrees, 353 U.S. 953 (1957), but also by the negotiation and enforcement of interstate compacts. Our law therefore has recognized the relevance of state boundaries in the allocation of scarce water resources. Third, although appellee's claim to public ownership of Nebraska ground water cannot justify a total denial of federal regulatory power, it may support a limited preference for its own citizens in the utilization of the resource. In this regard, it is relevant that appellee's claim is logically more substantial than claims to public ownership of other natural resources. Finally, given appellee's conservation efforts, the continuing availability of ground water in Nebraska is not simply happenstance; the natural resource has some indicia of a good publicly produced and owned in which a State may favor its own citizens in times of shortage. See Reeves, Inc. v. Stake, 447 U.S. 429 (1980). A facial examination of the first three conditions set forth in § 46–613.01 does not, therefore, indicate that they impermissibly burden interstate commerce. Appellants, indeed, seem to concede their reasonableness.

Appellants, however, do challenge the requirement that "the state in which the water is to be used grants reciprocal rights to withdraw and transport ground water from that state for use in the State of Nebraska"—the reciprocity provision that troubled the Chief Justice of the Nebraska Supreme Court. Because Colorado forbids the exportation of its ground water,[17] the reciprocity provision operates as an explicit barrier to commerce between the two States. The State therefore bears the initial burden of demonstrating a close fit between the reciprocity requirement and its asserted local purpose.

The reciprocity requirement fails to clear this initial hurdle. For there is no evidence that this restriction is narrowly tailored to the conservation and preservation rationale. Even though the supply of water in a particular well may be abundant, or perhaps even excessive, and even though the most beneficial use of that water might be in another State, such water may not be shipped into a neighboring State that does not permit its water to be used in Nebraska. If it could be shown that the State as a whole suffers a water shortage, that the intrastate transportation of water from areas of abundance to areas of shortage is feasible regardless of distance, and that the importation of water from adjoining States would roughly compensate for any exporta-

17. Colo.Rev.Stat. § 37–90–136 provides as follows:

"For the purpose of aiding and preserving unto the state of Colorado and all its citizens the use of all ground waters of this state, whether tributary or nontributary to a natural stream, which waters are necessary for the health and prosperity of all the citizens of the state of Colorado, and for the growth, maintenance, and general welfare of the state, it is unlawful for any person to divert, carry, or transport by ditches, canals, pipelines, conduits, or any other manner any of the ground waters of this state, as said waters are in this section defined, into any other state for use therein."

tion to those States, then the conservation and preservation purpose might be credibly advanced for the reciprocity provision. A demonstrably arid state conceivably might be able to marshall evidence to establish a close means-end relationship between even a total ban on the exportation of water and a purpose to conserve and preserve water. Appellee, however, does not claim that such evidence exists. We therefore are not persuaded that the reciprocity requirement—when superimposed on the first three restrictions in the statute—significantly advances the State's legitimate conservation and preservation interest; it surely is not narrowly tailored to serve that purpose. The reciprocity requirement does not survive the "strictest scrutiny" reserved for facially discriminatory legislation.

III

Appellee's suggestion that Congress has authorized the States to impose otherwise impermissible burdens on interstate commerce in ground water is not well-founded. The suggestion is based on 37 statutes in which Congress has deferred to state water law, and on a number of interstate compacts dealing with water that have been approved by Congress.

* * * Neither the fact that Congress has chosen not to create a federal water law to govern water rights involved in federal projects, nor the fact that Congress has been willing to let the States settle their differences over water rights through mutual agreement, constitutes persuasive evidence that Congress consented to the unilateral imposition of unreasonable burdens on commerce. In the instances in which we have found such consent, Congress' " 'intent and policy' to sustain state legislation from attack under the Commerce Clause" was " 'expressly stated.' "

* * *

JUSTICE REHNQUIST, with whom JUSTICE O'CONNOR joins, dissenting.

* * *

In my view, [the] cases appropriately recognize the traditional authority of a State over resources within its boundaries which are essential not only to the well-being, but often to the very lives of its citizens. In the exercise of this authority, a State may so regulate a natural resource so as to preclude that resource from attaining the status of an "article of commerce" for the purposes of the negative impact of the Commerce Clause. It is difficult, if not impossible, to conclude that "commerce" exists in an item that cannot be reduced to possession under state law and in which the State recognizes only a usufructuary right. "Commerce" cannot exist in a natural resource that cannot be sold, rented, traded, or transferred, but only *used*.

* * *

NOTES

1. How would you advise a state that was intent on prohibiting exports to go about drafting legislation that will pass constitutional muster? What changes in state law may be necessary?

2. *New Mexico's Attempts to Prevent Exports to Texas.* Justice Stevens' opinion offers states some hope that interstate transfer restrictions and perhaps even prohibitions will be found constitutional. New Mexico immediately tried to exploit this "window of opportunity" in its efforts to stave off a "water raid" by El Paso, Texas. El Paso obtains most of its water supplies from an interstate aquifer, the Hueco Bolson, underlying New Mexico and Texas. El Paso estimated that by 2010 the aquifer would become too salty for a primary water supply, and after considering various alternatives decided to augment its supplies from two aquifers that support agricultural uses in adjacent New Mexico. The city filed under New Mexico law to appropriate water in two designated underground basins in the southwestern part of the state. That law, since repealed, prohibited the transfer of water out of the state, and the state engineer denied the applications. N.M.Stat.Ann. § 72–12–19 (repealed 1983) was challenged by El Paso as unconstitutional. New Mexico attempted to defend by showing that it was a "demonstrably arid state" where water needed for human survival was that water needed to prevent a long-term, statewide shortage for all users. Evidence was produced to show that the state as a whole would have a 626,000 acre-foot shortage by 2020, but the district court would not buy this reading of *Sporhase:* "Outside of fulfilling human survival needs, water is an economic resource." El Paso v. Reynolds, 563 F.Supp. 379 (D.N.M.1983).

New Mexico then repealed its flat export prohibition and enacted the following statute:

APPLICATIONS FOR THE TRANSPORTATION AND USE OF PUBLIC WATERS OUTSIDE THE STATE.

A. The state of New Mexico has long recognized the importance of the conservation of its public waters and the necessity to maintain adequate water supplies for the state's water requirements. The state of New Mexico also recognizes that under appropriate conditions the out-of-state transportation and use of its public waters is not in conflict with the public welfare of its citizens or the conservation of its waters.

B. Any person, firm or corporation or any other entity intending to withdraw water from any surface or underground water source in the state of New Mexico and transport it for use outside the state * * * shall apply to the state engineer for a permit to do so. * * *

C. In order to approve an application under this act, the state engineer must find that the applicant's withdrawal and transportation of water for use outside the state would not impair existing water rights, is not contrary to the conservation of water within the state and is not otherwise detrimental to the public welfare of the citizens of New Mexico.

D.　In acting upon an application under this act, the state engineer shall consider, but not be limited to, the following factors:

(1) the supply of water available to the state of New Mexico;

(2) water demands of the state of New Mexico;

(3) whether there are water shortages within the state of New Mexico;

(4) whether the water that is the subject of the application could feasibly be transported to alleviate water shortages in the state of New Mexico;

(5) the supply and sources of water available to the applicant in the state where the applicant intends to use the water;　and

(6) the demands placed on the applicant's supply in the state where the applicant intends to use the water.

* * *

F.　The state engineer is empowered to condition the permit to insure that the use of water in another state is subject to the same regulations and restrictions that may be imposed upon water use in the state of New Mexico.

* * *

N.M.Stat.Ann. § 72–12B–1

The statute was challenged by El Paso. El Paso v. Reynolds, 597 F.Supp. 694 (D.N.M.1984) (*El Paso II*), rejected two of the city's arguments that the statute discriminated against interstate commerce but accepted the third. El Paso first argued that the "conservation within the state" standard prohibited all transfers because, by definition, exported water cannot be conserved or kept within the state. The court reasoned that "water within the state" did not mean that all water must be retained in-state. It further found that because the state had a tradition of public interest review, "it cannot be concluded that the conservation and public welfare criteria are on their face meaningless as applied to in-state uses." 597 F.Supp. at 699. El Paso next argued that the "public welfare of the citizens of New Mexico" standard was intrinsically discriminatory and precluded even-handed regulation of water use. The court's rejection of this argument was quite different from its conclusion in *El Paso I:*

A state may favor its own citizens in times and places of shortage. *Sporhase,* 458 U.S. at 956–957. Of course, this does not mean that a state may limit or bar exports simply because it anticipates that one day there will not be enough water to meet all future uses. Even some of the most water-abundant states predict shortages at some future date. The preference envisioned by the Supreme Court must be limited to the times and places where its exercise would not place unreasonable burdens on interstate commerce relative to the local benefits it produces.

* * *

New Mexico need not wait until the appropriate time and place of shortage arises to enact a statute limiting exports. The State may enact a law to provide for future contingencies. If facially valid, any constitutional attack on such a statute for violation of the Commerce Clause must await its application.

597 F.Supp. at 701.

The possibility of a congressional or compact solution to the El Paso–New Mexico conflict is discussed in Wyatt L. Brooks & Valerie M. Fogleman, Note, *New Mexico Continues to Study Water Embargo Measures: A Reply to the State Water Law Study Committee*, 16 Tex.Tech. L.Rev. 939 (1985).

In 1986, a statewide study recommended that New Mexico take a new approach to controlling exports. It concluded that the state should enter the intrastate and interstate water markets directly as a market participant by engaging in large-scale state appropriations of unappropriated groundwater. Water Resources Research Institute and University of New Mexico Law School, State Appropriation of Unappropriated Groundwater: A Strategy for Insuring New Mexico a Water Future (1986).

After ten years of litigation, El Paso settled the case by withdrawing its claims to New Mexico groundwater. In exchange, El Paso received the cooperation of New Mexico to conduct regional water studies to be coordinated through a joint commission with members from El Paso and New Mexico. In 1992, the commission approved a study of the feasibility of conveyance, treatment, and distribution of Rio Grande Project surface water for the southern New Mexico and El Paso area. Until recently, El Paso (like other western cities) considered such water—historically dedicated to agriculture—to be off-limits for conversion to urban uses. But throughout the West the historical urban-agricultural alliance favoring development of new supplies is splintering. El Paso is now required to develop a regional strategy to augment its water use by utilizing Texas-based water resources. The strategy will: (1) increase the capacity of its well field along the Rio Grande; (2) implement water conservation programs; (3) increase access to additional Bureau of Reclamation Rio Grande Project surface water; and (4) clarify water rights through adjudication of the Rio Grande from the New Mexico line to the Fort Quitman gauging station. See A. Dan Tarlock & Darcy Alan Frownfelter, *State Groundwater Sovereignty After Sporhase: The Case of the Hueco Bolson*, 43 Okla.L.Rev. 27 (1990).

3. The power of a state to prevent interstate transfers of water arose in connection with proposals during the 1970s to transport Rocky Mountain coal to other areas of the country through coal slurry pipelines. Slurry is composed of roughly equal parts of pulverized coal and water. A slurry pipeline is an efficient means of transporting coal, but western states feared that the water requirements for several

projected pipelines could hamper agricultural production. Environmentalists suggested that the pumping necessary to supply the pipelines' demands could damage groundwater reserves in the Northern Great Plains. See Nancy T. Reed, Comment, *An Analysis of Technical and Legal Issues Raised By the Development of Coal Slurry Pipelines*, 13 Houston L.Rev. 528 (1976). At least two states have responded to these concerns by restricting the use of appropriated water outside the state. Wyo.Stat. § 41–3–115(B) (Cum.Supp.1986) prohibits the use of water in amounts greater than 1000 acre-feet per year for coal slurry pipelines outside the state "without the specific prior approval of the legislature." The tension between state and federal interests in waters available for slurry pipelines is discussed in Clyde O. Martz & Stanley L. Grazis, *Interstate Transfers of Water and Water Rights—The Slurry Issue*, 23 Rocky Mtn.Min.L.Inst. 33 (1977).

4. Although the dormant Commerce Clause limits state efforts to restrict interstate water marketing, congressional legislation may govern such transactions and permit them, even when they are undertaken by a state. In 1982, the state of South Dakota granted a permit to the ETSI Pipeline Company for consumptive use of 50,000 acre-feet of water per year from the 23 million acre-foot Oahe Reservoir located on the mainstream of the Missouri River in South Dakota. ETSI intended to use the water to transport coal by slurry pipeline from Wyoming to the Gulf Coast. ETSI also obtained a water service contract from the Bureau of Reclamation and a pumping permit from the Army Corps of Engineers. The proposal first met a state court challenge. Then the downstream states of Iowa, Missouri, and Nebraska brought a lawsuit in federal district court in Nebraska to block the diversion from Lake Oahe. The issue, then, was whether Congress intended Oahe Reservoir to be a reclamation facility subject to the water marketing authority of the Secretary. The Supreme Court found that the Secretary of Interior lacked authority under the 1944 Flood Control Act to make a contract allowing the state to use (and sell) water for industrial purposes, and thus held the contract void. ETSI v. Missouri, 484 U.S. 495, (1988).

ETSI is the first significant case interpreting the Flood Control Act of 1944, 33 U.S.C.A. §§ 701–709 (Pick–Sloan Act), under which the development of the upper basin of the Missouri River was undertaken. Five new dams, with large reservoir capacity, were authorized by the legislation for multiple purposes, including aid of navigation downstream, flood control downstream and reclamation in the upstream states of North and South Dakota, Montana and Wyoming. The Pick–Sloan Act combined two rival proposals of the Bureau of Reclamation and U.S. Army Corps of Engineers. See generally, Henry C. Hart, The Dark Missouri (1957). As such it represented a compromise between upstream and downstream interests, between federal and state control over the waters within their boundaries, and finally between the Corps of Engineers, whose primary functions are flood control and navigation and the Bureau of Reclamation, whose primary purpose is aiding irrigation. See generally, John P. Guhin, *The Law of the Missouri*, 30 S.D.L.Rev. 347 (1985).

A question not reached in *ETSI* is whether a state can immunize itself from dormant or negative commerce clause review by claiming unappropriated water as the state's and selling it.   The basis of the immunity would be the market participation doctrine.   Recall Justice Stevens' citation of Reeves, Inc. v. Stake, 447 U.S. 429 (1980), in *Sporhase.*   The state of South Dakota, which had owned a cement plant since 1919, responded to the excess demand for cement created by a regional construction boom by giving in-state purchasers preference over out-of-state purchasers.   A Wyoming ready-mix distributor, who had purchased cement for twenty years before being denied service in 1978, challenged the preference as unconstitutional.   A five to four majority held that the decision to prefer in-state residents in the sale of state-produced goods did not violate the commerce clause because the state was acting in a proprietary capacity and "[t]here is no indication of a constitutional plan to limit the abilities of the states themselves to operate freely in a free market."   The Supreme Court continues to adhere to the market participation doctrine.   White v. Massachusetts Council of Constr. Employees, Inc., 460 U.S. 204 (1983).

C. RIGHTS RESERVED FOR INDIAN AND PUBLIC LANDS

In the nineteenth century, the national policy was to use and distribute the public lands—virtually all the lands west of the Mississippi River—to encourage settlement and development of the nation. Lands were made available under the mining and homesteading laws. Other laws provided for the distribution of public lands to states for the benefit of education and for other purposes.   See Gates, History of Public Land Law Development (1968).

Individuals taking up mining claims or homesteads could establish water rights under the emerging common law doctrine of prior appropriation.   The doctrine was the product of a consensus that recognized certain realities of the West.   If an arid region with waterways that were few and far between was to be developed, there could be no prohibition on moving water to lands separated from the streams. Security for otherwise precarious investments was provided by recognizing the best right to water in the person who was first to appropriate it and put it to a beneficial use.   First customs, then judicial decisions, and finally statutes of the western states recognized the prior appropriation doctrine.   A series of federal enactments in 1866, 1870, and 1877 recognized the validity of state and local laws and customs in allocating water on and across the public lands.

In Chapter Three, pages 157–59, supra, we traced the triumph of the idea that the pioneers should not be treated as trespassers on the public domain but rather as the beneficiaries of federal grants that had ripened into fees.   When a member of the California Supreme Court, Stephen Field adopted the trespass theory; but "when a member of the supreme court of the United States, gives up his former stand, and, now that the war is over, becomes a strong supporter of the theory of the pioneers regarding the obligations of the Federal Government." 1 Samuel A. Wiel, Water Rights in the Western States 109 (3d ed. 1911). Field construed the Act of 1866 and subsequent acts to validate existing uses based on local custom. The leading opinion is Jennison v. Kirk, 98 U.S. (8 Otto) 453 (1878) which Wiel described as "merely a condensation of the Congressional Globe report of Senator Stewart's (the Nevada sponsor of the Act of 1866) speech in the Senate * * * " Another westerner, Justice Sutherland, went farther and held that the Desert Land Act, 43 U.S.C.A. §§ 321–339 (as amended), resulted in a severance of water from the public lands, leaving unappropriated waters of non-navigable sources open to appropriation for use by the citizens of the territories or states. California–Oregon Power Co. v. Beaver Portland Cement Co., 295 U.S. 142 (1935), page 167, supra.

For many years, the trend of judicial decisions, as well as political philosophy, was to defer to state law in the use of waters on the public lands. This was consistent with the then-reigning public land policy of disposal. Little attention was given to the question of what water rights attached to the federal lands and to the Indian lands that were not to be transferred to settlers. If the public lands were to be distributed eventually, this was not a great concern. Further, the dominant Indian policy in the period was one of assimilation. Until at least the 1830s, it was widely assumed that Indians would become extinct as a separate people through the forces of civilization. For a lucid exposition of the relationship between Indian policy and nineteenth century thought, see Brian W. Dippie, The Vanishing American (1982). The Indian land base was being diminished and former Indian lands opened up for settlement. Indians confined to increasingly smaller reservations were expected eventually to learn the ways of a civilized society and to meld with the larger society. Part of the civilizing plan for Indians was the development of skills in agriculture. If these purposes were to succeed, and if reservations in many parts of the arid West were to be habitable, even as temporary homes, water would be needed. Further, by the late nineteenth century, it was apparent that some federal lands would be needed for federal purposes and would have to be retained from disposal. In some cases these federal purposes would demand water.

It was necessary to reconcile an early deference to state water law with the need for water to fulfill national purposes on Indian reservations and federal public lands that were kept or set aside for particular purposes. In United States v. Rio Grande Dam & Irrigation Co., 174 U.S. 690 (1899), the Supreme Court said that the states' power to create water rights in streams within their borders was subject to two limitations:

> First, that in the absence of specific authority from Congress a State cannot by its legislation destroy the right of the United States, as the owner of the lands bordering on a stream, to the continued flow of its waters; so far at least as may be necessary for the beneficial uses of the government property.

Id. at 703. The second limitation was the federal power to protect the navigable capacity of streams. Few people then perceived the great potential for conflict between the use of water pursuant to the prior appropriation doctrine and the future needs for water on Indian lands or on the public lands that were reserved for a particular government purpose.

The government was vigorously pursuing a policy of dividing Indian tribal land holdings among individual Indians. On these allotments, which are similar to homesteads, Indians were to learn to farm and become self-sufficient. The policy of allotting the Indians' collectively-held tribal lands in severalty was consistent with the American ideal of the yeoman farmer. It became apparent early, however, that many of the lands distributed to Indians under the allotment policy were unsuitable for agriculture without irrigation. This was discovered earlier with respect to many of the western homestead lands taken up by non-Indians who organized themselves to press for federal assistance with irrigation projects. The heavy involvement of the United States government in western water development, beginning in the 1880s, created the prospect of comprehensive water distribution schemes that could monopolize the waters of many streams.

Funding and political support for Indian irrigation projects lagged far behind non-Indian projects. The proponents and the beneficiaries of projects developed under the Reclamation Act, pages 681–89, supra, were mostly non-Indians. Although the Reclamation Service itself recognized in its early reports the potential for neglect and loss of Indian lands for lack of water, little attention was given to the subject; and virtually no mention was made of the need for water on federal lands. The collision course of the reclamation program and of American Indian policy should have been evident. The National Water Commission found:

> With the encouragement, or at least the cooperation, of the Secretary of Interior—the very office entrusted with protection of all Indian rights—many large irrigation projects were constructed on streams that flowed through or bordered Indian Reservations, sometimes above and more often below the Reservations. With few exceptions the projects were planned and built by the Federal Government without any attempt to define, let alone protect, prior rights that Indian tribes might have had in the waters used for the projects * * *. In the history of the United States Government's treatment of Indian tribes, its failure to protect Indian water rights for use on the Reservations it set aside for them is one of the sorrier chapters.

U.S. National Water Commission, Water Policies for the Future—Final Report to the President and to the Congress of the United States 474–75 (1973).

The possibility of conflict between Indian and non-Indian uses crystallized in Winters v. United States, 207 U.S. 564 (1908), page 764, infra, in which the Supreme Court held that when the United States sets aside an Indian reservation, it impliedly reserves sufficient water to fulfill the purposes of the reservation. The Court further held that the priority date of Indian reserved rights does not depend on when the rights are put to a beneficial use, but on when the reservation was established. Since most Indian reservations were created at an early date by federal treaties, agreements, statutes or executive orders, the *Winters* doctrine placed rights of indeterminate quantities higher on the ladder of priorities than the established appropriations of non-Indian settlers in the vicinity who depended on the same water sources.

The federal government's commitment to retaining and using federal lands for specific purposes such as parks, wildlife refuges, and forests, increased the possibilities for conflict with state-created water rights. Although the earliest conflict to reach the Supreme Court, and the one leading to the creation of the doctrine of reserved rights, was in the context of an Indian reservation, the same principles ultimately were to apply to reserved public lands. It was half a century later, however, before doubts about the applicability of the reserved rights doctrine to federal lands, as opposed to Indian lands, were laid to rest in Arizona v. California, 373 U.S. 546 (1963), page 769, infra. In fact, there have been only a few actual conflicts between the use of water rights on federal public lands and the use of state-created water rights.

The most difficult and persistent questions concerning rights recognized by the courts for Indian lands and federal reservations have been how to quantify those rights and how to integrate them with state water rights. Because of the McCarran Amendment, a federal statute consenting to state jurisdiction and waiving sovereign immunity, adjudication of federal rights is ordinarily in state courts. Quantification suits are proceeding in nearly all of the western states in an attempt to determine the magnitude of reserved rights that exist and to make the necessary accommodations so that there will be maximum certainty for water users.

1. Nature and Extent of Reserved Rights

In 1874, a vast area had been set aside in Northern Montana for the Great Blackfeet Indian Reservation. In 1888, the reservation was broken up into smaller parcels, one of which became the Fort Belknap Reservation. The breakup of the reservation allowed other lands to be opened for settlement by non-Indians. In the early 1890s non-Indians who had moved into the area began establishing communities and diverting water out of the Milk River. The federal government, through the Bureau of Indian Affairs, had established a Fort Belknap Indian Irrigation project which drew waters from the Milk River. Thus, Indians on the Fort Belknap Reservation, located on the south side of the Milk River, also began using the waters of the Milk River for irrigation. The competition for water made it difficult for both Indians and non-Indians to thrive, so the settlers moved their diversions upstream, leaving the Indians without a sufficient supply.

The Bureau of Indian Affairs then called upon the Department of Justice for assistance in protecting the Indians' rights. The United States Attorney in Montana sought an injunction against the non-Indian water users. He realized that he could not use the prior appropriation doctrine as the basis for the injunction because the non-Indians produced evidence that they had begun appropriating the water under Montana law four days before the Indian irrigation project, which had attempted to establish rights under Montana law as well. See Daniel McCool, Command of the Waters: Iron Triangles, Federal Water Development, and Indian Water 38 (1987).

Thus, the U.S. Attorney's theory was based on other grounds. In part, he argued that the reservation had riparian rights. He also asserted that the Milk River, as part of the Fort Belknap Reservation, was never a source of public water and that to deprive the reservation of water would violate treaties between the Indians and the government. In making the latter argument he asserted the supremacy of federal law, arguing that state legislation cannot destroy the federal government's ability to carry out federal purposes, a principle that was recognized in United States v. Rio Grande Dam & Irrig. Co., supra. The U.S. Attorney's strategy was not endorsed by Washington, D.C. Indeed, at the same time the U.S. Attorney in Montana was asserting the riparian doctrine, the United States Department of Justice was arguing in Kansas v. Colorado, 206 U.S. 46 (1907), page 833, infra, that riparian rights were not the law in western states, and instead, that the United States government had sanctioned and approved the prior appropriation doctrine there. See Norris Hundley, *The Winters Decision and Indian Water Rights: A Mystery Reexamined,* 13 W.Hist.Q. 17 (1982).

The injunction sought by the United States Attorney was granted, not based on riparian rights but on the treaty claim. The case was affirmed in the Ninth Circuit Court of Appeals and by the Supreme Court. Interestingly, the opinion was written by Justice Field's successor, Justice McKenna, a self-educated California lawyer.

WINTERS v. UNITED STATES

Supreme Court of the United States, 1908.
207 U.S. 564, 28 S.Ct. 207, 52 L.Ed. 340.

This suit was brought by the United States to restrain appellants and others from constructing or maintaining dams or reservoirs on the Milk River in the State of Montana, or in any manner preventing the water of the river or its tributaries from flowing to the Fort Belknap Indian Reservation.

* * *

The allegations of the bill, so far as necessary to state them, are as follows: On the first day of May, 1888, a tract of land, the property of the United States, was reserved and set apart "as an Indian reservation as and for a permanent home and abiding place of the Gros Ventre and Assiniboine bands or tribes of Indians in the State (then Territory) of Montana, designated and known as the Fort Belknap Indian Reservation." The tract has ever since been used as an Indian Reservation and as the home and abiding place of the Indians. * * *

Milk River, designated as the northern boundary of the reservation, is a non-navigable stream. Large portions of the lands embraced within the reservation are well fitted and adapted for pasturage and the feeding and grazing of stock, and since the establishment of the reservation the United States and the Indians have had and have large herds of cattle and large numbers of horses grazing upon the land within the reservation, "being and situate along and bordering upon said Milk River." Other portions of the reservation are "adapted for and susceptible of farming and cultivation and the pursuit of agriculture, and productive in the raising thereon of grass, grain and vegetables," but such portions are of dry and arid character, and in order to make them productive require large quantities of water for the purpose of irrigating them. * * * It is alleged with detail that all of the waters of the river are necessary for all those purposes and the purposes for which the reservation was created, and that in furthering and advancing the civilization and improvement of the Indians, and to encourage habits of industry and thrift among them, it is essential and necessary that all of the waters of the river flow down the channel uninterruptedly and undiminished in quantity and undeteriorated in quality.

It is alleged that "notwithstanding the riparian and other rights" of the United States and the Indians to the uninterrupted flow of the waters of the river the defendants, in the year 1900, wrongfully entered upon the river and its tributaries above the points of the diversion of the waters of the river by the United States and the Indians, built large and substantial dams and reservoirs, and by means of canals and ditches and waterways have diverted the waters of the river from its channel, and have deprived the United States and the Indians of the use thereof. And this diversion of the water, it is alleged, has continued until the present time, to the irreparable injury of the United States, for which there is no adequate remedy at law.

The allegations of the answer, so far as material to the present controversy, are as follows: * * *

That the individual defendants and the stockholders of the Matheson Ditch Company and Cook's Irrigation Company were qualified to become settlers upon the public land and to acquire title thereto under the homestead and desert land laws of the United States. And that said corporations were recognized and exist under the laws of Montana for the purpose of supplying to their said stockholders the water of Milk River and its tributaries, to be used by them in the irrigation of their lands.

* * *

That for the purpose of reclaiming the lands, and acting under the laws of the United States and the laws of Montana, the defendants, respectively, posted upon the river and its tributaries, at the points of intended diversion, notices of appropriation, stating the means of diversion and place of use, and thereafter filed in the office of the clerk and recorder of the county wherein the lands were situated a copy of the notices, duly verified, and within forty days thereafter commenced the construction of ditches and other instrumentalities, and completed them with diligence and diverted, appropriated, and applied to a beneficial use more than 5,000 miners' inches of the waters of the river and its tributaries, or 120 cubic feet per second, irrigating their lands and producing hay, grain and other crops thereon. * * *

MR. JUSTICE MCKENNA, after making the foregoing statement, delivered the opinion of the court.

* * *

The case, as we view it, turns on the agreement of May, 1888, resulting in the creation of Fort Belknap Reservation. In the construction of this agreement there are certain elements to be considered that are prominent and significant. The reservation was a part of a very much larger tract which the Indians had the right to occupy and use, and which was adequate for the habits and wants of a nomadic and uncivilized people. It was the policy of the Government, it was the desire of the Indians, to change those habits and to become a pastoral and civilized people. If they should become such the original tract was too extensive, but a smaller tract would be inadequate without a change of conditions. The lands were arid and, without irrigation, were practically valueless. And yet, it is contended, the means of irrigation were deliberately given up by the Indians and deliberately accepted by the Government. The lands ceded were, it is true, also arid; and some argument may be urged, and is urged, that with their cession there was the cession of the waters, without which they would be valueless, and "civilized communities could not be established thereon." And this, it is further contended, the Indians knew, and yet made no reservation of the waters. We realize that there is a conflict of implications, but that which makes for the retention of the waters is of greater force than that which makes for their cession. The Indians had command of the lands and the waters—command of all their beneficial use, whether kept for hunting, "and grazing roving herds of stock," or turned to agriculture and the arts of civilization. Did they give up all this? Did they reduce the area of their occupation and give up the waters which made it valuable or adequate? And, even regarding the allegation of the answer as true, that there are springs and streams on the reservation flowing about 2,900 inches of water, the inquiries are pertinent. If it were possible to believe affirmative answers, we might also believe that the Indians were awed by the power of the Government or deceived by its negotiators. Neither view is possible. The Government is asserting the right of the Indians. But extremes need not be taken into account. By a rule of interpretation of agreements and treaties with the Indians, ambiguities occurring will be resolved from the standpoint of the Indians. And the rule should certainly be applied to determine between two inferences, one of which would support the purpose of the agreement and the other impair or defeat it. On account of their relations to the Government, it cannot be supposed that the Indians were alert to exclude by formal words every inference which might militate against or defeat the declared purpose of themselves and the Government, even if it could be supposed that they had the intelligence to foresee the "double sense" which might some time be urged against them.

Another contention of appellants is that if it be conceded that there was a reservation of the waters of Milk River by the agreement of 1888, yet the reservation was repealed by the admission of Montana into the Union, February 22, 1889, c. 180, 25 Stat. 676, "upon an equal footing with the original States." The language of counsel is that "any reservation in the agreement with the Indians, expressed or implied, whereby the waters of Milk River were not to be subject of appropriation by the citizens and inhabitants of said State, was repealed by the act of admission." But to establish the repeal counsel rely substantially upon the same argument that they advance against the intention of the agreement to reserve the waters. The power of the Government to reserve the waters and exempt them from appropriation under the state laws is not denied, and could not be. The United States v. The Rio Grande Ditch & Irrigation Co., 174 U.S. 690, 702 (1899); United States v. Winans, 198 U.S. 371 [1905]. That the Government did reserve them we have decided, and for a use which would be necessarily continued through years. This was done May 1, 1888, and it would be extreme to believe that within a year Congress destroyed the reservation and took from the Indians the consideration of their grant, leaving them a barren waste—took from them the means of continuing their old habits, yet did not leave them the power to change to new ones.

Appellants' argument upon the incidental repeal of the agreement by the admission of Montana into the Union and the power over the waters of Milk River which the State thereby acquired to dispose of them under its laws, is elaborate and able, but our construction of the agreement and its effect make it unnecessary to answer the argument in detail. For the same reason we have not discussed the doctrine of riparian rights urged by the Government.

Decree affirmed.

NOTES

1. Cases and commentators generally agree that the effective date of the reservation—whether by treaty, Act of Congress, or executive Order—should be regarded as the priority date of the water rights necessary to fulfill the purposes of that reservation. However, under a theory of "aboriginal rights," when the land reserved is part of a tribe's traditional homeland, it can be argued that Indian water rights date back to "time immemorial" and are thus superior to any right held by a non-Indian. See, e.g., the Consent Decree in United States v. Gila Valley Irrigation Dist. (Globe Equity # 59), June 29, 1935; William Veeder, *Indian Prior and Paramount Rights of the Use of Water,* 16 Rocky Mtn.Min.L.Inst. 631 (1971); U.S. National Water Commission, Water Policies for the Future 473 (1973) ("Where the Reservation is located on lands aboriginally owned by the Indian tribe, their water rights may even be said to have existed from time immemorial"); and United States v. Adair, 723 F.2d 1394, 1414 (8th Cir.1983), page 797, infra.

2. In *Winters,* the Court said that "the power *of the Government* to reserve the waters and exempt them from appropriation under state

laws is not denied and could not be." 207 U.S. at 577 (emphasis added.) From the perspective of federal Indian law, it is axiomatic that—in the context of treaties—it is the tribe that reserves rights not explicitly granted away. See David H. Getches, Charles F. Wilkinson & Robert F. Williams, Federal Indian Law, Cases and Materials, chap. 11 (3d ed. 1993).

In other words, as Justice McKenna wrote in United States v. Winans, a precursor of *Winters* dealing with fishing rights, "the treaty was not a grant of rights to the Indians, but a grant of rights from them—a reservation of those not granted." 198 U.S. 371, 381 (1905). Language in *Winters* tends to support this theory. The Court held that the absence of an explicit reservation of water rights by the Indians on lands they ceded so the government could open them for non-Indian homesteading—land that would also be valueless without irrigation— created a "conflict of implications." However, the Court concluded that the implication of a "retention of waters is of greater force than that which makes for their cession," because the Indians would not have voluntarily given up their "command of the lands and the waters" which made them "valuable or adequate." 207 U.S. at 576.

3. After *Winters*, a 10,425 acre irrigation project was constructed on the Fort Belknap Reservation to allow the tribes to enjoy their water right, which amounts to the approximate annual natural flow of the Milk. The Milk is an international river that originates in Glacier National Park. As part of the Boundary Waters Treaty of 1909, the United States was awarded 75% of the Milk's flow and Canada received similar rights to the Saint Mary's River which also originates in the Park and flows almost due north into Alberta. In 1946 the Bureau of Reclamation built a dam and reservoir on the Milk some fifty miles upstream from the reservation. The tribe's natural flow right was recognized in a Bureau of Reclamation–Bureau of Indian Affairs operating agreement; the agreement gave the tribes an additional $\frac{1}{7}$ interest in the waters of the Milk stored behind Fresno Dam near Havre, Montana. (The right does not include waters of the Saint Mary's River diverted into the Milk.) Between 1983 and 1985 there was a severe drought in Montana, and by July of 1985 the entire natural flow of the Milk had dried up and the tribes used up their full $\frac{1}{7}$ interest in the Fresno Reservoir. The Bureau of Indian Affairs acceded to the Bureau of Reclamation's request to close the Fort Belknap Irrigation Project diversion. In August of that same year "Due to insufficient water and fear of 'water pirates' who might divert the water before the Tribes could receive it, BOR and BIA decided not to release any water and the Fort Belknap Irrigation Project remained closed." Gros Ventre and Assiniboine Tribes of Fort Belknap Indian Community of the Fort Belknap Indian Reservation v. Hodel, No. CV–85–213–GF (D.Mont. August 22, 1985), Defendant's Motion to Dismiss, p. 10. The tribes immediately filed suit to protect their senior *Winters* rights, but August rains made it possible for BOR and BIA to agree to a temporary schedule of reservoir releases. The suit was dismissed without preju- dice in July, 1986.

4. Is the case wrong? One Indian historian thinks that *Winters* was contrary to the expectations of the assimilation movement. That movement wanted to give the Indians a chance to adopt non-Indian values but expected that the resources of the Indians who failed this test would be quickly shifted to non-Indian settlers. Frederick B. Hoxie, A Final Promise: The Campaign to Assimilate the Indians, 1880–1920, at 171 (1984).

ARIZONA v. CALIFORNIA

Supreme Court of the United States, 1963.
373 U.S. 546, 83 S.Ct. 1468, 10 L.Ed.2d 542, decree entered
376 U.S. 340, 84 S.Ct. 755, 11 L.Ed.2d 757 (1964).

BLACK, J. * * *

CLAIMS OF THE UNITED STATES

In these proceedings, the United States has asserted claims to waters in the main river and in some of the tributaries for use on Indian Reservations, National Forests, Recreational and Wildlife Areas, and other government lands and works. While the Master passed upon some of these claims, he declined to reach others, particularly those relating to tributaries. We approve his decision as to which claims required adjudication, and likewise we approve the decree he recommended for the government claims he did decide. We shall discuss only the claims of the United States on behalf of the Indian Reservations.

The Government, on behalf of five Indian Reservations in Arizona, California, and Nevada, asserted rights to water in the mainstream of the Colorado River. The Colorado River Reservation, located partly in Arizona and partly in California, is the largest. It was originally created by an Act of Congress in 1865, but its area was later increased by Executive Order. Other reservations were created by Executive Orders and amendments to them, ranging in dates from 1870 to 1907. The Master found both as a matter of fact and law that when the United States created these reservations or added to them, it reserved not only land but also the use of enough water from the Colorado to irrigate the irrigable portions of the reserved lands. The aggregate quantity of water which the Master held was reserved for all the reservations is about 1,000,000 acre-feet, to be used on around 135,000 irrigable acres of land. Here, as before the Master, Arizona argues that the United States had no power to make a reservation of navigable waters after Arizona became a State; that navigable waters could not be reserved by Executive Orders; that the United States did not intend to reserve water for the Indian Reservations; that the amount of water reserved should be measured by the reasonably foreseeable needs of the Indians living on the reservation rather than by the number of irrigable acres; and, finally, that the judicial doctrine of equitable apportionment should be used to divide the water between the Indians and the other people in the State of Arizona.

The last argument is easily answered. The doctrine of equitable apportionment is a method of resolving water disputes between States. It was created by this Court in the exercise of its original jurisdiction over controversies in which States are parties. An Indian Reservation is not a State. And while Congress has sometimes left Indian Reservations considerable power to manage their own affairs, we are not convinced by Arizona's argument that each reservation is so much like a State that its rights to water should be determined by the doctrine of equitable apportionment. Moreover, even were we to treat an Indian Reservation like a State, equitable apportionment would still not control since, under our view, the Indian claims here are governed by the statutes and Executive Orders creating the reservations.

Arizona's contention that the Federal government had no power, after Arizona became a State, to reserve waters for the use and benefit of federally reserved lands rests largely upon statements in Pollard's Lessee v. Hagan, 3 How. 212 (1845), and Shively v. Bowlby, 152 U.S. 1 (1894). Those cases and others that followed them gave rise to the doctrine that lands underlying navigable rivers within territory acquired by the Government are held in trust for future States and that title to such lands is automatically vested in the States upon admission to the Union. But those cases involved only the shores of and lands beneath navigable waters. They do not determine the problem before us and cannot be accepted as limiting the broad powers of the United States to regulate navigable waters under the Commerce Clause and to regulate government lands under Art. IV., § 3, of the Constitution. We have no doubt about the power of the United States under these clauses to reserve water rights for its reservations and its property.

Arizona also argues that, in any event, water rights cannot be reserved by Executive Order. Some of the reservations of Indian lands here involved were made almost 100 years ago, and all of them were made over 45 years ago. In our view, these reservations, like those created directly by Congress, were not limited to land, but included waters as well. Congress and the Executive have ever since recognized these as Indian Reservations. Numerous appropriations, including appropriations for irrigation projects, have been made by Congress. They have been uniformly and universally treated as reservations by map makers, surveyors, and the public. We can give but short shrift at this late date to the argument that the reservations either of land or water are invalid because they were originally set apart by the Executive.

Arizona also challenges the Master's holding as to the Indian Reservations on two other grounds: first, that there is a lack of evidence showing that the United States in establishing the reservations intended to reserve water for them; second, that even if water was meant to be reserved the Master has awarded too much water. We reject both of these contentions. Most of the land in these reservations is and always has been arid. If the water necessary to sustain life is to be had, it must come from the Colorado River or its tributaries. It can be said without overstatement that when the Indians were put on these reservations they were not considered to be located in the most desirable area of the Nation. It is impossible to believe that when Congress created the great Colorado River Indian Reservation and when the Executive Department of this Nation created the other reservations they were unaware that most of the lands were of the desert kind—hot, scorching sands—and that water from the river would be essential to the life of the Indian people and to the animals they hunted and the crops they raised. In the debate leading to approval of the first congressional appropriation for irrigation of the Colorado River Indian Reservation, the delegate from the Territory of Arizona made this statement:

> "Irrigating canals are essential to the prosperity of these Indians. Without water there can be no production, no life; and all they ask of you is to give them a few agricultural implements to enable them to dig an irrigating canal by which their lands may be watered and their fields irrigated, so that they may enjoy the means of existence. You must provide these Indians with the means of subsistence or they will take by robbery from those who have. During the last year I have seen a number of these Indians starved to death for want of food." Cong.Globe, 38th Cong., 2d Sess. 1321 (1865).

The question of the Government's implied reservation of water rights upon the creation of an Indian Reservation was before this Court in Winters v. United States, 207 U.S. 564, decided in 1908. Much the same argument made to us was made in *Winters* to persuade the Court to hold that Congress had created an Indian Reservation without intending to reserve waters necessary to make those reservations livable. The Court rejected all of the arguments. * * * The Court in *Winters* concluded that the Government, when it created that Indian Reservation, intended to deal fairly with the Indians by reserving for them the waters without which their lands would have been useless. *Winters* has been followed by this Court as recently as 1939 in United States v. Powers, 305 U.S. 527. We follow it now and agree that the United States did reserve the water rights for the Indians effective as of the time the Indian Reservations were created. This means, as the Master held, that these water rights, having vested before the Act became effective on June 25, 1929, are "present perfected rights" and as such are entitled to priority under the Act.

We also agree with the Master's conclusion as to the quantity of water intended to be reserved. He found that the water was intended to satisfy the future as well as the present needs of the Indian Reservations and ruled that enough water was reserved to irrigate all the practicably irrigable acreage on the reservations. Arizona, on the other hand, contends that the quantity of water reserved should be measured by the Indians' "reasonably foreseeable needs," which, in fact, means by the number of Indians. How many Indians there will be and what their future uses will be can only be guessed. We have concluded, as did the Master, that the only feasible and fair way by which reserved water for the reservations can be measured is irrigable acreage. The various acreages of irrigable land which the Master found to be on the different reservations we find to be reasonable.

* * *

The Master ruled that the principle underlying the reservation of water rights for Indian Reservations was equally applicable to other federal establishments such as National Recreation Areas and Forests. We agree with the conclusions of the Master that the United States intended to reserve water sufficient for the future requirements of the Lake Mead National Recreation Area, the Havasu Lake National Wildlife Refuge, the Imperial National Wildlife Refuge and the Gila National Forest.

* * *

NOTES

1. *Federal lands.* Should non-Indians who were establishing water uses based on appropriations have been surprised when the Supreme Court in Arizona v. California decided that the *Winters* doctrine applied to federal lands as well as Indian lands? Eight years before deciding Arizona v. California, the Court held that a reservation of federal land for particular purposes (not merely public land available for disposition and general purposes) removes sources of water on the land from appropriation. Federal Power Comm'n v. Oregon, 349 U.S. 435 (1955).

2. *Quantities set.* The Supreme Court's decree in Arizona v. California, 376 U.S. 340 (1964), specified quantities of water reserved for various Indian reservations and federal lands along the Colorado River. The tribes were awarded about 900,000 acre-feet of water a year. More than 79,000 acre-feet a year was reserved for federal lands including the Havasu Lake National Wildlife Refuge, the Imperial National Wildlife Refuge, and the Lake Mead National Recreation Area. The quantities, of course, were not based on former use of water. On the Fort Mojave Reservation, for instance, the largest amount of land ever irrigated before the decision had been twenty-three acres, and only one family lived there in 1957. But the tribe now makes use of an average of 77% of its 123,000 acre-feet entitlement. On the other hand, some Colorado River tribes still use virtually no water.

3. *Quantities revised.* In 1979 the tribes whose reservations are located along the Colorado River moved to intervene on their own behalf in Arizona v. California and to reopen the case, in which the Supreme Court maintained continuing jurisdiction. They had been represented by the United States Department of Justice in the earlier litigation, but alleged that the government claimed too little irrigable acreage. They claimed rights to an expanded allocation of water based on arguments that irrigable acreage had been calculated erroneously and that circumstances had changed. 439 U.S. 419 (1979). A Court-appointed special master recommended that the tribes' annual entitlement to water be increased by about thirty-five percent—317,000 acre-feet—because of the United States' failure to claim all the irrigable acreage which the tribes owned. The Supreme Court allowed only a slight expansion of the tribes' entitlement—about 10,000 acre-feet. 460 U.S. 605 (1983). This represents additional water attributable to the

final resolution of boundary disputes that were left open by the Court in its 1964 decree.

The Supreme Court specifically refused to allow greater allocations to remedy the failure of the Department of Justice, as the tribes' representative, to claim all of the acreage that was actually irrigable. In striking down the tribes' claims that they had been inadequately represented, the Court noted a "strong interest in finality" where "[c]ertainty * * * with respect to water rights in the Western United States" is at stake. The Court concluded that "[t]he doctrine of prior appropriation, the prevailing law in the western states, is largely a product of the compelling need for certainty in the holding and use of water rights." 460 U.S. at 620.

Reliable irrigation figures for Indian lands are difficult to ascertain, since much irrigated reservation land is owned or leased by non-Indians. The best available estimates are that between 500,000 and 600,000 acres of all Indian-owned lands are under irrigation. The five lower Colorado River tribes have committed some 700,000 acre-feet to irrigate about 100,000 acres. See Reid P. Chambers & John E. Echohawk, *Implementing the Winter's Doctrine of Indian Reserved Water Rights: Producing Indian Water and Economic Development without Injuring Non–Indian Water Users?*, 27 Gonz.L.Rev. 447, 457 (1991/92). Do the Indian tribes have any legal remedies for the loss of water rights not claimed by the United States in Arizona v. California? Do non-Indians whose rights may be rendered less valuable by the quantification and exercise of reserved rights have any remedy? Should they?

4. *Quantification and equity.* The magnitude of potential Indian reserved water rights claims is tremendous. The possibilities of disruption of established non-Indian uses created great uncertainty for appropriative rights perfected after reservations were established. Furthermore, many tribes have not yet asserted all their rights. One minimum estimate of Navajo reserved rights based on an irrigable acreage formula is two million acre-feet (maf) a year, with a potential of 50 maf. William A. Back & Jeffrey S. Taylor, *Navajo Water Rights: Pulling the Plug on the Colorado River,* 20 Nat.Resources J. 71, 74 & n. 12 (1980). Other estimates range as high as 15 million acre-feet—the entire flow of the Colorado River in most years. See Indian Water Rights in the West 26 (Western States Water Council 1983). In two negotiated settlements, the Navajo Nation agreed to defer asserting its reserved rights in exchange for federal irrigation projects initially intended to irrigate some 110,630 acres but is currently irrigating only some 60,000 acres. See Chambers & Echohawk, supra, and the discussion of Indian water settlements, pages 820–22, infra.

How can Indians be treated justly in determining and protecting their rights? What equities do non-Indians have as claims to inchoate rights are raised that may conflict with their water uses?

The National Water Commission made several recommendations to deal fairly with Indian reserved rights without causing dislocations to non-Indian uses. Consider this one:

Recommendation No. 14–5: Congress should make available financial assistance to Indian tribes which lack the funds to make economic use of their water to permit them to make economic use of it. In addition, Congress should enact legislation providing that on fully appropriated streams the United States shall make a standing offer of indefinite duration to Indian tribes to lease for periods not to exceed 50 years any water or water rights tendered by the Indian owners at the fair market value of the interest tendered.

National Water Commission, Water Policies for the Future—Final Report to the President and to the Congress of the United States 481 (1973).

5. *Winters* turned eighty-five years old in 1993. In 1911 water lawyers could read in Samuel A. Wiel, Water Rights in the Western States, that: "The Supreme Court of the United States says in Winters v. United States that the right of the reservation to water flowing through it, even in the absence of actual use thereon (if necessary for use in the future), cannot be destroyed by private appropriators who first put it to use under local law so permitting, even in States following the Colorado doctrine which ignore the proprietary rights of the United States as riparian proprietary in other respects." 1 Wiel at 239.

6. *Practicably Irrigable Acreage.* The special master in the 1963 litigation of Arizona v. California recommended and the Court accepted the argument that reserved rights of the tribes in question should be determined based on the amount of practicably irrigable acreage (PIA) on the reservations. The approach is based on the master's determination, from historical information showing that the purpose of the Colorado River Indian reservations was to enable the tribal members "to develop a viable agricultural economy." Adjudications to quantify Indian reserved rights are being pursued in dozens of cases throughout the western states. Litigation is typically expensive and time-consuming because the parties must hire not only lawyers but experts in soils, hydrology and engineering to determine how much practicably irrigable acreage the reservations contain. Economics also plays a role in determining whether certain irrigable land should be counted as practicably irrigable. Is it "practicable" to irrigate land that requires expensive delivery systems? Should the economics of reservations be calculated by looking at the reservation as a whole or by studying individual parcels?

After Arizona v. California, 373 U.S. 546 (1963), page 769, supra, was reopened, the special master found that economic feasibility was part of the determination of whether land is practicably irrigable. The master's 1982 report noted that many of the lands the 1962 master's report found to be practicably irrigable could not be cultivated profitably under the best of circumstances. The master rejected state contentions that a benefit-cost analysis must show a margin of profit. Instead, the master found it to be sufficient that benefits are equal to costs. The master also rejected the argument that practicability should be determined based on nineteenth century farming technology. The master's determinations on these points were not challenged.

Many "benefits" to Indian tribes from water rights relate to future security that, if evaluated today, would have a discounted present value of zero. Should such benefits be considered? Is it appropriate to use the economies of heavily subsidized non-Indian reclamation projects (i.e., cost per acre irrigated or per acre-foot of water) as a benchmark for defining the economic feasibility of developing Indian water? A new consciousness of water conservation is moving some states to change their laws to require more efficient water use. See pages 209–27, supra. Should the standard of efficiency be the same as that which applies in the state in question at the time of the adjudication?

7. *Other standards for quantifying rights.* Most Indian water rights claims are based on the PIA formula, but what purposes other than agriculture might the United States and the tribes have had in setting aside an Indian reservation? See Cappaert v. United States, 426 U.S. 128 (1976), and United States v. New Mexico, 438 U.S. 696 (1978), page 787, infra, suggesting that water could also have been reserved for a non-agricultural purpose. Cf. Nevada v. United States, 463 U.S. 110 (1983) (rejecting the Pyramid Lake Paiute Tribe's claim for water for a fishery on grounds of res judicata). See also U.S. National Water Commission, Water Policies for the Future 476 (1973) ("Indian Reservations created for other types of occupations may have water rights measured by different formulas."). Would those purposes command greater quantities of water than would be needed for agriculture?

The purposes of many Indian reservations are stated generally in treaties, statutes or executive orders. Presumably every reservation was meant to provide a permanent homeland where a tribe could become economically self-sufficient and govern itself. The Supreme Court in *Winters* referred to the general purposes of encouraging "habits of industry" and "advancing the civilization and improvement of the Indians." But see In re General Adjudication of All Rights to use Water in the Big Horn River System, 835 P.2d 273 (Wyo.1992), page 808, infra (rejecting a master's recommendation to quantify rights based on "homeland" purpose).

8. *Use of quantified rights for other purposes.* Can reserved rights quantified based on the original purpose of the reservation be put to other uses (e.g., mining, power generation, recreation, municipal uses)? The special master in Arizona v. California stated that the fact that the practicably irrigable acreage formula had been used "does not necessarily mean, however, that water reserved for Indian Reservations may not be used for purposes other than agriculture and related uses." The Supreme Court later acknowledged this. 439 U.S. 419, 422 (1979). Several of the Colorado River tribes have put their water to more productive uses than agriculture. Interestingly, most of the agricultural development on the reservations—and use of water—is actually by non-Indians. Nationally, non-Indians produce 69% of Indian farm land income and use 78% of all irrigated reservation lands.

9. *Pueblo rights.* When the State of New Mexico instituted suit to adjudicate rights in tributaries of the Rio Grande, Indian pueblos asserted reserved rights to all the water they needed for irrigation. Indians living on pueblo lands trace their tenure centuries back to before the Spanish and Mexican governments ruled the area. Titles recognized by these predecessor sovereigns had been confirmed by the United States, consistent with the government's promise to respect pre-existing titles in the Treaty of Guadalupe Hidalgo, 9 Stat. 922 (1848). See generally Charles T. Dumars et al., Pueblo Indian Water Rights (1984). The court held that because, unlike other tribes, pueblos held fee title to their land, the reserved rights doctrine was not applicable. New Mexico v. Aamodt, 537 F.2d 1102 (10th Cir.1976), cert. denied 429 U.S. 1121 (1977). It ruled, however, that the water rights of the pueblos were prior to the water rights of all non-Indians whose land ownership was recognized under 1924 and 1933 Acts of Congress that confirmed the pueblos' land titles. It reasoned that a "recognition of any priority date for the Indians later than, or equal to, a priority date for a non-Indian" would violate the mandate of Congress. 537 F.2d at 1113. The result, then, was essentially what it would have been if *Winters* had applied. The court then remanded the case to the district court, suggesting that it consider the applicability of Spanish or Mexican law. In a subsequent decision, 618 F.Supp. 993 (D.N.M.1985), the court confirmed that pueblo Indians held aboriginal title to their traditional lands and retained prior rights to use water thereon, absent specific legislation by Congress to the contrary. Moreover, the pueblos' right to use water extended to all water of a stream system necessary for domestic and irrigation uses, except where explicitly terminated by the Pueblo Lands Act of 1924. As a result, the pueblos had priority to irrigate all irrigable acreage within the boundaries of lands reserved by Executive Order or Congressional statute, subject to prior uses established before the creation of the reservation. Applying this rule, the court said that rights would attach only to lands that had been irrigated between 1846–1924. This, it found to be about 10% of the amount of water recommended by the master. Findings and conclusions, dated April 29, 1987.

California also recognizes "pueblo water rights" tracing to Spanish and Mexican law. See page 566, supra. The Treaty of Guadalupe Hidalgo by which Mexico ceded its holdings to the United States assures continued respect for property rights vested prior to the 1848 treaty. Thus, those whose title traces to Spanish land grants which predated Mexican rule have a *Winters*-type water right. The California grants were for pueblos that were to produce agricultural supplies for the presidios. In City of Los Angeles v. City of San Fernando, 537 P.2d 1250 (Cal.1975), the California Supreme Court looked to the purpose of the pueblo (now Los Angeles) to find that Spanish law provided rights to sufficient water for its present and future needs:

> The pueblo was deliberately located to take maximum advantage of the Los Angeles River as a source of water for irrigation and the orders for the pueblo's founding included detailed provisions for an irrigation dam and canals. These circumstances strongly suggest a

governmental policy of assuring the pueblo a supply of water sufficient for its maintenance and growth, at least in the absence of any other town or settlement of comparable importance competing for the same water supply.

537 P.2d at 1275.

2.　Jurisdiction to Determine Reserved Rights

UNITED STATES v. DISTRICT COURT IN AND FOR EAGLE COUNTY

Supreme Court of the United States, 1971.
401 U.S. 520, 91 S.Ct. 998, 28 L.Ed.2d 278.

MR. JUSTICE DOUGLAS delivered the opinion of the Court.

Eagle River is a tributary of the Colorado River; and Water District 37 is a Colorado entity encompassing all Colorado lands irrigated by water of the Eagle and its tributaries. The present case started in the Colorado courts and is called a supplemental water adjudication under Colo.Rev.Stat.Ann. 148–9–7 (1963). The Colorado court issued a notice which, *inter alia,* asked all owners and claimants of water rights in those streams "to file a statement of claim and to appear * * * in regard to all water rights owned or claimed by them." The United States was served with this notice pursuant to 43 U.S.C.A. § 666.[1] The United States moved to be dismissed as a party, asserting that 43 U.S.C.A. § 666 does not constitute consent to have adjudicated in a state court the reserved water rights of the United States.

The objections of the United States were overruled by the state District Court and on a motion for a writ of prohibition the Colorado Supreme Court took the same view. 169 Colo. 555, 458 P.2d 760. The case is here on a petition for certiorari, which we granted. 397 U.S. 1005.

We affirm the Colorado decree.

It is clear from our cases that the United States often has reserved water rights based on withdrawals from the public domain. As we said in Arizona v. California, 373 U.S. 546, the Federal Government had the authority both before and after a State is admitted into the Union "to reserve waters for the use and benefit of federally reserved lands." Id., at 597. The federally reserved lands include any federal enclave. In

---

1. 66 Stat. 560, 43 U.S.C.A. § 666(a), provides:

"Consent is given to join the United States as a defendant in any suit (1) for the adjudication of rights to the use of water of a river system or other source, or (2) for the administration of such rights, where it appears that the United States is the owner of or is in the process of acquiring water rights by appropriation under State law, by purchase, by exchange, or otherwise, and the United States is a necessary party to such suit. The United States, when a party to any such suit, shall (1) be deemed to have waived any right to plead that the State laws are inapplicable or that the United States is not amenable thereto by reason of its sovereignty, and (2) shall be subject to the judgments, orders, and decrees of the court having jurisdiction, and may obtain review thereof, in the same manner and to the same extent as a private individual under like circumstances: *Provided, That no judgment for costs shall be entered against the United States in any such suit.*"

Arizona v. California we were primarily concerned with Indian reservations. Id., at 598–601. The reservation of waters may be only implied and the amount will reflect the nature of the federal enclave. Id., at 600–601. Here the United States is primarily concerned with reserved waters for the White River National Forest, withdrawn in 1905, Colorado having been admitted into the Union in 1876.

The United States points out that Colorado water rights are based on the appropriation system which requires the permanent fixing of rights to the use of water at the time of the adjudication, with no provision for the future needs, as is often required in case of reserved water rights. Since those rights may potentially be at war with appropriative rights, it is earnestly urged that 43 U.S.C.A. § 666 gave consent to join the United States only for the adjudication of water rights which the United States acquired pursuant to state law.

* * * [T]he first clause of § 666(a)(1), read literally, would seem to cover this case for "rights to the use of water of a river system" is broad enough to embrace "reserved" waters.

The main reliance of the United States appears to be on Clause 2 of § 666(a) which reads:

"* * * for the administration of such rights, where it appears that the United States is the owner of or is in the process of acquiring water rights by appropriation under State law, by purchase, by exchange, or otherwise."

This provision does not qualify § 666(a)(1), for (1) and (2) are separated by an "or." Yet even if "or" be read as "and", we see no difficulty with Colorado's position. Section 666(a)(2) obviously includes water rights previously acquired by the United States through appropriation or presently in the process of being so acquired. But we do not read § 666(a)(2) as being restricted to appropriative rights acquired under state law. In the first place, "the administration of such rights" in § 666(a)(2) must refer to the rights described in (1) for they are the only ones which in this context "such" could mean; and as we have seen they are all-inclusive, in terms at least. Moreover, (2) covers rights acquired by appropriation under state law and rights acquired "by purchase" or "by exchange," which we assume would normally be appropriative rights. But it also includes water rights which the United States has "otherwise" acquired. The doctrine of *ejusdem generis* is invoked to maintain that "or otherwise" does not encompass the adjudication of reserved water rights, which are in no way dependent for their creation or existence on state law. We reject that conclusion for we deal with an all-inclusive statute concerning "the adjudication of rights to the use of water of a river system" which in § 666(a)(1) has no exceptions and which, as we read it, includes appropriative rights, riparian rights, and reserved rights.

It is said that this adjudication is not a "general" one as required by Dugan v. Rank, 372 U.S. 609, 618. This proceeding, unlike the one in *Dugan,* is not a private one to determine whether named claimants have priority over the United States. The whole community of claims is involved and as Senator McCarran, Chairman of the Committee reporting on the bill, said in reply to Senator Magnuson: "S. 18 is not intended * * * to be used for any other purpose than to allow the United States to be joined in a suit wherein it is necessary to adjudicate all of the rights of various owners on a given stream. This is so because unless all of the parties owning or in the process of acquiring water rights on a particular stream can be joined as parties defendant, any subsequent decree would be of little value."

* * *

Affirmed.

NOTES

1. Dugan v. Rank, 372 U.S. 609 (1963) is cited in the principal case. As a result of the Central Valley Project (described at page 705, supra), water flow in the San Joaquin River near plaintiff's property was severely diminished. Plaintiff sought to enjoin local officials of the United States Bureau of Reclamation from diverting the water. The United States was joined as a party defendant. The Supreme Court in *Dugan* held that the McCarran Amendment was not applicable in that case:

> * * * Rather than a case involving a *general* adjudication of "all of the rights of various owners on a given stream," S.Rep. No. 755, 82d Cong., 1st Sess. 9 (1951), it is a private suit to determine water rights solely between the respondents and the United States and the local Reclamation Bureau officials. In addition to the fact that all of the claimants of water rights along the river are not made parties, no relief is either asked or granted as between claimants, nor are priorities sought to be established as to the appropriative and prescriptive rights asserted.

372 U.S. at 618.

2. Once it proceeds with its claims in state court under the McCarran Amendment, is the United States subject to procedural requirements that may prevent the assertion of certain federal claims? The United States filed reserved water rights claims in state court after losing the principal case. One such federal claim was for 200,000 acre-feet per year for Naval Oil Shale Reserves with priority dates of 1916 and 1924. The claim described the source of waters as "the Colorado and White rivers and water tributary thereto, which are located in or on the [oil shale reserves]." In fact, no part of the reserves was actually located on the rivers, the nearest point to the Colorado River being about one-half mile away. In 1983, the claims had not yet been ruled upon and the federal government sought to amend its application to specify that it asserted the right to divert its water at a particular point on the Colorado River mainstem. The motion to amend was granted, but the water court held that the claims were new ones, not amendments to the original claims (which, if proved, would have had 1916 and 1920 priorities). The Colorado Supreme Court affirmed. United States v. Bell, 724 P.2d 631 (Colo.1986). Thus, only federal claims made in or prior to the year of the *Eagle County* decision (1971)

have a potential priority date as of the date of the original reservation. Later claims are untimely and can only have priority as of the year in which the application is filed. This way of handling reserved rights claims is similar to the Colorado court's handling of private appropriative claims with old priority dates that are not filed in the first available adjudication after the adjudication law was passed. The court might have allowed the United States to amend the claim that related back if the first claim had put others on notice that water might be taken on the mainstem which was not "in or on" the lands in question.

The United States Supreme Court has not ruled on the extent to which such state procedural rules may preclude or limit assertions of reserved rights. It has ruled that the McCarran Amendment's waiver of sovereign immunity, which specifically exempts the U.S. from a "judgment for costs," did not require the government to pay filing fees (totalling over $10 million) in an Idaho adjudication. United States v. Idaho, 113 S.Ct. 1893 (1993).

3. Neither the McCarran Amendment nor *Eagle County* specifically addressed the issue of Indian reserved rights. The amendment consented to suits only where "the United States is the owner of * * * water rights." Tribal water rights and other property are only held in trust for tribes, and tribes are themselves sovereign. The U.S. therefore objected to claiming rights for Indian lands in the Colorado adjudication.

In Colorado River Water Conservation District v. United States, 424 U.S. 800 (1976), the Court decided that the McCarran Amendment created state court jurisdiction to adjudicate Indian reserved rights as well as federal rights. The Court found that "not only the Amendment's language, but also its underlying policy, dictates a construction including Indian rights in its provisions." 424 U.S. at 810. Likewise, its "legislative history demonstrates that the McCarran Amendment is to be construed as reaching federal water rights reserved on behalf of Indians. It was unmistakably the understanding of proponents and opponents of the legislation that it contemplated water rights reserved for Indians." 424 U.S. at 818. See also Arizona v. San Carlos Apache Tribe, 463 U.S. 545 (1983) (holding that the McCarran Amendment extended state jurisdiction even to states whose constitutions "disclaim all right and title to * * * [Indian] lands" and promised that those lands "shall remain under the absolute jurisdiction and control of the United States."

Not only did *Colorado River* extend the McCarran Amendment's reach to include Indian reserved rights, but it also fashioned a doctrine of federal court abstention for cases involving concurrent adjudication of water rights in a state forum, in apparent deference to the policies underlying the McCarran Amendment. In *Colorado River,* a federal case was pending before the state case commenced. The Court cited the litigants' ready access to the state's comprehensive regulatory scheme and convenient forum, as well as the McCarran Amendment's policy against piecemeal adjudication as reasons for its deference to the state adjudicative process. See Martin H. Redish, Federal Courts: Cases, Comments, and Questions 807–20 (2d ed. 1989).

4. Can the federal government be compelled to assert reserved rights? In Sierra Club v. Andrus, 487 F.Supp. 443 (D.D.C.1980), the Sierra Club argued that the United States had a public trust duty to participate in a state water rights adjudication in southern Utah because proposed energy development projects threatened to jeopardize the future assertion of reserved rights. The district court held that although the issue was not ripe, "in the event of a real and immediate water supply threat to the scenic, natural, historic or biotic resource values of the Glen Canyon National Recreation Area or the Grand Canyon National Park, the Secretary [of Interior] must take appropriate action." Id. at 448. The Sierra Club appealed only the district court's refusal to decide if the Federal Land Policy and Management Act, 43 U.S.C.A. §§ 1701–1784, "confers by implication federal reserved water rights." In the meantime, the United States did join the state proceeding. The court of appeals expressed grave doubts about instructing the United States to take a particular position in litigation and rejected the Club's argument that reserved rights attach in the absence of a withdrawal of land from the public domain and reservation of the land for a specific use. Sierra Club v. Watt, 659 F.2d 203, 206 (D.C.Cir.1981).

SIERRA CLUB v. YEUTTER

United States Court of Appeals, Tenth Circuit, 1990.
911 F.2d 1405.

Before LOGAN and TACHA, CIRCUIT JUDGES, and THEIS, SENIOR DISTRICT JUDGE.

TACHA, CIRCUIT JUDGE.

* * *

I.

Sierra Club commenced this litigation in 1984 against the Secretary of Agriculture and the Chief of the Forest Service. In its second amended complaint, the Sierra Club stated that the United States had been joined in various water rights adjudications in the Colorado state courts. The complaint alleged that the United States had not claimed any federal reserved water rights based on the Wilderness Act ("wilderness water rights") for the twenty-four wilderness areas on national forest lands. * * *

The district court denied the motion to dismiss [based on lack of jurisdiction]. Sierra Club v. Block, 615 F.Supp. 44 (D.Colo.1985).

In a subsequent decision, * * * Sierra Club v. Block, 622 F.Supp. 842 (D.Colo.1985), the court held that "federal reserved water rights do exist in the designated Colorado wilderness areas." The court held, however, that although the federal defendants are under a "general duty under the Wilderness Act to protect and preserve all wilderness resources," "[t]here is, however, no specific statutory duty to claim reserved water rights in the wilderness areas even though Congress impliedly reserved such rights in order to effectuate the purposes of the Act * * *." The court ruled that it was without power to order the

Attorney General to initiate litigation to obtain such rights in the Colorado state court proceedings. The court explained that under the doctrine of separation of powers, it could not order the executive to litigate the wilderness water rights in the absence of a statute requiring the executive to do so. Id. (quoting Sierra Club v. Department of the Interior, 424 F.Supp. 172, 175 (N.D.Cal.1976)).

    * * * The court noted that reserved water rights represent only one alternative available to the federal defendants to fulfill their statutory duty to preserve wilderness water resources. After concluding that the briefs and administrative record were not adequate to evaluate fully Sierra Club's assertion that reserved water rights were the only means to protect water resources, the court remanded the matter to the federal defendants with directions ordering them to "come forward with a memorandum explaining their analysis, final decision, and plan to comply with their statutory obligations * * *."

* * *

    The district court addressed these contentions in a third decision. See Sierra Club v. Lyng, 661 F.Supp. 1490 (D.Colo.1987). The court reaffirmed its earlier holding that federal reserved water rights exist under the Wilderness Act. The court held that the first report submitted by the Forest Service was "deficient in the kind of detail necessary to conduct a satisfactory review" of the agency's decision not to adjudicate federal reserved water rights based on the Wilderness Act. * * * Accordingly, the court struck the first report and ordered the Forest Service to submit a proper plan.

    Thereafter, the Forest Service submitted a new plan, which analyzed the status of existing absolute and conditional water rights on and above the wilderness areas. * * *

    The second report outlined a number of options the Forest Service could use to protect wilderness water values. These included: administrative land use controls; recommendations to the President, Congress, and other agencies; recommending assertion of reserved water rights under the Organic Administration Act of 1897, 30 Stat. 34; and recommending the assertion of reserved water rights under the Wilderness Act. * * *

II.

    The first issue we address is whether this case is properly before us. * * *

    Review of the Forest Service's inaction is available only if its inaction is irreconcilable with the Act's mandate to preserve the wilderness character of the wilderness areas. Determining whether the statutory mandate is so threatened requires evaluation of the extent and immediacy of the alleged harm, possible agency responses, and the probable efficacy of such responses. Because of the contextual nature of such an inquiry, we must determine whether the challenge is ripe for adjudication at this time.

The law of ripeness was authoritatively restated by the Supreme Court in Abbott Laboratories v. Gardner, 387 U.S. 136, 87 S.Ct. 1507, 18 L.Ed.2d 681 (1967). * * *

We begin our ripeness analysis by applying the two factor *Abbott Laboratories* test. Under the fitness for judicial resolution factor, the Court in *Abbott Laboratories* considered both the legal nature of the question presented and the finality of the administrative action in making its decision. One aspect of the question presented by Sierra Club—whether the Wilderness Act creates federal reserved water rights—is undoubtedly legal. See, e.g., United States v. New Mexico, 438 U.S. 696, 698, 98 S.Ct. 8012, 8013, 57 L.Ed.2d 1052 (1978) (scope of federal reserved water rights turns on congressional intent); Cappaert v. United States, 426 U.S. 128, 188, 96 S.Ct. 2062, 2069, 48 L.Ed.2d 523 (1976) (reserved water rights can arise by implication from reservations of land). The other aspect of the question presented to us—whether federal reserved water rights are necessary to preserve the wilderness characteristics of the wilderness areas—is either a question of fact or a mixed question of law and fact. Although Sierra Club submitted affidavits alleging that federal reserved water rights are necessary to preserve the wilderness characteristics of the Colorado wilderness areas, the Forest Service's second report generally denies the existence of any threat to the wilderness areas, and asserts that other administrative measures could adequately address the preservation of wilderness characteristics. Where disputed facts exist and the issue is not purely legal, greater caution is required prior to concluding that an issue is ripe for review.

In assessing the fitness for judicial resolution factor of the *Abbott Laboratories* test, we also consider the finality of the Forest Service's conduct. Administrative finality is interpreted pragmatically. *Abbott Laboratories,* 387 U.S. at 149, 87 S.Ct. at 1515–16. An administrative decision is final when it is definitive rather than tentative, when it has a "direct and immediate * * * effect on the day-to-day business" of the parties, and when it has "the status of law" and requires immediate compliance.

* * *

In light of these cases, the finality of the Forest Service's action in this case in uncertain. The Forest Service's principal position is not that federal reserved water rights do not exist, but rather that their assertion at this time is unnecessary and possibly counterproductive. Indeed, the Forest Service stated in the second report that the assertion of federal reserved water rights based on the Wilderness Act was a possible option. It is thus difficult to say that the Forest Service has reached a "final decision" given its possible acceptance of a wilderness water right in an appropriate case.

Even if we were to rule in favor of Sierra Club's request for a declaratory judgment that the Wilderness Act creates federal reserved water rights, the Forest Service is not obligated to assert those rights in the absence of a threat to the wilderness characteristics of the Colorado wilderness areas. Sierra Club could thus be forced to litigate once again to show that the Forest Service's inaction violated the preservation duty imposed by the Act.   * * * In this case, because of our limited scope of review, the possibility that the Forest Service's position may change when presented with an actual case of imminent harm, and the possibility of piecemeal litigation, we find that this case is not fit for judicial resolution at this time.

We next apply the second factor of the *Abbott Laboratories* test, which turns on the hardship to the parties of withholding judicial consideration. We conclude that delaying consideration until there is a more imminent threat to wilderness water values does not impose a substantial hardship on the parties. Such delay benefits the government by allowing it to pursue its alternative program of protecting wilderness water values. Nor does such a delay prejudice Sierra Club, which can seek judicial review when a threat to wilderness statutory mandate is imminent.

Deferring a decision is even more compelling given the provision in Colorado water law permitting parties asserting a claim to water rights to intervene in a general water rights adjudication during that calendar year while still preserving their relative priority date vis-a-vis the other parties in the adjudication. See U.S. v. Bell, 724 P.2d 631, 641–42 (Colo.1986) (en banc); Colo.Rev.Stat. § 37–92–306 (1973). When and if a water development claim that may threaten wilderness water values is filed, and the Forest Service does not assert a federal reserved water right based on the Wilderness Act, and furthermore such failure to assert the reserved water right is irreconcilable with the Forest Service's duty to protect wilderness characteristics, then the Sierra Club may either intervene in the state water proceeding as appropriate under state law or may seek judicial review of the Forest Service's failure to act in federal court. At that time the record will be more fully developed and the courts can better determine whether the Forest Service's proposed alternatives to the use of wilderness water rights are adequate to reconcile its actions with its obligations under the Act. If the proposed alternatives are not adequate, appropriate corrective orders can be issued.

Our conclusion is bolstered by the speculative and contingent nature of the harm in this case. Because of the limited scope of review provided by the Wilderness Act, only agency conduct that is irreconcilable with the statutory mandate to preserve the wilderness characteristics of the Colorado wilderness areas will invoke judicial review. Yet Sierra Club has not even contended that the wilderness water values are themselves imminently and directly threatened in this case. Instead, Sierra Club contends only that the federal reserved water rights that protect these wilderness water values are threatened by the operation of the Colorado postponement doctrine,[7] which may subor-

---

7. Briefly stated, the Colorado postponement doctrine provides that holders of senior conditional water rights (which are similar to federal reserved water rights, may lose their priority to junior conditional appropriators who adjudicate their rights first if the senior conditional appropriators do not intervene in the same calendar year. See Bell, 724 P.2d at 641–42; Colo.Rev.Stat. § 37–92–306. For example, if a senior conditional appropriator with a priority date of 1907 did not appear in an

dinate the priority of wilderness water rights if the Forest Service fails to assert the rights in the state water courts.

Sierra Club has not, however, shown that even if the alleged federal reserved water rights created under the Wilderness Act are threatened, that then the wilderness water values themselves are threatened. Nor does that conclusion inevitably follow. *First,* federal reserved water rights, as creatures of federal law, are protected from extinguishment under state law by the Supremacy Clause, U.S. Const. art. VI. See United States v. City & County of Denver, 656 P.2d 1, 34–35 (Colo.1983) (en banc); Navajo Development Co. v. Sanderson, 655 P.2d 1374, 1379 (Colo.1982) (en banc). *Second,* even if federal reserved water rights are subject to postponement under Colorado law as held by *Bell,* there is no guarantee that the point of any diversion will be above or within the wilderness areas, where the direct impact of such change in water rights status would be the greatest. Absent a diversion within or above the wilderness area, it is difficult to see what harm might befall the wilderness water values that a wilderness water right could prevent. *Third,* the Forest Service contends that there are either adequate administrative controls in place that will prevent diversions above or within wilderness areas or that geographical features render such diversions or projects impractical in areas within or above the wilderness areas. *Fourth,* there is no guarantee that any diversion which might occur in or above a wilderness area would even have a noticeable impact on wilderness water values. The mere statement of the contingencies that must occur before Sierra Club's asserted harms to wilderness water values will occur even if there are water appropriations underscores the speculative and hypothetical nature of this issue. Based on these considerations, we conclude that there is simply no showing of a harm with the necessary degree of magnitude or imminence that would justify a finding that the Forest Service's conduct is irreconcilable with its duty to preserve the wilderness characteristics of the wilderness areas. Accordingly, we find that judicial intervention is inappropriate at this time.

* * *

Finally, we note that our determination is supported by the Supreme Court's recent decision in *Lujan,* 497 U.S. 871, 110 S.Ct. 3177. In *Lujan,* the National Wildlife Federation sought to challenge the Department of the Interior's "land withdrawal review program," which consisted of hundreds of administrative decisions reclassifying federal lands. The Court emphasized:

> a regulation is not ordinarily considered the type of agency action "ripe" for judicial review under the APA until the scope of the controversy has been reduced to more manageable proportions, and its factual components fleshed out, by some concrete action applying the regulation to the claimant's situation in a fashion that harms or threatens to harm him.

adjudication started by a junior conditional appropriator with a priority date of 1976, the junior appropriator's conditional right would become absolute on adjudication and have priority over the senior appropriator's conditional right.

Id. at 891, 110 S.Ct. at 3190. The Court then reviewed the nature of the challenged "program" and determined that because the program included hundreds of individual administrative decisions that it was neither final agency action nor ripe for judicial review.

* * *

III.

This case is not ripe for adjudication because the harm which is the basis of Sierra Club's claim to reviewability is speculative and contingent, the issues are not fit for judicial resolution, and prudential concerns counsel forbearance. The district court therefore erred in granting declaratory judgment that the Wilderness Act created federal reserved water rights. Accordingly, we DISMISS the appeal, VACATE the judgment of the district court and REMAND with directions to dismiss the complaint as not ripe for adjudication.

THEIS, SENIOR DISTRICT JUDGE, concurring.

* * * It is obvious to me that if and when any future threat to the wilderness areas results from the Forest Service's refusal to assert implied water rights, the very assumption of review under this standard should be a fair indication of the decision to follow. Congress withdrew and reserved such areas for the express purpose of providing "for the protection of these areas [and] the preservation of their wilderness character," 16 U.S.C. § 1131(a), and commanded that they "be devoted to the public purposes of recreation, scenic, scientific, educational, conservation, and historical use." Id. at § 1133(b). Unless one can take seriously defendant-intervenors' suggestion that Congress created the wilderness areas with such specific language, but did not intend to reserve enough water to fulfill their central purpose, I believe that the conclusion of the district court may well be vindicated in the appropriate case.

The opinion also observes that Colorado's postponement doctrine will not defeat any implied rights to wilderness waters reserved by the federal government under the Wilderness Act. Supra at note 7 and accompanying text. Thus, the intentional refusal or "benign neglect," Sierra Club v. Block, 622 F.Supp. 842, 865 (D.Colo.1985), of the federal government timely to adjudicate the issue of prior reserved rights to wilderness waters should not operate to extinguish any superior federal rights. If Forest Service inaction becomes incompatible with its statutory mandate to protect and preserve the wilderness character of these areas, "the Sierra Club may either intervene in the state water proceeding * * * or may seek judicial review * * * in federal court." I read this statement as a repudiation of defendants' argument that under the McCarran Amendment, 43 U.S.C. § 666, entertainment of this issue in federal court would never be appropriate in the face of ongoing stream adjudications in state court.

NOTES

1. Given its acknowledged status as a trustee for Indian tribes, does the United States have less discretion over whether and to what

extent it will assert Indian reserved water rights? See, for example, Judge Gesell's classic admonition regarding the Secretary of the Interior's trust responsibility in Pyramid Lake Paiute Tribe of Indians v. Morton, 354 F.Supp. 252 (D.D.C.1972), supplemented by 360 F.Supp. 669 (D.D.C.1973), reversed 499 F.2d 1095 (D.C.Cir.1974), cert. denied, 420 U.S. 962 (1975). In Nevada v. United States, 463 U.S. 110 (1983), the Supreme Court declined to correct the underlying inequity spawned by early disregard for the trust responsibility and refused to allow the tribe itself to reopen the adjudication. It cited the value of not disturbing non-Indian expectations implicit in notions of finality and res judicata in water rights decisions. In the Truckee–Carson–Pyramid Lake Water Rights Settlement Act of 1990, Title II of Pub.L. No. 101–618, 104 Stat. 3294, codified at 16 U.S.C.A. § 668dd, Congress intervened to accomplish what the Interior Department and courts refused to do—assure more water for Pyramid Lake. See generally Bonnie G. Colby et al., *Mitigating Environmental Externalities through Voluntary and Involuntary Water Reallocation: Nevada's Truckee–Carson River Basin,* 31 Nat.Resources J. 757 (1991); and Joseph R. Membrino, *Indian Reserved Water Rights, Federalism and the Trust Responsibility,* 27 Land & Water L.Rev. 1 (1992).

2. The Wild and Scenic Rivers Act of 1968 is the only federal statutory acknowledgment that reserved rights exist for instream flows. 16 U.S.C.A. §§ 1271–1287. The Act is designed to protect free flowing rivers from incompatible development projects and to provide for the management of land along the river corridor. Rivers may be designated for inclusion within the system either by an Act of Congress or by the Secretary of Interior's approval of state legislation nominating a river for inclusion. The Act provides:

> (c) Designation of any stream or portion thereof as a national wild, scenic or recreational river area shall not be construed as a reservation of the waters of such streams for purposes other than those specified in this Act, or in quantities greater than necessary to accomplish these purposes.

> (d) The jurisdiction of the States over waters of any stream included in a national wild, scenic or recreational river area shall be unaffected by this Act to the extent that such jurisdiction may be exercised without impairing the purposes of this Act or its administration.

16 U.S.C.A. §§ 1284(c), (d). If the United States fails to claim reserved rights for a wild and scenic river in a McCarran Amendment adjudication, should a court order it to do so?

3. Intent to Reserve

UNITED STATES v. NEW MEXICO
Supreme Court of the United States, 1978.
438 U.S. 696, 98 S.Ct. 3012, 57 L.Ed.2d 1052.

Mr. Justice Rehnquist delivered the opinion of the Court.

The Rio Mimbres rises in the southwestern highlands of New Mexico and flows generally southward, finally disappearing in a desert sink just north of the Mexican border. The river originates in the upper reaches of the Gila National Forest, but during its course it winds more than 50 miles past privately owned lands and provides substantial water for both irrigation and mining. In 1970, a stream adjudication was begun by the State of New Mexico to determine the exact rights of each user to water from the Mimbres. In this adjudication the United States claimed reserved water rights for use in the Gila National Forest. The State District Court held that the United States, in setting the Gila National Forest aside from other public lands, reserved the use of such water "as may be necessary for the purposes for which [the land was] withdrawn," but that these purposes did not include recreation, aesthetics, wildlife preservation, or cattle grazing. The United States appealed unsuccessfully to the Supreme Court of New Mexico. Mimbres Valley Irrigation Co. v. Salopek, 90 N.M. 410, 564 P.2d 615 (1977). We granted certiorari to consider whether the Supreme Court of New Mexico had applied the correct principles of federal law in determining petitioner's reserved rights in the Mimbres. We now affirm.

I

The question posed in this case—what quantity of water, if any, the United States reserved out of the Mimbres River when it set aside the Gila National Forest in 1899—is a question of implied intent and not power. In California v. United States, [438 U.S. 645, 653–63 (1978), page 715, supra,] we had occasion to discuss the respective authority of Federal and State governments over waters in the Western States. The Court has previously concluded that whatever powers the States acquired over their waters as a result of congressional acts and admission into the Union, however, Congress did not intend thereby to relinquish its authority to reserve unappropriated water in the future for use on appurtenant lands withdrawn from the public domain for specific federal purposes. Winters v. United States, 207 U.S. 564, 577 (1908); Arizona v. California, 373 U.S. 546, 597–598 (1963); Cappaert v. United States, 426 U.S. 128, 143–146 (1976).

Recognition of Congress' power to reserve water for land which is itself set apart from the public domain, however, does not answer the question of the amount of water which has been reserved or the purposes for which the water may be used. Substantial portions of the public domain *have* been withdrawn and reserved by the United States for use as Indian reservations, forest reserves, national parks, and national monuments. And water is frequently necessary to achieve the purposes for which these reservations are made. But Congress has seldom expressly reserved water for use on these withdrawn lands. If water were abundant, Congress' silence would pose no problem. In the arid parts of the West, however claims to water for use on federal reservations inescapably vie with other public and private claims for the limited quantities to be found in the rivers and streams. This competition is compounded by the sheer quantity of reserved lands in the Western States, which lands form brightly colored swaths across the maps of these States.[3]

The Court has previously concluded that Congress, in giving the President the power to reserve portions of the federal domain for specific federal purposes, *impliedly* authorized him to reserve "appurtenant water then unappropriated *to the extent needed to accomplish the purpose of the reservation.*" *Cappaert*, 426 U.S., at 138 (emphasis added).

While many of the contours of what has come to be called the "implied-reservation-of-water doctrine" remain unspecified, the Court has repeatedly emphasized that Congress reserved "only that amount of water necessary to fulfill the purpose of the reservation, no more." *Cappaert*, 426 U.S., at 141. Each time this Court has applied the "implied-reservation-of-water doctrine," it has carefully examined both the asserted water right and the specific purposes for which the land was reserved, and concluded that without the water the purposes of the reservation would be entirely defeated.[4]

This careful examination is required both because the reservation is implied, rather than expressed, and because of the history of congres-

---

3. The percentage of federally owned land (*excluding* Indian reservations and other trust properties) in the western States ranges from 29.5% of the land in the State of Washington to 86.5% of the land in the State of Nevada, an average of about 46%. Of the land in the State of New Mexico, 33.6% is federally owned. General Services Administration, Inventory Report on Real Property Owned by the United States Throughout the World as of June 30, 1974, at 17, 34, and App. I, table 4. Because federal reservations are normally found in the uplands of the Western States rather than the flatlands, the percentage of water flow originating in or flowing through the reservations is even more impressive. More than 60% of the average annual water yield in the 11 western States is from federal reservations. The percentages of average annual water yield range from a low of 56% in the Columbia–North Pacific water resource region to a high of 96% in the Upper Colorado region. In the Rio Grande water resource region, where the Rio Mimbres lies, 77% of the average runoff originates on federal reservations. C. Wheatley, C. Corker, T. Stetson, & D. Reed, Study of the Development, Management and Use of Water Resources on the Public Lands 402–406, and table 4 (1969).

4. * * *

In *Cappaert*, Congress had given the President the power to reserve "objects of historic and scientific interest that are situated upon the lands owned or controlled by the Government." American

Antiquities Preservation Act, 34 Stat. 225, 16 U.S.C.A. § 431 et seq. Pursuant to this power, the President had reserved Devil's Hole as a national monument. Devil's Hole, according to the Presidential Proclamation, is " 'a unique subsurface remnant of the prehistoric chain of lakes which in Pleistocene times formed the Death Valley Lake System' "; it also contains " 'a peculiar race of desert fish, and zoologists have demonstrated that this race of fish, which is found nowhere else in the world, evolved only after the gradual drying up of the Death Valley Lake System isolated this fish population from the original ancestral stock that in Pleistocene times was common to the entire region.' " 426 U.S. at 132. As the Court concluded, the pool was reserved specifically to preserve its scientific interest, principal of which was the Devil's Hole pupfish. Without a certain quantity of water, these fish would not be able to spawn and would die. This quantity of water was therefore impliedly reserved when the monument was proclaimed. Id., at 141. The Court, however, went on to note that the pool "need only be preserved, consistent with the intention expressed in the Proclamation, to the extent necessary to preserve its scientific interest. * * * The District Court thus tailored its injunction, very appropriately, to *minimal need*, curtailing pumping only to the extent necessary to preserve an adequate water level at Devil's Hole, thus implementing the stated objectives of the Proclamation." Ibid. (emphasis added).

sional intent in the field of federal-state jurisdiction with respect to allocation of water. Where Congress has expressly addressed the question of whether federal entities must abide by state water law, it has almost invariably deferred to the state law. See California v. United States. Where water is necessary to fulfill the very purposes for which a federal reservation was created, it is reasonable to conclude, even in the face of Congress' express deference to state water law in other areas, that the United States intended to reserve the necessary water. Where water is only valuable for a secondary use of the reservation, however, there arises the contrary inference that Congress intended, consistent with its other views, that the United States would acquire water in the same manner as any other public or private appropriator.

* * *

II

A

* * *

The United States contends that Congress intended to reserve minimum instream flows for aesthetic, recreational, and fish-preservation purposes. An examination of the limited purposes for which Congress authorized the creation of national forests, however, provides no support for this claim. In the mid- and late–1800's many of the forests on the public domain were ravaged and the fear arose that the forest lands might soon disappear, leaving the United States with a shortage both of timber and of watersheds with which to encourage stream flows while preventing floods. It was in answer to these fears that in 1891 Congress authorized the President to "set apart and reserve, in any State or Territory having public land bearing forests, in any part of the public lands wholly or in part covered with timber or undergrowth, whether of commercial value or not, as public reservations." Creative Act of March 3, 1891, 26 Stat. 1095, 1103, 16 U.S.C.A. § 471 (repealed 1976).

The Creative Act of 1891 unfortunately did not solve the forest problems of the expanding Nation. To the dismay of the conservationists, the new national forests were not adequately attended and regulated; fires and indiscriminate timber cutting continued their toll. To the anguish of Western settlers, reservations were frequently made indiscriminately. President Cleveland, in particular, responded to pleas of conservationists for greater protective measures by reserving some 21 million acres of "generally settled" forest land on February 22, 1897. President Cleveland's action drew immediate and strong protest from Western Congressmen who felt that the "hasty and ill considered" reservation might prove disastrous to the settlers living on or near these lands.

Congress' answer to these continuing problems was three fold. It suspended the President's Executive Order of February 22, 1897; it carefully defined the purposes for which national forests could in the future be reserved; and it provided a charter for forest management and economic uses within the forests. Organic Administration Act of June 4, 1897, 30 Stat. 31, 16 U.S.C.A. § 473 et seq. In particular, Congress provided

"*No national forest shall be established, except to improve and protect the forest within the boundaries, or for the purpose of securing favorable conditions of water flows, and to furnish a continuous supply of timber for the use and necessities of citizens of the United States;* but it is not the purpose or intent of these provisions, or of [the Creative Act of 1891], to authorize the inclusion therein of lands more valuable for the mineral therein, or for agricultural purposes, than for forest purposes." 30 Stat. 35, as amended, 16 U.S.C.A. § 475 (1976 ed.) (emphasis added).

The legislative debates surrounding the Organic Administration Act of 1897 and its predecessor bills demonstrate that Congress intended national forests to be reserved for only two purposes—"[t]o conserve the water flows and to furnish a continuous supply of timber for the people." 30 Cong.Rec. 967 (1897) (Cong. McRae). See United States v. Grimaud, 220 U.S. 506, 515 (1911). National forests were not to be reserved for aesthetic, environmental, recreational, or wildlife-preservation purposes.

"The objects for which the forest reservation should be made are the protection of the forest growth against destruction by fire and ax, and preservation of forest conditions upon which water conditions and water flow are dependent. The purpose, therefore, of this bill is to maintain favorable forest conditions, without excluding the use of these reservations for other purposes. They are not parks set aside for nonuse, but have been established for economic reasons." 30 Cong.Rec. 966 (1897) (Cong. McRae).

Administrative regulations at the turn of the century confirmed that national forests were to be reserved for only these two limited purposes.

Any doubt as to the relatively narrow purposes for which national forests were to be reserved is removed by comparing the broader language Congress used to authorize the establishment of national parks. In 1916, Congress created the National Park Service and provided that the

"fundamental purpose of said parks, monuments, and reservations * * * is to conserve the scenery and the natural and historic objects and the wild life therein and to provide for the enjoyment of the same * * * unimpaired for the enjoyment of future generations." National Park Service Act of 1916, 39 Stat. 535, 16 U.S.C.A. § 1 et seq.

* * *

B

Petitioner's claim that Congress intended to reserve water for recreation and wildlife-preservation is not only inconsistent with Congress' failure to recognize these goals as purposes of the national forests, but would also defeat the very purposes for which Congress did create the national forest system.

* * *

C

In 1960, Congress passed the Multiple–Use Sustained–Yield Act of 1960, 74 Stat. 215, 16 U.S.C.A. § 528 et seq., which provides

"It is the policy of Congress that the national forests are established and shall be administered for outdoor recreation, range, timber, watershed, and wildlife and fish purposes. The purposes of Sections 528 to 531 of this title are declared to be supplemental to, but not in derogation of, the purposes for which the national forests were established as set forth in the [Organic Administration Act of 1897.]"

* * * While we conclude that the Multiple–Use Sustained–Yield Act of 1960 was intended to broaden the purposes for which national forests had previously been administered, we agree that Congress did not intend to thereby expand the reserved rights of the United States.

* * * Without legislative history to the contrary, we are led to conclude that Congress did not intend in enacting the Multiple–Use Sustained–Yield Act of 1960 to reserve water for the *secondary* purposes there established.[22]   A reservation of additional water could mean a substantial loss in the amount of water available for irrigation and domestic use, thereby defeating Congress' principal purpose of securing favorable conditions of water flow.   Congress intended the national forests to be administered for broader purposes after 1960 but there is no indication that it believed the new purposes to be so crucial as to require a reservation of additional water.   By reaffirming the primacy of a favorable water flow, it indicated the opposite intent.

III

What we have said also answers the Government's contention that Congress intended to reserve water from the Rio Mimbres for stockwatering purposes.   The United States issues permits to private cattle owners to graze their stock on the Gila National Forest and provides for stockwatering at various locations along the Rio Mimbres.   The United States contends that, since Congress clearly foresaw stockwatering on national forests, reserved rights must be recognized for this purpose. * * *

While Congress intended the national forests to be put to a variety of uses, including stockwatering, not inconsistent with the two principal purposes of the forests, stockwatering was not itself a direct purpose of reserving the land.   If stockwatering could not take place on the Gila National Forest, Congress' purposes in reserving the land would not be defeated.   * * *

---

22. We intimate no view as to whether Congress, in the 1960 Act, authorized the subsequent reservation of national forests out of public lands to which a broader doctrine of reserved water rights might apply.

IV

Congress intended that water would be reserved only where necessary to preserve the timber or to secure favorable water flows for private and public uses under state law. This intent is revealed in the purposes for which the national forest system was created and Congress' principled deference to state water law in the Organic Administration Act of 1897 and other legislation. * * *

MR. JUSTICE POWELL, with whom MR. JUSTICE BRENNAN, MR. JUSTICE WHITE, and MR. JUSTICE MARSHALL join, dissenting in part.

I agree with the Court that the implied reservation doctrine should be applied with sensitivity to its impact upon those who have obtained water rights under state law and to Congress' general policy of deference to state water law. I also agree that the Organic Administration Act of 1897, 30 Stat. 11, cannot fairly be read as evidencing an intent to reserve water for recreational or stockwatering purposes in the national forests.

I do not agree, however, that the forests which Congress intended to "improve and protect" are the still, silent, lifeless places envisioned by the Court. In my view, the forests consist of the birds, animals, and fish—the wildlife—that inhabit them, as well as the trees, flowers, shrubs, and grasses. I therefore would hold that the United States is entitled to so much water as is necessary to sustain the wildlife of the forests, as well as the plants. I also add a word concerning the impact of the Court's holding today on future claims by the United States that the reservation of particular national forests impliedly reserved instream flows.

I

My analysis begins with the language of the statute. The Organic Administration Act of 1897, as amended, 16 U.S.C.A. § 475, provides in pertinent part:

> "No national forest shall be established, except to improve and protect the forest within the boundaries, or for the purpose of securing favorable conditions of water flows, and to furnish a continuous supply of timber for the use and necessities of citizens of the United States; * * *."

Although the language of the statute is not artful, a natural reading would attribute to Congress an intent to authorize the establishment of national forests for three purposes, not the two discerned by the Court. The New Mexico Supreme Court gave the statute its natural reading in this case when it wrote:

> "The Act limits the purposes for which the national forests are authorized to: 1) improving and protecting the forest, 2) securing favorable conditions of water flows, and 3) furnishing a continuous supply of timber." Mimbres Valley Irrigation Co. v. Salopek, 90 N.M. 410, 412, 564 P.2d 615, 617 (1977).

Congress has given the statute the same reading, stating that under the Organic Administration Act of 1897 national forests may be established for "the purposes of improving and protecting the forest, securing favorable conditions of water flows, or to furnish a continuous supply of timber * * *." H.R.Rep. No. 1551, 86th Cong., 2d Sess., 4 (1960).

* * * It is inconceivable that Congress envisioned the forests it sought to preserve as including only inanimate components such as the timber and flora. Insofar as the Court holds otherwise, the 55th Congress is maligned and the Nation is the poorer, and I dissent.

II

Contrary to the Court's intimations, * * * I see no inconsistency between holding that the United States impliedly reserved the right to instream flows, and what the Court views as the underlying purposes of the 1897 Act. The national forests can regulate the flow of water—which the Court views as "the very purpose for which Congress did create the national forest system" * * *—only for the benefit of appropriators who are downstream from the reservation. The reservation of an instream flow is not a consumptive use; it does not subtract from the amount of water that is available to downstream appropriators. Reservation of an instream flow therefore would be perfectly consistent with the purposes of the 1897 Act as construed by the Court.

I do not dwell on this point, however, for the Court's opinion cannot be read as holding that the United States never reserved instream flows when it set aside national forests under the 1897 Act. The State concedes, quite correctly on the Court's own theory, that even in this case "the United States is not barred from asserting that rights to minimum instream flows might be necessary for erosion control or fire protection on the basis of the recognized purposes of watershed management and the maintenance of timber." Brief for Respondent. Thus, if the United States proves, in this case or others, that the reservation of instream flows is necessary to fulfill the purposes discerned by the Court, I find nothing in the Court's opinion that bars it from asserting this right.

NOTES

1. In *New Mexico,* the Supreme Court relied heavily upon one of the few cases in which the government asserted non-Indian reserved rights that were in direct conflict with established uses under state water law, Cappaert v. United States, 426 U.S. 128 (1976), discussed in footnote 4 of the principal case. Devil's Hole, a deep cavern in Nevada containing an underground pool inhabited by a unique species of desert fish, was reserved as a national monument by a presidential proclamation in 1952. In 1968, the Cappaerts, who own a ranch nearby, began pumping groundwater coming from the same source as the water in Devil's Hole, thereby reducing the water level in the underground pool to levels that endangered the fish. The United States sought an injunction to limit the pumping, which the district court granted and the court of appeals approved. The Supreme Court, in addition to affirming the lower courts by holding that sufficient water had been reserved to maintain the level of the underground pool, discussed the reserved rights doctrine:

This Court has long held that when the Federal Government withdraws its land from the public domain and reserves it for a federal purpose, the Government, by implication, reserves appurtenant water then unappropriated to the extent needed to accomplish the purpose of the reservation. In so doing the United States acquires a reserved right in unappropriated water which vests on the date of the reservation and is superior to the rights of future appropriators. Reservation of water rights is empowered by the Commerce Clause, Art. I, § 8, which permits federal regulation of navigable streams, and the Property Clause, Art. IV, § 3, which permits federal regulation of federal lands. The doctrine applies to Indian reservations and other federal enclaves, encompassing water rights in navigable and nonnavigable streams.

* * *

In determining whether there is a federally reserved water right implicit in a federal reservation of public land, the issue is whether the Government intended to reserve unappropriated and thus available water. Intent is inferred if the previously unappropriated waters are necessary to accomplish the purposes for which the reservation was created. See, e.g., Arizona v. California, supra, 373 U.S., at 599–601; Winters v. United States, supra, 207 U.S., at 576. Both the District Court and the Court of Appeals held that the 1952 Proclamation expressed an intention to reserve unappropriated water, and we agree. The Proclamation discussed the pool in Devil's Hole in four of the five preambles and recited that the "pool * * * should be given special protection." Since a pool is a body of water, the protection contemplated is meaningful only if the water remains; the water right reserved by the 1952 Proclamation was thus explicit, not implied.

* * *

The implied-reservation-of-water-rights doctrine, however, reserves only that amount of water necessary to fulfill the purpose of the reservation, no more. Arizona v. California, supra, 373 U.S., at 600–601. Here the purpose of reserving Devil's Hole Monument is preservation of the pool. Devil's Hole was reserved "for the preservation of the unusual features of scenic, scientific, and educational interest." The Proclamation notes that the pool contains "a peculiar race of desert fish * * * which is found nowhere else in the world" and that the "pool is of * * * outstanding scientific importance * * *." The pool need only be preserved, consistent with the intention expressed in the Proclamation, to the extent necessary to preserve its scientific interest. The fish are one of the features of scientific interest. The preamble noting the scientific interest of the pool follows the preamble describing the fish as unique; the Proclamation must be read in its entirety. Thus, as the District Court has correctly determined, the level of the pool may be permitted to drop to the extent that the drop does not impair the scientific value of the pool as the natural habitat of the species sought to be preserved. * * *

Id. at 138–41.

The events preceding and following the *Cappaert* decision have been summarized:

> The 1960s witnessed the beginning of major physical changes in Ash Meadows [near the southern Nevada desert wetland area occupied by the pupfish], as a large farming operation came to the area. With cultivation of the land and installation of an extensive irrigation system, the water level in the springs decreased. This activity was well on its way toward causing the extinction of the endangered Devil's Hole pupfish and several other endemic species until a Supreme Court decision in 1976 limited the withdrawal of groundwater in Ash Meadows. This court decision forced the farming operation to close.
>
> In 1980, a land development company bought the farming operation's approximately 13,000 acres of land and promptly announced plans for the construction of its first 4000–lot subdivision, one of several it intended to develop in Ash Meadows. With the construction of roads and the clearing of land adjacent to springs, several of the endangered plants and animals were pushed to the brink of extinction. Fortunately for the wildlife, these activities allowed conservationists to invoke the protective measures of the Endangered Species Act of 1973. And once the destructive actions of the developers had been halted. The Nature Conservancy, a national conservation organization, began discussions with the owning company to purchase its land in Ash Meadows. In 1984, The Nature Conservancy purchased the 12,614 acres of Ash Meadows held by the developer and subsequently sold it to the US Fish and Wildlife Service. This land plus additional public domain lands in the area are now part of the recently established Ash Meadows National Wildlife Refuge.

James D. Williams & Ronald M. Nowak, *Vanishing Species in Our Own Backyard: Extinct Fish and Wildlife of the United States and Canada,* in The Last Extinction 107, 127–28 (Les Kaufman & Kenneth Mallory eds., 1986). The relationship between the federal Endangered Species Act and water law is explored at pages 739–841, supra.

2. Does *New Mexico* rule out reserved rights for instream flows on the public lands? In United States v. Denver, 656 P.2d 1 (Colo.1982), the Colorado Supreme Court held that recreational boating was clearly not within the purposes of the Dinosaur National Monument, pursuant to the federal Antiquities Act of 1906, 16 U.S.C.A. § 431 (which protects "objects of historic and scientific interest"), but remanded the question of "whether the reservation purpose of the Monument includes preservation of fish habitats." 656 P.2d at 36. On remand, the water court reviewed the documents leading up to the Monument's creation and found that "neither the Presidential Proclamation nor the relevant underlying documents contemporaneous with its issuance suggests that fishes or other wildlife were thought by the President to be of scientific, biological, or historic importance at the time the reservation was made." In the Matter of the Application for Water Rights of the

United States of America in Dinosaur National Monument, District Court, Water Division No. 6, Colorado, Case No. W–85 (March 21, 1985).

The *Denver* case also ruled that the U.S. Forest Service could present evidence on the amount of water needed for "channel maintenance" for the purpose of "preserving favorable conditions of water flows." In one trial court, the United States then attempted to show (with evidence from the field of fluvial geomorphology) that certain flushing flows were necessary to maintain the stream channel and thereby to "conserve the water flows" consistent with the Forest Service Organic Act. The water court rejected the claim finding that there was "little evidence of observed ill effects" on the channel from years of irrigation diversions and water storage. Further, the court was unimpressed with the expert testimony and theories saying they "gave a scientific tone to what was essentially speculation." According to the court, if a claim of reserved rights for instream flows for channel maintenance is to succeed it will be "only to a reasonable degree consistent with both the requirements of stream flows and the necessities of efficient irrigation and domestic use." In the Matter of the Amended Application of the United States of America for Reserved Water Rights in the Platte River, District Court, Water Division No. 1, Colorado, Case No. W–8439–76 (February 12, 1993).

UNITED STATES v. ADAIR

United States Court of Appeals, Ninth Circuit, 1983.
723 F.2d 1394, cert. denied 467 U.S. 1252.

Before KILKENNY, GOODWIN and FLETCHER, Circuit Judges.

FLETCHER, Circuit Judge:

I

BACKGROUND

A. *History of the Litigation Area*

The Klamath Indians have hunted, fished, and foraged in the area of the Klamath Marsh and upper Williamson River for over a thousand years. In 1864 the Klamath Tribe entered into a treaty with the United States whereby it relinquished its aboriginal claim to some 12 million acres of land in return for a reservation of approximately 800,000 acres in south-central Oregon. This reservation included all of the Klamath Marsh as well as large forested tracts of the Williamson River watershed. Treaty between the United States of America and the Klamath and Moadoc Tribes and Yahooskin Band of Snake Indians, Oct. 14, 1864, 16 Stat. 707. Article I of the treaty gave the Klamath the exclusive right to hunt, fish, and gather on their reservation. Article II provided funds to help the Klamath adopt an agricultural way of life. 16 Stat. 708.

For 20 years, until 1887, the Klamath lived on their reservation under the terms of the 1864 treaty. In 1887 Congress passed the General Allotment Act, ch. 119, 24 Stat. 388 (1887) which fundamentally changed the nature of land ownership on the Klamath Reservation.

Prior to the Act, the tribe held the reservation land in communal ownership. Pursuant to the terms of the Allotment Act, however, parcels of tribal land were granted to individual Indians in fee. Under the allotment system, approximately 25% of the original Klamath Reservation passed from tribal to individual Indian ownership. Over time, many of these individual allotments passed into non-Indian ownership.

The next major change in the pattern of land ownership on the Klamath Reservation occurred in 1954 when Congress approved the Klamath Termination Act. Under this Act, tribe members could give up their interest in tribal property for cash. A large majority of the tribe chose to do this. In order to meet the cash obligation, in 1961, the United States purchased much of the former Klamath Reservation. The balance of the reservation was placed in a private trust for the remaining tribe members.

* * * In 1973, to complete implementation of the Klamath Termination Act, the United States condemned most of the tribal land held in trust. Payments from the condemnation proceeding and sale of the remaining trust land went to Indians still enrolled in the tribe. This final distribution of assets essentially extinguished the original Klamath Reservation as a source of tribal property.

* * *

B. Proceedings in the District Court

In September of 1975, the United States filed suit in federal district court seeking a declaration of water rights within the Williamson River drainage [within the former Klamath Reservation]. In January of 1976, the State of Oregon initiated formal proceedings under state law to determine water rights in the Klamath Basin including that portion of the Williamson River drainage covered by the Government's suit. Later in 1976, the State of Oregon moved to intervene as a defendant in the United States suit. The Klamath Tribe also moved to intervene in the federal suit as a plaintiff. Both motions were granted. Subsequently, the State, joined by the individual defendants, moved for dismissal of the federal court water rights adjudication in favor of the state proceeding under the rule announced by the Supreme Court in *Colorado River Water Conservation District v. United States,* [page 780, supra]. The district court in effect denied the defendants' motion to dismiss when on November 14, 1977, it entered a Pretrial Order to govern the conduct of the federal suit.

This order, in listing the issues to be decided, significantly limited the nature of the federal proceeding. The district court did not agree to decide any question concerning the actual quantification of water rights. * * *

III

WATER RIGHTS

The district court declared reserved water rights within the litigation area to the Klamath Tribe, the Government, individual Indians, and non-Indian successors to Indian land owners.

A. *A Reservation of Water to Accompany the Tribe's Treaty Right to Hunt, Fish, and Gather*

Article I of the 1864 treaty with the Klamath Tribe reserved to the Tribe the exclusive right to hunt, fish, and gather on its reservation. This right survived the Klamath Termination Act * * *. The issue presented for decision in this case is whether, as the district court held, these hunting and fishing rights carry with them an implied reservation of water rights.

1. *Reservation of Water in the 1864 Treaty*

* * * *New Mexico* and *Cappaert,* while not directly applicable to *Winters* doctrine rights on Indian reservations, *see* F. Cohen, *Handbook of Federal Indian Law* 581–85 (1982 ed.), establish several useful guidelines. First, water rights may be implied only "[w]here water is necessary to fulfill the very purposes for which a federal reservation was created," and not where it is merely "valuable for a secondary use of the reservation." Second, the scope of the implied right is circumscribed by the necessity that calls for its creation. The doctrine "reserves only that amount of water necessary to fulfill the purpose of the reservation, no more." * * *

Article I of the Klamath Treaty expressly provides that the Tribe will have exclusive on-reservation fishing and gathering rights. * * * In view of the historical importance of hunting and fishing, and the language of Article I of the 1864 Treaty, we find that one of the "very purposes" of establishing the Klamath Reservation was to secure to the Tribe a continuation of its traditional hunting and fishing lifestyle. This was at the forefront of the Tribe's concerns in negotiating the treaty and was recognized as important by the United States as well.

At the same time, as the State and individual defendants argue, Articles II through V of the 1864 Treaty evince a purpose to convert the Klamath Tribe to an agricultural way of life. Article II provides that monies paid to the Tribe in consideration for the land ceded by the treaty "shall be expended * * * to promote the well-being of the Indians, advance them in civilization, *and especially agriculture,* and to secure their moral improvement and education." A similar focus on agriculture is reflected in the language of Articles III, IV and V. It is apparent that a second essential purpose in setting aside the Klamath Reservation, recognized by both the Tribe and the Government, was to encourage the Indians to take up farming. * * * Neither *Cappaert* nor *New Mexico* requires us to choose between these activities or to identify a single essential purpose which the parties to the 1864 Treaty intended the Klamath Reservation to serve. * * * A water right to support game and fish adequate to the needs of Indian hunters and fishers is not a right recognized as a part of the common law doctrine of prior appropriation followed in Oregon. Indeed, one of the standard requirements of the prior appropriation doctrine is that some diversion of the natural flow of a stream is necessary to effect a valid appropriation. But diversion of water is not required to support the fish and game that the Klamath Tribe take in exercise of their treaty rights. Thus the right to water reserved to further the Tribe's hunting and fishing purposes is unusual in that it is basically non-consumptive. * * * The holder of such a right is not entitled to withdraw water from the stream for agricultural, industrial, or other consumptive uses (absent independent consumptive rights). Rather, the entitlement consists of the right to prevent other appropriators from depleting the streams waters below a protected level in any area where the non-consumptive right applies. * * *

2. Effect of the Klamath Termination Act on the Tribe's Hunting and Fishing Water Rights

In 1954, Congress terminated federal supervision of the Klamath Tribe. * * * The state and individual appellants now argue that the Termination Act also abrogated any water rights reserved by the 1864 Treaty to accompany the Tribe's right to hunt and fish. Appellants contend that when federal supervision was terminated, former reservation lands were sold at full market value without limitations on use. * * * They conclude that recognition of a reserved water right to sustain the Tribe's hunting and fishing rights would impose a servitude or limitation on the use of former reservation lands in contravention of the Termination Act policy of unencumbered sale.

Appellants' argument, however, overlooks the substantive language of the Termination Act,[20] the canons of construction for legislation affecting Indian Tribes, and the implications of our [previous] decision. Section 564m(a) of the Termination Act provides, "[n]othing in sections 564–564w of this title shall abrogate any water rights of the tribe and its members." * * * This provision admits no exception, nor can it be read to exclude reserved water rights. Congress presumably was aware of the importance of such rights to Indian tribes at the time it drafted section 564m of the Klamath Termination Act. In sum, we agree with the district court that the water rights reserved to the Klamath Tribe by Treaty in 1864 were not abrogated by enactment of the Klamath Termination Act in 1954.

3. Priority of the Water Right Reserved to Accompany the Tribe's Treaty Right to Hunt and Fish

The district court found that the Tribe's water right accompanying its right to hunt and fish carried a priority date for appropriation of

---

20. Appellants cite language from subsection 28(c) of the 1958 amendments to the Termination Act, 72 Stat. 817. Subsection (c) details the method for appraising the fair market value of Klamath Reservation lands: "each appraiser shall estimate the fair market value of such forest units and marshlands *as if they had been offered for sale on a competitive market without limitation on use* * * *." Id. (emphasis added.) These appraisal instructions cannot be read to dictate the substantive conditions of termination.

time immemorial. United States v. Adair, 478 F.Supp. at 350. The State and individual appellants argue that an implied reservation of water cannot have a priority date earlier than establishment of the reservation. The Government and the Tribe argue that a pre-reservation priority date is appropriate for tribal water uses that pre-date establishment of the reservation. We have been unable to find any decisions that squarely address this issue. We therefore begin our analysis by turning to well-established principles of Indian treaty interpretation and Indian property rights for guidance. * * * Foremost among these is the principle that "the treaty is not a grant of rights to the Indians, but a grant of rights from them—a reservation of those not granted." Further, Indian treaties should be construed as the tribes would have understood them. And any ambiguity in a treaty must be resolved in favor of the Indians. A corollary of these principles, also recognized by the Supreme Court, is that when a tribe and the Government negotiate a treaty, the tribe retains all rights not expressly ceded to the Government in the treaty so long as the rights retained are consistent with the tribe's sovereign dependent status. * * * In 1864, at the time the Klamath entered into a treaty with the United States, the Tribe had lived in Central Oregon and Northern California for more than a thousand years. This ancestral homeland encompassed some 12 million acres. Within its domain, the Tribe used the waters that flowed over its land for domestic purposes and to support its hunting, fishing, and gathering lifestyle. This uninterrupted use and occupation of land and water created in the Tribe aboriginal or "Indian title" to all of its vast holdings. * * * The Supreme Court has specifically held that the Tribe had aboriginal title to timber on the Klamath Reservation. * * * The Tribe's title also included aboriginal hunting and fishing rights, and by the same reasoning, an aboriginal right to the water used by the Tribe as it flowed through its homeland. * * *

With this background in mind, we examine the priority date attaching to the Klamath Tribe's reservation of water to support its hunting and fishing rights. In Article I of the 1864 Treaty the Tribe expressly ceded "all [its] right, title and claim" to most of its ancestral domain. * * * In the same article, however, the Tribe reserved for its exclusive use and occupancy the lands that became the Klamath Reservation, the same lands that are the subject of the instant suit. * * * There is no indication in the treaty, express or implied, that the Tribe intended to cede any of its interest in those lands it reserved for itself. * * * Nor is it possible that the Tribe would have understood such a reservation of land to include a relinquishment of its right to use the water as it had always used it on the land it had reserved as a permanent home.

* * * Further, we find no language in the treaty to indicate that the United States intended or understood the agreement to diminish the Tribe's rights in that part of its aboriginal holding reserved for its permanent occupancy and use. Accordingly, we agree with the district court that within the 1864 Treaty is a recognition of the Tribe's aboriginal water rights and a confirmation to the Tribe of a continued

water right to support its hunting and fishing lifestyle on the Klamath Reservation. * * * Such water rights necessarily carry a priority date of time immemorial. The rights were not created by the 1864 Treaty, rather, the treaty confirmed the continued existence of these rights. * * * To assign the Tribe's hunting and fishing water rights the later, 1864, priority date argued for by the State and individual appellants would ignore one of the fundamental principles of prior appropriations law—that priority for a particular water right dates from the time of first use. Furthermore, an 1864 priority date might limit the scope of the Tribe's hunting and fishing water rights by reduction for any pre–1864 appropriations of water. This could extinguish rights the Tribe held before 1864 and intended to reserve to itself thereafter. Thus, we are compelled to conclude that where, as here, a tribe shows its aboriginal use of water to support a hunting and fishing lifestyle, and then enters into a treaty with the United States that reserves this aboriginal water use, the water right thereby established retains a priority date of first or immemorial use.[22] * * *

B.   Water Rights of Successors-in-Interest to Klamath Indian Allottees

* * *

1.   Indian Successors to Allotted Reservation Lands

* * * The scope of Indian irrigation rights is well settled. It is a right to sufficient water to "irrigate all the practicably irrigable acreage on the reservation."

* * * Individual Indian allottees have a right to use a portion of this reserved water. Moreover, the full measure of this right need not be exercised immediately. As with rights reserved to the Tribe, water may be used by Indian allottees for present and future irrigation needs.[25]

This right is limited here only by section 14 of the Klamath Termination Act, 25 U.S.C. § 564m (1976). This section provides, first, that "[n]othing in [The Termination Act] shall abrogate any water rights of the tribe and its members," and second, that "the laws of the State of Oregon with respect to abandonment of water rights by non-use shall not apply to the tribe and its members until fifteen years after the

---

22. In the present case, the Klamath Tribe, as we have noted, has depended upon the waters in question to support its hunting and fishing activities for over 1,000 years. It would be inconsistent with the principles we follow in today's decision to hold that the priority of the Tribe's water rights is any less ancient than the "immemorial" use that has been made of them. See United States v. Shoshone Tribe, 304 U.S. 111, 117, 58 S.Ct. 794, 798, 82 L.Ed. 1213 (1938); F. Cohen, *Handbook of Federal Indian Law* 591 & n. 100 (1982).

25. The water rights of Indian irrigators, as the district court noted, are subordinate to the Tribe's right to water for support of its hunting and fishing lifestyle.

478 F.Supp. at 346. This hierarchy among Indian water rights arises, not from any implication in the 1864 treaty that the purpose of hunting and fishing should predominate over any of the other purposes for which the Klamath Reservation was established, but rather from the analytically separate question of what priority date for appropriation the various water rights reserved in the treaty carry. Analysis of this latter question, under the unique circumstances of this case, leads to the conclusion that the Tribe's hunting and fishing water rights carry an earlier priority date for appropriation, because of historical use, than do water rights for irrigation.

date of the proclamation [of termination]." Id. The State and individual appellants argue that the second part of section 564m was meant to apply all Oregon water law, except that respecting abandonment of water rights by non-use, to the Tribe immediately upon the proclamation of termination.

* * *

In order to effectuate the Termination Act's explicit command that Klamath water rights survive unimpaired, we must interpret the second part of section 564m to mean that starting in 1976, fifteen years after the proclamation of termination in 1961, reserved water actually appropriated for use by members of the Tribe on allotments, could be lost under Oregon laws "with respect to abandonment of water rights by non-use." However, no other provision of Oregon water law that might preclude appropriation of the full measure of Klamath reserved water rights may be applied to the Tribe or its members consistently with the unequivocal language of protection in the first sentence of section 564m. To hold otherwise would sanction destruction of treaty rights in the absence of the required express Congressional approval.

2. *Non–Indian Successors to Allotted Reservation Lands*

The district court held that:

a non-Indian successor to an Indian allottee acquires an appurtenant right to water for the actual acreage under irrigation when he gets title from his Indian predecessor. The priority date of that right is 1864.

The non-Indian also acquires a right, with an 1864 priority date, to water for additional acreage which he, with reasonable diligence, may place under irrigation.

478 F.Supp. at 349.

The sole claim raised by the Tribe in its cross-appeal is to this aspect of the district court's decision.

The claim, however, is foreclosed by our recent decision in Colville Confederated Tribes v. Walton, 647 F.2d at 42. There we held the "[t]he full quantity of water available to the Indian allottee thus may be conveyed to the non-Indian purchaser." The limitations on this transfer, recognized in *Colville* are, first, that the non-Indian successor's right to water is "limited by the number of irrigable acres [of former reservation lands that] he owns," id., and second, that the non-Indian purchaser may lose the right to that quantity of water through non-use. Thus, citing the district court's opinion in the instant case, in *Colville,* we limited a non-Indian successor to lands allotted to a member of the Colville Tribe to the amount of water used by the Indian predecessor plus additional water that "he or she appropriates with reasonable diligence after the passage of title." * * *

NOTES

1. Several other courts have held that Indian tribes possess reserved water rights to minimum flows. Saying that it was applying the *New Mexico* test, the Ninth Circuit Court of Appeals recognized that the specific purposes of Indian reservations "were often unarticulated," and that because "the general purpose, to provide a home for the Indians, is a broad one [it] must be liberally construed." Colville Confederated Tribes v. Walton, 647 F.2d 42 (9th Cir.1981), cert. denied 454 U.S. 1092 (1981), page 823, infra. The court then looked at the Colville Tribes' traditional dependence on fishing for salmon and trout and the economic and religious importance of fishing. The court found that preservation of the tribes' fishing grounds was a purpose for creating the reservation in addition to the agricultural purposes. Consequently, the court held that the tribes had a reserved right to sufficient water to maintain a fishery in Omak Lake (as a replacement for the fishery it lost when the Columbia River was dammed). See also Colville Confederated Tribes v. Walton, 752 F.2d 397 (9th Cir.1985), cert. denied 475 U.S. 1010 (1986); United States v. Anderson, 736 F.2d 1358 (9th Cir.1984); Muckleshoot Indian Tribe v. Trans–Canada Enterprises, Ltd., 713 F.2d 455 (9th Cir.1983), cert. denied 465 U.S. 1049 (1984).

Is it "necessary to fulfill the purposes of the reservation" to allow reserved water rights with early priority dates to pass to non-Indian purchasers of allotments? For differing views see Richard B. Collins, *Indian Allotment Water Rights*, 20 Land & Water L.Rev. 421 (1985) and David H. Getches, *Water Rights on Indian Allotments*, 26 S.D.L.Rev. 405 (1981).

2. Should private persons who use federal lands be able to use the reserved water right of the federal government? For instance, suppose a timber contractor with a federal timber cutting permit wishes to use water in connection with the timber operation or a concessionaire in a National Park needs water to operate a campground or hotel. See United States v. Denver, 656 P.2d 1, 34 (Colo.1982). What limitations might there be on private use of federal reserved water rights? If the United States lawfully transfers a portion of a federal reservation to a private individual, does a portion of the federal reserved rights that attach to that land pass with it?

3. Should Indian tribes be able to sell or lease water held by them under reserved rights to non-Indians for use off the reservations? See page 819, infra.

NOTE: FEDERAL POWERS, RESERVED AND NONRESERVED FEDERAL WATER RIGHTS

Basis of Reserved Rights

The Supreme Court in Arizona v. California said that there was "no doubt about the power of the United States * * * to reserve water rights for its reservations and its property." The basis primarily relied upon by the Court in *Arizona*, was the Property Clause, which provides that "The Congress shall have Power to dispose of and make all needful Rules and Regulations respecting the Territory or other property belonging to the United States * * *." U.S. Const. art. IV, § 3, cl. 2. At one time in the nineteenth century, the United States owned almost all of the land, and all of the water appurtenant to that land, in sixteen of the seventeen western states. The federal government thus possessed the constitutional power to dispose of this land and water. The Court also cited the Commerce Clause of the Constitution, which gives Congress powers over navigable waters. The same clause gives Congress extensive power over Indian affairs, including Indian reservations, speaking of authority "to regulate Commerce * * * with the Indian Tribes." In addition, reserved rights for Indian reservations may be based on the treaty power found in article II, § 2, cl. 2, which furnishes sufficient power to establish reservations by treaty.

Initially, the federal government took no action regarding western water on the public lands. Early western settlers, when faced with a need for water, simply took what they needed. The Mining Act of 1866, 43 U.S.C.A. § 661, validated these uses, as it confirmed water rights recognized by custom and local law, and provided that pre–1866 appropriative rights would not be defeated by riparian claims of federal patentees.

In 1877, Congress passed the Desert Land Act, providing that the right to the use of water should depend upon prior appropriation, and that all water not appropriated should "remain and be held free for the appropriation and use of the public * * *." 43 U.S.C.A. § 321. The Act severed appropriated water from the public domain, and the states and territories were permitted to establish water rights systems allocating rights to use water according to their laws. See California Oregon Power Co. v. Beaver Portland Cement Co., 295 U.S. 142, 158, 164 (1935), page 167, supra. Unless and until rights to those waters are actually appropriated by individuals under state law, however, there is nothing preventing the United States from putting the water to use itself, thereby precluding future appropriations by others. To the extent the U.S. decides to use the unappropriated water, then, it becomes unavailable for appropriation under state law. The question is more difficult when the U.S. decides to commit its land to water-demanding purposes but does not actually start using the water.

The reserved right doctrine holds that when the United States withdraws land from the public domain, that is, sets it aside for particular federal purposes like a park, forest, or military base, it impliedly reserves unappropriated water sufficient for the purposes of the reservation. At that point, the federal government effectively revokes its permission for the state to allocate rights in the water as granted under the Desert Land Act. Any water appropriated as of the date of the reservation is, however, unavailable to the United States unless it compensates the prior appropriators. The water "reserved" by the United States can be used by private parties until the United States decides to put it to use, but they are junior in priority to the federal government. Their uses can be disputed, and if the water is later put to use by the federal government, the junior appropriators are owed no compensation, since they had no rights superior to the United States in the waters they were using.

Suppose the United States has not reserved land for purposes that require water but it needs to use water to carry out some federal program. The government does not have reserved water rights for the program. In United States v. New Mexico the Court insisted that rights are reserved by the United States only to the extent they are needed to fulfill the primary purposes for which the reservation was established. Thus, the government may not rely on reserved rights for any water needed to fulfill "secondary" purposes, or for water needed to carry out statutory programs and management mandates on and off federal lands. Surely the federal agencies may proceed to acquire water rights under state law. They have done so extensively throughout the country, especially in connection with federal public lands.

Must the government adhere to all the requirements of state law as it proceeds to appropriate water within the state system? It seems clear that any water rights appropriated by the United States will have a priority as of the date they are actually perfected. The early date of reserved rights is not available. But suppose the state system involved an administrative determination that could deny or limit the quantity of rights sought by the land manager. Or suppose the land manager sought water for a purpose not recognized as a beneficial use by the state system (e.g., for instream flows in a state where such rights are not allowed). A traditional preemption analysis applies to these situations. The question in each instance is whether Congress, exercising a constitutionally enumerated power, intended to preempt state water law. The issue is usually whether state action would frustrate "the accomplishment and execution of the full purposes and objectives of Congress." Laurence H. Tribe, American Constitutional Law 481 (1988), citing Hines v. Davidowitz, 312 U.S. 52 (1941). Thus, state action may be ousted by the operation of a federal program, or it may intrude upon a traditionally federal field. The first step is to look at the statutes granting management authority to the agency or official. Because these statutes usually do not specifically grant authority to appropriate water for a particular use, it is necessary to look at the broader purposes of the program or reservation of land, or other statement of the agency's mission. Congressional intent must be determined in light of these statutes and, where the words are unclear, their legislative history and the circumstances in which Congress acted.

There has been considerable debate within the Executive Branch as to the extent to which the government can and should assert that its non-reserved water rights claims preempt state water law. A 1979 Interior Department Solicitor's opinion that took an expansive view of the preemptive scope of federal water claims (86 Interior Dec. 553) was rejected in a later administration. The later position was embodied in a memorandum from the Office of Legal Counsel, United States Department of Justice, entitled "Federal Non–Reserved Water Rights," dated June 17, 1982. The memorandum concludes "the federal non-reserved water rights theory * * * does not provide an appropriate legal basis for assertion of water rights by federal agencies in the Western states."

However, the memorandum does not reject such rights under all circumstances. Instead, it says that the relevant issues are: (1) did Congress intend to exercise its constitutional powers to preempt state water law; and (2) if it did, what is the scope of the preemption? The memorandum also commented that the effect of Congress' traditional deference to state water law can best be understood as establishing a "presumption" to be read into the language and legislative history of federal statutes that authorize the management of federal lands—i.e., that in the absence of evidence to the contrary, it will be presumed that Congress did not intend to alter or affect its policy of deference to state water law. Therefore, as a general rule, it will be assumed that Congress intended federal agencies to acquire water rights in accordance with state law and contemplated that a state could deny some federal uses of water. Further, public land management statutes like the Federal Land Policy and Management Act (FLPMA), 43 U.S.C.A. §§ 1701–1782, were not intended by Congress to preempt state water law. The memorandum cautioned, however, that the Mining Acts and the Desert Land Act did not automatically "cede to the states control over the federal government's use of water for federal purposes and programs." Rather those acts only authorized state control of private appropriations of unappropriated water on federal lands.

Although the phrase "non-reserved" rights has been used to describe the administrative authority delegated by Congress to control water quantity in furtherance of federal land management purposes, that term can be characterized as "singularly unhelpful" and lacking in content when phrased in the negative. See Charles F. Wilkinson & H. Michael Anderson, *Land and Resources Planning in the National Forest*, 64 Or.L.Rev. 1, 232 (1985). The United States follows state water law in appropriating water rights, but when it is unable to comply with provisions of that law and still carry out federal purposes, state law may be preempted. The policy debate is over how vigorously the Executive will act in asserting preemption.

Consider several possible federal needs for water. In which cases do reserved rights exist? In which must the government proceed to acquire water rights entirely according to state law? In which may aspects of state law be avoided in order to acquire water rights?

1. The Department of Defense needs water to serve barracks built on a military reservation.

2. The Forest Service seeks instream flow rights for fish and wildlife purposes in a national forest, but state law does not recognize instream flows as a beneficial use.

3. The Park Service seeks to convert state-permitted agricultural rights it purchased from a farmer to instream flow rights for a national park, but state law allows instream flow rights to be held only by a state agency.

4. The Bureau of Land Management (BLM) seeks water rights to maintain a fishery in a stream on unreserved lands in a state that does not recognize instream flows as a beneficial use.

5.   The Forest Service desires to use water to irrigate a "community garden" operated by employees and their families who live within a national forest.

4. Quantification

As the authority of state courts to adjudicate reserved rights was clarified, states and non-Indian water users pressed for determinations that would provide them with certainty. State court adjudications of federal and Indian reserved rights are proceeding throughout the West. So far, only one such case has dealt with the issues of the existence, priority, and quantity of Indian reserved rights. It also provided an opportunity for the United States Supreme Court to revisit its practicable irrigable acreage standard announced in Arizona v. California. A quantification was made, but uncertainty persists as to a number of issues.

IN RE GENERAL ADJUDICATION OF ALL RIGHTS TO USE WATER IN THE BIG HORN RIVER SYSTEM

Supreme Court of Wyoming, 1988.
753 P.2d 76, affirmed sub nom. Wyoming v. United States,
492 U.S. 406, 109 S.Ct. 2994, 106 L.Ed.2d 342 (1989).

Before BROWN, C.J., and THOMAS, CARDINE, and MACY, JJ., and HANSCUM, DISTRICT JUDGE.

I INTRODUCTION

This appeal is from the district court's order adjudicating rights to use water in the Big Horn River System and all other sources within the State's Water Division No. 3.   * * *

The primary drainage system in the division is the Wind River–Big Horn River which originates in northern Fremont County and leaves the Division at the Wyoming–Montana border in northern Big Horn County.   * * *

The history of the Big Horn Basin for purposes of this case begins in the early 1800's when explorers, trappers and traders began traveling into northwestern Wyoming, part of the vast hunting grounds of the peripatetic Shoshone Indians. Neither group encroached on the other and relations were friendly. Nonetheless, in 1865, the United States, hoping to preserve the peace and stability, reached an agreement delineating the area within which the Eastern Shoshone roamed, a 44,672,000 acre region comprising parts of Wyoming, Colorado and Utah. Following the Civil War, as the westward movement gained momentum, the United States government realized the size of the region set aside for Indians only was unrealistic, and on July 3, 1868, executed the Second Treaty of Fort Bridger with the Shoshone and Bannock Indians, establishing the Wind River Indian Reservation.

* * *

B. *Procedural History of the Instant Litigation*

On January 22, 1977, Wyoming enacted § 1–1054.1, W.S.1957 (now § 1–37–106, W.S.1977), authorizing the State to commence system-wide adjudications of water rights. The State of Wyoming filed the complaint commencing this litigation and naming the United States as a defendant on January 24, 1977, in the District Court of the Fifth Judicial District of Wyoming.

* * *

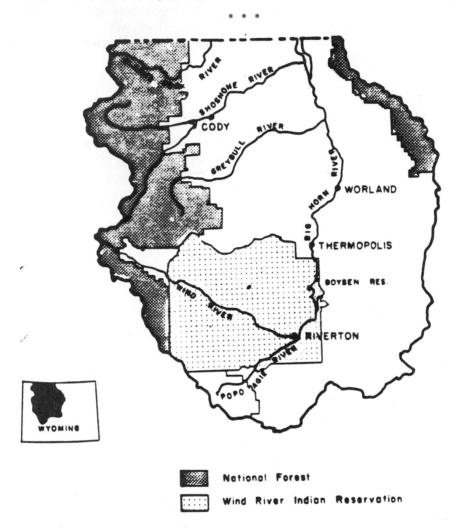

National Forest

Wind River Indian Reservation

WATER DIVISION NO. 3

Source Tom Kinney, Supervisor
Water Division III, General Adjudication,
State Engineers Office

The special master signed his 451–page Report Concerning Reserved Water Right Claims by and on Behalf of the Tribes in the Wind River Reservation on December 15, 1982, covering four years of conferences and hearings, involving more than 100 attorneys, transcripts of more than 15,000 pages and over 2,300 exhibits.

The report recognized a reserved water right for the Wind River Indian Reservation and determined that the purpose for which the reservation had been established was a permanent homeland for the Indians. A reserved water right for irrigation, stock watering, fisheries, wildlife and aesthetics, mineral and industrial, and domestic, commercial, and municipal uses was quantified and awarded.

* * *

The State of Wyoming, the United States, the Shoshone and Arapahoe Tribes, and numerous private parties presented objections to the master's report, and on May 10, 1983, Judge Joffe entered his Findings of Fact, Conclusions of Law and Judgment approving that portion of the master's report awarding reserved water rights for practicably irrigable acreage within the Wind River Indian Reservation and refusing to accept that portion of the master's report recommending an award of reserved water rights for other than agricultural purposes.

* * *

The treaty establishing the Wind River Indian Reservation, Treaty of Ft. Bridger, 15 Stat. 673 (1869), is silent on the subject of water for the reservation. Yet both the district court and the special master found an intent to reserve water. We affirm.

* * *

IV PURPOSES OF THE WIND RIVER INDIAN RESERVATION

The government may reserve water from appropriation under state law for use on the lands set aside for an Indian reservation. Winters v. United States, supra 207 U.S. 564, 28 S.Ct. 207. A reserved water right is implied for an Indian reservation where water is necessary to fulfill the purposes of reservation. United States v. Adair, 723 F.2d 1394, 1409 (9th Cir.1983), cert. denied sub nom. Oregon v. United States, 467 U.S. 1252, 104 S.Ct. 3536, 82 L.Ed.2d 841 (1984). The quantity of water reserved is the amount of water sufficient to fulfill the purpose of the lands set aside for the reservation. * * * We have already decided that Congress intended to reserve water for the Wind River Indian Reservation when it was created in 1868, and we accept the proposition that the amount of water impliedly reserved is determined by the purposes for which the reservation was created.

The special master's finding that the principal purpose for the creation of the reservation was to provide a permanent homeland for the Indians is not a factual determination. The master determined the purpose of the Indian reservation from the face of the treaty as a matter of law. Where the contract is unambiguous, the meaning or intent is derived from the instrument itself as a matter of law. * * * The district court ascertained the purpose of the reservation from the treaty itself, stating: "On the very face of the Treaty, it is clear that its purpose was purely agricultural." This legal determination is fully reviewable by this court.

A. *The Treaty*

The Treaty with the Shoshones and Bannacks, July 3, 1868, provides in pertinent part:

* * *

"ARTICLE IV. The Indians herein named agree * * * they will make said reservations their permanent home, and they will make no permanent settlement elsewhere; but they shall have the right to hunt on the unoccupied lands of the United States so long as game may be found thereon, and so long as place subsist * * *.

* * *

"ARTICLE VI. If any individual belonging to said tribes * * * shall desire to commence farming, he shall have the privilege to select * * * a tract of land within the reservation of his tribe * * * which tract * * * shall cease to be held in common * * *.

* * *

"ARTICLE VII. In order to insure the civilization of the tribes entering into this treaty, the necessity of education is admitted, especially of such of them as are or may be settled on said *agricultural reservations* * * *.

"ARTICLE VIII. When the head of a family or lodge shall have selected lands and received his certificate as above directed, and the agent shall be satisfied that he intends in good faith to commence cultivating the soil for a living, he shall be entitled to receive seeds and agricultural implements for the first year * * * and for each succeeding year he shall continue to farm, for a period of three years more * * *.

"And it is further stipulated that such persons as commence farming shall receive instructions from the farmers * * * and whenever more than one hundred persons on either reservation shall enter upon the cultivation of the soil, a second blacksmith shall be provided * * *.

"ARTICLE IX. * * * the United States agrees to deliver at the agency house on the reservation [items of clothing].

" * * * and in addition to the clothing herein named, the sum of ten dollars shall be annually appropriated for each Indian roaming and twenty dollars for each Indian engaged in agriculture, for a period of ten years, to be used by the Secretary of the Interior in the purchase of such articles as from time to time the condition and necessities of the Indians may indicate to be proper.

* * *

"ARTICLE XII. It is agreed that the sum of five hundred dollars annually for three years from the date when they commence to cultivate a farm, shall be expended in presents to the ten persons of said tribe, who in the judgment of the agent, may grow the most valuable crops for the respective year." (Emphasis added.)

The court in Colville Confederated Tribes v. Walton, supra 647 F.2d 42, did not mandate that a single purpose for the reservation be found. Rather, the court applied the specific purpose test outlined in United States v. New Mexico, supra 438 U.S. at 702, 98 S.Ct. at 3015, in an Indian reserved water case and found two primary purposes: "to provide a homeland for the Indians to maintain their agrarian society," 647 F.2d at 47, for which practicably irrigable acreage was the measure, and to preserve the "tribes' access to fishing grounds." 647 F.2d at 48. * * * In United States v. Adair, supra 723 F.2d at 1408, the ninth circuit agreed that non-Indian federal reservation reserved water rights cases only provide useful guidelines to Indian reserved water rights.

* * *

Considering the well-established principles of treaty interpretation, the treaty itself, the ample evidence and testimony addressed, and the findings of the district court, we have no difficulty affirming the finding that it was the intent at the time to create a reservation with a sole agricultural purpose. Indian treaties should be interpreted generously, * * * and should not be given a crabbed or restrictive meaning. McClanahan v. State Tax Commission of Arizona, supra 411 U.S. at 176, 93 S.Ct. at 1264. Nor should treaties be improperly construed in favor of Indians, for " '[W]e cannot remake history,' " Rosebud Sioux Tribe v. Kneip, supra 430 U.S. at 615, 97 S.Ct. at 1377, and courts should not distort the words of a treaty to find rights inconsistent with its language.

Article 7 of the treaty refers to "said agricultural reservations." Article 6 authorizes allotments for farming purposes; Article 8 provides seeds and implements for farmers; in Article 9 "the United States agreed to pay each Indian farming a $20 annual stipend, but only $10 to 'roaming' Indians"; and Article 12 establishes a $50 prize to the ten best Indian farmers. The treaty does not encourage any other occupation or pursuit. The district court correctly found that the reference in Article 4 to "permanent homeland" does nothing more than permanently set aside lands for the Indians; it does not define the purpose of the reservation. Rather, the purpose of the permanent-home reservation is found in Articles 6, 8, 9, and 12 of the treaty.

* * *

The fact that the Indians fully intended to continue to hunt and fish does not alter that conclusion.

Agreements subsequent to the treaty acknowledge the continuance of non-agricultural activities on the reservation. The reports of the Indian agents are replete with descriptions of and plans for other activities. Yet not one of the cited reports neglects to report also on the progress of the farming and ranching operations. The primary activity was clearly agricultural.

B. *Fisheries*

Reserved water rights for fisheries have been recognized where a treaty provision explicitly recognized an exclusive right to take fish on the reservation or the right to take fish at traditional off-reservation fishing grounds, in common with others.

* * *

Instream fishery flows have also been recognized where the Indians were heavily, if not totally, dependent on fish for their livelihood. United States v. Adair, supra 723 F.2d at 1409; Colville Confederated Tribes v. Walton, supra 647 F.2d at 48. In the case at bar, the Tribes introduced evidence showing that fish had always been part of the Indians' diet. The master, erroneously concluding that a reserved right for fisheries should be implied when the tribe is "at least partially dependent upon fishing," awarded an instream flow right for fisheries. The district court, however, finding neither a dependency upon fishing for a livelihood nor a traditional lifestyle involving fishing, deleted the award. The district court did not err. The evidence is not sufficient to imply a fishery flow right absent a treaty provision.

C. *Mineral and Industrial*

The Tribes were denied a reserved water right for mineral and industrial development. All parties to the treaty were well aware before it was signed of the valuable mineral estate underlying the Wind River Indian Reservation. The question of whether, because the Indians own the minerals, the intent was that they should have the water necessary to develop them must be determined, of course, by the intent in 1868. Neither the Tribes nor the United States has cited this court to any provision of the treaty or other evidence indicating that the parties contemplated in 1868 that a purpose of the reservation would be for the Indians to develop the minerals. The fact that the Tribes have since used water for mineral and industrial purposes does not establish that water was impliedly reserved in 1868 for such uses. The district court did not err in denying a reserved water right for mineral and industrial uses.

D. *Municipal, Domestic and Commercial*

A reserved water right for municipal, domestic and commercial uses was included within the agricultural reserved water award. Domestic and related use has traditionally been subsumed in agricultural reserved rights. See, e.g., United States ex rel. Ray v. Hibner, supra 27 F.2d at 911 (the treaties fixed the rights of the Indians—"to a continuous use of a sufficient amount of water for the irrigation of their lands, and domestic purposes"); United States v. Powers, supra 305 U.S. at

533, 59 S.Ct. at 347 ("waters essential to farming and home making"). Practicably irrigable acreage (PIA) was established as the measure of an agricultural reserved water right in Arizona v. California, supra 373 U.S. at 601, 83 S.Ct. at 1498. The special master there indicated that PIA was the measure of water necessary for agriculture and related purposes. The court properly allowed a reserved water right for municipal, domestic, and commercial use.

E. *Livestock*

For the reasons stated above, the district court did not err in finding a sole agricultural purpose for the reservation or in subsuming livestock use within that purpose.

F. *Wildlife and Aesthetics*

The special master awarded 60% of historic flows for wildlife and aesthetic uses, consistent with his determination that the purpose of the reservation was to be a permanent homeland. The district court deleted this award, reciting not only that the purpose was solely agricultural, but that insufficient evidence had been presented to justify an award for these uses. The district court did not err in holding that the Tribes and the United States did not introduce sufficient evidence of a tradition of wildlife and aesthetic preservation which would justify finding this to be a purpose for which the reservation was created and for which water was impliedly reserved.

The district court did not err in finding a sole agricultural purpose in the creation of the Wind River Indian Reservation. The Treaty itself evidences no other purpose, and none of the extraneous evidence cited is sufficient to attribute a broader purpose.

V SCOPE OF THE RESERVED WATER RIGHT

A. *Groundwater*

The logic which supports a reservation of surface water to fulfill the purpose of the reservation also supports reservation of groundwater. See Tweedy v. Texas Company, 286 F.Supp. 383, 385 (D.Mont.1968) ("whether the [necessary] waters were found on the surface of the land or under it should make no difference"). Certainly the two sources are often interconnected. See § 41–3–916, W.S.1977 (where underground and surface waters are "so interconnected as to constitute in fact one source of supply," a single schedule of priorities shall be made).

Acknowledging the above, we note that, nonetheless, not a single case applying the reserved water doctrine to groundwater is cited to us. The ninth circuit indicated that groundwater was reserved in United States v. Cappaert, 508 F.2d 313, 317 (9th Cir.1974). The United States Supreme Court, however, found the water in the pool reserved for preservation of the pupfish was not groundwater but surface water, protected from subsequent diversions from either surface or groundwater supplies. Cappaert v. United States, supra 426 U.S. at 143, 96 S.Ct. at 2071. * * *

The district court did not err in deciding there was no reserved groundwater right. Because we hold that the reserved water doctrine does not extend to groundwater, we need not address the separate claim that the district court erred in determining that the State owns the groundwater. The State has not appealed the decision that the Tribes may continue to satisfy their domestic and livestock needs (part of the agricultural award) from existing wells at current withdrawal rates; therefore, we do not address that question.

B. *Exportation*

The district court held that "[t]he Tribes can sell or lease any part of the water covered by their reserved water rights but the said sale or lease cannot be for exportation off of the Reservation." The Tribes did not seek permission to export reserved water, and the United States concedes that no federal law permits the sale of reserved water to non-Indians off the reservation. Because of our holding on the groundwater issue, we need not address the separate constitutional attack on the prohibition of exportation of groundwater.

* * *

VI QUANTIFICATION

A. *The Measure*

The measure of the Tribes' reserved water right is the water necessary to irrigate the practicably irrigable acreage on the reservation. In Arizona v. California, supra 373 U.S. at 600–601, 83 S.Ct. at 1498, a needs test was rejected as too uncertain, the Court opting instead for practicably irrigable acreage as the measure of a tribal agricultural reserved water right. Two subsequent non-Indian reserved water right cases, Cappaert v. United States, supra 426 U.S. 128, 96 S.Ct. 2067, and United States v. New Mexico, supra 438 U.S. at 702, 98 S.Ct. at 3015, indicate that necessity is the measure of a reserved water right. And in Washington v. Washington State Commercial Passenger Fishing Vessel Association, supra 443 U.S. at 686–687, 99 S.Ct. at 3075, the Court recognized the propriety of reducing the Indians' proportion of the fish harvest as their needs diminished. Nonetheless, the Court declined the invitation to re-examine the PIA standard in Arizona v. California, supra 460 U.S. at 625–626, 103 S.Ct. at 1394–1395, and reaffirmed the value of the certainty inherent in the practicably irrigable acreage standard. The district court was correct in quantifying the Tribes' reserved water right by the amount of water necessary to irrigate all of the reservation's practicably irrigable acreage.

B. *Future Lands*

The Tribes and the United States claimed a reserved water right for lands on the reservation not yet developed for irrigation, but which were in their view, practicably irrigable acreage. Counsel for the State, the Tribes and the United States agreed upon a definition of practicably irrigable acreage: "those acres susceptible to sustained irrigation at reasonable costs." The determination of practicably irrigable acreage involves a two-part analysis, i.e., the PIA must be susceptible of sustained irrigation (not only proof of the arability but also of the engineering feasibility of irrigating the land) and irrigable "at reasonable cost."

The United States presented evidence on all these factors to support its ultimate claim for 53,760 practicably irrigable acres (210,000 acre-feet/year), and Wyoming presented evidence in opposition. * * *
The Amended Judgment and Decree * * * resulted in the total final award being 48,097 acres.

   1. Arability

* * *

The master determined that the arable land base was 76,027 acres. Wyoming claims on appeal that the arability investigation did not meet Bureau of Reclamation Standards for 60% of the land as to the depth to barrier, maximum slope, hydraulic conductivity, barrier definition and maximum drain spacing standards. The special master accepted the approach of the United States as meeting its burden of establishing the land base for the determination of arability. There was substantial evidence to support this determination, and looking, as we must, only to the evidence of the United States, we affirm the master's finding of 76,027 acres of arable land base.

   2. Engineering Feasibility

* * *

The master did not abuse his discretion in accepting the engineering feasibility work which incorporated 35% project efficiencies rather than a 50% project efficiency. * * *

The master determined that practicably irrigable acreage should be based on present standards.

* * *

VIII   MONITORING OF THE DECREE BY THE STATE ENGINEER

The issue of whether the state engineer may monitor the decree is a controversy conferring jurisdiction upon this court. * * * The decree entered in the instant case does not require application of state water law to the Indian reservation. The decree recognizes reserved water rights based on federal law. The role of the state engineer is thus not to apply state law, but to enforce the reserved rights as decreed under principles of federal law. This court is also cognizant of the fact that exercise of the reserved water rights are intimately bound up with the state water rights of off-reservation users. The state water appropriators are not in a position to jeopardize the decreed rights of the Tribes. The decree only requires the United States and the Tribes first to turn to the state engineer to exercise his authority over the state users to protect their reserved water rights before they seek court assistance to enforce their rights; it does not preclude access to the courts. Incidental monitoring of Indian use to this end has carelessly been termed "administration" of Indian water by the state engineer. Should the state engineer find that it is the Tribes who are violating the decree, it is clear that he must then turn to the courts for enforcement of the decree against the United States and the Tribes and that he cannot simply close the headgates. Any fear that the state engineer may be unfair must be dispelled by Article 1, § 31 of the Wyoming Constitution which provides that the State "shall equally guard all of the various [water] interests involved." The state engineer has sworn to uphold this constitution. Thus it is readily apparent that the provisions authorizing the state engineer to monitor reserved water rights contemplate neither the application of state law nor the authority to deprive the Tribes of water without the assistance of the courts in a suit for the administration of the decree.

* * *

The district court did not err in including provisions giving the state engineer authority to enforce the decree against state appropriators.

* * *

THOMAS, JUSTICE, dissenting with whom HANSCUM, DISTRICT JUDGE, joins.

I differ from the majority with respect to three propositions and must dissent from the disposition made in the majority opinion. Except for my three points of difference, I am in accord with the resolution of this case as set forth in that opinion. My three points of difference are: first, I do not agree that reserved water rights, to the extent that they properly are recognized under the reserved rights doctrine, should be limited in the manner suggested by the majority opinion; second, I believe that there should be a pragmatic limitation on the standard for quantification, the practicably irrigable acreage, which would eliminate those lands from the quantification formula which only could be irrigated by the construction of some future water project; and third, but most important, I do not believe that the reserved rights doctrine is applicable to that portion of the lands lying north of the "Big Wind River," i.e., the ceded portion of the Wind River Indian Reservation.

* * *

NOTES

1. The decision resulted in a quantification of the tribe's reserved rights amounting to over 500,000 acre-feet. After the state petitioned for U.S. Supreme Court review, the tribes cross-petitioned on several grounds. What grounds would you raise as tribal attorney? Certiorari was granted solely on a ground urged by the state: that the PIA standard should not have applied to the case. The case was briefed and argued on that point, but the court divided equally, with Justice O'Connor not participating. Does the PIA standard appear vulnerable?

2. The Court in *New Mexico* said that the quantity of water reserved at the time of a federal reservation, and thus available under the reservation doctrine, is strictly limited to that amount necessary to fulfill the original purposes of the withdrawal. The Court emphasized that water was reserved only to the extent that "the purpose of the reservation would be entirely defeated" without the water. Does the Court's reference to the purposes at the time of the reservation imply that the PIA standard set in Arizona v. California must be determined in light of nineteenth century technology? Is the standard itself subject to review to the extent that it calls for water quantities in excess of an amount necessary to prevent defeat of the original purposes of the reservation? In light of the broad purposes of Indian reservations, is the restrictive language in *New Mexico* limited to non-Indian federal reservations?

3. Shortly after the Wyoming Supreme Court's decision, the tribes closed the headgates to the Crowheart Irrigation Unit of the Wind River Indian Reservation thus severely restricting the water of the non-Indian irrigators. The tribes contended that the non-Indian irrigators had used more water than had been allotted to them. In February of 1989, Wyoming's Governor and the tribes resolved the dispute in a one-year agreement in which the state paid approximately $5 million and the tribes agreed to limit their exercise of *Winters* rights. In times of shortage, the tribes would share equally with other water users in restricting their use of water, regardless of priority. The state also agreed to improve the water works projects serving the reservation and to look into water storage sites.

Then, in April of 1990, when the agreement with the state expired, the tribes issued an "Instream Flow Permit" to the Shoshone and Northern Arapahoe Tribes for a term of six months authorizing the dedication of 252 cfs of water from the Wind River that had been quantified for future agricultural project uses into instream flows for fisheries, groundwater recharge, and habitat restoration and enhancement, among other things. This again restricted the available water for non-Indian irrigators, who claimed that the decree did not authorize use of the tribes' water for instream flow. The state argued that the tribes' attempt to convert their reserved water rights to instream flows would severely damage many non-Indian junior appropriators in the area.

When the Wyoming State Engineer declined to enforce tribal "Instream Flow Permits," the tribes asked the state district court to appoint a special master to resolve the conflict over the tribes' right to apply their water rights to instream flows and, ultimately, to hold the State Engineer in contempt of court. Based on the report of the special master, the district court declared that the tribes were entitled to use their reserved water rights on the reservation as they deemed advisable, including instream flow use, without regard to Wyoming water law. Furthermore, the district court appointed the tribal water agency to administer water rights of Indians and non-Indians on the reservation, instead of the State Engineer.

On appeal, the Wyoming Supreme Court, in a deeply divided plurality opinion, held that its 1989 decision (*Big Horn I*) had already determined that instream flow was not an allowable use of water on the Wind River Indian Reservation, which had been created exclusively for agricultural purposes and not for fisheries. The decision allowed the tribes to change the use of their own quantified rights from the present use in agriculture to instream flow uses. However, *Big Horn II* precluded them from changing the purpose of rights quantified for future agricultural projects to instream flows when doing so would deprive non-Indian appropriators of their use rights. The decision also found it improper for the lower court to assign the State Engineer's statutory duty of administering state water rights to the tribal agency. In the General Adjudication of All Rights to Use Water in the Big Horn River System, 835 P.2d 273 (Wyo.1992). The tribes decided for both strategic and practical reasons not to seek review of the decision in the U.S. Supreme Court.

Now, major non-Indian irrigators affected by the decision are seeking to have their priority dates changed from 1906—when the irrigation districts acquired land from the Wind River Indians—to 1868—the year of the original treaty from which the reservation's rights are dated. In a 1990 ruling, the Wyoming Supreme Court held that purchasers of water rights from tribal interests were entitled to the same priority date, as long as the land to which the right was appurtenant had been in continuous irrigation.

4. Can the Wind River tribes sell or lease the right to use quantified reserved rights outside the reservation? Questions have been raised about whether the reserved rights held by Indians can or should ever extend to selling water for uses outside the reservation. Indian property cannot be sold or leased without congressional consent. See 25 U.S.C.A. § 177. Several settlements of *Winters* doctrine water rights approved by Congress have included provisions for the tribes to market their water off the reservation. See pages 820–22, infra.

Should there be any conditions placed on Indian off-reservation water marketing? What protection should there be for junior appropriators injured by the transfer? Should there be protection imposed for the tribe's benefit? Off-reservation water marketing could limit future generations of Indians in their possibilities for maintaining economic security and cultural integrity. Can a transfer of water to non-Indians who may become dependent upon it be truly temporary? If a transfer is not temporary, what are the effects on Indian society? See generally Lee H. Storey, Comment, *Leasing Indian Water Off the Reservation: A Use Consistent with the Reservation's Purpose,* 76 Cal.L.Rev. 179 (1988); Karen M. Shapiro, *An Argument for the Marketability of Indian Reserved Water Rights: Tapping the Untapped Reservoir,* 23 Idaho L.Rev. 277 (1986–87); and Christine Lichtenfels, Comment, *Indian Reserved Water Rights: An Argument for the Right to Export and Sell,* 24 Land & Water L.Rev. 131 (1989).

NOTE: QUANTIFICATION OF INDIAN RESERVED
WATER RIGHTS WITHOUT LITIGATION

One possible alternative to litigation of Indian reserved rights is congressional quantification. Several bills have been introduced in Congress that would lead to quantification of reserved rights, but they all have died before coming to a vote. Indian tribes differ widely in the economic and cultural importance that they place on water. Furthermore, reservations are located in areas of varying climates and where competing non-Indian demands are quite different. These factors auger against a generic solution to Indian reserved water rights claims. Congressional quantification, even done on a tribe-by-tribe basis may be difficult to achieve fairly given the fact that politically weak and unsophisticated tribes may be pitted against interests powerful enough to move Congress to act. See Charles DuMars & Helen M. Ingram, *Congressional Quantification of Indian Reserved Water Rights: A Definitive Solution or a Mirage?*, 20 Nat.Resources J. 17 (1980); and Judith B. Jacobson, *A Promise Made: The Navajo Indian Irrigation Project and Water Policies in the American West*, Cooperative Thesis # 119, Univ. of Colo. (1989).

States, tribes, and the federal government are increasingly turning to negotiation as a means of resolving Indian water rights issues and quantifying Indian reserved rights. Often the negotiations commence in the course of litigation. In some cases litigation may be useful to fix quantification, but can not solve practical problems that are best left for negotiated solutions.

Negotiated settlements are attractive to all parties as a way of avoiding the enormous transaction costs of water rights litigation. The *Big Horn* adjudication (page 808, supra) cost the state of Wyoming alone more than $7 million in legal fees. In addition, a negotiated solution can provide for delivery of "wet water" to Indians—not just paper water rights that result from a courtroom victory. In many cases, the non-Indian parties can persuade the federal government to provide them with facilities and other benefits as well.

Indian water settlements have received mixed reviews. See, for example, Lloyd Burton, American Indian Water Rights and the Limits of the Law (1991). Describing the early Navajo and Uintah–Ouray deferral agreements, Burton concludes that: "It appears in retrospect that the tribes either deferred or surrendered potent, senior, and superior rights to a great deal of water in return for promises made but not yet fulfilled * * * or for economic development that has proved largely illusory." Id. at 69.

Without understanding the motives of the participants, it is impossible to judge the "success of negotiations." Indian tribes usually seek to retain intact their water rights and the sovereignty they need to exercise, to protect, and to use those rights. Non–Indian water users and state water administrators generally seek certainty of rights and maximum protection of existing uses, particularly by appropriators junior to the tribe whose interests are exposed in litigation. The federal government seeks to mollify political constituencies allied with non-Indians and state authorities, but within the constraints of its trust responsibility to the tribes. Some officials have been reluctant to commit the government to expenditures beyond the cost of defending litigation.

Where—as in the West—water is a scarce and already over-appropriated resource, one might expect negotiated settlements to be a zero-sum game. In fact, and not surprisingly, the lubricant that allows seemingly intractable conflicts to come "unstuck" is federal money, used either to fund water projects that produce more water by adding storage capacity, or to provide tribal development funds that enable tribes to take advantage of their rights by putting some of their water to use on the reservation.

On June 21, 1989, President Bush signed the Puyallup Tribe of Indians Settlement Act of 1989 (Pub.L. No. 101–41, § 2, 103 Stat. 83) and issued a policy statement announcing that disputes involving Indian water rights would be resolved through negotiation rather than litigation. The Department of the Interior then published criteria for structuring such settlements (55 Fed.Reg. 9223, Mar. 12, 1990) apparently making negotiated settlements the rule rather than the exception for quantifying Indian rights and dealing with related issues.

The thrust of official policy is to provide a framework for negotiating settlements of Indian water rights within which: 1) the United States can participate in a manner consistent with its trust responsibilities to the tribes; 2) Indians receive benefits commensurate with the claims they may release as part of a settlement; 3) Indians obtain the ability to realize value from the confirmed water rights resulting from a settlement; and 4) the costs of the settlement are appropriately shared by its beneficiaries. Id.

Indian tribes have objected to Interior's settlement criteria on philosophical, substantive, and procedural grounds. First, they fail to acknowledge the extent to which the present situation is a direct result of the federal government's deliberate disregard for Indian reserved rights from 1908 (when *Winters* was handed down) to 1963, when the Supreme Court reaffirmed the existence of those rights in Arizona v. California. Second, the settlement criteria were developed without formal consultation with the tribes.

The Native American Rights Fund (NARF) filed formal objections to the criteria, insisting that: 1) the dispositive measure of settlements negotiated under the ambit of the federal trust responsibility must be the "best interests of the tribe;" 2) tribal interests are best served by settlements which convert water rights into an income stream for the tribe; 3) no tribe should bear—either directly or indirectly—the costs of conferring federal benefits on non-Indian water users who became dependent on the use of Indian water rights (despite adequate notice that such reliance was not justified); 4) tribal interests are best served by negotiated settlements that promote "win-win" outcomes and generate increased goodwill within the affected community; and 5) no tribe should bear any costs of a settlement that results in the surrender of Indian rights to secure water for non-Indian users. NARF also encouraged reducing transaction costs by adopting more flexible and less time-consuming procedures. See Eileen Shimizu, *Indian Water Rights: An Examination of the Current Status of the Department of Interior's Guidelines and the Opposition to Them,* 30 Fed.B.News & J. 88 (1991). A socio-economic response to issues underlying the federal settlement policy is offered in Michael R. Moore, *Native American Water Rights: Efficiency and Fairness,* 29 Nat. Resources J. 764 (1989).

Between 1982 and 1993, Congress had approved negotiated settlements of Indian water issues affecting 21 reservations. They reveal a pattern of common features. Nearly all guaranteed a specific quantity of water to the tribes. Several provide for water to be supplied from a federal project. Virtually all create trust funds of mostly federal money for tribes to invest in water development or economic development activities. The funds range from $6 million to over $150 million. Nearly all allow for some tribal water marketing, though provisions are usually drafted to specify limits on the amount, the lessee (or purchaser), or the place of use. See John A. Folk–Williams, *Environmental Dispute Resolution: the Use of Negotiated Agreements to Resolve Water Disputes Involving Indian Rights,* 28 Nat.Resources J. 63 (1988); and Reid P. Chambers & John E. Echohawk, *Implementing the Winters Doctrine of Indian Reserved Water Rights: Producing Indian Water and Economic Development without Injuring Non–Indian Water Users?,* 27 Gonz.L.Rev. 447 (1991). For an excellent summary of current issues, see John E. Thorson, *Proceedings of the Symposium on Settlement of Indian Water Rights Claims,* 22 Envtl.L. 1009 (1992).

While Lloyd Burton and others have feared the worst from negotiations pitting under-represented and arguably unsophisticated tribes against the powerful interests that oppose them, Chambers and Echohawk conclude that the results have been largely beneficial. In no case has the quantity of a tribe's claimed *Winters* rights been diminished. See Jana L. Walker & Susan M. Williams, *Indian Reserved Water Rights,* 5 Nat.Resources & Env't, Spring 1991, at 6. Negotiated agreements have produced almost $693 million for tribes. Furthermore, off-reservation use and marketing of Indian water under the agreements allows tribes to reap economic benefits when water is not needed for on-reservation uses, though it is subject to limiting conditions and state water transfer laws. See Steven J. Shupe, *Indian Tribes in the Water Marketing Arena,* 15 Am. Indian L.Rev. 185 (1990). Non–Indian interests have begun to benefit from greater certainty, from federal projects and expenditures for their use, and, in most cases, the availability of additional water supplies.

5. Tribal Water Management

While most litigation involving Indian water rights has been concerned with the quantity of water reserved under *Winters,* or with the jurisdiction of state or federal courts to hear such cases, a separate issue concerns governmental authority to regulate water use. The question is: under what circumstances do state or tribal governments have authority to regulate and manage water rights of Indians and non-Indians within reservation boundaries?

There is strong legal precedent requiring state deference to federal and tribal jurisdiction over Indians and Indian property within reservation boundaries. Many non-Indians live within Indian reservations and, indeed, own or lease land there. As tribes have begun to clarify their reserved rights entitlements and to develop economically, they have also become more sophisticated in their ability to manage resources. Economic necessity and the availability of professional assistance have encouraged them to enact tribal water codes and to hire administrative, technical, and enforcement staffs to deal with water resources within reservation boundaries. In many cases, they have not limited their asserted jurisdiction to Indians, but have purported to extend it over all persons using water within the reservation. See Susan M. Williams, *Indian* Winters *Water Rights Administration: Averting New War,* 11 Pub. Land L.Rev. 53 (1990).

The exclusive right of Indian tribes to regulate Indians within Indian country is well-established. Tribes may also regulate non-Indian land. More difficult questions arise, however, when tribes regulate water use by non-Indians on non-Indian land located within reservation boundaries. In Colville Confederated Tribes v. Walton, 647 F.2d 42 (9th Cir.1981) (*Walton II*), the court found that the state had no authority to regulate non-Indian users of a water source located entirely within reservation boundaries. Applying the test from Montana v. United States, 450 U.S. 544 (1981), the *Walton II* court found that, since the stream system was critical to the development of reservation resources and thus to the lifestyle of reservation residents, state regulation would interfere with tribal sovereignty. Likewise, since the water source had no impact on state-managed water resources located off-reservation, the state had little genuine interest in regulating that source.

By contrast, in United States v. Anderson, 736 F.2d 1358 (9th Cir.1984), the same court reached an opposite result, ruling that the state, and not the tribe, had regulatory authority over use of excess water by junior non-Indian appropriators located on the reservation. Since the water source was located substantially off the reservation and the water being used was in excess of the tribe's own needs, regulation of junior users had no "direct effect on the political integrity, the economic security, or the health or welfare of the tribe," the criteria announced by the Court in *Montana.* The state's interest in developing and maintaining a comprehensive water program weighed in favor of state regulatory authority over non-Indian users. See Tribal Water Management 64 (American Indian Resources Institute 1988).

Most Indian water rights settlement agreements have failed to deal fully with water rights administration and jurisdiction. This phenomenon is explained by some commentators as follows:

> Many of the water quantity settlements have adopted an approach that delays or avoids altogether the difficult issues of water administration * * *. This "jurisdictional finesse" is particularly appropriate for settlements on reservations with substantial nonmember populations, where issues of water management have

roots in history and complex, checkerboard landholdings. In the Colorado Ute * * * and 1986 Fort Peck settlements, for example, the parties deferred issues of water administration until the final stages of discussion, when water allocations had been established. In the 1990 Pyramid Lake settlement, the parties left water administration issues (including selection of an agency or court to oversee operation of the Truckee River and its reservoirs) for negotiation by the states and Interior in a later operating agreement.

The jurisdictional finesse approach is supported by judicial insistence that water administration issues not be reached until water rights are first quantified in a stream adjudication. As a consequence, Indian water administration issues are only arising now. For example, in [*Big Horn I*, page 808, supra], the state court effort to quantify tribal reserved water rights took more than fifteen years, but did not resolve administration questions * * *. Now the state engineer asserts primary jurisdiction over the tribes' effort to change use of the reserved water right from agricultural to instream use. In a similar vein, in the Carson, Walker, and Truckee River decrees, the federal courts turned to the state engineer to make preliminary rulings on transfer applications, including those of tribes.

Peter W. Sly & Cheryl A. Maier, *Indian Water Settlements and EPA*, 5 Nat. Resources & Env't, Spring 1991, at 23, 24–25.

STEVEN J. SHUPE, WATER IN INDIAN COUNTRY: FROM PAPER RIGHTS TO A MANAGED RESOURCE

57 U.Colo.L.Rev. 561, 577 (1986).

* * *

C. Impediments to Tribal Water Regulation

* * * Two unresolved issues continue to create uncertainty for tribes wanting to regulate the use of water on the reservation. * * *

1. Non–Indian Water Use

The land ownership pattern within many Indian reservations is a patchwork of tribal lands and parcels owned by various individuals. This checkerboarding was spawned by the General Allotment Act of 1887 wherein many tracts of reservation lands were distributed to individual tribal members. Subsequently, many of the allotments passed into non-Indian ownership, as did other tribal lands that had been deemed "surplus" by the government and opened to homesteading.

This patchwork of land ownership has created a complex pattern of Indian and non-Indian water use within many reservations. This, in turn, led to controversy over which government, tribal or state, has jurisdiction to regulate water use of non-Indians on the reservation. One specific issue that has reached the courts is whether water rights permits issued by the state to non-Indians on the reservations are valid. Tribes have argued that such permits are of no effect and that appropriators, both Indian and non-Indian, must follow tribal law in order to establish a valid right to use water on the reservation. Tribal authority to allocate and regulate limited supplies, they argue, extends not only to tribal water rights reserved under the *Winters* doctrine, but also includes any waters within the reservation.

* * *

2. The Secretarial Moratorium

In [*Walton* and *Anderson*], both the Spokane and Colville tribal governments had enacted water codes in order to assert their regulatory control over reservation water. On many reservations, such codes can be an important tool for implementing tribal policies and effectuating comprehensive water management. Numerous tribes, however, are currently inhibited from utilizing this tool due to the longstanding requirement that their codes receive the approval of the Secretary of the Interior.

In 1934, Congress passed the Indian Reorganization Act (IRA) to stem the erosion of tribal strength that had resulted from the previous allotment policy. Many tribal governments reorganized under the IRA provisions and adopted model constitutions. These IRA constitutions typically contained the provision that all codes enacted by the tribal government needed approval of the Secretary of the Interior in order for them to be valid.

In 1975, Interior Secretary Morton sent a two-paragraph memorandum to the Commissioner of Indian Affairs stating that "any tribal ordinance, resolution, code or other enactment which purports to regulate the use of water on Indian reservations" and which requires approval for its validity shall be automatically disapproved.[105] The moratorium on code approval was to remain in effect until the Department of the Interior promulgated rules providing guidelines for the adoption of tribal water codes. The Secretary expressed his concern that, without such rules, independent tribal water codes "could lead to confusion and a series of separate legal challenges which might lead to undesirable results."

On March 7, 1977, Interior Secretary Andrus published proposed rules regarding the adoption of tribal water codes. Under the proposed rules, the Secretary of the Interior must approve a tribal water code if it comports with certain conditions. First, the code must afford procedural due process to all water users on the reservations. This includes

---

105. Memorandum from the Sec'y of the Interior, Rogers C.B. Morton, to the Comm'r of Indian Affairs (Jan. 15, 1975):

As you know, the Department is currently considering regulations providing for the adoption of tribal codes to allocate the use of reserved waters on Indian reservations. Our authority to regulate the use of water on Indian reservations is presently in litigation. I am informed, however, that some tribes may be considering the enactment of water use codes of their own. This could lead to confusion and a series of separate legal challenges which might lead to undesirable results.

I ask, therefore, that you instruct all agency superintendents and area directors to disapprove any tribal ordinance, resolution, code, or other enactment which purports to regulate the use of water on Indian reservations and which by the terms of the tribal governing document is subject to such approval or review in order to become or to remain effective, pending ultimate determination of this matter.

establishing a method for a just distribution of water that ensures that all those similarly situated will be given an equal opportunity to make beneficial use of supplies. Second, it must provide aggrieved persons with the opportunity to seek judicial review of administrative decisions made under the code. Third, the tribe must demonstrate its capacity to administer the code. Fourth, the code must comport with pertinent federal laws and not regulate water use within federal irrigation projects in Indian Country. Finally, and importantly, the code is limited to administering only tribal water rights under the *Winters* doctrine, and cannot regulate other waters of the reservation.

This final condition was particularly offensive to tribes, as was a provision that empowered the Secretary to enact and enforce a water code on the reservation if the tribe failed to act. Many state interests were also dissatisfied by the proposed rules. As a consequence, the Secretary did not attempt to finalize them.

The next set of proposed rules was published in early 1981. They were very similar to the 1977 provisions, including limitation of tribal code jurisdiction exclusively to the regulation of reserved *Winters* rights. Also, they spelled out the rights of non-Indians who had obtained former allotments. The rules further provided that the tribe could not prevent existing water users, Indian or non-Indian, from using the tribe's reserved rights "until such time as an authorized tribal permittee or the tribe is prepared to make beneficial use of such reserved water." These 1981 proposed rules were more palatable to state interests, but they were never issued in final form either. Consequently, the moratorium on tribal water code approval remains in effect, bringing uncertainty to tribes that desire to implement water management systems.

Tribes have responded to the moratorium in a variety of ways. Some have chosen to ignore it and enforce water codes without Secretarial approval. Others are attempting to manage waters without enacting an ordinance or code that requires Secretarial approval. In one instance, a tribe has argued successfully for an exemption from the moratorium and is currently drafting a water code for Secretarial review.[112] The next section of this article discusses the various strategies and administration techniques which tribes are currently pursuing in order to manage and control important water resources.

III. TRIBAL WATER MANAGEMENT STRATEGIES

* * * As the focus shifts from paper rights to a managed resource, numerous tribes are addressing the many questions involved in comprehensive water management. Among the decisions to be made are: what kind of water administration office to establish, whether to create a permit system, and how best to regulate groundwater use. There is a century of state experience in this field for tribes to assess in evaluating water management strategies. Also, tribal decisionmakers are ensuring that any water administration system on their reservation is

---

112. The United States acquiesced to a provision in the Fort Peck/Montana Compact that the tribes be allowed to enforce a water code applicable to the use of reservation waters by tribal members.

designed to accommodate the customs and culture of the tribal members.

As discussed in the following sections, different tribes are currently at various stages of the process. Some, such as those at the Umatilla, Navajo, and Colville reservations, are already implementing their water policies through comprehensive water codes and sophisticated offices. Others are still in the formative stages and are only beginning to assess alternatives for managing tribal water resources.

A. *The Umatilla Experience*

The Confederated Tribes of the Umatilla Indian Reservation began their water management process in the 1970's by assessing the reservation's water resources and how they were being used. The process involved a number of scientific investigations, including both field work and document review. Specifically, the tribes compiled streamflow data, inventoried wells on the reservation, compiled diversion and other water use records, and monitored groundwater fluctuations in critical areas.

In addition to the physical inventory, the tribes analyzed how water rights in the area were being administered by the State of Oregon. Specific areas of dissatisfaction arose from the tribes' findings that state permits were being issued for large irrigation wells despite evidence that the aquifer was in an overdraft condition. It also appeared to the tribes that diversion permits for surface waters were still being approved by the state in the overappropriated Umatilla River basin. These findings helped motivate the tribe to assert regulatory authority over water resources within the reservation boundaries.

* * *

A key component of the management strategy on the Umatilla reservation is the interim water code. * * *

The code established a regulatory system under which water users, both Indian and non-Indian, are required to apply for permits. A focus of the code is the amelioration of groundwater problems associated with overuse of aquifers in portions of the reservation. Any proposed well drilling or modification to an existing well receives close scrutiny under the tribal program before it is permitted or denied. Since Oregon asserts authority over non-Indian well permitting, potential jurisdictional conflicts exist that have yet to be litigated or otherwise resolved.

B. *The Navajo Regulatory System*

* * * In July, 1983, the council consolidated authority for water management under a new Division of Water Resources created to achieve numerous water policy objectives.

Five departments, employing more than two hundred people, were created within the Division to achieve these objectives. First, the Water Management Department has primary authority to regulate and manage water on the reservation and the responsibility to inventory water resources and use. It employs a groundwater geologist, soil scientist, hydrologist, water quality specialist, and other personnel to perform its duties.

Second, the Department of Water Development is the construction arm of the Division. It constructs all wells on the reservation as well as structures relating to flood control, irrigation water distribution, and impoundments.

The third department, Operations and Maintenance, is responsible for repair of water distribution facilities and the installation and repair of the many windmills needed by the Navajo people for pumping groundwater.

The Department of Planning and Design applies its economic and engineering expertise to create, assess, and implement various water development strategies. It also pursues water conservation practices in conjunction with the Navajo Young Adult Conservation Program.

Finally, the Department of Agriculture, within the Division of Water Resources, provides technical assistance on irrigation and other matters to ranchers and farmers throughout Navajo lands.

In 1984, the tribal council enacted the Navajo Nation Water Code which asserts authority "over all actions taken within the territorial jurisdiction of the Navajo Nation which affect the use of water within the Navajo Nation." * * *

The code became effective on August 2, 1984. Within one year from that date, all persons desiring to divert water from any source on the reservation were required to file an application for a water use permit. Water users, both Navajo and non-Navajo, generally have responded favorably to this requirement, and the tribe is in the process of issuing numerous water permits. Initially, some energy companies operating on Navajo lands did not respond, but following the *Kerr–McGee* decision, they too filed for water use permits. Also, to date, none of the three states affected by this assertion of jurisdiction has initiated a legal challenge to the code.

C. The Colville Program

* * * As seen above in the *Walton* case, the Colville tribes have enacted a water code with judicially recognized authority over reservation water use. In addition, the tribes have been very active in pursuing comprehensive water quality control.

Through the efforts of their leaders, the Colville tribes were selected by the EPA for a pilot program involving the control of water pollution in Indian Country. Under this program, the tribes received financial and technical support to assess water quality problems caused by timber harvesting, mining, irrigation return flows, and other potential sources of nonpoint pollution. Following extensive scientific investigation, the tribes enacted measures designed to minimize pollution of reservation waters. These measures included a Mining Practices Water Quality Act, an Onsite Wastewater Treatment and Disposal Code, a Forest Practices Water Quality Act, and Water Quality Standards for streams running through the reservation.

[T]he State of Washington recognized the desirability of coordinating its water quality programs with those of the tribes. As a consequence, the tribes and the state entered a cooperative agreement for water quality control.

* * * The state will undertake primary enforcement efforts of its regulations on fee lands within the reservation, while the tribes maintained jurisdiction over the remainder of the reservation.

Phase Two of the agreement provides for enforcement of both state and tribal regulations by a person or persons designated by the state and employed by the tribes. * * *

NOTES

1. The question of whether a tribal water code applies to non-Indians must be resolved on a case-by-case basis. In Holly v. Confederated Tribes & Bands of the Yakima Indian Nation, 655 F.Supp. 557 (E.D.Wash.1985), a federal district court dealt with the Yakima Tribal Code:

> The Code in question is comprehensive, purporting to regulate all waters underlying, arising upon or flowing through or along the border of the Reservation. To determine whether the Yakima Nation's sovereign power is sufficient to apply its Code to nonmembers of the Tribe using excess waters on fee lands requires analysis under Montana v. United States, 450 U.S. 544 (1981). While Indian tribes possess inherent sovereign power over their members and their territory, due to their "original incorporation into the United States," exercise of tribal power beyond that necessary to protect tribal self-government is deemed inconsistent with its "dependent status". Therefore, such inherent power was held not to survive without express congressional delegation. Because tribes may not exercise power inconsistent with this diminished sovereign status, Indians have lost the right to govern nonmembers residing within Reservations except in certain instances. One exception exists where nonmembers enter into consensual relationships with a tribe or its members. More importantly in this case, a tribe also retains inherent power to civilly regulate the conduct on non-Indians on fee lands "when that conduct threatens or has some direct effect on the political integrity, the economic security, or the health or welfare of the tribe." 450 U.S. at 566.

> Significantly, in a case arising in this district, the reviewing court held that conduct threatening the health or welfare of an Indian tribe may include conduct involving the tribe's water rights. *Walton II*, 647 F.2d at 52. In *Walton*, a non-Indian's water appropriation imperiled the Colville Confederated Tribes' downstream use of agricultural and fisheries water. On the other hand, a contrary conclusion was reached, under different circumstances, in a later action also initiated in this district. See, generally, United States v. Anderson, 736 F.2d 1358, 1365 (9th Cir.1984) (political and economic welfare of the Spokane Tribe unaffected by the conduct of nonmembers using excess water on fee land).

Here, for purposes of this motion, it is undisputed that surplus waters exist and are used by non-Indians on Reservation fee land and off the Reservation. As the facts demonstrate, the state has met its burden of demonstrating a peaceful co-existence of the non-Indian water users with the Tribes. The [defendants have] not come forward with facts to show existence of a material factual question with respect to whether non-Indian conduct related to non-Indian use of excess waters threatens the political integrity, economic security, or health and welfare of the Tribes. Nor have the non-Indians entered into agreements or dealings with the Tribes with a result of subjecting themselves to tribal civil jurisdiction. Consequently, the inescapable conclusion is the Yakima Nation has not retained the power to regulate excess water use by nonmembers on their fee land within or without the Reservation. It follows, then, that the Code is invalid to the extent it purports to bestow upon the Yakima Nation civil regulatory jurisdiction over non-Indian use of surplus waters.   * * *

The Ninth Circuit Court of Appeals affirmed in Holly v. Totus, 812 F.2d 714 (9th Cir.1987) with no published opinion.

2. Most of the federal environmental laws give tribes the ability to assume the same type of primacy over the administration and enforcement of those laws that is available to states. See Clean Water Act, 33 U.S.C.A. § 1377; Safe Drinking Water Act, 42 U.S.C.A. § 300j–11; Federal Insecticide, Fungicide and Rodenticide Act, 7 U.S.C.A. § 136u; Comprehensive Environmental Response, Compensation and Liability Act, 42 U.S.C.A. § 9626.

Chapter Eight

INTERSTATE ALLOCATION OF WATER

John Wesley Powell, after his pioneering exploration of the Colorado River, urged that political boundaries follow the divides between river drainages. Report on the Lands of the Arid Region of the United States, With a More Detailed Account of the Lands of Utah, (1879). He foresaw that the West's success, perhaps its survival, would depend on the ability of people to cooperate in the allocation and development of water. Powell's vision was largely ignored as counties were laid out and as state boundaries were drawn. Few western state lines coincide with the divides between watersheds; most are straight lines drawn on a map. In several cases they are the centerline or edge of a river, providing rich fodder for conflicts over the respective interests of neighboring states in the waterway.

As a result, disputes abound among states that share common waterways along their borders or within their territories. Many relate to allocation of rights to use the resource. Others concern pollution in one state that affects another. These battles have often been fought in courts, leaving to federal judges the task of dividing the waters or controlling their use. In a number of cases the disputant states have taken another approach, bargaining with one another to reach agreement in the form of an interstate compact, which must be ratified by the United States Congress. A third means of interstate water allocation, congressional action, has been used only once, in the apportionment of the waters of the Colorado River.

The chore of allocating rights of states, or individuals in more than one state, to use shared waterways raises a variety of questions. What court has jurisdiction over a waterway that is in more than a single state? Should it matter what legal systems for water allocation are applied within the individual states? Of what importance is it that water use commenced earlier in one state than in another? Is it significant that water is used to produce more economic benefit in one state than the other? How can a slower developing state plan for future needs and expansion?

Thus, resolution of interstate conflicts over rights in streams is a *sine qua non* of major development, whether conducted by private enterprise or by the state or federal government. Until state claims have been reduced to definite rights in specified quantities of water, private capital cannot afford the investment risk, states will have difficulty selling bonds, and even the federal government will not authorize projects.

A. ADJUDICATION

Disputes over rights to use interstate waters have regularly been resolved by courts. If the dispute is between individuals on both sides of a state line, problems arise of jurisdiction over the person and the subject matter. In the usual case of an upstream user (in State A) interfering with a downstream user (in State B), the latter can enter the courts of State A and obtain personal service on the defendant, or can go into federal district court on diversity of citizenship jurisdiction (assuming the requisite jurisdictional amount is in controversy), similarly obtaining personal service on the defendant within State A.

Jurisdiction over the subject matter raises a conceptual problem, since the court's decree affects a water right not only in State A but also in State B, where the court's writ does not run, whether it be a federal or a state court. Bean v. Morris, 221 U.S. 485 (1911), page 837, infra, offers guidance on this question.

States also find themselves parties in conflicts over water uses. Such disputes are adjudicated in the United States Supreme Court, which under art. III, § 2, cl. 2 has original jurisdiction in "all cases * * * in which a state shall be a party." The Supreme Court's original jurisdiction has been invoked in disputes on the Arkansas, Colorado, Connecticut, Delaware, Laramie, Mississippi, North Platte, Rio Grande, Vermejo and Walla Walla Rivers.

In its original jurisdiction, the Supreme Court acts in the capacity of a trial court, although it never takes evidence. The proceeding commences with the filing of a complaint, which is then subject to various motions including a motion to dismiss. If the complaint survives the motion stage, the respondent state is required to answer and then, typically, a special master is appointed to take evidence, prepare findings of fact and conclusions of law, and recommend a decree. The Court then considers the matter on exceptions to the master's report. Usually the Court writes an opinion and enters a decree, and the Court may or may not agree with the master. New Jersey v. New York, 283 U.S. 336 (1931), page 839, infra, illustrates interstate stream adjudications by the Court.

The Supreme Court has developed its own common law in exercising its jurisdiction over interstate water disputes. The Court has announced the doctrine of "equitable apportionment" for allocating rights to use waters among states. A line of cases spanning eighty years has set forth the several considerations the Court will weigh in making its apportionments. The cases culminate in Colorado v. New Mexico, 467 U.S. 310 (1984), page 851, infra.

The evolution of federal common law in interstate disputes over water pollution has been affected by extensive federal water quality legislation. Milwaukee v. Illinois and Michigan, 451 U.S. 304 (1981), held that the federal common law of nuisance in the area of water quality was preempted by the 1972 Amendments to the Federal Water Pollution Control Act (Clean Water Act). International Paper Co. v. Ouellette, 479 U.S. 481 (1987), confirmed that analysis and held that, since the Clean Water Act had preempted interstate nuisance law, the only state law applicable to a pollution point source was that of the state in which the point source was located. Most recently, Arkansas v. Oklahoma, 112 S.Ct. 1046 (1992), page 854, infra, held that the extent to which the water quality standards of a downstream state are incorporated into an EPA permit and applied against a polluter in an upstream state depends on the exercise of EPA discretion. Thus, as will become more apparent below, while the need for a federal common law arises from differences in the levels and types of pollution controls imposed within neighboring states, the problems of authority and uniformity can be addressed in federal pollution control laws.

KANSAS v. COLORADO

Supreme Court of the United States, 1906.
206 U.S. 46, 27 S.Ct. 655, 51 L.Ed. 956.

MR. JUSTICE BREWER, * * * delivered the opinion of the court. * * *

Turning now to the controversy as here presented, it is whether Kansas has a right to the continuous flow of the waters of the Arkansas River, as that flow existed before any human interference therewith, or Colorado the right to appropriate the waters of that stream so as to prevent that continuous flow, or that the amount of the flow is subject to the superior authority and supervisory control of the United States. * * * [W]hen the States of Kansas and Colorado were admitted into the Union they were admitted with the full powers of local sovereignty which belonged to other States, * * * and Colorado by its legislation has recognized the right of appropriating the flowing waters to the purposes of irrigation. Now the question arises between two States, one recognizing generally the common law rule of riparian rights and the other prescribing the doctrine of the public ownership of flowing water. Neither State can legislate for or impose its own policy upon the other. A stream flows through the two and a controversy is presented as to the flow of that stream.

[W]henever, * * * the action of one State reaches through the agency of natural laws into the territory of another State, the question of the extent and the limitations of the rights of the two States becomes a matter of justiciable dispute between them, and this court is called upon to settle that dispute in such a way as will recognize the equal rights of both and at the same time establish justice between them. In other words, through these successive disputes and decisions this court is practically building up what may not improperly be called interstate common law. This very case presents a significant illustration. Before either Kansas or Colorado was settled the Arkansas River was a stream running through the territory which now composes these two States. Arid lands abound in Colorado. Reclamation is possible only by the application of water, and the extreme contention of Colorado is that it has a right to appropriate all the waters of this stream for the purposes of irrigating its soil and making more valuable its own territory. But the appropriation of the entire flow of the river would naturally tend to make the lands along the stream in Kansas less arable. It would be taking from the adjacent territory that which had been the customary natural means of preserving its arable character. On the other hand, the possible contention of Kansas, that the flowing water in the Arkansas must, in accordance with the extreme doctrine of the common law of England, be left to flow as it was wont to flow, no portion of it being appropriated in Colorado for the purposes of irrigation, would have the effect to perpetuate a desert condition in portions of Colorado beyond the power of reclamation. Surely here is a dispute of a justiciable nature which must and ought to be tried and determined. If the two States were absolutely independent nations it would be settled by treaty or by force. Neither of these ways being practicable, it must be settled by decision of this court.

* * *

This changes in some respect the scope of our inquiry. It is not limited to the simple matter of whether any portion of the waters of the Arkansas is withheld by Colorado. We must consider the effect of what has been done upon the conditions in the respective States and so adjust the dispute upon the basis of equality of rights as to secure as far as possible to Colorado the benefits of irrigation without depriving Kansas of the like beneficial effects of a flowing stream.

* * * [W]e are justified in looking at the question not narrowly and solely as to the amount of the flow in the channel of the Arkansas River, inquiring merely whether any portion thereof is appropriated by Colorado, but we may properly consider what, in case a portion of that flow is appropriated by Colorado, are the effects of such appropriation upon Kansas territory. For instance, if there be many thousands of acres in Colorado destitute of vegetation, which by the taking of water from the Arkansas River and in no other way can be made valuable as arable lands producing an abundance of vegetable growth, and this transformation of desert land has the effect, through percolation of water in the soil, or in any other way, of giving to Kansas territory, although not in the Arkansas Valley, a benefit from water as great as that which would enure by keeping the flow of the Arkansas in its channel undiminished, then we may rightfully regard the usefulness to Colorado as justifying its action, although the locality of the benefit which the flow of the Arkansas through Kansas has territorially changed. * * * May we not consider some appropriation by Colorado of the waters of the Arkansas to the irrigation and reclamation of its arid lands as a reasonable exercise of its sovereignty and as not unreasonably trespassing upon any rights of Kansas? And here we must notice the local law of Kansas. * * *

"The use of water by a riparian proprietor for irrigation purposes must be reasonable under all the circumstances, and the right must be exercised with due regard to the equal right of every other riparian owner along the course of the stream.

"A diminution of the flow of water over riparian land caused by its use for irrigation purposes by upper riparian proprietors occasions no injury for which damages may be allowed unless it results in subtracting from the value of the land by interfering with the reasonable uses of the water which the landowner is able to enjoy.

* * *

As Kansas thus recognizes the right of appropriating the waters of a stream for the purposes of irrigation, subject to the condition of an equitable division between the riparian proprietors, she cannot complain if the same rule is administered between herself and a sister State. * * *

Comparing the tables of population it will be perceived that both the counties in Colorado and Kansas made a considerable increase in the years from 1880 to 1890; that while the Colorado counties continued their increase from 1890 to 1900, the Kansas counties lost. As the withdrawal of water in Colorado for irrigating purposes became substantially effective about the year 1890, it might, if nothing else appeared, not unreasonably be concluded that the diminished flow of the river in Kansas, caused by the action of Colorado, had resulted in making the land more unproductive, and hence induced settlers to leave the State. As against this it should be noted, as a matter of history, that in the years preceding 1890, Kansas passed through a period of depression, with crops largely a failure in different parts of the State. But, more than that, in 1889 Oklahoma, lying directly south of Kansas, was opened for settlement and immediately there was a large immigration into that territory, coming from all parts of the West, and especially from the State of Kansas, induced by glowing reports of its great possibilities. The population of Oklahoma, as shown by the United States census, was, in 1890, 61,834, and in 1900, 348,331.

Turning to the tables of the corn and wheat products, they do not disclose any marked injury which can be attributed to a diminution of the flow of the river. While there is a variance in the amount produced in the different counties from year to year, it is a variance no more than that which will be found in other parts of the Union, and although the population from 1890 to 1900 in fact diminished, the amount of both the corn and wheat product largely increased. Not only was the total product increased, but the productiveness per acre seems to have been materially improved. Take the corn crop, and per acre, it was, in 1890, 12 bushels and a fraction; in 1895, 21 and a fraction, in 1900, 15, and in 1904, 28 bushels. Of wheat, the product per acre in 1890 was nearly 15 bushels; in 1895 it was only about 3 bushels. (For some reason, while that was a good year for corn, it seems to have been a bad year for wheat.) But in 1900 the product per acre rose to 19 bushels, and in 1904 it was 12 bushels.

These are official figures taken from the United States census reports, and they tend strongly to show that the withdrawal of the water in Colorado for purposes of irrigation has not proved a source of serious detriment to the Kansas counties along the Arkansas River. It is not strange that the western counties show the least development, for being nearest the irrigation in Colorado, they would be most affected thereby. At one time there were some irrigating ditches in these western counties, which promised to be valuable in supplying water and thus increasing the productiveness of the lands in the vicinity of the stream, and it is true that those ditches have ceased to be of much value, the flow in them having largely diminished.

It cannot be denied in view of all the testimony (for that which we have quoted is but a sample of much more bearing upon the question), that the diminution of the flow of water in the river by the irrigation of Colorado has worked some detriment to the southwestern part of Kansas, and yet when we compare the amount of this detriment with the great benefit which has obviously resulted to the counties in Colorado, it would seem that equality of right and equity between the two States forbids any interference with the present withdrawal of water in Colorado for purposes of irrigation.

* * *

Summing up our conclusions, we are of the opinion * * * that the appropriation of the waters of the Arkansas by Colorado, for purposes of irrigation, has diminished the flow of water into the State of Kansas, that the result of that appropriation has been the reclamation of large areas in Colorado, transforming thousands of acres into fertile fields and rendering possible their occupation and cultivation when otherwise they would have continued barren and unoccupied, that while the influence of such diminution has been of perceptible injury to portions of the Arkansas Valley in Kansas, particularly those portions closest to the Colorado line, yet to the great body of the valley it has worked little, if any, detriment, and regarding the interests of both States and the right of each to receive benefit through irrigation and in any other manner from the waters of this stream, we are not satisfied that Kansas has made out a case entitling it to a decree. At the same time it is obvious that if the depletion of the waters of the river by Colorado continues to increase there will come a time when Kansas may justly say that there is no longer an equitable division of benefits and may rightfully call for relief against the action of Colorado, its corporations and citizens in appropriating the waters of the Arkansas for irrigation purposes.

The decree which, therefore, will be entered will dismiss the bill of the State of Kansas as against all the defendants, without prejudice to the right of the plaintiff to institute new proceedings when ever it shall appear that through a material increase in the depletion of the waters of the Arkansas by Colorado, its corporations or citizens, the substantial interests of Kansas are being injured to the extent of destroying the equitable apportionment of benefits between the two States resulting from the flow of the river. * * *

NOTE

In an earlier case, Kansas v. Colorado, 185 U.S. 125 (1902), the first water rights case over which the United States Supreme Court exercised original jurisdiction, Kansas alleged that Colorado diversions had caused irreparable damage to crops and livestock. After further evidence was presented in 1907, the Court decided the principal case.

After the 1907 decision, several Kansas ditch companies sued Colorado ditch companies to adjudicate priorities. When attempts at settlement failed, Colorado sued to enjoin Kansas and the ditch companies from bringing suit against Colorado ditch companies. Colorado v. Kansas, 320 U.S. 383 (1943). The Court again held that the benefit to Colorado outweighed the injury to Kansas, and ruled for Colorado. After the first three lawsuits, Kansas and Colorado, with congressional permission, entered into the Arkansas River Compact in 1948, the same year the John Martin Reservoir (located on the Arkansas River in Colorado) was completed. See Mark J. Wagner, Note, *The Parting of the Waters—The Dispute Between Colorado and Kansas Over the Arkansas River,* 24 Washburn L.J. 99 (1984).

In March 1986, Kansas presented a fourth suit in its running dispute over Colorado's alleged illegal diversion of water. The suit alleged that Colorado had "materially depleted" the river's flow contrary to the commitments made in the 1948 Compact. The suit claimed that three Colorado activities resulted in violations of the Compact: post-compact well development; operation of a winter water storage program on the Arkansas River; and operation of Trinidad Reservoir on the Purgatoire River, the major southern tributary of the Arkansas. On Kansas' motion, the trial was bifurcated into a liability and a remedy phase. Trial of the first phase to a special master sitting in California began on September 17, 1990. After 141 days of trial, it concluded on December 16, 1992. The trial had been delayed by a nine-month recess to allow Kansas to replace its chief technical witness who was admitted to a psychiatric hospital after collapsing during cross-examination. The special master's report is expected in late 1993.

BEAN v. MORRIS

Supreme Court of the United States, 1911.
221 U.S. 485, 31 S.Ct. 703, 55 L.Ed. 821.

MR. JUSTICE HOLMES delivered the opinion of the court.

This suit was brought by the respondent, Morris, to prevent the petitioners from so diverting the waters of Sage Creek in Montana as to interfere with an alleged prior right of Morris, by appropriation, to two hundred and fifty inches of such waters in Wyoming. Afterwards the other respondent, Howell, was allowed to intervene and make a similar claim. Sage Creek is a small creek, not navigable, that joins the Stinking Water in Wyoming, the latter stream flowing into the Big Horn, which then flows back northerly into Montana again, and unites with the Yellowstone. The Circuit Court made a decree that Morris was entitled to 100 inches miner's measurement, of date April, 1887, and that, subject to Morris, Howell was entitled to one hundred and ten inches, of date August 1, 1890, both parties being prior in time and right to the petitioners. 146 Fed.Rep. 423. On appeal the findings of fact below were adopted and the decree of the Circuit Court affirmed by the Circuit Court of Appeals. 159 Fed. 651; 86 C.C.A. 519.

It was admitted at the argument that but for the fact that the prior appropriation was in one State, Wyoming, and the interference in another, Montana, the decree would be right, so far as the main and important question is concerned. It is true that some minor points were suggested, such as laches, abandonment, the statute of limitations, &c., but the findings of two courts have been against the petitioners upon all of these, and we see no reason for giving them further consideration. So we pass at once to the question of private water rights as between users in different States.

We know no reason to doubt, and we assume, that, subject to such rights as the lower State might be decided by this court to have, and to vested private rights, if any, protected by the Constitution, the State of Montana has full legislative power over Sage Creek while it flows within that State. Kansas v. Colorado, 206 U.S. 46. Therefore, subject to the same qualifications, we assume that the concurrence of the laws of Montana with those of Wyoming is necessary to create easements, or such private rights and obligations as are in dispute, across their common boundary line. Missouri v. Illinois, 200 U.S. 496, 521. Rickey Land & Cattle Co. v. Miller & Lux, 218 U.S. 258, 260. But with regard to such rights as came into question in the older States, we believe that it always was assumed, in the absence of legislation to the contrary, that the States were willing to ignore boundaries, and allowed the same rights to be acquired from outside the State that could be acquired from within. * * *

There is even stronger reason for the same assumption here. Montana cannot be presumed to be intent on suicide, and there are as many if not more cases in which it would lose as there are in which it would gain, if it invoked a trial of strength with its neighbors. In this very instance, as has been said, the Big Horn, after it has received the waters of Sage Creek, flows back into that State. But this is the least consideration. The doctrine of appropriation has prevailed in these regions probably from the first moment that they knew of any law, and has continued since they became territory of the United States. It was recognized by the statutes of the United States, while Montana and Wyoming were such territory, Rev.Stat., §§ 2339, 2340, p. 429, Act of March 3, 1877, c. 107, 19 Stat. 377, and is recognized by both States now. Before the state lines were drawn of course the principle prevailed between the lands that were destined to be thus artificially divided. Indeed, Morris had made his appropriation before either State was admitted to the Union. The only reasonable presumption is that the States upon their incorporation continued the system that had prevailed theretofore, and made no changes other than those necessarily implied or expressed.

It follows from what we have said that it is unnecessary to consider what limits there may be to the powers of an upper State, if it should seek to do all that it could. The grounds upon which such limits would stand are referred to in Rickey Land & Cattle Co. v. Miller & Lux, 218 U.S. 258, 261. So it is unnecessary to consider whether Morris is not protected by the Constitution; for it seems superfluous to fall back upon the citadel until some attack drives him to that retreat. Other matters adverted to in argument, so far as not disposed of by what we have said, have been dealt with sufficiently in two courts. It is enough here to say that we are satisfied with their discussion and confine our own to the only matter that warranted a certiorari or suggested questions that might be grave.

Decree affirmed.

NEW JERSEY v. NEW YORK

Supreme Court of the United States, 1931.
283 U.S. 336, 51 S.Ct. 478, 75 L.Ed. 1104.

MR. JUSTICE HOLMES delivered the opinion of the Court.

This is a bill in equity by which the State of New Jersey seeks to enjoin the State of New York and the City of New York from diverting any waters from the Delaware River or its tributaries, and particularly from the Neversink River, Willowemoc River, Beaver Kill, East Branch of the Delaware River and Little Delaware River, or from any part of any one of them. The other rivers named are among the headwaters of the Delaware and flow into it where it forms a boundary between New York and Pennsylvania. The Delaware continues its course as such boundary to Tristate Rock, near Port Jervis in New York, at which point Pennsylvania and New York are met by New Jersey. From there the River marks the boundary between Pennsylvania and New Jersey until Pennsylvania stops at the Delaware state line, and from then on the River divides Delaware from New Jersey until it reaches the Atlantic between Cape Henlopen and Cape May.

New York proposes to divert a large amount of water from the above-named tributaries of the Delaware and from the watershed of that river to the watershed of the Hudson River in order to increase the water supply of the City of New York. New Jersey insists on a strict application of the rules of the common law governing private riparian proprietors subject to the same sovereign power. Pennsylvania intervenes to protect its interests as against anything that might be done to prejudice its future needs.

We are met at the outset by the question what rule is to be applied. It is established that a more liberal answer may be given than in a controversy between neighbors members of a single State. Connecticut v. Massachusetts, 282 U.S. 660. Different considerations come in when we are dealing with independent sovereigns having to regard the welfare of the whole population and when the alternative to settlement is war. In a less degree, perhaps, the same is true of the quasi-sovereignties bound together in the Union. A river is more than an amenity, it is a treasure. It offers a necessity of life that must be rationed among those who have power over it. New York has the physical power to cut off all the water within its jurisdiction. But clearly the exercise of such a power to the destruction of the interest of lower States could not be tolerated. And on the other hand equally little could New Jersey be permitted to require New York to give up its power altogether in order that the River might come down to it undiminished. Both States have real and substantial interests in the River that must be reconciled as best they may be. The different traditions and practices in different parts of the country may lead to varying results, but the effort always is to secure an equitable apportionment without quibbling over formulas.

This case was referred to a Master and a great mass of evidence was taken. In a most competent and excellent report the Master adopted the principle of equitable division which clearly results from the decisions of the last quarter of a century. Where that principle is established there is not much left to discuss. The removal of water to a different watershed obviously must be allowed at times unless States are to be deprived of the most beneficial use on formal grounds. In fact it has been allowed repeatedly and has been practiced by the States concerned.

New Jersey alleges that the proposed diversion will transgress its rights in many respects. That it will interfere with the navigability of the Delaware without the authority of Congress or the Secretary of War. That it will deprive the State and its citizens who are riparian owners of the undiminished flow of the stream to which they are entitled by the common law as adopted by both States. That it will injuriously affect water power and the ability to develop it. That it will injuriously affect the sanitary conditions of the River. That it will do the same to the industrial use of it. That it will increase the salinity of the lower part of the River and of Delaware Bay to the injury of the oyster industry there. That it will injure the shad fisheries. That it will do the same to the municipal water supply of the New Jersey towns and cities on the River. That by lowering the level of the water it will injure the cultivation of adjoining lands; and finally, that it will injuriously affect the River for recreational purposes. The bill also complains of the change of watershed, already disposed of; denies the necessity of the diversion; charges extravagant use of present supplies, and alleges that the plan will violate the Federal Water Power Act, 16 U.S.C.A. §§ 791–823 (but see U.S.Code, Tit. 16, § 821 [16 U.S.C.A. § 821])*, interfere with interstate commerce, prefer the ports of New York to those of New Jersey and will take the property of New Jersey and its citizens without due process of law.

The Master finds that the above-named tributaries of the Delaware are not navigable waters of the United States at and above the places where the City of New York proposes to erect dams. Assuming that relief by injunction still might be proper if a substantial diminution within the limits of navigability was threatened, United States v. Rio Grande Dam & Irrigation Co., 174 U.S. 690, 709, he called as a witness General George B. Pillsbury, Assistant Chief of Engineers of the United States Army, who was well acquainted with the River and the plan, and who, although not speaking officially for the War Department, satisfied the Master's mind that the navigable capacity of the River would not be impaired.   * * *

---

* 16 U.S.C.A. § 821 reads:
Nothing contained in this chapter shall be construed as affecting or intending to affect or in any way to interfere with the laws of the respective States relating to the control, appropriation, use, or distribution of water used in irrigation or for municipal or other uses, or any vested right acquired therein. [Eds.]

With regard to water power the Master concludes that any future plan of New Jersey for constructing dams would need the consent of Congress and of the States of New York and Pennsylvania and, though possible as a matter of engineering, probably would not pay. He adds that there is no such showing of a present interest as to entitle New Jersey to relief. We have spoken at the outset of the more general qualifications of New Jersey's rights as against another State. The Master finds that the taking of 600 millions of gallons daily from the tributaries will not materially affect the River or its sanitary condition, or as a source of municipal water supply, or for industrial uses, or for agriculture, or for the fisheries for shad. The effect upon the use for recreation and upon its reputation in that regard will be somewhat more serious, as will be the effect of increased salinity of the River upon the oyster fisheries. The total is found to be greater than New Jersey ought to bear, but the damage can be removed by reducing the draft of New York to 440 million gallons daily; constructing an efficient plant for the treatment of sewage entering the Delaware or Neversink (the main source of present pollution,) thereby reducing the organic impurities 85% and treating the effluent with a germicide so as to reduce the Bacillus Coli originally present in the sewage by 90%; and finally, subject to the qualifications in the decree, when the stage of the Delaware falls below .50 c.s.m. at Port Jervis, New York, or Trenton, New Jersey, by releasing water from the impounding reservoirs of New York, sufficient to restore the flow at those points to .50 c.s.m. We are of opinion that the Master's report should be confirmed and that a decree should be entered to the following effect, subject to such modifications as may be ordered by the Court hereafter.

1. The injunction prayed for by New Jersey so far as it would restrain the State of New York or City of New York from diverting from the Delaware River or its tributaries to the New York City water supply the equivalent of 440 million gallons of water daily is denied, but is granted to restrain the said State and City from diverting water in excess of that amount. The denial of the injunction as above is subject to the [conditions concerning effluent treatment and reservoir releases in the preceding paragraph].

2. The diversion herein allowed shall not constitute a prior appropriation and shall not give the State of New York and City of New York any superiority of right over the State of New Jersey and Commonwealth of Pennsylvania in the enjoyment and use of the Delaware River and its tributaries.

* * *

6. Any of the parties hereto, complainant, defendants or intervenor, may apply at the foot of this decree for other or further action or relief and this Court retains jurisdiction of the suit for the purpose of any order or direction or modification of this decree, or any supplemental decree that it may deem at any time to be proper in relation to the subject matter in controversy.

* * *

NOTES

1. The decree was amended in 1954, 347 U.S. 995, to allow increased diversions after completion of the Cannonsville Reservoir, but the decree required at such time a minimum flow at Montague (which became the measuring point in place of Point Jervis). Who bears the risk of a drought under the initial and amended decrees?

2. After two hurricanes caused extensive flooding, a congressionally-mandated study recommended a new location for the mainstem reservoir anticipated in the decree. Eventually the four states entered into a compact responding to the new conditions and varying the terms of the decree, and they added the federal government as a party. The compact is briefly discussed at pages 869–70, infra.

A. DAN TARLOCK, THE LAW OF EQUITABLE APPORTIONMENT REVISITED, UPDATED, AND RESTATED

56 U.Colo.L.Rev. 381, 385–400 (1985).

The Court first announced its power to apportion equitably interstate streams in *Kansas v. Colorado*.[15] This seminal case arose when Kansas sued Colorado to enjoin Colorado diversions on the Arkansas River. The Court rejected both Kansas' argument that Colorado could not use the river and Colorado's argument that territorial sovereignty gave it the right to deplete the entire flow of the stream, in favor of a sharing rule. Kansas, then a dual system state, argued both that priority of settlement and the riparian rule that "the owners of land on the banks are entitled to the continual flow of the stream * * * " gave it the right to relief. In addition to its assertion of territorial sovereignty, Colorado, the originator of pure prior appropriation, asserted the right to the full flow as a riparian making a reasonable use, but further confused the issue by invoking a classic prior appropriation defense. Kansas, it said, was not entitled to any water because its call would be futile; the Arkansas was a dry stream through western Kansas. Colorado prevailed and Kansas's complaint was dismissed without prejudice.[18] Each state, the Court held, had an equal right to use the flow, and Colorado's irrigation withdrawals were reasonable under the common law of riparian rights and did not exceed her rights, whatever they were, under the doctrine of equitable apportionment because Colorado had developed faster than Kansas:

> Official figures taken from the United States census reports * * * tend strongly to show that the withdrawal of the water in Colorado for purposes of irrigation has not proved a source of serious detriment to the Kansas counties along the Arkansas River. * * *

15. 206 U.S. 46 (1907).

* * *

18. Kansas was subsequently unsuccessful in reopening the decree in light of increased Colorado withdrawals. Colorado v. Kansas, 320 U.S. 383 (1943). In 1948, the two states negotiated a compact, Kan. Stat. Ann. § 82a–520 (1977), but the dispute between the two states is on-going and it is not clear whether the compact provisions or the doctrine of equitable apportionment will control future litigation. See Note, *The Parting of the Waters—The Dispute Between Colorado and Kansas Over the Arkansas River*, 24 Washburn L.J. 99 (1984).

It cannot be denied in view of all the testimony * * * that the diminution of the flow of water in the river by the irrigation of Colorado has worked some detriment to the southwestern part of Kansas, and yet when we compare the amount of this detriment with the great benefit which has obviously resulted to the counties in Colorado, it would seem that equality of right and equity between the two States forbids any interference with the present withdrawal of water in Colorado for purposes of irrigation.

* * *

III.   1907–1945: BARRIERS TO RELIEF AND THE INTEGRATION OF LOCAL AND FEDERAL COMMON LAW

A.   Barriers to Relief: Political Question, the Eleventh Amendment and Lack of Ripeness

To make equitable apportionments, Supreme Court jurisdiction had to be sustained against two challenges. First, states argued that despite the express recognition of original jurisdiction in the Constitution, the issues were non-justiciable because they were political. Second, they argued that the eleventh amendment, which bars suits by citizens of one state against another state, precluded original actions for equitable apportionment simply to protect holders of state-created rights. At the same time that the Court eliminated these two per se barriers to jurisdiction, it imposed a major limitation on original jurisdiction suits. An action may be dismissed for lack of ripeness if there is insufficient proof of injury.

* * *

Missouri v. Illinois [42] was the first case to set a high standard of injury as a prerequisite to Supreme Court relief. In an epic environmentally unsound public works project, Illinois reversed the flow of the Chicago River to flush Chicago's sewage into the Illinois River, a tributary of the Mississippi, instead of treating and discharging it into its frontyard—Lake Michigan. Alarmed, Missouri sued to protect the health of residents of St. Louis and other riparian cities. Missouri invoked the common law rule that a riparian had a right to the flow of a stream unimpaired in quality and quantity. To dismiss Missouri's suit, a higher standard of proof than would be applied to a suit for equitable relief between private parties was articulated: "Before this Court ought to intervene the case should be of serious magnitude, clearly and fully proved, and the principle applied should be one which the Court is prepared deliberately to maintain against all considerations on the other side." [43] Relief was not warranted on the facts.

* * *

In 1931 the Court similarly dismissed Connecticut's attempt to prevent a Massachusetts transbasin diversion to benefit Boston. [46] Con-

42. 200 U.S. 496 (1906).
43. Id. at 521.

46. Connecticut v. Massachusetts, 282 U.S. 660 (1931).

necticut relied on the strict common law rule that all uses outside of the watershed were per se unreasonable,[47] but the Court found at least three reasons to dismiss the action. Connecticut, the lower riparian state, failed to prove any injury and thus the case arguably fell within the more "modern" common law rule that only transwatershed diversions that actually caused injury to downstream riparians were actionable.

Four years later, the Court applied its high standards of injury to a familiar western water law doctrine, and dismissed a suit by Washington against Oregon because the former's call would be futile.[50]

B. Standards for Equitable Apportionment

Once the Court accepts original jurisdiction and appoints a master to take the evidence, the issue becomes what law to apply. The Court initially rejected local law as the basis for an apportionment, then accepted it as the basis among states that followed the same law, and finally downgraded local law to a "guiding principle." Fair allocation rather than consistency with locally generated expectations became the touchstone of equitable apportionment. Local law remains, however, central to an equitable apportionment inquiry. Although the Court has never been very precise about the source of the law of equitable apportionment, its early decision makes it clear that the grant of original jurisdiction requires a federal law and a federal law that will not allow one state to use its law to gain an unfair advantage over another. The use of local law as a basis for allocation is thus not compelled by the constitution. But local law may serve as a source of principles to apply since a federal common law must of necessity examine the most relevant sources of substantive law.

In 1911, in Bean v. Morris, [221 U.S. 485 (1911), page 837, supra], Justice Holmes enforced priorities on an interstate stream on the theory that when all states through which it flowed had adopted the same system of water law, they estopped themselves from asserting the power to ignore out-of-state priorities. * * *

Eleven years later, Wyoming's action against Colorado to protect prior Wyoming irrigators from the upstream state's proposed diversions of the Laramie River produced the Court's first substantive decision and required the Court to begin integrating state water laws into the federal doctrine of equitable apportionment. In the Laramie litigation, Wyoming successfully urged the application of *Bean* to counter Colorado's argument—prophetic in light of subsequent developments in the state—that priority is a rule of the past, not of the future.[59] The Court upheld Wyoming's priority and awarded it, with minor qualifications, 272,000 out of the river's 288,000 acre feet of dependable supply. Colorado's argument that it could put the water to more beneficial use because the site of the proposed trans-watershed diversion, the Cache

---

47. Stratton v. Mt. Hermon Boys' School, 216 Mass. 83, 103 N.E. 87 (1913).

50. Washington v. Oregon, 297 U.S. 517 (1936).

59. Wyoming v. Colorado, 259 U.S. 419 (1922). * * *

La Poudre Valley, was more developed was not seriously considered, although it had carried the day for the state in *Kansas v. Colorado*.

While *Wyoming v. Colorado* has been criticized because it freezes existing, and presumably inefficient, uses in place to the detriment of future, presumably more efficient, uses, the Court's reasoning may actually lead to better conservation practices. Undoubtedly, the rigid adherence to prior appropriation throughout a large river basin might produce inefficiencies. However, there is a strong case for reliance on a modified doctrine of prior appropriation, as the Court has done, on smaller streams. First users build up legitimate expectations of security, and subsequent users can not claim surprise when prior uses are protected. Recognition of prior uses need not freeze all existing uses. It operates more to place the burden of water conservation on new users. This is a difficult but not impossible burden to discharge as the Court's most recent equitable apportionment case, *Colorado v. New Mexico*, [page 846, infra] illustrates.   * * *

New York City's plans to divert water from the Delaware River watershed produced the Court's major equitable apportionment case among riparian states, and although the Court stressed that its primary objective was an equitable apportionment, again the decision was based primarily on local law.   * * *   Justice Holmes began by saying, in an oft-quoted phrase, that "[t]he different traditions and practices in different parts of the country may lead to varying results, but the effort is always to secure an equitable apportionment without quibbling over formulas." But he in fact made a riparian apportionment.   * * *

New Jersey v. New York is a creative adaption of the law of riparian rights to interstate conflicts. Historically, instream uses have been of greater importance compared to consumptive uses in riparian states, and the Court gave full weight to this aspect of riparianism by apportioning the most valuable attribute of the river, its base flow, and it gave full weight to another core riparian concept, preservation of the status quo among similar users. The decree required that the essential benefits of the flow, pollution dilution and salt water intrusion prevention, be preserved as a condition to New York City's withdrawals from the watershed for consumptive uses.

The importance of riparian principles and marginal reductions in base water levels is also illustrated by the litigation over Illinois's reversal of the Chicago River and construction of a channel to link Lake Michigan with the Mississippi. Illinois was able to fend off challenges by downstream states, but was not as successful in defending the necessary diversions from Lake Michigan to flush Chicago's sewage against challenges by the Great Lakes states that the diversions impaired navigation of the lakes.*   * * *

Dust bowl conditions in the Great Plains produced the Court's most complex equitable apportionment and statement of current doctrine. To protect the flow of the North Platte River for irrigation purposes,

* [Wisconsin v. Illinois, 281 U.S. 179   (1930).]
(1929), affirmed *per curiam*, 281 U.S. 696

Nebraska sued the upstream state of Wyoming, which impleaded Colorado.[71] Relying on *Wyoming v. Colorado*, Nebraska alleged that the dependable natural flow of the river during irrigation season on a critical reach of the river had long been over-appropriated. The case also involved federal and state claims to water stored in Wyoming reservoirs for the benefit of Wyoming and Nebraska users. Nebraska did benefit substantially from the litigation, but the Court departed from the application of the rule of priority followed in *Wyoming v. Colorado*. Writing for the majority, Justice Douglas concluded that strict adherence to the doctrine of prior appropriation may not be possible if justice and equity are to be done among states, and substituted the following and oft quoted multifactor standard of equitable apportionment:

> So far as possible those established uses should be protected though strict application of the priority rule might jeopardize them. Apportionment calls for the exercise for an informed judgment on a consideration of many factors. Priority of appropriation is the guiding principle. But physical and climatic conditions, the consumptive use of water in the several sections of the river, the character and rate of return flows, the extent of established uses, the availability of storage water, the practical effect of wasteful uses on downstream areas, the damage to upstream areas as compared to the benefits to downstream areas if a limitation is imposed on the former—these are all relevant factors.

NOTE

If the United States has interests in water, such as reserved rights to water for public lands, it must be joined in an equitable apportionment suit as an indispensable party. This can be a formidable barrier to adjudication of interstate claims. Arizona sued California for an equitable apportionment of the lower Colorado River. As discussed in the next section of this chapter, the waters of the river had been apportioned between states of the upper basin and states of the lower basin by the 1922 Colorado River Compact, but an allocation was not made among the states in each basin. Arizona's suit to effect such a division among the lower basin states was dismissed because the United States, which had extensive land holdings, was an indispensable party and had not consented to be sued. *Arizona v. California*, 298 U.S. 558 (1936). A later adjudication, in which the United States consented to be sued, resulted not in an equitable apportionment, but in a finding that Congress had already apportioned the river among the lower basin states by the Boulder Canyon Project Act of 1928. *Arizona v. California*, 373 U.S. 546 (1963), page 886, infra.

COLORADO v. NEW MEXICO

Supreme Court of the United States, 1982.
459 U.S. 176, 103 S.Ct. 539, 74 L.Ed.2d 348.

JUSTICE MARSHALL delivered the opinion of the Court.

* * *

---

71. Nebraska v. Wyoming, 325 U.S. 589 (1945). * * *

I

The Vermejo River is a small, nonnavigable river that originates in the snow belt of the Rocky Mountains in southern Colorado and flows southeasterly into New Mexico for a distance of roughly 55 miles before it joins the Canadian River. The major portion of the river is located in New Mexico. The Colorado portion consists of three main tributaries that combine to form the Vermejo River proper approximately one mile below the Colorado-New Mexico border. At present there are no uses of the water of the Vermejo River in Colorado, and no use or diversion has ever been made in Colorado. In New Mexico, by contrast, farmers and industrial users have diverted water from the Vermejo for many years. * * *

In 1975, a Colorado corporation, Colorado Fuel and Iron Steel Corp. (C.F. & I.), obtained in Colorado state court a conditional right to divert 75 cubic feet per second from the headwaters of the Vermejo River. C.F. & I. proposed a transmountain diversion of the water to a tributary of the Purgatoire River in Colorado to be used for industrial development and other purposes. * * *

The Special Master found that most of the water of the Vermejo River is consumed by the New Mexico users * * *. He thus recognized that strict application of the rule of priority would not permit Colorado any diversion since the entire available supply is needed to satisfy the demands of appropriators in New Mexico with senior rights. Nevertheless, applying the principle of equitable apportionment established in our prior cases, he recommended permitting Colorado a transmountain diversion of 4,000 acre-feet of water per year from the headwaters of the Vermejo River. * * *

Explaining his conclusion, the Special Master noted that any injury to New Mexico would be restricted to the Conservancy District, the user in New Mexico furthest downstream, since there was sufficient water in the Vermejo River for the three other principal New Mexico water users, Vermejo Park, Kaiser Steel, and Phelps Dodge. He further found that the "Vermejo Conservancy District has never been an economically feasible operation."

* * *

We conclude that the criteria relied upon by the Special Master comport with the doctrine of equitable apportionment as it has evolved in our prior cases. We thus reject New Mexico's contention that the Special Master was required to focus exclusively on the rule of priority. * * *

II

Equitable apportionment is the doctrine of federal common law that governs disputes between States concerning their rights to use the water of an interstate stream. Kansas v. Colorado, 206 U.S. 46, 98 (1907); Connecticut v. Massachusetts, 282 U.S. 660, 670–671 (1931). It is a flexible doctrine which calls for "the exercise of an informed judgment on a consideration of many factors" to secure a "just and equitable" allocation. Nebraska v. Wyoming, 325 U.S. 589, 618 (1945). We have stressed that in arriving at "the delicate adjustment of interests which must be made," ibid., we must consider all relevant factors * * *.

The laws of the contending States concerning intrastate water disputes are an important consideration governing equitable apportionment. When, as in this case, both States recognize the doctrine of prior appropriation, priority becomes the "guiding principle" in an allocation between competing States. But state law is not controlling. Rather, the just apportionment of interstate waters is a question of federal law that depends "upon a consideration of the pertinent laws of the contending States and *all other relevant facts.*" Connecticut v. Massachusetts, supra (emphasis added).

In reaching his recommendation the Special Master did not focus exclusively on the rule of priority, but considered other factors such as the efficiency of current uses in New Mexico and the balance of benefits to Colorado and harm to New Mexico. New Mexico contends that it is improper to consider these other factors. It maintains that this Court has strictly applied the rule of priority when apportioning water between States adhering to the prior appropriation doctrine, and has departed from that rule only to protect an existing economy built upon junior appropriations. Since there is no existing economy in Colorado dependent upon the use of water from the Vermejo River, New Mexico contends that the rule of priority is controlling. We disagree with this inflexible interpretation of the doctrine of equitable apportionment.

Our prior cases clearly establish that equitable apportionment will protect only those rights to water that are "reasonably required and applied." Wyoming v. Colorado, 259 U.S. 419, 484 (1922). Especially in those Western States where water is scarce, "[t]here must be no waste * * * of the 'treasure' of a river. * * * Only diligence and good faith will keep the privilege alive." Washington v. Oregon, 297 U.S. 517, 527 (1936). Thus, wasteful or inefficient uses will not be protected. Similarly, concededly senior water rights will be deemed forfeited or substantially diminished where the rights have not been exercised or asserted with reasonable diligence.

We have invoked equitable apportionment not only to require the reasonably efficient use of water, but also to impose on States an affirmative duty to take reasonable steps to conserve and augment the water supply of an interstate stream. In *Wyoming* v. *Colorado*, Wyoming brought suit to prevent a *proposed* diversion by Colorado from the Laramie River. This Court calculated the dependable supply available to both States, subtracted the senior Wyoming uses, and permitted Colorado to divert an amount not exceeding the balance. In calculating the dependable supply we placed on each State the duty to employ "financially and physically feasible" measures "adapted to *conserving and equalizing* the natural flow." 259 U.S., at 484 (emphasis added). Adopting a position similar to New Mexico's in this case, Wyoming objected to a requirement that it employ conservation measures to facilitate Colorado's proposed uses. The answer we gave is especially relevant to this case:

> "The question here is not what one State should do for the other, but how each should exercise her relative rights in the waters of this interstate stream. * * * Both States recognize that conservation within practicable limits is essential in order that needless waste may be prevented and the largest feasible use may be secured. This comports with the all-pervading spirit of the doctrine of appropriation and takes appropriate heed of the natural necessities out of which it arose. We think that doctrine lays on each of these States a duty to exercise her right reasonably and in a manner calculated to conserve the common supply."

We conclude that it is entirely appropriate to consider the extent to which reasonable conservation measures by New Mexico might offset the proposed Colorado diversion and thereby minimize any injury to New Mexico users. Similarly, it is appropriate to consider whether Colorado has undertaken reasonable steps to minimize the amount of diversion that will be required.

In addition, we have held that in an equitable apportionment of interstate waters it is proper to weigh the harms and benefits to competing States. In *Kansas* v. *Colorado*, where we first announced the doctrine of equitable apportionment, we found that users in Kansas were injured by Colorado's upstream diversions from the Arkansas River. Yet we declined to grant any relief to Kansas on the ground that the great benefit to Colorado outweighed the detriment to Kansas. Similarly, in *Nebraska* v. *Wyoming*, we held that water rights in Wyoming and Nebraska, which under state law were senior, had to yield to the "countervailing equities" of an established economy in Colorado even though it was based on junior appropriations. We noted that the rule of priority should not be strictly applied where it "would work more hardship" on the junior user "than it would bestow benefits" on the senior user. The same principle is applicable in balancing the benefits of a diversion for *proposed* uses against the possible harms to existing uses.

We recognize that the equities supporting the protection of existing economies will usually be compelling. The harm that may result from disrupting established uses is typically certain and immediate, whereas the potential benefits from a proposed diversion may be speculative and remote. Under some circumstances, however, the countervailing equities supporting a diversion for future use in one State may justify the detriment to existing users in another State. This may be the case, for example, where the State seeking a diversion demonstrates by clear and convincing evidence that the benefits of the diversion substantially outweigh the harm that might result. In the determination of whether the State proposing the diversion has carried this burden, an important consideration is whether the existing users could offset the diversion by reasonable conservation measures to prevent waste. This approach comports with our emphasis on flexibility in equitable apportionment and also accords sufficient protection to existing uses.

* * *

IV

The flexible doctrine of equitable apportionment clearly extends to a State's claim to divert water for future uses. Whether such a diversion should be permitted will turn on an examination of all factors relevant to a just apportionment. It is proper, therefore, to consider factors such as the extent to which reasonable conservation measures by existing users can offset the reduction in supply due to diversion, and whether the benefits to the State seeking the diversion substantially outweigh the harm to existing uses in another State. We remand for specific factual findings relevant to determining a just and equitable apportionment of the water of the Vermejo River between Colorado and New Mexico.

It is so ordered.

JUSTICE O'CONNOR, with whom JUSTICE POWELL joins, concurring in the judgment.

* * *

Colorado would have the Court assess the Conservancy District's "waste" and "inefficiency" by a new yardstick—i.e., not by comparing the economic gains to the District with the costs of achieving greater efficiency, but by comparing the "inefficiency" of New Mexico's uses with the relative benefits to Colorado of a new use. * * *

Today the Court has also gone dangerously far toward accepting that suggestion. The Court holds, *ante*, at 186, that it is appropriate in equitable apportionment litigation to weigh the harms and benefits to the competing States. It does so notwithstanding its recognition that the potential benefits from a *proposed* diversion are likely to be speculative and remote, and therefore difficult to balance against any threatened harms, and its concession that the equities supporting protection of an existing economy will usually be compelling.

* * * Where, as here, however, no existing economy in Colorado depends on the waters of the Vermejo and the actual uses in New Mexico rank in equal importance with the proposed uses in Colorado,[6] the difficulty of arriving at the proper balance is especially great.

* * * Protection of existing economies does not require that users be permitted to continue in unreasonably wasteful or inefficient practices. But the Court should be moved to exercise its original jurisdiction to alter the status quo between States only where there is *clear and convincing evidence*, that one State's use is unreasonably wasteful. * * *

---

6. According to Colorado, the diverted water would be used "in industrial operations at coal mines, agriculture, timbering, power generation, domestic needs and other industrial operations. * * *" Reply Brief for Colorado 8.

NOTE

Justice Marshall held that the equitable apportionment doctrine required not only efficient water use, but also imposed "on states an affirmative duty to take reasonable steps to conserve and augment the water supply of an interstate stream." Justice O'Connor took issue with this point in her concurring opinion. Was such a duty apparent prior to the decision in *Colorado I*?

COLORADO v. NEW MEXICO

Supreme Court of the United States, 1984.
467 U.S. 310, 104 S.Ct. 2433, 81 L.Ed.2d 247.

JUSTICE O'CONNOR delivered the opinion of the Court.

[The Court reviewed the decision in Colorado v. New Mexico, 459 U.S. 176 (1982), page 846, supra ("*Colorado I*").]

* * *

[W]e found the Master's report unclear and determined that a remand would be appropriate.

* * *

Requiring Colorado to present clear and convincing evidence in support of its proposed diversion is necessary to appropriately balance the unique interests involved in water rights disputes between sovereigns. The standard reflects this Court's long-held view that a proposed diverter should bear most, though not all, of the risks of erroneous decision * * *. * * * In addition, the clear-and-convincing-evidence standard accommodates society's competing interests in increasing the stability of property rights and in putting resources to their most efficient uses * * *. In short, Colorado's diversion should and will be allowed only if actual inefficiencies in present uses or future benefits from other uses are highly probable.

With these principles in mind, we turn to review the evidence the parties have submitted concerning the proposed diversion. As our opinion noted last Term, New Mexico has met its initial burden of showing "real or substantial injury" because "*any* diversion by Colorado, unless offset by New Mexico at its own expense, [would] necessarily reduce the amount of water available to New Mexico users." Accordingly, the burden shifted on remand to Colorado to show, by clear and convincing evidence, that reasonable conservation measures could compensate for some or all of the proposed diversion and that the injury, if any, to New Mexico would be outweighed by the benefits to Colorado from the diversion. * * *

A

To establish whether Colorado's proposed diversion could be offset by eliminating New Mexico's nonuse or inefficiency, we asked the Master to make specific findings concerning existing uses, supplies of water, and reasonable conservation measures available to the two

States. After assessing the evidence both States offered about existing uses and available supplies, the Master concluded that "current levels of use primarily reflect failure on the part of existing users to fully develop and put to work available water." Moreover, with respect to reasonable conservation measures available, the Master indicated his belief that more careful water administration in New Mexico would alleviate shortages from unregulated stockponds, fishponds, and water detention structures, prevent waste from blockage and clogging in canals, and ensure that users fully devote themselves to development of available resources. He further concluded that "the heart of New Mexico's water problem is the Vermejo Conservancy District," which he considered a failed "reclamation project [that had] never lived up to its expectations or even proved to be a successful project, * * * and [that] quite possibly should never have been built." Though the District was quite arguably in the "middle range in reclamation project efficiencies," the Master was of the opinion "that [the District's] inefficient water use should not be charged to Colorado." Furthermore, though Colorado had not submitted evidence or testimony of any conservation measures that C.F. & I. would take, the Master concluded that "it is not for the Master or for New Mexico to say that reasonable attempts to conserve water will not be implemented by Colorado."

We share the Master's concern that New Mexico may be overstating the amount of harm its users would suffer from a diversion. Water use by appropriators along the Vermejo River has remained relatively stable for the past 30 years, and this historic use falls substantially below the decreed rights of those users. Unreliable supplies satisfactorily explain some of this difference, but New Mexico's attempt to excuse three decades of nonuse in this way is, at the very least, suspect. Nevertheless, whatever the merit of New Mexico's explanation, we cannot agree that Colorado has met its burden of identifying, by clear and convincing evidence, conservation efforts that would preserve any of the Vermejo River water supply.

For example, though Colorado alleged that New Mexico could improve its administration of stockponds, fishponds, and water detention structures, it did not actually point to specific measures New Mexico could take to conserve water. * * * Similarly, though Colorado asserted that more rigorous water administration could eliminate blocked diversion works and ensure more careful development of water supplies, it did not show how this would actually preserve existing supplies. Even if Colorado's generalizations were true, they would prove only that some junior users are diverting water that senior appropriators ultimately could call; they would not prove that water is being wasted or used inefficiently by those actually diverting it. * * *

Colorado's attack on current water use in the Vermejo Conservancy District is inadequate for much the same reason. Our cases require only conservation measures that are "financially and physically feasible" and "within practicable limits." * * * A State can carry its burden of proof in an equitable apportionment action only with specific evidence about how existing uses might be improved, or with clear evidence that a project is far less efficient than most other projects.

Mere assertions about the relative efficiencies of competing projects will not do.

Finally, there is no evidence in the record that "Colorado has undertaken reasonable steps to minimize the amount of the diversion that will be required." Nine years have past since C.F. & I. first proposed diverting water from the Vermejo River. Yet Colorado has presented no evidence concerning C.F. & I.'s inability to relieve its needs through substitute sources. Furthermore, there is no evidence that C.F. & I. has settled on a definite or even tentative construction design or plan, or that it has prepared an economic analysis of its proposed diversion. Indeed, C.F. & I. has not even conducted an operational study of the reservoir that Colorado contends will be built in conjunction with the proposed diversion. It may be impracticable to ask the State proposing a diversion to provide unerring proof of future uses and concomitant conservation measures that would be taken. But it would be irresponsible of us to apportion water to uses that have not been, at a minimum, carefully studied and objectively evaluated, not to mention decided upon. Financially and physically feasible conservation efforts include careful study of future, as well as prudent implementation of current, water uses. Colorado has been unwilling to take any concrete steps in this direction.   * * *

B

We also asked the Master to help us balance the benefits and harms that might result from the proposed diversion. The Master found that Colorado's proposed interim use is agricultural in nature and that more permanent applications might include use in coal mines, timbering, power generation, domestic needs, and other industrial operations. The Master admitted that "[t]his area of fact finding [was] one of the most difficult [both] because of the necessarily speculative nature of [the] benefits * * * " and because of Colorado's "natural reluctance to spend large amounts of time and money developing plans, operations, and cost schemes. * * * " Nevertheless, because the diverted water would, at a minimum, alleviate existing water shortages in Colorado, the Master concluded that the evidence showed considerable benefits would accrue from the diversion. Furthermore, the Master concluded that the injury, if any, to New Mexico would be insubstantial, if only because reasonable conservation measures could, in his opinion, offset the entire impact of the diversion.

Again, we find ourselves without adequate evidence to approve Colorado's proposed diversion. Colorado has not committed itself to any long-term use for which future benefits can be studied and predicted. Nor has Colorado specified how long the interim agricultural use might or might not last. All Colorado has established is that a steel corporation wants to take water for some unidentified use in the future.

By contrast, New Mexico has attempted to identify the harms that would result from the proposed diversion. New Mexico commissioned some independent economists to study the economic effects, direct and indirect, that the diversion would have on persons in New Mexico.

* * * New Mexico, at the very least, has taken concrete steps toward addressing the query this Court posed last Term. Colorado has made no similar effort.

* * * We have only required that a State proposing a diversion conceive and implement some type of long-range planning and analysis of the diversion it proposes. Long-range planning and analysis will, we believe, reduce the uncertainties with which equitable apportionment judgments are made. If New Mexico can develop evidence to prove that its existing economy is efficiently using water, we see no reason why Colorado cannot take similar steps to prove that its future economy could do better.

* * *

JUSTICE STEVENS, dissenting.

* * *

[Justice Stevens reviewed the record and found ample evidence to support the conclusion that New Mexico was using its share of the river wastefully and that additional conservation measures were available to New Mexico.]

* * *

Colorado is correct when it states that "New Mexico should not be permitted to use its own lack of administration and record keeping to establish its claim that no water can be conserved. That position, if accepted by the Court, would encourage states to obscure their water use practices and needs in order to avoid their duty to help conserve the common supply." Last Term we explicitly rejected New Mexico's inflexible interpretation of the doctrine of equitable apportionment under which priority would not merely be a guiding principle but the controlling one. * * *

NOTE

After the two *Colorado v. New Mexico* decisions, what would your advice be to a state concerned about protecting its share of an interstate stream, in regard to planning? In regard to water management and conservation?

Modern litigation among states invoking the original jurisdiction of the Supreme Court to adjudicate rights to protect interstate waterways from pollution by dischargers in another state tends to be dominated by tort principles and federal pollution statutes rather than the notions of equitable apportionment discussed in New Jersey v. New York, page 839, supra.

ARKANSAS v. OKLAHOMA

Supreme Court of the United States, 1992.
___ U.S. ___, 112 S.Ct. 1046, 117 L.Ed.2d 239.

JUSTICE STEVENS delivered the opinion of the Court.

* * *

I

In 1985, the City of Fayetteville, Arkansas, applied to the EPA, seeking a permit for the City's new sewage treatment plant under the National Pollution Discharge Elimination System (NPDES). After the appropriate procedures, the EPA, pursuant to § 402(a)(1) of the Act, 33 U.S.C. § 1342(a)(1), issued a permit authorizing the plant to discharge up to half of its effluent (to a limit of 6.1 million gallons per day) into an unnamed stream in northwestern Arkansas. That flow passes through a series of three creeks for about 17 miles, and then enters the Illinois River at a point 22 miles upstream from the Arkansas–Oklahoma border.

The permit imposed specific limitations on the quantity, content, and character of the discharge and also included a number of special conditions, including a provision that if a study then underway indicated that more stringent limitations were necessary to ensure compliance with Oklahoma's water quality standards, the permit would be modified to incorporate those limits. App. 84.

Respondents challenged this permit before the EPA, alleging, *inter alia,* that the discharge violated the Oklahoma water quality standards. Those standards provide that "no degradation [of water quality] shall be allowed" in the upper Illinois River, including the portion of the River immediately downstream from the state line.

Following a hearing, the Administrative Law Judge (ALJ) concluded that the Oklahoma standards would not be implicated unless the contested discharge had "something more than a mere *de minimis* impact" on the State's waters. He found that the discharge would not have an "undue impact" on Oklahoma's waters and, accordingly, affirmed the issuance of the permit.

On a petition for review, the EPA's Chief Judicial Officer first ruled that § 301(b)(1)(C) of the Clean Water Act "requires an NPDES permit to impose any effluent limitations necessary to comply with applicable state water quality standards." [3] He then held that the Act and EPA regulations offered greater protection for the downstream State than the ALJ's "undue impact" standard suggested. He explained the proper standard as follows:

> "[A] mere theoretical impairment of Oklahoma's water quality standards—i.e., an infinitesimal impairment predicted through modeling but not expected to be actually detectable or measurable should not by itself block the issuance of the permit. In this case, the permit should be upheld if the record shows by a preponderance of the evidence that the authorized discharges would not

---

3. Section 301(b)(1)(C) provides, in relevant part, that

"there shall be achieved—

* * *

"(C) not later than July 1, 1977, any more stringent limitation, including those necessary to meet *water quality standards * * * established pursuant to any State law or regulations * * ** or required to implement any applicable water quality standard established pursuant to this chapter." 33 U.S.C. § 1311(b)(1)(C) (emphasis supplied).

cause an actual *detectable* violation of Oklahoma's water quality standards." Id., at 117a (emphasis in original).

On remand, the ALJ made detailed findings of fact and concluded that the City had satisfied the standard set forth by the Chief Judicial Officer. Specifically, the ALJ found that there would be no detectable violation of any of the components of Oklahoma's water quality standards. The Chief Judicial Officer sustained the issuance of the permit.

Both the petitioners in No. 90–1262 (collectively Arkansas) and the respondents in this litigation sought judicial review. Arkansas argued that the Clean Water Act did not require an Arkansas point source to comply with Oklahoma's water quality standards. Oklahoma challenged the EPA's determination that the Fayetteville discharge would not produce a detectable violation of the Oklahoma standards.

* * *

II

Interstate waters have been a font of controversy since the founding of the Nation. E.g., Gibbons v. Ogden, 9 Wheat. 1, 6 L.Ed. 23 (1824). This Court has frequently resolved disputes between States that are separated by a common river, see, e.g., Ohio v. Kentucky, 444 U.S. 335 (1980), that border the same body of water, see, e.g., New York v. New Jersey, 256 U.S. 296 (1921), or that are fed by the same river basin, see, e.g., New Jersey v. New York, 283 U.S. 336 (1931).

* * * Among these cases are controversies between a State that introduces pollutants to a waterway and a downstream State that objects. See, e.g., Missouri v. Illinois, 200 U.S. 496 (1906). In such cases, this Court has applied principles of common law tempered by a respect for the sovereignty of the States. In forging what "may not improperly be called interstate common law," Illinois v. Milwaukee, 406 U.S. 91, 105–106 (1972) (*Milwaukee I*), however, we remained aware "that new federal laws and new federal regulations may in time pre-empt the field of federal common law of nuisance." Id., at 107.

In Milwaukee v. Illinois, 451 U.S. 304 (1981) (*Milwaukee II*), we held that the 1972 Amendments to the Federal Water Pollution Control Act did just that. In addressing Illinois' claim that Milwaukee's discharges into Lake Michigan constituted a nuisance, we held that the comprehensive regulatory regime created by the 1972 Amendments pre-empted Illinois' federal common law remedy. We observed that Congress had addressed many of the problems we had identified in *Milwaukee I* by providing a downstream State with an opportunity for a hearing before the source State's permitting agency, by requiring the latter to explain its failure to accept any recommendations offered by the downstream State, and by authorizing the EPA, in its discretion, to veto a source State's issuance of any permit if the waters of another State may be affected. *Milwaukee II*, 451 U.S., at 325–326.

In *Milwaukee II*, the Court did not address whether the 1972 Amendments had supplanted *state* common law remedies as well as the federal common law remedy. See id., at 310, n. 4. On remand, Illinois argued that § 510 of the Clean Water Act, 33 U.S.C. § 1370, expressly preserved the State's right to adopt and enforce rules that are more stringent than federal standards. The Court of Appeals accepted Illinois' reading of § 510, but held that that section did "no more than to save the right and jurisdiction of a state to regulate activity occurring within the confines of its boundary waters." Illinois v. Milwaukee, 731 F.2d 403, 413 (CA7 1984), cert. denied, 469 U.S. 1196 (1985).

* * * This Court subsequently endorsed that analysis in International Paper Co. v. Ouellette, 479 U.S. 481 (1987), in which Vermont property owners claimed that the pollution discharged into Lake Champlain by a paper company located in New York constituted a nuisance under Vermont law. The Court held the Clean Water Act taken "as a whole, its purposes and its history" preempted an action based on the law of the affected State and that the only state law applicable to an interstate discharge is "the law of the State in which the point source is located." Id., at 487, 493. Moreover, in reviewing § 402(b) of the Act, the Court pointed out that when a new permit is being issued by the source State's permit-granting agency, the downstream state

> "does not have the authority to block the issuance of the permit if it is dissatisfied with the proposed standards. An affected State's only recourse is to apply to the EPA Administrator, who then has the discretion to disapprove the permit if he concludes that the discharges will have an undue impact on interstate waters. § 1342(d)(2) * * *. Thus the Act makes it clear that affected States occupy a subordinate position to source States in the federal regulatory program." Id., at 490–491.

Unlike the foregoing cases, this litigation involves not a State-issued permit, but a federally issued permit. To explain the significance of this distinction, we comment further on the statutory scheme before addressing the specific issues raised by the parties.

III

The Clean Water Act anticipates a partnership between the States and the Federal Government, animated by a shared objective: "to restore and maintain the chemical, physical, and biological integrity of the Nation's waters." 33 U.S.C. § 1251(a). Toward this end, the Act provides for two sets of water quality measures. "Effluent limitations" are promulgated by the EPA and restrict the quantities, rates, and concentrations of specified substances which are discharged from point sources. See 33 U.S.C. §§ 1311, 1314. "[W]ater quality standards" are, in general, promulgated by the States and establish the desired condition of a waterway. See 33 U.S.C. § 1313. These standards supplement effluent limitations "so that numerous point sources, despite individual compliance with effluent limitations, may be further regulated to prevent water quality from falling below acceptable levels." EPA v. California ex rel. State Water Resources Control Board, 426 U.S. 200, 205, n. 12 (1976).

The EPA provides States with substantial guidance in the drafting of water quality standards. See generally 40 CFR pt. 131 (1991) (setting forth model water quality standards). Moreover, § 303 of the Act requires, *inter alia*, that state authorities periodically review water quality standards and secure the EPA's approval of any revisions in the standards. If the EPA recommends changes to the standards and the State fails to comply with that recommendation, the Act authorizes the EPA to promulgate water quality standards for the State. 33 U.S.C. § 1313(c).

The primary means for enforcing these limitations and standards is the National Pollution Discharge Elimination System (NPDES), enacted in 1972 as a critical part of Congress' "complete rewriting" of federal water pollution law. *Milwaukee II*, 451 U.S., at 317. Section 301(a) of the Act, 33 U.S.C. § 1311(a), generally prohibits the discharge of any effluent into a navigable body of water unless the point source has obtained an NPDES permit. Section 402 establishes the NPDES permitting regime, and describes two types of permitting systems: state permit programs that must satisfy federal requirements and be approved by the EPA, and a federal program administered by the EPA.

Section 402(b) authorizes each State to establish "its own permit program for discharges into navigable waters within its jurisdiction." 33 U.S.C. § 1342(b). Among the requirements the state program must satisfy are the procedural protections for downstream States discussed in *Ouellette* and *Milwaukee II*. See 33 U.S.C. §§ 1342(b)(3), (5). Although these provisions do not authorize the downstream State to veto the issuance of a permit for a new point source in another State, the Administrator retains authority to block the issuance of any state-issued permit that "is outside the guidelines and requirements" of the Act. 33 U.S.C. § 1342(d)(2).

In the absence of an approved state program, the EPA may issue an NPDES permit under § 402(a) of the Act. (In this case, for example, because Arkansas had not been authorized to issue NPDES permits when the Fayetteville plant was completed, the permit was issued by the EPA itself.) The EPA's permit program is subject to the "same terms, conditions, and requirements" as a state permit program. 33 U.S.C. § 1342(a)(3). Notwithstanding this general symmetry, the EPA has construed the Act as requiring that EPA-issued NPDES permits also comply with § 401(a). That section, which predates § 402 and the NPDES, applies to a broad category of federal licenses, and sets forth requirements for "[a]ny applicant for a Federal license or permit to conduct any activity including, but not limited to, the construction or operation of facilities, which may result in any discharge into the navigable waters." 33 U.S.C. § 1341(a). Section 401(a)(2) appears to prohibit the issuance of any federal license or permit over the objection of an affected State unless compliance with the affected State's water quality requirements can be insured.

IV

* * * The parties have argued three analytically distinct questions concerning the interpretation of the Clean Water Act. First, does the Act require the EPA, in crafting and issuing a permit to a point source in one State, to apply the water quality standards of downstream

States? Second, even if the Act does not *require* as much, does the Agency have the statutory authority to mandate such compliance? Third, does the Act provide, as the Court of Appeals held, that once a body of water fails to meet water quality standards no discharge that yields effluent that reach the degraded waters will be permitted?

In this case, it is neither necessary nor prudent for us to resolve the first of these questions. In issuing the Fayetteville permit, the EPA assumed it was obligated by both the Act and its own regulations to ensure that the Fayetteville discharge would not violate Oklahoma's standards.

* * * As we discuss below, this assumption was permissible and reasonable and therefore there is no need for us to address whether the Act requires as much. Moreover, much of the analysis and argument in the briefs of the parties relies on statutory provisions that govern not only federal permits issued pursuant to §§ 401(a) and 402(a), but also state permits issued under § 402(b). It seems unwise to evaluate those arguments in a case such as this one, which only involves a federal permit.

* * * Our decision not to determine at this time the scope of the Agency's statutory *obligations* does not affect our resolution of the second question, which concerns the Agency's statutory *authority*. Even if the Clean Water Act itself does not require the Fayetteville discharge to comply with Oklahoma's water quality standards, the statute clearly does not limit the EPA's authority to mandate such compliance.

* * * Since 1973, EPA regulations have provided that an NPDES permit shall not be issued "[w]hen the imposition of conditions cannot ensure compliance with the applicable water quality requirements of all affected States."[10] 40 CFR § 122.4(d) (1991); see also 38 Fed.Reg. 13533 (1973); 40 CFR § 122.44(d) (1991). Those regulations—relied upon by the EPA in the issuance of the Fayetteville permit—constitute a reasonable exercise of the Agency's statutory authority.

Congress has vested in the Administrator broad discretion to establish conditions for NPDES permits. Section 402(a)(2) provides that for EPA-issued permits "[t]he Administrator shall prescribe conditions for such permits to assure compliance with the requirements of [§ 402(a)(1)] and *such other requirements as he deems appropriate.*" 33 U.S.C. § 1342(a)(2) (emphasis supplied). Similarly, Congress preserved for the Administrator broad authority to oversee state permit programs:

> "No permit shall issue * * * if the Administrator * * * objects in writing to the issuance of such permit as being outside the guidelines and requirements of this chapter." 33 U.S.C. § 1342(d)(2).

The regulations relied on by the EPA were a perfectly reasonable exercise of the Agency's statutory discretion. The application of state

---

10. This restriction applies whether the permit is issued by the EPA or by an approved state program. See 40 CFR § 123.25 (1991).

water quality standards in the interstate context is wholly consistent with the Act's broad purpose, "to restore and maintain the chemical, physical, and biological integrity of the Nation's waters." 33 U.S.C. § 1251(a). Moreover, as noted above, § 301(b)(1)(C) expressly identifies the achievement of state water quality standards as one of the Act's central objectives. The Agency's regulations conditioning NPDES permits are a well-tailored means of achieving this goal.

* * * Notwithstanding this apparent reasonableness, Arkansas argues that our description in *Ouellette* of the role of affected States in the permit process and our characterization of the affected States' position as "subordinate," indicates that the EPA's application of the Oklahoma standards was error. We disagree. Our statement in *Ouellette* concerned only an affected State's input into the permit process; that input is clearly limited by the plain language of § 402(b). Limits on an affected State's direct participation in permitting decisions, however, do not in any way constrain the *EPA's* authority to require a point source to comply with downstream water quality standards.

Arkansas also argues that regulations requiring compliance with downstream standards are at odds with the legislative history of the Act and with the statutory scheme established by the Act. Although we agree with Arkansas that the Act's legislative history indicates that Congress intended to grant the Administrator discretion in his oversight of the issuance of NPDES permits, we find nothing in that history to indicate that Congress intended to preclude the EPA from establishing a general requirement that such permits be conditioned to ensure compliance with downstream water quality standards.

Similarly, we agree with Arkansas that in the Clean Water Act Congress struck a careful balance among competing policies and interests, but do not find the EPA regulations concerning the application of downstream water quality standards at all incompatible with that balance. Congress, in crafting the Act, protected certain sovereign interest of the States; for example, § 510 allows States to adopt more demanding pollution-control standards than those established under the Act. Arkansas emphasizes that § 510 preserves such state authority only as it is applied to the waters of the regulating State. Even assuming Arkansas's construction of § 510 is correct, cf. id., at 493, that section only concerns *state* authority and does not constrain the *EPA's* authority to promulgate reasonable regulations requiring point sources in one State to comply with water quality standards in downstream States.

* * * For these reasons, we find the EPA's requirement that the Fayetteville discharge comply with Oklahoma's water quality standards to be a reasonable exercise of the Agency's substantial statutory discretion.

V

* * * The Court of Appeals construed the Clean Water Act to prohibit any discharge of effluent that would reach waters already in

violation of existing water quality standards. We find nothing in the Act to support this reading.

* * *

VI

* * * The Court of Appeals also concluded that the EPA's issuance of the Fayetteville permit was arbitrary and capricious because the Agency misinterpreted Oklahoma's water quality standards.

* * *

* * * In sum, the Court of Appeals made a policy choice that it was not authorized to make. Arguably, as that court suggested, it might be wise to prohibit any discharge into the Illinois River, even if that discharge would have no adverse impact on water quality. But it was surely not arbitrary for the EPA to conclude—given the benefits to the River from the increased flow of relatively clean water and the benefits achieved in Arkansas by allowing the new plant to operate as designed—that allowing the discharge would be even wiser. * * *

Accordingly, the judgment of the Court of Appeals is

Reversed.

NOTE: INTERSTATE POLLUTION REMEDIES

Preemption of Federal Tort Law. In Section II of the Court's unanimous decision in *Arkansas*, Justice Stevens traced the evolutionary interaction between the common law—both state and federal—and congressional enactments pertaining to water pollution. For all practical purposes, the Court in Milwaukee v. Illinois and Michigan, 451 U.S. 304 (1981) (*Milwaukee II*), arrested the development of a federal common law of torts to fill in gaps left by antipollution regulatory programs. The decision states that "federal courts, unlike state courts, are not general common law courts and do not possess a general power to develop and apply their own rules of decision," citing Erie v. Tompkins, 304 U.S. 64, 78 (1938). This rationale for the decision is troubling, since it was traditionally assumed that the power to develop a federal common law of interstate water allocation and pollution came from either the constitutional grant of original jurisdiction or an act of Congress. See Martin H. Redish, Federal Jurisdiction: Tensions in the Allocation of Judicial Power 79–107 (1980).

In fact, Judge Friendly argued in a law review article that *Erie* did not impeach the constitutionality of the development of a federal common law. He pointed out that Hinderlider v. La Plata River and Cherry Creek Ditch Co., 304 U.S. 92 (1938), page 870, infra, decided the same day as *Erie*, stands for the proposition that "the Constitution can well be deemed to *require* that the federal courts should fashion a law when the interstate nature of the controversy makes it inappropriate that the law of either state should govern" (emphasis added). Friendly, *In Praise of Erie and of the New Federal Common Law*, 39 N.Y.U.L.Rev. 383, 408 n. 119 (1964). But cf. Note, *Federal Common Law and Interstate Pollution*, 85 Harv.L.Rev. 1439 (1972).

In an earlier phase of the litigation, Illinois v. Milwaukee, 406 U.S. 91 (1972) (*Milwaukee I*), the Supreme Court based the availability of a common law remedy on both its original jurisdiction to hear interstate equitable apportionment actions and on congressional pollution control statutes. The Clean Water Act (CWA) was passed after *Milwaukee I* but before *Milwaukee II*, however. *Milwaukee II* found nothing in the Act to indicate that Congress intended to preserve federal common law remedies. Indeed, it found that a system of federal statutory standards would be fundamentally at odds with allowing separate federal common law remedies that might result in different standards being applied. See generally A. Dan Tarlock, *Upstream, Downstream: Rationalizing Different State Water Quality Standards on Interstate Streams*, 37 Rocky Mtn.Min.L.Inst. 23–1 (1991).

State Law Remedies. If the federal common law of nuisance is preempted by a statutory scheme, can similar actions be pursued under state law? Section 510 of the CWA allows states to impose stricter limits on pollutant discharges than apply under federal standards. Suppose that a polluter discharges a pollutant in State A that injures citizens of State B. Can the victims sue in the state courts of State B and apply the state law of State B? In Ohio v. Wyandotte Chemicals Corp., 401 U.S. 493 (1971), the state of Ohio brought an original action against a corporation for dumping mercury into Lake Erie in Michigan. The Court declined to take original jurisdiction, suggesting that Ohio could exercise long-arm jurisdiction to obtain adequate relief in its own courts. In such an action, what law would apply?

After the decision in *Milwaukee II*, Illinois sought the same type of relief in U.S. District Court that it had pursued in the Supreme Court, but this time under Illinois statute and common law. The case was consolidated with a class action commenced in the Northern District of Illinois by the state Attorney General against the City of Hammond, Indiana, which was dumping raw sewage into Lake Michigan and was thereby allegedly causing a public and private nuisance under Illinois law. In *Milwaukee III*, the Seventh Circuit said that "in the ordinary interstate tort, the Constitution does not preclude the application of one state's law to afford a remedy for acts done in another state and producing injury within the forum state." Illinois v. Milwaukee, 731 F.2d 403, 411 n. 3 (7th Cir.1984), cert. denied, 469 U.S. 1196 (1985). However, it also held that the issue here was "the equitable reconciliation of competing uses of an interstate body of water, Lake Michigan." As a result, "the very reasons that the Court gave for resorting to federal common law in Milwaukee I [the need for equitable apportionment] are the same reasons that the state claiming injury cannot apply its own law to out-of-state dischargers now." 731 F.2d 403.

The Court resolved this issue in International Paper Co. v. Ouellette, 479 U.S. 481 (1987), but not by resorting to federal common law. Instead, the Court held that the CWA preempted an action based on Vermont tort law alleging a cause of action for nuisance caused by a polluter discharging effluents on the New York side of Lake Champlain. The Court found that the CWA preempts suits based on the laws of an affected state to curb pollution originating in another state.

Thus, it limited the effect of § 510 to allowing state laws stricter than federal laws to be applied only by the polluting state. It is interesting that the CWA has little provision for dealing with interstate pollution. Therefore, the Court in *Ouellette* noted that the Vermont plaintiff could still bring a nuisance claim based on New York statutory or common law inasmuch as stricter standards could be imposed by the source state, according to the Court's interpretation of the CWA.

Equitable Apportionment. Apparently lost in the volley of *Milwaukee* litigation was any serious consideration of equitable apportionment. After federal tort remedies were ruled out, the parties went scurrying for courts in which to bring a state law tort suit.

The law of equitable apportionment is a kind of federal common law that is well-accepted in interstate water litigation. Are interstate water pollution cases effectively cases that seek to "apportion" the right to use waters shared by two or more states? One "use" is to carry away discharged pollutants and it competes with uses in a neighbor state—drinking water, recreation, other pollutant discharge. Indeed, a remedy for pollution is to leave more water in the stream. Recall that the Supreme Court in New Jersey v. New York, page 839, supra, required reductions in diversions and additional releases from reservoirs to prevent harm to water quality. The theory and basis for the decision was equitable apportionment, not tort.

An allocation of waters was not specifically sought in *Milwaukee II* or in Arkansas v. Oklahoma. Are remedies like those in *New Jersey* still viable where present or future actions in one state cause or exacerbate a pollution problem? Is the federal common law of equitable apportionment preempted by the Clean Water Act (that targets the discharge of effluent, not the availability of water to dilute concentrations of effluents)? In other words, did Congress intend to apportion the use of interstate waters when it set up the scheme in the Clean Water Act?

B. INTERSTATE COMPACTS

Interstate compacts are contractual arrangements, like treaties, that are used to carry out the objectives of two or more states. The Supreme Court has indicated several times its reluctance to adjudicate interstate stream disputes and has urged the parties to resolve their differences by compact. Compacts are authorized by art. I, § 10, cl. 3 of the Constitution. The clause, however, requires Congress' consent to the compact.

There are dozens of interstate compacts dealing with water allocation, pollution control, flood control, project development and basin planning in interstate waters. Interstate stream compacts that allocate water among the signatory parties vary in their terms from an apportionment of a percentage of streamflow to a requirement that a certain quantity of water be delivered at a specified point on the stream.

Apportioning the rights of states to use interstate waters by compact offers flexibility that may not be available in judicial apportionment. Furthermore, adjudication may not be available because the Supreme Court generally refuses jurisdiction unless there is imminent injury, a condition that does not usually arise until a stream is overappropriated. Thus, compacting states can anticipate their respective future needs and provide for them. This is essential to long range planning by the respective states. The United States may also be a party to an interstate compact to represent the government's needs for federal lands or other national interests.

Compact formation generally begins with congressional authorization of negotiation, often providing for a federal representative to participate. States then commence negotiations, usually after passing enabling legislation designating their negotiators. Negotiations may take many years. The final step is for Congress to consent, a requirement of the compact clause, which states: "No state shall, without the consent of Congress * * * enter into any agreement or compact with another state, or with a foreign power. * * * "

Many compacts require the establishment of commissions or similar agencies to deal with matters of compact administration. Often the commissioners are appointed by the governors of the participating states and a federal member who may not have a vote. Commissions allocating waters between states have much administrative power, relegating enforcement to the courts. Some recent compacts, like the Delaware River Compact, delegate considerable power to a compact agency. However, the Colorado River Compact, page 873, infra, created no compact agency at all. The enforcement problems of ordinary compacts are multiplied when the federal government is a signatory, for the question remains unresolved whether congressional consent to such a compact binds future Congresses in, say, the exercise of commerce clause powers that may be contrary to the compact provisions.

Notwithstanding their promise, compacts can leave many problems unresolved. Compact negotiations succeed only because difficult points are plastered over with ambiguity. Some compacts are based on errors of fact, but once the compact is accepted it is nearly impossible to get the parties to agree to changes. Compacts may be difficult to enforce because the United States is sometimes regarded as an indispensable party, but it cannot be sued without its consent. Furthermore, enforcement suits can be expensive and lengthy because they are usually within the original jurisdiction of the Supreme Court of the United States. Compacts often lack the flexibility to deal with changing conditions and they cannot be easily amended.

The classic study of the compact is Felix Frankfurter & James M. Landis, *The Compact Clause of the Constitution—A Study in Interstate Adjustments*, 34 Yale L.J. 685 (1925). A useful supplement is Frederick Lloyd Zimmerman and Mitchell Wendell, The Interstate Compact Since 1925 (Council of State Governments, 1951). The United States Department of the Interior published a reference book: T. Richard Witmer, Documents on the Use and Control of the Waters of Interstate and International Streams: Compacts, Treaties and Adjudications (1956). See also Jerome C. Muys, Interstate Water Compacts: The Interstate

Compact and Federal-Interstate Compact, National Water Commission
Legal Study No. 14 (1971).

STATE ex rel. DYER v. SIMS

Supreme Court of the United States, 1951.
341 U.S. 22, 71 S.Ct. 557, 95 L.Ed. 713.

Mr. Justice Frankfurter delivered the opinion of the Court.

After extended negotiations eight States entered into a Compact to
control pollution in the Ohio River system. See Ohio River Valley
Water Sanitation Compact, 54 Stat. 752. Illinois, Indiana, Kentucky,
New York, Ohio, Pennsylvania, Virginia and West Virginia recognized
that they were faced with one of the problems of government that are
defined by natural rather than political boundaries. Accordingly, they
pledged themselves to cooperate in maintaining waters in the Ohio
River basin in a sanitary condition through the administrative mechanism of the Ohio River Valley Water Sanitation Commission, consisting
of three members from each State and three representing the United
States.

The heart of the Compact is Article VI. This provides that sewage
discharged into boundary streams or streams flowing from one State
into another "shall be so treated, within a time reasonable for the
construction of the necessary works, as to provide for substantially
complete removal of settleable solids, and the removal of not less than
forty-five per cent (45%) of the total suspended solids; provided that, in
order to protect the public health or to preserve the waters for other
legitimate purposes, * * * in specific instances such higher degree of
treatment shall be used as may be determined to be necessary by the
Commission after investigation, due notice and hearing." Industrial
wastes are to be treated "to such degree as may be determined to be
necessary by the Commission after investigation, due notice and hearing." Sewage and industrial wastes discharged into streams located
wholly within one State are to be treated "to that extent, if any, which
may be necessary to maintain such waters in a sanitary and satisfactory condition at least equal to the condition of the waters of the
interstate stream immediately above the confluence."

Article IX provides that the Commission may, after notice and
hearing, issue orders for compliance enforceable in the State and
federal courts. It further provides: "No such order shall go into effect
unless and until it receives the assent of at least a majority of the
commissioners from each of not less than a majority of the signatory
States; and no such order upon a municipality, corporation, person or
entity in any State shall go into effect unless and until it receives the
assent of not less than a majority of the commissioners from such
state."

By Article X the States also agree "to appropriate for the salaries,
office and other administrative expenses, their proper proportion of the
annual budget as determined by the Commission and approved by the
Governors of the signatory States. * * * "

The present controversy arose because of conflicting views between officials of West Virginia regarding the responsibility of West Virginia under the Compact.

The Legislature of that State ratified and approved the Compact on March 11, 1939. W. Va. Acts 1939, c. 38. Congress gave its consent on July 11, 1940, 54 Stat. 752, and upon adoption by all the signatory States the Compact was formally executed by the Governor of West Virginia on June 30, 1948. At its 1949 session the West Virginia Legislature appropriated $12,250 as the State's contribution to the expenses of the Commission for the fiscal year beginning July 1, 1949. W. Va. Acts 1949, c. 9, Item 93. Respondent Sims, the auditor of the State, refused to issue a warrant upon its treasury for payment of this appropriation. To compel him to issue it, the West Virginia Commissioners to the Compact Commission and the members of the West Virginia State Water Commission instituted this original mandamus proceeding in the Supreme Court of Appeals of West Virginia. The court denied relief on the merits, 134 W.Va. [278], 58 S.E.2d 766, and we brought the case here, 340 U.S. 807, because questions of obviously important public interest are raised.

The West Virginia court found that the "sole question" before it was the validity of the Act of 1939 approving West Virginia's adherence to the Compact. It found that Act invalid in that (1) the Compact was deemed to delegate West Virginia's police power to other States and to the Federal Government, and (2) it was deemed to bind future legislatures to make appropriations for the continued activities of the Sanitation Commission and thus to violate Art. X, § 4 of the West Virginia Constitution.

Briefs filed on behalf of the United States and other States, as *amici*, invite the Court to consider far-reaching issues relating to the Compact Clause of the United States Constitution. Art. I, § 10, cl. 3. The United States urges that the Compact be so read as to allow any signatory State to withdraw from its obligations at any time. Pennsylvania, Ohio, Indiana, Illinois, Kentucky and New York contend that the Compact Clause precludes any State from limiting its power to enter into a compact to which Congress has consented. We must not be tempted by these inviting vistas. We need not go beyond the issues on which the West Virginia court found the Compact not binding on that State. That these are issues which give this Court jurisdiction to review the State court proceeding, 28 U.S.C. § 1257, needs no discussion after Delaware River Comm'n v. Colburn, 310 U.S. 419, 427.

Control of pollution in interstate streams might, on occasion, be an appropriate subject for national legislation. * * * But, with prescience, the Framers left the States free to settle regional controversies in diverse ways. Solution of the problem underlying this case may be attempted directly by the affected States through contentious litigation before this Court. * * *

Indeed, so awkward and unsatisfactory is the available litigious solution for these problems that this Court deemed it appropriate to emphasize the practical constitutional alternative provided by the Compact Clause.

* * *

The growing interdependence of regional interests, calling for regional adjustments, has brought extensive use of compacts. A compact is more than a supple device for dealing with interests confined within a region. That it is also a means of safeguarding the national interest is well illustrated in the Compact now under review. Not only was congressional consent required, as for all compacts; direct participation by the Federal Government was provided in the President's appointment of three members of the Compact Commission. Art. IV; Art. XI, § 3.

But a compact is after all a legal document. Though the circumstances of its drafting are likely to assure great care and deliberation, all avoidance of disputes as to scope and meaning is not within human gift. Just as this Court has power to settle disputes between States where there is no compact, it must have final power to pass upon the meaning and validity of compacts. It requires no elaborate argument to reject the suggestion that an agreement solemnly entered into between States by those who alone have political authority to speak for a State can be unilaterally nullified, or given final meaning by an organ of one of the contracting States. A State cannot be its own ultimate judge in a controversy with a sister State. To determine the nature and scope of obligations as between States, whether they arise through the legislative means of compact or the "federal common law" governing interstate controversies (Hinderlider v. La Plata Co., 304 U.S. 92, 110) is the function and duty of the Supreme Court of the Nation. Of course every deference will be shown to what the highest court of a State deems to be the law and policy of its State, particularly when recondite or unique features of local law are urged. Deference is one thing; submission to a State's own determination of whether it has undertaken an obligation, what that obligation is, and whether it conflicts with a disability of the State to undertake it is quite another.

The Supreme Court of Appeals of the State of West Virginia is, for exclusively State purposes, the ultimate tribunal in construing the meaning of her Constitution. Two prior decisions of this Court make clear, however, that we are free to examine determinations of law by State courts in the limited field where a compact brings in issue the rights of other States and the United States.

* * * The issue before us is whether the West Virginia Legislature had authority, under her Constitution, to enter into a compact which involves delegation of power to an interstate agency and an agreement to appropriate funds for the administrative expenses of the agency.

That a legislature may delegate to an administrative body the power to make rules and decide particular cases is one of the axioms of modern government. * * * The Compact involves a reasonable and carefully limited delegation of power to an interstate agency. Nothing in its Constitution suggests that, in dealing with the problem dealt with by the Compact, West Virginia must wait for the answer to be dictated by this Court after harassing and unsatisfactory litigation.

* * *

The State court also held that the Compact is in conflict with Art. X, § 4, of the State Constitution and for that reason is not binding on West Virginia. This section provides:

> "No debt shall be contracted by this State, except to meet casual deficits in the revenue, to redeem a previous liability of the State, to suppress insurrection, repel invasion, or defend the State in time of war; but the payment of any liability, other than that for the ordinary expenses of the State, shall be equally distributed over a period of at least twenty years."

The Compact was evidently drawn with great care to meet the problem of debt limitation in light of this section and similar restrictive provisions in the constitutions of other States. Although, under Art. X of the Compact, the States agree to appropriate funds for administrative expenses, the annual budget must be approved by the Governors of the signatory States. In addition, Article V provides: "The Commission shall not incur any obligations of any kind prior to the making of appropriations adequate to meet the same; nor shall the Commission pledge the credit of any of the signatory States, except by and with the authority of the legislature thereof." In view of these provisions, we conclude that the obligation of the State under the Compact is not in conflict with Art. X, § 4 of the State Constitution.

Reversed and remanded.

* * *

NOTES

1. The Court said that it was not answering the "inviting" question of whether a state which is signatory to a compact can withdraw from its obligations at any time. However, in ruling that it has supervening authority to interpret state law alleged to be in conflict with an interstate compact, the Court does "reject the suggestion that an agreement solemnly entered into between States * * * can be unilaterally nullified, or given final meaning by an organ of one of the contracting States." Has the Court decided the issue that it said it was avoiding?

2. The principal case arose on review of a state court decision. Do federal courts have jurisdiction to interpret compacts in the first instance? Is such interpretation a federal question within the meaning of 28 U.S.C.A. § 1331(a) (i.e., arising "under the Constitution, laws, or treaties of the United States")? League to Save Lake Tahoe v. Tahoe Regional Planning Agency, 507 F.2d 517 (9th Cir. 1974), cert. denied 420 U.S. 974 (1975), says yes, but several cases reach contrary results. E.g., Port Auth. Bondholders Protective Comm'n v. Port of New York

Auth., 270 F.Supp. 947 (S.D.N.Y. 1967); Delaware River Joint Toll Bridge Comm'n v. Miller, 147 F.Supp. 270 (E.D. Pa. 1956); Rivoli Trucking Corp. v. American Export Lines, 167 F.Supp. 937 (S.D.N.Y. 1958).

3. Is every interstate agreement a "compact" requiring congressional consent? Does the Court in *Dyer* shed light on the question? An earlier case suggested that consent is required only for agreements that exercise the political power of states. Virginia v. Tennessee, 148 U.S. 503, 518–19 (1893).

To forestall possible diversions from the Great Lakes, the Great Lakes states' governors and the premiers of Ontario and Quebec signed the Great Lakes Charter in 1985. Principle IV of the Charter imposes the international law concept of prior notice and consultation on the states and provinces before the unilateral approval by any party of a major new or increased consumptive withdrawal in the basin. The Charter also commits the states and provinces to exchange data and to develop parallel water management programs to implement the Charter. The Charter does not constitute an interstate compact, since it was never ratified by Congress, nor is it a binding treaty. It was merely an agreement between the executive officers of several states and provinces and was not enacted by any legislative body. As an agreement between several states and the provinces of a foreign country, not the countries themselves, it cannot constitute an international agreement. The intent of the Charter is embodied in law to the extent that each of the states and provinces adopts and maintains domestic legislation implementing it. See Ann Rodgers, The Limits of State Activity in the Interstate Water Market, 21 Land & Water L.Rev. 357, at 362–63 n. 29 (1986). While the Charter has not been approved by Congress as either an interstate compact or international treaty, it has contributed to a proliferation of environmental legal institutions in the basin and has improved intra-basin cooperation. See Barry Rabe and Janet Zimmerman, Cross-Media Environmental Integration in the Great Lakes Basin, 22 Envtl.L. 253 (1992).

Congress has been supportive of the will of the parties to the Charter. In 1986, it prohibited new Great Lakes diversions unless the governors of littoral states consent to them. 42 U.S.C.A. § 1926d–20. Twice Great Lakes governors have blocked proposed diversions. In the drought summer of 1988, Governor James Thompson of Illinois proposed and then withdrew a unilateral plan to increase the state's Lake Michigan diversion, limited by Supreme Court decree, to support barge traffic on the Illinois and Mississippi rivers. See Valiante and Muldoon, *Annual Review of Canadian–American Environmental Relations*, 1 Int'l Envt'l Affairs 289 (1989). In 1992, Governor John Engler of Michigan rejected a plan by a small northern Indiana community to dilute natural fluoride in its wells by adding Lake Michigan water. 9 U.S. Water News 1, July, 1992, at 1.

4. Interstate compacts are often entered into to avoid the risks of an equitable apportionment, but a compact may also follow a Supreme Court decree. In 1930 the Supreme Court apportioned the flow of the

Delaware River among New York, Pennsylvania, New Jersey, and Delaware. New Jersey v. New York, 283 U.S. 336 (1931), page 839, supra. The decree allowed New York state to supply New York City by transwatershed diversions from tributaries of the Delaware in the Catskills, subject to several conditions. The Delaware River Basin Compact, Pub. L. 87–328, 75 Stat. 688 (1961), provided that the decree of 1954 may not be changed without the unanimous consent of the parties to the lawsuit, except that the basin commission (made up of one representative from each signatory state—New York, New Jersey, Pennsylvania, Delaware—and the United States) could declare an emergency and thereafter, upon unanimous vote, vary the terms of the decree during the emergency. The emergency powers of the compact have been employed to reduce the delivery obligations and diversions and to require releases to the river from storage.

5. The legal force of an interstate compact as federal law, as the supreme law of the land, "trumps" any conflicting law of signatory states. Hinderlider v. La Plata River and Cherry Creek Ditch Co., 304 U.S. 92 (1938). In *Hinderlider,* the state engineer administered water rights perfected under Colorado law by withholding water from in-state appropriators in order to satisfy delivery requirements mandated by the La Plata River Compact between Colorado and New Mexico. Pursuant to the compact, the state engineer curtailed diversions entirely from time to time, rotating deliveries between users in the two states. The Colorado Supreme Court held the compact to be unconstitutional, as enabling an infringement on vested private property interests.

The U.S. Supreme Court reversed. Since the La Plata was an interstate watercourse being beneficially used in both states, its waters must be equitably apportioned between the two. A compact is a constitutional means of effecting an equitable apportionment and therefore it is binding on the citizens of both states. Further, giving discretion to state officials to rotate uses rather than making a continuous equal division was a "detail" within Congress constitutional power. Finally, the Court in *Hinderlider* concluded that Colorado users had not been divested of a compensable property interest because the state could allocate only its equitable share of the interstate watercourse and therefore any allocations in excess of that equitable share could not have created a vested property right subject to "taking."

6. Assume that River A and River B both rise in Colorado and flow into New Mexico. Invoking the doctrine of equitable apportionment, a compact allocates all the water of River A to Colorado and all the water of River B to New Mexico. Plaintiff has an adjudicated appropriative right on River B in Colorado senior to some users on River A, but the state engineer shuts down the plaintiff's headgate pursuant to the compact. Is plaintiff entitled to relief?

7. Who is responsible for the satisfaction of Indian water rights in an equitable apportionment or compact adjudication? Arizona has estimated that the claims of the Navajo Reservation could be as high as 15 million acre-feet per year. In Arizona v. California, in a portion of the decision reprinted at page 769, supra (see also page 886, infra), the

special master held that Indian rights were present perfected rights (having priority over virtually all others) and must be satisfied by the state in which the reservation lies. Arizona's total apportionment under compacts and the Supreme Court's interpretation of federal statutes is 2.8 million acre-feet. If tribal claims approach or exceed a state's apportionment, should all states sharing the waterway share responsibility for satisfying those rights? Is the satisfaction of Indian claims a federal responsibility since the federal government has a trust responsibility to the tribes to protect their water rights? See generally A. Dan Tarlock, *One River, Three Sovereigns: Indian and Interstate Water Rights*, 22 Land & Water L.Rev. 631 (1987).

DAVID H. GETCHES, COMPETING DEMANDS FOR THE COLORADO RIVER
56 U.Colo.L.Rev. 413, 415–20 (1985).

In the early years of the twentieth century, Southern California's growing need for federal assistance in building delivery facilities for Colorado River water came into conflict with the desire of states in the Upper Basin to secure the right to develop River water for future needs. Rich farms in California's Imperial Valley were irrigated with water brought from the River by a canal through Mexico. The Imperial Irrigation District sought the security of an "all-American" canal that would not leave the Valley's farmers at the mercy of Mexico. The federal government began investigating the possibilities. At the same time, rapidly expanding Los Angeles was feeling the need for new sources of electric power and anticipating new water needs. Leaders in the Upper Basin states, especially Colorado, objected. They knew that they would eventually need to develop Colorado River water to meet the needs of growing areas like Denver. They feared that if California were allowed to develop the River's water first, it would perfect a better legal claim. Their fears were justified by contemporary jurisprudence.

In 1922 it was reasonable to assume that the United States Supreme Court would recognize greater legal rights in a state that developed water first than in a state developing later. The Court allocates waters of interstate streams by the principle of "equitable apportionment." The Court applied the doctrine of prior appropriation in a 1922 equitable apportionment between Colorado and Wyoming, both of which use prior appropriation to allocate water within the states. Interstate apportionment of the Colorado River under that approach could have resulted in the Upper Basin states getting very little water.

The 1922 Colorado River Compact was intended to strike an accommodation between the expanding demands of the Lower Basin and the desire to preserve adequate water for future use in the less developed Upper Basin, the source of virtually all the River's water. Compacts had been used to settle or avoid conflicts between states on other issues since the signing of the Constitution, but the Colorado River Compact was the first compact negotiated to resolve claims to an interstate stream. The Compact enabled construction of storage facilities to protect the Lower Basin from floods and allowed the Lower Basin to use water needed for a growing population. The Upper Basin states relied on the Compact to prevent River water from being monopolized by California and Arizona through the establishment of legal priorities.

Under the Compact * the waters of the Colorado River were apportioned on an essentially equal basis between the Upper Basin states—Colorado, Utah, Wyoming, and New Mexico—and the Lower Basin states—Arizona, California and Nevada. The Compact guaranteed the Lower Basin states a flow of 75,000,000 acre-feet over a progressive series of ten-year periods. The drafters intended that Article III(a) would give each Basin, Upper and Lower, an average of 7,500,000 acre-feet a year. In addition, under Article III(b) the Lower Basin may consume another 1,000,000 acre-feet in years when flows permit. Article III(e) allows the faster developing Lower Basin to use any water the Upper Basin cannot use. Further, under Article III(c), the two basins are to share equally any burden that might be imposed to deliver water to Mexico, an obligation later set at 1,500,000 acre-feet annually.[8]

The water apportioned to the two basins was later allocated to individual states. In 1949, the Upper Colorado River Basin Compact gave each Upper Basin state a percentage share of that Basin's apportionment.[9] California, Arizona, and Nevada, however, were unable to agree on how to divide the Lower Basin share. After years of intense dispute and litigation, Congress enacted legislation making federal financing of Hoover Dam contingent on a prescribed Lower Basin allocation formula. Later the Supreme Court found that the Act had effectively apportioned the water.[10]

* * *

The allocation scheme in the 1922 Compact was to give the two basins equitable shares of available water. It is now apparent that the apportionment was made on the incorrect assumption that there would be an average annual flow of at least 16,000,000 acre-feet. Data spanning three centuries, however, reveal an average annual flow of only about 13,500,000 acre-feet. Furthermore, annual flows have been erratic, ranging from 4,400,000 acre-feet to over 22,000,000 acre-feet. The erroneous assumption about average flows resulted in the Lower Basin's being guaranteed substantial minimum deliveries by the Upper Basin, leaving far less water available for Upper Basin use than the negotiators apparently expected.

---

* Excerpts of the Compact are reprinted at pages 873–75, infra.—Eds.

8. The obligation to Mexico was quantified in the Treaty with Mexico, T.S. No. 994, 59 Stat. 1219 (1944).

9. Upper Colorado River Basin Compact, ch. 48, 63 Stat. 31, 33 (1949). The states received the following shares: Colorado, 51.75%; Utah, 23%; Wyoming, 14%; New Mexico, 11.25%; Arizona, 50,000 acre-feet.

10. Arizona v. California, 373 U.S. 546 (1963). The Court held that allocation of the Lower Basin share is governed by the Boulder Canyon Project Act, 43 U.S.C. §§ 617–617f (1982). The Act gives Arizona 2.8 million acre-feet, California 4.4 million acre-feet, and Nevada 300,000 acre-feet of the first 7.5 million acre-feet. Deliveries in excess of such amounts are apportioned 46 percent to Arizona, 50 percent to California and 4 percent to Nevada.

The Compact contemplates storage facilities to smooth out fluctuating flows and to allow for the average annual usage described in Articles III(a) and III(b). Adequate storage exists on the River to protect Lower Basin Compact entitlements except in the most severe and prolonged drought. Lake Mead, behind Hoover Dam, can hold 27,400,000 acre-feet. Lake Powell has a capacity of 25,000,000 acre-feet. Together, all reservoirs in the Colorado River system have a storage capacity of 62,489,200 acre-feet. With sixty percent of this storage effectively inaccessible to Upper Basin users, however, the burdens of cyclical water shortages fall largely on the Upper Basin. These inherent burdens, as well as practical limits on Upper Basin storage, should inform Compact interpretation. For instance, Article III(e) says that the Upper Basin may not withhold water from Lower Basin uses unless it can "reasonably be applied to domestic and agricultural uses." But the provision should not be read to preclude storage of water to meet future compact delivery requirements under Article III(d) or for reasonably foreseeable Upper Basin needs.

THE COLORADO RIVER COMPACT

The States of Arizona, California, Colorado, Nevada, New Mexico, Utah, and Wyoming, having resolved to enter into a compact under the Act of the Congress of the United States of America approved August 19, 1921 (42 Stat. 141) and the Acts of the Legislatures of the said States, have through their Governors appointed as their Commissioners * * * who, after negotiations participated in by Herbert Hoover appointed by The President as the representative of the United States of America, have agreed upon the following articles:

Article I

The major purposes of this compact are to provide for the equitable division and apportionment of the use of the waters of the Colorado River System; to establish the relative importance of different beneficial uses of water; to promote interstate comity; to remove causes of present and future controversies; and to secure the expeditious agricultural and industrial development of the Colorado River Basin, the storage of its waters, and the protection of life and property from floods. To these ends the Colorado River Basin is divided into two Basins, and an apportionment of the use of part of the water of the Colorado River System is made to each of them with the provision that further equitable apportionments may be made.

Article II

As used in this compact—

(a) The term "Colorado River System" means that portion of the Colorado River and its tributaries within the United States of America.

(b) The term "Colorado River Basin" means all of the drainage area of the Colorado River System and all other territory within the

United States of America to which the waters of the Colorado River System shall be beneficially applied.

* * *

(e) The term "Lee Ferry" means a point in the main stream of the Colorado River one mile below the mouth of the Paria River.

(f) The term "Upper Basin" means those parts of the States of Arizona, Colorado, New Mexico, Utah, and Wyoming within and from which waters naturally drain into the Colorado River System above Lee Ferry, and also all parts of said States located without the drainage area of the Colorado River System which are now or shall hereafter be beneficially served by waters diverted from the System above Lee Ferry.

(g) The term "Lower Basin" means those parts of the States of Arizona, California, Nevada, New Mexico, and Utah within and from which waters naturally drain into the Colorado River System below Lee Ferry, and also all parts of said States located without the drainage area of the Colorado River System which are now or shall hereafter be beneficially served by waters diverted from the System below Lee Ferry.

(h) The term "domestic use" shall include the use of water for household, stock, municipal, mining, milling, industrial, and other like purposes, but shall exclude the generation of electrical power.

Article III

(a) There is hereby apportioned from the Colorado River System in perpetuity to the Upper Basin and to the Lower Basin, respectively, the exclusive beneficial consumptive use of 7,500,000 acre-feet of water per annum, which shall include all water necessary for the supply of any rights which may now exist.

(b) In addition to the apportionment in paragraph (a), the Lower Basin is hereby given the right to increase its beneficial consumptive use of such waters by one million acre-feet per annum.

(c) If, as a matter of international comity, the United States of America shall hereafter recognize in the United States of Mexico any right to the use of any waters of the Colorado River System, such waters shall be supplied first from the waters which are surplus over and above the aggregate of the quantities specified in paragraphs (a) and (b); and if such surplus shall prove insufficient for this purpose, then the burden of such deficiency shall be equally borne by the Upper Basin and the Lower Basin, and whenever necessary the States of the Upper Division shall deliver at Lee Ferry water to supply one-half of the deficiency so recognized in addition to that provided in paragraph (d).

(d) The States of the Upper Division will not cause the flow of the river at Lee Ferry to be depleted below an aggregate of 75,000,000 acre-feet for any period of ten consecutive years reckoned in continuing progressive series beginning with the first day of October next succeeding the ratification of this compact.

(e) The States of the Upper Division shall not withhold water, and the States of the Lower Division shall not require the delivery of water, which cannot reasonably be applied to domestic and agricultural uses.

* * *

[Paragraph (f) provides for further apportionment "of the waters of the Colorado River System unapportioned by paragraphs (a), (b) and (c)" after 1963 if either Basin reaches its total beneficial consumptive use under (a) and (b). Paragraph (g) allows any two signatory states to call for such an equitable apportionment.]

Article IV

(a) Inasmuch as the Colorado River has ceased to be navigable for commerce and the reservation of its waters for navigation would seriously limit the development of its Basin, the use of its waters for purposes of navigation shall be subservient to the uses of such waters for domestic, agricultural, and power purposes. If the Congress shall not consent to this paragraph, the other provisions of this compact shall nevertheless remain binding.

(b) Subject to the provisions of this compact, water of the Colorado River System may be impounded and used for the generation of electrical power, but such impounding and use shall be subservient to the use and consumption of such water for agricultural and domestic purposes and shall not interfere with or prevent use for such dominant purposes.

(c) The provisions of this article shall not apply to or interfere with the regulation and control by any State within its boundaries of the appropriation, use, and distribution of water.

* * *

Article VII

Nothing in this compact shall be construed as affecting the obligations of the United States of America to Indian tribes.

Article VIII

Present perfected rights to the beneficial use of waters of the Colorado River System are unimpaired by this compact. Whenever storage capacity of 5,000,000 acre-feet shall have been provided on the main Colorado River within or for the benefit of the Lower Basin, then claims of such rights, if any, by appropriators or users of water in the Lower Basin against appropriators or users of water in the Upper Basin shall attach to and be satisfied from water that may be stored not in conflict with Article III.

All other rights to beneficial use of waters of the Colorado River System shall be satisfied solely from the water apportioned to that Basin in which they are situate.

NOTES

1. Some of the questions arising over interpretation of the Colorado River Compact include the following:

a. Suppose that beneficial consumptive uses in the upper basin average 3.5 million acre-feet (maf) annually, while beneficial uses in the lower basin average 7.5 maf annually. The states in the lower basin have plans to increase their beneficial consumptive uses by 2 maf. Do such plans violate the compact?

b. When flows are sufficient to satisfy a total of 15 maf of consumptive uses in both basins and the lower basin has beneficial consumptive uses of 8.5 maf and the upper basin 3.0, there would be a surplus of 3.5 maf of the upper basin's allocation in the mainstream at Lee Ferry. The Mexican Treaty obligation is 1.5 maf. Can the upper basin withhold in reservoir storage all but 750,000 acre-feet (half of the Mexican obligation) of the remaining 3.0 maf? Consider both Articles III(c) and III(e).

c. If it takes the release of 2.0 maf at Lee Ferry to supply 1.5 maf at the Mexican border, what responsibility is borne by the two basins regarding the loss?

d. Assume the upper basin has delivered only 70 maf to the lower basin over the preceding 10 year period. While the lower basin's agricultural and domestic uses have been satisfied, the lower basin demands delivery this year of 5 maf from the upper basin, beyond its annual demand for beneficial consumptive uses, to be used to generate electric power at Hoover Dam (the revenue from which repays the lower basin's financial obligations to the U.S.). Does the compact require the delivery even if the reservoirs are low and the upper basin would have to reduce its agricultural uses to supply the water?

e. Suppose the upper basin has delivered 75 maf over the preceding 10 year period but had, in addition, stored 15 maf in Lake Powell (the reservoir behind Glen Canyon Dam). All domestic and agricultural uses in both basins have been satisfied. The lower basin demands delivery to Lake Mead of one-half of the supply stored in Lake Powell for use in generating electric power. What result under the compact?

f. The Gila River joins the mainstream of the Colorado near the Mexican border. It produces more than 2 maf of water a year, much of which flows beneath its bed and is extracted by wells. Nearly all of the annual flow is consumed in Arizona so that no water actually flows into the mainstream. Should the water produced by the Gila be considered in satisfaction of the lower basin's apportionment? Should it diminish the upper basin's obligation to deliver 75 maf each ten years? Should it be counted against the lower basin's allowable annual consumptive use? Should the Gila's waters be considered available to meet obligations to deliver water to Mexico?

2. Many questions of interpretation of the Colorado River Compact have been avoided by adoption of "operating criteria" for the two major reservoirs on the Colorado River—Lake Mead, behind Hoover Dam, and Lake Powell, behind the Glen Canyon Dam. Congress, in Section 602(a) of the Colorado River Basin Project Act of 1968, imposed a hierarchy of priorities on the release of water stored in Lake Powell, required that storage in Lake Powell be equalized with that in Lake Mead, and authorized the Secretary of the Interior to promulgate

implementing regulations. The Secretary subsequently adopted long-range operating criteria for Glen Canyon Dam which require minimum annual releases from Lake Powell of 8.23 maf (consisting of the lower basin's 7.5 maf plus Mexico's .75 maf, less the 20,000 acre-feet annual flow of the Paria River, which enters the mainstream below Glen Canyon Dam but above Lee Ferry). Does this depart from the compact delivery requirements?

3. Could the upper basin successfully assert that the compact should be voided or reformed because of a mutual mistake of fact (for lower average flows than were supposed in 1922)? The prolonged history of Texas v. New Mexico, 446 U.S. 540 (1980), is instructive. Texas and New Mexico entered into the Pecos River Compact in 1948, and based New Mexico's required deliveries to Texas on "the 1947 condition" of the river. That condition was defined in terms of inflows into the basin and projected outflows therefrom, based on New Mexico's water uses in 1947. This "inflow-outflow method" was recommended by the Compact Engineering Advisory Committee and incorporated in a manual that was in turn made part of the compact itself.

> Since the manual was incorrect, calculations made in accordance with it operated to understate New Mexico's annual delivery obligation. The Compact Commission (composed of one voting representative from each state and one nonvoting federal representative) became aware of the mistake, but became hopelessly deadlocked over how to resolve the matter.

Texas then sued, alleging that New Mexico owed it 1.2 million acre-feet of water for the years 1950 through 1972. The Court subsequently ruled at 462 U.S. 554 (1983) that it could not restructure the Compact Commission to break the tie, but remanded the case to a master with directions to develop and retroactively apply an accurate rendition of the "inflow-outflow method." Over the objections of both parties, the Court accepted the resulting master's report in its entirety. 467 U.S. 1238 (1984).

By applying the corrected methodology, the master, Charles J. Meyers, determined that New Mexico's cumulative "water debt" to Texas was 340,100 acre-feet for the years 1950 through 1983, to which "water interest" was to be applied. 482 U.S. 124 (1987). While the master presumed that the debt would be paid by means of increased water deliveries over the following ten years, New Mexico sought the option of a cash settlement. The Court enjoined New Mexico to comply with the compact, remanding to the master the issue of whether New Mexico should be allowed to retire its obligation using money rather than water. New Mexico estimated damages to Texas at $5.3 million, but Texas estimated them at $49.7, with the cumulative benefit to New Mexico at nearly $1 billion. The two states ultimately agreed to a stipulated judgment under which New Mexico paid Texas $14 million.

4. One danger of seeking reformation of an interstate compact based on mutual mistake of fact is uncertainty as to the outcome. Once a compact is subjected to the scrutiny of the Supreme Court, the parties in effect lose control of its contents—even as to the definition of terms.

For example, in Oklahoma v. New Mexico, 111 S.Ct. 2281 (1991), Oklahoma and Texas brought an original action alleging that New Mexico had been violating the Canadian River Compact by storing and diverting more than its share of water.

The compact gave New Mexico exclusive rights to water "originating" above the La Concha Dam, but limited New Mexico to 200,000 acre-feet of water originating below the dam. To avoid the need to measure below-dam waters, the compact limited New Mexico's storage capacity below La Concha to 200,000 acre-feet. However, New Mexico had increased its storage capacity beyond that limit and was using it to capture water that originated above La Concha Dam, but had seeped under or spilled over the dam.

In a 5–4 decision, the Court first concluded that the language of the compact was sufficiently ambiguous to justify an examination of the negotiating history to determine the true intentions of the parties. The Court then held that, based on the practicalities at the time, "storage capacity" actually meant "stored water," and that water seeping around or spilling over La Concha Dam should be treated as having originated (entered the stream) *below* the dam.

Given the many ambiguities and the massive but conflicting record associated with the Colorado River Compact, it is not surprising that the states of the upper basin have been extremely cautious about opening the potential Pandora's box of a court reformulation of the compact. How might the results of the known mistake be more favorable to the upper basin than would the implications of its correction? What are the risks to the upper basin if the Court applies equitable apportionment standards to the adjudication?

NOTE: GLOBAL WARMING AND INTERSTATE ALLOCATION

Long-term droughts stress many intra- and interstate allocation regimes, but projected global warming scenarios potentially introduce even higher levels of uncertainty and conflict. Because of "greenhouse gas" emissions such as CO_2, methane, NO_x, and CFCs, many experts predict that average global temperatures will rise from .5 to 1.5 degrees centigrade within the next few decades. The consequences of the various global climate change scenarios for water allocation are highly uncertain. For example, runoff in the Colorado River Basin could rise, fall or remain the same depending on the balance between temperature and precipitation changes.

Water law, especially the prior appropriation doctrine, is designed to allocate the right to use water during droughts. Many scientists predict greater extremes of rainfall and drought rather than a simple shift to a warmer, stable climate. John Firor, *The Heating of the Climate*, 1 Colo.J.Int'l Envtl. L. & Pol'y 29, 38 (1990). However, scientists currently distinguish between climate variability and global climate change. The former implies a climate norm and fluctuations on either side of it; the latter implies a permanent climatic shift and the establishment of a new norm. Global warming may change the global water budget by increasing precipitation in some regions while others become drier.

There may be heightened competition for diminished water supplies in both the West and Midwest. In California, for example, there may be less snow in the mountains, and what snow does fall may melt and run off during the winters rather than the springs and summers. Annual deliveries to the California State Water Project could decline by 7% to 15%. At the same time, global warming may cause the demand for electricity to increase by 4% to 6% over the expected increase without global warming. In addition, warmer temperatures could increase spring runoffs recreating the pattern of flooding followed by inadequate summer supplies that the conservation era set out to rectify with the construction of large carry-over storage reservoirs. Growing competition between municipal and industrial water use and agricultural water use will exacerbate existing supply shortfalls in dry, populated areas. Environmental values will be threatened by sea level rise, which will inundate wetlands, and there may be wildlife losses from the stressed inland wetlands and other habitats from water shortages. See generally W. Reid and M. Trexler, Drowning the National Heritage: Climate Change and Coastal Biodiversity in the United States (1991) and Daniel B. Botkin, *Global Warming: What It Is, What Is Controversial About It, and What We Might Do in Response to It*, 9 UCLA J.Envtl. L. & Pol'y 119, 136–37 (1991). The stability of currently water-rich areas is threatened as well. In the eastern portion of the country supplemental irrigation might be necessary to grow crops now supported by rain. Soils will be drier and surface moisture decreased because of increased evaporation.

The current policy debate is between adaptation and mitigation strategies. Proponents of adaptation over mitigation argue that water allocation institutions can adapt to global warming by the enforcement of existing priorities and markets that shift water from agriculture to municipal and industrial uses. Adaptation strategies pose new challenges for the United States Corps of Engineers and the Bureau of Reclamation. Changed runoff patterns will create pressure to operate reservoirs differently. There may be increased demand for the dedication of more storage space in Bureau of Reclamation reservoirs to flood control at the expense of hydropower and consumptive use releases if runoffs occur earlier in the year. In severe sustained droughts, it may not be possible both to generate power and to satisfy calls for irrigation and municipal supplies. Further, the release of water for navigation on rivers such as the Missouri may accentuate the economically perverse priorities in existing allocation regimes and accelerate pressures to modify the allocation regime.

Interstate and international allocation regimes may be less adaptable to climate change than state allocation systems, resulting in uncontemplated inequities. For example, on the Colorado River, the upper basin delivery obligation is the same—an average of 7.5 million acre-feet per year—regardless of flows in the river, leaving the upper basin with little or nothing in prolonged dry periods. The treaty with Mexico requires that the United States deliver 1.5 million acre-feet annually.

Article X allows the United States' delivery duty to be relaxed in the case of extraordinary drought or a serious accident to the irrigation system of the United States in "proportion as consumptive uses in the United States are reduced." Would a continued decrease in available supply allow the United States to modify its delivery obligation on a long-term basis? See Gretta Goldenmann, *Adapting to Global Climate Change: A Study of International Rivers and Their Legal Arrangements*, 17 Ecology L.Q. 741, 762–66 (1990).

C. CONGRESSIONAL APPORTIONMENT: THE SPECIAL CASE OF THE COLORADO RIVER

Apportionment of the Colorado River between the upper and lower basins in the Colorado River Compact was to provide the upper basin states (Colorado, Utah, Wyoming and New Mexico) with sufficient water for their later development. But it did not resolve differences over allocation of the lower basin states' (Arizona, California and Nevada) share among themselves. Likewise, it did not specify how the upper basin states were to share their apportionment of the river. The sparsely populated, slower developing upper basin states were able to work out an agreement allocating percentages of the upper basin share to each state in a 1949 Upper Basin Colorado River Compact. See page 873, supra.

Agreement among the lower basin states on an allocation of their water was frustrated by intense conflicts that raged on for years. California wanted extensive development of the river to provide a stable supply of water for the Imperial Valley (which had been irrigated since the early 1900s) and to provide a new supply for the rapidly growing city of Los Angeles. Arizona also wanted development and envisioned a project to bring Colorado River water to central Arizona. But Arizona was extremely fearful of California's taking a disproportionate share of the lower basin supply. Consequently, Arizona withheld its agreement to the compact pending resolution of its concerns. Furthermore, Arizona was able to thwart California's attempts to develop Colorado River water. Year after year, beginning in 1922, members of the California congressional delegation introduced bills to authorize the construction of a Boulder (later Hoover) Dam. Arizona prevented their enactment, principally through the efforts of Senator Carl Hayden who resorted to a variety of tactics, including filibuster.

Finally, a compromise was arranged in the Senate resulting in the Boulder Canyon Project Act which became law June 25, 1929. The Act overrode the resistance of Arizona to signing the compact, allowing it to become effective upon approval of any six states, so long as California was one of them. With that approval, work on Hoover Dam could begin. Whether intended or not, the Boulder Canyon Project Act became the first, and only, legislative allocation of interstate waters. Arizona v. California, 373 U.S. 546 (1963), page 886, infra, held that Congress had the power to apportion the water of a navigable interstate stream among the states that touch the stream. However, the decision did not face the question of whether Congress can create legal interests in favor of one state in navigable (or non-navigable) streams within another state and not crossing into the favored state—as is the case with the Gila River.

As you read the following excerpts from the Boulder Canyon Project Act, consider whether Congress intended to apportion waters between California and Arizona when it passed the Act in 1928.

THE BOULDER CANYON PROJECT ACT
Pub. L. No. 642, 45 Stat. 1057 (1928).

Be it enacted by the Senate and House of Representatives of the United States of America in Congress assembled, That for the purpose of controlling the floods, improving navigation and regulating the flow of the Colorado River, providing for storage and for the delivery of the stored waters thereof for reclamation of public lands and other beneficial uses exclusively within the United States, and for the generation of electrical energy as a means of making the project herein authorized a self-supporting and financially solvent undertaking the Secretary of the Interior, subject to the terms of the Colorado River compact hereinafter mentioned, is hereby authorized to construct, operate, and maintain a dam and incidental works in the main stream of the Colorado River at Black Canyon or Boulder Canyon adequate to create a storage reservoir of a capacity of not less than twenty million acre-feet of water and a main canal and appurtenant structures located entirely within the United States connecting the Laguna Dam, or other suitable diversion dam, which the Secretary of the Interior is hereby authorized to construct if deemed necessary or advisable by him upon engineering or economic considerations, with the Imperial and Coachella Valleys in California, the expenditures for said main canal and appurtenant structures to be reimbursable, as provided in the reclamation law, and shall not be paid out of revenues derived from the sale or disposal of water power or electric energy at the dam authorized to be constructed at said Black Canyon or Boulder Canyon, or for water for potable purposes outside of the Imperial and Coachella Valleys: *Provided, however,* That no charge shall be made for water or for the use, storage, or delivery of water for irrigation or water for potable purposes in the Imperial or Coachella Valleys; also to construct and equip, operate, and maintain at or near said dam, or cause to be constructed a complete plant and incidental structures suitable for the fullest economic development of electrical energy from the water discharged from said reservoir; and to acquire by proceedings in eminent domain, or otherwise, all lands, rights-of-way, and other property necessary for said purposes.

* * *

Section 4(a)

This Act shall not take effect and no authority shall be exercised hereunder and no work shall be begun and no moneys expended on or in connection with the works or structures provided for in this Act, and no water rights shall be claimed or initiated hereunder, and no steps shall be taken by the United States or by others to initiate or perfect any claims to the use of water pertinent to such works or structures unless and until (1) the States of Arizona, California, Colorado, Nevada, New Mexico, Utah, and Wyoming shall have ratified the Colorado River compact, mentioned in section 13 hereof, and the President by public proclamation shall have so declared, or (2) if said States fail to ratify the said compact within six months from the date of the passage of this Act then, until six of said States, including the State of California, shall ratify said compact and shall consent to waive the provisions of the first paragraph of Article XI of said compact, which makes the same binding and obligatory only when approved by each of the seven States signatory thereto, and shall have approved said compact without conditions, save that of such six-State approval, and the President by public proclamation shall have so declared, and, further, until the State of California, by act of its legislature, shall agree irrevocably and unconditionally with the United States and for the benefit of the States of Arizona, Colorado, Nevada, New Mexico, Utah, and Wyoming, as an express covenant and in consideration of the passage of this Act, that the aggregate annual consumptive use (diversions less returns to the river) of water of and from the Colorado River for use in the State of California, including all uses under contracts made under the provisions of this Act and all water necessary for the supply of any rights which may now exist, shall not exceed four million four hundred thousand acre-feet of the waters apportioned to the lower basin States by paragraph (a) of Article III of the Colorado River compact, plus not more than one-half of any excess or surplus waters unapportioned by said compact, such uses always to be subject to the terms of said compact.

The States of Arizona, California, and Nevada are authorized to enter into an agreement which shall provide (1) that of the 7,500,000 acre-feet annually apportioned to the lower basin by paragraph (a) of Article III of the Colorado River compact, there shall be apportioned to the State of Nevada 300,000 acre-feet and to the State of Arizona 2,800,000 acre-feet for exclusive beneficial consumptive use in perpetuity, and (2) that the State of Arizona may annually use one-half of the excess or surplus waters unapportioned by the Colorado River compact, and (3) that the State of Arizona shall have the exclusive beneficial consumptive use of the Gila River and its tributaries within the boundaries of said State, and (4) that the waters of the Gila River and its tributaries, except return flow after the same enters the Colorado River, shall never be subject to any diminution whatever by any allowance of water which may be made by treaty or otherwise to the United States of Mexico but if, as provided in paragraph (c) of Article III of the Colorado River compact, it shall become necessary to supply water to the United States of Mexico from waters over and above the quantities which are surplus as defined by said compact, then the State of California shall and will mutually agree with the State of Arizona to supply, out of the main stream of the Colorado River, one-half of any deficiency which must be supplied to Mexico by the lower basin, and (5) that the State of California shall and will further mutually agree with the States of Arizona and Nevada that none of said three States shall withhold water and none shall require the delivery of water, which cannot reasonably be applied to domestic and agricultural uses, and (6) that all of the provisions of said tri-State agreement shall be subject in all particulars to the provisions of the Colorado River compact, and (7) said agreement to take effect upon the ratification of the Colorado River compact by Arizona, California, and Nevada.

* * *

Section 5

That the Secretary of the Interior is hereby authorized, under such general regulations as he may prescribe, to contract for the storage of water in said reservoir and for delivery thereof at such points on the river and on said canal as may be agreed upon, for irrigation and domestic uses, and generation of electrical energy and delivery at the switchboard to States, municipal corporations, political subdivisions, and private corporations of electrical energy generated at said dam, upon charges that will provide revenue which, in addition to other revenue accruing under the reclamation law and under this Act, will in his judgment cover all expenses of operation and maintenance incurred by the United States on account of works constructed under this Act and the payments to the United States under subdivision (b) of section 4. Contracts respecting water for irrigation and domestic uses shall be for permanent service and shall conform to paragraph (a) of section 4 of this Act. No person shall have or be entitled to have the use for any purpose of the water stored as aforesaid except by contract made as herein stated.

* * *

Section 6

That the dam and reservoir provided for by section 1 hereof shall be used: First, for river regulation, improvement of navigation, and flood control; second, for irrigation and domestic uses and satisfaction of present perfected rights in pursuance of Article VIII of said Colorado River compact; and third, for power. The title to said dam, reservoir, plant, and incidental works shall forever remain in the United States, and the United States shall, until otherwise provided by Congress, control, manage, and operate the same, except as herein otherwise provided: * * *

NOTES

1. The tri-state compact authorized in Paragraph 2 of § 4(a) was never agreed upon. Can the terms of the proposed compact aid in the interpretation of paragraph 1 of § 4(a)?

2. In what ways does the Act modify or determine the meaning of the Colorado River Compact?

3. Is an apportionment of water between Arizona and California made in the Act? If not, in what tribunal and on what basis would such apportionment be made traditionally?

4. Does the Act delegate power to the Secretary to apportion water to Arizona and California? What standards control the exercise of that power?

The following article summarizes the events between the passage of the Boulder Canyon Project Act and its definitive interpretation in Arizona v. California, page 886, infra.

CHARLES J. MEYERS, THE COLORADO RIVER
19 Stan.L.Rev. 1, 39–43, 51–53 (1966).

* * * In its first suit [169] Arizona sued the Secretary of the Interior and all six of the other Colorado River Basin states to enjoin the building of Hoover Dam and the All-American Canal, to stop the formation and performance of contracts for delivery of water from the projected reservoir, and to declare the Colorado River Compact and the Project Act unconstitutional. The case was heard by the Supreme Court on the plaintiff's bill of complaint and defendants' motions to dismiss. Holding that the Boulder Canyon Project Act was a valid exercise of congressional power under the commerce clause, the Court dismissed the bill without prejudice to a later suit for relief if the dam should be operated so as to interfere with Arizona's rights. Apart from its significance to the parties, the case has a general importance since the Supreme Court, for the first time, upheld congressional power under the commerce clause to authorize construction of multipurpose dams on navigable streams.[170] While the Court preserved the fiction that a navigation purpose would be served, it recognized that other purposes not authorized by the navigation power would also be served, primarily the generation and sale of electric power. On this foundation rest many mighty dams that dry up the stream below, thus destroying navigability entirely, if indeed any ever existed.

In its second suit [171] Arizona changed tactics. Conceding that there was as yet no interference with her water rights (Hoover Dam was under construction but had yet to be closed in), Arizona alleged that such interference was threatened in the future. In order to prepare for the lawsuit to come, she sought to commence an action to perpetuate testimony relating to her interpretation of the Project Act and the compact. In essence, Arizona relied upon the act and compact and desired to obtain and record testimony favorable to her construction of each—namely, that the article III(b) water was intended to belong exclusively to Arizona. This bill was dismissed, one ground being that the testimony sought to be preserved would be inadmissible as evidence of the meaning of the compact and the act.

After this rebuff events moved rapidly. In 1934 work began on Parker Dam, the diversion point for the Colorado River Aqueduct. (The aqueduct was designed to carry about 1.3 million acre-feet of water per year to the southern California coastal plain.) Claiming that

---

169. Arizona v. California, 283 U.S. 423 (1931).

170. See Morreale, *Federal Power in Western Waters: The Navigation Power*

and the Rule of No Compensation, 3 Natural Resources J. 1, 10–11 (1963).

171. Arizona v. California, 292 U.S. 341 (1934).

construction of the dam, which had one foot on Arizona soil, was unauthorized, Arizona's governor sent troops to halt the work.[172] The United States sued for an injunction in the Supreme Court, but lost when the Court determined that Congress had not authorized the dam.[173] Within months after the decision Congress specifically authorized the dam,[174] and Arizona withdrew her troops.

In November of 1935 Arizona filed suit for a general equitable apportionment of the unappropriated water in the river.[175] The United States had not consented to be sued and was not a party. The Court dismissed the complaint without reaching the merits, holding that joinder of the United States was indispensable.

Upon the rendition of this judgment, Arizona found herself stymied. She could secure no judicial relief until the United States consented to be sued. She had not ratified the Colorado River Compact and had no contract for delivery of water from Lake Mead. Her rival, California, on the other hand, had contracts calling for the delivery of water from the main stream to satisfy 5.362 million acre-feet of consumptive use per year, and work was going forward in California on projects which would enable her to make full use of this water.

For nearly ten years Arizona was beset by drought and racked with dissension over the proper course of action.[178] The agricultural interests of central Arizona suffered greatly from lack of water but also feared the effect that compact ratification might have on the Gila supply. Finally, Arizona did what she had to do—she ratified the compact and obtained a contract for the delivery of water from the main stream to supply 2.8 million acre-feet of consumptive use per year.

Unfortunately for Arizona, a contract for water and the actual receipt of water are two very different things. For another ten years she struggled in vain to obtain federal authorization and financing of the works necessary to bring water to her central farming region. Every step of the way she was fought by California, who had a telling argument in the enormous cost of the Central Arizona Project—roughly one billion dollars. Bills to authorize the project were introduced in the 79th, 80th, 81st, and 82d Congresses, and, while some passed in the Senate, all failed in the House, where California was immensely more powerful than Arizona.

The endless squabbling must have tried the patience of Congressmen from other states. For that reason and probably because of genuine unwillingness to consider a project of such magnitude when rights to the water involved were in dispute, the responsible House committee resolved in 1951 that consideration of the Central Arizona Project "be postponed until such time as use of the water in the lower Colorado River Basin is either adjudicated or a binding and mutual

172. D. Mann, The Politics of Waters in Arizona 85–86 (1963).

173. United States v. Arizona, 295 U.S. 174 (1935).

174. Act of Aug. 30, 1935, 49 Stat. 1039.

175. Arizona v. California, 298 U.S. 558 (1936).

178. Mann, *op. cit. supra* note [172], at 86–88.

agreement as to the use of the water is reached by the States of the lower Colorado River Basin." [180]

For thirty years the states had been unable to reach agreement, and no evidence exists of a serious effort to do so after the committee's resolution. A little more than a year later, apparently with an understanding that the United States would intervene to give the Court jurisdiction, Arizona filed another original suit in the Supreme Court in an effort to get a judicial determination of her water rights. Nearly four years were devoted to the filing of pleadings and motions, the holding of pretrial conferences, and the preparation and entry of a pretrial order. On June 14, 1956, twenty-six years after Arizona made her first attempt to obtain an adjudication of her water rights in the Colorado, the trial on the merits began before a Special Master.

* * * [Four and one half years later, on December 5, 1960, the Special Master] filed his final report with the Supreme Court, having heard some 106 witnesses (who filled 22,500 pages of transcript) and having received volumes of exhibits numbering in the hundreds. In addition, depositions were taken from 234 witnesses, filling a transcript of 3,742 pages, on a minor dispute between Arizona and New Mexico. The final report (with a proposed decree) ran 433 pages.

Coming then before the Supreme Court, the case was first argued for sixteen hours in the 1961 term and then, with the retirement of Mr. Justice Whittaker, was set for reargument in the 1962 term. By the time the second argument was held, Mr. Justice Frankfurter had also retired; so the bench contained two new Justices, Goldberg and White. Both voted with the majority, providing the necessary difference in the five-to-three division (Mr. Chief Justice Warren not participating). The Supreme Court gave its judgment on June 3, 1963,[182] and entered the decree on March 9, 1964.[183]

ARIZONA v. CALIFORNIA

Supreme Court of the United States, 1963.
373 U.S. 546, 83 S.Ct. 1468, 10 L.Ed.2d 542, decree entered
376 U.S. 340, 84 S.Ct. 755, 11 L.Ed.2d 757.

MR. JUSTICE BLACK* delivered the opinion of the Court.

* * *

The Special Master appointed by this Court found that the Colorado River Compact, the law of prior appropriation, and the doctrine of equitable apportionment—by which doctrine this Court in the absence of statute resolves interstate claims according to the equities—do not control the issues in this case. The Master concluded that, since the Lower Basin States had failed to make a compact to allocate the waters among themselves as authorized by §§ 4(a) and 8(b), the Secretary's contracts with the States had within the statutory scheme of §§ 4(a), 5,

---

180. *Master's Report* 131 n.3.

182. 373 U.S. 546 (1963).

183. 376 U.S. 340 (1964).

* Justice Black was a Senator when the Boulder Canyon Project Act was passed in 1928.—Eds.

and 8(b) effected an apportionment of the waters of the mainstream which, according to the Master, were the only waters to be apportioned under the Act. The Master further held that, in the event of a shortage of water making it impossible for the Secretary to supply all the water due California, Arizona, and Nevada under their contracts, the burden of the shortage must be borne by each State in proportion to her share of the first 7,500,000 acre-feet allocated to the Lower Basin, that is, $^{4.4}/_{7.5}$ by California, $^{2.8}/_{7.5}$ by Arizona, and $^{.3}/_{7.5}$ by Nevada, without regard to the law of prior appropriation.

Arizona, Nevada, and the United States support with few exceptions the analysis, conclusions, and recommendations of the Special Master's report. These parties agree that Congress did not leave division of the waters to an equitable apportionment by this Court but instead created a comprehensive statutory scheme for the allocation of mainstream waters. Arizona, however, believes that the allocation formula established by the Secretary's contracts was in fact the formula required by the Act. * * *

California is in basic disagreement with almost all of the Master's Report. She argues that the Project Act, like the Colorado River Compact, deals with the entire Colorado River System, not just the mainstream. This would mean that diversions within Arizona and Nevada of tributary waters flowing in those States would be charged against their apportionments and that, because tributary water would be added to the mainstream water in computing the first 7,500,000 acre-feet available to the States, there would be a greater likelihood of a surplus, of which California gets one-half. The result of California's argument would be much more water for California and much less for Arizona. California also argues that the Act neither allocates the Colorado River waters nor gives the Secretary authority to make an allocation. Rather she takes the position that the judicial doctrine of equitable apportionment giving full interstate effect to the traditional western water law of prior appropriation should determine the rights of the parties to the water. Finally, California claims that in any event the Act does not control in time of shortage. Under such circumstances, she says, this Court should divide the waters according to the doctrine of equitable apportionment or the law of prior appropriation, either of which, she argues, should result in protecting her prior uses.

* * *

I.

ALLOCATION OF WATER AMONG THE STATES AND DISTRIBUTION TO USERS.

We have concluded, for reasons to be stated, that Congress in passing the Project Act intended to and did create its own comprehensive scheme for the apportionment among California, Arizona, and Nevada of the Lower Basin's share of the mainstream waters of the Colorado River, leaving each State its tributaries. Congress decided that a fair division of the first 7,500,000 acre-feet of such mainstream waters would give 4,400,000 acre-feet to California, 2,800,000 to Arizona, and 300,000 to Nevada; Arizona and California would each get one-half of any surplus. Prior approval was therefore given in the Act for a tri-state compact to incorporate these terms. The States, subject to subsequent congressional approval, were also permitted to agree on a compact with different terms. Division of the water did not, however, depend on the States' agreeing to a compact, for Congress gave the Secretary of the Interior adequate authority to accomplish the division. Congress did this by giving the Secretary power to make contracts for the delivery of water and by providing that no person could have water without a contract.

A. *Relevancy of Judicial Apportionment and Colorado River Compact.*—We agree with the Master that apportionment of the Lower Basin waters of the Colorado River is not controlled by the doctrine of equitable apportionment or by the Colorado River Compact. It is true that the Court has used the doctrine of equitable apportionment to decide river controversies between States. But in those cases Congress had not made any statutory apportionment. In this case, we have decided that Congress has provided its own method for allocating among the Lower Basin States the mainstream water to which they are entitled under the Compact. Where Congress has so exercised its constitutional power over waters, courts have no power to substitute their own notions of an "equitable apportionment" for the apportionment chosen by Congress.* Nor does the Colorado River Compact control this case. Nothing in that Compact purports to divide water among the Lower Basin States nor in any way to affect or control any future apportionment among those States or any distribution of water within a State. That the Commissioners were able to accomplish even a division of water between the basins is due to what is generally known as the "Hoover Compromise."

> "Participants [in the Compact negotiations] have stated that the negotiations would have broken up but for Mr. Hoover's proposal: that the Commission limit its efforts to a division of water between the upper basin and the lower basin, leaving to each basin the future internal allocation of its share."

And in fact this is all the Compact did. However, the Project Act, by referring to the Compact in several places, does make the Compact relevant to a limited extent. To begin with, the Act explicitly approves the Compact and thereby fixes a division of the waters between the basins which must be respected. Further, in several places the Act refers to terms contained in the Compact. For example, § 12 of the Act adopts the Compact definition of "domestic," and § 6 requires satisfaction of "present perfected rights" as used in the Compact. Obviously, therefore, those particular terms, though originally formulated only for the Compact's allocation of water between basins, are incorporated into

---

* The Court does not give the Constitutional basis for Congressional apportionment at this point in the opinion; the justification appears 20 pages later in one off-hand sentence (373 U.S. at 587): "[The Project] * * * Act was passed in the exercise of congressional power to control navigable water for purposes of flood control, navigation, power generation, and other objects, and is equally sustained by the power of Congress to promote the general welfare through projects for reclamation, irrigation, or other internal improvements." (Citing the 1931 decision in *Arizona v. California* and the *Gerlach* case, page 705, supra.) Eds.

the Act and are made applicable to the Project Act's allocation among Lower Basin States. The Act also declares that the Secretary of the Interior and the United States in the construction, operation, and maintenance of the dam and other works and in the making of contracts shall be subject to and controlled by the Colorado River Compact. These latter references to the Compact are quite different from the Act's adoption of Compact terms. Such references, unlike the explicit adoption of terms, were used only to show that the Act and its provisions were in no way to upset, alter, or affect the Compact's congressionally approved division of water between the basins. They were not intended to make the Compact and its provisions control or affect the Act's allocation among and distribution of water within the States of the Lower Basin. Therefore, we look to the Compact for terms specifically incorporated in the Act, and we would also look to it to resolve disputes between the Upper and Lower Basins, were any involved in this case. But no such questions are here. We must determine what apportionment and delivery scheme in the Lower Basin has been effected through the Secretary's contracts. For that determination, we look to the Project Act alone.

B. *Mainstream Apportionment.*—The congressional scheme of apportionment cannot be understood without knowing what water Congress wanted apportioned. Under California's view, which we reject, the first 7,500,000 acre-feet of Lower Basin water, of which California has agreed to use only 4,400,000, is made up of both mainstream and tributary water, not just mainstream water. Under the view of Arizona, Nevada, and the United States, with which we agree, the tributaries are not included in the waters to be divided but remain for the exclusive use of each State. Assuming 7,500,000 acre-feet or more in the mainstream and 2,000,000 in the tributaries, California would get 1,000,000 acre-feet more if the tributaries are included and Arizona 1,000,000 less.

California's argument that the Project Act, like the Colorado River Compact, deals with the main river and all its tributaries rests on § 4(a) of the Act, which limits California to 4,400,000 acre-feet "of the waters apportioned to the lower basin States by paragraph (a) of Article III of the Colorado River compact, plus not more than one-half of any excess or surplus waters unapportioned by said compact. * * * " And Article III(a), referred to by § 4(a), apportioned in perpetuity to the Lower Basin the use of 7,500,000 acre-feet of water per annum "from the Colorado River System," which was defined in the Compact as "that portion of the Colorado River and its tributaries within the United States of America."

Arizona argues that the Compact apportions between basins only the waters of the mainstream, not the mainstream and the tributaries. We need not reach that question, however, for we have concluded that whatever waters the Compact apportioned the Project Act itself dealt only with water of the mainstream. In the first place, the Act, in § 4(a), states that the California limitation, which is in reality her share of the first 7,500,000 acre-feet of Lower Basin water, is on "water of and from the Colorado River," not of and from the "Colorado River

System." But more importantly, the negotiations among the States and the congressional debates leading to the passage of the Project Act clearly show that the language used by Congress in the Act was meant to refer to mainstream waters only. Inclusion of the tributaries in the Compact was natural in view of the upper States' strong feeling that the Lower Basin tributaries should be made to share the burden of any obligation to deliver water to Mexico which a future treaty might impose. But when it came to an apportionment among the Lower Basin States, the Gila, by far the most important Lower Basin tributary, would not logically be included, since Arizona alone of the States could effectively use that river. Therefore, with minor exceptions, the proposals and counterproposals over the years, culminating in the Project Act, consistently provided for division of the mainstream only, reserving the tributaries to each State's exclusive use.

* * *

C. *The Project Act's Apportionment and Distribution Scheme.*— The legislative history, the language of the Act, and the scheme established by the Act for the storage and delivery of water convince us also that Congress intended to provide its own method for a complete apportionment of the mainstream water among Arizona, California, and Nevada.

* * *

In the first section of the Act, the Secretary was authorized to "construct, operate, and maintain a dam and incidental works * * * adequate to create a storage reservoir of a capacity of not less than twenty million acre-feet of water * * *" for the stated purpose of "controlling the floods, improving navigation and regulating the flow of the Colorado River, providing for storage and for the delivery of the stored waters thereof for reclamation of public lands and other beneficial uses * * *," and generating electrical power. The whole point of the Act was to replace the erratic, undependable, often destructive natural flow of the Colorado with the regular, dependable release of waters conserved and stored by the project. Having undertaken this beneficial project, Congress, in several provisions of the Act, made it clear that no one should use mainstream waters save in strict compliance with the scheme set up by the Act. Section 5 authorized the Secretary "under such general regulations as he may prescribe, to contract for the storage of water in said reservoir and for the delivery thereof at such points on the river * * * as may be agreed upon, for irrigation and domestic uses. * * *" To emphasize that water could be obtained from the Secretary alone, § 5 further declared, "No person shall have or be entitled to have the use for any purpose of the water stored as aforesaid except by contract made as herein stated." The supremacy given the Secretary's contracts was made clear in § 8(b) of the Act, which provided that, while the Lower Basin States were free to negotiate a compact dividing the waters, such a compact if made and approved after January 1, 1929, was to be "subject to all contracts, if any, made by the Secretary of the Interior under section 5" before Congress approved the compact.

These several provisions, even without legislative history, are persuasive that Congress intended the Secretary of the Interior, through his § 5 contracts, both to carry out the allocation of the waters of the main Colorado River among the Lower Basin States and to decide which users within each State would get water. The general authority to make contracts normally includes the power to choose with whom and upon what terms the contracts will be made. When Congress in an Act grants authority to contract, that authority is no less than the general authority, unless Congress has placed some limit on it. In this respect it is of interest that in an earlier version the bill did limit the Secretary's contract power by making the contracts "subject to rights of prior appropriators." But that restriction, which preserved the law of prior appropriation, did not survive. It was stricken from the bill when the requirement that every water user have a contract was added to § 5. Significantly, no phrase or provision indicating that the Secretary's contract power was to be controlled by the law of prior appropriation was substituted either then or at any other time before passage of the Act, and we are persuaded that had Congress intended so to fetter the Secretary's discretion, it would have done so in clear and unequivocal terms, as it did in recognizing "present perfected rights" in § 6.

* * *

The argument that Congress would not have delegated to the Secretary so much power to apportion and distribute the water overlooks the ways in which his power is limited and channeled by standards in the Project Act. In particular, the Secretary is bound to observe the Act's limitation of 4,400,000 acre-feet on California's consumptive uses out of the first 7,500,000 acre-feet of mainstream water. This necessarily leaves the remaining 3,100,000 acre-feet for the use of Arizona and Nevada, since they are the only other States with access to the main Colorado River. Nevada consistently took the position, accepted by the other States throughout the debates, that her conceivable needs would not exceed 300,000 acre-feet, which, of course, left 2,800,-000 acre-feet for Arizona's use. Moreover, Congress indicated that it thought this a proper division of the waters when in the second paragraph of § 4(a) it gave advance consent to a tri-state compact adopting such division. While no such compact was ever entered into, the Secretary by his contracts has apportioned the water in the approved amounts and thereby followed the guidelines set down by Congress. And, as the Master pointed out, Congress set up other standards and placed other significant limitations upon the Secretary's power to distribute the stored waters. It specifically set out in order the purposes for which the Secretary must use the dam and the reservoir:

> "First, for river regulation, improvement of navigation, and flood control; second, for irrigation and domestic uses and satisfaction of present perfected rights in pursuance of Article VIII of said Colorado River compact; and third, for power." § 6.

The Act further requires the Secretary to make revenue provisions in his contracts adequate to ensure the recovery of the expenses of construction, operation, and maintenance of the dam and other works within 50 years after their construction. § 4(b). The Secretary is directed to make water contracts for irrigation and domestic uses only for "permanent service." § 5. He and his permittees, licensees, and contractees are subject to the Colorado River Compact, § 8(a), and therefore can do nothing to upset or encroach upon the Compact's allocation of Colorado River water between the Upper and Lower Basins. In the construction, operation, and management of the works, the Secretary is subject to the provisions of the reclamation law, except as the Act otherwise provides. § 14. One of the most significant limitations in the Act is that the Secretary is required to satisfy present perfected rights, a matter of intense importance to those who had reduced their water rights to actual beneficial use at the time the Act became effective. § 6. And, of course, all of the powers granted by the Act are exercised by the Secretary and his well-established executive department, responsible to Congress and the President and subject to judicial review.

* * *

III.

APPORTIONMENT AND CONTRACTS IN TIME OF SHORTAGE.

We have agreed with the Master that the Secretary's contracts with Arizona for 2,800,000 acre-feet of water and with Nevada for 300,000, together with the limitation of California to 4,400,000 acre-feet, effect a valid apportionment of the first 7,500,000 acre-feet of mainstream water in the Lower Basin. There remains the question of what shall be done in time of shortage. The Master, while declining to make any findings as to what future supply might be expected, nevertheless decided that the Project Act and the Secretary's contract require the Secretary in case of shortage to divide the burden among the three States in this proportion: California $4.4/7.5$; Arizona $2.8/7.5$; Nevada $3/7.5$. While pro rata sharing of water shortages seems equitable on its face, more considered judgment may demonstrate quite the contrary. Certainly we should not bind the Secretary to this formula. We have held that the Secretary is vested with considerable control over the apportionment of Colorado River waters. And neither the Project Act nor the water contracts require the use of any particular formula for apportioning shortages. While the Secretary must follow the standards set out in the Act, he nevertheless is free to choose among the recognized methods of apportionment or to devise reasonable methods of his own. This choice, as we see it, is primarily his, not the Master's or even ours. And the Secretary may or may not conclude that a pro rata division is the best solution.

It must be remembered that the Secretary's decision may have an effect not only on irrigation uses but also on other important functions for which Congress brought this great project into being—flood control, improvement of navigation, regulation of flow, and generation and distribution of electric power. Requiring the Secretary to prorate shortages would strip him of the very power of choice which we think

Congress, for reasons satisfactory to it, vested in him and which we should not impair or take away from him. For the same reasons we cannot accept California's contention that in case of shortage each State's share of water should be determined by the judicial doctrine of equitable apportionment or by the law of prior appropriation. These principles, while they may provide some guidance, are not binding upon the Secretary where, as here, Congress, with full power to do so, has provided that the waters of a navigable stream shall be harnessed, conserved, stored, and distributed through a government agency under a statutory scheme.

None of this is to say that in case of shortage, the Secretary cannot adopt a method of proration or that he may not lay stress upon priority of use, local laws and customs, or any other factors that might be helpful in reaching an informed judgment in harmony with the Act, the best interests of the Basin States, and the welfare of the Nation. It will be time enough for the courts to intervene when and if the Secretary, in making apportionments or contracts, deviates from the standards Congress has set for him to follow, including his obligation to respect "present perfected rights" as of the date the Act was passed. At this time the Secretary has made no decision at all based on an actual or anticipated shortage of water, and so there is no action of his in this respect for us to review. Finally, as the Master pointed out, Congress still has broad powers over this navigable international stream. Congress can undoubtedly reduce or enlarge the Secretary's power if it wishes. Unless and until it does, we leave in the hands of the Secretary, where Congress placed it, full power to control, manage, and operate the Government's Colorado River works and to make contracts for the sale and delivery of water on such terms as are not prohibited by the Project Act.

* * *

MR. JUSTICE HARLAN, whom MR. JUSTICE DOUGLAS and MR. JUSTICE STEWART join, dissenting in part.

I dissent from so much of the Court's opinion as holds that the Secretary of the Interior has been given authority by Congress to apportion, among and within the States of California, Arizona, and Nevada, the waters of the mainstream of the Colorado River below Lee Ferry. I also dissent from the holding that in times of shortage the Secretary has discretion to select or devise any "reasonable method" he wishes for determining which users within these States are to bear the burden of that shortage. (In all other respects Mr. Justice Stewart and I—but not Mr. Justice Douglas—agree with and join in the Court's opinion, though not without some misgivings regarding the amounts of water allocated to the Indian Reservations.)

In my view, it is the equitable principles established by the Court in interstate water-rights cases, as modified by the Colorado River Compact and the California limitation, that were intended by Congress to govern the apportionment of mainstream waters among the Lower Basin States, whether in surplus or in shortage. *A fortiori*, state law was intended to control apportionment among users within a single State.

The Court's conclusions respecting the Secretary's apportionment powers, particularly those in times of shortage, result in a single appointed federal official being vested with absolute control, unrestrained by adequate standards, over the fate of a substantial segment of the life and economy of three States. Such restraint upon his actions as may follow from judicial review are, as will be shown, at best illusory. Today's result, I venture to say, would have dumbfounded those responsible for the legislation the Court construes, for nothing could have been farther from their minds or more inconsistent with their deeply felt convictions.

The Court professes to find this extraordinary delegation of power principally in § 5 of the Project Act, the provision authorizing the Secretary to enter into contracts for the storage and delivery of water. But § 5, * * * had no design resembling that which the Court now extracts from it. Rather, it was intended principally as a revenue measure, and the clause *requiring* a contract as a condition of delivery was inserted at the insistence not of the Lower but of the Upper Basin States in an effort to insure that nothing would disturb that basin's rights under the Colorado River Compact. There was no thought that § 5 would give authority to apportion water among the Lower Basin States. * * *

It is manifest that § 4(a), on which the Court so heavily relies, neither apportions the waters of the river nor vests power in any official to make such an apportionment. The first paragraph does not *grant* any water to anyone; it merely conditions the Act's effectiveness on seven-state ratification of the Compact or on six-state ratification, plus California's agreement to a limitation, i.e., a *ceiling*, on her appropriations. The source of authority to make such appropriations must be found elsewhere. And the second paragraph of § 4(a), suggesting a particular interstate agreement, similarly makes no apportionment of water among the States and delegates no power to any official to make such an apportionment. * * *

This history bears recapitulation. *First*, the law of appropriation, basic to western water law, was greatly respected, and the solution of interstate water disputes by judicial apportionment in this Court was well established and accepted. *Second*, the problems created by these doctrines as applied in *Wyoming* v. *Colorado* were narrow ones, not requiring for their solution complete abrogation of well-tried principles; existing law was quite adequate to deal with all questions save those Congress expressly solved by imposing a ceiling on California. *Third*, Congress throughout the dispute exhibited great reluctance to interfere with the division of water by legislation, because of a deep and fundamental mistrust of federal intervention and a profound regard for state sovereignty, shared by many influential members. *Finally*, when Congress was forced to legislate with respect to this problem or face defeat of the entire Project Act, it chose narrow terms appropriate to the narrow problem before it, and even then acted only indirectly to require California's consent to limiting her consumption.

It is inconceivable that such a Congress intended that the sweeping federal power which it declined to exercise—a power even the most avid partisans of national authority might hesitate to grant to a single administrator—be exercised at the unbridled discretion of an administrative officer, especially in the light of complaints registered about "bureaucratic" and "oppressive" interference of the Department which that very officer headed. It is utterly incredible that a Congress unwilling because of concern for States' rights even to limit California's maximum consumption to 4,400,000 acre-feet without the consent of her legislature intended to give the Secretary of the Interior authority without California's consent to reduce her share even below that quantity in a shortage.

* * *

THE LACK OF STANDARDS DEFINING THE LIMITS OF THE SECRETARY'S POWER.

* * * How is the burden of any shortage to be borne by the Lower Basin States? This question is not decided; the Court simply states that the initial determination is for the Secretary to make.

What yardsticks has Congress laid down for him to follow? There is, it is true, a duty imposed on the Secretary under § 6 to satisfy "present perfected rights," and if these rights are defined as those perfected on or before the effective date of the Act, it has been estimated that California's share amounts to approximately 3,000,000 acre-feet annually. This, then, would be the floor provided by the Act for California, assuming enough water is available to satisfy such present perfected rights. And the Act also has provided a ceiling for California: the 4,400,000 acre-feet of water (plus one-half of surplus) described in § 4(a).

But what of that wide area between these two outer limits? Here, when we look for the standards defining the Secretary's authority, we find nothing. Under the Court's construction of the Act, in other words, Congress has made a gift to the Secretary of almost 1,500,000 acre-feet of water a year, to allocate virtually as he pleases in the event of any shortage preventing the fulfillment of all of his delivery commitments.

The delegation of such unrestrained authority to an executive official raises, to say the least, the gravest constitutional doubts. See Schechter Poultry Corp. v. United States, 295 U.S. 495; Panama Refining Co. v. Ryan, 293 U.S. 388; cf. Youngstown Sheet & Tube Co. v. Sawyer, 343 U.S. 579, 587–589. * * *

NOTES

1. The Meyers article argues that the Court was correct in finding an intent to apportion 7.5 maf of mainstream water but expresses doubt about the Court's conclusion that Congress intended to delegate power to the Secretary to deal with lesser amounts as his discretion should prescribe.

2. Although the Congress had never apportioned an interstate stream, its authority was not questioned. Is the facile treatment of the issue, noted by the editors in the footnote on page 888, supra, satisfactory?

3. The leading historian of the Colorado River, Norris Hundley, Jr., Water and the West: The Colorado River Compact and the Politics of Water in the American West 270 (1975), concluded that the Court misread the legislative history:

> While some congressmen thought that Congress was infringing upon states' rights by even suggesting a lower-basin pact, Pittman strenuously disagreed. "If California and Nevada and Arizona do not like this agreement," he explained, "they do not have to approve it." "All I have in mind," he protested, is "trying to save six or seven months' time." If the lower-basin states were to enter into an agreement that already had congressional approval, he observed, then they would not have to return later to Congress for approval. "I may not be accomplishing anything; but Arizona seems to be wedded to a certain plan. If the California Legislature does not like it, it does not put us in any worse fix than we are in if we do not adopt it."

> Congress agreed, and Pittman's proposal was incorporated into section 4(a) of the bill. Thirty-five years later the U.S. Supreme Court would misconstrue this action and decide that the Boulder Canyon Act provided a statutory apportionment of the waters of the lower Colorado. In 1928, however, Congress appeared confident that it was merely suggesting a way in which the lower states *might* settle their problem themselves.

NOTE: THE CENTRAL ARIZONA PROJECT

Whether intended or not, the Court's finding in 1963 that Congress had allocated the waters of the Colorado River in 1928 by means of the Boulder Canyon Project Act helped clear the way for further development of the river for the benefit of Arizona.

As early as the 1940s, the importation of Colorado River water into central Arizona was advanced as a solution for the state's groundwater overdraft problem. In 1947, the Bureau of Reclamation completed a feasibility study of the Central Arizona Project (CAP), which called for annually pumping 1.5 maf of water some 2100 feet uphill from the Colorado River into an aqueduct that would carry it over 330 miles to Phoenix and Tucson. The CAP was to consist of three main transportation facilities—the Granite Reef Aqueduct, running from Parker Dam on the Colorado River to the Phoenix area; the Salt–Gila Aqueduct, affording delivery to Pinal County; and the Tucson Aqueduct, completing the project by extending it to Tucson.

Arizona vigorously supported the CAP and for years sought its approval in Congress. California—realizing that its demand for water exceeded its allocation and fearing that CAP would further impinge its future growth—tenaciously opposed it. However, once the Court in Arizona v. California affirmed Arizona's entitlement to 2.8 maf annually, California's concern shifted from maximizing the amount of its own allocation (which the Court set at 4.4 maf) toward assuring the certainty of its delivery.

As a result, an accommodation was reached in the Colorado River Basin Project Act of 1968 (P.L. 90–537). In exchange for California's support of the project, the priority of CAP's upstream diversion was specified as being junior to California's downstream entitlement to 4.4 maf. The CAP therefore must suffer all cutbacks necessary in a shortage.

The support of the upper basin was secured through the inclusion of several other water projects in the authorization package—including the Animas–La Plata, Dolores, Dallas Creek, West Divide, and San Miguel projects in Colorado, which were to be built concurrently with CAP—and increased funding for the Dixie Project in Utah. When passed, the bill committed almost $2 billion to the mammoth package.

It took almost 18 years from the time of the authorization to complete the basic works for CAP. The estimated final cost for CAP alone will exceed $4 billion, making it the most expensive Bureau of Reclamation project in the nation. The later appropriations were difficult to obtain. Further, the Carter administration invoked a provision of the 1968 Act which banned use of CAP water in areas that did not effectively control the expansion of groundwater use for agricultural irrigation. This led to the passage of the Arizona Groundwater Management Act in 1980, pages 538–57, supra. However, since the CAP began delivering water, its price has caused Arizonans to avoid it. In 1991, less than one third of the 1.5 maf capacity was utilized. Arizona is now studying how to pay for the expensive, oversized project and what to do with the water it delivers. Meanwhile, of the five Colorado projects, two have been built (Dolores and Dallas Creek), two have apparently died (San Miguel and West Divide), and the Animas–La Plata project remains embroiled in litigation.

DAVID H. GETCHES, WATER ALLOCATION DURING DROUGHT IN ARIZONA AND SOUTHERN CALIFORNIA: LEGAL AND INSTITUTIONAL RESPONSES

(NRLC Research Report Series, Nat. Resources L. Center, Univ. of Colo. Sch. of L., January 1991, at 1–3).

A Heavy Dependence on Water

Despite the scarcity of its indigenous natural water supplies, the study area is populated by over 19 million people, about five-sixths of them in Southern California; the area includes the fastest growing cities in the nation. The expansion of human population in the area has accompanied intense economic activity. Much of the activity is water-dependent, including massive production of agricultural goods requiring heavy irrigation. In half a century of almost uninterrupted prosperity and growth there have been few concessions to the area's aridity.

The most obvious natural fact about the region, its dryness, has had little impact on the livelihoods or lifestyles of the people settling there. Indeed, the area abounds with outward manifestations of denial of its aridity. Green lawns and exotic plantings imported from humid climes are the hallmarks of suburban living. Golf courses have proliferated. Fountains and artificial lakes grace residential developments, places of business and government buildings. The area has not attempted to find alternate, less water-intensive ways to satisfy its economic goals, its aesthetic needs, recreational demands, environmental concerns and other objectives.

The government agencies and special districts charged with providing the area with adequate water historically succeeded in keeping supply ahead of demand. Until the last decade they insulated consumers from pressure to restrict usage. And there has always been sufficient water available to accommodate population growth in the region. Engineering ingenuity supported by public investment has created facilities to move water long distances and to store enough to smooth out annual fluctuations in precipitation. Political action and interstate accords have secured rights to use definite quantities of water in Southern California and Arizona vis a vis other states and Northern California.

The region has not yet confirmed the limits of its ability to grow. It is, however, struggling to cope with the economic, social and environmental symptoms of rapidly expanding population. The area managed to keep water supplies ahead of growing demand by importing new water and exceeding safe groundwater pumping levels locally. Recently, however, governments and water suppliers in Arizona and Southern California have recognized that encouraging consumers to reduce water demand can relieve some of the pressure to develop new supplies which are increasingly difficult and costly to find.

Cyclical droughts have occasionally broken the illusion of security, reminding water consumers that some uses are more important than others. Legal principles for allocation of water are frequently invoked to determine which combination of streams, aquifers and reservoirs will provide water in a particular year. But ordinarily there is no apparent difference felt by consumers from one year to the next. Only in extraordinary episodes, such as the Southern California dry spell of 1988–1990, have supplies been so low that a few local curtailments in use have been necessary. Yet these droughts have been less severe, shorter and less widespread than the droughts revealed in tree ring studies that reveal historical precipitation patterns.

The moderately severe, multi-year dry spells the area has experienced in the post-war years, since demand has so dramatically increased, have caused localized minor intrusions on lifestyle—brown lawns, reduction in car washing, attention to leaky plumbing. These episodes have aroused considerable citizen concern in recent years. In Southern California the effects have been confined to a few communities but, because of the publicity, for the first time in seventy years water is being perceived as a potential restraint on the quality of life and on ability to expand. In Arizona, precautionary legal reductions in per capita use in urban areas and controversy over retirement of agricultural uses to provide more water for urban growth have raised Arizonans' consciousness of the finite nature of water in the desert and its linkages to population growth and lifestyle.

NOTE: MEETING FUTURE DEMAND IN
THE COLORADO RIVER BASIN

Dreams of Augmentation. Continued projections of shortfalls in the ability of the Colorado River to supply all of the basin's future expectations has inspired far-ranging dreams of ways to augment the river's natural flows, both with additional dams and with ambitious schemes to import water from other basins. The more notable proposals included:

• The Southwest Water Plan: Proposed by Secretary of the Interior Udall shortly after the decision in Arizona v. California was announced, the plan called for building two additional dams (Bridge Canyon and Marble Canyon) at either end of the Grand Canyon National Monument, the Central Arizona Project (CAP), an experimental desalinization plant in California, and a proposal to divert the waters of wild rivers of Northern California as far south as Arizona, at a cost of $2.4 billion. Only the CAP survived the subsequent debate.

• Snake-Colorado Project: Five million acre-feet of water would be brought south through eastern Oregon to the lower Colorado at a cost of $3.2 billion.

• Western Water Plan: Fifteen million acre-feet would be brought through an elaborate system of pumping stations and reservoirs from the Columbia River to Lake Mead on the Colorado at an estimated cost of $11 billion.

• NESCO Plan: A $20 billion fiberglass pipeline would follow the continental shelf of California, carrying four million acre-feet of north coast river water to serve population centers along the coast.

• North American Water and Power Alliance: Water supplies would move from as far north as the Yukon River through Canada, connecting with major rivers there and then linking waterways from coast to coast to augment supplies at a cost of some $200 billion.

A variety of ideas to augment Colorado River water supplies from sources other than imports were also discussed by the states. One possibility was massive cloudseeding. Extensive testing was needed to determine whether sufficient additional water could be produced to justify the expense of the program. Augmentation research was authorized in the 1968 Colorado River Basin Project Act. Protectionist sentiment in the Columbia River Basin led the late Senator Henry Jackson to press for and obtain a moratorium on further federal research or planning for transbasin diversions from that area. The Missouri River Basin was studied by private industry considering oil shale development in the upper basin states.

Though the importation schemes have generally died, drought in California in the 1990s sparked new suggestions for importation of Alaskan water using an offshore pipeline or single-hulled oil tankers retired from service after the Exxon Valdez oil spill.

There is still sufficient water in the basin to satisfy most present beneficial uses, considering the availability of groundwater in Arizona and California, and the inefficient uses of water in agriculture. In the long run, however, continued growth of population and consequent water demand cannot be sustained at present levels, forcing consideration of growth management. For the immediate future, the essential problem may be the present allocation of the existing supply of water. California is the fastest growing and hardest hit by scarcity. Most efforts at reallocation are accordingly focused there. The most promising approaches have been water marketing, salvage, and exchange agreements under which the Metropolitan Water District of Southern California (MWD) obtains the right to use Colorado River water allocated to other users.

Southern California has sought to develop new water supplies to compensate for about a million acre-feet of water a year in excess of its apportionment that it was able to use before the Central Arizona Project was completed. It looked to completion of the vast California State Water Project by construction of a peripheral canal to divert water from the Sacramento-San Joaquin Delta that would otherwise flow into San Francisco Bay. But when the state's voters soundly defeated a proposal to build the canal in 1982, the growing Los Angeles area had to look elsewhere.

Water Salvage: MWD–IID. The MWD is the major water wholesaler for all of Southern California and the major municipal contractor for California's apportionment of Colorado River water. MWD has been forced to examine and consider a gamut of potentially available alternative sources of water.

The Imperial Irrigation District (IID) serves rich agricultural lands in the southernmost portion of California and is the largest single contractor for Colorado River water in the state. One court observed that IID "has occupied a position of great strength, discretion and vested right in a geographical part of the country that is 'far western,' embracing a philosophy that is independent in every sense of the word. Recent trends in water-use philosophy and the administration of water law have severely undermined the positions of districts such as IID." Imperial Irrigation District v. State Water Resources Control Board, 275 Cal.Rptr. 250, 266 (1990). IID was under orders from the State Water Resources Control Board to stop its wasteful use of irrigation water.

After lengthy negotiations, IID concluded an agreement with MWD that solved IID's immediate problems and provided more municipal water for MWD. The agreement finessed all the asserted obstacles to marketing Colorado River water that were posed by the "Law of the River" and California water law.   Under the "Water Conservation Agreement Between the MWD of Southern California and IID" of December 1989, the IID agreed to conserve 100,000 acre-feet per year, which MWD can divert through its facilities upstream.   In return, MWD agreed to pay IID $220 million in direct and indirect costs of the water conservation program, including lining ditches and canals, constructing new regulating reservoirs, and installing automatic control structures to regulate water flow throughout the system.

Is the agreement a transfer?   Is it a sale or lease of a water right? Part G provides:

> IID and MWD recognize that they have differences of opinion over various legal questions relating to the transfer of certain water and entitlement of junior priorities to certain water, but each wishes to go forward with the Agreement embodied herein without regard to current or future legal differences, and both agree that nothing herein is intended to or should have the effect of adding to or subtracting from the legal position heretofore or hereafter taken by either, as is more specifically set forth in Article VI hereof.

Under the Seven Party Agreement, by which seven large water users in California defined their relative priorities to California's share of Colorado River water that was made available upon completion of the Hoover Dam, any water not used by a higher priority user goes to the next party in line.   Since IID holds the second and third priorities, while MWD holds the fourth and fifth, MWD could argue that it is entitled to water conserved by IID at no cost.   Thus, Article VI, Section 6.2(d) of the 1989 agreement explicitly waives any potential claim by MWD that saved water reverts to the stream and is thus available for use by those with lower priorities, and estops MWD from claiming that IID forfeited any right by its participation in the agreement.

Yet, other questions remain.   For example, what happens after the MWD–IID agreement ends?   Article VI, Section 6.1 provides that all water claimed by IID—including conserved water—may be used by IID in "any lawful manner."   If IID conserves more water using its own funds or through changing crop use, may MWD claim that this water is now available for use by those with lower priorities?   Section 6.2 provides that the agreement does not "limit or restrict the rights held by either Party by contract or law to divert or use Colorado River water," and precludes either party from using the agreement as the basis for any legal argument.   Why?

Another similar effort at conserving Colorado River water so that it may be used for other purposes is the congressionally authorized lining of the All–American Canal that serves IID.   A complication resulting from the project is the adverse effect of conservation measures on Mexican irrigators, who have been relying on seepage from the All–American Canal for over 100,000 acre-feet of water annually that they pump from wells just south of the border.   Do these users have potential legal or political claims?   See Douglas Hayes, *The All–American Canal Lining Project: A Catalyst for Rational and Comprehensive Groundwater Management on the United States–Mexico Border*, 31 Nat.Resources J. 803 (1991).

Exchanges and Groundwater Storage. MWD is also considering a variety of arrangements to transfer, exchange, and store water to extend its reliable supplies. The Coachella Valley groundwater storage program allows MWD to "bank" Colorado River water underground in the depleted aquifers of two desert districts. Under the agreement negotiated with the Coachella Valley Water District, MWD delivers water from the Colorado River aqueduct for recharge into the Coachella Valley groundwater basin. During dry years, MWD will cease deliveries to Coachella and receive water from the California State Water Project (SWP) to which Coachella Valley users would otherwise have been entitled. Meanwhile, Coachella Valley users will pump groundwater, previously replenished by MWD's Colorado River water. A similar project is being studied in the IID. Another arrangement with the Arvin–Edison Water Storage District in the Central Valley provides for MWD to store its SWP water in the district during wet years and to receive Arvin–Edison's dry year entitlements from the SWP while farmers pump the stored water.

MWD's other projects include several short-term purchases from San Joaquin Valley water agencies. Negotiations are underway to turn some into long-term arrangements. MWD has also proposed that the Palo Verde Valley Irrigation District, holder of the most senior water rights in California to the Colorado River, reduce irrigated acreage, freeing up some 100,000 acre-feet of water for MWD to use in dry years.

Interstate Water Banking and Markets. In the depths of the 1988 to 1992 drought, California suggested the establishment of an escrow account, into which it would pay cash for the privilege of using water in excess of its allotted maximum under the compact. In turn, the cash would be distributed among the states of the upper basin to promote conservation and purchase water rights in order to make water available. Second, California suggested that the upper basin states establish a water bank, through which existing laws permitting the intrastate sale and transfer of water rights could be harnessed to make additional water available for interstate transfer.

Finally, there is a significant convergence in the thinking of academics, economists, and water rights experts that individual water rights marketing is both long overdue and essential to achieving a more efficient beneficial use of the total water resource. Arizona's difficulty in paying for CAP project water led to a 1993 agreement providing that MWD and Las Vegas will pay Arizona to store up to 100,000 acre-feet of CAP water in aquifers. In dry years, Arizona will pump and use the stored groundwater while MWD and Las Vegas may take an equivalent amount of the CAP entitlement directly from the river. In addition, water apportioned to the upper basin states is under-utilized—providing an obvious source of supply for downstream markets.

Salinity. The amount of usable water for Southern California ultimately will be limited by water quality in the Colorado River. An already complex legal setting for allocation of the Colorado is further complicated by the fact that salt concentrations may render the river's waters practically useless by the time water reaches the lower basin states and Mexico. Upper basin uses increase salinity because depletions for consumptive uses and evaporation result in less water being available to dilute salts in the river. Repeated irrigation diversion and return flows result in the addition of salts leached from the land.

The following excerpt provides a look at efforts to control Colorado River salinity—efforts that have avoided the ultimate question of allocating responsibility for salinity control among specific states.

TAYLOR O. MILLER, GARY D. WEATHERFORD, AND JOHN E. THORSON, THE SALTY COLORADO

24–26, 30–31, 36–39, 41–45, 51–52, 65, 72–75, 77 (1986).

In 1961 saline concentrations of about 6,000 mg/l in the drainage water of the Wellton-Mohawk division of the Gila Project in Arizona caused Colorado River water flowing across the border to Mexico to reach 2,700 mg/l. Salt buildup in the groundwater had previously led to the reduction of Wellton-Mohawk farming in the 1930s and 1940s, prompting the importation of cleaner Colorado River water in the mid-1950s under a federal project. Importation of the new irrigation water, however, resulted in a rise in the salt-laden groundwater table. This development prompted an additional federal project to pump saline water from beneath the lands and convey it out of the area to the Colorado River just north of the Mexican border. The effects of this new salt loading were exacerbated when the filling of Lake Powell behind the Glen Canyon Dam reduced river flows in the lower basin. Mexico expressed alarm and outrage at the resulting rise in salinity of Colorado River waters it received. It publicized crop losses in the Mexicali Valley and claimed the 1944 U.S.-Mexico treaty guaranteeing water delivery to Mexico was being violated.

The 1944 treaty contained no express water-quality guarantee, but the United States negotiated a five-year agreement with Mexico in 1965 involving the bypassing of the drainage water around Mexico's diversion point above Morelos Dam. After extended negotiations and two interim agreements, an accord was reached in August 1973. Under Minute 242 of the International Boundary and Water Commission, the United States agreed that about 1.36 million acre-feet of the waters delivered to Mexico above the Morelos Dam would maintain an average annual salinity of not more than 115 parts per million (ppm), plus or minus 30 ppm, over the annual average salinity at Imperial Dam.

* * *

Subsequently Congress passed the Colorado River Basin Salinity Control Act in 1974 (PL 93–320) [43 U.S.C.A. § 1592 et seq.] authorizing the secretary of the interior not only to implement the international accord, but also to undertake a basin-wide program to control salinity in the Colorado River. Title I of the act contained provisions authorizing construction of a desalinization plant at Yuma, Arizona, to treat Wellton-Mohawk water; lining of the Coachella Canal in California;

extending the Wellton-Mohawk bypass canal; and implementing a groundwater pumping program in the border area. Title II of the statute authorized a salinity control program for areas in the basin upstream of Imperial Dam. Four projects were authorized for construction under Title II, and 12 others were authorized for planning.

* * *

In 1965 Congress had passed the Water Quality Act, calling for states to establish water-quality standards and plans. As part of the implementation of this mandate, the states of the Colorado River basin were given until 1969 to develop salinity standards including numeric criteria for total dissolved solids (TDS). Citing unresolved scientific questions, the states opposed the setting of numeric criteria for TDS, chlorides, sulfates, and sodium in the Colorado River. In 1968 the federal government backed off, committing the subject to study.

A report issued in 1971 by the newly created Environmental Protection Agency (EPA) advised the basin states to take the steps necessary to establish a numeric objective for salinity concentration.
* * *

* * * The basin states then organized themselves into a Colorado River Basin Salinity Control Forum, aiming for the development and adoption of such criteria by the fall of 1975. In December 1974 EPA published a regulation requiring the basin states to adopt numeric criteria that, together with an implementation plan for their achievement, would maintain salinity at or below the flow-weighted annual average for 1972 in the Colorado's lower main stem. About the same time, EPA's general counsel interpreted the 1972 amendments to require each state in the basin to adopt salinity standards, and for a short time agency policy called for setting of standards at state lines.

The basin states adamantly opposed state-line standards, arguing instead for a basin-wide approach. They finally prevailed in 1976, when EPA and the states agreed on the numeric criteria [for salt levels that] were set not at state lines but solely at three lower-basin locations. The standards also included an implementation plan that described actions to be taken to achieve the numeric criteria.

* * *

The Clean Water Act requires state and EPA review of water-quality standards at least once every three years. These reviews are coordinated in the basin states by the regional Salinity Control Forum.
* * *

In 1977 the Environmental Defense Fund (EDF) filed a lawsuit seeking, among other things, to compel EPA to set state-line salinity standards and to emphasize on-farm water conservation to achieve salinity control. A decision adverse to EDF was issued in 1981. [Environmental Defense Fund v. Costle, 657 F.2d 275 (D.C. Cir. 1981).] In its ruling, the court deferred to EPA and the states concerning the adequacy of the EPA-approved standards and the salinity control plan. * * *

Salinity control projects are usually grouped into three general problem types:

- Irrigation sources (with salt pickup by return flows);

- Point sources (localized natural saline springs, abandoned oil wells, or geysers); and

- Diffuse sources (where a combination of natural seeps, runoff and irrigation, grazing, and other management practices in a comparatively large area results in increased downstream salinity).

The basic control strategies are:

- To reduce water contact with saline geologic formations by controlling the amount of irrigation water applied and by reducing seepage from irrigation canals, laterals, and ditches;

- To intercept discharges for saline surface water and groundwater into tributary streams by pumping, diversions, vegetation management, industrial use, or other means.

* * *

Irrigation management usually requires only small amounts of structural work and involves a cooperative effort by USDA and landowners to improve efficiency. Once an improved irrigation system is operating, it is the responsibility of the irrigator to continue. Typical practices include head ditch lining and automated gates, land leveling, more efficient irrigation devices, and irrigation scheduling.

* * *

Control of point sources and diffuse sources frequently involves intercepting saline waters and routing them away from the river system. Unlike the techniques used to deal with irrigation sources, this approach requires disposal or reuse of saline waters, which can be accomplished through deep well injection, evaporation in ponds, desalinization, or use in industrial facilities (such as for power-plant cooling). In one current project requiring saline water disposal at Paradox Valley in southwestern Colorado, saline groundwater will be pumped to prevent its discharge into the Dolores River. Pumped waters will then be injected into one or more deep disposal wells. In all cases, state water rights must be addressed prior to undertaking interception and disposal phases of point source control projects.

Though large reductions in salt loading from point and diffuse sources seem possible (from 1 to 1.6 million tons per year), the required initial engineering and structural work and the disposal costs tend to make them more expensive than irrigation source control projects. The Bureau of Reclamation estimates that all agricultural source projects plus the Paradox Valley project would reduce salt loading by up to 1.2 million tons per year and lessen salt concentration at Imperial Dam by 120 mg/l. Construction costs for these projects have been estimated at between $690 and $770 million (in 1981 dollars). To remove significantly more salt, relatively more expensive projects involving the disposal or reuse of the saline water would be required.

* * *

Yuma Desalting Plant

The Yuma facility, a reverse osmosis desalinization plant, will treat drainage flows from the Wellton-Mohawk District prior to their return to the river just upstream from the Mexican diversion point. Currently these waters are bypassed around Mexico's diversion point just below the border near Yuma and discharged into the Gulf of California. These bypassed drainage waters are then replaced, for purposes of meeting U.S. delivery obligations, with other water from upstream storage, from floodwaters, and from canal lining and groundwater pumping measures provided in Title I of the Salinity Control Act.

The Yuma plant will be one of the largest in the world, with a capacity of 72 million gallons per day (roughly equivalent to a municipal wastewater treatment plant serving a city of 720,000). It will produce 78,000 acre-feet of water per year, including a small amount of raw drainage water that will be blended with the plant's output. It will cost an estimated minimum of $225 million to build and about $20 million annually to operate. This translates to a high cost of $326 per acre-foot of delivered water (in 1983 dollars). The plant is scheduled to go into operation in 1989.

The salinity standard for deliveries to Mexico required under the U.S.-Mexico agreement has been met since Minute 242 went into force, and it could continue to be met simply by continuing to route Wellton-Mohawk drainage water around Mexico's diversion point, at little additional cost. This option is not a favored long-term solution, however, because the bypassed water does not count against the treaty's obligation to deliver a total of 1.5 million acre-feet annually to Mexico. Treated water produced by the Yuma plant, on the other hand, will count toward required deliveries to Mexico and thus free up an equivalent amount of water for use above the border. This factor could assume significance as water demand increases, or during droughts. The particular constituency for the Yuma plant thus is composed principally of lower-priority users who would lose water in times of shortage.

On-farm and Structural Measures Undertaken in the Grand Valley Area of Colorado and Uinta Basin of Utah

The 76,000 acres irrigated in Grand Valley near Grand Junction, Colorado, have been estimated to add approximately 580,000 tons of salts to the river annually. Work is under way by the Bureau of Reclamation to reduce on-farm seepage from unlined canals and laterals and by USDA to improve water management by installing underground pipelines, lining canals and ditches, land leveling, and irrigation scheduling. The project, when completed, is projected to decrease salt loading by 290,000 tons per year (or 29 mg/l less salinity at Imperial Dam) with a total investment of $230 million. A similar project has been launched in the Uinta Basin in Utah. The projections there are for a reduction in salt loading of 90,000 tons at a cost between $28 million and $89 million. Monitoring by Reclamation and USDA indicates that the combined effect in 1983 of the completed portions of the two projects was to reduce salt loading by about 49,700 tons per year.

* * *

Salinity control projects are to be selected according to their "cost effectiveness"—that is, the amount of salinity reduction per dollar spent to construct and operate the project. This is not a "cost-benefit" analysis that attempts to compare costs of the project with its benefits—that is, the damages that would be avoided by reducing Colorado River salinity. * * *

* * *

Costs for the on-farm USDA projects are partially shared by farmers, who generally pay 30 percent of project costs for irrigation improvements. The upper and lower basin development funds are expected to contribute 30 percent of the remaining 70 percent federal share of the implementation costs. All other on-farm measures are charged to the USDA budget. The federal portion of Wellton-Mohawk's on-farm measures comes from the Bureau of Reclamation's budget.

The power sales contracts for Hoover Dam, due to expire in 1987, recently were renegotiated. The contracted amounts of long-term contingent power were modified to reflect an increase in capacity to the states of Arizona, California, and Nevada. The results of this planned uprating program will increase the overall capacity of Hoover's power plant from 1,450 to 1,837 megawatts. In accordance with the Hoover Powerplant Act of 1984 (PL 98–381), the new contracts will include a surcharge for salinity control. California and Nevada users will pay the equivalent of 2.5 mills per kilowatt hour for salinity control. Arizona users will pay an additional 4.5 mills until the amortization of the Central Arizona Project is complete, when that state's charge will drop to 2.5 mills, which can then be used both for salinity control and other authorized uses.

* * *

Evaluating the progress of the salinity control program requires an assessment of the probability of future events as much as it does a retrospective look at what has been accomplished. The inherent difficulty of predicting the future is compounded by the fact that the experience of the last 15 years may not be representative of future conditions. The salinity control program began in an atmosphere of controversy and international tension and was preceded by significant salinity increases. The subsequent decline of salinity levels in the 1970s is thought to be partly related to the effect of the filling and operation of basin reservoirs, particularly Lake Powell and Flaming Gorge Reservoir. The Bureau of Reclamation is continuing to pursue further research to better understand and predict the long-term effects of reservoir operations.

Above-average precipitation and river flows have also held salinity levels in check. The 1983 average of 710 mg/l at Imperial Dam was the lowest since the mid-1950s. Wet conditions, of course, can quickly give way to prolonged dry periods. Despite indications of some relief from the salinity problem, most of the players in the salinity control program continue to base their evaluations of the problem on projected increases in salinity. * * *

A working rule of thumb adopted by planners is that about 1.2 million of the 9 million tons of salt projected to be transported by the river system without controls must be removed to achieve compliance with the standards after the year 2000. Colorado River Simulation System projections indicate that perhaps another 500,000 tons would need to be removed to meet the standards in 2020. The total program assembled by the Bureau of Reclamation in cooperation with other agencies and the forum exceeds this 1.2-million-ton goal by almost a million tons. Because the program is just getting under way, however, it is too early to judge how well it will work in practice. Overall program implementation strategy is being developed now.

So far, total salt removal amounts to about 110,000 tons per year from the Meeker Dome, Grand Valley, and Uinta Basin projects. Removal of another 1,364,000 tons per year has been projected to result from completion of the balance of the projects authorized for construction by the Salinity Control Act together with the on-farm projects currently in progress. These projects could be completed or under way by the mid-1990s assuming continued federal budgetary support and the absence of any insurmountable technical or institutional obstacles.

* * *

Three principal factors determine how salty the water will be at various points along the lower Colorado: development (mostly in the upper basin), runoff from the upper basin, and land and water management practices affecting the natural and human-caused sources of salt. * * *

The inflow of saline water into the Colorado can be prevented by intercepting those flows and then retaining them by reuse, storage, or evaporation. In the latter case, the salts are no longer in solution and must be managed in some environmentally acceptable manner. Salt pickup can be reduced through more efficient irrigation management or by taking irrigated acreage out of production. It is possible, though unconfirmed, that the timing of soil-leaching activities and reservoir releases could reduce salinity effects downstream. Dilution can be achieved by importing water low in salt into the basin, augmenting runoff through weather modification, reducing evaporation, or limiting the transbasin exportation of high-quality headwaters. These physical means of salt control appear in various degrees and mixes in the following policy strategies.

Retiring or Reforming Existing Development

One of the most effective strategies, where socially and politically acceptable, could be cessation of irrigation in areas of high-saline pickup. The phase-out could be accomplished gradually through public condemnation or negotiated public or private purchase. A public buyout of 6,000 agriculturally marginal acres in the Wellton-Mohawk District was authorized by Congress as part of the Salinity Control Act of 1984. Economic justification, though not political support, existed for the retirement of even more acreage there.

The potential for the purchase of upper-basin farmland and associated water rights by lower-basin municipalities has been discussed, but changes in the "law of the river" would first be required. If interstate water leasing were allowed in the basin, for example, substantial salt control might be attainable through the retirement of upper-basin acreage.

* * *

Limiting the Scale, Type, and Location of New Development

Given the lessons learned and the public cost imposed by past development in the basin, we have the choice of influencing future development decisions in ways that reduce the salinity. Some sites—such as those overlying mancos shale—ought not to be developed or expanded unless the saline drainage can be retained safely away from the river system. Where new development does occur, the costs of salt control could be required to be "internalized" by appropriate levels of government.

* * *

Limiting or Recalling Exports

The exportation of pure headwaters out of the basin denies the river system dilutive flows. The choice can be made not to allow further exportations. To "recall" exports already made or relied on would involve the public acquisition of water rights and substantial political resistance, leaving it as a choice that would not likely be available except where water exchanges were possible or dire salinity and drought conditions existed.

Controlling Natural Sources

Natural discharges of salinity are currently the largest contributors of salts. Where the sources are discrete—springs and arroyos, for example—the choice is whether to divert or to retain the saline flows. In some instances this possibility could become a mitigation project required of water project developers. * * *

Augmenting the Flow

The amount of dilutive flow can be increased through weather modification, which has been attempted on a limited scale, through vegetation management, or through the importation of water from another basin. For augmented flow to improve the salinity picture, however, the additional runoff must be dedicated to in-stream flows and not consumed. * * *

Attempting to Influence the Timing and Effects of Salinity Impacts

Within the limits of other project purposes and user economics, water use might be more consciously managed to time the inputs of salt, so that the concentrating or diluting effects occur when the system can best absorb the effects. Under this strategy, salt control could be factored in with other objectives for water project operations.

* * *

Desalting Before Use

Like importation, the alternative of desalinization remains prohibitively expensive at present. Despite millions of dollars of research, demonstration, and application, costs still have not been reduced below about $300 per acre-foot. The Yuma plant, originally estimated to cost $77 million to build and $10 million per year to operate, is now estimated to be facing more than $226 million in construction costs and a yearly operation expense of $20 million, resulting in a treatment cost of approximately $326 an acre-foot (in 1983 dollars). Operating costs for desalinization are tending to rise in part because of the significant energy requirements of the process. * * *

Finally, another strategy besides salinity reduction would be to develop ways to use higher-salinity water. Certain crops, including some grains, are known to be salt-tolerant but are not as profitable to grow. Research is under way concerning opportunities to grow and use more salt-tolerant crops. New methods might also be found to use higher-salinity water in municipal and industrial processes. * * *

Increases in salinity have resulted largely from an extensive effort to reclaim arid lands for crops. Irrigation development has long ranked as the dominant item on the water management agenda. Hydroelectric power production and sales have helped to subsidize these developments. Some additional water development already promised to participants in the interstate coalition—particularly Utah, Colorado, and Arizona—awaits construction or completion. These old promises, including those to Indian tribes, are now competing with the modern demand for economic efficiency, environmental quality, and leisure-time recreation. Water decision making must moderate the old and new commitments.

NOTE: CONGRESSIONAL ALLOCATION OF THE CARSON AND TRUCKEE RIVERS

In 1990, Congress apportioned the waters of the Carson and Truckee rivers that originate on the eastern slope of the Sierra Nevada Mountains in California and flow into Nevada where they eventually drain into Great Basin sinks. These rivers had been effectively apportioned by a series of lawsuits, adjudications and agreements. Congress basically ratified this de facto apportionment when it adopted the

Truckee–Carson–Pyramid Lake Water Rights Settlement Act, Pub.L. No. 101–618, 104 Stat. 3294 (1990). The Act is the most precise and comprehensive congressional settlement of a longstanding interstate water dispute. See John Kramer, *Lake Tahoe, the Truckee River, and Pyramid Lake: The Past, Present and Future of Interstate Water Issues,* 19 Pac.L.J. 1339 (1988).

The focus of the Act is a four-way, intra-Nevada dispute among the Pyramid Lake Paiute Tribe, which wants increased Truckee River flows to preserve and restore native fisheries, the Truckee–Carson Irrigation District, which holds most water rights on the lower Truckee, the Sierra Pacific Power Company, which supplies water to the growing cities of Reno and Sparks, and environmental interests seeking to maintain flows into the Lahontan Valley wetlands. A byproduct of this settlement is the apportionment of these two interstate rivers.

A series of agreements, lawsuits, and adjudications spanned almost a century, but the two states had never formally apportioned the waters. California and Nevada began compact negotiations in 1956, negotiated one in 1965, and approved it in 1969–70. Congress refused to ratify it because of federal government, tribal and California state senatorial opposition, but eventually the tribe, the federal government, and the cities of Reno and Sparks reached an agreement that Congress ratified. The legislation made the same allocation of the Truckee as provided in the compact. Lake Tahoe basin diversions are limited to 34,000 acre–feet per year; California gets 23,000 acre–feet, and Nevada 11,000 acre–feet. Notably both surface and groundwater are included in this allocation.

Most of the Truckee is used in Nevada and allocated by the 1944 Orr Ditch decree. United States of America v. Orr Ditch Co., Equity Docket No. A3 (D.Nev.1944). The settlement preserves these prior uses by limiting California to 32,000 acre–feet of gross diversions from surface and groundwater in the Truckee River basin. Maximum annual surface diversions are limited to 10,000 acre–feet. All future California commercial and irrigation withdrawals are junior to all Nevada beneficial uses for the maintenance and preservation of the Pyramid Lake fishery. The apportionment contains novel features such as the protection of return flows from sewage treatment plant discharges and the allocation of water used for winter snow-making.

INTAKE WATER COMPANY v. YELLOWSTONE RIVER COMPACT COMMISSION

United States Court of Appeals, Ninth Circuit, 1985.
769 F.2d 568, cert. denied 476 U.S. 1163, 106 S.Ct. 2288, 90 L.Ed.2d 729 (1986).

J. Blaine Anderson, Circuit Judge:

* * *

The Yellowstone River Compact fixes the water usage of all waters of the Yellowstone River Basin. It was enacted by Congress on October 10, 1951. Act of Consent to the Yellowstone River Compact, 65 Stat. 663, Ch. 629, Pub.L. 231 (1951). The signatory states, Montana, Wyoming and North Dakota, approved the Compact and codified it in their laws prior to congressional ratification. The Yellowstone River Compact Commission is charged by Congress with implementation of the Compact.

In June, 1973, appellant Intake appropriated 80,650 acre feet per year of Yellowstone River water. Intake planned construction of a diversion works, including a reservoir near Dawson, Montana. Some of the water was to be diverted outside the Yellowstone Basin for use elsewhere in Montana and North Dakota and thus outside the jurisdiction of the Compact.

Intake challenged the validity of Article X of the Compact, contending that it discriminated against, unreasonably impeded and exerted an undue burden on the flow of interstate commerce in violation of the Commerce Clause of the Constitution. Art. I, § 8, cl. 3. Article X of the Compact restricts interbasin or interstate transfer of Yellowstone River waters, providing that:

> No waters shall be diverted from the Yellowstone River Basin without unanimous consent of all the signatory states:

> * * *

Intake alleges that Article X of the Compact, as state law, places a constitutionally impermissible burden on inter-state commerce by requiring unanimous consent of the signatory states for out-of-basin transfers of Yellowstone River water. Appellees, while not challenging the sufficiency of this argument, contend that: the Yellowstone River Compact was approved by Congress; because it was approved by Congress, it is federal, not state, law for purposes of Commerce Clause objections; therefore, the Compact cannot, by definition, be a state law impermissibly interfering with commerce but is instead a federal law, immune from attack.

The three-judge district court, in a well-reasoned decision, concluded that appellees' argument was the compelling one. Intake Water Co. v. Yellowstone River Compact Commission, 590 F.Supp. 293, 296–97 (1983). On the basis of that reasoning, we agree.

When Congress approved this compact, Congress was acting within its authority to immunize state law from some constitutional objections by converting it into federal law. Cuyler v. Adams, 449 U.S. 433, 438, 101 S.Ct. 703, 706, 66 L.Ed.2d 641 (1981). Accord, NYSA-ILA Vacation & Holiday Fund v. Waterfront Comm'n of New York Harbor, 732 F.2d 292 (2d Cir.), cert. denied, 469 U.S. 852 (1984). Nor can there be any question as to whether Congress in fact approved the state law from which immunity from Commerce Clause attack is claimed: The Compact was before Congress and Congress expressly approved it.

We find additional support for this holding in the Supreme Court's recent decision of Northeast Bancorp Inc. v. Board of Governors of the Federal Reserve System, 472 U.S. 159 (1985). There, the Court rejected the argument that regional limitations contained in Massachusetts and Connecticut statutes burdened interstate commerce. The Court held: "When Congress so chooses, state actions which it plainly authorizes are invulnerable to constitutional attack under the Commerce Clause." 472 U.S. at 174.   Thus, as a federal law, the Compact authorizes those actions included within its provisions.

* * *

TASHIMA, DISTRICT JUDGE, concurring:

* * *

* * * The real issue raised by appellant is what inference should be drawn from an essentially silent congressional record, which is the case here.   Neither the Act of Consent to the Yellowstone River Compact, nor its legislative history, discloses that Commerce Clause immunity was expressly considered.   Appellant contends that such a silent record compels the conclusion that Congress, in approving a compact, intended not to immunize it from Commerce Clause attack.

By rejecting appellant's contention, we merely ascribe to Congress the intent plainly to be inferred from its action, *i.e.*, that it intended to do what it did—approve the Yellowstone River Compact without reservation.

NOTE

It is well established that Congress may expressly consent to state legislation affecting interstate commerce that would otherwise be unconstitutional.   E.g., Prudential Insurance Co. v. Benjamin, 328 U.S. 408 (1946).   Likewise, congressional consent to an interstate compact may immunize the compact's restrictions from Commerce Clause attack.   Is a state law that is intended to implement an interstate compact also immunized from attack under the Commerce Clause because of congressional approval of that compact?   In 1984, an entrepreneur unveiled an ambitious plan to export water from the Yampa River in Colorado to water-short San Diego by simply "appropriating" it in Colorado under state law and leaving it in the river to be used in San Diego.   Colorado law allows a water export upon a showing that it will not deprive Coloradans of the beneficial use of water and that it will not impair the state's ability to comply with interstate apportionments pursuant to compacts.   Colo.Rev.Stat. § 37–81–101(3)(a).   Unlike the Yellowstone River Compact, the Colorado River Compact is silent on taking water out of the basin.   However, the San Diego scheme would have resulted in 10% of Colorado's total apportionment being used in California.   If a Colorado water court denied approval to the proposal on the grounds that it would interfere with the interstate allocation scheme, would the Colorado law as applied offend the Commerce Clause as interpreted under *Sporhase*, pages 748–55, supra?

Appendix A

TABLE OF WATER EQUIVALENTS

1 gallon	=	8.34 pounds
	=	231 cubic inches
	=	0.134 cubic foot
1 million gallons	=	3.07 acre-feet
1 million gallons per day (mgd)	=	1,120 acre-feet per year
	=	1.55 cubic feet per second
	=	694.4 gallons per minute (gpm)
1 cubic foot	=	7.48 gallons
	=	62.4 pounds
1 cubic foot per second (cfs)	=	646,317 gallons per day
	=	448.8 gallons per minute
	=	1.98 acre-feet per day
	=	38.4 miner's inches (CO)
	=	40 miner's inches (AZ, CA, MT, NV, OR)
	=	50 miner's inches (ID, NE, NM, ND, SD, UT)
1 miner's inch	=	.02–.028 c.f.s. (depending on state)
1 acre-foot (af)	=	325,851 gallons
	=	43,560 cubic feet
1 inch of rain	=	27,200 gallons per acre
	=	113 tons per acre

METRIC CONVERSION FACTORS

Multiply:	By:	To Obtain:
foot (ft)	0.3048	meter (m)
cubic foot per second (cfs)	0.02832	cubic meter per second (m^3/s)
mile (mi)	1.609	kilometer (km)
acre	0.405	hectare (ha)
acre-foot (af)	1,233.	cubic meter (m^3)
gallon	3.785	liter (l)
million gallons per day	3,785.	cubic meter per day

Appendix B

SOURCES OF WATER LAW AND RESOURCES LITERATURE

1. Introduction

Water allocation, especially in the West, has inspired lawyers, historians, economists and others to write about water resources issues. The literature runs from classic late nineteenth and early twentieth century legal treatises to rich, technical studies and impassioned polemics. We include the sources that have been most useful to us along with some general comments about their significance and quality. This bibliography includes sources of answers to issues raised in this book, as well as sources that provide the full context to understand the drama of water resources allocation.

2. The Law

Old and new treatises abound. Henry Philip Farnham, The Law of Waters and Water Rights (1904) is the oldest and the first major treatise that is national in scope. It is still cited by courts, especially in riparian jurisdictions. A concise treatment of the law of each state is National Water Commission, A Summary–Digest of State Water Laws (Richard L. Dewsnup and Dallin W. Jensen eds. 1973). For students who want to do further reading in water law: David H. Getches, Water Rights in a Nutshell (2d ed. 1990); A. Dan Tarlock, Law of Water Rights and Resources (1988) (one volume survey with annual updates); and Waters and Water Rights (Robert Beck ed.) (multi-author, multiple volume treatise).

The other treatises are regional. Samuel Charles Wiel, Water Rights in the Western States (3d ed. 1911) and Clesson Selwy Kinney, A Treatise on the Law of Irrigation and Water Rights and the Arid Region Doctrine of Appropriation of Water (2d ed. 1912) are the two standard treatises on western water law. Wiel is the superior analytical work and courts continue to refer to it for basic and arcane points of law. Kinney is a useful source on the law of prior appropriation in its formative period and is essential reading to catch the spirit of those who converted the West to irrigation farming. A water law scholar in the U.S. Department of Agriculture, Wells A. Hutchins, capped his 62–year career of the study of western water institutions with the post-humous publication of a three-volume treatise, Water Rights Laws in the Nineteen Western States (completed by Harold H. Ellis and J. Peter DeBraal 1971). The work is somewhat repetitive, but contains a wealth of information and insights into western water law and the development of law in each state.

In addition to the national or regional treatises, there are some very useful state treatises. Frank B. Maloney, Sheldon J. Plager and Fletcher N. Baldwin, Jr., Water Law and Administration: The Florida Experience (1968) is an essential source of information about Florida's water, and riparian rights in general. Thanks to the efforts of the pioneering water resources law scholar at the University of Wisconsin, Jacob Beuscher, there is a good treatise on Wisconsin law, Harold H. Ellis et al., Water–Use Law and Administration in Wisconsin (1970). Wells Hutchins published a series of Department of Agriculture monographs on the law of water rights of various western states, and these useful volumes are in many law libraries. Other books that are helpful in understanding the water laws of specific states include: Robert I. Reis, Connecticut Water Law: Judicial Allocation of Water Resources (1967) and Charles W. Wixom and Karl F. Zeisler, Industrial Uses of Water in Michigan (1966). California law is described for the practitioner in Harold E. Rogers and Alan H. Nichols, Water For California: Planning Law & Practice Finances (2 vols. 1967). Statutes, treatises, forms and cases relating to Colorado water law are collected in Colorado Water Laws (George Radosevich ed. 1979). A recent work focuses on modern Colorado water problems. Tradition, Innovation and Conflict: Perspectives on Colorado Water Law (Lawrence J. MacDonnell ed. 1986).

Joseph K. Angell, A Treatise on the Right of Property in Tidewaters and in the Soil and Shores Thereof (1847) was the first major American work on the law of navigable waters. Moses M. Frankel, Law of Seashore Waters and Water Courses: Maine and Massachusetts (1969) is a modern book on the same subject.

Water law casebooks are also an important source of law. Indeed, the very first American casebook on any subject was Angell on Water Courses (1824). There are two current, national water law casebooks besides this book: a recent revision of the pioneering effort of the late Dean Frank J. Trelease, the most prominent water law scholar of the post-World War II generation, Frank J. Trelease and George A. Gould, Water Law (4th ed. 1986); and a new book, Joseph L. Sax, Robert J. Abrams, and Barton Thompson, Legal Control of Water Resources (1992). Jacob H. Beuscher, Water Rights (now James B. McDonald and Jacob H. Beuscher, Water Rights (2d ed. 1973)) was the first effort to focus a casebook around midwestern and eastern issues.

3. History

Classical scholars may find a 1905 publication by a Topeka, Kansas lawyer to be interesting reading. Eugene F. Ware, Roman Water Law: Translated from the Pandects of Justinian. The book has been reprinted by Fred B. Rothman & Co.

The development of western water law is tied to the history of the settlement and development of the West. Bernard DeVoto's trilogy, Course of Empire (1952), Across the Wide Missouri (1947), Year of Decision: 1846 (1943), is a fine introduction to the politics of the opening of the West. The relationship between land, climate and human institutions was first comprehensively explored in Walter Prescott Webb's The Great Plains (1931). Frederick Jackson Turner's successor at Harvard, Frederick Merk, summed up a life of teaching about the West in History of the Western Movement (1978), in which the role of water development is covered extensively. William L. Graf, Wilderness Preservation and the Sagebrush Rebellions (1990) surveys the history of public land and water resources management from the failed efforts to establish a scientific national irrigation policy in the 1870s and 1880s to the failure of the Sagebrush Rebellion in the 1980s to cause the divestment of federal lands.

Books about the history of water law and water development have begun to appear with increasing frequency. For example, Robert G. Dunbar, Forging New Rights in Western Waters (1983) is a very readable introduction to the history of the development of water law. Michael C. Meyer, Water in the Hispanic Southwest: A Social and Legal History 1550–1850 (1984) is an inquiry into the Spanish origins of irrigation. Water in the American West: Essays in Honor of Raphael J. Moses (David H. Getches ed. 1988) is a balanced evaluation of many aspects of western water development.

Much of western water law and practice is a product of the irrigation movement. Donald J. Pisani, From the Family Farm to Agribusiness: The Irrigation Crusade in California and the West 1850–1931 (1984) is now the standard history. Until recently federal water policy was based on multiple-purpose river basin development. The standard (and excellent) history of the origins of this idea is Samuel P. Hays, Conservation and the Gospel of Efficiency: The Progressive Conservation Movement 1890–1920 (1959). The role of the counter-preservation tradition in natural resource thinking is traced in Roderick Nash, Wilderness and the American Mind (3d ed. 1982). Beatrice H. Holmes, A History of Federal Water Resources Programs, 1800–1960 (U.S. Dep't of Ag. Misc. Pub. No. 1233, 1972) and History of Federal Water Resources Programs and Policies, 1961–1970 (U.S. Dep't Ag. Misc. Pub. No. 1379, 1979) are very useful sources of information about the growth of federal involvement in water management.

Donald Worster has written a provocative critical history of western water development, Rivers of Empire: Water, Aridity, and the Growth of the American West (1985).

Environmental histories of the West and the Nation now being written stress the adverse consequences of man's effort to mold nature rather than to adapt to natural conditions. The model articulation of the idea that "[m]an might limit the demands he makes on a basin's water processes" is Henry C. Hart's study of the taming of the Missouri, The Dark Missouri (1957). Joseph M. Petulla, American Environmental History: The Exploitation and Conservation of Natural Resources (1977) is an adequate introduction for the nonspecialist. An important new environmental history, not directly related to water, is William Cronon's Changes in the Land: Indians, Colonists, and the Ecology of New England (1983), which traces the early roots of the creation of private property in resources held in common by the public.

Edward Goldsmith and Nicholas Hildyard, The Environmental and Social Effects of Large Dams (1984) is a critical Sierra Club book survey of the consequences of a technology that we have perfected in the United States and exported world-wide. Richard L. Berkman and W. Kip Viscusi, Damming the West (1973) is an earlier Nader exposé of the Bureau of Reclamation.

Individual rivers, specific projects, and states have attracted scholarly attention. The Colorado River has inspired its own literature. Norris Hundley's Water and the West: The Colorado River Compact and the Politics of Water in the American West (1975) and Dividing the Waters: A Century of Controversy Between the United States and Mexico (1966) provide a rich history of the 1922 Compact, the Boulder Canyon Project Act and our relations with Mexico. His most recent work is The Great Thirst: Californians and Water 1770s–1990s (1992). A River No More: The Colorado River and the West (1981) by Phillip L. Fradkin is an artful blend of history, law, ecology, and social commentary. R. Martin, A Story That Stands Like a Dam: Glen Canyon and the Struggle for the Soul of the West (1989) focuses on one of the two major dams on the river. In 1983 a group of scholars and water specialists gathered at the Bishop's Lodge in Santa Fe, New Mexico to assess the Colorado River Compact, and the conference produced New Courses for the Colorado River: Major Issues for the Next Century (Gary D. Weatherford and F. Lee Brown eds. 1986). Dean Mann, The Politics of Water in Arizona (1963) tells how that state developed its dependence on Colorado River water for future growth. Francis J. Welsh, How to Create a Water Crisis (1985) carries the story forward with a well-documented dissection of the federal bailout of Arizona, the Central Arizona Project. Conflicts over the use of the water supply of the Owens Valley have been central to California water law. William L. Kahrl, Water and Power: The Conflict over Los Angeles' Water Supply in the Owens Valley (1982) is a fine chronology of the on-going conflict. Abraham Hoffman, Vision or Villainy: Origins of the Owens Valley–Los Angeles Water Controversy (1981) is also good. Ira Clark, Water in New Mexico: A History of Its Management and Use (1987) traces the influence of environmental values in that state.

In the 1950s and 1960s, Rivers of America, a series of histories of individual river basins was published. Among the best are Paul Horgan, The Great River: The Rio Grande in North American History (1954) and Stewart H. Holbrook, The Columbia River (1965). Tim Palmer, The Snake River: Window to the West (1991) continues this tradition. Eastern water allocation problems are the subject of Roscoe C. Martin, Water for New York: A Study in State Administration of Water Resources (1960). Preston J. Hubbard, Origins of the TVA: The Muscle Shoals Controversy, 1920–1932 (1961) examines the origins of our most famous experiment with a river basin authority.

Controversies over whether to destroy white water for a dam often produce case studies. Among the best are Elmo R. Richardson, Dams, Parks and Politics: Resource Development and Preservation in the Truman–Eisenhower Era (1973); B. Andrews and M. Sansone, Who Runs the Rivers: Dams and Decisions in the New West (1983); and

Thomas J. Schoenbaum, The New River Controversy (1979), a good case study of the use of the Wild and Scenic Rivers Act to block a FERC license.

There is a substantial body of "crisis" literature that predicts a water shortage, surveys wasteful uses and pollution practices, and calls for reform. Books include James C. Wright, The Coming Water Famine (1966); William A. Ashworth, Nor Any Drop to Drink (1982); Fred Powledge, Water: The Nature, Uses, and Future of Our Most Precious and Abused Resource (1982); Frank B. Moss, The Water Crisis (1967); and David A. Francko & Robert G. Wetzel, To Quench Our Thirst: The Present and Future Status of Fresh Water Resources of the United States (1983).

4. Official Documents

Water policy is always being studied at the federal and state levels. Two classic reports are John Wesley Powell's Report on the Lands of the Arid Region of the United States, With a More Detailed Account of the Lands of Utah (1879), and Elwood Mead's U.S. Dep't of Agriculture, Office of Experiment Stations, Report of Irrigation Investigations in California, Bulletin S. Doc. 108 (1901). James R. Kluger, Turning on the Water With a Shovel: The Career of Elwood Mead (1992) is a good biography of this pivotal figure. The 1962 Belknap Press of Harvard University's edition of Powell, edited by Wallace Stegner, is the edition of Powell most used by scholars today. Stegner's Beyond the Hundredth Meridian: John Wesley Powell and the Second Opening of the West (1954) is the standard biography of Powell and a classic book on the West.

Among the most important modern government studies are the three volumes, A Water Policy for the American People, Ten Rivers in America's Future, and Water Resources Law, The Report of the President's Water Resources Policy Commission (1950); and Water Policies For the Future, Final Report to the President and to the Congress of the United States by the National Water Commission (1973). Water Policies For the Future is the most searching analysis of state and federal water policy to date and frames the policy debate in a still-poignant manner. A 1968 National Academy of Sciences Study, Water and Choice in the Colorado Basin: An Example of Alternatives in Water Management is a high-powered model of water policy analysis. Forecasts of future water demands are summarized in State and National Water Use Trends to the Year 2000, A Report Prepared By the Congressional Research Service of the Library of Congress for the Committee on Environment and Public Works, U.S. Senate, S. No. 96–12, 96th Cong., 2d Sess. 227–297 (1980).

The Water Science and Technology Board of the National Academy of Sciences and National Research Council, formed in 1982, has published several reports of interest, including Water Transfers in the West: Efficiency, Equity, and the Environment (1992) and Irrigation–Induced Water Quality: What Can Be Learned from the San Joaquin Valley Experience (1989).

5. Economics

As in other areas, economists have had a major influence on the debate about water allocation policy. Among the modern classics are Otto Eckstein, Water–Resource Development: The Economics of Project Evaluation (1958); John V. Krutilla and Otto Eckstein, Multiple Purpose River Development: Studies in Applied Economic Analysis (1958). Jack Hirshleifer, James C. DeHaven and Jerome W. Milliman, Water Supply: Economics, Technology and Policy (1960). Economics and Public Policy in Water Resource Development (Stephen C. Smith and Emery N. Castle eds. 1964) remains an important collection of papers on the use of economic analysis to guide water development decisions. Arthur Maass and Raymond L. Anderson, * * * And the Desert Shall Rejoice: Conflict, Growth, and Justice in Arid Environments (1978) is a worthwhile recent evaluation of reclamation. Charles W. Howe, Benefit–Cost Analysis for Water System Planning (1971) is a fine introduction to formal cost-benefit analysis. Professor Howe's important work on water transfers includes Charles W. Howe and K. William Easter, Interbasin Transfers of Water: Economic Issues and Impacts (1971). Terry L. Anderson, Water Crisis: Ending the Policy Drought (1983) is a popular introduction to current market-based reform proposals. Z. Willey, Economic Development and Environmental Quality in California's Water System (1985) applies economic analysis to propose an environmental and marketing reform agenda for that state. Richard W. Wahl, Markets for Federal Water: Subsidies, Property Rights, and the Bureau of Reclamation (1989) is a blueprint for a reformed, market-oriented Bureau. In the late 1980s mainstream resource economists began to incorporate the concept of "sustainable development." Noteworthy texts include David W. Pearce and R. Kerry Turner, Economics of Natural Resources and the Environment (1990) and David W. Pearce et al., Sustainable Development: Economics and Environment in the Third World (1990).

6. Political Science

Political scientists have devoted considerable effort to explaining the "logic" of federal subsidies. The effect of state water attitudes on western state legislatures is examined in Helen M. Ingram, Nancy K. Laney and John R. McCain, A Policy Approach to Political Representation: Lessons from the Four Corners States (1980). Professor Ingram's earlier book, Patterns of Politics in Water Resource Development (1969), is a revealing study of the formation of a coalition to secure congressional funding for a basin-wide development project—in this case the Colorado River Basin Project Act. Merrill R. Goodall, John D. Sullivan and Timothy DeYoung, California Water: A New Political Economy (1978) is the major study of the role of the special districts in water allocation and distribution. Also of interest are David Lewis Feldman, Water Resources Management: In Search of an Environmental Ethic (1991), surveying the tension between the development mission of the water agencies and environmental protection, and William Blomquist, Dividing the Water (1992).

7. Law Reviews

Water law articles and student comments and notes can be found in all law reviews. The greatest concentration of academic writing is in two specialized journals, the University of Wyoming's Land and Water Law Review and the University of New Mexico's Natural Resources Journal; an additional source that includes frequent attention to water issues is the University of Colorado Law Review.

A journal, Rivers, is devoted to technical and policy issues related to river preservation and instream flow protection.

8. Popular Literature

Marc Reisner, Cadillac Desert: The American West And Its Disappearing Water (1986) is a lively and critical account of the ability of the Bureau of Reclamation to develop and hold power in the West. This book was followed by Marc Reisner and Sarah Bates, Overtapped Oasis: Reform or Revolution for Western Water (1990). Another popular book, The Milagro Beanfield War (1976), part of a trilogy by John T. Nichols, chronicles the conflicts between wealthy developers and local farmers in the Southwest. The late Wallace Stegner's The American West As Living Space (1987) sums up this great author's thoughts on how the West should be used. Charles Wilkinson has carried forward Stegner's thinking in two recent books, The Eagle Bird: Mapping a New West (1990) and Crossing the Next Meridian (1992).

*

INDEX

References are to Pages

†